S0-ABO-206

Management Information Systems

**Solving Business Problems
with Information Technology**

Fourth Edition

Gerald V. Post
University of the Pacific

David L. Anderson
Northwestern University

**McGraw-Hill
Irwin**

Boston   Burr Ridge, IL   Dubuque, IA   Madison, WI   New York   San Francisco   St. Louis
Bangkok   Bogotá   Caracas   Kuala Lumpur   Lisbon   London   Madrid   Mexico City
Milan   Montreal   New Delhi   Santiago   Seoul   Singapore   Sydney   Taipei   Toronto

The McGraw·Hill Companies

MANAGEMENT INFORMATION SYSTEMS:
SOLVING BUSINESS PROBLEMS WITH INFORMATION TECHNOLOGY
Published by McGraw-Hill/Irwin, a business unit of The McGraw-Hill Companies, Inc., 1221 Avenue of the
Americas, New York, NY, 10020. Copyright © 2006, 2003, 2000, 1997 by The McGraw-Hill Companies, Inc.
All rights reserved. No part of this publication may be reproduced or distributed in any form or by any means,
or stored in a database or retrieval system, without the prior written consent of The McGraw-Hill Companies,
Inc., including, but not limited to, in any network or other electronic storage or transmission, or broadcast for
distance learning.
Some ancillaries, including electronic and print components, may not be available to customers outside the
United States.

This book is printed on acid-free paper.

1 2 3 4 5 6 7 8 9 0 WCK/WCK 0 9 8 7 6 5

ISBN 0-07-111638-9

To Our Parents

About the Authors

Gerald V. Post   *University of the Pacific*

Dr. Post is a professor of information systems at the University of the Pacific's School of Business. Jerry holds a Ph.D. in economics and statistics from Iowa State University. He earned his post doctorate from Indiana University's Graduate School of Business and earned a B.A. in mathematics and economics from University of Wisconsin—Eau Claire. Jerry has worked as a freelance programmer and software designer for various companies. He has published numerous papers that explore security, systems development, and evaluation issues in MIS. He is also the author of *Database Management Systems: Designing and Building Business Applications.* When he is not tied to the keyboard, he can be found riding one of his bikes.

David L. Anderson   *Northwestern University*

Dr. Anderson is a technology and security professional at a leading provider of health care insurance in the Chicago metropolitan area. He also serves as an adjunct professor at Northwestern University. David received his law degree from George Washington University and is a member of the Ohio, District of Columbia, federal, and U.S. Supreme Court Bars. He earned his M.B.A. from the University of Michigan, his M.S. in computer science and electrical engineering from Northwestern University, and his doctorate in educational administration from Harvard University.

Prior to his current position, David served as a project management specialist at Hewitt Associates, a strategic planner at ISSC/IBM Corporation, a corporate information access planner at Continental Bank, and a senior consultant at Andersen Consulting (now Accenture).

David also serves as an adjunct professor at the Kellstadt Graduate School of Business at DePaul University. He has served as an assistant professor of management information systems at the Loyola University Graduate School of Business and at Wheaton College.

David is the author of *Managing Information Systems: Using Cases within an Industry Context to Solve Business Problems with Information Technology* and (with James Pannabecker) *Guide to Financial Privacy: Regulatory Impact on Technology.*

Brief Contents

Preface   xii

Acknowledgments   xx

1   Introduction   2

PART ONE
Information Technology Infrastructure   37

2   Information Technology Foundations   38

3   Networks and Telecommunications   74

4   Database Management   122

PART TWO
Operations   163

5   Computer Security   164

6   Transactions and Operations   198

7   Enterprise Integration   234

8   Electronic Business   272

PART THREE
Tactics and Strategies   313

9   Teamwork   314

10   Business Decisions   348

11   Strategic Analysis   394

PART FOUR
Organizing Businesses and Systems   441

12   Systems Development   442

13   Organizing MIS Resources   492

14   Information Management and Society   526

GLOSSARY   577

ORGANIZATION INDEX   589

SUBJECT INDEX   592

Contents

Preface   xii

Acknowledgments   xx

Chapter One
Introduction   2

Introduction   3
What Is MIS?   4
The Importance of Information Technology   5
    Productivity   5
    Teamwork and Communication   6
    Business Operations and Strategy   7
The Role of the Internet in Business   7
So You Want to Be a Manager   8
    Traditional Management and Observations   8
    Making Decisions   9
Business and Technology Trends   10
    Specialization   11
    Management by Methodology and Franchises   11
    Merger Mania   12
    Decentralization and Small Business   13
    Temporary Workers   13
    Internationalization   15
    Service-Oriented Business   16
Reengineering: Altering the Rules   16
Management and Decision Levels   18
    Operations   18
    Tactics   19
    Strategy   20
An Introduction to Strategy   21
    Searching for Ideas   21
    Strategy Example: Baxter Healthcare   22
Summary   24
Key Words   25
Web Site References   25
Additional Readings   25
Review Questions   26
Exercises   26
Cases: The Fast-Food Industry   27

PART ONE
INFORMATION TECHNOLOGY
INFRASTRUCTURE   37

Chapter Two
Information Technology Foundations   38

Introduction   39

Types of Data   40
    Object Orientation   40
    Numbers and Text   42
    Pictures   44
    Sound   45
    Video   46
    Size Complications   46
    Data Compression   47
Hardware Components   47
    Processors   48
    Input   52
    Output   53
    Secondary Storage   55
Operating Systems   56
Computers in e-Business   57
    What Is a Browser?   57
    What Is a Server?   58
Application Software   58
    Research: Databases   59
    Analysis: Calculations   59
    Communication: Writing   60
    Communication: Presentation and Graphics   60
    Communication: Voice and Mail   62
    Organizing Resources: Calendars and Schedules   62
    The Paperless Office?   63
    Open Software   63
Summary   64
Key Words   65
Web Site References   65
Additional Readings   65
Review Questions   66
Exercises   66
Cases: The Computer Industry   68

Chapter Three
Networks and Telecommunications   74

Introduction   75
Network Functions   76
    Sharing Data   76
    Sharing Hardware   81
    Sharing Software   83
    Voice and Video Communication   83
Components of a Network   84
    Computers   84
    Transmission Media   85
    Connection Devices   91
Network Structure   92
    Shared-Media Networks   92

Switched Networks   93
Enterprise Networks   93
Standards   95
The Need for Standards   95
The Changing Environment   95
Internet TCP/IP Reference Model   96
The Internet   98
How the Internet Works   98
Internet Addresses   100
Internet Mail   102
Access to Data on the Internet   103
Internet 2   104
Wireless Networks and Mobile Commerce   105
Unsolicited Commercial e-Mail   106
Global Telecommunications   107
Technical Problems   108
Legal and Political Complications   109
Cultural Issues   109
Comment   110
Summary   110
Key Words   111
Web Site References   111
Additional Readings   111
Review Questions   112
Exercises   112
Cases: Wholesale Suppliers   114

Chapter Four
Database Management   122

Introduction   123
Relational Databases   123
Tables, Rows, Columns, Data Types   124
The Database Management Approach   126
Focus on Data   127
Data Independence   127
Data Integrity   127
Speed of Development   128
Control over Output   128
Queries   129
Single-Table Queries   129
Computations   131
Joining Multiple Tables   133
Examples   134
Views   136
Designing a Database   137
Notation   138
First Normal Form   139
Second Normal Form   139
Third Normal Form   140
Database Applications   142
Data Input Forms   142
Reports   145
Putting It Together with Menus   146

Database Administration   148
Standards and Documentation   148
Testing, Backup, and Recovery   149
Access Controls   150
Databases and E-Business   150
Summary   151
Key Words   152
Web Site References   152
Additional Readings   152
Review Questions   153
Exercises   153
Cases: Pharmaceuticals   155

PART TWO
OPERATIONS   163

Chapter Five
Computer Security   164

Introduction   165
Threats to Information   166
Disasters   167
Employees and Consultants   168
Business Partnerships   169
Outsiders   170
Viruses   170
Spyware   173
Computer Security Controls   173
Manual and Electronic Information   174
Data Backup   174
User Identification   175
Access Control   176
Single Sign-On and Lack of Standards   177
Additional Security Measures   178
Audits   178
Physical Access   178
Monitoring   179
Hiring and Employee Evaluation   179
Encryption   179
Single Key   180
Public Key Infrastructure   181
Computer Forensics   183
e-Commerce Security Issues   183
Data Transmission   183
Spoofing Sites   185
Wireless Networks   186
Carnivore, Echelon, and Escrow Keys   186
Theft of Data from Servers   187
Denial of Service   187
Firewalls and Intrusion Detection   188
Privacy   189
Summary   189
Key Words   190
Website References   190

Additional Readings 190
Review Questions 191
Exercises 191
Cases: Professional Sports 192

Chapter Six
Transactions and Operations 198

Introduction 199
Data Capture 200
    Point of Sale 201
    POS Advantages 203
    Process Control 203
    Electronic Data Interchange (EDI) 205
Elements of a Transaction 209
    Vendor Perspective 209
    Customer Perspective 210
    Transaction Fees 210
    Government Perspective 212
    Risk Mitigation in e-Commerce 212
International Issues 213
Payment Mechanisms 214
Data Quality 216
    Data Integrity 216
    Multitasking, Concurrency, and Integrity 217
    Data Volume 218
    Data Summaries 218
    Time 219
Production Management 220
    Production Issues 220
    Distribution and Inventory Control 221
Summary 222
Key Words 223
Web Site References 223
Additional Readings 223
Review Questions 224
Exercises 224
Cases: Retail Sales 225

Chapter Seven
Enterprise Integration 234

Introduction 235
Integration in Business 237
Enterprise Resource Planning 239
    International Environment 242
    Financial Accounting 242
    Logistics 242
    Human Resource Management 243
    Integration 243
The Role of Accounting 244
    Input and Output: Financial Data and Reports 245
    Purchases, Sales, Loans, and Investments 246
    Inventory 246
    The Accounting Cycle 246
    Process: Controls, Checks, and Balances 247

Human Resources and Transaction Processing 247
    Input: Data Collection 247
    Output: Reports 248
    Process: Automation 249
Supply Chain Management 249
    SCM Changes the Focus 250
    SCM Challenges 251
    The Role of XML: Integration across Systems 253
Customer Relationship Management 254
    Multiple Contact Points 254
    Feedback, Individual Needs, and Cross Selling 255
    CRM Packages 255
Summarizing ERP Data 258
    Digital Dashboard and EIS 258
    How Does an EIS Work? 258
    Advantages of an EIS 260
Transaction Accuracy: Sarbanes-Oxley 260
Summary 261
Key Words 262
Web Site References 262
Additional Readings 262
Review Questions 262
Exercises 263
Cases: Automobile Industry 264

Chapter Eight
Electronic Business 272

Introduction 273
The Production Chain 276
    Disintermediation 277
    Business to Consumer 278
    Business to Business 284
Increasing Sales and Reducing Costs 286
    *Prepurchase, Purchase, and Postpurchase
    Support 286*
    Search Engines 287
    Traditional Media and Name Recognition 287
    Web Advertisements 287
    Web Site Traffic Analysis 289
    Privacy 291
e-Commerce Options 291
    Simple Static HTML 291
    Single-Unit Sales 293
    Web Commerce Servers 295
    Web Hosting Options 297
    Content Management Systems 297
Mobile Commerce 298
Taxes 298
Global Economy 299
Analysis of Dot-Com Failures 301
    Pure Internet Plays 301
    Profit Margins 302
    Advertising Revenue 302
Summary 303
Key Words 304

Additional Readings 304
Review Questions 305
Exercises 305
Cases: Entrepreneurship 307

PART THREE
TACTICS AND STRATEGIES 313

Chapter Nine
Teamwork 314

Introduction 315
Communication 316
　　e-Mail, Instant Messaging, and Voice Mail 317
　　Web Pages and Blogs 319
　　Scheduling and Project Management 319
　　Conferences and Meetings 320
　　Mobile Systems 321
Collaboration 321
　　Shared Documents and Changes 321
　　Version Control 323
　　Information Rights Management 323
　　Workflow 324
　　Group Decision Support Systems 325
Knowledge Management 326
　　Organizational Memory 327
　　Service Processes 327
Microsoft SharePoint 328
　　Communication and Scheduling 329
　　Collaboration 331
　　Workflow 333
　　Knowledge Management 334
Summary 335
Key Words 336
Web Site References 336
Additional Readings 336
Review Questions 337
Exercises 337
Cases: Package Delivery 338

Chapter Ten
Business Decisions 348

Introduction 349
It Is Hard to Make Good Decisions 350
　　Human Biases 351
　　Models 352
Data Warehouse 355
Online Analytical Processing (OLAP) 356
Decision Support System 358
　　Marketing Forecasts 359
　　Human Resources Management 360
Geographical Information Systems 361
　　Maps and Location Data 362
　　Example 363

Data: Data Mining 364
Expert Systems 365
　　Specialized Problems 365
Building Expert Systems 368
　　Knowledge Base 369
　　Rules 369
　　Creating an ES 370
　　Limitations of Expert Systems 371
　　Management Issues of Expert Systems 372
Specialized Tools 372
　　Pattern Recognition and Neural Networks 372
　　Machine Vision 375
　　Language Comprehension and Translation 375
　　Robotics and Motion 376
Machine Intelligence 377
DSS, ES, and AI 378
The Importance of Intelligent Systems in e-Business 379
　　Agents 380
　　Support and Problem-Solving Applications 381
Summary 382
Key Words 383
Web Site References 383
Additional Readings 383
Review Questions 383
Exercises 384
Cases: Financial Services Industry 386

Chapter Eleven
Strategic Analysis 394

Introduction 395
The Competitive Environment 397
External Agents 397
　　Buyers 398
　　Suppliers 399
　　Rivals, New Entrants, and Substitutes 399
　　Government Regulations 401
IS Techniques to Gain Competitive Advantage 401
　　Barriers to Entry 401
　　Distribution Channels 402
　　Switching Costs 404
　　Lower Production Costs 404
　　Product Differentiation and New Products 405
　　Quality Management 406
　　The Value Chain 407
The Search for Innovation 408
　　Research 408
　　Engineering and Design 409
　　Manufacturing 410
　　Logistics and Supply 410
　　Marketing 410
　　Sales and Order Management 411
　　Service 411
　　Management 412
Costs and Dangers of Strategies 412
　　High Capital Costs 413

When the Competition Follows 414
Changing Industry 414
Sharing Data 415
Government Intervention 415
The Role of Economics 417
Entrepreneurship 417
Idea 418
Strategy 418
Research 422
Plan 422
Strategy, Competition, and Market Analysis 423
Forecasts, Cash Flow, and Investment Budget 423
Marketing 425
Organization and Timetable 425
Implementation 425
Ownership Structure 426
Financing 426
Accounting and Benchmarks 427
Flexibility 428
Starting an e-Commerce Firm 428
Summary 429
Key Words 430
Web Site References 430
Additional Readings 430
Review Questions 431
Exercises 431
Cases: The Airline Industry 433

PART FOUR
**ORGANIZING BUSINESSES AND
SYSTEMS 441**

Chapter Twelve
Systems Development 442

Introduction 443
Building Information Systems 445
Custom Programming 445
Outsourcing and Contract Programmers 446
Assemble Applications from Components 446
Purchase an External Solution 448
Systems Development Life Cycle 448
The Need for Control 448
Introduction to SDLC 449
Feasibility and Planning 449
Systems Analysis 450
Systems Design 451
Systems Implementation 452
Maintenance 454
Evaluation 455
Strengths and Weaknesses of SDLC 455
Alternatives to SDLC 457
Prototyping 457
*Developing Systems Requires Teamwork: JAD
and RAD 457*

Extreme Programming 459
Open Source Development 459
End-User Development 461
Development Summary 462
Process Analysis 463
Input, Process, Output 463
Divide and Conquer 464
Goals and Objectives 465
Diagramming Systems 465
Summary: How Do You Create a DFD? 468
Object-Oriented Design 469
Properties and Functions 469
Object Hierarchies 470
Events 470
Object-Oriented and Event-Driven Development 471
Distributed Services 471
Summary 472
Key Words 473
Web Site References 473
Additional Readings 473
Review Questions 474
Exercises 474
Cases: Government Agencies 477

Chapter Thirteen
Organizing MIS Resources 492

Introduction 493
Managing the Information Systems Function 494
MIS Roles 495
Hardware Administration 496
Software Support 497
Network Support 497
Software Development 498
Support for End-User Development 498
Corporate Computing Standards 498
Data and Database Administration 499
Security 501
Advocacy Role 501
MIS Jobs 502
Outsourcing 503
MIS Organization: Centralization and
Decentralization 506
Hardware 506
Software and Data 508
Personnel 509
Recentralization with Intranets 512
Networks 512
Hardware 514
Data 514
Conflict Management 515
Summary 516
Key Words 517
Web Site References 517
Additional Readings 517

Review Questions   517
Exercises   518
Cases: The Energy Industry   520

Chapter Fourteen
Information Management and Society   526

Introduction   527
Individuals   528
    Privacy   529
    Privacy Laws and Rules   535
    Anonymity   536
Jobs   536
    Loss of Jobs   537
    Physical Disabilities   538
    Telecommuting   539
Business: Vendors and Consumers   539
    Intellectual Property   540
    Balance of Power   544
Education and Training   545
Social Interactions   546
    Social Group Legitimacy   546
    Access to Technology   546
    e-Mail Freedom   548
    Liability and Control of Data   548
Government   549
    Government Representatives and Agencies   549
    Democracy and Participation   549

    Voting   549
    Information Warfare   551
    Rise of the World-State?   552
Crime   553
    Police Powers   553
    Freedom of Speech   554
Responsibility and Ethics   554
    Users   555
    Programmers and Developers   555
    Companies   556
    Governments   556
A Summary of Important Computer-Related Laws   557
    Property Rights   558
    Privacy   561
    Information Era Crimes   563
Summary   564
Key Words   565
Web Site References   565
Additional Readings   566
Review Questions   566
Exercises   566
Cases: Health Care   568

Glossary   577

Organization Index   589

Subject Index   592

Preface

Managers and Information Technology

Today, everyone uses computers. But does everyone use them efficiently? How many business people turn to a spreadsheet when a database would be a better tool? Do managers understand how information technology can solve business problems? As a future manager, do you know about all of the technologies that businesses are using? Can you spot a business problem and identify possible information technology solutions?

Over the past decade, technology has changed many jobs. Competition and an economic downturn have caused companies to cut costs wherever possible. In many cases, that means reducing the number of employees. In the past few years, companies have used technology to alter and even eliminated management jobs. Twenty years ago, new college graduates could get entry-level jobs as manages, often performing relatively simple analytical tasks or summarizing data. Today, software does those jobs and generates detailed information on demand for executives.

If you want a job as a manager, you need to know how to use information technology. But it is not simply a matter of knowing how to use a word processor or spreadsheet. You need to use the technology to collaborate with other workers, to analyze data, and to find ways to improve your organization.

Continual changes in IT present two challenges: learning to use it and finding new opportunities to improve management. Most students have taken a hands-on course that teaches them how to use a computer. Many expect the introductory MIS course to be more of the same—hands-on computer usage tied to specific needs. However, there are more complex and interesting problems to be solved. Managers need to apply their knowledge of IT tools to solve management problems and find new opportunities to improve their organizations. The focus of this book is to investigate the more complex question: How can information technology be used to improve management and make companies more efficient or better than their competitors?

About the Book

Features That Focus on Solving Problems

Each chapter contains several unique features to assist in understanding the material and in applying it to analyze and solve business problems. Each chapter focuses on a specific type of problem. These problems are highlighted by the introduction and demonstrated in the business cases. The text dissects the problems and explores how technology can be used to solve the problems.

- **What You Will Learn in This Chapter.** A series of questions highlight the important issues.
- **Lead Case.** An introductory, real-world case illustrates the problems explored in the chapter.
- **Trends.** Sidebar boxes present the major changes, brief history, or trends that affect the topics in the chapter.
- **Reality Bytes.** Brief applications, mini-cases, and discussions emphasize a specific point and highlight international issues, business trends, or ethics. They also illustrate problems and solutions in the real world.

- **Technology Toolboxes.** A short example and description of a software tool that can be used to help managers solve specific problems. They provide a hands-on example of specific projects. Students are encouraged to follow the exercises and use the software tools to build the examples.
- **Chapter Summary.** A brief synopsis of the chapter highlights—useful when reviewing for exams.
- **A Manager's View.** A short summary of how the chapter relates to managers and to the overall question of how information technology can improve management.
- **Key Words.** A list of words introduced in the chapter. A full glossary is provided at the end of the text.
- **Review Questions.** Designed as a study guide for students.
- **Exercises.** Problems that apply the knowledge learned in the chapter. Many utilize common application software to illustrate the topics.
- **Additional Reading.** References for more detailed investigation of the topics.
- **Web Site References.** Web sites that provide discussions or links to useful topics.
- **Industry-Specific Cases.** In-depth discussion of the lead case and several other companies. Each chapter highlights a specific industry and compares different approaches to the problems faced by the firms.

Chapter	Case Focus: Industry
1	Fast Food
2	Computer Hardware
3	Wholesale Trade
4	Pharmaceutical Industry
5	Professional Sports
6	Retail Sales
7	Automobiles
8	Entrepreneurial Business
9	Package Delivery
10	Financial Services
11	Airlines
12	Government Agencies
13	Energy
14	Health Care

Goals and Philosophy

- All of the chapters emphasize the goal of understanding how information technology can be used to improve management. The focus is on understanding the benefits and costs of technology and its application.
- Emphasis is on the importance of database management systems. Increasingly, managers need to retrieve data and utilize a DBMS to investigate, analyze, and communicate.
- Emphasis is also placed on the importance of communication, teamwork, collaboration, and integration of data. Understanding information technology requires more than knowledge of basic application packages. Students need to use and understand the applications of groupware technologies.
- In-depth cases illustrate the use of technology. By focusing each chapter on a specific industry, students can understand and evaluate a variety of approaches. Many cases illustrate companies varying over time, so students can see the changes occurring in business and understand the evolving role and importance of information technology.

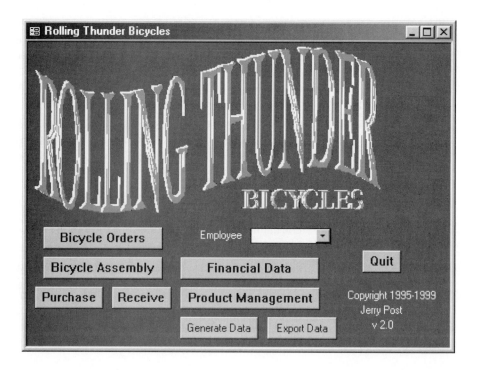

- The Rolling Thunder Database, a medium-size, detailed database application of a small business, is available on disk. Specific exercises are highlighted in each chapter. The database contains data and applications suitable for operating a small (fictional) firm. It also contains data generation routines so that instructors can create their own scenarios.

This Book Is Different from Other Texts

First, this book is a business text designed for an upper division or M.B.A. course, so it does not have the hundreds of step-by-step instructions to show students how to use a particular piece of software. It addresses the more difficult question of how to use information technology to solve business problems. Consequently, this text focuses on business issues first.

Second, this book is not simply a dictionary or encyclopedia that defines technology terms in one or two sentences. Students need to understand the various technology tools and see how they actually solve business problems. This book uses detailed cases to show the business problems and the technological solutions to illustrate each chapter. It also contains in-depth explanations of various technology issues, showing their strengths and weaknesses. Where possible, these tools are also demonstrated with hands-on applications, through the accompanying databases and through the Technology Toolboxes.

Learning Objectives

After finishing the book, students should be able to evaluate common business problems and identify information technology solutions that could help an organization. Students should be able to explain their choices and point out potential problems or issues.

Anyone who teaches this material knows that this learning objective is difficult to meet—because of the huge number of possible issues and the flexibility required in analyzing problems. To meet the objective, smaller and more concrete goals are presented in each chapter. Each of these is spelled out as a series of questions at the start of the chapter. By the end of each chapter, students should be able to provide intelligent answers to the various questions.

The book provides several tools to achieve its objectives. The industry cases and Reality Bytes show business problems and how organizations have attacked them. The body of the text explains the problems in more detail and focuses on the strengths and weaknesses of the various tools used to solve similar problems. The Technology Toolboxes and chapter exercises show students how to apply the tools and concepts to solve problems.

Changes to the Fourth Edition

1. **Focus on Business Problems.** MIS is a business class, so students need to begin with the business perspective and then see how technology can solve the problems. The chapters emphasize this focus by beginning with a series of questions. Specific, real-world cases highlight aspects of these problems so that students see the problems in context. The chapter then addresses the questions and demonstrates how technology can be used to solve the problems. Each chapter begins with a set of questions that will be addressed—providing students with a direct learning objective. The questions also serve to increase student curiosity, by raising issues that they are not likely to have considered before. Several chapters have been restructured and the overall book has been reorganized to emphasize the business focus.

2. **Technology Toolboxes.** Hands-on demonstrations have been integrated into the chapters in the Technology Toolbox examples. The exercises briefly show how to use information technology tools to solve specific problems. The examples are kept small so that students can work on them in a short lab, or instructors can demonstrate them as part of a class. Some of the toolboxes have more detailed explanations in e-book appendixes on the Student CD.

Chapter	Appendix
1	Finding Information on the Internet
	Choosing a Search Engine
2	Voice Input
	Creating Effective Charts
3	Creating Web Pages
	Transferring Files on the Internet
4	Building Forms in Access
	Creating Database Reports
5	Encrypting e-Mail
	Assigning Security Permissions
6	Paying for Transactions
	Handling EDI Transactions
7	Selecting an ERP System
	Designing an Executive Information System
8	Using Commerce Server Software
	Choosing Web Server Technologies
9	Meeting Online with NetMeeting
	Collaborating with SharePoint
10	Browsing Data with a Pivot Table
	Forecasting a Trend
11	Locating Customers with a GIS
	Creating a Business Plan
12	Analyzing Businesses
	Programming a New Function in Excel
13	Defining e-Mail Rules
	Managing Projects
14	Working in a Global Environment
	Navigating e-Government

3. **Collaboration and Teamwork.** Some of the biggest changes in software and technology in the last few years have been designed to improve collaboration and teamwork. It is critical that managers be able to use these tools, and they are not taught in typical

introductory tools courses. This text covers these tools in Chapter 9 and uses Technology Toolboxes to demonstrate the basic features. In addition, each chapter contains teamwork exercises designed for collaboration by a group of students. Ideally, students would be able to use the collaboration tools while participating in these exercises.

4. **New Cases and Reality Bytes.** All of the chapter cases and most of the Reality Bytes examples have been replaced or rewritten. The book contains over 100 new Reality Bytes cases. The cases have a tighter focus and are tied to the specific problems in each chapter.

Organization of the Text

The text is organized into four sections to explore answers to the question of how information technology can improve management.

- Part One. Information Technology Infrastructure
- Part Two. Operations
- Part Three. Tactics and Strategies.
- Part Four. Organizing Businesses and Systems

The organization of the text is based on two features. First, each chapter emphasizes the goal of the text: applying information technology to improve management and organizations. Second, the text is organized so that it begins with concepts familiar to the students and builds on them.

Each chapter is organized in a common format: (1) the introduction ties to the goal and raises questions specific to that chapter, (2) the main discussion emphasizes the application of technology and the strengths and weaknesses of various approaches, and (3) the application of technology in various real-world organizations is presented in the end-of-chapter cases.

Organization	
Chapter 1:	Introduction
Part One:	Information Technology Infrastructure
Chapter 2:	Information Technology Foundations
Chapter 3:	Networks and Telecommunications
Chapter 4:	Database Management
Part Two:	Operations
Chapter 5:	Computer Security
Chapter 6:	Transactions and Operations
Chapter 7:	Enterprise Integration
Chapter 8:	Electronic Business
Part Three:	Tactics and Strategies
Chapter 9:	Teamwork
Chapter 10:	Business Decisions
Chapter 11:	Strategic Analysis
Part Four:	Organizing Businesses and Systems
Chapter 12:	Systems Development
Chapter 13:	Organizing MIS Resources
Chapter 14:	Information Management and Society

Chapter 1 (Introduction) remains an introduction to MIS and provides an explanation of the goals—emphasizing the text's focus on how technology can help managers perform their jobs and improve the companies they manage.

Chapter 2 (Information Technology Foundations) reviews the basic issues in personal productivity and hardware and software. It emphasizes recent issues such as the growing importance of wireless devices. It also discusses issues in choosing computers used in e-business such as the importance of scalability in servers.

Chapter 3 (Networks and Telecommunications) explains the role of networks in managing businesses. It also explains the foundations of the Internet, so students can understand how problems can arise on the Internet and why certain technologies have evolved to solve them.

Chapter 4 (Database Management) explains the importance of database systems in business. The focus remains on managers' roles and uses of databases, such as querying databases and building reports.

Chapter 5 (Computer Security) focuses on the business problems and threats. It explains the various tools and the fact that business managers are critical in helping maintain computer security.

Chapter 6 (Transactions and Operations) raises the main issues in operations and transaction processing, particularly payment mechanisms. In addition to the traditional issues, it focuses on transaction elements and data quality.

Chapter 7 (Enterprise Integration) is a complete chapter on ERP systems. It includes the role of accounting and HRM systems as well as supply chain management and customer relationship management. The goal is to show managers how the systems are used to solve common business problems.

Chapter 8 (Electronic Business) describes the various ways that companies can use the Internet to extend their businesses. It includes traditional e-commerce applications, as well as Web services and mobile commerce.

Chapter 9 (Teamwork) explains the increasing importance of teamwork and collaboration tools. Managers need these tools in almost any business, and almost no other textbooks even talk about them. Here, an entire chapter explains the problems that need to be solved and shows how the various tools support communication, collaboration, and knowledge management.

Chapter 10 (Business Decisions) begins with the basic importance of using analytical tools to make decisions. It then explains how basic tools help managers evaluate data, from decision support systems to data mining. Expert systems are introduced to show how computers can make more advanced decisions. Specialized tools and topics in artificial intelligence research are used to show how more intelligent software can solve even relatively complex problems.

Chapter 11 (Strategic Analysis) explores in detail how information systems are used to support the functional business areas to help gain a competitive advantage. The chapter also explores how IT helps entrepreneurs create new businesses.

Chapter 12 (Systems Development) looks at systems design and various development alternatives. It examines the challenges faced in developing software and the continuing movement to commercial off-the-shelf software.

Chapter 13 (Organizing MIS Resources) looks at the issues involved in the organization and management of MIS resources. In examining MIS roles, it also presents job opportunities. The chapter discusses how wireless, intranets, and Web services are having important effects on the structure and management of IT resources.

Chapter 14 (Information Management and Society) is an expanded discussion of the impact of IT on society—particularly the effects of the Internet. It investigates the issue of privacy versus business, social, and governmental needs. It examines the potential changes in a global society that is increasingly linked online.

The Support Package

No text is complete without a well-rounded and value-added support package. Our support package is designed to ease your teaching burden by providing you with a Web site full of valuable information, as well as an Instructor's Resource CD-ROM that includes a test bank and easy-to-use test generating software, an Instructor's Manual complete with teaching tips and answers for end-of-chapter material, application databases, and PowerPoint presentations.

Online Learning Center at www.mhhe.com/post

As in previous editions, the Web site for the fourth edition contains a wealth of valuable information and supplements for both the instructor and the student. The Online Learning Center (OLC) builds on the book's pedagogy and features with self-assessment quizzes, the glossary, and a collection of useful Web links.

Instructor's Resource CD-ROM

The Instructor's Resource CD-ROM is available to adopters and offers the following resources for course presentation and management.

Instructor's Manual

The Instructor's Manual includes answers to all end-of-chapter review questions and exercises, as well as teaching notes for the industry-specific cases. Teaching notes and ties to the PowerPoint slides are also included for each chapter.

Test Bank

The test bank contains a variety of challenging and accurate true/false, multiple choice, and fill-in-the-blank questions. The included computerized testing software is fully networkable for LAN test administration, but tests can also be printed for standard paper delivery or posted to a Web site for student access.

PowerPoint Presentations

The PowerPoint presentations are ready for you to use in class. Lecture notes and overheads are available as slide shows in Microsoft PowerPoint format. The slides are organized by chapter and can be rearranged to suit individual preferences.

Rolling Thunder and Other Databases

Several databases and exercises are available on disk. The instructor can add new data, modify the exercises, or use them to expand on the discussion in the text.

The Rolling Thunder database application is available in Microsoft Access format. It is a self-contained application that illustrates many of the MIS concepts presented in the text, and it enables students to examine any facet of operating a small company. The Instructor's Manual includes further guidance on how to incorporate this innovative tool into your course.

McGraw-Hill Irwin Supplements

Problem Solving Video Vignettes

Three separate segments show how a growing beverage company comes to terms with problems and opportunities that can be addressed with database systems, telecommunications technology, and system development. Use the questions that follow each segment to inspire discussion or test students' critical thinking skills.

MIS Case Videos

Additional videos demonstrate analysis, design, implementation, and maintenance of information systems, and business process reengineering. It is available to adopters at no extra cost. See your McGraw-Hill Irwin sales representative for details.

MBA MIS Cases

Developed by Richard Perle of Loyola Marymount University, these 14 comprehensive cases allow you to add MBA-level analysis to your course. Find out more at www.mhhe.com/primis.

Application Cases for MIS

Looking for a more substantial hands-on component? The Fifth Edition of Application Cases in MIS (ISBN 0072933631) by James Morgan is the proven answer.

MISource

MISource uses a three-pronged approach—*Teach Me, Show Me,* and *Let Me Try*—to provide students with the core skills and understanding of important computer concepts for the Microsoft Excel, Access and PowerPoint programs. Consequently, you spend less time reviewing fundamental software skills. The MISource CD also includes the three aforementioned beverage company video vignettes and accompanying questions.

Online Courses

Content for the Fourth Edition is available in webCT, Blackboard, and PageOut formats to accommodate virtually any online delivery platform.

Packaging Options

McGraw-Hill Irwin has a huge selection of IT products that can be packaged with this text to meet the needs of your course—three different application software series of manuals and CDs on the Microsoft Office suite, Internet Explorer and Netscape products, programming languages, and Internet literacy. For more about our discount options, contact your local McGraw-Hill sales representative or visit our Web site at www.mhhe.com.

Acknowledgments

Like any large project, producing a book is a team effort. In developing this book, we have had the privilege of working with dedicated professionals. The contributions of many people have resulted in an improved book and have made the process enjoyable.

First, we thank our students over the years, who encouraged us to explore new technologies and to focus on how IT can benefit students, managers, and organizations. Second, we are indebted to the reviewers listed below, who offered many improvements and suggestions. Their ideas and direction substantially improved the book.

Robert Chi
California State University—Long Beach

Dr. Les Pang
University of Maryland

Syama Chaudhuri
University of Maryland, University College

Weiqi Li
University of Michigan—Flint

Kenneth Rowe
Purdue University

Dr. Peggy M. Beranek
University of Colorado, Colorado Springs

Henry Waldron
Rutgers University

G. Shankar
Boston University

Rex Karsten
University of Northern Iowa

Karen Williams
University of Texas at San Antonio

Dr. Warren L. Dickson
University of Central Oklahoma

Roy Dejoie
Purdue University—West Lafayette

Dr. Dorothy G. Dologite
Baruch College, City University of New York

Dr. Dennis L. Williams
California Polytechnic State University, San Luis Obispo

Spera Georgiou
De Anza College

Floyd Ploeger
Texas State University—San Marcos

Finally, this text has been substantially improved through the dedication and professionalism of the editors and staff at McGraw-Hill Irwin. It is a pleasure to work with people like Paul Ducham, Marlena Pechan, and Liz Farina, whose guidance, support, ideas, and answers to innumerable questions were invaluable to the project.

Management Information Systems

CHAPTER ONE

Introduction

Chapter Outline

Introduction

What Is MIS?

The Importance of Information Technology

   Productivity

   Teamwork and Communication

   Business Operations and Strategy

The Role of the Internet in Business

So You Want to Be a Manager

   Traditional Management and Observations

   Making Decisions

Business and Technology Trends

   Specialization

   Management by Methodology and Franchises

   Merger Mania

   Decentralization and Small Business

   Temporary Workers

   Internationalization

   Service-Oriented Business

Reengineering: Altering the Rules

Management and Decision Levels

   Operations

   Tactics

   Strategy

An Introduction to Strategy

   Searching for Ideas

   Strategy Example: Baxter Healthcare

Summary

Key Words

Web Site References

Additional Reading

Review Questions

Exercises

Cases: The Fast-Food Industry

What You Will Learn in This Chapter

- How can MIS help you in your job?
- What is MIS?
- Why is information technology important? Why do all business majors need to study it?
- What are e-commerce and e-business? Is e-business increasing or decreasing?
- Do you know what a manager does? Do you know what a successful manager will do in the future?
- How is business changing? What will managers need to know in the future?
- Does technology alone improve a business?
- How do you break businesses into smaller pieces to analyze them?
- Why are strategic decisions so difficult?
- How do you begin searching for competitive advantage?

What do customers want? McDonald's Corporation has sold billions of hamburgers. Beginning in 1955 with a single drive-in in Des Plaines, Illinois, McDonald's has grown to today's system of more than 25,000 restaurants across 115 countries. As a brand, McDonald's is synonymous with a quality product at a reasonable price. Equally important, McDonald's markets itself as more than a place to get a hamburger. Ronald McDonald, Happy Meals, the clean restaurants, and each new product or promotional theme add to the fun that brings more than 40 million customers of all ages to its restaurants around the world each day.

Eighty percent of worldwide McDonald's are franchised. Each restaurant must meet strict requirements to make it the same as all others. This ensures that each time you drive or walk into a McDonald's, no matter where you are, the Big Mac that you order will always be the same taste, size, weight, and quality. It will also be competitively priced.

Legal contracts, quality standards, and performance specifications direct the individual restaurants in the effort to keep all the food orders the same. What most individuals do not think about when they walk or drive into McDonald's is that McDonald's management information system (MIS) plays a critical role in ensuring the quality and consistency of each sandwich. McDonald's Corporation maintains a strict requirement that food be fresh and not stored more than a limited amount of time. MIS applications direct managers in the management of employees and the ordering and tracking of hamburgers, buns, potatoes, and soft drinks.

Competition is fierce in the fast-food industry. The top chains have been struggling over the last several years to find a way to attract new customers. McDonald's experimented with changing menus. It altered its in-store system to focus on the "Made for You" campaign. Concerns about healthy food have led the company to try new foods and new ways of cooking. Following in the footsteps of Starbucks, McDonald's is offering wireless Internet access to customers for a fee. But is that what McDonald's customers really want? Will you go to McDonald's, pay money for a connection to the Internet, and then hang around to buy more food?

Introduction

How can MIS help you in your job? This is the ultimate question that you must continually ask and answer as you pursue a management career. This book explores many variations of this question and some useful answers. Of course, at the start of the class, you are probably also wondering why you need to study technology. This first chapter shows you that managers cannot survive today without technology. As computers and software become more powerful and take over an increasing number of jobs, you need to be the manager who knows how to use the technology to move the company forward. You do not want to be the manager who is replaced by the technology.

Almost all companies, including fast-food restaurants, rely on information technology. Managers need information to run the day-to-day operations, to improve the operations, and ultimately to gain a competitive advantage. In the fast-food setting, how do you know what your customers want? You need data to evaluate trends, predict responses, and plan ahead.

Welcome to the information age. Going shopping? As a consumer, you have instant access to millions of pieces of data. With a few clicks of the mouse button, you can find anything from current stock prices to video clips of current movies. You can get product descriptions, pictures, and prices from thousands of companies across the United States and around the world. Trying to sell services and products? You can purchase demographic, economic, consumer-buying-pattern, and market-analysis data. Your firm will have internal financial, marketing, production, and employee data for past years. This tremendous amount of data provides opportunities to managers and consumers who know how to obtain it and analyze it to make better decisions.

TRENDS

Economies, businesses, people, and societies all change over time. A century ago, people were farmers and laborers. Most businesses were small. Technologies changed and people moved to cities and manufacturing jobs. Technology changed again, and the importance of the service sector grew. Although digital computers were invented in the early 1940s, it was not until the 1960s and 1970s that they became affordable for most businesses. At first, most companies used information technology to solve easy problems such as transaction processing. Before computers, companies needed hundreds of bookkeepers in the back office tracking sales, updating ledgers, and summarizing data by hand. As hardware prices dropped in the 1980s and 1990s, businesses integrated personal computers into management. Networks—and today, the Internet—made it easier to share data and communicate. Information technology not only changes jobs but also changes the way companies are organized. If you want a job in business, you need to know how to use these technologies to become a better manager and to improve the business. Remember that technology can perform amazing tasks. Businesses no longer need people to perform many of the menial middle-management tasks. Instead, businesses need managers who can think, adapt, and creatively find new solutions.

There is no question that the use of computers in business is increasing. Walk into your local bank, grocery store, or fast-food restaurant and you will see that the operations depend on computers. Go into management offices and you will find computers used to analyze marketing alternatives, make financial decisions, and coordinate team members around the world. Watch people walking around in any city and half of them will be talking on cell phones. Wireless devices are spreading into our work lives—both voice and Internet services. As a manager, how can you use these technologies to improve your business, increase sales, and gain an edge on your competitors? Because technology changes rapidly, how do you know what tools to buy? Is it worth the money and risk to buy the latest technology? Can you rebuild your company to use the technologies? Should you rebuild your company? What do the customers want and how will they respond to technology? These are questions that managers face every day. The questions are challenging and the answers are hard to find. This book lays out a framework for analyzing your business problems and evaluating technology solutions.

What Is MIS?

What is MIS? The first step in learning how to apply information technology to solve problems is to get a broader picture of what is meant by the term *management information system.* You probably have some experience with using computers and various software packages. Yet computers are only one component of a management information system. A **management information system (MIS),** or *computer information system (CIS),* consists of five related components: hardware, software, people, procedures, and collections of data. The term **information technology (IT)** represents the various types of hardware and software used in an information system, including computers and networking equipment. The goal of MIS is to enable managers to make better decisions by providing quality information.

The physical equipment used in computing is called **hardware.** The set of instructions that controls the hardware is known as **software.** In the early days of computers, the **people** directly involved in MIS tended to be programmers, design analysts, and a few external users. Today, almost everyone in the firm is involved with the information system. **Procedures** are instructions that help people use the systems. They include items such as user manuals, documentation, and procedures to ensure that backups are made regularly. **Databases** are collections of related data that can be retrieved easily and processed by the computers. As you will see in the cases throughout the book, all of these components are vital to creating an effective information system.

So what is information? One way to answer that question is to examine the use of information technology on three levels: (1) data management, (2) information systems, and (3) knowledge bases. **Data** consists of factual elements (or opinions or comments) that de-

REALITY BYTES   Data, Information, Knowledge, and Wisdom

Consider the case of a retail store that is trying to increase sales. Some of the data available includes sales levels for the last 36 months, advertising expenses, and customer comments from surveys.

By itself, this data may be interesting, but it must be organized and analyzed to be useful in making a decision. For example, a manager might use economic and marketing models to forecast patterns and determine relationships among various advertising expenses and sales. The resulting information (presented in equations, charts, and tables) would clarify relationships among the data and would be used to decide how to proceed.

It requires knowledge to determine how to analyze data and make decisions. Education and experience create knowledge in humans. A manager learns which data to collect, the proper models to apply, and ways to analyze results for making better decisions. In some cases, this knowledge can be transferred to specialized computer programs (expert systems).

Wisdom is more difficult to define, but it refers to the ability to learn from experience and adapt to changing conditions. In this example, wisdom would enable a manager to spot trends, identify potential problems, and develop new techniques to analyze the data.

scribe some object or event. Data can be thought of as raw numbers or text. Data management systems focus on data collection and providing basic reports. **Information** represents data that has been processed, organized, and integrated to provide insight. Information systems are designed to help managers analyze data and make decisions. From a decision maker's standpoint, the challenge is that you might not know ahead of time which information you need, so it is hard to determine what data you need to collect. **Knowledge** represents a higher level of understanding, including rules, patterns, and decisions. Knowledge-based systems are built to automatically analyze data, identify patterns, and recommend decisions. Humans are also capable of **wisdom,** where they put knowledge, experience, and analytical skills to work to create new knowledge and adapt to changing situations. To date no computer system has attained the properties of wisdom.

To create an effective information system, you need to do more than simply purchase the various components. Quality is an important issue in business today, particularly as it relates to information systems. The quality of an information system is measured by its ability to provide exactly the information needed by managers in a timely manner. The information must be accurate and up-to-date. Users should be able to receive the information in a variety of formats: tables of data, graphs, summary statistics, or even pictures or sound. Users have different perspectives and different requirements, and a good information system must have the flexibility to present information in diverse forms for each user.

The Importance of Information Technology

Why is information technology important? Why do all business majors need to study it? Productivity is the bottom-line issue in information technology. Workers are expensive, difficult to manage, and hard to remove. Information technology continues to decline in price with increased power and capabilities. Programmers are more creative, and new tools are being developed to solve more complex problems. Organizations that use information technology to reduce costs and provide better service can thrive. If you want a job in management, you must learn to use the technologies. But it is not as simple as knowing how to use a spreadsheet and a word processor. You have to understand how businesses work and determine how technology can be used to improve the business.

Productivity

An enormous amount of data is available to managers—generated internally and externally. It is impossible to deal with this volume of data without information technology. The era of "pure" managers who simply direct other people is gone. Managers today must be capable of performing the tasks within their area of expertise. For example, accounting managers still practice accounting, lawyers handle cases, and financial managers still track investments. In

Problem: How do you find information on the Internet? The Internet is huge and getting bigger. It contains an enormous number of pages. Content is provided by millions of organizations—each using different formats and terms.

Tools: Internet search engines were created specifically to crawl the Web and capture key words from the billions of pages they find.

> General purpose search engines
>> Google, Vivisimo, MSN, Lycos, Altavista
>
> Human supervised category searches
>> Yahoo, Looksmart
>
> Meta-searches across multiple engines
>> Webcrawler, Dogpile
>
> Encyclopedia
>> Wikipedia.org
>
> Dictionary
>> Bartleby
>
> Phone book
>> Switchboard, Superpages
>
> Products
>> Mysimon, Cnet
>
> Government data
>> CIA.gov (World Factbook)
>>
>> Fedstats.gov (main data source)
>>
>> SEC.gov (EDGAR corporate filings)
>
> Other (and often better)
>> Your library databases

Choosing the right starting point can be critical to a successful search. Obtaining the most number of hits is not as important as a site that returns accurate results. The main search companies constantly refine their methods to improve the accuracy. Remember the following hints when you are searching:

1. Google is currently the most popular search site and often returns the most hits.

2. Vivisimo is a new system that organizes the results into categories.

3. Yahoo and Looksmart contain sections that are categorized by humans. If you have only a vague idea of your search topic, start with the categories.

4. Sometimes it is best to search an encyclopedia (wikipedia.org), dictionary (bartleby.com), a phone book (switchboard.com), the CIA World Factbook (www.cia.gov/cia/publications/factbook), or government statistics (fedstats.gov).

5. Many sites are not indexed by the search engines. For example, searching for products often requires specialized search engines (mysimon.com or cnet.com) that scan the databases of various online stores.

6. Check specialist magazine sites for targeted information. For example, use fortune.com to find information on the largest companies.

7. The most accurate sources are not free. University libraries provide access to huge commercial databases.

Quick Quiz: Where would you begin your search to answer the following questions?

1. How many Internet users are there in Tanzania?

2. How much revenue did Heinz earn last year?

3. What is the lowest price on a 21-inch LCD monitor?

4. Where are the best surfing beaches in Hawaii?

5. How many students applied to your school last year?

6. Which movie won the Oscar for best picture last year?

other words, managers do two jobs: perform basic day-to-day functions, as well as plan, organize, and communicate.

Firms are increasingly required to improve productivity, which means that each year managers must increase production without increasing the number of workers. Information technology is critical to this improvement process, enabling employees to perform more tasks, getting work done faster at a lower cost. Figure 1.1 shows the productivity index from the Bureau of Labor Statistics. Workers at the end of 2003 produced 14 percent more than they did at the start of 2000, and 31 percent more than they did 10 years earlier. As a manager, it is critical that you understand two implications of this trend. First, you have to use information technology to stay competitive. Today, computers are almost always cheaper than people. Second, at the current productivity rate of about 5 percent per year, the productivity index would double in 14 years, which means that in a little over a decade, a firm could produce the same output with half the number of workers. What happens to the other half of the workers? Chapter 14 addresses the economic issue in more detail, but you are going to be better off if you are one of the workers who understands and uses the technology.

Teamwork and Communication

Teamwork is a key element in business. Teamwork means that tasks are divided among team members. You are responsible for completing specific items. You are also responsible for helping the other members of the team to find the best solution to the problems. Teamwork requires cooperation, but with technology, it no longer means that the teams have to work

FIGURE 1.1

Productivity is an index of the amount of work per employee. There is a 31 percent increase in output over the decade shown, with almost half of that (14 percent) in the last four years.

Source: http://www.bls.gov/news.release/prod2.t02.htm.

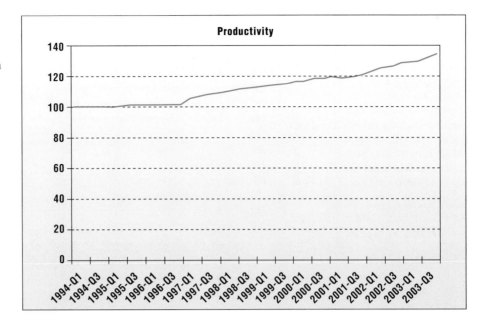

in the same room. Your team members may participate from around the world. Even if everyone is in the same room, you need technology to organize and share the contributions.

At a minimum, you already know how to use a word processor and a spreadsheet to write reports and analyze data. Do you know what changes have been made to these tools in the last few versions? The most important changes have been support for collaboration tools that make it easier to share documents and work as teams. Working on a team is difficult. Not only do you have to produce your own work, but you also have to communicate closely with the group to see what problems and answers they have encountered and determine how to integrate all of the pieces. Chapter 9 explores these problems and examines some of the tools available to help you.

Business Operations and Strategy

Information technology is increasingly critical to the daily operations of a business. Obviously, online businesses cannot live without technology, but neither can the local grocery store, bank, or many other businesses. Computers process sales, handle payments, and place new orders. They also analyze the sales data and help set prices and predict trends. Information technology is also used to create new products and services or to provide unique features to existing products. These new features can give your company a strategic advantage and help the company grow.

The Role of the Internet in Business

What are e-commerce and e-business? Is e-business increasing or decreasing? Electronic commerce, or **e-commerce (EC),** denotes the selling of products over the Internet. These sales can be from a business to consumers **(B2C)** or from one business to another **(B2B).** For a while in 1999, some people believed that e-commerce would become the dominant form of business—where everyone bought all items over the Internet. Thousands of firms and Web sites were created, trying to become the dominant firm in some niche. The group was called **dot-coms** because almost all had an Internet address of something.com. Many of the firms received huge amounts of funding from venture capitalists and experienced surprisingly high prices for their stock. Some foolish people predicted a new economic world. But beginning in mid-2000, thousands of these firms failed. Most had enormous expenses and huge losses. Many had been taking losses on every item they sold. And foolish people predicted the end of e-commerce.

FIGURE 1.2

Retail and B2C e-commerce data in the United States. Although e-commerce sales are only 1.5 percent of the total, the percentage has been steadily increasing—despite the crash of the dot-coms in 2000 and 2001. Notice the seasonal peak in the fourth quarter—as more people go online to purchase holiday gifts.

Source: http://www.census.gov/mrts/www/current.html.

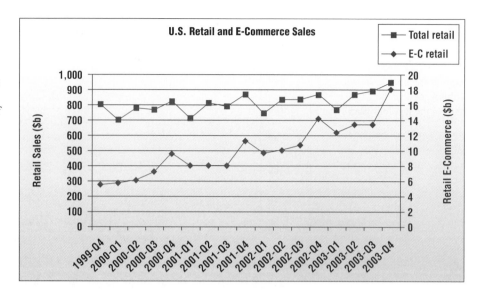

E-business is a more general term that encompasses e-commerce but also includes using the Internet for other business tasks, such as teamwork, communication, and new business services. As Internet technologies improve, more firms are offering e-business services—such as digital maps, remote data backup, and supply chain management.

Despite the crash of the dot-coms, it is important to remember that e-commerce and e-business are increasingly valuable tools for more traditional firms. For example, when the Webvan grocery delivery company failed, a traditional giant grocery and drug retailer (Albertson's) picked up many of the customers with its online service. Figure 1.2 shows the continued growth, and e-commerce and e-business have a large role to play in the future of many companies. As with any technology, you must strive to find profitable solutions. Chapter 8 discusses e-commerce and e-business in more detail.

So You Want to Be a Manager

Do you know what a manager does? Do you know what a successful manager will do in the future? Answer: The good ones work their tails off. But what exactly does a manager do? Managers actually have many tasks, and the roles depend on the culture of the organization, the style of top managers, and the skills of the individual manager.

Traditional Management and Observations

If you think of a traditional manager, you would consider tasks such as organizing work, planning jobs, and controlling workers. ("Joe, go peel those potatoes.") However, when observed at their jobs, managers appear to spend most of their time in meetings, talking on the phone, reading or preparing reports, discussing projects with their colleagues, explaining procedures, and participating in other activities that are difficult to fit into the traditional framework.

Henry Mintzberg, a psychologist who studies management, classifies managerial tasks into three categories: (1) interpersonal, (2) informational, and (3) decisional. Interpersonal roles refer to teaching and leading employees. Informational tasks are based on the transfer of information throughout the organization, such as relaying information to subordinates or summarizing information for executives. Decisions involve collecting information, evaluating alternatives, and choosing directions that benefit the firm.

Other researchers have studied managers and developed alternative classifications. Fred Luthans uses three classifications of management activities. He indicates that approxi-

REALITY BYTES   Improving Searches

Most people are familiar with the search process on Google and the other search engines. Google scans pages on the Internet and builds a giant index. Using a variety of approaches, it assigns weights to the various pages that are indexed. For example, pages that are pointed to by multiple sources are considered better matches. But many people continue to have difficulty finding information on the Internet. In fact, many people have trouble finding information on their own computers. Search engines, such as Google, can return thousands of pages, and it is up to the user to figure out which ones are truly relevant.

Some companies are offering new features. For example, Vivisimo (vivisimo.com) provides software that organizes and sorts the results of a search. Vivisimo's technology is used by intelligence agencies to organize data and can be purchased for use within your own company. Raul Valdes-Perez, cofounder of Vivisimo, Inc., notes that "we enliven the otherwise deadening process of searching for information." He compares the search process to a giant library. The

search engine returns hundreds of books and throws them in a pile on the floor. Vivisimo acts as a librarian and instantly categories the results so you can see which sites are related. The categories are built on the fly to match the contents of the documents.

Another company, Grokker, not only creates the categories but also creates a graphical depiction of the results. The main documents are shown as connected circles. Subcategories appear as smaller circles. You can click on each circle to zoom in and see the detail. Grokker (from Groxis, Inc.) is not a search engine but an add-on that provides the additional analysis. It can also be used to organize and sort files on your hard drive. The CEO, R. J. Pittman, notes that "search has to evolve. It can't just be Google sitting there with a stash of places they've crawled on the Web. People are becoming more astute and demanding better results, and they're demanding a more powerful search experience."

Source: Adapted from "Better Search Results Than Google?" CNN.com, January 5, 2004.

mately 50 percent of a manager's time is spent on traditional management activities (planning, organizing, and controlling), 30 percent in formal communications, and 20 percent in informal networking. Formal communications include attending meetings and creating reports and memos. Informal networking consists of contacts with colleagues and workers that tend to be social in nature but often involve discussions regarding business and jobs.

Making Decisions

In many ways managers expend a lot of their effort in making decisions or contributing information so others can make decisions. When you look at courses offered for future managers, you will find a focus on administration, human behavior, quantitative modeling and problem solving, decision theory, and elements of business ethics and globalization. Typically, these courses are designed to help managers solve problems and make decisions. However, if you ask managers how much time they spend making decisions, they are likely to say that they seldom make decisions. That seems like a contradiction. If managers and executives do not make decisions, who does?

In many organizations, day-to-day decisions are embodied in the methodology, rules, or philosophy of the company. Managers are encouraged to collect data and follow the decisions that have resulted from experience. The managers are directly involved in the decision process, even though they may not think they are making the final choice.

The broader **decision process** involves collecting data, identifying problems, and making choices. Making a decision also requires persuading others to accept the decision and implement a solution. With this broader definition, many of the tasks performed by managers are actually steps in the decision process. Meetings, phone calls, and discussions with colleagues are used to collect data, identify problems, and persuade others to choose a course of action. Each of these steps may be so gradual that the participants do not think they are actually making decisions.

Because of the subtlety of the process and the complexity of the decisions, it is often difficult to determine what information will be needed. Decisions often require creativity. Because data generally need to be collected *before* problems arise, it is challenging to design information systems to support managers and benefit the organization. One important job of management is to examine the need for information and how it can be used to solve future problems.

Business and Technology Trends

How is business changing? What will managers need to know in the future? A key issue in management is that you must always work in the future. If you spend all of your time running around trying to solve today's problems by putting out fires, you will never succeed. You must plan for tomorrow and build the structure and processes to handle the day-to-day tasks.

Even without the Internet, management and companies are changing. The most important change is the move away from the traditional hierarchical structure to a team-based approach. Most of today's large companies developed years ago when communications were limited and there were no computers. Most adopted a military-inspired hierarchical command structure illustrated in Figure 1.3. The top-level managers set policy and directed the vice presidents to carry out the mission of the company. Sales staff dealt directly with customers, collected data, and passed it to middle managers. The middle managers organized and summarized the data and passed it up the chain. Little data was shared among the middle and lower levels.

In contrast, because information technology makes it easy to share data, it offers the ability to alter the way companies are organized and managed. Figure 1.4 shows the new approach. This method focuses on teamwork and a shared knowledge of all relevant data. Some teams, like sales and accounting, will have ongoing tasks. Other task forces will be formed to solve new problems—often created from managers across the company. Managers can expect to participate in many teams, essentially at the same time. Data can be obtained and shared through the information system, meetings can be held online, and documents and comments can be circulated electronically.

This structure enables companies to be run with a smaller number of managers. Each manager is more productive because of the tools and the ability to perform many jobs. Another strength of this approach is that it is easy to use consultants and temporary workers for short-term projects. In today's legal climate, it is exceedingly difficult to fire workers, so firms often use temporary workers for individual projects. Permanent workers, supple-

FIGURE 1.3

In a traditional organizational structure, lower-level managers deal with customers and collect basic data. Middle-level managers analyze the data, create reports, and make suggestions to upper-level managers. The higher-level managers make decisions and set rules to guide the other managers.

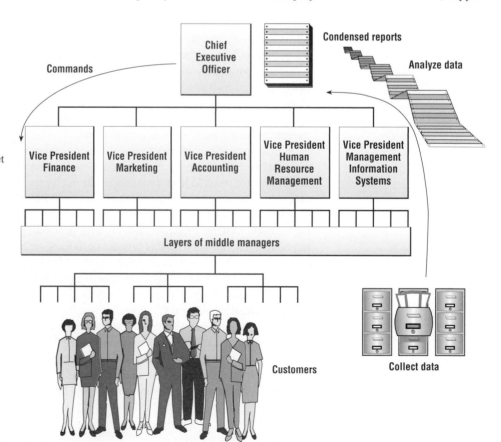

FIGURE 1.4

In the last few years, many companies have moved toward a more decentralized form of management. They have removed the middle layers of management and replaced them with smaller teams. Franchises and smaller teams have become the primary service contact with customers. Information sharing becomes crucial in this environment. Teams communicate directly and share data across the company.

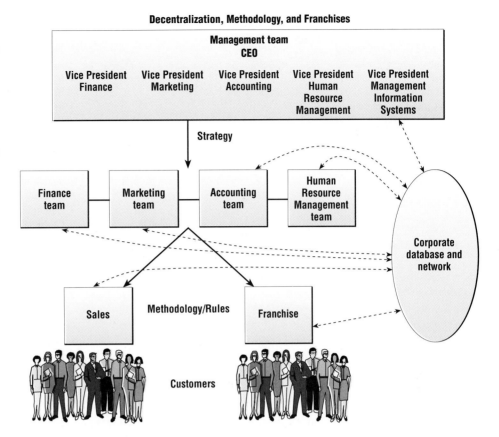

mented with specialized temporary talent, can organize a team. The team disbands when the project is finished.

As described in Figure 1.5, seven fundamental trends have been driving the economy and changing businesses: (1) specialization, (2) management by methodology, (3) mergers, (4) decentralization and small business, (5) reliance on temporary workers, (6) internationalization, and (7) the increasing importance of service-oriented businesses. These trends will be discussed throughout the text to illustrate how they affect the use of information systems and how managers can use information systems to take advantage of these trends. Tightening job markets also means that managers must continually work on self-improvement. To survive, you must provide value to the organization.

Specialization

Adam Smith described the advantages of specialization and division of labor in manufacturing more than 200 years ago. These concepts are now being applied to managers. As functional areas (such as marketing or finance) become more complex, they also become more specialized. Area managers are expected to understand and use increasingly sophisticated models and tools to analyze events and make decisions. As a result, the demand for managers with specific technical skills is increasing, while the demand for general business managers is declining. First you get a job as an accountant (or whatever your specialty is), then you become a manager. This trend is reflected in MIS by the large number of specialized tools being created and the increased communication demands for sharing information among the specialists.

Management by Methodology and Franchises

Specialization's advantage is that it reduces management tasks to smaller problems. Using specialization coupled with technology, firms have reduced many management problems to a set of rules or standard operating procedures. Day-to-day problems can be addressed with a standard methodology. For example, the manager's guidebook at Wal-Mart or at Mrs. Fields Cookies explains how to solve or prevent many common problems. These rules were created by analyzing the business setting, building models of the business, and then

FIGURE 1.5
Changes occurring in the business world affect the use of information technology. These trends and the implications are discussed throughout the book. Managers who understand these trends and their relationship with technology will make better decisions.

Business Trend	Implications for Technology
Specialization	• Increased demand for technical skills • Specialized MIS tools • Increased communication
Methodology and franchises	• Reduction of middle management • Increased data sharing • Increased analysis by top management • Computer support for rules • Reengineering
Mergers	• Four or five big firms dominate most industries • Need for communication • Strategic ties to customers and suppliers
Decentralization and small business	• Communication needs • Lower cost of management tasks • Low maintenance technology
Temporary workers	• Managing through rules • Finding and evaluating workers • Coordination and control • Personal advancement through technology • Security
Internationalization	• Communication • Product design • System development and programming • Sales and marketing
Service orientation	• Management jobs are information jobs • Customer service requires better information • Speed

creating rules by anticipating decisions and problems. This approach gives less flexibility to the lower-level managers but encourages a standardized product, consistent quality, and adherence to the corporate philosophy.

Management by methodology also allows firms to reduce their number of middle managers. By anticipating common problems and decisions, there is no need to call on trained managers to solve the daily problems. Franchises like McDonald's or Mrs. Fields Cookies carry this technique one level further by making the franchisee responsible for the financial performance of individual units. The common management tasks, however, are defined by the central corporation.

Merger Mania

Up to the late 1800s and early 1900s, most businesses were small, having markets limited to small geographic regions. A brief history of industrial organization reveals four waves of mergers in the United States: (1) the horizontal mergers of the late 1800s epitomized by the oil and banking industries; (2) the vertical integration of the early half of the 20th century, illustrated by the oil, steel, and automobile companies; (3) conglomerate mergers of the 1950s and 1960s, in which firms like IT&T (an international telecommunications giant) acquired subsidiaries in many different industries (including a bakery!); and (4) giant horizontal mergers of the late 1990s. All of these mergers arose to take advantage of economic power, but technology made them possible. Without communication (telegraph and telephones earlier, computer networks later), firms could not grow beyond a certain size because managers could not monitor and control lower-level workers.

The most recent mergers have been impressive in terms of the size of the firms and the sectors involved. The banking industry was one of the first to begin consolidation. Relax-

REALITY BYTES · Do You Have What It Takes to Succeed?

Mike Roper opened a Quiznos Sub franchise in a Chicago suburb in 2000—right before the restaurant industry hit a big-time slump. Yet he increased sales by 40 percent in the second year. The International Franchise Association says that every eight minutes, a new franchise outlet is added to the 320,000 in the United States. How can yours be different? How can you succeed? Mike notes that "when you have your own money on the line, you act a little differently. You tend to be a little more aggressive on the day to day." For his grand opening, he went door-to-door to all businesses within a three-mile radius and handed out free bags of chocolate chip cookies and dis-count coupons. On opening day, he faxed the businesses to tell them he was open. Whenever business slows down, or competitors open a nearby store, he distributes more cookies and coupons. He also treats his employees differently. In an industry with 200 percent turnover, 12 of his first 16 employees still work for him. He offers his employees medical and retirement benefits and has even helped them buy cars. He believes that if he treats employees well, they will treat the customers better.

Source: Adapted from Shirley Leung, "Secrets of My Success," The Wall Street Journal, December 15, 2003.

ation of federal restrictions quickly led to large regional and national banks. The telecommunications industry also experienced several changes, such as the ABC-Disney and AOL-Time/Warner merger between telecommunications and entertainment industries. Telephone, Internet, and cable companies also were fertile ground for mergers, such as MCI and WorldCom or AT&T and TCI. The horizontal mergers in the petroleum, food production, automobile, and grocery industries represented major consolidations of operations as well. Some of these combinations crossed international boundaries (e.g., Daimler and Chrysler). Some of these trends were fueled by the high stock market valuations, which provided capital to the successful firms and punished the weaker ones.

One of the important keys to these mergers was the improved capability of information and communication technology. Without the IT structure, it would be exceedingly difficult to manage these combined firms. Most of the combinations also resulted in a loss of middle-management jobs. The remaining workers relied on technology to improve their productivity. The newly centralized firms also relied on communication technology to provide customer service across the country.

Decentralization and Small Business

Strangely, businesses today are becoming both larger and more decentralized. The goal of decentralization is to push the decision-making authority down to the level that deals with the customer. The top managers set strategy and establish projects across the organization. The lower-level managers and salespeople solve problems and make decisions to improve sales and negotiate with customers. The gap between these groups is bridged by information technology. Companies no longer need hundreds of middle-level managers to organize data and interpret top management commands. In the past, with limited information technology, small divisions were expensive to maintain because of the cost of collecting and processing the basic accounting and operating data.

Within a firm, operations can be decentralized into teams of workers. In this situation, departments operate relatively independently, "selling" services to other departments by competing with other teams. They often perform work for outside firms as well—essentially operating as an independent business unit within the corporation. The main goal of decentralization is to push the decisions and the work down to the level of the customer, to provide better customer service and faster decisions. Information systems enable executives to gather and manipulate information themselves or with automated systems. As a result, there is less need for middle managers to prepare and analyze data.

Temporary Workers

So what happens to the people who are no longer needed as middle-level managers? At various times in the past, some companies provided a form of lifetime employment for their workers. As long as workers continued to do their job and remained loyal to the company,

REALITY BYTES The Web Is International and Multilingual

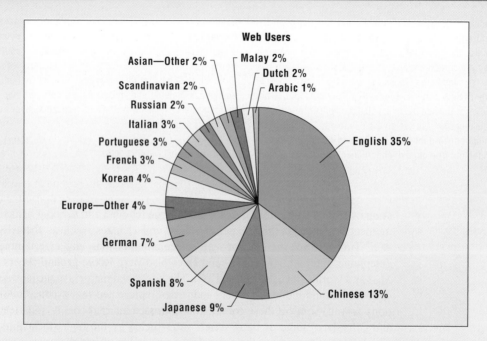

Web Users

- Asian—Other 2%
- Malay 2%
- Scandinavian 2%
- Dutch 2%
- Russian 2%
- Arabic 1%
- Italian 3%
- English 35%
- Portuguese 3%
- French 3%
- Korean 4%
- Europe—Other 4%
- German 7%
- Spanish 8%
- Japanese 9%
- Chinese 13%

Web browser settings report the language on the computer to the server, providing a measure of the dynamic Web population. Languages on the Internet are beginning to reflect the distribution of languages in the real world.

Source: http://www.glreach.com/globstats/, March 2004.

their jobs were secure. Even in more difficult times, when employees were laid off, they were often encouraged (through extensions of unemployment benefits) to wait until the economy improved and they could be rehired. Companies in other nations, especially Japan, had stronger commitments to workers and kept them on the payroll even in difficult times.

Today, in almost every industry and in many nations (including Japan), all jobs are at risk. To compensate, companies increasingly rely on a temporary workforce. Individuals are hired for specific skills and tasks. When these basic tasks are completed, the employees move on to other jobs. Increasingly, even executives are hired because of their specific expertise. Consultants and other professionals are hired on a contract basis to solve specific problems or complete special assignments.

In many ways, it is more difficult to manage a company that relies on temporary workers. Special efforts must be made to control quality, keep employees working together, and ensure that contract provisions are met. Technology can play an important role in these situations. It can improve communications, maintain easy (but controlled) access to data and contracts, and help to institute corporate standards. The Internet is beginning to play this management role—finding contract workers, negotiating the work, and distributing the finished products.

To you as a worker, the loss of middle-management jobs and reliance on temporary workers should be scary. It means more competition for jobs—particularly higher-level careers. To obtain higher-level jobs, you will need to possess more analytic skills than other potential employees. Even as a manager, you will need your own competitive (professional) advantage. Along with additional education, your use and knowledge of technology can give you an advantage.

Internationalization

Several events of the early 1990s demonstrated the importance of international trade: closer ties forged with the European Union, creation of the North American Free Trade Area (NAFTA), and the continued relaxation of trade restrictions through the General Agreement on Tariffs and Trade (GATT) and the World Trade Organization (WTO). Although barriers to trade remain, there is no doubt that the international flow of trade and services plays an increasingly important role in many companies. Even small firms are buying supplies from overseas and selling products in foreign markets. Trade also brings more competition, which encourages firms to be more careful in making decisions.

As Figure 1.6 shows, the role of exports and imports has expanded rapidly in the United States since 1970. In European nations, international trade is even more important. Today, internationalization is a daily fact of life for workers and managers in almost every company. Even small businesses have links to firms in other nations. Many have set up their own production facilities in other nations. Much of this global expansion is supported by technology, from communication to transportation, from management to quality control.

Communication facilities are one of the most prominent uses of information technology to support the move to international operations. Communication technology is especially important for service industries such as consulting, programming, design, marketing, and banking. Several years ago, services were often considered to be nontradable goods because they tended to have high transportation costs, making them difficult to export. Today, improved communication facilities through the Internet have made certain types of services easy to export. For example, financial institutions now operate globally. Today, software development has a growing international presence. Many U.S. firms are turning to programmers in Ireland, India, and Taiwan. Through the use of programmers in India, for example, a U.S.-based firm can develop specifications during the day and transmit them to India. Because of the time difference, the Indian programmers work during the U.S. night and the U.S. workers receive updates and fixes the next morning.

Internationalization also plays a role in selling products. Groups of countries have different standards, regulations, and consumer preferences. Products and sales techniques that work well in one nation may not transfer to another culture. Information technology can track these differences, enabling more flexible manufacturing systems that can customize products for each market.

FIGURE 1.6

By almost any statistic, in almost every nation, the level of international trade has increased dramatically during the last 20 years. International trade brings more choices, more competition, more data, more complexity, and more management challenges.

Source: http://www.bea.doc.gov/bea/dn/nipaweb/index.asp.

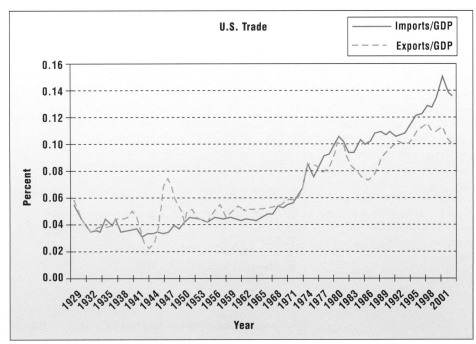

The increased competition created by internationalization and decentralization requires corporations to be more flexible. Flexibility is needed to adapt products to different markets, choose suppliers, adopt new production processes, find innovative financing, change marketing campaigns, and modify accounting systems. Firms that attain this flexibility can respond faster to market changes, catch opportunities unavailable to slower firms, and become more profitable.

Service-Oriented Business

Another trend facing industrialized nations is the move toward a service-oriented economy. As shown in Figure 1.7, in 1920 the U.S. census showed 29 percent of the employed were in farming. By 1990, that figure had shrunk to 3 percent. In the early 1900s, people were afraid that this trend would cause food shortages throughout the United States and the world. Improvements in technology in the form of mechanization, transportation, growing techniques, chemicals, and crop genetics proved them wrong.

A similar trend in manufacturing has produced the same consternation. Although the number of workers employed in manufacturing has varied over time, it is clear that the largest increase in jobs has been in the management, clerical, and service sectors. In 2000, 25 percent of the jobs were in manufacturing, with 73 percent in service and management jobs. The largest increase in new jobs has been in the management, clerical, and service sectors.

These trends represent changes in the U.S. economy and in demographics such as age characteristics of the population. The importance of the management, clerical, and service sectors has to be considered when we examine how MIS can benefit a firm and its workers. The goal is to gain a competitive advantage through better customer service. Even manufacturing companies are beginning to focus their efforts around the concept of providing services to the customer.

Reengineering: Altering the Rules

Does technology alone improve a business? Many companies are managed by rules and procedures. It would be virtually impossible to do otherwise—the cost of an intense evaluation of every single decision would be overwhelming. Hence, upper-level managers establish procedures and rules and an organizational structure that automatically solve typical problems. More complex problems are supposed to be identified by managers and forwarded up the chain of command for answers.

FIGURE 1.7

Over time, Americans have moved from agricultural to manufacturing to service and management jobs. Management and service jobs are often dedicated to collecting and analyzing data. Just as the decline of workers in agriculture did not create a shortage of food, the relative decline in manufacturing did not create a shortage of products.

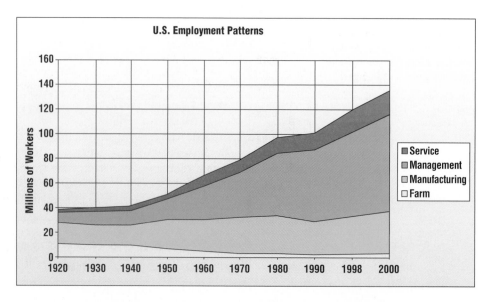

REALITY BYTES   MIS Job Trends

The California technology job market was hit hard by the dot-com crash in the early 2000s. Coupled with the rise in offshoring, many job seekers are wondering whether MIS jobs will exist in the future. Yet all forecasts indicate a future demand for technology workers—retirements by the baby-boom generation, few new students studying MIS and CIS, and continued demand for new features and new technology. But the nature of the jobs will likely change from those of the 1990s. Employers today want workers who understand the business aspects of technology: how the project can improve the business and increase profits, how to understand business needs, and how to collaborate and work with teams. Rajiv Donde, CIO of VantageMEd Corp., recommends that technology students seek degrees in business to broaden their knowledge. Just understanding computers is not enough. Ultimately, companies need to develop the right tools to solve business problems.

Source: Adapted from Loretta Kalb, "Tools of Success," The Sacramento Bee, March 1, 2004.

This type of management creates a fixed approach to operations and to solving problems. However, the business environment rarely remains constant. Over time, new technologies are introduced, new competitors arrive, products change, old markets shrink, and new markets arise. At some point, firms that have been guided by relatively static methodologies find their methods no longer match the marketplace. Hence, they decide to **reengineer** the company: beginning from scratch, they identify goals along with the most efficient means of attaining those goals, and create new processes that change the company to meet the new goals. The term *reengineering* and its current usage were made popular in 1990 by management consultants James Champy and Michael Hammer. Many of the underlying concepts have been in use for years.

Sometimes reengineering is undertaken by internal management as a means to improve the company. For example, in the early 1990s, Compaq Computer altered its strategy and reengineered its operations and management to cut millions of dollars in costs and save the company. But in 2000, Dell Computer's just-in-time and made-to-order production system dominated the industry. Unable to alter the company fast enough, Compaq was ultimately purchased by Hewlett-Packard.

Sometimes reengineering is forced on the company when it is taken over by another corporation. In a few rare cases, managers continually evaluate the firm to make several small changes instead of relying on a major overhaul.

Reengineering can be a highly complex process, requiring thousands of hours of time to analyze the company and its processes. In addition to the complexity, reengineering often faces resistance because it results in a change in the organization's structure, which affects the authority and power of various managers.

Like any management technique, reengineering is not guaranteed to work. A report by CSC Index, a major reengineering consulting company that surveyed 497 large companies in the United States and 124 in Europe, noted that 69 percent of the American and 75 percent of the European companies have already undertaken reengineering projects. Several of these projects have not been successful. CSC Index notes that three factors are necessary for success: (1) overcome resistance by managers who are afraid of losing jobs or power, (2) earn strong support by upper management, and (3) aim high and go for major changes instead of small rearrangements.

Often the point of reengineering is to rebuild the company so that it can make better use of technology. Simply placing computers into a firm, or just buying replacement computers, does not provide competitive advantages. The key to technology is to restructure the operations and management to reduce costs and make better decisions. For example, in the 1980s, replacing a secretary's typewriter with a personal computer had some benefits. But firms ultimately gained more benefits by giving personal computers to managers and eliminating the secretary. Today, you might consider simply updating those personal computers. However, building an information system that provides easy-to-read, up-to-the-minute data to top management makes it possible to eliminate the lower-level managers and still make better decisions.

REALITY BYTES | IT Budgets

A survey by Merrill Lynch in 2002 revealed that on average, companies spend 5 percent of their total revenue on IT projects. Over 60 percent of them are trying to reduce that number. In terms of growth areas, companies were targeting more money for storage and services in 2003. Spending on personal computers and networks was steady or declined in 2003. Most CIOs were feeling pressured to maintain operations with the reduced spending. In general, expansion and new projects were limited.

Source: Adapted from Juan Carlos Perez, "CIOs: 2003 IT Budgets under the Gun," *Computerworld*, December 9, 2002.

One of the challenges of reengineering is that the proposals can seem drastic. What do you mean you want to eliminate half of the corporate-level employees!? But being driven out of business by a leaner, lower-cost competitor is always a worse situation.

Management and Decision Levels

How do you break businesses into smaller pieces to analyze them? To understand management, reengineering, and information systems, it helps to divide the organization into three decision levels: strategy, tactics, and operations. Each level has unique characteristics which use different types of support from information technology. These levels were explained by Robert Anthony in 1965. In 1971, Gorry and Scott Morton added a detailed explanation of how information systems at that time could support the various levels of management. Figure 1.8 is an updated picture of the typical pyramid shape of most organizations involving operations and tactical and strategic decisions. As is typical with most management models, there are many gray areas and the lines are not absolute.

The power of the model is that it makes it easier to solve business problems. With any problem, your goal is to identify the primary management level. Once you know the level, it is easier to focus on the types of solutions that will be relevant. For example, if a company is having basic problems with its day-to-day accounting, you would focus on improving the data collection—and worry later about strategic tools and problems with competition. As you read the cases and Reality Bytes throughout this book, you should identify the primary level of each problem.

Operations

The *operations level* consists of day-to-day operations and decisions. In your first job, you will typically concentrate on the problems that arise at this level. For example, in a manufacturing firm, machine settings, worker schedules, and maintenance requirements would represent management tasks and decisions at the operational level. Information technology

FIGURE 1.8
There are three primary levels of decisions in business. Business operations consist of tasks to keep the business operating on a day-to-day basis. Tactical decisions involve changes to the firm without altering the overall structure. Strategic decisions can alter the entire firm or even the industry. Information system tools exist to help with each type of decision.

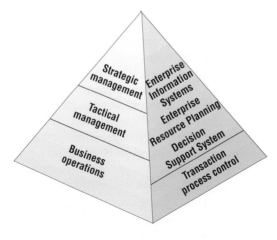

at this level is used to collect data and perform well-defined computations. Most of the tasks and decisions are **well-structured,** in the sense that they can be defined by a set of rules or procedures. For example, a clerk at Wal-Mart follows the procedures in the guidebook to deal with typical operations. Common problems are anticipated, with actions spelled out in the guidebook. Computer security is an increasingly important problem—for both individuals and companies. Chapter 5 examines the major threats and tools available to protect your assets.

As summarized in Figure 1.9, managers in other disciplines—such as accounting, marketing, or finance—also face operational decisions. Personal productivity tools like spreadsheets, word processors, and database management systems help managers collect and evaluate data they receive on a daily basis. The use of these tools is reviewed in Chapter 2.

An important task at the operations level is to collect data on transactions and operations; hence **transaction processing systems** are a crucial component of the organization's information system. The data collected form the foundation for all other information system capabilities. As discussed in Chapter 6, an important characteristic of transaction processing systems is the ability to provide data for multiple users at the same time. A special class of transaction processing software designed for factory operations is called *process control* software. Chapter 7 shows how modern **enterprise resource planning (ERP)** software extends the concepts of transactions across the organization.

Database management systems are increasingly used to control data and build systems to share data. Their role is explained in Chapter 4. Chapter 3 shows how communication networks are used to provide access to data throughout the organization. Increasingly managers work in teams—either with workers in the same department or across departments and sometimes companies. Sophisticated software tools are being developed to help integrate data in these collaborative arrangements. These integration tools and *enterprise resource planning systems* are described in Chapter 7. Operational decisions are often the easiest to understand. They deal with structured problems over relatively short periods of time.

Tactics

As you move up in your career to project leader or department manager, you will encounter a different level of decision making, where the types of problems will depend on your specialization, but some common features will stand out. At the *tactical level,* decisions typically involve time frames of less than a year. As shown in Figure 1.10, these decisions usually result in making relatively major changes but stay within the existing structure of the organization.

A manufacturing tactical-level decision might involve rearranging the work area, altering production schedules, changing inventory methods, or expanding quality control measures. These changes require time to implement and represent changes to the basic methods of the firm. What distinguishes them is that they can be made without altering the overall characteristics of the organization. For example, in most cases, expanding quality control measures does

FIGURE 1.9

Each functional area of management faces the three categories of decisions and problems. A few examples are presented here.

Sector	Operations	Tactics	Strategy
Production	• Machine settings • Worker schedules • Maintenance schedule	• Rearrange work area • Schedule new products • Change inventory method	• New factory • New products • New industry
Accounting	• Categorize assets • Assign expenses • Produce reports	• Inventory valuation • Depreciation method • Finance short/long term	• New General Ledger system • Debt vs. equity • International taxes
Marketing	• Reward salespeople • Survey customers • Monitor promotions	• Determine pricing • Promotional campaigns • Select marketing media	• Monitor competitors • New products • New markets

Technology Toolbox: Finding Information on the Internet

Problem: By now, you have performed many searches on the Internet. How successful have you been? If your search terms are too vague, you receive too many hits to be useful. If you do not include enough search terms, you get no hits.

Tools: Boolean searches are a powerful tool available on many search engines. Generally called "Advanced" searches, they enable you to specify how multiple words should be combined using AND and OR conditions.

As an example, you need to find information about corporate takeovers that were saved by a white knight merger. First you enter the phrase "white knight" into the search engine (Google). Using quotation marks treats both terms as a phrase that must appear as a single unit. Slightly dismayed, you find 126,000 pages, and only a few seem relevant. Adding the word *corporate* to the list you still get 12,000 hits. Looking through a few pages, you notice that pages you do not want seem to be about hackers, Australia, and a company called White Knight Resources. Since you do not want those pages, switch to Advanced Search mode and enter those four words in the "without" section. In the search, removed words are preceded by a negative sign. This search results in 701 matches. You can reduce the count slightly by removing "history" as well. You can further restrict searches by language and date.

"white knight"   126,000

"white knight" corporate   12,000

"white knight" corporate

    –hackers –groups –Australia –resources 5,080

"white knight" corporate merger

    –hackers –groups –resources   701

"white knight" corporate merger

    –hackers –groups –resources –history –Australia   655

Be sure you understand how your favorite search engine treats individual words. By forcing words to be included (AND or all words) you reduce the number of matches. By combining words with OR (at least one) you increase the number of matches. Removing words (without) helps discard pages that you know you do not want. For large or vaguely defined topics, it is often easier to narrow the search with these exclusionary words.

Quick Quiz: See how long it takes you to find answers to the following questions.

1. How many times has Pierce Brosnan played James Bond?
2. What is the current stock price for Radio Shack?
3. Where can you get free copies of the GIS data files to draw the counties of your state?
4. Who finished second in the 2004 Tour de France?
5. Where can you bid on property auctioned from the New York Police impound?

not require the firm to expand into new industries, build new facilities, or alter the structure of the industry. Much of the information for making tactical decisions comes from the transaction records that have been stored in the computer. Computer tools to help analyze this type of data are called **decision support systems (DSSs)** and are described in detail in Chapter 10.

Other types of problems that involve more complex models occur in business. For instance, **diagnostic situations** consist of spotting problems, searching for the cause, and implementing corrections. Examples of these situations include responding to problem reports from operations to identify the cause of the problem and potential solutions. For instance, a marketing manager might be asked to determine why the latest marketing approach did not perform as well as expected. Tactical-level decisions tend to involve specialized problems and can often be solved with the help of an expert. Chapter 10 presents **expert systems (ES)** to make this knowledge more accessible to an organization.

Strategy

The next step on the pyramid moves up the corporate ladder to executive-level decisions. Although you may never be a CEO, you might be in a position to advise upper-level manage-

FIGURE 1.10

Each decision level affects the firm in different ways. Each level uses and produces different types of information.

Decision Level	Description	Example	Type of Information
Strategic	Competitive advantage, become a market leader Long-term outlook	New product that will change the industry	External events, rivals, sales, costs quality, trends
Tactical	Improving operations without restructuring the company	New tools to cut costs or improve efficiency	Expenses, schedules, sales, models, forecasts
Operations	Day-to-day actions to keep the company functioning	Scheduling employees, ordering supplies	Transactions, accounting, human resource management, inventory

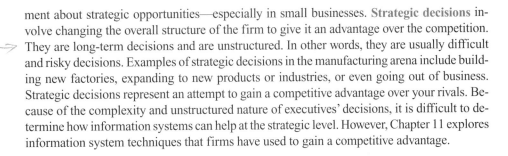

REALITY BYTES   Health Care Supply Chain Costs

Basic medical supplies account for 25 percent of a hospital's operating costs. Throw in the logistics and management costs, and the total rises to 35 or 40 percent. Much of the ordering process is fragmented and uncontrolled. Physicians often buy preferred brands from random vendors, instead of ordering the items on the contracted list. Few hospitals have an integrated computer system that can identify these problems. David Youndt, chief operating officer at Hospital Logistics, Inc., notes that "hospitals and clinics tend to want to focus the dollars they have on patient care. They're not going to channel their capital budget into supply chain." Broadlane Inc., a health care software and services company, tracked all of the purchases at one of its clients for a year. It found that the multihospital chain spent eight times what it should have—if all the items had been purchased at the discount contract prices. The problem is compounded because many of the large multihospital chains have grown through mergers. The limited computer systems that they do have cannot share data across the hospitals. Allina Hospitals and Clinics in Minneapolis with 11 hospitals and clinics exemplifies the problems. While upgrading their systems to provide year 2000 compliance, the organization installed a suite of integrated systems from Lawson Software. Managers found that only 50 percent of the supplies were purchased on the discount contracts. The IT department cleaned the data and analyzed it to understand where the discrepancies were. By tracking purchases down to individual departments and buyers, Allina was able to reach its goal of 70 percent purchases on contract. The organization saved almost $4.5 million.

Source: Adapted from Julia King, "Health Care's Major Illness," Computerworld, May 10, 2004.

ment about strategic opportunities—especially in small businesses. **Strategic decisions** involve changing the overall structure of the firm to give it an advantage over the competition. They are long-term decisions and are unstructured. In other words, they are usually difficult and risky decisions. Examples of strategic decisions in the manufacturing arena include building new factories, expanding to new products or industries, or even going out of business. Strategic decisions represent an attempt to gain a competitive advantage over your rivals. Because of the complexity and unstructured nature of executives' decisions, it is difficult to determine how information systems can help at the strategic level. However, Chapter 11 explores information system techniques that firms have used to gain a competitive advantage.

An Introduction to Strategy

Why are strategic decisions so difficult? How do you begin searching for competitive advantage? In all industries, competition is challenging. Firms are constantly searching for ways to gain an advantage over their rivals. Finding these opportunities is hard: it requires extensive knowledge of the industry, and it requires creativity. Managers also have to be willing to take risks to implement strategic options. Strategic uses of IT often involve the use of new technology and development of new software. Being the first company to implement a new idea can be risky. However, it can also bring substantial rewards.

Strategic uses of IT are discussed in detail in Chapter 11 because you need to understand the technology before trying to use it to solve difficult problems. On the other hand, to stimulate the imagination needed for creativity, it helps to begin thinking about the basic ideas right from the start. Many cases throughout the book illustrate how firms have used technology to gain substantial advantages. These examples should help you solve other problems. If you can recognize a pattern or similarity between your problem and actions taken by other firms, it may help you create a solution.

Searching for Ideas

Michael Porter noted that often the first step in searching for competitive advantage is to focus on *external agents*, or entities that are outside the direct control of your company.

Porter's Five Forces model shown in Figure 1.11 illustrates the typical external agents: customers, suppliers, and rivals. You should also look at the role of government as an external agent. Competitive advantages can be found by producing better quality items or services at a lower cost than your rivals. Also, many firms have strengthened their positions by building closer ties with their suppliers and customers.

It is hard to find revolutionary ideas that alter the entire industry, and every firm in the world is constantly searching for that next big idea. Not only do you have to come up with the best idea, but you have to do it before someone else tries the same (or better) strategy. Then, because new strategies involve significant changes, and often high costs, you have to be able to persuade the other managers that your idea will succeed.

Strategy Example: Baxter Healthcare

Hospitals use a large amount of routine supplies such as bandages and antiseptics. Originally, they purchased them from various suppliers, held them in inventory, and distributed them throughout the hospital as they were needed. This relationship is shown in Figure 1.12. American Hospital Supply (AHS) was one of these suppliers. To gain an advantage over their competitors, AHS created a new system and made an offer to the hospital managers. AHS placed computer terminals in hospital locations where the supplies were used (emergency, operating rooms, nursing stations, etc.). As shown in Figure 1.13, these terminals were connected to the AHS computer.

As hospital personnel removed supplies, they recorded them on the terminals. The computer kept track of the amount of supplies in each location. A list would be printed at the warehouse, and drivers delivered the necessary supplies to each location in the hospital. Monthly usage statistics were sent to the hospital.

The hospital gained because the facility did not need to maintain extra inventory, which saved money and space. Fewer hospital employees were required, because the supplies were delivered directly to the needed locations. Additionally, the hospital received detailed usage records.

To offer this service, AHS incurred higher costs—largely the cost of creating and maintaining the information system. What did AHS gain in return? As long as it was the only company offering this service, AHS gained a competitive advantage by providing a new service. Hospitals were more likely to choose AHS over the rivals. But what would happen if a competitor created a similar system? Would the hospitals stay with AHS or switch to the rivals?

Although the answer depended on the prices, hospitals had a strong incentive to stay with AHS. They would encounter various switching costs if they chose another supplier. For example, daily operations would be disrupted while the system was changed. Employees

FIGURE 1.11
In analyzing strategies, Michael Porter focuses on the five forces: threat of new entrants, threat of substitute products or services, bargaining power of suppliers, bargaining power of buyers, and rivalry among existing competitors. Competitive advantage can be obtained by using these forces or altering the relationships between these external agents.

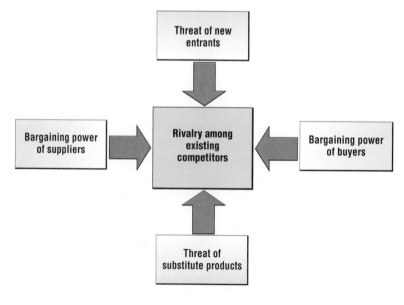

FIGURE 1.12

American Hospital Supply began as an intermediary that bought various medical supplies and distributed them in bulk to hospitals. The hospital distributed supplies throughout its facility and was responsible for maintaining its own inventory.

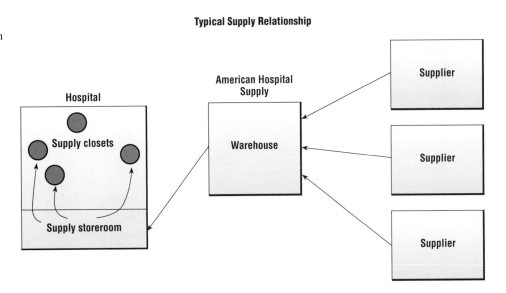

Typical Supply Relationship

would have to be retrained to use the new system. Managers who used the monthly usage reports would have to adapt to the new system. A rival would have to offer strong price advantages to overcome these costs.

In 1985, Baxter Healthcare, a large manufacturer of supplies, purchased AHS. Of course, over time Baxter had an incentive to cut its costs to maintain higher profits. In the process their delivery service might suffer. Some hospitals apparently experienced problems and returned to in-house stock rooms to eliminate shortages of basic supplies. In 1996, Baxter spun off Allegiance Corporation as a separate unit. Today, Allegiance is a subsidiary of Cardinal Health, one of the three main health care distributors in the United States (Owens & Minor and McKesson are the other two).

Today, as shown in Figure 1.14, the entire medical supply chain industry is attempting to build an online Web service system. Ideally, miniature electronic auctions would take place each day. The supplier systems would automatically monitor the hospital needs and compete to resupply them. Most of the monitoring and bidding could take place automatically on the Internet. The best bid would win each day, and the hospitals would not be tied to a single supplier. Yet all transactions and payments would be automated, holding costs down for all parties.

FIGURE 1.13

American Hospital Supply changed the industry by providing a just-in-time inventory delivery service. Supplies then were delivered directly to where they are used within the hospital. AHS could offer this system only by maintaining a computer link between supply usage and the local warehouse. The computer data also provided summary reports to management. By purchasing AHS, Baxter Healthcare gained immediate access to that sales data.

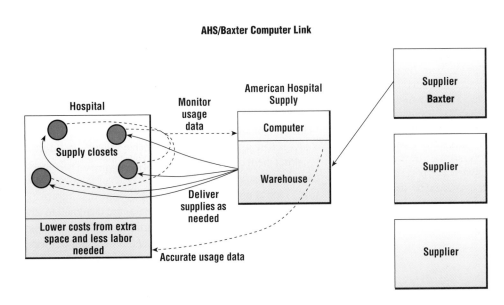

AHS/Baxter Computer Link

FIGURE 1.14
Moving to the Internet. Today, competition could be increased by connecting the hospitals and suppliers through a B2B Internet auction. The daily hospital data could be listed on a private auction site, and the supplier computer system would automatically bid for each job. The winning bidder would deliver supplies as usual, but different suppliers might win the bidding each day.

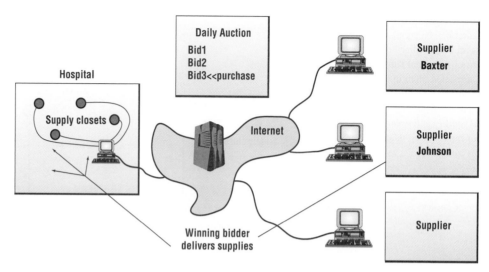

Summary

Information technology is altering jobs, businesses, and society. Managers who understand and use this technology will be able to improve companies and advance their personal careers. Information systems consist of hardware, software, people, procedures, and collections of data. These components work together to provide information and help managers run the firm, solve problems, and make decisions. Studying information systems will also teach you to analyze business operations and solve problems.

A Manager's View

How do you manage and control a firm? In the 1950s, an army of back-office workers and managers were required just to record the basic data for the firm. Today, a good information system helps you manage a small company or a large empire with fewer workers. The workers that remain are those who use the technology intelligently to solve business problems. Regardless of your area of expertise, as a manager you have to be able to analyze and interpret data. You also have to communicate and share your work with teammates. Information technology provides the tools you need to solve common business problems.

The role of a manager is changing, but at a basic level all managers spend time organizing resources, planning, motivating workers, and communicating with other employees and managers. Several business trends will affect individual jobs, business operations, and society. Important trends include specialization, management by methodology and franchising, decentralization, the increased importance of small businesses, the use of temporary workers and consultants, the growing international scope of business, and the rise in service-oriented businesses. Information technology is used to support these trends and provide new management alternatives.

As is true of many problems, management and information technology can be studied by breaking them down into smaller pieces. The three basic levels to management are operations, tactics, and strategies. The operations level is concerned with day-to-day operations of the firm. Tactics involve changes and decisions that improve operations but do not require a major restructuring of the firm. Strategies are designed to give a firm a competitive advantage.

Strategy typically involves examining external forces: rivals (competitors within the industry), customers, suppliers, potential new competitors, and potential substitute products or services. Information technology can be used to strengthen links strategically between customers and suppliers. It can also be used to create new products and services and to improve the quality of the operations.

Key Words

B2B, *7*
B2C, *7*
data, *4*
database, *4*
decision process, *9*
decision support system (DSS), *20*
diagnostic situation, *20*
dot-com, *7*
e-business, *8*
e-commerce (EC), *7*

enterprise resource planning (ERP), *19*
expert system (ES), *20*
hardware, *4*
information, *5*
information technology (IT), *4*
knowledge, *5*
management information system (MIS), *4*
people, *4*

procedures, *4*
reengineering, *17*
software, *4*
strategic decisions, *21*
structured decisions, *19*
switching costs, *22*
transaction processing system, *19*
wisdom, *5*

Web Site References

General Searches

AltaVista	www.altavista.com
AskJeeves	www.ask.com
Dogpile	www.dogpile.com
Google	www.google.com
Web Crawler	www.webcrawler.com
Vivisimo	www.vivisimo.com
Yahoo	www.yahoo.com

People and Businesses

Anywho	www.anywho.com
Infospace	www.infospace.com
Knowx	www.knowx.com
Securities and Exchange	www.sec.gov
SuperPages	www.superpages.com
Switchboard	www.switchboard.com
Whitepages	www.whitepages.com

Reference

American Heritage dictionary	www.bartleby.com/61/
Britannica (encyclopedia)	www.britannica.com
CIA World Factbook	www.cia.gov/cia/publications/factbook/
Encarta (encyclopedia)	www.encarta.com
FedStats	www.fedstats.gov
Translation dictionaries	www.freedict.com
Wikipedia	www.wikipedia.org

Additional Readings

Anthony, Robert N. *Planning and Control Systems: A Framework for Analysis.* Cambridge: Harvard University Press, 1965. [Early MIS.]

Booker, Ellis. "Baxter Gets PC Smart, Ousts Dumb Terminals." *Computerworld,* April 3, 1989, p. 33. [Baxter Healthcare.]

Gorry, G. A., and M. Scott Morton. "A Framework for Management Information Systems." *Sloan Management Review,* Fall 1971, pp. 55–70. [Early MIS.]

"Health-Care Guys Can Make Good on Retail IT." *PC Week,* August 21, 1995, p. 11. [Baxter Healthcare.]

Leavitt, Harold J., and Thomas L. Whisler. "Management in the 1980s." *Harvard Business Review,* November 1958, pp. 41–48. [Prediction of decline in middle management.]

Luthans, Fred. *Organizational Behavior: A Modern Behavioral Approach to Management.* New York: McGraw Hill, 1973. [Management.]

Mintzberg, Henry. *The Nature of Managerial Work.* New York: Harper & Row, 1973. [Management.]

Nash, Jim. "Just What the Doctor Ordered." *Computerworld,* June 1, 1992, p. 79. [Baxter Healthcare.]

Porter, Michael. *Competitive Strategy: Techniques for Analyzing Industries and Competitors.* New York: Free Press, 1980. [Strategy.]

Sloan, Alfred. *Adventures of a White-Collar Man.* New York: Doubleday, 1941. [Management.]

Review Questions

1. What is the main purpose of MIS?
2. Why do students who are not MIS majors need to study MIS?
3. What are e-commerce and e-business?
4. What are the roles of managers in a modern company?
5. Describe how seven basic trends in today's business environment are related to MIS.
6. Describe the five components of a management information system.
7. How has the management structure of many businesses changed in the past decade—largely due to reengineering?
8. Describe the three basic levels of management decisions.
9. How can an understanding of the levels of management decisions help you solve business problems?
10. How are information systems used at the various levels of business management?
11. How do you begin the search for strategic uses of information systems?

Exercises

1. Find a local company that has international purchases or sales. Determine how the orders are processed and the payments made.
2. Choose a company and describe three decisions that must be made: one at the operations level, one tactical, one strategic. Be specific.
3. Choose a company and read its two most recent annual reports. Summarize the company's strategy and goals for the coming year.
4. As an entrepreneur, you decide to open a fast-food restaurant. You can purchase a franchise from one of the established corporations (as discussed in the McDonald's case) or create your own restaurant. Compare the choices by identifying the decisions you will face with each approach. What data will you need to collect?
5. Interview a recent graduate in your major (or a relative or friend). Find out what they do at their jobs on a daily basis. Ask what his or her managers do. Do managers have operations tasks to perform as well as management duties? For instance, does a manager in an accounting firm work on tax returns?
6. Think of a part-time job you have or have had. How does your manager break down his or her time among the categories of communication, traditional management, networking, and human resource management? What issues have you felt your manager has dealt with effectively? On what issues could your manager spend time to improve?
7. Review business magazines, newspapers, and Web sites. Find two organizations and identify a specific business problem that each one faces. Classify the problem as operations, tactics, or strategies.

Technology Toolbox

8. What was the name of the Martian rover that successfully landed in early 2004?
9. How many cell phones are in use in Peru?
10. What is the tallest mountain in South America?
11. Currently, what are the most common search words on the Internet?
12. List the names of the two senators from your state and when their terms expire.

Teamwork

13. Choose an industry. Have each team member select one company within the industry and find information about the size of that company. Also, find information about the use of information technology within the company. Write a single-page summary for each company. Combine the results into a report, and write a paragraph summarizing the level of competition within the industry.

14. Choose an industry. Have each team member select one company within the industry and find the number of employees at that company for the two most recent years. Compare the total number of employees to see if the total has increased, and to see which firms are growing the fastest. Compare the industry results to those in the rest of the class.

15. Find two companies that have merged within the last two years. Split the team into two groups and have each group track the products and workers from one of the companies. Summarize the changes to the management and production structures.

Rolling Thunder Database

16. Install the Rolling Thunder Bicycles database. Look through the various forms. List each of the main forms and briefly describe the purpose of the form.

17. Using the Rolling Thunder help files or the description available on the Rolling Thunder Internet site (http://jerrypost.com/rollingthunder), describe the goals of the firm and outline the basic operations.

18. Using Internet sources, identify the competitors to Rolling Thunder Bicycles.

19. Using Internet, financial, and government sources, estimate the size of the market (total sales and number of bicycles) for quality bicycles.

20. Locate at least five sources for additional information about bicycles and bicycle components on the Internet. List and briefly describe the Web sites.

Cases: The Fast-Food Industry

The Industry

What do customers want? Look at the sales for the major fast-food restaurants, and you see increases by many companies. Look at the Standard and Poor's restaurant stock market index, and investors agree. In 2003, the index was up 37.5 percent, compared to a 24.8 percent rise in the S&P 1500. Since an aging, wealthier population favors dining in full-service restaurants, the casual-dining sector is gaining share from fast-food restaurants. This trend is projected to continue as the population ages. Many restaurant chains, especially those in the fast-food sector, will increase their focus on healthy food initiatives to attract customers and reduce the impact of obesity-related lawsuits. Increased diversity in menus will help to reduce the dependence on industry price discounting, enabling operating margins to further expand. The introduction of new restaurants will likely slow in the overstored U.S. fast-food market. Most fast-food restaurants are looking to international expansion to lead to growth.

During the past two decades, the percentage of U.S. food dollars that has gone to eating out has increased substantially. A greater percentage of people, particularly women, are working more, leaving less time available to prepare food at home. Overall sales have increased based on three factors:

- The opening of new stores.
- Higher contributions from older restaurants.
- Acquisitions of other chains or selective sites.

But over the past several years, fast-food sales gains have lagged behind those of the full-service sector, due in part to ferocious competition, fierce price discounting, and reduced same-store sales and profitability. In January 2003, both McDonald's and Burger King changed management teams. Both companies have focused on rebranding efforts to recast their dowdy image and less reliance on price discounting as a means to drive traffic. In 2004, the CEO of McDonald's died of a heart attack, but it is likely the changes he instituted will continue.

What Do Customers Want?

Most of the fast-food restaurants have tested a variety of options to find what customers want. Originally, McDonald's was successful because it promised the same level of service and quality regardless of where you traveled. But incomes increased

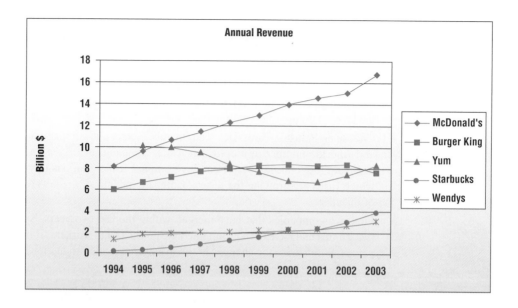

Annual Revenue

and health became an important issue. Do customers still want the same things? How can the big fast-food chains identify what customers want? How can they respond quickly enough?

New Concepts: Quick Casual

The first generation to grow up with fast food has now reached their mature, high-income years. To meet their needs, "quick casual," limited, self-service restaurants are geared toward adults. They feature "upscale" menus, with more healthful items such as gourmet soups, salads, and sandwiches. In some quick-casual units, workers take orders from behind the counter as customers proceed in a line toward the register. In others, they take orders at a counter where customers pay for the food, which is then prepared and delivered to the customer's table. Checks, averaging between $6 and $9, are higher than in traditional limited-service units, but lower than in full-service casual dining restaurants.

The most successful and most visible of the quick-casual chains is Panera Bread Company. An operator of bakery/cafés, Panera's system sales now surpass $800 million. The company plans to add another 100 to 150 units annually over the next several years. Other implementers of this concept include:

McDonald's	Boston Market, Chipotle Mexican Grill
Wendy's	Baja Fresh Mexican Cuisine
Yum! Brands	Yan Can Chinese Restaurant

Focus on Health

The American culture has become significantly more health-conscious and litigious over the past decades. This culture has resulted in lawsuits focused on the responsibility for obesity-related health problems faced by consumers, particularly children. Plaintiffs have sought remedies such as menu changes, nutritional labeling, advertising restrictions, and monetary damages. In response to this strong customer demand, many restaurant chains have begun to make significant

changes in their menu offerings. Applebee's International signed a deal with Weight Watchers International Inc. in July 2003 to develop a menu for diet-conscious individuals. In February 2003, Darden Restaurants opened its first Seasons 52 unit, a test concept offering low-calorie menu items.

The fast-food industry has introduced even more dramatic changes, perhaps because it has the most to lose from consumer perceptions of the healthfulness of its food offerings and from potential lawsuits. In August 2003, Wendy's announced that it would promote four meal combinations from items already on the menu that would have less than 10 grams of fat. Wendy's also added another salad offering to its menu. Burger King and Jack in the Box have focused on salad, chicken, and turkey offerings to revamp their menus.

McDonald's has developed a wide range of "Healthy Lifestyle" programs, including the addition of menu offerings that the company believes will attract health-conscious consumers. It has also developed new Happy Meals that include yogurt, milk, vegetables, or fruit, depending on the end market. In 2002, McDonald's changed its cooking oils to reduce the amount of trans-fatty acids in its fried foods. In June 2003, it phased out animal-growth-promoting antibiotics in its meat supply. McDonald's has also sought to promote nutritional education and awareness among its customers. In May 2003, the company formed its Global Advisory Council on Healthy Lifestyles, consisting of experts such as doctors, educators, and athletes in the areas of fitness, nutrition, and active lifestyles. The group is commissioned to help guide the company toward activities that promote balanced, healthy lifestyles among its customers. McDonald's has also begun to collaborate with the World Health Organization and the U.S. Department of Health and Human Services to educate consumers on the importance of nutrition and fitness. The company has educated consumers by printing brochures directing them to the nutritional information on its corporate Web site.

The Future

The restaurant industry generally depends on the economy. When people work, they have less time and more money, so they vote for convenience. As long as costs stay low, the industry should continue to do well. Costs are heavily dependent on labor and food. Companies tend to lock in food costs for up to a year, so they are less affected by short-term swings in prices. Labor costs depend on the overall economy. The question of what customers want is difficult to answer. And the answer changes over time. Information systems can help identify sales patterns. They can also help control costs and reduce order lags with suppliers. But analyzing the data requires a keen eye and experience.

Case: McDonald's

What do customers want? In *The Customer Connection,* John Gusapari suggests that one goal is to meet customers' expectations. You accomplish this by creating value. Creating quality is not just a matter of reducing defects but of providing customers with something they value. McDonald's (ticker: MCD) has a clear definition of customer needs and expectations. Its formula is QSC: quality, service, and cleanliness (Band 1989). Transaction quality, defined from a customer's perspective, means paying for a product or service in a way that makes the customer feel good about doing business with a company.

According to Harry Beckwith, customer definition is essential to success in marketing (Beckwith 2003). Beckwith viewed McDonald's as an example of a classic, but simple, excellent service model. However, he feels that they have recently taken their eye off the ball, forgetting their formula for success. Beckwith feels their mistake is that they have been thinking that fast food is a food business. Beckwith focuses instead on the "fast" part of the definition: It is a time and convenience business. In Beckwith's opinion, McDonald's has made the menu choices too complex costing customers too much time. Beckwith does not feel that people go to McDonald's for the menu.

Corporate Summary

McDonald's Corporation serves more than 46 million customers daily from 31,000 fast-food restaurants in over 120 countries. In 2003 there were 13,602 restaurants in the United States and 17,614 in other countries. McDonald's maintains its competitiveness through substantially uniform menus and standard operating processes. The company has expanded through partner brands in additional market segments including Boston Market, Chipotle Mexican Grill, Donato's Pizza, and (in the UK) Pret A Manger. McDonald's operates all of its restaurants under joint venture agreements. In 2002, McDonald's annual report showed the mix was (although only company stores recorded as revenue):

Franchised restaurants:	17,864	62 percent of sales
Company-owned	9,000	28 percent of sales
Affiliated	4,244	10 percent of sales

Systemwide sales were $46 billion in 2003, up 11 percent from $41.5 billion in 2002. International business contributed 45 percent of operating income in 2003. In 2003, comparable store sales rose in the United States and Latin America, but fell elsewhere. New product offerings have helped with a strong rebound in sales since April 2003. Current operating priorities with goals of a 6 to 7 percent growth in earnings include:

- Fixing operating inadequacies in existing restaurants.
- Taking a more integrated and focused approach to growth by emphasizing increasing sales, margins, and returns in existing restaurants.
- Ensuring the correct operating structure and resources aligned behind it.
- Focusing priorities on benefits for customers and restaurants.

Turnaround Under Way

Jim Cantalupo, one of the architects of McDonald's highly successful worldwide expansion in the 1990s, was lured out of retirement to run the company. He assembled a youthful and energetic management team, led by president and chief operating officer Charles Bell, to revamp the company's fortunes. Under this new leadership, the company embarked on a strategic plan to return to positive sales growth and income trends. To accomplish this goal, the company shifted its focus away from expansion and toward the improvement of existing operations. Tragically, Jim died of a heart attack in April 2003.

McDonald's began to address concerns that its menu had become stale and irrelevant to today's consumer. McDonald's introduced new products, including salad offerings, the McGriddle breakfast sandwich, and increased Happy Meal options. Even though management believes that excessive price discounting has diminished the company's brand image, the company plans to maintain the 99-cent Value Meal offering. In relation to the brand image, the public's perception of the quality, service, and cleanliness at McDonald's units has suffered over the last several years. The company has lagged behind its peers in consumer attitude toward these areas. To improve overall customer satisfaction, the company has refocused on its quality, service, cleanliness (QSC) program. This program gauges performance at each location through customer satisfaction studies and "mystery shoppers," who pose as customers and score each unit's performance in various categories. The company has also taken a harder line with franchisers who do not perform to expectations.

McDonald's must also reinvigorate the company's franchise base. Franchisees run more than 70 percent of McDonald's 31,000 restaurants worldwide and account for a similar level of systemwide sales. In recent years, many franchisees have been demoralized by declining profits caused by company-mandated discounting, a proliferation of stores that has cannibalized individual store sales, and the overall lack of a coherent national advertising program. Retaining hardworking, entrepreneurial store owners is paramount to reinvigorating the company's health.

McDonald's began to reap benefits from its new strategies in early 2003. The company had seen its profitability deteriorate in the United States during 2001 and 2002 because of operational shortcomings and sales trends that were significantly below the industry average. In the second quarter of 2003, driven by new product offerings and improved marketing effectiveness, same-store sales jumped 4.9 percent, year-to-year. While these sales results are only an important first step in reviving McDonald's image, the company must show tangible improvement in its customer satisfaction scores to maintain momentum. New products may lure customers through the doors, but high degrees of customer satisfaction are often the key to keep them coming back.

Enhancing Information Technology through Project Management

To improve the project success rates on information technology projects, McDonald's has developed an apprenticeship program for prospective project managers, combining classroom theory, on-the-job learning, and support from mentors. McDonald's is accomplishing this program in association with the Computer Technology Industry Association (CompTIA), six other companies, and a $2.8 million grant from the Department of Labor. The goal is to develop a National Information Technology Apprenticeship System aimed at building skills and credentials around specific business-technology functions.

The grant enables CompTIA to build four career tracks in areas that it feels are prime for IT apprenticeships: IT generalist, project manager, security, and database. The grant also provides funds to implement Web-based processing of applications and certification. Over the next five years, CompTIA has committed matching funds of nearly $3.8 million to develop the system's infrastructure, skill standards and work processes, and marketing strategies to encourage large-scale private sector adoption.

The Labor Department awarded CompTIA a grant of $550,000 through December 2002 to assess whether apprenticeships would work in the IT industry and to develop one apprenticeship track for the IT generalist. Success with that led the Labor Department to award a $475,000 second-round grant through December 2003 to develop additional apprenticeship tracks, including IT project management, and to test them in pilot companies such as McDonald's. The latest round of funding enables the Labor Department to expand on these original efforts.

Application of the Internet to Solving Business Problems

One of the ways that McDonald's has used the Internet is to provide information to customers to deal with the fat content of their meals. While this is in some way a response to attorneys and consumer groups that have criticized the industry for fattening America, McDonald's is using Internet technology to better disseminate information about the nutritional properties of their menu items. In 2003, McDonald's revamped its www.mcdonalds.com Web site to better explain the nutritional values of the chain's foods.

Among the most graphically sophisticated nutrition tools on the Internet, "Bag a McMeal" enables users to drag up to five McDonald's menu items from pull-down lists into a virtual bag. Once completed, the users receive a cumulative nutrition profile covering calories, fat, cholesterol, and sodium, among other information. A "Customize an Item" feature enables consumers to obtain a nutrition profile for a special order, such as a McChicken sandwich without mayonnaise or a Big Mac without cheese or sauce. "Bag a McMeal" uses multiple pull-down lists and drag-and-drop functionality to generate a nutrition profile for a complete meal of up to five items. The goal is to provide additional educational resources to demonstrate the range of options and service sizes available to make it easy to fit McDonald's into a balanced diet.

According to McDonald's representative Lisa Howard, the Web-surfing public has found value in the dynamic nutrition databases. "There are from 160,000 to 200,000 unique visitors to the nutrition section of McDonalds.com each month," Howard said. "We've seen it spike [upward]" since the new Web tools were put in place, she added. According to Howard, "We continue to look at new and innovative ways to communicate with customers, like in-store kiosks" (Brewin 2003).

Reaction to the Web-based nutrition information has been critical. "If [the chains] were really serious about doing a better job at giving consumers information, diners would have that information at the point of decision in the restaurant," said Jeff Cronin, director of communications for the Washington, D.C.–based Center for Science in the Public Interest. "Now the [nutrition] brochures are hard to read and hard to find and sometimes altogether absent. Few consumers would leave their place in the drive-thru or counter line to find and read a poster with nutrition information before ordering, and many fewer are likely to go to a Web site before making a decision." National Restaurant Association officials and representatives of some other trade groups have countered this argument by asserting that restaurateurs provide what consumers want, not what restaurateurs think consumers should eat. They believe menu board notices are unnecessary, since many chains already provide interested consumers with printed brochures or Web site pages containing nutrition information for regular menu items.

Given the debate about practicality and accessibility, information about nutrition can be stored in large, centralized, and easily updated databases that many consumers can tap into through the Internet. Such data can be presented in ways that enable Web surfers to personalize searches and "drill down" through multiple layers of details to get as little or as much insight into a topic as desired. Many restaurant companies have ignored such dynamic Internet presentation plans in favor of merely presenting at their Web sites the same nutrition information tables contained in printed brochures.

McDonald's may be considering ways to leverage its Web site technology in such a fashion, company spokeswoman Howard said. "We continue to look at new and innovative ways to communicate with customers—that is certainly something we might look at."

Implementing Wireless Technology

Many restaurants view the public-access Wi-Fi "hot spot" technology as essential for attracting customers. But what is still unclear is how much businesses can charge customers to use the Wi-Fi links—or whether they should simply provide the Internet and e-mail access capabilities for free with the hope that increased sales of food, drinks, and other products will offset the cost of the technology.

McDonald's launched a Wi-Fi pilot project at 75 restaurants in the San Francisco Bay area in mid-2003 through a deal with Austin-based Internet access provider Wayport Inc. Mark Jamison, vice president of business strategy and development at McDonald's, said the company would use the San Francisco trial and similar ones in Chicago and New York to evaluate potential pricing models for the service and Wi-Fi technology's ability to attract customers. The end result is that McDonald's plans to equip several hundred restaurants in the United States with Wi-Fi connections by 2004. McDonald's charges $4.95 for two hours of Wi-Fi access at the San Francisco locations, but customers who buy a meal can use the technology for free.

But will customers really go to a restaurant because it has wireless access? Consider the opinion of Matthew Nuss of the Valencia Group, a Houston-based hotel operator: "Wireless, in our opinion, is the next running water. It has become part of the infrastructure of a hotel" (Wright 2003). On the other hand, McDonald's is using an outside company (Wayport) to set up and run the Wi-Fi operations. McDonald's is also benefiting from the technology. It is using the same Internet connection to run its cashless payment and credit card systems. Basically, it is turning communications with the stores into a revenue-generating operation (Brewin 2004).

Seattle-based Starbucks Corp. launched Wi-Fi service in its U.S. cafés in August 2002 and offers access in about 2,000 locations. Users have to sign up for the service with Bellevue, Washington–based T-Mobile USA Inc., whose prices start at $19.99 per month. Lovina McMurchy, director of Wi-Fi business and alliances at Starbucks, said the company plans to stick with that approach. But she added that Wi-Fi hot-spot deployment is "a learning experience" for businesses and said it's hard to tell how different pricing plans or free services will play out. At this point, a lot of companies are still just "dabbling" in Wi-Fi through pilot projects, McMurchy said.

Questions

1. How does McDonald's use technology to learn what customers want?
2. How does information technology reduce management costs?
3. Will Wi-Fi increase sales? Will you pay for Wi-Fi access at McDonald's?
4. Does the franchise model make it more difficult to implement information technology solutions? Explain.
5. Is it more important for information technologies to reduce costs or provide new services?

Case: Burger King

Burger King (private) is the second largest fast-food chain in the United States, with more than 8,000 locations and $8.4 billion in systemwide sales in fiscal year 2003. Worldwide, the restaurant has 35,000 employees, 1,500 franchisees, and scores of key suppliers. However, Burger King has encountered difficulties over the last few years. According to *Nation's Restaurant News* (*NRN),* the company's market share among quick-service sandwich chains dropped from 15.03 percent in 2000 to 13.68 percent in 2002. In 2004, Wendy's basically matched Burger King sales.

In the fall of 2002, Burger King was sold to a private investment group for approximately $1.5 billion. Many analysts believed the change in ownership would improve the chain's management focus and vision, increasing its competitiveness in the marketplace. Brady Blum, formerly a senior executive of Darden Restaurants Inc., was hired as CEO to engineer a turnaround. Burger King now seeks to recast its brand image by focusing on its grilling processes and retooling its menu, while downplaying its previous emphasis on discounts. The new strategy has yet to provide the desired results, however. The chain has acknowledged that negative same-store sales trends continued into the first six months of 2003.

Standardized Point-of-Sale Terminals

New point-of-sale (POS) terminals from NCR Corp. have provided more than 130 Burger King restaurants in Canada with a standard method of order taking and data entry. Burger King Corp. has already installed NCR's Compris food service software, support services, and RealPOS 7454 terminals in more than 600 company-owned restaurants in the United States. It is wrapping up deployment in its 259 company locations in Canada, the United Kingdom, and Mexico. The goal of the deployment is to streamline equipment across corporate-owned restaurants around the globe, according to Michael Lingswiler, director of technical services with Burger King. "The drive behind this is standardization. The NCR platform provided the functionality, and given where they are in the market, is able to provide for future releases" (Hilson 2003).

A standard interface for all restaurants enables changes in the menu or special promotions to be easily linked with the corporation's back-end systems. Training can be standardized and deployed across all regions of the company. Simplicity, durability, and environmental friendliness are important in these fast-paced environments. Prior to the standardization effort, Burger King had a mixture of NCR and non-NCR equipment in their restaurants. Typically, these terminals have a life cycle of about three years. While franchise restaurants are responsible for their own POS hardware/software selections, they often adopt the corporate-owned model for ease in purchase and maintenance.

Computer Security

Given its worldwide status, Burger King wanted to use automation to help it efficiently assign and manage the identities and network privileges tied to enterprise and online initiatives. "In our opinion it is a necessity," says Burger King's chief information officer, Rafael Sanchez. Such tools are needed "because every organization has legacy systems, and most legacy systems have their own security" (Liddle October 2003). In 2003, the installation of Oblix NetPoint software for enterprise Web access and identity management purposes was the latest development in a sweeping Burger King information technology project. That undertaking, for which Burger King involved consultant Pricewaterhouse-Coopers, is aimed at improving internal network security and controls over financial statements and enhancing the chain's performance by better empowering employees and improving relationships with franchisees and vendors.

According to Burger King officials and Pricewaterhouse-Coopers documents, the latter two goals can be achieved by making available to field personnel, franchisees, and suppliers certain business support applications and information once accessible only by select headquarters or regional staff. Such information sharing can take place through an Internet portal that might also benefit Miami-based Burger King by acquiring additional higher-quality operations information from franchisees, a PricewaterhouseCoopers case study of the project suggested.

Oblix NetPoint supports "single sign-on" for network users, or the consolidation of user-ID and password information for multiple Web-based applications or applications with Web front ends. It works with the Active Directory feature of Microsoft's Windows Server to streamline and automate several of the steps needed to make changes to user identity information and access privileges. The NetPoint software supports self-registration by users and the delegation of some administrative duties to certain classes of end users, such as department heads. It also ties access and privileges administration into a user organization's workflow routine. That makes possible scenarios such as one in which network ac-

cess is immediately revoked for any employee subject to a termination notice from the company's human resources department.

Under the former security plan at Burger King, different legacy applications required or permitted administrators to create log-in IDs or passwords different from those used for other programs. That, CIO Sanchez says, made it possible for individual users to wind up with multiple log-on IDs or passwords or both. In the Burger King information technology realm "a person may have access to from five to 15 different applications," Sanchez explains. Those programs, he adds, include such things as basic network access and applications tied to sales, finance, and franchise-related matters.

Sanchez says he or someone else in his department had to change log-on IDs and password information and access privileges for a variety of applications whenever an employee joined the company, left the company, was given additional responsibilities, or was stripped of duties. Because disgruntled terminated employees are a potential threat to company resources accessible via a network, Sanchez says of the old security plan, "I had to pray that whoever provided access [to the employee in question] let me know about the termination." Creating an identity management infrastructure "allows you to manage the [network] environment a lot more efficiently," Sanchez says. "Everyone has one user ID and password for everything they use."

According to Sanchez, under the new system the "primary user of a particular application," such as a department head, assigns access and privileges to people within his or her sphere of influence. Such assignments, however, must be in keeping with the protocols and security parameters established by the configuration of NetPoint and the underlying identity management infrastructure, he indicates. "Dealing with outside communities—that is where we will use the power of Oblix [NetPoint] for self-administration," Sanchez remarks, referring to resources he expects to save by delegating administration of identity and privileges to suppliers and franchise groups with extranet access. The concept, he says, is that he might say to a supplier, "I'll give you access for up to 20 people, but the internal assignment within your company is your responsibility."

Human resources "can clue us [to personnel changes] in house, but when your partners are outside, it becomes even more difficult" to determine who should have access or who should have access terminated, Sanchez observes. Burger King's goal, Sanchez reports, is to reduce the time spent administering network security, while increasing the company's ability to implement new security strategies. To help achieve that goal, the Miami-based chain used Pricewaterhouse-Coopers to help build a modern directory and identity management infrastructure.

Among other things, Burger King will use its new identity management capabilities to help support portal access to the company's SAP R/3 suite of applications. Offering a wide range of end users access to business support software through a portal with solid identity management underpinnings "allows us to extend the applications to the outer edge" of the Burger King universe, Sanchez says. "Technologies like identity management that drive costs down and increase employee, franchisee and [business] partner satisfaction give companies in the restaurant industry a competitive edge," Sanchez states. Because the use of NetPoint will reduce to one the number of log-on IDs and passwords used by Burger King employees, it should be easier for those workers to remember that information. And that, Sanchez says, should

help reduce costs, or at least the workload, associated with the chain's information technology help desk.

Questions

1. Why is security so important to Burger King?
2. Why is technology standardization so critical?
3. Do all franchises need to worry as much about security, or just the fast-food industry?

Case: Wendy's

Driven by expansion and new product offerings, U.S. annual sales gains at Wendy's (ticker: WEN) Old Fashioned Hamburgers outpaced those of McDonald's from 1998 through the end of 2002. According to *Nation's Restaurant News,* Wendy's market share in the quick-service sandwich sector rose to 11.4 percent in 2002, from 10.3 percent in 2000. While the company's expansion enabled it to continue capturing market share in 2003, same-store sales at its restaurants were down, year to year, through July. This decline was due to a change in comparisons from 2002 and competitive pressures, particularly from a recovering McDonald's.

The company has sustained its image as selling high-quality products in the quick-service sector and continues to enhance its reputation for offering a diverse selection of sandwiches. The company has also maintained industry-leading customer satisfaction scores. Future plans include an increase in national advertising spending targeting the growing number of Hispanics and late-night customers. Though the company has stalled for the near term, its strong brand image has prepared it for the longer term.

Customer Cards

Under the direction of Scott McClenahan, Wendy's in Redwood City, Utah, is collaborating with Visa USA in a payment card acceptance pilot test. Wendy's is using a Verifone Omni 3200 customer-activated, credit-card-payment terminal on the front counter and a Verifone Everest terminal at the

menu board in the drive-through. In configuring the Everest for the drive-through, Verifone developed a weatherized case for the terminal and attached a MagTek dual-head "dip" card reader to minimize instances of incorrect insertion that could slow transactions. The drive-through Everest terminal served as a remote link to the countertop Omni model. The two units were connected by a cable that ran underground from the restaurant to the outdoor terminal at vehicle-window height near a red LED order-confirmation board.

To keep transaction times as low as possible, most quick-service chains have limited their initial tests of card acceptance to credit cards and "check cards" that can be processed without requiring card users to sign receipts or enter personal identification numbers. As a result, drive-through point-of-order payment terminals often came without numeric keypads. The latest card-acceptance platforms combine a payment terminal supporting PIN-based debit transactions with LCD order-confirmation systems. A 2.4-gigahertz, wireless transmitter with encryption capabilities from AeroComm is now being used to transfer payment terminal data to the POS system.

Questions

1. Why has Wendy's been more successful at identifying customer desires than Burger King?
2. How do most customers pay for fast food? How much are they willing to pay in service charges to use ATMs in the restaurant?

Case: Yum! Brands

After several years of closing unprofitable stores and selling company-owned units to franchisees, Yum! Brands Inc. (ticker: YUM) has shown renewed vigor. The owner of the KFC, Pizza Hut, and Taco Bell brands acquired the Long John Silver's and A&W restaurant brands in 2002 as part of its multibranding restaurant strategy. The company is aggressively expanding internationally as well, particularly in China, Mexico, Korea, and the United Kingdom. The company's diversified portfolio has enabled Yum! Brands to successfully grow its business despite difficulties that may occur with any one of its restaurant brands. Through late August 2003, strength at Taco Bell had helped to offset difficulties at

KFC, while overall profitability was aided by a weaker dollar. Today, Yum! Brands, with 33,000 restaurants in five major chains and 2002 sales of $7.8 billion, is the world's largest restaurant operator in terms of units.

The restaurants are trying to lift traffic and sales around the world by adding ambience, quality, and service to a business that largely ignores such niceties. Emphasis is placed upon training at the counter and upgrading the restaurants in terms of equipment and food. The average checks in the restaurants are $3 to $4 at Taco Bell and $5 to $7 at KFC.

While the burger chains duke it out on price, KFC, Pizza Hut, and Taco Bell are adding and emphasizing better food, which, in the case of KFC's roasted chicken, at least, also means lighter fare. Yum restaurants are pushing higher-priced items to bolster dine-in business. Among them: Pizza Hut's Chicago Dish pizza ($13) and Taco Bell's popular Southwest Steak Border Bowl ($3.50).

The new CEO, David Novak, began an overhaul in 2000 in response to customer feedback. Customers bluntly told the chains their service was shoddy, their food subpar, and their restaurants, in some cases, shabby (Wells 2003). Novak, aged 50, still fumes when he recalls answering a call on Taco Bell's toll-free complaint line in early 2001. A woman named Michelle complained bitterly about getting the wrong $3.60 order and a lot of attitude. "I can assure you Michelle would be justified to tell everyone she sees about how poorly she was treated," Novak exploded in an e-mail to restaurant managers after the call. "This is the kind of word-of-mouth that kills us."

David Novak hopes that acting on this feedback will make the company stronger. Employees at all the chains around the world now attend training four times a year at which customer-service initiatives are hammered home. They also get evaluated, in part, on how they treat customers and react to problems when they arise. Novak is pushing to slice service times, particularly at Taco Bell and KFC. At Taco Bell a timer installed at drive-through windows beeps after 60 seconds. This is the time in which an employee is supposed to spend taking and filling an order. Novak blames some of the lingering problems at the restaurants on former owner PepsiCo. He feels Pepsi emphasized marketing at the expense of quality food, service, and atmosphere. "It wasn't our schtick," PepsiCo President and Chief Financial Officer Indra Nooyi answers. "The restaurant business wasn't our schtick."

David Novak is orchestrating this dramatic shift to civilize the fast-food experience. At Taco Bell, where food is delivered to its 6,444 U.S. restaurants premade, new $1,450 grills are being installed to cook new menu entries on-site. Restaurants in the Mexican-themed chain are also paying $16 million more a year for better-quality beef, tortillas, and beans. The company is developing higher-end ideas, such as Yan Can, the name of four new Asian-themed restaurants in California created with Arthur Ho, a Hong Kong–based franchisee of KFC, and chef Martin Yan of PBS Yan Can Cook fame. Average sales at these restaurants exceed $35,000 a

week, compared with just under $20,000 a week at a typical Taco Bell. Yum! Brands is also combining Pizza Hut with a fast-casual chain called Pasta Bravo in test markets.

Some Taco Bell franchisees argued against paying more for the new ingredients. "I didn't think our customer base was that discerning," says Ned Kirby, a franchisee in Noblesville, Indiana. "But they noticed the better food and didn't resist the higher prices" (Wells 2003). Not every trial restaurant is successful. Bell Grille was an experimental restaurant the company opened in Garden Grove, California, to test higher-end menu items, such as smoothies. According to Emil Brolick, president of Taco Bell, it was short-lived, because the food did not fit in with the restaurant, which looked like a regular Taco Bell.

Novak is also pushing to pair the different Yum! Brands restaurants in multibranded units, which offer unit sales that are 20 percent higher than that of stand-alone restaurants. With just 1,870 twofers open, the goal is to have 6,000 by 2007. Novak has focused on new designs for the multibranded units, emphasizing what traditionally makes fast-casual chains popular. The new designs include inviting lighting with sleek sconces that are conducive to reading or hanging out. Whimsical murals fuse the personalities of two restaurants when they are combined into one unit. "Fast-casual chains make a statement. They spend little on advertising but a lot on the dining experience. If we apply this kind of thinking to our category we think it will give us some edge" (Wells 2003).

Given the weakness in the market sector and the focus on fast-food companies' vulnerability to new lawsuits, Yum's stock has recently fallen. Since 1997, revenue has sagged from a high of $9.7 billion. Since that time, operating income has more than tripled to $891 million in 2001. Debt has been slashed from $4.6 to $2.1 billion. Emphasis continues to be placed on refurbishing the restaurants themselves in a concentrated program.

Questions

1. How does Yum! Brands use information technology to improve efficiency?

2. With the mix of restaurants, how could Yum! Brands use IT to determine the best store combinations and selection of items to sell?

Case: Starbucks

Starbucks (ticker: SBUX) is committed to offering the highest quality coffee and the Starbucks Experience while conducting its business in ways that produce social, environmental, and economic benefits for the communities in which it does business. In addition to its retail operations, the company produces and sells bottled Frappuccino coffee drinks, Starbucks DoubleShot coffee drink, and a line of super premium ice creams through its joint venture partnerships. The company's brand portfolio provides a wide variety of consumer products. Tazo Tea's line of innovative premium teas

and Hear Music's exceptional compact discs enhance the Starbucks Experience through best-of-class products. The Seattle's Best Coffee and Torrefazione Italia Coffee brands enable Starbucks to appeal to a broader consumer base by offering an alternative variety of coffee flavors.

Starbucks has grown to 7,225 retail stores from only 125 stores in September 1991. Starbucks purchases green coffee beans for more than 50 blends and varieties from coffee-producing regions worldwide. All green coffee beans purchased are of the Arabica species, which is of higher quality than the Robusta species typically found in supermarket coffees. Starbucks custom roasts the coffee beans to exacting standards. To add sales margins, the company stores offer a wide selection of coffee-making equipment, accessories, pastries, and confections.

In fiscal year 2003, retail stores accounted for 84 percent of net sales. Stores are typically clustered in high-traffic, high-visibility locations in each market. This includes office buildings, downtown and suburban retail centers, and kiosks placed in building lobbies, airport terminals, and supermarkets. In fiscal year 2002 the retail store sales mix by product type was 77 percent beverages, 13 percent food items, 6 percent whole bean coffees, and 4 percent coffee-related hardware items.

Starbucks has expanded its retail business by increasing its share in existing markets and opening stores in new markets in which it sees an opportunity to become the leading specialty coffee retailer. The company opened a net total of 602 company-owned stores in fiscal year 2003 and planned to open a similar number in fiscal year 2004. Starbucks has tried to use its Specialty Operations, which accounted for 16 percent of total revenues in fiscal year 2003, to develop the Starbucks brand outside the company-owned retail store environment. Starbucks has licensing agreements (35 percent of specialty revenues) with prominent retailers in North America, Central America, Europe, and Asia. The company has about 5,600 food service accounts (27 percent), whereby it sells whole bean and ground coffee to various coffee distributors, hotels, airlines, and restaurants. Starbucks has a licensing agreement (13 percent) with Kraft, Inc., which markets and distributes the company's whole bean and ground coffees in the U.S. grocery channel. In addition, the company sells its coffee products through warehouse club accounts (13 percent) and through mail order and online (7 percent) (Standard and Poor's, Starbucks annual report).

In the fourth quarter 2003, Starbucks acquired Seattle Coffee Company, which includes Seattle's Best Coffee and Torrefazione Italia coffee brands, for $72 million. In the first nine months of fiscal year 2003, the company repurchased 2.8 million common shares of stock for $61.2 million.

Stored-Value Card

Brian Cyrnes, senior vice president and chief information officer, is proud of the coffeehouse chain's stored-value, customer loyalty-enhancing Starbucks Card and Duetto. The new Duetto offering is a combination Starbucks Card and Visa credit card. This was accomplished by keeping an eye toward offering the best service and value, while targeting competitive advantages, speed-to-market issues, and enterprisewide integration. The launch follows the success of the reloadable Starbucks Card, of which more than 11 million have been activated since the card began in November 2001. A Starbucks Visa credit card, incorporating the stored-value feature, was launched in association with Bank One in March 2003.

The Starbucks Card program was run by an outside vendor, ValueLink, a First Data Corporation. First Data is an electronic payment service specialist. Customers buy the cards in dollar amounts to be redeemed like cash at the checkout line. ValueLink processes the transactions and manages an off-site database for the system. The program is already "a big loyalty winner." Starbucks redeemed 11 million cards worth $41 million in the recent second quarter. Starbucks outsourced the processing because it felt it lacked the knowledge to develop a complex customer service program on its own.

Wi-Fi Technology

Based on its experience at thousands of Starbucks Coffee outlets, Starbucks is convinced that providing Internet access to guests will build customer loyalty and sales. As a result, Starbucks is forging ahead with deployment of wireless local area networks, as other food service chains accelerate rollouts or expand tests of the technology. Starbucks Corp. launched Wi-Fi service in its U.S. cafés in August 2003 and now offers access in over 2,000 locations. Users have to sign up for the service with Bellevue, Washington-based T-Mobile USA Inc., a unit of Deutsche Telekom, whose prices start at $19.99 per month. The T-Mobile HotSpot service is backed by reliable high-speed T-1 connections that can accommodate the full spectrum of applications from checking e-mail to viewing rich multimedia and video. T-Mobile HotSpot window signs are visible near the entrance of all participating Starbucks locations. A complete list of stores can be found by visiting the Starbucks store locator on www.starbucks.com/hotspot and selecting "Wireless HotSpot Stores" as the Store Type.

Today the chain has fee-based hot spots managed by strategic partner T-Mobile International at about 2,600 of its 3,854 company-operated coffee bars. The goal is to install hot spots in about 70 percent of the retail sites operated by the company. Size, seating capacity, and the demographics of a market all determine which stores will incorporate the technology. Starbucks looked at a number of alternatives in terms of how to provide in-store Internet access, but decided wireless was the way to go to provide access without disrupting the other customers. The chain did not want to become known as an "Internet café" littered with cabling and other hard-wired network paraphernalia.

The wireless service is already paying dividends at Starbucks. The company charges customers about $6 an hour for the T-Mobile service. The typical wireless user stays for 45 minutes. Of the nonwireless users, 70 percent spend 5 minutes or less at the store; the remaining 30 percent linger for about 20 minutes. "We certainly believe that means they buy more coffee and food. The real exciting thing for us about the hot-spot service is that it is bringing people into our stores at different times of the day, and hot-spot users are staying longer," Nick Davis, Starbucks spokesman, remarked (Liddle August 2003). Typically, a Starbucks unit is busiest from 6 A.M. to 9 A.M., so building traffic later is a positive development. About 90 percent of hot spot users arrive after 9 A.M., and that group, on average, spends about 45 minutes online and in the stores.

In the attempt to leverage its wireless network installations further, Starbucks in 2004 began testing possible synergies between its hot spot strategy and the distribution of product by its music industry holding, Hear Music. To spur additional hot spot registrations and publicize Hear Music's "Artist's Choice" compact disc of Sheryl Crow's favorite songs by other recording stars, Starbucks' hot spot users were given Web access to audio clips of the songs and Crow interviews on the CD. They were permitted to download three complete songs from the compilation product.

Starbucks and the Sundance Film Festival

In addition to being the official coffee at the 2004 Sundance Film Festival, Starbucks worked closely with the Sundance Institute to sponsor the 2004 festival, as well as bring the excitement of the Sundance Film Festival experience directly to customers in its stores. Throughout the month of January, customers who visited their favorite participating Starbucks location with a Wi-Fi (802.11b)-enabled notebook computer or Tablet PC experienced the passion and inspiration of the 2004 Sundance Film Festival firsthand. By simply launching the Internet browser on their device, customers watched exclusive filmmaker interviews, behind-the-scenes video clips, and film trailers for free prior to logging on to the T-Mobile HotSpot wireless broadband Internet service.

Customers who logged on to the T-Mobile HotSpot service received a free day pass to the Sundance Online Film Festival—the online extension of the 2004 Sundance Film Festival. The free day pass enabled Starbucks customers to access the Sundance Online Film Festival, where they could cast a vote for their favorite animation and short subject films while in the comfort of any participating Starbucks location. Independent film aficionados and consumers did not have to be in Park City to experience the festival—they only needed to find the nearest T-Mobile HotSpot-enabled Starbucks to access the exclusive content.

Starbuck's sponsorship of the film festival enabled them to add value to the T-Mobile HotSpot service in their stores by giving their customers the ability to interact directly with digital entertainment. Since Starbucks has sponsored film festivals large and small, this next step enabled the company to share their enthusiasm for independent film directly with their customers.

Questions

1. Has Wi-Fi access improved sales and profits at Starbucks?
2. Given the huge number of stores, how could Starbucks use information technology to determine where to open new stores and which ones to close?

Additional Reading

Band, William. "Quality: I Know It When I See It." *Sales & Marketing Management in Canada,* Vol. 30(2), February 1989, pp. 36–38.

Beckwith, Harry. "10 Questions with . . . Harry Beckwith." *Journal of Financial Planning,* Vol. 16(10), October 2003, pp. 12–15.

Brewin, Bob. *Computerworld,* Vol. 37(28), July 10, 2003, p. 1.

Brewin, Bob. "McDonald's to Supersize Use of Wi-Fi Connections." *Computerworld,* April 19, 2004.

Hilson, Gary. "Hardware Fit for a King: Restaurant Chain Upgrades POS Terminals across Canadian Locations in Quest for Standardization." *Computing Canada,* Vol. 29(3), February 14, 2003, p. 19.

Liddle, Alan J. "Operators Chew on Ways to Offer In-Store Internet Access." *Nation's Restaurant News,* Vol. 37(32), August 11, 2003, pp. 1, 69.

Liddle, Alan J. "BK Seeks Simplification of Complex Network, Online Identity Management Process." *Nation's Restaurant News,* Vol. 37(40), October 6, 2003, p. 36.

Wells, Melanie, "Happier Meals." *Forbes,* Vol. 171(2), January 20, 2003, pp. 76–78.

Wright, Maury. "Combo, Please." *EDN,* Vol. 48(16), July 24, 2003, pp. 95–96, 98.

Summary Industry Questions

1. What information technologies have helped this industry?
2. Did the technologies provide a competitive advantage or were they quickly adopted by rivals?
3. Which technologies could this industry use that were developed in other sectors?
4. Is the level of competition increasing or decreasing in this industry? Is it dominated by a few firms, or are they fairly balanced?
5. What problems have been created from the use of information technology in this industry, and how did the firms solve the problems?

PART ONE

Information Technology Infrastructure

2 INFORMATION TECHNOLOGY FOUNDATIONS

3 NETWORKS AND TELECOMMUNICATIONS

4 DATABASE MANAGEMENT

What are the main features and tools of information systems?

How is information technology changing and how do you evaluate and choose technologies for business? How do you share information and collaborate? How do you store and retrieve data?

These are fundamental questions that any manager needs to be able to answer. Information technology forms the foundations of management information systems. As a manager, you need to understand what technologies are available today and how they are likely to change tomorrow. Although you do not have to be able to build your own computer, you need to understand the trends and limitations of computing equipment.

Networks are critical in most organizations today. The Internet continues to expand into professional and personal lives. Managers should understand how wired and wireless technologies can be used to share data and communicate. Particularly in terms of the Internet, you need to be able to evaluate emerging technologies and evaluate costs.

Database management systems are probably the most important tools in business today. Managers can no longer rely on programmers to answer business questions. Instead, you need to know how to retrieve data and build reports from central databases.

CHAPTER TWO

Information Technology Foundations

Chapter Outline

Introduction

Types of Data

Object Orientation

Numbers and Text

Pictures

Sound

Video

Size Complications

Data Compression

Hardware Components

Processors

Input

Output

Secondary Storage

Operating Systems

Computers in e-Business

What Is a Browser?

What Is a Server?

Application Software

Research: Databases

Analysis: Calculations

Communication: Writing

*Communication: Presentation and
Graphics*

Communication: Voice and Mail

*Organizing Resources: Calendars and
Schedules*

The Paperless Office?

Open Software

Summary

Key Words

Web Site References

Additional Reading

Review Questions

Exercises

Cases: The Computer Industry

What You Will Learn in This Chapter

- Are your computers and software out of date?
- What are the basic objects that computers process? How do computers handle music and video?
- What are the main components of a computer?
- Why is the operating system so important?
- How does the Internet change the role of computers?
- What are the main software applications used in business?

Should you buy new computers? How is information technology changing and how do you evaluate and choose technologies for business? These are difficult questions to answer for any business. Buying one new computer is not the problem—replacing hundreds or thousands of computers is expensive. One of the keys to changing technology is that buying a computer is not a one-time event. Organizations need to plan on buying new machines on a regular basis. Of course, you also have to think about how to dispose of the old computers.

The computer industry is driven by change and growth. An interesting feature of computers is that they have a short shelf life. A computer that sits unsold for a few weeks quickly becomes obsolete as more powerful or cheaper machines are introduced. From a manufacturer's perspective, this pattern of change is difficult to handle. It is even harder when you realize that people often want to try out a computer first. At one time, Dell tried to sell computers through retail stores, but had to give up. Dell's solution has become a driving force in the industry. Dell tightly manages the supply chain and builds each machine to order. Components such as disk drives, processors, and cases are purchased in bulk—often with long-term contracts. The majority of the components are delivered in small just-in-time batches to manufacturing facilities. The individualized machines are built and formatted for each specific customer. Dell holds costs down by minimizing inventory and producing the exact products ordered by customers. Dell risks losing sales to retail stores, but the company knows it will make a profit on every machine.

Which options should you choose on a computer? Do you need the fastest processor, a huge amount of RAM, and a monster disk drive? Where can you cut performance slightly and save money? These questions are hard enough for buyers to answer, but cause headaches for vendors. Again, Dell's made-to-order process reduces the risks. But vendors like eMachines (now owned by Gateway) and Hewlett-Packard have shown that with accurate predictions, it is possible to capture a substantial slice of the retail market. The key is to have the combination of features that are demanded by customers, at the right price.

Getting rid of old computer equipment could involve almost as big a decision as purchasing a new computer. California and Massachusetts have banned computer equipment from landfills. Europe and Japan have relatively strict recycling laws. Vendors are struggling to create recycling programs. Dell has committed to increasing the recycling rates by offering new programs that embed the cost of recycling into the new equipment. Other vendors will take back old equipment for a fee of $30 to $50.

Introduction

Are your computers and software out of date? Your employees are upset. They say their computers are out of date, and Microsoft has released three newer versions of the Office software. But do they really need new computers and software? Or do they just want new computers because some other department has new ones? If you decide to buy new machines, what should you buy? The biggest, fastest, most expensive? Or the smallest and most portable? Figure 2.1 shows the challenge of the choices. Does software really change, or should you stick with older versions? These questions can be difficult to answer because technology continually changes and business needs change. Each decision depends on the specific needs of the organization and must be continually reevaluated. To make better decisions, it helps to understand some fundamental characteristics of the hardware and software. These decisions become even more complex and critical when you have to evaluate servers and other computers used to run the entire company.

Why should you care how computers work? After all, it is easy to use a photocopy machine without understanding how it works. Automobiles cost more than most computers, yet you can buy an automobile without knowing the difference between a manifold and a muffler. You can also make telephone calls without understanding fiber optic cables and digital transmissions.

FIGURE 2.1
Information technology changes constantly. Change makes it difficult to choose products and control costs as you upgrade over time. As a manager, you have to evaluate the technology features and choose options that provide the functions you need while minimizing costs.

On the other hand, when you buy an automobile you need to decide if you want options such as power windows, a turbo charger, or a sunroof. Similarly, many options are available for telephone services. If you do not understand the options, you might not end up with the car, telephone service, photocopier, or computer that you need. Or you could end up paying extra money for services that you will not use. To choose among the various options, you need to know a little about how computers work. Many features are particularly important when evaluating computers to use as Web servers in e-business.

Computers are typically discussed in terms of two important classifications: hardware and software. *Hardware* consists of physical items; *software* is the logical component such as a set of instructions. Of course, many functions can be provided in either software or hardware, and a computer user often cannot tell which has been used, and most often does not care. The one main difference is that it is easier to make changes to software than to hardware—especially since software patches can be transmitted across the Internet.

Types of Data

What are the basic objects that computers process? How do computers handle music and video? To a computer user, the most important aspect of the computer is the data that it handles. Today, computers are used to process five basic types of data: numbers, text, images, sound, and video. Because of limited speed and storage capacity, early computers could handle only simple text and numbers. Just recently have computers become fast enough and inexpensive enough to handle more complex sound and video data on a regular basis. As computers continue to improve, these new capabilities will alter many aspects of our jobs and society.

As always, the business challenge is using technology to add value. For example, putting music and video footage in an accounting presentation might be entertaining, but in many cases it would not add value to the presentation itself. On the other hand, holding meetings with digital video links could save money by eliminating travel for a face-to-face meeting. You need to understand the concepts and characteristics of these technologies so that you understand their merits and costs and learn to identify worthwhile uses.

Object Orientation

One of the most important concepts to understand with computers is that all data are represented as **binary data.** The computer processor can only handle binary data in the form of bits. Processors operate on groups of bits at a time. The smallest group of 8 bits is called a *byte.* The industry often refers to the maximum number of bits that a processor can handle.

TRENDS

The first computers were simple pieces of hardware. Like all computers, they had to be programmed to produce results. Programming these machines was a time-consuming task, because all of the pieces were connected by individual wires. Programming the computer consisted of rearranging the wires to change the way the pieces were connected. As computer hardware improved, it became possible to program the processor without having to change the internal wiring. These new programs were just a list of numbers and short words that were input to the machine. These lists of commands were called *software,* because they were easier to change.

Programmers soon learned that some tasks needed to be performed for most programs. For example, almost every program needs to send data to a printer or retrieve information stored on a disk drive. It would be a waste of time if every programmer or user had to write a special program to talk to the printer. By writing these common routines only once, the other programmers could concentrate on their specific applications. As a result, every computer has a basic collection of software programs called an *operating system.* The operating system handles jobs that are common to all users and

programs. It is responsible for controlling the hardware devices, such as displays, disk drives, and printers.

As machines became faster and added new capabilities, operating systems evolved. These new capabilities have changed the way the computer is used. The early computers could recognize only individual characters and numbers, so keyboards were used to type information for the computer. Printers that could handle only characters and numbers were the only way to get output from the computer. Eventually, television screens were used for output, but most of this output remained as characters. With the introduction of microcomputers, low-cost graphics hardware allowed the video screens to display pictures that were created by the computer. Today's operating systems are graphical, which enables users to work with pictures and icons. Inputs are changing to graphics, sound, and video.

The Internet changed everything by focusing on networks and sharing data. The Web changed everything by making the browser the most important display device. Increasingly, software and data are stored on Web servers. Users rely on browsers installed on a variety of clients—from desktops to handheld computers, PDAs, and cell phones.

Common machines use 32-bit processors, but the industry is slowly shifting to 64-bit processors. A 64-bit processor can process 8 bytes of data in one operation. Of course, people do not deal very well with bits (or even bytes). Our real-world data consists of analog objects such as numbers, text, images, sound, and video. Computers need **input** devices to convert these objects into bits. **Output** devices then change this data back to a form that humans can understand. Figure 2.2 illustrates the five basic data types.

Software development has strongly embraced the concept of *object orientation.* The designers create objects for each software package. Each object has its own *properties* and *methods* or *functions.* Users can change properties and call them predefined functions. The five fundamental objects form the foundation for most software packages. These objects are being integrated into newer operating systems. The operating system enables you to organize and search for objects based on their properties and contents.

Each of the basic data types has its own characteristics. Numbers have a precision and usually a scaling factor. Text has a typeface and display size, as well as appearance attributes such as bold, underline, and italic. Pictures can be described by their resolution and the number of colors. Digitized sound is based on a specified sampling and playback rate, and fits into frequency and amplitude ranges. Video combines the attributes of pictures with a frames-per-second definition.

Along with the attributes, several predefined functions can operate on each data type. Basic functions dealing with numbers include totals, calculations, and comparisons. Standard methods to manipulate text include searching, formatting, and spell-checking. Methods dealing with pictures involve artistic alterations such as color or lighting changes, rescaling, and rotation. Existing functions for sound and video are often limited to recording, playback, and compression/decompression.

Most application packages create their own objects as combinations of the basic data types. For example, graphs consist of numbers, text, and pictures. As a result, all of the attributes and functions that apply to the base types also apply to derived graph objects. Hence, graphing packages can perform calculations on numbers, select fonts for displaying text, and enable you to set colors and rotation for the graph. Other applications, such as slide shows, provide additional functions, like controls for how one slide is replaced by another (e.g., fades, dissolves, and wipes). The point is, once you understand the properties and

FIGURE 2.2

Five basic types of data. Because processors deal with only binary data, each format must be converted or digitized. Computer peripheral devices are used to convert the binary data back to the original format.

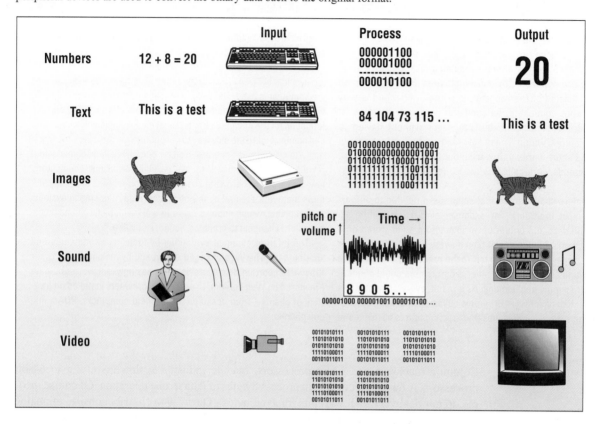

FIGURE 2.3

Numeric precision. If you tell a spreadsheet to display two decimal digits, it performs the additions in the full precision of the data—and displays the data in the right column. If you really want two-digit precision, you should use the Round (x,2) function to round off the data before adding—giving the results in the middle column.

Precision	Round Off before Add	Round Off after Add
5.563	5.56	5.56
0.354	0.35	0.35
6.864	6.86	6.86
12.781	12.77	12.78

functions of the basic data types, you can learn how to use any new application by concentrating on the new objects, their attributes, and functions. This approach is especially true since many applications are designed and built using object-oriented methods.

Numbers and Text

Numbers and text are still the most common types of computer data used in business—for example, each cell in a spreadsheet can display a number or text (labels). Most business reports consist of tables of numbers with supporting text.

As shown in Figure 2.3, you must be careful with round-off—particularly within spreadsheets. Consider the first column of numbers with three decimal digits. What happens when the format command tells a spreadsheet to display those numbers in the third column with only two decimal places? The computer will perform the addition first and round off the displayed result, which means the total will appear to be incorrect. If you really want only two digits of precision, you should use the Round function to convert each number before it is added, as shown in the second column. Precision of calculations is important in business. For example, the 1999 European Union standards require that all monetary conversions be computed to six digits to the right of the decimal point.

FIGURE 2.4

Typefaces fall into two main categories: serif and sans serif. Serifs are little curls and dots on the edges of letters. They make text easier to read; however, san serif typefaces are useful for overheads and signs because the added white space makes them easier to see from a distance. Ornamental typefaces can be used for headlines. Size of fonts is measured in points. Characters in a 72-point font are about one inch tall, and most books and newspapers use a font between 10 and 12 points.

Typeface Classification

Sans serif	Arial 20
	Courier 18 (monospace)
Serif	Garamond 24
	New Century Schoolbook 16
	Times 22
Ornamental	B r a g g a d o c i o 18
	Brush Script 20

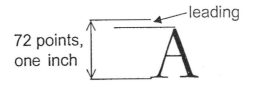

72 points, one inch — leading — A

Since processors can handle only binary data, how can they deal with text? The answer is that they assign a number to each character in the alphabet, which raises a very important, but tricky, question: How many letters are there in the alphabet? The question is tricky because you need to first ask: Which alphabet? Until the 1990s (or later), most computer systems were based on an English-language assumption that there are only 26 letters in the alphabet (plus uppercase letters, numbers, and punctuation). The key to numbering the alphabet is that all hardware and software vendors have to agree to use the same numbering system. It is a little hard for everyone to agree on a system that only displays English characters. Consequently, most computers today support the **Unicode** system. Unicode is an international standard that defines character sets for every modern language and even most dead languages.

A key feature of Unicode is that it can handle oriental languages such as Chinese and Japanese that use ideograms instead of characters. The challenge with ideograms is that each language contains tens of thousands of different ideograms. Character-based languages like English used to be handled by storing one character number in one byte. But one byte can only hold 256 (2^8) numbers—which is not enough to handle ideograms. Consequently, Unicode uses two bytes to count each character or ideogram, enabling it to handle 65,536 (2^{16}) ideograms in each language. It also has the ability to switch to three bytes if even more characters or ideograms are needed.

Why do you care? Remember the increasing importance of international trade. If you build a computer system or database that needs to be used around the world, make sure that you use the Unicode character set so you can collect data in multiple languages. Unfortunately, many systems by default still use the older character systems, and you have to deliberately change the settings to ensure you can handle other languages.

Figure 2.4 illustrates one of the more important properties of text: its typeface. You can choose from several thousand typefaces to achieve a desired style. Be careful with your choices. Some choices are obvious; for example, do not use a script typeface to write a business report. Also, serif fonts are typically used for printed material, and sans-serif fonts are used for very small or very large presentations. Other choices are more subtle and may require the assistance of a professional designer. You will also have to choose font sizes. The basic rules of thumb are that most printed text is displayed at 10 to 12 points. It is also useful to know that letters in a 72-point font are approximately one inch tall.

REALITY BYTES — Communication Requires More Than a PowerPoint Slide

Many graphics artists, designers, and communicators have suggested that PowerPoint is bad because people focus too much on trivial effects and nothing on the content. Peter Norvig, engineering director at Google, Inc., created a sensation with his PowerPoint parody of Lincoln's Gettysburg Address. "People are asking whether, ultimately, PowerPoint makes us all stupid, or does it help us streamline our thoughts. My belief is that PowerPoint doesn't kill meetings. People kill meetings. But using PowerPoint is like having a loaded AK-47 on the table: You can do very bad things with it." Vincent Cerf, who helped define and create the Internet and is now an executive at MCI, notes that PowerPoint often gets in the way of communication because people are distracted. He is fond of observing that "power corrupts and PowerPoint corrupts absolutely." Yet PowerPoint lives on. David Byrne, lead singer of the 1970s group the Talking Heads, notes that it is easy to use. He believes PowerPoint does have an intrinsic bias—indoctrinating users to present things simply. He also created a book and DVD utilizing PowerPoint as an artistic medium.

Source: Adapted from "Does PowerPoint Make Us Stupid?" *CNN Online*, December 30, 2003.

Pictures

Pictures, graphics, and icons are used to display graphs and charts. Pictures are sometimes used as backgrounds or as **icons** in presentations that are used to help the audience remember certain points. In fact, almost all of the computer work that you do today is based on a graphical perspective. Video screens and printers are designed to display everything, including text, in a graphical format. The graphical foundation provides considerably more control over the presentation. For example, you can change the appearance of characters or combine figures and graphs in your reports.

Two basic ways to store images are bitmap and vector formats. The easiest to visualize is bitmap (or raster or pixel) format. A **bitmap image** is converted into small dots or *pixels* (*picture elements*). If the picture is in color, each dot is assigned a (binary) number to represent its color. This method is often used to display photographic pictures where subtle changes in color (such as blends) are important. Bitmap pictures are evaluated in terms of the number of colors and resolution of the picture. **Resolution** is often measured in *dots per inch (dpi)*. You will encounter certain problems with bitmap images. Consider what happens if you create a bitmap picture in a square that has 50 pixels per side. How do you make the image larger? Use larger dots? Then the lines are very rough. How can you stretch the picture into a box that is 100 by 200 pixels? Although these operations are possible, they do not usually produce good results.

Historically, each graphics software package created its own file format for saving image files. Hence, it is easy to find more than 50 different formats on one computer. These differences cause problems when you attempt to exchange files. Your colleagues might not have the same graphics software and might not be able to convert your images correctly. With the Web, it is crucial that everyone is able to read the same graphics files. Hence, two major formats are used for sharing image files: GIF and JPEG. GIF files tend to be smaller, but they support only 256 colors. Hence, GIF files are often used for icons, while JPEG files are used for more realistic photographs. A third standard (PNG) began gaining acceptance in 1998. PNG files combine the advantages of both GIF and JPEG formats. However, remember that all three of these formats are bitmap formats.

When you need to change the size of pictures and keep fine lines and smooth edges, it is better to store pictures in vector format. **Vector images** consist of mathematical descriptions instead of dots. In most cases, they take up less storage space than bitmaps. For example, a line is described by a statement such as: "line from (0,0) to (10,10) in yellow." Do not worry: You do not have to be a mathematician to use vector images. Most of the current drawing packages store their work in vector format. Web browsers are beginning to support a new Internet vector image (SVG: scalable vector graphics) format that provides for faster image transfers and scalable images.

Graphics devices—including displays, printers, digital cameras, and scanners—are evaluated largely in terms of resolution. Resolution is commonly measured by the number of

FIGURE 2.5

Resolution: The image on the left has twice the resolution as the image on the right. In total, the higher resolution image has four times (two squared) the number of pixels and provides more precise lines—particularly diagonal lines.

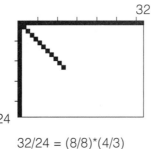

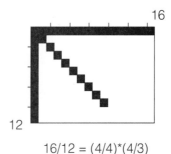

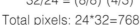

32/24 = (8/8)*(4/3)
Total pixels: 24*32=768

16/12 = (4/4)*(4/3)
Total pixels: 16*12=192

FIGURE 2.6

Resolution examples: Video screens use the 4/3 aspect ratio from the older television standard. HDTV uses a wider 16/9 ratio and about 2.5 times the resolution of the original VGA/TV screen. Final resolution values depend on the physical size of the screen or paper.

Video	Pixels
VGA	640 × 480
XGA	1024 × 768
SXGA	1280 × 1024
UXGA	1600 × 1200
HDTV	1920 × 1080

Printing	
Method	**Pixels/Inch**
Fax	100–200
Ink jet	300–700
Laser	600–1200
Typeset	2400

5-Megapixel Camera (2592 × 1944)	
Print Size	**Pixels/Inch**
3″ × 4″	648
4″ × 5″	486
8″ × 10″	243

pixels (or dots) per inch. Figure 2.5 shows the importance of resolution. Doubling the number of pixels per inch delivers much finer lines—particularly for diagonal lines. But doubling the resolutions results in four times the number of total pixels—which requires substantially more memory and processing time to handle.

Figure 2.6 shows resolutions for some common devices. Notice how the resolution of a photograph declines when it is printed in a larger size. Print resolutions less than 300 pixels per inch (ppi) are grainy and jagged. A similar effect occurs with video screens. On the other hand, operating systems through Windows XP draw text characters with a set font size. Increasing the resolution results in smaller text. For example, if you have a monitor with a physical diagonal measure of 16 inches, an SVGA resolution produces 80 pixels per inch, so the dot on an i is 1/80 of an inch. Increasing the resolution to UXGA creates 125 ppi, so every character and dot shrinks to a little over half the original size (64 percent). The newer releases of Windows are scheduled to solve this problem by separating the size of the fonts from the resolution. Screen displays will behave the way printers do now, so that increasing the resolution will leave the text the same height but provide sharper characters with finer details.

Sound

Digitized sound is increasingly important for computer users. For example, you can use music to add emphasis and entertainment to a presentation. More important, you can use your computer to send voice mail messages and to store notes with your e-mail and documents. Tools exist to convert text to voice—so you can have your computer read your e-mail messages over the phone. Increasingly, voice input is being used both to control the computer and for dictation. Increased storage capacity and declining costs make it easier for sound to be stored in digital format.

As shown in Figure 2.7, sound consists of two basic components: volume (amplitude) and pitch (frequency). These two values are changed over time to produce words and music. To digitize sound, volume and pitch are measured several thousand times per second. The resulting binary numbers are stored in sequence. The challenge is to sample the source often enough so no important information is lost. Synthesizers convert the sampled numbers back into music or speech and play them through amplifiers and speakers.

Most audio applications store sound by digitizing the sound waves. These files can become very large, depending on the quality. If you tell the computer to sample the sound more often, you will get a higher quality recording, but it can take considerably more

FIGURE 2.7

Sound sampling: At a specific point in time, the system measures frequency and amplitude using 16-bit numbers. The quality of the sample is largely determined by the number of times per second the audio is measured. The CD standard is 44,100 times per second.

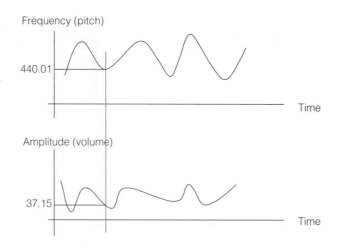

Frequency (pitch)

440.01

Time

Amplitude (volume)

37.15

Time

storage space. For example, compared to high-quality recordings used in CDs, the MP3 standard results in a substantially smaller file with a decrease in quality that most people cannot detect. An even more efficient method of storing music is to file it in the musical instrument data interchange (MIDI) format. MIDI is a method of specifying music based on the musical notation and instrument, so it is substantially more efficient. A version of this method was designed for the MP4 standard, but this standard has not been widely adopted.

Video

The use of computerized video is still in its infancy. Several recent technological changes are lowering the cost of digitized video, which will ultimately increase its use in business. For years, people have talked about sharing video applications, but the hardware, software, and networks could not handle the data. For instance, physicians can send images to specialists for consultation. Engineers can use video transmissions to diagnose problems remotely. Managers can carry on face-to-face conversations. Computer imaging tools also make it easier for workers to create animated presentations for demonstrations or for analyzing designs and layouts.

Although it is possible to convert motion picture and television signals to binary form, the conversion results in a tremendous amount of data. The process is similar to that for single pictures, except standard movies display 24 frames (images) per second, while U.S. televisions display 30 frames per second. Digital video signals also enable you to alter the image. In fact, it is now common to create entire digital scenes that never existed in nature. These techniques are commonly used in marketing. They are also used by engineers to develop and market-test new products.

Size Complications

To understand the importance of the five types of data, it helps to examine the size of each type. For many years, computers predominantly handled numbers and limited text. Over time, usage has gradually changed to include images, sound, and video. The more complex data types require much greater storage space, processing power, and transmission capacity.

Consider a typical single-spaced printed page. An average page might contain 5,000 characters. A 300-page book would hold about 1.5 million characters. Now, consider a picture. At 300 dots per inch, a full 8.5- by 11-inch page would require a little over a million bytes if it were scanned in black and white. A photograph in a base resolution with 16 million colors (24 bits per pixel) would require 18 **megabytes** (million characters) of storage space.

Sound and video require considerably more storage space. Remember that thousands of numbers are being generated every second. A typical CD holds 700 megabytes of data, which can store 72 minutes of stereo music. At lower quality, the current standard for digitizing telephone conversations generates 64 kilobits per second, almost half a megabyte per minute. Video generates approximately 3 megabytes of data every second. Figure 2.8 summarizes the basic size characteristics for the standard data types.

FIGURE 2.8

Size complications: Lossy compression results in substantially less data but at a lower quality. A text file is compressed with a Zip folder. An image is compressed with JPEG from high to low quality. Sound is compressed with a WAV file (44.1 kbps) and WMA (64 kbps). Video is compressed with the DV standard and WMV at 6383 kbps.

Object	Raw	Compressed	Lossy
Text and numbers	5 KB/page	2.3 KB/page	N/A
Image (300 dpi, 24-bit color, 4 × 6 in.)	6.32 MB	2.4 MB	78–245 KB
Sound (44.1 KHz stereo)	170 KB/sec	100 KB/sec	0.01 KB/sec
Video (NTSC 30 fps, stereo sound)	25 MB/sec	3.7 MB/sec	1 MB/sec

FIGURE 2.9

Data compression: Storing every single pixel requires a huge amount of space. Compression looks for patterns. For example, instead of storing 1,000 black dots in a row, it is much shorter to store a note that says 1,000 black dots come next.

Data Compression

Storing every single pixel in a photograph takes a huge amount of space at higher resolutions. Data compression techniques scan the data looking for patterns. The photograph in Figure 2.9 provides an example. Instead of storing several thousand black dots for the bottom row of the picture, the compression algorithm would store a short note that the picture repeats 1,000 black pixels. Some systems, such as the JPEG method, support lossy compression. In these cases, patterns are matched as long as the pixels are "close" to an existing match. When you compress the data, you get to select how close of a match to allow. For example, with a tight match, the system might allow a very dark gray pixel to count as black, but might not allow a dark blue one to match a black pattern. Lossy compression methods are commonly used to transmit photographs, audio files, and videos.

Hardware Components

What are the main components of a computer? As a manager, you need to understand the basic features of hardware. You do not have to be a computer-repair expert, but you need to understand the fundamental structure and characteristics of the computer components. The most important first step is to recognize that declining prices rule this industry. Because of technological advancements and standardization you know that you can buy a new computer next year that is faster than the one you just bought today. Instead of worrying about your "new" computer becoming obsolete, just accept that you will be able to buy a faster computer next year, which raises the questions: How often should you buy a new computer and what features should you buy? The answers to these questions change over time and depend on your specific uses, but as long as you understand how to evaluate the major components, you will be able to make a rational decision.

Along with declining prices, one of the most important trends in hardware is the shrinking size. But regardless of the size, computers consist of four basic component devices to handle: input, output, processing, and secondary storage. Of course, each category has hundreds of options so that you can tailor the computer to your specific needs. One trend that you have to remember is that the hardware industry changes rapidly, especially for small systems. Most computers that you buy today will have a short economic life—perhaps only three years. At the end of that time, each component will have changed so much that typically you will want to replace the entire computer.

The relationship among the four components is summarized in Figure 2.10. Note that the process subsystem consists of **random access memory (RAM)** and at least one processor. In many ways, the **processor** is the most important component of the computer. It carries out instructions written by various programmers. It uses RAM to temporarily store instructions and data. Data and instructions that need to be stored for a longer time are transferred to secondary storage. The capabilities, performance, and cost of the computer are affected by each of these components.

One of the interesting aspects of computers is that the various components operate at different speeds. The processor is the fastest of the group and its performance is measured in **nanoseconds** (billionths of a second). Processors are even faster than RAM. As a result, processors contain separate memory caches embedded in the chip. When the processor asks for data items from RAM, it loads a large chunk of data at one time so that it can fetch related items from its internal cache to save time. Secondary storage devices are substantially slower. Because most disk drives are mechanical, performance time is measured in **milliseconds** (thousandths of a second). Divide those numbers, and you see that the processor is a million times faster than the disk drive! Of course, humans are even slower—most people type a couple of characters per second. Why do these speed differences matter? It means the processor can be told to do multiple tasks at the same time. While you are typing, the processor can take a fraction of its time to store your keystroke, then retrieve some data from the disk drive, then send an item to the printer, then add some numbers together, and finally return to get another keystroke.

Processors

Processors come in a wide variety of formats. Some computers use one processor that consists of a single silicon chip. Others use several different chips to make up one processor. Still other computers use multiple processors. The critical point to remember is that each type of processor is unique. Each manufacturer creates its processor in a certain way and designs it

FIGURE 2.10

Computer performance and capabilities are highly dependent on the peripheral devices. Most computers will use several devices in each of the four major categories. Technological progress in one area often results in changes to all four types of components.

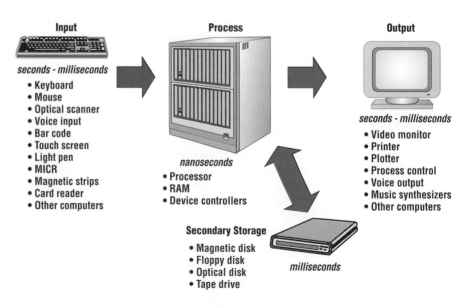

Input

seconds - milliseconds

- Keyboard
- Mouse
- Optical scanner
- Voice input
- Bar code
- Touch screen
- Light pen
- MICR
- Magnetic strips
- Card reader
- Other computers

Process

nanoseconds

- Processor
- RAM
- Device controllers

Output

seconds - milliseconds

- Video monitor
- Printer
- Plotter
- Process control
- Voice output
- Music synthesizers
- Other computers

Secondary Storage

- Magnetic disk
- Floppy disk
- Optical disk
- Tape drive

milliseconds

REALITY BYTES Building Processors and Memory Chips

Building processors and memory chips involves growing silicon crystals and slicing them into wafers. The internal circuits are then etched onto these wafers using chemical deposition techniques. The catch is that cramming more storage on a chip requires finer and finer circuit lines. Common RAM chips in 1994 held 4 megabits of data, with leading-edge chips at 16 megabits. Because of capital costs, manufacturers will only produce new chips if they can gain four times the amount of storage.

In 2001, common processor and RAM chips were being created with lines that were 0.12 microns (about 1/200,000 of an inch) wide. A micron is one millionth of a meter.

Using conventional laser lithography to etch patterns onto the chip becomes difficult as the lines get smaller. Conventional meth-ods rely on a mask to cover parts of the chip, which is then exposed to laser light that removes a photo-resistive material from the un-covered sections. The main difficulty with small sizes is that the light waves are too wide. Modern chip technology relies on ultraviolet rays because they are narrower, but they are still 0.193 microns wide. Manufacturers are experimenting with smaller wave x-rays or electron beams.

A second problem is that the etching size is coming closer to the size of a single molecule, which brings in quantum physics effects, where atoms randomly "tunnel" through barriers.

Researchers are working with new materials and entirely new technologies, such as biocomputers, to overcome the physical lim-its of the existing process.

to follow a specific set of instructions. For instance, a processor made by Intel works differently than one made by Motorola (used in Apple computers). As a result, instructions written for one processor cannot be used directly by the other processor. Note that some companies (especially in the personal computer world) produce "clones" of the leading chip manufacturer. For example, Advanced Micro Devices and Cyrix/IBM make chips that are compatible with Intel processors and can run the same programs. Conversely, when Intel develops a new chip, like the Itanium, it must be careful to provide backward compatibility, so that the millions of existing programs can continue to run on the new processors.

You can check on the status of your processor and its various tasks by opening the Task Manager. Right-click on the Windows menu bar and select the Processes tab, but be careful not to end any of the processes or your computer might crash. Most of the time the System Idle Process will be the main user—which means the processor is simply waiting. You can also watch the performance chart to see the total demands placed on your processor. If you find that the processor is consistently in heavy use, you should consider buying a new machine. More likely, there is something wrong with your computer and you should check it for viruses and spyware software described in Chapter 5.

The Evolution of Processors

Figure 2.11 shows the approximate measure of Intel processor performance over time, as indicated by an index value (estimated SysMark). The exponential increase in performance arises because the industry has been able to follow Moore's Law: the number of components placed on a chip doubles every 18 months. But three potential problems are facing the chip industry: (1) light waves are too wide to draw increasingly smaller lines; (2) when the components shrink to the size of a couple of atoms, the electronic properties no longer behave the same (quantum effects); and (3) the power requirements and heat generation increase dramatically.

For at least two decades, the IT industry has lived with and relied on this increasing performance (and reduction in costs). Eventually, this pattern will stop—possibly within 10 or 20 years. With luck and research, the industry will develop entirely new technology that will produce even greater performance. But in any case, managers need to monitor technical developments and be prepared for substantial changes.

Random Access Memory

As processor speed has improved, RAM has become a crucial factor in system performance. Because disk drives are mechanical, they are the greatest bottleneck in a computer system. Hence, modern operating systems try to hold as much data as possible in RAM. Although RAM speeds have remained relatively constant in the last few years, RAM price has

REALITY BYTES   Is It Getting Hot in Here?

The latest, fastest processors gain their performance by packing transistors closer together and driving them with a faster clock rate. These techniques quickly generate large amounts of heat. Temperatures inside a PC can reach 70 degrees Celsius (158 degrees Fahrenheit). Manufacturers are looking for ways to keep the components cool—heat shortens the life of the components. One company, Asia Vital Components (AVC) of Taiwan, specializes in cooling products and has $250 million (USD) a year in revenue. Exotic devices include cooling pipes for laptops and magnesium cases to dissipate heat faster, although moving heat to the case of a laptop is not always a good thing for customers. There are at least two reports of

gentlemen suffering burn blisters from using notebook computers on their laps. In the meantime, Intel has changed its focus. Instead of continually pushing the envelope for higher speeds, the highly successful Centrino laptop chipset was specifically designed to generate less heat and consume less power. Shekhar Borkar, director of circuit research at Intel, notes that "with the Centrino's success, you can expect in the future for us to learn from this exercise and impact our future desktop lines."

Source: Adapted from "Overheated PCs Mean Hot Business for Cooling Firms," *CNN Online,* June 4, 2004.

FIGURE 2.11

To assist buyers, Intel provides a measure of its own processors. The rating is an index that measures relative performance. A processor with a rating of 2 would generally be about twice as fast as a processor with a rating of 1. Of course, other devices also influence the overall system speed, so just buying a faster processor does not guarantee that your machine will fun faster.

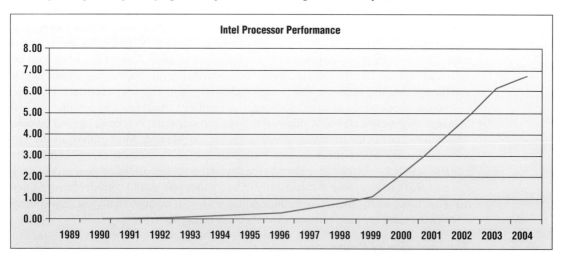

dropped substantially. In relative terms, RAM is virtually free. For a few hundred dollars, you can easily buy enough RAM to hold several applications and their data in RAM at one time.

Connections

Even if two computers have the same basic components, it is still possible for one machine to be substantially faster than the other. The reason is that the components need to exchange data with each other. This communication requires an electrical connection. Most computers have special slots that form the connection between add-on boards and the processor *bus.* Various manufacturers make boards that fit into these slots. The processor can exchange data with these other devices, but it is constrained by the design of the bus. For example, even if a processor can handle 64 bits of data at a time, the bus might not have the connections to allow it to transfer that much data at a time. Each computer manufacturer has to choose how to design the bus. Standards enable users to exchange cards and devices from one computer to another. The problem is that a bus designed for today's computers will eventually become obsolete as the processor improves. At some point, the standards need to be changed. In the personal computer market, standards for the bus have been gradually evolving. For several years, the industry has relied on an Intel-sponsored design known as the *Personal Computer Interconnect (PCI)* bus. PCI was also designed to make it easier for users to set up their computers. Over time, manufacturers have increased the transfer speeds of PCI, but it is increasingly a limitation in computer performance.

Vendors are developing new technologies to connect computers and components. The IEEE 1394 or firewire standard is commonly used to transfer data from video equipment, but is also used to connect disk drives to the computer. USB 2.0 is a similar standard used to connect peripherals including disk drives and RAM drives. Fiber channel and serial ATA are used to connect disk drives at high speeds. Ultra-wideband wireless (UWB) might eventually be used to connect devices at high speeds without using cables. For example, you could tell your video camera to send the signal to your television simply by setting it next to the TV and pushing a button.

Why are these technologies important? Because they enable you to create new types of computers where the components can be placed in different locations, sometimes even miles away. For example, users can carry substantially smaller devices if they do not need to carry disk drives, or if additional processing can be instantly obtained from distant machines.

Parallel Processors

In the past, when processors were more expensive, designers used only one processor in a machine. Today, many computers contain multiple processors. Although it can be a desirable feature, you must be careful when evaluating parallel-processing machines. If a computer has four processors, it is tempting to say that the machine is four times faster than a computer with only one processor. Indeed, many computer companies advertise their computers this way. Can a computer with four processors really do your job four times faster? The answer is that it depends on your job. Consider an example: A computer with two processors has to add two sets of numbers together. Each processor works on one pair of numbers and finishes in half the time of a single processor. Now, the same two computers have to work the problem in Figure 2.12.

Notice that the second calculation depends on the outcome of the first one. The second one cannot be computed until the first one is finished. Even if we assign one processor to each calculation, the parallel-processing machine will take just as long as the single processor.

Massively parallel machines can include thousands of processors. They are used for some highly specialized applications. For example, governments use them to break codes; physicists use them to simulate large-scale events such as nuclear explosions and weather patterns; computer artists use them at special-effects studios, such as Industrial Light & Magic, to create movies. This concept has been extended with the use of **grid computing,** where thousands or millions of separate computers are assigned portions of a task. The search for extraterrestrial intelligence (SETI) project is the most famous example using a grid approach. Users are encouraged to download a small program that runs in the background on the computer. The program retrieves portions of radio-astronomy data from an Internet site and scans them looking for patterns. The millions of participating computers provide a huge (free) resource to process data that could not be handled by any other method. Using similar software, the grid concept can be applied to business and scientific applications. A company could use existing clerical computers or, since personal computers are so inexpensive today, could buy hundreds of machines and tie them together to handle large databases.

FIGURE 2.12

Some computations must be performed in sequence, so there is little to be gained with multiple parallel processors. In this example, the second computation (yyy) must wait for the first one to finish.

```
  23        xx
+ 54      + 92
-----     -----
  xx       yyy
```

Today's computers take advantage of multiple processors in more subtle ways. Most computers today utilize a separate graphics processor to draw items on the screen. It is a sophisticated processor with its own RAM that handles complex three-dimensional calculations. The 2005 (or 2006) version of Windows will take advantage of this processor and off-load all drawing tasks to the graphics processor—creating faster graphics and enabling special effects within applications.

Input

Because of the variety of data types, many input devices are available. The purpose of an input device is to convert data into electronic binary form. Keyboards are the most common method of entering new text and data. Note that you can purchase different types of keyboards to suit individual users. For example, some keyboards enable you to change the layout of the keys. Keyboards have their own feel; some individuals prefer sensitive keys requiring a light touch while others like stiffer keys to support their hands.

Ergonomics is the study of how machines can be made to fit humans better. One of the main conclusions of this research in the computer area is that individuals need to be able to adjust input (and output) devices to their own preference. Forcing people to adapt to rigid devices can lead to complaints and even physical injuries. Since the mid-1980s, many workers have encountered a disabling condition known as *repetitive stress injury,* which some people claim results from extended use of tools that do not physically match the worker.

Although there is limited scientific study of these injuries and their causes, some people have found relief after ergonomic changes to their work environment. Complaints typically involve back pain, eye strain, headaches, arm and shoulder pain, and finger or wrist pain due to carpal tunnel syndrome. Common ergonomic suggestions include adjustable chairs, footrests, armrests, adjustable keyboards, high-resolution low-flicker monitors, and improved lighting. Of course, all of these adjustments cost money—especially if they are added as an afterthought. The key to the problem is to evaluate individual requirements and adjust the environment *before* installing computers.

Pointing Devices

With the increased use of graphics and pictures, it is common for computers to use pointing devices for input. A mouse is the most popular device in use today, although light pens, touch screens, and digitizer tablets are heavily used in some applications. Touch screens are commonly used for displays that involve customers or other atypical computer users. Many tourist bureaus, hotels, and shopping areas use computer displays with touch screens to give directions to visitors. Besides the fingerprints, the biggest problem with touch screens is that the tip of your finger is often too large to be a useful pointer. For more detailed use, an engineer who is designing a wiring diagram for an automobile would use a digitizer tablet with a special pen to draw fine lines and select individual points that are close together.

Scanners

When you are dealing with pictures, it is often helpful to have a scanner convert a paper-based image into digital (bitmap) form. For certain types of images (line drawings and text), vector tracing software can convert the bitmap image into vector form.

The quality of a scanner is measured by the number of pixels per inch that it can distinguish as well as the number of colors. Most scanners can read at least 600 dots per inch. More dots mean you get finer lines and sharper pictures.

Scanners also can be used to input text and data into a computer. The scanner first converts the page into a picture of dots. Then **optical character recognition (OCR)** software examines the picture and looks for text. The software checks each line and deciphers one character at a time. Although OCR software is improving, it is not 100 percent accurate. Some systems automatically look up each word in a dictionary to spot conversion errors and improve accuracy. Even then, users report about a 95 percent accuracy rate—which is highly dependent on the quality of the original document.

Pen-Based Systems

A new category of computers is being created. Some handheld, notebook-size computers use a pen as the primary input device. The pen is used to point to objects on the screen, make changes to documents, and even write notes. In some cases, the machines can convert handwriting to computer text—much like OCR converts typed papers. Of course, deciphering individual handwriting is much more difficult than reading typed characters, and the accuracy of data can be limited. Despite the hype about potential applications for traveling managers (and salespeople), the first versions of pen-based computers did not sell well. As processors, storage, and display technology and telecommunications improve, we will probably see more acceptance of pen-based handheld computers.

Sound

Sound is initially captured with a microphone that converts sound pressure waves into electrical signals. A *sampler* then converts these signals into numeric data that can be stored on the computer. Musical **synthesizer** technology is used to convert the numbers back to electrical signals that can be heard with speakers. Sound boards can be purchased for personal computers that contain both the sampler and synthesizer technology. Digital sound conversion occurs on almost every long distance telephone call you make. Your voice is converted to 1s and 0s to be sent across fiber-optic telephone lines.

Speech Recognition

As long as computers have existed, individuals have dreamed of being able to talk to them and have their words translated into text. Today, computers can digitize and record speech, and they can convert spoken words into computer text. Some problems still exist, and the systems need to be trained to a specific user. Common problems include the use of homonyms, variations in speech patterns or dialects, and the effects of punctuation on meaning.

Initially, speech recognition systems were adopted by occupations that require note taking along with two hands to do the job. Quality control inspectors and surgeons use them regularly. As performance continues to improve, we will see an expanded use of speech recognition systems among all users. Ultimately, speech recognition will be a key element in dealing with computers. Keyboards do not work well in a wireless environment. They are too large to be portable and hard to use.

Video Capture

As technology improves, companies are increasingly adding video clips to presentations. Digital video transmissions are also being used for communication. Because computer monitors and television sets are loosely based on the same technology, it would seem easy to merge the two. However, computer monitors deal with different types of video signals. Computers need special video boards to convert and display TV signals on the computer monitor. These cards accept standard coaxial video output from a VCR, camcorder, and television receiver. Not only can the signal be displayed on a monitor, but it can also be converted to digital form and saved or replayed. Digital video offers substantial improvements over traditional video signals. But several nations have different standards for digital video, and the signals are not directly compatible with computer formats. Consequently, you will continue to need conversion devices.

Output

Most people are interested in two types of output: video and paper copy. Video output is created by a video card and displayed on a monitor. Computer projection systems for meetings and presentations use high-intensity light to project an image onto a screen. In addition to resolution, they are evaluated by the intensity of the light, measured in lumens. Other display technologies have been developed including heads-up displays for cars, personal projection systems that project an image from special glasses, and electronic ink that displays text and images on flexible displays.

Technology Toolbox: Voice Input

Problem: You are a slow typist or need to use your hands for other tasks.
Tools: A voice input system is built into Microsoft Office. You need a decent microphone to use it, and a headset microphone is recommended because it minimizes external noise. The system is relatively easy to set up, but it takes a half hour to train it so that it recognizes your voice. Remember that no voice system is perfect, so you will still have to edit the text that it enters. You can find information on speech recognition in the Office help system by searching on the "speech" key word.

You can install the speech recognition software within either Word or the Microsoft Windows Control Panel. Within Word, select Tools/Speech.

From the Control Panel, select Add/Remove Programs, find Office and click Change. Use Add or Remove Features and find the option to add Speech under the Alternative User Input. Once the software is installed, you have to train it. Follow the installation instructions to perform the basic training. To improve recognition accuracy, you should also take the time to read at least one of the additional training documents. Once the system is installed and trained, you can dictate text into an Office document. Remember that the system works better if you dictate complete sentences.

The voice toolbar enables you to turn the microphone off, so that you can speak to someone else or cough. Notice that it also enables you to switch between Dictation and Voice Command modes. The help system provides additional information about command mode and the additional things that you can say to control the computer with voice. For example, in Voice Command, you can say the word "font" followed by the name of the font to change the font in use. You can also start other programs and select items on the menu. The help documentation includes information on commands you can use during dictation. Some of the common commands are in the table.

Command	Character/Result
period or dot	.
comma	,
new line	Enter
new paragraph	Enter twice
open paren or open parenthesis	(
close paren or close parenthesis	)
force num, pause, digits	numbers (for several numbers in a row)
spell it or spelling mode, letters	spell out a word
microphone	turn microphone on or off
correct that	change or delete the last phrase entered
scratch that	delete the last phrase entered
go to top	move to top of the document (or use bottom)
move up	move up one line (also accepts down, left, and right)
backspace	delete one character to the left
select word	select a word (or use phrase with several options)

Quick Quiz: Use the Help system to find the commands for the following:

1. !, ?, #, $
2. Make a word boldface or italic.
3. Print the current page.

The other common output device is the printer. Printers come in many different forms. The most common formats are laser and ink jet, where the output is created by printing dots on the page. Common resolutions include 600 dpi and 1200 dpi lasers. In contrast, standard typesetters, such as those that are used to print books, operate at resolutions of at least 2,400 dots per inch. Again, higher-resolution devices are more expensive. Also, the increased amount of data being displayed takes longer to print (for the first copy).

FIGURE 2.13

Printer evaluations. Printers are
evaluated in terms of initial cost,
cost per page, resolution, and
speed. There are many types of
printers, led by laser, ink jets, and
dot matrix printers. Prices vary
depending largely on speed and
resolution. Technological changes
are leading to new varieties of
printers that can produce full
color at a cost of around 5 cents
to 10 cents per page.

Printer	Initial Cost (dollars)	Cost per Page (cents)	Quality (dots/inch)	Speed (pages/min)
Laser: B&W	400–50,000	0.6–3	600–1,200	4–8–17–100+
Laser: Color	900+	5–75	600–1,200	0.5–8
Ink jet	100–500	5–150	300–720	0.1–4

Laser printers operate much like photocopiers. In fact, newer copiers include hardware to connect to a local network so the departmental copier can function as a high-speed printer. From your desktop, you can tell the printer to make multiple copies and collate and staple them—at speeds of over 70 pages per minute. As noted in Figure 2.13, the initial cost is usually only a minor component of a printer's price. It is more important that you look at the cost per page—particularly for color copies.

Secondary Storage

Why are there secondary storage devices? Why not just store everything in high-speed RAM? The main reason is that standard RAM is dynamic—which means that the data disappears when the power is turned off. The second reason is cost: a 160-GB drive costs less than $100. Even at today's relatively low prices, the equivalent amount of RAM would cost several thousand dollars.

Hard disk drives are the most common method of secondary storage. The primary drawback to disk drives is that data transfer is limited by the physical need to spin the disk and to move the read/write heads. Besides being slower, mechanical processes are sensitive to movement and deteriorate faster than pure electronic systems. Consequently, several manufacturers have developed static memory chips that hold data for portable devices—like Sony's memory stick. USB drives are a popular method for transporting data and have quickly replaced floppy disk drives. The main drawback to static memory is that the write speeds are quite slow. In many cases, it takes longer to store a file onto a static RAM drive than to write it to a hard disk. For example, a fast USB drive can write 5 megabytes per second, while an average disk drive can write 30 megabytes per second. However with no moving parts and a tiny physical size, the USB drives are a convenient way to carry some pretty big files.

Except for prices (declining) and capacity (increasing), typical secondary storage devices have changed little during the last few years. Secondary storage is needed to hold data and programs for longer periods. Secondary storage is evaluated by three attributes: capacity, speed, and price. Figure 2.14 shows the values for different types of storage.

With the increasing importance of data, companies are searching for ways to prevent loss of data by providing continuous backups. One straightforward method is to install an extra disk drive and keep duplicate copies of all files on this *mirror drive*. If something goes wrong with one of the drives, users simply switch to the other drive. A second method of protecting data is known as a **redundant array of independent drives (RAID).** Instead of containing one large drive, this system consists of several smaller drives. Large files are split into pieces stored on several different physical drives. At the same time, the pieces can be duplicated and stored in more than one location. In addition to the duplication, RAID systems provide faster access to the data, because each of the drives can be searching through its part of the file at the same time.

On personal machines, even if you do not want to spend the money for a RAID solution, it can be a good idea to buy two hard drives instead of one large drive. Particularly for data-intensive applications like video editing, it is wise to put the operating system and application software on one drive and place the data files on the second drive. Two drives are better than one because the computer can retrieve the data simultaneously from both drives. In fact, video and large database applications often benefit from using three drives: one for the system, one for the main data, and one to hold temporary files. Putting everything on one drive forces the computer to trade between tasks and wait for the single drive to spin to the proper location.

FIGURE 2.14

Secondary storage comparison: Hard drive prices and speed make them the best choice for secondary storage. Tapes make good backup systems because of the cost per gigabyte and 50 to 100 gigabyte storage per tape, but the sequential storage makes it harder to retrieve data.

Drive	Capacity (gigabytes)	Speed (write MB/s)	Initial Cost (dollars)	Cost/GByte (dollars)
Magnetic hard	80–320	30–50	80–300	0.50
USB drive	0.064–1	1–5	40–350	350
Tape	250–2,000	2–20	300–5,000+	0.50–1.00
CD-ROM	0.700	2–5	50	0.70
DVD	4.77–9.0	2–5	50–500	0.30

Magnetic tapes are also used to store data. Their biggest drawback is that they can only store and retrieve data sequentially. That means you have to search the tape from the beginning to find any data. A single tape can hold 20 to 100 gigabytes of data. Compression can double or triple the capacity of a single tape, driving the cost per gigabyte from $0.50 down to $0.20 or lower. Because of these two features, tapes are most commonly used to hold backup data.

With the increased use of images, sound, and video, there is a need for substantially greater storage capacity for data files. Optical disks have provided substantial capacity at relatively low costs. The optical (or magneto-optical) disk drive uses a laser light to read data stored on the disk. **CD-ROM** stands for *compact disc read-only memory,* the format used to store music CDs. The ROM portion of the name means that you can only read data from the disk. A special machine is required to store data on a CD-ROM. One side of a CD can hold 700 megabytes of data, and blank disks are inexpensive. The biggest drawback is that saving data to a CD is relatively slow.

The **DVD (digital video disk** or **digital versatile disk)** is a significantly better technology. DVD was created to distribute digitized video. Compared to CD, the strengths of DVD are (1) increased capacity, (2) significantly faster access speeds, and (3) standards for audio, video, and computer data. A basic DVD holds 4.77 GB of data. However, the commercial DVDs for movies can hold as much as 9 GB of data by using an advanced writing technique. Personal DVD writers with this double capacity are becoming available, but the technology scares the movie studios, so the drives will likely have some type of copy limitations.

Operating Systems

Why is the operating system so important? Computers follow instructions called software that are written by programmers. Every computer needs one special type of software known as the *operating system.* The **operating system** is software that is responsible for communication among the hardware components. The operating system is also a primary factor in determining how the user deals with the machine.

Historically, each computer manufacturer created its own operating system tailored for that specific hardware. Proprietary operating systems caused many problems; in particular, changing vendors typically required purchasing new application software. AT&T researchers began to solve this problem when they created a hardware-independent operating system known as *UNIX.* This operating system was designed to work with computers from many different manufacturers. However, UNIX is not a complete standard, and application software must generally be rewritten before it can function on different computers.

Today, fewer operating system choices exist. Personal computers generally run a version of Microsoft Windows. However, a version of UNIX is available for personal computers. AT&T essentially released the source code for UNIX to the public. Linus Torvalds used the code to create an inexpensive and relatively popular version for personal computers. His base versions are called Linux. Apple computer also adopted the UNIX foundation with its OS X operating system. Most midrange computers and many servers also run an operating system derived from UNIX. Notably, both Sun (Solaris) and IBM (AIX and Linux) focus on UNIX versions for their servers. IBM also continues to support some older, proprietary

REALITY BYTES   Can You Reduce Costs with Open-Source Software?

Many companies have been struggling to reduce technology costs. One area that offers substantial cost reductions is to switch to open-source software. In particular, companies have moved many server-based applications to Linux software. Amazon.com began the process in 2000 by switching its Web servers to Linux. Over the following four years, more server applications were converted. In early 2004, the company announced that the last of its applications had been ported to the lower-cost system. Switching from Sun UNIX servers to HP ProLiant servers running Linux, the company noted

that it cut its technology expenses by 25 percent to $16 million. Over the holiday season, the new system processed the shipment of over 1 million packages a day and processed 20 million inventory updates each day. The new system represents an architectural shift, from a system that scales vertically to a horizontally scalable approach. The server farm method also provides fault tolerance—if one machine crashes, the others pick up the slack.

Source: Adapted from Sean Gallagher, "Amazon.com at LinuxWorld: All Linux, All the Time," *eWeek,* January 21, 2004.

operating systems. For servers and midrange systems, you still typically use the operating system provided by the hardware manufacturer.

The battle over operating systems continues today. At least some portion of Microsoft's market strength is tied to its ownership and control of the desktop operating system (Windows). Yet the standardization of the operating system has made it possible for vendors to create thousands of useful software applications. The relatively open platform has encouraged the development of thousands of new hardware devices that can be easily installed in millions of computers worldwide. Yet the common operating system has also made it easier for hackers and viruses to attack millions of machines. And many smaller companies are concerned about the ability to compete against a company as firmly entrenched as Microsoft.

Computers in e-Business

How does the Internet change the role of computers? The Internet and the Web changed computing and business in several ways. Beyond the issues of connectivity, the key feature of the Web was the introduction and acceptance of the browser. To see its importance, you need simply look at the Microsoft antitrust case, where the integrated browser played a critical role. The reason the browser is so important is that it has become the standard display mechanism. Increasingly, applications are being built that rely on the services of the browser. When the browser becomes the most important display device, then nothing else matters. For example, developers no longer care what type of computer you use: IBM or Apple; desktop, laptop, handheld personal digital assistant (PDA), or cell phone. As long as your equipment supports the major browser standards, you will be able to use the applications.

What Is a Browser?

At heart, browsers are simply software display devices. They read incoming files, recognize the data type, and display the data as instructed. The data could be text, images, sound, or even video. However, the sound and video are usually handled by an add-in component for the browser because standards are still evolving.

To add more interactivity, browsers also have an internal programming language. Developers can include program code that gives detailed instructions to the browser and reacts to changes users make. For example, when users move the cursor, the code can highlight an object on the browser. Browser code is also used to check user data. This code runs entirely on the local machine, but can send data in batches to the Web server.

The beauty of the browser approach is that it standardizes the way data is displayed, so that everyone is free to choose any hardware and software platform they prefer. Since browsers are relatively easy to implement and do not require huge amounts of hardware, they can be built into smaller, portable devices. Combined with the wireless Internet possibilities, these new devices have the ability to change the business world.

As technology and the Internet become more important in our lives and businesses, portability becomes increasingly critical. Even the portability offered by laptops is useful. For example, you might need to pull up sales data in a meeting or take some work home with you. In other cases, even more portability is needed. Tablet PCs and PDAs provide the ability to access the Internet and your corporate servers as long as you can find a network connection. Wireless connections are available in many locations, but still have limited range. Newer cell phones offer greater connectivity to the Internet from any major city or transportation area in the world. As people demand greater continuous access to the Internet, portable devices become more important. At the same time, the servers that store the data and provide the major processing will also become more important.

What Is a Server?

So you want to run a Web site? Being a participant in the Internet and running a browser is one thing. Running a Web server is completely different. Establishing an e-business requires that you either run a server or pay someone to run it for you, so you should understand some of the main issues in Web servers.

Technically, almost any reasonably up-to-date PC can function as a Web server. A Web server is essentially a piece of software that monitors the full-time Internet connection and delivers the requested pages. But to perform e-business tasks, the server also needs to evaluate programmed Web code and interact with a database.

In most cases, the primary issue with Web servers is scalability. The goal is to build a server inexpensively enough to make the application profitable, yet capable of expanding to handle increased demands of the future. It does not take much hardware to handle a simple Web site. Even a laptop can be used—but do not expect it to handle many simultaneous hits or complex database processing.

In terms of hardware, the primary characteristics that you want in a Web server are (1) scalability, (2) easy backup, and (3) easy maintenance. One solution to all of these problems is splitting the major computer components into separate pieces. For example, server farms use multiple small computers instead of one large machine. A storage area network (SAN) can be built using fiber channel connections to a set of external disk drives. If a processor or disk drive needs to be replaced, it can be hot-swapped—each individual component can be shut down and replaced without shutting down the rest of the system. Similarly, new processors and drives can be added without disrupting the others—and the system automatically identifies the changes and uses the hardware. These types of systems provide a relatively inexpensive solution to the three goals. But managing the system requires a sophisticated operating system and Web server software.

Application Software

What are the main software applications used in business? The main reason for buying a computer is its application software. It is good software that makes your job easier. Regardless of your job, you will always perform certain tasks. As a manager and decision maker, you first have to gather data (research). Then you analyze the data and determine alternatives (involving calculations). Next you will make decisions and implement them (requiring writing, communication, and organizing resources). Each of these tasks can be supported by computer resources. The trick is to use the appropriate tools for each task. The objective is to use the tools to make you more productive in your job.

The catch is that productivity is a slippery problem in business—especially with respect to computer tools. One measure of productivity involves efficiency: Can you perform tasks faster? A second, more complicated measure of productivity involves effectiveness: Can you make better decisions? Early uses of computers focused on improving efficiency by au-

REALITY BYTES   Personal Computer Sales

In the fourth quarter of 2003, Hewlett-Packard (HP) sold more personal computers worldwide than any other company, but Dell held the lead for the entire year. Presumably, HP made the gain by selling through retail channels, compared to Dell's overall lead in sales to businesses. In the quarter, HP shipped 7.5 million PCs worldwide, an increase of 21 percent from the same quarter in the prior year. Dell was only slightly behind with 7.1 million sales. Total worldwide shipments in the fourth quarter were 48.4 million, according to research firm Gartner. For the entire year, Dell shipped 25.8 million computers.

HP was second with 25 million machines. Total worldwide shipments for 2003 were 152.6 million according to IDC or 168.9 million according to Gartner. (Gartner includes some unbranded and self-assembled computers that IDC does not count.) The other large producers were IBM, Fujitsu Siemens, and Toshiba. Gateway and eMachines combined sales were just under 1 million units.

Source: Adapted from Tom Krazit and Robert McMillan, "HP Regains Lead in PC Shipments in Q4," *Computerworld,* January 15, 2004.

tomating manual tasks. The tools were often justified on the basis of decreased labor costs. Today, managerial uses often focus on effectiveness, which is harder to measure.

An important concept to remember with application software is that it was created by teams of designers and programmers. In the "old" days, when software was custom-written for specific companies and users, users could tell the designers how the software should behave. Today, we are moving rapidly to off-the-shelf software that is created to support the needs of millions of different users. In creating the software, designers had to make thousands of decisions about what the software should do and how it should appear. Sometimes their final choices might seem strange, and software does not always work the way you might prefer. Some issues can be resolved by customizing the software to your particular situation. Other times, just remember that you acquired the software for a tiny fraction of the price you would have paid for custom software.

Research: Databases

Almost any job involves workers searching for information. This search could involve any of the five basic types of data. Computers have made it substantially easier to find, compare, and retrieve data. Two important strengths of a *database management system (DBMS)* are the ease of sharing data and the ability to search for data by any criteria. In terms of productivity, a DBMS can both make you more efficient and improve your decisions. It improves efficiency by providing easier and faster data retrieval. By providing more complete access to data, a DBMS helps ensure that your decision incorporates all relevant data.

One complication with research is that you must first determine where the information is located. It could be located on your personal computer, the group's networked server, the company's central computers, a computer run by the government, or one purchased from another company. Unless all of these databases are connected, you must first determine which database to search. Today, along with numbers and text, DBMSs can handle large text files, pictures, sound, and video. DBMSs form the foundation of almost all business applications. Chapter 5 focuses on the use of database management systems.

Analysis: Calculations

Almost everyone performs computations in a job. Although simple calculators are useful, they have some drawbacks. For example, it is difficult to go back and change a number entered previously. Also, calculators cannot save much data, and it is hard to print out the results. Finally, because of their small screens, they can display only a few numbers at a time. Spreadsheets were initially designed to overcome these limitations. These features are designed to make you more efficient at making calculations.

Most people find spreadsheets useful because their disciplines began with models on paper that used columns and rows of numbers. For instance, most accounting systems and financial models were designed for ledgers in this way. Whenever software mimics the way you already work, it is easier to learn.

REALITY BYTES   International Notations

Most applications today have the ability to use characters that are not found in the U.S. alphabet. For instance, in France or Mexico, you might need to use an acute mark (é). However, different software packages handle the characters differently, so you might have trouble converting a document from one word processor to another or to a different computer. For example, if a French subsidiary is using WordPerfect and the Canadian headquarters is using Microsoft Word, they can both print reports using the special characters. However, the document might change when the Canadian users attempt to retrieve a French document electronically.

Furthermore, if you work for an international organization, remember that people in different countries write dates differently. For example, 5/10/93 means May 10, 1993, in the United States but would be interpreted as October 5, 1993, in Europe. Most word processors enable you to choose how automatic dates should be displayed.

Numbers are also handled differently in European nations. The use of commas (,) and points (.) is reversed from the U.S. version where commas separate thousands and the decimal point delineates the fractional component. (The number 126,843.57 in the United States should be denoted as 126.843,57 in Europe.)

You also need to be careful with currencies in spreadsheets. When you transfer documents to other languages or fonts, be sure to check any currency symbols. A few systems will automatically change the symbol to the local units (e.g., change $ to £), but unless the numbers are converted by exchange rates, these changes would be incorrect.

Spreadsheets have many additional features. Graphs can be created with a couple of mouse clicks. Most packages enable users to modify the graphs by adding text, arrows, and pictures. Spreadsheets also perform various statistical and mathematical analyses. You can perform basic matrix operations such as multiplication and inversion. Statistics capabilities include multiple regression to examine the relationships among different variables. Linear programming can be used to search for optimum solutions to problems. These additional features are designed to help you make better decisions by providing more powerful decision-evaluation tools.

Communication: Writing

The primary gain from word processing is increased efficiency. Word processors improve communication by making it easier to revise text, find writing errors, and produce legible reports. Word processors today also include a spell-checker, a thesaurus, and a grammar-checker. Although they are not the same as having a human editor correct your writing, they are all useful tools for writers. Grammar-checkers use standard measures to estimate the reading difficulty level of your writing. For instance, if you write an employee policy manual, you want to make sure that an average employee can understand it. Most word processors also have outline tools that help you organize your thoughts and rearrange a document, improving the communication.

The proliferation of word processors creates additional advantages. At some point, a company finds that almost all of its reports, data, and graphs are being created and stored on the computer. If this transition is handled carefully, managers can use the computer to search for any prior reports or data. It also becomes easier to send reports and notes to other managers. It sounds as though companies would use less paper and rely on electronic transmissions. Most organizations have not made it to this stage yet, and some people believe we never will. In fact, the use of personal computers has dramatically increased the usage of paper by U.S. companies.

Communication: Presentation and Graphics

In many cases, the difference between a good report and an outstanding report is the presence and quality of the artwork. Graphs and pictures are used to communicate information and feelings. Charts and graphs are easy to create, store, and modify using graphics software. Even if you are not an artist, you can buy **clip art** that was created by someone else and use it in your reports or charts. By using existing art libraries, you can create reports and presentations in a few hours. In the past, reports and presentations took days or weeks to finish by a staff of artists. By improving the appearance, a well-designed graphic can also improve communication and decision making.

Technology Toolbox: Creating Effective Charts

Problem: You need to create a chart that users can understand.
Tools: Spreadsheets contain powerful tools for creating charts; however, you must be careful when using the tools to ensure that the features are used to make the chart more informative and easier to read.

The first step in creating a chart is to enter the data correctly and perform any needed transformations. Second, choose the correct type of chart to emphasize your message. Third, clean up the chart and make sure it contains the proper title and labels. The table shows the main purpose for each chart type and the common mistakes made by novices.

Chart Type	Purpose	Most Common Mistakes
Bar or column	Show category values	Too many series
		Unreadable colors
		Not zero-based
Pie	Compare category percentages	Too many observations/slices
		Unreadable features/3-D
		Poorly labeled
Line	Show trends over time	Too many series
		Poor or missing legend
		Not zero-based
Scatter	Show relationship between two variables	Poor choice of variables
		Not zero-based

One major mistake that is common to all chart types is to use excessive ornamentation. As Edward Tufte points out in his book *The Visual Display of Quantitative Information,* graphing software offers many temptations that should be avoided. Make sure that every option you choose highlights the main purpose of the chart. Avoid cluttering your graph with excess lines, images, or garish color schemes. The goal of any design is to strive for elegance.

Creating a chart in Excel is straightforward. In this example, export the sales by model by month from Rolling Thunder Bicycles. Open the generated spreadsheet and select all of the data cells. Click the chart button and build the line chart. To simplify the chart, remove the Hybrid and Tour models. Enter the titles, and change the line settings to make it easier to read.

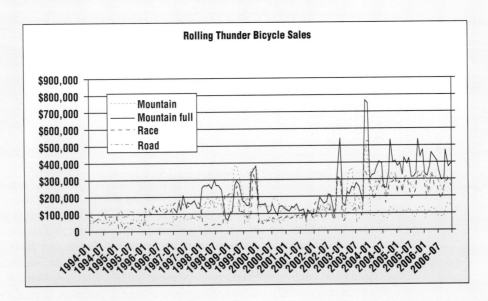

Quick Quiz: Create the following charts:

1. Use the export data form in Rolling Thunder Bicycles to generate sales by state. Create a column chart and a pie chart for this data. Briefly explain why one chart is better than the other.

2. Using Bureau of Labor Statistics data, plot the unemployment rate and the hourly wage rate over three years.

To create or modify your artwork, you need a graphics package and an input device such as a mouse that enables you to draw on the computer screen. Most commercial artists use scanners so they can draw an original on paper and convert it to computer form. The digitized form enables you to make very precise changes, since you can *zoom* into a specific area. Zooming is helpful if you need to force lines to meet exactly or you want to make changes to small items, such as eyelashes on a person.

Color often presents problems to computer artists. Colors on display screens are usually different from those generated by the printer. If you are serious about exact color matching, the Pantone® color standard is supported by some printers (especially those used by commercial print shops), graphics software, and monitors. By choosing colors according to these definitions, you are assured of getting the precise color on the final copy. Some software packages also support color separation. In modern four-color presses, color is created based on four different masks (cyan [blue], magenta [red], yellow, and key [black]—abbreviated CMYK). Other colors are created by blending portions of these colors, as controlled by the masks. Software that supports color separation can use a special machine to print the separate masks, which go directly to a commercial printing press.

Although you do not have to be an artist to incorporate artwork into your reports and documents, you do need an element of artistic sensibility. The goal is to use art to enhance your presentation, not clutter it. Knowing what looks good and using restraint are signs of artistic talent. Remember that faster does not always mean better. Use some of the time savings to put more thought into your presentations.

Communication: Voice and Mail

All jobs require communication—with coworkers, managers, and customers or clients. Word processors help with reports and memos, but much of our communication is less formal. Everyone is familiar with answering machines for telephones. Businesses have taken this concept a step further by using voice mail systems. **Voice mail** systems record messages much like an answering machine, but they store the messages in digital form on computers. They usually give the caller control over where the message is sent. Most people in the United States have dealt with systems that direct you to press buttons on the telephone to make choices. Some voice mail systems enable you to send the same message to several people. Some systems also enable you to skip messages or fast-forward to the end.

Networked computers can be used to send messages directly to other users. These **electronic mail (e-mail)** systems are typically used to send written notices to various people. They can be used to send pictures, facsimiles (faxes), or even voice messages if the computers have sound boards and speakers. The basic problem with any communication system is that sooner or later it becomes cluttered with junk mail. One of the advantages of text e-mail is that the recipient can have the computer scan the messages to search for items that are important or interesting. With the appropriate *mail filters,* junk mail can be discarded automatically. Messages also can be retrieved and stored for future reference or forwarded to other people.

Organizing Resources: Calendars and Schedules

An important task of managers is to organize company resources so that they are used most effectively. An important function is scheduling workers. Schedules for line workers entail making sure that there are enough employees to get the job done, but no extra employees. Schedules involving managers typically involve meetings and require trade-offs between competing demands for a manager's time. Several software tools are available to improve both types of scheduling and make more efficient use of the human resources.

Most managers spend a considerable amount of time in meetings. In fact, it becomes difficult to keep track of appointments, set up new meetings, and reschedule meetings. The process is even more difficult when some participants are traveling or are based in another city or country. Several software packages store appointments and schedules on electronic calendars. Electronic calendar and scheduling software enables data to be shared with other people. For instance, each person in a department would use the electronic calendar to keep

REALITY BYTES Hidden Information in Documents

Microsoft Word is a powerful tool with many complex features. To support all of these features, a tremendous amount of information is stored within the document. Much of that information you do not see, but could cause you problems if you send someone the electronic copy. SCO received tremendous negative press in 2003 and 2004 when it claimed to own the rights to the UNIX (and Linux) source code. In 2004, it filed a suit against DaimlerChrysler via a Microsoft Word document. A CNET News reporter wandered through the document and found that the case had originally been drawn up against Bank of America in California.

A powerful feature in Word is the ability to track changes (Tools/Track Changes). This option keeps the original text, but displays the changes, so you can ultimately decide which version to keep. Similarly, you can tell Word to keep saving older versions of the entire document (File/Versions) each time the document is revised. The files also tend to keep the names of everyone who worked on the document. Wired News analyzed a Word document circulated by California Attorney General Bill Lockyer urging a crack down on file sharing. The analysts found that the text had been edited or reviewed by an official of the Motion Picture Association of America.

If you really have to share the original document with others, make sure that markup and earlier versions have been deleted. You can also use File/Remove Hidden Data to clean up the majority of these hidden items. But it might not remove everything. You could convert the document to a different format, such as Adobe's portable document format (PDF). Although you probably do not need to be paranoid with every document, you should consider these extra steps for sensitive documents.

Source: Adapted from Stephen H. Wildstrom, "Don't Let Word Give Away Your Secrets," *Business Week*, April 16, 2004.

track of his or her personal, departmental, and corporate appointments. To schedule a meeting with departmental members, the manager selects an approximate time, specifies the priority of the meeting, and fills in the participants, location, and subject information. The calendar software then searches each personal calendar for the best time for the meeting. It overrides lower-priority meetings and places the complete meeting notice on each person's calendar in a matter of seconds. Employees have to check their calendars periodically to see whether meetings have been added or changed.

The Paperless Office?

You might think that with increased use of electronic data, there would be less need for paper. So far, the opposite has happened. According to *The Economist,* in the 1990s in Britain the use of paper increased by 65 percent over 10 years. From 1993 to 1998, despite the growth in use of personal computers and the Internet, paper usage increased by 13 percent. Worldwide, paper use doubled from 1982 to 1998. Some people might argue that electronic capabilities helped hold down the increased use of paper, but there is little evidence to support this claim.

Why would the use of paper increase? First, corporate information systems and the Internet have made it easier to create and distribute information. Second, the current electronic displays are generally not as readable or as portable as paper copies. Consequently, people retrieve the data they want and print it out.

Today, electronic displays are approaching the point where they might eventually be able to replace paper copies. Screen resolution has been a big factor in readability. Conventional monitors operate at about 100-dpi resolution. Newer technologies will produce 200-dpi resolutions, which will produce good quality text at traditional book sizes. Portability is also improving, although battery life is still an important issue.

There are still unresolved issues about future compatibility. Properly cared for, paper documents will last for decades. While electronic data can survive for years on CDs or DVDs, the hardware and software to read them may disappear in a short time.

Open Software

It is difficult and time consuming to create software. Commercial vendors spend billions of dollars researching customer needs, developing software, and updating and revising the code. For a few decades, major software development has been performed by large corporations that hire thousands of programmers and sell the software for a profit. Microsoft alone spends over $6 billion a year on research and development. On the other hand, the marginal cost of a software product is almost zero. Almost all of the expenses are front-end fixed costs, except for marketing, distribution, and dealing with customers.

In the past few years, led by visionaries such as Richard Stallman with GNU and Linus Torvalds with Linux, a new approach to software development has arisen. Complex programs have been created using the volunteer talents of thousands of programmers around the world. The result is software specifically developed to be distributed free of charge for anyone to use. The operating system Linux is a popular example, but several application packages exist as well.

As a manager, you will eventually have to answer the question of whether you should use open-source software or continue to rely on commercial packages. The answers are difficult, and discussions are often tinged with religious fervor. Although "free" seems like a good price, how much do you really pay for software? Today, the Windows operating system price is largely embedded in the cost of buying a new computer. On the other hand, more expensive packages such as the Office suite, graphics editor, or database management system can represent large sums of money.

Other issues in open-source software remain unresolved. Often the open-source packages have minimal support and can be harder to use. Certainly, novices find the Linux/UNIX operating system difficult to learn. Issues about security are unresolved. With thousands of programmers working on millions of lines of code, it might be possible for someone to sneak in a tiny, but nasty, routine. On the other hand, with thousands of people looking through the code, the problem might be caught early. You also need to consider whether the open-source programs will be around for a long period of time. With no real income stream, can they survive? Will the leaders remain in charge? These are important questions to ask any software vendor, but the risks are slightly higher with open-source programs. On the other hand, you do get copies of the source code, so in theory, you could edit and maintain the software indefinitely by yourself. But how many managers or companies have that ability?

Summary

One of the original purposes of computers was to make it easier to perform basic tasks. Over time, as computers have become more powerful, they have come to support increasingly complex tasks. Today, in addition to increasing efficiency, computers can help you make better decisions. One major change to computers is the type of data routinely processed. The five major types of data are numbers, text, images, sound, and video. To handle more sophisticated data and more difficult tasks, computer hardware and software have grown increasingly complex.

To choose a computer that best meets your needs, you must evaluate the four basic hardware components: input, processor, output, and secondary storage devices. Each component is measured by slightly different characteristics. Input devices are selected based on the specific task (such as a keyboard for typing, mouse for pointing, or a microphone for voice input). Processors are often selected based on speed and price. Output device quality is appraised by resolution and color capabilities as well as initial and ongoing costs. Secondary storage is evaluated based on speed, capacity, and price.

A Manager's View

Technology constantly changes. New features are added every day to hardware and software. How do you know which features to buy and which to ignore? The key is to evaluate the features of the main components and to understand how you will use the computer. Given the declining prices of processors, RAM, and secondary storage, it is relatively easy to buy a reasonable computer today for most common business applications. When you get to issues of portability or Web servers, you need to evaluate the choices more carefully.

Application software is the primary source of improved productivity. Packages exist to assist in research, analysis, communication, and organizing resources. Database management systems are used for research and data sharing. Spreadsheets and other analytical tools assist in calculations. Word processors, drawing packages, voice mail, and e-mail are used for communication. Electronic calendars and scheduling software are used to help organize human resources.

Key Words

binary data, *40*
bitmap image, *44*
CD-ROM, *56*
clip art, *60*
digital video/versatile disk (DVD), *56*
electronic mail (e-mail), *62*
ergonomics, *52*
grid computing, *51*

icons, *44*
input, *41*
megabyte, *46*
milliseconds, *48*
nanoseconds, *48*
operating system, *56*
optical character recognition (OCR), *52*
output, *44*
processor, *48*

random access memory (RAM), *48*
redundant array of independent drives (RAID), *55*
resolution, *44*
synthesizer, *53*
Unicode, *43*
vector image, *44*
voice mail, *62*

Web Site References

Free News Sources

Associated Press	wire.ap.org
CNN	www.cnn.com
Ecola	www.ecola.com
ESPN	espn.go.com
Fox News	www.foxnews.com
Internet News	www.internetnews.com
MSNBC	www.msnbc.com
News.com	www.news.com
Newshare	www.newshare.com
USA Today	www.usatoday.com
United Press International	www.upi.com
Wired	www.wired.com
ZDNet	www.zdnet.com

Almost Any Magazine or Newspaper (many charge for access)

Business 2.0	www.business2.com
Fortune	www.fortune.com
The Economist	www.economist.com
Wall Street Journal	wsj.com
Washington Post	www.washingtonpost.com

Additional Readings

Adams, S., R. Rosemier, and P. Sleeman. "Readable Letter Size and Visibility for Overhead Projection Transparencies." *AV Communication Review,* 1965, pp. 412–417. [An early discussion of creating good presentations.]

"Science: The Numbers Game." *Time,* February 20, 1988, pp. 54–58. [Short history of computers.]

Simonds, D., and L. Reynolds. *Computer Presentation of Data in Science: A Do It Yourself Guide.* Boston: Kluwer Academic, 1989. [Ideas for presentations.]

Review Questions

1. List and describe the five basic types of data. How much space would it take to store a typical example of each type of data?

2. What are the primary hardware components in a computer?

3. How do the various computer components affect the speed of the computer?

4. What problems might arise if everyone in a company used a different operating system?

5. How does the use of Web browsers change the way applications operate?

6. What issues are important when selecting servers for e-business applications?

7. Briefly describe five tasks you expect to perform in your job as a manager and list the application tool you will use.

8. What will it take for people to adopt a paperless office?

9. How do computers improve productivity in communication? What is the difference between increased efficiency and increased effectiveness (better decisions)?

Exercises

1. What are the current prices of disk drives ($/GB) and RAM ($/MB)?

2. If you want to build a relatively high-level computer from parts, what parts would you buy and how much will they cost?

3. Find a computer running a version of the Linux operating system (or read the documentation), and outline the problems that might arise if you want everyone in your company to use it as a desktop operating system.

4. Find a tablet PC that has the highest-rated battery life. Is the life sufficient to use the tablet in a business setting? If not, how could you compensate for the problems?

5. Find a high-resolution digital photograph. Using photo editing software, save several copies of the photo in JPEG format with different levels of compression. At what point do you begin to notice the photograph quality degrade? Compare the file sizes as well. Print the photo (a black and white print is fine) and compare the results to the original.

6. Estimate the storage space (number of bytes) required for each of the following items:

    a. A telephone book with 10,000 entries consisting of names, addresses, and phone numbers. Use your phone book to estimate the average length of an entry.

    b. A fax transmission of a 30-page report at high resolution (200 by 200 bits per inch). What is the raw size? What is the size if you can use a compression algorithm that reduces each page to one-twentieth the original size?

    c. A 4- by 6-inch color photograph scanned in high resolution at 2,400 dots per inch and 16 million colors (24 bits for color). How far (percentage) would you have to compress this image to fit into 4 MB of available RAM?

    d. A 15-minute explanation of a spreadsheet recorded with the PC audio recorder. Make and save a 30-second recording and use the file size to estimate a 15-minute recording.

    e. Your favorite half-hour television show in digital form. How many bytes of storage would it take? Extra credit: How much space would it take if you remove the commercials? (*Hint:* Time the commercials.)

7. Research state-of-the-art video displays. What are the best resolutions you can find? At what price? What additional capabilities exist (e.g., three-dimensional)?

Technology Toolbox

CO2Ex08.txt

8. You are trying to decide on raises for your departmental employees. The accompanying table lists the performance evaluations they received along with an estimate of the percentage raises that you wish to give. To review your spreadsheet skills, enter the formulas necessary to complete the table, including the totals and averages. Also, create a graph that displays the percentage raise and the performance evaluation for each employee. (One extra credit point is given for identifying all of the employees.)

	A	B	C	D	E	F
1	Name	Salary	Evaluation	Raise%	Raise	New Salary
2	Mandelbrot	117000	6.4	6		
3	Gardner	94000	5.3	5		
4	Thom	72400	2.7	8		
5	Russell	67200	8.5	3		
6	Whitehead	51200	7.2	1		
7	Goedel	41700	4.5	5		
8	Hardy	39800	3.9	4		
9	Cauchy	29800	7.2	2		
10	Ramanujan	39400	6.4	8		
11	Gauss	24500	7.9	9		
12	Euler	18900	5.8	5		
13		total	average	average	total	total

9. A spreadsheet is an important tool that can be used to manage your personal finances. A simple plan that you can implement is a personal balance sheet. The top of the balance sheet includes your income. In it you can list all of the money that you have coming in each month. The bottom of the balance sheet is your expenses. Using it, you can list all the expenditures that you were required to make each month. Your instructor has a disk with a sample outline that you can fill in with your personal data. Of course, you can enter additional lines in each category.

 CO2Ex09a.xls, CO2Ex09b.xls

   a. An important part of financial analysis is the ability to compare your financial statement to those of others. Several sample worksheets are included on the sample disk. Examine several worksheets. They are each listed by student name. How do these worksheets compare to your income and expenses?

   b. Graph the most significant items in your worksheet. These would include those items that seem to have the most variance or the widest range of dispersion. What difficulties occur when you graph these items against the totals in each category?

10. Set up speech recognition on your computer and train it. Choose a paragraph of text and dictate it into Word. Do not make corrections to the text as you dictate it. When you have finished, copy the paragraph and make the corrections to the copy. Count the number of mistakes, and hand in both paragraphs.

11. Identify the best chart to use for the following datasets, and give a brief justification for your choice:

   a. Sales by department for the last five years.
   b. Sales by employee for the last month.
   c. Production data for output quality and percent of carbon.
   d. Share of sales to five nations.
   e. Total customer billings by employee for the last 24 months.

12. Find at least two data series from the government (try www.fedstats.gov) and plot them. Briefly explain any patterns or trends.

 Teamwork

13. Split the team into two groups. Each person in one group should find and price the most expensive personal computer that can be used for business applications. Each person in the other group should find and price the least expensive computer. Compare the results to determine how far apart the prices are and identify the components that cause the greatest price differentials.

14. Each person should research a printer that could be used to print all of the work done by a group of 30 people who sometimes print (or copy) 200,000 pages per month. Each person should then outline the benefits and costs of the printer selected. Combine the results and, as a group, select the best printer and explain your recommendation.

15. Select a common application tool (word processor, spreadsheet, and so on). Each person on the team should read the documentation or search the Web and identify one feature that he or she has not used before. Create an example that uses this feature. Write a short note describing the feature and its benefits, including a brief tutorial on how to use it. Combine the notes into a document and share it with the team. Have each team member vote on the usefulness of each topic and reorganize the document so that the most useful features are listed first.

16. Have each person on the team create a one-page description of a job they have had. Use a template to set styles for the body text, a main heading, and second-level headings. Each document must use these styles. Combine the individual pages, and then change the template slightly and verify that all pages contain the same styles.

17. Have each person on the team find an example of a good chart and a bad chart using newspapers and the Internet. Combine the results from each person into a document so that each person can vote on the best and worst charts.

18. Using your e-mail client, set up a distribution list so that you can send mail to everyone on your team. Use the calendar system to set a meeting time and send the message to each person on the list.

Rolling Thunder Database

19. Using the Export Data form, copy the data to a spreadsheet and create graphs for the following situations. (Choose the type of graph you feel is best suited to present the data.)
    a. Sales by model type.
    b. Sales by month.
    c. Sales by model type for each month.
    d. Sales by state.
    e. Sales by employee by month.

20. Using the existing forms, enter data for a new bicycle order.

21. Find at least two other bicycles (e.g., on the Internet or from a dealer). Create a spreadsheet comparing the features and costs with a similar bicycle built by Rolling Thunder Bicycles.

22. Using the Export Data form, copy the data to a spreadsheet and compute the average profit margin for each type of bicycle for two different years. Comment on any differences that you find.

23. Assume you have to give a presentation to the marketing manager. Create a slide show to compare the sales of each model type for the last two years.

Cases: The Computer Industry

The Industry

How often should you replace a personal computer? Hardware and software are continually changing. To run new software and take advantage of new peripherals such as DVD players or huge drives, you often need to purchase new computers. Typically, personal computers are replaced after three years. Yet firms can often delay purchasing new computers in a weak economy to save money. All of these decisions affect the industry, and overall sales can skyrocket one year and die down the next. The industry is also driven by brutal competition. Between Dell's quest for low prices and efficient production, and relentless price cuts by Chinese, Taiwanese, and Korean manufacturers, PCs have largely become commodity items.

Where do you buy PCs? Some people like to physically see the items they buy and be able to take them home immediately, so there is some incentive to sell computers in retail stores. But remember that PCs have a limited shelf life. A model can become obsolete in a few weeks, and its value can drop in a matter of days. How can a retailer stock items when they depreciate so quickly? Stores can try to forecast demand, but if the economy drops, people may stop buying and the store will be stuck with obsolete computers. Yet selling strictly by mail order means that you might miss out on sales to a relatively large market.

These conflicts have caused considerable grief to computer firms over the last few years. Dell, the leading mail-order/ Internet vendor, at one time tried retail sales and gave up. Gateway tried to ride the middle line by running its own retail

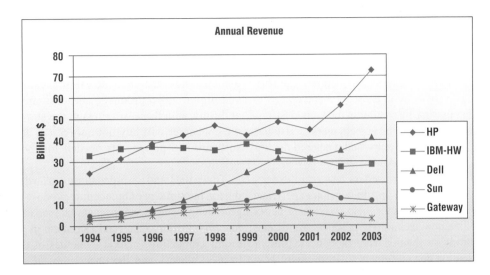

Annual Revenue

stores. It, too, lost money and closed the stores. Apple has begun opening a few retail stores to demonstrate new electronics products (mostly music).

After several years of dismal growth, demand for personal computers increased in 2003 and 2004. PC unit shipments in both the second and third quarters of 2003 were higher than expected. Consumer buying remained strong, and a transition from desktop computers to notebooks has helped to fuel growth in the category. As of 2004, there were few signs of any meaningful recovery in corporate purchases of PCs. As the economy improves, and provides increased profits, businesses are expected to increase their purchases of technology. Furthermore, as the average age of the existing machines increases, companies will begin to replace their computers.

Aggressive price competition is a significant factor in stimulating demand. Vendors have reported disappointing PC revenues due to price competition. Competitive pricing pressures continue to drive pricing decisions. In addition, business pressures have not recovered. Consumer demand for notebook computers has also driven demand.

International sales are an increasingly important element in growth for the major computer vendors. Growth in Europe and the Middle East has seen an 18.7 percent year-to-year increase in PC shipments for the third quarter of 2003. This growth was built on the robust sales of portables, which rose 51 percent in consumer and business demand. Aggressive price competition was a significant factor in stimulating demand.

The top five PC vendors—Dell, Hewlett-Packard Co., International Business Machines Corporation, Fujitsu Siemens Computers, and Toshiba Corporation—all experienced year-over-year unit growth in the third quarter of 2003. Toshiba was the only one of the five not to experience double-digit year-to-year growth according to data from IDC. A large percentage of the growth in the personal computer market is in the sale of network servers.

Worldwide server unit shipments rose 17.5 percent in the second quarter of 2003, following nine quarters of year-over-year declines. Revenues remained about flat, however, reflecting price competition. In the second quarter of 2003, unit shipment growth was led by a 21 percent gain in both the Linux and Windows markets. Linux servers grew 42 percent, recording the fastest growth in the server market, albeit from a smaller base. The Windows server market, which represents the largest segment based on units, saw unit shipments advance by 21.7 percent in the second quarter of 2003. On a revenue basis, sales of these servers grew 11.5 percent to $3.1 billion. Meanwhile, the UNIX server market remained the largest on a revenue basis, but continued to show declines in revenue. The UNIX server market witnessed a 5.2 percent revenue decline to $4.3 billion in the second quarter of 2003. IBM led the overall server market on a worldwide basis in the second quarter of 2003, with a 30.4 percent share of market revenues, up from 27.7 percent in the same quarter in 2002. IBM reported revenue growth of 10.1 percent, well above the 0.2 percent growth recorded for the industry, as it gained market share in the UNIX environment. The weak corporate spending environment continues to plague the server market. Tight technology budgets have caused a shift in server spending toward lower priced systems. This trend continues to restrict the industry's overall revenue growth.

The top firms continue to fight for dominance in the industry, but the weaker firms are attempting to gain ground by consolidating. In 2004, Gateway purchased eMachines. In the process, Gateway fired most of its existing managers and replaced them with managers from eMachines.

The Consumer Electronics Market

The PC vendors are attracted to the appealing growth projections for consumer electronics markets. LCD television sales were expected to jump 50 percent worldwide in 2003 to $3.5 billion and rise to $9.2 billion in 2005 (iSuppli Corporation). Although LCD TV prices have dropped considerably, margins are still considered attractive. Low-priced 22-inch LCD TVs in 2004 cost around $1,400, about half of what they cost in 2003. Attractive margins may soon draw even more new entrants to the market. Chinese manufacturers are expected to aggressively focus on this market with significantly lower prices.

In 2003, Gateway, Dell, and H-P announced plans to enter the television market as well as other consumer electronics markets in which they had not previously had product offerings. In October 2003, Dell launched its entry into the flat-panel television and digital music player markets. Gateway launched its plasma TV offering in early 2003 and claims to be the biggest selling plasma TV vendor in the United States. Gateway has also entered the digital camera market. H-P has made digital cameras for several years, and it entered the liquid crystal display TV market in August 2004.

Both H-P and Gateway are focused on new retail experiences to attract customers. H-P wants to develop experience centers in certain retail footprints to help consumers better understand and utilize new technology products. As of late October 2003, Gateway overhauled its retail stores to present a more attractive setting for customers to learn about new technologies and to try systems before buying them.

Apple Computer had success with its retail outlets in 2003. Its stores are located in high-traffic areas, such as upscale malls, near sizable Apple customer bases. Apple's concept has been to create a setting where salespeople can demonstrate some of the new digital camera, digital music, and digital video products, and customers can experience and work with these offerings in the store. The hope is that the consumer will buy not only a new PC but also all the software and peripherals needed for the complete digital solution.

Given the trend toward maturing growth rates in the PC industry, the strategy of broadening product lines to tap higher-growth opportunities appears to be reasonable. However, the margin benefits to the vendors remain in question, given the highly competitive market dynamics of the consumer electronics industry and the uncertainty of growth projections and product life cycles.

Case: Dell

Dell has posted rapid sales growth since July 1994, when it discontinued retail channel sales to focus exclusively on its direct business. After entering the market for Windows-based workstations in 1997, the company quickly became the world's leading supplier. As of the first quarter 2003, Dell was the world's largest PC maker, retaking the title from Hewlett-Packard Company which, with its May 2002 acquisition of Compaq Computer, became Dell's largest rival. The present corporate title was adopted in July 2003. Desktop computer systems make up the largest segment (53 percent) of the business. Dell ranked first in the United States and second worldwide in desktop shipments in calendar 2002.

The company is a direct marketer of PCs, including desktops, notebooks, servers, workstations, storage, printers, handhelds, and portable projectors. The company's enterprise systems (20 percent 2003 total net revenues, 19 percent 2002) include workstations, servers, and storage and network switches. Dell's PowerEdge servers are used in networked environments to distribute files, database information, applications, and communication products. Its PowerApp Servers are new appliance servers aimed at Web-related workloads.

The company's higher margin notebooks and portables (27 percent) include the Latitude product lines for corporate users, and the Inspiron line for consumers and small businesses. Dell ranked first in the United States and second worldwide in notebook computer shipments in calendar 2002.

Dell offers services that include professional consulting, custom hardware and software integration, and network installation and support. Manufacturing sites include Austin, Texas; Limerick, Ireland; Penang, Malaysia; and Xiamen, China.

Dell is aggressive in pricing its products. As a direct seller of PCs, Dell benefits because it can pass lower component costs through to customers faster than its rivals. As such, it can lead the competition in price cuts. The company strategy includes the ability to gain market share by leveraging its position as the low-cost producer in the PC industry. Dell's market share gains over the past year reflect the successful implementation of this strategy. This strategy is cramped, however, by the rapid growth in component prices.

Keys to Success

Much of Dell's success has been credited to the built-to-order model. Nothing is manufactured until someone buys it. This reduces inventory holding time to three to five days. Dell also applies this just-in-time approach to its marketing efforts. Advertising dollars and resources are focused on the segments that are growing the most. For example, the fourth quarter is always focused on the holiday gift season for consumers. Quarters 2 and 3 are focused on the public sector when schools and the government begin their buying cycles.

While Dell has always sold to the education market, in 1996 the sector became more interesting, thanks to the federal government's E-Rates program that provided from $2.5 billion to $3 billion per year to subsidize schools' technology budgets. Apple had previously addressed this market by engaging in "emotional marketing," pitching warm and fuzzy computing to teachers in the hope that they would lobby their schools. In contrast, Dell had realized that computers in the schools had moved from freestanding desktop tools to nodes in an increasingly complex web of technology that included wireless networks, handheld devices, software, and servers. While Apple advertised personal creativity, Dell marketed standardization and commoditization. Dell did not go to its education buyers and say, "We'll sell you desktops and laptops." Instead they offered solutions including education software, packages, and IT services. They addressed storage and the leverage of the existing technology. This approach proved to be more compelling for people with limited budgets and no resources or staff.

Perhaps Dell's most important weapon was its huge customer database, the result of Dell's sales model. This provides a direct relationship with the customer. Since it sells directly, Dell can get immediate feedback from customers before, during, and after the sales process. Dell courts such feedback, maintaining a Platinum Council of buyers to offer their insight at the executive level, and also inviting customers to work with product development teams in a direct feedback loop.

Due to tight supply chain management, Dell's made-to-order model is also a financial gold mine. Dell orders and receives components as they are needed to build a machine. The computer is shipped within a few days, and the customer is charged. But Dell does not have to pay the suppliers until 30 days later. So Dell earns interest on the revenue for a couple of weeks before it pays suppliers.

Database Applications to Better Service Customers

Valerie Hausladen knew that she could get Dell's customer database to work harder. "I used to be more of a traditional marketing person," she says. "But I learned that unless I could measure and show ROI on marketing, my budget kept getting cut. I realized at Dell, you have to be able to show results" (Kuchinskas 2003). Hausladen set up a pilot program to test whether better customer relationships could be established in the interactive channel. Smaller Dell accounts were initially targeted in three areas: health care, K–12 schools, and colleges and universities.

Dell divides its accounts into the three categories of acquisition, development, or retention. Development accounts are those that the company thinks could grow, or that are not spending all their budgets on Dell products. The tactical goal of the campaign was to get the name of one buying decision maker for each account. The strategic goal was "to become more actionable on how the company served customers with right information at the right time" (Kuchinskas 2003). The implementation goal was to send laptop information to customers who were interested in laptops and server info to server buyers.

Dell's database group went to work. They analyzed Dell's customer list to establish benchmarks. To find out if Dell knew a decision maker at an organization, they analyzed job titles, asked salespeople, and even called the customer to ask. They also began outreach via e-mail and direct mail, renting mailing lists and building and refining the Dell customer database through opt-in methods.

To implement the program, Web portals were built for each of the customer verticals, offering tools and information to aid them in their technology decisions. This was aided by the fact that the three Knowledge Centers—those for K–12, for institutions of higher education, and for government purchasers—were similar in their application. The visual identity and content for the Web pages were crafted to serve as a "virtual account executive" for each market.

The direct mail campaign focused on two goals. First was the desire to alert customers to deals and sell more products.

Second was the effort to improve information in the customer database and turn names into relationships. When customers registered on the Knowledge Center sites to read content or request e-newsletters, they also selected products they were interested in from a list. The next time Dell communicated with them, it focused on the items they had checked. The Dell team set up a control group to measure the effects of their marketing and define subsequent benchmarks. Dell began to see results from this database marketing effort in 2002. The short-term gains included the maximization of tactical elements such as response rates. This included the establishment of 5,000 new accounts in eight months. The Web interface lets the marketers compare different campaigns, different media, and calculate the current ROI. Three years into the program, Dell's information-rich database contains at least one key decision maker for each account. The goal is to expand this list to the names of five key decision makers for each location in the database.

Dell addresses the budget-conscious public sector market by talking to them about getting what they need, supporting them, and saving them money. In direct mail, e-mails, and on the Web, it uses a straightforward style and packs its communications with information. The postcards are not fancy. They include a couple of generic hardware close-ups and text. They follow a simple formula: one close-up of the product, another that shows the entire case, a photo of smiling customers, and lots of text, with prices prominently featured.

All this leads back to the Knowledge Center Web page, where Dell is building a deep resource that offers quick links to shopping, customer service, and technical support backed by articles that can help Dell's customers evaluate, plan, and use technology more effectively. They are also integrated with more offers, sweepstakes, and discounts. Every time a customer clicks within a newsletter, navigates around a Knowledge Center, or responds to a postcard electronically or via a call center, the choices are recorded in Dell's customer database. Over time, the Knowledge Center begins to appear differently from the one encountered by another education decision maker. This system results in a more interesting interaction with Dell each time the customer comes to the Web page.

Dell has Rerouted its U.S. Support Calls to the United States

In November 2003, Dell rerouted calls from its U.S.-based users to a U.S.-based call center instead of to its facility in India. Some customers had complained about the quality of the help they had received from the offshore center. Support operations for Dell's Optiplex line of desktop PCs and its Latitude notebooks were moved back to facilities in Texas, Idaho, and Tennessee.

Ned May, an analyst at the market research firm IDC, said he had heard criticisms from corporate IT managers about the support they were getting from Dell's call center in Bangalore, India. Barry French, a Dell spokesman, said a portion of the calls from U.S. PC users would still go to India, where support has been handled since mid-2001. He indicated that Dell may shift all of the support back offshore at some point. "We are increasing the number of people we have providing support in India," he said. "Dell has a number of call centers around the world, and we will continue to optimize those to provide the best customer experience" (Brewin 2003).

Questions

1. Is the pace of technological change slowing? Can a business wait longer now to refresh computers?

2. How is information technology critical to Dell's success?

3. What is the current status of Dell's recycling program and is it successful?

4. Why is Dell expanding into consumer electronics and corporate networking products?

5. Is there a limit to the number of computers Dell can sell through its current methods? Should it reconsider retail sales?

Case: Gateway

Gateway directly sells personal computers. Gateway also sells digital technology products, including the Gateway plasma TV. Gateway gained market share in the PC industry until the second half of 2000. Since that time, its rapid growth has reversed. In 2002, Gateway estimated its market share to be 6 percent, but the company still believes it has a strong presence in the U.S. consumer market. In early 2001, management reviewed its operations and discontinued unprofitable revenue streams beginning in the second quarter of 2001 with roughly $200 million per quarter. In the third quarter of 2001, it exited its international operations. In March 2003, management planned to save $400 million annually from workforce cuts, cost programs, and a reduction in the number of its stores.

In the beginning, Gateway focused on providing high-end personal computers at relatively low prices. The company led the industry consolidation through the 1990s and dominated PC sales for a time. Based in South Dakota, the company featured a cow motif as a means to create a brand identity. Eventually, its headquarters was moved to San Diego. In 1997, Gateway introduced an innovative extension of its traditional business model. Instead of relying on developing customers solely through the Internet, Gateway opened 37 Gateway Country stores in which customers could test-drive PCs. One of the goals was to expand sales of consumer electronics goods such as printers, cameras, and eventually plasma televisions. After several years of expansion, the company began closing certain stores. As of December 31, 2002, Gateway had 272 retail stores in the United States, down from 327 at the end of 2000. In the first quarter of 2003, the company closed another 80 stores. In 2004, Gateway acquired eMachines largely in exchange for stock. Ted Waitt, founder and chairman, quickly replaced Gateway management with eMachines managers. In April 2004, the new management shut down all of the remaining Gateway retail stores (Zimmerman 2004).

In 1997, Gateway also launched its Internet service. In October 1999, the company announced a strategic alliance with America Online, calling for Gateway to package AOL service into all its computers. AOL was to invest $800 million in Gateway over two years, including $150 million in AOL stock. In December 2001, Gateway extinguished its convertible note to AOL through the issuance of 50,000 shares of Series C redeemable convertible preferred stock. This resulted in an extraordinary gain of $4.3 million, net of tax.

Realizing the price competitiveness in technology, Gateway was among the first PC vendors to shift its focus to "beyond-the-box revenues." These revenues incorporate the sales of software and peripherals, Internet access, financing, and warranty and training revenue. In 2002, these sales were $692 million, down from $1.2 billion in 2001 and $1.9 billion in 2000. These sales have wide margins. Several categories offer recurring revenue streams. Gateway reported a net loss of $0.95 per share in 2002.

The merger with eMachines appears to represent a refocusing on the "value" end of the computer spectrum. Originally, eMachines succeeded by building standard computers in China and beating the cost of equivalent Hewlett-Packard machines by $150. As PCs become a commodity industry, people are less interested in the raw technology. Instead, certain features become important, such as more memory or larger disk drives. John Hui, the owner of eMachines, explained that "they created what we called a 'value formula' that Wayne [Inouye] developed at Best Buy. They attach value to every single component of a PC. They can at any time tell you if you use, let's say, a DVD-RW versus a CD-ROM how much more the consumer is willing to pay. Now that has nothing to do with the cost. Because it's the value that the consumer will attach to every single component. For example, how much is the consumer willing to pay for a 512MB system versus a 256? They can attach value to it, because the consumer knows they can easily buy the memory and stick it in themselves. But the memory prices go up and down everyday. So they have a certain perceived value. And when that perceived value is high and the cost is low, that's when eMachines would put those components in there." Inouye became CEO of Gateway after the merger (Zimmerman 2004).

Questions

1. Why did the Gateway stores fail?

2. Can Gateway survive? What will it have to do to regain profitability?

Case: Sun

Sun is in the No. 3 spot in server technology, with 13.5 percent of the market, well below the 16.6 percent market share the company recorded a year earlier. As a result of this decline, revenues fell 18.7 percent. Sun has focused on the UNIX market where it is the No. 1 vendor. Founded in 1982, Sun Microsystems invented the workstation. It continues to rely on the concept that the network is the computer. Sun is a leading supplier of networked computing products, including workstations, servers, and storage products that primarily use Sun's own Scaleable Processor Architecture (SPARC) microprocessors and its Solaris software. Computer systems accounted for 55 percent of net revenues in 2003; network storage products, 14 percent; support services, 25 percent; and professional services, 7 percent.

Sun's workstations are primarily used for engineering applications (CAD/CAM), desktop publishing, software development, and other applications that need a moderate amount of computing power and high-quality graphics capabilities. In terms of computing power, workstations fall between PCs and minicomputers. UNIX has been the most common operating system for workstations, but Microsoft's Windows XP has posed a formidable challenge. Sun's workstations range from low-cost UltraSPARC-based workstations to high-end, multiprocessor color graphics systems. Sun servers can be used for file sharing, letting users access data distributed across multiple storage devices and networks, or as computer resources, to distribute computer-intensive applications across multiple processors.

In June 2000, Sun shifted its focus to include storage, launching its StorEdge T3 line, as well as software and services to enhance its storage solution offerings. In 2002, Sun introduced Solaris 9, the latest upgrade of its popular UNIX operating system. Its features include identity management and enhanced security and manageability.

Sun has concentrated on software development as well. It invented the Java object-oriented programming language. Java has attracted significant interest in the software development industry because of its portability; software created in Java can run on any type of system. As a result, it is a popular tool for designing software for distribution over the Internet.

Sales at Sun have been weak for the past few years as customers realize that Intel-based personal computers can now perform as effectively as workstations and midrange servers, at a substantially lower upfront cost. In 2004, Sun received $1.6 billion in a settlement with Microsoft over the use of Java. Yet Sun lost $0.75 billion in just one quarter of that year and was forced to lay off 9 percent of its workforce. In 2004,

Sun began selling Intel- and AMD-based workstations that can run the Windows and Linux operating systems. But it is not clear that Sun can compete in the low-end and midrange markets.

Questions

1. Can Sun survive? How will it compete against Linux and generic PCs?
2. Since much of the world has accepted Java as a Web-based programming language, can Sun make any money from it?

Additional Reading

Boslet, Mark. "Sun Microsystems Posts Big Loss in 3Q as Sales Slump." *The Wall Street Journal,* April 16, 2004.

Brewin, Bob. "User Complaints Push Dell to Return PC Support to U.S." *Computerworld,* Vol. 37(48), December 1, 2003, p. 6.

Guth, Robert A. "Microsoft Settles Another in String of Antitrust Suits," *The Wall Street Journal,* April 20, 2004, p. B5.

Kuchinskas, Susan. "Data-Based Dell, Adweek Magazines' Technology." *Marketing,* Vol. 23(6), September 2003, pp. 20–23.

Plamondon, Scott. "PC Recycling Made Easier." *PC World,* December 29, 2003.

Skillings, Jonathan. "Dell to Get Green with PC Recycling." *News.Com,* May 16, 2002.

Zimmerman, Michael R. "Why the eMachines Model Is Paying Off." *eWeek,* April 18, 2004.

Summary Industry Questions

1. What information technologies have helped this industry?
2. Did the technologies provide a competitive advantage or were they quickly adopted by rivals?
3. Which technologies could this industry use that were developed in other sectors?
4. Is the level of competition increasing or decreasing in this industry? Is it dominated by a few firms, or are they fairly balanced?
5. What problems have been created from the use of information technology in this industry and how did the firms solve the problems?

CHAPTER THREE

Networks and Telecommunications

Chapter Outline

Introduction

Network Functions

Sharing Data
Sharing Hardware
Sharing Software
Voice and Video Communication

Components of a Network

Computers
Transmission Media
Connection Devices

Network Structure

Shared-Media Networks
Switched Networks
Enterprise Networks

Standards

The Need for Standards
A Changing Environment
Internet TCP/IP Reference Model

The Internet

How the Internet Works
Internet Addresses
Internet Mail
Access to Data on the Internet
Internet 2
Wireless Networks and Mobile Commerce
Unsolicited Commercial e-Mail

Global Telecommunications

Technical Problems
Legal and Political Complications
Cultural Issues
Comment

Summary

Key Words

Web Site References

Additional Reading

Review Questions

Exercises

Cases: Wholesale Suppliers

What You Will Learn in This Chapter

- What is the value of a single computer?
- Why are computer networks so important in today's businesses?
- What components do you need to install to create a network?
- Why does it matter how your computer is connected to the network?
- How is it possible that you can connect your computer to a network at the office, at home, or while on the road, even overseas?
- What is the Internet, how is it controlled, and how does it work?
- What problems are you likely to encounter if you need to connect to a supplier in a different country?

How do suppliers connect to customers? Owens & Minor sells thousands of products to hospitals. It is one of three large companies in the market, competing with Cardinal Health (which owns the system built by American Hospital Supply). Like other wholesalers, Owens & Minor exists in a highly competitive environment with low margins. Whether you call it logistics or supply chain management, buyers continually search for ways to reduce their purchasing costs. Companies like Owens & Minor use information technology to reduce inventories throughout the purchasing system. By building links with customers and suppliers, Owens & Minor can immediately react to changes in demand and plan the most efficient method to deliver supplies.

Introduction

What is the value of a single computer? This question almost sounds like the old Buddhist Zen koan: What is the sound of one hand clapping? You do not need to debate the complexities of Zen to understand that the value of computers is multiplied by connecting them and sharing information. How do you place orders with your suppliers? Call or fax them? Send them orders by postal mail? All of these methods are slow and expensive. It is more efficient to connect with a network. It is difficult to run a company today without a computer network. Imagine what would happen if your network failed? How are you going to get any work done with no e-mail, instant messenger, file transfer, or Internet access? You could use the telephone, cell phone, or fax. But what happens if your phone system also uses the Internet? How do you share information? How can you fix the network problems? As shown in Figure 3.1, companies today use internal networks and the Internet to improve communications and create new business structures.

FIGURE 3.1

Networks: Managing an organization requires communication and teamwork. Networks facilitate teamwork and create opportunities for new organizational structures. The Internet makes it easy to connect to customers and suppliers—creating new opportunities and new business relationships.

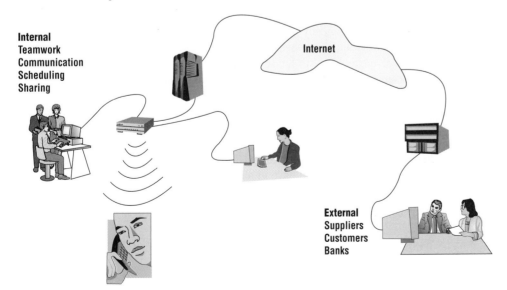

Internal
Teamwork
Communication
Scheduling
Sharing

Internet

External
Suppliers
Customers
Banks

Communication is important to companies both internally and externally. Internally, communication is used to keep the business running as one cohesive organization. Messages and data constantly travel among workers and managers. Workers collect data and share it with colleagues and summarize it for managers. Managers use the data to make decisions and change the organization. Changes are implemented as new policies and procedures, resulting in messages that are distributed throughout the company. External communications are important for many reasons including collecting data about customers and suppliers and providing information to shareholders and governmental agencies.

Sharing data and resources can cause problems. For example, security must be addressed to determine who should be able to use and change the data. These concerns are multiplied in an international environment because national governments may impose constraints on how companies can use the data they collect.

The objective of a network is to connect computers transparently, so that the users do not know the network exists. The network provides access to data on central computers, departmental computers, and sometimes other workers' personal computers. Networks can create shared access to fax machines, modems, printers, scanners, and other specialized hardware. To the user, it does not matter where these devices are located. The network makes them work the same as if they were on any desktop. The Internet expands these capabilities across the world. Wireless makes the services available to you wherever you travel in major cities.

Network Functions

Why are computer networks so important in today's businesses? Most companies did not seriously begin installing networks until the early 1990s. The Internet expanded into the commercial world in the mid to late 1990s. Perhaps the better question is: Why did it take so long? The answer: cost. To understand the value of networks, you need to look at the business applications and new procedures that have been created with networks. Then, you can start thinking about the future networks and new applications—particularly wireless and mobile applications.

Sharing Data

Sharing data is one of the most obvious uses of networks and it can make profound changes in the way an organization works. Managers can see customer and marketing data immediately as it is collected. Employees in one department can easily share data with other departments. A network facilitates the use of teams. In particular, it enables informal teams to spring up throughout the company to solve problems as they arise. Instead of waiting for a higher-level manager to appoint a team, employees can use the network to ask questions, notify others involved, and find in-house experts. A **local area network (LAN)** is commonly used to connect computers and share data within a company.

Transactions

One of the most important reasons for connecting computers is the ability to share data. Consider a retail store with five checkout registers. Each register is actually a computer. If these computers are not connected, it is difficult to compute the daily sales for the store. At the end of the day, someone would have to manually collect the data from each computer and enter it into another computer. Also, imagine what would happen if a customer asked a clerk to determine whether a product was sold out. The clerk would have to check with each of the other clerks or perhaps call the storeroom.

As shown in Figure 3.2, e-commerce consists of a transaction system with the Internet as the network and customer browsers as the client computers. The product data and sales transactions are stored in the central database connected to the Internet. Using a central database provides inventory data to customers. When a customer asks whether an item is in stock, the Web site can provide the answer. Managers can get daily sales figures from any

TRENDS

The telephone system was originally designed to transmit sound by converting sound waves into electrical signals. Certain limitations were built into the system to keep costs down. An important feature of the phone system is its ability to handle multiple phone calls on one line. In the very early days of telephony, phone calls were connected by giant switchboards that required separate physical connections for each call. Over time, these switchboards were replaced with electronic switches. Today, the switches are the heart of the phone system network. Most of the switches in the United States are actually dedicated computers. To carry voice calls, the switches first convert the electrical signal into packets of digital data. These packets are then sent to the appropriate destination.

Another major change is the use of cellular telephones. In the 1980s, cellular telephone networks were installed in U.S. cities. By 2000, most of these systems were replaced with digital networks that could begin to handle data. The 3G system being built today will handle voice and high-speed data equally well.

A more recent trend that will affect personal communications is the rapid growth of cable television, which is accessible to over 60 percent of U.S. households. In 1996, the government removed almost all barriers in the telecommunications industry. Cable companies are working on providing Internet access and more interactive features.

The defining trend of the 1990s was the use of the Internet. From 1994, commercial use of the Internet grew exponentially. Substantial improvements were made in browsers, Web site capabilities, and transmission speed. Technologically, the Internet is simply a large global network created by the acceptance of standards. In practice, the Internet capabilities have the power to change society.

The next wave is wireless access—both high-speed connections within a company and Internet access to cell phones and PDAs wherever you travel. These changes offer new ways of doing business and the potential to change society. Hundreds of opportunities exist in this new world, but the costs and complications can destroy a company.

FIGURE 3.2

Network for transaction processing: Networks are often used to collect data in a central database. From there, the data can be queried and analyzed by managers. E-commerce sales represent transactions across the Internet.

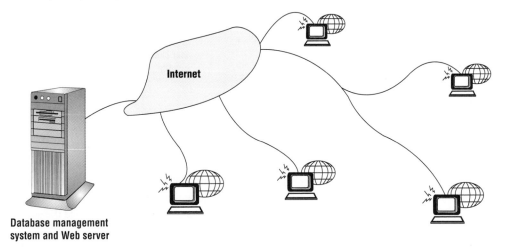

Database management system and Web server

location with a Web browser and an Internet connection. Payments and bills can also be handled directly online.

Decisions and Searches

Many types of data need to be shared in a company. Consider a situation in which a manager is told to close down 3 out of 200 stores. Selecting those stores can be a tough decision. It requires knowing sales volume for every store and projected future sales as well as operating costs. The manager will bring this basic information to a personal computer to create graphs and evaluate models. It is possible to collect all of the data from each store by hand and enter it into the computer. However, it is much more efficient when the manager can simply transfer the data directly from the central database to the personal computer. Not only is this method faster, but it prevents errors. The database should have the most recent information. Furthermore, all managers will use the same data. A portion of a network for making decisions and sharing work with team members is illustrated in Figure 3.3. Without

FIGURE 3.3

Network for decisions and collaboration: The file server holds basic data and software tools. Managers retrieve data and create reports. The reports can be shared with other managers. With collaborative software, revisions are automatically tracked and combined to form the final document.

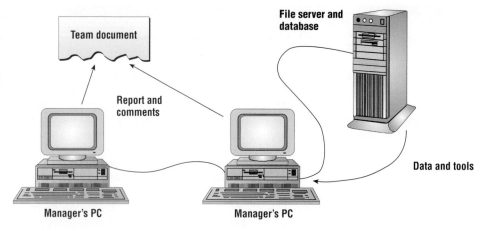

FIGURE 3.4

Networks for communication: With e-mail, a server holds the mail until the recipient logs on and can receive the message. Because several servers might be involved and each makes backup copies, e-mail messages are hard to delete.

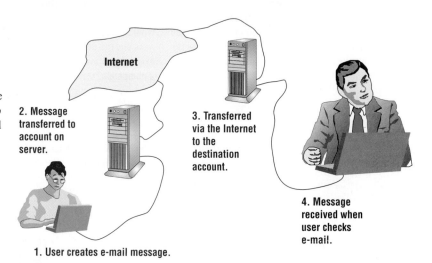

networks and centralized data sharing, many companies experience problems when managers have different versions of the data.

Messages

Most people are familiar with electronic mail, or **e-mail.** With e-mail, you can send a message to any person with a mail account. Many people have come to prefer e-mail contacts to phone calls. As shown in Figure 3.4, e-mail messages are asynchronous since the sender and recipient do not have to participate at the same time. A mail server holds the message until the user logs in and retrieves the e-mail. Moreover, users can create mailing lists and send a message to many people at one time. Messages can be stored, retrieved, and searched for later usage. In most systems, the computer can automatically notify you when the recipient reads your message. You never have to worry about whether your message was received. Voice mail systems, which resemble answering machines, have some of these same advantages. However, e-mail takes less space to store. More important, e-mail can be scanned electronically to search for key topics.

There are some drawbacks to e-mail. For one, some people are still reluctant to use computers, so they do not check the computer often enough to keep up with their mail. Another problem is that in 1991, the U.S. courts ruled that public transmission systems such as e-mail are not subject to the same legal protections for privacy as paper mail and phone calls. Unless the laws are rewritten, therefore, it is legal for employers (and almost anyone else) to read everyone's e-mail messages. Of course, the fact that it is legal does not make it ethical. The best solution to open communication systems is to encrypt the messages. Most word processors and spreadsheets make it easy to encrypt the files when they are saved. An interesting twist on this situation is that some courts have ruled that public officials *cannot*

REALITY BYTES   Video Bandwidth Needs

In the increasingly digital world, you need to connect devices that carry data, voice, music, and video. The home presents the greatest market, but the technologies will also be useful in business. Some companies are working on wireless solutions. Ultra-wideband offers the possibility of transferring files directly from a video camera to a television without wires—but only over a short distance. Wi-Fi wireless offers some possibilities but has limited quality of service (QOS), is subject to interference, and has a limited bandwidth. Ladd Wardani, an executive of Entropic and president of the Multimedia over Cable Alliance (MoCA), notes that high-definition television signals represent a tremendous increase in bandwidth—requiring from 20 to 40 megabits per second for one channel. To handle the increased demands, Entropic is building devices that turn in-house coaxial television wiring into a high-speed network. The company foresees the ability to let you begin watching a television program in one room, pause the program with a remote using a digital video recorder, and then watch the rest of the show in a different room.

Source: Adapted from Don Clark, "Electronics Giants See New Future for Old Coaxial Cable," *The Wall Street Journal*, January 5, 2004.

encrypt their messages; in fact, in some situations, it is illegal for public officials to communicate via e-mail at all.

Web Sites, Newsgroups, and Chat Rooms

Web sites are essentially bulletin boards that are used to make information available to many people over the Internet. **Intranet** sites are similar in that they use Internet technologies but employ security methods to restrict access to internal users. Web sites can be interactive and retrieve customized information from a database. **Extranets** are sites specifically designed for companies that partner with your organization. For example, your suppliers can log into a special section to check on your production schedule, pick up technical specifications, or bid on jobs. Intranets and extranets use the same technologies as the common Internet, but are limited to special groups of users.

Discussion sites and chat rooms allow users to post information as well as search for specific topics. Chat rooms do not usually store comments, but discussion sites provide databases and links so users can maintain a string of related messages. Discussion systems are generally more organized than simple e-mail and store the data in one location to make it easier to find. Chat rooms are more interactive than e-mail, since they display messages as they are written.

A **newsgroup** is an Internet feature similar to a discussion site in that it carries comments from many people. It is designed to be copied from server to server so that the comments are available to a wide audience. Internet newsgroups are useful when you are searching for people with experiences similar to your own. However, they are a bad place to put company information.

Overall, the purpose of these systems is to enable people to send and retrieve electronic messages from others. The difference lies in the level of central control and monitoring. More highly monitored newsgroups are generally more accurate and more valuable in business. For example, the HRM department could run a newsgroup to provide information about benefits. Employee questions and answers could be posted in the newsgroup or on a Web site, because answers to one person might be valuable to many other employees.

Most students today are familiar with **instant messaging (IM).** But have you thought about the possible business uses as a manager? When you are working on a team project, you can establish IM connections with each team member. As problems or questions arise, you can quickly type in a message and share ideas. Yes, you could use e-mail, but then you have to wait for everyone to check for new mail. Yes, you could use the phone, but phone calls are more disruptive. If someone is busy working, he or she can ignore the IM for a few minutes to finish a section. Similarly, if you are working late at night, you can quickly see which of the other team members are also online, so you know that you can ask a question without having to call everyone just to see if they are in.

A Web log or **blog** is an interesting variation of a Web site. It is essentially a diary on any topic posted on a special Web site (check out www.blogger.com) for everyone to read.

Although most blogs are based on personal or political topics, the concept offers some interesting business uses. The same technology could be used by managers to keep a log of the daily issues, problems, and solutions. Other managers in the company could skim the logs to see if problems arising in one area might cause problems in their own sections. Similarly, if a manager encounters a problem, he or she could search the blogs for similar problems, ideas on how to approach it, or even solutions that worked in the past. In essence, the blogs become a knowledge base that is accessible to other managers. Of course, the sites would be secured so that only managers within the organization could read them.

Calendars and Scheduling

Managers spend a great deal of time in meetings. Yet sometimes the greatest challenge with meetings is finding a time when everyone can get together. Several software packages use computer networks to solve this problem. As shown in Figure 3.5, managers enter planned meeting times and scheduled events into their personal electronic calendar file, where each event is assigned a priority number. For example, a time allotted for a haircut would be given a low priority; a meeting with a supervisor would receive a higher rating. If the CEO wants to set up a meeting, the CEO tells the computer which people are to be included, sets a priority level, and gives an approximate time. The computer then uses the network to check everyone else's schedule. When it finds an open time (overriding lower priority events if needed), it enters the meeting into each person's calendar. These systems can be useful when managers carry PDAs that are connected to a wireless network.

Teamwork and Joint Authorship

In any job, it is rare for one person to work alone. Most businesses are arranged as teams. Within the teams, individual people are given specific assignments, and each team member contributes to the final product. For instance, the marketing department might have to prepare a sales forecast for the next six months. Each person could work on a specific sales region or product category. These individual pieces would then be merged into a single document. If the computers are networked, the manager's computer can pull the individual pieces from each of the individual computers. Also, each team member can be given access to the others' work to ensure that the reports use the same data and assumptions.

Groupware includes software that enables several people to work on the same document. Each individual computer has access to the master document. When one person makes a change to the document, the change is highlighted for everyone to read and approve. With existing international networks, each person might be located in a different country. E-mail systems can work as simple groupware tools by routing copies of files to everyone on the team. More sophisticated tools are included in Web sites built by systems like Microsoft's SharePoint. These tools are discussed in greater detail in Chapter 9.

FIGURE 3.5

Sharing calendars: With the appropriate software, you can open your calendar to other members of your team. A team member can check the calendar and have the software find a common open time for a meeting.

8:00	Mgt meeting
8:30	(open)
9:00	Staff meeting
9:30	Staff meeting
10:00	New meeting

Backup

Another important reason for sharing data over computer networks is that most people are not very good at maintaining backup copies of their work—especially on personal computers. If each computer is attached to a network, there are two ways to set up an automatic backup system for individual personal computers. The older method relies on individual workers saving their data files to a central file server. The network manager then makes daily (or hourly) backups of the data on the central server. A few companies even provide this service over the Internet. For a monthly fee, you can transfer your files to their server, giving you a backup copy—plus they keep backup tapes for the server.

A newer method is significantly safer because it is virtually automatic and does not require users to remember to transfer their files. It does require users to leave their machines running. At a predetermined time, a central computer with a large backup capacity connects to the individual machines and copies the files that have changed. This data is then stored somewhere safe (such as a tape or optical disk). If a computer or a person accidentally deletes a file, the backup computer can restore the file and send it back to the personal computer. With the communication network, the backup process is almost completely automatic.

Sharing Hardware

Networks also enable workers to share expensive hardware. For example, networks are used to provide users access to special output devices, such as high-speed printers, plotters, or color printers. Networks can be used to give people access to special computers, such as when an engineer needs to use a high-speed supercomputer.

Printers

A common use of networks is to give users access to high-speed, high-quality printers. Even if each computer has a small personal printer attached, some jobs need to be handled by a high-speed laser printer. Many modern copiers now function as network printers and can collate and staple large quantities of documents. Similarly, at $3,000 each it would be expensive to buy color laser printers for everyone who might need one, yet it might be reasonable to buy one for a department to share. With a network, users can choose from among two or three different printers by selecting them on the screen. Figure 3.6 shows some of the hardware devices that are often shared.

Another advantage is that if one printer breaks down, users can send their jobs to another printer on the network. Think about what happens if there is no network and your printer breaks down. You have to copy the file to a USB drive and interrupt someone else's work to borrow their computer to send the file to another printer. What happens if you are using a special software package that no one else has on his or her computer? You will probably

FIGURE 3.6

Networks for sharing hardware: The workstations use the server to perform backups. Files are picked up by the server and transferred to tape. The LAN administrator can reload a tape and restore files as needed. Networks are often used to share printers and storage devices. Networks can be used to share access to supercomputers—even if they are in a different city or different country.

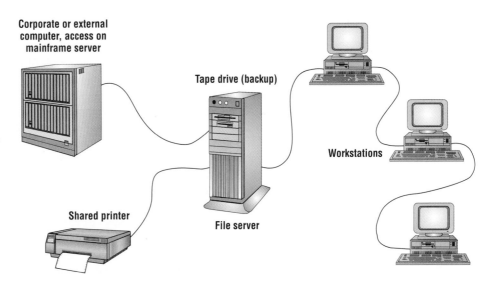

REALITY BYTES   Bandwidth Is Scarce for Everyone

The U.S. defense department loves its unmanned spy planes. The high-tech equipment carries video cameras and now guns. The planes can be flown into dangerous areas to provide detailed reconnaissance. Other versions of the planes cruise invisibly at high altitudes and can be used as relay stations or with high-resolution cameras to cover wide areas of the battlefield. Through the planes, the remote pilot can talk to battlefield commanders and pilots flying F-15s. In 2002, the Pentagon budgeted $1 billion to add 37 more to its fleet. The only drawback is that it will not be able to fly them all. The planes rely on satellite communications for their command and information systems. With a serious shortage of commercial and military satellites, there is insufficient bandwidth to fly more than a few of the Predators at one time. One Global Hawk alone uses 500 megabits per second. Between 1998 and 2002, only 275 satellites out of 675 launches reached space. In Afghanistan in 2002, the Pentagon had access to six Predators and two Global Hawks (the higher flying planes). But the lack of bandwidth meant they could fly only two Predators and one Global Hawk at the same time. In 2000, the Defense Science Board forecast that the military would need 16 gigabits per second of bandwidth to fight a major war in 2010. Today, the classified number is substantially higher. Between 2004 and 2006, the Pentagon will launch three new satellites, but in total they will provide a maximum of 7.5 gigabits of bandwidth.

Source: Adapted from Greg Jaffe, "Military Feels Bandwidth Squeeze as the Satellite Industry Sputters," *The Wall Street Journal,* April 10, 2002.

have to physically move a printer from another computer desk to yours, connect the hardware, print your document, and return the printer. When you are on a network, you simply select a different printer from a list displayed on your computer and go pick up the output.

Several e-commerce printing companies enable you to send your large print jobs over the Internet and have the boxes of papers shipped to you. All of the setup, pricing, and payment can be handled over the Internet.

Storage Devices

The arguments used for network printer sharing can be applied to sharing storage devices. If you have huge data files that you want to share across the organization, it is best to put them in a central location and provide network access to everyone who needs them. The central location makes it easy to upgrade the drives, provide sufficient capacity, and control the access rights and monitor security. A specialized **storage area network (SAN)** is often used to provide vast amounts of flexible storage. The disk drives are separated from the computers and connected by a high-speed network using fiber channel or similar connections. Physically separating the secondary storage from the computer box makes it easy to expand the capacity, provide redundancy, and move the drives to safer locations. Because of the high transfer speeds across the SAN, the drives appear as simple local devices to the computer, so no software changes are needed.

Special Processors and Grid Computing

Special computers that are relatively expensive can be attached to a network to save costs and make it easier for users to access these machines. Parallel-processing computers and other supercomputers can perform calculations thousands of times faster than ordinary computers, but they are expensive. Consider a small engineering company. For the most part, the engineers use their workstations to develop their designs. They occasionally need to run simulations or produce detailed graphics images. Both of these tasks could take many hours to perform on individual client computers. The company can cable each engineer's workstation to a network that can access a supercomputer. When an engineer needs to perform high-speed calculations, the job is sent directly to the supercomputer. The results are returned via the network to the workstation so they can be added to the final report. More likely, a university could own the supercomputer, and the firm would lease time to run each job. If the network is designed properly, it makes no difference where the machine is located.

Grid computing extends the concept of parallel processing—instead of having multiple processors in one computer, you simply attach multiple computers together across a network. Remember that personal computers are relatively fast and inexpensive. When you can buy a new computer for $500, it becomes possible to build a huge amount of computing power by purchasing hundreds or thousands of computers and spreading the work across all of them. Of course, it requires special software to split up the computing job and coordinate it across all of the computers.

Sharing Software

Networks have been used at different times to share software. When disk space was expensive, it was cheaper to put one copy of the software on a server and download it to each computer as it was needed. Today, several firms have been working on a system that stores software on Internet servers, where client computers use Web browsers to connect to the server and run the software.

The main advantages of running software on a central server are that (1) it is easier to install and update and (2) the client computers can be small and low-cost, which makes it particularly useful for PDAs and cell phones. The main drawback is network performance and reliability. If the network is slow or the server crashes, no one can use the software.

Voice and Video Communication

A major cost of telecommunications in business is for telephone calls. Despite the total expenditures, there is little doubt about the value of communication and phones. Phone calls are almost always cheaper than in-person visits. With the rapidly declining costs of phone calls, cost is less of an issue. Even cellular phone costs are dropping rapidly; some experts predict that within a few years, almost all calls will be made over the cellular networks instead of traditional phone lines.

Newer technologies are emphasizing the value of routing all communication over a single Internet-based network, often called **voice over Internet protocol (VoIP).** With this technology, your telephone becomes a device on the Internet and conversations are digitized and sent over the Internet along with all other traffic. Figure 3.7 illustrates the process. Your voice conversation is split into packets, mixed with other data traffic, and routed to its destination over the Internet, where the computer/phone on the other end puts the packets in the proper order and re-creates the conversation. **Packets** are a key feature of modern networks. A packet consists of a chunk of data, a destination address, and a source address. Additional data can be added by the network equipment to facilitate routing of the packets.

With improvements in technology and faster transmission of data at lower costs, it is becoming feasible to run full-service networks to each desk. These links enable workers to communicate with others using voice, pictures, computer data, or video across the same line. Although these links are technically feasible today, they are somewhat expensive. As Internet speeds improve and costs continue to decline, you will have more opportunities to use these technologies. Currently, one of the greatest difficulties with using these technologies over the Internet is that you may randomly experience delays from some link. But newer versions of the Internet protocols are being released that support guaranteed levels

FIGURE 3.7

Packet-switched networks operate by partitioning all messages into small packets. Each packet contains a destination and source address, along with sequencing instructions. The packets can be separated and set over different routes. At their destination, the original message is automatically restored by the network. Packets provide efficient use of transmission networks because they can mix packets and route transmissions over empty routes.

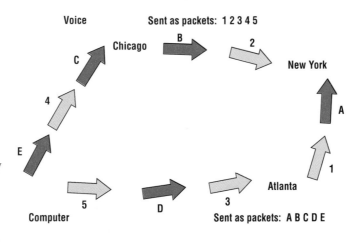

of service. Soon you will be able to conduct video meetings by reserving a certain level of speed at a set time. Today, several companies are making phones that run VoIP on wireless networks. Much like a laptop, the phone connects to the wireless access point, digitizes your voice, and sends it across the Internet to its destination. With either wireless or wired VoIP, you need to sign a service contract with a company to convert your Internet calls back to the regular telephone system if you want to call someone with only a traditional phone.

Components of a Network

What components do you need to install to create a network? As networks have become more important, the components are increasingly built into the machines. However, you still face many decisions about which technologies to use and how to solve problems, so all managers should understand the basic elements of a network shown in Figure 3.8. Each of these components (computers, transmission medium, and connection devices) is discussed in greater detail in this section.

Computers

Virtually any type of computer device can be connected to a network. The earliest computer networks consisted of one computer with several terminals and printers attached to it. These networks were fairly simple, because the one computer performed all of the work. Substantially more problems are involved in connecting several computers together. For starters, each computer needs to know that the others exist and that they have a specific location (address) on the network. The computers need to know how to send and receive information from each other. To work together, they need connection devices (LAN cards) and special software.

Computers attached to networks tend to perform one of two functions: servers or clients. *Servers* are computers that store data to be used by other computers attached to the network. *Clients* are computers used by individual people. Sometimes a computer is used as both a client and a file server. Networks where many of the machines operate as both clients and servers are called **peer-to-peer networks.**

Servers

A wide range of servers exists today—from a simple PC to huge, expensive specialized computers. The main questions you face in choosing a server are the operating system and the issue of scalability, and the two questions are intertwined. **Scalability** is the ability to easily move up to greater performance—without having to rewrite all of your existing applications. Figure 3.9 shows two common methods used to provide scalability: (1) a vendor-provided range of servers from low-cost machines to handle small loads, to midrange, to high-capacity computers that can handle thousands of users simultaneously; and (2) inte-

FIGURE 3.8

Network components: Networks require a transmission medium and each device connected must have a network card to make the connection. Connecting to the Internet requires a router or switch and usually a firewall to block certain types of messages. Computers are often classified as workstations or servers. The distinction is blurring, but servers are dedicated to sharing data and files.

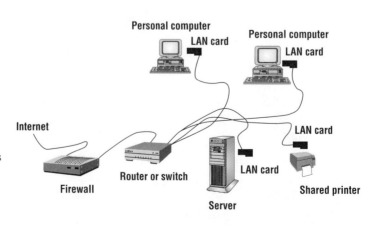

FIGURE 3.9

Server scalability: Two common methods of providing easy expansion of performance are (1) to purchase a faster performance server within the same product family, and (2) to build a server farm where the workload is automatically distributed across machines and new low-cost servers can be added at any time.

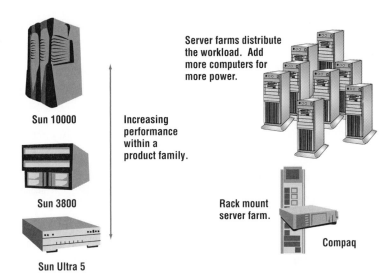

gration technology that enables the workload to be distributed across hundreds or thousands of small servers, known as a **server farm.**

Both approaches have their benefits. The single server is easier to configure and administer. The server farm can be expanded easily and cheaply without disrupting the existing applications. The operating system software is crucial to making a server farm work efficiently. Several vendors sell enterprise versions of software that assigns applications to the least-busy server and makes it easier to manage the server farm.

Client Computers

The networked computers could be any type of machine. Because individual people at their own desks typically use these computers, they are often called *client computers*. These computers need to access the network and be able to send information to at least one other computer. A **network interface card (NIC)** (or LAN card) is installed in each computer. These cards are connected together by some transmission medium (e.g., cable). In addition, these computers might have to be configured to connect to the network and set security parameters. Client computers today include laptops and PDAs that can be connected with wireless networks to enable workers to maintain connections and share data while they move around the building.

Many of the mobile devices have limited capabilities and essentially run browsers, e-mail, and calendars. Hence, more of the processing is done on the server, and the mobile device is only responsible for displaying data and basic user interface tasks. This type of environment is considerably different from the situation where all workers have desktop machines capable of handling large amounts of the processing. The thin-client PDAs rely on the server, while the desktop applications simply use the server for basic data sharing. Developing applications for this new environment requires some major changes in design, programming, and security—issues that will be explained in detail in other chapters.

Transmission Media

All communication requires a transmission medium. As illustrated in Figure 3.10, common methods include electric wires, light waves, and radio waves. Each method offers certain advantages and disadvantages, so they are designed for specific applications. Installation costs for all types of cables are high, and most organizations are unwilling to throw away old cable and install a totally new system.

Electric Cables

The two basic types of electric cables are twisted pair and coaxial. *Twisted pair* is the oldest form of electrical wiring. Since electricity must travel in a closed loop, electrical connections require at least two wires. Twisted-pair wires are simply pairs of plain copper

FIGURE 3.10

Signals can be sent via several types of media. They can be carried by electricity, light waves, or radio waves. All of these methods have advantages and disadvantages. Fiber-optic cabling offers the fastest transmission rates with the least interference, but because it is relatively new, the initial cost tends to be higher.

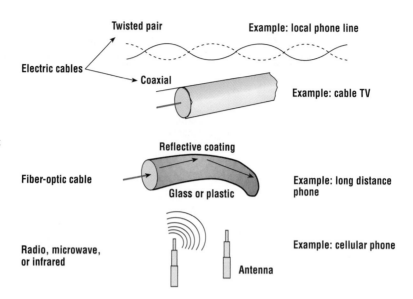

wires. Telephone cables are the most common example of twisted-pair wires in households. Because of the cost, most businesses have already installed twisted-pair wires—typically a specific version known as Cat 5. Cat 5 wiring consists of four pairs of wires, and generally two pairs (4 wires) are used for most typical networks. Because of the extensive use of Cat 5 cables, the network industry has invested considerable research into maximizing the data that can be carried over that type of cable. However, the newer high-speed transmissions systems might require better cables. The Cat 5e (enhanced) standard would be the minimum for installing new cables, and depending on price and location, you might consider Cat 6 or the proposed Cat 7, which is heavily shielded.

Twisted-pair wires have certain disadvantages. This type of cable cannot carry much information at one time. Plus, data transmitted on unshielded twisted-pair wires is subject to interference from other electrical devices. Interference can distort or damage a telecommunications signal. For instance, it is best to avoid running twisted-pair wires next to electric power lines and electric motors, because these devices produce electromagnetic radiation that can interfere with the signal. On the other hand, it is possible to put several twisted pairs into one cable at a relatively low cost. Sending portions of the message along each wire can increase the overall transmission speed.

Coaxial cables were designed to carry more information than twisted pairs, with lower chances of interference. *Coaxial cable* (often shortened to *coax*) consists of a central wire surrounded by a nonconductive plastic, which is surrounded by a second wire. The second wire is actually a metallic foil or mesh that is wrapped around the entire cable. This shielding minimizes interference from outside sources. Cable television signals are transmitted on coaxial cables. Coax is capable of carrying more information for longer distances than twisted pair.

Fiber Optics

A relatively recent invention (early 1970s) in communication uses light instead of electricity. Because light generally travels in a straight line, it could be difficult to use for communication. Fiber-optic cable allows light to travel in straight lines but still be bent around corners. A fiber-optic cable consists of a glass or plastic core that is surrounded by a reflective material. A laser light (typically infrared) is sent down the cable. When the cable turns, the light is reflected around the corner and continues down the cable. Fiber-optic cable provides the advantages of high capacity with almost no interference. The limitation in using fiber is the higher cost of the cable and the cost of the connectors and interface cards that convert computer electrical signals into light. For example, NICs for coaxial or twisted-pair cables can be purchased for around $20, whereas NICs for fiber-optic lines that run directly to personal computers cost around $700 (in 2004). A study by Partha Mitra and Jason

REALITY BYTES   Excess Capacity

Partly because of crazy predictions of Internet growth, partly because of economies of scale, and partly because of improved technologies, several long-haul data-transmission companies overbuilt when installing fiber-optic cables. In late 2002, only 2.7 percent of the fiber was being used—a whopping 97.3 percent was dark. Over time, economics prevailed and bandwidth prices dropped—at a rate of 65 percent per year. Many of the large telecommunications firms filed for bankruptcy. The bankruptcy filings generally erased the debts of the companies—enabling them to charge even lower prices when returning.

Prior to 1995, telecommunications companies could send the equivalent of 25,000 one-page e-mails per second over one fiber-optic line. By 2002, advances in technology enabled them to send 25 million messages over the same line—an increase of one thousand times. The new technology, called dense-wave division multiplexing (DWDM), effectively splits light into multiple colors—enabling the companies to send different messages on each color frequency.

Source: Adapted from Yochi J. Dreazen, "Wildly Optimistic Data Drove Telecoms to Build Fiber Glut," *The Wall Street Journal*, September 26, 2002; and Dennis K. Berman, "Technology Races Far Ahead of Demand and the Workplace," *The Wall Street Journal*, September 26, 2002.

Stark showed that even fiber-optic cables have limits. The theoretical capacity of a single fiber-optic cable is at least 100 terabits per second (*The Economist* June 28, 2001 or *Nature* June 28, 2001). Although it is possible to run fiber optics directly to your desktop, it is rarely worth the expense. Fiber-optic connections are used for long distances or when connecting buildings. Twisted pair runs cannot exceed 90 meters (295 feet); anything longer should use fiber-optic connections. Similarly, any connections that run outside or near electrical motors should use fiber-optic connections.

Radio, Micro, and Infrared Waves

Radio, microwave, and infrared transmissions do not require cables. These communication methods are called **broadcasts.** Any receiver or antenna that lies in its path can pick up the signal. However, infrared transmissions and some microwaves require clear line-of-sight transmission. The major advantage of broadcast methods is portability. For example, computers can be installed in delivery vehicles to receive information from corporate headquarters. On a smaller scale, individuals can carry around laptops and PDAs and remain connected to the network. These computers can communicate with each other and with a central database via a broadcast network. For example, physicians in hospitals can carry small computers that automatically receive information for each patient when the physician enters the room. Any instructions can be sent directly from the physician's computer to the nursing station. In the business world, you can carry a PDA or tablet that maintains contact on the Internet to retrieve e-mail or scan Web sites while you are in meetings, other offices, or a client's office.

Broadcast media have two primary drawbacks. First, it is more important to provide security for the transmissions. Second, broadcast transmissions carry a limited amount of data. The two problems are related. Because it is a broadcast method, the signals sent by one computer can be received by any other computer within range. There is no way to prevent other computers from physically receiving the signal. The most common solution is to encrypt the wireless transmissions, but encryption increases the number of bits sent, which slows the transmissions.

The problem of limited capacity arises because only a small number of radio frequencies can be used to carry data. Most of the radio and television frequencies are already being used for other purposes. Figure 3.11 shows some of the major frequency allocations in the United States. The Federal Communications Commission (FCC) allocated the personal communication service (PCS) bands in late 1993 for use by personal communication devices such as laptop computers and personal digital assistants (PDAs). To provide these frequencies, the FCC had to take them away from existing users. Imagine what would happen if computers suddenly started sending information over the same radio frequency as that used by your favorite radio station. You would not be able to hear the voices on the radio, and the computers would miss most of their data because of the interference.

REALITY BYTES   How Much Are You Willing to Pay?

Third generation (3G) mobile phones introduced to Europe in 2004 offered some interesting features. Alcatel SA, the French telecommunications giant, announced a deal with the cable channel Eurosport to develop sports TV for cell phones. Eurosport director Arjan Hoekstra noted that the company already broadcasts in 18 languages around the world and has the technology in place to broadcast to cell phones, but "it's a question of whether the consumer's ready to pay for it. Nobody really knows—but we certainly hope so." The 3G operator 3 began selling Premiership football highlights to British fans in late 2003. The company also began streaming live 24-hour coverage of "Big Brother" to Swedish sub-scribers in January 2004. The company sold 60,000 sessions in the first two weeks.

Other features introduced in 2004 include multimedia messaging services (MMS) as an extension to the popular SMS text system. With MMS, users can send pictures, video, animation, music, and add their own voice comments. Of course, mobile games are also expected to be popular. Mobile operators are also developing payment systems so users can purchase digital content from any provider and pay for it on their next wireless bill.

Source: Adapted from "New-Wave Cell Phones Arriving in Europe," *CNN Online,* February 26, 2004.

FIGURE 3.11

Electromagnetic frequency spectrum: Communication techniques are essentially the same for all media, because all waves physically have similar properties. However, the different frequencies affect the communication performance. Shorter wavelengths (higher frequencies) can carry more data. Some waves can travel longer distances. Others are more susceptible to interference. In any case, there are a finite number of frequencies available for communication. Hence, the frequency spectrum is allocated by governmental agencies.

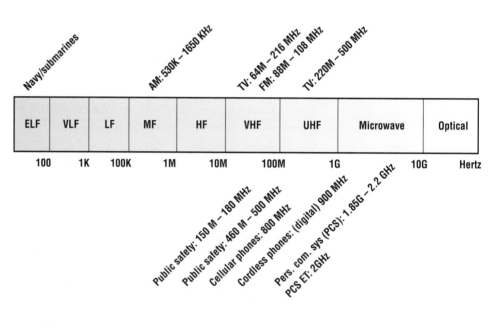

All governments allocate the frequency spectrum for various uses, such as radio, television, cellular phones, and garage door openers. The PCS frequencies were auctioned off to the highest bidders in 1994, raising more than $65 billion. The frequency problem is even more complicated when the signals might cross political boundaries. As a result, most broadcast telecommunications issues are established with international cooperation. Some of the overcrowding problems are being mitigated through the use of digital transmissions that cram more calls and more data into the same amount of frequency space.

Despite these problems, an increasing amount of business communication is being carried over radio networks. The International Telecommunication Union reports that in 2002, both Taiwan and Luxembourg averaged about 105 cell phone users per 100 people! In comparison with broadband Internet connections, Korea leads the way with 21.9 subscribers per 100 inhabitants, followed by Hong Kong with 14.6. Although wireless Internet connections are not yet as fast as broadband connections, it is substantially less expensive to reach people with wireless connections. Already, in many nations, the number of cell phone subscribers exceeds the number of fixed telephone subscribers.

Transmission Capacity

As shown in Figure 3.12, transmission capacity is often measured in millions of bits per second. Each transmission medium has a different maximum capacity. Twisted pair can be relatively fast for short distances, but fiber optic is substantially better for longer distances.

Glance at the frequency spectrum allocation in any country and you will find few openings for new services. Yet new wireless technologies need more bandwidth. In the recent past, spectrum has been reallocated from smaller users and consolidated for technologies like cell phones. One big area that offers possibilities is the television spectrum. In addition to encompassing a large bandwidth, the particular frequencies are good at passing through buildings. In 1997, broadcasters were given $70 billion of new spectrum to prepare for digital television broadcasts. In exchange, they were supposed to switch to digital by 2006 and release the older frequencies. Due to "weasel" clauses in the agreement, and delays by the broadcasters, this exchange is not likely to happen. The Federal Communications Commission (FCC) and Commerce Department are pushing the broadcasters to move faster or give up some of the spectrum. Having spent millions on lobbyists to obtain the current agreement, broadcasters are not budging. But technology lobbyists are hopeful. Peter K. Pitsch, an Intel Corp. lobbyist, notes that broadcasters face "a lot more powerful interest on the other side now. If you look at the information technology industry, two or three years ago we were almost nowhere when it came to spectrum debates. Now, we are right in the middle of things in a big way."

Source: Adapted from Jube Shiver, Jr., "Plan for Spectrum Is Making Waves," *The Los Angeles Times,* May 7, 2004.

FIGURE 3.12

Transmission capacity: Fiber-optic cables have the greatest capacity and they are immune to most traditional interference. However, they are expensive to install and repair. Most firms use twisted-pair or wireless connections within buildings and fiber-optic cables to connect buildings. You can purchase almost any Internet connection speed that you are willing to pay for. Leased line rates are negotiable and depend on distance and degree of local competition.

Local Area Networks		
Name	**Format**	**Speed (mbps)**
10Base-T	Twisted pair	10
100Base-T	Twisted pair	100
Gigabit Ethernet	Twisted pair	1,000
Wireless LAN	Wireless	11
Wireless LAN future	Wireless	54
LAN/fiber FDDI	Fiber optic	100
LAN/fiber ATM	Fiber optic	155
LAN/fiber future	Fiber optic	10,000

Internet Connections			
Name	**Format**	**Speed (mbps)**	**Estimated Cost**
Dial-up	Twisted pair	0.05	$20/month
DSL	Twisted pair	1.5 down/0.13 up	$50/month
Cable modem	Coaxial	1.5 down/0.26 up	$50/month
Satellite	Microwave	1.5 down/0.05 up	$50/month
Wireless	Microwave	1.5	$70/month
Wireless/future	Microwave	20–50	
T1-lease	Twisted pair	1.544	$500–$1,000/month
T3-lease	Fiber optic	45	$4,000–$10,000/month
ATM	Fiber optic	155	Negotiable
OC-3	Fiber optic	155	$16,000–$20,000/month
OC-12	Fiber optic	622	$35,000–$70,000/month
OC-48	Fiber optic	2,500	
OC-192/future	Fiber optic	10,000	

Getting a faster Internet connection is primarily an issue of cost. Fiber-optic cable might also carry a high installation cost if there are no fiber-optic connection points near your office.

The effect of the transmission capacity is shown in Figure 3.13. For small text and data files, the speed is not critical. Even slow dial-up lines can transfer a full page of text in a short time. The problem arises when you want to transfer more complex data like photos or even video. This figure shows why designing Web pages carefully is still so important. When over 75 percent of your clients are using dial-up lines, you need to limit pages to around 50,000 bytes, which takes at least 8 seconds to download. Most people will not wait more than 15 seconds for a page to load. Now you can see why Internet video is so bad.

FIGURE 3.13

Importance of transmission
capacity: Text is not a problem
even for slow dial-up lines, but
images and video can be slow
even over relatively high-speed
Internet connections.

	Text	Image	Video 10 Sec
Bytes	10,000	500,000	15,000,000
Bits	80,000	4,000,000	120,000,000
Seconds			
Dial-up 50 kbps	1.6	80	2,400
DSL 1.5 mbps	0.05	2.67	80
LAN 10 mbps	0.008	0.4	12
LAN 100 mbps	0.0008	0.04	1.2
Gigabit 1 gbps	0.00008	0.004	0.12

FIGURE 3.14

Shared connections: Some
networks rely on sharing the
transmission medium with many
users. Sharing means computers
must take turns using the
network. Sometimes one or two
highly active users can slow
down the network for everyone,
so you will not really get the
listed transmission capacity.

With shared connections, machines have to take turns, and congestion can slow down all connections.

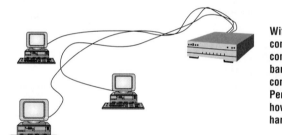

With switched connections, each computer has the full bandwidth of the connection at all times. Performance depends on how fast the switch can handle connections.

Even with video at broadband speeds of 1.5 mbps, site designers have to restrict the video to small sizes (one-fourth of a TV screen or smaller) and slower frame rates (as low as 15 frames per second). These two actions cut the video size by at least ⅛ (¼ size * ½ frames). At that size, the 10 seconds of video could be sent in 10 seconds (80/8), which just barely matches the speed of the original video and assumes that the viewer actually gets the full bandwidth.

Shared Connections

Figure 3.14 shows that transmission times become more important when more than two computers are involved, and when you want to send more than one item. For example, think about what will happen if you share a slow (2 mbps) wireless network with 10 other users—and everyone tries to retrieve a complex image at the same time. The networks are designed to handle multiple users, but heavy usage by a few people can slow down the connection for everyone.

Originally, most local area networks used shared lines; but as usage and data complexity have increased, firms have moved to switched networks. With a switched network, each person has sole use of the wire run between the computer and the switch, providing faster throughput even for large numbers of users.

This issue can be particularly important for Internet connections. By nature, the Internet is a shared system—many links in the connections are shared lines. But consider two common broadband connections: DSL and cable modem. **Digital subscriber line (DSL)** is a system offered by phone companies using the twisted-pair phone line into your house. **Cable modems** are shared Internet connections offered by the cable television company on a channel of the coaxial cable into your house. The DSL line is not shared between your house and the phone company. On the other hand, the cable modem connection between your house and the cable company is usually shared, so your performance might depend on the usage by your neighbors. Ultimately, the connections are shared once they reach the phone or cable company, so in a carefully designed network, there might not be much difference—since your ultimate performance will depend on all of the other connections on the Internet at that time. DSL and cable connections are often referred to as **broadband** connections because they have the ability to transfer more data at one time.

Wireless radio connections always use a shared medium. Radio spectrum is very limited and it must be shared. In fact, advanced sharing techniques are responsible for the higher speeds that are available now. Figure 3.15 shows how modern wireless systems use spread spectrum techniques to utilize the available bandwidth as completely as possible for maximum transmission capacity. All communications are broken into tiny packets that can be sent in a short time slot. At a given time, the transmitter searches for an open frequency. If all are being used, the transmitter waits for the next time slot and sends on an open frequency. The recipient monitors all allocated frequencies and identifies packets with its address.

Connection Devices

To reduce overall traffic, larger organizations often find it beneficial to build the corporate network from a set of smaller networks. Both large and small companies use similar techniques to connect their networks to the Internet. Figure 3.16 shows a common configuration. Computers within a building or smaller area are linked into a hub, switch, or router. This interconnection device is then linked to the backbone, which is typically a fiber-optic line.

If you look at the physical box, it can be difficult to tell the difference between a hub, router, and switch. However, internally, they function quite differently, and you need to understand those differences to decide how a network should be configured. Hubs are the simplest connection devices. They essentially act like a giant junction box. Any device connected to a hub shares all of the lines with the other devices. It is just a mechanism to plug several computers together. Switches and routers actually examine every packet that passes through them and decide where to send each packet. They are actually specialized computers that can be programmed to identify network problems and intelligently route traffic to the fastest route.

Routers and switches are crucial to improving efficiency in large networks. In many respects, a router works like a post office. It examines the destination address of each packet of information and selects the best way to send that packet. Routers improve performance by choosing the path of the message and segmenting large networks into smaller pieces. For example, router segments might be assigned to each department of a large company, where each department has its own server. Most of the messages stay within the specific department, so they do not take up bandwidth across the entire company. Only messages that truly need to be sent to other areas will be transmitted outside the departmental segment. *Switches* perform a similar task but isolate communications down to one line. So

FIGURE 3.15

Spread spectrum: Radio networks share the scarce airwaves by breaking communications into small packets that are sent at different frequencies and time slots. In a given time slot, if one frequency is not available, the transmitter shifts to the next frequency. If all frequencies are being used, the transmitter must wait for the next time slot.

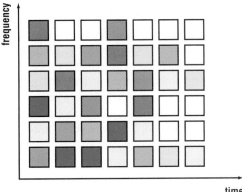

FIGURE 3.16

Connecting networks: Several challenges arise if you build an enterprise network. An enterprise network often connects many smaller networks established in different departments, buildings, or even nations. The hardware and software components must follow standards so they can communicate. An MIS team has to manage the overall structure to maximize efficiency, avoid duplication, and solve problems.

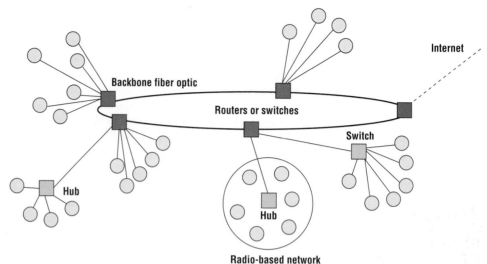

your communication would have full use of a line for a period of time. Modern routers combine the function of both switching and routing to take advantage of both techniques.

Network Structure

Why does it matter how your computer is connected to the network? Two primary methods are used to connect computers: shared-media networks and direct connections on switched networks. Arguments continually arise over which type of network is better, and often there is no one right answer. Most modern networks consist of both types of connections.

Shared-Media Networks

As shown in Figure 3.17, computers in a shared-media network can be connected to a common wire. They might also use the same radio frequency space. The main advantage of a shared-media network is that it is cheaper to install one wire (or share one frequency) than to run separate wires from each computer back to a central location. In many ways, a shared-media network is like a room full of people trying to talk to each other. The limitation of sharing the media (the air in the room) is that only one person or computer can talk at a time. As a result, *protocols* are needed to establish rules of behavior to avoid common problems. The protocols need to cover four situations: (1) providing a means to address each recipient and sender, (2) determining who is allowed to talk (initiate a conversation), (3) determining how long a single sender can talk at one time, and (4) specifying what to do if there is a *collision* when two machines (or people) try to talk at the same time.

Ethernet is one of the earliest protocols to resolve these problems. It has been standardized by several national and international standard-setting bodies so that a network can be built from equipment provided by different vendors. The Ethernet protocol is also known as CSMA/CD, which stands for *Carrier-Sense, Multiple-Access/Collision Detection.* In this system, any LAN card is allowed to transmit on the network, but first it must examine the media to see whether another card is currently transmitting (carrier-sense). If so, the second card must wait until the line is clear. Users are prevented from tying up the line for extended periods by restricting the length of time each card can transmit at any one time. One of the biggest drawbacks to CSMA/CD is that as the number of users increases, there will be more collisions. With many collisions, the computers end up spending more time detecting collisions and waiting than they do transmitting. It is also the reason why a high-speed medium is important to this method. The faster that every transmission can be sent, the sooner the line is clear and ready for the next user.

FIGURE 3.17
Shared-media (Ethernet) network: Each device is connected to a common transmission medium. Only one device can transmit at a time. Standards define when a device can transmit, how to specify a device, and how to tell whether the line is busy.

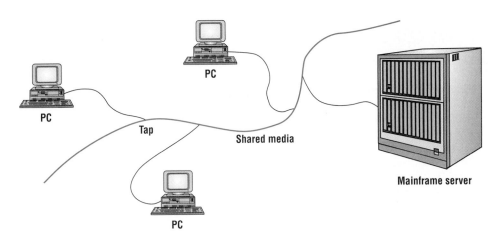

FIGURE 3.18
Switched network: Each device is connected independently to a switch. The switch rapidly transfers each packet to the desired destination.

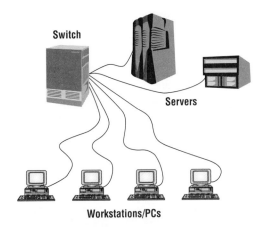

Switched Networks

Switched networks originally evolved from the telephone system. Initially, each telephone had its own direct connection wire to the phone company switchboard. As shown in Figure 3.18, each computer has a connection to a switch. The switch is a specialized high-speed computer that examines each packet of data and transfers it to the appropriate destination. The performance of the network depends on the speed of the switch. In general, switches are faster than shared-media networks (such as those using hubs) because each computer gets full capacity on the line. But keep in mind that it often costs more money to install all of the cables.

Most modern networks are combinations of switched and shared-media. Within buildings and individual offices, where you have to run lines to each machine anyway, it makes sense to install a switch. Communications between buildings are carried over a shared-media connection—using fiber-optic cables.

Enterprise Networks

Many large companies have hundreds of local area networks. Connecting personal computers is only the first step in building a telecommunications system. The next step is to facilitate communication across the company and interconnect the LANs. A network that connects various subnetworks across a firm is called an *enterprise network*.

Several types of data need to be collected and shared throughout a company. Basic transaction-processing data such as accounting and HRM data need to be collected and aggregated for the firm. Management decisions and questions need to be communicated with all employees. Planning documents and forecasts are often prepared by interdisciplinary teams.

Although it is easy to agree that all computers in a company should be able to share data, several problems arise in practice. Various departments often use different hardware,

REALITY BYTES   Broadband Access and Competition

"We ought to have universal, affordable access to broadband technology by the year 2007. And then we ought to make sure that as soon as possible thereafter consumers have plenty of choices." President Bush in 2004 seems to understand the importance of communication technology and the need for competition. In June 2003, 20.6 million homes and small businesses subscribed to high-speed Internet access. About 13.7 million of those were through cable modems, compared with 7.7 million through phone company DSL

systems. But there is still limited price competition with only two main providers. Customers have some limited choices with wireless access in some cities, but technical hurdles need to be cleared before that technology can compete. Despite Bush's sentiments, federal government policy and support for high-speed access and competition remain minimal.

Source: Adapted from "Bush Wants Cheap High-Speed Internet Access for All by 2007," *CNN Online,* March 26, 2004.

FIGURE 3.19

Enterprise network: Switched networks within buildings are connected by shared-media fiber-optic cables. Distant offices and subsidiaries can be connected over the Internet.

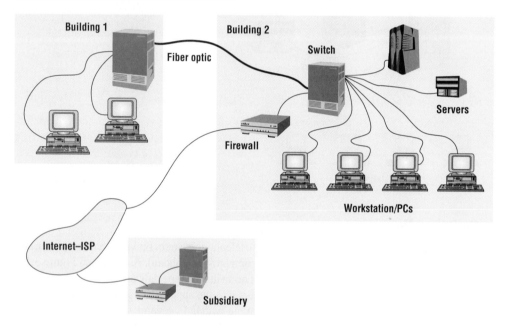

software, and network protocols. It becomes more difficult to identify the cause of problems in a network as it becomes larger. Likewise, adding more components tends to slow down all transmissions. Network management issues multiply. Small tasks such as assigning usernames and maintaining passwords become major chores when there are thousands of users and hundreds of file servers. Security becomes increasingly complex, especially when corporate data is carried across public networks. Upgrading network components can become a nightmare, resulting in either complete replacement across the firm or incompatibilities between some divisions. Even simple network functions like e-mail can quickly bog down a system when there are 50,000 users.

Enterprise networking requires a combination of standards and special hardware and software to translate data from one system to another. It also requires investing in more network personnel to install, upgrade, and manage all of the components.

As shown in Figure 3.19, as enterprise networks spread across large distances, they tend to involve wide area networks. A *wide area network (WAN)* differs from a LAN because of the geographical distance that it covers. More specifically, a WAN involves links that are controlled by public carriers (e.g., telecommunication companies). Few individual firms can afford to build their own long-distance networks. Although some companies do have their own satellite connections, it is almost impossible for a company to install its own cables for any distance. Instead, you can lease lines from the phone company. It is possible, but expensive, to lease point-to-point lines used only by your company. Today, it is often easier and cheaper to have each office connect to the Internet. The drawback is that data sent over the Internet is open and might be intercepted by others. In this case, you can install encryption software on each system to create a **virtual private network (VPN).** All of your Internet transmissions are automatically encrypted. Users see the network as one connected set of computers, regardless of their location. A VPN requires special encryption software or hardware at both ends of the network. It is commonly used for managers who want to work from home and connect to the company network.

Standards

How is it possible that you can connect your computer to a network at the office, at home, or while on the road, even overseas? Standards are agreements among vendors, customers, and nations. If everyone follows the standards, equipment can be connected, data can be shared, and you can connect your computer to the network anywhere in the world. But evolving technologies and competition significantly complicate these tasks. Setting standards and moving to new ones is always a challenging task.

The Need for Standards

Standards are important with networks. There are many different types of computers and various network types. Each computer and network company has its own idea of which methods are best. Without standards, there is no way to connect computers or networks produced by different vendors. Standards are also supposed to protect the buyers from obsolescence. If you install network equipment that meets existing standards, you should be able to buy products in the future that will work with it.

Unfortunately, there are many standard-setting organizations. Each major country has its own standards organization such as ANSI, the American National Standards Institute. There are several international organizations, such as ISO and the ITU (International Telecommunications Organization, renamed from CCITT), charged with defining computer and communication standards. In addition, manufacturers of computers and telecommunications equipment try to define their own standards. If one company's products are chosen as a standard, they gain a slight advantage in design and production.

It is not likely that typical managers will be involved in the issues of setting and choosing communication standards. Yet, as a consumer, you need to be aware that there are many standards and sometimes variations on the standards. (In this industry, the word *standards* does not mean there is only one way to do something.) When you are buying telecommunications equipment, the goal is to purchase equipment that meets popular standards. It is not always easy to decide which standards will become popular and which ones will be abandoned.

A Changing Environment

Why are there so many standards? It would be far simpler if everyone could agree to use one standard and build products that are compatible. The problem with this concept is that technology is continually changing. Thirty years ago, phone companies never considered using digital transmission over fiber-optic cables, which is the dominant form of long-distance transmission used today.

As each technology is introduced, new standards are created. Yet we cannot discard existing standards because it takes time for firms to convert to the new technology. Besides, as manufacturers gain experience with a technology, they add features and find better ways to use the products. These alterations usually result in changes to the standards. An additional complication is that many companies are modifying their products at the same time. It is hard to determine in advance which changes are worthwhile and should be made standards.

Problem: You need to share information with others on the Internet.

Tools: Several tools exist to create Web pages, but at heart, Web pages are simply text files. The pages are written in the **hypertext markup language (HTML)**. HTML consists of a few dozen tags that tell the browser how to display a page. A simple page can be written as:

```
<HTML>
<HEAD><TITLE>Sample HTML Page</TITLE>
<BODY>
<H1>Section One</H1>
<P>This is a sample paragraph on a sample page.</P>
</BODY>
</HTML>
```

You can memorize the various tags, or you can use an editor to simply type the text and let it generate the tags. However, if you are creating pages for the Internet, avoid using document editors like Microsoft Word because the additional material it inserts makes the pages considerably larger than necessary.

Web pages display images using the IMG SRC='myfile.jpg'> tag. You must be careful when creating image files to store them in a standard format: (1) graphics interchange format (GIF), (2) joint photographic exports group (JPEG), or (3) portable network graphics (PNG). You must be even more careful to watch the size of the file. A modern digital camera can create photographs that are 15 megabytes! Think about how long it would take a browser to download a file that large. In general, you must keep the total size of a page below 100 kilobytes.

Links are created with the anchor tag: <a href='annual.html'>Annual Results</a>. The text or image between the starting and ending tags will be displayed to the user. Clicking on the link opens the file shown in quotes.

When you are creating an entire Web site, you need to use a style sheet. A style sheet contains a list of styles (fonts, sizes, colors, margins, and so on) that will be applied to the various elements on a page. For instance, you could specify that the main heading style (H1) would use an Arial typeface at 14 points in blue. The power of the style sheet is that all styles are defined in one place. By changing the style only once, every page on your site that is linked to that style sheet will automatically be displayed with the new style.

HTML is easy to use, but if you need more precise control over the page layout, you should use Adobe's **portable document format (pdf)**. You can buy software that saves documents in this format. Browsers can download the Acrobat reader free from Adobe's Web site. This method is commonly used to distribute detailed documents such as tax forms and posters.

Quick Quiz: Search the Web, or create a document and View the source to do the following:

1. Display a word or phrase in boldface.
2. Link a style sheet to an HTML page.
3. Display a table with three rows and four columns.
4. Display a numbered list of five items.
5. Display an icon in GIF format with a transparent background.

The net result is that standards can be useful, but managers have to be careful not to rely too much on a standard. First, remember that even if two products support a standard, they still might not work well together. Second, if you choose a standard for your department or company, remember that technology changes. Corporate standards should be reevaluated every year or so to make sure they are still the best solution.

Internet TCP/IP Reference Model

If you want to understand the details of how the Internet works, it is best to begin with the TCP/IP reference model. As shown in Figure 3.20, the reference model breaks the process into four layers: application, transport, Internet, and subnet. Breaking the process into separate layers is critical to building large networks. Each layer can be handled independently of the others. For example, at the physical layer, replacing a wired connection with a wireless one should not affect any of the higher layers. The physical layer devices simply have to provide the same functionality to the Internet layer.

Notice that moving down, each layer takes the data from the prior layer and adds header and trailer information. This additional data is necessary for each layer to perform its function, but it means that more data must be transferred. For example, even if your physical connection can transmit data at 10 mbps, a 10-megabit file cannot be transferred in one second. Depending on the application and the network details, the overhead from the layers can be 20 percent or higher.

Subnet/Physical Layer

The purpose of the subnet or physical layer is to make the connection between two machines and physically transfer bits of data. It is directly related to hardware. There are standards to specify constraints on voltage, type of wire, frequency of signals, and sizes of physical con-

FIGURE 3.20

TCP/IP reference model: The model illustrates how data from an application like e-mail is turned into packets at the transport layer, routed to the destination at the IP layer, and physically transferred as bits at the physical layer.

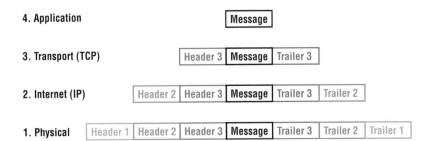

nectors. Raw data bits are transferred at this stage. Many different technologies exist, including wireless, wired, and fiber-optic lines.

Internet/Network Layer

The Internet layer is concerned with routing messages to the appropriate location. In particular, it selects the appropriate path for a message in networks where there is a choice. Its main advantage is that it separates the higher layers from the physical transmission of data. The network layer handles connections across different machines and multiple networks. The Internet Protocol (IP) is the standard used in routing packets on the Internet network. With IP, each packet is treated independently of the others and each can follow a different route to the destination. Each machine must have a globally unique address, so a mechanism is established to assign numbers to machines. The current version of IP (IPv4) is creating problems because addresses are only 32 bits long—and the world is running out of numbers. The newer IPv6 standard supports 128-bit addresses, but it will take time to phase in the new system. Newer servers and hosts support the IPv6 protocol (e.g., Windows XP); but it will take time to update all of the routers on the Internet. In the meantime, most companies are using intermediate steps to allocate the IPv4 numbers.

Global standards are required to ensure compatibility of networks and efficient routing of data. The Internet Corporation for Assigned Names and Numbers (ICANN) and the Internet Engineering Task Force (IETF) are publicly run organizations in charge of establishing many of these standards. Both organizations are heavily dependent on volunteers and rely on public comments to design new standards.

Transport Layer

The transport layer is responsible for dividing the application data into packets and providing logical connections to the network. The transport control protocol (TCP) is commonly used on the Internet to handle these connections. TCP supports multiple applications at the same time by creating numbered ports. For example, e-mail is usually transferred through port 25, and Web data through port 80. TCP sends the data packet to the specified port on the desired machine. TCP on the host machine listens to these ports and sends the incoming data to the appropriate application server. TCP also monitors the packets to see if any are lost in transmission. If so, the recipient machine can request that the missing packet be re-sent, providing a highly reliable connection between two machines.

The Internet also supports the user datagram protocol (UDP), which is a highly simplified transport method. Most important, it does not guarantee that a packet will be transferred. Generally, users do not get to choose between TCP and UDP. This choice is made by the software developer at the network level. But why would anyone choose UDP when there is no assurance that the packets will be delivered? The main reason is speed. Because UDP is so simple, it adds only a tiny overhead to each packet, which makes it useful for large transfers of data, such as large files and streaming multimedia. If necessary, the application can check at the end to ensure that all data was transferred.

Application Layer

The application layer consists of tools and services for the user. Typical Internet applications include e-mail, file transfer protocol (FTP), and Web browsing with the hypertext transfer protocol (HTTP). These systems work because developers have agreed to follow basic standards.

With the TCP/IP reference model, applications are responsible for incorporating authentication and compression. Not having a standard underlying method for handling security has caused some problems with TCP/IP. Few applications actually have any security, several incompatible variations of security systems have been created, and hackers have been able to write programs that attack the underlying, unprotected layers. Security is one of the main problems being addressed in IPv6 and Internet2.

The Internet

What is the Internet, how is it controlled, and how does it work? The Internet is a loose collection of computer networks throughout the world. It began as a means to exchange data among major U.S. universities (NSFnet of the National Science Foundation) and connections to various military organizations and U.S. defense suppliers (Arpanet of the Advanced Research Projects Agency). No one knows how many computers or networks are currently connected by the Internet. The numbers have been increasing exponentially since the early 1990s, so any number is likely to be wrong within a few days. To give you some idea of the Internet's astounding growth, in January 1993, there were 1.313 million host computers. In January 1994, there were 2.217 million hosts located in more than 70 countries. In 2000, Telecordia estimated that the Internet had exceeded 100 million hosts. In 1994, over 20 million people had access to at least e-mail services. As of mid-1994, commercial use (as opposed to university and government use) accounted for 50 percent of the Internet usage. By 2004, over 500 million people worldwide had access to the Internet. Measuring the Internet is difficult, since machines are not always connected. Most studies use some type of survey to estimate the size.

What exactly is the Internet? At heart, the Internet is just a communication system for computers. It is defined by a set of standards that allow computers to exchange messages. The most amazing aspect of the Internet is that there really is no single person or group in charge. Anyone who wishes to connect a computer to the Internet simply agrees to pay for a communication link—via an Internet service provider (ISP)—and to install communications hardware and software that supports the current Internet standard protocols. The person or company is given a base address that allows other computers to identify users on the new computer. Standards are defined by a loose committee, and addresses are controlled by another small committee. The committees are convened purely for the purpose of speeding the process; all decisions are up to the organizations connected to the network. Participation in the Internet is voluntary, and there are few rules, just standard practices and agreements. From a business or consumer viewpoint, there are two primary aspects to the Internet: establishing a connection and using the Internet.

How the Internet Works

The Internet is a communication system; it is a method of connecting computers together. So the first step in determining how the Internet works is to understand how your computer connects to others. As shown in Figure 3.21, the Internet has a hierarchy of service providers. Individuals pay a local **Internet service provider (ISP)** for access to the Internet. In turn, local ISPs pay an upstream *network service provider (NSP)* for access to their systems and features. Each connection must be made over a communication link. Local links are typically made over telephone wires, but cable companies also provide service over their coaxial lines. A few companies provide satellite connections. Some wireless providers exist, but availability, features, and pricing vary by location. Most ISPs also utilize phone company lines to connect to their NSP, but they lease dedicated, full-time lines that provide faster service. The largest NSPs (Tier 1) also provide backbone service. That is, they route communications over their own fiber-optic lines that are installed across the United States. Increasingly, NSPs are also phone companies. Some started as phone companies and expanded into the Internet; others started with the Internet and gradually offered voice services.

You should understand the foundations of the Internet, because someone has to pay for each connection. Current pricing policies are to charge for the initial communication link

FIGURE 3.21

Internet connections: Each computer must be connected to others. The Internet has a connection hierarchy. Companies and individuals typically use phone company lines to connect to an ISP. The ISP connects to an NSP, which routes data over the high-speed backbone network to the destination NSP, down to the other ISP, and to the final computer. Each step may involve several computers.

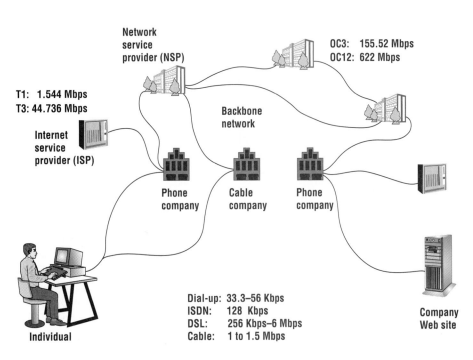

FIGURE 3.22

Leading Internet providers: There are thousands of ISPs and cable companies. This list provides only some of the large companies in each category.

Backbone Providers	
AT&T	Sprint
GTE	MCI
Qwest	

Network Service Providers	
AT&T	Qwest
Cable & Wireless	Sprint
IBM	UUNet

Phone Companies
Regional Bell operating companies (RBOCs)
Competitive local exchange carriers (CLECs)

Cable Companies
AT&T
Cablevision
Regional

Satellite
Direct Satellite
Starband

Leading Internet Service Providers
America Online
Microsoft Network
EarthLink
AT&T WorldNet

and for the point-of-contact Internet service. For example, an individual pays the phone company for the local phone line and pays the ISP for basic services. The ISP pays the phone company for the next link and pays the NSP for access services. Figure 3.22 lists some of the largest providers in each category. You can check with them for current prices and services.

The charging mechanism is similar for companies that wish to establish Web sites. The catch is that the costs are higher because the company needs faster communication services. The phone company charges more money for a faster link (e.g., $500 to $1,000 per month for a T1 line). The ISP also charges more money for the increased traffic because it needs faster equipment and faster connections to the NSP.

The Internet service connection business is completely based on economies of scale. The high-speed fiber networks (OC3 and OC12) can handle a vast number of transmissions, but they carry a high fixed cost. The backbone providers make money by selling smaller increments of bandwidth to the ISPs, which incorporate a sufficient profit. Many of the NSPs are backbone providers and increasingly they also offer ISP services.

Internet Addresses

To use the Internet, each machine (host) must have an address. Currently, these addresses are 32-bit numbers, typically written as 4 bytes separated by dots. For example, your machine might be assigned 161.6.28.18 as an address. However, 32-bit numbers will identify a maximum of 4 billion machines, about half in practice because some values cannot be assigned. Hence, an Internet committee designed a new numbering system consisting of 128 bits, which allows for several millions of numbers to be assigned to every person likely to live on the planet. The new system is known as **IPv6** and will be phased in gradually.

In part because IPv6 is not widely in use yet, companies are using other techniques to assign numbers. **Network address translation (NAT)** is commonly used by businesses and even home users today. With NAT, your house (or office) might be assigned one Internet address that connects to a router. The router then assigns completely different numbers to all of the machines in the home or office. No one outside this miniature network can directly access any of the computers. When a local computer requests a page or service from the Internet, the router tags the address so it can identify which machine made the request. All replies are returned to the same port, and the router directs the connection to the original machine. Essentially, the router translates or changes the internal addresses into the single external number. This approach provides slightly better security and it reduces the number of real IP addresses needed. However, it makes it more complicated for outside computers to connect with your machine. In particular, it causes complications if you want to use groupware or peer-to-peer systems across the NAT router.

NAT also makes it considerably more difficult to track down individual users on the Internet. If you receive a message (spam) from someone, or want to find the true owner of a Web site, you begin with only the shared IP address. This address will point you to the company that hosts the original user. You can find the hosting company by entering the IP address at one of the registry sites, such as www.arin.net. But to find the specific person, the hosting company (or university) will have to provide you with detailed records of who was using the computer at the specific time. Most of these organizations will reveal the information only (if they kept historical records) when presented with a court order. This process makes it more difficult and expensive to track down fraud and illegal activities on the Internet.

Of course, numbers are difficult for most people to remember. So the Internet utilizes a system where a **domain name system (DNS)** server converts names to numbers. Anyone can apply for a name and pay a nominal fee (e.g., $35 per year) to use that name. Of course, names must be unique, so sometimes disagreements arise over popular names. Names are followed by a suffix such as .com, .edu, or .gov. Several newer suffixes were added in 2002 and 2003, but the .com and .net suffixes are still the most coveted. One interesting feature of the names is that each country is given a specific suffix. Some of the countries sell names using their unique suffix. For example, the small nation of Tuvalu allows companies to use its suffix (.tv) for a fee.

As a business, you will need to register your domain name to make it accessible to other users. Several companies act as registrars and you pay them to officially link your name to your IP address. In terms of data, the connection is ultimately performed with the DNS system, and you can either run your own DNS computer or pay another company to handle the updates. Figure 3.23 shows that DNS registration is a critical element to electronic commerce. Registration provides a tie between the Internet world and the real world. A second

REALITY BYTES   Tying the Internet to the Real World

The domain name system (DNS) is a key element of the Internet. At its core, it is a simple system that translates domain names (microsoft.com) into IP addresses (207.46.250.222). But it is also the major link between the Internet and the business world. Companies that register domain names have to pay for the name, and they have to provide real-world contacts and addresses. In the Internet world, you can identify machines based on the IP address. Given this number, you can use the DNS registry to identify the name of the company or person who owns the IP address. In theory, you can then identify the real-world contact responsible for the computer. The registrars maintain a Whois database that lists the details. In practice, many people lie on the DNS registration forms. Of course, spammers and miscreants lie because they do not want to be caught. But the publicly accessible Whois database presents more difficult problems. Anyone who owns a domain name will have their address and contact information displayed to the public. If you are running a business, this is probably a good practice—to reduce fraud and ensure that firms are legitimate. If you are an individual

person, you might not want to list your home address and phone number. Even worse, the Whois registry has been a prime source of e-mail addresses for the spammers. Congress has proposed a bill that would make it a federal crime to provide false information when registering a domain name. Some people are concerned that this law would reduce citizen rights by making it difficult to be anonymous.

In some ways, today's Internet business world is like the early days of business—you simply did not trust anyone you did not know. As economies grew, states learned to control fraudulent businesses by requiring them to register. Today, legitimate businesses are registered with at least one state government and must file annual forms and provide legal contact information. Most of this data is accessible online. Is it really any different to require people to file legitimate contact information for online registrations?

Source: Adapted from Declan McCullagh, "Privacy Reduction's Next Act," *CNet,* February 9, 2004.

FIGURE 3.23

Domain name registration: Internet entities are anchored to the real world through the DNS registration and their ISP. But some firms lie on their registration, and some ISPs are controlled by unethical people.

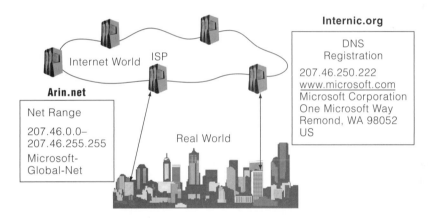

tie is provided by the connection of the firm to its ISP. In a legal situation, the ISP can be forced to reveal the true identity and address of its client. A third anchor is created when a company installs a digital security certificate. The certificate authority verifies the real-world identity of the client and binds it to the certificate.

You can use the Whois facilities of the domain registrars (e.g., NetworkSolutions, or Internic.org) to look up the registration data. You can use the Internet registries to identify ISPs based on the IP address. These registries are organized by geographical location and include arin.net (America), ripe.net (Europe), and apnic.net (Asia). However, some ethically challenged people lie on their DNS registrations. A few even more ethically challenged people operate ISP services specifically to support spammers and hackers. As a consumer, the answer is relatively easy: never, ever send money to a company that lies on its DNS registration!

If you want to run your own Web site, you will want to create and register your own domain name. The exact IP address will be given to you by your hosting ISP, but you have to register for the domain name that will be linked to the address. This registration information is kept in global Whois databases. For example, you can use the networksolutions.com database to enter a Web site name and retrieve the registered owner of the site. When you register a site name, you are supposed to provide accurate information on your name, address, and phone number. However, at this point in time, the registrars have been weak at verifying the data. The resulting misleading information makes it difficult to track down

Problem: You need to transfer data files to a Web site.

Tools: It is relatively easy to transfer files from your computer to another computer connected on a local area network. Assuming that you have the proper security permissions, you can see the other computer as if it were another disk drive and drag-and-drop the file. But no company is going to open its network to allow you to do the same thing across the Internet. So, how do you transfer files to a Web server if it is not located on your LAN?

Surprisingly, given how frequently people need to transfer files, this question does not yet have a good answer. An older method still used in some situations is the **file transfer protocol (FTP)**. Your Web browser probably supports drag-and-drop with ftp. For example, you could enter an address like ftp://myserver.com/www, and the browser will connect and display a list of files in the specified folder. Then you can drag-and-drop your files or an entire folder onto the folder window and it will be transferred to the server. The drawback to FTP is that passwords and files are sent in the clear and might be intercepted by hackers. So most companies block FTP transfers. Most companies today require that you transfer files using secure FTP tools that automatically encrypt login and file data. These systems require your client computer to have special software that matches the server's encryption.

Another approach that is relatively common in commercial hosting is Microsoft's FrontPage Extensions. The server owner installs the extensions on the server. You have to buy compatible client software (such as FrontPage or Visual Studio) that will establish an encrypted connection to the server. The software is easy to use and generally enables you to transfer the entire set of files by clicking one button. However, Microsoft is phasing out these extensions in favor of the new SharePoint services.

The Internet community has developed the Web distributed authoring and versioning (WebDAV) service to help solve the problems of sharing files. As an open standard, it is available on many servers. If you have an account on a server that has WebDAV enabled, you can use the Internet Explorer to connect and transfer files. Just be sure to use the File/Open command, enter the name of the site, and check the box to "Open as a Web Folder." WebDAV is an extension of the HTTP protocols, so it supports secure login and can take advantage of common encryption tools.

The other approach to transferring files to a corporate server is to establish a VPN connection first so that all communications are encrypted. Then you are free to use FTP or any other common protocol inside the VPN tunnel because no one can intercept and decrypt the messages.

Connection	Strengths	Weaknesses
FTP	Inexpensive and easy to use	No security
FrontPage	Very easy to use with secure login	Limited availability and users have to purchase client software
WebDAV	Internet standard and can be secure	Web server security is weaker by allowing directory browsing
VPN	Very secure	Need to purchase server and client software and requires extra setup steps

Quick Quiz:

1. Which methods can you use to transfer files to a university server?

2. Why is FTP considered a security threat?

3. What other objections exist to FrontPage?

spammers and other owners of fraudulent sites. In a sense, the Internet today is like the business world in the 1800s—any fly-by-night scammer can set up a business Web site. In the business world, this situation was partly solved by requiring businesses to obtain licenses and register with the government. If you have any doubts about the validity of a company, you should check to ensure that the business is legally registered with the state government. Most states have searchable online databases and provide free access through the office of the secretary of state.

Internet Mail

One of the most popular features on the Internet is electronic mail. Virtually every machine on the Internet is capable of sending and receiving mail for registered users. As long as all participants have the appropriate software, they can send files, pictures, even sound as their message. One company even sells an Internet "phone" system that enables two people to talk to each other using the Internet links. Another sells a service that enables you to transfer real-time video images—as long as both sides have a video camera and appropriate software.

The Internet offers two other services similar to e-mail: discussion groups (listserv) and newsgroups (news). Discussion groups send electronic journals to anyone who "sub-

REALITY BYTES   IRC: The Original Chat Room

Most people think of e-mail and the Web when they think about the Internet. Internet Relay Chat (IRC) is older than the Web and considerably older than current messaging systems. It is a real-time chat system that can be accessed from any computer on the Internet. It supports text and peer-to-peer file transfers. Today, although a few legitimate users of IRC remain, it is often used for piracy and hacking. For example, hackers often communicate with their zombie computers through IRC. To use IRC, you need client software, available from sites such as www.mirc.com. Then you connect to a public or private server and join a channel. You can also obtain software to set up your own IRC server, using it for either public communications or simply to share among your friends or business partners.

Source: Adapted from Seth Schiesel, "The Internet's Wilder Side," *The New York Times,* May 6, 2004.

scribes" to the list. Typically, there is no fee for subscribing. Editors control the "publication" of a group. Comments are sent first to the editor, who decides whether to include them. Newsgroups are similar, but more open. Anyone can submit a comment at any time to a newsgroup, which represents a giant, global bulletin board. There are thousands of established topics, ranging from science to alternative lifestyles to anything you can imagine. The comments are usually uncensored and might or might not be accurate. Some people have found newsgroups useful for addressing complex computer problems. With millions of people on the Internet, there is a good chance that someone else has already encountered your problem and might have a solution. Newsgroups and Web sites provide useful tools to managers, especially to small business managers who have limited resources.

Although messages on the Internet tend to be uncensored, be careful. If you somehow manage to insult a few thousand people, you could find yourself immersed in hundreds of thousands of mail messages that overwhelm your computer account. Also, avoid using the Internet for personal use while working for a company. In the United States, companies have the legal right to monitor your messages. In extreme situations, the computer manager can revoke accounts from people who abuse the system. Even more important, some hiring managers have been known to search the Internet for messages that you posted—to check you out before making a job offer.

Access to Data on the Internet

Anyone with a computer connected to the Internet has the ability to give other users access to data stored on that computer. Read that sentence again. The owner has control over the data. Unless someone specifically grants you access to data, it is basically illegal to try and get the data, or even to use the person's computer.

The World Wide Web is a first attempt to set up an international database of information. As discussed in Chapter 1, today's challenge lies in finding the information you want. Sites are built as pages that contain links to other pages. Making a choice in one page will usually connect you to another computer on the Internet and bring up its WWW pages. From there you can look at library catalogs, pictures, or whatever information is provided by that Web server. The initial versions of the Web were developed at CERN, the European particle-physics laboratory, where the staff wanted to make it easier for researchers to share their work.

The easiest access to the Web is with a browser such as Internet Explorer or Netscape. Browsers present a page of information that contains links to other pages on the Web. The page can contain text, graphics, video, and sound clips. By selecting highlighted words, you can move to other systems, trace topics, and transfer data. Pictures are displayed automatically, and most operations can be completed by selecting items with a mouse.

Because the Internet is so large and is growing rapidly, it can be difficult to find useful data. Furthermore, organizations are constantly changing the type of information they provide. The data available is constantly changing, making it impossible to provide an up-to-date listing. So how do you find anything on the Internet?

REALITY BYTES   Who Is Hogging All of the Bandwidth?

In any organization, there is a limited amount of bandwidth—partic- ularly to the Internet or to external offices. Bandwidth is expensive and companies try to prevent employees (and students) from wast- ing it. LandAmerica Financial Group in Richmond, Virginia, has 10,000 employees worldwide in 700 different offices. The company was spending more than $1 million a year on bandwidth costs—and users were still complaining that applications were too slow. They tried reducing internal bandwidth demands by using the Citrix termi- nal server system—where most processing is done on the server, and each connection needs only about 10K bytes of bandwidth. The demand was still too high, and user sessions kept crashing. Finally, the company brought in Packeteer—a hardware and software sys- tem that monitors every packet transmitted on the network. More important, it enables the network department to place limits on the network traffic based on the content of the packet and on the user or destination. LandAmerica also installed a data compression util- ity from Packeteer to reduce the transfer time for a large database replication task. LandAmerica spent about $200,000 on six con- trollers from Packeteer, but saved more than $50,000 a month in re- duced bandwidth costs. Throw in the improved productivity from the users because of no delays, and the decision was clearly cost ef- fective.

Many universities use Packeteer to shape the traffic on their In- ternet connections. Instead of banning peer-to-peer file sharing, the system simply gives them low priority—conserving bandwidth for more critical tasks.

Source: Adapted from Anthony O'Donnell, "Packeteer Unclogs LandAmerica's Pipes," *Insurance & Technology,* May 18, 2004.

Search engines, off-line advertising, and word of mouth are the most popular methods of finding information on the Internet. Several search engines exist, and new ones arrive every day. Most have their own quirks and strengths; but no engine indexes more than about 30 percent of the content on the Web.

One of the biggest issues on the Internet is identifying reliable data. Anyone can say al- most anything on a Web page, but that does not make it true. Problems tend to arise in ar- eas like medicine and finance. A healthy dose of skepticism is required when retrieving information from an open network. Reputation of the source becomes an important factor.

Internet 2

Originally, the U.S. government funded much of the Internet design and development. By 1995, the U.S. government had discontinued almost all funding, and the Internet was largely financed and controlled by private organizations. From 1994, the commercial use of the In- ternet increased exponentially. In 1996, 34 university participants decided that they needed faster connections (the number of participants expanded to 100 in 1999 and to 205 in 2003). With the support of the government and industry, they began creating Internet 2 (http://www.internet2.edu). When the original Internet was developed, most traffic was simple text, and the bulk of the communications were via e-mail. There was little need for high-speed connections, and delays in delivering e-mail did not matter since most people did not read their mail immediately.

The two most important proposed features of Internet 2 are high-speed connections and quality-of-service provisions. The overall objective is to provide a transmission network that can support full-speed video and other high-bandwidth applications. To understand the change, consider that most existing "high-speed" Internet connections are in the range of 1 mbps to 50 mbps. The Internet 2 calls for gigabit connection points and a *minimum* con- nection of 155 mbps.

A related, but more fundamental, change is the ability to specify a desired level-of- service quality. Currently, if traffic increases on the Internet, all communications slow down. This situation is annoying but not troublesome for simple tasks like sending e-mail. On the other hand, full video transfer requires a constant minimum level of transmission ca- pacity. So participants need a mechanism to tell all components that a specific set of mes- sages should take priority to receive a certain level of service. Some people have suggested that the system should enable participants to pay a fee to gain their desired levels of serv- ice, for each type of message. For example, basic e-mail messages would be free if there is no rush in delivering them. But to reserve a time slot for videoconferencing, participants would pay an additional fee. Then all of the Internet 2 components would give the video

REALITY BYTES   Do You Need IPv6?

To connect to the Internet, every computer must have a unique address. This address is a number. In the case of the current Internet protocol (version 4), addresses are 32-bit numbers, usually written in dotted-decimal form, such as 209.177.135.229. But a 32-bit number can only take on values between 0 and 4 billion. In practice, the Internet reserves several ranges of addresses for special purposes, so there are approximately 2 billion Internet addresses available. About 75 percent of the available addresses have already been assigned to U.S.-based Internet service providers. China, with a population of over 1 billion people, has been assigned 38.5 million addresses. Throw in the fact that every cell phone today, and most refrigerators and other appliances tomorrow, will be connected to the Internet. Is there a problem?

Actually, without two major tricks, there would already be major battles over reallocating IP addresses. First, many companies have implemented network address translation (NAT), so that all machines within the company (or your home) are given internal numbers. When you request an external Internet connection, your computer is assigned a temporary IP number that is sent to the outside world. Second, most Web hosting companies utilize a single IP address to service Web sites for multiple companies. The server resolves the specific site based on its name instead of the IP address.

The problem with NAT is that it makes it difficult to connect computers. Standard Web browsing is handled properly. Peer-to-peer applications, collaborative software, and multi-person games do not work as well. Sometimes, they do not work at all, because your computer is unable to locate the specific machine hiding behind a translator.

The Internet engineers have developed a more modern system known as IPv6 (version 5 was never released). IPv6 uses a 128-bit address space—providing enough unique numbers so that the world will never run out of addresses, ever. But longer addresses mean that the entire Internet infrastructure has to be upgraded, including your computer, your operating system, and all of the routers on the Internet. In theory, most newer machines already have the necessary upgrades. But without a pressing need, companies are going to be reluctant to switch. Asian nations, and parts of Europe, are leading the way on the transition to IPv6. But some tools enable both IPv6 and IPv4 to coexist, so the United States could lag and stick with IPv4. The U.S. Department of Defense has tried to lead the switch, but it remains to be seen whether companies will follow.

Source: Adapted from Simson Garfinkel, "Internet 6.0," *Technology Review,* January 7, 2004.

packets a higher priority. So far, there has been no agreement on whether additional fees should be charged, or on how the quality-of-service issues can be resolved. Although the system is being designed for academic and government users, the industry participants (e.g., Cisco) ultimately intend to transfer any useful technologies to the commercial Internet. Businesses could find many uses for high-speed connections and service-quality guarantees. For starters, better video transfer may finally open the way for desktop videoconferencing to replace travel to meetings.

Wireless Networks and Mobile Commerce

Beginning with cell phones in the 1990s people and businesses have become fascinated with wireless communication. Wireless Internet and mobile commerce have the potential to revolutionize the Internet, business, and society. Technologically, wireless is different from the traditional Internet in only two ways: (1) the transmission medium is microwave radio, and (2) the client devices are smaller with smaller screens and less computing power. Yet wireless connections open thousands of new possibilities. The client devices can consist of anything from enhanced cell phones to PDAs and digital tablets. It is highly likely that the functions of these devices will converge to form some type of digital notepad with Internet and cell phone capabilities. Many new cell phones even have digital cameras built in, offering the possibility that all of your data needs can be handled through one small device.

To date, the wireless communication presents the greatest challenges. The base cell phone network is too slow to support most applications. In most places, data transfers on cellular frequencies are slow, ranging from 14.4 kbps to 100 kbps. The 3G system (third generation cell phone) is being designed to handle data at speeds from 56 kbps to 2 mbps. The problem, as anyone with a cell phone knows, is the limited coverage area offered by wireless connections. Although major cities offer reasonable coverage, cell phones often have trouble deep within buildings and in smaller cities and rural areas. While you might not be concerned about the need to establish a wireless Internet connection in the backwoods, what happens if you rely on the system for purchases and you end up in a town that does not support your system?

REALITY BYTES   Wireless Broadband

Cable modems and DSL are nice, but they are not portable. Wi-Fi is useful but has a maximum range of about 300 feet. Yes, you can find hot spots at various locations. But what if you could have wireless broadband access across the United States in every major city? Verizon is piloting a new service in Washington, D.C., called BroadBand Access based on a new cell phone technology called Evolution-Data Optimized (EV-DO). The service will provide download speeds between 300 and 700 kbps. Verizon plans to roll out the service na-tionwide in 2005. The one drawback is the price: scheduled to be $80 per month for unlimited Internet access. Upload speeds are also slow—around 50 kbps. Despite the price, it will offer incredible mo-bility and flexibility for users who travel. You will have a full-time con-nection to the Internet.

Source: Adapted from Walter S. Mossberg, "Verizon Is Crossing the U.S. with Speedy, True Wireless Access," *The Wall Street Journal*, April 8, 2004.

FIGURE 3.24

Location knowledge in m-commerce: Businesses could contact potential customers on learning their location through the wireless system.

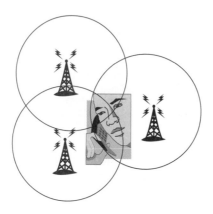

Some of the more interesting possibilities of m-commerce come from the ability to use the phone to find and pay for virtually anything you might need. Rather than rely on credit cards or cash, your cell phone could record all of your transactions and give you complete instantaneous access to your data. But an incredibly reliable and secure system must exist before consumers will trust it.

Another interesting possibility for m-commerce comes from the ability to use location to identify potential customers. Figure 3.24 shows that it is relatively easy to identify a person's location based on the way the cellular system works using signal strength and trian-gulation. In fact, the federal government requires that cell phone systems provide caller location within a couple hundred feet—primarily for use in 911 emergency calls. But the wireless providers can easily make this data available to anyone.

Think about the business opportunities that this system could provide, even from the perspective of a consumer. As you walk into a mall, you could enter your shopping list into a browser on your phone, which would contact all of the local stores for prices and availability, and then provide a local map and directions to each item. You could enter notes and make your selection through the browser, then press a couple of keys and pur-chase the items. Similarly, some companies have proposed a system that would automat-ically notify you when a "buddy" is within a certain range of your phone, such as in the next store.

Businesses would have even more opportunities to collect data on customers, such as sending advertising to your phone and tracking the number of browsers versus buyers. But marketing systems would have greater knowledge of exactly what products and features each customer wants. For instance, the systems could offer a mini-survey to each customer who chooses to buy a competitor's product to find ways to improve products. Of course, the privacy aspects are scary. They will be examined in Chapter 14.

Unsolicited Commercial e-Mail

Junk e-mail, or **spam,** is an increasingly annoying problem. Many companies capture e-mail addresses and sell them to other companies that send out unwanted messages. These

REALITY BYTES   Pervasive Spam

On January 1, 2004, the federal CAN-SPAM law took effect, creating rules to be followed by senders of unsolicited commercial e-mail (spam). The initial results are not promising. At the end of 2003, estimates indicated that 60 percent of all e-mail traffic was spam. For the first week in 2004, Postini, Inc., a company that provides e-mail filtering, noted that almost 85 percent of the 1 billion pieces of e-mail it handled was spam. Brightmail, another spam-filtering company, observed that junk e-mail was holding steady at 60 percent of the traffic it handled. Likewise, AOL noted little change in 2.4 billion pieces of e-mail a day that it blocks. AOL's spam fighting group did notice that there was approximately a 10 percent shift in sources to overseas IP addresses. There is still some hope that the spammers will wake up when they are sued for millions of dollars by the big ISPs.

Source: Adapted from Jonathan Krim, "Spam Is Still Flowing into E-Mail Boxes," *The Washington Post,* January 6, 2004.

messages take up space on company networks and computers and make it more difficult for users to deal with legitimate messages. You should get in the habit of automatically deleting unsolicited messages—largely because the information they contain is highly unlikely to be true, and because they might contain viruses. Sometimes, you can set up e-mail filters that automatically read your mail and focus on the topics you have chosen. They cut down on the amount of junk e-mail messages, but they need more sophistication to be useful.

In 2003, the United States enacted the CAN-SPAM Act, which makes many types of e-mail illegal. For example, commercial mail must indicate that it is an advertisement, it must be sent from a legitimate address, it must contain the real name and address of the company, and it must contain a working opt-out mechanism. If you select to opt out of receiving more messages, the company must honor your request within 10 days. This opt-out provision is the most contested aspect of the law. It effectively requires consumers to opt out of thousands of different e-mail lists. Worse yet, most of the opt-out links provided on spam are phony. If you click one of those links, the spammer uses it to recognize that it is a valid e-mail address and simply sends you more spam. Of course, these actions are now illegal—but that does not help you when the spammer uses false registration data and hides behind servers hosted in China. As a consumer, you have to identify which opt-out links and companies are legitimate and which are frauds. From a business perspective, the law is relatively friendly. You are free to send e-mail to potential customers—as long as you abide by the details of the law and make sure you include an opt-out system.

Global Telecommunications

What problems are you likely to encounter if you need to connect to a supplier in a different country? Business firms are becoming more dependent on international markets. This internationalization increases the demands on the telecommunications system. The international transmission of data is becoming part of the daily business routine. A manufacturing company may have factories in several different countries, with the headquarters located in yet another country. Supplies have to be sent to factories. Finished and intermediate products have to be tracked. Customer demands have to be followed in each country. Quality control and warranty repair information have to be followed from the supplier through the factory and out to the customers. Financial investments have to be tracked on stock markets in many countries. Different accounting and payroll rules have to be provided for each country. Basic accounting and financial data have to be available to management at any time of day, in any part of the organization.

Creating networks across international boundaries creates many problems. Some of the complications are technical, some are political or legal, and others are cultural.

REALITY BYTES   The Digital Divide Is Narrower than You Think

The International Telecommunication Union (ITU) is a major player in setting standards and supporting cooperation around the world. As one of their roles, they have developed the Digital Access Index (DAI) to help measure the information technology capabilities within a nation. It combines eight variables in five basic areas: availability of infrastructure, affordability of access, educational level, quality of communication services, and Internet usage. Michael Minges of the ITU reflected on the choice of variables by noting that "until now, limited infrastructure has often been regarded as the main barrier to bridging the Digital Divide. Our research, however, suggests that affordability and education are equally important factors." The ITU released a report in late 2003 based on 2002 data that ranks nations based on the DAI. Based on the index, nations were grouped into four categories: high, upper, medium, and low access. The entire list is available on the ITU Web site. The results are somewhat surprising.

High Access			Upper Access		
1	Sweden	0.85	26	Ireland	0.69
2	Denmark	0.83	27	Cyprus	0.68
3	Iceland	0.82	28	Estonia	0.67
4	Korea (Rep.)	0.82	29	Spain	0.67
5	Norway	0.79	30	Malta	0.67
6	Netherlands	0.79	31	Czech Republic	0.66
7	Hong Kong	0.79	32	Greece	0.66
8	Finland	0.79	33	Portugal	0.65
9	Taiwan	0.79	34	UAE	0.64
10	Canada	0.78	35	Macao	0.64
11	United States	0.78	36	Hungary	0.63
12	United Kingdom	0.77	37	Bahamas	0.62
13	Switzerland	0.76	38	Bahrain	0.60
14	Singapore	0.75	39	Saint Kitts and Nevis	0.60
15	Japan	0.75	40	Poland	0.59

Source: Adapted from http://www.itu.int/newsarchive/press_releases/2003/30.html.

Technical Problems

The biggest technical complication is that each country may have its own telecommunications standards. For example, in the western European nations, the telephone systems are managed by governmental agencies called postal telephone (PTT) companies. Because PTTs are publicly run, national governments have a habit of insisting that communication equipment be purchased from manufacturers within their own nation. Despite the standards, there are still technical incompatibilities among the various nations.

In developing nations, the communications equipment may be antiquated. The older equipment will not be able to handle large amounts of data transfers, and there may be an unacceptable number of errors. Also, the government-controlled power supplies may not be reliable enough to run computers and network equipment.

One possible way to avoid the public telecommunications hassles is to use microwave transmissions through satellites. This approach can be more reliable but can be expensive unless you have huge amounts of data to transfer. For developing nations located in the Southern Hemisphere, there may not be adequate satellite coverage. Many of the satellite channels available to developing nations are used and controlled by the individual governments. It is generally not economically feasible to put up a new satellite, and most governments would object if you attempted to bypass their control.

To transmit more than simple text and numbers, there are more potential problems to consider. The United States, Europe, and Pacific Rim nations all have different video standards. Televisions made for the U.S. market, therefore, will not function in Europe. If a company creates a multimedia marketing presentation in the United States, it will probably be difficult to show it to clients in France. These incompatibilities are about to get worse with the introduction of high-definition television (HDTV) or digital television. Each of the national groups is working with a different technique.

Legal and Political Complications

Some important problems can be created when a firm wants to transmit information across national boundaries. These transfers are called **transborder data flows (TBDFs).** The problem arises because the information has value to the sender. Because it has value, some governments have suggested that they would like to impose a tariff or tax on that value. Besides the cost of the tariff, the issue raises the possibility that the national governments may want to monitor the amount and type of data being transferred. Most businesses are reluctant to allow anyone that much access to their information. Some countries go further—for example, France made it illegal to encrypt data.

Another important issue revolves around typical marketing data about customers. It is common for marketing departments to maintain huge databases. These databases contain customer names, addresses, phone numbers, estimated income levels, purchases, and other marketing information. Problems have arisen because the western European nations have much stricter laws concerning privacy than the United States. In most European nations, it is illegal to sell or trade customer data to other companies. It must also be stored in protected files that cannot be seen by unauthorized employees or outsiders. In most cases, it is the responsibility of the company to prove it is meeting the requirements of the law. In many cases, this requirement means that customer data must be maintained on computers within the original nation. Also, this data cannot then be transmitted to computers in other countries. As a result, the multinational company may be forced to maintain computer facilities in each of the nations in which it does business. It also needs to impose security conditions that prevent the raw data from being transmitted from these computers.

There is one more important political issue involving international computer centers. Many nations, especially the developing nations, change governments quite often, as well as abruptly. There are many nations where terrorist activities are prevalent. Oftentimes, large multinational companies present tempting targets. Because computer centers tend to be expensive, special security precautions need to be established in these countries. Probably the most important step is to keep the computer center away from public access. Several U.S. security specialists publish risk factors and suggested precautions for each country. They also provide security analysis and protection—for a fee.

A host of other political complications affect any multinational operation. For example, each nation has different employment laws, accounting rules, investment constraints, and local partnership requirements. Most of these can be surmounted, but they usually require the services of a local attorney.

Cultural Issues

All of the typical cultural issues can play a role in running multinational computer networks. The work habits of employees can vary in different nations. It may be difficult to obtain qualified service personnel at some times of day or night. These issues can be critical for computer networks that need to remain in operation 24 hours a day. In many nations, it is still considered inappropriate to have female managers when there are male subordinates. Collecting information may be exceedingly difficult or even culturally forbidden. In some countries, you will lose a customer if you try to obtain marketing data such as age and income.

In some nations, the connections between suppliers and customers are established by culture. For instance, in Japan, distribution of products is handled by only a few large firms. These companies have established relationships with the suppliers and retail outlets. In any country,

REALITY BYTES   More Spam, a Worldwide Problem

Asia has led the way in many cell phone innovations, and spam is no exception. Japanese users on the DoCoMo system send and receive an average of 10 short message service (SMS) messages a day. Users in Japan and Hong Kong are increasingly being hit with spam messages. Most spammers randomly generate the e-mail type addresses and send out thousands of messages at a time. Many are fraudulent. Some ask people to send money to a specified bank account. Marketers have begun targeting the medium and are sending short messages to phones offering discount "coupons."

SMS text messages are popular in Asia and tend to receive immediate attention. Chi-wing Chan, regional director for telecommunications at a marketing company (TNS), notes that "people like to receive messages. They think it's cool. When you get an SMS message you deal with it immediately, but for e-mails it just feeds into your e-mail box." In January 2004, cell phone users in China sent 10 billion messages during the eight-day Lunar new year.

Europe has relatively strong privacy laws. Its antispam law specifically forbids commercial e-mail unless the recipient has opted in. Nonetheless, 53 percent of the e-mail in Europe is spam. Although the number is slightly lower than the 60 percent for the United States, European officials are not happy. Much of the spam appears to be originating from the United States, and Europe wants the United States to crack down. Brightmail, a U.S. company that provides filtering services, notes that 79 percent of the messages in January 2004 originated in North America. About 80 percent of the messages are written in English, or at least attempt to be in English, given the poor grammar and weak translations of many of the messages. The real issue is that there is no international cooperation or organization for identifying and prosecuting spammers.

Source: Adapted from Brandon Mitchener, "Europe Blames Weak U.S. Laws for Surge in the Region's Spam," *The Wall Street Journal,* February 3, 2004; and "Spam Invasion Targets Mobile Phones," *CNN Online,* February 4, 2004.

it can be difficult for an outside firm to create a relationship between suppliers and customers. Trying to build computer networks with the various companies could cause severe repercussions. The established firms may think you are trying to steal their knowledge or information.

Comment

Creating international data networks can lead to many problems. There is no easy solution to many of these problems. However, international networks do exist and they will increase in the next few years. In many cases, firms have to operate in the international environment in order to succeed. There is no choice. The company must build international telecommunications networks.

As the European Union increases the amount of interdependence between western and eastern European nations, there will be even more reasons for companies to operate in many nations. The same holds true for the conversion of the eastern European nations to market economies. The companies that take the lead in international computer networks will face many problems, but if they succeed, they will create the foundation necessary to be the leaders in their industry.

Summary

One of the most important concepts in MIS is the necessity of sharing data. Networks today are based on the Internet protocols and provide data transfers as well as applications through Web browsers. Networks are used to send messages (e-mail), share experiences (discussion groups and Web sites), schedule meetings (electronic calendars), and share teamwork.

A Manager's View

Choosing the correct network options is difficult. It requires knowing how the network will be used and understanding the detailed options available. Just as computers need to be updated and replaced, network components need to be upgraded. The goal of telecommunications is to remove location as a factor in management and decisions. As bandwidth increases and wireless access becomes more widely available, you can create entirely new business structures. Managers and companies that are prepared to take advantage of these changes can become more efficient and competitive.

Advances in the cell phone and wireless industries are enabling convergence of phones and data access through wireless network connections. Wired networks still form the backbone of our networks and provide better connections and faster data transfers. Internet costs are determined by the local phone companies that control the pricing of the last mile, and by the long-distance companies that own the nationwide fiber-optic network. To establish a business connection to the Internet (to run a server), you need to lease a communication line from a local provider (in most cases the phone company) and also pay an ISP for access to the Internet. Higher-capacity connections cost more money, but economies of scale make it profitable for the large providers to resell access to smaller businesses.

The telecommunications facilities and prices on which we rely in industrialized nations are not always available in other countries. Moreover, there are incompatibilities between equipment produced for various nations. Political restrictions are another source of complications when transferring data across international boundaries.

Key Words

blog, *79*
broadband, *91*
broadcasts, *87*
cable modems, *90*
digital subscriber line (DSL), *90*
domain name system (DNS), *100*
e-mail, *78*
extranet, *79*
file transfer protocol (FTP), *102*
grid computing, *82*
groupware, *80*
hypertext markup language (HTML), *96*

instant messaging (IM), *79*
Internet service provider (ISP), *98*
intranet, *79*
IPv6, *100*
local area networks (LANs), *76*
network address translation (NAT), *100*
network interface card (NIC), *85*
newsgroup, *79*
packets, *83*
peer-to-peer networks, *84*

portable document format (pdf), *96*
scalability, *84*
server farm, *85*
spam, *106*
standards, *95*
storage area network (SAN), *82*
transborder data flows (TBDFs), *109*
virtual private network (VPN), *95*
voice over Internet protocol (VoIP), *83*

Web Site References

Financial News and Quotes

Big Charts	www.bigcharts.com
Bloomberg	www.bloomberg.com
Dun & Bradstreet	www.dnb.com
Global Financial Data	www.findata.com
Reuters	www.reuters.com
SEC Edgar	www.sec.gov
Motley Fool	www.fool.com
Wall Street Journal	wsj.com

Discount Online Trading

Ameritrade	www.ameritrade.com
Harris Direct	www.harrisdirect.com
E*Trade	www.etrade.com
Fidelity	www.fidelity.com
Quick & Reilly	www.quickandreilly.com
Charles Schwab	www.schwab.com

Additional Readings

"The Capacity of Optical Fibre." *The Economist,* June 28, 2001. [Theoretical capacity of fiber-optic cables.]

"The Internet, Untethered." *The Economist,* October 13, 2001. [Special section on wireless issues with examples from Japan.]

Kahn, J. M., and K. P. Ho. "Communications Technology: A Bottleneck for Optical Fibres." *Nature,* June 28, 2001, pp. 1007–1009. [Theoretical capacity of fiber-optic cables.]

Kahn, Robert E. "The Role of Government in the Evolution of the Internet." *Communications of the ACM,* August 1994, pp. 15–19. [Early days of the Internet.]

Kurose, James F., and Keith W. Ross. *Computer Networking: A Top-Down Approach Featuring the Internet.* Boston: Addison Wesley Longman, 2001. [Technical details on networking and TCP/IP.]

Waltner, C. "Meet Your Connection." *Fortune Technology Review,* Summer 2001, pp. 59–66. [Discussion of business Internet connection costs and options.]

Wiggins, R. "How the Internet Works." *Internet World,* Vol. 8(10), 1996. [Basic explanation of terms and connection points.]

Review Questions

1. How are networks used to share data?
2. Why do businesses use networks to share hardware?
3. What is the value in sharing calendars electronically?
4. List the main components of a network.
5. List the types of transmission media that are available. How do they compare in transmission rates and cost?
6. What are the main advantages and drawbacks to wireless networks?
7. Explain the concept of an enterprise network.
8. Why are standards so important in networks?
9. In what way have phones and computers converged? Why is this convergence occurring?
10. How does the Internet work? What type of service do you need to set up a Web server and how much will it cost?
11. What applications might exist for mobile commerce? Why would people use Internet access instead of just a voice call?
12. Why is Internet service so slow at your house (apartment)?
13. What is the Internet2 and how will it affect businesses?
14. What problems arise with global telecommunications?

Exercises

1. Find a hub or switch and build a small network. If available, connect it to the Internet. Keep notes on the steps you took to build the network.
2. Using the Internet, find at least two software packages that will back up data across a LAN. Briefly explain how the software functions and what components need to be installed. Estimate the price of the software for a network of four servers and 100 clients.
3. Research the current status of 3G for cellular phones. In what countries is 3G available? What features are provided? What are the data transfer rates?
4. Identify the primary organizations in charge of establishing standards for the Internet. Provide the name of the organization, its location, and its current president/leader.
5. Assume you want to start an e-business. What steps do you have to take to obtain and establish a domain name for the business? How much will it cost?
6. Choose two existing Web site names. To make it more interesting, one of them should be from a spam site. Use the Internet resources to obtain as much information about the company and owner as you can. Note, you should also check the office of the appropriate secretary of state.
7. Check vendor advertising and identify the costs and speed of the following services:
   a. DSL from the phone company.
   b. Cable modem.
   c. Cell phone Internet access.
   d. Dial-up Internet access.
   e. Wireless access at a local hot spot.

Technology Toolbox

8. Create three Web pages that are linked. Include at least one image.

9. Create a style sheet for at least two Web pages and demonstrate how the look of the site can be changed by altering the style sheet.

10. Create a simple Web page using Microsoft Word and save it. Create a similar page using either straight HTML or an HTML editor such as FrontPage. Compare the two files and comment on the differences.

11. Find three Web hosting companies and identify the file transfer methods supported by each company. Does the company charge extra for some methods?

12. Research the additional file transfer features offered by WebDAV. Briefly explain how these features would be useful to managers.

Teamwork

13. Each team member should interview at least five people to identify (a) how many e-mail messages they send a day, (b) how much time they spend (or number of messages sent) on IM, (c) how many cell phone text messages they send per day. Also collect basic personal data such as gender and approximate age. Combine the results from all team members and comment on any patterns.

14. Have each person on the team set up a folder and assign permissions so that other team members can share data on that folder. Each person should write a short statement describing the steps involved, then transfer the file to the other folders. Combine the statements into one document.

15. If a network is available with Microsoft Outlook (or similar package) on each client, add each team member to the Contacts list. Each person should enter a few items in a personal calendar to block out some times for one week. Then share the calendars and use the system to schedule a meeting.

16. Use an IM system to add each team member. Find a time when everyone can work on a project to create an outline of the chapter that lists the major headings and a one- or two-line description of the section. Split the task up so each person takes a couple of sections. While the group is working, each person should interrupt another with an IM message. In addition, each person should interrupt someone else with either a phone call or a face-to-face meeting. At the end of the document, add a brief comment about the differences between the two interruptions.

17. Interview managers, friends, or family members who have jobs and identify where their primary files are stored. Are they stored on local computers, on a department file server, or at a more distant location? Who is responsible for backup? What is the process for recovering lost files? Combine each result into a document. Create a table and a chart to summarize the results. Write a short paragraph suggesting improvements.

Rolling Thunder Database

18. Design a network for the Rolling Thunder Bicycle Company. Identify who will need access to the network; how many workstations you will need (and where to place them); the data, input forms, and reports users will need. Using the existing data, estimate the storage requirements and transmission needs. Specify how changes and growth will affect the type of network needed.

19. Describe how the Internet could be used to increase sales at Rolling Thunder Bicycles.

20. Rolling Thunder Bicycles wants to expand international sales. What changes would need to be made to the application? What problems would you expect to encounter, and how would you overcome these potential problems?

21. The manager of Rolling Thunder Bicycles wants to access the database from home. Describe some options of how this could be done. What potential problems might arise?

22. If you have access to laptops and a wireless network, test the database running over a wireless connection. If five or six people want to use the system with wireless devices, what problems might arise? Do some research: Is there a system that can help?

Cases: Wholesale Suppliers

The Industry

Wholesale suppliers are the original business-to-business providers. In many ways, they are like any other manufacturer or retailer. The difference is that their primary customers are other businesses. Selling to other businesses often means that the company supplies bulk items, but some wholesalers specialize in small, hard-to-find items. Some wholesalers provide commodities, such as raw chemicals. That raises one of the big challenges: differentiating your company from the competitors. What makes one company's products different from the others? In most cases, it is not the product that matters, but the customer service. Sometimes location is a key aspect to providing service, so small firms can survive by carving a local niche. But the big firms often have an advantage in economies of scale, driving costs down by serving large geographical regions through distribution centers. Some of the large commodity providers are global in scope. But size raises a new set of problems: managing a global company that has grown through multiple mergers. Communicating within the company is difficult enough. Communicating a consistent message to customers can be exceedingly hard.

Payments are another challenging issue for wholesalers. Manufacturers often squeeze vendors by stretching payments to the future. Small firms often pay the price in these cases, because it puts pressure on their cash flow when they do not receive payment for 90 days. Technology cannot always solve this problem because it is a power balance between vendor and customer. However, it can at least track the payment history and make the entire process transparent to both sides.

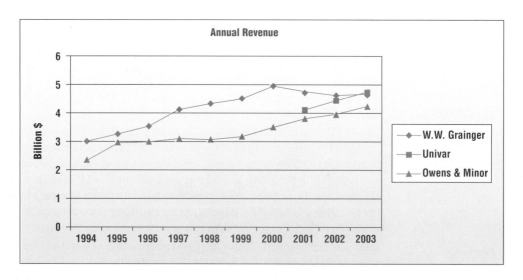

B2B E-Commerce

Communication is the entire purpose of electronic networks. Internal networks are useful for collaboration and coordinating employees. For customers, the big leap in the last decade has been e-commerce—particularly business-to-business (B2B) sites. B2B sites can be set up by one company, focused on providing a single interface for its customers. Alternatively, it might be a site shared across the industry by multiple suppliers and many customers. Several auction-based Web sites were created around 2000 to increase competition and make it easier for customers to find and purchase various items. Many of these sites later failed; however, a few remain in some key industries. Both sellers and purchasers have to decide what type of B2B site works best for each type of product.

A shared site can be run by a neutral party, with costs shared by everyone. Hence, it can be easier for smaller firms to participate. But auction-based sites tend to drive down the prices of commodities, so sellers might not want to use them.

From the perspective of the buyers, they might prefer a tighter relationship with one or two suppliers. If you compete only on the basis of price, suppliers might not be responsive when crises arise. Ultimately, one of the big questions for buyers is how much of the logistics they want to handle themselves, versus how much they want to outsource to the vendors.

Logistics

Distribution is a key factor in the wholesale industry. Suppliers need to get products to the customers. Sometimes the products are bulky. In the case of chemicals, they might be volatile and difficult to transport. But that is the point of customer service by the supplier. On the other hand, logistics involves more than just transportation. It includes tracking orders and payments, timing the deliveries, finding rare products, tracking shipments, and recording everything in a format that can be shared. Elemica is a multi-vendor Web site for the chemical industry. Its Web site notes that an average international shipment requires 6 participants, 20 documents, and between 4 and 12 weeks of time. One of Elemica's selling points is a software tool to track the entire process and integrate the data between the supplier and purchaser enterprise resource planning (ERP) systems.

Wholesalers also have to make difficult decisions about inventory levels. Increasingly, through just-in-time ordering systems, manufacturers have pushed inventories back to the suppliers. Consequently, suppliers have to continually evaluate and forecast customer demands, compare them with world supply levels, and determine how much to stock of each item in every location. Linking to customer databases can be a useful step, because it enables suppliers to quickly spot trends and make more accurate forecasts (Babcock 2003).

Additional Reading

Babcock, Charles. "Distribution: Distributors Look to 'Crystal Balls.'" *Information Week,* September 22, 2003.

Elemica Web site: http://www.elemica.com/servlet/page?_pageid=57,87&_dad=elemica&_schema=ELE MICA

Case: Owens & Minor

Founded in 1882, Owens & Minor (ticker: OMI) is a leading distributor of medical and surgical supplies to hospitals in the United States. It is also a health care supply chain management company that can run the entire logistics side for hospitals. The company distributes almost 120,000 products from over 1,000 suppliers. It has 41 distribution centers and a total of 3,200 employees distributing products to about 4,000 customers (annual report). The company purchases medical items in bulk from suppliers and stores them in its warehouses, which are close to customers. Most warehouses deliver within a 200-mile radius. Customers can order through a variety of systems, including a stockless, automated system where Owens & Minor employees deliver individual items as needed. Although the company purchases items from almost all of the medical manufacturers, about 16 percent of the net sales in 2003 consisted of products from Johnson & Johnson and 14 percent from subsidiaries of Tyco International, which includes the Kendall Company (annual report). Its major nationwide competitors are Cardinal Health (whose roots lie with American Hospital Supply Corporation) and McKesson.

Delivering Supplies

Until 1998, O&M was simply delivering supplies to hospitals. In that year, the company was hit with the loss of substantial revenue when HCA Inc., the biggest health care provider in the United States, decided to take its business to another company—immediately reducing O&M's revenue by 11 percent. The company decided that the answer was to go beyond simply selling and delivering products. It needed to provide entire supply chain management tools to hospitals. The company estimates that hospitals spend an additional 40 percent of their supply costs just managing the logistics, tracking orders, and restocking. David Guzman, hired as CIO in 2000, notes that "there's only so much blood you can squeeze from a turnip in terms of the product price. But there's a lot you can do with the logistics costs" (Kontzer 2003). Consequently, O&M decided to extend itself deeper into the supply chain on both the hospital and manufacturer ends. CEO Bilmer Minor III notes that "our business has been built on supply-chain services and customer service. We realized our difference would be based on providing information" (Kolbasuk 2001).

Logistics Services

As a distributor, O&M understands the importance of networks for connecting to customers and suppliers. The company survives on price differentials—buying products at discounts from manufacturers and distributing them to hospitals. With fierce competition, it has to use technology to hold down costs to make a profit—about 1 percent on sales (Stahl 2004).

One challenge that O&M faces is that its customers (hospitals, nurses, and physicians) are several years behind in technology. Craig Smith, president of O&M, estimates they are as much as 20 years behind. Smith believes that radio frequency identification (RFID) chips can make a substantial difference by helping hospitals track everything they own from beds to drugs. "We're headstrong into RFID. It will have a significant impact on our business" (Stahl 2004).

Beyond the simple warehouse and transportation services, O&M has created several tools to help hospitals reduce their costs. The OMSolutions division is a professional services unit that handles consulting and outsourcing to help hospitals reduce costs. The team handles everything from stockroom and process redesign within a hospital to outsourced management of supplies (annual report). The CostTrack system is another tool to help customers analyze their costs. Using activity-based costing, the system shows customers exactly how much each step of the purchasing process is costing. It enables hospitals to then choose exactly which parts of the process they want to outsource to O&M. In 2003, 32 percent of O&M sales were generated through the CostTrack system (annual report).

One big problem that hospitals face is that they buy supplies from many sources. As much as 50 percent of the purchases are direct from manufacturers. Other items might be purchased from multiple suppliers and distributors. So O&M developed the Wisdom2 analytical tool. It collects all purchasing data from a hospital and makes it available as a single dataset. It tracks purchases from competitor suppliers as well as directly from the manufacturers. Judy Springfield, director of corporate standardization and contracting at Baylor Health Care System (a nine-hospital network), says that "we've just been dying for data" (Kontzer 2003). The Wisdom2 system provides the detailed data she wants, across all of the purchases, and even puts it into a spreadsheet. Wisdom and Wisdom2 are also useful to O&M directly.

Ultimately, Owens & Minor would like to simplify the ordering process even more—to the point of automated replenishment. If the system can forecast usage rates, O&M employees could deliver new items to the hospital and track the entire process, without needing a separate order from the hospital. CIO Guzman thinks the process is feasible: "You'd be surprised how remarkably predictable demand is in the healthcare system. And I don't mean in general. I mean system by system. Massachusetts General is different from Stanford Hospital, but Stanford in its own right is predictable, as is Massachusetts General" (Kontzer 2003).

O&M also uses technology and networks to improve its operations. Remember that margins are extremely tight, and saving costs is critical. A new warehouse-management system in 2001 that uses wireless technology to guide workers increased productivity by 20 percent (Kolbasuk 2001). Notice that O&M manages to record over $4 billion of sales a year with only about 3,200 total employees.

New Systems

To provide new services, Owens & Minor needed new systems. But before building new systems, the company first needed to consolidate its information technology team. In 2002, the company canceled an outsourcing contract with IBM and expanded an arrangement it had with Perot Systems. The goal was to consolidate data centers to save costs, but also to begin creating new technology systems (Vijayan 2002). The company's main goal is to redesign the legacy systems so they use Web services to integrate all of the components. Ultimately, every information system the company has will need to connect to the OMDirect Web portal. Integrating the systems is still difficult and requires a new system architecture that uses XML to transfer the data. Guzman notes that "you can't go out and buy Web services. It's clear you have to be the one to build [them]" (Murphy and Bacheldor 2003), so the process is scheduled to take three years.

Security

With any network system, and particularly with Internet-based systems, security is a critical factor—particularly in the health care industry. At one level, security today is relatively straightforward: identify each resource and user, and then assign the appropriate permissions to users. Except that with thousands of users and hundreds of applications, it is expensive to manage the tasks. Owens & Minor has more than 12 administrators who are dedicated to managing, adding, and deleting employee and customer access rights (Hulme 2003). And the company has to be extremely careful to monitor access rights to ensure they are correct and that they are updated as employees change jobs or leave the company. To simplify the process, O&M is consolidating the identity databases onto a single centralized Microsoft Active Directory repository. Active Directory (AD) runs on Microsoft servers and holds user credentials. It can be accessed by a variety of applications and services. Users essentially login to AD, and the system authenticates the user to other applications. O&M is also using IdentityMinder from Netegrity Inc. to transfer the user rights into the 20 or 30 applications accessed by each user. Paul Higday, chief architect for O&M, notes that "what this will allow us to do is set up a user based on what they're allowed to access with a single click instead of having to manually add each account" (Hulme 2003).

Questions

1. How does Owens & Minor use networks and information systems to reduce costs?
2. Given the innovations by American Hospital Supply in the 1980s, why are hospitals not even more integrated into the supply chain?
3. How are logistics services different from simply delivering supplies?
4. How will RFID affect the use and purchasing of hospital supplies? Will the technology be widely accepted?

Additional Reading

Ante, Spencer E. "Owens & Minor." *BusinessWeek,* November 24, 2003, p. 92.

Hulme, George V. "Identity Checkpoint." *Information Week,* January 20, 2003.

Kolbasuk McGee, Marianne. "Supply Chain's Missing Link." *Information Week,* September 17, 2001.

Kontzer, Tony. "Owens & Minor Takes Supply Chain Deeper." *Information Week,* September 22, 2003.

Murphy, Chris, and Beth Bacheldor. "Tying It All Together." *Information Week,* March 17, 2003.

Stahl, Stephanie. "Prescription for Change." *Information Week,* February 2, 2004.

Vijayan, Jaikumar. "Owens & Minor Axes IBM for Perot." *Computerworld,* July 29, 2002.

Case: W. W. Grainger

Founded in 1927 in Chicago, W. W. Grainger (ticker: GWW) is in an interesting industry. The company supplies products to other businesses for maintenance, repair, and operations (MRO). The products include janitorial supplies, lightbulbs, and bolts. But the repair side can include any number of unique parts or tools used to repair equipment, from gaskets to pumps. The company estimates the U.S. market for MRO to be $100 billion a year, giving Grainger about a 5 percent share of the market—the largest of any competitor. About 90 percent of the market is filled by local and regional suppliers, and Grainger's strategy is to capture market share from these fragmented rivals. In 2003, the company had 575 sales outlets backed by 17 distribution centers and carried more than 500,000 different products (annual report).

As a distributor and supplier, Grainger makes money on the price differential by purchasing items in bulk and selling them at a markup to customers. But the markup is small. However, Grainger is expanding into the logistics market. The company estimates that about 40 percent of the total procurement cost comes from trying to locate and purchase MRO products. One of Grainger's competitive strengths is the number of products it carries and makes available almost immediately at any of its stores. Customers need to know that Grainger will carry the parts and supplies they need, regardless of the manufacturer. Parts that are not stocked in the local branches can usually be shipped for next-day delivery out of the distribution centers. To strengthen its local presence, Grainger is adding more showrooms and warehouse capacity across the United States. The goal is to have an outlet within 20 minutes of most businesses and institutions (annual report).

Of course, it does not make sense to carry products that rarely sell, so Grainger has to carefully choose the products that it holds in inventory. The company also works closely with manufacturers to reduce cycle times so that they can quickly refill warehouses or custom-order products if needed. Grainger manages the inventory problem by using multiple channels. Its 3,700-page CD-ROM catalog describes 82,000 products. Its Web site offers more than 200,000 products. When customers need more specialized repair parts, Grainger's Parts division can obtain more than 2.5 million parts from its suppliers. The FindMRO division is even more specialized and can track down over 5 million facilities maintenance products (annual report). George Rimnac, vice president and chief technologist at Grainger, observes that "many of the products we sell are products our customers didn't know they needed until today" (Pratt 2001).

The FindMRO division demonstrates a key element of Grainger's success: its knowledge base. Between its systems and workers, the company is extremely successful at finding parts, including chemicals to fuel Universal Studios' fog machines. This knowledge has a huge value to Grainger. A typical online order is worth $250 with small profit margins. Orders on FindMRO average $1,200 and 80 percent of the items are shipped directly from the manufacturer—giving Grainger an immediate profit (Sviokla 2001).

Grainger has been adversely affected by the transfer of manufacturing from the United States to other nations. The company has countered this shift somewhat by focusing on health care and government agencies—which cannot easily move offshore. At the same time, the company is expanding its purchases from lower-cost offshore suppliers—particularly for house brands ("Top Distributor" June 2003).

Logistics Services

Selling to businesses and government agencies is a key component to growth for Grainger. But Grainger knows that simply offering them products is not good enough. Grainger has developed sophisticated information tools to help customers analyze and replace their purchasing systems. The company's Integrated Supply division is a professional services group that will reengineer a customer's stockroom and provide a just-in-time inventory system.

Like other distributors, Grainger was hurt by the economic downturn of 2001 and 2002. Although sales revenue declined, the company used its supply chain software to boost its profit margins, resulting in an increase in net income (Konicki 2002). The company also expanded its investments in warehouses and information technology. Rimnac observes that "if you have financial resources, a recession is a good time to invest so when the rebound comes you can excel" (Konicki 2002). After another decline in sales in 2002, yet a continued improvement in profits, CEO Richard L. Keyser commented that "we remain committed to improving service to our customers as they continue to look for ways to reduce costs. Enhancements to our logistics network and local availability of the right products will provide higher levels of service. Our initiatives should accelerate sales growth as more customers experience this improved service" ("Lower Sales" August 2003).

To combat these changes, Grainger is expanding into additional services. In 2001, the company opened an on-site branch at Florida State University. It followed by opening a second on-site branch at Langley Air Force Base in 2002.

In 1996, Grainger took on a more in-depth role at the American Airlines facility at the Dallas/Fort Worth airport. The company essentially took over all janitorial and MRO services for the facility. With its success, two years later, the contract was extended to cover the nearby American Airlines headquarters building. In 2003, the company ran integrated supply programs for more than 40 customers. Large customers with over $2 million a year in MRO purchases from Grainger are eligible for the program. Grainger customizes the service for each company, but essentially, Grainger identifies the inventory needs and handles everything from ordering to stocking and might even include an on-site center distributing products to employees. At American Airlines, Grainger was able to substantially reduce the amount of MRO inventory sitting around. At the same time, facility worker complaints about not having the necessary tools available disappeared (Fraza 2003).

Grainger experimented with several Web sites and e-business approaches before reaching its current configuration. In 1999, the company had multiple Web divisions, including OrderZone (a marketplace), FindMRO (a search site for hard-to-find parts), and MROverstocks (an auction site). It also had relationships with logistics sites such as Ariba and Commerceone as well as several other e-marketplaces. Carol Rozewell, vice president research director at research firm

Gartner Inc., noted that "Grainger customers were confused. They offered such a wide variety of products, customers needed guidance to navigate [the Web sites]" (Maddox 2002). Ultimately, Grainger killed off all of the sites except the company's main site (grainger.com) and the FindMRO site that is accessed only through the main site. But Grainger spent more than $180 million on Internet technologies and took a $23.2 million charge, followed by a $13.4 million write-off of digital properties (Maddox 2002). The main Web site was redesigned to make it easier and faster to use.

Internal Systems

Despite the growing importance of Web-based sales and in-house ties to customers, Grainger is also emphasizing increased sales through its local branches. Pushing products more efficiently through the local stores is the main reason for the $200 million redesign of Grainger's distribution system (Buss 2002).

One step Grainger took to improve efficiency was to install an SAP R/3 ERP system in 1999. Unfortunately, Grainger had several problems installing and configuring the system. For example, the ERP software miscounted the items on hand—partly because of problems in the transaction-processing subsystem. In the first year alone, the system cost Grainger $19 million in lost sales (Stedman 2000). Ultimately, Grainger got the system fixed and consolidated its financial data onto a single system. One of the problems Grainger had was trying to connect too many outside products to the SAP system. In 2003, the company began phasing out the old systems and using standard SAP components instead. Jarnail Lail, vice president of business systems, observed that the move enabled the company to reduce the number of outside consulting firms from 100 down to 10 (Colkin Cuneo 2003).

Despite the integrated enterprise resource planning system, Vice President of Finance Laura Brown wants more. In particular, she wants to be able to match sales figures with expense data in real time (Colkin and Whiting 2002). The principles of the Sarbanes-Oxley Act are scaring financial managers and executives who want to ensure that the numbers the systems are spitting out are true representations of the business finances.

Questions

1. How is Grainger's business different from that faced by Owens & Minor?

2. Why did Grainger's initial Web approach using multiple sites fail?

3. Grainger's problems implementing its ERP system are often cited for being unusually severe. Why did Grainger experience so many problems?

4. How does Grainger support local stores as well as online sales? Why is that approach successful for Grainger but not for Dell?

Additional Reading

Buss, Dale. "The New Deal." *Sales and Marketing Management,* June 2002, Vol. 154(6), pp. 24–29.

Colkin, Eileen, and Rick Whiting. "Inadequate IT?" *Information Week,* September 9, 2002.

Colkin Cuneo, Eileen. "Less Is More in Software." *Information Week,* January 13, 2003.

Fraza, Victoria. "Making Integrated Supply Work." *Industrial Distribution,* April 2003, Vol. 92(4), p. 69.

Konicki, Steve, and Eileen Colkin. "Optimism's Back!" *Information Week,* March 25, 2002.

"Lower Sales, Higher Earnings." *Industrial Distribution,* August 2003, Vol. 92(8), p. 34.

Maddox, Kate. "Growing Wiser." *B to B,* September 9, 2002, Vol. 87(9), pp. 1, 2.

Pratt, Mary K. "Maintenance, Repair and Operations." *Computerworld,* February 26, 2001.

Stedman, Craig. "ERP Woes Cut Grainger Profits." *Computerworld,* January 7, 2000.

Sviokla, John. "Knowledge Pays." *Information Week,* February 15, 2001.

"Top Distributor Talks Business." *Industrial Distribution,* June 2003, Vol. 92(6), p. 46.

Case: Univar: Van Waters & Rogers

Van Waters & Rogers is a respected name in the chemical supply industry. Established in Seattle in 1924 by George Van Waters and Nat S. Rogers, the company grew through acquisitions to become the largest wholesale provider of chemicals in the United States and Canada. Through international mergers, the company is also a major (but not the largest) supplier in Europe. In 1973, the company changed its official name to Univar, but kept the esteemed Van Waters & Rogers name on its local units. In 1986, the company acquired McKesson Chemical to extend its reach across the United States. Starting in 1991, the company began a series of mergers and acquisitions in Europe, forming Univar Europe. The rest of the chemical supply industry was consolidating at the same time.

In 1996, Royal Pakhoed, a major worldwide player in liquid chemicals, purchased the shares of Univar it did not already own. In 1999, Royal Pakhoed merged with its major competitor (Royal Van Ommeren) and created Royal Vopak. The growth continued with the purchase of Ellis & Everard in 2001, giving Vopak a substantial market share in the United Kingdom and Ireland. However, with the global economic downturn after 2001, all chemical suppliers were suffering. In 2002, Vopak spun off the chemical and distribution assets and reestablished Univar as an independent company. Univar is a Dutch company, listed on the Euronext Amsterdam stock exchange as UNIVR. Its headquarters is in Rotterdam, but major administrative offices remain in Bellevue, Washington (company history Web site). Largely because of the economic recession of 2003 and the high prices for oil (a major ingredient for many chemicals as well as a factor in transportation costs), all of the major chemical suppliers have suffered. Analysts estimate that Vopak has invested about $1 billion in Univar. Shortly after stock was issued in the new Univar company, its shares fell to €5.6, which gave the company a valuation of only about €150 million, less than one-fifth of that billion dollars (Tilton 2002).

Univar has progressed through considerable turmoil with the various mergers and the flat economies. In the early 1990s, the company tried to centralize management and run its distribution centers using a hub-and-spoke system. Analysts have pointed out that the system worked poorly and sales suffered. With the purchase by Vopak, the Van Waters & Rogers division was moved back to a decentralized approach, with more responsibility pushed to regional directors and a focus on specific product segments. In the late 1990s, the company moved more operations out to multiple local warehouses (Morris 1996). The multiple acquisitions during the late 1990s and early 2000s did not really help sales in the short run. Managers and investors faced huge uncertainties about what was going to happen next.

Initially, splitting the company back from Vopak appears to have helped. Sales for 2003 increased 9 percent to 1.62 billion. However, much of that gain was due to currency effects from the 40 percent Euro appreciation. (In the chart on page 114, Univar's sales have been converted to dollars using a single exchange rate to eliminate the exchange-rate effects.) Sales in North America were flat and hampered by the manufacturing slowdown and the rise in oil prices (Van Arnum 2003). A key step in the mergers was to consolidate the European operations under a single brand. Managing the company globally instead of regionally is a second imperative. As part of Vopak, the strategy had been to balance regional storage with distribution. John Phillpotts, president of Univar Europe, notes that "we never operated commercially as a global business before. For the last 18 months, we've had no distractions about where the company is going or who's going to own it. Chemical distribution is all we talk about now" (Young 2004).

E-Business

Univar has followed two approaches to e-business. The company is part of the consortium that drives Elemica, the chemical industry Web site. Univar also runs its own B2B Web portal, ChemPoint. The ChemPoint site is also designed to support smaller chemical manufacturers and highlight new products. In particular, the site is aimed at providing distribution services to chemical producers. Customers place orders through the site, and Univar handles the distribution—linking electronically to Yellow Transportation, its main less-than-truckload (LTL) carrier. Chad Steigers, managing director of ChemPoint.com, notes that there are still some difficulties getting companies to adopt electronic transactions. The goal of many firms is to increase productivity. His

firm is looking to more technology to encourage the use of e-business. "We think, for example, RFID will be a major factor especially in the chemical arena" (Cottrill 2003). Ultimately, buyers should be able to place an order, and then track it all the way through shipping, storing, and delivery.

ChemPoint focused on ensuring a broad market by signing up at least one supplier for each type of chemical, with the goal of providing buyers with a dependable source. Reliability and reduction of search costs are important factors for many of the hard-to-find chemicals (Cuny 2001).

When the ChemPoint site was started, it faced intense competition. As Chad Steigers, managing director, pointed out in 2000, "There are 25 trading companies that offer auctions of chemicals. We think that will drop down to two or three." At the time, the Web site had 127 customers and sold 1.3 million products provided by 2,200 suppliers, amounting to $24 million in transactions a year (Seideman 2000). The emphasis on specialty chemicals and distribution are key elements that have kept the site active today. Steigers observes that "e-distribution is a new segment for the industry. We're the only ones focused on the less-than-truckload segment of the specialty and fine chemicals market, which is about a $70-billion/year niche" (Fuller 2000).

Univar also participates in Elemica, an electronic marketplace for the huge chemical producers and distributors. The site was set up at the end of 2000, primarily to facilitate long-term contracts. It was also designed to assist firms with financing and transportation issues. The decision to avoid spot market auctions was probably due to the competing systems already in development (most of them have since failed) (Rosencrance 2000). Because of the emphasis on large sales, Elemica is emphasizing the ability to connect ERP systems between buyers and sellers. Larger purchasers can transmit orders, receive confirmations, and transfer the data directly into their accounting ERP systems (www.elemica.com).

Internal Network Technologies

The global nature of Univar makes it more difficult to manage the company. Even across the United States, the battles between centralization and decentralization led to sales problems. Dealing with multiple offices around the world, in a company that now sees itself as a single global entity, can be difficult and expensive. To improve communications without increasing travel costs, Van Waters & Rogers turned to PlaceWare's hosted collaboration system (now owned by Microsoft and renamed LiveMeeting). The system provides voice and video to any desktop that is connected to the Internet. It also has shared drawing boards, chat facilities, and the ability to show slides. It can also store a presentation for later playback if some people cannot make the initial meeting. In one example, Van Waters & Rogers used it for a strategy meeting between a team in North America and one in Switzerland to discuss a product rollout (Agnew 2000). The system is also used for training and general meetings. Ron Miazga, the human resources training director, notes that the system has been well-received and cost effective. However, building training sessions takes some practice, since "you have to make the presentations very media intensive. You should ask a polling question every three to five minutes. You have to change the screen every minute or so to hold their attention" (Agnew 2000).

Questions

1. Why does decentralization at Univar require more use of networks?

2. Why does Univar pursue a multiple-site e-commerce strategy, and why does it work for Univar and not for Grainger?

3. Why are some customers reluctant to adopt electronic ordering for chemicals?

Additional Reading

Agnew, Marion. "Collaboration on the Desktop." *Information Week,* July 10, 2000.

Corporate History Web site: http://www.univarcorp.com/ourhistory.htm.

Cottrill, Ken. "Overcoming Inertia." *Traffic World,* January 27, 2003, p. 1.

Cuny, Tim, and Marvin Richardson. "Redefining Business: Proving Grounds." *Information Week,* February 12, 2001.

Fuller, John. "Vopak Launches ChemPoint.com." *Chemical Week,* March 15, 2000, Vol. 162(11), p. 56.

Morris, Gregory D. L. "Pakhoed's VW&R Buy Accelerates Expansion." *Chemical Week,* October 16, 1996, Vol. 158(39), p. 60.

Rosencrance, Linda. "Twelve Chemical Companies Are Setting Up Online Exchange." *Computerworld,* May 17, 2000.

Seideman, Tony. "E-Marketplace Vision Collides with Reality." *InformationWeek,* June 6, 2000.

Tilton, Helga. "Analysts Positive on More Focused Univar." *Chemical Market Reporter,* November 18, 2002, Vol. 262(18), p. 19.

Van Arnum, Patricia. "North American Distributors, Wait and See." *Chemical Market Reporter,* November 24, 2003, Vol. 264(18) p. FR3.

Young, Ian. "European Unification Takes Shape at Univar." *Chemical Week,* May 19, 2004, Vol. 166(17), p. 22.

Summary Industry Questions

1. What information technologies have helped this industry?

2. Did the technologies provide a competitive advantage or were they quickly adopted by rivals?

3. Which technologies could this industry use that were developed in other sectors?

4. Is the level of competition increasing or decreasing in this industry? Is it dominated by a few firms, or are they fairly balanced?

5. What problems have been created from the use of information technology and how did the firms solve the problems?

CHAPTER FOUR

Database Management

Chapter Outline

Introduction
  Relational Databases
  Tables, Rows, Columns, Data Types
The Database Management Approach
  Focus on Data
  Data Independence
  Data Integrity
  Speed of Development
  Control over Output
Queries
  Single-Table Queries
  Computations
  Joining Multiple Tables
  Examples
  Views
Designing a Database
  Notation
  First Normal Form
  Second Normal Form
  Third Normal Form
Database Applications
  Data Input Forms
  Reports
  Putting It Together with Menus
Database Administration
  Standards and Documentation
  Testing, Backup, and Recovery
  Access Controls
Databases and e-Business
Summary
Key Words
Web Site References
Additional Reading
Review Questions
Exercises
Industry: Pharmaceuticals

What You Will Learn in This Chapter

- How do you store and retrieve the vast amount of data collected in a modern company?
- Why is the database management approach so important to business?
- How do you write questions for the DBMS to obtain data?
- How do you create a new database?
- How do you create business applications using a DBMS?
- What tasks need to be performed to keep a database running?
- Why are databases so important in e-business?

How do you store and retrieve huge amounts of data? Eli Lilly is a giant pharmaceutical company. Creating new drugs requires enormous efforts in research. Getting drugs approved takes years and dozens of lawyers. Except for the occasionally unique blockbuster, selling a drug requires delicate, but expensive, marketing. All three areas benefit from the use of information technology, particularly database systems. Evaluating chemicals, searching the huge database of existing results, and tracking progress generate huge amounts of data and require sophisticated analytical systems. Tracking clinical trials, the paperwork, and the progress of drugs through various agencies requires nontraditional databases and support. Marketing is a relatively new area for pharmaceutical companies, and they are still looking for ways to sell such complex products. Sometimes problems arise, such as when Lilly accidentally included the e-mail addresses of 669 subscribers to its prozac.com service in a message to 700 users.

Introduction

How do you store and retrieve the vast amount of data collected in a modern company? Airlines have a difficult problem: they need to track every seat and passenger on every flight. Thousands of people might be trying to book the same flight at the same time, but the system can never sell the same seat to different people. Many other business problems have similar characteristics. All of the accounting and payroll data, sales, and purchases have to be saved for any company. Database management systems were specifically designed to solve these problems. As shown in Figure 4.1, the primary elements of a database system are to collect and store data, produce reports, and provide data to answer business queries. Today, database systems form the foundation of almost every business application. What database features do you need as a manager? How can you retrieve the data stored by the system? How can you create reports?

A **database management system (DBMS)** is one of the most important tools in business and MIS. The systems have changed the way that computer applications are developed, and they are changing the way that companies are managed. The database approach begins with the premise that the most important aspect of the computer system is the data that it stores. The purposes of a database management system are to provide shared access to the data, answer questions, and create reports from the data.

A crucial factor with databases is that they can become massive. Several companies such as American Express and UPS have indicated that their databases contain several terabytes (trillions of bytes) of data. Even small companies deal with databases with megabytes (millions of bytes) of data. The size of the database greatly affects its performance and the ability of users to find the data they need. Large databases need to be designed and maintained carefully to ensure that they run properly.

Another important characteristic of databases is that they are designed to help users examine the data from a variety of perspectives. Instead of simply printing one type of report, they enable users to ask questions and create their own reports. Figure 4.2 illustrates how a DBMS is used in an organization. It collects data for transaction processing, creates reports, and processes ad hoc queries for managers. Figure 4.2 also indicates that databases usually require programmers to define the initial database and maintain programs to perform basic operations. The overall design is controlled by the database administrator.

Relational Databases

The goal of a relational DBMS is to make it easy to store and retrieve the data you need. All data is stored in **tables,** which consist of **columns** with **rows** of data. Each table has a name

TRENDS

In the 1960s and 1970s, companies typically built their own transaction-processing systems by writing programs in COBOL. These programs consisted of millions of lines of code. Each program created and used its own set of files. As companies expanded, more programs were created—each with its own format for files. Whenever a manager wanted a new **report** or additional information, a programmer had to modify the old code or create a completely new program.

A database management system (DBMS) presents a different approach to data, reports, and programming. The most important task is to define and store the data so authorized users can find everything they need. Report writers and input screens make it easy to enter data and create reports without relying on programmers. Data is stored in a special format so that it can be shared with multiple users.

In the early 1970s, E. F. Codd created a flexible approach to storing data, known as the **relational model,** that avoided these problems. Today, relational databases are the dominant method used to store and access data. Relational databases have a **query system** that enables managers to get answers to questions without relying on programmers.

Early databases were designed to handle business types of data, such as customer names and account data. Some modern database systems can store entire books, pictures, graphs, or even sound clips as types of data. A few companies are working on **object-oriented** DBMSs that enable users to create their own data types and continue to manipulate and search the data.

When E. F. Codd created the relational database model, he deliberately introduced new terms to describe the way that databases should store information. His terms are *attribute, tuple,* and *relation.*

FIGURE 4.1

Without a database management system (DBMS), data can be scattered throughout the company, making it more difficult to share information. Inconsistent data, duplication, and errors are common. A DBMS collects data from many sources and maintains data through a common interface. Data definition, access, consistency, and security are maintained by the DBMS.

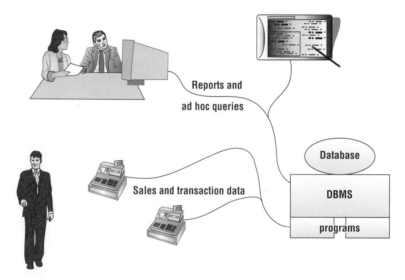

and represents objects or relationships in the data. For instance, most businesses will have tables for customers, employees, orders, and inventory.

Besides storing data, a modern DBMS has several useful tools. Input screens are built to help users enter data. Reports can be created by laying out data, text, and graphics on the screen—often with no programming. You can get answers to questions with a query language or even by pointing to tables and data on the screen. You can establish security conditions by granting or denying access to portions of the data. Most systems include an application generator that can tie input screens, queries, and reports together with a menu system. A complex application can be created by typing a few titles on the screen, without writing a single line of traditional program code.

Tables, Rows, Columns, Data Types

If you understand how spreadsheets work, it is easy to comprehend relational databases. A single spreadsheet consists of rows and columns of data. Each column has a unique name, and a row contains data about one individual object. A database consists of many of these tables that are linked by the data they contain.

REALITY BYTES   Database Terminology

Although Codd's terms are precisely defined mathematically, they can be confusing. As a result, many people use the slightly easier words: *column, row,* and *table.*

Before relational databases, several different terms were used to refer to the various parts of a database. The problem is that many of the terms had several definitions. Common terms include *field, record,* and *file.* You should avoid these terms.

FIGURE 4.2

MIS employees and databases: The database administrator is responsible for defining and maintaining the overall structure and data. Programmers and analysts create applications and programs that collect data and produce reports. Business operations generate data that fills the database. Managers use the application programs and ask ad hoc questions of the data.

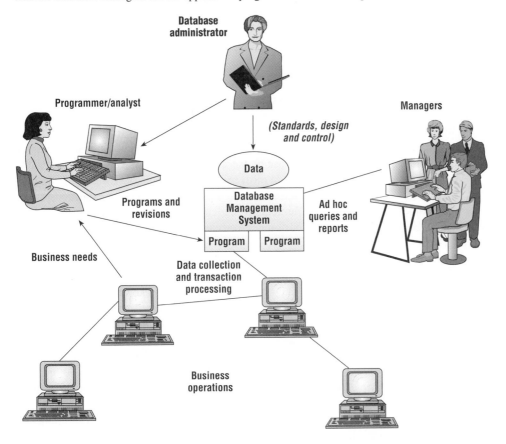

In a database, each table contains data for a specific entity or object. For example, most companies will have a table to hold customer data. There are certain attributes or characteristics of the customers that you want to store. In Figure 4.3, each customer is assigned a unique CustomerID and has a name, address, and city. In practice, there will be more columns.

Figure 4.3 also illustrates one of the most important features of a database system: Relational databases are specifically designed to allow many tables to be created and then combined in interesting ways. If you had only one table, you could use a spreadsheet or virtually any filing system, assuming it could handle the number of rows you needed. However, most business problems involve data stored in different tables. In the example, customers can place many different orders. Each order is stored in a separate line in the Orders table.

FIGURE 4.3
Creating table definitions: Tables are defined so that they can be linked by common columns. For a given row in the Orders table, you can find the corresponding customer data by locating the row with the machine phone number. In practice, this matching is handled by the DBMS query system.

Customer Table

CustomerID	Name	Address	City
12345	Jones	123 Elm	Chicago
28764	Adamz	938 Main	Phoenix
29587	Smitz	523 Oak	Seattle
33352	Sanchez	999 Pine	Denver
44453	Kolke	909 West	Denver
87535	James	374 Main	Miami

Orders Table

OrderID	CustomerID	Date	Salesperson	Total Sale
117	12345	3/3/06	887	57.92
125	87535	4/4/06	663	123.54
157	12345	4/9/06	554	297.89
169	29587	5/6/06	255	89.93

Notice that the tables are joined or linked by the CustomerID column. The CustomerID is the **primary key** column in the customer table. Each row in a table must be different from the rest; otherwise, it is a waste of space. Consequently, each table must have a primary key. A primary key is a set of one or more columns that uniquely identifies each row. If someone gives you a key value (e.g., 12345), you can immediately locate the appropriate row and find the rest of the data for that entity (name, address, city).

Each primary key value must be unique, but that is hard to guarantee with most common identifiers. In some cases, you might use phone numbers, but what happens if a customer moves and gets a new phone number? In most cases, it is safest to have the computer generate identifier values that are guaranteed to be unique. However, do not expect customers (or salespeople) to memorize these numbers. The identifiers are simply used in the database to ensure there is a way to separate customers. You can always use names or phone numbers to look up other data for customers.

More complex tables require multiple columns to identify a row. These keys are called **composite keys.** They represent many-to-many relationships. For example, a typical order system requires an OrderItem table that contains two columns as keys: OrderID + ItemID. Both columns are keyed because many items can be ordered at one time (so ItemID is keyed), and an item can be ordered at many different times (so OrderID is keyed).

Unlike a spreadsheet, each database column can contain only one type of data at a time. For example, in the Date column you can store only dates. You would not be allowed to put names or totals in this column. Most relational databases were designed to hold business types of data. The basic choices are text, dates (and times), numeric, and objects (graphics, video, and sound). Some systems enable you to be more specific about how to store numeric data. For instance, you might want to store data with only two decimal places for monetary values. Whenever possible, dates should be stored in a date format instead of text. That way you can perform arithmetic on the values. For example, a formula like (today + 30) could be used to find a due date that is 30 days from today.

The Database Management Approach

Why is the database management approach so important to business? In many ways, the database approach has revolutionized the way information systems function and altered the way businesses operate. Originally, all programs handled their own data in separate files. It took enormous coordination and documentation to try and make the multiple programs work together. The DBMS changes everything by focusing on the data instead of the programs. Its primary purpose is to store and share the data.

Focus on Data

The database management approach is fundamentally different from the older programming methods. Whenever someone needs a computer application, the first step is to identify the data that will be needed. Then a database management system is used to store the data. It takes care of storing the raw data, as well as information about that data. Everything you want to know is stored within the DBMS, not in an application program. This situation is illustrated in Figure 4.4. The goal of the DBMS approach is to collect accurate data and make it available to users. The system should also minimize unnecessary duplication of data.

Data Independence

Defining the data separately from the programs is called **data independence**. The main advantage is that it is possible to change the data without having to change the programs. For instance, you might want to add a second phone number to the customer data. With a DBMS, you can make this change, and it will not affect any of the existing programs. Similarly, the reports can be modified without having to change the data. That means when the programmer is called in at 3 A.M., she has to change only one program. All the other programs will be unaffected. Besides making the programmer's life easier, the database is more likely to be accurate and there will be less duplication of data.

Data independence means that the data and programs are separate, which makes it possible to alter the database tables as needed, without destroying the programs. As the business grows, you might decide to collect additional data, such as keeping track of sales by salesperson or by sales route. As the company expands and changes, the underlying tables can be expanded and new tables can be added—without interfering with the existing tables or current programs. Just be careful to avoid deleting tables or removing entire columns. Of course, as the business changes, managers will undoubtedly want to modify the reports to add the new information.

Data Integrity

Data integrity is an important consideration in designing and maintaining databases. Data integrity means that the database holds accurate, up-to-date data. In the airline case, it means not selling the same seat to two different people. If there are business limits on certain values, the database should force the data entry to abide by those rules. For example, prices will always be positive numbers. Another integrity concept is the importance of identifying missing (null) data. Computations should be able to skip missing data. From a manager's viewpoint, an important integrity design element is naming columns carefully. The columns should have names and descriptions so that the users understand what is stored in the database. If a column is simply labeled *Revenue,* users might wonder if that means revenue from all products, all divisions, the current year, or perhaps just monthly totals. All of this information is stored with the database in the data dictionary.

An important component of database integrity is that the data needs to be consistent. For example, consider a table that describes products for sale. Perhaps the products are grouped into categories (cleaning supplies, paper goods, clothing, etc.). Each item belongs

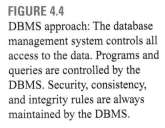

FIGURE 4.4
DBMS approach: The database management system controls all access to the data. Programs and queries are controlled by the DBMS. Security, consistency, and integrity rules are always maintained by the DBMS.

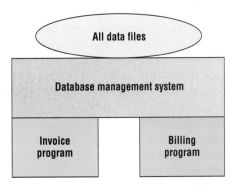

REALITY BYTES   Betting on Data

A casino deals with a tremendous amount of data from many sources. The Borgata Hotel Casino and Spa in New Jersey uses industry standard applications on IBM's DB2 to handle reservations and track transactions in the hotel and the casino. The organization uses Microsoft SQL Server as a data warehouse that collects data from the IBM system. The casino developed a business intelligence project that uses the Data Transformation Service and OLAP processing. The system is used to forecast hotel occupancy, customer visits, and correlate the data against demographic characteristics for marketing. Borgata also created a Web site to handle the 40,000 job applications, book interview times, and handle the entire process without paper.

Source: Adapted from Brian Fonseca, "Casino Hits Database Jackpot with SQL Server," *eWeek,* May 31, 2004.

to only one category. What happens if the categories are not entered consistently? The *Cleaning Supplies* category might be entered as just *Cleaning,* or maybe as *Clean Supplies,* or even *Cl Sup.* These variations in the data make it difficult to search the table based on that category because the user would have to know all of the variations. A good DBMS supports rules that can be used to minimize these problems. However, when dealing with databases, it is good practice to be careful when you enter data to ensure that your entries are consistent.

Speed of Development

It is possible to create an entire database application without having to write a single line of traditional programming code. As a result, an application can be built in a fraction of the time it would take to create it by writing COBOL programs. Studies indicate that most systems can be created 10 times faster using a DBMS—if the data already exists in the database. As the commercial database products—such as Oracle, SQL Server, and DB2—continue to add features, they can be used to solve even more complex problems.

Keep in mind that it is possible to use traditional programming tools such as COBOL in conjunction with the DBMS. If complex reports or complicated calculations are involved, it is sometimes easier to use a traditional programming language. These programs retrieve the base data from the DBMS and print their own reports or store computed values in the database for later use.

One of the most important steps of developing a solution is to break the problem into smaller pieces. One major piece of any problem is the data. A DBMS makes this portion of the problem easier to solve. By putting the DBMS in charge of maintaining the data, keeping track of security, automatically supporting multiple users, and printing reports, the developer can concentrate on solving the specific business problems. By starting from scratch with COBOL, each of these features would have to be rewritten for every application that was designed, which would be expensive.

Control over Output

Another strong advantage of database management systems is their ability to provide many different views of the output. In fact, a primary objective of the relational database approach is to store the data so that users can retrieve it any way they need. The other feature of databases is that they are designed to make it easy to combine related data. An older programming-file approach generally limits the user to using data in only one way.

With a DBMS, output can be created from report writers, which make it easy to format the data; some systems even draw graphs. The other common method of retrieving data is to use a query language such as query by example (QBE) or SQL discussed in the next section. Queries enable managers to search for answers to questions without using a programmer to write special programs.

Queries

How do you write questions for the DBMS to obtain data? Most of the time, managers work with databases that have been created by someone else. You will need to learn how to retrieve data to answer questions. It might be nice to be able to ask questions in a natural language (such as English), but it turns out to be hard to make computers understand these questions and you might not always be certain that the answer is what you asked for. A DBMS provides at least one method of asking questions and retrieving data. Two common methods are QBE and SQL. **SQL** is an international standard method for retrieving data from database management systems. It is supported by most of the major commercial relational database management systems. By the way, according to the standard, the name SQL is just three letters and not an acronym. **QBE** stands for **query by example** and is a visual method of examining data stored in a relational database. You ask questions and examine the data by pointing to tables on the screen and filling in templates. Queries can only answer questions for which you have collected the appropriate data.

Regardless of the method used to look up information in a database, there are four basic questions you will answer, as listed in Figure 4.5. It does not matter in which order you think of the questions. With some methods (such as QBE), it is easier to choose the tables first. With other methods (such as SQL), it is sometimes easier to choose the output first. In many cases, you will switch back and forth among the four questions until you have all of the components you need. As you learn more about databases, keep these four questions handy and write down your answers before you attempt to create the query on the DBMS.

Single-Table Queries

Consider a simple customer table that contains columns for CustomerID, Name, Phone, Address, City, State, and AccountBalance. Each customer is assigned a unique number that will be used as a primary key. The AccountBalance is the amount of money the customer currently owes to our company. The table with some sample data is shown in Figure 4.6.

Query by Example

Query-by-example systems that were designed for graphical user interfaces (GUIs) are especially easy to use. Microsoft's Access illustrates a common approach. The basic mechanism is to make selections on the screen—typically by pointing to them with a mouse. You then fill out a template like the one shown in Figure 4.7.

With a QBE approach, you will first be asked to choose the table that contains the data you want to see. You will be given a list of tables in the database and you select the one you

FIGURE 4.5

Four questions to create a query: You will always have to answer these four questions. In many cases, there will be only one table (or view), so the second and last questions are easy.

Four Questions to Create a Query
• What output do you want to see?
• What tables are involved?
• What do you already know (or what constraints are given)?
• How are the tables joined together?

FIGURE 4.6

A sample table for customer data: CustomerID is the primary key and is used to uniquely identify each customer.

Customer				
CustomerID	**Name**	**Phone**	**City**	**AccountBalance**
28764	Adamz	602-999-2539	Phoenix	526.76
87535	James	305-777-2235	Miami	255.93
12345	Jones	312-555-1234	Chicago	197.54
44453	Kolke	303-888-8876	Denver	863.39
33352	Sanchez	303-444-1352	Denver	153.00
29587	Smitz	206-676-7763	Seattle	353.76

FIGURE 4.7

Query by example for the customer table: Checking the Show box ensures that the column will be displayed when the query is run. Conditions are entered in the Criteria row. Conditions entered on the same row are connected by an "AND" clause. Conditions on separate rows are combined with an "OR" clause.

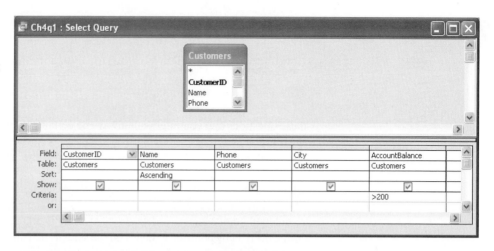

FIGURE 4.8

Query by example: List the customers from Denver with an AccountBalance of more than $200. Results of the query can be sorted in Ascending or Descending order. Multiple levels of sorts are created by selecting additional columns. You will use multiple column sorts when the first column contains several identical values. For example, sort by City, Name.

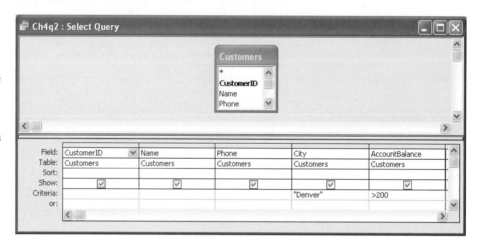

need. Once you have selected the table, you choose the columns that you want to display in the result. You use the QBE screen to specify totals, sort the results, and place restraints (criteria) on the data.

Most of the time, you will want to see only some of the rows of data. For instance, you want a list of customers who owe you the most money. You decide to restrict the listing to customers who have account balances greater than $200. With QBE, you enter the appropriate restriction in the column as shown in Figure 4.8. You can specify other conditions for the other columns. Placing them on the same row means they will be interpreted as AND conditions. If conditions are placed on separate rows, results will be computed for rows that match at least one of the criteria (OR condition). Figure 4.8 shows the QBE screen, which tells the DBMS to display the ID, City, and AccountBalance for customers who live in Denver and have account balances of more than $200.

If you are searching a text column, you might want to look for a single word or part of a word in a sentence. The pattern-matching command called LIKE enables you to search for parts of text. For example, to assign customer accounts alphabetically to your salespeople, you might need a list of customers whose names start with the letter S. In the name column, you would enter the constraint: LIKE "S*". The asterisk (*) will match any characters that follow the letter S. You also can use a question mark (?) wildcard character to match exactly one character. Note that many database systems use the SQL standard percent sign (%) and underscore (_) instead of * and ?.

Another useful condition is the BETWEEN statement. If you have a table of orders and want to get a list of orders placed in June and July, you can enter the condition for Order-Date: BETWEEN #6/1/2006# and #7/31/2006#.

One additional feature of relational databases is useful. In many cases, data will be missing from your database. Perhaps you do not have the phone numbers of all of your customers. Or maybe the marketing department has not yet set a price for a new product. Missing data is represented by the NULL value in relational databases. So if you want a list of all the customers where you do not know their phone numbers, you can enter the condition for the phone column: IS NULL.

SQL

Another method of retrieving data from a DBMS is with the query language SQL. Although some people find SQL more difficult to learn, it has two advantages. First, it is a standard language that is supported by many different database systems, so the commands will work the same in many situations. Second, it is easier to read than QBE, so it is easier for your colleagues to understand your queries.

SQL is a moderately complex language. There are only a few major commands in SQL, but each command can have several components. You will use only a few simple SQL statements. You can take a database class to learn more SQL details. You will start by looking at data in a single table to introduce the SELECT statement. Then you will learn how to combine data from several tables.

The standard command for retrieving data in SQL is SELECT. To be clear, you will write SQL command words in uppercase, but you can type them into the computer as lowercase. The simple form of the command is shown in Figure 4.9. The four parts are written on separate lines here to make the command easier to read.

The first step is to decide which columns you want to see. These columns can be listed in whatever order you want. The column names should be separated by commas. If you want to see all the columns, you can use the key word ALL or an asterisk (*). Next, you need to know the name of the table. The SQL command to retrieve all of the customer data is SELECT * FROM Customers. The result can be sorted by adding the ORDER BY clause. For example, SELECT * FROM customers ORDER BY City.

To get a list of customers who live in Denver with account balances greater than $200, you need to add a WHERE clause. The command becomes SELECT * FROM Customers WHERE (AccountBalance > 200) and (City = "Denver"). Notice the similarity to the QBE command. Of course, with SQL, you need to remember (and type in) the names of the tables and columns. NULL values and BETWEEN commands are also available in SQL.

Computations

Many business questions involve totals or other calculations. All database systems have some mechanism to perform simple calculations. However, these facilities are not as complex as those available in spreadsheets. On the other hand, the database versions are generally easier to use and can operate on millions of rows of data. Typical functions are listed in Figure 4.10.

FIGURE 4.9
The SQL SELECT command: This command is used to retrieve and display data. It is the foundation of many of the other SQL commands.

SELECT	columns
FROM	tables
JOIN	matching columns
WHERE	conditions
ORDER BY	column {ASC | DESC}

FIGURE 4.10
QBE and SQL can both perform calculations on the data. In addition to these aggregation functions, new columns can be created with standard algebraic operators (+ − */).

SUM	total value of items
AVG	average of values
MIN	minimum value
MAX	maximum value
COUNT	number of rows
STDEV	standard deviation
VAR	variance of items

FIGURE 4.11

Query by example overall AccountBalance average for the Customer table: This query counts the number of rows (CustomerID) and computes the overall average of the account balance.

FIGURE 4.12

QBE AccountBalance average for Denver customers for the Customer table: This query computes the average account balance for those customers living in Denver.

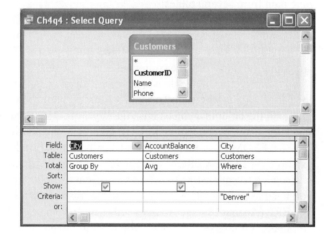

Query by Example

Although most database management systems provide a means to compute totals and averages, there is no standard method for entering the commands. Typically, the commands are displayed on a menu. Access uses an extended grid, which is shown in Figure 4.11. You point to the row you want to calculate and type in the desired function. The example shows how to get the number of customers and the average account balance.

Calculations are generally combined with the selection criteria. For instance, you might want the average account balance for all customers who live in Denver. The QBE screen for this question is displayed in Figure 4.12. The only change you have to make is to type *Denver* into the city column. Combining selection clauses with calculations enables you to answer many different questions.

Another useful feature is the ability to divide the rows into groups and get subtotals or other calculations for each group. If you know there are 10 cities in the database, you could run the average account balance query 10 different times to get the values for each city. An easier method is to use the GROUP BY option and run the query once. This time, instead of specifying the city, you indicate that cities are to be treated as groups. Then the DBMS will find the average account balance for each city. You do not even have to know which cities are in the database. The GROUP BY method used by Access is shown in Figure 4.13.

SQL

SQL can also perform simple calculations. If you have columns for Price and QuantitySold, the value of items sold can be found by computing SELECT Price * QuantitySold. The standard functions listed in Figure 4.10 are available. To compute the total of the accounts, you would enter SELECT SUM(AccountBalance) FROM Customers.

FIGURE 4.13

Subtotal calculations: One powerful capability of query systems is the ability to compute summary statistics for subsets (groups) of data. This query computes the average account balance for customers and lists the results for each city in the database.

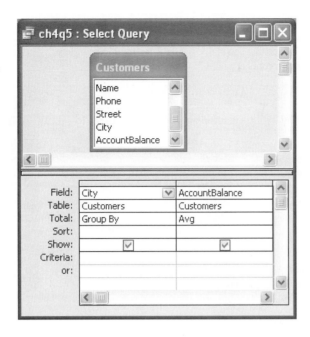

The GROUP BY clause is also available. The command becomes SELECT AVG(AccountBalance) FROM Customers GROUP BY City. Although it might be more difficult to remember the command and the column names, using SQL has two advantages over QBE. First, SQL is a defined standard. The commands you learn for one DBMS will generally work the same on another DBMS. Second, SQL statements are sometimes easier to read. Some QBE commands are not easy to understand, especially if selection criteria are connected by AND or OR commands displayed on separate lines. Many QBE systems automatically build the corresponding SQL statement for you. It is a good idea to check this statement to make sure you placed the conditions correctly on the form.

Joining Multiple Tables

The true strength of a database management system lies in its ability to combine data from several tables. Part of the Customer table is shown in Figure 4.14, with additional tables that show a list of orders placed by those customers and the salespeople involved.

Notice that the tables were designed so they can be connected. For example, the Orders table can be connected to the Customers table by matching the CustomerID (abbreviated as CID to save space). The Orders table can be matched to the Salespeople table through the SalespersonID (SID). Once you have joined the tables together, the database system retrieves and displays the data as if it were stored in one table.

The chief advantage to using multiple tables is that you can connect tables that have a one-to-many relationship. For example, each salesperson may be associated with many different orders. Instead of repeating the salesperson information on every order, you only need to include the salesperson's ID (SID) number. Joining the tables together tells the DBMS to automatically look up the corresponding data from the Salespeople table.

Query by Example

Most people find that database systems that use graphical QBE commands to join tables together are much easier to use than straight SQL commands. With a DBMS like Access you join the tables together by pointing to the column name in one table and dragging it to the matching column in the other table. The DBMS displays the connection between the two columns. Whenever you want to retrieve data from more than one table, you must first join them together.

SQL

In SQL, connections between tables are typically made with the INNER JOIN clause in the FROM statement. For example, to join the Customers and Orders tables by equal customer

FIGURE 4.14

Multiple tables: The true power of a database lies in the ability to combine data from multiple tables. Actual databases can have hundreds or thousands of related tables. Notice that each table is related to another table through matching columns. You should be able to draw lines between column labels that will connect each of the tables.

Customers

CID	Name	Phone	City	AccountBalance
12345	Jones	312-555-1234	Chicago	$197.54
28764	Adams	602-999-2539	Phoenix	$526.76
29587	Smitz	206-656-7763	Seattle	$353.76
33352	Sanchez	303-444-1352	Seattle	$153.00
44453	Kolke	303-888-8876	Denver	$863.39
87535	James	305-777-2235	Miami	$255.98

Salespeople

SID	Name	DateHired	Phone	Commission
255	West	5/23/75	213-333-2345	5
452	Zeke	8/15/94	213-343-5553	3
554	Jabbar	7/15/91	213-534-8876	4
663	Bird	9/12/93	213-225-3335	4
887	Johnson	2/2/92	213-887-6635	4

Items

ItemID	Description	Price
1154	Corn Broom	$ 1.00
2254	Blue Jeans	$12.00
3342	Paper Towels—3 rolls	$ 1.00
7653	Laundry Detergent	$ 2.00
8763	Men's Boots	$15.00
9987	Candy Popcorn	$ 0.50

Orders

OrderID	CID	SID	OrderDate	Amount
117	12345	887	3/3/2006	$ 57.92
125	87535	663	4/4/2006	$123.54
157	12345	554	4/9/2006	$297.89
169	29587	255	5/5/2006	$ 89.93
178	44453	663	5/1/2006	$154.89
188	29587	554	5/8/2006	$325.46
201	12345	887	5/28/2006	$193.58
211	44453	255	6/9/2006	$201.39
213	44453	255	6/9/2006	$154.15
215	87535	887	6/9/2006	$563.27
280	28764	663	5/27/2006	$255.32

ItemsSold

OID	ItemID	Quantity
117	1154	2
117	3342	1
117	7653	4
125	1154	4
125	8763	3
157	7653	2
169	3342	1
169	9987	5
178	2254	1

numbers and get the combined data, use the command SELECT * FROM Customers INNER JOIN Orders ON Customers.CustomerID = Orders.CustomerID.

Notice that both tables must be listed in the FROM statement. Always remember that if you list more than one table, the tables must be joined. The dot before the column (CustomerID) separates the table name from the column name (table.column). You can use this form any time you type in a column name, but it is only required when there might be confusion about which table the column is in. In the example, both tables have a column called CustomerID. To keep them straight, you have to specify which table you want to use.

Examples

You now have the basics to begin asking questions of the data. Start with an easy one. Which customers (CustomerID) have placed orders since June 1, 2006? The query and result are shown in Figure 4.15. Notice that customer number 44453 has placed two orders. Some systems will show you the order number twice; others will automatically delete the duplicates.

It can be difficult to remember each customer's number, so it is better to use the customer name and have the DBMS automatically look up the customer number. This second query is shown in Figure 4.16. Note that the Customer table is joined to the Orders table by the matching values of CustomerID.

Now, try a more complicated query: List the salespeople (sorted alphabetically) with the names of the customers who placed orders with that salesperson. This question sounds dif-

FIGURE 4.15

QBE and SQL: Which customers have placed orders since June 1, 2006? QBE and SQL are based on the same fundamental concepts. You build each query by asking the same four basic questions.

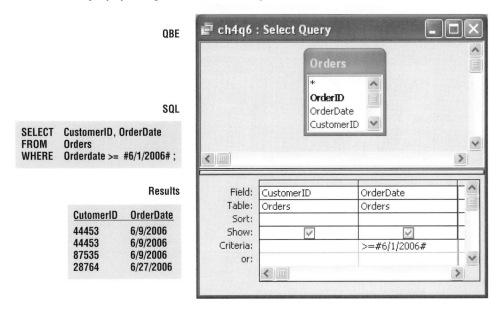

QBE

SQL

```
SELECT   CustomerID, OrderDate
FROM     Orders
WHERE    Orderdate >= #6/1/2006# ;
```

Results

CutomerID	OrderDate
44453	6/9/2006
44453	6/9/2006
87535	6/9/2006
28764	6/27/2006

FIGURE 4.16

Multitable queries. Queries that use more than one table are slightly more complex. Because columns can have any name, you must tell the database system how the tables are connected. What are the names of the customers who placed orders since June 1, 2006?

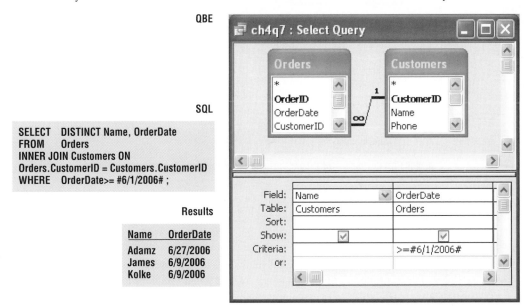

QBE

SQL

```
SELECT   DISTINCT Name, OrderDate
FROM     Orders
INNER JOIN Customers ON
Orders.CustomerID = Customers.CustomerID
WHERE    OrderDate>= #6/1/2006# ;
```

Results

Name	OrderDate
Adamz	6/27/2006
James	6/9/2006
Kolke	6/9/2006

ficult, but the command is easy when you join all three tables together. The query and the result are shown in Figure 4.17. Notice there is no entry for the salesperson (Zeke) who has no orders at this point.

One more example and you should be ready to work on problems by yourself. Say your firm is thinking about opening a new office in Miami, and your manager wants to know the total amount of orders placed from customers who live in Miami. This command uses the SUM function and is shown in Figure 4.18.

FIGURE 4.17

Mulitable queries with several joins: More complicated queries follow the same basic rules. Note that some database management systems can automatically switch displays between QBE and SQL. This feature is useful so that you can check the joins and the criteria to be sure they are being interpreted correctly: salespeople (sorted alphabetically) along with the names of customers who placed orders with that salesperson.

SQL

```
SELECT   DISTINCT Salespeople.Name,
         Customers.Name
FROM     Salespeople INNER JOIN (Customers INNER JOIN Orders ON
         Customers.CustomerID=Orders.CustomerID)
         ON Salespeople.SalespersonID = Orders.SalespersonID
ORDER BY Salespeople.Name ;
```

Results

SalesName	Cust.Name
Bird	Adamz
Bird	James
Bird	Kolke
Jabbar	Jones
Jabbar	Smitz
Johnson	James
Johnson	Jones
West	Kolke
West	Smitz

QBE

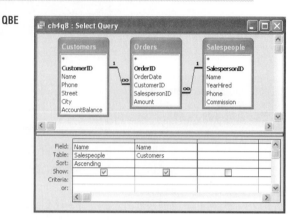

FIGURE 4.18

Computations and subsets: Totals and other computations can be entered on the QBE form. Be careful about the WHERE criteria. In this example, we want the condition to be applied to each data line, so we specify the WHERE label. Some systems might try to apply the condition to the overall total, which would use the SQL HAVING label. What is the total amount of orders placed from customers who live in Miami?

QBE

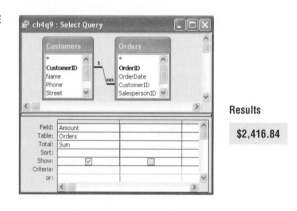

Results

$2,416.84

SQL

```
SELECT   SUM(Amount)
FROM     Orders
         INNER JOIN Customers ON Orders.CustomerID = Customers.CustomerID;
```

Views

There is one important feature of queries that you will find useful. Any query can be saved as a **view.** For example, if you have a complex query that you have to run every week, you (or a database specialist) could create the query and save it as a view with its own name. The important point is that the view can now be treated like any other table. In the example, you might define a view that combines the tables for customers, orders, and salespeople, and call it SalesOrders. Then, to get the total sales from customers in Miami, you run the query on the SalesOrders view and you no longer have to worry about joining tables because the query has already performed the step.

The advantage of views is that you can look at the data in different ways without having to duplicate the data. As a manager, you can create complex views so your employees can look up information using much simpler commands. Think of a view as a mirror. If you stand in front of a three-way mirror in a clothing store, you get different views of yourself although there is still only one person.

Designing a Database

How do you create a new database? Database management systems are powerful tools with the ability to present data in many ways. They are used by managers to answer many different types of questions. However, this flexibility is not automatic. Databases need to be carefully designed; otherwise, managers will not be able to get the information they need. Poor design also leads to unnecessary duplication of data. Duplication wastes space and requires workers to enter the same data several times. **Normalization** is an important technique to design databases.

To understand the process of normalization, consider a small example. You want to build a database for a small video rental store. You begin by thinking about who will be using the database and identifying what data they will need. Consider the situation of the checkout clerks. They first identify the customer, then record each movie to be rented. The computer should then calculate the amount of money due along with any taxes. Figure 4.19 shows a sample input screen that might be used.

The important point to note is that the data will have to be stored in more than one table. Each entity or object on the form will be represented by a separate table. For this example, there are four objects on the form: Customers, Videos, Rental, and VideosRented.

Before explaining how to derive the four tables from the form, there are some basic concepts you need to understand. First, remember that every table must have a primary key. A primary key is one or more columns that uniquely identify each row. For example, you anticipated problems with identifying customers, so each customer is assigned a unique ID number. Similarly, each video is given a unique ID number. Note that you might have more than one copy of each title, so you have also assigned a copy number to each video. There is one drawback to assigning numbers to customers: you cannot expect customers to remember their number, so you will need a method to look it up. One possibility is to give everyone an ID card imprinted with the number—perhaps printed with a bar code that can be scanned. However, you still need a method to deal with customers who forget their cards.

The second aspect to understand when designing databases is the relationships between various entities. First, observe that there are two sections to the form: (1) the main rental that identifies the transaction, the customer, and the date, and (2) a *repeating section* that lists the videos being rented. Each customer can rent several different videos at one time.

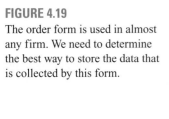

FIGURE 4.19

The order form is used in almost any firm. We need to determine the best way to store the data that is collected by this form.

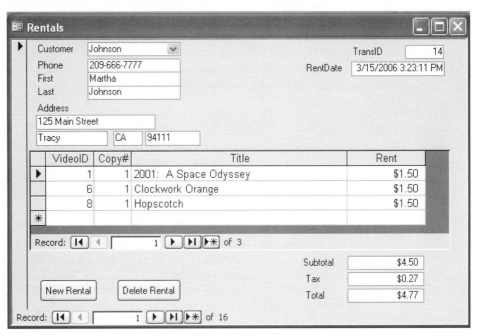

REALITY BYTES   Internationalization: Zip Codes

Databases often contain addresses (of customers, suppliers, employees, etc.) that typically use zip codes. In the United States, zip codes typically consist of five digits, so it is tempting to set up a Zip-Code column that restricts input to five integers. However, bulk mail is often cheaper if it uses nine-digit zip codes (zip + 4).

Even more important, if your addresses might someday include international data, you have to be more careful in column restric-tions. For instance, Canadian and British postal codes include al-phabetic characters in the middle of the code. Some areas (such as Hong Kong) do not use any postal codes.

Similarly, when you set up databases that include phone num-bers, be sure to allocate enough space for area codes. If interna-tional phone numbers will be listed, you need to add three extra digits on the front for the international country code.

FIGURE 4.20

Notation for tables: Table definitions can often be written in one or two lines. Each table has a name and a list of columns. The column (or columns) that makes up the primary key is underlined.

Customer (<u>CustomerID</u>, Phone, FirstName, LastName, Address, City, State, ZipCode)

CustomerID	Phone	LastName	FirstName	Address	City	State	ZipCode
1	209-666-7777	Johnson	Martha	125 Main Street	Tracy	CA	94111
2	209-888-6464	Smith	Jack	873 Elm Street	Merced	CA	94109
3	209-777-7575	Washington	Elroy	95 Easy Street	Lodi	CA	93111
4	209-333-9494	Adams	Samuel	746 Brown Drive	Sutter's Creek	CA	93998
5	209-474-4746	Rabitz	Victor	645 White Avenue	Ione	CA	92881
6	209-373-4746	Steinmetz	Susan	15 Speedway Drive	Jackson	CA	92115
7	209-888-4474	Lasater	Les	67 S. Ray Drive	Valley Springs	CA	92322
8	209-452-1162	Jones	Charlie	867 Lakeside Drive	Walnut Creek	CA	94102
9	209-222-4351	Chavez	Juan	673 Industry Blvd.	Lockeford	CA	93221
10	209-444-2512	Rojo	Maria	88 Main Street	Angels Camp	CA	95411

There is a *one-to-many* relationship between the Rental and the VideosRented sections. As you will see, identifying one-to-many relationships is crucial to proper database design.

In some respects, designing databases is straightforward: There are only three basic rules. However, database design is often interrelated with systems analysis. In most cases, you are attempting to understand the business at the same time the database is being de-signed. One common problem that arises is that it is not always easy to see which relation-ships are one-to-many and which are one-to-one or many-to-many.

Notation

It would be cumbersome to draw pictures of every table that you use, so you usually write table definitions in a standard notation. The base customer table is shown in Figure 4.20, both in notational form and with sample data.

Figure 4.21 illustrates another feature of the notation. You denote one-to-many or re-peating relationships by placing parentheses around them. Figure 4.21 represents all the data shown in the input screen from Figure 4.19. The description is created by starting at the top of the form and writing down each element that you encounter. If a section contains repeating data, place parentheses around it. Preliminary keys are identified at this step by underlining them. However, you might have to add or change them at later steps. Notice that CustomerID is marked with a dashed line to indicate that in the RentalForm, it is not the primary key, but it might be used as a key in another table. Because TransID is unique for every transaction, there is no need to make CustomerID a key. You can already see some problems with trying to store data in this format. Notice that the same customer name, phone, and address would have to be entered several times.

Remember that some repeating sections are difficult to spot and might consist of only one column. For example, how many phone numbers can a customer have? Should the Phone column be repeating? In the case of the video store, probably not, because you most likely want to keep only one number per customer. In other businesses, you might want to

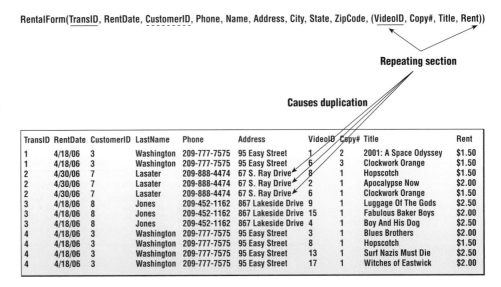

FIGURE 4.21

Converting to notation: The basic rental form can be written in notational form. Notice that repeating sections are indicated by the inner parentheses. If we actually try to store the data this way, notice the problem created by the repeating section: Each time a customer checks out a video, we have to reenter the phone and address.

RentalForm(TransID, RentDate, CustomerID, Phone, Name, Address, City, State, ZipCode, (VideoID, Copy#, Title, Rent))

Repeating section

Causes duplication

TransID	RentDate	CustomerID	LastName	Phone	Address	VideoID	Copy#	Title	Rent
1	4/18/06	3	Washington	209-777-7575	95 Easy Street	1	2	2001: A Space Odyssey	$1.50
1	4/18/06	3	Washington	209-777-7575	95 Easy Street	6	3	Clockwork Orange	$1.50
2	4/30/06	7	Lasater	209-888-4474	67 S. Ray Drive	8	1	Hopscotch	$1.50
2	4/30/06	7	Lasater	209-888-4474	67 S. Ray Drive	2	1	Apocalypse Now	$2.00
2	4/30/06	7	Lasater	209-888-4474	67 S. Ray Drive	6	1	Clockwork Orange	$1.50
3	4/18/06	8	Jones	209-452-1162	867 Lakeside Drive	9	1	Luggage Of The Gods	$2.50
3	4/18/06	8	Jones	209-452-1162	867 Lakeside Drive	15	1	Fabulous Baker Boys	$2.00
3	4/18/06	8	Jones	209-452-1162	867 Lakeside Drive	4	1	Boy And His Dog	$2.50
4	4/18/06	3	Washington	209-777-7575	95 Easy Street	3	1	Blues Brothers	$2.00
4	4/18/06	3	Washington	209-777-7575	95 Easy Street	8	1	Hopscotch	$1.50
4	4/18/06	3	Washington	209-777-7575	95 Easy Street	13	1	Surf Nazis Must Die	$2.50
4	4/18/06	3	Washington	209-777-7575	95 Easy Street	17	1	Witches of Eastwick	$2.00

FIGURE 4.22

A table that contains repeating sections is not in first normal form. If we try to store data in this form, we are faced with the question of deciding how many videos might be rented at one time. We will waste a lot of space with missing data.

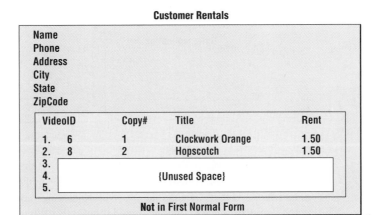

Customer Rentals

Name
Phone
Address
City
State
ZipCode

VideoID	Copy#	Title	Rent
1. 6	1	Clockwork Orange	1.50
2. 8	2	Hopscotch	1.50
3.			
4.	{Unused Space}		
5.			

Not in First Normal Form

keep several phone numbers for each client. Data normalization is directly related to the business processes. The tables you design depend on the way the business is organized.

First Normal Form

Now that you have a way of writing down the assumptions, it is relatively straightforward to separate the data into tables. The first step is to split out all repeating sections. Think about the problems that might arise if you try to keep the repeating VideosRented section with the customer data. If you design the database this way, you would have to know how many videos could be rented by each customer, because you would have to set aside space beforehand. If you do not choose enough space, you will have to throw out transaction data. If you set aside too much, there will be wasted space. Figure 4.22 illustrates the problem.

The answer to this problem is to pull out the repeating section and form a new table. Then, each movie rented by a customer will fill a new row. Rows do not have to be preallocated, so there is no wasted space. Figure 4.23 uses the notation to show how the table will split. Notice that whenever you split a table this way, you have to bring along the key from the prior section. Hence, the new table will include the TransID key as well as the VideoID key. When a table contains no repeating sections, you say that it is in *first normal form*.

Second Normal Form

Even if a table is in first normal form, there can be additional problems. Consider the RentalLine table in Figure 4.23. Notice there are two components to the key: TransID and VideoID. The nonkey items consist of the Copy#, Title, and the Rental rate for the movie.

FIGURE 4.23
Splitting a table to solve problems: Problems with repeating sections are resolved by moving the repeating section into a new table. Be sure to include the old key in the new table so that you can connect the tables back together.

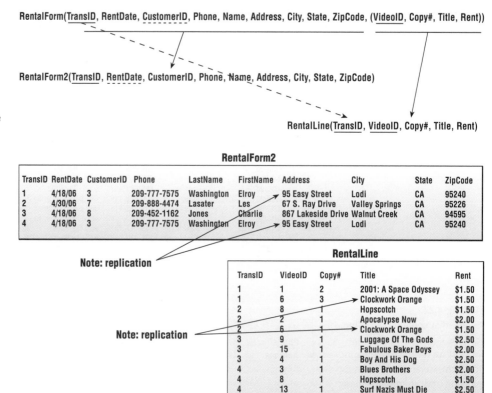

If you leave the table in this form, consider the situation of renting a movie. Every time a movie is rented (new TransID), it will be necessary to enter the VideoID, Copy#, *and* the title and rental rate. It means that you will be storing the video title every time a video is rented. Popular movies might be rented thousands of times. Do you really want to store the title each time?

The reason you have this problem is that when the TransID changes, the movie title stays the same. The movie title depends only on the VideoID. It is tempting to say that the same problem arises with respect to the rental rate. Indeed, in some video stores, the rental rate might depend only on the VideoID. However, what if the store offers discounts on certain dates, or to specific customers? If the rental rate can vary with each transaction, the rate would have to be stored with the TransID. The final choice depends on the business rules and assumptions. For now, assume that rental rates are like the title and depend only on the VideoID.

When the nonkey items depend on only part of the key, you need to split them into their own table. Figure 4.24 shows the new tables. When each nonkey column in a table depends on the entire key, the table is in *second normal form.*

Third Normal Form

Examine the RentalForm2 table in Figure 4.23. Notice that because the primary key consists of only one column (TransID), the table must already be in second normal form. However, a different problem arises here. Again, consider what happens when you begin to collect data. Each time a customer comes to the store and rents videos, there will be a new transaction. In each case, you would have to record the customer name, address, phone, city, state, and zip code. Each entry in the transaction table for a customer would duplicate this data. In addition to the wasted space, imagine the problems that arise when a customer changes a phone number. You might have to update it in hundreds of rows.

The problem in this case is that the customer data does not depend on the primary key (TransID) at all. Instead, it depends only on the CustomerID column. Again, the solution is to place this data into its own table. Figure 4.25 shows the split.

FIGURE 4.24

Second normal form: Even though the repeating sections are gone, we have another problem. Every time we enter the VideoID, we have to reenter the title. That would waste a lot of space. There is a more serious problem: If no one has rented a video yet, we have no way to find its title since it is not yet stored in the database. Again, the solution is to split the table. In second normal form, all nonkey columns depend on the whole key (not just part of it).

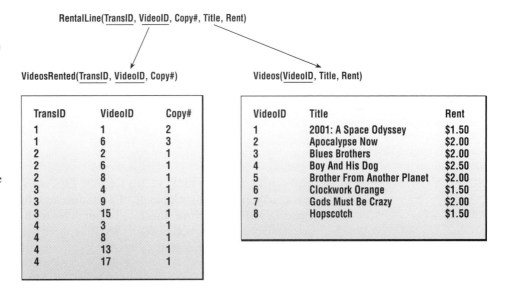

RentalLine(TransID, VideoID, Copy#, Title, Rent)

VideosRented(TransID, VideoID, Copy#)

Videos(VideoID, Title, Rent)

TransID	VideoID	Copy#
1	1	2
1	6	3
2	2	1
2	6	1
2	8	1
3	4	1
3	9	1
3	15	1
4	3	1
4	8	1
4	13	1
4	17	1

VideoID	Title	Rent
1	2001: A Space Odyssey	$1.50
2	Apocalypse Now	$2.00
3	Blues Brothers	$2.00
4	Boy And His Dog	$2.50
5	Brother From Another Planet	$2.00
6	Clockwork Orange	$1.50
7	Gods Must Be Crazy	$2.00
8	Hopscotch	$1.50

FIGURE 4.25

Third normal form: There is another problem with this definition. The customer name does not depend on the key (TransID) at all. Instead, it depends on the CustomerID. Because the name and address do not change for each different TransID, we need to put the customer data in a separate table. The Rentals table now contains only the CustomerID, which is used to link to the Customers table and collect the rest of the data.

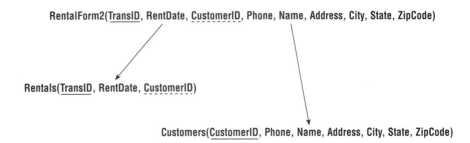

RentalForm2(TransID, RentDate, CustomerID, Phone, Name, Address, City, State, ZipCode)

Rentals(TransID, RentDate, CustomerID)

Customers(CustomerID, Phone, Name, Address, City, State, ZipCode)

Rentals

TransID	RentDate	CustomerID
1	4/18/06	3
2	4/30/06	7
3	4/18/06	8
4	4/18/06	3

Customers

CustomerID	Phone	LastName	FirstName	Address	City	State	ZipCode
1	209-666-7777	Johnson	Martha	125 Main Street	Tracy	CA	95304
2	209-888-6464	Smith	Jack	873 Elm Street	Merced	CA	95340
3	209-777-7575	Washington	Elroy	95 Easy Street	Lodi	CA	95240
4	209-333-9494	Adams	Samuel	746 Brown Drive	Sutters Creek	CA	95685
5	209-474-4746	Rabitz	Victor	645 White Avenue	Ione	CA	95640
6	209-373-4746	Steinmetz	Susan	15 Speedway Drive	Jackson	CA	95642
7	209-888-4474	Lasater	Les	67 S. Ray Drive	Valley Springs	CA	95226
8	209-452-1162	Jones	Charlie	867 Lakeside Drive	Walnut Creek	CA	94595
9	209-222-4351	Chavez	Juan	673 Industry Blvd.	Lockeford	CA	95238
10	209-444-2512	Rojo	Maria	88 Main Street	Angels Camp	CA	95221

Splitting the table solves the problem. Customer data is now stored only one time for each customer. It is referenced back to the Rentals table through the CustomerID.

The four tables you created are listed in Figure 4.26. Each table is now in *third normal form*. It is easy to remember the conditions required for third normal form. First: There are no repeating groups in the tables. Second and third: Each nonkey column depends on the whole key and nothing but the key.

Note in Figure 4.26 that you could technically split the Customers table one more time. Because zip codes are uniquely assigned by the post office, the city and state could be de-termined directly from the zip code (they do not depend on the CustomerID). In fact, most

FIGURE 4.26

Third normal form tables: There are no repeating sections and each nonkey column depends on the whole key and nothing but the key. This figure also shows the relationships between the tables that will be enforced by the DBMS. When referential integrity is properly defined, the DBMS will ensure that rentals can be made only to customers who are defined in the Customers table.

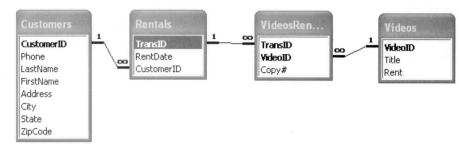

mail-order companies today keep a separate ZipCode table for that very reason. For our small video firm, it might be more of a nuisance to split the table. Although you can purchase a complete zip code directory in computer form, it is a very large database table. For small cases, it is often easier to leave the three items in the Customer table and use the database to assign default values so clerks can simply press ENTER and accept the common values.

Database Applications

How do you create business applications using a DBMS? Database systems typically have tools to help build applications. The tools make it relatively easy to create input forms and reports. Even if you never learn how to design a database, or become a programmer, you can learn to use these tools to build small applications and customized reports.

Data Input Forms

Rarely is data entered directly into the database's tables. Instead, input forms are used to enter some data automatically and to present a screen that is easier for users to understand. It is common to use colors and boxes to make the screen easier to read. Input screens can be used to perform calculations (such as taxes). Longer descriptions and help screens can be included to make it easier for the user to remember what goes in each column. A sample form is shown in Figure 4.27.

Many times, input screens look like existing paper forms. Consider a typical order form, which first collects customer information such as name and address. It also contains lines for items ordered, descriptions, and prices. These are usually followed by subtotals and totals. If these forms exist on paper, it is easy to create them as a DBMS input screen. If you are creating a completely new form, it helps to draw it on paper first to get a feel for what you want it to look like.

Most input forms begin as a screen that is empty except for a menu line or some other help message. Three types of information can be placed on an input screen: (1) simple text, (2) input blanks, or (3) data retrieved from the database. A Windows-based DBMS can also include pictures, graphs, sound, and video.

Paper forms have labels to tell the user what is supposed to be entered into each blank. For instance, many paper forms ask for a name: NAME ____. The label (NAME) tells you what you are supposed to enter on the blank line. A DBMS input form works much the same way. The first step is to type in the various labels. Move the cursor to a spot on the screen and type in a label or sentence that will tell the user what needs to be entered.

Most database systems automatically enter some types of data, such as the current date. If necessary, users can change the date, but it saves time by enabling them to press ENTER to accept the displayed value. The same situation holds for sequential items like order numbers, where the DBMS can automatically generate each unique order number.

After you have typed in the basic labels, the next step is to add the data-entry boxes. Just as you would type a blank line on a paper form, you need to tell the DBMS exactly what data will be entered by the user. For instance, move the screen cursor to a position next to the Date label, and then tell the DBMS to enter data at that point. You will specify the name

REALITY BYTES   How Much Data Do You Have?

Between 2001 and 2003, the size of the largest databases in the world more than doubled. The workload figures also increased dramatically. So, who has the most data? France Telecom's decision support database handles 29.2 terabytes of data. In terms of transaction processing, the UK's Land Registry holds 18.3 terabytes. The interesting aspect of the 2003 voluntary survey data is that the decision support databases are now larger than the transaction-processing systems. However, the Stanford Linear Accelerator Center (SLAC) wins top prize for total data—most of it held on tapes. The system handles 828 terabytes of data.

In terms of processing, the Bureau of Customs and Border Protection wins the top workload prize by processing 51,448 transactions per second. The system tracks hundreds of thousands of passengers and shipments a day. The Experian Marketing Services

database won the record for processing the 887 concurrent queries. The system uses an Oracle DBMS and Sun Fire servers.

Monster databases present several challenges. It is not simply a matter of increasing the storage space—the entire system has to be designed to handle the increased processing, searching, and sorting demands. Jose Amando-Blanco, production DBA for Verizon, discusses his 5.3 terabytes of transaction data in a Microsoft SQL Server database. "You want to double your data, but you need to keep the same performance that the customer representatives are used to. You need to be more proactive in finding out what the hot spots are on the database and which stored procedures are being called the most."

Source: Adapted from Matt Hicks, "Survey: Biggest Databases Approach 30 Terabytes," *eWeek,* November 8, 2003; and www.wintercorp.com.

FIGURE 4.27

DBMS input forms: Input forms are used to collect data from the user and perform basic computations. Subforms or scrolling regions are used when there is a one-to-many relationship.

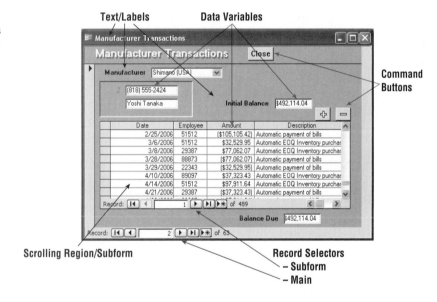

of the column where the data will be stored. You can also specify default values. A **default value** is a value that is automatically displayed by the computer. For the case of the date, the DBMS will let you enter a name like Date() that will display the current date.

When a DBMS prints out data, it can be formatted in different ways. You can control the way the data is displayed by using a format command. A date might be displayed as 10/24/2006 by entering the format MM/DD/YYYY. There are several common date formats; most firms tend to use one standard format. Note that many European firms use a format that is different from the common ones used in the United States.

The next section of the order form contains basic customer information. This data is stored in the Customer table, not the Orders table. When you select the Orders table, you might have to indicate that the Orders and Customer tables are connected to each other by the phone number. Now, place the text labels on the screen (customer name, address, etc.). Then place a data entry box after each label.

Next, you can add the Sales table; it is connected to the Orders table by the order number. Type in the column names for Item#, Description, Price, and Quantity. The DBMS input form will define this part of the table as a **scrolling region** or subform. To users, this subform will behave somewhat like a spreadsheet. They can see several rows at a time, and keys (or the mouse) will move the screen cursor up and down as users enter data into any row.

Technology Toolbox: Building Forms in Access

Problem: Every month you have to create a report that uses several new pieces of data. You have an assistant to help enter data, but need to create a system that is simple to use.

Tools: Most DBMSs have a forms builder tool to quickly generate forms. In Microsoft Access, the Form Wizard is easy to use, as long as the tables are defined correctly.

It is relatively easy to make forms to enter and edit data for a single row at a time. You can quickly build a form to edit data for a single customer. Start the Form Wizard, select the Customer table and all of its columns by moving them to the right-side column. Work through the remaining selections by choosing design options. If you do not like the result, you can always delete the form and start over. When the form is complete, use it to enter data for a couple of customers.

The Form Wizard can build more complex forms, such as the Sale form that includes data from the tables: Sale, Customer, SaleItem, and Item. You need to be cautious in choosing columns. Start the Form Wiz-

ard and choose all columns from the Sale table. Then choose most of the columns from the SaleItem table, but do not include the SaleID. The SaleItem table represents the repeating section. If you include the SaleID, it will waste space by displaying the same value on every row. Next, choose columns from the Customer table, but do not include the CustomerID. You should not include the CustomerID column from the Customer table, because you will not use this form to add new customers. Keep your forms relatively simple, so each form has a clear purpose. Finally, select any desired columns from the Item table (Description, Color, Price, and so on). Once again, do not include the ItemID column from the Item table, because you will not use this form to add items. Once the columns have been selected, follow the prompts to finish building the form.

To make the form easier to use, you will want to switch to Design View and rearrange the items on the form so they are grouped in a layout that is easier to read.

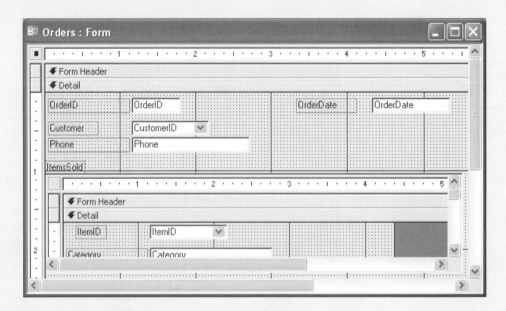

Look at some of the problems with the form. To enter a new sale, you will have to enter the CustomerID. Did you memorize all of the CustomerID values? Instead, delete the CustomerID text box. Select the Combo box in the Toolbox and click on the form where the CustomerID box used to sit. Follow the Wizard prompts to select the Customer table; choose at least the CustomerID and Name columns. On the last screen, make sure you mark the option to store the result in the CustomerID column. Test the result. This procedure displays all of the cus-

tomers in the drop-down box. When you select a customer, the corresponding CustomerID is transferred to the CustomerID column in the Customer table.

Quick Quiz:

1. Create a simple customer form and enter data to test it.
2. Create a basic order form and add a combo box to select customers.

The only items entered in the Sales table are the Item# and the Quantity ordered. The Description and Price can be found by creating a look-up in the Items table. If the clerk using this screen types in the item number, the description and price will appear. With a good DBMS, it is possible to define a pop-up form or combo box in case the clerk does not know the number. This way, by pressing a certain key, a table listing each Item# and Description will be displayed in a window on the screen. The clerk can then scroll through the list to find the item.

Reports

Most of the time, the data listed in one table is not complete enough to help managers make decisions. For example, a listing of a Sales table might provide only phone numbers, item numbers, and the quantity ordered. A more useful report would print sales grouped by customer. It would also compute total sales for each customer. Because this report relies on data from several tables, it is best to base the report on a view.

The view for the sales report example needs four tables. An OrderReport view is created that joins the Customer table to Orders by CustomerID, Orders to ItemSold by OrderID, and ItemsSold to Items by ItemID. The DBMS will have a "create report" option to create the sales report. The report will be based on the OrderReport view. The report writer consists of a blank screen. You can put simple text statements anywhere on the page. You also can place data values on the page, and you can compute totals and make other calculations.

Most reports can be broken into categories. For example, there might be report titles that appear only at the front of the report (such as cover pages). Other information—such as the report title, date, and column labels—will be repeated at the top of each page. All of these items are called **page headers.** Similarly, there can be **page footers** at the bottom of each page. Reports may also contain group **breaks.** For instance, the sales report needs subtotals for each customer, so you need to break the report into subsections for each customer. Generally, you can specify several levels of breaks. For instance, you might break each customer order into totals by date. Each break can have a *break header,* a **detail section,** and a *break footer.* In the example shown in Figure 4.27, the customer name is printed on the break header. There is a detail line that lists the item information. The subtotals are displayed on the break footers. The report design or layout is illustrated in Figure 4.28. The report with sample data is printed in Figure 4.29.

To create this report, you first tell the DBMS that the report will contain one break based on customer phone number. You also define the variable *extended,* which is price multiplied by quantity. Now you move the cursor to the top of the screen and type in the titles for the top of the page. Then place each column and variable on the report. You can format each item to make it look better. For example, you might want to format dates as MM/DD/YYYY so that all four digits of the year are displayed. Similarly, you can add dollar signs to the subtotals and totals.

When you have finished creating the report, you can print it. When you print this report, it should be sorted by customer name. The DBMS will also enable you to print the report so that it contains data just for one month. Notice that only five or six lines are needed to create a complex report. Without the DBMS report writer, it would take a programmer several hours to create this report, and it would be much harder to make changes to it in the future.

FIGURE 4.28

DBMS report writers: Reports are created in sections. The report header is printed one time at the top of the report. Data in the page header section is printed at the top of every page. There are corresponding page footers and report footer. Primary data is printed in the detail section. Data can be organized as groups by creating breaks. Titles are often printed in the break header with subtotals in the break footer.

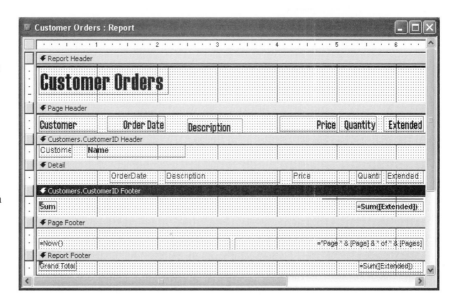

FIGURE 4.29
Sample report: Reports are often printed by groups or breaks with subtotals for each group. With a report writer, the layout, typefaces, and computations are easy to change.

Customer Orders

Customer		Order Date	Description	Price	Quantity	Extended
12345	Jones					
		3/3/2006	Corn Broom	$1.00	2	$2.00
		3/3/2006	Laundry Detergent	$2.00	4	$8.00
		3/3/2006	Paper Towels, 3 rolls	$1.00	1	$1.00
		4/9/2006	Laundry Detergent	$2.00	2	$4.00
		5/23/2006	Corn Broom	$1.00	1	$1.00
Sum						**$16.00**
28764	Adamz					
		6/27/2006	Blue Jeans	$12.00	1	$12.00
		6/27/2006	Paper Towels, 3 rolls	$1.00	3	$3.00
Sum						**$15.00**
29587	Smitz					
		5/6/2006	Candy Popcorn	$0.50	5	$2.50
		5/6/2006	Paper Towels, 3 rolls	$1.00	1	$1.00
		5/8/2006	Men's Boots	$15.00	1	$15.00
		5/8/2006	Paper Towels, 3 rolls	$1.00	4	$4.00
Sum						**$22.50**
44453	Kolke					
		5/1/2006	Blue Jeans	$12.00	1	$12.00
		6/9/2006	Blue Jeans	$12.00	1	$12.00
		6/9/2006	Candy Popcorn	$0.50	5	$2.50
		6/9/2006	Paper Towels, 3 rolls	$1.00	2	$2.00
Sum						**$28.50**
87535	James					
		4/4/2006	Corn Broom	$1.00	4	$4.00
		4/4/2006	Men's Boots	$15.00	3	$45.00
		6/9/2006	Blue Jeans	$12.00	1	$12.00
		6/9/2006	Laundry Detergent	$2.00	1	$2.00
Sum						**$63.00**
Grand Total						$145.00

Putting It Together with Menus

If you are creating a database for yourself with just a couple of input screens and reports, you can probably quit at this point. On the other hand, for more complex databases or for projects other people will use, it would be wise to make the system easier to use. *Application generators* are tools that enable you to combine the various features into a single application. The resulting application can be used by selecting choices from a menu, much like users do with commercial software. The important design feature is that you can create the entire application without writing any programming commands.

Consider a simple example. As a manager, you need a sales report printed every day that shows the best-selling items. Every week you want a list of total sales for each employee to bring to your sales meetings. You also send letters to your best customers every month offering them additional discounts. You want to put your secretary in charge of printing these reports, but you do not have time to explain all the details about how to use the database program. Instead, you create a simple menu that lists each report. The secretary chooses the

Problem: Your company has a large database that contains the information you need. However, you need to produce a relatively complex report every month based on data in that database.

Tools: A database Report Wizard can help you build reports with a visually oriented tool that makes it easy to create the layout and subtotals that you want.

If you need in-line computations, such as price * quantity, it is generally easiest to create a query that performs these simple calculations and selects the columns you will need on the report. Just create a query, test the data, and save it as a view. Then open the Report Wizard and select the saved view. Otherwise, you can select individual tables and choose the columns you want from each table.

The key to understanding reports is to use the groupings and levels correctly. First, identify the data that you want to see at the most detailed level. For example, you might want to see individual sale items. In creating the underlying query, make sure you select the tables and columns necessary to display the detail level you need. Sometimes, you will want to use subtotals in the query, but many times you will simply let the report writer create the totals—it all depends on what you want to see at the detail level. The next decision is to identify what groupings and levels you need. For instance, you might want to see a list of items ordered by each customer, so you set a grouping by customer. Alternatively, you might want to see a list of orders by each customer, so you set groupings for customer and then for order.

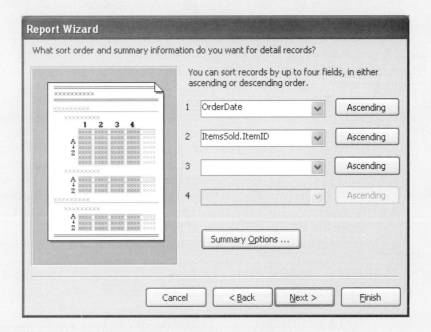

The Form Wizard contains an option to compute totals for the numeric columns. The button to select this option is easy to miss, so look carefully. Once the Wizard creates the design, you will still have to set properties to improve the format and layout of the report. You can also add new text boxes to compute other values. For example, to create a total, just place a text box in the desired footer and enter the formula =Sum(Value), using whatever column you want to total.

Creating reports is detail work. It takes time to get the layout and the format right. It takes a sense of design to make the report look good. Remember that the goal is to present the important information so that it can be found quickly.

Quick Quiz:

1. Create a report that prints all of the items ordered by each customer.

2. Create a report that prints each customer, followed by the orders for that customer.

3. Create a report that displays a chart of total sales by customer.

desired report from the list. Some reports might ask questions, such as which week to use. The secretary enters the answers and the report is printed.

The first step in creating an application is to think about the people who will use it. How do they do their jobs? How do the database inputs and reports fit into their job? The goal is to devise a menu system that reflects the way they work. Two examples of a first menu are shown in Figure 4.30. Which menu is easier for a clerk to understand? The one that best relates to the job. Once you understand the basic tasks, write down a set of related menus. Some menu options will call up other menus. Some will print reports; others will activate the input screens you created.

FIGURE 4.30

FIGURE 4.30
Designing menus for users:
Which menu is easier for a
secretary to understand? When
designing applications, you
should organize the application
to match the processes users
perform.

Main Menu	Customer Information
1. Set Up Choices	Daily Sales Reports
2. Data Input	Friday Sales Meeting
3. Print Reports	Monthly Customer Letters
4. Utilities	
5. Backups	Quit

Once you know how you want the menu structure to appear, you fill in the menu templates in the application generator. To create a menu, you type in a title and fill in the choices. Then you assign an action to each choice. Usually you just pick from a list of actions and type in specific data such as the name of the report and how you want it sorted. When you are finished, the application generator creates the application.

Database Administration

What tasks need to be performed to keep a database running? Managing a database can be a complex job. Often there are hundreds of choices that need to be made when the database is designed. Someone needs to be in charge of defining the data, making sure that all useful facts are captured, and managing security for this valuable asset. Databases have to be evaluated and fine-tuned on a regular basis. Someone has to keep track of these maintenance changes and decide when major updates should be installed. A **database administrator (DBA)** is usually appointed to manage the databases for the firm. The DBA needs to know the technical details of the DBMS and the computer system. The DBA also needs to understand the business operations of the firm.

The database administrator is responsible for all operations involving the database. These duties include coordinating users and designers, establishing standards, and defining the data characteristics. When new programs are created, the DBA makes sure they are tested and documented. The DBA also schedules backups and recovery, and establishes security controls.

In a few large companies, an additional person known as the *data administrator* (*DA*) is charged with overseeing all of the data definitions and data standards for the company. In this case, typically several DBAs are used to monitor and control various databases. The DA is responsible for making sure data can be shared throughout the company.

Standards and Documentation

In any company of moderate size, many different databases will be used by hundreds of workers. These databases were created at different points in time by teams of employees. If there are no standards, each piece will be unique, making it difficult to combine information from multiple databases or tables. The marketing department may refer to *customers,* whereas management calls them *clients.* The DBMS needs to know that both terms refer to the same set of data. Also, someone has to determine the key values for each table. Consider the Customer table. One department might assign identification numbers to each customer, another department might use customers' phone numbers, and a third department might use the customer names. To prevent confusion and to be able to combine information, it is best for all users to use only one of these methods to identify the customers.

Many standards are related to the database process. It is easier to use a database if all input screens have similar characteristics. For instance, the base screen might use a blue background with white characters. Data that is entered by the user will be displayed in yellow. Similarly, certain function keys may be predefined. ESC might be used to cancel or escape from choices. F1 might be used for help and F3 to display a list of choices. If each application uses keys differently, the user will have a hard time remembering which keys do what with which database.

A woman in County Cork, Ireland, gives birth to a baby. A few days later, she receives two letters from the Department of Health and Children informing her that her newborn baby has been issued a personal public service (PPS) number, and stating that benefit payments will be deposited directly into her bank account. As a result of the Civil Registration Modernization Program, the registration process has dropped from several months to a few days. Under the old system, every record had to be filed by hand at a local office. Anyone needing copies of a birth certificate had to go to the original office in person and wait in line while a clerk searched through paper files, a process spelled out in laws beginning in 1845. Vera Dervan, who led the modernization project, noted that with the old process, people sometimes had to give the same information to government agencies six different times.

With the assistance of Accenture, the Irish government built a new database of its birth, marriage, and death registrations. Over the course of three years, workers scanned 5 million documents going back to 1845, affecting 25 million people. All of them are recorded in an indexed online database. When someone applies for a passport, the passport office can look up documentation in the database—so people will not have to obtain paper copies of their birth certificates. Validating the integrity of the data has been a high priority for the project to ensure its continued value. The entire project was run by three people. In peak periods when the documents were scanned and validated, only 28 people were needed.

Source: Adapted from "Life Preserver," *The Wall Street Journal,* December 5, 2003.

Likewise, it is helpful to standardize certain aspects of reports. It might be necessary to choose specific typefaces and fonts. Titles could be in an 18-point Helvetica font, whereas the body of reports could be printed in 11-point Palatino. To provide emphasis, subtotals and totals could be printed in boldface, with single and double underlining, respectively.

One of the crucial steps in creating a database is the definition of the data. Many important decisions have to be made at this point. Besides the issues of what to call each item, the DBMS has to be told how to store every item. For instance, are phone numbers stored as 7 digits, or should they be stored as 10 digits, or perhaps stored with the 3-digit international calling code? Postal zip codes pose similar problems. The United States uses either a five-digit or nine-digit zip code, but is considering adding two more digits. Other countries include alphabetic characters in their codes. Someone has to determine how to store this information in the manner that is best for the company.

There are many other aspects of database design that need standards to make life easier for the users. However, whenever there are standards, there should be a mechanism to change these standards. Technology always changes, so standards that were established five years ago are probably not relevant today. The DBA constantly reviews and updates the standards, and makes sure that employees follow them.

Even though databases are easy to use, they would be confusing if the designers did not document their work. Picture a situation where you want to find information about customers but the designers named the table *Patrons.* You might never find the information without documentation.

Documentation can assume many forms. Most DBMSs allow the designers to add comments to each table and column. This internal documentation can often be searched by the users. Many times it can be printed in different formats so that it can be distributed to users in manuals. Because it is maintained in the database along with the data, it is easy to find. It is also easy for the designers to add these comments as they create or change the database, so the documentation is more likely to be current. It is up to the DBA to ensure that all designers document their work.

Testing, Backup, and Recovery

One advantage of the DBMS approach is that it provides tools such as report writers and application generators that end users can employ to create their own systems. Although it is easier for users to create these programs than to start from scratch, the programs still need to be tested. Corporate databases are extremely valuable, but only if the information they contain is accurate. It is the responsibility of the DBA to keep the information accurate, which means that all software that changes data must be tested.

Most companies would not survive long if a disaster destroyed their databases. For this reason, all databases need to be backed up on a regular basis. How often this backup occurs depends on the importance and value of the data. It is possible to back up data continuously. With two identical computer systems, a change made to one can be automatically written to the other. If a fire destroys one system, the other one can be used to continue with no loss of information. Obviously, it is expensive to maintain duplicate facilities. Many organizations choose to back up their data less frequently.

The main point of backup and recovery is that someone has to be placed in charge. Especially in small businesses, there is a tendency to assume that someone else is responsible for making backups. Also, remember that at least one current copy of the database must be stored in a different location. A major disaster could easily wipe out everything stored in the same building. There are some private companies that for a fee will hold your backup data in a secure, fireproof building where you can access your data any time of the day.

Access Controls

Another important task in database administration is the establishment of security safeguards. The DBA has to determine which data needs to be protected. Once basic security conditions are established, the DBA is responsible for monitoring database activity. The DBA tracks security violation attempts and monitors who is using the database. Because there are always changes in employees, removing access for departed employees and entering new access levels and passwords can be a full-time job.

Databases and E-Business

Why are databases so important in e-business? Many people still think of Web sites as simple pages of text with a few images. But e-business requires interaction with customers and the company data. Consequently, most e-business Web sites are connected to databases. In e-commerce, customers want to know if a product is in stock—this information is in the database. Similarly, customer, order, and shipping data have to be maintained and shared throughout the company. Other e-business sites use databases to provide services, store transaction data, and provide search and matching capabilities.

Designing an e-business database is no different than traditional business applications. However, the technologies for building Web-based applications are still evolving. Currently, two leading systems are being developed: Sun is championing a Java-based approach known as J2EE, and Microsoft is building the .NET platform. Databases are the heart of both systems, and both are server-based technologies designed to build interactive Web sites. Unfortunately, the two systems are completely independent and incompatible. If you build an application to run with one approach, you would have to completely rewrite it to use the other method.

Because the two approaches are so different, if you are building an e-business system, one of your first actions is to select one of these systems. In most cases, the J2EE approach runs on UNIX-based computers, but some versions exist for Microsoft-based systems. The Microsoft approach will probably only run on Microsoft servers, but some companies are experimenting with building versions that run on UNIX systems. Because the two systems are both new, it is difficult to evaluate them on technical grounds. The Microsoft approach offers a little more flexibility with its support for multiple languages. Microsoft .NET also provides a complete development environment with several easy-to-use tools that make it relatively easy for beginners to create database-oriented Web sites.

The basic approach is shown in Figure 4.31. Web developers create script pages that interact with the database. When customers request a page, the server executes the associated program script. The script sends queries to the database and retrieves the desired data. For

FIGURE 4.31

E-business database: When a customer requests a page, the server runs a script program that interacts with the database by sending queries and formatting the data to build a new Web page.

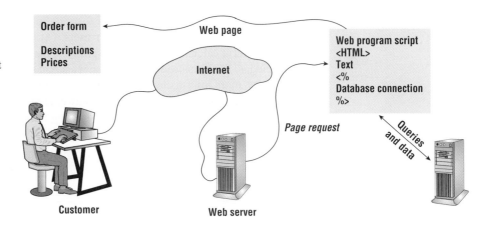

example, the script might retrieve product descriptions, prices, and in-stock status. The data and images are added to the Web page and sent to the customer, who sees only the simple results.

Generally, the database runs on a separate server—which reduces the load on the Web server and makes it easier to handle backups and other database maintenance chores. However, with increasingly powerful servers, one server can handle smaller applications.

Summary

Everyone needs to search for information. Computers make this job easier, but someone must set up and maintain the databases to ensure their integrity. There are many ways to search databases, and relational database management systems are a popular method. They are increasingly used as the foundation of the information system. They make it easy to share data among users while maintaining access controls. Equally important, the databases are easy to alter as the organization changes. Sophisticated databases can handle all the data types in use today, not just simple numbers and text.

A Manager's View

Every business has to store data. Every manager needs to do research. Sometimes you will have to summarize and evaluate transaction data. Sometimes you will use external databases to evaluate the industry and your competitors. Database management systems provide important capabilities to managers. One of the most useful is a query language, such as QBE or SQL, that enables you to answer questions without the need for hiring an MIS expert. A DBMS also speeds the development of new systems and provides basic features such as report writers and input forms.

It is relatively easy for users to obtain data using SQL or query-by-example tools. Because SQL is a recognized standard query language, it is worth remembering the basic elements of the SELECT command. The syntax is easy (SELECT columns, FROM tables, WHERE conditions, ORDER BY columns). Just remember that whenever you use more than one table, they must be joined by related columns.

An important step in databases is to design them correctly. The trick is to split the data into tables that refer to exactly one concept. Most organizations have a database administrator to help users create the initial database tables, define standards, establish access rights, and perform backups and testing. Once the tables have been defined, users can create input screens, reports, and views by using graphical tools to draw the desired items on the screen.

It is important to choose the right tool for each job. Databases excel at handling huge amounts of data and sharing it with other users. On the other hand, spreadsheets are designed to perform calculations and create graphs. One indication that a problem should be solved using a DBMS instead of a spreadsheet is that several tables of data are involved.

Every day, more information is stored in commercial databases. In many ways, they are becoming the libraries of the future. Almost any type of reference data you can imagine can be searched electronically. Just remember that you have to pay to access this data, so you have to design your search strategies carefully to save money.

Key Words

breaks, *145*
column, *123*
composite keys, *126*
data independence, *127*
database administrator (DBA), *148*
database management system (DBMS), *123*
default value, *143*

detail section, *145*
normalization, *137*
object-oriented, *124*
page footers, *145*
page headers, *145*
primary key, *126*
query by example (QBE), *129*
query system, *124*

relational model, *124*
report, *124*
row, *123*
scrolling region, *143*
SQL, *129*
table, *123*
view, *136*

Web Site References

Database References

Computerworld data management links	http://zones.computerworld.com/bmc
CIO data management	www.cio.com/research/data/index.html
eWeek Database	http:www.eweek.com/category2/ 0,1738,1237934,00.asp

Car Shopping Services

America's Automall	wws.automall.com
Autobytel	www.autobytel.com
Dealer Net	www.dealernet.com
Edmunds	www.edmunds.com
Kelley Blue Book	www.kbb.com
MSN	autos.msn.com
Vehix	www.vehix.com

Additional Readings

Disabatino, Jennifer. "NHL Scores with Database on Draft Day." *Computerworld,* July 9, 2001. [NHL uses a database to provide more information and cut hours off the time to draft players.]

Fox, Prim. "Tax Filing Gets Connected to the Web." *Computerworld,* August 8, 2001. [The importance of connecting databases to the Web even for governments.]

Mayer, Merry. "New DNA Database Extends the Long Arm of Law Enforcement." *Government Computer News,* October 19, 1998, p. 47. [Government database to identify criminals.]

Post, Gerald. *Database Management Systems: Designing and Building Applications.* New York: Irwin/McGraw-Hill, 2002. [How to design databases and use them to build business applications.]

Sliwa, Carol, Lee Copeland, and Don Tennant. "Dead Voters in Florida?" *Computerworld,* November 13, 2000. [Only 10 states have an online central voter registration database, and 16 have no state database at all.]

Tiboni, Frank. "FEMA Automates Property Inspection Scheduling." *Government Computer News,* November 9, 1998, p. 14. [Emergency agency uses telephone registration and database to help disaster victims in less time.]

Trombly, Maria. "Schwab Database Glitch Cuts Users Off from Some Information," *Computerworld,* February 13, 2001. [The importance of database availability and reliability.]

Review Questions

1. How is data stored in a relational database?
2. How does data independence make it easier to design and maintain computer applications?
3. What four questions do you need to answer in order to create a database query?
4. How do you join tables with QBE? With SQL?
5. How do you enter restrictions or constraints with QBE? With SQL?
6. How do you perform computations with QBE? With SQL?
7. Would you prefer to use QBE or SQL to access a database? Why?
8. What tasks are performed by a database administrator?
9. Why are forms (input screens) important in a relational database?
10. Do you think users can create their own reports with a DBMS report writer? What limitations does it have?
11. Why are standards important in a database environment?
12. Why is a DBMS important for e-business?

Exercises

CO4Ex15.mdb

It is best to answer the first 15 exercise questions using a DBMS, but if one is not available, you can use the tables in Figure 4.14 and write your queries by hand. If you have a DBMS that handles both QBE and SQL, you should do the exercise with both methods.

1. List the customers who live on Main Street (in any city).
2. List the customers who have an account balance between $200 and $600, sorted by account balance in descending order.
3. What is the total amount of money owed us by customers who live in Denver?
4. How many orders were placed in May?
5. What is the smallest order ever placed (in terms of dollar amount)?
6. Which salesperson sold the most expensive item in May?
7. What was the best day in terms of highest total value of orders?
8. Calculate the total commissions owed to salesperson West. (*Hint:* You need to compute the total of commission multiplied by order amount.)
9. Get the name and phone number of customers who bought blue jeans in June 2006.
10. Who is the best salesperson?
11. Which customer bought the most number of brooms?
12. Which salespeople placed orders in June?
13. In which city did the company sell the most brooms?
14. What is the lowest price item available for sale?
15. Who was the first customer (made the earliest purchase)?
16. A friend of yours has just opened a photofinishing operation. She wants you to create a database system to help her run the business. The basic processing is straightforward: A customer drops off or mails in one or more rolls of film. A clerk records the basic data on the customer and the film. The rolls are assigned a number, sorted, and run through the processor. Processing varies slightly depending on the type of film, film speed, and processing options. Your friend wants to keep track of which clerk performed the processing and match the names with any complaints that might arise. She also wants to offer a frequent-buyer program to reward the most active customers. It

is also important to track the chemical usage for the processing—both to keep track of orders and expenses, and to make sure the processors always have fresh chemicals. The clerks are also responsible for cleaning the processing equipment. Create a set of normalized tables for this company. Identify attributes where possible. (*Hint:* Obtain a film mailer that lists various options.)

17. You have been hired by an environmental consulting company (ECC) that specializes in creating environmental impact statements (EISs) for large projects. It needs a database to track the progress of each EIS. The company is particularly concerned about tracking public comments, questions from state and federal officials, and the responses to all of these comments. All comments are scanned and stored as digital files. Create a list of normalized tables needed to build this database.

EIS Project #: Date initiated: Date ECC involved: Date ECC finished:	Client Principal contact Phone Contact address City, State, ZIP	Phone Billing address City, State, ZIP
Site location: Latitude Site address: Site description	Longitude City	State ZIP
Proposed development description	Proposed activities (standard list) Drain wetlands Fill Build roads Store waste	

Comments and Responses						
Date Received	Category	Source	File	Response Date	Person	Title

Technology Toolbox

18. Create an input screen that enables a clerk to update information and add new customers to the database.

19. Using the tables in the chapter, create an order-entry input screen that can be used by a clerk who knows nothing about databases.

20. Create an inventory report that lists all of the products; group them by category; and, within each category, sort them by ID number.

21. Create the customer order report that is described in the chapter. (*Hint:* First create a view that joins the appropriate tables together.)

22. Create a start-up form that can be used as a menu. Begin in Design View and add buttons that open the other forms and reports. Use colors or images to enhance the appearance of the form.

Teamwork

23. Select a business. Each person should choose five entities (objects) that might be used as database tables. Identify primary keys for each table. Share your tables with the rest of the team and combine the results to one set of consistent tables.

24. As a team, identify features on a Web site that would indicate that it has a database behind it. Using this discussion, each person should find at least three Web sites that rely on a DBMS. Combine the results into a team report.

25. Assume that you need to buy a DBMS for a midsize company. Research the components needed and have each person find information and evaluate a DBMS package. Try to identify costs as well as strengths and weaknesses of the package. Share the individual results and create a report that makes a recommendation.

26. With the cooperation of a local small business, create a database for that company. Note that you should verify the initial layout of the tables with your instructor or someone who has studied database design. Assign specific forms and reports to individual team members and combine the pieces.

27. Each team member should write up three business questions related to either the C04Ex15.mdb or Rolling Thunder database. Exchange the questions with the other team members, and then create the queries to answer each question. Share your answers.

Rolling Thunder Database

Create queries to answer the following questions. (*Difficulty level: 1 = easiest.*)

28. List the customers who live in Colorado. *(2)*
29. How many employees does the firm have? *(2)*
30. List the bikes shipped to Oregon in December 2004. *(1)*
31. What is the most number of race bikes ever assembled (StartDate) in one day? *(3)*
32. Which employee has painted the most mountain bikes? *(3)*
33. What is the total estimated cost of components of all bikes ordered in October 2004? *(3)*
34. Which paint color was most popular on mountain bikes in 2003? *(3)*
35. List the phone numbers for all California customers who bought race bikes from Ochirbat in November 2004. *(2)*
36. What is the most expensive race bike built? *(2)*
37. What is the most popular crank installed on race bikes in 2005? *(3)*
38. Assuming that a race frame weighs two pounds, what is the total weight of the lightest race bicycle built in 2005? (*Note:* Component weights are in grams, so be sure to convert them.) *(4)*
39. How many mountain bikes, or full suspension mountain bikes, larger than 17 inches (FrameSize) were sold in Florida in 2003? *(2)*
40. What is the total salary cost? *(2)*
41. What is the average price Rolling Thunder Bicycles paid for Shimano XT derailleurs (rear)? *(4)*
42. On average, shipping costs are what percentage of the total order for merchandise purchased in August 2004? *(3)*
43. List the component items that had *no* sales in July 2005. *(5)*
44. On average, which costs more, tires for road bikes or tires for mountain bikes? *(3)*
45. Compute the sales by model type by month for all years. *(5)* (*Hints:* Use Crosstab and Format (date, "yyyy-mm").)
46. What percentage of sales came through retail stores in December 2001? *(4)* (*Hint:* Use two queries and compute the percentage with a calculator.)
47. List all of the retail bicycle stores in your state. *(2)*

Cases: Pharmaceuticals

The Industry

The pharmaceutical industry has received considerable attention in the past few years. Several organizations, including the AARP, have criticized the industry for price increases on name-brand drugs that exceed the inflation rate. The AARP reported that prices have increased by 6 to 7 percent a year in 2002 and 2003 (Kaufman and Brubaker 2004). Prescription drugs often form a significant percentage of household budgets for elderly retirees. Yet the pharmacy industry notes that identifying and testing a new drug is expensive. On average, it takes 10 to 15 years and costs $800 million to bring one new drug to the market. And only one in five potential drugs makes it through the entire process. The industry spent an estimated $33.2 billion on R&D in 2003 (PhRMA 2004). In the same report, the industry observes that 10.5 percent of total health care dollars in the United States are spent on prescription drugs.

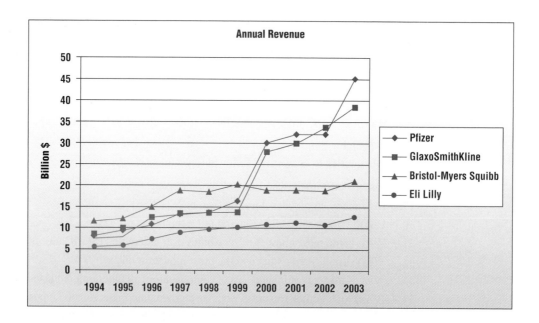

Drug Prices

The combination of high research costs, high risk, and the need to make a profit makes it difficult to set public policy. Profits encourage additional research and development to create new drugs. High prices keep the drugs out of the reach of some people who need them. Some governments have imposed price controls in an attempt to keep prices lower for patients. Canada presents an interesting example. Because trade with Canada is relatively unrestricted, U.S. patients have turned to Canadian pharmacies to fill their prescriptions. Even some state and local governments have tried to save costs by purchasing drugs from Canada, where the prices are held down by government rules (Schiavone 2003). Drug companies have staged an all-out battle to prevent the purchase of drugs from other countries. GlaxoSmithKline went as far as stopping sales to Canadian pharmacies (CNN 2003).

In 2004, the U.S. government introduced a Medicare insurance policy for purchasing name-brand prescription drugs. Participants have to sign up for the plan and pay a specified amount. The policies are sold by private companies, and the terms vary. Essentially, the policy covers a certain level of drug costs. However, with the copayments, limits on total value, and rising prices, it is not clear how many people will be able to benefit from the plan.

Research and Development

Research and development is a difficult process. Many times, luck and accidents play a role in creating new drugs. Yet companies need a huge infrastructure to take advantage of that luck. Research requires people and labs. Increasingly, it also needs information technology—in the form of databases, analytical tools, and collaboration software.

Finding a potential drug is only the first step (research). Development requires extensive testing, finding ways to de-

liver the drug with minimal side effects, and manufacturing it cheaply and consistently to narrow tolerances.

A pharmaceutical firm has to recover all costs within the life of a patented drug. Once the patent expires, the drug can be manufactured generically, and the inventing firm no longer makes any money. Since 2000, several of the leading firms have suffered substantial declines in revenue as their patents expired on several blockbuster drugs.

An interesting twist on pharmacy research arose in 2004. A couple of firms, particularly GlaxoSmithKline, were charged with withholding research data. All potential drugs have to go through clinical human trials to identify the specific gains and evaluate potential side effects. The drug companies provide the results of the studies to the Federal Drug Administration (FDA), which has to give final approval to the drug. In at least some cases, negative research was withheld. Many of the trials are somewhat secretive—neither patients nor physicians can be allowed to know which patients have the specific drugs. Consequently, it is relatively easy to bury negative results and only publish the positive ones. Of course, easy is not the same thing as ethical. As a result of substantial publicity in 2004, several agencies, companies, and people are pushing for a national registry of clinical trials—before they are started. This way, everyone can check on the progress—both good and bad (Martinez 2004).

Genetics is playing an increasing role in drug discovery and testing. Several specialist firms (e.g., Genentech) have been struggling for several years to use genetic modifications techniques to create completely new drugs. A few of the drugs have been successful, but the subsector has not yet matched its early promises.

Marketing

Pharmaceutical firms have substantially pushed the boundaries of drug marketing in the last decade. Originally, the firms relied on publications in medical journals to highlight the success of their drugs. Of course, sales representatives made direct calls to physicians to point out the results, offer comparisons with existing drugs, and answer basic questions. These activities are still important to the industry. However, the industry changed enormously when it began marketing drugs directly to consumers. The FDA has relatively strict rules about the contents of these ads, and it routinely monitors the ads and requires companies to alter the ads. Nonetheless, physicians are now bombarded with questions from patients about a new drug they saw on television. Of course, patients rarely read the fine print—telling about the side effects—and few can make comparisons among the various drugs. So, physicians have to spend time explaining their choices. The pharmaceutical industry points out that increased communication between doctor and patient is a good thing. But there remain many unresolved questions about the effectiveness of the campaigns—other than to boost pharmacy company profits.

Information Technology Needs

The pharmaceutical industry runs on data, information, and knowledge. The research departments generate and need to scan enormous amounts of data. They experiment and produce papers that disseminate knowledge. Researchers need to collaborate and share this data and knowledge. But the size of the companies, the variety of products, and the geographical dispersion all add complications. Additional data comes from physicians and even customers. On top of the research data, the marketers need to track salespeople, physician contacts, and marketing plans. The legal staff needs to monitor progress, evaluate patent documents, and shepherd thousands of documents through the FDA approval process. On top of all that, the CFO and CEO have to run the business—watching the financial data and creating the standard business reports.

Additional Reading

"GlaxoSmithKline Stops Selling Drugs to Canadian Pharmacies." *CNN Online,* January 21, 2003.

Kaufman, Marc, and Bill Brubaker. "Study: Drug Prices Outpace Inflation." *The Washington Post,* May 25, 2004.

Martinez, Barbara. "Spitzer Charges Glaxo Concealed Paxil Data." *The Wall Street Journal,* June 3, 2004.

Pharmaceutical Research and Manufacturers of America (PhRMA). *Pharmaceutical Industry Profile 2004.* Washington, DC: PhRMA (http://www.phrma.org/publications/publications/2004-03-31.937.pdf).

Schiavone, Louise. "Governments Eye Canada for Cheap Drugs," *CNN Online,* October 16, 2003.

Case: Eli Lilly and Company

Eli Lilly (ticker: LLY) is one of the leading pharmaceutical companies. Founded in 1876, the firm now has more than 46,000 employees (www.lilly.com). Like other pharmaceutical firms, Lilly is dependent on revenue from blockbuster drugs. When patent protection expires for a blockbuster drug, as it did for Lilly's Prozac in the early 2000s, revenue and profits drop. The challenge for companies is to fill the pipeline with new drugs that will provide a new revenue stream. Research and development are key elements in this process. But finding new blockbuster drugs that solve a major medical problem is not easy. Lilly, like the other firms, is turning to biotechnology to help create and test new drugs. Lilly's genetically engineered insulin has been one of the first successes in this new line of research. Lilly is also hoping to capitalize on the erectile dysfunction sales by heavily advertising its Cialis drug directly to consumers.

Research and Development

R&D is critical to generating profits. But R&D has become considerably more complicated. Research is no longer performed by one or two scientists working alone in a lab. Instead, Lilly has thousands of researchers working on various projects. Each of the compounds being created needs to be shared across the company. Collaboration has become a critical success factor. Throw in the fact that most of the large companies have expanded through mergers. Now, how do you combine the systems and the people to provide effective collaboration? Charles Cooney, codirector of the Program on the Pharmaceutical Industry at MIT, observes that "R&D is useless unless it can be integrated into a bigger picture that helps you convert leads to drug candidates. The difficulty for the CIO is getting the team to work between the various disciplines needed to integrate the information in order to create knowledge" (Overby 2002).

Genetics is an increasingly important factor in pharmacy, and it adds many complications. Lilly, as well as the other firms, is looking at a future where drug selection may be tailored to a patient's DNA. Some drugs are more effective when specific genes are present. This level of knowledge will require a tremendous amount of information flow—both in R&D and in marketing.

Information Technology

Information technology with its connections to customers provides a new way to evaluate drug effects. All drugs go through scientific trials where physicians carefully monitor patients and evaluate side effects. But testing on a few hundred or even a thousand subjects does not always provide complete information. Historically, drug firms have relied on physicians to evaluate and report on effectiveness and side effects. Lilly's drug Strattera was the first nonstimulant treatment for children with attention-deficit hyperactivity disorder. On the basis of early trials, the company knew that sleepiness could be a side effect. To evaluate the drug when it was released to customers, Lilly designed a customer relationship management system to track customer contacts through its call center. With the feedback from actual customer use, the company was able to identify that the sleepiness was minimized if the drug was taken at a meal and at night. Sidney Taurel, Lilly's CEO, notes that "we've seen that IT makes you more effective. It's a big shift. We've changed to seeing IT as an enabler of effectiveness" (Murphy 2004).

"Big shift" is right. When Lilly hired Tom Trainer as its first CIO in 1994, he found a mess—with 17 different IT organizations and minimal use of computers for business. By the time Trainer left in 1999 to head global IT for Citigroup, the technology had improved considerably. But IT was still largely used to reduce costs. CFO Charlie Golden says, "We had gone through quite a change in our perspective and strategy in IT. It was important to try to sort through what it would take to continue to change, but also to make IT a more integral part of our strategy" (Ewalt 2003). Roy Dunbar was chosen as the new CIO. He began as a pharmacist, had some business experience, but little experience with information technology. With some intense education, and a lot of humility, Dunbar learned the foundations of information systems. His ultimate charge was to find ways to use technology to support the strategy of the firm. For that, he needed everyone to start with a business perspective. One of the key tools his team created in 2000 was the Molecule Library. It is a knowledge management system that makes it easy for researchers to find information about chemical compounds being worked with in the company's pipeline. The system reduces research time from days to minutes. Another new tool, the Sample Identification Database, functions as a registry of all compounds being developed. The Gene Anatomy Made Easy (Game) project helps scientists identify DNA analysis without requiring expert help. Shaving a few hours a week off the research time of every scientist can help get projects to market earlier, saving billions of dollars in costs (Ewalt 2003).

In 2001, the IT department began expanding its use of SAP (its enterprise resource planning system) to improve connections to suppliers and customers. Combining the company's shipping, billing, and sales data makes it easier to track sales and keep on top of billing problems. The company also implemented a sales management system to provide better information to salespeople.

Coming from the pharmacy side of the business, Dunbar knew that it was critical for the scientists to not only understand the value of the technology but also define and shape it to make it useful. He notes that "even as the projects move into production, it's senior-level scientists who are championing the new tools and evangelizing about their benefits" (Overby 2002). To improve communication between the IT staff and scientists, the IT development teams hold meetings at least once every two weeks between the two groups. Moreover, Dunbar doubled his IT department staff to 2,700 people, with an emphasis on hiring people with dual computer science and biology or chemistry degrees. In 2003, Mike Heim was appointed as the new CIO. Mike began his career at Lilly as a systems analyst in 1979.

Marketing

Developing a new drug is only the first step to making a profit. Companies also have to convince physicians to prescribe the drugs. With competition, and a huge array of new drugs, physicians need to evaluate the benefits and side effects. In the past, drug companies had sales representatives call on physicians. But Brian Weed, global marketing and sales IT directory for Lilly, points out that "doctor's offices are closing their doors to pharmaceuticals sales representatives and citing HIPAA and privacy concerns as reasons" (Greenemeier 2003).

Sales force management and customer relationship management software are becoming more important at the pharmaceutical firms. Salespeople need to tell a consistent story to physicians. In terms of patients, Lilly is encouraging customers to contact the drug firm directly, instead of first going to their physician (Greenemeier 2003). The direct contacts can be beneficial in building brand awareness. As Lilly learned with Strattera, the call centers can provide more immediate feedback on actual usage and side effects. Ultimately, the process might require tighter links between the patients, physicians, and pharmaceutical firms, but those are not yet on the drawing boards.

Questions

1. How does Eli Lilly use databases to improve efficiency?
2. What types of data does Lilly store in its databases?
3. How could Eli Lilly use additional information technology in marketing?

Additional Reading

Ewalt, David M. "Roy Dunbar." *Information Week,* December 15, 2003.

Greenemeier, Larry. "Pharmaceutical Makers Turn to CRM." *Information Week,* October 29, 2003.

Murphy, Chris. "Answers That Matter." *Information Week,* February 2, 2004.

Overby, Stephanie. "They Want a New Drug." *CIO,* October 15, 2002.

www.EliLilly.com/about/highlights.html

Case: GlaxoSmithKline

GlaxoSmithKline (ticker: GSK) is one of the leading global pharmaceutical firms. Created through the merger of several firms over the past decade, it is headquartered in England and has over 100,000 employees worldwide. Like the other large pharmaceutical firms, GlaxoSmithKline (GSK) is suffering from the transition of its blockbuster drugs to generic status.

It could easily lose $3 billion to $4 billion in revenue from its antidepressants Wellbutrin and Paxil and the antibiotic Augmentin ("Business: Glaxo" 2004). Because the company is headquartered in England, but almost half of its sales are in the United States, profits have suffered from the 35 percent depreciation of the dollar in 2003–2004. Nonetheless, CEO Jean-Pierre Garnier is optimistic. Through the mergers, he was able to trim $6 billion in costs. He has rearranged the research teams into divisions focused on specific areas (cancer, AIDs, and so on). More important, the company has 80 new products in the pipeline and half have reached advanced stage clinical trials ("Business: Glaxo" 2004).

GSK faces other issues. In 2004, the New York attorney general, Eliot Spitzer, filed suit against GSK for concealing negative data about Paxil. Spitzer contends that of all the studies Glaxo performed, only one generated the results they wanted to promote the drug. "Their effort to suppress the other studies was harmful and improper to the doctors who were making prescribing decisions and it violated the law" (Martinez 2004). The primary concern is that Paxil might lead to suicidal behavior if used in children under 18 years of age. Glaxo notes that Paxil was never approved for use by children in the United States and was not promoted that way. Glaxo spokesperson Mary Anne Rhyne notes that "there are many, many studies each year. It's impractical to believe that every company in the industry will be able to publish from every study" (Martinez 2004). But Glaxo's problems are compounded by a couple of internal memos. One noted that the company would have to "effectively manage the dissemination of these data in order to minimize any potential negative commercial impact." Another stated that "it would be commercially unacceptable to include a statement that efficacy had not been demonstrated" (Martinez 2004).

In response to these problems, several organizations have called for a clinical trial registry to track the progress of all trials and outcomes. The leading pharmaceutical companies are also backing the registry. However, the process is not that simple. Many of the Phase 1 trials are designed to test for side effects and do not focus on efficacy. So, some drugs might not appear to be useful. Some companies have noted that the National Institute of Health already maintains an online registry (www.clinicaltrials.gov), and it could be expanded to include results from all Phase III trials (Hovey 2004).

Information Technology in Research

In one sense, pharmaceutical R&D is similar to a university. Sharing knowledge within the organization is a key factor. The company generates and acquires information in the form of documents—some electronic, some in paper. GSK built a centralized library system (Lynx) to give researchers imme-

diate access to the documents. The system provides access to over 2,000 electronic journals. Requests for paper books or articles are handled by librarians, who first try to locate the appropriate title within one of the company's nine libraries. If it is not available, they check with their outside suppliers. Of course, the company would prefer to digitize all paper documents, making it simpler to deliver the information, plus make it available to other users later. However, copyright limits the number of documents that can be digitized and prevents the company from disseminating them (Delaney 2003).

Genetics, particularly individual differences among patients, is one of the big target areas for pharmaceutical firms. Glaxo has forged a relationship with First Genetic Trust to study how variations in individual DNA can affect the efficacy and side effects of various drugs. Glaxo even built a proprietary high-speed network to communicate with First Genetic Trust. The company uses data mining and huge databases to compare drug effects across individuals. The main system runs on several HP 16L-Series 9000 UNIX servers. The company uses commercial applications to enable patients to provide informed consent and specify how their genetic data can be used. In general, only the genetic data without personal patient identifiers is given to Glaxo researchers (Greenemeier 2002).

Questions

1. How does information technology help Glaxo in its research?

2. Would a national database of clinical trials prevent the problems that Glaxo had with approval of its Paxil drug?

3. Assuming that new drugs are developed that are tailored to specific DNA markers, how would you build an information system to take advantage of this data? How will you handle the privacy issues?

Additional Reading

"Business: Glaxo's Big Challenge." *The Economist,* May 15, 2004.

Delaney, Emma L. "Glaxosmithkline Pharmaceuticals Research and Development." *Interlending & Document Supply,* Vol. 31(1), 2003.

Greenemeier, Larry. "Genetic Research Drives High-End Computing." *Information Week,* February 18, 2002.

Hovey, Hollister H. "J&J Adds Its Support for Idea of Clinical Trial Registry." *The Wall Street Journal,* June 18, 2004.

Martinez, Barbara. "Spitzer Charges Glaxo Concealed Paxil Data." *The Wall Street Journal,* June 3, 2004.

Case: Bristol-Myers Squibb

Bristol-Myers Squibb (ticker: BMY) has headquarters in New York City and employs about 44,000 people worldwide.

One of the company's recent innovations was the development of TAXOL to treat breast cancer. The company was able to create a synthetic compound that duplicated the original drug derived from the bark of the Pacific Yew (an endangered tree). In 2004, Bristol-Myers Squibb was approved to market the genetically created drug Erbitux in conjunction with Im-Clone Systems. You might remember the drug as the one that led Martha Stewart to be found guilty of lying to SEC investigators. Bristol-Myers Squibb also sells many consumer-level products (www.bristolmyers.com).

Research Data

Laboratory equipment today is generally automated. Often, it can be controlled by computers and most machines generate data that can be collected by computers. The catch is that machines can generate enormous amounts of data. BMY was having trouble keeping up with the amount of data generated. The BioAnalytical Sciences (BAS) group turned to the Scientific Data Management System (SDMS) developed by Nu-Genesis Technologies Corporation. The system collects all incoming data and reports and archives them to a central repository—which frees up the hard drives on the local workstations. The data and reports are then available to other researchers from a secure Web site. The system also provides access to the binary data, which is needed for compliance with federal laws. The system enables researchers to tag the raw data by researcher, project, analytical method, and so on. It collects data from diverse systems and makes the data accessible via a common interface. The BAS group connects to over 100 instruments in two sites in New York and New Jersey. The central server also backs up two main servers. Because the system consolidates historical data, it makes it easy for researchers to compare current results to older analyses. Data is stored in a secure Oracle database and marked with time-stamp and audit trail data so everything can be tracked. In a six-month pilot test, the system generated 5,000 reports. The system automates most data management tasks, freeing up time by researchers and IT administrators. More important, it enables greater collaboration because the data and reports are accessible throughout the company, regardless of the geographic location or software installed on a specific machine (DeVincentis 2002).

Knowledge is critical to pharmaceutical researchers. And knowledge is vastly more complex than simple data. How can a researcher in one location quickly find an expert in another division of the company? How does the research in one area compare to that by another department? Bristol-Myers Squibb purchased tools from LexiQuest to help solve these types of problems. LexiQuest is a linguistic search specialist, providing the ability to search based on information instead of just key words. LexiQuest Guide uses language-recogni-

tion technology to search documents based on everyday language. It semantically analyzes each document to evaluate its content. The two companies are also building a custom dictionary and search system to handle the specific terms used in pharmaceutical research (Jezzard 2001). In essence, the system reads the documents, enabling it to provide a more precise match to researcher requests. By providing more accurate and faster responses, researchers can save considerable time. And time is critical when you need to bring a new drug to the market.

Business Operations

Pharmaceutical firms are pressured by expiring patents, government attempts to reduce drug costs, and increased competition. Like any business, they are turning to information technology to reduce costs and improve the business operations. Bristol-Myers Squibb is turning to the Web for its purchasing needs. It acquired Ariba's Buyer e-procurement software in 2000, saving over $90 million a year within the first year. The system standardizes purchasing methods. Employees who need to buy something, such as a PC, check the suppliers and options on the Web site. Then a request for quote (RFQ) is posted on the Ariba network and suppliers bid for the contract. Employees can also use the system to purchase smaller items directly. The system aggregates the purchases where possible and orders in bulk. In 2001, as much as 16 percent of sales orders were conducted over the system (Yasin 2001).

Questions

1. Can machines replace lab workers and scientists in conducting experiments and evaluating data? What problems might arise and how would you minimize the risks?

2. How does Bristol-Myers use information technology to reduce costs—particularly in purchasing?

3. Why is a central research database system so important to Bristol-Myers?

Additional Reading

DeVincentis, John, "Performance, Speed Improve with Scalable SDMS." *R&D,* October 2002.

Jezzard, Helen. "LexiQuest Aids Drug Co." *Information World Review,* December 2001.

www.bms.com/aboutbms/content/data/ourhis.html

Yasin, Rutrell. "E-Procurement Is Drug for Bristol-Myers Squibb." *InternetWeek,* June 11, 2001.

Case: Pfizer

With over $45 billion in sales, Pfizer (ticker: PFE) is the largest of the pharmaceutical firms (www.pfizer.com). As a research organization, the company has produced some well-

known brands, including prescription drugs such as Celebrex, Diflucan, Lipitor, and Viagra. It also has a big presence in the consumer market with Benadryl, e.p.t., Listerine,

Neosporin, and Rolaids, among others. The company has seven blockbuster drugs each generating over $1 billion a year in sales. It has 130 potential drugs in the pipeline (Overby 2002).

The company faces many of the same problems as the other pharmaceutical companies. One of the biggest issues is how to integrate data and knowledge across the company—particularly when growth came through mergers.

Walter Hauck, vice president of worldwide informatics at Pfizer, knew he faced a huge problem in trying to integrate the many research departments. He needed to create tools that would support collaboration not only among the scientists but also among the lawyers and marketers who bring the drugs to market. He began with an ambitious task: integrate all of the changes at once. At La Jolla Labs in California, his IT team introduced one new application a week for six months. The scientists almost rebelled, saying that the sheer number of changes was taking away time from their research. Hauck heard similar complaints from many other divisions: "It was a lot of change to drop on people while expecting them to continue to deliver" (Overby 2002). With little control over introducing new tools, some employees were asked to sit through training sessions on the same product multiple times. Hauck knew it was time to implement a change management strategy. One of the keys was to standardize the process by creating a checklist, making sure that the business units needed the changes and understood the value. The lists also ensured that the developers captured the feedback and evaluated the pilot tests accurately.

Pfizer also tried to help employees by creating a new application to enter expense reports. But the new system was harder to use than paper forms, help calls increased, and many people stopped using it. Joseph C. Schmadel Jr., senior director of business technology, observed that "that was an indication to us that something was wrong." To solve the problem, Pfizer brought in netNumina, Inc., a consulting firm, to rethink the user interface. By rebuilding the user screens and linking them to the back-end reporting system, the system became easier to use and still collected the necessary data. The system also creates a digital dashboard that provides summary statistics for executives (Weiss 2004).

Integrating data is critical to a company as large as Pfizer. The company had 14 different financial systems and wanted to combine the data into a data warehouse. The IT group built a data warehouse as a central repository, and then built links to each of the individual systems. But the IT department quickly encountered a problem. Each of the systems had different definitions for the data. It took months to clean up the data so that it could be combined and managed as a single source. Danny Siegel, senior manager of business technology, says, "We saw that we had to put in place some rigorous data standards. This kicked off a six-month, totally non-technical effort to devise a set of standards that allow users to slice and dice data in whatever context they need it" (King 2003).

Because Pfizer has acquired or partnered with many companies since the introduction of computerized database management, the company has a staggering amount of legacy data. The difficulty is "to get the data into a shape where it can be easily accessed by researchers that span the globe and be nimble enough to be able to accept new data and new systems as more companies come in via mergers and acquisitions. In addition, they need to convince scientists that what they have is not just an archive of past experiments but also a rich resource of information for future drugs" (Derra 2004).

Pfizer, like many other pharmaceutical companies, is pushing to become more efficient in drug discovery, and is looking to its legacy data as a source of useful information and insights into new drug development. But the sheer number of legacy systems within even one research facility is overwhelming. Bhooshan Kelkar, PhD, advisory software engineer at IBM Life Sciences, Dallas, says that the comments of a colleague speak to the enormity of the issue. "He was working with a big pharmaceutical company last year and reported that they had 500 legacy applications just in their discovery and clinical area. . . . It was costing them 50% of their IT budget every year, just in maintenance and reconciliation of different legacy systems. That is huge." The key to unlock the power of mining legacy systems will be a combination of robust systems, standard methods, consistent data, and cultural change from within the drug discovery environment (Derra 2004). While the task is daunting, it is essential to new drug development to effectively catalog all the known compounds within Pfizer's extensive library in order to rapidly develop new pharmaceuticals or delivery methods. Transferring all of the corporation's legacy data to a common format is the best possible way for researchers to have quick access to important older data.

This same need for a universal data standard for collecting, sorting, and processing clinical trial data for FDA submission is currently occupying the entire pharmaceuticals industry. But the data-collection standards have been slow to catch on. However, in June 2004, a consortium of American pharmaceutical companies debuted a data-interchange standard for electronically submitting drug-approval applications to the U.S. Food and Drug Administration. This could speed the entire drug-review process, reducing the time between submission and FDA approval. The major pharmaceutical companies—including Eli Lilly, Merck, Aventis, and Pfizer—are the sponsors of the move, under the heading of the Clinical Data Interchange Standards Consortium (CDISC). Among the standards are a universal file structure and submission form, both within XML programming. CDISC previously developed standards for collecting lab data and clinical-trial data such as patient information. Those are designed to simplify the collection of clinical-trial data by pharmaceutical companies and the contract research organizations—such as Quintiles Inc.—that drug makers hire to manage clinical trials (Whiting 2004). The FDA will not require CDISC standards for drug-approval applications, but it has endorsed CDISC's efforts.

Questions

1. Why did Hauck introduce so many new applications at one time? Why was it such a failure? Could you have predicted that outcome?

2. Why does Pfizer have so many different research systems and why is it so difficult to integrate them? What information technology tools might help?

3. How did Pfizer manage to have so many different financial systems?

Additional Reading

Derra, Skip. "Legacy Systems: More Than Old Data in the Attic." *Drug Discovery and Development,* May 1, 2004.

King, Julia. "Business Intelligence: One Version of the Truth." *Computerworld,* December 22, 2003.

Overby, Stephanie. "They Want a New Drug." *CIO,* October 15, 2002.

Weiss, Todd. "Pfizer Case Study: Hiding Complex Apps behind User-Friendly Interfaces." *Computerworld,* March 9, 2004.

Whiting, Rick. "Standards May Speed Approval of New Drugs." *Information Week,* June 14, 2004.

Summary Industry Questions

1. What information technologies have helped this industry?

2. Did the technologies provide a competitive advantage or were they quickly adopted by rivals?

3. Which technologies could this industry use that were developed in other sectors?

4. Is the level of competition increasing or decreasing in this industry? Is it dominated by a few firms, or are they fairly balanced?

5. What problems have been created from the use of information technology and how did the firms solve the problems?

PART TWO

Operations

5 COMPUTER SECURITY

6 TRANSACTIONS AND OPERATIONS

7 ENTERPRISE INTEGRATION

8 ELECTRONIC BUSINESS

How are information systems used to handle common business operations?

How do you protect data? How do you process transactions and what problems will arise? How do you integrate data across the organization and with suppliers and customers? How can the Internet be used to improve businesses?

Protecting computers and data today is no longer the job of just some arcane security director. Because of the network-based threats, it is everyone's responsibility to be aware of potential problems and maintain good computing habits.

A hundred years ago, few large businesses existed. As firms became larger, owners needed a way to manage and control the huge number of employees. Managers needed assistance with hundreds of daily operational decisions. Information technology provides the means to both share and protect data. It is relied on today to collect transaction data.

Firms, even large ones, are increasingly creating enterprise systems that store financial and transaction data in a common central format—making it available to managers throughout the company.

The Internet offers new ways to extend companies into relationships with suppliers and customers. As a manager, you need to use information technology to reduce costs, create new sales opportunities, and organize the company.

CHAPTER FIVE

Computer Security

Chapter Outline

Introduction
Threats to Information
    Disasters
    Employees and Consultants
    Business Partnerships
    Outsiders
    Viruses
    Spyware
Computer Security Controls
    Manual and Electronic Information
    Data Backup
    User Identification
    Access Control
    Single Sign-On and Lack of Standards
Additional Security Measures
    Audits
    Physical Access
    Monitoring
    Hiring and Employee Evaluation
Encryption
    Single Key
    Public Key Infrastructure
Computer Forensics
e-Commerce Security Issues
    Data Transmission
    Spoofing Sites
    Wireless Networks
    Carnivore, Echelon, and Escrow Keys
    Theft of Data from Servers
    Denial of Service
    Firewalls and Intrusion Detection
Privacy
Summary
Key Words
Web Site References
Additional Reading
Review Questions
Exercises
Cases: Professional Sports

What You Will Learn in This Chapter

- How do you protect your information resources?
- What are the primary threats to an information system?
- What primary options are used to provide computer security?
- What non-computer-based tools can be used to provide additional security?
- How do you protect data when unknown people might be able to find it or intercept it? What additional benefits can be provided by encryption?
- How do you prove the allegations in a computer crime?
- What special security problems arise in e-commerce?
- If you have to track everyone's computer use to improve security, what happens to privacy?

How do you keep data secure? Any professional football team has dozens of coaches and players—whether it is American football or European soccer, the characteristics are similar. Teams win through cooperation—that means everyone needs to share information. Coaches create playbooks, players provide feedback, and scouts identify weaknesses in opposing teams. All of this information has to be shared—so teams increasingly put the data onto computers. But securing this data is critical. Imagine the problems that arise if an opposing team gets a copy of the latest player health reports and new plays. Yet there are dozens of players and coaches, most of whom are not computer experts (to put it politely, since you really do not want to insult a 300-pound linebacker). Plus, coaches and players are sometimes replaced or switch teams.

Teams increasingly have to offer more data to fans. Some stadiums are now offering wireless networks. But security again becomes critical. How do you keep the fans from accidentally interfering with the coaching networks? What other threats can you think of? Hundreds of things can go wrong with technology, and someone has to be responsible for protecting the systems and creating contingency plans to handle problems.

Introduction

How do you protect your information resources? What are the major threats? Figure 5.1 presents some of the issues: outside hackers, people intercepting data, attacks on the server, physical threats to the equipment (including natural disasters such as fire), and internal threats from employees, as well as privacy issues such as abuse of personal data. Who stole more money in 2003 (or almost any other year): teenage hackers or CEOs? Computer security has to prepare for both of these threats and others.

There is little doubt that business use of computers is increasing—to the point where e-commerce businesses require all of the components to be functioning 24 hours a day. In this environment managers need to know what threats they face and what technologies exist to protect the systems.

Because of the complexity and size of the systems, computer security is difficult. Advances in encryption and biometrics have provided powerful tools. But, ultimately, security comes down to people. If a worker is careless with passwords, or a programmer makes a mistake, or a network engineer falls behind on updates, or an auditor fails to test an account, holes are created that can be exploited by a thief or miscreant.

On the other hand, organizations can go overboard with security rules. If you have a document that you wish to prevent anyone else from seeing, it is possible to absolutely guarantee that no one can read it: simply burn it and scatter the ashes. Of course, you will not be able to read it anymore either. The point is that computer security is a balance—you must protect the data but still enable workers to do their jobs.

Encryption plays an important role in protecting systems. It can also be used to authenticate the sender of a message. A key aspect of security and encryption is the need to identify users. Consequently, the flip side of many security policies is the loss of privacy.

As more business data and more of our consumer lives go online, computer security and privacy become even more important to everyone. Hundreds of horror stories are created every year as unscrupulous people find new ways to steal or destroy data. To learn to protect computer data, you must first understand the threats. Encryption plays several important roles in protecting data and in identifying users. However, the newer systems require that people trust the companies creating the security systems.

TRENDS

Security has been an issue for thousands of years, from the simple substitution ciphers of Caesar to the importance of codes and code breaking in World War II. As more data was moved to computers, several complications arose. One of the biggest obstacles has been the need to identify people. Passwords have been the most common method, but they cause many problems. Newer technologies are available, but they require standards and people will have to agree to use them. Since security requires identifying people, increased emphasis on security can result in a reduction in privacy. Firms have collected data on consumers for years, but only recently have technologies advanced to the point where it is relatively inexpensive and easy to collect and analyze data on millions of consumers. Despite

Hollywood's portrayals, the greatest security threats come from insiders. On the other hand, it used to be difficult to attack servers and required programmers with a deep knowledge of the system. Today, with millions of computers connected to the Internet, it is relatively easy for beginners to download code from a site and run automated attacks against known bugs in operating systems. This technique is commonly used for creating denial-of-service attacks on Web sites. As e-commerce expands in importance, it becomes increasingly critical to develop a more robust Internet protocol that can identify and stop denial-of-service attacks. Many security tools exist to protect servers and to encrypt data transmissions, but it is difficult to stop denial-of-service attacks that rely on flooding the server.

FIGURE 5.1

Security and privacy are important issues in the Internet era. People can intercept data and attack servers directly and indirectly, and companies routinely monitor all transactions.

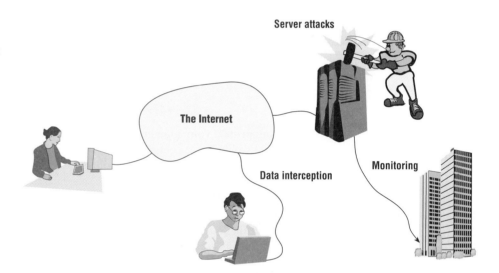

The Internet and e-commerce add some challenging aspects to security. E-commerce requires that portions of the computer systems be available to consumers and other businesses. Greater business benefits are generated when Web sites are integrated with corporate data—such as inventory levels, so customers can determine if an item is in stock. Yet, allowing public access to these systems creates greater security risks. Furthermore, since the Internet is a shared public network, data needs to be protected in transmission—to ensure it is not intercepted or altered. Wireless networks are even more open to eavesdropping and interception. Because of the public nature of the Internet, even a well-protected system can be brought down with denial-of-service attacks.

Tightening security can easily lead to a loss of privacy. One way to improve security is to completely identify every person and every activity performed. But even completely honest people are not willing to give up that much privacy. So, security faces another trade-off. These trade-offs are important, but they make the job harder for the corporate security expert.

Threats to Information

What are the primary threats to an information system? Many potential threats exist to information systems and the data they hold. The complicated aspect is that the biggest information threat is from legitimate users and developers. Purely by accident, a user might enter incorrect data or delete important information. A designer might misunderstand an important function and the system will produce erroneous results. An innocent programming mistake could result in incorrect or destroyed data. Minor changes to a frail system could result in a cascading failure of the entire system.

You can detect and prevent some of these problems through careful design, testing, training, and backup provisions. However, modern information systems are extremely complex. You cannot guarantee they will work correctly all of the time. Plus, the world poses physical threats that cannot be avoided: hurricanes, earthquakes, fires, and so on. Often, the best you can do is build contingency plans that enable the company to recover as quickly as possible. The most important aspect of any disaster plan is to maintain adequate backup copies. With careful planning, organization, and enough money, firms are able to provide virtually continuous information system support.

A second set of problems arises from the fact that as technology changes, so do criminals. Today, only a desperate person would rob a bank with a gun. The probability of being caught is high, and the amount of money stolen is low. Not that we wish to encourage anyone to become a thief, but the computer offers much easier ways to steal larger amounts of money.

It is important to determine the potential threats to computer security described by Figure 5.2. Some tools have made it easier for outsiders to attack companies over the Internet, but by far the biggest issues remain the people inside the company and viruses.

Disasters

Fortunately, fires, floods, hurricanes, and other physical disasters do not happen too often. But when a disaster does hit a company's data center, it could destroy the company. Without advance preparations, the loss of a data center could shut down the operations. How long can a modern company survive without transaction processing?

Today, there are many ways to plan for and recover from disasters. A common method today is to contract with a disaster recovery services provider. As shown in Figure 5.3, you can contract with service providers to access their commercial recovery facilities in the event of a disaster. One common level of support, called a **hot site,** consists of a fully configured computer center. Specific computer equipment is already installed and ready for immediate use. When the MIS staff declares a disaster, they install the backup tapes on the hot-site computers and use telecommunication lines to run the day-to-day operations. Another alternative is to contract for a **cold site,** which provides fully functional computer room space, without the computer equipment. If a disaster occurs, either the company or the disaster recovery services provider can arrange for the necessary equipment to be shipped to the cold site. However, there might be a delay of several days before the new data center will be operational, so a cold site is often used in conjunction with a hot-site contract.

FIGURE 5.2

Threats to information: By far, the most serious threats are from insiders—employees, mistakes, consultants, and partnerships. Businesses have to trust insiders to stay in operation, but you need to put limits on the access to data. It is possible for outsiders to break into most computer systems, but it is fairly difficult. Viruses are a serious threat to both data and security in general.

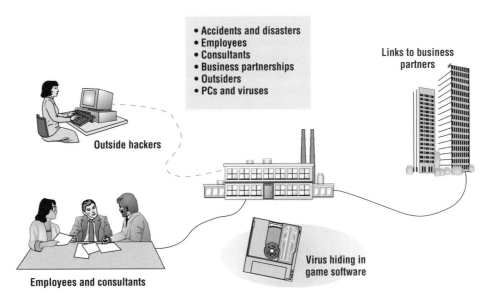

- Accidents and disasters
- Employees
- Consultants
- Business partnerships
- Outsiders
- PCs and viruses

Links to business partners

Outside hackers

Employees and consultants

Virus hiding in game software

FIGURE 5.3

Disaster planning: (1) You have to back up your data. (2) You can contract with a disaster facility to have a site ready. (3) Create a detailed plan to move your MIS people and restore the system. (4) If a disaster strikes, shift the business network to the temporary facility. (5)Rebuild the original data center.

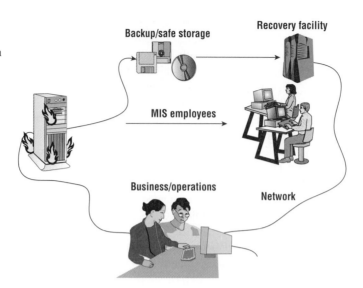

For computer operations that absolutely must never be interrupted, some firms utilize a backup computer that is continuously running to maintain a complete copy of the daily operations. All data is maintained simultaneously at both locations. If problems arise with one machine, the second one takes over automatically. Specialty firms are now offering these **data mirroring** facilities. The outside firm is sent copies of all your data as it is generated. The firm makes backup copies and provides virtually instantaneous renewal of service if something interferes with your main computer.

Employees and Consultants

Employees are the heart of any company. Companies function and succeed by trusting their employees. Although almost all employees are honest and diligent, there is always the chance that one employee will use the company's knowledge, experience, and trust to misappropriate resources.

It can be difficult to identify people who might cause damage to the firm. Many companies today use psychological tests, background checks, and random drug tests to indicate potential problems. Most companies are wary of employees whose employment has been terminated. Businesses follow specific steps when employees leave, being particularly careful to remove the employees' access to company computers.

A more complicated problem arises with MIS employees. Programmers and analysts have to be trusted. Without them, there would be no software. However, it is generally best if the programmers are not the users of the program. Companies enforce a separation of duties among staff programmers and users. Think about what might happen if a bank teller was also responsible for writing the computer program used by tellers. It would be easy to use the computer to steal money from different accounts. Auditing transaction-processing systems is an important task for auditors.

Unscrupulous programmers have also been known to include "time bombs" in their software. Whenever the software runs, it checks a hidden file for a secret word. If the programmer leaves the company, the secret word does not get changed. When the program does not find the correct word, it starts deleting files. On large projects, these bombs can be impossible to spot (until they go off). Keeping good backups can usually minimize the damage. As a related side note, the software industry is pushing states to adopt a new set of laws (UCITA) that makes it legal to include a shutdown time bomb if a software company has a dispute with a business that uses its software.

Another danger area is that programmers might include a trap door or secret password that allows them to gain access to the software even if they leave the company. Sometimes these trap doors are installed innocently, to enable programmers to make corrections faster. The important point is to make sure they are removed when the system is permanently installed.

REALITY BYTES — Have You Lost Your Identity Yet?

The government includes several crimes in the category of identity theft. In particular, theft of credit cards is included. Consequently, federal statistics show that $437 million was lost to identity theft by Americans in 2003. Identity theft is not always reported to the police, but even so, the number of complaints increased by 33 percent from 2002. The Federal Trade Commission (FTC) estimates that one in eight U.S. adults was affected by identity theft in 2003.

Internet-related fraud increased even more—by 51 percent. Many were victims of scams from Web sites and spam e-mail. How-ever, auction fraud was the most prevalent complaint. Removing the extreme cases of million-dollar reported losses, half of the complaints involved less than $228.

The good news is that after December 4, 2004, you will be able to receive a free credit report once a year. This federal law makes it easier to monitor your credit activity and spot potential problems.

Source: Adapted from "FTC: Identity Theft, Tech Fraud Up," *CNN Online,* January 23, 2004.

An interesting class of threats to securing your data arises from negligence instead of deliberate actions by the users. For instance, employees might accidentally delete data. Or carrying disks, tapes, or even laptop computers past magnetic fields can sometimes damage the files. In these cases, the best bet is to have backups readily available. More complicated problems arise when laptop computers are lost or even stolen. In addition to the data stored on the machines, the files often hold passwords for corporate computers. Many laptops provide passwords and encrypt the data to minimize these problems. One other problem that falls into this category is a warning to be careful about how you dispose of old tapes, disks, and computer equipment. Businesses run similar risks when they send computer equipment out for repairs.

In general, the best way to minimize problems from employees stems from typical management techniques. Hire workers carefully, treat employees fairly, have separation of jobs, use teamwork, and maintain constant checks on their work. Consultants present the same potential problems as employees. However, consultants tend to be hired for a short time, so the firm knows even less about them than about regular employees. Consultants are generally used for specialized jobs, so there may not be any internal employees who can adequately monitor their work.

Business Partnerships

As computers spread throughout every aspect of business, many companies share their data. For example, General Motors asks its suppliers to provide all information electronically. This electronic data interchange (EDI) means that business information is processed faster and with fewer errors. The problem is that in many cases, it means GM gives other companies considerable access to GM's computers and vice versa. For instance, if GM is thinking about increasing production, the managers might want to check supplier production schedules to make sure the suppliers could provide enough parts. To do it electronically, GM needs access to the suppliers' computers. To participate in business today, you must trust your partners. However, you have limited ability to evaluate all of their employees.

The issue of partnerships becomes more important in an Internet world of software. Increasingly, firms are providing services over the Internet—where the software and your data reside on a service provider's Web site. A good example is NetSuite, which is an **application service provider (ASP)** that processes all of your accounting needs on its Web site. The main advantages of an ASP are that (1) experts set up and run the site so you do not have to hire specialists, (2) storing the data on the Web means it is accessible to your employees wherever they have Web access, and (3) you can start small and scale up to a reasonable size without hassles. A potential drawback is that all of your financial data is stored on a site run by someone else. Of course, the reputation of the ASP depends on protecting your data and maintaining security, so it is probably safer than what a small business could handle independently; however, you should still investigate the ASP security procedures.

REALITY BYTES   New Technology, New Criminals

The U.S. government argues that Internet gambling is illegal—so there are few or no sites based in the United States. Other nations are far more open to gambling. In fact, a case is being made that if the United States blocks access to foreign gambling sites, it will be a restraint of international trade. Regardless of the status, international gambling is big business. Sports sites in the United Kingdom and elsewhere enable people to place bets on almost anything—including American sports.

Apparently, sporting events offer a lucrative target for a new breed of criminals. Before the 2004 Super Bowl, several sites were threatened by organized criminals demanding extortion. They threatened to attack the sites' servers with a denial-of-service attack unless "protection" money was paid. The potential damage was huge, because many people would place bets during a short period of time. Alistair Assheton, manager of a company that runs several sites, including www.BetGameDay.com, says that "we were first targeted in September and have been under intermittent attack ever since." In the week before the Super Bowl, he received a threat by e-mail demanding $30,000. Jeffrey Weber, who writes an online newsletter about the industry, notes that an outage of a few hours could result in the loss of up to a million dollars. Weber believes some smaller sites have paid up, figuring it would be cheaper than to face the loss. Law enforcement experts believe the threats are the work of professional criminals or gangs with experience in shakedown schemes. Security experts indicated that the gangs are probably based in eastern Europe and Russia.

Source: Adapted from "Shakedown of Gambling Sites before Super Bowl," *CNN Online,* January 30, 2004.

Outsiders

There is some threat from outsiders who might dial up your computer and guess a password. Using some common sense can minimize most of these threats. For example, in the 1980s, some groups gained access to computers because the operators never changed the default password that was shipped with the computer! The Internet causes additional problems because it was designed to give other people access to your machines. The key lies in providing people with just the level of access they need. The biggest problems today arise from a group labeled *script kiddies,* who download system scanning/attack software from the Internet and randomly search computers for holes. Another major problem with passwords is a technique hackers call *social engineering.* A hacker calls up a victim (you), tells some story, and convinces you to reveal your password. Never give your password to anyone.

In theory, modern computer security systems are effective and can prevent most outside attacks. The problem is that operating systems are complex software programs that have errors. Experts search these systems to find the errors, and ultimately, the vendor fixes the errors. However, this process can result in dozens of patches a year. Some businesses do not keep up with the patches, and some patches interfere with other programs and are not applied. Consequently, there can be thousands of systems connected to the Internet that suffer from published flaws. Software downloaded from the Internet can automatically search for these flaws and provide access even to inexperienced hackers. One key to protecting your servers is to make sure they have all the current operating system patches.

Viruses

Microsoft Office software presents a major point of vulnerability because the tools support a macro programming language called Visual Basic for Applications. This language is a powerful feature that enables MIS departments and other software vendors to automate many tasks—such as synchronizing calendars and contact lists with multiple devices. The problem is that a programming language can also be used to create programs that steal or destroy data.

These programs can be hidden inside a document, slide show, database, or e-mail message. One particularly dangerous threat comes in the form of a software program called a **virus.** As illustrated in Figure 5.4, a computer virus is a small program that hides inside a program attached to an e-mail message. If you open the attachment, the macro program runs and the virus tends to do two things: (1) it sends itself to everyone in your contact list using your name, and (2) it attaches itself to other files in your computer. At some point, the nastier viruses then delete all of your files, or send your files to a Web server. Some writers

Technology Toolbox: Encrypting E-Mail

Problem: You often need to send messages to other employees on your team and want to protect the messages so no one can intercept and read them.

Tools: You can encrypt and digitally sign your e-mail by installing a digital certificate. There are two main steps: (1) obtain a digital certificate, and (2) install the certificate in your browser and e-mail client. Verisign, Thawte (owned by Verisign), and PGP provide certificates. Thawte and PGP both provide free certificates for personal use, while Verisign charges an annual fee. Verisign and Thawte have a relatively simple process to automatically install keys into your browser. PGP requires a few more steps to generate a key, but documentation is available for several systems. Once you have the certificate installed in your browser, you can see the details from the menu:

Tools/Internet Options, select the Content tab, and click the Certificates button.

You can use the certificate to digitally sign your messages and to encrypt them, but the process depends on your e-mail client. Microsoft Outlook is commonly used in business and can automatically sign and encrypt every message, or you can individually encrypt only some messages. In most cases, you will want to select the messages to be encrypted—unless you use the account strictly for critical business.

When you create a new message in Microsoft Outlook, click the Options button, then the Security Settings button to check or set digital signing and encryption. The two check boxes at the top of the Security Properties page control whether the message will be encrypted and signed. Signing a message is straightforward.

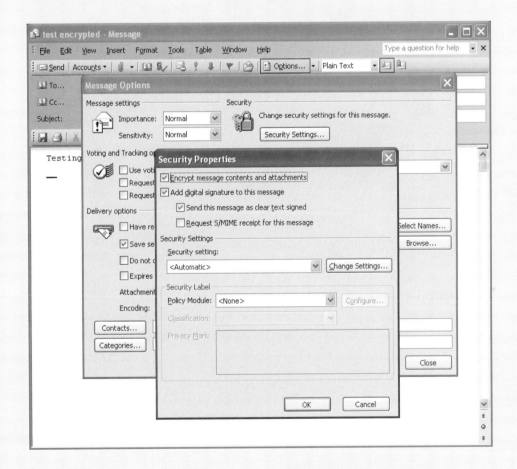

Encrypting a message is slightly trickier. How do you get the public key of the person receiving the message? The easiest method is to have the person send you a signed message. Outlook will identify and store the public key in a separate certificate. Then you will be able to check the box that encrypts messages sent to that person.

Note that the free and low-cost certificates do not exactly validate who you are. At best, they authenticate the e-mail address that you registered. If you want a recipient to verify your name, you have to follow a more complicated (expensive) process. Verisign has different classes of certificates

to match your registration to you. Thawte has the Web of Trust. PGP does not have a mechanism to link your digital life to your real life.

Quick Quiz:

1. Check the Thawte site and describe the steps needed to obtain and install a certificate.

2. Search the Internet for PGP and describe the steps needed to generate and install a certificate.

FIGURE 5.4

Virus activity: Once a virus is loaded on your machine, you will need an antivirus software package to remove the virus. Several versions are available at low cost. A virus can come from any software that supports executable code. Attachments sent through e-mail are currently the most common method of being infected.

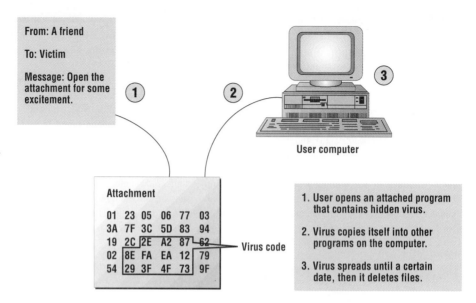

From: A friend

To: Victim

Message: Open the attachment for some excitement.

User computer

Attachment

01	23	05	06	77	03
3A	7F	3C	5D	83	94
19	2C	2E	A2	87	62
02	8E	FA	EA	12	79
54	29	3F	4F	73	9F

Virus code

1. User opens an attached program that contains hidden virus.

2. Virus copies itself into other programs on the computer.

3. Virus spreads until a certain date, then it deletes files.

FIGURE 5.5

Spyware: Software loaded into your computer captures keystrokes, Web sites you visit, or other personal information. It transfers the data to a Web site run by a company or hacker who steals your money. The problem is particularly dangerous on public computers that are used by several people.

Hacker

Capture keystrokes

Password

Credit card

Password

make a distinction and call a program a worm if it simply replicates itself but is not designed to cause any damage.

A virus can be picked up from many sources, but e-mail attachments are the prevalent method today. Antivirus software will search your computer for known viruses. Even so, firms continue to experience problems with viruses. As shown in Figure 5.5, viruses and worms are the most common attack faced by companies today. Although the survey does not show it, virtually every company experiences several virus attacks every year. Antivirus software can help clean files once a virus is identified, but it has not proven very useful in stopping attacks—particularly since new viruses are created every day. In 1999, software virus costs were estimated to be slightly under $8 billion in the United States alone.

Today, it is easy to create a virus—simply find a virus software kit on the Web, make a few changes, and send it to someone. You would need only minimal technical skills. Of course, it is illegal to create and release viruses and other destructive software (in most nations).

The best way to stop a virus is to avoid running software acquired from the Internet and to never open script attachments sent to you by e-mail—even if they appear to come from a friend. Be cautious, because some attachments that appear to be pictures are actually virus scripts. Vendors are beginning to work on e-mail filters that can block script attachments, but they tend to be heavy-handed and also block useful files.

Ultimately, the most important step with viruses is to make certain that you always have current backup files. Then, even if a virus deletes your files, you can recover the data, run

REALITY BYTES   Spyware Invasion

Most people have learned that viruses can be nasty—they use your computer to infect others and can delete or damage your files. But there are other nasty programs out there. You can pick up these spyware programs in the same way you get infected with viruses. They sneak in from software or even Web sites. The difference is that instead of damaging your files, they collect data and send it back to someone else. Senator Ron Wyden from Oregon exaggerated only slightly when he proposed legislation to regulate spyware: "Snoops and spies are really trying to set up base camp in millions of computers across the country." Some spyware is relatively benign and simply tracks your activities to deliver ads targeted to your interests.

Other versions log your keystrokes and send them to criminals hoping to steal your passwords. Many people have actually agreed to allow Web sites to install spyware programs on their computers. Well, if "agree" means they did not read the fine print on the Web site. One site, WhenU.com, noted that its ad software was installed more than 100 million times. Of course, it was uninstalled 80 million times. Claria Corp. claims that its Gator advertising system (often installed with music sharing programs) is installed on 45 million computers—but has been removed 155 million times in five years.

Source: Adapted from David Bank, "What's That Sneaking into Your Computer?" *The Wall Street Journal,* April 26, 2004.

an antivirus software package, and remove the virus. It will cost you time, but at least you will save the data.

Spyware

Trojan horses are an old threat to security. Named from the fabled war where the Greeks hid soldiers inside a wooden horse, the basic concept is to hide malicious code inside other programs. Viruses are often distributed with a Trojan horse. **Spyware** is a similar concept—but instead of destroying files, the spyware takes residence inside your computer. It then captures all of your activities, such as Web sites visited, passwords entered, and credit card numbers. As shown in Figure 5.5, periodically, the spyware software sends the information to a Web site, where it is collected by a company or a hacker.

Viruses, worms (essentially viruses that do not destroy data), Trojan horses, and spyware are often called **malware,** because they are designed to do bad things to your computer system. Spyware tools are particularly dangerous on public computers—such as those at Internet cafés, print shops, or libraries. Someone could install the software and capture all of your keystrokes and passwords. You should avoid entering passwords and credit card data on computers that are shared with the public. Today, you can download software that scans your machine for spyware. You can also use the Windows Task Manager to show you what processes are currently running on your computer. If you recognize a malware tool, you can stop the process to shut it down. But you have to be careful, because a standard computer runs many processes. You need to decipher the cryptic names of the processes to understand which ones are good and which ones are bad. It is usually best to use a spyware tool—which contains a list of the known malware tools.

Computer Security Controls

What primary options are used to provide computer security? Transaction and accounting data is clearly valuable to a company and needs to be protected. Computer security systems need to protect against three general problems: (1) unauthorized disclosure of information, (2) unauthorized modification, and (3) unauthorized withholding of information. As an example of the first problem, you would not want hackers to get access to your customers' credit card data. An example of the second problem would be employees modifying their payroll records to change their pay rates. The third problem is less obvious, but just as important. Imagine what would happen if you needed to look at the latest inventory to decide how much to reorder, but the computer refused to give you access. This problem is often referred to as **denial of service (DoS)** and is a difficult problem faced by Web sites.

Manual and Electronic Information

Protection of information is a topic that has existed forever. Not surprisingly, the strongest developments in security have come from the military. The armed services lead the way in both manual and electronic security. Military funding has paid for much of the development of computer security. Because manual security precautions existed long before computers, the initial work in computer security focused on applying these older techniques. Nevertheless, some major differences arise from storing information electronically.

To see the complications added by electronic storage of information, consider a hypothetical case of two spies looking for a letter. Juan has gained access to a personal computer, but Mike is in a musty basement library full of paper files. Mike is not even sure he is in the right place. There are thousands of documents in the basement, and the letter might even be stored in some other building. The computer that Juan is searching is large enough to hold all of the company's information, so he only has to look in one place. For his search, Juan just uses the computer database. In seconds, he finds what he wants. He copies the letter to a disk, turns off the machine, and walks out the door. Mike is still walking up and down aisles in the basement trying to read file tags with his flashlight. When he finally finds the letter, he uses his trusty spy camera to take pictures of the letter, hoping they will be legible. Now he has to put the letter back exactly as he found it so no one can tell he copied it.

Obviously it is much easier to locate and copy data stored on computers. Even more important, it is easier to change the data. In many cases, data on computers can be changed without anyone knowing that the file was altered. The Internet makes it even easier for people to steal huge amounts of electronic data.

Data Backup

The most important aspect of any security plan is to protect the data through formal backups. A company can recover from almost any problem—as long as the data is available. If you lose transactions data, you lose part of the company.

As shown in Figure 5.6, with a formal backup plan, data is transferred to a transportable format (usually tapes or DVD drives). The data must be stored off-site to protect it from local disasters. That means you need a plan to rotate the data so that the off-site backups remain up to date. One solution is to make complete backup tapes once a week, and then just send incremental change data over the Internet. Large organizations have several options because they probably have offices in many locations that can swap data. Smaller businesses can use commercial data storage facilities. Just remember to move the data far enough away so that if a disaster hits the business, the backup data will not be affected. This rule is particularly important for areas subject to hurricanes and floods.

FIGURE 5.6

Data backup: Backup is critical to security. Off-site backups are needed to recover from disasters. Mirrored sites are used when extreme reliability is needed. PCs can be backed up over the network.

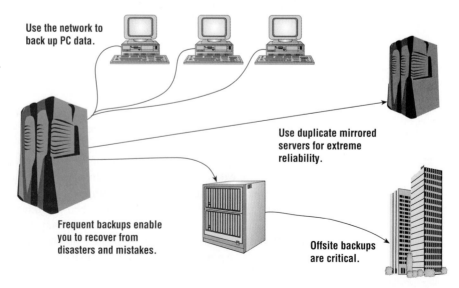

Use the network to back up PC data.

Use duplicate mirrored servers for extreme reliability.

Frequent backups enable you to recover from disasters and mistakes.

Offsite backups are critical.

Data stored on personal computers is often difficult to back up. Users are not very conscientious about making copies, so few people have daily backups of their work. Networks can help, because users can store their data on network drives, which can be backed up on a regular schedule by the MIS department. Some software even automatically transfers data from personal computers to the network, so users do not need to remember to transfer it.

Along the same lines, if you want to keep your computer running—particularly servers—you need to install an **uninterruptible power supply (UPS).** A UPS is basically a large battery that is constantly recharged from the power outlet. The computer always runs off the battery, so if power fails, the computer keeps running. A UPS provides only a few minutes of power, but it protects the server during typical brownouts and short outages. If the power outage is extended, you will have time to shut down the machine safely or switch to auxiliary generators.

User Identification

One difficulty with providing computer security lies in identifying the user. In a manual security system, a guard can be used to physically identify each person by asking to see identification. There are few vision systems available for computers, and they are expensive. The most common method of identifying users to computers is with a password.

Passwords

Each user is given an account name and a password that are known only to the computer and the user. If someone correctly enters both the name and the password, the computer assumes it must be the user. This method is cheap, fast, and does not require too much effort by the user. However, there are problems. The biggest difficulty is that users are afraid of forgetting their password, so they choose words that are easy to remember. Unfortunately, passwords that are easy to remember tend to be obvious to other people. For instance, *never* use the words *password* or *secret* as a password. Similarly, do not use the names of relatives, pets, or celebrities. Most of these can be obtained by looking in a phone book or asking someone you know. In fact, you should not use any actual words. Most people use only a couple thousand words in typical conversation. The goal is to make it hard for someone to guess the password. You need to choose passwords from the largest possible set of characters and numbers. Two other rules about passwords: Change them often and never write them down. If you forget a password, the system administrator will let you create a new one. For additional security, many computer systems require users to change their passwords on a regular basis, such as every 30 or 60 days.

One drawback to passwords is that you need too many of them. Everything from ATM cards to phone calls to computer accounts uses passwords or *personal identification numbers (PINs).* It is difficult to remember several different passwords, especially if you choose random letters and numbers and change them often. With so many passwords, it is tempting to write them down, which defeats their purpose. Some computer network security systems use a **Kerberos** server. Users log in once and the security server provides authentication to all of the authorized servers. This system is built into the newer Windows servers and simplifies access to local computers. At this point in time, it is not used for access to Internet sites.

Passwords are not a perfect solution to identifying users. No matter how well they are chosen or how often they are changed, there is always a chance that someone could guess the password. They are so risky that U.S. government top-secret information is stored on computers that cannot be connected to phone lines or the Internet. By physically preventing outsiders from using the computers, there is a smaller chance that the information could be compromised.

Password Generators

Password generators are small electronic cards that users carry that generate new passwords every minute. The same system is embedded on the main computer. When you want to log in, you simply enter the number on the card. Since the password is changed every minute,

REALITY BYTES   Who Are You?

Many of the technologies in biometrics have been around for a decade, but adoption has been slow. With the increased governmental attention to security, many people expected biometrics to take off. Yet others are wary of the potential loss of privacy. Some point to the problems with inaccuracies and lack of standards. In 2004, the U.S. Department of Homeland Security selected Accenture to help design and build its controversial U.S. Visitor and Immigrant Status Indicator Technology (US-VISIT). Budgeting begins at $1 billion a year for three years. In the initial phase, the system will include electronic fingerprint scanners and cameras at 115 U.S. airports and 14 seaports. The United States is also encouraging other nations to implement biometrics into machine-readable passports. Yet many people have unrealistic expectations of biometric systems. Andy Amanovich is cofounder of Imagis Technologies and sells facial-recognition software. He points out that much of his time is spent damping customer expectations. "I think there really is a hope out there that you can take a database with the names of 1,000 al-Qaida terrorists, wipe off the sand, and start matching those names to faces as they pass through an airport." But this level of technology is probably decades away. A much-touted system (FaceIt) was used in Tampa, Florida, from 2001 to 2003 to try and find criminals by scanning all faces in the Ybor City entertainment district. In the two-year trial, it did not make a single positive identification. Dr. Joseph Atick, whose company Identix owns the current version of FaceIt, understands the complications of using biometrics to identify people: "This is not an industry you can be neutral about. This is an industry that changes the way people travel and provide information to one another. If you're out of touch with people's attitudes about it, you're going to face significant resistance. If on the other hand you're going to provide a beneficial service, you're better aligning yourself with where society is heading."

Source: Adapted from Sam Williams, "The Curse of the Biometric Future," *Salon,* February 26, 2004.

you do not have to worry about anyone guessing it or intercepting it. On the other hand, you have to carry around the card.

Biometrics

Biometrics is a field of study that attempts to identify people based on biological characteristics. The most promising devices are fingerprint and handprint readers. There are even devices that recognize the pattern of your iris (the colored ring surrounding the pupil of your eye). These systems work with a simple camera that can be installed cheaply. They are being tested now for identification at airports and in ATMs. The Canadian government is building a large-scale system to handle customs check-in for returning Canadian citizens.

As costs decline, the biggest drawback to biometric security devices is a lack of standards. In 2000, Microsoft bought a company to develop a set of standards to handle biometric devices within the Windows operating system. If this system gets implemented and accepted by the industry, it will be much easier to use biometric devices for all user identification needs.

Biometric security devices have some important advantages. The user does not have to remember anything or carry keys around. They are reasonably accurate and difficult to fool by an unauthorized person. But the industry still needs standards so that the security information can be transferred securely and validated by the final server.

Access Control

As long as the computer can identify each user, you can control access to any piece of data. As manager of the marketing department, you could allow other managers to read the sales data but not change it. Similarly, as shown in Figure 5.7, the accounting department could allow managers to see the accounts payable data, but only the accounting department would be able to modify the data and write new checks. With a good security system, it is possible for the human resources manager to allow employees to look up work phone numbers in the corporate database but not to see salaries or other confidential information.

The common access controls available are read, write, execute, and delete. With these security features, the owner of the information can give other users exactly the type of access they need.

As a creator of data, it is your responsibility to set the appropriate access permissions. Today, most of your files will be shared through a Web site. You can set aside different di-

REALITY BYTES   Password Generator Cards

Remembering passwords is painful. Users today have dozens of passwords, and for security reasons the passwords need to be long and include nonalphabetic characters, making them impossible to remember. In 2004, Microsoft signed a deal with RSA, a leading security provider, to integrate its two-factor login system into Windows. The SecurID card generates a unique password every 60 seconds that is synchronized with a central server. With the integrated login, users will be able to insert the card and enter a four-digit PIN that will log them into the personal computer and establish a link to the corporate network. In bulk, the license and the cards cost about $20 per person per year. RSA estimates that the system is currently used in 48 million desktops. The integrated login would also be used to protect the user's laptop. If it was lost or stolen, no one would be able to login without the SecurID card.

Source: Adapted from William M. Bulkeley, "Microsoft, RSA Reach Security Pact," *The Wall Street Journal,* February 24, 2004.

FIGURE 5.7

Access control: In Windows, right-click the folder or file to set its properties. Under the Security tab, you can set permissions to any person or group.

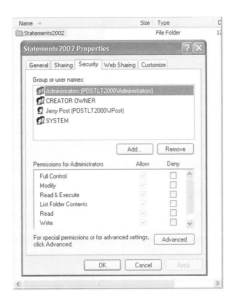

rectories for each group of users and assign permissions to each directory. To avoid accidents, you generally do not give anyone delete permissions. Your main choice is which users should be able to read the data, and which ones need to be able to change it. Of course, if multiple people have permission to change a document, you should set the document to track changes so you can see who made each change.

Single Sign-On and Lack of Standards

As more business activities get shifted online, you will notice that you need dozens of passwords. You need to use different passwords, because you do not want to use the same password at some new Web site that you use for your bank. Do you trust the operators of every Web site? Even if they do not steal your password, do they protect it? Similar issues arise in companies that have multiple Web-based applications. They might not be interconnected, so you have to continually log in to various applications. As a result, you end up with too many passwords. Figure 5.8 shows how the **single sign-on** approach is designed to minimize some of these problems. Within a company, it is possible to set up a server dedicated to handling your login. Other applications can then verify who you are from that central server. Once you are signed into the network, you have access to the many applications used in the company.

In some ways, it would be nice if this feature could extend to Web sites across the Internet. Once you have logged into your machine, it could authenticate you to other computers on the Internet. This way, you would need only one password—or perhaps even a biometric scanner attached to your laptop. At this point in time, the world is not even close to this solution. The problem: lack of standards. Few standards exist for collecting, storing, or sharing

FIGURE 5.8

Single sign-on: You log into the network through a central security server. Resources that you wish to access such as a database or Web server identify you by contacting the security server. The goal is to reduce the number of passwords needed and make it easier to manage the security system by centralizing the logins.

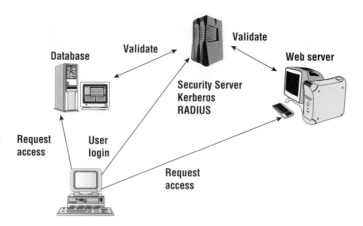

authentication data. Even if you buy a fingerprint reader for your laptop or PDA, it cannot be used to verify your identity to external Web sites. So far, almost no work has been done on developing standards to support this level of authentication. The lack of standards is less important within a single company. Within a company, the MIS department has the authority to create and define its own standards, which gives it the ability to purchase and create software so that it can all be integrated. But it will likely be several years before everyone sits down and agrees to the standards needed to share authentication information across the Internet.

Additional Security Measures

What non-computer-based tools can be used to provide additional security? A fundamental issue in computer security is that logical controls are never enough to protect the computer. For example, anyone who has physical access to the computer can either circumvent the security controls or destroy the data. Besides, many employees have extended access to the data and applications. To be safe, you need to implement some standard business policies.

Audits

Accountants have long known that in order to maintain security over data, it is necessary to perform audits. There are too many ways for unscrupulous people to make changes to stored information. Audits are used to locate mistakes and to prevent fraud. Existing criminology practice states that in many cases, the threat of getting caught (by an audit) will convince most people to be more careful and to avoid fraudulent behavior. The same principles extend to security audits. By monitoring computer activity, auditing financial records, and periodically checking to see whether everyone is obeying security regulations, users are encouraged to follow the security guidelines of the company.

Of course, audits cost money and they interfere with the daily operations of the firm. As a result, it is important to schedule audits carefully and to keep an eye on the costs as well as the potential benefits. There are several professional organizations (such as the EDP Auditors Association) designed to help security employees learn more about the latest technologies and to teach them what to look for in audits. The American Institute of Certified Public Accountants (AICPA) also provides standards and audit guidelines that are useful at combating fraud.

Physical Access

Because it is so difficult to provide logical security to a computer, other mechanisms have been developed. Many of them rely on controlling physical access to the computer. For instance, computers and terminals should be kept in controlled areas. They must certainly be kept away from visitors and delivery people. Many types of locks and keys can be used to

REALITY BYTES   Steganography

Today, when privacy has disappeared and the U.S. government monitors international calls, faxes, and e-mails—and uses satellites to watch activities around the world—how could terrorists secretly set up the plan to hijack airplanes and crash them? By most accounts, those particular terrorists avoided using most electronic communication systems, relying on hand-to-hand messages among trusted members. Yet encryption technologies today are readily available to anyone, technologies that are difficult or impossible to break. Some experts speculate that terrorist organizations can use steganography, hiding secret messages within other communications. The British made use of these tricks in World War II. BBC public broadcasts often carried secret messages to agents, such as announcing a "secret" number within a weather forecast. Only the spies would

know that the temperature for a certain town on a specific day would have a secret meaning. The huge volume of messages also makes it difficult to identify specific threats in advance. Scouring files stored on Internet servers, federal authorities have found copies of hundreds of e-mail messages sent over a month before the attack from personal and public library computers. The messages in Arabic and English indicate a plan for the attack. Modern steganography can hide messages inside images or other computer files. Free "stego-tools" can be found on the Internet. While bin Laden–funded terrorists have used this technique in the past, so far no one has found evidence of its use in the September 11 attacks.

Source: Adapted from Lisa M. Krieger, "How Technology Is Used to Mask Communications," *Mercury News,* October 1, 2001.

protect terminals and personal computers. Similarly, all documents should be controlled. Paper copies of important reports should be shredded. All financial data is routinely audited by both internal and external auditors. Sometimes hidden control data is used to make sure procedures are followed.

Monitoring

Another effective security provision is to monitor access to all of the data. Most computers can keep track of every change to every file. They can keep a log of who accesses each file. They track every time someone incorrectly enters a password. An audit trail of every file change can be provided to management. That means it is possible to find out who changed the salary data, what time it was changed, and from which terminal.

Remember that every device connected to the Internet is given a unique number as an address. Every Web site that you visit can track this number. In some cases, you can only be identified down to the company you work for, but in many situations, companies can monitor exactly what each machine is doing at any time. Additional software can be installed on computers to provide even more detail—including storing all keystrokes.

Hiring and Employee Evaluation

Because insiders raise the greatest security issues, it makes sense to be careful when you hire employees. Employers should always check candidates' references. In more extreme situations, employers can check employee backgrounds for criminal records. There are several instances of disgruntled employees causing security problems. In many cases, the best security solution is to establish close relationships with your employees and encourage teamwork. Employees who work closely together can defuse potential problems and informally monitor the work of other employees. Figure 5.9 notes that several Web sites will search public records to perform basic background checks for small businesses. Validating social security numbers is an important step for many U.S. businesses.

Encryption

How do you protect data when unknown people might be able to find it or intercept it? What additional benefits can be provided by encryption? Encryption is the foundation of many aspects of security. For example, encryption protects messages sent across the Internet and protects files stored on servers. Cryptography has been around for thousands of years, but computers have radically altered the types of codes available. One important

FIGURE 5.9

Employee background checks are important. For a fee, several Web sites help small businesses perform basic background checks to verify SSNs and check public criminal records.

➤ Audits
➤ Monitoring
➤ Background checks:

http://www.casebreakers.com/

http://www.knowx.com/

http://www.publicdata.com/

FIGURE 5.10

Single-key encryption: Both the person who encrypts the message and the person who decrypts it use the same key. The systems are fast, but it is difficult to safely distribute the key.

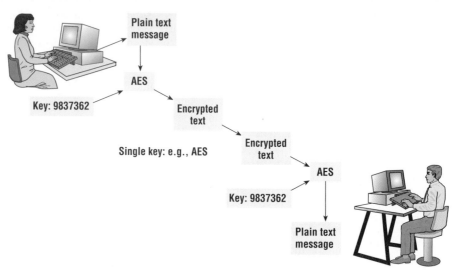

feature to remember in terms of cryptography and computers is the concept of **brute force** attacks. If a hacker knows the algorithm method used to encrypt a message, it might be conceivable to have a computer test every possible key to decode the message. The essence of stopping a brute force attack is to have a key that is so long that it would take hundreds of years to try every combination. The problem is that computers get faster every year. So encryption technologies that were secure 20 years ago can be broken in hours today.

Encryption should be seriously considered for any communications that are sent between computers. Without encryption, it is relatively easy for unauthorized people to deliberately or accidentally read or change the messages. Encryption is available with many personal computer software packages. Almost all spreadsheets and word processors permit you to encrypt your file when you save it. To read it back, you have to enter the correct password. You also can find encryption packages on the Internet that will protect your e-mail messages.

Single Key

For many years, single-key encryption codes were the only systems available. Figure 5.10 shows the basic steps required to encrypt and decrypt a message with a single-key system. Both the sender and receiver have the software that handles the encryption and decryption. Both people also need to have the same key, which is the difficult part. How do you deliver a secret key to someone? And if you can deliver a secret key, you might as well send the message the same way.

On the other hand, single-key systems are fast. They can encrypt or decrypt a message with almost no delay. Since the late 1970s, most of the business world standardized on the

Data Encryption Standard (DES). However, this system only supported keys of 56 bits, and by 2000, messages encrypted with DES were broken in about 24 hours by brute force attacks in various contests. Triple DES was popular for a while—essentially encrypting the message three times. But in 2001, the U.S. government chose a new method known as the **Advanced Encryption Standard (AES)** because it is fast and users have a choice of a key length of 128, 192, or 256 bits. Keep in mind that longer keys make the message more secure (harder to break by brute force) but increase the time it takes to encrypt and decrypt the message.

Public Key Infrastructure

Public key infrastructure (PKI) is a substantial leap in encryption technology. The method arose from a military–political question. Given a U.S. embassy in the middle of a foreign nation that can intercept all communications, how can a secret message be transmitted out of the embassy when there is no way to exchange a secret key? The answer was found by two mathematicians (Diffie and Hellman) and later refined into a system (and company) named after three other mathematicians (RSA: Rivest, Shamir, and Adleman). The solution is to create an encryption system that uses two keys: a **public key** and a **private key.**

Dual Key Encryption

The essence of a dual-key system is that it takes both keys to encrypt and decrypt a message. Whichever key is used to encrypt the message, the other key must be used to decrypt it. Figure 5.11 illustrates the process. The beauty of the system is that anyone can be given your public key—in fact, this key can be published in a directory. Then, whenever someone wants to send you a secure message, he or she simply uses the RSA algorithm and your public key. At that point, the message is gibberish and can only be decrypted using your super-secret private key. No one can read or alter the message. However, someone could destroy it before it reaches you.

Today's Web browsers use this method to encrypt credit card transmissions. The Web server sends your browser a public key. The browser encrypts the content and sends it across the Internet. Only the Web server can decrypt the contents—using the private key. A similar system called **Pretty Good Privacy (PGP)** is available on the Internet to encrypt e-mail messages.

The one drawback to dual-key encryption systems is that they tend to be slow—particularly for long messages. One common solution is to use dual-key encryption to establish the identity of the parties and to exchange a one-time secret key to be used for the rest of the transmissions. The single-key system is fast and protects the transmitted data, and the initial dual-key system makes it possible to distribute the secret key without anyone stealing it.

Authentication

A second aspect of dual keys has even more uses. PKI can be used for **authentication.** Consider the case where Alice works for a bank, and she receives a message that claims to be

FIGURE 5.11

Dual-key encryption: Alice sends a message that only Bob can read. With a dual-key system, one key encrypts the message, the other decrypts it. Once Bob's public key is applied to the message, only Alice's private key will retrieve the message. Keys are usually very large prime numbers.

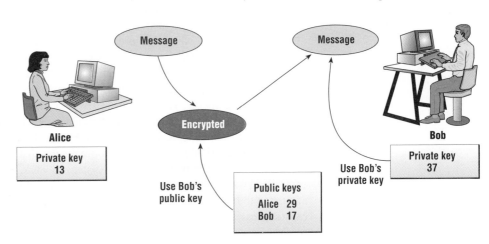

FIGURE 5.12

Dual-key encryption for message authentication: Bob sends a message to Alice at the bank. Using his private key ensures that the message must have come from him. Using Alice's public key prevents anyone else from reading the message.

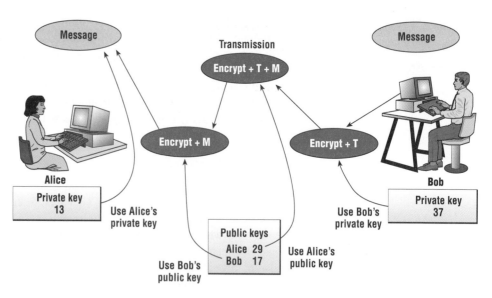

from Bob, and it says to pay you $1 million. How does Alice know that the message is authentic and not forged by you? Consider the case where Bob does want to pay you some money (but only $100).

Figure 5.12 shows the answer. To make sure that only Alice can read the message (and that no one else can modify it), Bob encrypts it with her public key. To ensure that the message is authentic, Bob also encrypts it with his private key. Remember that the keys always work in pairs. When Alice receives the message, she uses Bob's public key and her private key to decrypt it. If the message is decrypted correctly, then it was not modified in transit, and it could only have come from Bob. This process is used to create **digital signatures.** In 2000, the federal government passed a law declaring digital signatures to carry the same legal authority as a traditional signature for legal purposes.

Certificate Authorities

The proper name for dual-key encryption is public key infrastructure (PKI). Why is the word *infrastructure* so important? Think about how a hacker might attack the system in Figure 5.12. What if Bob did not know much about technology and encryption? So, posing as Bob, you create a private key and publish the public key in a directory under Bob's name. Then you send your e-mail message to the bank pretending to be Bob, using "his" public key and asking the bank to pay you $1 million. The message decrypts fine, and Alice believes the message is legitimate. Similar problems can arise by impersonating the bank.

To make the PKI system work, it is critical that the directory of public keys accurately represents the people indicated. So, some organization needs to be in charge of the public directory, and people who wish to use it need to verify their identity before registering a public key. At the moment, this task is handled only by Verisign, a public company—with virtually no regulation or rules. Verisign issues **digital certificates** that verify the identity of the person who generated the public key. Companies and individuals can purchase these certificates, and you are supposed to verify your identity before receiving the certificate. However, in 2001, Verisign announced that it accidentally issued a digital certificate to an imposter who claimed to be from Microsoft. Eventually Verisign caught the mistake and invalidated the certificate, but the incident points out that the process is far from foolproof. The troubling point is that for the PKI system to work, the certificates and keys must be controlled by a trusted organization. Other companies (including the U.S. Post Office) have attempted to become trusted **certificate authorities,** but so far none have been economically successful.

> ## REALITY BYTES   Forensic Investigations
>
> Catching a criminal is only the first step in a long legal process. You have to be able to prove the crime in a court of law. Technology-based crimes present an entirely new type of evidence, and police investigators need to be trained to perform the investigation and handle the data properly. In the UK, only 1,000 of the nation's 140,000 police officers are trained to handle digital evidence. Fewer than 250 have advanced computer forensics skills. Several companies, such as 7Safe Ltd., have sprung up to provide training. The best of the in-spectors can work for Britain's National Hi-Tech Crime Unit, which also hunts online criminals. In May 2004, the NHTCU arrested 12 people allegedly involved in a case where a Russian crime gang used a phishing scheme to steal hundreds of thousands of pounds from UK bank customers.
>
> **Source:** Adapted from "Cyber-Sleuthing the Latest in High-Tech Crime Fighting," *CNN Online*, May 26, 2004.

Computer Forensics

How do you prove the allegations in a computer crime? Sometimes, stopping computer attacks is not good enough. You want to catch the crooks or attackers and have them charged with the appropriate crime. The problem is that you have to be extremely careful when you collect evidence that will be used in a criminal case. In particular, the investigator has to be able to guarantee the authenticity of the evidence from the moment it is collected to when it is presented in court. This process can be tricky with digital evidence. It is not a task for amateurs. You have to bring in a professional investigator to handle the evidence correctly. Of course, few police departments have people trained in computer crime, and they are probably busy chasing murderers and drug dealers.

Some private companies help with investigations, but make sure you contact your lawyers and the prosecuting attorneys early in the process. Several technical companies exist to help examine computer evidence, such as recovering data from hard drives and decrypting files. Throughout the entire process, you have to keep good records. Most actions have to be logged; and be sure to record the date, time, and people involved. Also, remember that computer logs and backup tapes often get recycled after a certain time, so be sure to maintain secure copies.

e-Commerce Security Issues

What special security problems arise in e-commerce? E-commerce uses the same security technologies available to any business. However, some aspects of e-commerce are more sensitive and require more careful security planning. These issues are highlighted in this section, with a discussion of the common solutions.

Data Transmission

Although security is an issue with all computer networks, the Internet presents a special challenge. In particular, the Internet is not owned by anyone and is really just a loose connection of computers. Virtually anyone can connect a computer to the Internet—even serving as a host computer or a router.

Because of the design and size of the network, messages are rarely sent directly from one computer to another. In almost all cases, messages are passed through several other computers or routers on the way to their destination. As indicated in Figure 5.13, it is possible for someone to join the Internet and spy on all conversations that pass through that section of the network. Unprotected credit card numbers sent over the Internet could be intercepted and used illegally.

Problem: You need to share some files with members of the marketing department.

Tools: Windows XP Professional has the ability to set detailed security permissions on folders and files. In a student lab, you might not have permissions to create folders and set file permissions. Also, you might have to change an option to set detailed security. By default, this level of security is often turned off on home machines. Open My Computer, select Tools/Folder Options from the menu and click on the View tab. Scroll to the bottom of the Advanced settings and uncheck the option: Use simple file sharing. Click the OK button and browse to a location where you want to put the shared folder. Create the new folder.

In a business setting, the users and groups have probably already been created by the network administrator. If you need to create groups and users, use the Start menu/All Programs/Administrative Tools/Computer Management. If you do not see the administrative tools, you need to enable it by setting the properties of the main taskbar, or use Start/Run: compmgmt.msc/s. Right-click the Users icon and select New User. Make up a username and password for a user. Repeat this until you have three sample users. (If the users are already defined on the network, you can skip this step.) Right-click the Groups icon and select New Group. Name it Marketing and provide a description. Click the Add button and enter the usernames of the three users you just created.

Return to your folder and right-click the folder icon and select the Sharing and Security option. Click the option to share the folder and name it Marketing. Click the Permissions button and Remove the Everyone group. Add the new Marketing group and assign Read permission. Click the Apply button, then click the Security tab. Click the Add button and enter the Marketing group so they have read access. Click the Add button and enter the name of one of the users. Give this person Modify (and Write) permissions. This user will be able to read and change files stored in this folder—the others will only be able to read them. Log on as one of the new users and testing the file permis-

sions. Note, if you are familiar with command-line commands (DOS), you can use the runas command without logging off. When you are finished, remove the Marketing group and users using the Computer Management tool.

Quick Quiz:

1. Why is it important to define groups of users?

2. Why is it important to delete this test group and users when you are finished?

FIGURE 5.13

Internet security concerns: Data passes through many unknown servers. Any machine connected could read the data, destroy it, or fabricate a different message. Encryption techniques are available but not yet employed by the mainstream of Internet users. Rapidly changing automatic password generators are available for secure logins across insecure networks.

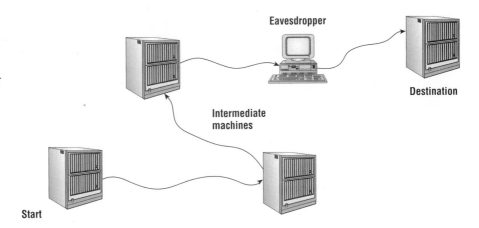

Of course, with the huge volume of data on the Internet, there is probably only a slight chance that someone will notice one particular transaction. But automated tools could be written to monitor all packets that transfer through one piece of the Internet; so the odds of someone stealing data are higher than they first appear.

Today, this aspect of Internet security is relatively easy to handle: simply encrypt your transmissions. Web transactions and e-mail can automatically be encrypted with a secure server. If you want to run an e-commerce site, you pay the money to Verisign for a digital certificate. Your Web server software has a special program to load the encryption identifiers. For transmissions you wish to protect, you move the Web pages into a special directory. From that point, your Web server and the customer's browser automatically handle the data encryption. Most Web sites use dual-key encryption through a system known as **secure sockets layer (SSL).** The Web site owner purchases a digital certificate and configures the server pages to run from a protected folder. When the client browser connects to these pages, the server sends its public key to enable encryption automatically.

To improve security for workers who need to connect to computers across the Internet, many companies have created a **virtual private network (VPN).** A VPN encrypts all transmissions before they are sent across the Internet. Using this technology, it is safe for employees to work from home using high-speed Internet connection. The encryption protects the data just as securely as having a local wired connection. In a sense, VPN creates a secure tunnel from your computer to the company's server.

Spoofing Sites

Breaking into protected computers is difficult and requires patience. Many hackers are lazy or in a hurry, so the easiest solution is to trick employees or customers. An increasingly common approach is to set up a fake site that looks like the original. For example, an attacker can quickly create a partial Web site that looks identical to a large banking site. Then the attacker spams millions of people and makes up a story about errors in their accounts. The spam message contains a link to the fake Web site, where customers are asked to enter their real username and passwords. The attacker collects this data and uses it to log into the real site and steal money.

Alert customers can spot the fraud immediately, because the URL in the browser will be wrong—it will not contain the correct name of the bank. For example, instead of www.bankofamerica.com, the link might be bankofamerica.xyzzz.kr. Moreover, it is highly unlikely that the fake site will have a security certificate, so the little lock will not be displayed in the browser frame, and the URL reference will use http:// instead of https:// for secure sockets. Of course, many customers are not alert enough to catch these details.

Banks and other large companies routinely scan spam and online sites searching for these spoofed sites. The sites are generally shut down quickly with the international cooperation of various governments and agencies. Creating a spoof site is a serious crime in most countries.

REALITY BYTES   Gone Phishing

Thieves have developed a new tool to steal your money. Called "phishing," they create a Web site that looks similar to a large company's such as Citicorp or EarthLink. Then they spam everyone with a phony message saying you need to log in and verify or change your personal data, including account numbers, passwords, and PINs. EarthLink receives about 40,000 calls or e-mails a month from subscribers who received a fraudulent message. Citibank maintains a permanent link on their Web site (www.citibank.com) informing peo-ple about current phishing attacks and asking users to report any problems. Because of the severity of the problem, Citibank reacts quickly to track and shut down phishing sites—anywhere in the world. Earthlink is developing an antiphishing tool that automatically blocks known phishing sites.

Source: Adapted from "EarthLink Fights Data-Stealing Websites," *CNN Online*, April 14, 2004.

Wireless Networks

Wireless networks add an extra challenge to security because the radio waves are accessible to anyone within a certain distance of the antenna. Two primary types of wireless systems exist today: (1) private LANs that you install at your company and (2) public networks that offer shared access to millions of people (such as the cellular phone system). The public networks are similar to the Internet. If you want to protect your transmissions, you will have to encrypt your messages. Some of the digital phones offer encryption, but the systems are sometimes weak. But it is better than the old days of analog cell phones, where anyone with a scanner could eavesdrop on your phone calls.

Private wireless LANs can create more problems, because a stranger might sit outside your building and connect to your network. Early implementers of wireless LANs experienced these problems when they failed to activate all of the security features. Wireless LANs generally require a password to allow users to connect to the network. They can also encrypt all transmissions to prevent others from intercepting the transmissions. The only catch with encryption is that it slows down the transmission, and wireless networks are relatively slow already. So you have to make a trade-off decision: do you want faster wireless communications or a more secure network? The encryption technology in older wireless systems has several well-known flaws. If you need to seriously encrypt wireless transmissions, you need to use a VPN or a secure sockets layer connection through the server.

Carnivore, Echelon, and Escrow Keys

An interesting twist to interception of data transmissions is government involvement. In the United States, for years the government has had wiretap capabilities to force the phone company to intercept and record voice calls—with the permission of a judge. Digital and computer transmissions make this task more difficult. So, the federal government has been working on systems to intercept and decode data.

One public system revealed in 2000 is an FBI-sponsored computer system known as Carnivore. (In 2001, it was renamed DCS-10000, but most people still call it by the more colorful name.) Essentially, it is a computer with special software that can be installed at an ISP to capture all Internet traffic from a specified person. The system is supposed to be used with the permission of a judge to reduce criminal activities, and it is supposed to capture data only from the alleged criminal.

Echelon is a more secret project run internationally by the NSA in cooperation with Canada, the UK, Australia, and New Zealand. The government has not officially acknowledged its existence, but the foreign press (and several government committees) have investigated portions of it. It is a system that intercepts a variety of communications, including faxes, e-mail messages, international phone calls, and cellular phones in several nations (by law, it is not supposed to be used in the United States). Several powerful computers evaluate the intercepted data and search it for key words to search for terrorist and illegal drug activity.

Along the same lines and for the same reasons, the NSA created a special encryption system similar to dual-key encryption. However, it had a unique twist: every encryption key

FIGURE 5.14

Escrow keys: The U.S. government is concerned that citizens and foreigners will use encryption for "undesirable" purposes, such as spying and committing crimes. The National Security Agency created a secret method of encrypting messages, including digital phone transmissions. Every encryption device can be broken with two special keys (numbers) that are held in escrow by judicial or governmental agencies. On receiving court permission, police would be able to decrypt any message or conversation.

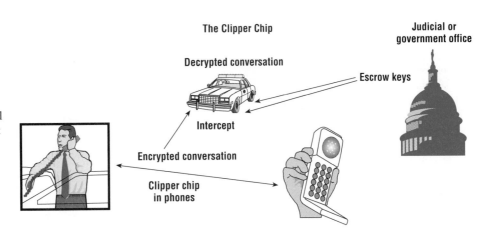

has two escrow keys that can be used to decrypt any message. The system was originally created for digital cell phones. The cell phones can automatically encrypt the transmissions. But the security organizations wanted the ability to get a wiretap authorization to intercept phone calls in certain cases. Figure 5.14 shows how the police would collect the escrow keys from a judge. Entering the key numbers into a special receiver would decrypt the conversation without the user's knowledge. For a short time, the U.S. government thought about requiring that only escrow-key encryption be legal. But this requirement would have destroyed the international sales of most U.S. products, because businesses in other nations would not trust the U.S. government. The technology still exists and is used in some products, but most consumers would avoid it—if they knew it was being used.

Theft of Data from Servers

Because of the powerful encryption systems available, interception of transmissions is a relatively minor problem—as long as you use the encryption techniques. Instead, the servers connected to the Internet have become tempting targets. Several incidents have been reported of hackers stealing millions of records of customer credit card data from e-commerce firms. While credit laws protect consumers, the loss of a credit card is still painful and time consuming. In addition, the e-commerce firm faces liability issues if it did not adequately secure the data.

Securing servers uses the same technologies as any computer system: (1) make sure the latest operating system patches have been applied, (2) set access control rights to the smallest number of people possible, (3) encrypt the sensitive data, (4) hire trusted employees, and (5) monitor access to the sensitive data. A sixth step (firewalls) is explained in a later section. In 2000, Visa added some details and expanded this list to 12 principles that all Internet firms are supposed to follow. At some point, the rules might become mandatory, but any e-commerce firm needs to be careful about protecting servers and customer data.

Denial of Service

Denial-of-service attacks have gained importance in the last few years. The essence of an e-commerce site is the ability to reach customers 24 hours a day. If someone floods the site with meaningless traffic, then no one can use the service and the company may go out of business. Several variations of DoS have been used in the past couple of years, sometimes dragging down large chunks of the Internet at one time. Most of the techniques take advantage of flaws in the Internet protocols or in their implementation on a particular type of server. Figure 5.15 illustrates the process. A hacker breaks into some weakly protected computers and loads a special program that is hidden. On a signal, the machines all send requests to the targeted server. With some known Internet design flaws, these messages can be multiplied so that a few thousand messages become millions and bog down the server. This type of attack is hard to trace to the original source unless investigators find monitor logs on the zombie machines. Several Internet sites provide simplified instructions on how to perform these attacks, so even weak hackers or "script kiddies" can create havoc.

FIGURE 5.15
Denial-of-service attack: A bored hacker first breaks into weakly protected homes and school systems and loads a hidden program on thousands of machines. At a signal, all of the zombie machines send messages to the server, preventing everyone else from using it.

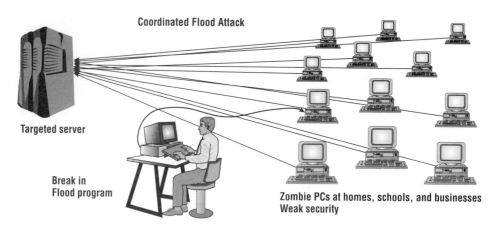

Coordinated Flood Attack

Targeted server

**Break in
Flood program**

**Zombie PCs at homes, schools, and businesses
Weak security**

FIGURE 5.16
Firewalls: Firewalls are packet analyzers that are used to keep local data from moving to the Internet and to limit the actions allowed in from the Internet. Firewalls examine each packet of data on the network and block certain types to limit the interaction of the company network with the Internet.

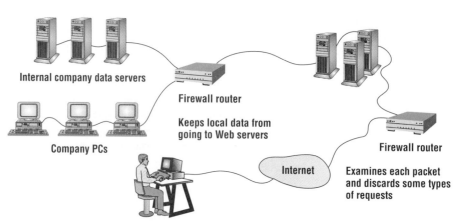

Internal company data servers

Firewall router

**Keeps local data from
going to Web servers**

Company PCs

Internet

Firewall router

**Examines each packet
and discards some types
of requests**

Firewalls and Intrusion Detection

The Internet and e-commerce add some complications to protecting company data. You need to give customers access to some important company data to provide the best e-commerce site. For example, customers like to know if an item is in stock before they place an order. To offer this service, you need to connect your Web server to your company inventory system. But any time you open a connection from the Internet to your company data, you have to be extremely careful to control that interaction. Security access controls and database security controls are two important provisions.

Beyond access control, simply connecting your company computers to the Internet could cause problems within the network itself. You do not want company network traffic being sent to the Internet, and you do not want outsiders to be able to see your internal computers—giving them the chance to try and break into your servers. Figure 5.16 shows how firewalls are used to isolate sections of the network. **Firewalls** are essentially routers that examine each packet of network data passing through them and block certain types to limit the interaction of the company network with the Internet.

The Internet protocols were designed as an open network to transport many types of data and to enable computers to connect in many different ways. For example, servers have logical ports on which they listen for requests. Since only a few of these ports are used for common Internet activities, the firewall is configured to block all of the other ports to prevent outsiders from finding a back way into one of your servers. Security experts configure the routers, but as a manager, you need to make sure your company is using them. Also, you will find that some tasks you want to do will be blocked by the firewalls. Usually, these restrictions are for your own safety, but sometimes security analysts go a little overboard and block useful features. This trade-off between user access and company security is an ongoing problem. It often arises because the security tools are not sophisticated enough, so security personnel choose to block everything.

REALITY BYTES   Is Your Computer a Zombie?

Spammers and computer hackers today use viruses and other known attacks to take over personal computers connected to the Internet. Machines that are connected full-time on cable modem or DSL lines are particular favorites. Machines that have not been upgraded with the latest patches are favorite targets. Once the machine is compromised, spammers use them to launch millions of e-mail messages that cannot be traced back to the original source. Hackers use them for denial-of-service attacks. Many people are unaware that their machines have been compromised. Some ISPs, including Comcast, are cutting off service for these zombie computers. On one day, the Internet Storm Center recorded scanning activity indicating a virus infection coming from 10,000 machines on the Comcast network. SenderBase, a company that monitors e-mail transmissions, showed 40 Comcast customers who have sent more than 100,000 messages per day, with some sending as many as 1 million messages. Comcast claims to be aware of the problem, and it has procedures for alerting customers and helping them clean up the infections.

Source: Adapted from Paul Roberts, "Comcast Cutting Off 'Spam Zombies,' " *Computerworld*, March 9, 2004.

An **intrusion detection system (IDS)** is a combination of hardware and software that continuously monitors the network traffic. The hardware is similar to that used in a firewall, but instead of blocking the packets, it performs a more complex analysis. The systems use a set of rules to monitor all Internet traffic and search for patterns. For instance, a common attack often begins with a sweep of a target's network to look for open ports. The IDS observes this repeated scanning, blocks the requests, identifies the source, and sends a warning to the security manager. An IDS is an effective monitoring tool, but the cheaper ones tend to generate too many false warnings.

Privacy

If you have to track everyone's computer use to improve security, what happens to privacy? Computer security is a complex topic. One of its most challenging aspects is that many of the tools available to improve security can also reduce individual privacy. For example, a single sign-on system used across the country could be used to track people through their purchases, when and where they used a computer, when they passed through toll booths or boarded planes, or almost anything else. Even without single sign-on, the security systems enable companies to track detailed usage by employees and customers.

These issues are explored in detail in Chapter 14. For now, you need to remember that many proposed security controls scare even honest people—because of the loss of privacy. As a businessperson, you must be aware of these problems and establish policies to minimize the effects and keep customers happy.

Summary

Companies have to trust employees, consultants, and business partners, but this group presents the greatest security threats. Natural disasters are a threat to the physical assets, but their business damage can be minimized by having up-to-date backups and a disaster plan with arrangements to run operations off-site if a disaster strikes. The Internet provides more avenues of attack for outsiders—particularly from viruses spread through e-mail messages. The best defenses are to install all current operating system patches, to assign access rights carefully, and to monitor the computer usage with an intrusion detection system. However, denial-of-service attacks are particularly hard to prevent.

Encryption protects data during transmission. It is particularly useful for sending credit card data over the Internet. It can also be used to provide digital signatures that authenticate users to validate the source of messages.

A Manager's View

Computer security is a critical issue for any company. For Web-based businesses, careful controls and continual vigilance are mandatory. Information systems have many potential weaknesses and threats. But overall, electronic security can be stronger than any other form—if it is maintained by experts. Encryption is a key component in securing systems, communications, and protecting privacy. The drawback to security is that it imposes limits on employees and customers. Some tasks become more difficult and some loss of privacy occurs. To protect corporate and personal data, we have to be able to trust the people who collect the data.

Key Words

Advanced Encryption Standard (AES), *181*	digital certificate, *182*	public key, *181*
application service provider (ASP), *169*	digital signature, *182*	secure sockets layer (SSL), *185*
authentication, *181*	firewall, *188*	single sign-on, *177*
biometrics, *176*	hot site, *167*	spyware, *173*
brute force, *180*	intrusion detection system (IDS), *189*	uninterruptible power supply (UPS), *175*
certificate authority, *182*	Kerberos, *175*	virtual private network (VPN), *185*
cold site, *167*	malware, *173*	virus, *170*
data mirroring, *168*	Pretty Good Privacy (PGP), *181*	
denial of service (DoS), *173*	private key, *181*	

Website References

Computer Crime

CERT	www.cert.org
Computer Crime Research Center	www.crime-research.org
Computer Security Institute	www.gocsi.com
FBI: Internet Fraud Complaint Center	www.ifccfbi.gov
Interpol	www.interpol.int/Public/TechnologyCrime/
National Fraud Information	www.fraud.org
National Infrastructure Protection Center	www.nipc.gov
National Security Agency	www.nsa.gov
National White Collar Crime Center	www.cybercrime.org
SEC Internet enforcement	www.sec.gov/divisions/enforce/internetenforce.htm
Virtual Librarian crime links	www.virtuallibrarian.com/legal/org.html

Additional Readings

Bequai, August. *Technocrimes.* Lexington, MA: Lexington Books, 1989. [Security Pacific and other cases.]

Faltermayer, Charlotte. "Cyberveillance." *Time,* August 14, 2000, p. B22. [Worker monitoring statistics.]

Forno, Richard, and William Feinbloom. "PKI: A Question of Trust and Value." *Communications of the ACM,* June 2001, Vol. 44, No. 6. [A good summary of the difficulties of trusting public key certificate authorities.]

Feig, Christy. "Medical Privacy Rules to Take Effect." CNN, April 12, 2001, http://www.cnn.com/2001/HEALTH/04/12/medical.privacy.index.html?s=2 [Notice of new federal medical privacy rules.]

Harriss, H. 1999. "Computer Virus Attacks Have Cost Businesses $7.6 Billion in 1999." *Computer Economics,* report dated June 18, 1999. (http://www.info-ec.com/viruses/99/viruses_062299a_j.shtml) [Increased costs of virus attacks.]

Oakes, Chris. "Privacy Laws Aim to Protect the Hunters as Well as the Hunted." *International Herald Tribune,* March 23, 2001. [Good analysis of European Union privacy controls.]

Thurman, Mathias (pseudonym). "What to Do When the Feds Come Knocking." *Computerworld,* June 4, 2001, p. 62. [Situation where hacker used a stolen laptop to attack other systems, and computer logs helped show the employee was innocent.]

Whiteside, Thomas. *Computer Capers: Tales of Electronic Thievery, Embezzlement and Fraud.* New York: Crowell, 1978. [Early cases of computer fraud and abuse.]

http://csrc.nist.gov/encryption/aes/ [Reference source for AES algorithm.]

http://www.visabrc.com/doc.phtml?2,64,932,932a_cisp.html [Reference to Visa CISP security.]

Review Questions

1. What are the primary threats to information processed by computers?
2. How do viruses spread over the Internet? How do you stop them?
3. What methods are available to identify computer users?
4. What are access controls and how are they used to protect information?
5. What threat are audits trying to protect against?
6. What are the advantages and disadvantages of dual-key encryption compared to single-key encryption?
7. How can dual-key encryption be used to authenticate a message?
8. What are the main issues in protecting e-commerce Web sites?
9. Why are certificate authorities so important in a public key infrastructure?
10. Why are wireless transmissions more of a security problem than wired systems?
11. What is a denial-of-service attack? Why is it so important in e-commerce? Why is it so difficult to prevent?
12. What is a firewall and how does it protect a company from Internet attacks?

Exercises

1. Find information on two biometric devices. Identify the costs and the steps required to install them. Can they be used for identification over the Internet?
2. Find and download a free trial copy of a personal intrusion detection system, and install it on a PC connected to the Internet full-time (school connection, DSL, or cable modem). Let the system run for a few days and record how many potential attacks it records.
3. Search the Internet for tools that might be used to attack computers. Do not download them! Do not attempt to use them! Just list the sites and a brief description of the tools.
4. Obtain a tool that searches for spyware and check your computer. If you have permission on a public machine (lab or library), run the tool on it. Write a brief report of any problems you found.
5. Use the Windows Task Manager to list all of the active processes on your computer. Search the Internet to identify the purpose of each process.
6. Assume you have a server with about 120 gigabytes of data. Identify the hardware and software you could use to make backups. Be sure to specify the price and estimate the amount of time it will take to back up the data.
7. Identify a tool (hardware or software) that provides VPN security. Briefly describe it and estimate the costs for implementing it at a company with 50 employees who want to access the company's servers while traveling.

 Technology Toolbox

8. Install a digital security certificate on your computer and send a digitally signed message to your instructor.
9. Read the information on the Thawte Web site about how users can be authenticated

(Web of Trust). Briefly explain how the system works. Do you think this is a secure and reliable system?

10. Research the current status of the U.S. Post Office EPM mail system. Explain what it does and how it is different from encrypted e-mail.

11. If you have the appropriate network permissions, or using your own computer, create the Marketing group and three users on your computer. Create a folder and set the permissions so that the Marketing group can access the files in the folder. Add your instructor to the group and include a test file that he or she can read.

12. Check the security permissions on your computer—particularly the My Documents folder (or wherever you store most of your files). Is the folder secure or should you set different permissions?

Teamwork

13. Get a copy of PGP (or sign up for a free e-mail encryption key at Thawte). Write an e-mail message and send an encrypted copy to the other members of your team.

14. Create a subdirectory on a computer that enables you to set access rights. Select a user or group and set permissions so members of that group can read the data but cannot change it. All other users (except yourself) cannot read the data.

15. Conduct a small survey of students (not in your MIS class). Find out how often they back up their data, the last time they updated their operating systems, and how many of them have been infected by a virus in the last 6, 12, and 24 months.

16. Your B2C company needs a privacy policy for data collected on the site. Remember that if you violate the policy, you could be fined. Have each person find an existing privacy policy. Compare the policies by matching sections and provisions. Use the combined results to create a new policy.

17. Create a simple chart in a spreadsheet and encrypt it. Send a version to each person on your team using a different password key so that they can add a couple of rows of data and return it. Combine the results into one spreadsheet. Comment on any problems you encountered.

18. Each person should save a small Word document and encrypt it with a password. Exchange files with others in the group and see if you can guess the passwords to open the file. At least one person should pick a relatively easy password.

Rolling Thunder Database

19. What privacy problems might exist at Rolling Thunder? What rules or procedures should you enact to avoid problems? Write a privacy statement for the company.

20. If Rolling Thunder Bicycles adds an Internet site to order bicycles and deal with customers, what security procedures should be implemented to protect the data?

21. Research the costs and steps involved in setting up a secure Web server for Rolling Thunder that can be used to sell bicycles over the Internet.

22. Write a disaster plan for Rolling Thunder. Identify how the backup tapes will be handled and the type of system you will need if a natural disaster hits.

Cases: Professional Sports

The Industry

Professional sports raise billions of dollars a year in the United States and around the world. Actually, European professional soccer teams usually top the lists in terms of revenue. In the United States, baseball teams brought in $3.6 billion in revenue in 2001 ("MLB" 2002), basketball teams $2.7 billion in 2003 ("NBA" 2004), and football teams almost $5 billion in 2002 (Ozanian 2003). These numbers include gate receipts as well as other revenue sources such as television payments. Of course, the teams also have enormous costs in the form of player (and coach) salaries. In total, sports franchises are the most popular segment of the entertainment industry. If you add in the amount spent on gambling (where it is legal, of course), sports are incredibly popular.

Information systems play several roles in sports management. Coaches, players, and scouts use information systems to track performance and opponents, store game files, diagram plays, and communicate information. IT is also used in the front office to sell tickets and merchandise. Like any other business, administrators have to derive financial information and evaluate customers and suppliers. Because of the popularity of the Internet and the role of television, sports teams have also begun to implement sophisticated networks within the stadiums for use by high-end customers.

Since the teams generally use networks to share information during games, security is critical. Any public networks have to be built separately from the team networks. Fans might be frustrated if a public network crashes or is hacked, but a team could be severely crippled if its main coaching system goes down or is compromised.

Additional Reading

"MLB." *Forbes,* April 15, 2002.

"NBA Valuations." *Forbes,* February 9, 2004.

Ozanian, Michael K. "Showing You the Money." *Forbes,* September 15, 2003.

Case: Professional Football

Football requires a large number of players, and that means a team needs a large number of coaches. The information technology system becomes relatively more complex to handle the increased number of users and machines. Brian Wright, IT director for the Chicago Bears, notes that "the NFL in general is looking closely at security and how best to protect the information in our business. One of the things we identified was the need for better user authentication" (Vijayan 2004). The team installed a USB authentication key that staff members use to log onto the network. They must also enter a PIN. The strength of the dual-factor authentication is that the PIN is relatively easy to remember, but outsiders cannot hack into the network because they would need the physical USB key.

The Denver Broncos focused on providing more information for fans—particularly the fans who watch the game from the luxury box seats. The IT department installed flat panel touch screens and a high-speed network into every box. Using the GamePlus system, fans can touch the screen and bring up the view from any camera in the stadium. Rick Schoenhals, IT director for the Broncos, notes that "I just know technology is gaining a bigger place in sports venues and sporting events. We're opening a new venue and we don't want to find out someone who opened next week is doing these great things with technology and we're not doing it. We can't be complacent in any area, including technology" (George 2002). The GamePlus system consists of 135 screens. The Broncos are trying to offset some of the costs by selling corporate sponsorships that display logos throughout the game. Because Denver was the first team to implement this type of system, the costs were relatively high.

Local area and wide area networks are important to improve communication within football teams, and many teams were early adopters. The Carolina Panthers installed a 100-mbps network in 1997. Roger Goss, MIS manager for the Panthers, comments on the speed by noting: "We needed that because the coaches create complex graphics, like playbook diagrams and game plans, and download them from servers to workstations" (Wallace 1997). The team also uses frame-relay links to other teams and to the NFL office. The connection is used to share statistics and to notify the league about trades and waivers. With 83 users, the system is heavily used on Monday to Wednesday when the coaches are creating and distributing game plans, and scouting reports arrive for the next opponent.

Sports teams are increasingly aware that fans want up-to-the-minute information on many aspects of the game. In 2000, the Washington Redskins created a Mobile Flash application to offer team news via Web-enabled cell phones and PDAs. Fans can sign up to receive daily e-mail messages about trades, statistics, and player injuries. The Redskins were the first NFL team to implement the wireless system—although others provide e-mail newsletters.

When the New England Patriots built a new 68,000-seat stadium in 2002, the network was a critical element. The voice and data networks alone cost about $1 million. The network uses Nortel Passport switches with a gigabit Ethernet backbone. It links 80 luxury suites and provides more than 2,000 ports at 100 mbps. The network is important to the teams and the fans. It is also important for renting the stadium to businesses during the week. Pat Curley, the IT director, notes that "no other stadium has this setup. It makes it very exciting, and very challenging" (Cummings 2002). The network supports the various coaching and scouting systems used by teams. The Patriots scouts use notebook computers with comments and data uploaded to the central servers for the coaching staff. The coaching system also stores digitized video so coaches can watch specific plays. Curley notes that the coaching system runs on a separate LAN. She says, "We've designed everything to be separate so that people who need Internet bandwidth, such as the suite users and press, will have access but it won't conflict with or steal our bandwidth. Plus, it's more secure" (Cummings 2002).

Data security often extends beyond the digital world. Minnesota Vikings player Michael Bennet learned that the hard way in 2003. He received credit card statements with bills from various convenience stores. But the card did not really belong to him. Instead, an off-duty police officer working as a security guard for the team had stolen various documents from players and applied for credit cards in their names. The identity thief was caught in part from video surveillance tapes taken at one of the stores where he used the card. Several other well-known athletes have had problems with identity theft as well (ESPN 2003).

Questions

1. How can well-known stars protect themselves from identity theft?
2. What threats exist for portable computers used for scouting and how can those risks be minimized?
3. Would fans pay for mobile access to games? How much? What type of network would be needed to handle the data?

Additional Reading

Copeland, Lee. "Redskins Tackle Wireless Access." *Computerworld,* October 31, 2000.

Cummings, Joanne. "Network of Champions." *Network World,* July 22, 2002.

ESPN. "Vikings QB Culpepper, Four Others Were Victims," August 20, 2003.

George, Tischelle. "Football Fans See Games from a New Angle." *Information Week,* January 30, 2002.

Vijayan, Jaikumar. "Chicago Bears Boost Network Defenses." *Computerworld,* May 28, 2004.

Wallace, Bob. "LAN Blitz Sharpens Panthers' Claws." *Computerworld,* September 29, 1997.

Case: Basketball

The summer of 2003 was not a good year for the electricity grid in the northeastern United States. A combination of errors caused the international loop around Lake Erie to overload and shut down the power grid for the entire Northeast. Jay Wessel, the IT director for the Boston Celtics, was attending a picnic at 4:30 p.m., and he notes that when the grid crashed, "every cell phone and pager in the place went off" (Kontzer 2003). Because most of the blackout was focused in New York, he lost only some e-mail servers. Other teams had entire systems shut down. But it convinced Wessel to look into ways to provide backup in case his facility lost power. The problem he encountered is that most backup facilities were also located in the same areas. He notes that "it doesn't really do me any good to back up my data 10 miles away" (Kontzer 2003). Like many other businesses, Wessel is also looking for solutions to the problems with virus and worm attacks. By keeping systems patched, his losses have been minimal, but he is frustrated with the frequency of patches required.

The Women's NBA teams have added a new twist to marketing basketball. When the Portland Trail Blazers acquired a new team in 2000, management turned to a CRM system to target sales to season ticket holders. They also merged demographic data from external marketing lists and Ticketmaster. Tony Cesarano, database marketing manager, notes that the system significantly improved the efficiency of the sales team and was able to sell 6,400 season tickets in four months. He notes that "in the past, we would have manually keyed the WNBA sales information into a Microsoft Excel spreadsheet, which would have been time-consuming and could have introduced inaccuracies into the database" (Baron 2000). The Trail Blazers are using customer relationship management (CRM) tools to boost sales of season tickets for the men's team. The system has consolidated the data that used to be scattered on spreadsheets of the 50 sales and marketing employees. It tracks individual ticket holders as well as corporate customers. One of the big gains was to minimize overlap, where multiple salespeople often called on the same prospects. The system has proved useful in managing requests by ticket holders to change their seat locations. It can quickly bring up unsold or released seats as well as track priority values of important customers. The organization ultimately expanded the system to their Web site. Cesarano notes that the process is complicated: "We'll have to manage a much larger volume of data coming off the Web. We'll also have to figure out how to clean up the data, to make sure that we're using only useful, legitimate, and accurate data" (Baron 2000).

The NBA in total boasts a fan base of over 50 million people for the 29 teams. In an attempt to boost the level higher, the NBA installed a customer relationship management system from E.piphany. Bernie Mullin, senior vice president of marketing, notes that "we're going to have a 360-degree view of the fans and customers of the NBA. We've never had that before at the league or team level" (Songini 2001). The system pulls data from all of the customer-interaction points: ticket sales, All-Star nomination ballots, the NBA store Web site, individual team databases, and the NBA store in New York. The main focus is to place the data into a data warehouse and provide analytical tools to sell more tickets. The plan is to track sales by various events to answer questions such as whether certain teams provide bigger draws, or if some months or days draw bigger crowds. The main NBA office in Secaucus, New Jersey, has about 1,000 employees. The NBA has several data collection and online systems to maintain. Two staffers attend each game with touch screen laptops to collect data. The data is transferred back to the main system at headquarters in real time. It can be used by fans to create custom highlight reels.

The Orlando Magic also implemented CRM software to help boost ticket sales. A primary focus of their system is to identify and track customer complaints. If customers have problems, the system can direct them to the appropriate vendor and monitor vendor compliance with contracts. Julie Gory, fan relations and retail manager, notes that "we are a watchdog department that looks at things from a fan's perspective. Whatever happens from when the fan leaves their driveway—everything from parking, the cleanliness of the restrooms—when we hear of issues, we make notes and input them to GoldMine and can review them on whatever basis we want" (Songini 2002). Gory decided not to use the NBA CRM software because it was too expensive—the NBA was going to charge them about $100,000. The system was also more complex and harder to use.

Video is critical to coaches and players. Digital video provides enormous benefits over tape because it can be edited and indexed quickly. The New Jersey Nets were the first team to implement a comprehensive system from Ark Digital Technologies. The system lets coaches quickly grab the clips they want based on various statistics. Ark CEO Alan Kidd notes that "during halftime, coaches could show clips of the first half by type, for example, jump shots or post positioning" (Kreiser 2002). Ark has also created a digital video coaching system. The system can show basic drills. Ultimately, it can be coupled with the game-day videos so players can go to a Web site and compare their performance with the drills (www.arkdigitalsystems.com).

Questions

1. What privacy issues arise from the NBA using a CRM system to track customer purchases?

2. How can the CIO of a basketball team provide backup facilities for a small-to-medium-sized network?

3. How long will it take for digital video coaching technology to be implemented at the college level?

Additional Reading

Baron, Talila. "Team Scores with Apps That Net Ticket-Buyers." *Information Week,* February 21, 2000.

Goff, Leslie. "NBA's IT Team Makes Play with Web, CRM Initiatives." *Computerworld,* June 11, 2001.

Kontzer, Tony. "Data Backup: Rethinking the Unthinkable(s)." *Information Week,* August 18, 2003.

Kreiser, John. "Virtual Coaching." *Information Week,* July 22, 2002.

Songini, Marc L. "NBA Shoots for Data Analysis." *Computerworld,* May 28, 2001.

Songini, Marc L. "Orlando Magic Shoot for Customer Satisfaction." *Computerworld,* December 5, 2002.

Case: Baseball

Sports fans, particularly in baseball, are often crazy about souvenirs. They will collect almost anything. So, it is not surprising that outdated copies of baseball contracts found their way to an e-Bay auction set up by Scott Gaynor, a sports memorabilia dealer. Bob Tufts, who played for the San Francisco Giants and the Kansas City Royals in the early 1980s, found that his contracts were among those offered for sale. While there is nothing illegal per se about the sale, there was an important twist: As employee contracts, most of the documents contained the social security numbers of the players. With some big-name players in the group (read "money"), the risks were quite high. Tufts observed: "I'm shocked to find out how easy it is for people to get their hands on files like these" (Rovell 2003). With a home address, the social security number, and a guess at a mother's maiden name, criminals could have created fake bank accounts. The commissioner's office requested that the auction be stopped and the contracts returned. Some of the bids had reached $200 before the items were pulled.

The Internet is increasingly important for attracting fans to all sports. Since baseball has been number-intensive for years, Web sites are an important source of data on games and players. In 2001, all major league baseball teams agreed to consolidate and standardize their Web sites. All of the sites are now run from the MLB servers. All sites were given a common look. An interesting aspect to the change is that revenue from sales on the site is split across all of the teams. Bud Selig, the commissioner, observed that "the most significant part of our whole Internet activity was the unanimous vote to share the revenue. That was a very dramatic change in think-

ing, because disparity is the biggest problem we have" (Wilder 2001). Bob DuPuy, chief legal officer in the commissioner's office, adds that "of course, we agreed to share revenues that don't currently exist. I don't think we could do it at a later date when there was revenue disparity" (Wilder 2001). The site is operated by a separate company created by the team owners and run in New York City. The new organization was initially funded with $1 million a year for three years from each of the 30 teams ($30 million a year). In a somewhat risky move, the MLB site sells video access to games. The risk is that it could alienate traditional television broadcasters—who provide a substantial part of baseball revenues. But the site is still subject to local blackout rules, and the picture quality is not even close to television standards. So, its market would most likely consist of out-of-area fans.

Season tickets present interesting problems for clubs and fans. About 80 percent of them are owned by corporations—particularly the luxury suites. Robert McAuliff, CEO of Season Ticket Solutions, notes that "season ticket holders . . . miss 25 to 50 percent of games every year" (Rosencrance 2001). The challenge for teams is that filling seats increases revenue through sales of food and souvenirs. The challenge for fans is that they want to efficiently use their investments. The Arizona Diamondbacks, as well as other teams, have purchased software that enables season ticket holders to manage their seats. The Web site allows ticket holders to check on who is using the tickets, and which dates still have seats available.

Web casting ball games is an interesting legal and marketing area. Are people willing to pay for Web broadcasts? Do they want to select specific games? (Currently, MLB offers a subscription but only to specific games.) Would such a system encroach on television broadcasts? Is there a profit? Many of these questions remain unanswered, and it is not clear that anyone is seriously addressing them yet. In 2000, William Craig and George Simons created a company and the iCraveTV Web site in Canada. The company picked up signals from 17 broadcast stations in the United States and Canada, digitized the signals, and offered them for free on its server. Rebroadcasting signals is legal in Canada. But it is a violation of U.S. copyright laws. The company was quickly sued by several U.S. sports agencies as well as the Motion Picture Association of America, because the company did not block the signals to U.S. customers. The company quickly made an out-of-court settlement and shut down the site (McGeever 2000). So, many questions remain about whether fans want to see Internet, or even cell phone, video of games. And, if so, how much they might be willing to pay and whether those fees would offset any lost television advertising revenue.

Questions

1. How are player privacy rights different from average citizens?

2. What procedures can be implemented to help protect players from identity theft?

3. What are the benefits and drawbacks to centralizing the team Web sites for MLB?

4. How could a team provide individual customized access to baseball games via the Internet?

Additional Reading

McGeever, Christine. "Webcaster under Fire." *Computerworld,* January 21, 2000.

Rosencrance, Linda. "Watching the Bottom Line from Box Seats." *Computerworld,* August 6, 2001.

Rovell, Darren. "Confidential Information Pulled from Online Auction." *ESPN,* June 17, 2003.

Wilder, Clinton. "Redefining Business: A New Game Plan." *Information Week,* April 9, 2001.

Summary Industry Questions

1. What information technologies have helped this industry?

2. Did the technologies provide a competitive advantage or were they quickly adopted by rivals?

3. Which technologies could this industry use that were developed in other sectors?

4. Is the level of competition increasing or decreasing in this industry? Is it dominated by a few firms, or are they fairly balanced?

5. What problems have been created from the use of information technology and how did the firms solve the problems?

CHAPTER SIX

Transactions and Operations

Chapter Outline

Introduction

Data Capture
  Point of Sale
  POS Advantages
  Process Control
  Electronic Data Interchange (EDI)

Elements of a Transaction
  Vendor Perspective
  Customer Perspective
  Transaction Fees
  Government Perspective
  Risk Mitigation in e-Commerce

International Issues

Payment Mechanisms

Data Quality
  Data Integrity
  Multitasking, Concurrency, and Integrity
  Data Volume
  Data Summaries
  Time

Production Management
  Production Issues
  Distribution and Inventory Control

Summary

Key Words

Web Site References

Additional Reading

Review Questions

Exercises

Cases: Retail Sales

What You Will Learn in This Chapter

- How do you handle the huge amount of data generated from transactions and operations?
- How do you efficiently collect transaction data?
- What are the major elements and risks of a transaction?
- Why are transactions more difficult in an international environment?
- How can customers pay for products and why do you need new payment mechanisms?
- How do you ensure that the transaction data is accurate?
- Can your company be more efficient and productive?

How do retail stores handle transactions? Wal-Mart has grown to become not just the largest retailer but the largest company in the world. Each store is huge and sells hundreds of thousands of items a day. Each sale has to be recorded with absolutely no errors. Moreover, the store has to monitor sales and choose which products to order. Then it must monitor the progress of incoming items, compare the received items to each order, and resolve problems and errors. Wal-Mart has succeeded because it uses information technology to handle these operations at the lowest possible cost.

A retailer that focuses on low prices can never rest. It must continually search for new ways to reduce costs, improve store management, and choose the correct products to sell at the best price. Being the biggest provides several advantages—notably in terms of negotiations with suppliers. For these reasons, Wal-Mart is one of the companies leading the transition to radio frequency identification (RFID) chips. Initially, Wal-Mart is asking major suppliers to place the passive tags on pallets and major crates. The primary advantage is that the receiving docks can quickly scan incoming shipments and match the products to the individual orders. RFID tags carry more information and are easier to read than traditional bar codes.

FIGURE 6.1

Transaction processing: Transaction processing involves collecting data from the business operations and from external partners. Electronic commerce can be used to handle consumer and business transactions over the Internet.

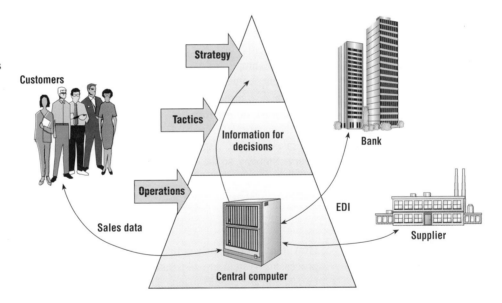

Introduction

How do you handle the huge amount of data generated from transactions and operations? This question has been asked repeatedly for centuries. In fact, it has driven the organizational structure of companies. What were firms like in the 1800s or earlier? Most were small proprietorships. As firms became larger, how could they handle the thousands of daily transactions? Hierarchical structures evolved to collect data at the point of sale, summarize it, and move it up the chain of command to the CEO. Figure 6.1 shows how transactional data is exchanged with customers, suppliers, manufacturing, and banks, and summarized for higher-level decisions. However, when you have computers today that can capture all of the operations data automatically, do you still need this hierarchical structure?

TRENDS

Because of legal ramifications, businesses have always collected data about transactions. Accounting systems play an important role in collecting and analyzing transaction data. Through the 1960s, most business computers were primarily producing basic accounting reports. Raw data was punched into the computer by hand, and the computer produced totals and updated the general ledger. In effect, the computer was used as a giant calculator to automate the production of printed reports similar to those used before the advent of computers. The primary reason for using the computer was speed and accuracy. It was justified because it was cheaper and less error-prone than hiring thousands of people to produce the reports.

As computer capabilities increased in the 1970s, the most important change was to use the computer to collect the raw data. In retail sales, the cash register was replaced with a computer terminal and a bar code scanner. Whenever a customer purchased an item, the transaction data was immediately sent to the main computer. This automation eliminated the need to hire a person to enter the data at the end of the day. Together with fewer errors, these online transaction systems provided better service to the customer. Because sales were recorded immediately, the sales clerk could quickly determine whether an item was in stock. The systems also provided virtually instantaneous sales data to the managers. If some item was selling rapidly, the system could tell the employees to restock that item on the shelves.

The 1980s and 1990s resulted in more integration. Transaction data was made available to managers throughout the company. One goal was to combine the systems across the company into an enterprise system that enabled managers to examine all aspects of the business.

In many respects, electronic commerce and mobile commerce are simply new transaction systems. In these systems, the customer selects a product and enters purchase information directly into the vendor's computer system. Yet new transaction systems can change the entire economy.

Whenever two people make an exchange, it is called a *transaction*. Transactions are important events for a company, and collecting data about them is called **transaction processing.** Examples of transactions include making a purchase at a store, withdrawing money from a checking account, making a payment to a creditor, or paying an employee.

Because transactions generally involve an exchange of money, it is critical that the data be protected during transmission and stored carefully so that it cannot be altered. It is also critical that the data be saved so that managers can verify the data if any conflicts arise. Also, the sales and purchase data form the foundation of the accounting and financial systems of every company, so the system must be able to produce the standard reports.

Data Capture

How do you efficiently collect transaction data? The basic components of a transaction-processing system are illustrated in Figure 6.2. The focus is twofold: accomplishing the transaction and capturing data. Data capture consists of gathering or acquiring data from the firm's operations and storing data in the computer system. Entering data into the computer can be time consuming and difficult. For instance, banks have invested heavily in automating the collection and recording of transaction data. Yet because many transactions are based on paper, clerks still spend considerable time entering data. First, tellers enter the data into their terminals. Then a bank staff reads the dollar value written on checks and deposit slips. The bank staff works through the night, typing the amount into a machine that codes the number on the bottom of the check so it can be read by other computers.

As the volume of transactions increased, businesses looked for faster and more accurate ways to get data into the computer. Four basic methods are used to collect data, depending on its source. The data-collection method consumers are most familiar with is **point of sale (POS),** where the sales register is actually a computer terminal that sends all data to a central computer. On assembly lines, robots and manufacturing equipment can collect data, such as quality control measures, and return it to a computer. Typically the computer also can send control instructions to these machines. This exchange of data between manufacturing machines and computers is known as **process control.** The third way to collect data automatically involves the exchange of information with organizations outside the firm, especially suppliers and customers. Instead of dealing with paper records such as purchase or-

REALITY BYTES Verifying Transactions

Parmalat is a large food products company headquartered in a small town in Italy. It began with a focus on milk and cheese and grew to a large empire that supplied grocery stores across Europe. In 2003, everything fell apart when several "financial irregularities" were revealed. A key element in the accounting scandal involved bank accounts by the Bonlat Financing Corp., a Parmalat subsidiary in Cayman with Bank America. According to corporate records, audited by the Italian branch of the Grant Thornton accounting firm, the Bonlat account allegedly held $5 billion in cash and securities. There was no money in the account, and the initial indications reported that Parmalat had a $13 billion black hole in its accounts. Ian John-

son, a Grant Thornton partner in Grand Cayman, notes that "this office didn't do any audits for Parmalat entities. How they went about the audits, we have no information." While it is almost certain that fraud was involved in the Parmalat case, most observers would agree that the auditors should have been able to verify simple bank account assets. Bank accounts and other transactions with external parties are a primary anchor point in auditing. It is difficult to cook the books when they have to reconcile against the records of a third party.

Source: Adapted from "Parmalat's Cayman Islands Books a Work of Fiction," *Caribbean Net News,* January 15, 2004.

FIGURE 6.2

Data that is captured at the operations level is used throughout the firm to make decisions. If there are problems in the data or in providing access to the data, all of the decisions will suffer.

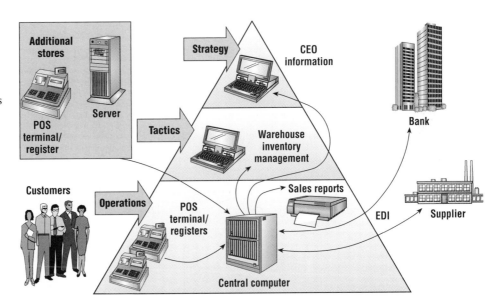

ders, it is possible to send orders electronically through a process called **electronic data interchange (EDI).** The fourth method is to have the customers select products and enter data directly into the electronic commerce Web site. This fourth method offers the potential of reducing errors and costs—if the Web sites are built carefully and if the customers are motivated and capable of selecting the products themselves.

Point of Sale

Several devices have been created to capture data at the point of the sale. Some companies rely on keyboards to enter data, but high-volume areas have switched to bar code scanners. All consumers are familiar with bar code scanners that read the universal product codes (UPCs). The scanner reads the code and sends it to the computer, which looks up the corresponding name and price. The computer prints the receipt, stores the sale information, and automatically decreases the inventory count.

Another type of scanner is used by the U.S. Postal System—**optical character recognition (OCR)**—to read handwritten zip codes, allowing mail to be processed and sorted faster. Even so, the post office hires thousands of workers to type in data that the scanners cannot read. Banks use a process called **magnetic ink character recognition (MICR)** to process checks and deposit slips. MICR readers are more accurate than straight OCR because they pick up a stronger signal from magnetic particles in the ink. A few companies

REALITY BYTES   Grocery Clerks Are Expensive

Grocery stores survive on small margins and high volume. Bar code scanners were a big step in improving the efficiency of the checkout process. In the 1990s, several stores began experimenting with self-checkout stations. Customers pass their items over a scanner and place them in a bag. The system weighs each product to make sure it was scanned. The goal was to reduce the cost of the human clerks. In 2004, grocery stores are implementing the technology to go even further. Several stores are experimenting with wireless scanners, either attached to the grocery cart or handheld. Customers scan items as they put them in the cart. The portable systems track the running total, display instant coupons, and can suggest related products. The computer can even personalize its coupons and suggestions. If you bought ice cream several weeks ago, it can offer a discount on that item when you return to the store. Albertson's CTO Bob Dunst notes that "our customers tell us they feel they save 15 to 20 minutes in a shopping trip." The grocery chain is experimenting with the system in some of its Chicago-area Jewel stores, as well as some in its Boise home market, and piloting the program in more than 100 stores in the Dallas–Fort Worth area. Other chains, including Ahold's Stop & Shop division and Supervalu Inc.'s Bigg's superstores, are testing similar technologies. To pay for the items, customers simply scan their credit or debit cards. Random spot checks and video surveillance are used to reduce theft.

Source: Adapted from Michelle Higgins, "Grocery Shopping Enters a New Age," *The Wall Street Journal,* March 30, 2004.

FIGURE 6.3

Data that is captured at the operations level is used throughout the firm to make decisions. If there are problems in the data or in providing access to the data, all of the decisions will suffer.

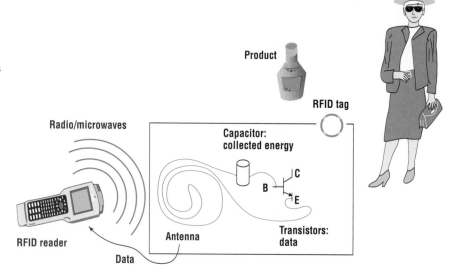

are using speech recognition technology to enable workers to enter data by speaking to the computer. Speech recognition enables the users to enter data while leaving their hands free to do something else.

The newest data-acquisition technology is **radio frequency identification (RFID).** Bar codes have two major limitations: (1) They hold a limited amount of data, and (2) even the best scanners have trouble reading them. Basic bar codes can hold 10 digits, but 5 of those are used to identify the manufacturing company, which leaves only 5 digits for the actual product. As a consumer, you have certainly encountered bar codes that are difficult to read. RFIDs are small chips about the size of a grain of rice that consist of an antenna and some transistors. When the scanner sends a radio signal to the chip, the antenna receives it and uses the radio waves to power the transistors and return the stored data by modifying the scanner wave. For several years, people have implanted the chips in their dogs in case the pet becomes lost and loses his or her collar. The capacity and range of RFID chips depend on the frequency (low, high, or ultra-high). The ultra-high frequency chips can be read from the greatest distance (12 feet with a maximum of 40) but hold only 12 bytes of data. The high-frequency chips are typically scanned at less than a foot (with a maximum of 10 feet), but can hold from 8 to 10,000 bytes of data. The ability to read the tags from a distance provides a substantial advantage in supply chain or warehouse environments. Figure 6.3 shows that you no longer have to scan each item from a few inches. You can walk down the aisles with a reader and quickly pick up and distinguish the RFID tags from hundreds of products at a time. The main drawback to RFID at the moment is that the tags are relatively expensive—starting at $0.50 each. But if you have to count inventory in a store or warehouse several times a year, the RFID tags could save you substantial time and money, plus provide improved accuracy.

Wal-Mart and the U.S. Department of Defense are pressing suppliers to put the tags on all items shipped to Wal-Mart. Using their dominant market position, Wal-Mart is asking suppliers to bear the cost of the tags. However, at this point in time, it is probably not economically feasible to include the tags on small, low-price items. Instead, the tags will probably be placed on pallets or boxed shipments. RFID tags at this level will probably not be useful in the store itself, but it will help to identify items received and track them through the supply chain delivery system.

Ultimately, if tags become cheap enough to place on all items, retail stores might be able to radically alter their format. For instance, scanners could be embedded in shopping carts or doorways. Customers would simply select the items and get an immediate price and running total. Payment could be virtually automatic as well, so customers could skip the checkout lanes. Cart-based systems could also suggest related products or direct customers to aisles with similar products. Sound far-fetched? Albertsons (a grocery chain) began experimenting with these tools in some of its Chicago stores in 2003.

Some privacy advocates have argued against RFID tags on the grounds that if all of your clothes contained these tags (as originally proposed by Benetton), it would be possible to track individual people. However, the limited range of the scanners, coupled with the ability to deactivate or remove the tags, can reduce or eliminate this problem.

POS Advantages

Several advantages arise from using automated data entry. Directly capturing data means fewer errors occur because the machines make fewer mistakes. However, sometimes it is not easy to collect data at the source. POS systems also have built-in error detection methods to make certain the numbers are read correctly. By collecting the data immediately, it is easier to find and correct mistakes. If a clerk using a POS system enters an incorrect product number (or the scanner reads it incorrectly), the error can be caught immediately.

With POS data collection, the computer performs all necessary computations immediately. Hence, the job is easier for clerks and fewer errors will occur. For example, a retail store might give discounts to certain customers. With a POS system, the employees do not have to keep track of the customers or discounts, because the computer can look up the discounts and apply them automatically. Similarly, prices are maintained and changed by the computer. To hold a sale, you simply change the price in the computer (one place) and put up a new sign. Of course, when there are thousands of items and prices, there are still plenty of opportunities for errors.

POS systems also can provide better service to customers. Because the sales data is captured immediately, the managers and clerks always know the inventory levels. If a customer calls to learn whether a product is in stock, the clerk can instantly determine the answer. With most systems, it is possible to tell the computer to hold that item until the customer picks it up. Some companies even connect their store computers together. If you find that one store has run out of a particular item, the clerk can quickly check the other stores in the area and tell one to hold the item for you.

Process Control

Manufacturing firms often deal with a different type of data. Most factories use machines that can be connected to each other and to computers. The computers can exchange data with the production machines. If you want to alter your product, you would need to change the manufacturing settings on several different machines. If the production line has 10 machines, each with 5 control items that need to be set, it could take several hours to reset the entire production line. Even a minor change in the product means that someone has to set

REALITY BYTES   Micropayments

Although many people believe everything on the Internet should be free, economics notes that money creates incentives for new applications. A big problem with payments is the cost of the overhead. For large purchases, the cost is acceptable—even at one or two percentage points. But for small items, costing about a dollar, the overhead charges are too high—at about 25 cents. Ron Rivest, a pioneer in encryption, started a company called Peppercoin (www.peppercoin.com) with a radical approach to small payments. Instead of running a credit card charge for every sale, the system statistically samples the transactions and pays the vendor based on those results. Over time, with thousands or millions of transactions, the costs average with only a small error. The customer is still billed in exact amounts, but the vendor payments might vary.

BitPass is another new micropayment company that claims to enable the sales of items for as little as 10 to 50 cents. Over the years, several companies have created innovative tools for micropayments, but few survived. One issue is whether consumers even care. Joe Cunningham, marketing manager for Clear Channel Radio, testing the BitPass system, noted that "it's an easy chance to monetize some things we wouldn't offer for free." His company offered digital images and videos from backstage at concerts. On the other side, Walter Nirenberg, vice president for sales at Yaga, a company that handles online payments for archival contents, notes that "no merchant is going to meet their revenue goals with micropayments. We see them as an e-commerce enabler. But if your entire business were predicated on them, you'd have a microbusiness."

Source: Adapted from Anne Eisenberg, "A Virtual Cash Register Rings Up Tiny Transactions," *The New York Times,* January 7, 2004.

FIGURE 6.4

Process control is the control of production machines from centralized computers. The computers monitor data from the machines and make continual adjustments. The central control enables designers to specify all production settings from one location.

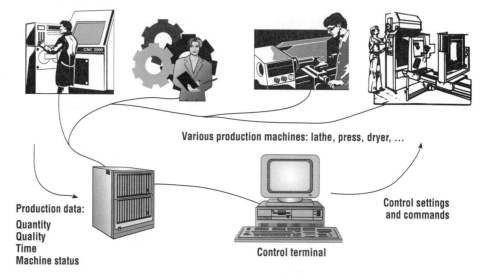

Various production machines: lathe, press, dryer, …

Production data:

Quantity
Quality
Time
Machine status

Control terminal

Control settings and commands

each of the machines correctly. By connecting the machines to a computer, the computer can store the appropriate settings. When you make a change in the product, the computer sends the correct settings to all the machines. Computers are often used to monitor the progress of the production line. The data is used to identify problem spots and to help the firm meet production goals. Figure 6.4 illustrates the basic concept of individual machines controlled from one location.

Technology also can be used to collect data from manufacturing machines. With this communication, the computer can constantly monitor production levels. Managers can keep track of hourly and daily production, and even track individual products. If a customer wants to check on the progress of a special order, the manager can determine how much of the product has been produced and when it is likely to be completed.

Process control computers can also be used to monitor quality in the manufacturing process. Sensors can automatically measure almost any characteristic. They can check for items such as thickness, weight, strength, color, and size. These measurements can then be passed to a computer. If the computer notices a trend or a major problem, it can notify the operators. In some operations, the computer can send messages to the machine causing the problem and reset its controls to correct the problem automatically.

REALITY BYTES   Will RFID Replace Bar Codes?

Metro Group is a large German retailer with more than 2,300 stores in 28 countries. In early 2004, the company announced to its top suppliers that it would require RFID tags on pallets and cases shipped to the central warehouses after November 2004. In one store in Rheinberg, the company is pilot testing item-level RFID tags for items such as razor blades, cream cheese, and shampoo. So far, the technology has shown some significant advantages, but is less than perfect. The tags can generally be read through boxes and plastic cases. But the company says it is obtaining only 96 percent accuracy for hanging garments. The tags are also expensive, costing 25 to 50 cents each. Hans Joachim-Korber, the CEO of Metro, is taking a long-run view of the process. He expects it to be at least a decade before RFID is universally adopted, and it will take time before it is used at the item level. "We don't care about that. We have to start. In the end, it will replace the bar code."

Source: Adapted from Carol Sliwa, "German Retailer's RFID Effort Rivals Wal-Mart's," *Computerworld,* January 19, 2004.

Two basic difficulties exist with process control. First, the large number of machines makes it difficult to establish standards, making it harder to connect the various machines together. Second, production machines can produce an enormous amount of data. Some machines can generate billions of bytes of data per hour. This large amount of data requires efficient communication lines, high-speed computers, and a large storage capacity. Despite these complications, process control can provide enormous advantages. It enables companies to change production processes and alter products faster and more often. It provides better information and control over quality. It enables manufacturers to create products that match the needs of individual customers.

Electronic Data Interchange (EDI)

EDI is a form of automated data entry that supports operations by transferring documents between firms electronically. The essence of EDI is the ability to transfer data among computers from different companies. The goal is to connect to suppliers so that production orders can be sent automatically at substantially lower cost than traditional paper-based systems. Two basic methods are used to accomplish the transfer: (1) send the data directly from one computer to the other or (2) send the data to a third party that consolidates the data and sends it to the proper location. Early EDI implementations were based on direct connections as individual firms experimented with the technology. In both methods, there are two important considerations: establishing the physical links and transferring data in a format compatible to all users.

For EDI to work, each company must translate its data into a form that can be used by the other companies. If one company like Sears or GM takes the lead and requires suppliers to send data via EDI, then they are free to define the base transaction objects. Suppliers must translate their objects into the appropriate EDI structure. Yet a supplier might need links to several customers. If each customer used different EDI definitions, the supplier must have a conversion system for each link. Someday it might be possible to create standards for EDI connections, forcing everyone to conform to one type of data definition. Although there is some progress in this area, firms with existing EDI systems will be reluctant to spend the money to convert their data.

Data conversion might sound like an easy task, but it is complicated when the transaction systems were created over long periods of time and were poorly documented. In many cases, the programmer might have to search major portions of the corporate systems to find the appropriate data definitions. Once the appropriate data is found, it can be hard to modify. Existing programs might expect the data to maintain specific formats. Making changes to the data can require rewriting other programs.

The concept of EDI is closely tied to **supply chain management (SCM),** which revolves around purchasing, but also incorporates just-in-time delivery, searching for competitive pricing, and controlling and monitoring quality. Web sites and search engines make it easier for businesses to find unique products and tools.

FIGURE 6.5

EDI can be built from individual pair-wise links over proprietary connections. If the majority of transactions are between two companies, this method will work fine. If companies deal with many different suppliers or larger customers, this method can cause problems when each link requires conversion to a different format.

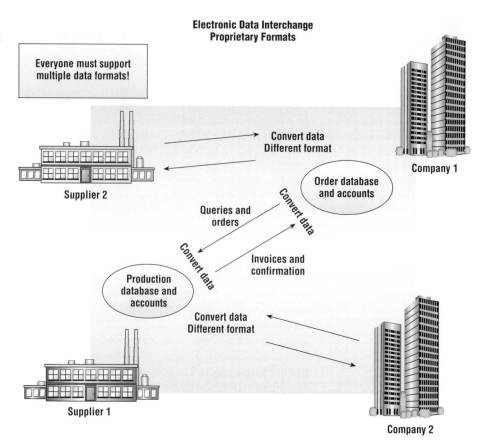

Electronic Data Interchange Proprietary Formats

Proprietary EDI

As displayed in Figure 6.5, most of the early EDI systems were created independently: one large company required suppliers to provide data and accept orders electronically. The goal was to cut the costs of transactions and speed up the ordering process. EDI arrangements also enabled manufacturers to improve quality control and to implement just-in-time inventory systems. Suppliers were "encouraged" to adopt the EDI systems by threatening a loss of sales if the vendors did not comply.

With proprietary systems, the lead firm establishes the standards in terms of the hardware and the types and format of data to be exchanged. From the standpoint of the lead firm, these controls ensure that they are able to connect to each supplier with one standard technique.

To a supplier, proprietary systems created by one company can lead to problems. Imagine what happens when the supplier sells to several firms, and each firm requires the use of a different EDI system. In addition to the hassles of providing data in the proper format for each customer, the supplier's employees would have to learn how to use several different systems. Purchasers face similar problems unless all of their suppliers follow a standard.

Commercial EDI Providers and Standards

Multiple proprietary systems lead to confusion and higher costs. Consequently, companies have formed groups to define common methods to exchange data among companies. As shown in Figure 6.6, third-party providers (such as banks) have begun operating as clearinghouses for EDI transactions. In both cases, the objective is to establish common hardware and software requirements so that any company following the standards can share data with other companies.

Communication standards enable firms to share the data and automate basic transactions. However, to provide useful information, companies need to integrate this data into their management information systems. Sending purchase orders over phone lines is faster than using traditional mail, but firms can gain more advantages if the resulting data can be tied directly to their internal accounting systems.

FIGURE 6.6

When many firms need to exchange data with several other firms, it is best if they can agree to a common EDI transaction format. In some cases, a central or regional firm can coordinate transfers among all parties. This method is especially beneficial to small firms.

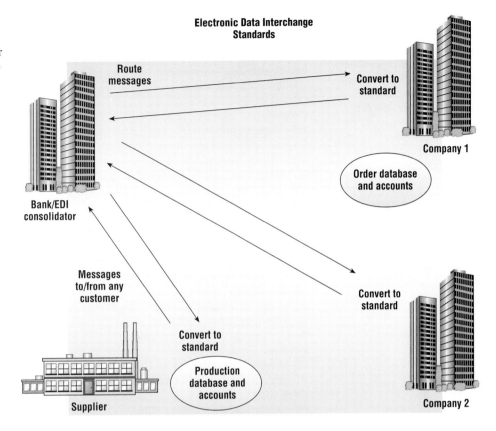

Electronic Data Interchange Standards

FIGURE 6.7

EDI standards: UN Edifact and U.S. ANSI X12 standards are similar in format; each message consists of segments and detailed data lists. Each message, segment, and data element is defined by numbers from a predefined list of possible transactions. There are substantial differences in the numbering system used for the segments and data.

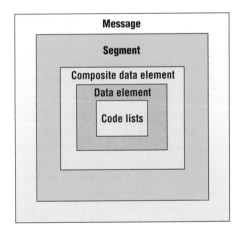

Two primary standards exist for EDI messages. The UN sponsors the Edifact standard; the United States defined the ANSI (American National Standards Institute) X12 definition. Figure 6.7 shows the overall structure of an EDI message. A significant difference between the standards is in the numbering system used to represent the types of messages, segments, and data elements. Figure 6.8 presents a partial list of the segment types available in the X12 standard. The standards also specify the exact format of the data required in each segment type.

Additional Features and Problems

Taken to its full capabilities, EDI enables firms to electronically handle all communications among other firms. It enables managers to create and review orders without relying on paper printouts. Having data available electronically means that several people can work with the same form at the same time. In most companies, purchase orders and invoices are examined and altered by several people. If the form is processed on the computer, each person

FIGURE 6.8

Sample segment codes for ANSI X12: A partial list of the codes used within X12 EDI messages. Only the number is transmitted. Each segment specifies the format of the additional data.

104—Air Shipment Information
110—Air Freight Details and Invoice
125—Multilevel Railcar Load Details
126—Vehicle Application Advice
127—Vehicle Buying Order
128—Dealer Information
129—Vehicle Carrier Rate Update
130—Student Educational Record (Transcript)
131—Student Educational Record (Transcript) Acknowledgment
135—Student Loan Application
139—Student Loan Guarantee Result
140—Product Registration
141—Product Service Claim Response
142—Product Service Claim
143—Product Service Notification
144—Student Loan Transfer and Status Verification
146—Request for Student Educational Record (Transcript)
147—Response to Request for Student Educational Record (Transcript)
148—Report of Injury or Illness
151—Electronic Filing of Tax Return Data Acknowledgment
152—Statistical Government Information
154—Uniform Commercial Code Filing
161—Train Sheet
170—Revenue Receipts Statement
180—Return Merchandise Authorization and Notification
186—Laboratory Reporting
190—Student Enrollment Verification

has access to the data at the same time. It is also much easier to store and search the electronic data. Eventually, even prices and negotiations could be handled electronically, making it much easier to sort and compare bids from various suppliers.

Some unresolved issues with EDI's security and ethics need further consideration. What happens when a company denies that it placed an order? How do you protect the communication links so people cannot intercept orders? Reading, changing, or deleting your competitor's orders could destroy its business. Although these actions are illegal, they can be difficult to prevent or uncover. Privacy issues also arise in conjunction with EDI. If consumer transactions are captured electronically and stored, an enormous amount of personal information will be available. What will prevent a company from acquiring or selling a list of all the items you purchase along with your salary and your home address? These questions and solutions are addressed in more detail in Chapter 4.

Using the Internet for EDI

The entire purpose of EDI is to share data with business partners. Sharing data requires a communication link and standards that define how the data will be interpreted. The ANSI and Edifact definitions describe how the data should be organized. However, communication links are equally important. Increasingly, companies are using the Internet as a primary link to other firms. The main strength of the Internet is that it is widely available throughout the world. Standardization enables any firm to participate at a low cost.

Web sites are used to advertise and display information about products and their availability. Search engines enable companies to find components and potential suppliers quickly. EDI transactions such as orders and request-for-prices can be handled over the Internet as e-mail messages. The Internet can also host secure communication channels between two partners. These links can be used for high-volume exchanges of data.

The one catch with the Internet is that currently there are no service guarantees. While messages are rarely lost, they might be delayed. Periodically, various segments of the Internet become overloaded and it can be difficult to transfer data. If these interruptions are

FIGURE 6.9

XML for EDI: Data is sent in a standard format that is easy for computers to parse and read. Industry groups have been establishing standard formats and tags for exchanging EDI data within their industries.

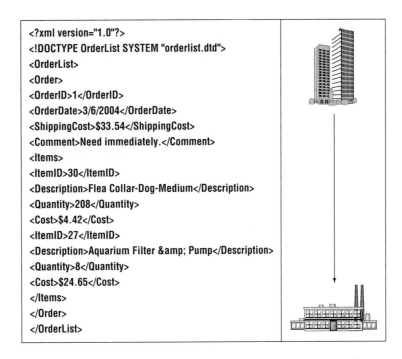

```
<?xml version="1.0"?>
<!DOCTYPE OrderList SYSTEM "orderlist.dtd">
<OrderList>
<Order>
<OrderID>1</OrderID>
<OrderDate>3/6/2004</OrderDate>
<ShippingCost>$33.54</ShippingCost>
<Comment>Need immediately.</Comment>
<Items>
<ItemID>30</ItemID>
<Description>Flea Collar-Dog-Medium</Description>
<Quantity>208</Quantity>
<Cost>$4.42</Cost>
<ItemID>27</ItemID>
<Description>Aquarium Filter &amp; Pump</Description>
<Quantity>8</Quantity>
<Cost>$24.65</Cost>
</Items>
</Order>
</OrderList>
```

infrequent, you could resort to manual methods such as fax machines and telephone calls. Plans for improving the Internet include the ability to specify (and purchase) dedicated bandwidth, so that companies can ensure a certain level of service. So far, the strengths of the Internet far outweigh the potential drawbacks. The newer version of the Internet protocol (IP.v6) is defined to have the ability to request a specified level of service, but firms have been reluctant to spend the money to upgrade to this system.

Extensible markup language (XML) was developed in the last couple of years to provide better Internet support for EDI. At its foundations, XML is a tag-based document that contains data. As shown in Figure 6.9, the tags indicate the type of data contained within the document. The document can have a hierarchical structure similar to the EDI standards, such as Order–OrderItem–Product. Various industry groups have been establishing standard document formats (data type definition or DTD) for common documents within their industries. Many software packages can read and write XML documents, so companies can use diverse hardware and software and still communicate easily.

Elements of a Transaction

What are the major elements and risks of a transaction? Transactions are a critical foundation of modern economic societies. In many ways, transactions define and enable different types of societies and cultures. A transaction consists of an exchange of a product or service for money. Consequently, there is always a risk that something might go wrong in the exchange. Figure 6.10 summarizes the transaction risks that are borne by the vendor, the customer, and the government. The laws and culture determine how these risks are minimized.

Vendor Perspective

At heart, a vendor cares about only one fundamental aspect of transactions: receiving the money. This simple statement has several complicating factors: (1) the payment might never arrive, (2) the payment might be fraudulent, (3) the customer might repudiate the transaction and withhold the money, or (4) the government might invalidate the transaction.

In older times, these risks were minimized through personal reputation of the customer and money based on precious metals. More recently, in our mobile, anonymous society,

REALITY BYTES   How Much Does That Cost?

Debit cards are popular with consumers, accounting for 15 percent of total spending and hundreds of billions of dollars. In 2001, Visa processed more debit card transactions than credit cards. The costs for a merchant to accept debit cards vary, but there are some standard costs. The terminal and printer to accept debit and credit cards carry an initial cost of about $500. The merchant will also need a key-pad for the customer to enter a PIN, and it costs about $200 plus a $50 setup fee. Every payment mechanism carries transaction fees; some of them can be negotiated with the merchant bank. Costs for either debit or credit cards typically range from 1 to 3 percent of the sale.

Source: Adapted from Betsy Butler, "Debit Card Use Escalating; Merchant Cost Plans Vary," *Columbus Business First,* September 20, 2002.

FIGURE 6.10

Transaction risk factors: Risk elements and causes vary depending on the transaction method. Laws and business procedures are created to minimize these risks, so new laws are needed when transaction methods change.

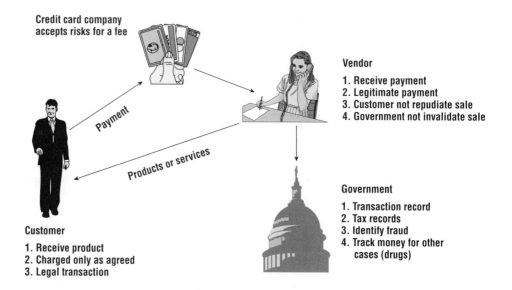

Credit card company accepts risks for a fee

Payment

Products or services

Vendor
1. Receive payment
2. Legitimate payment
3. Customer not repudiate sale
4. Government not invalidate sale

Government
1. Transaction record
2. Tax records
3. Identify fraud
4. Track money for other cases (drugs)

Customer
1. Receive product
2. Charged only as agreed
3. Legal transaction

credit card companies have stepped in to assume much of this vendor risk—for a price. The credit card companies and credit bureaus provide identification and personal reference services. Under the proper conditions, the card companies effectively guarantee payment to the merchant. The conditions primarily consist of (1) keeping good transaction records and (2) identifying the customer through either a magnetic swipe of the card or a signature.

Customer Perspective

In some ways, customers face a more complex set of risks. Their primary concern lies in receiving the identified value for their money. Specifically, they want to be sure that (1) they receive the product or service that they ordered, (2) they are charged only the amount they agreed to pay, and (3) the transaction is legal—for example, not stolen goods that could be confiscated.

In older times, these risks were small when customers shopped at local stores, could physically examine the goods, and paid in cash. Identification and reputation of the merchant were critical. Even so, fraud was a problem. Again, credit card companies stepped in to reduce much of this risk. Today, credit card companies warranty products, ensure delivery, and validate the merchants.

Transaction Fees

While often invisible to consumers, the fee for using a credit card consists of a percentage of the transaction cost paid by the merchant. Of course, economics shows that the price of the product reflects a portion of this fee, so the consumer and merchant both bear the cost. The cost depends on the size of the merchant, the card company, and the size of

Technology Toolbox: Creating EDI Transactions

Problem: How do you send an EDI statement to a customer?

Tools: Several vendors provide EDI software that enables you to create standard transactions to send to customers. Most large retail companies require all vendors to send transactions using EDI standards. To a novice, the EDI process seems complicated. Essentially it consists of a series of messages. To ensure that messages are received, each major message requires a confirmation message. For example, a standard purchase order sent by a customer is carried in an EDI 850 document. You must then acknowledge receipt of the document with an EDI 997 (receipt envelope confirmation) message. This message can be automated since it simply indicates that your machine received the original purchase order. Later, when you accept the purchase order, you must return an EDI 855 (vendor acknowledgment) document. You can often include changes in this reply document, such as item numbers or prices.

You need to handle three basic steps to process EDI documents. First, you have to be able to connect to the customer or supplier. Some companies use the Internet to establish connections; others use a private value added network (VAN). A VAN requires you to pay an annual fee (about $500) along with a fee for each message (about $0.15). Second, you need software that creates outgoing documents in the proper format. Several software packages exist, but before you buy and install one, make sure that it can connect to the proper network and can read and write documents in the formats you need. Third, you need to handle the incoming messages and send the outgoing ones. If you are managing a small company, you will probably want to use a graphical-based system that shows you each message. Then assign a person to handle the system. Larger companies will want to find a system that integrates with the internal information system and automatically translates documents and checks data against the internal database.

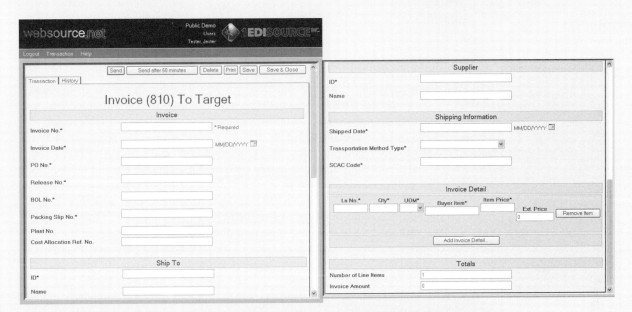

Some systems, like the one from www.1edisource.com, support graphical and Web-based tools that make it easy for a person to enter common business data. After a one-time setup, the system automatically converts the messages to the proper format and sends them on the established connection.

Quick Quiz:

1. Why would customers require the use of a VAN instead of the Internet?

2. Even for relatively large companies, what are the advantages of using people to enter data and read EDI messages instead of an automated system?

3. Using the Internet, find at least five companies that provide EDI software.

the transaction. Typical fees are 1.5 to 5 percent, with minimum costs of 1 to 2 dollars per transaction.

What about payments by check instead of credit card? In this case, the vendor bears a relatively high risk that the check is invalid or will be refused for insufficient funds. While there are laws against check fraud, the merchant would experience high costs to recover the money. Consequently, vendors generally contract with specialist firms to validate and process checks. Again, the merchant pays a fee to transfer this risk to another company.

FIGURE 6.11

Risk mitigation in e-commerce: Encryption verifies the identity of the vendor and protects the data in transmission. Credit card companies accept risks for the consumers but not for the vendors. Huge vendor databases of credit card data are tempting targets and need to be protected by the vendor.

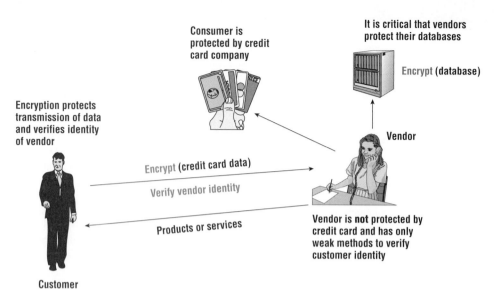

Government Perspective

When discussing transactions, many people forget about the perspective of the government or society. Yet several government organizations have a strong interest in transactions to protect various members of society. The primary interests include (1) an auditable record of transactions and financial statements for the protection of investors, (2) a record of taxable transactions for the collection of sales tax, (3) identification and tracking of fraudulent transactions, and (4) general tracking of money used in transactions to monitor other types of crimes, such as drugs and terrorism.

Most government interests are established by laws and administrative rules that are enforced through manual audits of financial documents. Some data is collected from transaction partners, such as the $10,000 cash reporting rule in the United States. On the other hand, governments are rapidly becoming aware of the jurisdictional problems inherent in electronic commerce. The most prominent issue is the inability of states to force out-of-state firms to collect sales taxes for them.

After a few embarrassingly huge fraud cases in the upper echelons of companies in the early 2000s, Congress got tired of hearing CEOs trying to avoid criminal charges by saying they did not know anything about the problems created by their underlings. So, Congress passed the Sarbanes-Oxley Act that requires executives to take responsibility for all financial reports. The top executives have to certify that the accounting reports accurately represent the status of the firm. The act has scared many executives—not enough to give up their huge salaries and pensions—but they are beginning to search for ways to validate the transaction and financial systems. It is no longer sufficient to just record transaction data—now firms have to institute processes and ensure that people follow them to guarantee that the correct data is being recorded.

Risk Mitigation in e-Commerce

The transaction risks in e-commerce are similar to those of traditional commerce, but with a couple of twists because of the network connection. The Internet is an open network where messages can be intercepted and transferred at will. Consequently, it is challenging for the merchant and customer to verify the other's identity. Similarly, both merchant and vendor need to be concerned about the transfer of money and digital products. Because these two issues stem from the same cause (the insecure network), they have both been solved through the use of strong encryption methods. These techniques are described in Chapter 5. They are commonplace on the Internet today, and consumers and vendors face minimal risk from the interception of data. Figure 6.11 shows that encryption can protect the transmission and storage of credit card data, but vendors still assume several risks because the only method they have to identify customers is by the credit card data. Some vendors attempt to reduce this risk by shipping products only to the home address corresponding to the customer's credit file.

The risks of nonpayment or nondelivery are more difficult to solve. They have been particularly challenging in an international environment where governmental jurisdiction and enforcement are not effectively defined. For the most part, consumers are still protected if they use a credit card to pay for a product. However, the consumer may still find it hard to prove that a product was not received. On the other hand, e-commerce businesses have virtually no protection from fraud. The credit card rules specifically exclude mail orders, telephone orders (MOTO), and Internet orders. The card companies will assist merchants in identifying invalid cards, but will not guarantee the transaction. This issue is important because the Gartner Group (Trombley 2000) estimates that credit card fraud is 12 times higher for online merchants—with about 1.1 percent of all online transactions fraudulent.

Technically, it is relatively easy to use encryption to verify the identity of the merchant and the customer in any transaction. In fact, the common Web encryption system works because the merchant buys a digital certificate from an encryption company. Customers could obtain similar certificates or digital signatures, but they have little incentive to do so, since the credit card companies protect them.

With today's encryption systems, transmission risks are relatively minor. Two far more serious risks are (1) theft of consumer data from the vendor's computer and (2) alteration of the purchase documents by either the merchant or the customer (repudiation).

The risk of theft is real and has happened to several vendors. The potential target is huge: thousands or millions of validated credit card numbers—all accessible via the Internet. The only effective solutions are for vendors either to keep the card numbers off-line or to encrypt them and bury the encryption key.

The second risk arises because digital orders are easy to alter. The solution is to create electronic orders that cannot be altered. Again, this solution requires encryption. In this case, the customer and the vendor both need a digital certificate. When both parties encrypt the order, it cannot be altered later.

International Issues

Why are transactions more difficult in an international environment? In the early stages of e-commerce, several people suggested that the Internet's global reach would make it easy even for small businesses to sell products internationally. However, several factors interfere with international sales. Some are traditional (such as shipping and tariffs), while others are unique to the Internet.

Figure 6.12 summarizes some of the major points involving sales into other nations. Jurisdiction for dispute resolution is a major issue. Nations have many different laws and cultures. Tactics (and content) that might be commonplace in one country could be illegal in another nation. Gambling is a classic example. The United States might ban gambling on the Internet, but how can it enforce that law? If a U.S. citizen has a dispute with an overseas casino, there would be few options to protect the consumer. Similarly, fraud and Web attacks can easily originate from several different nations. Varying laws and lack of coordination make it difficult to identify and prosecute the perpetrators.

Privacy and encryption present additional challenges. The European Union has privacy rules that are substantially stricter than those of other nations, and it does not want international companies transferring personal data to computers outside of the Union. Likewise, governments sometimes control encryption, which makes it more difficult to prevent common transaction problems on the Internet. For many years, the United States forbade the export of strong encryption technology (even though similar technologies already existed worldwide). Only in 2001 did the United States begin to allow software to be shipped with strong encryption. Consequently, international customers could never be sure that their transactions were secure, since the weaker encryption systems could be broken in a matter of hours. On the other hand, France does not allow citizens to use encryption at all.

FIGURE 6.12

Some international issues in e-commerce: Jurisdiction is a big issue with different laws and cultures. Customers can use credit cards to mitigate risks, but people in many nations do not use them.

Jurisdiction questions for disputes.
    Collection and payment for sales.
        Currently rely on credit cards.
        Many people do not use credit cards.
        Does not protect vendor.
    Coordinate and stop fraud.
    Control harassment, spamming, and denial-of-service attacks.
Encryption restrictions.
    U.S. classifies as munitions.
    France does not allow citizens to use encryption at all.
Different privacy rules.
Nations have differing perspectives of "offensive" content.

FIGURE 6.13

Payment mechanisms: Credit cards do not protect merchants and have high transaction costs, so they cannot be used for low-price items. Several systems have been created to provide the desired characteristics, but customers have not yet been willing to adopt them.

Credit card drawbacks

  High transaction costs
  Not feasible for small payments
  Do not protect the merchant

Characteristics needed

  Low enough costs to support payments less than $1
  Secure transmission
  Secure storage
  Authentication mechanism
  Easy translation to traditional money

Alternatives

  Mobile phone bill
  Smart cards

Payment Mechanisms

How can customers pay for products and why do you need new payment mechanisms? Payment mechanisms must change along with the changes in transactions. Years ago, when purchases were made locally, currency was the primary method of settling transactions. Eventually, as banks stabilized and gained respect (and government guarantees), transactions were settled by checks. Business transactions (particularly internationally) are often settled with letters of credit from banks. In the United States, many payments have migrated to credit cards.

From a consumer standpoint, credit cards are easy, available, provide short-term loans, and offer protection from fraud and errors. Figure 6.13 shows the drawbacks to credit cards and lists the characteristics desired from a new payment mechanism. From an e-commerce merchant perspective, credit cards offer only minimal support and are expensive. From the perspective of a mobile-commerce merchant, credit cards will be unacceptable because the transaction costs are too high to support small payments.

From a theoretical perspective, e-commerce payment mechanisms should be easy to create. In fact, dozens have been proposed or started in the past few years. None of them have garnered enough support to be successful.

Several companies have proposed alternative payment mechanisms. As illustrated in Figure 6.14, most involve the use of a trusted third party (like a bank). **Digital cash** is an example, where buyers can make anonymous purchases over a network, and sellers are assured of receiving payment. Consumers transfer real money to the third party and receive one-time-use digital cash numbers. These numbers can be given to a vendor, who returns them to the third party for an account credit. Other methods use the third party to verify the authenticity of the buyer and seller. The third party completes the transaction by transferring the money between accounts.

FIGURE 6.14

Digital cash payment mechanism: Large payments or monthly payments can be made through most banks in the form of real money in checking accounts. These methods can be cumbersome and expensive for small transactions. Several companies have proposed standards for the creation of digital cash. The goal is to create an electronic form of money that can be verified, is inexpensive to use, can support anonymity, and cannot be easily counterfeited.

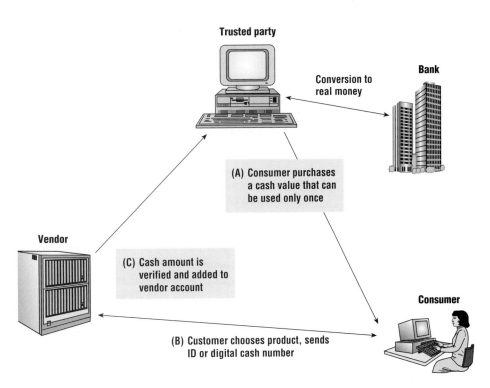

A few other payment mechanisms are used by customers that rely on e-mail messages to transfer money using traditional credit card or checking accounts, for example, PayPal (X.com corporation), Billpoint (Wells Fargo Bank), eMoneyMail (Bank One), and c2it (Citicorp). However, in most cases, the transaction costs for these mechanisms are still too high for low-price transactions.

Mobile commerce offers one possibility for handling small transactions: put the cost on the customer's cell phone bill. Most phone bills already contain lists of small transactions, and the total monthly fee is high enough to pay using traditional mechanisms. As long as the vendor builds up enough credits with the phone company, the transaction costs on that side will be reasonable. Currently, the biggest potential drawback is the limited security. Phone numbers are easy to find, although a 4-digit PIN would improve security a little. Requiring physical access to the phone will provide more security, until the phone is lost or stolen.

At a minimum, encryption requires that the vendor obtain a digital certificate. The most secure systems require the consumer to obtain a digital certificate to authenticate the identity of the consumer. Most consumers are reluctant to pay the cost in money and time to obtain a personal digital certificate. As an alternative, credit card companies are pushing smart cards, which can contain customer authentication information. But these cards require new scanning hardware, and merchants and vendors are generally unwilling to pay for the new hardware.

In summary, electronic payment mechanisms are still in their infancy. It could take years for a standard to evolve and be accepted by enough merchants and customers to be important. In the past, governments have borne the costs of creating and printing money. Today, most seem unwilling to become involved, and they have left the mechanisms to the private sector—which is more focused on developing a system that provides profits to the issuing authority, instead of developing a system that would be widely accepted.

Even for traditional businesses, **bill presentation and payment** mechanisms can make life easier and save money. Service businesses in particular can benefit because they tend to bill clients on a regular basis. The goal is to send all bills electronically and provide a simple method for clients to transfer funds to your account. If clients are large businesses, they may wish to use existing EDI or banking systems to transfer money. Smaller customers with smaller payments will generally prefer the newer online payment systems like BillPay because they have lower costs to the customers.

The electronic systems save time because the bills can be created automatically from the in-house billing system. They do not have to be printed or mailed. Customers can feed the data into their own accounts payable systems and create electronic payments with only a few review steps. The payment data, and any disputes, can be processed electronically and automated.

Data Quality

How do you ensure that the transaction data is accurate? Transaction-processing systems can become quite complex. Problems are going to occur in any system—especially because all business organizations change over time. That means the computer system has to change to match the business. It is virtually impossible to change the system at exactly the same time as the business, so problems will occur. Other problems arise simply because the systems are so complex. Many processes involve humans who make mistakes. If you understand what types of problems might arise, they will be easier to solve.

The key to data quality is to focus on quality throughout the process. At input, data should be collected as close to the source as possible. For processing, data should be available to all users in a form they can use without having to reenter the data. In terms of output, reports should be linked to the databases so they always use the most recent data. Figure 6.15 lists the primary measures of data quality that you need to consider. In examining an information system, if you detect any of these problems, they are clues that you should search for ways to improve the transaction-processing system.

Data Integrity

One of the most important concepts in information processing is the issue of data integrity. **Data integrity** means keeping data accurate and correct as it is gathered and stored in the computer system. There is little value in an information system that contains out-of-date or inaccurate data. A common complaint among shoppers today is that stores using bar code scanners might have a different price in the computer than the amount displayed on the shelf. It is easy to change prices in the computer; it is more difficult to change the signs in the store. Shoppers will feel cheated if the computer tries to charge them a higher price than the amount listed on the shelf. Some states, such as Michigan, have passed laws requiring that the scanned price cannot be higher than the amount listed on the package or display. Similar errors cause problems when the computer shows more items in stock than actually exist.

The first step to ensure data integrity lies in its capture. Each item must be correctly entered and the complete information recorded. It is sometimes possible to check the data as it is entered. Item code numbers usually include a check number that is based on the other digits. In the item code 548737, the first five digits add up to 27, so the number 7 is included as the last digit. If the person or machine makes a mistake entering one of the digits, they

FIGURE 6.15

Maintaining data quality is crucial to managing a firm. There are several problems that make it difficult to build good transaction-processing systems.

Data Quality Attribute	Description and Problems
Integrity	Errors in data entry. Missing data. Failure to make updates.
Multitasking–concurrency	Data altered by two people at the same time, creating incorrect results.
Volume	Cost, difficulty of searching, transmission costs, errors harder to find, system overload.
Summaries	Too much detail is overkill when you only need summaries. With only summaries, you cannot recover the details.
Time	Many reports and decisions are subject to deadlines. Different departments getting data at different times can cause sequencing errors and additional delays.

REALITY BYTES   Garbage In, Garbage Out

Garbage In, Garbage Out (GIGO) is an old saying in the computer industry. It means that the value of your databases and information is only as good as the data that gets entered. Sometimes data problems are accidental, sometimes an issue with design. Other times, it can be a more serious problem. Drew Pooters was stunned when he found his Toys "R" Us store manager in Albuquerque altering payroll records. The manager was altering time records, deleting hours to cut their paychecks and make his store's profits higher. Mr. Pooters quit and eventually landed a job managing a Family Dollar store. There, top managers for the chain ordered him to hold employee hours under a certain amount each week. His district manager even showed him how to use a trick to delete some hours electronically. When he refused, the district manager erased the hours herself. Ex-

perts report that time shaving is widespread in America today and has resulted in an increasing number of lawsuits. Lawsuits exist against Family Dollar, Pep Boys, and Wal-Mart. Individual suits have been settled against some Taco Bell outlets in Oregon and Kinko's in New York. All of the chains have policies against altering records and will fire managers caught changing the data. But the pressure to alter records is huge—when management pay is based on the bottom line. Since the records are electronic and have few safeguards or security features, they are easy to change. Unless the employee maintains photocopied records, it is difficult to prove.

Source: Adapted from Steven Greenhouse, "Time Records Often Altered, Job Experts Say," *The New York Times,* April 4, 2004.

will probably not add up to 7, so the computer can immediately determine that there is an error. Sophisticated methods exist to catch mistakes involving more than one digit.

Even with machine entry of data, validity problems can arise. What happens when a shipment arrives but the receiving department forgets to record it? The same problem occurs when a clerk holds an item for a customer and does not record it in the computer. Data integrity can be destroyed by indiscriminately allowing people to change the numbers in the computer. It is one of the main reasons for creating secure computers and controlling access to each piece of information.

Multitasking, Concurrency, and Integrity

A useful feature offered by more sophisticated operating systems is the ability to perform more than one task at a time. In many situations it is useful to have several jobs running at the same time. What happens if you are searching a huge database and your boss calls and asks you for a sales figure? With a multitasking computer operating system, you could switch to a new program, look up the number, and allow the database to continue searching in the background.

If you use a multitasking operating system, it is important that your application software understand that other applications might be running at the same time. Each application needs to protect its data files from concurrency problems. **Concurrency** arises when applications attempt to modify the same piece of data at the same time. If two people are allowed to make changes to the same piece of data, the computer system must control the order in which it processes the two requests. Mixing the two tasks will result in the wrong data being stored in the computer. These problems can be avoided by only using software that was specifically written for multiuser (or multitasking) computers.

Consider the case of a mail-order firm shown in Figure 6.16. On the left side, customer Sanchez sent a payment on his account. At the same time the clerk begins to process the payment, Sanchez calls a second clerk and places a new order. The figure shows what happens if both transactions continue and interfere with each other. What should the final balance be? Does the computer have the correct number?

To solve this problem, the application program must know that several people might try to access the same piece of data at the same time. The software locks out all users except one. When the first process is finished, the other users can try to gain access again. To keep data accurate, applications used by many people at the same time must be written to handle these concurrency problems. Early personal computers were designed for only one user, so much of the software did not prevent concurrency problems. Software designed for computer networks generally handles this issue. When you use this software, you will occasionally receive a message that says a piece of data you desire is currently being used by

FIGURE 6.16

Concurrency and data integrity: Multiuser and multitasking systems can cause problems with concurrent changes to data. Two processes cannot be allowed to change the same data at the same time. Most systems will lock out transaction B until transaction A is completed. If a system becomes very busy, you can sometimes encounter delays while you wait for other users to finish their changes.

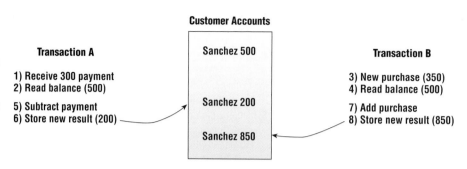

another person. If you get this message, simply wait for a few minutes and try again. When the first person is finished, you should be able to proceed.

Data Volume

A common problem experienced by a growing business is the increase in the amount of data or data volume. Consider the huge databases handled by Information Resources, which processes data from supermarket checkouts, or United Parcel Service, which tracks every package every day.

As the business grows, there will be an increase in the number of transactions. As the price of a computer drops, more applications are placed on the computer. Additional transactions become computerized. Several problems can be created from this increase: (1) processing overload or system slowdowns, (2) greater difficulty in making sure the data is accurate, (3) insufficient storage within the computer system, and (4) data not captured fast enough.

Visa International processes more than 6 billion electronic transactions a year. By the year 2000, the company was handling 15 billion annual transactions. There are 18,000 banks offering Visa cards, used by 10 million customers. So much data is generated on a daily basis that Visa cannot keep transaction data online beyond six months. All older records are moved to backup storage, making them inaccessible for additional research or decisions.

Sloppy practices and huge datasets can lead to inaccurate data. As the system slows down or the computer runs out of storage space, people avoid using it, so data is no longer up to date. With the increase in volume and the computerization of new types of data, it is more difficult for programmers and managers to check the data. If parts of the computer system are too slow, data may not be captured fast enough. As a result, some data might be lost. A tremendous amount of information is stored in raw data. The raw data could be analyzed to offer new services or improve the quality of existing services. However, the huge volumes require too much storage space and too much processing time.

Careful planning is required to avoid these problems. At best, new computers and storage usually take a month or two to purchase. It could take a year or more to evaluate and purchase a large, expensive central computer. The MIS department would like to forecast the demands that will be placed on the computers at least a year in advance.

Data Summaries

Another situation is commonly encountered in transaction-processing systems. In almost any company today, managers complain of having too much data. Consider the situation of a marketing manager who needs to determine the best way to increase sales for the next year. Think of the amount of data that is readily available. The firm's transaction-processing system can provide detailed records on sales of every item every day, by each salesperson, broken down by city, for at least the last five years. Scanner data from marketing research firms lists itemized sales by grocery store for every product. There is also internal data from consumer surveys, production, and responses to promotions. Demographic data is available from the government.

Technology Toolbox: Paying for Transactions

Problem: As a business, how do you get paid?

Tools: Many mechanisms have been proposed to handle payments, from cash to credit cards to cell phones. For decades, checks were the dominant payment mechanism in the United States. Only recently has it been possible to use electronic checks—essentially a direct debit to your checking account based on the routing numbers. Each method has potential advantages and drawbacks. As a businessperson, you might be tempted to accept as many methods of payment as possible, so you do not shut out potential customers. However, many of the methods have setup and fixed costs, so it can be expensive to accept everything.

Any payment method essentially has three main costs to the business: (1) fixed setup costs, (2) transaction costs as a fixed number and a percentage of the price, and (3) the expected loss from fraud or the cost of an insurance system. Often, there is an implicit cost to train employees in the proper procedures as well, which increases as you try to accept more variations of payments.

Payment Method	Fixed Cost	Fixed Fee	Discount Fee	Fraud/Insurance
Cash	Low except for security	$0.00	0%	Physical security
Check—physical	$20/month	$0.25	1.7%	Included
Check—electronic	$20/month	$0.25	2.5%	Included
Credit card—physical	$10/month Minimum $25	$0.25–$0.50	1.6%	Covered: 0.08% fraud average
Credit card—electronic	$30–$50/month Minimum $25	$0.25–$0.50	2.6%–4%	Not covered: 0.25% fraud average
Debit card	Setup/keypads	$0.35–$0.55	0%–2%	None
PayPal	None	$0.30	2.2%–2.9%	Covered for physical shipments

The transaction costs and risk are all paid by the seller. Merchant banks usually charge a monthly document or connection fee, and sometimes a one-time setup fee. A fixed cost per transaction is common, as well as a percentage of the sale. Customers often prefer credit cards, although in 2002, 15 percent of U.S. purchases were made with debit cards, and that number is increasing rapidly. Debit cards are useful to brick-and-mortar merchants because of the lower transaction costs and minimal risk. However, they are rarely accepted for online commerce because of the potential risk to consumer accounts. Checks and credit cards carry similar transaction costs today—when you factor in the insurance coverage for insufficient fund checks. One challenge with most of the payment mechanisms is that merchant banks usually require a monthly minimum fee charge. If your firm has few sales through the system, you will still have to pay $25 per month. For small companies just starting out in business, this fee can be expensive.

Quick Quiz:

1. Why have consumers rejected most electronic payment mechanisms?
2. What additional fees are charged for international transactions?
3. What happens if a customer refutes a charge?

To deal with this much data, managers are forced to rely on summaries. The marketing manager may see only a list of sales totals by each salesperson. That total might or might not include merchandise that was returned. Imagine what happens if returns are *not* included in the totals, but the manager believes that they were included. An unethical salesperson could sell extra merchandise to a friend (boosting the totals) and then return the merchandise the same day (because the returns are not subtracted from the list).

The problem multiplies as the information travels through different levels in the organization. Higher-level managers in the firm deal with data that has gone through several types of summarizing at each lower level. By the time they finally receive the information, the reports might not contain the data that is needed. The details might have been deleted or the summaries might carry the wrong set of information.

Time

Time is another aspect of information quality in transaction-processing systems. The information system must furnish the information at the time it is needed for decision making. An information system that is overloaded or not producing properly summarized data will not be able to provide information at the right time. Consider the data needed to file tax forms. The government has a time limit for filing tax forms. Managers would be understandably upset if their computer system could not produce the annual accounting reports in time to calculate taxes. Similarly, it is difficult to place orders for new merchandise when the only available data is a three-month-old sales report.

Problems with timeliness generally arise because data is not captured early enough. The sales report might be delayed because too many people are needed to enter the data and make some of the computations. A POS system could provide a detailed sales list almost instantly. Other delays arise when the system cannot distribute data to everyone at the same time, so reports end up sitting on someone's desk.

Production Management

Can your company be more efficient and productive? Sometimes this question is easy to answer—if you have been losing money. But perhaps you are manager of an organization that has been successful and profitable. Many companies have been successful for years and continue to operate the same way they always have. This practice might not be bad in every case, but the concept of **continuous quality improvement** dictates that you should always look for improvements—no matter how successful you have been. New production and information technologies are introduced continuously. Any one of these technologies might give you the ability to leapfrog your competition, or it might give your competitors the ability to squeeze you out of the market.

As shown in Figure 6.17, information technology has several important uses in production management. It is important to track orders, shipments, and all steps in the production process. The **bill of materials** is an important concept in manufacturing. It records the components that were used to manufacture a finished product. Data on it is used to trigger deductions in inventory of parts and signal the addition of the final product to finished inventory. These actions impact the accounting ledgers, so recording the proper amounts and time is important. Similarly, quality control measures are taken at several steps in the process—particularly with the receipt of supplies and the shipment of finished products. Detailed quality measures during the production process are used to identify processes, machines, and employees that need improvement.

Production Issues

Manufacturing in large scale presents several problems and issues to management. As shown in Figure 6.18, consider the case of a clothing manufacturer with several factories.

FIGURE 6.17

Production management: Production of goods and services generates considerable information. Purchase orders are placed with suppliers, internal documents like the bill of materials record production, and shipping invoices record interactions with customers. Quality control measures are recorded at several steps in the process.

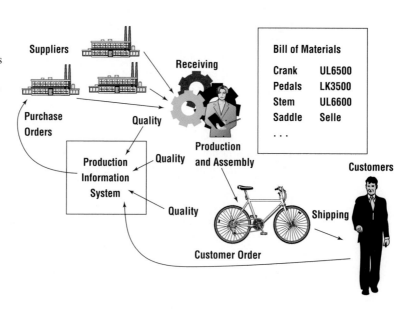

FIGURE 6.18

Production challenges: Multiple factories produce many items that are shipped to hundreds of customers. How do you schedule efficient production? How do you ensure the right products go to the correct locations?

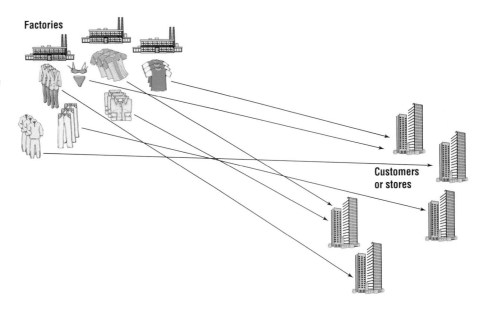

Each factory can produce multiple items and the company works with many factories. The items are collected and shipped to hundreds or thousands of customers and stores. How do you schedule efficient production? How do you ensure that the right products are shipped to the correct stores? These questions seem obvious, but they are critical. In the 1980s, the huge designer jean company Gitano self-destructed because it was unable to answer these two questions.

Obviously, information systems are a key component to the answers. But you need to make sure the processes are in place to collect the correct data in a timely manner. This data has to be available throughout the company so managers can monitor for problems and make the correct decisions. For instance, with only partial data, it might appear that a factory is idle, while complete data might show that it is scheduled to ramp up production as soon as supplies or new machines arrive. Collecting data in a manufacturing environment can be a difficult process. Most workers are busy trying to build products and are not interested in taking time to enter data into a computer. You need to define the processes and jobs to ensure that accurate data is also being recorded. You also need to automate as much of the data collection as possible. Some machines can transfer data directly into the information system, but often you need to assign the task to someone. This step is particularly important when things go wrong. You also might have to add bar codes or RFID tags to products so they can be counted and recorded automatically.

Once you have accurate data, you can usually purchase tools or hire experts to analyze the production processes and find improvements. The field of production operations management has many tools and models to organize and optimize production and scheduling.

Distribution and Inventory Control

A key mantra in today's business is that you do not want to hold inventory. **Just-in-time (JIT)** production was designed to eliminate parts inventories held by manufacturers. Instead, suppliers are asked to deliver parts exactly when they are needed. In one sense, the process shifts the inventory onto the supplier, because the supplier is penalized if it is late with shipments. But, ultimately, it reduces the number of products held in inventory because everyone along the supply chain is interested in minimizing the value of the stalled inventory. Instead, everyone forecasts production needs and delivers products by keeping them moving through the supply chain.

As shown in Figure 6.19, the **distribution center (DC)** is an important part of a modern supply system. Incoming bulk shipments are unloaded from the trucks and placed on high-speed conveyor systems. Bar code readers in the center of the DC read each box. Outgoing trucks are matched to a specific customer and store. The computer reads the customer order

FIGURE 6.19

Distribution center: Factories deliver products in bulk to the DC. High-speed conveyors read bar codes on the incoming boxes to split the products into smaller shipments and route them to trucks headed for individual stores.

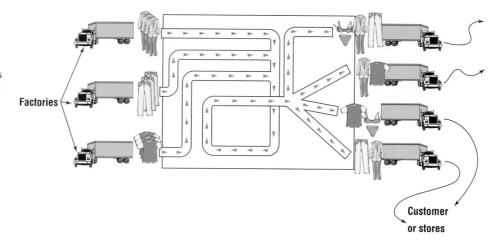

Factories

Customer or stores

list and routes the specified number of boxes of each item to every truck. When the trucks are loaded, they deliver the items to the designated customer and store. Additional savings are created by routing the same truck to the ship or rail yard freight docks to pick up an incoming bulk shipment. These trucks then deliver the bulk shipments on the left side of the DC in the diagram. Scheduling systems keep the trucks moving to maximize their capacity and to reduce deadhead or empty loads.

Distribution centers might be run by manufacturers, customers, or third-party transportation specialists. Wal-Mart is a leader in using the centers to reduce costs and deliver exactly the needed products to every store. Ultimately, you also need to match your shipment data against the customer receipts to ensure that your system is accurate and to compensate for shipping losses.

Summary

Every organization must perform certain basic operations: pay employees, manufacture products or services, pay bills, monitor revenue, and file government reports. Operations are relatively structured, short term, and easy to computerize. They form the foundation of the company. MIS supports operations by collecting data and helping to control the underlying processes.

A Manager's View

How do you keep up with the thousands or millions of transactions in a modern organization? Information systems have been developed to handle internal data from accounting, human resource management, and production. But the key to transactions is that they are interactions with outside companies. Interacting with other companies is complex and requires standards so everyone can communicate. Ordering and payment mechanisms are critical elements to reduce costs and improve accuracy. But standards are still evolving and you must investigate all options.

Transaction-processing systems are responsible for capturing, storing, and providing access to the basic data of the organization. The goal is to capture the transaction data as soon as possible. Common collection methods include point-of-sale devices, process control, electronic data interchange, and electronic commerce Web sites. Because data is the foundation for all other decisions, transaction-processing systems must maintain data integrity and minimize the threats to the data.

Transaction-processing systems are often difficult because they involve outside agents such as suppliers, banks, and customers. Exchanging data and money with outside organizations requires standards and solid communication fundamentals. EDI systems and the Internet help, but they are still evolving. Payment mechanisms ultimately need even more work. Several standard risks are faced by buyers, vendors, and the government. Online payment systems need work to control these risks.

Key Words

bill of materials, *220*
bill presentation and payment, *215*
concurrency, *217*
continuous quality improvement, *220*
data integrity, *216*
digital cash, *214*
distribution center (DC), *221*

electronic data interchange (EDI), *201*
extensible markup language (XML), *209*
just-in-time (JIT), *221*
magnetic ink character recognition (MICR), *201*
optical character recognition (OCR), *201*

point of sale (POS), *200*
process control, *200*
radio frequency identification (RFID), *202*
supply chain management (SCM), *205*
transaction processing, *200*

Web Site References

General Travel Reservations

Microsoft Expedia	www.expedia.com
One Travel	www.onetravel.com
Orbitz	www.orbitz.com
Sabre Travelocity	www.travelocity.com

Discounts

Bestfares	www.bestfares.com
Cheap Tickets	www.cheaptickets.com
Priceline	www.priceline.com
TravelHUB	www.travelhub.com

Individual Airlines

Alaska/Horizon	www.alaskaair.com
American	www.aa.com
America West	www.americawest.com
Continental	www.continental.com
Delta	www.delta.com
Frontier	www.frontierairlines.com
Jet Blue	www.jetblue.com
Northwest	www.nwa.com
Southwest	www.southwest.com
United	www.ual.com

Additional Readings

Anthes, Gary H. "When Five 9s Aren't Enough." *Computerworld,* October 8, 2001. [Challenges of transaction processing at Visa.]

Bleakley, Fred. "Electronic Payments Now Supplant Checks at More Large Firms." *The Wall Street Journal,* April 13, 1994, pp. A1, A9. [Costs of handling checks.]

Disabatino, Jennifer. "The Technology behind the Problem." *Computerworld,* October 22, 2001. [Transaction-processing difficulties in providing airline passenger data to the FBI.]

Loshin, Pete. "Transaction Processing." *Computerworld,* October 1, 2001. [Basic concepts of transactions.]

Trombley, M. "Visa Issues 10 'Commandments' for Online Merchants." *Computerworld,* August 11, 2000. [Visa's attempt to get vendors to protect credit card databases, and Gartner Group's estimate of online fraud.]

Want, Roy. "RFID: A Key to Automating Everything." *Scientific American,* January 2004. [The strengths and limitations of RFID with a good description of how it works.]

Winslow, Ron. "Four Hospital Suppliers Will Launch Common Electronic Ordering System." *The Wall Street Journal,* April 12, 1994, p. B8. [EDI for hospitals, including costs.]

Review Questions

1. Describe four methods of data capture.
2. What is electronic data interchange (EDI)? Why has EDI taken so long to catch on? Will businesses ever use EDI for all transactions?
3. What is the role of XML in EDI transactions?
4. What risks are involved in transactions? How are these risks handled in electronic commerce?
5. What is the government's role in transactions?
6. Why has it taken so long for new payment mechanisms to be adopted?
7. What is meant by the term *data quality*? Give three examples of problems with data quality.
8. Why is data volume an important issue in transaction-processing systems? Will newer, faster machines automatically solve the problem?
9. What is meant by *concurrency,* and why is it a problem in a multiuser environment?
10. What are the major information transaction elements in production management?
11. How are distribution centers used to reduce inventory, and what information is needed for them to operate efficiently?

Exercises

1. Choose an industry and research the use of EDI in that industry. Is it widely used? Explain the problems that exist. See if there is a B2B auction site for that industry. Has it been more successful than traditional EDI?
2. Using a DBMS, create two forms that enter data into the same table. Try to change the same row of data from each form and report how it handles the concurrent changes.
3. Research the costs and who pays them (a) if a customer reports that a charge is fraudulent and (b) if a vendor fails to ship a product to a customer.
4. Identify the primary government laws and rules that are designed to protect the government's interest in transactions.
5. Because of the importance of transactions, there are a large number of cases involving fraud and other legal problems with sales and other transactions. Pick an industry and find articles in business and trade journals that identify problems of this nature. How will computerization of the transactions affect fraudulent transactions? Why would the computerization make it easier or harder to detect these problems?

 Technology Toolbox

6. Find information on current proposals for at least three Internet-based payment mechanisms. Evaluate the strengths and weaknesses of the systems. Be sure to identify the transaction costs and who pays them.
7. Find information on the current fraud and chargeback levels with credit cards for online and traditional retail sales. Do the numbers vary by industry? If you are operating an online store with $10 million in annual sales, how much would you expect to lose to chargeback and fraud?
8. On the basis of the cost figures in the text, create a spreadsheet and compare the estimated annual costs for the various online payment mechanisms for three hypothetical companies. The first company sells digital content for about $20 each and anticipates about 5,000 sales per year. The second company sells music for $0.75 per song, but expects people to download and pay for 5 to 10 songs at a time. It anticipates 500,000 customers. The third company sells stereo and video equipment ranging from $400 to

$2,000 per item, and expects about 10,000 sales the first year. On the basis of the data, recommend a payment mechanism for each company.

9. Find three EDI vendors and identify how the data is transferred. In particular, does it support XML, X12, and Edifact? Also, what transmission networks are supported?

10. Find a major retailer and the EDI compliance rules they use. Briefly explain what happens if a vendor fails to follow some of the rules.

Teamwork

11. Have each team member visit a retail store in your area and determine how they handle transaction processing for sales. How many checkout counters are available at each store? By counting the number of customers in a 10- to 15-minute time interval, estimate the total number of sales transactions occurring for a given day. Combine the results and create charts to compare the stores.

12. From a list of at least 500 companies, each team member should randomly research one and identify the major operations of the firm. Identify the primary transactions.

13. Each team member should examine 10 random retail Web sites and identify whether the site sells to customers in different nations (list the nations). Combine the results from each person and compute the percentage of sites that ship internationally, and the list of nations. Are certain nations or regions absent from this list?

14. Create a short survey instrument and assign team members to interview groups of consumers to identify which payment mechanism they use the most, and identify how many have used alternative electronic payment systems such as PayPal, BillPoint, or eCheck. Combine the results and analyze the data for the group.

Rolling Thunder Database

15. Identify the major transaction-processing components in the system.

16. What features are used in the database and the forms to ensure quality of transaction data?

17. What additional data quality features should be added?

18. Explain how additional data quality features can be provided with training, procedures, and manual controls.

19. For each major transaction type, identify the sequence of steps that are performed and determine which ones are time critical.

20. For each major transaction type, estimate the frequency of the transaction and the volume of data involved.

21. Identify any transaction forms that could be improved to make them easier for clerks and other users.

22. Using the existing forms, perform the following tasks for Rolling Thunder:
    a. Take a bicycle order.
    b. Assemble a bicycle.
    c. Create a new purchase order.
    d. Record the receipt of purchases.

Cases: Retail Sales

The Industry

The retail sales industry includes a broad variety of products, but regardless of the product, several fundamental issues apply. You need to remember that retailers play three critical roles in selling products. The first is location—retail stores succeed by displaying and delivering products where the customers are lo-cated. The second is customer service. Many customers need help choosing products and need reassurance—particularly when buying large items. Retail stores also handle returns and take care of any problems that might arise with a product. The third major role played by retailers is to spread the sales risk. Generally, retailers purchase items in bulk. If the items do not sell, the retailer marks down the prices until they are sold. But

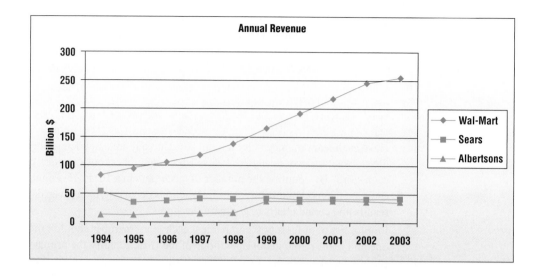

the retailer decides which items to carry and what final price to charge, so the retailer takes the loss if products do not sell well. These three services are important to manufacturers. As part of the economics of specialization, manufacturers can concentrate on building products, retailers can focus on customer service, and both firms come out ahead.

Transactions

Tracking sales of individual items and recording transactions are critical factors in retail sales. Originally, retail firms tracked final sales only for themselves. They used the information to help decide when to reorder and when to cut prices. Since the retailer sits in the middle between suppliers and customers, the retailer participates in several types of transactions. Consequently, retailers built important accounting and inventory systems. Recording transactions with customers is relatively easy in theory. The challenge is to keep the costs as low as possible, which is why retailers continually experiment with technology at the checkouts. The retail sales transactions also have to be accurate and secure. Because retailers are generally responsible for collecting sales taxes, the systems also have to maintain adequate audit trails for the state examiners. Retailers also have to track purchases from suppliers. The actual purchase is not that difficult to track, but they also have to monitor shipping and financing costs. Moreover, there are always special orders, and someone has to match received items to orders, monitor quality, and often track down missing or incorrect orders. Increasingly, retail stores also have to build transaction systems to handle the financial aspects as well. As more customers switch to digital payment systems (debit cards), retailers have to work with banks to validate card numbers, verify account balances, and transfer the transaction totals. The detailed financial system must also be able to go back and provide documentation for possible fraudulent transactions.

Supply Chain Management

Today, led by Wal-Mart, the emphasis is on the entire supply chain. A key aspect to reducing costs and improving the profit margin is to minimize the items held in inventory. Or, in retailer accounting language, maximizing inventory turnover. The ultimate goal might be a just-in-time replenishment system: just as a customer buys an item from the shelf, a new one shows up at the loading dock. Of course, this perfect system is almost impossible. But the profitable stores get closer every year. One key is the ability to forecast exactly which products customers are going to buy and then build a supply chain so that the right products are delivered on time. Transaction information is a key element in supply chain management. Retailers share their daily sales data with manufacturers, so manufacturers can forecast demand and fine-tune their delivery times.

Supply chains often suffer from what is called the bullwhip effect. A small increase in sales causes retailers to forecast an increase in demand and bulk order more of the product from their distributors. If the increase arises from several stores, the distributor also sees an increase in demand and orders more products. In the meantime, the stores perceive a shortage that is not being filled by the distributor, so they increase their orders even further—to hoard the product and ensure deliveries. The manufacturer sees a giant increase in demand and starts cranking up capacity. The initial small increase in demand has been magnified as it moves up the supply chain. Ultimately, the manufacturer overcompensates and the supply increases too far, raising costs for everyone and depressing prices as the retailers mark down the item to get rid of it. Of course, the fluctuating prices send the wrong signal to customers and can start the cycle all over again. One way to minimize the bullwhip effect is to make sure that all participants have access to the original data on customer demand and that everyone uses the same forecast. Retailers generally support this approach and share their sales data with manufacturers (Hugos 2003).

Of course, a large retail store carries tens of thousands of products and has a few thousand suppliers. So, the retail store needs to be able to integrate with thousands of different systems, or at least provide data in some common format. The massive volume of data also presents problems for storage, access, and transportation across networks. Ultimately, the stores that succeed in handling these data volumes at the least cost are the ones that have prospered.

Additional Reading

Hugos, Michael. "Essentials of Supply Chain Management [book excerpt]." *Computerworld,* March 24, 2003.

Case: Wal-Mart

Wal-Mart (ticker: WMT) represents a classic business technology case. Emphasizing customer service and low prices, the company pushes its suppliers hard. Founder Sam Walton realized early that computers would play an important role in these goals. In the mid-1960s, computers were used to handle basic accounting functions. Counting inventory was still painful because the tools were not available. It was not until 1983 that item-level bar codes were available on the majority of products. Each product was assigned an identifier or stockkeeping unit (SKU) and a standardized bar code. At that point, Wal-Mart installed point-of-sale terminals and was able to track inventory based on the sales. In 1987, the company used a satellite system to link all of the stores to company headquarters. The system enabled the company to compile real-time inventory data ("Dateline" September 2002). To reduce the inventory levels, Wal-Mart knew it needed to enlist the cooperation of its suppliers, so the company instituted the collaborative planning, forecasting, and replenishment (CPFR) program to share data with its suppliers. Pete Abell, retail research director at the AMR Research consulting firm, notes that Wal-Mart's "margins can be far lower than other retailers' because they have such an efficient supply chain." He estimates that the company pays 5 to 10 percent less than its competitors for products (Johnson 2002). The suppliers are willing to offer better prices to Wal-Mart because sharing the supply chain management reduces their costs as well. And it does not hurt that Wal-Mart is the biggest company in the world with almost $250 billion in annual sales and more than 1.2 million employees (www.fortune.com/global500).

Supply Chain Management

Wal-Mart led the industry in improving its supply chain to reduce costs. Its incredibly efficient distribution centers are one part of the story. Bulk shipments arrive from vendors at one side of the distribution center. For example, a large truck might be full of identical boxes of laundry detergent. The contents of the truck are unloaded and placed on a conveyor belt. The products are routed through the distribution center to the other side where a mixed load of multiple items is placed onto another truck. This load might contain some laundry detergent, toys, and clothes. The mixed load is then taken to a specific store. The computer-controlled distribution center knows exactly which items need to be shipped to each store and loads the trucks accordingly. The system runs by reading the individual bar codes and shifting products to different belts.

In 2003, Wal-Mart shocked many people when it announced that its top 100 suppliers would have to switch to radio frequency identification (RFID) chips in 2005. Initially, the RFID tags would apply only to pallet loads of products. The tags provide some significant advantages over bar codes in the warehouse. They can be read from farther away and do not require perfect line of sight. Multiple tags can be read at the same time (if boxes are stacked together). They are less susceptible to damage. An important issue is that they can contain more data. This last factor is important because it would enable Wal-Mart to electronically record and track the receipt of individual shipments. Bar codes allow it to track only the specific product. A person has to manually match the shipment with the specific order. The main drawback to the RFID approach is cost. Bar codes are essentially free, since they can simply be printed on the box or a label. RFID tags in 2003 cost around 50 cents each. Wal-Mart is hoping that by forcing suppliers to adopt the tags, the bulk demand will convince manufacturers to expand capacity and reduce prices through economies of scale. Wal-Mart's target is 5 cents per tag, and it anticipates that about 1 billion tags will be needed initially (Vijayan 2003).

It is risky to be on the leading edge of technology. Standards are not yet in place and costs are relatively high. The lack of standards is a substantial problem in the international marketplace. As of mid-2004, many Chinese manufacturers were waiting for an RFID standard to be approved before agreeing to use RFID tags. Consequently, some companies might end up having to add the RFID tags after the product reaches the United States (Sullivan June 2004). Several groups have also raised concerns about privacy issues if RFID tags are moved to individual products. Although the tags can be read from only a limited range of a few feet, some people expressed concerns about stores being able to track people by tags placed in their clothes. And if not enough suppliers and distributors install the hardware and software to take advantage of the tags, the entire experiment could be an expensive trial. Some "experts" were suggesting that as many as 50 percent of these trials would fail. Nonetheless, Linda Dillman, CIO of Wal-Mart, observed that the retailer believed it needed to stay on the leading edge of technology. It was important to try technologies that might help, even though the technology eventually might not be useful (Sullivan July 2004). Initial trials with Kimberly-Clark were successful. In April 2004, the company shipped pallets of its Scott paper towels with RFID tags through Wal-Mart's scanners. But Kimberly-Clark has been working toward the RFID system since 2001 (Bacheldor 2004).

Tighter Integration with Manufacturers

Procter & Gamble sells $40 billion of household products every year. You know most of their brand names. Despite the use of information technology and electronic ordering systems, Steve David, the CIO, pointed out that returns from retail stores cost P&G $50 million a year. Problems arise from incorrect orders, damaged products, and inaccurate shipments (Stahl 2003).

How can so many problems exist in an electronic system? One of the problems is that every company has a different description and ID number for every product. For example, P&G might have an internal ItemID for a tube of Crest toothpaste. But Wal-Mart will assign a different SKU to each specific size and flavor. The Wal-Mart database might even have a different description for the product than that used by Crest. Both companies probably have even more numbers to describe bulk orders or boxes of toothpaste. Relying on people to match the descriptions or to find items in a catalog or Web site is time consuming and easily causes errors. And manufacturers tend to continually introduce variations or new products and change the numbers. The consulting firm A.T. Kearney estimates that 30 percent of the information in catalogs is incorrect at any point in time (Konicki 2002). P&G alone sells around 60,000 different items.

One answer is to ensure that everyone uses a single standard description and ID of every product. But you have to get all of the manufacturers and retailers to agree to use the system, and someone has to pay for its maintenance. The current answer is the UCCnet registry. It is a not-for-profit subsidiary of the Uniform Code Council (UCC). Ultimately, it makes money by charging manufacturers and retailers an annual fee to use the system (www.uccnet.org). Each item listing contains 62 pieces of product data. By placing it in a single location, all merchants can synchronize their databases to the manufacturer's standard. Errors are reduced when everyone works from the same clean database (Meehan 2002).

With more accurate data, Wal-Mart can rely on EDI to place most of its orders—reducing the costs and time of having employees manually enter each order. EDI has been around since the 1980s, but it carried a high cost because most of the transactions were on private VAN networks that are expensive. In 2003, Wal-Mart began encouraging suppliers to switch to an Internet-based EDI system. To ensure security, most merchants are using the electronic data interchange Internet integration applicability statement 2 (AS2) standard. AS2 provides security through certificate-based encryption. Merchants and producers can use the system either through a Web browser or through low-cost client tools that will connect to their ERP systems (Scheier 2003).

Competition

Competition in discount retail is stiff. Wal-Mart has literally grabbed most of the market from other retailers. For comparison, look to Kmart—which was dominant through much of the nation before Wal-Mart. Because the company did not have the supply chain management systems, and because it did not have the data to forecast customer demand, its stores rarely had the products in stock that customers wanted. Ultimately, it filed for bankruptcy protection because it could not compete against Wal-Mart and Target. In 2000, the Kmart CEO announced that he would spend $1.4 billion on technology—more than the company had spent in an entire decade. The company burned through five CIOs in seven years and went without one for almost two years. The company also had to take a $130 million write-off of supply chain software and hardware that did not work properly. Although spending the money earlier on technology might not have saved Kmart, it is clear that it has provided a competitive advantage to Wal-Mart (Sliwa 2002).

Privacy

Wal-Mart collects a huge amount of transaction data—data that includes detailed information on everything customers purchase. Unless payment is made in cash, the Wal-Mart databases also identify the individual purchaser. This data can provide useful insights to manufacturers and marketing companies. In 2001, three retailers (CVS, Kmart, and Wal-Mart) decided to pool their pharmacy sales data and sell up-to-the-minute numbers to drug manufacturers—in exchange for a few million dollars in fees. However, Wal-Mart also made a decision to stop selling general sales data to market research companies. A Wal-Mart spokesman notes that "our competitors were getting more out of the third-party aggregation than we were, so it made more sense for us to stop" (Rendleman 2001).

Financial Transactions

On March 31, 2004, Wal-Mart spotted a problem: 800,000 shoppers were overcharged on their credit and debit cards. The transactions were double- or triple-billed due to a hardware error. First Data Corporation, which clears financial transactions for Wal-Mart, noticed the problem when reviewing one of its quality control logs. The company reversed the duplicate transactions, but Wal-Mart put up notices to customers to double-check their statements (D'Ambrosio 2004). First Data blamed the error on a computer glitch, but did not provide details.

Online

Wal-Mart has several online systems in place, but they provide only a tiny fraction of sales. Yet the site does get traffic. A test of the site for the 2003 holiday season showed that it was being used somewhat over its capacity—making it sluggish. The site was ranked 19th of 20 Web sites. Consumers had to wait an average of 54 seconds to complete an online transaction (Rosencrance 2003).

Somewhat surprisingly, in 2003, Wal-Mart introduced an online music service that charges 88 cents per song—11 cents less than the leading site by Apple. Songs are being provided by Anderson Merchandisers, which acquired Liquid Audio, one of the innovators in digital music. With a somewhat limited selection of songs, it remains to be seen whether customers will use the service (Bartels 2003).

IT Development

Unlike many of today's large companies, Wal-Mart tends to develop most of its own software. The company is leery of commercial packages because it does not want to be held hostage by the software vendor. The CIO of Wal-Mart also emphasizes that developers have to understand the user's tasks before creating software. Just developing something does not mean it will actually be used. Consequently, before the IT staff creates and deploys an application, developers have to work in the real job. For example, if someone is going to rewrite a point-of-sale application, he or she has to work for a couple of days as a cashier. That way, developers learn what issues are important and what problems need to be solved (Schrage 2003).

Questions

1. Why are some people upset about RFID tags? Are their fears justified?
2. What does the UCCnet project do and why is it so important to retailers?
3. Why did Wal-Mart stop selling some transaction data and will it affect the company in the future?
4. What is the role of Wal-Mart's Web site? Is it a useful tool?
5. Should Wal-Mart continue to rely on developing its own software?
6. What are the benefits and costs to having developers work in a functional area before creating new applications?

Additional Reading

Bacheldor, Beth. "Kimberly-Clark on RFID Trial: So Far, So Good." *Information Week,* May 17, 2004.

Bartels, Chuck. "Wal-Mart Begins Testing Online Music Service." *Information Week,* December 18, 2003.

"Dateline: A Timeline of Technology Advances at Wal-Mart." *Computerworld,* September 30, 2002.

D'Ambrosio, Dan. "800,000 Cards Overcharged at Wal-Mart." *Information Week,* April 5, 2004.

Johnson, Amy Helen. "A New Supply Chain Forged." *Computerworld,* September 30, 2002.

Konicki, Steve. "Shopping for Savings." *Information Week,* July 1, 2002.

Meehan, Michael. "UCCnet's Promise: Synchronized Product Data." *Computerworld,* June 10, 2002.

Rendleman, John. "Customer Data Means Money." *Information Week,* August 20, 2001.

Rosencrance, Linda. "Report: Some Retail Sites Strained by Online Shopping Surge." *Computerworld,* December 3, 2003.

Scheier, Robert L. "Internet EDI Grows Up." *Computerworld,* January 20, 2003.

Schrage, Michael. "Don't Trust Your Code to Strangers." *Computerworld,* September 18, 2003.

Sliwa, Carol. "IT Difficulties Help Take Kmart Down." *Computerworld,* January 28, 2002.

Stahl, Stephanie. "Editor's Note: Efficiency Leads to Lower Costs." *Information Week,* June 16, 2003.

Sullivan, Laurie. "China RFID Standards Are Eagerly Awaited by U.S. Manufacturers." *Information Week,* June 21, 2004.

Sullivan, Laurie. "RFID Will Go through Growing Pains." *Information Week,* July 2, 2004.

Vijayan, Jaikumar, and Bob Brewin. "Wal-Mart to Deploy Radio ID Tags for Supply Tracking." *Computerworld,* June 12, 2003.

Case: Sears, Roebuck and Co. and Lands' End

As one of the earliest mass merchandise stores, Sears (ticker: S) has a major place in the history of business in the United States. Richard Sears opened his first store in Chicago in 1887 selling watches and jewelry. In 1896, he began shipping the general catalog that made the company famous. In 1993, the company stopped distributing the general catalog because of the production and mailing costs. Its Craftsman tools and Kenmore kitchen appliances are household icons. In the 1980s and 1990s, Sears acquired several firms that were unrelated to its primary mission. For example, in 1981 it acquired the brokerage firm Dean Witter as well as the Coldwell Banker real estate company. By 2003, the company had divested all of those firms to concentrate on sales (www.searsarchive.com).

Gary Comer founded Lands' End in Chicago in 1963 with a couple of friends to sell yachting hardware. Over time, the company expanded into luggage, moved to rural Dodgeville, Wisconsin, and took off with direct sales of clothing through its catalogs, telephone operators, and the best guarantee in the business (www.landsend.com). In 2001, Lands' End had revenues of about $1.6 billion compared with $41 billion for Sears (Weiss 2002). In 2002, Sears purchased Lands' End for $1.9 billion. However, as a wholly owned subsidiary, the company remains relatively independent—even down to its information technology systems. The merger has had some interesting effects—partly on the success of Lands' End and the number of Lands' End executives who gained power at Sears.

Lands' End used technology to boost sales. In 2001, the company noticed that it was losing sales because products were not in stock. So, in 2002, the company built an inventory-management workbench. The data warehouse system uses an analytic engine to monitor sales and create reports. It automatically alerts sales managers when popular items need to be restocked. The system links to seven-year sales histories in the Lands' End IBM DB2 database. It even contains regional weather data so it can determine why sales of raincoats or parkas increased in an area. With its success, the company created another workbench to help with business-to-business sales, and a third one to help schedule workers in the warehouses (Whiting 2003). In addition, the Lands' End Web site introduced several innovative features.

Online

As a direct merchant, Lands' End presented several innovations. One of its more powerful tools is its virtual model. Customers enter some basic measurement data into the Web site and the system draws a 3-D model to match their body type. From that point, customers can have the model display combinations of the clothes to see how they might fit. Extending on its telephone-based personal services, the Web site also has a personal shopper service. When new styles are released, the personal shoppers recommend combinations to shoppers based on their preferences and prior purchases.

Lands' End built its company by establishing strong relationships with suppliers around the world. These ties enabled the company to offer custom clothing through its Web site. In 2001, the company began offering custom Chino pants for $54 online, compared with standard prices of $30 to $40. By 2004, the company was offering custom dress shirts or blouses, dress pants, and jeans as well. In addition to basic measurements, the Web site asks customers to choose among basic body types. The company then has the shirts or pants built to the specifications in a few days. The customization feature is useful because the top reason for returns is that clothing does not fit properly (Swanson 2001).

Lands' End quickly learned an important lesson about Internet sales: you still have to provide good customer service, so the Web interface does not necessarily save money. On the other hand, the level of service provided by Lands' End is amazing and generally exceeds that provided by most merchants. For example, a customer called to buy clothes for his wife for Christmas. He had already ordered a charcoal-gray blazer and slacks. He wanted to know if a skirt on a different page would match. The customer service representative put him on hold and quickly called a "personal shopper," who pulled both garments from a rack and compared them to see that they did not match. In 96 seconds, the service representative was back on the phone with the caller with a suggestion

for a different skirt that did match and a decision to ship the skirt at no extra shipping costs, since the first items were ordered a scant 12 hours earlier. Although the order was placed over the phone, the same level of service is available online. Bill Bass, vice president of electronic commerce, notes that "one of the great fallacies of the Internet is [that] you'll save on customer service costs because customers [will] serve themselves." But reducing service costs is not really an important issue to Lands' End. Instead, the company would like to reduce the cost of printing and mailing its 250 million catalogs—which accounts for 41 percent of its operating costs (King 1999).

The site also offers the ability to "shop with a friend." A customer shares a Web site with a friend in a different location. The two see the same products and can communicate via a chat session. To Lands' End, it is all part of customer service.

One of the tools that Lands' End needed help with is the search engine. Actually, few Web sites have had good search engines. Although companies like Google make their search engines available to commercial sites, they are designed to search static Web pages and not product databases. Specialty search companies such as EasyAsk and Endeca have created search engines that enable customers to ask questions in natural languages (e.g., English). The system then searches the database for the best matches (Sliwa 2002).

In 1999, Lands' End launched a global Web site, building the site on IBM's Websphere platform and partnering with Berlitz to handle the initial translations. By 2001, 14 percent of the total sales were outside of the United States. The first sites they added were Japan, the UK, and Germany. A few months later, they added Ireland, France, and Italy by cloning the UK site. Sam Taylor, vice president of international operations, notes that "to launch the French site, it cost us 12 times less than the UK site, and to launch Italy, it cost us 16 times less. That's the beauty of the Internet. It's so scalable" (Sliwa 2001). He also observed that it is considerably cheaper to reach customers via the Internet than through printing and mailing catalogs. However, he also pointed out that the company should not have created the Japanese site first. "There's nothing worse than when your programmers are making changes, and they look at the site to see if it works and they can't read it" (Sliwa 2001).

The Merger

Sears knew that its clothing division was in trouble, even though they sold $4.7 billion of apparel a year. And with the divestiture of its credit card and other unrelated operations, the executives knew that clothing sales had to be turned around. The merger with Lands' End, one of the most successful direct clothing merchants, gave them the opportunity to fix the problem. The Lands' End executives were given control over the Sears clothing department.

Although it was expected, trouble began brewing between the two cultures. The Lands' End group was used to making fast decisions informally. The Sears bureaucracy had multiple levels of red tape. Sid Mashburn, Lands' End's vice president of design and now design chief at Sears as well, refers to the main headquarters as "the Battlestar Galactica" and suggests giving out machetes at the door to cut through the ingrained procedures. He might have been referring to the 29,000 pages of company guidelines that Sears once had (Merrick 2004).

When the Lands' End merchandise was first brought into the 870 stores, sales were weak. Placing $139 cashmere sweaters next to $17 sweatshirts did not help sales of either item. Customers were confused about where to find items. Also, Lands' End executives did not have data on what items would sell, or characteristics of the shoppers. Several items had to be marked down at the end of the season to clear out the inventory.

Jeff Jones, originally chief operating officer at Lands' End, asked if he could purchase data mining software to analyze customer purchases. Executives said that Sears did not use those tools. After some behind-the-scenes negotiations, Jones was finally able to get the tools. Using the software, he was able to learn that the store needed to target more upscale customers—those with incomes of $50,000 to $100,000 or more. Other merchandising experts from Lands' End have been brought in to retarget all of the clothing lines and identify the primary customers. Mindy Meads led groups to picture an image of a representative customer for each of five brands of women's clothing sold at Sears. This routine exercise and the data mining were things that Sears had neglected for years (Merrick 2004).

Technology

In 2002, Sears purchased a huge storage area network from EM to handle a new customer relationship management database. The system will include 95 terabytes of new storage. It will be used to combine data from several inventory databases and existing data warehouses. The system is designed to give the company the ability to examine purchases by customers within the store and over time. As Jonathan Rand, director of merchandise planning and reporting, commented, the company needs to make sure "customers find the merchandise and service they want in our stores, while eliminating what they don't want faster than the competition" (Mearian 2002).

Because the Lands' End division continues to run as a separate subsidiary, Sears did not attempt to merge their information systems. Their Web site and internal systems remain as separate units. This decision minimizes interruptions and avoids causing problems with a system that has been successful.

At the same time, Sears realized that it needed to overhaul its own information systems. In 2003, Alan Lacy, the CEO of Sears, observed that "we've got too many point-of-sale systems, too many inventory systems, too many this, that, and the other thing, because we basically allowed for many, many years each business to do its own thing, which we're not going to do anymore" (Sliwa 2003). However, he also recog-

nizes the importance of keeping the successful Lands' End systems separate. In early 2004, Sears announced that it was installing 37,000 Internet-enabled IBM cashier terminals. The connected systems will enable Sears to provide additional types of customer service (McDougall 2004).

In 2004, Sears signed a $1.6 billion 10-year outsourcing contract with Computer Sciences Corporation (CSC). The main elements of the contract cover desktop services, servers, networks, and system management of the Sears.com Web sites. Management of the servers running the financial reporting and sales systems remains outsourced to IBM. The Lands' End operations remain completely independent (Weiss 2004).

Sears also made a decision to recentralize its IT staff. Up until 2003, the staff was split into the various business units such as human resources or credit. The company also moved to standardize its choice of hardware and software vendors. The overall goal was to reduce the number of disparate systems. Cheryl Murphy, vice president of IT operations and engineering, observed that "we're pulling the IT staffs together to get operational excellence and to drive that into the company. We want to find one way of doing things" (Rosencrance 2003).

Suppliers

Sears has been successful in its automotive division in building a relationship with Michelin. In a pilot test with GlobalNetXchange, Sears provides detailed real-time sales data to Michelin. Sears had planned a sale on Michelin tires in June 2002, but even before the sale began, Michelin spotted a problem. Sales earlier in the year had been higher than expected, and the sale would push even more tires out the door. Michelin was forecasting that it would be short 5,000 tires. Since Michelin had direct access to the sales and inventory data, and knew which sizes were selling, the company was able to increase production before the sale began. Hank Steermann, senior manager of supply chain for Sears, commented that "this is a way to manage the supply chain that is good for Sears, because we're fulfilling our commitment to customers, and it's good for the supplier, because they're selling more units than we'd planned" (Konicki 2002).

Questions

1. How can Sears use information technology to improve the sales of clothing—particularly the Lands' End items?

2. What are the benefits to centralizing the information systems and the IT staff at Sears?

3. Given the benefits of centralization, why does every Sears executive keep saying that they will not integrate the Lands' End systems with the Sears systems?

4. If Sears wanted to combine data from the Lands' End financial system with the main systems at Sears, how could they do it without actually merging the systems?

Additional Reading

King, Julia. "Service Needs Drive Tech Decisions at Lands' End." *Computerworld,* December 20, 1999.

Konicki, Steve. "Sears, Michelin Test Supply Chain." *Information Week,* July 1, 2002.

McDougall, Paul. "Ordering IT." *Information Week,* March 22, 2004.

Mearian, Lucas. "Sears to Build Huge Storage Network for CRM." *Computerworld,* January 24, 2002.

Merrick, Amy. "Sears Orders Fashion Makeover from the Lands' End Catalog." *The Wall Street Journal,* January 28, 2004.

Rosencrance, Linda. "New Sears VP of IT Operations Wants to Simplify IT Environment." *Computerworld,* May 16, 2003.

Sliwa, Carol. "Clothing Retailer Finds Worldwide Business on the Web." *Computerworld,* April 30, 2001.

Sliwa, Carol. "E-Retailers Seek Improved Search Engines." *Computerworld,* August 12, 2002.

Sliwa, Carol. "Sears CEO Says Company Will Standardize Technology." *Computerworld,* January 20, 2003.

Swanson, Sandra. "Lands' End Brings Custom-Made Pants Online." *Information Week,* November 6, 2001.

Weiss, Todd R. "Sears Buying Lands' End." *Computerworld,* May 13, 2002.

Weiss, Todd R. "Sears Inks $1.6B IT Outsourcing Services Deal with CSC." *Computerworld,* June 2, 2004.

Whiting, Rick. "The Data-Warehouse Advantage." *Information Week,* July 28, 2003.

Case: Albertsons

Albertsons (ticker: ABS) is the third largest grocery chain in America. Founded in 1939 by Joe Albertson, the company maintains its headquarters in Boise, Idaho. Until its 1999 merger with American Stores, Albertsons expanded through internal growth and creating new stores. The merger with American Stores gave it wider access in California and the Midwest. Some of the acquired stores maintain their original names, such as the Jewel-Osco grocery/drugstores in the Chicago area. In 2003, the company had around 2,300 retail stores and total revenue of $35 billion. The stores were supported by 17 distribution centers (annual report). Despite the mergers, Albertsons has seen total revenue decline since the 1999 fiscal year. In 2001, the company replaced the CEO by hiring Larry Johnston—who lost out in the GE competition to replace Jack Welch. Johnston quickly replaced most of the executive team. His stated emphasis is to reduce costs and streamline the company, but operating/administrative costs in FY 2003 were higher than they were in FY 1999. Johnston also closed several hundred stores—deciding to focus only on markets where the chain held the number one or two position. Fortunately for the company, federal regulators have not yet figured out the antitrust implications of that strategy. Overall, Steven Rhone, chief investment officer for Laird Norton Financial Group, which owns 25,000 shares, notes that "they have initiated some positive things, but the market has changed so dramatically, and in such a short period of time, that it's still behind its peers" (Stepankowsky 2002). Some analysts argue that trying to reduce costs by shrinking the company and selling off stores is not necessarily the best strategy. It might produce short-term profits but will hurt long-term market share and growth possibilities, particularly, in an environment where economies of scale and negotiation size are so important. Ross Margolies, manager of the Salomon Brothers Capital Fund, observes that "the supermarket industry is like France in World War I; you give up real estate and you never really get it back" (Blumenthal 2002).

Competitive Threats

The biggest threat to Albertsons (Kroger, Safeway and the other big grocers) is Wal-Mart. Wal-Mart now sells more groceries than any other chain in America. Its SuperCenter stores provide a one-stop market for customers, and the company is rolling out more of them every day (Gose 2002). With Wal-Mart's supply chain efficiencies and heavily advertised low-price strategy, customers flock to the stores. Oh yes, and Wal-Mart employees are not unionized.

Believe it or not, in some states (notably California) almost all of the grocery workers are members of unions—down to the checkout clerks and stockers. In addition to having wages substantially above minimum, the Wal-Mart workers also receive health care benefits. Facing the threat of Wal-Mart building SuperCenters in California, the grocery chains (Kroger, Albertsons, and Safeway) were trying to reduce wages. The unions went on strike in southern California, and Albertsons locked out workers at their stores. The strike lasted for 139 days. The resulting agreement mostly kept wages and benefits in place for existing workers, but allows the stores to pay new hires a substantially lower wage and lower benefits (Peltz 2004). But there is a serious question of how Albertsons (and the other chains) are going to compete against the lower costs of Wal-Mart.

Technology

Transactions processing is a key element to holding down costs in grocery stores—particularly when labor is expensive. Grocery stores were the first to implement bar codes and checkout scanners in the 1980s. Although bar codes provide better data, they do not significantly increase the speed of the checkout process. Someone still has to unpack the cart, move each item by hand over the scanner (sometimes multiple times to get it to read), and then pack the items into bags. Albertsons, like other chains, has experimented with self-service checkouts. Customers with a small number of items run them over the scanner or weigh them and place them into bags. Usually one clerk oversees four checkout stations. To reduce theft, the station weighs the bags as items are added and compares the weight to a known value. But the stations do not really change the checkout process, merely shift some of the work to the customers.

In 2004, Albertsons began testing self-service handheld scanners in several stores including 100 in the Dallas–Fort Worth area. Customers pick up a wireless handheld scanner on entering the store. They scan the items as they place them in their carts. The scanner maintains a running total and offers instant discount coupons. Customers can also order deli items and pick them up when they reach the deli. Customers register to use the scanners and include their payment data. Consequently, checkout is easy—they simply authorize the total amount when they leave the store by scanning an "end of trip" bar code at the checkout counter (Bacheldor 2004). Bob Dunst, chief technology officer at Albertsons, says that customers like the system: "Our customers tell us they feel they save 15 to 20 minutes in a shopping trip" (Higgins 2004). To reduce fraud, grocery chains use existing video surveillance systems and randomly check some shoppers.

Albertsons is also testing a new pricing mechanism in some stores—including a flagship store in Boise. The shelf tags were all replaced with tiny wireless LCD panels that are connected to the central computer. The manager can instantly change prices on any product by entering a new value into the computer. The technology gives managers the ability to price items on a day-to-day basis to reflect changing demand (company Web site). The LCD tags were available as early as 2001, but were relatively expensive—from $4 to $6 each. With tens of thousands of products in the store, the initial cost is high. However, it is almost impossible to change prices quickly using expensive employees. Besides, there are fewer pricing errors because the computer controls the price at both the shelf and the checkout. Software exists today that continually analyzes sales and inventory levels and automatically recommends price changes. To take full advantage of the system, the store really needs the LCD tags. Incorporating the prices into the inventory system also leads to better demand forecasting when the system needs to estimate the replenishment order (Heun 2001).

Following on the heels of Wal-Mart and Target, Albertsons is also experimenting with radio frequency identification (RFID) solutions in the supply chain.

The company did manage to replace its aging proprietary financial system with Oracle Financials in 2003 and 2004. In addition to providing a single consolidated view of the financial records, the system makes it possible for managers to examine trends in sales and in costs.

Questions

1. Will enough customers use the handheld scanners to make them profitable?

2. If there are 150,000 different items in a store, and LCD tags cost $5 each, how long will it take to recoup the cost of outfitting an entire store with the LCD tags? Remember that all employees are unionized, so assume average wages are at least $10 per hour. Write down any other assumptions.

3. Will new checkout technologies be enough to help Albertsons stay competitive against Wal-Mart? What can Albertsons do to stay alive?

Additional Reading

Bacheldor, Beth. "Albertson's Technology Brings Handhelds to Customers." *Information Week,* April 8, 2004.

Blumenthal, Robin. "Grocer on a Diet." *Barron's,* May 6, 2002, Vol. 82(18), p. 17.

Gose, Joe. "Supercenter Showdown." *National Real Estate Investor,* December 2002, Vol. 44(12), p. 14.

Heun, Christopher T. "Grocers Count on IT to Keep Cash Registers Ringing." *Information Week,* December 24, 2001.

Higgins, Michelle. "Grocery Shopping Enters a New Age." *The Wall Street Journal,* March 30, 2004.

Peltz, James F. "How the Supermarket Strike Was Settled." *The Los Angeles Times,* March 8, 2004.

Stepankowsky, Paula L. "Turnaround Bid by Albertson's Faces Challenges." *The Wall Street Journal,* December 26, 2002.

www.albertsons.com

Summary Industry Questions

1. What information technologies have helped this industry?

2. Did the technologies provide a competitive advantage or were they quickly adopted by rivals?

3. Which technologies could this industry use that were developed in other sectors?

4. Is the level of competition increasing or decreasing in this industry? Is it dominated by a few firms, or are they fairly balanced?

5. What problems have been created from the use of information technology and how did the firms solve the problems?

CHAPTER SEVEN

Enterprise Integration

Chapter Outline

Introduction

Integration in Business

Enterprise Resource Planning
  International Environment
  Financial Accounting
  Logistics
  Human Resource Management
  Integration

The Role of Accounting
  Input and Output: Financial Data and Reports
  Purchases, Sales, Loans, and Investments
  Inventory
  The Accounting Cycle
  Process: Controls, Checks, and Balances

Human Resources and Transaction Processing
  Input: Data Collection
  Output: Reports
  Process: Automation

Supply Chain Management
  SCM Changes the Focus
  SCM Challenges
  The Role of XML: Integration across Systems

Customer Relationship Management
  Multiple Contact Points
  Feedback, Individual Needs, and Cross Selling
  CRM Packages

Summarizing ERP Data
  Digital Dashboard and EIS
  How Does an EIS Work?
  Advantages of an EIS

Transaction Accuracy: Sarbanes-Oxley

Summary

Key Words

Web Site References

Additional Reading

Review Questions

Exercises

Cases: Automobile Industry

What You Will Learn in This Chapter

- How do you integrate data and systems?
- How do businesses combine data from operations?
- How do you combine data across functional areas, including production, purchasing, marketing, and accounting?
- How do you track and compare the financial information of a firm?
- What are the transaction elements in the human resources management system?
- How do you make production more efficient?
- How do you keep track of all customer interactions? Who are your best customers?
- How can a manager handle all of the data in an ERP system?
- How does the CEO know that financial records are correct?

How do you manage a huge organization? How can you integrate data from hundreds of divisions scattered around the world? Bill Ford, great-grandson of Henry, turned around the struggling manufacturer in the early 2000s. Along the way, he made an amazing discovery: it is more important to sell vehicles at a profit, instead of trying to just sell more at any cost. With hundreds of facilities, Ford, like the other automobile manufacturers, has an immense job of ordering parts, keeping factories scheduled, identifying cars and features that customers actually want, tracking production, monitoring sales, and designing for the future. Having pioneered the mass-production systems of the 1900s, Ford is only now learning to build a more flexible manufacturing system—where one plant can produce different car makes. Information technology plays a key role in making the factories and the entire operation more efficient.

Although the company is publicly held, the family exerts significant influence on it. After former chairman and CEO Donald Petersen rubbed the family the wrong way, he retired prematurely. Alex Trotman took the position in 1995 and hoped to retain the Ford family support. On January 1, 1999, the disappointed Ford family replaced Trotman as CEO with Jacques Nasser. Nasser came from the international side of Ford, which was experiencing strong sales. In 2001, a series of crises, capped by the Firestone tire recall on the Explorer, led to high tensions in Ford and in the industry. On October 29, 2001, Bill Ford, Jr., fired Jacques Nasser and installed himself as CEO.

Introduction

How do you integrate data and systems? Companies have many computer systems within the organization and need to connect with suppliers and customers. Think about the problems that arise if groups within the company (accounting, production, marketing, and so on) all have different databases. Figure 7.1 shows that enterprise systems are designed to solve these problems—by creating one giant database that is shared by everyone throughout the company. Of course, they are expensive and require considerable time and money to set up. But the benefits of an integrated system have convinced many companies to install them as the foundation of the modern information system.

Coordinating the many aspects of business requires a wide variety of information from many sources. Perhaps you need to make a decision about how to market a new product. You would retrieve a variety of customer data from the sales database. You would use reports from the production team and a collection of graphs created from the initial marketing surveys. You could use a spreadsheet to analyze this information along with various marketing strategies. Along the way, you would probably use accounting data to create graphs to display costs and projected profits for the various cases. Finally, you would use a word processor to create a formal report for your supervisors that describes the choices and your analysis. The report would contain your writing along with the graphs, spreadsheet tables, and some of the data.

Integrating data within the company is only the first step. Modern companies need to interact with customers, suppliers, banks, and other companies. You could hire thousands of people to handle the paperwork, or you could find a way to connect systems electronically. Yes, you still need salespeople and customer service representatives, but much of the day-to-day transaction work can be handled electronically.

A difficulty that arises when you are trying to integrate information is the diversity in hardware and software. For example, each software package uses its own format to store data files. As a result, there are more than 50 different formats for word processing documents. The problem multiplies rapidly when you consider that most of these formats change

TRENDS

Computer programs were initially small and performed simple calculations for a limited amount of data. For example, a system might store basic accounting journal data. Another system might hold the general ledger data, and a third might handle payroll. Gradually, computers became faster, drive space became cheaper, and more sophisticated programs were created to begin integrating data. Accounting packages were developed to handle all accounting information tasks, HRM systems handled all employee-related chores, and manufacturing systems dealt with production. Finally, with the introduction of powerful database systems, and hardware that can handle huge amounts of data, software vendors began developing completely integrated systems. These enterprise-level systems were designed from the ground up to handle all of the major information tasks of a company. By driving everything from a common database, the systems can be customized for almost any environment by rewriting the forms and reports. With extensive networks, data can be shared in real time from operations around the world. Beyond simple access to data, integrated systems make it possible to change the way the company operates.

FIGURE 7.1

To simplify management, firms are often split into departments. Yet they must be able to work as a single, integrated company. Information systems can help managers improve the integration and control of their firm.

Everyone in the company including managers, salespeople, and engineers needs access to the same data across the organization.

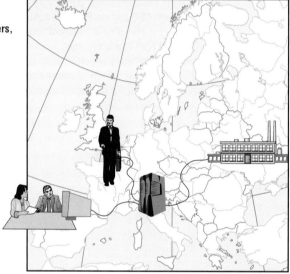

FIGURE 7.2

Sales report: Businesses create many different reports. Begin with this small excerpt of the daily sales report. It itemizes sales for each department.

Daily Sales Report				February 10, 2007
Department	**Item#**	**Q-Sold**	**Price**	**Value**
House	1153	52	2.95	153.40
	5543	13	0.59	7.67
W. Clothing	5563	1	87.32	87.32
	7765	4	54.89	219.56
	9986	2	15.69	31.38
Shoes	1553	2	65.79	131.58
	6673	1	29.39	29.39
Total Sales:				**660.30**

FIGURE 7.3

Returned merchandise: To evaluate customer service and quality, the store tracks returned merchandise and produces a daily report by item number.

Returned Merchandise Log			
February 10, 2007			
Item#	**Q**	**Price**	**Value**
1153	3	2.95	8.85
3353	6	27.59	165.54
4453	2	15.95	31.90
8878	1	24.95	24.95
Total	**12**		**231.24**

FIGURE 7.4

Commissions: Managers compute daily sales by employee and determine the commission based on each employee's commission rate.

Commissions					February 10, 2007
Emp#	Name	Dept	Sales	Rate	Amount
1143	Jones	House	543.95	5%	27.20
2895	Brown	M. Clothing	775.35	4%	31.01
4462	Smith	W. Clothing	1,544.52	5%	77.23
7893	Torrez	Shoes	876.93	6%	52.62
9963	Cousco	M. Clothing	589.47	5%	29.47

FIGURE 7.5

Final report: The weekly sales analysis report requires selecting and aggregating data from each of the other reports. The text, data, and graph are combined into a final document.

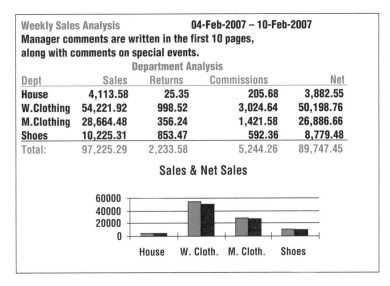

Weekly Sales Analysis   04-Feb-2007 – 10-Feb-2007

Manager comments are written in the first 10 pages, along with comments on special events.

Department Analysis

Dept	Sales	Returns	Commissions	Net
House	**4,113.58**	**25.35**	**205.68**	**3,882.55**
W.Clothing	**54,221.92**	**998.52**	**3,024.64**	**50,198.76**
M.Clothing	**28,664.48**	**356.24**	**1,421.58**	**26,886.66**
Shoes	**10,225.31**	**853.47**	**592.36**	**8,779.48**
Total:	97,225.29	2,233.58	5,244.26	89,747.45

Sales & Net Sales

with each software revision. To integrate these different types of information, you need software that can read many different file types, or the software needs to use a common format.

One trend in software is the adoption of enterprise systems that are designed to hold data in a central database. These systems provide consistent data across the company. A trend in personal productivity software is toward packages that work together by sharing data through links. When the underlying data changes, the software automatically picks up the new data and updates the document. The concept is similar to a spreadsheet formula that refers to other cells. The key difference is that you can refer to data in different programs, such as transferring data from a spreadsheet into a word processor. With a network, the data can be located in different departments throughout the business.

Integration in Business

How do businesses combine data from operations? The easiest way to understand the power of today's computer systems is to look at how integration has changed over time. Consider the relatively simple problem of integrating data within a department store. Figure 7.2 shows sales for one day. Figure 7.3 shows items returned for one day. Keep in mind that returns are probably handled by a separate desk. Figure 7.4 reports the commissions paid to each employee. As a manager, you want to monitor the profitability of each department. Figure 7.5 shows part of a typical analysis that combines the sales, subtracts the returns and commissions, and compares the sales over time. This example is relatively simple, but it is easy to follow over time.

As shown in Figure 7.6, in the 1960s and 1970s, computer systems were built for individual departments and areas within the company. In many companies, these systems became islands. They were focused on one task and did not share data with each other. For instance, the accounting department collected the basic transaction data and produced the necessary accounting reports. Anyone in the company who wanted to use this data relied on

FIGURE 7.6

FIGURE 7.6
Middle management over time: The methods used to create integrated reports have changed over the past three decades. With simple transaction systems, managers computed the totals, drew graphs, and had secretaries type the report. With the adoption of personal computers, middle managers (or their secretaries) reentered the data into spreadsheets and used a word processor to print the final report. With an integrated system, top managers can use a personal computer to query the database, draw the graphs, and produce the final report.

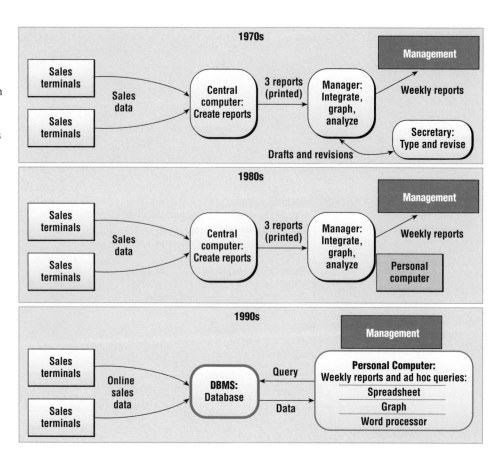

paper printouts of the standard reports. When spreadsheets arrived in the 1980s, the basic accounting numbers were often rekeyed into spreadsheets in other departments. Besides wasting employee time in retyping numbers that were already stored on a computer, this practice caused more errors from mistyping the data. Furthermore, consider that when the accounting department changes the numbers, some users of the data might not get the updated versions, and people would attempt to make decisions on the basis of outdated data. Notice that in the 1980s, the clerical support was replaced with PCs. As a manager, you are expected to write your own documents and create your own charts.

In the 1990s, organizations began the steps toward integration. The basic transaction is stored in a DBMS, and networks provide access to the database. More important, this integration makes it relatively easy to create automated tools that extract the desired data, display results in charts, and enable managers to quickly find the answers to basic questions. To some extent, this type of system means that the company no longer needs you: the middle manager. You might be interested to know that this trend was predicted in 1958 (Levitt and Whisler, *Harvard Business Review*). It just took 20 years longer than they anticipated for technology to be developed.

As shown in Figure 7.7, in the first decade of 2000, even more powerful integration tools are available. The goal of these tools is to integrate all of the data in the company, including ties to suppliers and customers. Again, the entire system runs on a DBMS; the difference lies in its reach and its capabilities. Tracking customers and working closely with suppliers are increasingly critical functions in business. Just collecting the data and billing customers or paying suppliers is not sufficient. You need to be able to analyze and compare the data. Who are your best customers? Which ones cost you the most? Which suppliers provide the best quality and are the most reliable? Answers to these questions can mean the difference between success and failure.

FIGURE 7.7

Integration with ERP: An ERP system can integrate almost all aspects of the company into one huge database. Either directly or through an executive information system, management can retrieve any report or piece of data by selecting options.

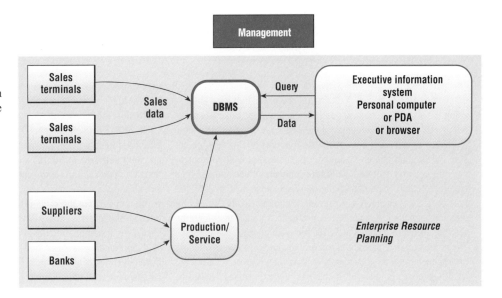

Enterprise Resource Planning

How do you combine data across functional areas, including production, purchasing, marketing, and accounting? Enterprise resource planning (ERP) is the current state of the art in integrated information in business systems. The systems incorporate data from financial accounting, logistics, and human resource management. The field is dominated by large, expensive software packages from companies such as SAP, Peoplesoft, and Oracle. The systems use databases, processes, and rules to provide up-to-the-minute data on the major financial issues in a firm. One of the key points of ERP systems is that they run on top of a DBMS; hence, all of the data is centralized and accessible via DBMS queries and reports.

As shown in Figure 7.8, ERP systems handle all of the financial accounting systems. They also emphasize purchasing, human resource management, and investment management. The systems are tailored for specific businesses and can focus on areas such as manufacturing, research and development, and retail sales.

One of the primary strengths of the ERP systems is that they were designed to handle data for large companies operating in an international environment. In the late 1990s, many companies chose to install commercial ERP systems, instead of trying to modify their existing systems to handle the year 2000 problem.

Computer use in most companies began with transaction-processing systems. Because transaction systems are structured and there is considerable experience at this level, it is a logical place to begin. However, it is also tempting to treat each transaction separately: (1) payroll services can be purchased from a specialized data processing company, so the data will be handled separately from the other corporate data; (2) a sales order-processing system might be constructed independently of the inventory control system; (3) process control systems to handle manufacturing tend to be isolated because the data (e.g., robotic control signals) are different from the data used in the rest of the company; (4) similarly, the corporate accounting system is often developed as a stand-alone product. Journal entries are created by copying data in reports produced by other systems. Although each of these transaction systems offers management advantages to their respective departments, it is difficult for managers to use data from other departments. Also, independent systems make it difficult for executives to share data and evaluate interrelationships between the departments.

The amount of data integration needed in a company often depends on the management structure of the firm. Some firms are highly decentralized, so that each business unit makes

REALITY BYTES   ERP Maintenance Fees

The purchase price of ERP software is only the beginning. Most companies also hire consultants to help tailor the software and develop the internal processes needed to improve the business operations. Of course, companies generally have to purchase new hardware as well. But once the system is running, the fees do not stop. All vendors charge maintenance fees that provide for technical support and software upgrades. Initially, these annual fees amount to about 15 percent of the original license cost. In 2004, the fees crept up to as much as 25 percent. For example, an Oracle ERP standard license cost was $3,995 per user. Annual fees would be $599 for software updates and $280 for product support—per user. These fees total 22 percent of the original cost. Hardware vendors charge maintenance and support fees as well.

The process is even more complex. Vendors release new versions of their base software every two to three years. They do not like to support old versions of the software and prefer to encourage customers to upgrade to the latest version. It is expensive to have programmers working on old versions. Consequently, ERP vendors either discontinue support for old products or increase the maintenance fees.

Of course, customers are often unhappy with these fees. In many cases, companies are content with their existing systems and do not want to pay the costs to upgrade. These costs generally include new hardware, plus retraining costs. If the upgrades are marginal, or the company does not need the new features, customers feel they are being unfairly pressured. A survey of SAP users published in 2003 by J. P. Morgan reported that only 28 percent of the companies believed SAP's most recent version "delivered value" over the current version.

In 2000, Esker SA, a French company that develops and sells fax and messaging software, installed Siebel Systems customer-management software for its 165 employees. In June 2003, Siebel Systems dropped support for the version Esker was using and offered to extend the support—at a cost of $94,000 per year—which was 50 percent more than the original price! Although Siebel was offering the upgrade for free, Esker's CEO Jean-Michel Berard estimated that hardware, training, and consultants would have cost $175,000. Berard presumably realized that these upgrade costs were not a fluke—he would undoubtedly face the same dilemma in another couple of years. Consequently, he switched vendors.

Salesforce.com offers a CRM system that runs entirely Web-based on its own computers. For a monthly fee, Salesforce.com handles all of the hardware and software as a service business. Customers simply connect with Web browsers. In a sense, this process represents a return to the days of the 1960s and 1970s when dozens of service-bureau companies ran computers and customers simply paid monthly fees to use the applications.

Source: Adapted from Kevin J. Delaney and David Bank, "Large Software Customers Refuse to Get With the Program," *The Wall Street Journal,* January 2, 2004.

FIGURE 7.8

Primary ERP functions: Each area has dozens of additional detailed functions. The real key is that all of the components are integrated. For example, any data entered into the HRM systems is immediately reflected in the financial reports.

Accounting
    All transaction data and all financial reports in any currency
Finance
    Portfolio management and financial projections
Human Resources Management
    Employees tracking from application to release
Production Management
    Product design and manufacturing life cycle
Supply Chain Management
    Purchasing, quality control, and tracking
Customer Relationship Management
    Contacts, orders, and shipments

---

its own decisions and functions independently of the others. Typically in these situations, only accounting data (profit/loss) are integrated and reported to upper management.

On the other hand, some organizations are much more integrated. In your economics courses you were shown the difference between vertically and horizontally integrated firms. Consider a vertically integrated firm such as an oil company that functions at different levels of production (including oil exploration, drilling, transportation, storage, and retail sales). Although an oil exploration team may not need access to daily fuel sales in New York State, they do need to forecast future demand for oil. Likewise, the retail sales division does not need to know the daily costs associated with drilling for oil, yet they might need to track deliveries and communicate with the corporate office.

Consider a horizontally integrated firm such as Wal-Mart with retail stores in many different cities. It achieves lower costs by combining the buying power of all its stores. By co-

Technology Toolbox: Selecting an ERP System

Problem: How do you select and evaluate ERP systems?

Tools: Several ERP systems and even more ERP consulting firms exist to give you choices and help you evaluate your options. Choosing a system is relatively difficult because of the costs. The cost of the hardware and software is high, but you face larger costs in converting from your existing system and redesigning your business processes. Once you have implemented a particular ERP system, it is difficult to switch to another vendor. So, you have to be careful to select a system that is going to work for your particular organization. Today, most large companies already have ERP systems, so the growth market lies with small and midsize businesses. Most of the ERP vendors are actively targeting this SMB market. Businesses within this category have to pay attention to the anticipated growth and scalability options of the software systems. For example, even small businesses can gain the advantages of ERP systems by leasing them from companies that host the software on Internet servers—you pay only a monthly fee.

In terms of technical business features, most of the large ERP systems are somewhat similar—offering the standard accounting, HRM, SCM, and CRM integration. However, you will find differences in ease of use, internationalization, and customization options. For a smaller business, one of the more important areas to look at is the quality of the predefined industry-specific application. Most ERP vendors provide shells that are customized for each industry, so it takes less time and money to set up the system for your company.

Planning Stage	Goals and Outputs
Initiation	Estimate costs, establish objectives, select team.
Initial planning	Initial vendor list and basic features (hardware platform, fees, internationalization, vendor size and stability, industry-specific support, and so on).
Requirements gathering	Identify business requirements. Detailed list of specifications, unit goals, and critical features. Evaluation criteria.
Demos and selection	Product demonstrations, ratings, and site visits.
Implementation	Customize applications, convert data, restructure company operations, define new processes, and train employees.

Selecting an ERP system is a time-consuming task, and you have to carefully evaluate the needs of the company. You will create lists of primary objectives and generate detailed specifications. You will endure hundreds of hours of vendor presentations and comparisons of databases, reports, and customization capabilities.

Then you have to implement the solution. Many companies work with a partner consulting firm that specializes in one ERP system. This detailed knowledge simplifies the conversion process because the consultant firm has experienced experts. But even midsize firms take six months to a year; larger operations can require a year or two. Most companies choose to implement ERP systems in stages—perhaps accounting first, followed by SCM and CRM. Even these packages can be split and implemented in smaller pieces.

Quick Quiz:

1. Assume you work for a midsize construction firm that does about 30 percent of its work internationally. Find at least three ERP vendors and outline the features they provide.

2. Assume you work for a large retail clothing firm with stores in most U.S. states. Identify the specific accounting and financial features you would want in an ERP system.

3. Assume you work for a regional manufacturer that makes parts for cars. Explain how you would select and evaluate an ERP system. Find an example of a system that would work.

ordinating sales, warehouses, and distribution, Wal-Mart can negotiate better prices with manufacturers. Moreover, Wal-Mart reduces operating costs by standardizing management practices (and information systems) across all the stores. By integrating information from all stores, it is easier for Wal-Mart to forecast customer demands. Also, by networking the store information systems, managers who experience higher sales of certain products can request shipments from stores that are not selling the item as rapidly.

Manufacturing firms can gain additional benefits from integrating data. Benefits like just-in-time inventory, total quality management, and mass customization can exist only with the tight integration of data. The National Bicycle Industrial Company of Japan illustrates how integrated data is used to provide customized products to mass markets.

REALITY BYTES   Real-Time Enterprise Computing

In 2000, Cisco was flying high. Based on stock valuation, briefly, it was the most valuable company in the world. With solid products and a substantial market share, it was widely admired. Cisco also touted its substantial information system—which was an advanced integrated system. In spring 2001, Cisco almost self-destructed. With the fallout in the telecommunications industry, orders evaporated and Cisco did not notice quickly enough. The company had to write off $1 billion in parts inventory that had been ordered to build products that were no longer needed. Despite increased sales for the year, Cisco lost another $2 billion in profits. Even the advanced integrated information system was not sufficient. Companies are now talking about real-time enterprise computing (RTEC) systems. RTEC systems not only integrate the internal systems but also tie to suppliers and customers, collecting and analyzing data in real time. All data is collected continuously, and financial statements and analysis are created at any time and are always up to date.

Source: Adapted from Michael S. Malone, "Internet II: Rebooting America," *Forbes,* September 10, 2001; and Scott Berinato, "What Went Wrong at Cisco?" *CIO Magazine,* August 1, 2001.

International Environment

Several ERP features are important to firms operating in an international environment. First, all menus and reports should be available in several languages, so clerks and managers can use the language they prefer. Second, the system should handle currency conversion automatically, so managers can view reports in any currency. Similarly, conversions should be capable of being fixed at a point in time, so that when items are transferred, they can be valued at the exchange rate in effect at that time, even if the rate changes later.

A more complex feature for the international environment is the ability to produce reports following the rules of individual nations. For example, a company with subsidiaries in many nations would need to produce reports that follow the rules (e.g., depreciation) for each specific nation and then produce consolidated reports following the rules of the home nation.

A third complicating factor arises from taxes. In addition to the rates, the rules and procedures vary by nation. The rules are particularly important for payroll and benefit applications. A good enterprise application automatically incorporates the rules for each nation and state.

Financial Accounting

The accounting system is a core feature of an ERP. Eventually, all transactions must be recorded in the general ledger accounts. The accounts fulfill the standards required by each nation. They are used to create the standard accounting reports. The systems provide flexibility by enabling managers to create their own subaccounts and subledgers, which are used to create reports on additional topics. An important feature of the accounting system is that standard accounting reports can be generated at any time for any section of the company. The ERP system automatically uses the most up-to-date data.

In addition to standard financial accounting, the systems manage assets and provide common treasury functions such as cash management. The systems also provide basic audit trails and other accounting controls. To make them easier to use, most ERP systems provide enterprise (or executive) information system (EIS) capabilities. Managers can examine data at virtually any level of detail. From summary values, they can drill down to more detail.

Logistics

Logistics consists of the operations required to purchase materials, deliver them to the warehouses and factories, and sell and distribute products. It incorporates traditional MRP analysis, quality control, accounts payable, and accounts receivable.

In today's manufacturing companies, logistics is an important component of just-in-time inventory and demand-driven production. Using an integrated system, the marketing department gets up-to-the-minute data on customer demands. Marketers can cooperate with designers and engineers to develop new products. The specifications can be transferred to

REALITY BYTES   Whatever Happened to B2B?

In the middle of the dot-com boom, billions of dollars were spent on B2B Web sites. "Visionaries" proclaimed that companies would radically alter their purchasing practices and move to online auction sites. Everything from office supplies to raw materials would be purchased through a competitive auction. Suppliers would be forced by competition to reduce prices, and costs would drop by cutting out the middlemen. More than 200 exchanges were rolled out each month from November 1999 to April 2000! Today, fewer than 200 survive. Carl F. Lehmann, an analyst at Meta Group, notes that "if you're trying to exploit economies of scale, you don't need to set up [online] markets; you need to analyze markets. All you have to do is put three good MBAs on the problem. But we learned that too late."

The systems that have survived are those funded by groups of companies to provide a specific purpose. For instance, Elemica, Inc., is an online exchange for the chemical industry that is used by Dow

Chemical company to reduce inventories and reduce the time spent dealing with orders. Elemica CEO Kent Dolby notes that a key element of their system is the ability to translate data from one client's computer to another's. "We wanted to get buyers' ERP talking to sellers' ERP. Some larger companies want to be very integrated and have a SAP or Oracle or Baan system. Others may be simple buyers working off Excel spreadsheets. We need to talk with all of them." Covisint has also been successful by playing a similar role for the automobile industry. Pantellos Group is a marketplace for large utility companies. Because of the nature of the industry, early on, they focused on reducing costs for their members. Cinergy Corp., a client of Pantellos, has received a 500 percent return on its investment in the exchange and a dramatic drop in errors.

Source: Adapted from Steve Ulfelder, "B2B Exchange Survivors," *Computerworld,* February 2, 2004.

the production machines and raw material orders can be generated for vendors. Purchasing and payments can be tracked and generated over EDI networks—including the Internet. As orders are generated and inventory levels change, the accounting data is automatically updated—providing instant analysis of profitability.

For service-oriented companies, logistics involves service management tasks. The ERP systems can track customers, identify repeat customers, monitor service contracts, help salespeople with call management, and handle automatic billing and accounts receivable issues.

Human Resource Management

Payroll is a complicated function, particularly in a multinational environment involving different rules and currencies. Even in a single state, the issues of benefits, state and federal rules, and legal issues arising from child support make handling payroll a complex task.

Today's HRM departments handle such additional tasks as recruitment, training, travel, and organizational planning. Each step must be documented and requires a variety of federal and state reports. In addition to these basic tasks, most of the major ERP systems enable HRM departments to offer Web access to basic data. For example, employees can use the Web to check on their taxes, change their withholding status, and sign up for benefit plans and training sessions.

Integration

Integration is probably the most important feature of the ERP systems. All the data is stored in a central database; hence, data is entered only one time (but into a double-entry accounting system). All reports are generated from the base data. Custom queries and reports can be generated through the DBMS.

Consider a simple example. A manufacturing plant takes an item from inventory. The system instantly adjusts the inventory quantity on hand. It also updates the financial value of the inventory holdings on the general ledger and any subledgers that utilize that figure. New orders can be triggered automatically with the orders and payments sent through common EDI mechanisms. All of the changes are made automatically. When managers request reports, the new data is automatically incorporated and displayed using current currency conversions.

The key point to remember is that all of the transactions and accounts are integrated. Managers can request reports by using any combination of data at any time—and each report will use the most up-to-date information.

FIGURE 7.9

ERP integration: Although data can be distributed, it is still integrated across the organization. Changes in one item (inventory) cause changes in all related databases. Reports are generated from current data.

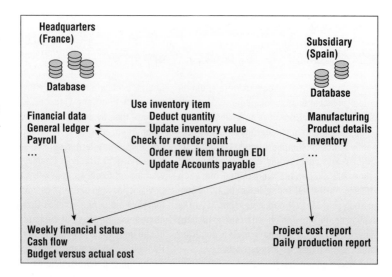

Most of the major ERP systems also utilize distributed hardware and software. Hence, the database can be split into many pieces stored in different locations. As changes occur in one location, they are automatically distributed across the network to the other locations. The company can add a subsidiary with its own processing support. Yet all of the new data is readily accessible to managers throughout the company.

Figure 7.9 provides a simple example of data integration. When a factory uses an inventory item, the system reduces the current inventory count. It also changes the inventory valuation in the general ledger. The item usage might trigger a purchase through the EDI system, which must also be recorded—along with the accounts payable change. Since the databases are shared across the organization, all changes are automatically included when new reports are generated.

Remember that all of the modules are integrated. So manufacturing schedules developed in the production module automatically provide data to the payroll system and personnel systems. Then the financial data (e.g., wages) is linked back to the general ledger, which provides updated data for all financial reports.

One important catch with an ERP system is that it requires changes to the way the company operates. In many cases, these changes can be good—for example, it forces everyone to follow the standard accounting procedures. In other cases, the ERP is too inflexible and interferes with the way the company operates. Managers have to carefully evaluate the trade-offs of integration and flexibility.

The Role of Accounting

How do you track and compare the financial information of a firm? Accounting systems are important because they extend throughout the company and because they focus on money. They are used to collect data and evaluate performance. Accounting systems also enable managers to combine the many divisions into an integrated picture of the entire company. Accounting systems also provide controls over the data to ensure accuracy and to prevent fraud. The primary purpose of accounting is to collect the financial data of the firm, ensure that it is accurate, and create standard reports. It is hard to capture all of the elements of an accounting system in one illustration, but Figure 7.10 summarizes the essential components of an accounting system. The accounting transaction system can be examined in terms of inputs, outputs, and processes.

If you are not going to be an accountant, why do you need to understand accounting, and why review it in an information systems book? The short answer is that the accounting information system provides the foundation data for the firm. The longer answer revolves around the fact that the accounting process is increasingly automated in companies. Al-

FIGURE 7.10

Transaction processing is a major function of the accounting system. The accounting system collects data throughout the company and produces consolidated (centralized) reports that are used for planning and management.

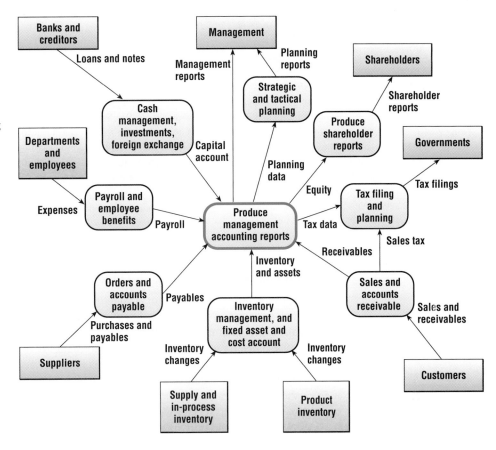

though the automation is a good thing in terms of reducing costs, it also means there is less need for pure accountants. As a result, all managers have to understand and analyze accounting data. You will have access to basic accounting data and reports directly from the computer. It will be your responsibility to monitor the changes and understand the effects.

Input and Output: Financial Data and Reports

Raw financial data is collected by the accounting department and stored in an **accounting journal.** Modern accounting requires the use of a double-entry system to ensure accurate data. In a double-entry system, at least two entries must occur for every transaction. Generally, one entry records the effect of the money (e.g., cash, accounts payable, accounts receivable), and the other refers to a specific category (e.g., sales, office expenses, commissions). Each entry includes the date, amount of money, account number, the name of the person or firm involved, perhaps a comment, and the name of the person making the entry. The journal's purpose is to record all the transactions.

Journal entries represent raw data. To be useful, this data must be transformed into information. The first step is to categorize the data by *accounts* or categories, which is the purpose of the **general ledger.** The ledger is a collection of accounts that break the data into specific categories. Common categories include *accounts receivable, accounts payable, inventory,* and *cash.* Although there are some standards, each company can define its own **chart of accounts,** which allows owners and managers to examine data on whatever categories are important to their firm.

For managers to make comparisons between divisions and other firms, accounting systems produce standardized reports. Most companies produce *balance sheets, cash flow statements,* and *income statements* every quarter. These reports are produced following standard accounting rules to enable owners, managers, and investors to compare the financial positions of various companies over time.

REALITY BYTES   Connecting Health Care Suppliers

In Dayton, Ohio, Premier Health Partners, Inc., oversees all purchasing, distribution, and warehousing for seven large health care facilities. It accomplishes these tasks through EDI connections directly to the health care computers. It even includes wireless access to applications. Usage data on supplies ranging from syringes to bed linens is collected and forwarded to Neoforma, Inc., which is a hosted marketplace to order and track purchases. The system has direct connections to over 300 health care supply vendors. Up-to-date information is provided on back orders within two hours. Sales and shipping data are integrated into the health care systems, so administrators can track all interchanges. The system hosted by Neoforma makes it possible to deliver similar benefits to even small offices. Michael McBrayer, senior vice president at dj Orthopedics in Vista, California, uses the system and observes that "nobody tracked what was going on [before]. Now administrators are running things more as a business. And they've got to know what's coming in, what's going out."

Source: Adapted from Pimm Fox, "Get Me Supply Chain, Stat!" *Computerworld,* December 15, 2003.

Purchases, Sales, Loans, and Investments

One of the primary purposes of accounting is to record the financial transactions with external organizations. In addition to collecting the raw data, the accounting system contains controls that minimize fraud by limiting access to the data. The system also creates summary and detail reports to monitor key information.

Managers often build **exception reports** into the accounting system that are triggered when some event occurs. If sales in some region suddenly drop, if there is a major increase in the cash balance, or if inventories fall below a defined level, a message will be sent to the appropriate manager. The manager typically responds by searching the recent summary reports for a possible cause.

Inventory

Most organizations need to control inventory carefully. Retail stores find it hard to sell items that are not in stock. Manufacturing firms need to receive and process parts as cheaply as possible. Inventory control consists of knowing exactly what items are available and where they are located. The system also needs to determine when to place new orders. It must then track the orders to make sure each item is delivered to the appropriate location at the right time. With EDI, the inventory control system can monitor current sales and automatically place orders with the supplier.

Manufacturing firms use these systems to implement just-in-time inventory control. The computer system monitors the current production requirements, keeps track of deliveries, and electronically sends orders to the suppliers. The suppliers then deliver the parts just as they are needed on the production line.

Automated inventory control systems also help identify and prevent theft. By recording all movement of items from receipt to sales to shipping, management knows exactly how many items exist. Consider a retail store like a bicycle shop. The computerized inventory notes that there should be three *Sigma computers* in stock. Yet when a customer asks to buy one, you notice there are only two left. If there is no mistake in your inventory report, you conclude that someone stole one of the items. Although the system did not prevent the speedometer from disappearing, it does show which items are susceptible to theft. It also helps control theft by employees, who will be less likely to steal if they know that the items are carefully monitored.

The Accounting Cycle

An important aspect of accounting systems is that they produce information in specific cycles. Firms are required to produce reports that reflect the financial condition of the firm at the end of every quarter. Accounting systems are based on these requirements. For the most part, managers operate from quarterly reports, with intermediate monthly reports for some items. Because of the volume of data in the detail, most companies keep only current statistics and summary reports on file. Older data is shuffled off the system to make room for the current numbers. As a result, managers may not have easy access to detailed data from prior years.

Process: Controls, Checks, and Balances

Double-Entry Systems

An important objective of accounting systems is to maintain the integrity of the financial data. The goal is to prevent mistakes and discourage fraud. Double-entry accounting provides a method to locate mistakes in data entry. If an amount is entered incorrectly, the account totals will not balance.

Because many transactions involve outside organizations, mistakes can be caught by sharing data. Every month firms receive a statement from the bank. The totals can be compared to changes in the firm's cash account. Similarly, companies typically send receipts when they receive payments from each other. Auditors periodically send verification requests to suppliers and customers to make sure the data was recorded correctly. EDI strengthens this approach, because transaction data is transmitted in computer form among the companies.

Separation of Duties

Another type of control is the separation of duties. A manager in the purchasing department might be responsible for choosing a supplier of parts. Only the accounting department can authorize the transfer of money to the supplier. The objective is to minimize fraud by requiring a potential thief to deal with multiple employees.

Many banks take this concept a step further. They require employees (especially tellers) to take their vacations every year. Several instances of fraud have been revealed when the employee was no longer at the job to keep the fraudulent mechanism running.

Audit Trails

An **audit trail** is important to accounting systems. It enables investigators to track backward through the data to the source. A cash flow statement might indicate that the company has spent twice as much money this month as last. To find out why, trace backward and find all of the raw entries that make up the number. Together with dates and amounts, the raw journal entries can contain the identity of the person responsible for the entry. By keeping this identification data, it is possible to list every article that affects an item on a report.

Human Resources and Transaction Processing

What are the transaction elements in the human resources management system? Every company has employees. Companies collect hundreds of pieces of data for each employee—some for management purposes, others because they are required by law. For years, the human resources (HR) department focused on filling out and storing forms. The enormous amount of paperwork alone begs for computerization just to cut down on storage space needed. Computerized databases also enable managers to find specific data on employees. Early HR software emphasized these two benefits. Modern HR software is expanding beyond simple forms to improving data collection and providing better analyses. To illustrate the problems presented by large-scale transaction-processing systems, consider the three areas of input, output, and processing.

Input: Data Collection

Figure 7.11 illustrates the basic components of a human resource management (HRM) transaction-processing system. Note that the system is even more complex because the data comes from all areas of the company. To understand how the HRM systems became so complicated, begin with the obvious data that needs to be collected: numbers related to the

FIGURE 7.11

Most employees know that human resources management (HRM) deals with payroll and benefits. But HRM also collects data and produces reports for a myriad of government requirements, oversees employee evaluations, and processes job applications. The department also handles training and education opportunities.

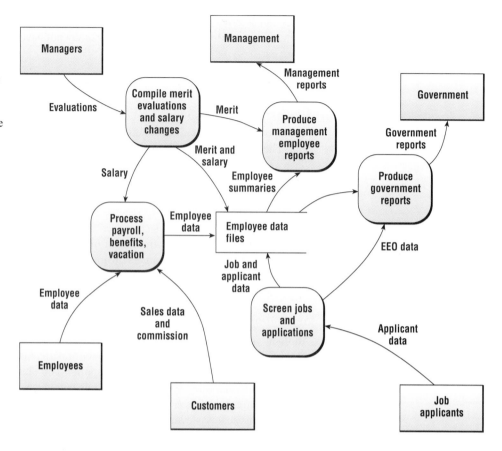

payroll. For hourly workers, the system needs to collect and monitor hours worked. For many sales tasks, the system must compute sales by employee to determine commissions. Professional service firms often ask employees to track their time in terms of billable hours for work that is charged back to clients. In all three situations, as the number of employees increases, it becomes increasingly difficult to collect all of these statistics and verify their accuracy. It also becomes harder to find specific pieces of data.

Think about paychecks you have received. In addition to the payment amount, there could be 10 to 20 other numbers on the pay stub. Companies monitor and report several types of payroll taxes, including federal, state, local, Social Security, and health. Also, firms monitor employee benefits, such as health care and retirement. Most firms also handle employee deductions for employee purchases, savings plans, stock purchases, parking, meal plans, and other options. In some situations, companies must garnishee wages and forward them to a third party.

Human resource departments also track days taken for vacations, personal time, and illness. In larger companies, HRM provides training courses and offers testing of critical skills. Employee attendance and performance data is stored and incorporated into evaluations.

With the increasing use of merit pay, the system must also track employee evaluations. Some performance measures are tied to productivity or output within the employee's department, so HR must relate employee work schedules to production and quality measures.

Most companies use a centralized HRM department to advertise job openings and to screen the initial applicants, verify credentials, and keep basic employment and hiring data.

Output: Reports

The human resources department also produces several reports related to payroll. Along with printing checks, HRM must provide expense reports and forecasts to the accounting system. Periodic reports are created for job vacancies and analyses of employee performance and morale.

HRM departments also spend a great deal of time creating reports for various government agencies. All companies must file various economic reports dealing with employment. Tax-withholding data must be filed regularly with federal, state, and local agencies. HRM departments create equal employment opportunity reports detailing characteristics of their workforce, job applicants, and hiring decisions. Then there are various reports required by the Occupational Safety and Health Administration (OSHA) regarding injuries and exposure to various hazards. If employees need to be certified, companies file aggregate reports with the various regulatory agencies. All of these reports have deadlines.

In addition to the standard reports, the human resources department is responsible for maintaining compliance with all relevant employment laws. Hence, HRM staff must continually monitor the employment data and evaluate it for exceptions and problems.

Process: Automation

The human resources department is a busy place. Keep in mind that the data and reports apply to every branch of the company. Even standard items such as paychecks become complicated when the company is split into several divisions scattered across the country. Also, remember that accuracy is crucial. Employees can become upset if their paychecks are wrong. Errors with government reports can lead to fines and lawsuits. Equally important, companies with good HRM departments are able to offer additional benefits to employees. With a good information system, they can offer cafeteria-style benefits where each employee selects a personal combination of benefits.

Small businesses have long complained about the burdens imposed by government reports and data collection. To alleviate some of the hassles and expense, several companies specialize in automating the data collection and report writing. Consider payroll: Because of the constantly changing laws, many companies rely on an outside agency to collect data and print the paychecks. One of the largest providers is Automated Data Processing (ADP). Even if a company chooses to maintain its own payroll records, it typically purchases the software from a third party instead of trying to keep up with the annual changes using internal programmers.

Several companies sell software that automates HRM data handling and produces government-required reports. From economics to equal employment to OSHA reports, the basic HRM reports are being computerized. You still need to collect the data in the proper format and convert it to the purchased software. In addition to saving time in producing reports, the packages often contain the essential government rules and can analyze the data to spot potential problems.

Some newer technologies are being used to simplify data gathering. In particular, companies are searching for ways to make it easier for workers to deal with the HRM department. A system created by PRC, Inc., uses touch-tone phones and a voice-response system to enable workers to make changes directly to their base information, like changing their address or tax withholding. Another approach is to install PC-based kiosks and use the Internet, so that employees can look up information, sign up for training classes, or modify their personal data whenever they wish. Other companies are using similar software and the corporate network to allow workers to perform basic HR tasks from their desks or from home using the Internet.

Supply Chain Management

How do you make production more efficient? Supply chain management (SCM) concentrates on the production side of ERP. It begins with logistics (purchasing and receiving components), through manufacturing configuration, and into distribution of the products. As shown in Figure 7.12, these factors involve a significant portion of the company, requiring integration of a huge amount of diverse data.

The key to understanding the value of SCM is to go back in time again to see how manufacturing evolved. From the 1920s through the 1970s, companies in many industries

FIGURE 7.12

Total data integration begins with the vendors, tracks data through all operations of the firm, and incorporates information from customers. Each area in the firm has easy access to data from any other location. This integrated data is used to make better decisions by enabling managers to focus on the big picture instead of on local solutions.

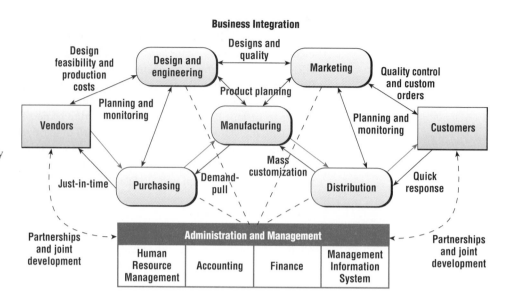

recognized the importance of economies of scale or mass production. The automobile industry presents the classic example. Producing thousands of identical cars enables the company to spread the huge fixed costs across a large base—leading to lower average costs. The huge scale enabled the car companies to negotiate better prices with suppliers and dealers, reducing costs even further. So, in the name of lower costs, the companies produced thousands to millions of identical items. They relied on the marketing departments for two critical purposes: (1) forecast consumer preferences in advance, and (2) convince consumers they need the products that were built. So, the car salesperson says, "Sure, we could order a car for you, but it will cost more and take months. You would really be happier with this car and you can drive it home today."

Of course, mass production has the potential for mass disaster. If you predict incorrectly, or cannot convince customers to buy the existing product, you end up dumping the products at sale prices. Remember that you have to clear the way for next year's models. More critically, mass production means that it is impossible to please all of the consumers—leaving a niche open for your competitors. A niche in the small-car market enabled Toyota to become one of the largest producers in the world.

SCM Changes the Focus

So how does SCM help? It can change the entire system. Mass production begins at the supply side and builds products as cheaply as possible to eventually sell to consumers. With a truly integrated supply chain, it is possible to start with the customers. The marketing department identifies exactly what each customer wants. The customized orders are entered into the system, and the engineering department evaluates the order, makes design changes as needed, and schedules production. Manufacturing knows each desired production date and organizes products to minimize production costs. Component orders are placed with suppliers electronically. On the day of production, as components arrive, they are scanned into the system and routed to the appropriate location. At the same time, payments are scheduled with the banks. As the parts arrive at each machine, the central process controller configures each machine correctly as the product moves through the assembly line. At the end of the production line, the product is labeled and shipped to the appropriate customer. The customer can be notified electronically and billed automatically.

Imagine how much easier it is to be in marketing now. Instead of convincing customers to buy what you have produced, you first find out exactly what they want, and that is what you sell them. It is not quite that simple, but at heart, that is the principle. **Mass customization** is the process of manufacturing products designed for specific consumers but using mass-production techniques to keep costs low. It can be done only if you have an integrated system. In many cases, it is not possible to produce exactly what the customer

REALITY BYTES   Mass Customization for Sofas

Buying furniture, particularly sofas, can be painful and time con-suming. Manufacturers and retailers like to sell customization, where you choose the style and fabric. The only drawback is that it generally takes months to get the finished product. England, Inc., a manufacturer owned by La-Z-Boy, Inc., located in New Tazewell, Tennessee, is shocking the industry by building 11,000 sofas and chairs a week and delivering them to the customer within three weeks. Customization for England means building 85 different styles and keeping 550 different fabrics in stock. It also requires pushing suppliers to deliver on time, approaching a just-in-time system. However, because shipping costs are so high, England cannot just build each item and ship it. Instead, the company begins by plotting out delivery schedules. From there, the plant managers organize the manufacturing of the hundreds of items, using computers to sched-ule each step, and bar-code the individual components to ensure they go to the right stage at the right time. The computer schedules production to match similar styles where possible, to minimize re-configuring the machines. Nonetheless, the production-run sizes are smaller than at its rivals, and prices are slightly higher.

Source: Adapted from Dan Morse, "Tennessee Producer Tries New Tactic in Sofas: Speed," *The Wall Street Journal,* November 19, 2002.

wants (after all, most customers want the world for free). And sometimes you have to pro-duce for groups of similar customers instead of a single consumer, but the principle is the same—use the integrated technology to provide as much customization as possible. For ex-ample, it might never be possible to produce a truly customized automobile economically, but customers might be satisfied with more choice of options.

JIT production is an example of how integrating information can change a production process. Japanese manufacturers created this method with low-tech *kanban* signals that conveyed information along the production line to the suppliers. Today, ERP systems can provide immediate information from all stages of production. This information can be made available to suppliers so they can schedule deliveries. The overall goal is to reduce produc-tion costs and eliminate bottlenecks by reducing the need for huge inventories.

SCM Challenges

SCM and integration are powerful tools. You might expect all firms to be using them heav-ily. But SCM has two serious obstacles: (1) cost and (2) establishing connections and agree-ments with outside firms. The issue of cost can be overcome—although the tools are expensive, if they can save enough money, the cost is acceptable. But that explains why smaller firms with fewer purchases might not be able to afford the technology. The second issue of building connections across multiple firms is far more difficult.

A key issue in SCM is connecting to suppliers electronically. It can also require con-nections to distributors and transporters. Each of these hundreds of companies could have different hardware and software. Plus, all companies involved have to worry about security issues. Sharing data is a more difficult problem than simply blocking all access. B2B e-commerce is an interesting solution proposed to solve some of these problems. In the late 1990s and early 2000s, several B2B auction sites were set up to coordinate purchasing and tracking of products within an industry. For example, Covisint was established by several automobile manufacturers to handle transactions for automobile components. Few of these electronic auction sites survived the dot-com crash. However, some are still supported and used in major industries, such as automobiles and steel.

To a typical consumer, purchasing seems like an easy process: you find a product and buy it. As shown in Figure 7.13, the reality is considerably more complex. Consider the pur-chase of a new item. First the buyer has to identify the purpose and individual features de-sired. Then the buyer identifies potential suppliers and sends a **request for proposal (RFP).** The suppliers select products that match the desired features and make proposals and bids for the sale. The buyer evaluates each request, selects a supplier, and negotiates a contract. From this point, the process is similar, even for repeat orders. The buyer generates a list of specific products, prices, and quantities, along with a desired delivery date. This purchase order is sent to the supplier, who verifies the orders and checks to make sure products are in stock and available for delivery. Any problems with prices or delivery times require

REALITY BYTES   Supply Chain Management for Toys

Toys present an interesting problem for supply chain management. The vast majority of them are sold in the final months of the year as holiday gifts. They often require days or weeks to build, and then several weeks to ship. Consequently, just-in-time production is not going to work. In fact, many toy makers would place their entire production orders in January and February for the coming year. Past holidays are littered with tales of products that suddenly became popular and in short supply. For example, in 1993, Bandai Inc. managed to ship only 600,000 Mighty Morphin Power Rangers—far below the estimated demand of 12 million units. Yet if a company overstocks stores or warehouses, prices drop and profits disappear.

LeapFrog Enterprises, Inc., had a huge success with its Little-Touch LeapPads in the 2003 holiday season. Early in the season, on Monday, August 11, Kevin Carlson, director of sales, received a pleasant surprise. In the first weekend of sales, his product sold 360 units. He was able to obtain the data instantly through ties into the sales systems at the big retailers (Wal-Mart, Target, Kmart, and Toys "R" Us). On the basis of that number, his forecasting software suggested he would need 700,000 units to meet the total demand—twice what he had planned to ship. So, while other companies were

unloading their final shipments, he challenged the Chinese factory to expand production. The company managed to get additional plastic molds, electronics, and special baby-drool-proof paper (Tyvek)—and started cranking out LeapPads around the clock. It took the company 12 months to build the first 350,000 LittleTouch toys. Scrambling, it built that same number in four months. Unlike the early sweatshops in China, the Capable Toys factory was designed to take advantage of supply chain management tools. Using a CAD-CAM design system, the company knows all of the design and manufacturing elements and was able to pinpoint a bottleneck with the metal molds used to create the plastic parts. The company built two new sets of molds (at a cost of several thousand dollars) and improved both, increasing the production speed and reducing failure rates. Tapping into its supplier database, the company was able to obtain the electronics components it needed. By the end of September, as demand increased, LeapFrog switched to air shipping—reducing the company's profit but getting the product to the stores.

Source: Adapted from Geoffrey Fowler and Joseph Pereira, "Behind Hit Toy, a Race to Tap Seasonal Surge," *The Wall Street Journal,* December 18, 2003.

FIGURE 7.13

SCM purchasing: Purchasing is considerably more complicated than it appears. It often requires several interaction steps with suppliers—even for existing relationships. Monitoring prices, quality, and timeliness is critical to both sides.

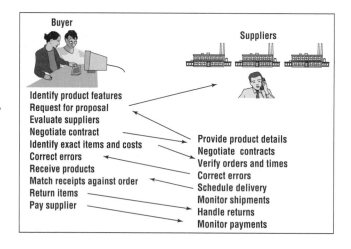

notifying the buyer and negotiating changes. Eventually, the products are shipped to the buyer along with an invoice detailing the items delivered. Of course, the buyer has to verify the quantity and quality of the items received. Any discrepancies are recorded and the seller is notified. Some items are returned. Ultimately, the seller sends a bill to the buyer detailing the amounts owed. On the accounting side, the appropriate accounts payable entries have to be made. Finally, the supplier has to be paid, and needs to monitor receipt of payments and match them against the bills.

One goal of an ERP system is to automate as many of these tasks as possible. Figure 7.14 shows a version of the PeopleSoft screen for a buyer or product planner. Other screens enable suppliers to connect and electronically pick up purchase orders or check on the status of deliveries and payments. All data is entered into a shared database. From the buyer's perspective, notice the scorecard that quickly indicates the status of several key variables. Additional tools on the page enable the buyer to check on the current inventory status of individual products. For example, she can quickly see if the company has too many items in stock for a particular product. Additional tools provide the ability to examine payments, shipments, problems or exceptions, and perform analyses on vendors and products.

FIGURE 7.14

PeopleSoft buyer's perspective: Notice the scorecard to indicate important performance variables. This page includes links to tools that help manage day-to-day tasks.

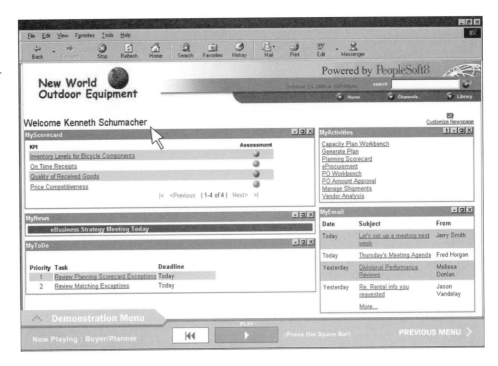

FIGURE 7.15

The role of XML: XML is used to transfer messages to diverse systems. Each system contains tools to read and write XML documents and convert the data into the appropriate internal database tables.

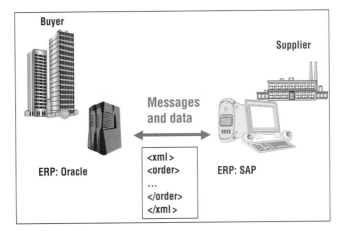

The Role of XML: Integration across Systems

The buyer–seller relationship points out a major challenge that remains to be solved: how do you exchange data electronically between buyers and sellers? Today, both the buyer and seller probably have ERP systems, but they might be from different vendors. Even if they are from the same vendor, they might not format data the same way. So, the buyer will ask the seller for a person to log in and check on the supplier data. Similarly, the seller will ask the buyer to log in and use its system.

As described in Chapter 6, XML is a tool that was established to help companies exchange data. As shown in Figure 7.15, ideally, each company would implement an interface that would accept and read XML documents sent from its partners. The machines could quickly parse the documents and transfer them into the required internal format. Internal functions could then schedule deliveries, check on shipments, or transfer payments.

Figure 7.16 shows a sample XML document. XML is the means to exchange data in a form that all computers can read. At least, that is the promise and hope. XML is still evolving and is still relatively expensive to implement because it often requires customized programming on both ends to handle the data. Software vendors are developing tools that incorporate XML automatically, and suppliers will be able to purchase the software needed to handle the multiple connections to customers.

FIGURE 7.16

XML document: XML is designed to transfer data between companies and computers. You can define any type of tag to describe the data.

```xml
<?xml version="1.0"?>
<!DOCTYPE OrderList(View Source for full doctype...)>
- <OrderList>
  - <Order>
      <OrderID>1</OrderID>
      <OrderDate>3/6/2001</OrderDate>
      <ShippingCost>$33.54</ShippingCost>
      <Comment>Need immediately.</Comment>
    - <Items>
        <ItemID>30</ItemID>
        <Description>Flea Collar-Dog-Medium</Description>
        <Quantity>208</Quantity>
        <Cost>$4.42</Cost>
        <ItemID>27</ItemID>
        <Description>Aquarium Filter & Pump</Description>
        <Quantity>8</Quantity>
        <Cost>$24.65</Cost>
      </Items>
    </Order>
  + <Order>
  + <Order>
  </OrderList>
```

EDI standards were originally developed to help companies share data with their partners, suppliers, and customers. But its progress stalled as firms found it difficult to build easy-to-use EDI systems that worked well with their internal systems and procedures. Initial EDI technologies also required that all transaction data be predefined and fit within the framework of the standards. Several firms began to realize that they needed a more flexible method of sharing data.

All of the data within an XML document is in a specified format and tagged so that a computer program can quickly read the file and identify the data and its purpose. Several companies, including IBM and Microsoft, are developing technologies to use XML to make it easier to share data across companies.

At its foundation, all data is transferred similarly to this example, but XML is considerably more powerful and more complex. Among other things, it supports a version of a style sheet to define and share the structure of the document (the tags). Several industry groups have created XML definitions for sharing data specific to their industry. These data templates make it easier for you to share data, and easier for programmers to develop applications that automatically send and receive the data. The main advantage of XML is that each message contains a description of the purpose of the data as well as the data itself. Hence, the receiving program can evaluate and understand what was sent.

Customer Relationship Management

How do you keep track of all customer interactions? Who are your best customers? Although customers are important to all businesses, the Internet and wireless applications add new dimensions to managing customer relationships. One problem is the expanding number of customer contact points, from sales representatives, to call centers, to Web sites, and wireless connections. Customers expect merchants and suppliers to remember actions and decisions that were made earlier—regardless of the method of contact. Consequently, companies need integrated systems that instantly provide all details of customer contacts. The new technologies also provide innovative methods to keep in touch with customers and identify their specific needs to sell additional products and services. Several software tools have been developed to improve **customer relationship management (CRM)**.

Multiple Contact Points

One of the greatest challenges facing a company today is the multiple sources of contact points with customers. Most of the original systems designed to handle these interactions are separate. Salespeople often keep their own records, Internet support systems may not be totally connected to the sales fulfillment centers, and faxes are rarely integrated into the online customer files. But customers assume that when they talk to one person, that person has records of all the prior interactions.

REALITY BYTES Customer Relationship Management at Dow

Dow Chemical had a problem: thousands of customers calling each day, with additional contacts through salespeople, faxes, and e-mail. Mack Murrell, director of Dow's Corporate Customer Interface Initiative notes that "Our customer memory, or ability to view a customer's interaction history, was not nearly good enough." Dow chose to implement customer relationship management software from Siebel. They began by providing a new system for the support call centers and moved to the sales force. All customer information is stored in a central repository, so salespeople can mine the database for leads or issues raised by customers. The system is also being linked to Dow's backend SAP ERP system. Ultimately, all employees should be able to retrieve customer data through the single system. Customers can use the eService application to check on

or update their orders using the Internet. Murrell summarizes their earlier issues: "Even a year ago, the left hand didn't always know what the right hand was doing. Soon, when a customer calls Dow for service, we'll know the customer's service history and order status before we even pick up the phone based on the caller ID." By reducing costs, the system has paid for itself, and Murrell anticipates "future increases in customer loyalty which will ultimately generate millions of dollars in profit."

Source: Adapted from Siebel eBusiness Applications Are the Catalysts for Dow's Improved Customer Service, Siebel White Paper, http://www.siebel.com/common/includes/case_study.shtm?pdfUrl=/downloads/common/case_studies/Manufacturing/pdf/Dow.pdf&coName=Dow%20Chemical%20Company.

At first glance, it appears that it would be straightforward to build an integrated application to hold all customer interaction data. Of course, it would be a lot of data and would take time to build the application. But the real challenge lies in getting everyone to enter all of the data. Consider the situation of a salesperson who has invested time and collected substantial data on product preferences and customer work environments. That information gives an advantage to the salesperson. Why would the salesperson be willing to share it?

Customers with multiple divisions and many different product tracks also add complications to CRM. The system has to be able to track transactions, questions, and issues by a variety of factors (date, product, company, person, and so on). The system also needs a sophisticated search routine so users can find exactly the pieces of data required.

Feedback, Individual Needs, and Cross Selling

The main purpose of CRM systems is to provide individual attention to each customer to improve sales. By tracking prior purchases, you understand the status of your customers. By providing new channels of communication, you improve the ability of customers to provide feedback to comment on products and services and to make suggestions for improvements. By identifying patterns in purchases, you can develop new ideas for cross selling. If a group of customers tends to purchase several products, you can search the CRM database to find customers with only part of the solution and have your salespeople demonstrate the advantages of the entire suite—using the other customers as examples and references.

The flip side to CRM is that collecting and coordinating substantial data about the customer can lead to privacy problems. As long as the data is secured and used internally, few problems arise. But firms still need to be sensitive to customer wishes about unsolicited contacts. In fact, customer privacy requests need to be part of the CRM system. The issues are more complex when the selling firm has multiple divisions, and each one wants to push new products to existing customers. The marketing staff needs to use the CRM system to coordinate and monitor all contacts.

Wireless applications provide even more options for CRM. Your salespeople can stay in constant contact with the corporate database. They can retrieve current shipping status or detailed customer information during a sales call. They can forward questions or comments, which can be analyzed and answered immediately.

CRM Packages

ERP systems often have a CRM component that provides a unified view of customer data. For example, as Figure 7.17 shows, sales managers can quickly check on the status of customer returns or any other transaction involving customers. When salespeople call on customers, they need to be able to quickly retrieve all of the recent transactions with that

Problem: How do you begin to understand the data collected by an ERP system?

Tools: Executive information systems or digital dashboards are designed to display summary data in real time. The systems usually begin by presenting a graphical overview using some primary measures of the organization. Executives and managers can quickly compare progress on key variables. They can then drill down and see more detailed statistics and even original transaction data such as orders.

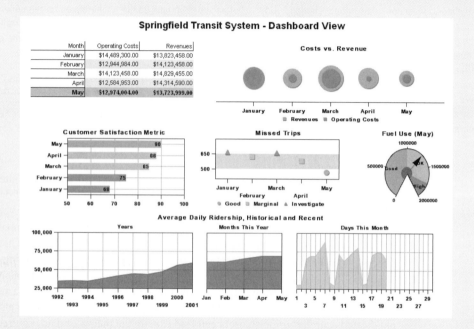

Springfield Transit System - Dashboard View

An EIS can be a powerful tool to follow the progress of the company. Most ERP systems have some type of software that makes it relatively easy to extract data and create an EIS. However, one of the most difficult tasks is to identify the key items that need to be displayed on the main form. Across industries, companies vary enormously in the outcomes managers need to follow. Even within an industry, firms and managers rarely agree on what items are the most important. Consequently, each company needs to develop an EIS customized for its executives.

One approach to identifying the desired elements in an EIS is to follow the balanced scorecard method proposed by Robert S. Kaplan and David P. Norton. They recommend a complete analysis beginning from the top to identify the main strategic goals and derive measures that fit into primary categories. For instance, you would typically need measures on financial, customer, internal data, and learning and change. The top managers cooperate to identify the main indicators of each variable.

Quick Quiz:

1. Assume you have been hired to help a regional law firm. What key elements might go on the main EIS screen?

2. Assume you have been hired to help an airplane manufacturer; design the main EIS screen.

3. To help design an EIS for a retail video store chain, briefly describe the screens and steps needed to identify stores that are performing below par and find possible causes of the problems.

Source: http://www.visualmining.com/ncs/projects/Examples/PerformanceDashboard/TransitMetrics.jsp

customer. Perhaps the customer had problems with a recent shipment, or perhaps they just placed a new order. The salesperson can review those activities before calling on each customer. Then the salesperson can investigate any problems or check on current status and provide immediate answers to customer questions. One of the biggest challenges with a CRM system is collecting the necessary data. An ERP system will have all of the basic transaction data—from the perspective of the main company. But will salespeople enter all of their personal data into the system?

Another important aspect of CRM is the ability to provide direct customer service. As shown in Figure 7.18, ERP systems have self-service portals that enable customers to check on order status, pay bills, order new products, contact salespeople and account man-

FIGURE 7.17
PeopleSoft CRM from a salesperson's perspective: Keeping all the customer interaction data in one location makes it straightforward for the salesperson to understand all of the company's associations with each customer.

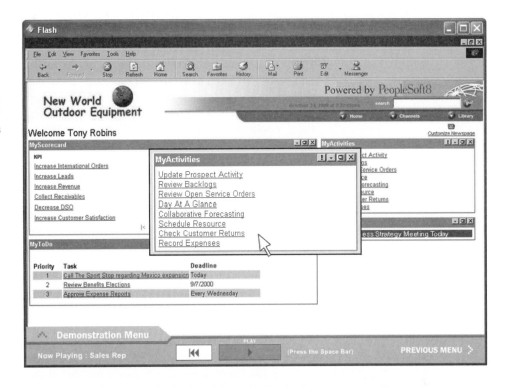

FIGURE 7.18
PeopleSoft CRM from a customer's perspective: The portal into the ERP system enables customers to check the status of various items, order new products, and contact the company.

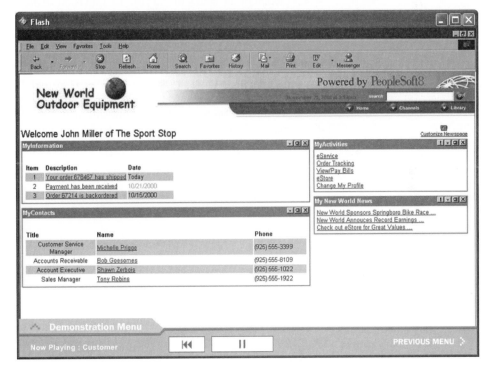

agers, check on company news and events, or ask for additional help. Although the page does not directly support XML, it does make it easy for customers to check on various transactions 24 hours a day. By encouraging customers to connect directly to your system, you obtain more accurate data and reduce costs. Of course, if your customer is the 800-pound gorilla in the industry, it is more likely that your salespeople will be spending time on the customer's ERP site.

Summarizing ERP Data

How can a manager handle all of the data in an ERP system? ERP systems result in huge databases containing an enormous amount of data. Since the data represents all aspects of business transactions, it contains incredibly valuable information needed to make key business decisions. But as a manager or executive, how do you find this information? Since it is stored in a relational DBMS, you could write queries to retrieve data. But after a little time, you will see that you often need the same data every day—so you can compare the progress of common items. Consequently, many ERP systems have special tools to retrieve this standard data and display it in a graphical format.

Digital Dashboard and EIS

One of the major challenges to any information system is to make it easy to use. This process is complicated because the decisions need to be provided to upper-level managers who have little time to learn complex applications, yet deal with huge amounts of diverse data. One approach is to build a portal that displays key data and graphs on one page. The page retrieves data from a data warehouse, the Internet, or even machines within a factory and displays graphs and warnings. Toolkits exist to help build this **digital dashboard**. The older term for this approach is an **executive information system (EIS)**. Figure 7.19 shows a sample digital dashboard that Honeywell is using to give plant managers a quick picture of the status of production lines.

Much like the dashboard on a car, the purpose of the main screen is to provide an overall picture of the status of the firm or a division or production plant. Managers can select the specific division and make comparisons to yesterday, last week, last month, or other locations. If there is a problem or a decision to be made, the executive can **drill down** to get more detailed data by pointing to another object. For example, if the main screen shows that current sales in the west region are low, the executive can focus on the west region and bring up the last few quarters of sales data. The EIS will graph the data to highlight trends. The manager can then dig deeper and bring up sales by departments or check the sales performance of each employee, highlighting unusually high or low sales figures. By pointing to customers, executives can get current profiles on the main customers and examine their recent purchases.

How Does an EIS Work?

For an EIS to work, it must be connected to the transaction-processing system or data warehouse, since it is the source of the data. Many of these systems are created with special soft-

FIGURE 7.19

Digital dashboard example: Like the gauges on an automobile dashboard, the digital dashboard presents a top-level graphical representation of the status of various elements. It is particularly useful for manufacturing environments, but can also be used in more service-oriented industries.

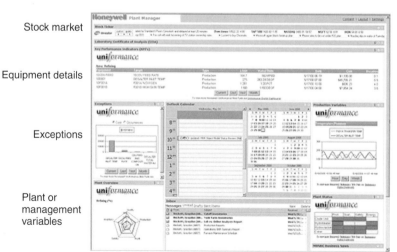

Stock market

Equipment details

Exceptions

Plant or management variables

Quality control

Products

Plant schedule

REALITY BYTES   One Hundred Bottles of Beer on the Wall

Dereck Gurden works for Sierra Beverage, one of about 700 U.S. distributors that work for Anheuser-Busch. His territory is 800 square miles in California's Central Valley. He delivers to a variety of stores—7-Eleven, Buy N Save, liquor marts, and restaurants. As he pulls into each location, he grabs his handheld PC and checks the basic data: accounts receivable, past sales, package placements, and information on displays. As he talks to the clients, he strolls the store, entering information about the competitor displays. With new orders entered, he plugs the PC into his cell phone and sends the orders and information back to the warehouse. From his perspective: "Honestly? I think I know more about these guys' businesses than they do. At least in the beer section."

Dereck is only one part of BudNet, a big reason why Anheuser's volume share of the $74.4 billion U.S. beer market is up to 50.1 percent. Anheuser collects data on every aspect of a beer purchase and constantly changes its marketing strategies to adjust to cultural and competitive trends. None of this technology existed until 1997 when August Busch III decided to make his company a leader in data mining. Initially, wholesalers began funneling data to Busch

in spreadsheets. When that became cumbersome, Busch developed the BudNet system. Overnight, Anheuser can collect and mine current data from every store in the nation and identify which brands are selling, how sales are responding to promotions, and generate new plans. Joe Patti, Anheuser's vice president for retail planning, describes a typical scenario: "Since Michelob Light serves as an official sponsor of the LPGA Tour, if someone asks how the brand is distributed on golf courses, we can quickly calculate our distribution and develop plans to address the courses that don't carry Michelob Light."

Combining the internal data with census demographics and scanner data from Information Resources Inc. enables Anheuser to tailor incredibly precise marketing campaigns. They can pinpoint data by individual stores and districts. Tequiza sells in San Antonio, but Bud Light is a mainstay in Peoria. Gay models appear on posters in San Francisco's Castro district but not in the Mission.

Source: Adapted from Kevin Kelleher, "66,207,896 Bottles of Beer on the Wall," *CNN Online*, February 25, 2004.

FIGURE 7.20

Executive information system: As industries become more competitive, managers search for ways to evaluate and improve the overall operations. Enterprise systems collect data from across the firm and make it available to managers and top executives. Executives can start with an overview of the firm and drill down to various levels and departments to get more detailed data.

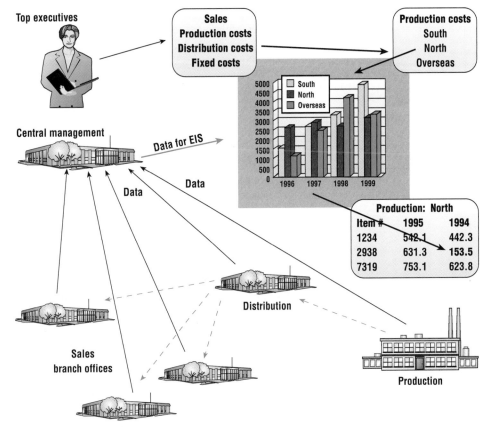

ware that simply grabs data from the corporate databases. In one sense, the EIS is a complex model of the firm. Figure 7.20 illustrates how executives can "visit" different divisions on the computer and retrieve the data immediately. For the EIS to be useful, the computer model must be a faithful representation of the actual company.

As a model, the EIS display has inputs of raw materials and people. Outputs are typically measured by traditional accounting standards of profits, costs, and growth rates. The EIS maintains budgets and forecasts and can compare them to actual values. The functions and processes are determined from the individual departments. For instance, there could be a production model that describes the manufacturing output. An EIS at McDonnell Douglas has a graphics screen that displays portions of airplanes as they are being built. As a wing is completed, it is drawn onto the computer model.

Advantages of an EIS

The primary goal of an EIS is to provide easy access to corporate data for the executives. Instead of waiting for a report, the top executives can retrieve the data as soon as it is available. Also, because all the data is accessible from the same system, it is easier to examine data from different departments to produce a better view of the big picture. Another useful feature is that the executive's use of the data is nonintrusive.

Imagine that you are CEO of a company, and you do not have an EIS. The monthly reports have just indicated that one of the warehouses is not running smoothly. You want to find out what the problems are. You suspect the warehouse manager is part of the problem, but you need to be sure. What do you do? The most direct approach is to go visit the warehouse. But what happens when you show up at the warehouse? It is likely that the manager and the workers will change the way they work. Your attempts to collect data have altered the way the system runs, so you will not get the information you wanted.

Other options include sending other people or asking for additional information via the chain of command. Although useful, these methods will be slower and the information you receive will be colored by the perceptions of the people collecting the data. For example, many people will try to focus on what they think you want to hear.

The EIS minimizes these problems by providing instant access to the corporate data. The executives can produce reports and examine departments without interfering with the operations of the company. Graphs can be created automatically. The executives can set up different scenarios or simulations. Most of these activities are accomplished simply by pointing to objects on the screen.

Transaction Accuracy: Sarbanes-Oxley

How does the CEO know that financial records are correct? After several huge corporate scandals in 2001 and 2002 (Enron, Worldcom/MCI, Tyco, and so on), Congress decided to try and stop some of the problems. In particular, high-level executives were pleading innocent claiming that they did not know about the problems. So, they passed the Sarbanes-Oxley Act, which requires top executives of public companies to sign a statement attesting to the validity of the annual financial statements. So, how does the CEO know if the transaction data and reports are correct?

The solution proposed by the accounting standards board (AICPA) is to require more independent audits and reviews of the audits. Accounting audits examine all aspects of the transaction-processing system: from data collection, to data storage security, to accuracy of calculations and reports. Auditors also check physical assets (particularly bank accounts) to ensure that the numbers listed on the financial statements tie to real-world data. As shown in Figure 6.19, bank accounts are a critical element of auditing because they are maintained by external companies. Similarly, inventory and customer sales are at least sampled to ensure that they match against the internal financial records. These external numbers help anchor the internal statements. For example, it is hard to falsify the books if you have to match the cash balance at the bank—but not impossible. Somehow the Italian dairy company Parmalat managed to list $5 billion in cash in a Cayman Island account from 2002 to 2004 that did not exist.

Auditors also focus on the transaction and reporting processes. Do standard procedures encourage the timely and accurate recording of all data? Do people follow the standard procedure? The generally accepted accounting practices (GAAP) were created to establish stan-

FIGURE 7.21

Financial audits: Verifying the quality of the data requires tying elements of the financial statements to externally validated numbers. Inventory can be physically counted. Customer sales can be sampled, and bank data must match the internal records.

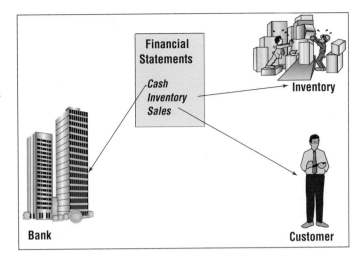

dards and guidelines for accounting procedures. Today, one of the purposes of accounting software is to encode these practices into the system. In one sense, corporate accountants and managers are given less flexibility. Yet from management's perspective, the software encourages everyone in the firm to follow the proper procedures. Of course, some companies and managers will find these procedures too restrictive. Particularly if the company uses highly individualized practices and nonstandard production techniques.

Summary

After decades of improving hardware and new software, even the largest companies are now able to integrate all of the data across the firm. Even when the firm has production and sales in multiple nations, ERP software makes it possible for managers and executives to get a complete up-to-date picture of the entire company. Equally important, this level of integration makes it possible to change the way the company operates. Instead of relying on mass production to lower costs, companies can focus on the customer and the market. Working from the customer perspective, the firm can produce the items and options desired by the market. This type of production is possible because the information is instantly available to production and to suppliers. Integrated data on customers improves relationships with customers by enabling companies to identify client needs and respond to problems faster.

A Manager's View

How can you improve a company's processes? By integrating all transaction information across the company, you gain the ability to change the way it works. By changing the way it works, you can reduce costs, increase production, and respond more quickly to market changes. By identifying your customers and tracking their needs, you can keep existing customers happy and make it easier to acquire new customers. By monitoring quality and tracking the internal processes and employee functions, you can improve quality and reward the best employees.

Integrating accounting, production, sales, and employee data makes it easier to identify bottlenecks, identify and reward the best employees, and gain a competitive advantage. Ultimately, the key to ERP systems is not the software—it is the integration and reengineering of the business operations that make your company better. The tools provide the ability to change the way the firm operates and to use these capabilities to find a better overall solution. Whether the firm manufactures products or is a service firm or governmental agency, you can find new ways to operate when everything is integrated.

Key Words

accounting journal, *245*
audit trail, *247*
chart of accounts, *245*
customer relationship
management (CRM), *254*
digital dashboard, *258*

drill down *258*
enterprise resource
planning (ERP), *239*
exception reports, *246*
executive information
system (EIS), *258*

general ledger, *245*
mass customization, *250*
request for proposal
(RFP), *251*
supply chain management
(SCM), *249*

Web Site References

Common Statistics
Bureau of Labor Statistics   www.bls.gov
Census Bureau   www.census.gov
FedStats   www.fedstats.gov
General Reference Sites
Congress   thomas.loc.gov/home/legbranch/
                                    legbranch.html
Congress   www.house.gov
                                    www.senate.gov
Congressional Quarterly   www.cq.com
Copyright Office   lcweb.loc.gov/copyright
Executive Branch   lcweb.loc.gov/global/executive/fed.html
IRS   www.irs.gov
Judicial   www.uscourts.gov
Legislative votes   www.vis.org/toolbox/default.aspx
Library of Congress   thomas.loc.gov
Patent Office   www.uspto.gov

Additional Readings

Harreld, Heather. "Extended ERP Reborn in B-to-B." *Infoworld,* August 27, 2001. [Updated perspective on ERP and new applications.]

Krill, Paul. "Data Analysis Redraws CRM Landscape." *Infoworld,* November 30, 2001. [CRM vendors and capabilities in sales analysis.]

"Never-Ending Story: Why ERP Projects Cause Panic Attacks." *Computerworld,* September 24, 2001. [ERP projects can cause problems when they are rushed.]

Songini, Marc L. "PeopleSoft Project Ends in Court," *Computerworld,* September 10, 2001. [Serious problems with an ERP installation at Connecticut General.]

Weston, Randy. "ERP Users Find Competitive Advantages." *Computerworld,* January 19, 1998, p. 9. [Summary of ERP benefits.]

Review Questions

1. What is meant by the concept of integrating information in business? Give an example of problems that can arise if business information is not integrated.
2. How do enterprise resource planning systems integrate data across the company?
3. What is the role of a DBMS in an enterprise resource planning system?
4. What are the primary features and capabilities of an enterprise resource planning system?
5. How do accounting and financial systems form the backbone of ERP systems?
6. Why are human resource management systems such an important component of ERP systems?
7. How does supply chain management enable a firm to change its structure and focus?
8. Why is customer relationship management so important? Why does it require an integrated system?
9. Why is an executive information system or digital dashboard so important to an ERP system?

Exercises

1. Find a balance sheet and income statement for a company (try the EDGAR system at www.sec.gov). Enter the major sections of each into two worksheets that link on the appropriate cells.

2. Research the rules and equations for computing payroll taxes in your locality. When were the rules or percentages changed last?

DeptStor.mdb

3. Using a DBMS, spreadsheet, and word processor, create the four reports shown in the introduction: daily sales report, returned merchandise log, commissions report, and weekly sales analysis. If possible, use tools that support dynamic integration.

4. Using current business publications, find an example of a company that is experiencing problems with integrating data. Alternatively, find an example of a company that has an excellent system for integrating information. Identify data that is shared dynamically and data that is shared through static copies. (*Hint:* Companies are more likely to report successes than problems, and be sure to check the MIS publications.)

5. If you have access to an ERP system, take a specific role (salesperson, production manager, customer, supplier, etc.) and use the system to enter data and check on the current status variables for your role.

6. Choose a manufacturing industry for consumer goods (for example, automobiles, bicycles, or refrigerators). Research the industry and identify what aspects follow mass production versus what operations follow mass customization strategies.

7. Choose a firm or industry that sells to other businesses (for example, air conditioners for retail stores). Research the industry and identify what aspects follow mass production versus what operations follow mass customization strategies.

Technology Toolbox

8. Find information on at least two accounting or ERP packages that could be used for a business with 100 to 150 employees. Identify the strengths and weaknesses of each package. Are the packages tailored to specific industries?

9. You need to select an accounting or ERP package for a small service business, such as a law firm or accounting firm. Identify the major features that you want to see in the accounting system.

10. You have been hired as a consultant to a small graphics design firm with 20 employees. Design a digital dashboard for the owner–manager to monitor the important variables of the company.

11. Make a list of the top five ERP vendors (if fewer than five exist, add some accounting system vendors). Identify their revenue, primary market, and major strengths.

12. Find an organization that uses a digital dashboard–executive information system. Identify the major components on the main screen, and briefly explain how the system is used to drill down to additional information.

Teamwork

13. Each team member should find an example of a company that implemented an ERP system. Briefly outline any problems encountered. Combine the papers and discuss why some companies had more problems than others.

14. Each team member should research one ERP system. Identify the internationalization features available. Assume you are running a midsize company with offices and operations in several European nations. Describe the benefits provided by these international features. Make a recommendation on which product to buy.

15. Choose an industry and have each team member find income and balance sheet data for a firm in that industry. Chart the revenue, net income, earnings per share, and assets for each of the firms for the last three years.

16. Interview or tour a local company as a team. Assign each person to a functional area (accounting, HRM, marketing, and so on). Write a report on how an ERP system could be used by the company to improve or change its operations.

17. You have been hired as a consultant to a midsize agricultural company that packs fruit and ships it to retail outlets. The fruit is grown under contract at regional farms. About 65 percent is sold to grocery and chains and fruit stores in the United States, while the rest is shipped overseas to high-end stores and restaurants. Design an ERP system with a digital dashboard for this company. Assign individual components to each team member. Be sure to identify potential problems and risks that might arise.

Rolling Thunder Database

18. Extract sales and cost data by model type and create a spreadsheet to analyze it. (*Hint:* Use the Extract Data form.) Write a short report discussing profitability and any trends. Include graphs to illustrate your comments. Your spreadsheet should look at monthly sales by model and monthly material costs by model. Be sure to compute profit margins and examine percentages.

19. Assume that Rolling Thunder is experiencing problems with quality control. Suddenly there are several complaints about the components. Write a report describing all of the data and reports we would need to help us resolve these problems.

20. Top management needs an analysis of purchases and deliveries from vendors. Begin by using queries to extract the appropriate data to create a basic spreadsheet. Write a report analyzing the data; include graphs to illustrate your points.

Vendor	Purchases Order Total $	Percent of Vendor Total	Received $	Receipts % of Purchase	Avg. # Days to Deliver

21. Describe how an ERP solution could improve operations at Rolling Thunder. What operations would you implement first?

22. Find an accounting or ERP system that would be appropriate for Rolling Thunder Bicycles. Identify the main features and approximate cost of the system.

23. Describe how Rolling Thunder Bicycles might use a supply chain management system. In particular, how would it integrate with its suppliers?

24. Describe or create a subsystem that could be used by the head of sales management to monitor and improve customer relationships and sales.

Cases: Automobile Industry

The Industry

Automobiles remain one of the most expensive, complex products sold to consumers. Manufacturing requires thousands of steps with parts acquired from hundreds of suppliers. And people buy cars for more than transportation—they are purchased based on image and style. As Ralph Szygenda, legendary CIO of GM, puts it: "GM is ultimately in the fashion business, and to win, the company needs the best cars and trucks, which we have, with more to come" (Szygenda 2003). Perhaps he was a bit optimistic. North American sales for 2003 dropped to 16.6 million vehicles. GM had the largest market share at 28.3 percent, followed by Ford (20.7), Daimler-Chrysler (12.8), Toyota (11.1), and Honda (8.1) (Warner 2004). The astonishing number is found in the 1960s when GM's market share was over 50 percent. However, the declining share is not all that it seems. Check the Web sites of the big three companies and you will quickly see that they have bought up several other brands over the past years. Dig a little deeper into GM's annual report and you will find that the company owns shares in Subaru, Suzuki, Fiat, and Daewoo, among others. Ford has similar arrangements with other companies.

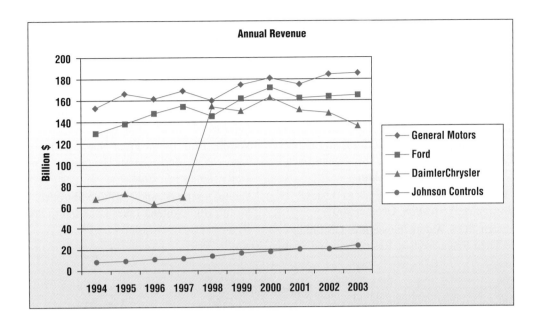

Annual Revenue

Most of the firms in the industry also face a huge problem they refer to as legacy costs. Over the years, the heavily unionized American firms promised huge pensions and health care benefits to their employees. Now, they face billions of dollars in fixed cost payments to retirees—costs that were never fully funded from prior operations. So, a substantial percentage of current sales revenue goes to paying these costs.

Competition

In general, the industry is highly competitive. It has been estimated that the Detroit big three have an excess production capacity of 2.5 million vehicles (Plunkett Research 2004). Total U.S. sales fell slightly in 2003 to 16.6 million new vehicles. Compounding the problem is the fact that many of the sales have been driven by deep discounts—either in price or in financing deals. At one point, in 1993, Ford pushed so hard to make the Taurus the number one selling car that it was giving discounts of $2,600—a considerable sum at the time. Most observers believe Ford was losing money on every car (White 2004).

At the same time that the American car companies appear to be suffering, you should note that only 40 percent of Americans can actually afford to buy new cars (National Independent Dealers Association). In 2001, the Bureau of Transportation Statistics reported sales of 8.6 million new passenger cars (not trucks) and 40.7 million used passenger cars (and 11 million new bicycles) (www.bts.gov). Used truck numbers are not reported, but in terms of new vehicles, cars make up about 50 percent of the total number of vehicles. In any case, sales of new vehicles account for about 17 percent of automobile sales. Globally, about 60 million vehicles were sold in 2003 (GM annual report).

Technology and Management

The ultimate question the automobile industry faces is: How do you manage such a large, complex company? In 2003, GM had 326,000 employees worldwide and revenues of $185 billion (annual report). The company ran 32 plants in North America alone (Garsten 2003). With multiple divisions, thousands of designers and engineers, and a recalcitrant union, how can you possibly determine what is going on, much less control it? As one of the largest companies in America for over 60 years, GM is an interesting case in management and mismanagement. The company was initially created by combining several independent brands. Alfred P. Sloan, who organized and ran the company in the 1930s, knew that with the information system available at the time, he could never control an organization that big. His decision was to let the divisions run somewhat independently, but report to a set of policy committees and central staffs in a system he called "decentralized operations and responsibilities with coordinated control" (Taylor 2004). All auto manufacturers have struggled in the last couple of decades with the question of how to control the huge organizations. As technology has improved, new options have been created that provide for increased central control across the entire organization. Tools such as global networks, CAD-CAM systems for engineers, workgroup and collaboration systems for managers, and enterprise resource planning systems for operations and finance make it possible to share data. Yet installing these systems is only the first step. You also have to change the way the company runs. And that can be difficult in an organization used to flexibility and defined ways of functioning that evolved over decades.

The automobile manufacturers have tested many variations of information technology over the past decade. The industry spent billions of dollars on telematics (integrating information systems into the vehicle). It has spent billions more on supply chain management and enterprise resource planning systems. Today, most of the $3 billion a year that GM and Ford spend on IT goes to operations—keeping the existing systems running (Piszczalski 2002). The companies have still not achieved total integration of their systems, and might never reach that state. But they are still interested in tools that can solve specific problems and provide gains in quality, cost reduction, and bringing new models to market faster.

Additional Reading

Garsten, Ed. "UAW May Sacrifice Jobs for Benefits." *The Detroit News,* September 8, 2003. http://www.niada.com/Industry_Information/ind_10key.htm

Piszczalski, Martin. "Auto IT Moves Back to Basics." *Automotive Design & Production,* October 2002.

Plunkett Research. "U.S. Automakers Suffer Declining Market Share/Their Response Is to Restructure and Seek Greater Efficiency Including Cutting Costs." http://www.plunkettresearch.com/automobile/automobile_trends.htm#1, 2004.

Szygenda, Ralph. "It's a Great Time to Be in I.T." *Information Week,* January 27, 2003.

Taylor III, Alex. "GM Gets Its Act Together. Finally." *Fortune,* March 21, 2004.

Warner, Fara. "Show Floor News: Detroit to Focus on Tastes as Its Market Share Decreases." *The New York Times,* January 5, 2004.

White, Joseph B., and Norihiko Shirouzo. "At Ford Motor, High Volume Takes Backseat to Profits." *The Wall Street Journal,* May 7, 2004.

Case: Ford

Ford (ticker: F) has presented several interesting cases in management over the years. Driven initially by Henry Ford's efficient adoption of mass production, the company dominated the automobile industry. Through all of the changes in the industry, technology, and finance, the company has largely remained under the control of the Ford family (40 percent of the voting stock). In October 2001, the family ousted Jacques Nasser and Henry's great-grandson, Bill Ford, became CEO. The firm struggled for a year, trying to recover from its earlier problems. One of the major changes implemented by Mr. Ford was an emphasis on profits—instead of raw sales numbers. Toyota is close to overtaking Ford and becoming the number two car company in the United States. Mr. Ford's comment: "I don't want to be the biggest. I want to be the best." With lower sales, Ford surpassed GM in profits for 2003 (White and Shirouzo 2004).

Revenue Decisions

The automobile industry is a classic case of mass production. Building thousands of identical cars and trucks reduces costs. But then you have to sell them. Does everyone want the exact same car or truck? In 2001 and 2002, Ford began to reevaluate its strategy, with a focus on identifying the source of profits. Why build 300,000 Tauruses if the company loses money on each car? In the process, the company found that it needed to track exactly which vehicles are selling, what features are in demand, and the details of regional preferences. Bill Ford promoted Lloyd Hansen to a corporate vice presidency in charge of overseeing revenue management—identifying exactly which products should be built. The company began analyzing data from existing sales channels. More important, it combined consumer Internet research data to identify regional choices. Mr. Hansen says that the company was surprised to find consumers in sunny states were interested in four-wheel drive pickups. "There was always this gut-feel paradigm that people who live in Texas, Florida, and California don't need a 4-by-4" (White and Shirouzo 2004). By shar-

ing the data with dealers, Ford increased shipments of the more expensive trucks. Ford uses the same information analysis to target discounts more precisely. With truck sales, Ford was able to increase revenue by $934 per vehicle from 2003 to 2004 (Taylor June 2004).

Think about the decisions required for revenue management. The key is that you have to decide exactly which products to produce tomorrow. You have dozens of cars and trucks, each with several trim variations. You have dozens of plants. You have some data on sales and profits. Should you produce 1,000 Ford Explorers that might generate $4,000 per vehicle in profits, or should you run 1,000 Focuses with lower profit margins. If you do run the Explorers, how much discount should you give to get them sold? Keep in mind that this is a $25 million decision that you have to make every day (White 2002).

Now, make the process even more complicated: what are your rivals going to do? If Cadillac offers a rebate on the Escalade, how will that affect sales of the Navigator? Should you match the discount, or accept the possibility of lower sales at higher profit margins? What is the probability that Cadillac will offer that rebate? More important, if you respond, will they retaliate and offer even larger discounts? Few models are actually this sophisticated today, but in reality, you need to forecast a huge number of variables to make these decisions.

Production Management

The system of mass production makes it difficult to respond to changes in demand. Forecasts are helpful, but Ford has worked hard to add flexibility into its production system. In particular, it is working to build different versions of cars from the same plant. At one time, each plant was designed to produce only one type of car. Today, plants need to be able to switch production so that when demand for crossover wagons increases, the company can stop producing sedans and build the high-demand cars instead. Toyota and Honda pioneered these practices, and Ford is still trying to catch up, but the company is making progress. Many of these changes are being implemented in the new Chinese plants. The goal is to put in only enough capacity to meet current demand, but enable the plants to expand quickly if demand takes off (White and Shirouzo 2004).

Of course, it always pays to improve efficiency in production. Ford's plant in Cuautitlan, Mexico, produces 300,000 to 400,000 cars and trucks a year. It uses a just-in-time production system, where suppliers deliver parts as they are needed on the line—instead of holding them in inventory. Until 2002, the partially completed vehicles were tracked through manufacturing and painting using paper identification sheets. But this manual system generated huge numbers of errors from lost, damaged, or switched sheets. Ford called on Escort Memory Systems from California and CAPTA from Mexico to convert the system using radio frequency identification (RFID) tags. Dealing with the electronically dirty manufacturing floor and the 220°C paint oven temperatures was a problem. The companies used high-temperature RFID tags with 48-byte memory and 1,200 bytes/second transfer rate. The tags were attached to the pallets that carry the vehicle bodies through the plant. Antennae were embedded in explosion-proof containers in the floor under the conveyor belts. As each skid passes over an antenna, the system reads it and feeds the information to the central control system (Johnson 2002).

In a fashion market, producing new models quickly is critical. Ford has reduced its development time by 25 percent from the late 1990s and is getting better by 10 percent a year. Still slower than Toyota, but Ford was able to produce a third of its new models in 30 months or less (Taylor February 2004).

Questions

1. How does Ford's information system help them reduce costs and add flexibility to the production line?

2. What data is provided by the ERP system that can be used to make tactical and strategic decisions?

3. What type of data does Ford need to know to build its forecasts and plan production levels? How does the ERP system provide this data?

Additional Reading

Johnson, Dick. "RFID Tags Improve Tracking, Quality on Ford Line in Mexico." *Control Engineering,* November 2002.

Taylor III, Alex. "Detroit Buffs Up." *Fortune,* February 9, 2004.

Taylor III, Alex. "Bill's Brand-New Ford." *Fortune,* June 28, 2004.

White, Joseph B. "Automobile Industry Is Using Science of Revenue Management to Sell Cars." *The Wall Street Journal,* May 5, 2002.

White, Joseph B., and Norihiko Shirouzo. "At Ford Motor, High Volume Takes Backseat to Profits." *The Wall Street Journal,* May 7, 2004.

Case: General Motors

General Motors (ticker: GM) began life as a diverse company—a collection of manufacturers loosely controlled through a central organization. It really has not changed much over the years, but it keeps trying.

Product Management and Marketing

Check out the GM Web site. The company lists nine major brands on its home page (now that Buick is gone). And that list does not include several European and Asian brands that are fully or partly owned by GM, such as Opel, Vauxhall, Daewoo, Fiat, Isuzu, and Suzuki (Plunkett Research 2004). Imagine trying to monitor the dozens of companies, product lines, and markets. One step GM is taking is an attempt to build a central European database encompassing clean data from Spain, the Netherlands, and the UK. Most of the work is being done for its Daewoo division. The goal is to create a consistent list of its 700,000 customers and prospects and make it available from its Amsterdam headquarters. Daewoo's UK direct marketing and e-commerce manager, Matthew Young, notes: "In Europe, it was apparent that we had no continuity or integration of style. This will also plug the hole in our cost efficiency" (GM Daewoo 2004).

Production and Collaboration

Production of automobiles is changing—particularly as the automotive technology changes. For example, the gas pedal in the 2004 Corvette is not mechanically connected to the engine. Instead, it is an electronic connection—much like the fly-by-wire Boeing 777 jet. Many cars have 30 wireless sensors in them, with plans for new models with over 50 devices in them. Tony Scott, chief technology officer at GM, notes that "we spend more per vehicle on software than we do on steel," and that software has to survive the 10-or-more-year life of the car (Sullivan 2003).

Implementing new technologies into automobiles is a complex task. Advances have to be evaluated, tested, and priced to match the level of the automobile. To handle the changing technologies and track which ones are being used in each vehicle, GM adapted a technology road mapping process developed at Saab (currently a subsidiary of GM). The basic process places the model year on the X-axis of a chart, and the Y-axis represents increasing performance. Individual projects are drawn on the chart to show if they are funded or unfunded, and when they started. Collecting the data for charts across the organization was not easy. Eventually, a database-driven Web site was created to hold the information about existing and planned projects, containing the description, budget, development stage, key personnel, cost, and planned applications. Even then, most divisions were reluctant to enter the appropriate data. So, GM forced divisions to enter data by explaining that if there was no data in the database, then the project must not be important, and it would not be funded. The process was useful for some groups, but avoided by others. The good news is that everyone could see how the various projects scattered across the company were related. For example, electronic steering was going to rely on the 42-volt electrical system (older cars use a 12-volt system), so the timing of the two projects had to match. The system also showed several redundant projects, which caused conflicts because everyone wanted the "other" project to be canceled (Grossman 2004). A powerful extension of the road mapping process was to extend it to suppliers. For example, by overlaying Motorola's road map, engineers could plan for future capabilities.

Automobile manufacturers are really assemblers and integrators. Each plant has thousands of suppliers who provide everything from individual bolts and glue to fully assembled cockpits and seats. Each of these companies has additional suppliers. How can anyone track the orders and solve problems if something goes wrong several layers deep into the supply chain? Product life cycle management (PLM) software presents one answer that is being used in the automotive world. The system enables GM to track the source of all components used in a product during its lifetime. It also provides information to the supply chain participants. Terry S. Kline, GM's global product development process information officer, notes that "in product development, IT projects like PLM have helped pare a billion dollars of cost over the past three years." But Kline also quickly notes that the system has also helped reduce the time-to-market from idea to product from 48 months to 18 months (Teresko 2004). About 80 percent of a car and as much as 70 percent of the design content come from outside the automobile company. PLM integrates the business information with the engineering (computer integrated manufacturing) data and shares it with other members of the supply chain.

Making the thousands of decisions and setting strategy is incredibly difficult. Rick Wagoner, the CEO, noted in 2004 that "we didn't do everything right over the last 12 years. About three times during that period you think you've got it, and then something else comes up. We made huge progress in '92, '93, '94, but then we started to pay the price because we had, out of necessity, underspent (on new products) during that tight period and didn't do that well on the revenue side. Then, in the last three or four years, we've run the business very well, but the pricing has been tough. So my lesson—these aren't complaints but an observation—is, Don't ever think you've got it licked, because you probably don't. This is not a one-step game. This is a multiple [year] thing, and it's hard, and you learn as you go along. The key thing is to remember what you've learned so you don't have to relearn it" (Taylor 2004).

Information Technology

Ralph Szygenda is already a legend at GM. As its first CIO in 1996, he inherited several problems. GM had tried to simplify its IT functions by outsourcing computer management to EDS—of course, the company wanted to keep the profits, so it purchased EDS. But the IT departments were still not running smoothly. Among other problems, it took the company 48 months to develop a new car. Szygenda went several steps further into outsourcing—by moving to a multivendor approach, forcing them to compete against each other, yet still cooperate to provide products that worked together. In the process, he slashed annual IT spending from $4 billion to $3 billion and installed 3-D virtual reality modeling software along with a collaborative infrastructure. Model development time dropped to 24 months. The time it takes to deliver a special-ordered vehicle dropped from 70 to 30 days. To control the outsourced components, Szygenda kept 2,000 IT managers in house. He observes that "when I first started doing this, people said you couldn't outsource critical aspects of the company, and I agree with that. Those 2,000 [managers] are the critical part, but the hands, arms, and legs of building IT can be outsourced" (Zarley 2003). Szygenda uses the 800-pound gorilla clout of GM to keep suppliers in line and encourage them to adopt standard procedures.

Technology has not always been successful at GM. In the 1990s, it installed a computerized system for dealers that required them to order cars 90 days in advance, and it made it difficult to change orders. In the meantime, GM announced that it wanted to take over 700 dealerships and run them centrally. Then, the ordering system crashed and sales plummeted for a month. The system was eventually fixed, but the two decisions alienated dealers. Jack Smith, ex-CEO of GM, notes that these and other problems were exacerbated by market manager Ron Zarrella, who was brought in as an outsider from Bausch & Lomb. Smith notes that the car business is unique, and an outsider might say, "That's really a dumb way to run." But the unfortunate thing is, that is the way it runs. There are some things you just have to live with (Taylor 2004).

Questions

1. How does GM's decentralized structure affect the implementation and use of ERP systems?

2. How does an integrated production and design system help GM design new cars?

3. Why is an integrated production system so important for building custom vehicles?

4. Will GM eventually be able to build a higher percentage of custom-ordered cars?

Additional Reading

Grossman, David S. "Putting Technology on the Road." *Research Technology Management,* March–April 2004.

Plunkett Research. "U.S. Automakers Suffer Declining Market Share/Their Response Is to Restructure and Seek Greater Efficiency Including Cutting Costs." http://www.plunkettresearch.com/automobile/automobile_trends.htm#1, 2004.

"GM Daewoo UK Leads Drive to First Pan-Euro Database." *Precision Marketing,* March 26, 2004.

Sullivan, Brian. "GM's Tony Scott on High-Tech Driving, Wireless Cars and Software Crashes." *Computerworld,* May 8, 2003.

Taylor III, Alex. "GM Gets Its Act Together. Finally." *Fortune,* March 21, 2004.

Teresko, John. "The PLM Revolution." *Industry Week,* February 2004.

Zarley, Craig. "Ralph Szygenda." *CRN,* December 15, 2003.

Case: Suppliers: Johnson Controls and Magna Steyr

Johnson Controls, Inc. (ticker: JCI), is one of thousands of suppliers in the automotive industry. The Milwaukee manufacturer sold $13.6 billion of components to the auto industry in 2001. It is a Tier 1 supplier of cockpits, which includes the dashboard, seats, and other interior elements. The company built nearly half of the cockpits for the 50 million vehicles built worldwide in 2001. The company relies on collaboration tools and networks to coordinate design and development. It is particularly important to catch design problems early. Solving problems at the design stage costs about one-tenth of what it will cost once the item reaches the prototype stage, and thousands less than trying to fix something once it hits the assembly line.

The company builds the cockpit for the Jeep Liberty using 35 different suppliers. To enable all of them to share data, JCI implemented a portal from MatrixOne. Each supplier can connect to MatrixOne, which converts data into the appropriate system. Suppliers that use one CAD system can still share with others that use a different system. Even ERP data can be exchanged across systems, so JCI and suppliers can track orders and inventory levels.

John Waraniak, executive director of e-speed at JCI, notes that the collaboration system has saved the company 80 percent on research and development and reduced costs by $20 million in the "core products portfolio." Engineers are also more productive because they can share designs electronically. He observes that "typically, engineers spend half their time engineering and the rest of the time they are looking for information. With the exchange, it's all brought together for them" (Hall 2002).

Magna Steyr is a major automotive supplier and engineering company. A key step in their engineering process is clash analysis. Engineers have to evaluate each part to make sure that it will not interfere with any others. Obviously, you cannot wait to build the car to test for interference. Magna installed Catia software from Dassault Systemes as part of a CAD program. The collaborative and virtual environment automatically evaluates designs from engineering teams. Installed on a high-speed IBM grid system, it still takes four hours to analyze an entire vehicle, but that is vastly better than the 72 hours it used to take manually. Engineers can run the system overnight and correct their designs in the morning. Laura Yandow, a grid sales executive at IBM, notes that "the ultimate benefit is that it has had a big impact on Magna's time to market" (Rosencrance 2004).

Questions

1. Why does Johnson need MatrixONe?
2. Why are integrated design systems so critical in creating today's vehicles?
3. How can design systems be improved through linkages with suppliers?

Additional Reading

Hall, Mark. "Portal Masks Integration Complexity." *Computerworld,* July 22, 2002.

Rosencrance, Linda. "IBM Offers Grid Computing for Automotive Design." *Computerworld,* March 31, 2004

Case: DaimlerChrysler

In 1999, when former Chrysler CEO Bob Eaton introduced the redesigned Jeep Grand Cherokee, he held up a bag that he claimed contained all of the parts that were carried over from the earlier design. He seemed proud of this huge design change. But the costs had to be enormous. Toyota saves billions of dollars by reusing as many components as possible. Reuse also leads to more flexible production and design, enabling Toyota to produce new vehicles in a few months instead of years (Taylor 2004).

Technology in Manufacturing

DaimlerChrysler (ticker: DCX) has 104 manufacturing plants in 37 countries. Communication among the 362,000 employees is challenging across those distances. The company uses videoconferencing and holds more than 100 meetings a day with the technology, saving it as much as $14 million a year in travel expenses. The engineering teams use Web portals to share work and check on business information (Niccolai 2004).

In 1998, after the merger of Daimler and Chrysler, Susan Unger was named CIO and head of global IT operations of the new company. In the middle of the dot-com hype, she notes that she "had a different message, which was that in the 'e-world,' you have to have business value. It was kind of funny at the time because I was a voice in the wilderness talking that way." Because of this focus, the company worked on B2B initiatives. Unger notes that many other companies have had to write off their Internet projects, but "we have had none because we were kind of religious about ROI (return on investment)" (Gibson 2004).

One of the big tools that DaimlerChrysler is implementing is DELMIA from Dassault Systemes AG. Unger points out that as the engineer designs a vehicle, they can use the tool to create "a virtual manufacturing environment—including your work cells, your line, your equipment—and simulate your workers installing a wiring harness or whatever else." The multiple divisions (Daimler, Chrysler, and Mitsubishi) all use an e-engineering portal to share CAD information.

DaimlerChrysler is also a big user of the Covisint automotive auction system. Sue Unger notes that in 2003, the company used the system for almost 200 separate bids, saving it between 15 and 20 percent compared to traditional prices. More important, the system simplified the purchase process, reducing the time from months to days (Gibson 2004).

Auto Sales and the Internet

In the middle of the dot-com boom, some people were forecasting that all car sales would be made online within 6 to 10 years. Today, most sales are still made in person—partly because people want to see, touch, and drive the cars. Yet Sue Unger reports that 90 percent of buyers use the Internet for research before shopping (Gibson 2004).

Although DaimlerChrysler is using incentives to try and gain market share for its primary models, Mitsubishi Motors is being hammered in the market. Their sales approach in 2002 did not help—when the company targeted first-time young buyers with a zero-zero-zero campaign. Essentially, even poorly qualified buyers could get new cars with nothing down and no payments for one year. Unfortunately, most of the cars had to be repossessed at the end of the year. In 2004, Mitsubishi tried to recapture market share through marketing. This time with a new twist—a return to Internet advertising. In 2001, the company abandoned Web ads as nonproductive. In 2004, the company is spending $6 million on the Web alone. DaimlerChrysler increased its Web spending by 30 percent in 2003 (Mangalindan 2004). Although the Mitsubishi campaign represents only 5 percent of its total advertising, the company believes the Web ads are more effective than other approaches. The key: targeted ads and quick ties to dealers. Tom Buczkowski of Silver Creek, New York, is one who responded to the new approach. Researching SUVs at the Autobytel site, he was presented with an ad from Mitsubishi. By signing up for a test drive, he won a $15 gas card. At the Mitsubishi site, he built a customized Outlander. The details and the personal data he entered were sent to the nearest dealer in minutes. The next day, the dealer called him and suggested a test drive. Mr. Buczkowski was impressed with the response. "If you get a response from somebody a day after the request, that's something you don't find too often anywhere else." He eventually bought a Mitsubishi.

Questions

1. How do integrated design systems solve typical problems that arise?

2. Check out the Web sites by the automobile manufacturers. Why are they so bad? As a customer, what additional features would you want to see?

Additional Reading

Gibson, Stan. "DaimlerChrysler CIO on the Road to IT Success." *eWeek,* May 3, 2004.

Mangalindan, Mylene. "After Wave of Disappointments, the Web Lures Back Advertisers." *The Wall Street Journal,* February 25, 2004

Niccolai, James. "DaimlerChrysler Sees Savings in RFID Tags." *Computerworld,* March 17, 2004.

Taylor III, Alex. "Detroit Buffs Up." *Fortune,* February 9, 2004.

Summary Industry Questions

1. What information technologies have helped this industry?

2. Did the technologies provide a competitive advantage or were they quickly adopted by rivals?

3. Which technologies could this industry use that were developed in other sectors?

4. Is the level of competition increasing or decreasing in this industry? Is it dominated by a few firms, or are they fairly balanced?

5. What problems have been created from the use of information technology and how did the firms solve the problems?

CHAPTER EIGHT

Electronic Business

Chapter Outline

Introduction

The Production Chain
  Disintermediation
  Business to Consumer
  Business to Business

Increasing Sales and Reducing Costs
  Prepurchase, Purchase, and Postpurchase Support
  Search Engines
  Traditional Media and Name Recognition
  Web Advertisements
  Web Site Traffic Analysis
  Privacy

e-Commerce Options
  Simple Static HTML
  Single-Unit Sales
  Web Commerce Servers
  Web Hosting Options
  Content Management Systems

Mobile Commerce

Taxes

Global Economy

Analysis of Dot-Com Failures
  Pure Internet Plays
  Profit Margins
  Advertising Revenue

Summary

Key Words

Web Site References

Additional Reading

Review Questions

Exercises

Cases: Entrepreneurship

What You Will Learn in This Chapter

- Should you move more business to the Internet? How can you use electronic business to increase sales and reduce costs?

- Why would you want to shift sales to the Internet? What problems might arise?

- How do you use the Internet to market goods and services?

- How do you create an EC Web site?

- How do portable Internet connections (mobile phones) provide new ways to sell things?

- When do consumers and businesses pay sales taxes on the Internet?

- Does the Internet create a global marketplace?

- Why did thousands of dot-com firms fail?

How can small firms use the Internet to improve their business? Petz Enterprises in Tracy, California, is a family-run company that specializes in income taxes. The company became a leader in providing software to professional accounting firms and storefront tax offices. The tax-accounting staff at Petz keeps up with the hundreds of tax-code changes made by the federal and state governments. It then writes the rules that compute the taxes and print the forms. As a closely held company, Petz does not report its financial data.

With the growth of the Internet, Leroy Petz, Sr., decided that the firm had to expand and create a system that could be used directly by individuals. The initial TaxBrain site attracted several respondents in the first two years. After it was given a substantial facelift, and backed by online advertising, the site became the third most popular tax site on the Internet. TaxBrain faces some serious competition with the well-known brands of H&R Block and TurboTax (Intuit).

Entrepreneurship, the development of new firms, is an idea that floats in the minds of many businesspeople. In 2003, over 500,000 new firms were started. On the other hand, almost the same number of firms were closed in the same time period. The Small Business Administration (SBA) reports that about two-thirds of new employer firms survive at least two years. Fifty percent survive past four years (Bounds 2004).

Information technology plays an important role in many small firms—because entrepreneurs need higher productivity. The Internet in some ways makes it easier to start or expand a business. In other ways, it increases the marketing and technical costs. And the Internet is certainly no guarantee of profits or success.

Introduction

Should you move more business to the Internet? How can you use electronic business to increase sales and reduce costs? In the late 1990s, the early days of the Web when millions of people first went online, thousands of companies were created to sell items on the Internet. Figure 8.1 shows some of the ways you can use the Internet in business. Billions of investment dollars were spent by these firms developing new ways to conduct business on the Internet. Some managers loudly proclaimed the dawn of the "new economy" and the death of "bricks-and-mortar" companies. In 2000 and 2001, many of these firms crashed. Some managers then proclaimed the Internet dead. Yet from the beginnings in the mid-1990s, sales using the Internet have increased—in most cases faster than retail sales in general. Likewise, new opportunities for sales between businesses and entirely new business opportunities are being created. The initial "irrational exuberance" (Alan Greenspan's term) and consequent crash highlight the importance of carefully addressing the question: exactly how can you use electronic business to make money? Wrong answers can be costly on both sides: wasting money on hopeless schemes or losing money by not using the Internet.

What is electronic business? E-commerce, or EC, can be hard to define. On the one hand, it could be defined as selling items on the Internet. But there are many aspects to business and many ways of using Internet technologies. Some writers refer to the broader concept as *e-business.* The main point is that EC represents considerably more functions than just putting up a Web site to describe or sell products. The fundamental goal of e-business is to increase sales and reduce costs by improving relationships with existing customers, and by reaching new customers and providing new services.

TRENDS

Largely because of transportation costs, consumers have been limited to purchasing products through local retail stores. Even for products produced elsewhere, it was generally cheaper to ship items in bulk to the retailer than to ship to individual customers. Plus, manufacturers and wholesalers did not want to deal with individual customers. They did not want to spend the money to create customer-service departments to handle thousands or millions of individual orders, returns, and complaints.

Eventually, shipping and transaction costs began to decline. Sears got its start and made its original reputation as a nationwide mail-order firm. Customers could now order thousands of products from a catalog and have them delivered. Over time, Sears found it profitable to build stores in thousands of cities and moved away from catalog sales. In the 1980s and 1990s, many other mail-order firms expanded to provide thousands of products direct from the manufacturer to the customer. While some people prefer shopping this way, only a fraction of total sales are made through mail-order companies. In 1998, mail-order sales were $356 billion, or slightly over 3 percent of GDP.

Around 1997, sales over the Internet started to become important, and by 1999, e-commerce was the hot topic in the nation. By 2001, over 50 percent of U.S. households had access to the Internet and e-commerce, promising access to millions of customers. Hundreds of dot-com firms were funded with venture capital and early IPOs to define new ways to interact with customers and businesses over the Internet. Hundreds of paper billionaires were created as stock prices were driven by expectations and hype. Some people were saying that bricks-and-mortar traditional firms were dead. But in late 2000 and early 2001, hundreds of the dot-com start-ups failed, laying off thousands of workers and crashing the technology sector of the stock market. Investors are wary, but the Internet continues.

Cell phones began with slow, poor quality analog signals that were gradually replaced with the second generation digital phones by 2000. The third generation wireless phone will handle data and Internet access as well as voice. Portable data access can create new opportunities in mobile commerce to improve contact with customers. Entirely new applications can evolve from virtually immediate contact.

FIGURE 8.1

Electronic commerce: The Internet is commonly used for sales from business to business and from business to consumer. Salespeople can use it to collect data and communicate with clients and the main offices. New Web-based businesses are being created to provide data and services.

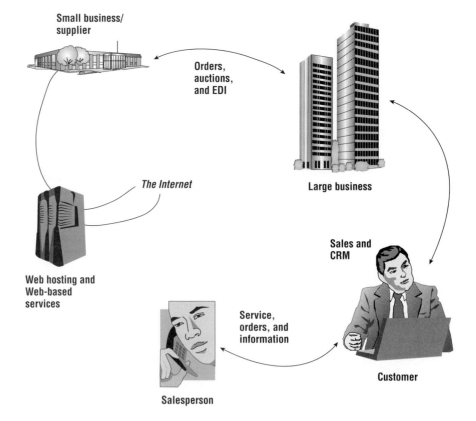

For at least the past 50 years, companies have followed and refined the modern business practices. These **business-to-consumer (B2C)** foundations were created to facilitate purchasing and distribution in a world with limited delivery systems and high communication costs. When the Internet changes these conditions, eventually the underlying structure will change. For example, retail stores for decades were small local firms where owners recog-

REALITY BYTES   How Can You Make Money Online?

"[People] are not paying for content for content's sake. To be able to charge, you need a service that's radically easier, faster and more fun than if it were free." Craig Sherman, chief marketing officer at MyFamily.com, Inc., a genealogy site, has derived a method for making money selling digital content on the Internet. In general, people are still reluctant to pay for basic information. On the other hand, sales of online content are increasing. The Online Publishers Association estimates that U.S. customers spent about $1.6 billion for online content in 2003, up from $1.3 billion in 2002. Much of the content is highly specialized: baseball games from distant cities, detailed product reviews from ConsumerReports.org, business news from *The Wall Street Journal,* or the contact information for a prospective

date on Match.com. *The Wall Street Journal Online* had 689,000 paying subscribers at the end of 2003.

Surprisingly, some sites have been successful selling news. ABC News and CNN charge for video content. ABC News saw subscriptions increase by 15 percent in 2003. Bernard Gershon, a senior vice president at ABCNews.com, observes that "you can't get high-quality news and video content on a PC unless you pay." There are many hurdles in selling digital content, including attracting customers, determining how much to charge, and minimizing customer churn. But sites are increasingly using subscriptions as an important source of revenue.

Source: Adapted from Michael Totty, "Making Them Pay," *The Wall Street Journal,* March 22, 2004.

FIGURE 8.2

E-commerce categories: E-commerce can be considered in the four categories shown. However, B2B and B2C are far more prevalent than consumer-led initiatives.

	Business	**Consumer**
Business	B2B	B2C
	EDI Commodity auctions	Consumer-oriented Sales Support
Consumer	C2B	C2C
	Minimal examples, possibly reverse auctions like PriceLine or contract employees sites	Auction sites (eBay), but many of these are dominated by small business sales

nized customer trends and ordered a specific mix of products. Wal-Mart took advantage of size in purchasing and distribution to create giant retail stores with a relatively standard mix of products. Theoretically, the Internet could bypass the retail stores completely. Mobile commerce offers even more potential to alter our existing economic institutions. Who needs credit cards and banks when all transactions are handled through your cell phone?

On the business side, just-in-time inventory and EDI were only the beginning of a revolution in changing the ordering systems of manufacturers. Electronic marketplaces and auctions enable businesses to find new suppliers and obtain supplies on short notice. Sellers can find new customers and negotiate prices without expensive sales visits.

You should remember one important point: EC is not just an issue with new firms. In many ways, existing firms have the most to gain from EC, because they can leverage their existing strengths. **Business to business (B2B)** is also critical for existing firms because it can reduce costs and provide new options to managing purchases. Finally, the interactive aspects of EC will become increasingly useful for intranets to improve internal operations and facilitate human resources management.

Figure 8.2 shows a broader classification of e-commerce that includes B2B and B2C as well as consumer-led initiatives. The consumer issues C2B and C2C make up a minor portion of e-commerce. It is not even clear that good examples of these categories exist. Some (e.g., *The Economist*) have suggested that PriceLine might represent a C2B perspective because it relies on a reverse auction technique, where customers enter a price and the "vendor" selects the highest offers. Although the auction method is slightly unusual, the effect of businesses offering products or services is not really any different from traditional commerce. A few employee contracting sites have arisen—particularly for programmers. Companies can post individual jobs, and workers can bid for them. Similarly, the job search sites might loosely be considered as C2B.

As for C2C, many writers place consumer auction sites like eBay in this category. While some of these auctions are consumer-to-consumer items, look carefully and you will see that many of the items are offered by small businesses or entrepreneurs. Many small firms, particularly those selling electronic items, use eBay to auction items in short supply or to sell a few items on a regular basis.

The entire world changes when commerce systems change. But will the economy really change that far? Did the mass failure of the EC firms in 2000 and 2001 really mean that consumers prefer the traditional systems? These are the questions that make life fun and add the risk to entrepreneurship. You must understand the fundamentals before you can create your own answers to these puzzles and help shape the future of business.

The Production Chain

Why would you want to shift sales to the Internet? What problems might arise? To understand the issues in EC, you must first understand the production chain. Shown in Figure 8.3, the strategic effects are important to EC. One of the key aspects in B2C e-commerce is the ability to bypass entire sections of the production chain. Consider the situation of airlines. In the 1960s and 1970s, airlines created giant reservation systems to handle flight bookings. The system consisted of the airlines' massive central computers and databases and travel agent terminals connected by a custom network. It was too expensive for customers to connect directly. Also, the systems were hard to use and travel agents needed special training. Agents were paid a commission based on the value of the flights booked through the reservation system paid by the airlines. With the advent of frequent-flyer miles, airlines encouraged consumers to book flights with the airline itself, bypassing the travel agent and saving the cost of the commission. But it is difficult to search for flights using the telephone. The Internet changed everything. Several travel sites and the airline sites them-

FIGURE 8.3

Production chain: The production chain is important to EC because EC offers the ability to skip elements of the chain. It also makes it easier to reach new customers at any level in the chain.

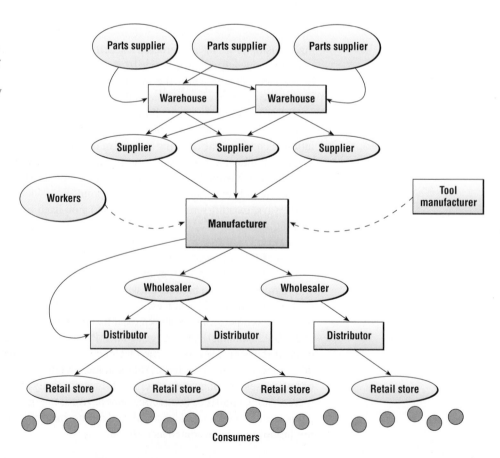

FIGURE 8.4

Disintermediation: The traditional production chain evolved because separate firms provided specialized functions more efficiently. E-commerce reduces costs and has the potential to circumvent various intermediaries. But disintermediation is a risky strategy.

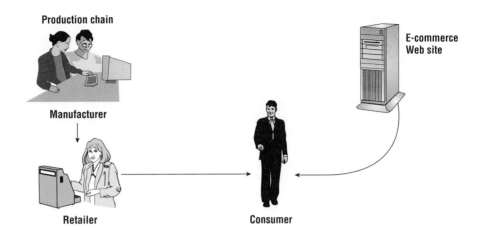

selves make it easy to find flights, compare prices, and purchase a ticket any time of day without the assistance of an overworked travel agent or salesperson. Tickets are merely electronic reservation numbers, where you simply show appropriate identification at the airport. On the production chain, the airlines (as service providers) bypassed the intermediaries to sell directly to the consumer—a process known as **disintermediation.**

A similar process can occur on the supplier side. Instead of wholesalers, purchasing agents and suppliers are forming B2B auction sites. Companies can sell or buy products and materials on a variety of Web sites. Instead of searching out buyers or sellers, businesses simply submit a bid on a Web site that covers the desired product.

Disintermediation

Today, it is rare for a company to be vertically integrated across the production chain. For example, most manufacturers rely on other firms to handle distribution and retail sales. In a sense, they choose to outsource these functions because of the costs. Over the last 50 years or so, firms have worked to become more efficient within their niche. As shown in Figure 8.4, e-commerce has the potential to change these relationships. By reducing the costs of dealing with individual customers, it becomes possible for firms to circumvent the retailers and sell directly to the end consumer. Since retail price markups can be in the range of 100 percent, the manufacturer has a strong incentive to sell directly to the public to capture some of this additional profit.

However, particularly in these early days of e-commerce, many manufacturers are reluctant to remove the retail role. Taking sales away from the established retail channel could alienate the retailers, who are currently responsible for almost all of the sales. If retailers decide to drop your product, and consumers are slow to switch to direct purchases, you may lose the market.

Interrelationship with the existing retail distribution channel is a critical factor in any e-commerce strategy. Removing an intermediary can increase your profits and can be used to reduce prices to capture more market share. But is the intermediary a critical component? Will your sales remain if you remove it? Are customers ready to switch to direct purchases? Some firms attempt to do both: keep sales through traditional channels and also provide direct e-commerce sales through a Web site. But they minimize competition and appease the retailers by charging the suggested retail price on the Web site. So, consumers can often find the product cheaper at a local store—which is willing to offer a discount on the list price.

In some situations, the reliance on the retail channel leads to strange conclusions. In early 2001, Compaq was producing a popular PDA with a color screen. But Compaq had trouble with production and demand was substantially higher than supply. Consequently, few retailers carried the product. Some of the businesses that were able to obtain the product did not bother to sell it at their local stores. Instead, they auctioned the units individually on eBay for several hundred dollars over the list price. Would Compaq have been better off auctioning the PDAs directly to consumers?

REALITY BYTES   Vendor Beware

Victoria Esposito owns an online computer-parts service company. In September 2001, someone placed an order for $11,000 of parts. She ran the order through the antifraud system provided by the card issuer: Capital One Financial Corporation. Initially, the system flagged the order saying that the destination address did not match the cardholder's address. Ms. Esposito called Capital One, and the credit card company told her the block was removed and she was free to ship the order. Ms. Esposito says she asked if there were any other warning signs and was told of no problems. After shipping the order, two weeks later, Capitol One told her the purchase was fraudulent and she would be charged for the entire loss! Ms. Esposito threatened the company with arbitration and says she no longer accepts cards from Capitol One. Capitol One issued a statement saying: "Understanding these risks, it was her choice to determine whether to process an order based on the information she had." It could have been worse. Credit card companies generally charge

merchants additional fees from $10 to $100 per transaction that is challenged by the cardholder. It is estimated that the card companies earn a total of $500 million a year from these fees. Several merchants have accused card companies of being lax on fraud and simply passing the costs back to merchants. Merchants often raise their prices to compensate. Online fraud is a growing problem since 25 percent of credit card charges are through mail-order or Internet sales where all risks are borne by the vendor. On the Web, 2.1 percent of total sales are fraudulent, versus 0.1 percent with traditional purchases. Visa and MasterCard are working on new programs ("Verified by Visa" and "MasterCard SecureCode") that will require customers to enter passwords for online transactions. However, it is not clear whether customers will adopt these cards.

Source: Adapted from Paul Beckett and Jathon Sapsford, "Tussle Over Who Pays for Credit-Card Theft," *The Wall Street Journal,* May 1, 2003.

Business to Consumer

When asked about e-commerce, most people think of B2C. We are all consumers, and it is easy to think about purchasing products and services over the Internet. But how is e-commerce different from traditional sales methods? And is it so different that consumers will not use it?

A couple of simple rules dominate marketing. First, consumers prefer instant gratification. Given a choice, with everything else equal, consumers will choose the product at hand over one that will be delivered later. Related to this rule, consumers will often buy items on impulse—simply because they are available and enticing. Second, consumers will prefer to pay a lower total price. While this rule seems obvious, it can be difficult in practice. Consumers need to know that the products being compared are equal. They need to know what other products or suppliers exist and their prices. And they need to be able to compare total prices (including taxes and transportation). Third, consumers prefer to see and touch many products before they buy them. The real challenge in marketing is analyzing the trade-offs when all conditions are not equal.

Ultimately, B2C e-commerce is relatively complex and needs to be evaluated in three major areas: (1) traditional products, (2) digital products, and (3) new services. Each of these issues has different features and different interactions with consumers and EC.

Products

In many ways, traditional products are the least likely to be successful in e-commerce—at least initially. Consider the four basic items on which people spend most of their income: food, clothing, shelter, and transportation. Distribution is the most critical issue with food. In the 1960s, when people lived closer together in central cities and small towns, neighborhood grocery stores provided basic food items within a short distance of many people. Yet these stores were inefficient because they could stock only a limited number of common items; and the delivery and inventory costs were high. Ultimately, large grocery chains that used their size to hold down costs, provide a large selection, and negotiate favorable terms with suppliers replaced the local stores. Consumers had to travel farther to these new stores, but they were more than willing to accept the distance to reduce costs. Small local stores were driven out. The two initial leading firms to sell groceries over the Internet were Peapod and Webvan. Customers place orders on the Web site and drivers drop off the purchases at a scheduled time, usually the next day. Customers pay a delivery charge for the service. Neither company was very successful in terms of profits. The increased costs, delivery time, and lack of ability to touch the items discourage customers.

A second way to look at EC and food is to realize that few families cook their own meals. Takeout from a variety of restaurants and even grocery stores is a popular substitute. Many restaurants—particularly pizzerias—deliver food on short notice with just a phone call. Would there be a reason to convert the phone system to an Internet connection? A few places do this, but many people still prefer phones. Theoretically, the Internet can provide menus and it is better at handling multiple customers at the same time. Furthermore, it could be used to provide feedback to the consumer—in terms of status of the order and when it will be delivered. But most restaurants are small businesses, and they have resisted building the infrastructure to provide these features.

Clothing offers more prospects for e-commerce. Selection is always an issue with local stores. No matter how large the store, it can carry only a small, targeted selection of styles and sizes. And larger selection means greater inventory costs. So, there might be room for an EC firm to sell a wide selection of products across the nation. In fact, several catalog mail-order firms concentrate on these markets. These mail-order companies have also been relatively successful at e-commerce. The one problem is that clothing sizes are not quite standardized. Hence, many shoppers—particularly women—prefer to try on clothing before purchasing it. Some leading sites like Lands' End have implemented electronic virtual models that enable customers to select items and see how they might look. But many people prefer touching the individual garments first. In fact, some manufacturers have sophisticated Web sites to display products, but direct interested consumers to local merchants instead of trying to complete the sale online.

Finding a home is always a difficult task. A medium-size city might have thousands of homes for sale at one point in time. It is hard to find and compare all of the details. The Internet has helped in some respects. Searching is an important strength of the Internet. Several real estate databases exist online to retrieve house listings based on a variety of items. However, almost no one would buy a house without seeing it in person; so the role of the Internet in this context is limited. At first glance, it would seem that real estate might be a prime opportunity for e-commerce. Real estate commissions are often priced at 6 percent of the sale price, which can be a high value for expensive houses. So there should be strong incentives for disintermediation—removing the commissioned agent from the middle of the transaction. But buyers often prefer to use agents, and agents control most of the existing online real estate search firms.

Transportation is more interesting because it can be a product (automobile) or a service (airplane or subway ticket). Airlines have done well with direct e-commerce sales. Yes, they have offended the traditional distribution channel (travel agents), but the people who travel the most have been willing to purchase tickets directly to save money and gain control over their choices.

Automobiles are more interesting. Few people are willing to buy new automobiles over the Internet, but Web sites offering searches for specific used cars are popular. Part of the difference is that consumers have greater bargaining power with used automobiles than with new ones, so the increased information on available cars gives them more leverage. If one owner or dealer offers a high price for a specific car, you can quickly find another one. New cars are more challenging because of the strong relationship between the few manufacturers and the dealers.

Most people want to test-drive a car before they buy it, so the manufacturers have a strong incentive to keep the dealer network. Many insiders also believe that the salesperson is critical to selling cars, by overcoming objections and talking people into buying cars when they hesitate. So, if dealers and showrooms are necessary, what is the value of e-commerce in selling a car? Both General Motors and Ford have experimented with online sales of new cars, with minimal success. Currently, the auto manufacturers prefer to sell through the dealers. A few states actually have laws that prohibit auto manufacturers from selling directly to the public. While the manufacturers want to keep the advantages of the dealers, they also want to find a more efficient method to distribute cars. Manufacturers have talked about an Internet-based build-to-order system, where customers could select options and cars would be made to order. A few larger regional dealers would maintain basic inventory to support test-drives. The advantage of this system would be to reduce inventories and

REALITY BYTES | FreshDirect, a New Online Grocer

Webvan blew through $2 billion in investor money without coming close to a profit. Peapod did not do much better. Grocery store chains Albertson's, Safeway, and Dutch Ahold now dominate the online grocery industry. That is no surprise since they dominate the bricks-and-mortar world. The online grocery sector is estimated at $1.6 billion a year in sales, but it is unlikely that any of these firms are making profits. The grocery stores fill orders by having clerks pick items off the shelves. They hope to cover their costs by charging delivery fees, perhaps a time saver for today's busy worker, but hardly a road to profitability.

FreshDirect, led by CEO Joe Fedele and chairman Jim Manzi (former CEO of Lotus Development), is following a radically different path. Located in New York City and focused solely on high-density areas, the company has rebuilt the grocery concept from the ground up. Running from a 300,000-square-foot facility in Queens, the company begins by purchasing directly from growers and butchers. Everything is made-to-order on the day it is needed. At midnight, orders from the Web are consolidated and routed to individual departments. The coffee shop knows exactly how many beans to roast, the baker how many cakes or quiches to make. A six-mile automated conveyor-belt system collects the individual items in bins controlled by bar codes and routes the final collections to the delivery points. Food is kept optimally fresh and customers are steered away from packaged goods to the fresh items and prepared meals where the margins are higher.

The company has the capacity to turn out as many as 20,000 orders a day and currently handles about 3,300 orders for 150,000 customers. But with an average order of almost $100, it sells about as much as two large supermarkets. The astounding difference is that it uses only one-fifth the inventory, and its perishable items inventory turns 197 times a year—compared to 40 at a typical supermarket. The company is close to profitability, but needs more volume. The entire concept at FreshDirect represents a major change in the grocery industry.

Source: Adapted from Erick Schonfeld, "The Big Cheese of Online Grocers," *Business 2.0,* February 2004.

---

enable manufacturers to build only the number of cars that are needed. The main drawback is the difficulty in configuring assembly lines quickly enough to hold costs down.

On the other hand, used cars present a different situation. Buyers have embraced the Internet as a method to locate used cars and compare prices. Sellers find it a useful tool to avoid the high prices of newspaper advertising—particularly since it is inexpensive to place photos on Web sites.

The point of these examples is that without substantial changes in behavior, people will continue to prefer the traditional sales mechanisms—particularly since these mechanisms have proven to be relatively efficient or are closely controlled by a group with a strong interest in maintaining the current system.

So, is the world really so bleak that B2C e-commerce is doomed to fail? What about Amazon.com, one of the larger retailers on the Internet? By selling commodities, they avoid the problem of choosing products. The latest best-selling novel is the same regardless of where it is purchased, so consumers do not need to see and touch it before purchasing it. Besides, Amazon.com can offer a wide selection of titles. It can also make it easier to find books and does a good job offering related products that might interest the consumer. But the concept is still hobbled by the distribution problem—it takes time to deliver a book or CD to the customer. So, online vendors like Amazon.com compensate by offering lower base prices than those found at a traditional local store. Consumers then have the choice of paying a higher price to obtain an item immediately, or waiting and paying a slightly lower price through EC. But can an EC firm make a profit with this model? To date, the answer has been no. Amazon.com, struggling to reduce costs, is slowly adopting many of the features of a traditional local store—minimize inventory by focusing on best sellers, and raise prices to a break-even point.

Internet EC Features

To find successful B2C strategies, you need to look at the features that the Internet provides that are superior to traditional stores. The most important ones are the (1) search technologies, (2) ability to quickly compare multiple products and vendors, (3) low costs for large amounts of information, (4) ability to reach a wide audience, and (5) ability to tailor responses to individual customers.

The essence of a profitable Web site for products is to identify items that can benefit most from these features. For example, specialty products can be hard to find. A few firms

REALITY BYTES   Return of Web Advertising

In the early days of the dot-com boom, many firms survived by selling advertising on their sites. Most of the ads were banner ads, which later evolved into pop-up ads. Then, the market crashed, and advertising dried up. Actually, advertising in the print world slowed substantially at the same time. Today, many of the advertisers are returning to the Internet—hopefully with more realistic expectations. Online advertising spending in 2003 was up 20 percent at $7.2 billion, which is still slightly below the $8.1 billion peak in 2000. Mitsubishi is a classic example. In 2001, the company abandoned Web advertising as wasteful. In 2004, despite declining sales and U.S. layoffs, the firm expanded its Web advertising—because it has found online ads to be effective at guiding surfers to the showroom. One of the keys is that Web advertisers have found ways to use the Internet to connect more closely with customers—including convincing them to part with their name and address. Brian Meehana, a Huffy Sports spokesman, notes the advantages: "You can build a relationship, ask them questions, have a back-and-forth [with consumers]. It's the

only medium you can do that in." Mitsubishi learned that the key is to get dealers to respond quickly to inquiries. Surfers who sign up for information have the data routed to the nearest dealer via e-mail. If the salesperson calls within a few hours, customers are more likely to respond. The only question is why it took them so long to figure that out.

Another important change in Web advertising revolves around the search engines. Google makes it easy for companies to "buy" key words. When a customer searches for a particular word or phrase, an ad is displayed on the right side of the results. Since the results and ad match the searcher's topic, surfers are more likely to click the ad. Similarly, auto manufacturers like Mitsubishi are finding that many customers are using the Internet automobile sites for research, and ads tied to those sites generate responses.

Source: Adapted from Mylene Mangalindan, "After Wave of Disappointments, the Web Lures Back Advertisers," *The Wall Street Journal,* February 25, 2004.

could reach a national audience using EC and capture most of the market by being easy to find and offering competitive prices.

Another approach is to offer products with many options that require customization. Dell has been successful at selling computers over the Internet by making it easy to configure and compare prices, and by using modern production technologies to hold costs down so that the EC solution highlights their prices.

Digital Products

Digital products are a field where e-commerce will eventually dominate. Already, many products are stored in digital format: music, news, books, movies, software, and games. In late 2000, many consumers found how easy it was to distribute digital music over the Internet using MP3 files and Napster—even though it was illegal. Digital content over EC meets two of the main consumer criteria: it is instantly available at any time, and costs should be lower since distribution costs are small. Furthermore, digital content is more portable than traditional CDs, DVDs, and books.

The main challenge to digital content revolves around intellectual property rights and laws. Digital content can be easy to copy and redistribute—depriving the owners (artists) of any reward. The risk is that free distribution of digital content would remove all incentive for artists and authors to invest time for which they receive nothing.

Several companies (particularly Microsoft and RealNetworks) are working on digital rights management systems to prevent unauthorized copying. Microsoft and Adobe both have systems in place for books. Most systems take advantage of the Internet. When a consumer purchases a digital product online, the purchase is recorded in a digital rights management server and issued a unique ID. From this point, the systems vary. Some work by periodically checking the Internet server as the product is used to verify that it is an authorized copy. In some systems, the generated ID can only work on the computer for which it was first created, so giving the file to someone else does not allow it to be played or viewed. Some systems enable users to transfer rights to another person; others do not.

Another challenge with digital products is the payment mechanism. The transaction costs on credit cards and checks are too high to enable low-price purchases, such as buying one song for a few cents. Until micro payment systems become accepted, it is difficult for sites to charge for content. Currently, subscriptions are the most common solution. One of the more successful sites is *The Wall Street Journal,* which charges an annual subscription fee to several hundred thousand subscribers. And even the *Journal* admits that it has

Technology Toolbox: Using Commerce Server Software

Problem: How do you quickly create an e-commerce Web site?

Tools: Several companies offer commerce server packages that enable you to set up and manage the major aspects of e-commerce. One readily available tool is Microsoft's Commerce Server. Commerce server software handles most aspects of the Web site, including a catalog management system for products, Web page creation, and a shopping cart for purchases. The system is designed to handle the most difficult Web site problems: high performance, scalability, and security. Specialist programmers designed the system to large numbers of simultaneous users. The system also handles multiple languages, currencies, tax rates, and shipping methods.

However, commerce server systems are not completely automatic. You must configure the system to establish your Web page style. You must also load and manage the catalog database. Microsoft has simplified some of these tasks by creating templates of commonly used sites. For example, you can load a retail Web site template and simply customize it for your business. Loading the catalog is relatively straightforward, but it takes time to enter data for all of the products. It takes even longer when you have to enter data in multiple languages. You can also extend your Web site by linking each product to additional information. For instance, you might include stories or pictures on how some customers used the products in the prior year. These stories or articles can encourage customers to find new applications for your products. The system can store customer data so that they can see their prior orders and save shipping addresses. With some additional programming, pages can be customized for individual users or groups of customers.

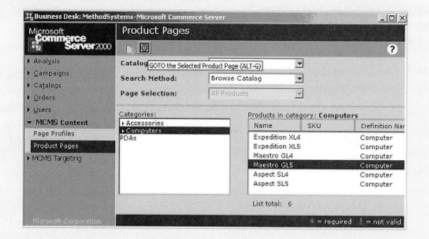

Analyzing sales data and evaluating customers are other important features offered by the commerce server software. In addition to typical Web logs, the system can show sales of products by category, type of customer, and time of day or week. Using the data, you can create marketing campaigns targeted to specific groups of customers or based on product categories.

The systems are extensible and can be programmed to interact with your back-end order fulfillment systems or with your internal product databases. At heart, the systems provide the functionality you need in an EC Web site with optimized software that can scale up to meet huge customer loads. Yet the system can be customized to meet the individual needs of each company. The drawback: price. As you scale up, you need to purchase additional software licenses. At an initial cost of around $5,000, the software is affordable for many situations. Even scaling up, it is probably cheaper than paying developers to build a similar system, but you should make a realistic evaluation of all costs before you purchase commerce software because it will be difficult to change the software later.

Quick Quiz:

1. Why is it better to purchase software than to create your own?
2. What main features do you want in a B2C website?
3. What detailed data do you want to examine in an e-commerce site?

difficulty preventing people from paying for one subscription and sharing it (although that would be in violation of the subscriber agreement.)

One difficulty with any protection system like the digital rights management schemes is that it is difficult to stop someone from breaking the system. Early software vendors in the 1980s learned the lesson that copy protection schemes were routinely defeated and removed. However, the digital millennium copyright act (DMCA) in the United States makes it illegal to break copy protection schemes. As a relatively new law, it remains to be seen whether this condition can be enforced. Also, the law does not apply to people outside the United States. DVD vendors pursued this issue in 2000 and 2001 when a group broke the encryption scheme used to slightly protect DVD movies. The Motion Picture Association of America (MPAA) has sued several companies in the United States for even linking to sites that list the decode algorithm, but the code remains on thousands of sites around the world. A major question exists in terms of whether copy protection schemes can survive.

New Services

Another way to look at e-commerce—particularly m-commerce—is to think about potentially new services that can exist only with the Internet or wireless technologies. For example, GM has been fairly successful with its OnStar system, which is essentially a wireless communication system from cars to a central service site. This new service helps sell cars, and it could not exist without current technologies.

Some Web sites are actually services in disguise. For example, 1800flowers sells flowers, but the company does not grow or ship the flowers. It contracts all of the details to other firms. What the main site really does is keep track of special event days, such as birthdays and anniversaries. It basically provides a reminder service and makes it easy to order products corresponding to those dates. Hundreds of other service-oriented sites exist, such as the ability to send greeting cards, share photographs, and file complaints about other companies.

The challenge with consumer-oriented service sites is to make money. The choices are (1) charge for the service, (2) sell related products, (3) sell advertising space, and (4) sell the service to another company. Many of the failed dot-coms chose option three. When the advertising market crashed, they could not cover their costs and went out of business. Option four is discussed in the B2B section. Selling related products is probably the easiest solution today. In this case, the service is simply another feature that will attract customers to your site. But the additional costs can make it harder to compete on the basis of price, so you have to be certain that customers really do value the service. The ability to charge for services is a significant obstacle to this type of e-commerce. M-commerce offers a greater potential. People are accustomed to paying for usage of their cell phone time. Also, the billing system is in place to handle relatively small transactions (less than a dollar). So, as an example, it might be possible to have a restaurant reservation system on mobile phones. Customers select a range of restaurants—by location or type of food—and your system searches for the most available time slot. The restaurants might fund this service, or perhaps you could charge a fee to customers to move them higher onto a wait list if they are in a hurry.

Price Competition

A primary concern expressed by many firms investigating e-commerce is the issue of price. The Internet makes it easy for people to search vendors and compare prices. This process is particularly easy for products that are the same (such as books, videos, and electronic equipment). Consequently, merchants are concerned that people will compare sites based only on price. Availability of the item will also make a difference. For example, check out the search agent on CNET (www.cnet.com) that displays prices and availability for a variety of electronic products.

Why are merchants concerned about price competition? First, the existing retail product chain was originally created so that retail outlets could provide personalized service and product information to customers. Vendors survived and grew based on their ability to provide customized information and support to local areas. Competing purely on price and availability changes the rules and requires a different type of merchant system. Second, if customers look only at price and availability, it is easy for a new firm to enter the market. The new firm simply slashes prices and sells products at a loss to attract customers. Of course, in the long run, the firm will fail—but so will the other firms. We could be good economists and assume that managers and owners are intelligent and will eventually learn to charge a price that does provide a profit. But it might take time for this new economy to evolve. This fear of irrational firms does have an element of truth. Amazon gained its market position primarily by offering substantial discounts on books. In fact, Amazon's finance officer made the remark in 2000 that he was surprised people were criticizing Amazon for not making a profit. He said that Amazon never intended to make a profit on sales. However, after the crash in e-commerce stock prices, Amazon has worked harder to cut costs.

Initially, the largest impact of Internet price competition will be on the retail firms. By minimizing the aspect of location, the primary strength of local firms is eroded. If customers are willing to wait for products to be delivered, then there is no longer a point in having thousands of small local stores. But that "if" is huge. The ultimate economy will depend on consumer preferences between price and the ability to receive a product immediately.

A few e-commerce firms have attempted to use the interactive features of the Internet to set prices dynamically. In an experiment, Amazon.com charged different prices to different customers. It was a relatively standard attempt to statistically evaluate price sensitivity to various products. However, when customers learned that others had obtained the same product for a lower price, they complained. Yet in traditional stores, customers routinely are charged different prices for the same items—for example, through coupons or negotiation. As shown in Figure 8.5, part of the fear is that the Internet might someday be used to force people to pay the highest amount they are willing to pay, as opposed to perfect competition price.

Business to Business

Business-to-business e-commerce has the potential to be substantially more important than B2C e-commerce. First, businesses tend to buy repeat items in bulk, so they do not need to test-drive or touch every product. Second, medium and large businesses already have high-speed connections to the Internet and rely on computer systems in their daily operations. Third, costs are becoming a driving factor, and technology can reduce the transaction costs and the number of errors.

Extended EDI

By simply offering the ability to sell products to other businesses, the Internet can be used for EDI. For materials and components that are purchased on a regular basis, EDI software can connect across the Internet to automatically monitor inventory and send orders to the appropriate company. For less frequent purchases, a buying firm could set up software to scan servers for prices, select the appropriate items, and place orders automatically.

Currently, few systems work this efficiently. Most require a human to collect data and place orders. Web sites make it easier to collect data on prices and availability, but every site has different search methods and different purchase screens. EDI software helps by following standards, but the companies involved must install and configure it.

XML is a more flexible method of sharing data with suppliers and customers. Eventually, the technology can be married with expert systems to provide more automated intelligence to handle ordering basic items and to monitor the progress of standard orders.

FIGURE 8.5

Dynamic pricing: The ultimate goal is to set individual prices for each consumer to capture the maximum price each is willing to pay, as opposed to the perfect competition price, where everyone pays the same price and some customers gain because they were willing to pay more.

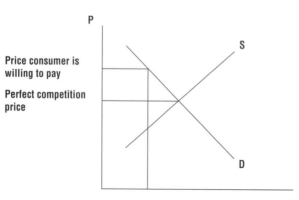

Auctions

From an economic perspective, B2B auctions are one of the most exciting tools created through e-commerce. In the past, companies purchased materials and supplies from a complex set of distributors and wholesalers, driven by in-person sales calls. Within this context, most manufacturers dealt with only one or two suppliers for each part. To hold down transaction costs, it was simpler to establish long-term relationships with a limited number of companies. Of course, it made it harder to ensure that the buyers were getting the best price. Competition helps hold down prices during the initial contract negotiations, but if anything changes in the ensuing year or two, it is difficult to renegotiate the contract. But in exchange, the buyer gains a more stable environment.

Economic theory shows that well-run auctions are the most efficient way to establish an efficient market price. To be well run, the auctions have to open to the widest range of participants, and everyone must have complete information on the items and prices. Several industry-specific auction sites have been established. One of the more successful sites involves the steel industry. Significant amounts of steel are still sold directly to manufacturers on long-term contracts. However, the auction sites make it easier for suppliers to unload specialty and overstocked inventory in a spot market. The auctions also give manufacturers the ability to monitor the spot market and availability of steel products, so that they can quickly pick up additional quantity.

For commodity items, auctions can hold down prices by improving competition and making price and quantity data available to all participants. Auctions are also useful for specialized products, when it is difficult to determine an asking price. Some companies have found that they can obtain higher prices for their products when they sell them at auction. Also, auction prices can change easily, so if there is a short-term jump in demand for your product, you will be able to capture the additional profit. Of course, you might have to accept lower prices the next day.

Distributed Services

XML is also creating opportunities for a new type of B2B e-commerce: Web sites that provide specific services that can be sold to other businesses. One example would be a Web site like Altavista (babel.altavista.com) that has an automated document translator. Figure 8.6 shows the basic concepts. The key is that the services are automated and simply called from your Web site. This arrangement is actually more of a peer-to-peer system than a client-server technology. You can create a Web site that uses services from many different companies. For example, you might create a Web site that pulls current stock price data from one site, performs some complex financial calculations on a second site, and converts currencies using a third site's exchange rates. All of these activities happen behind the page, so your users see only the final application.

The main advantage to this type of system is that experts can build objects and maintain and run the services on a Web site available to anyone willing to pay the service fee. In many

FIGURE 8.6

Distributed services: Firms can offer digital services over the Internet to other companies, such as document translation or reservation handling. With XML, the process is relatively automatic and can be billed for one-time and limited uses.

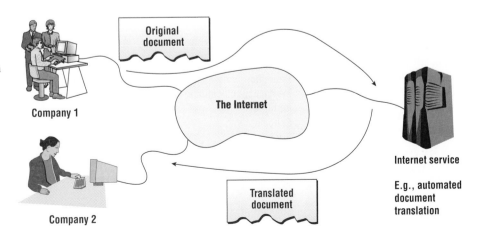

cases, the service fee could be a small per-usage value. So you could build a composite application that has state-of-the-art features and pay only for the actual usage of these features. The other alternative would be to license these technologies on an annual basis for a higher fee and run them on your own server, where you continually need to maintain and upgrade the services.

The technologies to support these services are still being developed. XML and the **simple object access protocol (SOAP)** are two important technologies. SOAP is a method of describing and activating services across the Internet. Ultimately, to make it easier to find services on the Internet, companies will want to register with a directory. IBM and Microsoft are pushing a directory called **universal description, discovery, and integration (UDDI)**. Details can be found at the www.uddi.org Web site. Registering a service makes it easier for other companies to find the service and connect to it.

Increasing Sales and Reducing Costs

How do you use the Internet to market goods and services? From a marketing perspective, the buying process has been defined in three basic steps: (1) prepurchase information gathering, (2) the purchase itself, and (3) postpurchase support. These steps are listed with examples in Figure 8.7. The Internet can support each of these areas. The level of support in each area depends on the industry, type of product, and capabilities of the customers. Note that the process differs depending on whether the customer is a retail consumer or another company. For example, sales to other companies are generally repetitive and typically require additional documentation and billing procedures.

Initially, basic servers simply presented static pages, with text and limited graphics that rarely changed. Even now, Network Solutions, the division of Verisign that handles site registrations, reports that over 90 percent of existing sites are only in the prepurchase phase. Gradually, more sophisticated services have been introduced that add a higher degree of interactivity. One of the most important features is the ability of the Web site to connect to the corporate databases.

Prepurchase, Purchase, and Postpurchase Support

In many ways, the purchase issue is a minor component. EC purchases currently offer only minor benefits compared to traditional phone orders. The main benefit to EC lies in providing additional support to customers before and after the sale. In particular, intelligent Web sites supported by expert systems can help customers select options and products or solve problems. For fixed development costs and relatively low monthly fees, the online systems can provide 24-hour support. Sales can be increased by providing more detailed information, helping customers customize their selections, and using an expert system to build cross sales. Costs are reduced because the system is automated. Sales and costs can

FIGURE 8.7

Electronic commerce: Web sites are commonly used to support the three main phases of marketing.

Prepurchase	Purchase	Postpurchase
Static data sites	Transmission security	Service
Promotion	User identification	Problem tracking
Product specifications	Product selection	Sales leads
Pictures	Payment validation	Resolve problems
Schematics	Order confirmation	Answer questions
Pricing		Product evaluation
FAQs		Modifications
Interactive sites		Tracking customers
Configuration		
Compatibility		
Complex pricing		

be further improved by providing after-sale support. Expert-system guided support can help customers solve problems faster. Any product design or production problems can be reported directly, giving you the chance to fix the product before it ships to more people.

Search Engines

Most people have used search engines to find information on the Internet. The searches are not always successful and tend to return a large number of sites unless the key words are specific and relatively unique. Nonetheless, search engines are an important method for potential customers to find your site.

One of your first objectives is to get your site listed and indexed on the major search engines. Each system uses a different process to search and categorize your site. All of the search engines have a Web page where you can register your Web site by entering the Internet address and a description of the purpose of the site. Eventually, your site will be added to the search engine list. Because of the human intervention, Yahoo is a minor exception. You can register with Yahoo, but it takes time for them to evaluate and classify your site. In some cases, they might choose to not list your site.

Some companies offer to register your Web site with the search engines for a fee. While this process might be convenient, it is rarely necessary. None of the search engines require a fee to register. The good search engines eventually find your site even if you do not register it at all. Some people claim to know tricks to make your page appear at the top of the search engine listings. Do not believe them. Read the Web site descriptions at the search sites for more useful advice. Basically, make sure your main page contains a precise description of the site's purpose. Include key words that consumers are likely to search for. Be as accurate as possible. Think like a customer and try searching for other sites. Look at the key words you used. Include them on your Web page.

In some cases, there is a way to get your site listed higher up in the search engine results. Many of the sites accept advertising payments to give higher priority to your site. You will have to carefully evaluate the costs and benefits of this approach compared to other advertising strategies.

Traditional Media and Name Recognition

To a consumer, name recognition of a company is an important element of buying products over the Internet. Trust is particularly critical when the consumer is not dealing face-to-face with the merchant. Depending on your target customers, it might be necessary to build this name recognition through advertising in traditional media (television, radio, or newspapers). Some early start-ups chose the splashy, but expensive, method of buying television spots during the Super Bowl to reach a large audience. If you do use traditional advertising, make sure that your Web site name is easy to remember and easy to type. Avoid words that are commonly misspelled.

Web Advertisements

Web advertising offers some potential advantages over traditional advertising. Ads can be delivered to specific audiences and to some extent controlled so that people continually see new ads. An original promise of Web ads was the ability to track the **click-through rate,** or the percentage of people who actually clicked on an ad and came to your site to get additional information. Initial reports placed click-through rates around 2 to 3 percent. By 2001, this rate had dropped below 1 percent. In the early stages of e-commerce, some sites survived on advertising revenue. As people became disappointed with the advertising response, spending for ads declined, and the chain effect helped drive the EC crash.

Figure 8.8 shows the estimated total advertising revenue by year as reported by the Interactive Advertising Bureau (IAB). The peak was in 2000 with the expansion of the dot-com boom. With its crash, many traditional companies pulled all Internet advertising. Despite the increasing use of the Web, advertisers and customers expressed disappointment with the initial Web advertising. Most of the early advertising consisted of banner ads that were static images displayed on a page. In 2003, advertisers began developing video-type

REALITY BYTES — Targeted Internet Ads

Several companies offer behavioral tracking and targeted ads on the Internet. Revenue Science, Inc., and Tacoda Systems, Inc., are two of the leaders. The systems combine personal data that people enter when registering for a site, or filling an application for a contest, along with tracking the Web sites visited. Eric Wheeler, director of OgilvyInteractive, notes the power of the systems: "Being able to refine messages based on who [readers] are and what they've done is incredibly powerful." Home and Garden Television signed with Tacoda to track the 36 million users who submitted entries for a dream-home contest. The technology will track customers across other sites owned by E. W. Scripps Co. and display ads based on the content they select. For example, ads from kitchen suppliers would be shown, as opposed to automobile ads. Several major newspaper sites are using the technology, including ESPN, *The Wall Street Journal,* and *The New York Times.* Publishers say they can charge premiums to advertisers of 10 to 100 percent or more for ads tied to behavioral tracking. The technology companies are downplaying the privacy aspects, claiming that the tracking stays within one company's sites, and the only personal data they use is zip code, age, and gender.

Source: Adapted from Carl Bialik, "More Web Sites Plan Ads Based on What Users Read," *The Wall Street Journal,* March 12, 2004.

FIGURE 8.8

Web advertising revenue: Revenue peaked with the dot-com boom in 2000, but began to recover in 2003 as advertisers found new ways to attract customers.

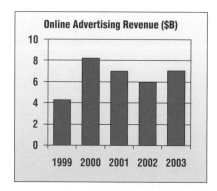

FIGURE 8.9

Web advertiser perspective: Advertisers want the biggest target audience possible. They need demographics about the Web site visitors, and they monitor response rates.

> Want viewers to see the ad.
> Want viewers to click through to the main site.
> Want to collect contact information from viewers.
> Need to match site demographics to target audience.
> Monitor response rates.
> Cost.

ads with Macromedia's flash, and they became more sophisticated about finding ways to get people to enter contact information. The goal today is to use the Internet to establish an interactive relationship with customers.

Advertiser Perspective

Figure 8.9 summarizes the perspective of advertisers—the ones who pay for the ads. They generally want the ads to be seen and to generate click-through responses. There is some argument that click-through rates are not an effective measure of advertising. Possibly the effect of an ad is to build an image or a brand name. Consumers might not need to purchase something immediately, but they might remember the ads later and use them to accept the validity of the company.

Increasingly, advertisers want to establish a relationship with the potential customers. Consequently, audience size and demographics are important to advertisers. In particular, advertisers are finding the most success in targeting specific sites. For instance, automobile manufacturers find it worthwhile to advertise on sites dedicated to automotive topics (such as vehix.com, Edmunds, and autobytel.com). Search engines are also an increasingly popular method of advertising. Targeted ads show up for specific searches. Users who enter "buy a car" into a search engine are highly likely to respond to an ad from a car manufacturer.

FIGURE 8.10

Web publisher perspective: There is money being spent on advertising, but your rates depend on volume and the ability to provide detailed demographic data. The daily tasks of sales and providing the ads are often handled by a third party like DoubleClick.

Income
    Cost per thousand viewings ($1–$50)
    Need volume (25,000 or 1,000,000 per month)
    Need demographics
Tasks
    Ad rotation software
    Tracking and monitoring
    Ad sales staff
    Billing
    Third party: DoubleClick

The IAB also helps coordinate the size of ads. It is much simpler for both advertisers and publishers if everyone uses a few standard types of ads. You should follow these standards as much as possible if you want to create an ad carried by other Web sites.

Web Site Publisher Perspective

In 2003, according to the IAB, Internet advertising spending for the year topped $7 billion. Many Web site publishers would like to get a share of that income. But keep in mind that according to the IAB, about 75 percent of online ad revenue goes to the top 10 Web site publishers. So, there is not much left for "your" share. The first catch is that you need a substantial volume of visitors to get anyone to consider your site. Probably at least 25,000 unique visitors a month, and 1 million would be a more likely minimum—since advertisers prefer larger audiences. Figure 8.10 shows some of the key points from a publisher's perspective.

One of the most difficult issues is obtaining the demographic data. You need some mechanism to identify your Internet users and to obtain some personal data from them. Of course, this data raises many privacy questions. Most sites find that they have to reward customers in some fashion to get them to provide personal demographic data, but it is often amazing how little is required to get customers to respond. Common tactics include random drawings for prizes or free trinkets. The other approach today is to have focused Web sites and then match the demographics against the existing public data. For example, antique car sites attract a particular demographic, while baby sites attract another group.

Handling Advertising

If you want to advertise on a site, how do you get started? If you have a popular Web site, where do you find advertisers? Like the traditional world of print, radio, and television advertising, the daily issues of handling the ads, monitoring placements, finding clients, and billing can be time consuming and expensive. Most sites choose a third party to perform these tasks, and DoubleClick is by far the largest such company. Of course, DoubleClick takes a portion of the ad revenue for its services. Figure 8.11 shows the intermediary role played by DoubleClick. The third party also simplifies the process for advertisers, since it would be difficult for a company to contract with hundreds of sites to place ads. One issue with using a central intermediary to place ads is that it is relatively easy to block ads from the central server. Check the Internet for information on how to add the DoubleClick sites to your hosts file and your computer will stop receiving any information from them.

Web Site Traffic Analysis

Even if you do not want to carry advertisements, analyzing traffic to your Web site is an important aspect of marketing. Among other questions, you want to know how many visitors arrive, what times the site is busy, which pages are most requested, and which outside sites commonly direct visitors to your site. All of this data and more is available by analyzing your server's Web logs. Most Web servers automatically maintain a detailed log of every single page request, the time it was requested, the amount of data transferred, and the IP address of the requesting user. These logs are stored as simple text files, but they are hard for people to read. Consequently, several companies, such as the one shown in Figure 8.12, sell software that retrieves the log, analyzes the data, and creates graphs to help managers understand the traffic.

FIGURE 8.11

Advertising consolidator: DoubleClick provides advertising services by functioning as a central point for both advertisers and publishers. DoubleClick handles the details of delivering the correct ads, tracking impressions, and collecting and distributing the money.

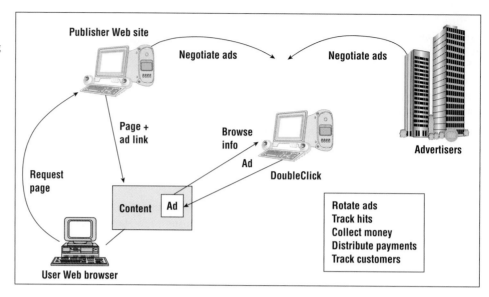

FIGURE 8.12

Web log analyzer: SurfStats is one tool that analyzes and displays the data captured whenever someone views a page on the server. The graphs make it easy to monitor which pages and files are most requested, when they are viewed, the IP address of the requester, and which site directed the user to your server.

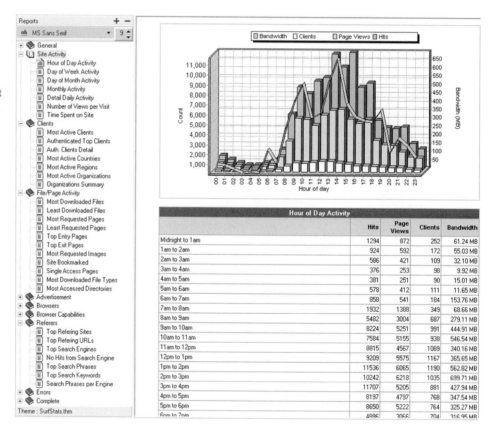

Hour of Day Activity	Hits	Page Views	Clients	Bandwidth
Midnight to 1am	1294	872	252	61.24 MB
1am to 2am	924	592	172	55.03 MB
2am to 3am	586	421	109	32.10 MB
3am to 4am	376	253	98	9.92 MB
4am to 5am	381	251	90	15.01 MB
5am to 6am	578	412	111	11.65 MB
6am to 7am	858	541	184	153.76 MB
7am to 8am	1932	1388	349	68.66 MB
8am to 9am	5482	3004	687	279.11 MB
9am to 10am	8224	5251	991	444.91 MB
10am to 11am	7584	5155	938	546.54 MB
11am to 12pm	8815	4567	1089	340.16 MB
12pm to 1pm	9209	5575	1167	365.65 MB
1pm to 2pm	11536	6065	1190	562.82 MB
2pm to 3pm	10242	6218	1035	699.71 MB
3pm to 4pm	11707	5205	881	427.94 MB
4pm to 5pm	8197	4797	768	347.54 MB
5pm to 6pm	8650	5222	764	325.27 MB
6pm to 7pm	4886	3066	704	316.95 MB

The statistics generated from the Web logs are useful to identify the most popular sections of your server and to spot problems with certain pages. For instance, you might find that a large number of users get halfway through your purchasing process, but few of them complete the actual transaction. Then you need to make your purchasing system faster or easier to use. The logs are also good at identifying which other sites, particularly search engines, direct viewers to your site. You can use this information to target advertising to similar sites.

Privacy

Privacy is the important flip side of advertising. The more serious privacy problems that have arisen were due to issues with advertising. The problem is the trade-off faced by advertisers. Companies want to target ads as closely as possible to people who are likely to care about and purchase the product. Hence, advertisers want to know a considerable amount of information about current customers and viewers of various Web sites. Yet collecting this data creates a loss of privacy for the customers.

DoubleClick has instigated one of the broader privacy problems. By routing so many ads through its servers, DoubleClick is able to track the Web pages visited by each of millions of Web browsers. At one point, DoubleClick wanted to sell this information along with demographic data on the individual consumers. Most consumers are not happy when a company tracks the sites they visit without informing them of the process. The basic premise of tracking demographic and customer data is that, by knowing more about the customer, it is easier to provide specific ads and data that might appeal to the customer and, in essence, fewer "junk" ads the viewer does not want.

e-Commerce Options

How do you create an EC Web site? Once you have decided that you want to participate in EC, you need to figure out how to create the site and get it hosted. In part because of the expense of maintaining a high-speed Internet connection, several companies have been created to provide alternative Web-hosting options. These hosting companies already have high-speed Internet connections, Web servers, databases, and management staff. They provide a variety of leasing options to host your site. One of the most important decisions to make regarding the Internet is where to locate the Web files. A variety of choices exists, and each method has different advantages, costs, and drawbacks. The choice of Web-hosting method depends on several characteristics of your business. Companies will often start with one option and move to other selections as they expand—particularly small firms or start-ups.

Ultimately, a major factor in the Web-hosting decision is the degree of integration you want to establish between the Web site and your existing business applications. Tighter integration generally means that you will have to run the Web site on your own servers. For example, if you want a retail Web page to display the current inventory level (to indicate if an item is in stock), the Web server will need to access your inventory database. If you can live with a lower level of integration, several options exist for hosting your application on another company's server, sometimes at very low cost.

Simple Static HTML

The most basic Web site consists of simple HTML pages—text and some images. These pages are generally fast to load, require minimal support from the server, and are relatively easy and inexpensive to host. For example, many Web providers offer free Web space. Most developers try to hold Web pages down to about 50KB per page, including graphics. The goal is to keep download times to an acceptable level even for dial-up users. A typical dial-up connection of 33 kbps will take about 12 seconds to download a 50KB page. A free Web site of 5 MB can hold about 100 pages of text and graphics. These basic Web sites cannot interact with the viewer. For example, you cannot accept form data or process credit cards. Similarly, the Web pages cannot interact with your internal databases. Generally, a single set of pages is made available to everyone, with little or no customization for individual users.

Although these relatively simple pages are easy to create, it is difficult to change them and keep them up to date. All changes must be made individually, and the developer must keep track of the details.

Consider the steps involved in creating a retail Web site with **static HTML** pages. You write a page that describes each product, including price and photo. You create a style for the site, adding fonts and colors. You can link the pages, probably using some type of index

FIGURE 8.13

Retail Web site with simple pages: Each product will generally be on a separate page, but each page must be created individually and linked by hand.

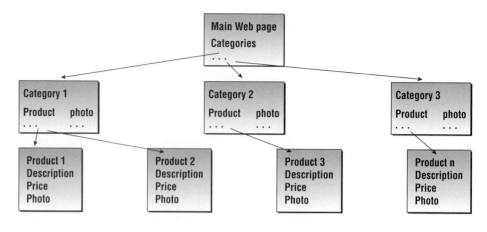

FIGURE 8.14

Order processing with static pages using a third-party processor: Clicking a link brings the customer to the card processor to enter card data and make the purchase.

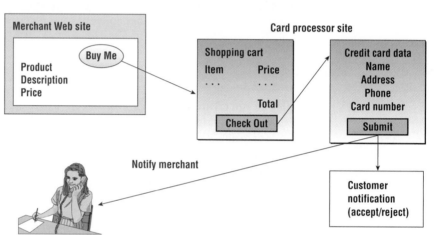

or a start page that lists major categories. With free hosting, it is rare to have a personalized search engine, so customers will need an easy method to find the products you are selling. Figure 8.13 shows the resulting hierarchical structure that you will have to follow. Each product will ultimately be displayed on a separate page. Each of these pages must be created individually, and links created by hand. To change any content, such as prices or descriptions, you must go to the desired page and make the change. This method may work for a small number of products, but as the number of products increases, it will become difficult for the developer to keep content and links up to date, and virtually impossible for users to find anything.

The other challenge with this Web structure is that the static Web server will not collect customer data, and because it cannot process form data, it is challenging to process a sale. One method is to use e-mail, where the customer enters product choices into a message that is e-mailed to your order-processing department.

Current technology offers a more sophisticated method to handle transactions. Regions Bank (http://www.goemerchant.com/buymebutton.htm) offers a third-party order-processing system called the Buy-Me Button. As shown in Figure 8.14, any merchant can paste this image onto a Web page and enter the product's description and price. By clicking on the button, the user is directed to a Web site that creates an electronic shopping cart. When finished shopping, the user can enter a credit card number using secure processing, and the Web site validates the card and sends the order to the merchant. Because all of the interactive processing occurs on the third-party site, the merchant's site can be run from a set of simple static Web pages. The merchant pays several fees for the service including fixed costs per month and per transaction. The merchant also pays a percentage of the transaction value.

Overall, the main advantage of this method is the price and simplicity of development. The static page site is often free. However, the merchant will have to pay for the credit-card processing site. The main drawback to this method is the difficulty in updating the data, and the related challenge for the customer in finding specific products. While it is possible to create these sites using a third-party credit-card processor, the method is realistic only if the merchant is selling a small number of products.

Single-Unit Sales

Some companies are interested in selling only a few individual items. If you want to experiment with the Internet, have a few unique items, or need to clear out a couple of items, it usually does not pay to set up a separate Web site—primarily because it would be hard to attract customers on a part-time basis. Two Internet alternatives exist: online auctions and Web services that specialize in single-unit sales.

The two methods are similar in their ability to attract customers. The most obvious difference lies in setting the price. At the auction sites, you sell to the highest bidder, although you can specify a minimum acceptable (reserve price).

Auctions

EBay.com is the best-known general **auction** site. The system operates similarly to newspaper classified advertising, but interactively enables potential buyers to bid on items. As highlighted in Figure 8.15, anyone can buy or sell products. The Web site lists the products and tracks the bids. At the end of the bidding period, the seller contacts the high bid and arranges shipment and payment.

One of the major difficulties with individual sales is authentication and ensuring that the transaction is handled properly. The buyer runs the risk that the seller is dishonest. If the seller ships the item before receiving payment, the buyer may never pay up. Most sellers are unwilling to accept this risk, so they generally require the buyer to send payment before the item is shipped. However, the buyer runs the risk of fraud. In 2000, eBay recognized the importance of this problem and added the ability for sellers to accept credit cards from any buyer (called Billpoint).

Several layers of pricing exist at auction sites. Generally, the seller must pay a fee to list the item and a second fee once it sells. If the item does not sell, the seller pays the first fee. The fee amounts depend on the value of the item being sold and on the options you choose. Read the fee schedules closely. For an average, figure $1 to list an item and about 3.5 percent of the value when it is sold. If you choose the credit-card billing option, the seller will generally pay another 3.5 percent of the selling price.

Several auction sites exist on the Internet. Some are general; others specialize in their choice of products. A special site even exists to list the auction sites (http://www. internetauctionlist.com). For a small retailer, probably the most important feature in choosing an auction site is the number of potential consumers who use the site that will be interested in your product. Perform a Web search to identify potential auction sites. Not many of the sites keep demographic profiles of the buyers; so you will have to examine the existing sales

FIGURE 8.15

Auctions: Good for unique items where you do not know what price to set. Economic efficiency depends on the number of participants and full information.

REALITY BYTES   eBay and Economics 101

In 2002, ReturnBuy, Inc., was making money on eBay liquidating unsold electronics items. It was selling so many items that for a while it was the largest seller on eBay. But the company managers quickly learned that offering more than a few dozen identical items crashed the price. In 2003, ReturnBuy went under. Walt Shill, former head of ReturnBuy, points out that "eBay is two inches deep and miles wide." Even eBay's CEO, Meg Whitman, observes that "if you want to move a thousand of the same computer in a day, eBay may not be one of the most effective channels." Several years ago, eBay pushed to sign on big retailers, hoping to pick up the sales of overstock and returned goods. Some companies, such as Sears and Sharper Image, continue to use eBay sales. Others, including Home Depot and Omaha Steaks, have pulled out, citing a lack of demand. EBay points out that the site is not really big enough yet. Ms. Whitman notes that "unless we can deliver sales of $20 million to $30 million it's probably not worth their time from an investment point of view."

EBay limits a seller to having no more than 10 identical auctions running at the same time. ReturnBuy got around that limit by bundling items and offering others for fixed prices. Nonetheless, the company found that it received acceptable (profitable) prices for only the first 20 percent of its merchandise. Callaway Golf experienced similar problems in demand. Initially, it offered limited sets of clubs received as trade-ins by buyers of new sets. Based on the early successes, it tied its inventory systems into eBay and tripled the number of clubs listed. It quickly became apparent that supply was outstripping demand, and the proportion of listings that found buyers dropped from 90 percent to 50 percent. Callaway's David Schofman notes that "we're not happy with their ability to move product in any kind of volume. We really hit the wall with them."

At the moment, eBay's core remains the small stores and entrepreneurs. The company estimates that of the 95 million registered users, 430,000 are full- and part-time sellers. These core sellers accounted for 95 percent of the $24 billion in transactions for 2003. To be in the top 10,000 merchants, you have to sell over $100,000 a year.

Source: Adapted from Nick Wingfield, "As eBay Grows, Site Disappoints Some Big Retailers," *The Wall Street Journal,* February 26, 2004.

FIGURE 8.16

Amazon.com zShops: Vendors list individual items. Consumers see zShops as the store and search for a product. Amazon.com can process the credit card–based purchase, and the vendor ships the product to the consumer. Vendors pay fees for listing items, selling them, and using the credit card processing.

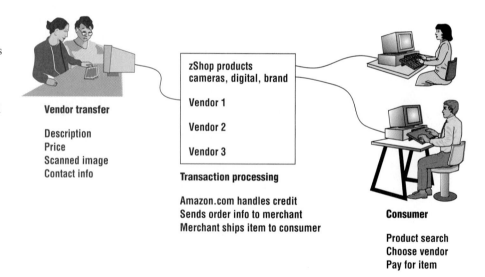

Vendor transfer

Description
Price
Scanned image
Contact info

zShop products
cameras, digital, brand

Vendor 1
Vendor 2
Vendor 3

Transaction processing

Amazon.com handles credit
Sends order info to merchant
Merchant ships item to consumer

Consumer

Product search
Choose vendor
Pay for item

carefully. Find some items similar to those that you want to sell and monitor the progress of the auctions.

Amazon.com MarketPlace

Amazon.com was one of the early e-commerce sites to enable small merchants to start Internet sales. As shown in Figure 8.16, the system (Amazon MarketPlace) enables merchants to sell items by setting a fixed price. Listing items for sale is similar to the auction process. The seller pays a fee for listing the item and a fee based on the selling price when the item is sold. The fees change over time, but are loosely $1 per item plus 6 to 15 percent of the item's value. Amazon also imposes some limits on the prices you can charge for various items. The company provides a bulk loading program to transfer all of the product descriptions and prices.

Amazon is essentially a Web mall that supports a number of sellers. Since the products show up in a regular search at Amazon, many customers do not know they are dealing with a third-party supplier. Consequently, although the costs are relatively high, the sellers gain instant credibility from the Amazon name. Other companies offer merchant mall services, but few have the name recognition and customer base provided by Amazon.

Auction versus MarketPlace/zShops

If you wish to sell a small number of items, then auctions and Amazon are a good option. The transaction and shipping costs tend to rule out low-priced items. On the other hand, buyers are somewhat leery of high-priced items from unknown sellers. For example, most people might consider buying a rare coin from a dealer but would be more reluctant to deal with an unknown independent seller.

If you have a small number of intermediate-priced items to sell, should you choose an auction site or Amazon? Auctions are particularly useful for unique items or items where you are uncertain of the value. The MarketPlace system has a good search engine and works well for small retailers who wish to maintain a continued presence on the Web. Auctions present a slight uncertainty in the final price. However, economic theory observes that an auction that is based on free information, and attracts all the relevant participants, will result in the highest price. One computer manufacturer that traditionally sold only through distributor channels tested this theory in 1999 by offering a limited number of machines at an auction site. All of them sold for higher prices than could have been obtained through traditional outlets. Keep in mind that if you have several products, you can always try multiple outlets and test the response.

Web Commerce Servers

Transactions on Web sites are often handled by Web commerce servers. These software programs provide all of the features needed to run a commercial Web site. As shown in Figure 8.17, the site can be run by a specialty hosting company, or you can run it on your own servers. The software is used by companies like Amazon to host multiple sites. You can also lease it from specialty hosting firms just to provide services for your company. The capabilities of the site depend on the features available in the software. As a vendor, you should examine the features of different site products to see which ones you need. Common software systems are available from Microsoft, Netscape, IBM, Intershop, and OpenMarket.

The Web hosting company provides a server, a connection to the Internet, an account for the hosting software, and credit card processing. The Web commerce server hosting software provides displays of your products, the ability to customize your store's displays, a search engine for your products, and the ability to process transactions securely. Some of the hosting software packages offer detailed customization options while others are more

FIGURE 8.17

Web commerce servers: The Web hosting company provides the servers, Internet connection, and commerce software that processes transactions. The merchant loads the database with product descriptions, images, and prices. The commerce software provides a typical retail experience.

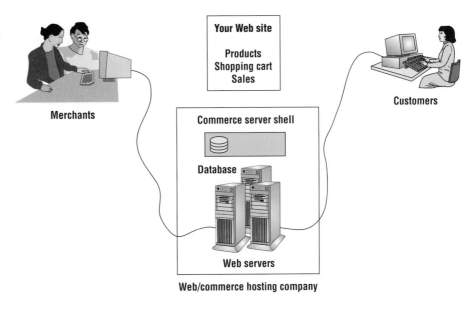

restrictive; but all of them provide the basic elements you need to create and run a retail Web site. The Web hosting company generally charges the retailer a setup fee, a fixed monthly fee, and a transaction fee—particularly for processing credit cards. The fees are highly variable and each company bases them on different parameters (such as number of products versus number of transactions). Minimal fees for a site that processes credit card transactions is around $150 per month, plus about 5 percent of the transaction as a credit card fee.

A Web mall is different from the Amazon.com MarketPlace model in several respects. The focus in MarketPlace is on the individual items. There is minimal opportunity to create the image of an individual store. In this case, MarketPlace is the store and thousands of merchants provide the products. With a Web mall, a business can establish a specific identity online and provide a collection of related products. In particular, you have the ability to obtain your own domain name. Customers can find your site directly as www.yourname.com, assuming that no one else is using yourname.com yet. Essentially, the Web mall approach makes it relatively easy for you to create a Web site that is independent and provides the basic functionality needed to sell products or services.

Application Service Providers

An **application service provider (ASP)** is a Web-based business that provides a specific service to other businesses. The service is very specific, and might or might not involve interactions with customers. For example, as shown in Figure 8.18, one company provides online accounting services for small businesses. For a monthly fee, you can enter all of your transaction data and generate standard reports. Other ASPs act as intermediaries in providing services. For instance, a few major companies provide Web-based real estate listing services. Other companies provide online reservations services for service businesses.

If you can find an ASP that provides the services you need, it will generally be easier and cheaper to use the services of the ASP than to create your own Web site. Competition should eventually give you greater choices in price and quality. Even if an ASP does not exist for the service you wish to provide, it might be possible to convince a firm to adapt their products or create a new service.

Advantages and Potential Problems

In general, commerce server sites and ASPs are a good way to get a quick start on the Internet. The software was created by experts, often involving thousands of hours of work. In most cases, it has been thoroughly tested and stress-tested to handle hundreds or thousands of simultaneous customers. In almost all cases, it will be cheaper to rent software instead of paying to develop it from scratch. Another nice feature is that it provides a standard interface for customers. Once customers learn how to use the standard systems, they will have no problems using your Web site.

FIGURE 8.18

Application service provider: The Web server runs an application that holds data for other businesses. The data may be exclusive to one business (e.g., accounting); it may be used to interact with other businesses (e.g., supplier auction site); or businesses may interact with consumers (e.g., real estate).

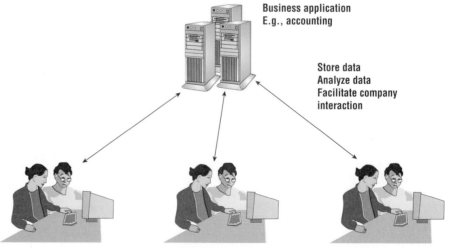

Businesses that lease the use of the application

Given these advantages, why would anyone want to choose an alternative? Three potential problems can arise with the commerce server and ASP software: (1) The software might not be flexible enough to provide the type of site you need, particularly for service operations. (2) Your site is almost always hosted on a server that is shared with other merchant sites—sometimes hundreds of other sites. A shared server raises the possibility of slower performance and increases the likelihood of server crashes. (3) It can be difficult to connect the Web server to your internal operations.

The question of sharing servers is complicated. If the Web hosting company has adequate facilities, including high-performance servers and backup plans, and if the commerce software is fast enough to handle multiple services, then a shared server does not present too many problems. In particular, if the Web hosting company stress-tests the server and Internet configuration, it should know the acceptable limits of sharing. However, as a merchant, keep in mind that the server performance is outside of your control. You might specify performance criteria in a contract, but it can be difficult to monitor the performance, and contracts do not necessarily prevent problems. Remember that Web site performance is one of the most critical factors for meeting the consumers' service requirements.

The other important issue in leased services and ASPs is that you lose most of the strategic benefits. Your business becomes "just another Web site." Hence, you have to differentiate your business based on price, selection, and service. It can be difficult to customize the Web service to provide additional features that might be used to attract and keep customers.

Web Hosting Options

Once you know the type of e-commerce site you wish to run, you need to select a hosting option. For simple sites, it is generally best to let someone else host the site. A few services still offer free hosting, but you might not like the conditions. Whenever you choose to outsource the Web hosting, several conditions become critical. Figure 8.19 outlines some of the major questions that you need to ask a Web service provider. Of course, the more features you want, the higher the monthly cost. Ultimately, most of your monthly cost comes down to whether you run on a separate server and the amount of data traffic. Remember that your hosting company must pay an ISP to carry greater traffic loads, and those costs will be passed on to you with a markup. The main benefit of using an outside hosting company is that it will handle all of the detailed technical issues automatically. The cost of hiring someone to set up and run your Web site and maintain security can be quite high.

On the other hand, the drawback to hosting your Web site outside the company is that it is more difficult to connect the site to your internal databases. If you want tighter integration and full control over the site, you ultimately need to run it yourself. You will also need to run a dedicated Internet connection to your servers.

Content Management Systems

If you have a small business with a Web site that sells only a few items, it is relatively easy to create and manage the Web site. On the other hand, you might have hundreds of products and need to change descriptions, photos, or prices on a regular basis. Or you might have thousands

FIGURE 8.19

Web hosting questions: Outsourcing your Web site hosting is popular, but be sure to ask these questions.

1. Will you have your own URL or just a subdirectory under someone else's name?
2. How much disk space will you have?
3. How much data transfer are you allowed? This number is critical as your traffic grows and is usually expressed in gigabytes per month.
4. How fast is the host's connection to the Internet, and have they oversold the capacity?
5. Will your site be on a shared server with other applications? If so, how many?
6. Will the company allow you to write server program code? What type of server and what limitations exist?
7. Will your application have database access?
8. Do you need a merchant server system?
9. What backup procedures are used?

of pages of content that need to be updated. For example, a service organization might include descriptions of services or analysis of recent events. Keeping pages up to date can require the participation of dozens or hundreds of workers to create and edit the content.

A **catalog management system** is designed to help you maintain a database of products for sale on Web sites. You enter product descriptions and prices on a local system and it updates the Web site catalog. The system has to recognize and know how to communicate with your commerce server software. The main strength of the catalog management system is that it focuses on the products and provides tools to group them into categories and change prices. It can then automate the Web server updates.

Web sites that focus on text pages instead of products are often more complicated. The pages can be written by hundreds of different employees. You want all of the pages to follow a standard style and to fit into your Web site's structure and search system. You cannot let hundreds of employees edit the Web site directly—it will be next to impossible to maintain consistency and security. A **content management system** is designed to make it easy for nonprogrammers to update content, maintain a consistent style, and keep track of changes to a Web site. The systems generally allow workers to create content using traditional editors such as Microsoft Word, and then convert the text into HTML and store it in the appropriate pages. They also track the revisions, so you know who changed each page and when it was modified. Most of the systems also maintain version control so you can switch back to an earlier version of a page if something goes wrong.

Mobile Commerce

How do portable Internet connections (mobile phones) provide new ways to sell things? In many ways, mobile commerce may not be much different from the existing Internet. Users will have cell phones, PDAs, and notebooks or touchpads with wireless connections to the Internet. However, for the near future, these appliances will have small, even tiny, screens. Also, until 3G wireless arrives, the data transmission speeds will be slow. From a technical standpoint, companies will have to rebuild their Web sites to support these devices. Each screen of data will have to be carefully designed, most graphics will have to be removed, and the page navigation will need to be simplified. Because the keyboards are hard to use, the Web sites will have to reduce the amount of data to be entered.

The real benefit of wireless connections is that they create new opportunities. If people are connected everywhere (or at least in the major cities), a vast amount of information becomes available at any time. Stores could instantly provide detailed product information to customer PDAs. For B2B sales, a salesperson could instantly retrieve data on competitor products, build charts, and transfer the presentation to the customer's system. Payments could be handled with wireless transfers of secure code, digital signatures, or even biometric data.

M-commerce will have an impact even on businesses that choose to stay with traditional sales methods. Consider a customer shopping for a product at a retail store. The customer can instantly get comparative price quotes from a dozen other sources and make an informed decision about whether to purchase the item electronically and wait for it to arrive, or to pay a premium to take the product home immediately.

Taxes

When do consumers and businesses pay sales taxes on the Internet? Sales taxes present a problem in the United States. Most states tax sales of products and services to obtain revenue to pay for public services. Many municipal governments add their own sales taxes to cover costs of local services. Consequently, there are over 7,800 separate tax districts. The system works reasonably well for small stores located in one district. But businesses that operate in more than one district must register and file tax forms within each district.

REALITY BYTES   Tax Districts

Vertex, Inc., is a company that sells software for use by companies that have stores in multiple states. Notably, the software computes sales taxes. Sales taxes might seem like a simple calculation: just multiply the price of an item by the tax rate. However, each state has different rates. Worse yet, counties and cities often throw in their own rates. Vertex estimates there are 7,800 different tax jurisdictions in the United States. And many of them change the rates each year. In 2001, the company recorded 771 increases. To make the process even more complex, some items are taxable in one jurisdiction and not in another. For instance, some states do not tax clothing or food. Sometimes the distinctions are interesting. The state of Connecticut has ruled that pumpkins are food items and nontaxable; unless they have decorations or markings on them, such as jack-o'lanterns, making them taxable. As a retailer, how do you keep track of all these changing details? Many of them pay Vertex.

Source: Adapted from "Tax Report: Sales-Tax Rates Increased Slightly Last Year," *The Wall Street Journal*, January 30, 2002; and www.vertexinc.com.

If the sales tax rate were the only issue, the situation might not be too bad. The difficulties multiply because each district has different categories of products and different taxable items. An item taxable within one district might not be taxed within a second. A third district might place the item in a different category and impose different taxes.

The interesting legal aspect of the taxes is that they are defined as use taxes on the citizens—and are supposed to be paid by consumers regardless of where the product was purchased. Since consumers are generally slow to volunteer payments, the states require businesses to collect the taxes and forward them to the appropriate agencies. This situation causes problems when the business is located in a different state. At various times, states have attempted to require out-of-state firms to collect the taxes, but the U.S. Supreme Court has always ruled that the U.S. Constitution clearly forbids the states from taxing interstate commerce. The fact that it is a constitutional issue is important, because it would require a constitutional amendment to change the situation. Congress has discussed creating a simpler tax system, but it is unlikely that it will pass as a constitutional amendment.

Local merchants often complain about the difficulty of competing with out-of-state firms that do not have to collect taxes. However, these same firms could sell in other states, so the issue could be neutral. Also, consumers who want to touch the product and bring it home immediately are still going to buy from local merchants. More important, state and local governments are concerned about losing their tax base. If consumers shift more of their purchases to e-commerce, the states will lose substantial revenue. For instance, consider the fact that Dell is one of the leading retailers of personal computers—relatively expensive items. Yet Dell has a physical presence in only a few states, so they do not collect taxes for most of the sales. This multibillion-dollar industry represents hundreds of millions of dollars of annual tax revenue to the states. Ultimately, states will have to increase other taxes to compensate for this lost revenue. Since most economists consider an income tax to be more progressive than sales taxes, the effect is not all bad.

Sales taxes on services are an even trickier issue. Since a large portion of the GDP is based on services instead of product sales, many states have begun taxing services. In 2003, Congress allowed the federal moratorium on Internet taxes to expire. States are now free to charge taxes on Internet connections. Just as you now pay several dollars a month in taxes and fees for telephone service, you might be asked to pay more for your Internet connection.

Global Economy

Does the Internet create a global marketplace? E-commerce has the potential to open up the global economy. Theoretically, anyone with access to the Internet can purchase products directly from anywhere in the world. However, actual practice cannot live up to the expectations of theory. Three major issues still limit international trade: (1) transportation costs, (2) national policies, and (3) payment and trust limitations.

Problem: How do your Web servers handle interaction and database tasks?

Tools: Web servers require special code engines to handle the interaction with users and the database. Three basic systems have evolved over time: Java (J2EE), PHP/PERL/PYTHON, and Microsoft.NET. Web sites today are built using one of these three technologies. There are major differences in the underlying technologies and philosophies of the three approaches, and some developers treat them as "religious" issues—which is a way of saying that proponents of each often argue over the relative merits of their choice of technology. As a manager, why do you care about the three technologies? The main answer is that you will probably have to make a decision between them if you develop a Web site. All three have evolved considerably over the past few years and will continue to improve.

Of the three, Microsoft's .NET is the newest and has some features that do not yet exist in the other methods. It is also considerably faster and more efficient at processing code and connecting to databases. It is also the most expensive. Java is probably the second most powerful technology. It has the advantage of being a standard that is supported by many vendors. Systems developed using standard Java code can be transferred to run on Web servers built using a variety of hardware and operating systems. Not only is the server code inexpensive, but the hardware and Web server software are inexpensive. The other approaches use scripting languages that have diverse features. Web sites built on these systems can be run on a variety of hardware and software platforms. In all three cases, you need to work closely with the hosting company to ensure that the proper hardware and software packages are installed.

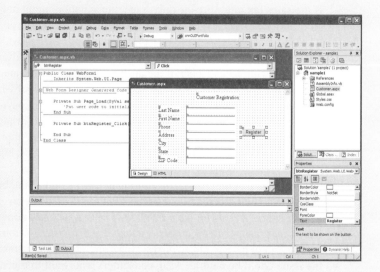

Building interactive Web sites generally requires custom programming to tell the server how to handle the customer responses. Development environments exist for Java and .NET that help programmers write the code. Most applications are built as Web forms where the user enters the data. This data is then transferred to the server, and the code behind the form examines the values. Based on the responses, the data can be stored in a database, e-mailed to someone, or additional pages can be returned to the user.

The differences between the systems lie in the capabilities of the underlying code and the amount of effort it takes to write the code and connect to database systems. Increasingly, vendors are developing libraries of code for the three systems that prepackage common procedures. These packages enable developers to build new applications faster and with fewer errors.

Quick Quiz:
1. Why would programmers become so attached to one system?
2. What are the advantages of choosing the most popular server technology?
3. What are the dominant costs of creating a Web site?

Transportation costs will always exist, but they can be relatively high for individual orders. International bulk shipments are considerably more economical, so there will always be an incentive for retailers to purchase in bulk and resell individual items. Transportation companies consolidate shipments to reduce costs, but customers often want products relatively quickly, and shipping by air is more expensive than shipping by sea.

Nations have many different policies and taxes regarding imports and exports. Most shipments have to go through a customs agent. Even digital products carry restrictions. A few nations attempt to monitor and control all Internet usage—to the point of insisting that all Internet traffic be channeled through government computers. An interesting case arose in 2001, when France filed suit against Yahoo (a U.S. company) to force Yahoo to prevent French citizens from buying or selling Nazi-related items. By French law, French citizens are not allowed to buy and sell Nazi items. The Yahoo auction site would enable the French to circumvent the law, so a French court ordered Yahoo to block the French from any transactions. Keep in mind that it would be virtually impossible for Yahoo to identify which items are Nazi-related, particularly if sellers do not use the word Nazi in their descriptions. It would also be difficult for Yahoo to continually monitor each bidder on every auction to see if the bidder is French. Consequently, Yahoo eventually banned all sales of Nazi-related items on its auction sites, even though a U.S. court ruled that France had no jurisdiction to collect a fine from Yahoo. The point of this case is that Yahoo had no physical presence in France, and it is unlikely that the French court had the jurisdiction to order Yahoo to stop the sales. Yahoo most likely complied because the company might someday want to establish a presence in France, at which time the judgment could become an issue.

But think about the consequences if every nation imposed its will on Internet sales. While individual nations do have the right to control sales within their territory, it would destroy e-commerce if every nation imposed its control on all Internet sales. As e-commerce increases in importance, more of these issues are going to arise, and firms will need to have technology ready to handle them.

Global e-commerce is evolving—from many nations, you can buy English rugby jerseys from British vendors. But the payment mechanisms need considerable work. Many U.S. Web sites will not accept overseas shipments because the risk is too great. Many companies will not sell to nations in eastern Europe, Southeast Asia, and the Middle East because the risks are even higher.

Analysis of Dot-Com Failures

Why did thousands of dot-com firms fail? This question is important because many people are concerned that e-commerce is inherently risky. From about 1996 to 2000, hundreds of dot-com firms were created, many in the San Francisco area. The excitement of the Internet led people to believe that these firms were the start of a new economy. Over-hyped statements were made about the death of the old economy and that traditional bricks-and-mortar firms would soon fail, to be replaced by an online world of competitive prices and advertisements tailored to individual customers. Entrepreneurs believed that if they could be the first firm to break into a category, and if they advertised heavily enough, they would automatically become the dominant player in the new economy. Many investors felt it was important to get in on the ground floor of these firms. IPOs were released daily; stock prices soared. Newly minted paper billionaires graced the covers of business magazines. And then investors woke up and the market crashed. The NASDAQ market index that covered many of these technology firms dropped from over 5,000 points to around 2,000 in less than a year. Pundits whipsawed to the other end of the spectrum and proclaimed the end of e-commerce. Of course, reality lies between the two endpoints, but it is worth examining some of the concepts of the time to understand the role of e-commerce in the future.

Pure Internet Plays

One of the first types of firms to fail followed a strategy known as **pure Internet plays,** where the e-commerce firm relies entirely on Internet transactions for money—with no ties to real products. Examples include sites that provide services to other sites, such as the search engines and Web advertising sites. Closely related sites include some that advertised and sold products over the Internet, but relied on other traditional companies to produce and deliver the products to customers.

These firms were at risk because they depended almost completely on Internet traffic and funds. When a few of the firms failed, it set off a domino effect that reduced cash flow at many other firms. Many of the firms were interlocked with the others through service agreements and advertising relationships.

REALITY BYTES   Pay Your DNS Bills

The Washington Post newspaper somehow missed renewing a payment on its domain name (WashPost.com). Because of the overdue bill, the domain name was delisted and readers, writers, and editors were unable to use the e-mail system that relies on the domain name. After identifying the cause, the newspaper quickly renewed the registration, and services were restored. The company was fortunate. Many of the domain registrars allow others to place a hold on a domain name that is not renewed. If you somehow do not renew a domain name, it could be immediately acquired by another company.

Source: Adapted from Todd R. Weiss, "Overdue Domain Registration Bill Stops e-Mail Access to Washington Post," *Computerworld,* February 6, 2004.

Profit Margins

Profit is an important issue for any firm. Yet many managers claimed that there was no need for traditional profits. This belief was endorsed by a market where IPOs were celebrated and stock prices on new firms jumped over $100 per share in the first day. These IPOs provided the cash that firms used to fund operations. In many cases, the goal of the firm was to advertise heavily and undercut prices in an attempt to build name recognition and capture market share. Even Amazon.com, one of the early entrants and cheerleader for e-commerce, gained its prominence by offering products at 30, 40, and 50 percent discounts. The CFO at Amazon once said that they never intended to make a profit. More recently, the firm has been working hard to reduce costs to achieve an operating profit. Much of the profit is the result of a change in strategy: substantially higher prices.

One of the challenges to measuring profits is that many different definitions of profit can be used, largely depending on which costs are included. But it is difficult to make a profit when products are sold for less than the cost of the item. It can be done, if additional revenue is received from other sources, such as advertising revenue, service contracts, or additional vendor payments. But, in the end, a firm must make a profit on operations or there is no point to continuing. In 2000, a McKinsey study revealed that only 20 percent of the e-commerce firms were making a profit on sales, and the top firms were actually traditional firms, such as mail-order companies.

Many of the early e-commerce firms attempted to establish market dominance through heavy advertising and large discounts. The plan was to use the name recognition to attract customers away from traditional firms and eventually increase prices to make a profit. The problem was that these firms still had to compete with traditional firms that already face considerable competition. In this crucible, the existing firms learned to squeeze costs. These efficiencies enable them to sell products at a profit and to fend off competitors during short-term attacks.

Advertising Revenue

As shown in Figure 8.20, Internet advertising revenue was a dominant factor in the failure of many of the early e-commerce firms. For some, the Internet appeared to be a new educational medium—much like television. Web sites would provide interesting or useful content that would attract viewers (often referred to as eyeballs). These sites would then sell screen space to other companies to use as advertising. The interactive nature of the Internet would also make it possible to track the effectiveness of the ads—both in terms of the number of times an ad was seen and in terms of the click-through rate for each ad.

This model does apply to some extent—the Interactive Advertising Board reported that U.S. Internet advertising revenue was $8.2 billion in 2000. However, only a handful of the top firms receive the lion's share of the revenue. Moreover, as click-through rates fell in 2000, advertisers began to believe that browsers no longer paid attention to the ads, so they began to question the value of advertising on the Internet and became particularly leery of smaller sites.

The situation was compounded by the fact that many of the firms followed some shaky accounting practices. For instance, advertising exchange agreements were often counted as rev-

FIGURE 8.20

Dot-com advertising crash: Many of the early firms were linked by agreements to advertise on other sites. With few actual sales, some firms ran out of investors' money and the outside advertising money dried up. The weak firms crashed, which cut off the advertising money to others, and the domino effect accelerated the crash.

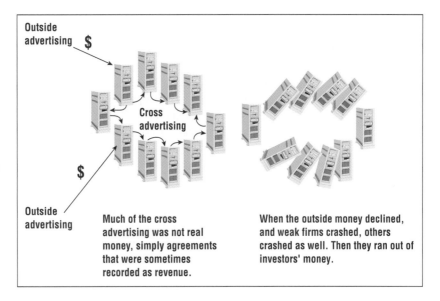

Outside advertising $

Cross advertising

Outside advertising $

Much of the cross advertising was not real money, simply agreements that were sometimes recorded as revenue.

When the outside money declined, and weak firms crashed, others crashed as well. Then they ran out of investors' money.

enue. Firm A would agree to carry advertisements for firm B in exchange for similar ads on B's site. Both sites recorded revenue from the advertisements—but never received any cash.

With the declining emphasis on advertising revenue, content providers are increasing their attempts to charge consumers for the content. According to a study by Jupiter Media Metrix, one of the leading e-commerce monitoring firms, in 1999 the top 100 firms were charging for only 6 percent of their content. In 2000, that number almost doubled to 11 percent. Almost all of these firms anticipate charging for some content by 2003. Some of the content is paid with service agreements, some through micro-payments for individual pieces of data.

Summary

E-commerce is a complex topic. On one hand, the Internet and mobile commerce simply represent new ways to interact with customers and handle transactions. On the other hand, they have the potential to change the economy and society. The production chain is a key issue in e-commerce. Businesses must decide whether the advantages of selling directly to customers are worth the loss of goodwill from distributors and retailers. The production chain also provides the means to evaluate EC alternatives from business to business or from business to consumer. EC also provides the ability to charge different prices to each customer through direct sales or auctions.

A Manager's View

Making money on the Internet is not easy, but it is possible. Internet sales are increasing faster than sales through traditional channels. The challenge is to use the Internet to increase your sales while still maintaining existing relationships. New services are being created and the sales of digital products are expanding. M-commerce offers the potential to provide another shift in business and society—but it will be a while before the hardware, networks, and software become widespread enough to make a difference. You need to understand how customers use Web sites to purchase products. Promoting your Web site and attracting customers is an increasingly important task, so you need to understand the role of search engines, advertising, and traffic analysis.

E-commerce can be analyzed in three phases: prepurchase, purchase, and postpurchase. The prepurchase phase consists primarily of advertising, providing specifications, and product configuration or selection. Purchase largely consists of handling the transactions, including verifying the customer, protecting the data transmissions, and handling the money transfer. Postpurchase support includes service, problem tracking, and cross selling.

Promoting Web sites is increasingly important. Search engines are an important means for potential customers to find sites, but many sites also need to advertise on other Web sites and on more traditional media. It is also important to analyze the Web site's traffic patterns to find out what pages are in demand and what sections do not work well.

Several types of e-commerce are in use, including simple static HTML pages to present information about products; single-unit sales using low-volume payment systems and auction sites; and Web malls and commerce server software for large product catalogs. Many firms choose to outsource the Web site hosting to a specialty company, but hosting your own servers makes it easier to integrate the Internet data with the other corporate data.

Mobile commerce is similar to e-commerce, but the wireless capabilities can provide some interesting applications—particularly for B2B e-commerce. Sales taxes and the Internet are a challenging problem for states. Ultimately, states will have to alter their tax systems. Similar problems arise on a global scale. Many issues involving customer authentication, payment validation, and national control need to be resolved before global e-commerce can seriously expand.

E-business and e-commerce mean more than just the dot-com firms that sell products. Many Internet-based business opportunities still exist, both within existing firms and for new companies. Joseph Schumpter, an economist, coined the term *creative destruction* to represent the dynamic changes required in a modern economy. A dynamic economy needs to have new firms to force the mainstream companies to respond to the pressure of new ideas. Firms that are set in their ways will ultimately fail. Entrepreneurs can work within larger organizations creating new products, but they generally choose to build entirely new firms. In any case, it takes solid ideas, good research, and an organized plan to succeed as an entrepreneur.

Key Words

application service provider (ASP), *296*	click-through rate, *287*	simple object access protocol (SOAP), *286*
auction, *293*	commerce server, *295*	static HTML, *291*
business to business (B2B), *275*	content management system, *298*	universal description, discovery, and integration (UDDI), *286*
business to consumer (B2C), *274*	digital rights management, *281*	
catalog management system, *298*	disintermediation, *277*	
	intellectual property, *281*	
	pure Internet plays, *301*	

Web Site References

Angel Investors and Venture Capital

Angel Investor Magazine	www.spencertrask.com
Business Finance	www.businessfinance.com
Inc Advice and Lists	www.inc.com/guides/finance/20797.html
National Venture Capital Association	www.nvca.org
Venture Capital Resource Directory	www.vfinance.com

Additional Readings

Borzo, Jeanette. "Online Micropayment Systems See New Interest but Face Old Hurdles." *The Wall Street Journal,* April 3, 2001. [Decline of e-commerce advertising revenue and increase in selling of content.]

Collett, Stacy. "Amid Turf Battle, Some Middlemen Call for Truce with Online Rivals." *Computerworld,* April 16, 2001. [Discussion of role of middlemen and disintermediation in e-commerce.]

Fireswick, Kris. "The e-Files." *CFO,* February 2001. [Comments and analysis of some lead managers of failed dot-coms.]

Matthews, Robert Guy. "Web Firm Lures Steel Giants." *The Wall Street Journal,* September 2, 1999. [Early auction site for the steel industry.]

Moss Kanter, Rosabeth. "The Ten Deadly Mistakes of Wanna-Dots." *Harvard Business Review,* January 2001. [Discussion of the e-commerce failures.]

National Mail Order Association. "1998 Mail Order Sales Results." 1999, http://www.nmoa.com/Library/1998sale.htm. [Statistics on mail-order sales.]

Regan, Keith. "Study: Era of e-Commerce Profits Underway." *EcommerceTimes,* June 20, 2001, http://www.newsfactor.com/perl/story/11381.html. [Summary of McKinsey study on e-commerce profits.]

"Shopping around the Web." *The Economist,* February 26, 2000. [Special section on e-commerce.]

Stone, Martha L. "U.S. Cell Phone Technology Lags Japan, Europe." mediainfo, June 7, 2000, http://www.mediainfo.com/ephome/news/newshtm/stories/060700n2.htm. [Statistics on cell phone usage in several nations.]

"Study: Four Sites Account for Half of Web Surfing." *CNN,* June 5, 2001. [Dominance of a few large firms in attracting users.]

Swisher, Kara. "Web Retailers Faced Death; Now Can They Handle Taxes?" *The Wall Street Journal,* April 9, 2001. [Summary of issues on e-commerce sales taxes.]

Review Questions

1. What are the potential benefits and costs to disintermediation that can be accomplished with e-business?

2. What Internet sales options exist beyond shipping traditional products to consumers?

3. How does EC differ in the three areas of prepurchase, purchase, and postpurchase?

4. What choices are available for promoting a Web site?

5. What standards exist in Web advertisements? How do Web advertisements affect customer privacy?

6. What options are available for building and hosting Web sites?

7. What will attract consumers to mobile commerce? What problems have to be overcome before it is successful?

8. Many people were concerned that by not requiring EC firms to collect sales taxes, traditional firms would eventually lose business and the states would suffer large declines in tax collections. Why did this scenario not happen? Might it still happen in the future?

9. What problems make it difficult for EC to be global?

10. Why did so many early EC firms fail? Could the same problems affect EC firms now and in the future? Does it mean that EC is dead?

Exercises

1. Find firms in three different industries that have used the Internet to disintermediate at least one level of the production chain. Were they successful? What problems did they encounter?

2. Identify the current state of the art in mobile commerce networks and handsets. What transmission speeds exist? What is the resolution on the video screens? What display languages do the leading devices support?

3. Find a firm that is providing an XML-based service. Describe the service and try to identify the costs.

4. Select a Web site and identify the prepurchase, purchase, and postpurchase elements.

5. Check with a Web advertising site and identify the cost to run an ad on the site. Specify the type of ad and the number of times to run.

6. Find a tool that you can use to analyze Web site traffic. If you can download a copy and have access to a server log, analyze the file and identify any trends.

7. Find a B2C product for sale on three Web sites: one based on simply HTML pages, one hosted on a commerce server, and one based on an auction or MarketPlace site. Briefly compare the descriptions, prices, and ease of use.

Technology Toolbox

8. Select one of the major Web server tools and identify how it handles multiple languages.

9. Find a reference that identifies the percentage of sites based on Microsoft Web servers.

10. Briefly explain how Java connects to a DBMS.

11. Find a content management system and describe its major features. What file formats does it support; that is, how do users create the content?

12. Find and compare at least two catalog management software packages. Which one seems easier to use? How many products can each one handle? Do they work with all Web sites, or only some commerce software packages?

Teamwork

13. Choose one common product available for purchase on the Internet and from local retailers (for example, a specific book, CD, or toy). Have each person find at least one Web site and one retail store that sells the product. Compare the prices of the item. Where is it easiest to purchase the product?

14. Choose a B2C industry in which you might start a business. Identify the primary Web site features that you would want to implement. Have each team member find a company that could host your Web site. Identify the features, tools, and costs of each firm. Which one would you recommend?

15. Have each person check with a different search engine to determine how to register your Web site and how much the site charges to list your site at the top of searches.

16. Have each team member select a dot-com firm that failed. Identify the amount of capital raised, the revenue generated, and the number of employees. Briefly describe the cause of the failure. Combine the results and identify any common patterns.

17. Have each person select an industry and research the use of the Internet in that industry. Focus on the production chain and identify any disintermediation that is being supported by Internet transactions. Combine the results and explain any differences across industries.

Rolling Thunder Database

18. Identify at least three areas in which Rolling Thunder Bicycles could profit from e-business. Be specific, and explain what technologies would have to be added (for instance, Web hosting).

19. Find at least five sites on which it would make sense to advertise Rolling Thunder Bicycles. As much as possible, identify the advertising costs and the demographics of the site visitors.

20. Develop a plan for expanding Rolling Thunder Bicycles into international sales. Be sure to identify any potential problems, and discuss how you will deal with them.

21. Develop a plan for creating a Web-based system for connecting to suppliers. What software would you need? How can you convince the suppliers to cooperate?

22. The management of Rolling Thunder Bicycles cannot decide on a Web strategy. For the three main approaches (simple HTML, auctions, and commerce server), list the primary strengths, weaknesses, and costs as they apply to this company. Make a recommendation and briefly explain your choice.

Cases: Entrepreneurship

The Industry

Entrepreneurship is the practice of starting a new business. The business might start small with one or two employees, become a large corporation, or anywhere in between. In many ways, the American economy has been driven by entrepreneurs, people with vision and independence, willing to take risks and try new ideas and new technologies. But starting a business requires more than just ideas and enthusiasm. It requires detailed organizational skills. The entrepreneur is responsible for creating all of the many procedures and rules that will keep the business running. You have to determine simple things like how the daily receipts get deposited each day and how employees are evaluated. You also have to determine all of the big-picture issues, such as the best way to counter a new plan by a competitor and keeping your customers happy. Several familiar companies began as small firms and grew to dominate their respective industries and even the economy. The large computer firms of IBM and Hewlett-Packard were once small companies. The Edward Jones brokerage firm was started by one man.

In 2000, slightly over 5 million corporations filed income tax returns in the United States, along with about 2 million partnerships and almost 18 million proprietorships. About 12 million of those proprietorships had less than $25,000 in receipts, compared to 1.2 million of the corporations and 1.1 million partnerships. Most of the corporations had receipts between $100,000 and $500,000. The total number of corporations increased from 3.7 million in 1990 to 5.0 million in 2000. At the same time, partnerships increased from 1.5 million to 2.1 million and proprietorships from 14.8 million to 17.9 million. The actual number of new firms created will be higher because the totals do not count the firms that disappeared in that time. Looking only at 1999 to 2000 (the most recent data available), the number of all firms increased by 559,000 (a 2.2 percent increase) (U.S. Census Bureau 2002, Table No. 732).

The Internet

The Internet raises the hopes of many of today's entrepreneurs. You can use it to reach a large audience—perhaps even worldwide. You can start small with a limited budget. But as the dot-com crash of the early 2000s shows, you still need a business plan. You need an idea that will generate profits. Even small expenses can overwhelm a company that has no sales revenue. People are still drawn by the examples of companies like Amazon.com, Yahoo, and Google. Of course, many forget about the hundreds of other Web start-ups that failed. Some of those companies actually had good ideas and plans. Part of their failure was due to timing—entrepreneurs and investors thought the world could be changed overnight.

Financing

Starting a business requires money—start-up capital. Depending on the industry, you might need to purchase buildings or equipment. You might have to pay programmers to develop software. You generally have to rent an office and rent or buy furniture. You most likely need to buy computers, along with office supplies. You might have to pay for licenses or patent fees. You most likely need to pay employees until the business generates enough cash to cover the day-to-day expenses. Several sources of funding exist, but most of them have drawbacks. If you can get by with small amounts of money, the best answer would be to save it and invest yourself, or with family members. Larger amounts of capital can be obtained from angel investors or possibly venture capital

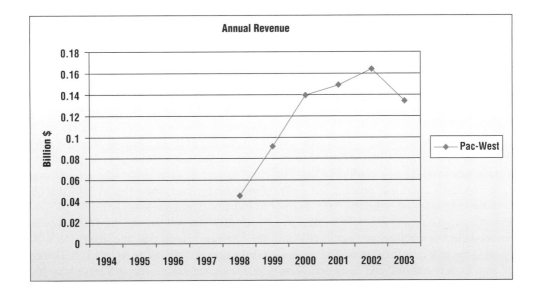

firms. Sometimes you can borrow money from a bank, but those amounts are generally limited to specific items such as inventory or capital goods that can be resold if your company fails to survive. No one gives you money for free. Banks require you to pay interest. Venture capital firms often ask you to give up some control, and they install a manager. In most cases, you give up some ownership, as the investors gain a negotiated percentage of your company.

Additional Reading

Bounds, Gwendolyn. "Lessons of Success—and Failure." *The Wall Street Journal,* July 12, 2004.

U.S. Census Bureau. *Statistical Abstract of the United States 2002.* Washington, DC: 2004 (http://www.census.gov/prod/www/statistical-abstract-02.html).

Case: Petz Enterprises Inc. (TaxBrain)

Leroy E. Petz, Sr., founded Petz Enterprises in 1964 in Tracy, California. Until 2000, the company specialized in providing tax software for accounting firms. The CrossLink package was commonly used by accountants to complete and print income tax returns for clients. The accounting firms, or local tax offices, buy the software annually and then use it to produce even complex returns for customers. The accountants provide advice and organize the customer's data. Clients often arrive with a shoebox full of receipts and the accountant has to sort it and categorize the data to determine what items are deductible and classify the income properly.

In 2000, the company realized that the Internet was going to become an important method for individuals to file taxes. The company created the TaxBrain Web site using its knowledge of the tax laws (company Web site).

CrossLink

As its original flagship product, CrossLink is an important source of revenue and name recognition. Petz has continued to improve the product over time to make it easier to use and to provide features that are useful to large tax-preparation offices. For example, returns that are filed electronically are initially evaluated by the IRS. If there are errors, the CrossLink package picks up the messages and integrates them into the form so that the tax preparer can quickly see the problems with a complete diagnostic statement. In 2001, the company also added the Tax Return Logging System. Petz notes that "tax offices with branches need to keep track of all tax returns. The Tax Return Logging System will track all returns that have been created, deleted, and changed" (McCausland and Lombardo 2001). The potential problem is that in a large company, a tax preparer hired in a remote location might use the software to generate a client's return, print it, and pocket the money. With the logging system, all use of the system is tracked.

In 2003, Petz rolled out a new approach—hosting the tax preparation software on its own site. Charles Petz, product development director, notes that the new product (VTax) "is a subset of our professional [CrossLink] product, but we're going after guys who have a lot of offices" ("Petz Enterprises" 2003). In particular, the system is geared for the hundreds of neighborhood electronic refund originators (EROs) that have sprung up in the past couple of years. The companies set up small storefront operations, and customers show up with their W2 form and basic financial information. Clerks enter the data into the system and give the clients an immediate refund. Of course, the refund is really a short-term loan and the actual refund is collected by the ERO, minus the interest and filing costs. The key is that the ERO practitioner has all of the data up-front to make the loan and can file the data immediately or hold it until later if additional information is needed. By using a hosted service, the ERO office needs only a simple computer with a Web browser and a basic Internet connection. Even better, all offices of the ERO have access to the form. A client could drop off paperwork at one site and return to a different one if needed. The system also prints detailed reports of activity by office. Originally, Petz anticipated 500 to 600 offices using the system. In the end, "it looks like we'll be closer to 2,000 locations," through 10 different EROs ("Petz Enterprises" 2003). Another strength of the hosted service is that the ERO can quickly set up a new office if demand is high.

TaxBrain.com

In 2000 and 2001, the TaxBrain site saw limited commercial success. For a flat fee of $24.95, individuals could file federal and state returns. The electronic filing fee was included in the cost. By filing electronically, filers could get a refund in as little as 10 days. Since they did not have to buy and install software, customers needed little computer knowledge. Mr. Petz noted that although the company did only limited marketing, "we saw over 10,000 hits a day and we have no idea how people found us" (McCausland and Lombardo 2001).

In 2002, Petz got more serious about the TaxBrain site. The company completely reworked the user interface to make it easier to use. It also began a more targeted marketing campaign to bring in more users and track where they were coming from. In November 2002, Petz observed that in the 2000 tax year, 130 million individual tax returns were filed, with 17.7 percent of those from off-the-shelf software. By 2005, he forecasted that percentage to drop to 7.1 percent. In 2000, 56.7 percent of individuals paid a professional to file their forms; his forecasts show that by 2005 that number will drop to 48 percent (press release 2002).

By 2003, the site was the third most popular tax system on the Internet, behind only the giants H&R Block and Intuit (TurboTax). At its peak on April 15, 2003, TaxBrain attracted 50,000 unique visitors (press release May 2003).

At the same time, the IRS saw a huge increase in the number of people filing returns electronically, with 53 million filed electronically in 2003 (IRS Web site). Leroy Petz, Sr., explains the popularity: "For millions of Americans, filing over the Internet is now accepted as the best way to go to beat the deadline. TaxBrain can help you get your taxes filed in less than an hour, provides assistance through live instant messaging chat and ensures your return is 'received' by the IRS with an official electronic reply." Petz also estimates that individuals "are saving more than $200 in time and professional fees doing their returns online" ("TaxBrain" 2004). Electronic filing is also better at catching errors, particularly since the IRS system catches most common problems and identifies them immediately. Overall, about 20 percent of paper returns have errors, while less than 1 percent of electronic returns have errors.

Although electronic filing is increasing, much of the growth is through third-party systems, such as the local offices and purchased software. For 2004, Petz initiated a larger marketing campaign. Leroy Petz, Sr., notes that "in order to make people more aware that they can prepare and file their taxes online, PEI is embarking on an aggressive media campaign to inform taxpayers of the ease, speed, and security of doing their taxes with TaxBrain. Our biggest challenge is demonstrating to the taxpaying public that it is truly easy" (press release December 2003).

Free Filing

Given the new IRS emphasis on electronic filing, along with the automated reporting system by employers and banks, many Americans are beginning to raise an important question: Why do they have to pay to purchase software or file electronically? Why not let the IRS develop the online software and make it available for free? To expert observers, the most immediate answer to the question is that the IRS has historically been terrible at developing software. The second issue is that the IRS might be tempted to provide tax advice. Although it might seem strange, many people could be better off using private advice instead of recommendations from the IRS. The IRS is likely to be considerably more conservative and has been known to ignore court cases that it has lost (Becker 2002). But over time, there is a possibility that the IRS could compete with the commercial providers.

In part to answer these questions, several of the commercial providers cooperated with the IRS in 2003 to offer the IRS Free Filing Program. The goal was to target the low-income and elderly populations. TaxBrain participated in 2003 and served 50,000 individuals. Strangely, in 2004, the IRS created a new rule that required all commercial providers to permanently flag every return that was filed through the program. The IRS apparently wanted to perform some type of analysis on these returns, but did not disclose the reasoning. Consequently, TaxBrain decided not to participate in the program—believing that it as an unnecessary invasion of privacy with a high risk to individuals (press release 2004).

TurboTax announced that it would continue to participate, but would ignore the IRS requirements and not flag the returns of those participating in the program (Wiles 2004). The IRS denied that taxpayer privacy might be compromised, but failed to provide an explanation. The IRS does note that it has always been able to tell how a return was prepared, whether it was by software, volunteer, or IRS walk-in location (Wiles 2004).

Questions

1. How can TaxBrain gain more customers and take market share from H&R Block and Intuit?

2. How does the CrossLink system give Petz an advantage with the TaxBrain site?

3. Should the IRS develop online tax software, possibly eliminating firms like H&R Block, Intuit, and Petz Enterprises?

4. By 2010, what percentage of people will file tax returns electronically? When this maximum is reached, how will Petz continue to grow?

5. Did Petz make the right decision with the Free File program? Should the company rejoin it?

Additional Reading

Becker, David. "IRS E-Filing Plans Worry Tax Industry." *News.Com,* March 11, 2002.

McCausland, Richard, and Carly Lombardo. "2001 Tax Software Odyssey Company Profiles: Petz Enterprises." *Accounting Technology,* October 2001, Vol. 17(9), p. 41.

"Petz Enterprises." *Accounting Technology,* October 2003, Vol. 19(9) p. 43.

Petz Press Release. "Petz Enterprises Sees Decreased Sales of Tax Software and Diminished Use of Professional Tax Preparers as Impact of New IRS Electronic Filing Initiatives." November 12, 2002; see www.taxbrain.com/about/news.

Petz Press Release. "Petz Enterprises Reports Record Tax Season." May15, 2003; see www.taxbrain.com/about/news.

Petz Press Release; "Is Your Neighborhood Tax Office Going the Way of the Dinosaur?" December 4, 2003; see www.taxbrain.com/about/news.

Petz Press Release. "For 2004, the TaxBrain Online Tax Center™ Is Not Participating in the IRS Free Filing Program." 2004, http://www.taxbrain.com/services/service_irsFreeFilingProgram.asp.

"TaxBrain Online Tax Center™ Braced for Blitz of Millions of Last-Minute Filers Using Internet to Beat April 15th Deadline." *BizWire,* March 19, 2004; see www.taxbrain.com/about/news.

Wiles, Russ. "IRS Free-Filing Rule Raises Ire." *Cincinnati Enquirer,* February 11, 2004; http://www.enquirer.com/editions/2004/02/11/biz_freefile11.html.

Case: Pac-West Telecomm, Inc.

Located in Stockton, California, Pac-West Telecomm (ticker: PACW) was founded in 1980 by Wally Griffin. The company is a competitive local exchange carrier (CLEC), which is a technical description for a telephone company that is not one of the original Bell companies. With the breakup of the telephone monopoly in 1986, the way was cleared for new firms to step in and provide voice and data services. Of course, it would be incredibly expensive to provide service to individuals, so the company focuses on communications for businesses. In particular, Pac-West dominates in providing data connections for Internet service providers and call centers. The company can provide one-stop service for all telecommunication needs, including voice and data (company Web site).

Internet Service Providers

Perhaps the most interesting service provided by Pac-West is its extensive telecommunications for West Coast ISPs. If you have a dial-up Internet account, you have to call a point-of-presence (POP) phone number. This number connects your modem to another modem, which is connected to a router and gets you on the Internet. But where is that modem and router located? One solution might be to put banks of modems in many cities and then connect them together. But that approach would require high-speed Internet lines in hundreds or thousands of locations even in small cities. Remember that most people want to dial local phone numbers to connect to the Internet. The solution Pac-West offers is to place telephone switches in these multiple areas. You dial that local phone, the switch transfers the call to one of Pac-West's SuperPOPs, which then connects to the Internet. Costs are reduced by consolidating the POP connections to a few locations. Reliability is higher because it is easier to provide multiple modems and backup facilities in the limited number of SuperPOPs.

Pac-West does not sell individual Internet connections. Instead, ISPs contract to use Pac-West's network. In 2000, over 90 ISPs were using the system, including Earthlink and Net-Zero (press release May 2000). The company had $95 million in revenue in 1999, followed by $139 million in 2000 (annual report). For the most part, Pac-West leases high-speed lines in bulk and then resells services to smaller firms. For example, in 2000, the company signed with Qwest for exclusive rights to an OC-48 optical transport ring from central to southern California. The line provides speeds of 2.4 gigabits per second ("Qwest" 2000). Jason Mills, vice president of network operations for Pac-West, notes that "ISPs and corporations need to focus on their core business, not building, financing and administering a widely distributed access network" (Alcatel).

In 2003 and 2004, several firms introduced data compression technology to reduce the time it takes to transfer data on dial-up lines. Pac-West installed this equipment on its servers and made it available to its ISP clients. With virtually no additional effort or change in technology, the ISPs could now offer faster access to individual customers. Wayne Bell, Pac-West's vice president of marketing and sales, observed: "The content acceleration technologies that are available through our partner program offer dial-up subscribers an Internet experience up to 5x faster than traditional dial-up, including web surfing, file downloads, and email, at a fraction of the cost of broadband alternatives, such as DSL, cable, and wireless. By partnering with our ISP customers to enhance their dial-up service, we help them improve customer satisfaction, reduce churn, and generate new revenue streams, particularly in areas where DSL, cable, and wireless are not available" (press release 2004).

Growth and the Telecommunications Crash

In 2001 and 2002, the telecommunications industry suffered a major collapse. In part, the crash was driven by the dot-com Internet crash. As firms failed, payments to Internet providers declined. But a big part of the telecommunications crash happened in the network side, when several large firms filed for bankruptcy. The problem was that they had overbuilt capacity. Anticipating huge and continued Internet expansion, some firms borrowed heavily to lay thousands of miles of fiber optic cables. When demand never materialized, they filed for bankruptcy. Pac-West avoided this fate. In 2002, Griffin noted that "we stayed out of fiber. We're not digging any holes in the ground. That's what kept us at a lower debt rating." Even so, with sales of $150 million in 2002, Pac-West lost $34.7 million ("Pac-West Telecomm" 2002).

Despite the challenges, Pac-West is still a substantial presence in the West Coast states. In 2004, Pac-West reported that it carries about 20 percent of the dial-up Internet traffic in California. It also carries over 120 million minutes of voice and data traffic per day (company Web site).

The Role of the FCC

The Federal Communications Commission (FCC) both through policy and through losing some court cases has caused some consternation among the CLECs. One FCC order phases out the line sharing policy that was imposed on the local telephone monopolies. These companies were originally required to offer a choice of ISPs to DSL subscribers. If you wanted a high-speed line, you had to pay the phone monopoly to handle the communication over the copper wire from your house to a switching facility. But you had a choice of using the phone company as the ISP to connect to the Internet or a third company. Dropping this rule most likely will result in less competition and possibly higher prices for DSL services (press release May 2003). If prices for DSL do increase, demand for higher-speed dial-up connections is likely to increase. So, Pac-West could benefit.

The other major shift in policy occurred when the U.S. Solicitor General refused to seek Supreme Court review of an FCC order that was overturned in a federal court. The original order gave the FCC the power to regulate prices for unbundled network elements (UNEs) from the local phone monopolies. The original monopoly breakup decree required that the phone companies lease lines and physical space to other companies so that they could connect to individual phone lines and offer new services. The FCC order enabled the agency to control the pricing for these leases. Since the order was overturned, the monopoly phone companies are now free to charge any price they choose. These increased costs have the potential to put rival CLECs out of business. However, John Sumpter, Pac-West's vice president of Regulatory, notes that "Pac-West does not employ UNEs in its current network architecture in any significant way, and therefore is not directly impacted by these actions." But he also gets a nice jab in at the same time: "Indirectly, however, perpetual regulatory confusion and biased decision making in favor of the former monopolies continue to impede the benefits of competition intended by the 1996 Telecom Act" (PRNewsWire 2004).

Investors

A company the size of Pac-West requires decent capitalization. Pac-West was a "closely held" company, which means it had only a few key stockholder investors. In 1998, an investment group led by Safeguard Scientifics acquired Pac-West for $115 million. The infusion of cash was primarily used to pay for expansions ("Technology Brief" 1998). Most of the money was provided by venture capital firms: Bay Alarm Co., SCP Private Equity Partners, William Blair Capital Partners, and TL Ventures.

In 2000, at the height of the Internet bubble, the group took Pac-West public with an initial public offering (IPO). The offering raised about $106 million, primarily targeted for capital expenditures and working capital (Postelnicu 2000). The company had profits of $3.6 million on revenues of $139 million in 2000. Although revenues increased in 2001 and 2002, the company suffered $34.8 million in losses in 2001. It recovered slightly to a $2 million profit in 2002. In 2003, the company downsized to reduce costs, and revenue plunged by almost 18 percent to $134.6 million with a net loss of $15 million (corporate annual report).

Adjusted for splits, Pac-West's stock price peaked at $40 a share early in 2000. Suffering from the dot-com crash and then the telecommunication industry meltdown, the stock plunged in 2001 and 2002. In 2003, the company was almost delisted from NASDAQ when its price fell below $1 per share. The company had planned a reverse stock split in 2003 to increase the price of its stock, but in August, the stock price had recovered sufficiently to meet the listing criteria (press release August 2003).

Questions

1. Can Pac-West survive? What will the company need to do to grow?

2. Since the industry is heavily regulated, what can the government do to encourage growth in firms like Pac-West? Should this growth be encouraged?

3. What ongoing information technology events will affect the growth and survival of Pac-West?

4. Can Pac-West make better use of information technology or the Internet to improve sales or reduce costs?

Additional Reading

Alcatel, http://www.businessweek.com/adsections/broadband/innovation/publicnet/alcatel.htm.

Pac-West Press Release. "Pac-West Telecomm Increases Revenues 114 Percent." May 1, 2000; see www.pacwest.com.

Pac-West Press Release. "Pac-West Telecomm Launches New Dial Broadband Service to ISPs." May 13, 2003.

Pac-West Press Release. "Pac-West Telecomm Regains Compliance with Nasdaq Listing Requirements." August 11, 2003.

Pac-West Press Release. "Pac-West Telecomm Launches Content Acceleration Partner Program." May 18, 2004.

"Pac-West Telecomm Earnings Down." *Sacramento Business Journal,* August 7, 2002.

Postelnicu, Andrei. "Pac-West Telecomm Inc." *Venture Capital Journal,* January 1, 2000.

PRNewsWire. "Pac-West Telecomm Anticipates No Direct Impact from Recent FCC Triennial Review Actions." June 10, 2004.

"Qwest Communications Awarded $24 Million Contract from Pac-West Telecomm for Optical Network Services." BizWatch, September 12, 2000.

"Technology Brief—SAFEGUARD SCIENTIFICS INC.: Investor Group to Acquire Pac-West Telecomm Inc." *The Wall Street Journal,* July 7, 1998.

Case: Jose Latour, Immigration Lawyer

Professional services such as a legal firm are an important element of entrepreneurship. Many of the firms are small and specialized. Jose Latour was running such a firm in Miami specializing in immigration law. By most measures, Latour was successful; he was winning many of his cases and his clients were happy. But he was unhappy. He was working 70 to 75 hours a week, under constant stress. His wife was working as the office manager, and the added pressure was stressing his marriage (Stuart 2002).

Then, at age 35, he decided to cut back. He hired two staff lawyers and an associate attorney. At the same time, he discovered the Internet and created USVisaNews.com to provide a resource to employers and potential immigrants. He initially played with it as a hobby; today, it dominates the world of immigration law. It contains thousands of pages on detailed legal questions, including forms, news stories that are updated daily, and question-and-answer sections. The site has raised Latour's $1.7 million firm into national prominence. Clients, both individuals and firms looking to hire immigrants, can use the Web site to find information and to contact the lawyers. In 1998, the firm gained $200,000 in new business from the Web site, and double that the next year. About 80 percent of its business is conducted over the Internet (Cisco 2000).

But the site is way more than just a marketing vehicle. The real key is that it changed the way the firm interacts with clients. Instead of long phone calls, much of the communication is via e-mail. The system automatically tracks e-mail messages by client and sequences them properly. The legal staff can easily follow each client's issues. The firm's eight-person staff receives an average of 300 messages a day and responds to every one on the same day.

Initially, Latour focused on finding immigrants work in the health care industry. With changing Medicare laws, and the new focus on the Internet, he found it more profitable to emphasize information technology jobs. Some of his clients are large high-tech firms that need to recruit specific skills. His firm handles the paperwork. The high-tech firms, and the computer-skilled immigrants, find it easy to communicate via e-mail.

The network overall is relatively simple. About a dozen computers are networked within the company via a LAN. Workers have access to each other's drives to share information. The main server is leased from a company that also provides a firewall. A Cisco 1600 router provides a connection through a T1 line to the Internet (Cisco 2000).

And Latour's stress levels? He reduced his workweek to 30 hours with the same income level. He lives with his wife on Key Largo, 400 miles from the office, and telecommutes. He observes that "I would not have continued to practice law but for the Internet" (Stuart 2002).

Questions

1. Why was the Internet so beneficial to Latour? Would other law firms experience the same benefits?

2. How did information technology change the operations within the firm?

3. Could other types of small businesses use similar techniques to increase sales or reduce costs?

Additional Reading

Cisco. 2000, *Growing with Technology Awards Finalist*. http://www.cisco.com/warp/public/cc/general/growing/virtual/lator_cp.pdf.

Stuart, Anne. "The Fourth Annual Inc Web Awards: Transformations." *Inc,* December 2002.

Summary Industry Questions

1. What information technologies have helped this industry?

2. Did the technologies provide a competitive advantage or were they quickly adopted by rivals?

3. Which technologies could this industry use that were developed in other sectors?

4. Is the level of competition increasing or decreasing in this industry? Is it dominated by a few firms, or are they fairly balanced?

5. What problems have been created from the use of information technology and how did the firms solve the problems?

PART THREE

Tactics and Strategies

9 TEAMWORK

10 BUSINESS DECISIONS

11 STRATEGIC ANALYSIS

How do information systems help managers make better decisions?

How does information technology help teams share information? Can computers make decisions? How can information systems make your company better than the competition?

Business decisions can be complex. Complexity can arise from several areas, including the use of huge amounts of data, difficult mathematical formulations, uncertain relationships, detailed linkages to multiple business units, and physical or procedural constraints. Middle-level managers in all functional areas face complex problems. Various models have been created to help you analyze these problems and evaluate alternative answers. Information technology provides several tools to help managers collect data, evaluate models, evaluate output, and make decisions.

Ongoing research into artificial intelligence has led to additional tools to tackle specific problems. Expert systems, robotics, and neural networks are sophisticated tools to solve complex problems.

Strategic analyses represent some of the most difficult decisions a manager can face. Strategy represents fundamental changes in the operations of the business. Information systems are used to search for useful changes. Information systems have also been useful in creating a competitive advantage.

CHAPTER NINE

Teamwork

Chapter Outline

Introduction

Communication

e-Mail, Instant Messaging, and Voice Mail

Web Pages and Blogs

Scheduling and Project Management

Conferences and Meetings

Mobile Systems

Collaboration

Shared Documents and Changes

Version Control

Information Rights Management

Workflow

Group Decision Support Systems

Knowledge Management

Organizational Memory

Service Processes

Microsoft SharePoint

Communication and Scheduling

Collaboration

Workflow

Knowledge Management

Summary

Key Words

Web Site References

Additional Reading

Review Questions

Exercises

Cases: Package Delivery

What You Will Learn in This Chapter

- How can information systems be used to support teams of workers?
- How many different ways are there to communicate with team members? Which method is best for each type of message?
- How can several people work on the same documents?
- How does an organization remember past events?
- Where can you find a system that provides these groupware capabilities?

How does technology help teams work together? Everyone has heard of FedEx—the company that invented overnight delivery of small packages. But FedEx is not alone; it must compete with several other large companies to earn your business. Being on time and at a reasonable price are important attributes to success. FedEx achieves its success through communication and teamwork. Downstream workers have access to information about incoming packages and can alter their schedules if necessary to provide better service.

Since 2000, with several mergers, FedEx has grown beyond overnight deliveries. The company now controls several package delivery and shipping carriers. It also acquired Kinko's in 2004. Information systems are used to integrate these operations and work closer with customers. Ultimately, to FedEx, teamwork entails identifying customer needs and finding new ways to solve problems.

Introduction

How can information systems be used to support teams of workers? Companies are increasingly approaching problems and decisions with teams, often built from members drawn from across the company. Workers can be members of several teams at the same time, and teammates might work in different parts of the country or around the world. Sharing information is a major element of teamwork, and networks are needed to transfer data and share resources. But beyond simple sharing, Figure 9.1 indicates that workers need to work collaboratively on a collection of project documents. Over the past few years, the standard personal productivity tools have gained features to support collaboration and sharing. Additional tools are available to stay in touch with teammates, discuss strategies, schedule meetings, and share research. As a manager, you need to use these tools on a regular basis to become more efficient. Microsoft SharePoint provides several tools to integrate communication and document sharing for teams of workers.

Teamwork is not an invention of the past couple of years. Most teams have developed methods to handle the collaboration needs of the group. Many organizations still use paper-based systems. Paper documents are photocopied and circulated for review. Individuals suggest changes and corrections, which are forwarded to one person. Meetings are held in person—people sometimes fly thousands of miles for meetings, everyone takes notes, and some people dominate the group discussions. Someday, people will look back and consider these systems to be quaint and inefficient.

FIGURE 9.1

Teamwork: Businesses increasingly rely on teams of workers that require coordination and shared documents. Several tools exist to help workers collaborate on common documents schedule meetings, and track changes.

TRENDS

Personal computers originally provided support for basic personal tasks—writing documents, computing totals, and drawing charts. In the 1990s, companies realized the importance of networks for sharing data. In the process, companies are beginning to realize that networks can change the way managers work. Instead of relying on rigid management hierarchies, small teams can be created to solve problems as they arise. Communication across networks makes it possible for teammates to be located anywhere within the company. Beyond the benefits of communication, can information systems do even more to support teams?

Look at the trends from another perspective for a minute. If you work for Microsoft, how many more features can be added to Word, Excel, and PowerPoint? Most people use only the basic elements in any of these tools. But what do managers need? How do people ac-

tually work with computers? Microsoft began seriously asking these questions before 2000. Researchers followed information workers to find answers. Bill Gates provided some answers in the New York unveiling of Office 2003. The typical information worker uses Office 4 hours a day. The typical tasks are e-mail (1+ hours), creating/authoring (2 hours), phone calls (1+ hours), data analysis (1+ hours), administrative (1+ hours), and meetings (2+ hours).

One of the biggest changes in Office software in the past couple of years has been the introduction of powerful tools to help groups of workers communicate and collaborate. Communication includes e-mail, scheduling, and task management. Collaboration includes working on shared documents, discussions, and meetings. These groupware features make it easier for teams to solve problems.

Teamwork revolves around two fundamental concepts: communication and collaboration. Teammates need to communicate on many topics, and you have several communication methods available today. One challenge is to choose the right communication method for each problem. Collaboration entails working together. Today, that means sharing electronic documents and tracking the revisions made to each document. More than simply combining changes, it also involves discussing why the changes were made. Collaboration also involves scheduling tasks and maintaining project schedules.

Software tools have existed for several years to help with the basic communication and collaboration tasks. The strengths of today's tools are the integration and focus on teamwork. Today, you can automate the business processes by automatically triggering messages and monitoring the schedules and the flow of documents through the company. One goal of these systems is to track the decisions, documentation, and discussions by everyone involved in a decision. If this knowledge is collected and indexed carefully, it can become the foundation of the organization's memory. If you need to solve a difficult problem, you could turn to this knowledge base to find similar problems, or suggestions from workers who faced the same problems.

Communication

How many different ways are there to communicate with team members? Which method is best for each type of message? Communication is a critical element in teamwork. You need to schedule meetings, discuss options, share and revise documents, and identify opinions. Because communication is so important to teams, several technologies are available. You can choose between simple meetings in the hall, phone calls or voice mail, e-mail and instant messaging, and online conferences, or full-blown team meetings. How do you choose the proper communication method?

As shown in Figure 9.2, one of the issues in organizing your daily work life is to manage the interruptions. Phone calls, e-mail messages, people walking into your office, and IM requests all break your concentration. One question you have to answer is to identify which method works best for you (and your teammates). Having multiple channels of communication gives you flexibility. Your goal is to prioritize each technology and method so that you accomplish your goals, yet still have time to work with the group. If possible, you might try to get the group to agree on the priorities of the main methods. Most organizations have a culture that establishes these priorities, but sometimes you need to discuss them so that everyone treats the channels with the same priority.

FIGURE 9.2

Communication interruptions: Which type of interruption is the least disruptive for you? Need to finish your work. Need to help the team.

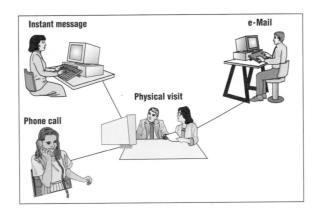

FIGURE 9.3

E-mail groupware: E-mail messages with attached documents are sent to team members. In this case, the build team sends requests for changes to the designers, who add more documents and forward the messages to the client and to the accountants for costing data and approvals.

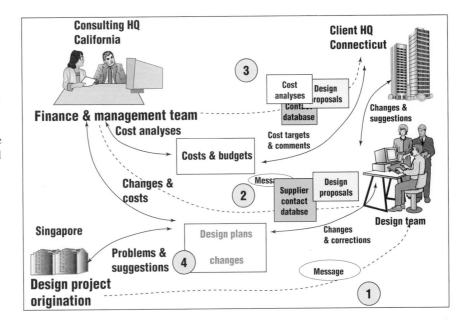

e-Mail, Instant Messaging, and Voice Mail

E-mail is a relatively common means of communicating. It has the fundamental advantage of being asynchronous, which means that the sender and receiver do not have to be connected at the same time. The recipient can pick up and reply to a message at any time. In a group context, e-mail is even more important because it is easy to send messages to the entire group. Moreover, the messages can be saved and organized so that they create a thread or history of a discussion. E-mail is also used to send documents as attachments.

As shown in Figure 9.3, e-mail systems such as Lotus Notes and Microsoft Exchange were originally advertised as **groupware** tools because of the support provided for attachments. The e-mail systems essentially become moving databases of documents. One of the drawbacks to this approach is that multiple copies of the documents are transferred continually with each message—placing higher demands on the network. It is also somewhat challenging to track versions and identify the current documents. Plus multiple people might be altering the same documents at the same time, so someone has to merge the final changes into a single document.

Instant messaging has become popular in the past few years—particularly with students. Most of the initial use has been among individuals in a social context. However, the technology can also be a time-saver for groups of workers. Each team member can add the others onto the buddy list. The ability to see if someone is online can save considerable time. If you encounter a problem while working, you could immediately see who might be available to answer questions. Yet if you are busy and receive an IM request, you can still choose to ignore it until you have time for a break.

Technology Toolbox: Meeting Online with NetMeeting

Problem: How can you meet with a few people online to discuss a document?

Tools: Several online meeting systems have been created to help you conduct a meeting for a small group. Microsoft NetMeeting is a free tool that is built into Windows XP. More sophisticated systems are available as stand-alone packages or as Web services, but they can be expensive. NetMeeting supports both voice and video connections as long as you have microphones and webcams.

To set up a meeting, each computer must have the software installed and configured. The easiest way to configure it is to use Start/Run/conf and follow the instructions. Then, one machine becomes the host by starting a call and selecting the host option. The person at this machine has to tell the others the address of the machine. The address can be given as the computer name, but it is usually best to use the numeric IP address of the host machine. The other participants call the host by starting NetMeeting on their computers and entering the IP address of the host machine. Note that most firewalls and network address translation (NAT) schemes will hide the host and make it unreachable.

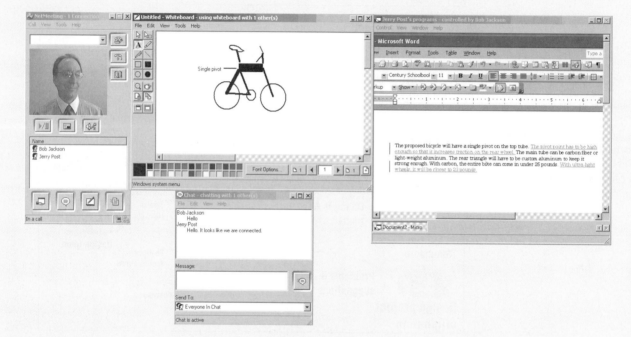

Once the meeting connections have been established, you can talk to the participants. A basic chat room is provided so that you can share written comments with others in the group. The whiteboard is a favorite of many people because you can simultaneously create or annotate a drawing. You can also share a document or almost any other software tool on your computer. Simply start the software, load the document, and use the Share button on the NetMeeting control panel. You can allow others to take control and make changes, but only one person can have control at a time. Remember that you need relatively fast connections to transfer voice and video. If the connection becomes overloaded, you might want to stop the video transmission.

Quick Quiz:

1. What problems are you likely to encounter if more than four or five participants try to use online meeting software?
2. Why is voice communication important in an online meeting?
3. Is a video connection critical to online meetings?

Voice mail systems were created so you can leave phone messages for people who are out of the office or talking to another person. Current voice mail systems have many advanced options, such as the ability to send the same message to multiple people, receive notifications when a message is retrieved, and archive messages for later use. The biggest drawback to voice mail is that some people leave long messages that you have to listen to before they get to the real point of the call. Long e-mail messages are annoying, but at least you can quickly scan the message to find the important elements. It is also difficult to search stored voice mail messages to find particular topics.

E-mail, voice mail, and IM are all push communication technologies. As a message sender, you choose when to place the message and contact the receiver. The other person did not necessarily ask to be contacted, so you are interrupting his or her work. Of the three methods, e-mail is the least intrusive since the recipient has to retrieve the messages and open each one. Because e-mail is less intrusive, you have to remember that any particular message might never actually be read. It could be buried in a stack of junk messages, or even lost or destroyed. Most systems enable you to ask for receipt confirmation when a message is opened. But these systems are not always automatic. The user can often override this request and tell the computer not to send the confirmation message. Voice mail messages suffer from the same issues and have similar controls. The point is that as the message sender, you need to understand the limitations of the tools. If you need confirmation of a message, it is your responsibility to follow up and make sure the message was received and understood.

Web Pages and Blogs

Web pages were initially created to share information among researchers. As a common platform, you can make files available to anyone on your team—regardless of where they are located or what equipment they are using. Most people are familiar with Web browsers and pages. Several tools help you create Web sites and update documents. Despite these tools, it is challenging to create Web sites and keep updating the pages. Web pages are generally seen as a client-pull technology. You create the Web pages and place them on the site. Team members can view or retrieve the documents, but there is no good mechanism for making changes or replacing the contents. In one sense, Web pages are a broadcast technology, where you can provide the same data to many people. Recognition of this feature makes it clearer when you should use Web sites for communication.

Web logs or blogs were created largely for individuals to use to create diaries on the Internet. The technology was largely developed to overcome the difficulties in creating and updating Web sites. A blog consists of a site framework that enables others to read your comments. A simple editing tool makes it easy to write daily or hourly comments and immediately post them to the Web. The process is simplified so you can focus on the content. It is also designed to save all of your earlier comments so people can trace the history. These tools could be used in a business or teamwork setting. They would provide a record of the team's actions and decisions. Each person could record current problems, solutions, and describe issues for discussion. Later, if questions arise, you can search the logs to find proposed solutions or learn exactly why a particular decision was made. Of course, you would restrict access to the logs. The big question is whether the team members will take the time to record their thoughts and relevant issues on a regular basis. Blog software is easy to use and you can find shareware implementations that can be installed for little or no cost; so it is relatively inexpensive to test the technology.

Scheduling and Project Management

Scheduling is a challenge with any team project. It is even more complicated when people work on several teams at the same time. Scheduling a meeting or conference is difficult and often requires several messages back and forth just to find a common time. Electronic calendar tools make this process a little easier. Teammates keep personal calendars that are shared with each other. Each person can check to see if there is an open time slot or use advanced tools to help find the best time for a meeting.

However, these tools can also make it harder to plan. If your schedule is constantly changing, you can waste time jumping between projects. For example, you might have a big project presentation scheduled for tomorrow, so you spend time organizing your notes. Then the meeting gets shifted because a higher priority event occurs. You have to rush around trying to collect and organize data for the new meeting.

Project management tools were created to help manage and control groups of workers on large projects. These tools are discussed in more detail in Chapter 13. The basic concept is that you define each task that needs to be accomplished and how these tasks depend on each other. For example, in construction, you must first lay the foundation before you can frame a building. If an earlier task gets delayed, it pushes back all of the dependent tasks. Project management software graphically shows the tasks and their dependencies. As tasks are completed or delayed, the schedule is updated and everyone can see the changes.

REALITY BYTES   Lord of the Team

The Lord of the Rings trilogy was one of the largest movies filmed in many years, and all three movies were created in 150 locations in an amazing 274 days. Director Peter Jackson was able to direct the movies in three primary locations using video communications from Polycom. Jackson linked all of the movie cameras into Polycom's videoconferencing system and each day could view footage over a high-speed line from the Pinewood editing studio in the UK; the main studio in Warkworth, New Zealand; or the on-location sites. Jackson could then suggest changes in lighting, camera angles, or character development. The film crew built a network of fiber optic and radio communications to feed the signals to the videoconferencing system. From there, the footage was transmitted via satellite to wherever Jackson was located. Operating in subzero temperatures in the winter and searing heat in the summer, the system made long-distance collaboration possible.

Source: Adapted from "Lord of the Rings Director Relies on Polycom Video Communications to Film Three Movies Concurrently," Polycom news release, December 18, 2003.

Conferences and Meetings

Face-to-face meetings are expensive. Even if everyone on the team works in the same building, a meeting requires everyone to stop their work, organize their presentations, and set aside most other communications during the meeting. If people have to travel to a meeting, the costs are considerably higher. Of course, sometimes the major point of a meeting is to create a deadline that forces everyone to organize their work and meet the project milestones.

Several electronic systems have been developed to support online conferences and meetings. At the high end, **video conference** systems provide real-time voice and video connections so people in different locations can hear and see each other. Videoconference systems require video cameras, microphones, and television displays at each location. For more realistic conferences, some systems use multiple cameras at each location or provide remote control over the cameras. The primary drawback to the systems is the bandwidth required to transmit realistic video data. Early systems used proprietary connections to ensure sufficient bandwidth. Newer systems can run across Internet connections, but require special configurations of routers to ensure the continuous availability of the required bandwidth. The problems multiply if the video signals have to be sent to multiple locations, so most systems operate point-to-point between two locations. Because of the bandwidth demands, a few private companies evolved to provide meeting rooms that can be rented for occasional long-distance meetings.

As bandwidth connections improve, lower-cost systems are being developed that enable you to set up videoconferences using personal computers and Web cameras. Be sure to test the systems first because low resolution cameras or slow-speed links can cause more distractions than benefits. While these systems do not give you the remote control capabilities of the big systems, they can support meetings from your desk. They are particularly useful for meetings with two or three participants.

If you do not need video, it is relatively easy to set up a telephone conference. Most phone systems have provisions to connect several people into one conversation. If your company system does not support these connections, you can pay a fee to an external company to host your phone call. Each participant simply calls a special number at the same time to join the conversation. Note that if you have several people in the same room participating in a phone call, you will have to use a special conference telephone. Polycom is one of the leading vendors. The phone has a speaker and robust microphone to pick up everyone's conversations. More important, it contains circuitry to eliminate audio feedback. Advanced versions of the phones also support **full duplex** communications, which means that you can interrupt someone speaking—because the phone transmits and receives at the same time.

Microsoft's Live Meeting is similar to NetMeeting in terms of features, but it is designed to handle as many as a few thousand participants. It is oriented to a broadcast approach. The video feed can be viewed by everyone. For reasonably sized groups, you can integrate telephone conferencing to handle interactive questions. The system also includes a standard chat tool if you do not want to deal with the telephone costs.

Live Meeting combines broadcast presentation with Web interaction. The presenter can share applications or the desktop with other participants. Team members can be given control to run an application or annotate a document. You can link in Web sites, where each participant can click on links and fill out forms. The polling tool enables you to quickly create questions and let the audience vote. The system also includes the popular electronic whiteboard where each person can contribute and draw in a different color. Of course, you will probably want to limit these interactive features if you are presenting to hundreds of people.

The system also includes a feedback system through a seating chart. At any time, a participant can click the seating chart to request that the presenter slow down or speed up, or to ask a question. The audience notes are displayed to the presenter on a color-coded status board. If you see many requests to slow down (red squares), you know you are going too fast. A useful feature of Live Meeting is that it records the presentation so you can save it on your Web site and customers can replay it later. For example, the Microsoft Office 2003 product launch is available for review from Microsoft.

Mobile Systems

Messaging and conferencing technologies are fairly well established for traditional environments and meetings. Of course, new features are added every year, so you need to keep up with the changes to see which options might be useful for your particular situation. On the other hand, the telecommunications world has changed markedly in the past decade. People now rely on cell phones, PDAs, and wireless Internet access, and want the ability to connect as they travel. As the cellular networks improve, mobile devices are gaining the ability to handle voice, data, and even video connections. At this point, the software does not really exist, but it is easy to forecast that mobile conferencing systems will be developed to work over mobile devices. Today you can use cell phones for voice conference calls. Ultimately, you should be able to add video and data transfer as well. So you will be able to hold meetings with teammates who are traveling in almost any major city.

Collaboration

How can several people work on the same documents? This question forms the heart of collaboration. One teamwork solution is to assign separate issues to each person. Working independently, each person creates documents that are then reviewed by the rest of the team. But some projects are not easily divided, and sometimes groups of people have to work together simultaneously.

Networks and e-mail systems make it possible to send documents to each person. But what if you need to identify the changes made by each person? Or what if you need to change directions and revert to an earlier version of a spreadsheet? And how do you handle issues in a hierarchical system where each person reviews a document and approves it before it can be forwarded to the next authority? With paper-based systems, these issues are generally handled by markups and handwritten margin notes. Microsoft Office contains several features that support electronic collaboration.

Shared Documents and Changes

Sharing documents is relatively easy with LANs and the Internet. Keeping track of when changes were made and who made them, or whether you have the current version of a document, is more difficult. One approach is to use IBM/Lotus Notes or Microsoft Exchange to continually e-mail new versions of documents to everyone in the group. Another approach is to create a central location to hold all of the team's shared documents. Microsoft's SharePoint system makes it easy to create Web-based projects and folders to hold team documents. The site is only accessible by invited team members. The folders hold Office documents that can be opened across standard Web connections. Using the Web connections

REALITY BYTES   Collaborating on Cars

Designing and building automobiles is a complex task involving thousands of people across many companies. Ford created the C3P collaboration system to link its CAD, management, engineering, and product information systems. Linking suppliers into the system provides important benefits to ensure everyone is working with a common set of parts and specifications. Ford also has a customer knowledge system (CKS) to provide real-time information and integration of customer and dealer data. General Motors built Supply-Power as a Web portal, enabling suppliers to interact with multiple GM organizations and subdivisions through a single point. Daimler-Chrysler expanded its IBM Lotus Notes system into an eCollaboration project. Its goal is primarily to link internal workgroup processes, but also aims to consolidate vehicle design, production, marketing, and logistics operations.

Source: Adapted from Linda Rosencrance, "Sharing Their Way to Speed and Profits," *Computerworld,* August 12, 2002.

FIGURE 9.4

Shared documents: By tracking changes, you can record the suggestions by each team member. The toolbar makes it easy to accept or reject the changes as they are merged into the final document.

makes it easy for team members to create and share documents. Placing the documents in a central location makes it easy to ensure that everyone has the most recent version.

Over the past few years, Microsoft has introduced several changes to the Office software suite. Cosmetically, the programs have not changed much in that time. However, some of the most important changes have been made to support teamwork. One of the most useful features is the ability to **track changes** in Word documents. Figure 9.4 shows an example. To see the power of this option, begin by creating a new document and typing a couple of sentences. Then choose the Tools/Track changes option. Now add a new sentence and delete or replace a few words from an existing sentence. As you make the changes, Word adds markup notes. You can send the document to other people on the team and all changes they make will be marked. When you get the document back, you can quickly see the changes that were made. The Reviewing toolbar contains icons to help you find the changes and accept or reject the changes with a single click.

The **protect document** options provide additional control over the document. You have the ability to control what changes (if any) other people can make. For instance, if you need to maintain consistency with other documents, you can prevent people from adding styles. You can also limit which team members can edit your document. Another option is to not allow people to change the actual document but give them the ability to add comments. Adobe Acrobat has similar features that enable you to specify the items that can be changed by other users. You can password-protect the document and limit users to entering form data or allow them to modify the document.

The ability to track changes and restrict changes is a powerful tool for teamwork. At some point in creating work you need to lock down the changes. Even if everyone initially contributes to a document, you need to freeze the changes so everyone can work forward from the same point. If people keep going back and changing costs or plans, it alters the rest of the project planning. The ability to perform these tasks electronically makes it easier to

FIGURE 9.5

Version control: Each revision of the document is saved individually along with comments. At any time, team members can roll back the changes and revert to an earlier version. Or they might simply refer to an earlier version and copy sections to be pasted into the current version.

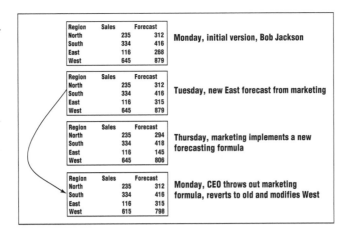

share documents. You no longer have to worry about having multiple copies floating around and trying to find them or trying to identify what changes were made.

Version Control

Version control is a powerful tool both for teams and for individual documents because it automatically saves every revision. Most documents need multiple revisions—whether they are text documents, spreadsheets, or artwork. Have you ever created a spreadsheet, made dozens of changes, and then realized that you were better off with the first version? Multiply this situation by the number of team members and throw in a changing environment. Your manager or client walks in and says that last week's version was much better. Version control systems save multiple copies of every document. As shown in Figure 9.5, each revision is saved independently along with comments and the name of the person who modified the document. At any time, team members can revert back to an earlier version. You can also open an earlier version and copy just a few elements and paste them into the current version.

Most version control systems work from a database. You **check out** a file when you want to change it. When you are finished making changes, you **check in** the file and add comments about the changes. The comments can be almost anything, but you want to add enough detail so others understand what was changed. The members of the team should discuss the types of comments and level of detail that you expect to see in the version control system. Ideally, the version control system should be integrated into your file server so that versions are automatically maintained, or at least the team members are reminded to check out/check in the documents.

Information Rights Management

What would happen if your marketing forecast containing your top customer list and expectations was delivered to your competitors? Or what if your employee list with salaries, bonuses, and manager comments was distributed throughout the company? Obviously, these are dangerous outcomes. How do you prevent them from happening? As explained in Chapter 5, you can store the documents on a server and assign access controls so only certain users can read or change them. But how do you prevent one of the authorized employees from copying the file to his or her laptop or e-mailing it to someone else? The standard solution is to simply trust your employees. But what if you need a more secure solution?

Information rights management (IRM) is one answer to these questions. The technologies are still evolving and few standards exist. The latest versions of Microsoft Office contain some tools to help you control access to documents. As shown in Figure 9.6, essentially every chosen document is protected through encryption, and the encryption keys are stored on a central server. The creator of the document gets to specify the list of people who can open or edit a document. These people are authenticated against the server list, and the server issues the appropriate decryption key to open the document with the specified permissions. Regardless of how the document was obtained (from the server, by e-mail, or

FIGURE 9.6

Information rights management: Each document is encrypted and the decryption keys are stored on a special server. Users must be connected to the network to exchange authorization identifiers and obtain the decryption key. The document is unlocked but users are allowed to perform only the specified tasks.

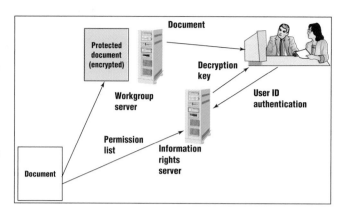

a copy on a USB drive), the user must first be authenticated against the information rights server before the decryption key will be issued. Furthermore, you can specify a list of permissions that limit what each user can do with the document. For example, you could prevent the use of cut-and-paste, or disable printing to make it more difficult for authorized users to make copies or spread the document.

The power of information rights management is that the permissions are enforced regardless of how the document was obtained. The main drawback is that you need a server to identify the users and provide the decryption keys. Microsoft provides a trial service to enable you to test the system, but ultimately, you would have to pay to install a Microsoft server to implement their system. To activate the Microsoft system, choose File/Permission within an Office document. With their own server, companies can create detailed customized permission schemes. The IRM scheme also enables you to set an expiration date for content. After the specified date users will not be allowed to decrypt the file.

Workflow

Workflow or **business process management (BPM)** is the concept that some actions have to be performed in a sequence. In particular, documents need to be delivered to and reviewed by various people in sequence. For a simple example, consider a purchase order. You need to purchase some equipment or software for your job. You begin by filling out a requisition form detailing the equipment and how it will be used. You forward the document to your supervisor, who might ask for some revisions or additional data. Once approved, it is forwarded to another manager or perhaps to the MIS department. With additional revisions and changes, the document is forwarded to purchasing and accounting. These departments create purchase orders and obtain responses and information from vendors. Some of the vendor information might be forwarded to you for verification or approval. Ultimately, the item is ordered, delivered, and installed. Remember that this was a "simple" purchase example. Team projects can be considerably more complex with more interactions and more approvals.

In the past, organizations created workflow systems using paper documents and internal procedures. Each document contained sign-off lines to indicate how the document was supposed to be circulated and to highlight the approvals. As shown in Figure 9.7, electronic workflow systems are being developed that provide similar features for electronic documents. Of course, you could just e-mail the document to everyone for approval, but standard e-mail messages do not provide the desired sequencing. Workflow systems work with e-mail but add the desired sequencing that you provide by filling out a sequenced list of addresses. Each person receives the message with attached documents. When finished with the document, the message is forwarded to the next person on the list. Ideally, the workflow system would provide feedback indicators to everyone on the list, so that you could check on the progress of individual items or get a list of items that are likely to show up on your desk in the next couple of days. Microsoft has embedded some workflow features into Office, but more sophisticated controls are available through specialized vendors such as Legato.

FIGURE 9.7

Business process management: A large purchase requires approvals and evaluations by several groups. Each event triggers tasks by others. An automated system can track the process and send messages to those involved as the process moves forward.

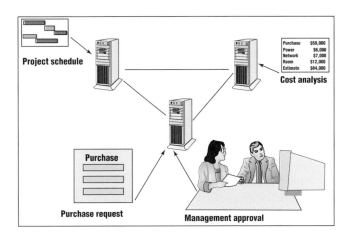

Group Decision Support Systems

How do groups make decisions? How can dozens of people present their ideas and questions? How can you keep track of the various statements and problems raised? Specialized tools such as a **group decision support system (GDSS)** were created to answer these questions. Most versions of a GDSS use a special meeting room, where each participant is seated at a networked computer. A facilitator operates the network and keeps the discussion moving in the right direction. Before the meeting, the primary decision maker meets with the facilitator to establish the objective of the meeting. They set up sample questions and design the overall strategy.

Typical meetings begin with a brainstorming session, where participants are asked to think of ideas, problems, and potential solutions. They type each of these into categories on their computers. The basic ideas and suggestions are stored in a database and shared with the group through the networked computers.

In terms of discussion and comments, the facilitator can choose individual items and project them on a screen for the entire group to analyze. Participants can write comments or criticisms of any idea at any time. This system is particularly helpful if many participants come up with ideas and comments at the same time. The computer enables everyone to enter comments at the same time, which is faster than waiting for each person to finish speaking.

Another feature of using the computer for the entry of ideas and comments is that they can be anonymous. Although each comment is numbered, they are not traced back to the original author, so people are free to criticize their supervisor's ideas. Anonymity reduces embarrassment and encourages people to submit riskier ideas.

At various points, the facilitator can call for participants to vote on some of the ideas and concepts. Depending on the software package, there can be several ways to vote. In addition to traditional one-vote methods, there are several schemes where you place weights on your choices. The votes are done on the computer and results appear instantly. Because it is so easy to vote, the GDSS encourages the group to take several votes. This approach makes it easier to drop undesirable alternatives early in the discussion.

One useful feature of conducting the meeting over a computer network is that all of the comments, criticisms, and votes are recorded. They can all be printed at the end of the session. Managers can review all of the comments and add them to their reports.

In theory, a meeting could be conducted entirely on a computer network, saving costs and travel time if the participants are located in different cities. Also, if it is designed properly, a GDSS can give each participant access to the corporate data while he or she is in the meeting. If a question arises about various facts, the computer can find the answer without waiting for a second meeting.

Perhaps the greatest drawback to a GDSS is that it requires participants to type in their ideas, comments, and criticisms. Most people are used to meetings based on oral discussions. Even if they have adequate typing skills, a GDSS can inhibit some managers.

Along the same lines, in a traditional meeting, only one person speaks at a time, and everyone concentrates on the same issues at the same time. With a GDSS, your focus is continually drawn to the many different comments and discussions taking place at the same time. People who type rapidly and flit from topic to topic will find that they can dominate the discussions.

In terms of costs, maintaining a separate meeting room with its own network and several computers can be expensive. Unless the facility is used on a regular basis, the computers will be idle a great deal of the time. When you factor in the costs for network software, the GDSS software, and other utilities, the costs multiply. One way to minimize this problem is to lease the facilities that have been established by a couple of universities and some companies (e.g., IBM).

The use of a GDSS also requires a trained facilitator—someone who can lead discussions, help users, and control the GDSS software on the network. Hiring an in-house specialist can be very expensive if there are only a few meetings a year. Again, using facilities from an outside agency can reduce this cost, but it means that someone outside your company is watching and controlling your meeting. Although most facilitators are scrupulously honest, there might be some topics that you do not want to discuss with nonemployees.

One way to overcome these limitations is to alter the approach to meetings. Instead of requiring everyone to get together at the same time in one room, meetings could be held via network discussion groups. Each participant could read messages, add comments, and vote on issues electronically at any time from any location. Again, the Internet offers possibilities to provide these facilities, but it could be a few years before organizations and managers can accept the changes required.

Knowledge Management

How does an organization remember past events? When an event arises similar to one you dealt with in the past, do the employees use the knowledge gained from the prior experience? What happens if several key managers leave your company? These questions are critical to reducing costs, maintaining continuity, and improving the organization. Every organization operates on some type of business processes. Some firms are highly structured and spell out detailed steps to follow in almost any situation. Other companies evolve implicit procedures over time. Many organizations make the same difficult decisions every month or every year. Difficult decisions can require the participation of dozens of employees and analysis of gigabytes of data. It would be nice if the organization could keep the knowledge gained from every decision and apply it to similar problems in the future. In the past, maintaining organizational knowledge was a key management factor in retaining and promoting key employees. But in medium-size and large organizations, turnover, distance, and the challenge of finding experts can make it difficult to maintain and share the knowledge. So, some companies have attempted to create **knowledge management (KM)** systems.

A KM is designed to store any type of data needed to convey the context of the decision and the discussion involved in making the decision. While the system might contain rules, it is primarily a giant database of easily accessible data for experts. KM systems are designed to organize information and to assist people in collaborative projects and research. The system can be relatively unstructured and often consists of many individual cases. Decision makers can search the system for cases with features similar to their current issues. The cases are cross-referenced so that a decision maker might research one aspect of a case and find a related issue. The links make it easy to explore the related issues, tying together a variety of concepts and identifying related problems or consequences.

Because the field is relatively new, the definition of KM is somewhat nebulous and many software vendors promote tools as useful for KM. One of the difficulties is that the decisions and knowledge required can be different for each organization. And organizations may approach decisions differently, so it is unlikely that a single tool will be useful to every company. Instead, each company needs to evaluate specific decisions to determine whether it

REALITY BYTES   Web Logs

Web logs (blogs) provide a relatively simple way to create content on the Internet. Essentially, users can type text into a journal and have it displayed and searchable on the Internet. A telephone study of 1,555 Internet users by Pew Internet in 2004 found that between 2 and 7 percent of adult Internet users in the United States keep their own blogs. Of those, only about 10 percent update them daily.

Source: Adapted from "Study: Very Few Bloggers on Net," *CNN Online,* March 1, 2004.

will be useful to explicitly collect the information and process knowledge that was involved in making the decision.

One of the biggest challenges with KM systems is creating an organizational environment that encourages decision makers to store their knowledge in the system. Initially, the system will have little data, and the early decision makers will have to spend a great deal of time organizing their discussions and creating the files and links necessary to make the system valuable in the future. Companies need to give managers enough time to consolidate their information and provide incentives to encourage them to help build the new system.

Organizational Memory

Organizational memory represents the knowledge held within the company and the processes and procedures used to perform the primary tasks. Imagine what would happen to an organization if all of the managers retired on the same day and all of the procedure books and documents were destroyed. All of the business processes would have to be reinvented. Sometimes reinventing new processes can result in more efficient systems (known as process reengineering). But it takes time to re-create all of the knowledge.

Now, think from a more positive perspective. How can information technology be used to improve organizational memory? Perhaps some events occur only rarely and no one remembers them. Or, perhaps employees try to re-create the wheel for every new event. If you can store the organizational memory in a searchable database and make it easy to use, employees can turn to it to obtain fast, accurate answers and even solutions to current problems.

One of the challenges to KM lies in getting everyone to use the system. Many times it is hard enough to solve a current problem. Most workers will complain about the lack of time to enter all of the issues into the computer. For that reason, KM has to become part of the groupware project. Employees need to store the information so that they can share it with teammates. Organizing it for future use is almost a secondary consideration. By using the system to gain immediate advantages (collaboration and instant access to data), employees will have an incentive to store the information—creating the organizational memory in the process.

Service Processes

Service firms probably have the most to gain from the use of a KM system. Production systems typically already have engineers and support firms testing new ideas and tracking problems. This production knowledge is often saved explicitly or discussed as a professional discipline. Service firms—such as lawyers, doctors, and financial institutions—have less specific processes. Often the service is dependent on one or two people within the firm.

As shown in Figure 9.8, documenting the processes makes it possible to improve the quality of the service. For example, a major premise of the ISO 9001 (and related) quality standard is that all processes need to be documented. You also need to assign measures that enable you to identify problem areas and measure your progress when you make changes. Theoretically, you could write all of the documentation and assessment on paper forms and stash them in a file cabinet. A more useful approach is to store all of the documents and assessment measures and comments in a KM system. The electronic system makes them available throughout the company so that everyone can find the appropriate process, can see the reasons and interactions for the process, and can suggest improvements.

Technology Toolbox: Collaborating with SharePoint

Problem: You need to collaborate on a project with several workers.

Tools: Several groupware and collaboration systems have been created in the last decade, but SharePoint is probably the easiest to configure and use since it is integrated with the standard Office suite. The biggest drawback to SharePoint is that you really need a departmental server running the latest version of Windows Server software. You also have to ensure that everyone has an account either on the server or on Active Directory. These issues are relatively minor in a business setting, but they can be a hurdle in an educational environment.

Once you have the server configured with the SharePoint extensions, you use the administration tools to create a new team site and add members. You can specify the role of each participant (browser, contributor, administrator, and so on). The system makes it easy to e-mail each person to notify them of the Web site group. When you configure the server, be sure to set up the e-mail server so participants can set alerts for changes.

You can configure the home page of the team Web site with the Modify options. For example, you can choose which items (Web parts)

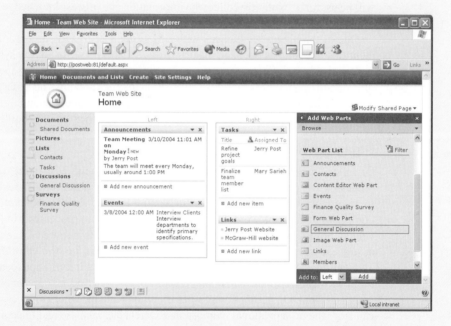

will be displayed and where they are located. The main page is essentially a portal for the team that organizes all of the work. Each person can also customize the home page with additional options. For example, you can have the page display all of the contacts or provide links to messages. Each day when you log on, you can check for urgent messages or examine the progress on the task list. Programmers can create additional Web parts and customize the data displayed on the site. Microsoft includes some pre-built parts such as weather or stock feeds from MSN. By customizing the home page for each project, workers can focus on the most important tasks and monitor progress. Additional features and the standard tools are only a couple of clicks away for any team site.

Quick Quiz:

1. Why would you want to configure the home page differently for different projects?

2. Is there a limit to the number of people you would want to place on a SharePoint team?

3. Research the two products and list the additional features provided by SharePoint Portal.

Microsoft SharePoint

Where can you find a system that provides these groupware capabilities? The benefits of the tools are relatively strong, but will it be expensive and require huge amounts of training to get workers to use these tools? In some cases, the answer is yes. Depending on your needs, you can buy specialized products in most of the groupware categories. On the other hand, Microsoft has integrated groupware tools with Office using the SharePoint product. SharePoint is a set of utilities that reside on a departmental server designed largely to share documents over the Web. Currently, Microsoft offers two version of SharePoint: (1) SharePoint Team Services is a "free" add-on with Office, and (2) SharePoint Portal is an expanded version that you must purchase separately. The discussion and capabilities described

FIGURE 9.8

Service process improvement: A major step in quality improvement is to document each step and provide an assessment measure. Ongoing evaluation of the processes and measures shows you what areas need improvement and measures your progress.

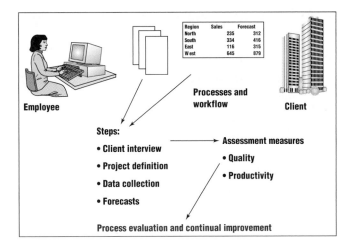

here are based on the free version. Although the tools may not be perfect, they are relatively inexpensive and easy to use. Consequently, you can install them and get employees using them fairly quickly. In terms of the cost, keep in mind that you will probably have to install a departmental server.

Most of the SharePoint tools use standard Web protocols, so authorized users can use them even when they are traveling. A special Web site has to be created to support the tools. Generally, this Web site should be run on a company server, using standard security precautions. If you want higher security, you can run the Web site as a secure site and encrypt the data transmissions. Small companies might consider obtaining the service from their ISPs. Participants are required to log in to the system, and security controls can specify detailed access rights.

Communication and Scheduling

It is always amazing to learn how difficult it is to contact everyone on a team. People work on many projects, at different times, in different locations. Consequently, even simple information can be hard to share. Basic announcements are useful for these situations. Announcements are short messages that are displayed to everyone—generally they are displayed prominently on the first page. Lists can be created to display timetables for tasks, contact names, or any other category needed by the group.

The power of sharing lists through a Web site is that members of the team can see the lists at any time. As authorized members make changes, everyone has access to the current data. Moreover, the lists can be organized and searched by various categories, such as deadline, project sponsor, or participant. Some standard lists exist in SharePoint, such as contacts and schedules. Additional lists can be created at any time. SharePoint also maintains e-mail contact lists for teammates and for any other core contacts that you need to share. This address book is easily accessible by everyone, and a single click launches your e-mail editor.

SharePoint also integrates an instant messenger service. While you are logged into the SharePoint system, it will show you a list of other team members and tell you if they are online. You can click on the name for each person online and send a quick message. As shown in Figure 9.9, SharePoint also includes a discussion system. Most people are familiar with Web-based discussion groups. Discussion administrators establish topics and can specify the roles of the other team members, such as the ability to read or reply to comments. Discussion groups are useful on team projects to discuss issues that arise. The strength of the computer-assisted discussion is that everyone has access to the comments, and the entire record is available if questions arise later. It also makes it easy to search for specific problems. Discussions can be created on any topic. Common business uses include overall comments on scheduling, sharing research information, and discussing problems that arise.

As shown in Figure 9.10, SharePoint also maintains a calendar that is tied to the task list. You can use the calendar as a simple project management system. The calendar shows

FIGURE 9.9

Discussion: You can create multiple discussion threads so all comments on a topic are grouped together. The system maintains the group memory, so teammates can check on the reasons for various decisions.

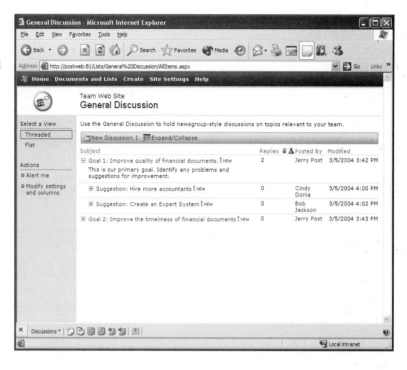

FIGURE 9.10

Project events and tasks: The internal calendar integrates with the event list. The task view is helpful for project management, so you can quickly see what tasks need to be completed and who is responsible for each task.

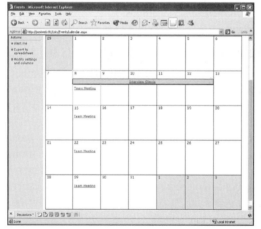

Event calendar

Task list

scheduled events. The task list enables you to assign and monitor tasks by employees. By scheduling tasks and assigning them to various workers, you can easily see which tasks are on schedule and which are falling behind. You can use the calendar and the task completion list to see if some employees need additional help. The system does not offer all of the features of a true project management system, but it displays the basic schedules and is easy to use.

Calendars are also useful for highlighting deadlines and meeting dates. SharePoint will also integrate with Microsoft Outlook, so meetings can be scheduled and automatic reminders will be generated for participants.

Surveys are useful for some business applications. In particular, they come in handy when designing new systems. Generally they are used to obtain a quick perspective on individual opinions. Paper surveys are a pain. Web-based surveys are easy to change, easy to

FIGURE 9.11
Create a survey: You add individual questions to the survey. They can have a variety of formats. After filling in the template for each question, users can enter data over the Web, and you can instantly see the responses on another Web page.

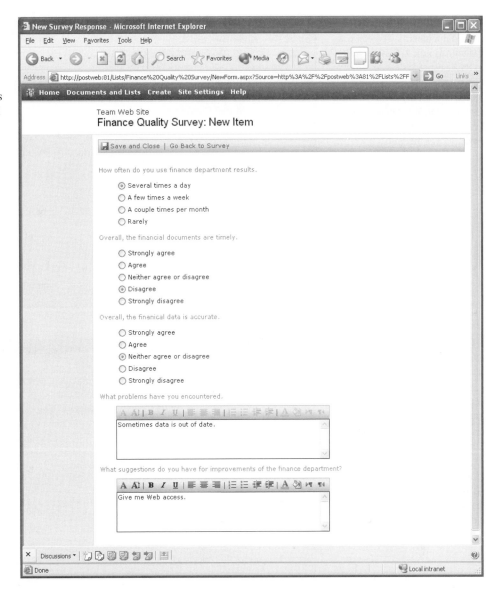

fill out, and can instantly report the data. As shown in Figure 9.11, SharePoint includes a basic survey-building tool. You simply write the questions by selecting a format, entering the question, and identifying the possible responses. When you post the survey to the Share-Point site, the other members of the team enter their selections. The results are immediately available. One advantage of the system is that the entire process is done through Web forms. Note that the surveys are not available to people unless they are registered in the group, so the technique does not work as well for public surveys. On the other hand, more sophisticated tools can be purchased from other companies to handle public surveys.

Collaboration

Until recently, most organizations shared files through shared directories on LANs or via e-mail. Document libraries are simply Web-based folders that hold a related collection of documents—such as all work on a particular project. The files are accessed across the Web, so they are accessible to team members anywhere in the world. Furthermore, the group leader can establish a template so that all documents have the same look.

As shown in Figure 9.12, once the site is set up, accessing the documents is easy—through the familiar File and Open commands. Generally, you will create a link to the directory in "My Network Places" so that you can find the documents with one click. In a team environment, it is important to store your files in a document library—instead of on

FIGURE 9.12

Shared documents: You can use the upload link to transfer a file to the server for sharing. You can also use the New Document link to add a Word document directly to the folder. You can open and save any existing document directly over the Web.

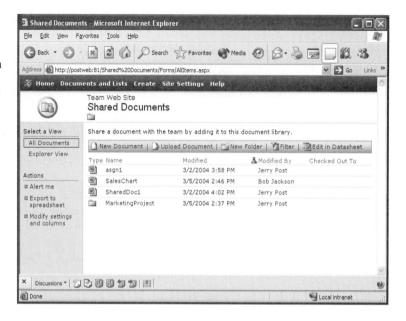

FIGURE 9.13

Tracking changes and adding discussions: Changes by each person are shown in a different color. Internal tools will help quickly integrate these changes into the final document. Discussion comments record the reasons for the changes as well as approvals by other managers. Also note the IM list of teammates on the right-hand side.

your personal machine. That way, everyone in the group can read and contribute to the work. Once the documents are stored in the shared library, some other powerful tools and options can be used to coordinate the team, as described in the next sections. Note that direct access to the documents generally requires that each team member have the most recent version of Office installed.

Have you ever tried to write a document with two or three people? SharePoint enables you to share the document, but you have to use the Tools/Track Changes option to lock the document so that it shows the changes by each person. Figure 9.13 shows the sample annotations. Observe that you can also embed a discussion within the document using the Tools/Online Collaboration option. The discussion comments are shown at the bottom of the document. The discussion makes it easy for you to write a longer explanation of the changes and to outline objectives and features. Colleagues can add comments or point out problems.

FIGURE 9.14

Configure library options: Use the server options to set up version control. You can also specify default templates so that all contributed documents follow a standard style. You can require that files be approved before they are made available to the team.

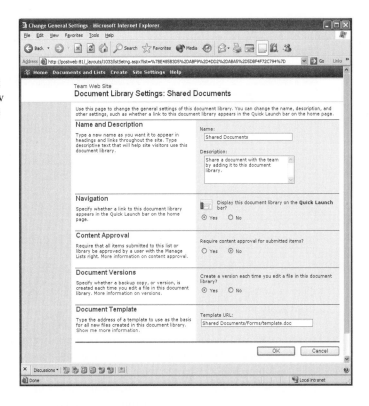

Also note that when you are logged in, the system shows you an IM list of the other teammates. It identifies which people are currently logged in online, and you can quickly send them a message if the need arises.

SharePoint can also handle version control. Moreover, version control systems support check in and check out of documents, so that only one person can edit a document at a time—minimizing the problem of needing to determine which change to keep. It also tracks who made the changes and which team member is currently using the document. If you want complete version control including the ability to automatically track changes, you will also need Visual Source Safe, Microsoft's version control software. As shown in Figure 9.14, you configure version control by setting the properties for the document library. You can also specify a default template for new documents to encourage teammates to apply a consistent style so documents look the same. Furthermore, you can require that documents be approved by the owner of the group site before they are made available to everyone.

The manual version control system requires each person to check out and then check in the document. When the document is checked out, others can read it but cannot alter it. When the document is checked in, you will be asked to provide a description of the changes. As shown in Figure 9.15, your comments are displayed in the version list. Users can see the version list at any time by selecting the option from the drop-down list for the file on the original document screen. From this version list, you can open prior versions to copy desired sections. Or you can delete an entire version, including the latest—causing the system to revert to the prior version. However, in general, you should avoid deleting versions—you never know when the changes or data might be useful. Instead, simply copy the older version, make the desired changes, and save it as the new version.

Workflow

Although it is not as sophisticated as specialized business process management systems, SharePoint provides a couple of tools to help with workflow. These tools integrate the features of communication and collaboration. Routing documents and messages is a useful workflow tool. For example, your manager probably wants to review recommendations that you make, purchasing managers are responsible for approving the purchase of major items, and important documents have to be approved by the legal department. Projects tend to have

FIGURE 9.15
Version control: Choosing the version option from the document library screen shows you the prior versions, who edited them, and the comments that were added. You can open prior versions to copy sections or simply revert to the prior version.

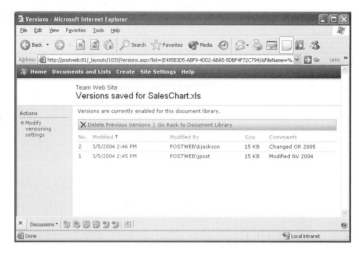

discrete steps. Sometimes the steps are as simple as obtaining an approval and comments from someone before proceeding.

In 2004, Microsoft moved the workflow component into the SharePoint Portal version. If you purchase this more advanced edition, you can attach a routing list to any document when you send it. The system delivers it to the first person on the list. When done, he or she clicks a button and it is sent to the next person on the routing list. Along the way, each person can add comments. These comments are stored in a discussion board associated with the document. Furthermore, the document can record changes and indicate who made them. Hence, everyone can see the final document, what changes were made, and comments on why the changes are important.

More complicated workflow rules can be created with lists, InfoPath, and Microsoft Project. All of these tools integrate with some minor programming. For example, a list can be created to describe the state of a document (draft, approved, final). Then various conditions and triggers can be applied to specify conditions for each state and how the document must be handled. For instance, two specific people must approve a document before it can leave the draft state and move to the next steps. Or, a document must have three completed and approved figures before it is considered to be complete. These rules require some effort to set up, but once established, the system enforces the basic procedures of the business. Moreover, team members can check on the progress of a project to see what steps remain or identify which team member is holding up a particular document.

Another powerful workflow technique is to add alerts to the shared items. As shown in Figure 9.16, you can set an alert so that you are notified when a document is changed. For example, you might need to obtain your supervisor's approval before continuing with a document. Save the document in the shared folder, notify the person that it is available, and then attach an alert to the document. When the document is revised, you will be notified by e-mail automatically. You can avoid bothering your manager, or wondering if he or she has gotten to the document yet. Note that you should inform everyone about these capabilities, partly so that they can take advantage of them, but also to minimize privacy issues.

Knowledge Management

Keeping all of the documents, discussions, messages, and schedules is a major step in creating a knowledge management system. If you hire new team members, they can quickly get up to speed by reading through the existing documents and discussions. If everyone was careful to place comments, objections, answers, and justifications in discussion lists, new workers (and managers) can see why decisions were made. Reading through real-time exchanges may be slightly boring, but it can be faster than pestering everyone else with questions. It is certainly better than operating without the knowledge.

Again, if you purchase the SharePoint Portal version, it includes some of the tools needed for a truly useful KM solution. It includes detailed index and search tools that pro-

FIGURE 9.16
Change alert: Almost all shared documents and lists support alerts. Whenever a document or folder is altered, an e-mail message will be sent to you. You can use alerts to track the progress of documents as they are revised by various people.

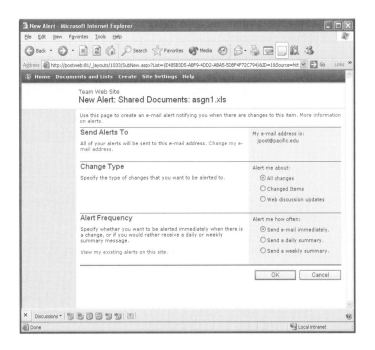

vide the ability for workers to search for similar events and decisions. It also makes it easier to create ad hoc links between the various documents. However, you might still need to add more capabilities with additional software or with people. Some of the limitations can be overcome with a little extra effort. For instance, you could periodically create summaries of the main issues. Create a document that explains the main points and include links to the detailed documents and discussion lists. The lack of a sophisticated search engine is a little harder to overcome. However, for really important cases, you could hire a librarian to categorize the documents and provide indexes that can be searched. These index documents would contain links to the other issues and would enable searchers to find information through cross listings.

Summary

Working together and sharing data are crucial in today's companies. MIS can help teams work better with tools designed to integrate data across an organization. Managers need to know how to use a variety of tools, from data sharing over networks, to dynamic linking, to groupware products.

A Manager's View

Teamwork is an increasingly important aspect of management. Integration of business units so they work together is another important issue. Effectively managed, the techniques can cut costs, improve quality, and improve response time. Communication and collaboration are key elements to the success of any team. Groupware tools support messaging and sharing documents. Business process management tools help automate collaborative processes by adding triggers and rules. Ultimately, storing all information on decisions contributes to the organizational memory, and the knowledge management system can help the company make better decisions.

Teamwork begins with communication, and information technology provides many ways to communicate, from voice mail, e-mail, instant messaging, Web pages, and blogs, to videoconferencing. As a communicator, one of your challenges is to choose the appropriate communication channel for the specific type of message. Teamwork also requires scheduling and task coordination. Electronic calendars and project management tools help everyone identify bottlenecks and keep projects on schedule. Meetings take big blocks of time from all managers, but they are often critical to communication and the success of a project. Electronic meeting systems make it possible to meet regardless of location. They also provide records of the meetings that can be reviewed or searched later.

Collaboration requires sharing documents and knowledge. Shared document features enable you to track changes made by all teammates. They also provide version control so you can recover elements deleted from earlier versions. Workflow software helps you control the sequence of events and when people will receive each document. Information rights management provides tools to limit the distribution of documents and control what people are allowed to do with each document. Ultimately, an important goal of teamwork systems is to collect all of the information used to make decisions and hold it as the organization's memory. This knowledge management system can then be used for future decisions and problem solving.

Microsoft SharePoint provides several tools to integrate the elements of the Office suite as well as communication and collaboration tools. The basic version makes it easy to share documents across the Web. It also maintains contact lists, events, and task items. All of the features are shared with teammates. Discussions can be created quickly on general topics or on specific documents. Surveys can record votes on critical issues.

Key Words

business process management (BPM), *324*
check in, *323*
check out, *323*
full duplex, *320*
group decision support system (GDSS), *325*

groupware, *317*
information rights management (IRM), *323*
knowledge management (KM), *326*
protect document, *322*

track changes, *322*
version control, *323*
videoconference, *320*
workflow, *324*

Web Site References

Teamwork Tools

Microsoft LiveMeeting	**www.microsoft.com/livemeeting**
Webex (Macromedia meeting)	**www.webex.com**
Version control comparison	**better-scm.berlios.de/comparison/comparison.html**
Microsoft SharePoint	**www.microsoft.com/sharepoint**

Knowledge Management

DestinationKM	**www.destinationkm.com**
KMWorld	**www.kmworld.com**
KMNetwork	**www.kmnetwork.com**
KMNews	**www.kmnews.com**
KMResource	**www.kmresource.com**

Additional Readings

Rosencrance, Linda. "Sidebar: A Collaborative Difference." *Computerworld,* January 26, 2004. [Using blogs as collaboration tools.]

Schlender, Brent. "Microsoft: The Beast Is Back." *Fortune,* June 11, 2001, pp. 75–86. [Outline of Microsoft's new ideas for integrating data.]

Verton, Dan. "Exostar's Collaboration Platform Takes Security to New Level." *Computerworld,* June 7, 2004. [External collaboration tool with powerful security controls.]

Weiss, Todd R. "Groove Touts Performance, Usability in Updated Virtual Office." *Computerworld,* July 8, 2004. [Alternative desktop collaboration software.]

Review Questions

1. What communication channels are available to teams? What are the strengths and weaknesses of each method?
2. What are the primary purposes of business meetings?
3. Why is it helpful to use collaboration tools when sharing documents?
4. Why is version control important to teams?
5. How is information rights management different from typical computer access controls?
6. What are the benefits of automating business process management?
7. What is the goal of a group decision support system?
8. How do groupware tools provide organizational memory?
9. What features are important in a knowledge management system?
10. What are the major features of Microsoft SharePoint?

Exercises

1. Find a specialized knowledge management software package and describe the major features.
2. Research and compare the scheduling and workflow features provided by either IBM/Lotus Notes or Microsoft Exchange. Explain how you could use these features as a manager.
3. Research the features of Cisco MeetingPlace and compare them to Microsoft's offerings. What hardware is required to implement Cisco's product?
4. What additional features are provided if you implement Microsoft's SourceSafe product within your team environment?
5. Identify a specific decision for which it would be helpful to use a group decision support system. Explain the benefits of using the GDSS for your problem.
6. Describe a business situation in which you would need to implement information rights management controls. Describe the specific rights you would assign.
7. How does Microsoft's InfoPath software support business process management?

Technology Toolbox

8. As a team project, if you have access to a SharePoint server, have one person create a small document that describes a computer that he or she might wish to purchase. Set change subscriptions on the document for each team member. Then over the next few days, have members make changes to the document, with suggestions for different components. As team members are notified of changes, they should check the suggestions and either accept or reject them by adding additional comments.
9. Assuming you have access to a server, set up a SharePoint Web site to discuss a specific problem. Create and share a couple of documents, set up a contact list, create a survey, and add a couple of tasks. Be sure to include your instructor or grader as a member of the team and send an e-mail invitation.
10. Pick a topic and set up a net meeting with three other people. Use the whiteboard to draw a figure. Save the chat screen and the whiteboard. If you have the hardware, test the voice (and video) capabilities.
11. Test NetMeeting over a dial-up connection with at least one other person. Compare the speed to a LAN connection. What capabilities work? Which ones would you avoid on the dial-up connection?
12. Identify the major features of a Web conferencing system such as Microsoft's Live Meeting. Find at least one company that will host a meeting for you. Identify the costs assuming you will need a presentation for 12 suppliers for two hours.

Teamwork

13. As a group project, assume that each person in the group is a manager of a different department. Each person creates a spreadsheet to list the salespeople in his or her department (4 to 10), their hours worked, total sales, and commissions. Compute the totals for each column. Once the individual spreadsheets have been created and stored

on separate computers, the group will create a composite spreadsheet that brings in the data from each individual spreadsheet. Compute the corporate total and draw pie charts for each column. If possible, use dynamic linking across the network to capture the data from the individual spreadsheets.

14. As a team project, if you have access to SharePoint, have one member create a document with a paragraph reviewing some recent movie. Create a distribution list and send the review to each person on the list, who can make changes to the document and add discussion comments before sending it to the next person on the list. If you do not have access to SharePoint, exchange the documents by e-mail.

15. As a project, each person should use the Internet and your library resources to find at least three uses of SharePoint or other groupware product in a real company. The team should work at the same time. At random intervals, interrupt other members of the team to ask questions, by phone, e-mail, instant messenger, or in person. At the end of the time, identify which method you personally found the most disruptive.

16. Have each person research the capabilities of a workflow/business process management system. Create a list of the major features and costs. Combine the results and try to identify the leading systems.

17. Connect as many people as possible using a single instant messenger or chat room system. As a topic, discuss a current movie. What problems do you encounter? Should you limit these types of meetings to a certain number of people? What would be the maximum?

Rolling Thunder Database

18. If you have access to a SharePoint server, set up a team site to discuss production issues. Generate queries to show production delays over time. Put the data into a spreadsheet and graph it. Create a discussion group for the spreadsheet and discuss possible reasons for any issues.

19. Describe the hardware and software Rolling Thunder should install so that all employees can coordinate schedules and conduct 15-minute meetings every day.

20. Inventory management has been a little out of line. Define a business process management plan for purchasing components from suppliers. Choose software that will enable you to set up the process.

21. Identify documents that Rolling Thunder should protect with an information rights management system and briefly describe the desired rights.

22. What information would you recommend placing in a knowledge management system for Rolling Thunder Bicycles?

23. Explain how version control would be useful for designing the bicycles at Rolling Thunder. Find software that could provide version control.

24. Find a task scheduling system that could be used to help schedule design and production at Rolling Thunder Bicycles.

Cases: Package Delivery

The Industry

The package delivery industry has changed dramatically over the past few years. In fact, today, it should probably be called the business logistics industry. Several large mergers have altered the industry. The competition among the remaining firms is intensifying. The primary players today are FedEx Corp., United Parcel Service (UPS), the United States Postal Service (USPS), and Deutsche Post (which owns DHL and Airborne).

To understand the changes, you need to understand how businesses operate today. The most important issue is that large companies operate in many locations, within the United States and around the world. This means that companies need to move supplies, assembled components, and finished products. Parts are moved from suppliers to assembly plants, and finished

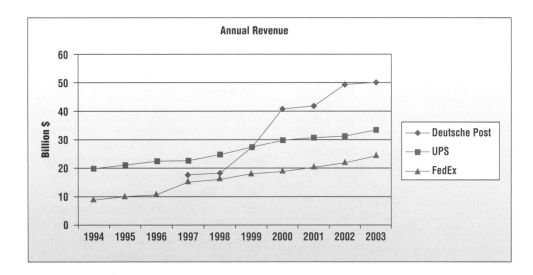

products are shipped to distribution centers and retail stores. Few firms today want to move their own products on their own trucks—it just does not pay. And smaller firms could never afford to own their own fleets. Instead, the large firms have focused on efficiency, time, and price to be able to provide a complete level of delivery services around the world. Today, that encompasses everything from freight handling (large shipments) to overnight packages (express delivery).

UPS was at the top of the revenue list in 2003 with slightly over $33 billion. DHL was second with $24 billion, closely followed by FedEx Corp. with $22.5 billion (Whiting 2003). However, USPS topped all of them with operating revenue of over $68 billion in 2003; but that includes money from its monopoly position to deliver letters to households (annual report).

Services and Information

In many ways, UPS was the leader in driving changes in the logistics industry. The company was initially formed to deliver merchandise from manufacturers to retail stores. This third-party service made it possible for manufacturers to increase their sales without having to build their own distribution centers. Even smaller companies now had direct access to sales across the United States. And all companies could use the system to ship short orders in a matter of days.

The industry has changed considerably over time as the firms have introduced new services and combined others. FedEx introduced the concept of next-day delivery. At a time when many people doubted there was demand for such a service, the company owned and then perfected the market. When computers became cheap enough, FedEx introduced package tracking—emphasizing that information was just as important as the package (FedEx Web site) (Ulfelder 2002). The other carriers struggled to provide the same service; but eventually UPS, USPS, and DHL, as well as a host of other firms, moved into next-day shipping. At the same time, FedEx began to move into ground and freight deliveries, shipping larger items across the country and delivering packages

to stores and individuals in a few days. FedEx grew largely by acquiring other firms. DHL has an interesting history—largely driven by one man: Larry L. Hillblom, who died in a plane crash in 1995. His focus was air delivery to islands and nations in the South Pacific, and for years, DHL dominated that international market.

Overall, the international market is a challenge for any shipping company, or even any company that wishes to ship packages around the world. Each nation has different customs requirements—in terms of forms, taxes, and even items that are banned. To make it more complex, most nations have their own definitions of items and terms. Complicating it even more, the rules tend to change over time. Now, if you are a manufacturer shipping only a single item to a single nation on a regular basis, you will eventually learn the procedures. But if you want to ship different items to multiple countries, how can you gain the knowledge you need?

Ultimately, the major shipping companies (not including USPS) have created huge online knowledge systems that automate most of the steps in shipping overseas. You simply fill out the declarations properly and their systems produce the necessary forms. UPS and FedEx have special facilities to notify customs agents when packages are arriving and produce detailed information on request. In 2003, the United States Department of Homeland Security (Bureau of Customs and Border Protection) proposed a regulation that all carriers have to notify officials of inbound cargos several hours before they arrive. The notice would have to be electronic so that the bureau could run computerized analyses on shipping data to spot potential terrorist threats or illegal shipments. DHL, UPS, and FedEx generally already meet this requirement. The DHL system is based on Open Harbor's global trade-management system that has over 8 million trade rules (Chabrow and Bacheldor 2003). Ultimately, it is likely that other major nations will require the same advance notice, and all of the carriers and software vendors are building systems to meet these demands. The key point is that shippers now offer much more advanced services. They are not simply ferrying packages—they are taking responsibility for the entire process.

Many companies today use these shipping firms as the first line of their logistics service. Even internal shipments between factories can be handled and tracked by UPS or FedEx. Particularly with the integration of freight, package, and overnight deliveries, companies can flexibly select and monitor their shipments. UPS and FedEx have divisions and special software to help companies use it as a complete transportation system. They can schedule deliveries for different times and days. They can even have UPS and FedEx integrate shipments. For example, if you buy a computer from Dell, the monitor might have been shipped from Asia, unloaded in a UPS warehouse, and then shipped directly to you—without first having to go to a Dell warehouse. And it would be shipped to arrive at the same time as the rest of the computer, which was shipped from the Dell assembly plant.

Competition

The major firms have consolidated to the point where they now offer essentially the same types of services. The declining costs of technology have made it possible for all of the firms to compete with information systems—for example, they all offer package tracking. The rivalry is fierce—particularly between FedEx and UPS. Both compete on the basis of global reach, quality, and price. Currently, DHL/Deutsche Post is not in the same league within the United States, but dominates in Europe and Asia. So, all firms have to focus on efficiency, and efficiency often requires automation—reducing the number of workers where possible and cutting times as much as possible. All of them have benefited from the increased level of shipping in the past decade. Will that trend continue? Or will it level off, forcing firms to compete harder to steal market share from each other? Information technology has played an enormous role in many aspects of the competition. From providing information for package tracking, to the knowledge bases for international shipping, to route scheduling, automation, and cost cutting.

Teamwork

These companies are huge, and they operate around the world. Moving packages and information quickly and efficiently in this environment requires tremendous teamwork. A large portion of the information technology is devoted to ensuring that everyone down the line knows exactly what is coming. When customers enter package data on the main Web site, the local driver knows what to pick up. Schedulers communicate in real time with drivers to alter routes as needed. The package data is provided to the central hub, which optimizes the plane loadings and flights. Data is sent to customs as well as to the local destination hubs, so drivers know the loads and routes for the next day. All through the process, customers are treated as team members and have access to the information. Customers include the shipper as well as the recipient. Firms that ship products can be notified of any problems before they become a disaster.

Additional Reading

Chabrow, Eric, and Beth Bacheldor. "Rules Could Force Shippers to Modernize." *Information Week,* July 28, 2003.

"FedEx Corporate History." http://fedex.com/us/about/today/history/.

Ulfelder, Steve. "Dateline: A Timeline of Technology Advances at Fedex and UPS." *Computerworld,* September 30, 2002.

Whiting, Rick. "Logistics & Transportation: Ship to Sure: Tracking in Real Time." *Information Week,* September 22, 2003.

Case: FedEx

The history of FedEx (ticker: FDX) is outlined on its Web site. Federal Express began with a paper that Frederick W. Smith wrote in 1965 while at Yale University. After serving in the military, Smith purchased Arkansas Aviation Sales in Little Rock in 1971. It officially began operations on April 17, 1973, with 14 small aircraft and delivered 186 packages to 25 cities. Deregulation of air cargo in 1977 enabled Federal Express to fly larger jets and the company grew rapidly. In 2004, the company had a daily lift capacity of more than 26.5 million pounds and the fleet travels 500,000 miles a day. The endpoint delivery vans log 2.5 million miles a day (company Web site). The company reached $1 billion in sales in 1983—a mere 10 years after start-up.

Mergers

In 1989, Federal Express purchased the Flying Tigers network—largely oriented to flights in the Pacific region, and giving Federal Express expertise in international shipments. In 1995, Federal Express acquired Evergreen International Airlines—largely because the acquisition gave it rights to deliver in China. In 1998, Federal Express expanded into ground deliveries by purchasing RPS (Roadway Package System, renamed Caliber System in 1996). The purchase of Caliber System also gave Federal Express Viking Freight. Federal Express expanded its freight system in 2001 by purchasing American Freightways. In 1999, FedEx acquired Caribbean Transportation Services, focusing on shipments to Puerto Rico. FedEx now has a full spectrum delivery system, from air shipping to large freight transfers to package delivery.

In 2000, FedEx acquired TowerGroup and World Tariff. This acquisition provided important knowledge and experience in handling international shipments. It provides customs clearance and electronic filing for all of the other divisions of FedEx, enabling FedEx to provide end-to-end transportation around the world.

The more surprising merger happened in February 2004 when FedEx acquired Kinko's Office stores. For several years, FedEx had a relationship with Kinko's, so that customers could drop off packages at the local stores. All 1,200 stores in 10 countries are digitally connected, making it possible to print documents nationally. The company evolved from neighborhood print shops into local business centers for mobile professionals and small businesses. The company also handles commercial print jobs.

Operations

The essence of package delivery seems easy—when you look at one package: pick up a package, transfer it to a plane, fly it to the nearest airport, put it on a delivery truck, and drop it off at the destination. The problem is that drivers have to pick up many packages, all of them have to be sorted, planes have to be loaded properly and flown to airports where you have landing rights, then packages have to be unloaded, re-sorted into delivery trucks, and the drivers have to get to multiple destinations. Now, you have to do all of that fast and at the lowest possible cost. And the mix of packages and destinations can change every day.

Scheduling and optimizing package handling and deliveries is a key element in the operations. In 1978, FedEx put voice radios in the trucks to assist and direct drivers. Only two years later, in 1980, the company launched a revolutionary proprietary wireless data network called Digitally Assisted Dispatch System (DADS). Dispatchers could send text messages to drivers. By reducing chatter and enabling drivers to check the messages when they needed, the system improved efficiency 30 percent in the first day (Ulfelder 2002). In 1986, the company adopted the wireless handheld SuperTrackers that capture data with bar code readers. The system is the foundation for tracking packages at every step and uploads data to the Customer Oriented Service and Management Operating System (COSMOS).

Tracking the package at every step in the process is critical to the operations. It provides information for the operations at the next stops, it provides data to the customers, and it makes it almost impossible to lose a package. On average, every FedEx package is scanned 23 times. Once a package is picked up and scanned, the data is transferred to the central computer. At the shipping hub, the computer routes the package to the proper conveyor belt. The package is loaded into an "igloo" container that fits the sloping sides of the plane. The container has a scan that represents all of the items held inside. While being routed to the proper container, each package is weighed and the billing corrected if necessary. The weights are also used to balance the loading of the plane. As the 160 planes land each night at the FedEx hub in Memphis, workers unload them within 20 minutes. Packages in the Memphis hub travel through a giant convey system to be routed to new planes or trucks to the nearest of 22 airports. The system scans 1,000 bar codes per minute. The hub alone generates about 900 MB

every two and a half hours (Brewin and Rosencrance 2001). The main FedEx hub in Memphis is a key element in the operations efficiency. FedEx can move 325,000 letters an hour through the hub, along with 125,000 small packages per hour. The average transit time is seven minutes (Brewin April 2004).

In 2003, FedEx rolled out a completely new handheld system. Dropping most of the proprietary technology, the PowerPad was developed by Motorola to run the Microsoft Pocket PC operating system. More important, the system uses the GPRS cellular wireless service from AT&T. It is designed to completely eliminate paperwork, saving couriers 10 seconds at each stop. Which adds up to $20 million in annual savings when you factor in the 3.5 million packages delivered a day (Brewin November 2002). GPRS has data rates between 20 and 40 kbps, which exceed the 19 kbps on the older FedEx network (Brewin March 2002). The PowerPad reduces errors by automatically checking zip codes. It can print labels through a label printer in the truck that is connected by Bluetooth radio. It even checks the weather at the destination so that the driver can notify the shipper of any potential delays. The PowerPad contains a third radio transmitter so that it can connect via WiFi to the networks at the FedEx hub.

Services

Providing global shipping is considerably more complex than simply transferring a package. Each nation has hundreds or thousands of different rules on tariffs and procedures for importing items. Increasingly, FedEx customers were asking for information on how to ship globally. FedEx began a project in 1997 and launched it in August 2000. Originally, the Web-based system arranged shipments between the United States, Canada, the United Kingdom, Hong Kong, and Puerto Rico. It was then expanded to 20 nations. The system runs on an Oracle database and provides the rules and appropriate import and export forms needed. It also lets shippers know about restrictions, embargoes, and licensing requirements. In February 2001, the Global Trade Manager system began computing government fees, duties, value-added tax (VAT), and other charges so that shippers can quickly estimate the total costs. Robert B. Carter, head of the division, notes that "Global Trade Manager makes it easier to ship internationally, which can be an intimidating experience. It allows customers to do import/export documentation in a straightforward fashion. . . . We are giving them [clients] access to technology they wouldn't otherwise have" (Rosencrance 2002).

In 2003, FedEx partnered with Cap Gemini Ernst & Young to offer detailed logistics services to companies of any size. Many large companies already outsource freight transportation (67 percent), and 42 percent outsource management of their distribution centers. But most firms still maintain control over the rest of the decision aspects of logistics and purchasing (Bacheldor 2003). The new offering from FedEx and Cap Gemini integrates software for transportation management, fulfillment management, supply chain event management, and business-to-business hub management. With the integrated tools, customers can examine and track shipments and warehouse or distribution center handling at the stockkeeping unit (SKU) or even serial number level. They will be able to see the movement of all products and obtain reports on all aspects of shipping, even though the entire process will actually be handled by FedEx. Douglas Witt, president of FedEx Supply Chain Services, notes that the system is important because "lack of visibility is a major issue for a lot of customers" (Bacheldor 2003).

Strategy

Battling head-to-head with UPS and forging entirely new ways of doing business have forced FedEx to focus on strategy. Technology plays a key role in its plans. But Smith is understandably cautious. He shies away from huge projects designed to alter everything. Instead, he says, "We try to do a lot of work on the front end, divide things into bite-size pieces, do things in a more evolutionary way" (Foley February 2, 2004). Exactly how Kinko's fits into that strategy is not completely clear yet, but it will probably take time for the value to be realized. FedEx CFO Alan Graf notes that "it diversifies our business. Kinko's is the back office for hundreds of thousands of businesses" (Foley February 9, 2004). Fred Smith notes only that it will enable both companies "to take advantage of growth opportunities in the fast-moving digital economy." Jim McCluskey, a FedEx spokesman, adds that it will enable FedEx to "push information electronically" for its clients (Brewin January 2004). If nothing else, the stores will raise the visibility of FedEx even higher—providing a convenient location for small business services and drop-off points for FedEx shipments. With the stagnant economy, a shift to digital documents, and a tight battle with UPS, the market for overnight delivery has leveled. FedEx is looking to the ground and international shipping to carry its growth forward. Furthermore, the company has to focus on costs to improve profits (Foley January 2004).

Teamwork

One of the challenges with growing through mergers is integrating all of the information systems. To maintain the existing efficiencies, FedEx chose to run the new divisions independently. But that means managers do not have a single view of customer data, and customers have to check multiple locations to find their shipping information. In 2004, FedEx began development of its Customer Fusion database. The package will pull data from all of the independent systems and make it available from a single point. The product is a computer messaging system that can talk to all of the individual applications. Larry Tieman, chief architect for the project, notes that "the message bus allows us to loosely couple the business application, apply the proper business rules, and build a unified application layer" (Sullivan 2004).

The company also created an integrated system for international managers in 2001. The international strategic information system (ISIS) uses a Web-based front-end query tool to integrate data from internal legacy systems for marketing, sales, and inventory. It then consolidates information for local agents into an Oracle database. The agents can then query the database and identify patterns such as the amount of shipping by industry. A key aspect of the system is to provide business intelligence data to local agents and FedEx managers. By sharing the same data and analysis, FedEx can better help the agents meet revenue targets (Dash 2001).

Questions

1. How does FedEx use information technology to improve teamwork and deliver packages more efficiently?

2. How can FedEx integrate data from its diverse companies to improve teamwork, without replacing all of the individual systems?

3. Why is wireless technology so important to FedEx?

Additional Reading

Bacheldor, Beth. "Better Visibility Along the Transport Chain." *Information Week,* September 29, 2003.

Brewin, Bob. "FedEx Expands Net Reach to Mobile Data." *Computerworld,* March 25, 2002.

Brewin, Bob. "Fedex: New Courier System Will Save $20M Annually." *Computerworld,* November 26, 2002.

Brewin, Bob. "Fedex to Use Kinko's Stores to Offer e-Services to Enterprise Customers." *Computerworld,* January 2, 2004.

Brewin, Bob. "Sidebar: FedEx vs. UPS: The Technology Arms Race." *Computerworld,* April 19, 2004.

Brewin, Bob, and Linda Rosencrance. "Follow That Package!" *Computerworld,* March 19, 2001.

Dash, Julekha. "FedEx Launches Global Business-Intelligence Application." *Computerworld,* May 28, 2001.

FedEx Web site: http://fedex.com/us/about/today/history/.

Foley, John. "FedEx Success Doesn't Come with Big IT Budget Increase." *Information Week,* January 12, 2004.

Foley, John. "Redefining What You Are." *Information Week,* February 2, 2004.

Foley, John. "Retail Plus: FedEx Buys Kinko's." *Information Week,* February 9, 2004.

Rosencrance, Linda. "FedEx Corp." *Computerworld, March 11, 2002.*

Sullivan, Laurie. "FedEx Achieves Fusion." *Information Week,* June 30, 2004.

Ulfelder, Steve. "Signed, Sealed and Delivered." *Computerworld,* September 30, 2002.

Case: United Parcel Service

The UPS (ticker: UPS) Web site has details on its history and growth. UPS began in Seattle in 1907 as a messenger service, with most deliveries made on foot by teenage boys. In 1913, the fledgling company acquired its first car: a Model T Ford. Merging with a couple of competitors, the company renamed itself Merchants Parcel Delivery and began focusing on delivering merchandise from the retail stores. The company also was the primary carrier of special delivery packages in Seattle for the U.S. Post Office. In 1919, the company expanded to Oakland, California, and adopted its current name: United Parcel Service. After World War II, retail shopping changed, as customers drove to malls and carried their own packages. UPS fought to provide common-carrier service in new areas, including Chicago. Expanding into competition with the U.S. Post Office raised regulatory issues, and the company fought many legal battles to win the right to deliver packages. In 1953, UPS began shipping cargo on existing airline flights. Yet package delivery had to remain inside a state to avoid regulation by the Interstate Commerce Commission (ICC). Fighting for three decades, the ICC finally granted UPS permission to deliver packages between Montana and Utah—in 1975. By 1985, the company was shipping packages by air to all 48 contiguous states and, in 1988, started its own airline. In 1993, to track the huge number of drivers and deliveries, and to keep up with FedEx, UPS introduced the handheld Delivery Information Acquisition Device (DIAD). In 1999, UPS joined the New York Stock Exchange.

Operations

Fighting competitors from day one, UPS pioneered efficiency in delivery—emphasizing the need to hold down costs and prices. Although UPS headquarters are in Atlanta, it runs its operations through its main Worldport hub in Louisville, Kentucky. The 4 million-square-foot facility handles over 100 planes a night, pushing 600,000 packages a day through the hub. Because of a limited labor pool and the desire to hold wages down, the facility emphasizes automation. It runs on almost 14,000 computer devices, including 30 terabytes of online storage and 5,500 miles of fiber-optic cable. It uses 122 miles of conveyor belts to move packages and sort them by bar code scanners as they fly by (Brewin April 2004). Most of the individual packages (93 percent) are identified by special bar codes. When shippers fill out the shipping labels on the UPS Web site, the system notifies UPS about incoming packages. Twice a day, this incoming information is used to create a sort plan that configures the hub to match the expected packages. The software Flexible Lineup Editor reorganizes the loading and unloading positions to optimize the package transfers. Packages are only touched twice by humans: once to be loaded onto the conveyor belts and once to be taken off and put into shipping containers (Brewin April 2004).

UPS also pays close attention to its drivers and their routes. Drivers are often monitored in terms of performance, and managers share tips on how to improve. In 2003, the company added a new software routing tool to plan the routes. Since most customers provide pickup data early in the day, the computer can plan the optimal route, speeding up the drivers while they make more stops and travel fewer miles. UPS CIO Ken Lacy estimates the system will reduce fleet miles in the United States by more than 100 million miles a year, saving about 14 million gallons of fuel (Brewin September 26, 2003).

UPS had thought about creating a massive routing system since at least the mid-1990s. The catch is that many people thought the problem was too big to solve. In computer science terms, the problem is called NP-complete because there is no perfect solution to analyze the entire delivery problem other than to examine every possible choice. And with trillions upon trillions of options, no machine could find the perfect solution. Operations research specialists studied the problem and found ways to narrow it down to just examining feasible solutions that are close to optimal. With research and faster machines, they managed to reduce the time to find a solution from 90 days down to three hours. By optimizing its primary routes, UPS was able to cut a day off its guaranteed delivery times for some routes, such as reducing shipping time from Los Angeles to New York from four days to three (Bacheldor 2004).

In 2003, UPS upgraded its handheld system to the DIAD IV terminal. The terminal contains a color screen and runs on Windows CE. In addition to the bar code scanner, it includes a global positioning system (GPS) receiver. It uses Bluetooth wireless to connect to a label printer in the van. When parked at the hub, the system connects to the local area network via a WiFi wireless connection. On the road, it uses a built-in cellular modem, so that drivers can connect to the network and provide immediate information to customers. Ultimately, the system will be able to use its Bluetooth radio to connect directly to customer computers. The GPS system will be particularly valuable in Europe, where drivers handle less frequent trips. In the United States, many companies require daily deliveries and pickups to fixed locations. But, the GPS system will also help route drivers for last-minute pickup requests (Brewin September 26, 2003).

Integrated Services

In 2001, UPS purchased the entire chain of 4,000 MailBoxes Etc. stores and renamed them The UPS Store. The chain provides UPS with local contact points for individual and small business pickups. But most of the stores are still run as franchises. The stores are eliminating the need for paper shipping forms. Customers simply enter the data into a kiosk PC (or have the clerk enter it), and it prints out the bar-coded label. In

2003, UPS took the interesting step of testing public-access WiFi in 66 of the retail stores in Chicago. Customers would pay either an hourly or monthly fee to connect their own laptops to the Internet through the WiFi connection. The demand for this service is still uncertain (Brewin September 11, 2003).

In 2002, UPS introduced a Web-based shipping solution to large customers with offices in multiple locations. The system enables employees to ship a package by simply entering the details in a Web site. The system automatically bills the company and provides a comprehensive report to managers. Best Buy is using the system to make it easy for employees in its stores to ship packages to other Best Buy locations or to send them directly to customers. Jim Hay, general transportation manager of small package solutions for Best Buy, observes that because employees do not have to handwrite the labels, "this saves 15 minutes per user per package. The biggest area of savings is in time and (in fewer) lost and misrouted packages due to poor handwriting or a bad address" (Rosencrance March 2002).

UPS began offering a useful service in early 2003 for exporters and importers. The company launched an electronic payment system called UPS Exchange Collect. Basically, UPS collects the money from the recipient/customer. Sellers are free to expand to new markets with unknown customers with minimal risk. UPS drivers will only deliver the product when they receive payment. When the shipper sends an item, the recipient is notified electronically. UPS then collects the money and delivers the package. The money is electronically sent to the seller. The system provides huge gains over the current system. Currently, shippers often wait 90 days for payment—and still run risks that the buyer will not pay. UPS will transfer the funds within 10 days (Rosencrance 2003).

UPS also provides expertise in shipping products internationally—in terms of handling forms and getting packages through customs. By identifying and controlling every package that UPS carries, the company's Worldport hub qualifies as a controlled building for the customs bureau. More important, the product information database is accessible to customs agents, who can scan it for potential problems. Any suspect packages are instantly rerouted within the Worldport hub to the customs office for detailed inspection (Rosencrance March 11, 2003).

In 2004, UPS introduced new tools for customers to use the system as a complete logistics solution. The Quantum View Manage software makes it easy for customers to identify all shipping information. In particular, customers can see all packages as a group, without needing to enter every tracking number. They can see exactly where packages are located, along with any reasons for delays. The system can even trigger alerts if problems arise and notify customer service automatically, or use automated delivery notices to send electronic invoices (Rosencrance 2004).

UPS demonstrated the true power of its integrated logistics system in 2004 by offering a new service to Toshiba. Toshiba outsources all laptop repairs to UPS Supply Chain Solutions. Broken laptops are sent by UPS to its Louisville hub where UPS engineers diagnose the problem, fix the laptop, and return it to its owner. Mark Simons, general manager of Toshiba's digital products division, notes that diagnosing and repairing computers is actually the easy part. Instead, "moving a unit around and getting replacement parts consumes most of the time. The actual service only takes about an hour" (James 2004). UPS has been helping Toshiba with repairs by performing an initial inspection since 1999. UPS has also been servicing Lexmark and Hewlett-Packard printers since 1996.

Questions

1. Does it make sense for UPS to move into the computer repair business?
2. How does the Quantum View system provide new revenue or profits for UPS?
3. How does UPS use the Internet to reduce costs?

Additional Reading

Bacheldor, Beth. "Breakthrough." *Information Week,* February 9, 2004.

Brewin, Bob. "UPS Delivers Public-Access Wi-Fi to Its Retail Outlets." *Computerworld,* September 11, 2003.

Brewin, Bob. "UPS Invests $30M in IT to Speed Package Delivery." *Computerworld,* September 26, 2003.

Brewin, Bob. "IT Drives the UPS Machine." *Computerworld,* April 19, 2004.

James, Geoffrey. "The Next Delivery? Computer Repairs by UPS." *Business 2.0,* July 2004.

Rosencrance, Linda. "UPS Launches CampusShip Shipping Tool." *Computerworld,* March 7, 2002.

Rosencrance, Linda. "UPS Uses Technology to Speed International Shipments." *Computerworld,* November 27, 2002.

Rosencrance, Linda. "New UPS Service Speeds Payments Between Exporters and Importers." *Computerworld,* March 11, 2003.

Rosencrance, Linda. "UPS Launches Quantum View Manage." *Computerworld,* February 4, 2004.

UPS Web site: http://www.ups.com/content/corp/about/history/index.html.

Case: DHL/Deutsche Post

DHL has an interesting history. The company was started and driven by Larry L. Hillblom, who loved to fly—particularly among the Pacific islands. Because of this love, DHL focused largely on international shipments and became a leader in Southeast Asia. After Hillblom died in a plane crash in 1995, a huge number of East Asian and Pacific Island women came forward and claimed that they had had children with Hillblom, and that he promised to support them. After hundreds of lawyers and several court battles, four children were shown to be his heirs by DNA testing, but several others received settlement money as well (Metropolitan News-Enterprise 2003). In 2003, DHL was purchased by Deutsche Post. With its strength in Europe, Deutsche Post and DHL provide a strong international solution to shipping (company Web site). In 2004, DHL announced a major commitment to expanding its operations in the United States. In addition to its international ties, the company wants to focus on competing with UPS and FedEx through highly visible trucks and a national marketing campaign (Press Release 2004).

DHL has one of the largest customs-clearance systems of any of the shipping companies. With over 8 million trade rules, the WorldWide Clearance System (WCS) helps millions of packages clear customs throughout Asia and Europe. The process is largely automatic for the shipper. Most items are shipped without intervention. If a problem arises, the system fires a message back to the shipper to handle it. As a result, the customer does not have to constantly monitor the process (Rosencrance 2003).

Teamwork

DHL does not have the huge amount of money to spend on IT that UPS and FedEx do. Consequently, it is rarely a leader. But it has made some smart moves in communications networks, and by waiting for prices to drop, it now has the ability to compete with the giants. Alan Boehme, director of business planning in 1998, noted that "the nice thing is Internet technology and the change it enables—inexpensive communication on an open, standards-based network—is like David's rock. I'm not going to say that DHL is going to kill the giant, but Internet technology is the great equalizer for any business" (Sliwa 1998). Actually, even before the Internet took off, DHL made some smart investments. In 1988, the company built a TCP UNIX-based network to connect its offices around the world. Their package tracking data is routed on the internal frame-relay based network. It uses object-oriented technology to integrate data regardless of whether it came from the Web site or the automated phone system. The worldwide network also connects programmers and developers so that they can share data electronically and work together even when they are scattered around the globe (Sliwa 1998).

In 2004, DHL expanded its operations to provide radio-frequency identification (RFID) technology and support to its customers. By tagging all packages, the company helps suppliers meet RFID requirements throughout Europe. As worldwide standards are developed, the company wants to expand the program globally. Clems Beckmann, managing director of corporate development at Deutsche Post, notes that "our goal is to become the core logistics supplier for RFID services worldwide" (Sullivan 2004).

Information Technology

One problem that DHL experienced in 2001 was that its pricing was too difficult for customers. It could take days for a sales representative to quote a price, and as long as two to three weeks to get final approval from management. Lacking the resources to develop the system themselves, DHL turned to Metreo Inc to automate the process. Going live in 2002, the system provides sales representatives with real-time customer data and pricing information based on the customer's shipment. Tied to the corporate network, the salesperson can suggest an optimal price and receive approval almost immediately, sealing the deal before the customer can be coaxed away by FedEx or UPS (Rosencrance 2002).

In 2002, DHL realized that it needed a new data center to consolidate its operations. Built in Scottsdale, Arizona, the system connects centers in Kuala Lumpur, Malaysia, and London. DHL's CIO, Steve J. Bandrowczak, noted that "DHL wanted to create a seamless single offering to our customers, like a single invoice or a single Web interface. In order to enable that global logistics business vision, we had to consolidate our IT infrastructure, which included the data center, our network backbone and our key global applications" (Rosencrance 2004).

In terms of development of applications, because of its global nature, DHL turned to offshore development early on. By hiring programmers in the UK, India, and Asia, it is able to develop critical applications throughout a 24-hour day. Colum Joyce, global e-business strategy manager based in Brussels, observed that "for us, large-scale development is not a hothouse environment, it's an everyday reality" (Gilhooly 2001). Using the time differences around the world, development effectively continues around the clock—something you cannot do very well if everyone is located in the same time zone. Plus, the lower turnover rates and low salaries for skilled overseas programmers help hold costs down. Finally, the multilingual and multicultural programmers can tailor the applications to specific nations.

Questions

1. How do RFID tags help Deutsche Post offer new services to customers?

2. What benefits does Deutsche Post gain by using offshore programmers?

3. How does the Deutsche Post information system make it easy for small businesses to ship internationally? Why is this important?

4. How can the Internet enable DHL to compete equally with FedEx and UPS?

Additional Reading

Deutsche Post Web site: http://www.dhl.com/publish/g0/en/about/history.high.html.

Gilhooly, Kym. "The Staff That Never Sleeps." *Computerworld,* June 25, 2001.

Metropolitan News-Enterprise. "Ninth Circuit Rejects Judicial Bias Claim in Dispute between Lawyers for Heirs of DHL Founder." February 7, 2003.

Press Release. "DHL Brings Competition and Choice to U.S. Express Delivery Business with New Campaign."

June 14, 2004, http://www.dhl-usa.com/about/pr/ PRDetail.asp?nav=&seq=664.

Rosencrance, Linda. "DHL Picks Metreo Software to Improve Efficiency." *Computerworld,* February 13, 2002.

Rosencrance, Linda. "Brief: DHL Expands Worldwide Clearance System to Europe." *Computerworld,* July 23, 2003.

Rosencrance, Linda. "DHL Reaps Massive Savings in Data Center Consolidation." *Computerworld,* March 15, 2004.

Sliwa, Carol. "Look Out, Goliath, David Has a Rock." *Computerworld,* June 15, 1998.

Sullivan, Laurie. "Logistics Providers Ready RFID Services." *Information Week,* June 28, 2004.

Summary Industry Questions

1. What information technologies have helped this industry?
2. Did the technologies provide a competitive advantage or were they quickly adopted by rivals?
3. Which technologies could this industry use that were developed in other sectors?
4. Is the level of competition increasing or decreasing in this industry? Is it dominated by a few firms, or are they fairly balanced?
5. What problems have been created from the use of information technology and how did the firms solve the problems?

CHAPTER TEN

Business Decisions

Chapter Outline

Introduction

It Is Hard to Make Good Decisions
  Human Biases
  Models

Data Warehouse

Online Analytical Processing (OLAP)

Decision Support System
  Marketing Forecasts
  Human Resources Management

Geographical Information Systems
  Maps and Location Data
  Example

Data: Data Mining

Expert Systems
  Specialized Problems

Building Expert Systems
  Knowledge Base
  Rules
  Creating an ES
  Limitations of Expert Systems
  Management Issues of Expert Systems

Specialized Tools
  Pattern Recognition and Neural Networks
  Machine Vision
  Language Comprehension and Translation
  Robotics and Motion

Machine Intelligence

DSS, ES, and AI

The Importance of Intelligent Systems in e-Business
  Agents
  Support and Problem-Solving Applications

Summary

Key Words

Web Site References

Additional Reading

Review Questions

Exercises

Cases: Financial Services Industry

What You Will Learn in This Chapter

- How do businesses make decisions?

- How do you make a good decision? Why do people make bad decisions?

- How do you find and retrieve data to analyze it?

- How can you quickly examine data and view subtotals without writing hundreds of queries?

- How does a decision support system help you analyze data?

- How do you visualize data that depends on location?

- Is it possible to automate the analysis of data?

- Can information technology be more intelligent? Can it analyze data and evaluate rules?

- How do you create an expert system?

- Can machines be made even smarter? What technologies can be used to help managers?

- What would it take to convince you that a machine is intelligent?

- What are the differences between DSS, ES, and AI systems?

- How can more intelligent systems benefit e-business?

How do you use information technology to make better decisions? Citigroup is one of the largest banks in the world. And the world part is important: the company operates in 101 countries. Running a global bank requires making thousands of decisions—from basic questions about approving loans to structuring mega-deals with huge corporations. Banks obviously adopted information technology early—to handle basic transactions. After all, money today is really just numbers in a computer. Banks, including Citigroup, have been slower to adopt technology to make decisions; but that reluctance has been changing in the last few years.

Citigroup is faced with competitive pressures as well as disruptions from economic fluctuations. It has attempted to reduce risk by spreading into multiple business areas, including insurance (Travelers), brokerage (Salomon Smith Barney), and investment banking. The company is one of the largest issuers of credit cards in the United States. With stagnant growth of the U.S. credit industry, Citigroup has expanded into South America and even China. Evaluating customers to minimize risk is a key aspect of the credit card industry.

FIGURE 10.1

Tactical decisions often require complicated analysis. Problems utilize forecasts, optimization, and in-depth analysis. Information systems provide support through data, modeling, and presentation tools. Managers use information system tools to build, evaluate, and maintain various models.

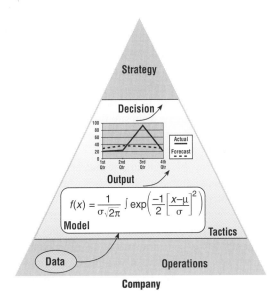

$$f(x) = \frac{1}{\sigma\sqrt{2\pi}} \int \exp\left(\frac{-1}{2}\left[\frac{x-\mu}{\sigma}\right]^2\right)$$

Introduction

How do businesses make decisions? As a manager, you will have access to huge amounts of data. How do you analyze it to understand what it means? How can information systems help you make better decisions? These questions are difficult to answer, but there is a much bigger underlying question. Why would companies need to hire you as a manager? Executives already have access to databases containing integrated data for the entire company. ERP systems can provide detailed data on any aspect of the business. EIS systems can show charts, summaries, and detailed data. As shown in Figure 10.1, what if computer systems can be built to analyze the data and make decisions? What job will you have?

Can computers make decisions? How can information systems help managers make decisions? Some business problems are straightforward. In these cases, developers simply create a set of rules or procedures that the computer can be programmed to follow. As long as the business behaves in a predictable manner, the rules apply and the computer can handle

TRENDS

Through the 1970s, computers were largely used to assist with transaction processing. Support for making decisions was generally limited to the basic reports produced from the data. Computers were too expensive and programming too difficult to be used by every manager. As personal computers became commonplace through the 1980s, managers began transferring data from the corporate central computers to their personal machines. Spreadsheets made it easier to analyze data, evaluate models, and create charts. In the 1990s, networks, improved spreadsheets, and better ties to databases made it possible to build more complex, interactive models and create forecasts.

Along with technology, improvements were made to modeling and analytical tools. Scientific advancements made it possible to add more intelligence to software tools. Data mining systems use statistical tools to semiautomatically evaluate data, searching for important relationships and clustering or classifying groups of data.

Expert systems evolved from early work on artificial intelligence. Focusing on narrow domains, these tools encode the rules of an expert to analyze data and suggest solutions. Today, thousands of expert systems are used to improve decisions and provide quick results 24 hours a day.

The study of human brains yielded clues that led to the development of neural networks. Today, neural networks are widely used in pattern matching applications. Humans are good at pattern recognition, and neural networks dramatically improve the ability of machines to perform these tasks.

Writers and researchers have long wondered whether machines can become intelligent. No one is close to an answer yet, but the new technologies mean that today's systems are more intelligent and can handle more complex problems than machines a few years ago. As the range of solvable problems increases, managers need to understand the capabilities and limitations of each method.

the details. However, many business problems are less structured and cannot be solved so easily. In addition, problems often involve data that is not well defined. For example, it is straightforward to create a computer system to handle inventory because the computer can easily keep track of item numbers and quantity sold. Consider the more difficult problem faced by a manager who has to decide where to locate a new plant. Some attributes are measurable, such as distance from suppliers, cost of land, and taxes. Other features are difficult to quantify: quality of the labor force, attitudes of government officials, and long-run political stability of the area.

Many problems involve nonnumeric data and complex interrelationships among the various factors. Without computers, businesses often call in experts or hire consultants to help solve these problems. Special software programs called **expert systems (ESs)** provide many of these features. From the beginning, researchers and computer designers have known that humans perform some tasks much better than computers can. These differences led researchers to investigate how people solve problems and investigate how humans think. The research into techniques that might make computers "think" more like humans is known as **artificial intelligence (AI).** There is some question as to whether it will ever be possible to build machines that can think the same way humans do. Nonetheless, the research has led to some useful tools that perform more complex analysis and can solve difficult problems. These tools attempt to mimic the processes used by humans in a simpler form that can be processed by a computer system.

The answer to the big question is yes, computers can make decisions in some situations. In other cases, the computer is a tool that helps you analyze the data. The level of support provided depends on the type of problem and on your skills as an analyst. As a manager, it is your responsibility to identify decisions that can be handled by machine systems and to recognize when these systems do not work.

It Is Hard to Make Good Decisions

How do you make a good decision? Why do people make bad decisions? Most businesses have evolved over time. In many cases, their business processes have been built and patched in response to various changes in the industry. The firms that made better decisions and changes survived, while the others failed. But the existing process might not be the most efficient. Consider the apparently simple process of farming. Farmers feed the animals and then sell them. The hard part is that the animals can be fed and housed many different ways—each with different costs. Should the animals be fed high-protein food that costs more and grows bigger animals faster, or should they be fed simple diets and take more time to mature? In the 1970s and 1980s, experts created software that analyzed these questions from the standpoint of minimizing the cost of feeding the animals. Using optimization methods, they were able to substantially reduce the production costs. But some experts have found it is possible to do even better by focusing on profits across the entire industry chain.

Even if you do have a system for making a better decision, you need to convince managers to use it. Many managers distrust new technologies and different answers, because they see an element of risk. A few companies have established a culture that focuses on continual improvement and growth. In these companies, managers are encouraged to explore new ideas and replace the existing processes.

Human Biases

Assume you have money to invest in the stock market. Someone shows you two companies. As shown in Figure 10.2, Company A's share prices have risen by 2 percent per month for the last year. The other's share price was flat for five months but has increased by 3 percent per month since then. Which stock do you buy? But wait a minute. How can you possibly decide based on the little information you have? It sounds silly, but people make these decisions with minimal data and no logical analysis every single day. When people make decisions this way, the results are going to be inconsistent and dangerous. But it is so much easier to make a snap decision, and so much harder to do the research and complex analyses to make the right decision.

Consider a true example: designing a new automobile. Assuming you have money, what kind of car would you buy? Sporty, luxurious, flashy, utilitarian, big, small? What color? How many doors? Now ask a few friends or relatives what they would buy. Will all of the answers be the same? Not likely. Now think about the problem from the perspective of an automobile manufacturer such as General Motors. What features are car buyers going to demand in two or three years? This classic marketing problem is difficult to solve. For years, GM used its multiple divisions to create separate identities that appealed to different segments of the population. Designers within each division focused on the preferences and lifestyles of their specific target. Most of that structure fell apart in the mid-1980s with the introduction of a completely new line of cars. At that time, the GM divisions introduced a new car model from four main divisions. Somewhat surprisingly, all four cars (Oldsmobile Cutlass Ciera, Pontiac J2000, Chevrolet Celebrity, and Buick Century) were virtually identical—down to the color. In effect, GM was assuming that millions of customers all wanted the same car.

FIGURE 10.2

Sample Decision: Do you invest your money in Company A or Company B? Be careful; it is a trick question.

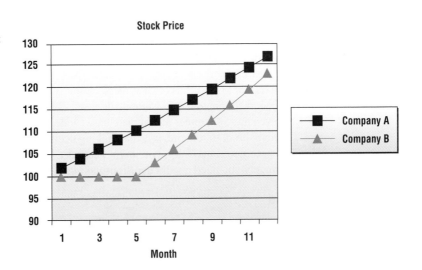

FIGURE 10.3

Biases in decision making: Without models, people tend to rely on simplistic "rules of thumb" and fall prey to a variety of common mistakes. These errors can be minimized with training and experience in a discipline. They can also be minimized by having computer systems perform much of the initial analysis.

Acquisition/Input		
Bias	**Description**	**Example**
Data availability	Ease with which specific instances can be recalled affects judgments of frequency.	People overestimate the risk of dying due to homicides compared to heart disease.
Illusory correlation	Belief that two variables are related when they are not.	Ask any conspiracy buff about the death of JFK.
Data presentation	Order effects.	First (or last) items in a list are given more importance.
Processing		
Inconsistency	Difficulty in being consistent for similar decisions.	Judgments involving selection, such as personnel.
Conservatism	Failure to completely use new information.	Resistance to change.
Stress	Stress causes people to make hasty decisions.	Panic judgments and quick fixes.
Social pressure	Social pressures cause people to alter their decisions and decision-making processes.	Majority opinion can unduly influence everyone else: mob rule.
Output		
Scale effects	The scale on which responses are recorded can affect responses.	Ask a group of people to rate how they feel on a scale from 1 to 10. Ask a similar group to use a scale from 1 to 1,000.
Wishful thinking	Preference for an outcome affects the assessment.	People sometimes place a higher probability on events that they want to happen.
Feedback		
Learning from irrelevant outcomes	People gain unrealistic expectations when they see incomplete or inaccurate data.	In personnel selection you see how good your selection is for candidates you accepted. You do not receive data on candidates you rejected.
Success/failure attributions	Tendency to attribute success to one's skill and failure to chance.	Only taking credit for the successes in your job.

In response to these problems, Barabba and Zaltman, two marketing researchers working with GM, analyzed decision making at General Motors and noticed that several common problems arose. In summary, they found that people are weak at making decisions. For example, people place too much emphasis on recent events, they tend to discard data that does not fit their prior beliefs, they follow rules of thumb instead of statistical analysis, and they choose outcomes based on wishful thinking. As shown in Figure 10.3, all of these problems and more influenced the decisions of designers at GM. In particular, they found that the designers tended to discuss ideas with their bosses in an attempt to identify management preferences that would help get a particular design approved. So cars were designed to the preferences of a few managers, instead of to the needs of customers. Despite attempts to improve, the fiasco eventually forced GM to eliminate the Oldsmobile division. The books written by Barabba and Zaltman discuss even more examples and human biases in decision making.

The main point to remember is that making decisions without a good model and process leads to poor decisions. Sure, you might get lucky for a while (like investors in the 1990s), but ultimately you need a solid decision-making process.

Models

Models are key aspects to any decision; they are simplifications designed to help you understand and analyze a problem. Many of the models you will use in business decisions were created by academics. You will be introduced to many of these models in other busi-

FIGURE 10.4

The four primary reasons for building and using models: Descriptive, graphical, and mathematical models can be used for each of these purposes. However, mathematical models tend to be emphasized for optimization and simulation.

Model Building
Understand the Process
Models force us to define objects and specify relationships. Modeling is a first step in improving the business processes.
Optimization
Models are used to search for the best solutions: minimizing costs, improving efficiency, increasing profits, and so on.
Prediction
Model parameters can be estimated from prior data. Sample data is used to forecast future changes based on the model.
Simulation
Models are used to examine what might happen if we make changes to the process or to examine relationships in more detail.

ness courses. As a manager, you are responsible for knowing that hundreds of models are available to help you make decisions, and for knowing which model best applies to the problem you are facing. Understanding and evaluating models is an important aspect of a business education.

Models often use drawings and pictures to represent the various objects. However, at heart they typically use mathematical equations to represent the process and the various relationships. For example, an operations engineer would model a machine as a mathematical formula that converts raw materials and labor into products. Using equations for each step of the production process, the engineer could search for ways to reorganize production to make it more efficient or to improve quality.

Models are used to help managers make decisions. Most businesses are far too complex for any single person to understand all of the details. Consequently, a variety of models may be created to present a simplified view of the business. In particular, one of the original purposes of accounting was to create a standardized model of the financial aspects of business. Another common model of business is the practice of dividing the company into functional areas. For example, a manager with experience in the finance department of one company can usually apply knowledge and problem-solving skills to finance departments in other companies and even other industries. The basic goals are summarized in Figure 10.4. Models help you simplify the world. They help you search for similarities in different situations. Models also enable managers to predict how changes might affect the business. As the decision maker, it is up to you to determine which models to use and to make sure they actually apply to the situation. Once you have selected the appropriate model, you apply whatever data you have, evaluate the results, and make the decision.

Prediction and Optimization

An important use of models is for **prediction**. If a model is reasonably accurate, it can be used to predict future outcomes. For instance, in the used automobile example it would be possible to estimate how the price of used cars changes over time.

Prediction first requires that you have a model that describes the situation. Then data is collected and statistical techniques are used to estimate the **parameters** of the model for the specific problem. Next you fill in any parameters that you already know, and the model provides a prediction. Prediction techniques such as regression and time series forecasting are used to examine the data, identify trends, and predict possible future changes. To use statistics effectively requires a model of the underlying system. For instance, to use regression methods you first identify the dependent variable and a set of possible independent variables. These choices come from the underlying model. Figure 10.5 illustrates how a spreadsheet or graphics package can be used to display the results of a forecast.

REALITY BYTES   Drowning in Data

Max Alexander had a problem he never anticipated—too many sales. Or, rather, too much sales data. As an executive of the Carphone Warehouse Group in the UK, he was responsible for analyzing sales data and prospects. As one of Europe's largest mobile phone retailers, the company already had substantial sales. In 2003, it started selling fixed-line services as well. Information poured in from telemarketers, the company's retail outlets, and grocery store chains that were comarketing the new services. Mr. Alexander notes that "we had sales updates every 15 minutes being pulled into ad hoc spreadsheets. You had to pore through reams and reams of data."

His answer was to install software from Fractal Edge of London. The visualization software collects that data and provides interactive charting. For Carphone, the software displays circles representing each of the sales marketing channels. Each circle is color-coded to show the sales performance. Clicking down through the circles provides more detailed data. Mr. Alexander believes the system is

helping him make better decisions more quickly. He also notes that he is spending 20 percent less time analyzing data.

Many other companies are turning to data visualization software to provide a more comprehensive view of the data. For example, J.P. Morgan Securities in London used software from Panopticon Software AB to create CreditMap. CreditMap displays a view of the corporate bond market by sector. New issues are displayed based on the size of the issue, with color representing its performance. Traders can see at a glance which sectors are hot, and the system uses drill-down capabilities to provide detailed information about each bond. Lee McGinty, European vice president of quantitative strategy at the firm, notes that "it can look a bit scary. But it's not half as scary as a thousand-row spreadsheet."

Source: Adapted from Jeanette Borzo, "Get the Picture," *The Wall Street Journal,* January 12, 2004.

FIGURE 10.5

Prediction model: Several statistical techniques exist for analyzing data and making forecasts. Two common methods are regression and moving averages. Both methods require substantial amounts of data. Choosing between the two requires some expertise in statistical analysis, but many times we display both methods to show a range of possible outcomes.

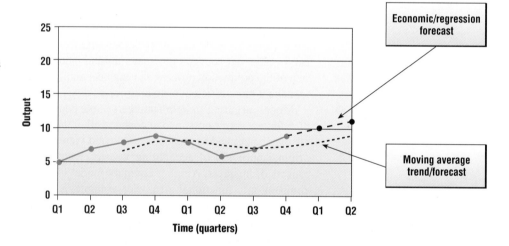

Optimization evaluates a model in terms of the inputs or control parameters and searches for the best solution. Optimization requires a detailed mathematical model. Several tools such as linear programming are used to find optimal values. Some optimization models have resulted in substantial savings in cost or increases in profit. Tasks that are repeated hundreds or thousands of times can often benefit through optimization modeling.

Simulation or "What-If" Scenarios

Simulation is a modeling technique with many uses. Once a model is created, managers use simulation to examine how the item being studied will respond to changes. With simulation, various options can be tested on the model to examine what might happen. For example, engineers always build models of airplanes and engines before they try to build the real thing. The models are much cheaper. In fact, most engineers today start with mathematical computer models because they are cheaper to create than physical models and can contain more detail. Moreover, they can perform experiments on models that would not be safe to perform in real life. For example, an engineer could stress a model of an airplane until it broke up. It would be dangerous and expensive to try such an experiment on a real plane. Similarly, a business model could examine what would happen if prices were increased by 20 percent, without worrying about losing real money.

FIGURE 10.6

Object-oriented simulation: A simple example of custom manufacturing. Each object (parts list, purchase order, etc.) and each process are defined in detail by the modeler. The simulation system generates orders, makes shipments, and orders inventory according to programmed rules. The simulator collects a wide variety of statistics that can be displayed graphically or in tabular reports.

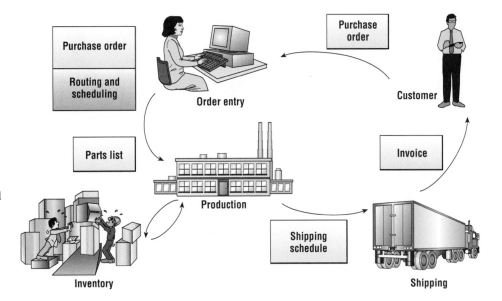

Most simulation models are mathematical instead of descriptive models, because they are easy to evaluate. Mathematical models contain parameters, or variables that can be controlled by the managers. For instance, you might use a spreadsheet to create an accounting model of an income statement and balance sheet. When you create the spreadsheet, production quantity and price of your products are controllable parameters that affect the income and profits of the firm. You could use the model to investigate decisions, like the effect on profits if you increase production. Costs will increase, but so will revenue from sales. The net result depends on the specific details of the firm and the model. Spreadsheets are often used to analyze small models and graph the results. More sophisticated simulation packages can support more complex analysis and will automatically create graphs and pictures to show interrelationships.

The more complex the model, the more alternatives that can be simulated. In the last example, a more detailed model might enable you to investigate alternatives such as increased overtime, hiring another shift, building additional plants, or subcontracting the work to another firm.

Object-oriented simulation tools developed in the last few years make it easy to create many simulations. As shown in Figure 10.6, you can place icons on the screen to represent various business objects. Behind each of these objects, you specify their behavior. For example, you would need to estimate the average number of customers that arrive in an hour and how long they are willing to wait for service. For physical processes like order entry, inventory, and shipping, you specify the number of transactions that can be handled in a given time. When all of the details have been entered, the system runs simulations and tracks statistics. You can change the parameters such as adding clerks to see what happens if you change the operations.

Data Warehouse

How do you find and retrieve data to analyze it? ERP and other transaction systems can provide enough data to bury you. But the transaction systems are designed to store data, not to search and analyze it. Relational databases turn out to be relatively slow when you need to analyze several gigabytes or even terabytes of data. If you do not have an ERP system, you have even greater problems trying to integrate and clean data from all of your systems. As shown in Figure 10.7, the answer is to create a separate **data warehouse** that extracts and stores the data in a clean, easy-to-analyze format. The process shown in Figure 10.7 is known as **extraction, transformation, and loading (ETL)**. Larger database management

FIGURE 10.7

Data warehouse: A data warehouse is commonly used as a method to provide data to decision makers without interfering with the transaction-processing operations. Selected data items are regularly pulled from the transaction data files and stored in a central location. DSS tools query the data warehouse for analysis and reporting.

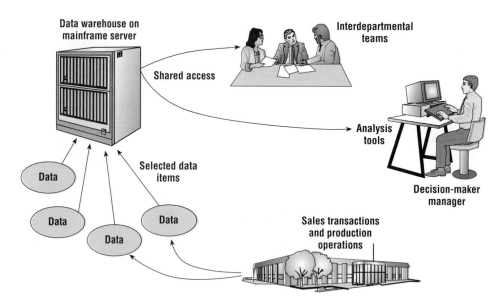

systems have specific tools and data storage methods to create data warehouses. Some companies also create specific **data marts** that are basically copies of a small portion of the data warehouse designed to feed a specific application. For instance, a financial data mart might be used by the accounting and finance department just to monitor investments and bank accounts.

Documenting the data is critical because managers have to understand what each item represents and they need to be able to find specific items. **Metadata** is used to describe the source data, identify the transformation and integration steps, and define the way the data warehouse is organized. A data warehouse represents a subset of the total data in the company. In most cases, it is a static copy that is refreshed on a daily or hourly basis. This type of system is relatively easy to use; managers do not have to learn data access commands (SQL or QBE). However, it is less flexible than using a database management system. Decision makers will be unable to get additional data or to compare the data in some previously unexpected way. The success of a data warehouse depends on how well the manager's needs have been anticipated.

Online Analytical Processing (OLAP)

How can you quickly examine data and view subtotals without writing hundreds of queries? Retrieving data and examining totals from different perspectives is an important part of making decisions. When the problem is unstructured and there is no existing mathematical model, it often helps to look at subtotals of data. This process is a major function of **online analytical processing (OLAP).** Most OLAP tools rely on a data warehouse to provide consistent data and fast access.

Most OLAP tools depict the data as multidimensional cubes. Managers use specific tools to examine various sections of the data. To illustrate the process, consider a simple example from a pet store database. Managers are interested in sales of merchandise. In particular, they want to look at sales by date, by the category of the item (cat, dog, etc.), and by the location of the customer. The attribute they want to measure is the value or amount of the items sold, which is the price times the quantity. Figure 10.8 shows how this small query could be pictured as a three-dimensional cube. The OLAP tools enable managers to examine any question that involves the dimensions of the cube. For instance, they can quickly examine totals by state, city, month, or category. They can look at subtotals for the different categories of products or details within individual states. The tools can provide detail items that can be pictured as a slice of the cube, or they can provide subtotals of any section.

FIGURE 10.8

Multidimensional cube for item sales: Managers are interested in various combinations of the dimensions. For example, total item sales of dog items in the last quarter. OLAP tools rapidly provide answers to questions involving any perspective of this cube.

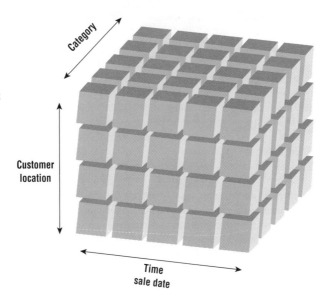

FIGURE 10.9

Microsoft pivot table report: Pivot tools make it easy for managers to examine cube data from any perspective, to select subsets of the data, to perform calculations, and to create charts.

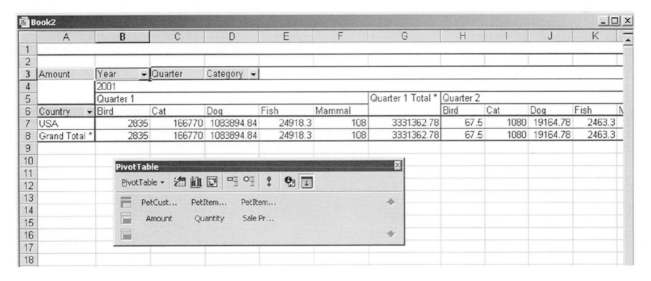

Although most DBMS vendors (including Microsoft, Oracle, and IBM) provide OLAP cube browsers, Microsoft provides Pivot Table interface that works with almost any DBMS or spreadsheet. A pivot table is an interactive interface to a multidimensional cube. A pivot table is created on the user's machine—most users will build pivot tables inside of Microsoft Excel. This tool has several options and provides a great deal of flexibility for the user.

The pivot table report for a pet store is shown in Figure 10.9. By clicking on a row or column dimension, managers can see details or subtotals. They can also select specific items to include in the subtotals. Managers even have the flexibility to drag the dimensions around—to move them from columns to rows, or to change the order of the summations. Additional options provide other statistics, such as averages. A powerful graphics option makes it easy to create charts—using the Excel interface that is familiar to most business managers. Data warehouses and pivot tables can also be used to create graphs and to feed data into other analytical software.

Problem: You and your manager need to analyze sales based on several attributes.

Tools: OLAP cube browsers are designed to make it easy for you to examine slices of the cube and examine a fact (sales) based on several dimensions. The big DBMS vendors sell cube browsers with their packages. However, you can also use the Microsoft Pivot Table that is built into Excel.

The Rolling Thunder Bicycle data provides a good example for a cube. The fact to be evaluated is the SalePrice. The more interesting dimensions are OrderDate, ModelType, and SaleState. The date presents a common problem: dates are really hierarchies. You might want to examine sales by year, or you might want to drill down and see sales by quarter or month. Some cube browsers make it easy to create this hierarchy. Excel does not create it automatically, but you can use a query to convert the date into the different dimensions. The qryPiv-

otAll query shows you how to compute the various year, month, and quarter fields.

In a new Excel worksheet, use the Data/PivotTable option to begin the process. Select the External Data Source option because the data comes from a DBMS. Follow the basic steps to get data from a Microsoft Access Database and select your copy of the Rolling Thunder database. In the Query Wizard, find the qryPivotAll query, and select all of its columns by moving them to the right side box. Follow the Next and Finish prompts to return the data to the spreadsheet. Avoid the sorting and filtering options.

The structure of the pivot table contains a space for row variables, column variables, page variables, and the main fact. Drag Year and YearMonth from the field list onto the table column location. Drag the ModelType and SaleState fields onto the row location. Finally, drag the SalePrice onto the main body of the table. You can place the remaining fields in the page location if you want to make them easy to find later.

$$y = 5897x + 156750$$
$$R^2 = 0.5198$$

Total Sales by Month

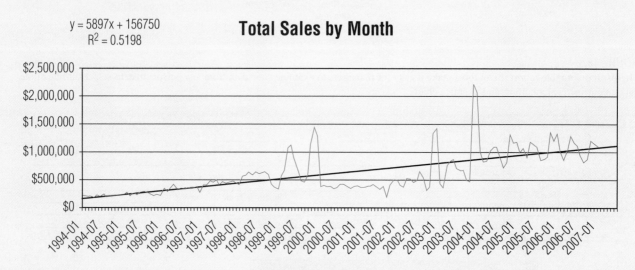

The fun part is playing with the cube. Select the Year heading and click the minus button to collapse the detail. Do the same with the ModelType or SaleState column. Watch as the totals are automatically updated. Drag the ModelType or SaleState field heading to swap the order. Collapse or expand the field to summarize or drill down into the data. You can just as easily expand only one year or one state.

Quick Quiz:

1. How is the cube browser better than writing queries?
2. How would you display quarterly instead of monthly data?
3. How many dimensions can you reasonably include in the cube? How would you handle additional dimensions?

Decision Support System

How does a decision support system help you analyze data? A **decision support system (DSS)** consists of three basic components: (1) data retrieval, (2) model evaluation, and (3) visualization of the results. Today, a data warehouse or OLAP cube is often used as the data source. The model is often developed by experts (usually consultants) and evaluated in a spreadsheet. The visualization component generally consists of charts, but more sophisticated time lines and schedules are used for complex problems.

To understand the value of a DSS, it is easiest to work with a couple of examples. Thousands of examples exist, but they often require detailed knowledge from a specialized discipline. On the other hand, most managers will need some familiarity with marketing and with human resources management. The examples are relatively small and you will cover

FIGURE 10.10

Common marketing data sources: There are three primary sources of marketing data: internal collections, specialty research companies, and government agencies. Detailed data is available on the industry, customers, regions, and competitors.

Internal	Purchase	Government
• Sales	• Scanner data	• Census
• Warranty cards	• Competitive market analysis	Income
• Customer service lines	• Mailing and phone lists	Demographics
• Coupons	• Subscriber lists	Regional data
• Surveys	• Rating services (e.g., Arbitron)	• Legal registration
• Focus groups	• Shipping, especially foreign	Drivers license
		Marriage
		Housing/
		construction

more complex models in other business classes. The principles are the same, and you can often use the same tools. Along the same lines, if you want to apply these models to real business problems, you will have to collect more data and add more features to the models.

Marketing Forecasts

Marketing departments are responsible for market research, sales forecasting, management of the sales staff, advertising, and promotion. In some firms they also process orders and manage the design of new products and features. Processing orders is essentially a transaction-processing task. The others involve tactical or strategic questions that are more complex, so we will focus on those tasks.

An enormous amount of data is available for market research. Figure 10.10 presents some of the common data available for marketing purposes. Internally, the marketing department maintains records of sales and basic customer attributes. With some firms, there can be a longer distance between the firm and the final customer. For instance, manufacturers typically sell products to wholesalers, who place the products in individual stores, where they reach the final customer. In these cases it is more difficult to identify customer needs and forecast sales. There will be delays in receiving sales data because the retailers and wholesalers typically place bulk orders. Furthermore, it is more difficult to identify customer preferences because their purchases are filtered through other companies. Marketing departments also have access to data that is collected by other firms. In a manufacturing environment, marketers might get raw sales data from the wholesalers and retailers. On the retail side, with the pervasiveness of checkout scanners, it is now possible to buy daily and hourly sales records from thousands of stores in various cities. This data contains sales of your products as well as rivals' products.

Marketing is often asked to forecast sales. Several different methods can be used, but a straightforward approach is to begin with statistical forecasts. Consider a simple example shown in Figure 10.11 for a fictional store that sells consumer products nationwide. The sales estimate is based on economics where sales are dependent on time and on consumers' income. As consumer income increases, they will be more likely to purchase the company's merchandise. Gross domestic product (GDP) will be used as a proxy for consumer income.

Notice the seasonal peaks in sales for each fourth quarter. It is important to capture this holiday sales effect. Since national GDP and household income have this same effect, you can build a model based on the relationship of your sales to GDP and time. The process is described in Figure 10.12, and all of the steps can be performed in a spreadsheet. Regression provides the estimate of the coefficients that describe the relationship between sales and GDP and time. The R-squared value is over 90 percent and all of the coefficients have high t-values, so it is a strong relationship. Forecasting the GDP is a little tricky, so most people just use government forecasts. But be careful to get nonseasonally adjusted values (which are difficult to find), so they show the quarterly cycle. You can also forecast the quarterly values yourself. The easy way to preserve the cycle is to forecast the quarters independently (all first quarters, all second quarters, and so on). Then plug these values in for the forecast, multiply by the estimated coefficients, and graph the result. It might not be

FIGURE 10.11

Sales forecast: Note the seasonal peaks in the fourth quarter. The points beyond quarter 40 are forecasts based on time and the relationship to income (GDP). This forecast requires that GDP predictions be made for each future quarter, but these values can often be obtained from government forecasts.

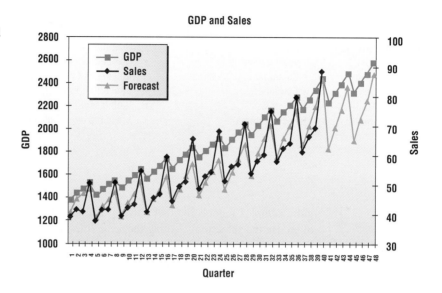

FIGURE 10.12

Forecasting process: All of these steps can be performed by a spreadsheet. To forecast the quarterly GDP values, simply split them into four columns, one for each quarter. Then use the spreadsheet's linear forecast tool to extend the columns.

Data:	Quarterly sales and GDP for 10 years.		
Model:	Sales = b0 + b1 time + b2 GDP		
Analysis:	Estimate model coefficients with regression.		
	Coefficients	**Standard Error**	**t Stat**
Intercept	-98.175	15.895	-6.176
Time	-1.663	0.304	-5.444
GDP	0.102	0.012	8.507
	Forecast GDP for each quarter.		
Output:	Compute sales prediction.		
	Graph forecast.		

quite as accurate as a full time-series estimation technique, but any business student can make it work, and it is much better than guessing or wishful thinking.

Human Resources Management

An important HRM task in any organization is the need to allocate raises. Using a merit pay system, each employee is evaluated on the basis of factors related to his or her job. Typically, each manager is given a fixed amount of money to allocate among the employees. The goal is to distribute the money relative to the performance appraisals, provide sufficient incentives to retain employees, and meet equal employment opportunity guidelines. Many of these goals are conflicting, especially with a finite amount of money available. To set the actual raises, managers need to examine the raw data. On the other hand, a graph makes it easier to compare the various goals.

A few specialized software packages can help you determine merit raises. However, as shown in Figure 10.13, it is possible to create a small system using a spreadsheet. A spreadsheet that can display a graph alongside the data tables is particularly useful. Assume that the company wishes to give a certain portion of the raise based on the average performance ratings. The amount of money per point (currently $100) can be changed. Each person can be given an additional market adjustment raise. The total departmental raises cannot exceed the allocated total ($10,000).

The goal is to fill in the market adjustment column so that the raises match the performance appraisals. As illustrated by the graph in Figure 10.14, the manager can evaluate both absolute dollar raise or the percentage increase. The total departmental raises should be

FIGURE 10.13

Merit pay analysis: With a merit system, salary increases should be related to performance evaluations (denoted r1, r2, r3). Managers are typically given a fixed pool of money to distribute among the employees. Employee raises should be based on merit evaluations, current salary, the salary range for the job. Market adjustments are often paid to attract workers in high-demand fields. A spreadsheet can be used to model the effects of various policies. In this example, the manager has allocated $100 for each merit percentage point. The rest of the money will be given as market adjustments. The effects of the adjustments can be seen in the graph displayed in the next figure.

| | | | | | Merit Pay | | | Raise Pool | | $10,000 | | |
| | Performance | | | Pct | Salary Range ($000) | | | Current | Merit | Market | Total | |
Name	r1	r2	r3	Perf	High	Low	Avg	Salary	$100	Adjust.	Raise	Raise%
Caulkins	9	7	6	73%	37.5	28.4	36.4	35.8	733		733	2.0%
Jihong	3	6	7	53%	18.9	15.4	16.3	17.9	533		533	3.0%
Louganis	8	7	7	73%	30.2	26.7	28.9	29.5	733		733	2.5%
Naber	9	8	8	83%	23.2	19.5	21.4	19.8	833		833	4.2%
Spitz	3	4	3	33%	22.4	17.3	18.4	17.5	333		333	1.9%
Weissmuller	5	4	6	50%	60.4	32.5	45.2	53.2	500		500	0.9%
Department	6	6	6		32.1	22.2	21.9	21.7	3665		3665	2.4%
Corporate	5	6	5		124	9.2	18.9	18.9				

FIGURE 10.14

Performance evaluation: Using a separate y-axis for the two types of data and overlaying line plots on the bar chart makes this graph easier to read. If this graph is dynamically linked to the salary table, the manager can make salary changes and instantly compare the raises to the performance ratings.

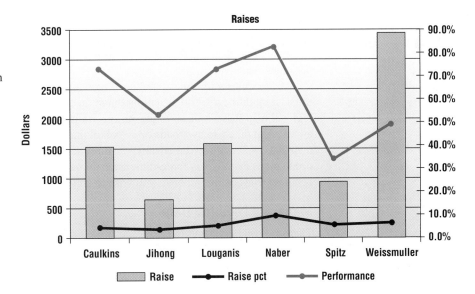

equal to $10,000. By displaying the graph next to the last columns in the spreadsheet, it is possible to watch the changes as you enter the data. This immediate feedback makes it easier to set the raises you prefer. Use of some type of DSS analytical system is helpful for identifying and minimizing illegal discrimination in salaries.

Geographical Information Systems

How do you visualize data that depends on location? Many aspects of business can benefit by modeling problems as geographical relationships. For instance, to choose the site of retail outlets, you need to know the location and travel patterns of your potential customers. Manufacturing can be made more efficient if you know the locations of raw materials, suppliers, and workers. Similarly, locations of distribution warehouses need to be chosen based on retail outlets, manufacturing facilities, and transportation routes. Thousands of other geographical considerations exist in business, such as monitoring pollution discharges, routing and tracking delivery vehicles, classifying areas for risk of crimes and fire, following

REALITY BYTES   GIS in the City

New York is a city of 8 million people, thousands of buildings, and hundreds of miles of roads. How can the government deal with the thousands of details? The Citywide Geographic Information Systems Utility helps with many of them. It is a combination of aerial photography, census figures, crime statistics, and data entered by the hundreds of civil agencies and utility companies. When hundreds of people called to report a loss of heat in the middle of winter, the system plotted their addresses and helped pinpoint where to place "heating centers" to help New Yorkers get through the problem. It records which streets have been paved, where the West Nile virus has appeared, and where the fire stations and police stations are located. All of the data can be overlaid on an interactive map that is detailed enough to show curb lines, trees, and even wires. Firefighters can instantly pull up the list of street closures and plot the fastest route to a fire. Building floor plans can be overlaid on the map, helping plan for emergencies or to estimate capacity limits.

Some workers are threatened by the technology. New York tested the system on Staten Island to see if it could improve the scheduling of garbage collection. When asked about the impact of the technology, Harry Nespoli, president of the sanitation workers' union, noted that he was not aware of the test. But he did not believe the software could be as effective as the current system. "We are not computers, you know. We are human beings," he said. "Does a computer get lunch time? Does a computer sprain his ankle? Does a computer die like one of my members did the other day? We have very, very efficient managers on this job. They came up through the ranks. They know the best way to pick up the garbage."

Source: Adapted from Brian Bergstein, "GIS Mapping Software Jolts City Governments," *eWeek,* February 1, 2004.

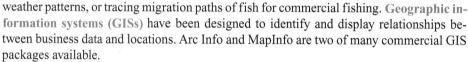

weather patterns, or tracing migration paths of fish for commercial fishing. **Geographic information systems (GISs)** have been designed to identify and display relationships between business data and locations. Arc Info and MapInfo are two of many commercial GIS packages available.

A GIS begins with the capability of drawing a map of the area in which you are interested. It might be a world or national map that displays political boundaries. It might be a regional map that emphasizes the various transportation routes or utility lines. It might be a local map that displays roads or even buildings. An oil exploration company might use a map that displays three-dimensional features of a small area. A shipping company could use ocean maps that display three-dimensional images of the ocean passageways. The level of detail depends on the problem you wish to solve.

Maps and Location Data

There are two basic ways to create and store the underlying maps: as pictures or as digitized map data. Digital map data provides the most flexibility. Besides being easier to change, digital maps enable you to zoom in and see more detail. Each item is stored by its location as measured by latitude and longitude and sometimes its elevation. Most U.S. digital maps are based on data that the Bureau of the Census created for the 1990 national census, known as TIGER. The Bureau of the Census has every road and house number entered into a giant database. Because of privacy reasons, they will not sell house locations, but you can get the range of street numbers for each city block. The U.S. Department of Defense has digital data available for many areas, including international locations, and often includes elevation data. The U.S. Geological Survey topographical maps are also being converted to digital systems. However, keep in mind that the systems being mapped are constantly changing, so even digital maps often contain missing, incomplete, or inaccurate data—as the United States learned when it accidentally blew up the Chinese embassy in Belgrade because the CIA maps were out of date.

Once you have the base maps, the objective is to overlay additional data on the maps. For example, you can obtain census data that displays average consumer characteristics such as income, house price, and number of autos within each geographic area. The GIS could be used to plot different colors for each income level. Next you can overlay the locations of your retail stores. If you are selling a high-price item such as a Cadillac, you want to locate the stores in areas of higher income.

Although you can buy base geographical data, how do you know the location of your retail stores? Or how do you plot the locations of delivery vehicles, or police cars, or trains? The easiest answer today is to use the **global positioning system (GPS),** which is a set of satellites maintained by the U.S. government. A portable receiver tuned to the satellites will identify your location in latitude, longitude, and elevation (if it can reach four satellites) within 50 feet. Several handheld units are available for a few hundred dollars. If you work for the Department of Defense, you can get receivers that will identify your location within a few millimeters, but you need appropriate security clearances to obtain these receivers. Currently, the government is broadcasting the higher-resolution signal to civilian receivers, but sometimes blocks it during emergencies. Civilian models that combine signals from U.S. and Russian satellites provide even better resolution, but cost about $8,000.

As a model, the GIS makes it easier to spot relationships among items. Visual presentations are generally easy to understand and are persuasive. A GIS can be an effective means to convince management that neighborhoods have changed and that you need to move your retail outlets. A GIS can also be used for simulations to examine alternatives. For example, a GIS oriented to road maps can compute the time it would take to travel by different routes, helping you establish a distribution pattern for delivery trucks.

Example

Consider the problem faced by a manager in a small retail chain that has stores located in 10 Florida cities. It sells a combination of hard goods (such as cleaning supplies, snack items, and drapery rods) and soft goods (mostly clothing). For the most part, profit margins for soft goods are higher than for hard goods. However, total sales of hard goods seem to be better than those of soft goods—except in certain stores. The manager has been unable to find a reason for the difference, but a friend who has lived in Florida longer suggested that there might be some geographical relationship. The basic numbers are presented in Figure 10.15.

Because there are only 10 cities, it might be possible to identify patterns in the data without using a GIS. However, an actual firm might have several hundred or a few thousand stores to evaluate. In this case, it is much more difficult to identify relationships by examining the raw data. It is better to use a GIS to plot the data. Different colors can be used to highlight large increases in sales. By overlaying this data with the population and income data, it is easier to spot patterns. In Figure 10.16 notice that there is a correlation between population and total sales. Also, notice that sales in the northern cities are concentrated more in hard goods than in the southern cities.

FIGURE 10.15

Geographic sales data: We suspect that sales of hard and soft goods are related to population and income. We also want to know whether there are regional patterns to the sales.

City	1990 Pop	2000 Pop	1990 per Capita Income	2000 per Capita Income	1990 Hard Good Sales (000)	1990 Soft Good Sales (000)	2000 Hard Good Sales (000)	2000 Soft Good Sales (000)
Clewiston	6,085	8,549	13,598	15,466	452.0	562.5	367.6	525.4
Fort Myers	45,206	59,491	16,890	20,256	535.2	652.9	928.2	1010.3
Gainesville	84,770	101,724	13,672	19,428	365.2	281.7	550.5	459.4
Jacksonville	635,230	734,961	15,316	19,275	990.2	849.1	1321.7	1109.3
Miami	258,548	300,691	16,874	18,812	721.7	833.4	967.1	1280.6
Ocala	42,045	55,878	12,027	15,130	359.0	321.7	486.2	407.3
Orlando	164,693	217,889	16,958	20,729	425.7	509.2	691.5	803.5
Perry	7,151	8,045	11,055	14,144	300.1	267.2	452.9	291.0
Tallahassee	124,773	155,218	14,578	20,185	595.4	489.7	843.8	611.7
Tampa	280,015	335,458	15,081	19,062	767.4	851.0	953.4	1009.1

FIGURE 10.16
Geographic-based data: It is difficult to display this much data without overwhelming managers. Notice that the sales (radar) graphs use size and shape to highlight total sales, and the changing sales mix. Income is color-coded in a smaller graph. Notice in the sales graphs that the northern counties experienced a greater increase in sales in hard goods compared to the southern counties.

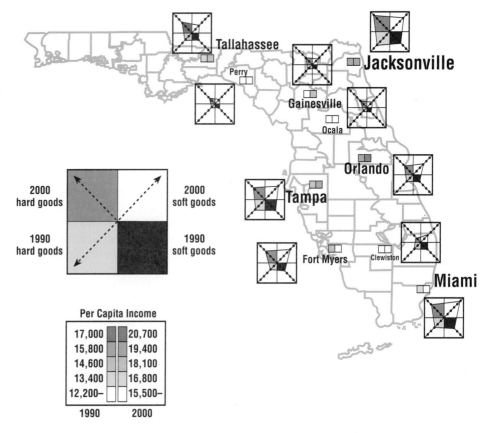

Data: Data Mining

Is it possible to automate the analysis of data? Many decision makers, particularly researchers, are buried in data. Transaction-processing systems, process control, automated research tools, even Web sites all generate thousands, millions, or even billions of pieces of data a day. Sure, you can retrieve the data into a data warehouse, run queries, or put it into a spreadsheet, but it is still difficult for humans to comprehend raw data.

Data mining consists of a variety of tools and techniques to automatically retrieve and search data for information. Originally, the term was somewhat derogatory because it represents an undirected search for relationships. Statistically, results obtained from nonscientific searches can be spurious and not repeatable. On the other hand, the tools can find minute comparisons that are not ordinarily found through traditional statistical methods. As the flood of data increases, more companies are turning to automated and semiautomated tools to help search databases and make it easier to visualize patterns. Additional models and research can then be used to investigate and validate the relationships.

Correlation is a key statistical tool that is leveraged in data mining. A data mining system can compute the cross correlation for all dimensions. High correlations provide a useful indicator of how one dimension (variable) affects another. Multiple regression is an extension of correlation where multiple dimensions (independent variables) are used to predict values for a dependent variable. The regression coefficients have long been used by statisticians to measure the importance of each attribute. Special data mining tools extend these concepts into nonlinear relationships, automatically searching for relationships between variables. For example, marketers could mine the sales data to determine which variables had the strongest impact on sales revenue, including price, quality, advertising, packaging, or collections of product attributes.

Clustering is another data mining technique. It tries to find groups of items that have similar attribute values. For example, a car manufacturer might find that younger buyers are

FIGURE 10.17
Market basket analysis: What items do people buy together? Data mining tools can examine each purchase to identify relationships. You can use this information to increase cross selling.

attracted to one car model, while older buyers tend to purchase a different model. These concepts are relatively easy to understand in two or three dimensions. The tools can search in higher dimensions, looking for groupings across dozens of attributes. The results are more difficult to interpret and act on, but can provide useful information in dealing with complex datasets.

One of the classic data mining tools is market basket analysis (or association rules). **Market basket analysis** was designed to address the question, What items do people tend to purchase together? Figure 10.17 shows the classic example that was identified by a convenience store. Managers found that on weekends, people often purchased both beer and diapers. This raises the immediate issue of how you can use the results. You might stock the items near each other to encourage people to buy both. Or you might place the items at opposite ends of an aisle—forcing people to walk past the high-impulse items such as chips. The tool is generic and is used by Amazon.com to show you books that were bought by other customers. If you are interested in the first book, you might also like the books that other people purchased along with that book. Tivo, the television recording system, uses a similar process to identify programs that you might be interested in watching. To illustrate the hazards of data mining, many people have reported interesting twists with Tivo. For instance, if you watch one movie for children, the system will begin to offer more shows geared toward children.

Several data mining tools have been built in the past few years. They are relatively easy to use, but you might want to review your statistics to help understand the results. One catch with the tools is that some of them can take time to run—even with fast machines, some complex analyses can take hours. For example, market basket analysis is relatively fast with pairs of items, but requires exponentially more computations and time if you attempt to compare more than two items at a time. A bigger problem is that the results might be meaningless or not reproducible. They might simply have arisen because of some random occurrence in the data. The bottom line is that you have to carefully evaluate each piece of information to make sure it is relevant and important.

Expert Systems

Can information technology be more intelligent? Can it analyze data and evaluate rules? Imagine your life as a top-notch manager. Coworkers perceive you as an expert and value your advice and problem-solving skills. You are constantly answering questions and there are always more problems than you can handle. You are using decision support systems and integrated information technology to perform your job better and more efficiently, but it is not enough. Can technology help you with more complex decisions and problem solving? From another perspective, when you encounter new problems with different, complex models, it would be helpful to have an expert assist you with applying and understanding the models. Yet experts or consultants are expensive and not always available. Can you somehow capture the knowledge and methods of experts and use technology to make this knowledge available to workers throughout the company?

Specialized Problems

Expert systems have proven useful for many problems. The goal of an expert system is to enable novices to achieve results similar to those of an expert. The users need to understand the basic problem, learn the terminology, and be able to answer questions. For example, a

REALITY BYTES   Can You Do This?

Have you heard of Stephen Thaler? On paper, he has written over 11,000 songs. He invented the Oral-B CrossAction toothbrush. He discovered substances harder than diamonds. But he did not really do all of these things himself. Instead, he created and patented the "Device for the Autonomous Generation of Useful Information." This device, called the Creativity Machine, is a computer program. In fact, this program created Thaler's second patent: the "Self-Training Neural Network Object."

In the 1980s, Thaler was working as a physicist at McDonnell Douglas Corp, where he used a laser to crystallize diamonds. He used customized neural networks to analyze his experiments. In 1989, he created a neural network and loaded in his favorite Christmas carols. He then created another program that started breaking the network connections in the first program and observed what happened. The system started randomly creating new connections and new carols based on fragments of the original data. He fine-tuned the system and realized that by introducing noise into the neural network, the system would create entirely new ideas. Building in self-criticizing functions enables the machine to select the best ideas and improve them, leading to new inventions.

Source: Adapted from Tina Hesman, "The Machine That Invents," *St. Louis Post-Dispatch,* January 25, 2004.

typical patient would not be able to use a medical expert system because the questions and terms would not make any sense.

Think of an expert system as a consultant in a box. The consultant can solve only certain specific problems. For example, perhaps a retail store manager needs to estimate buying patterns for the next few months. The manager might call a marketing consultant to survey buyers and statistically search for patterns. The consultant will ask questions to determine the basic objectives and identify problems. Similarly, a production manager might be having problems with a certain machine. The manager might call a support line or a repair technician. The advice in this situation will be quite different from the marketing example, because the topics (or domains) of the two problems are different. It would be difficult to create one computer program that could help you with both types of problems. On the other hand, there are similarities in the approach to the two problems. Computerized expert systems are designed to solve narrow, specialized problems. Each problem can be relatively complex, but it must be reasonably well defined. Many business problems fall into this category, and expert systems can be built for each problem.

Diagnostic Problems

Several problems in the world can be classified as diagnostic situations. These problems arise when the decision maker is presented with a set of symptoms and is asked to find the cause of the problem, as well as solutions. Consider a firm that uses a complex machine. If the machine breaks down, production stops until it is fixed. In addition, maintenance tasks have to be performed every day to keep the machine running. The company hires an engineer to perform these tasks. The engineer also knows which adjustments to make if various symptoms appear. This system has been working well, and the company wishes to expand to other locations with a franchise system. The problem is that there is only one engineer, and it would be too expensive to have a highly trained engineer at each location.

One possible solution would be to set up a phone link between the franchises and the engineer. One person at each franchise would be trained in the basics of the machine. If problems arise, the person could call the engineer. The engineer would ask specific questions, such as "What do the gauges show?" The answers will lead the engineer to ask other questions. Eventually, the engineer makes recommendations based on the answers.

Of course, if there are many franchises, the engineer will be too busy to solve all of the problems. Also, if the businesses are located in different countries, the time differences may not allow everyone enough access to the engineer. A better solution is to create a computerized expert system. All the expert's questions, recommendations, and rules can be entered into a computer system that is distributed to each franchise. If there is a problem, the on-site person turns to the expert system. The system asks the same questions that the engineer would and arrives at the same recommendations.

FIGURE 10.18
Expert system example from
ExSys: This sample expert
system acts as a knowledgeable
salesperson and asks questions
about how you intend to use a
digital video camera. Based on
your responses, it makes a
recommendation from several
cameras.

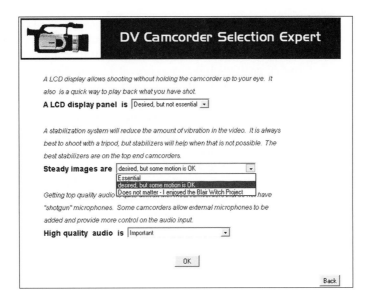

As shown in Figure 10.18, expert systems also have the ability to explain their recommendations. In more complex examples, while running the ES, the user can ask it to explain why it asked a particular question or why it arrived at some conclusion. The ES traces through the answers it was given and explains its reasoning. This ability helps the user gain confidence in the decisions, allows mistakes to be corrected, and helps the users remember the answer for future reference.

The business world offers many examples of diagnostic situations, such as identifying causes of defects, finding the source of delays, and keeping complex equipment running. The common characteristic is that you are faced with a set of symptoms, and you need to find the cause.

Speedy Decisions

Other situations can benefit from the use of expert systems. Even if a problem is not exceedingly complex, you could use an expert system to provide faster responses or to provide more consistent recommendations. Several advantages can be gained from making decisions faster than your competitors do. If you can identify a trend in stock prices before anyone else, you can make a higher profit. If you can answer customer questions faster, they will be more likely to shop with you in the future. If you can provide a loan to a customer sooner than anyone else, you will do more business.

Transaction-processing systems keep much of the basic data that you need to make decisions. Decision support systems help you analyze that raw data. Both of these tools enable you to make decisions faster than trying to make the decision without any computers. However, it still takes time for a human to analyze all of the information.

Consider the case of a bank loan. In order to get a loan, you go to the bank and fill out a loan application form. You tell the loan officer why you want the loan and provide basic data on income and expenses. Depending on the amount of money involved, the banker will probably check your credit history, get appraisals on any collateral, and perhaps get approval by a review officer or loan committee. All of these actions take time.

Now, consider the steps involved with a computerized process. First, you need to tell the bank that you want a loan. Instead of driving to the bank, you could use the telephone. With a push-button phone, you enter information directly into the bank's computer. The computer would give you a choice of loan types (car, boat, personal, etc.), and you push a button to select one. You enter the amount of money you want to borrow. The next step is to check your credit history. Your income, expenses, and credit record are available to the bank from national credit reporting agencies. The bank might also have its own database. The bank's computer could be connected to credit agency computers to collect additional data on your credit history.

To make the final decision, the bank needs a set of rules. These rules take into account the size of the loan, the value of the collateral, as well as your income, expenses, credit history, and existing loans. When the bank has determined the proper rules, the computer performs the analyses. If the bankers trust the rules, the computer could make the final decision. For example, there would be no need for a loan officer to be involved in simple decisions, such as making small car loans to customers with large savings accounts. With an expert system, a bank can cut the loan-approval period down to a few minutes on the phone.

Many other decisions need to be made rapidly. The first step in all of these cases is to make sure that the transaction-processing system provides the necessary raw data. The second step is to create a set of rules for making the decision. The difficulty lies in finding these rules. For some problems, there are well-defined rules that can be trusted. For other problems, the rules may not exist. In this case, the company will probably still need a human to make the final decision.

Consistency

The example of the bank loan demonstrates another advantage of expert systems. Business decisions are subject to a wide variety of nondiscrimination laws. An expert system can be used to provide consistent decisions. The rules followed by the ES can be set up to avoid illegal discrimination. Businesses also have credit ratings, which are often determined by Credit Clearing House (CCH). CCH uses an expert system to make the "easy" decisions, which speeds up the process by allowing humans to focus on the more complicated cases. It also leads to consistent application of the rules.

Consider the loan example. If each loan officer makes individual decisions, it is hard to determine whether they are consistent with corporate policy. Each individual decision would have to be checked to make sure it was nondiscriminatory. On the other hand, a committee could spend several weeks creating a set of lending rules that can be verified to be sure they are legal and ethical. As long as the bank employees follow the recommendations of the ES, the outcome should not be discriminatory. Because there should be few cases where the loan officer overrules the ES, managers will have more time to examine each of these circumstances.

Many business decisions need to be performed consistently to avoid bias and to treat people equally. Loans, pricing, raises, and promotions are some examples. However, there can be problems with using a computer system to enforce standards. The main difficulty lies in creating a set of rules that accurately describe the decisions and standards. For example, it might be useful to have a set of rules regarding raises and promotions, but think about what happens if an employee's job does not fit the basic rules. Organizations continually change, which means the rules have to be monitored and changed regularly.

Training

Training employees is closely associated with problems of consistency. All organizations must train employees. If the tasks are complex and the decisions highly unstructured, it can take years for employees to learn the rules and gain the experience needed to deal with problems. Two features of expert systems help employees learn. First, employees learn what questions need to be asked. In particular, after using the system for a while, certain groups of questions will occur together. Second, most expert systems have provisions for explaining their answers (and the motivation for each question). At any point, an employee can ask the expert system why it asked a certain question or why it reached a conclusion.

Building Expert Systems

How do you create an expert system? At first glance, you would suspect that expert systems are hard to create. However, except for one step, which is hard, tools exist to make the job easier. The area that causes the most problems when you are creating expert systems is finding a cooperative expert who fully understands and can explain the problem. Some problems are so complex that it is difficult to explain the reasoning process. Sometimes the expert may rely on vague descriptions and minor nuances that cannot be written down. Even though expert systems can deal with these types of problems, it might take too long to determine the entire process. Also, if you transfer the expert's knowledge to a computer, the expert might worry about losing his or her job.

Most expert systems are built as a knowledge base that is processed or analyzed by an inference engine. A **knowledge base** consists of basic data and a set of rules. In most situations, an *inference engine* applies new observations to the knowledge base and analyzes the rules to reach a conclusion.

The basic steps to create an expert system are (1) analyze the situation and identify needed data and possible outcomes, (2) determine relationships between data and rules that are followed in making the decision, (3) enter the data and rules into an expert system shell, and (4) design questions and responses. A **knowledge engineer** is often hired to organize the data, help devise the rules, and enter the criteria into the expert system shell, or supervise programmers as they create an expert system.

Knowledge Base

A knowledge base is more than a simple database. It consists of data but also contains rules, logic, and links among data elements. In most cases, it contains less structured and more descriptive data. For example, an ES for medicine might have a list of symptoms that contains items like "high temperature" and "intense muscle pain." This knowledge base is the reason why the problem must be narrow in scope. Even narrow, well-defined problems can require large amounts of information and thousands of rules or relationships. The real challenge in building expert systems is to devise the knowledge base with its associated rules.

There are three types of expert systems in use today. They are defined by how the knowledge base is organized: by rules, frames, or cases.

Rules

The heart of a rule-based ES is a set of logical rules. These **rules** are often complicated. Consider some of the rules that might be needed for an ES to evaluate bank loans, as shown in Figure 10.19. This example has been simplified to keep it short. There will usually be hundreds of rules or conditions to cover a wide variety of situations. Rules are often presented as IF . . . THEN . . . ELSE . . . statements. They can include Boolean conjunctions such as AND, OR, NOT. Figure 10.20 presents a portion of a **decision tree** that visually displays the rules.

The difficulty with any ES lies in determining these rules. Some of them will be easy. Others will be complex. Most of them will come from the expert. Unfortunately, most people do not usually express their thoughts in the form of these rules. Although we might

FIGURE 10.19

Sample rules for the bank loan: A portion of the business rules that are used to determine whether a person should get a loan.

First, compute the monthly income before taxes.
Next, compute the monthly payment of the loan.
If the payment is greater than 5% of income:
    Compute total of other loan payments.
    Compute payments as percent of monthly income.
    If this percent is less than 25%:
        If the new loan is less than 10%, make loan.
        Else:
            If total monthly expenses are less than 40% of income, make the loan.
            Else:
                If less than 50% and has been a customer for more than 5 years or if less than 60% and has been a customer for 10 years and has lived at the same address for 5 years, make the loan.

FIGURE 10.20

Decision tree for sample bank loan expert system: Parts of a knowledge base are often expressed as a decision tree. Each answer to a question leads to additional questions and eventually to a decision. Notice that questions sometimes require numeric answers but can also rely on subjective comments.

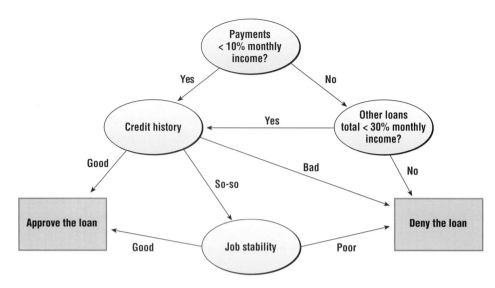

FIGURE 10.21

Bank loan sample screen: An expert system carries on a dialogue with the user. The ES asks questions and uses the answers to ask additional questions. The user can ask the ES to explain a decision or a question. Hence the ES can be used for training purposes.

> **Welcome to the Loan Evaluation System**
>
> What is the purpose of the loan? car
> How much money will be loaned? 10,000
> For how many years? 5
>
> The current interest rate is 10%.
> The payment will be $212.47 per month.
>
> What is the annual income? 24,000
>
> What is the total monthly payments of other loans?
> Why?
>
> Because the payment is more than 10% of the monthly income.
> What is the total monthly payments of other loans?
> 50.00
>
> The loan should be approved, because there is only a 2% chance of default.

follow rules of this sort, they can be difficult to express. It is even more difficult to re-member all the rules at one time. For instance, say you have lived in the same place for five years and a new person moves into the neighborhood. She asks you to describe the best ways to get to school, the mall, and the grocery store. Then she asks you for the best shortcuts if one of the roads is closed. This problem is relatively simple, but can you sit down right now and provide a complete list of all the rules?

Creating an ES

More commonly today, an ES is built from an expert system shell. This program provides a way to collect data, enter rules, talk to users, present results, and evaluate the rules. To cre-ate an ES, you must know what data you need and all of the rules. Once you express this knowledge base in the format used by the shell's inference engine, the shell takes care of the other problems. Many ES shells are available on a wide variety of computers; Jess and Clips are two common systems that are available free or at relatively low cost.

To understand how to create an ES, consider the bank loan example. A typical dialogue with the user (the loan clerk) appears in Figure 10.21. Notice that the ES begins by asking some basic information-gathering questions. The responses of the user are underlined.

REALITY BYTES   Time Pressure

For college basketball, the March playoffs represent a major goal. For Short's Travel Agency in Waterloo, Iowa, the playoffs present the ultimate time pressure and focused decision making. With only four days' notice for the women's teams and as little as two for the men's, the travel agency has to get 129 teams from their university to the playoff location. The NCAA picks up the costs of the travel—about $10 million—and consequently wants to keep costs down. It requires teams traveling less than 300 miles to take a bus. Others are supposed to fly on commercial airlines. Each team can bring 75 people (team, coaches, mascot, and so on). So, the travel agency has to find flights on short notice and issue tickets to each person. Some universities play games with the system, trying to get chartered flights instead of commercial. Throw in the fact that many destinations are in out-of-the-way locations (Missoula, Montana), add a few spring snowstorms, and you begin to understand the pressures. The company relies largely on the airline reservation systems to handle the technology needs. However, it did set up a Web site to enable teams to enter their rosters themselves.

Source: Adapted from Ron Lieber, "At NCAA Tourney, a Company in Iowa Is Called for Traveling," *The Wall Street Journal,* March 18, 2004.

Once the basic data is collected, the ES performs some computations and follows the built-in rules. Notice that the ES follows the rule that asks for the other loan payments. However, the loan clerk does not know about this rule, so he or she asks for clarification. This ability to ask questions is a powerful feature of expert systems.

Once you have collected all of the rules involved in the problem, you enter them into the ES shell. The shell lets you type in the questions you want to ask the user. You define the calculations and tell the shell how to look up any other information you need (e.g., the interest rates for auto loans). You then enter the conditions that tell the shell what questions to ask next. If there are many rules with complex interactions, it is more difficult to enter the rules into the shell. One advantage of ES shells is that you generally have to enter only the basic rules and data. As the user enters the data, the shell performs the calculations and follows the rules. The shell also automatically answers the user questions. You do not have to be a computer programmer to create an ES with a shell. With training, many users can create their own expert systems using a shell. However, there are many dangers inherent in ES development, so it helps to have someone evaluate and test the resulting system.

Limitations of Expert Systems

Expert systems are useful tools that can be applied to several specialized problems. However, several important drawbacks arise in their design and use. First, they can be created only for specific, narrowly defined problems. Some complex problems contain too many rules with too many interactions. It quickly becomes impossible to express all of the interrelationships. For example, it is currently impossible to create a medical diagnostic system that covers all possible diseases. However, smaller systems are in use that help determine drug dosages and other treatments such as radiation levels for cancer patients.

Another problem that users and designers have encountered is that it can be difficult to modify the knowledge base in an expert system. As the environment or problem changes, the expert system needs to be updated. The changes are relatively easy to make if they affect only a few rules. However, many expert systems use hundreds of interrelated rules. It is not always clear which rules need to be altered, and changes to one rule can affect many of the others. In essence, as the situation changes, the company is forced to completely redesign the expert system. In fast-changing industries, it would cost too much to continually redesign an expert system. In the lending example, a policy change based on monthly income would be relatively easy to implement. On the other hand, some changes in policy would force a complete redesign of the expert system. For instance, a bank might decide to grant loans to almost everyone but charge riskier people higher interest rates.

Probably the greatest difficulty in creating an expert system is determining the logic rules or frames that will lead to the proper conclusions. It requires finding an expert who understands the process and can express the rules in a form that can be used by the expert system.

Management Issues of Expert Systems

Creating and building an expert system involve many of the same issues encountered in building any other information system. For instance, the problem must be well defined, the designers must communicate with the users, and management and financial controls must be in place to evaluate and control the project.

However, expert systems raise additional management issues. Two issues are particularly important: (1) if an expert transfers knowledge to an expert system, is there still a need for the expert; and (2) what happens when the expert system encounters an exception that it was not designed to solve?

The answer to the first question depends on the individual situation. In cases where the problem is relatively stable over time, it is possible to transfer expert knowledge to software—enabling the firm to reduce the number of experts needed. If this action results in layoffs, the experts will need additional incentives to cooperate with the development of the system. In other cases, the firm will continue to need the services of the experts, to make changes to the ES and to solve new problems. Before starting an ES project, managers need to determine which situation applies and negotiate appropriately with the experts.

The second problem can be more difficult to identify. Consider what happens when workers rely on an expert system to make decisions, and management then cuts costs by hiring less-skilled workers. The new workers do not understand the system or the procedures—they simply follow decisions made by the rules in the ES. If an exception arises, the ES may not know how to respond or it may respond inappropriately. A customer then would be left to deal with an underskilled worker who does not understand the process and cannot resolve the problem.

Specialized Tools

Can machines be made even smarter? What technologies can be used to help managers? Research in artificial intelligence (AI) examined how humans are different from computers. This research led to tools that can be used for certain types of problems. Some of the ideas come from the early days of computers, but it has taken until now for machines to be developed that are fast enough to handle the sophisticated tasks. Ideas in AI have come from many disciplines, from biology to psychology to computer science and engineering.

Humans are noticeably better than computers in six broad areas: pattern recognition, performing multiple tasks at one time, movement, speech recognition, vision, and language comprehension. Some of these concepts are related, but they all represent features that would make machines much more useful. Even with current technological improvements, most observers agree that it will be several years before these features are available.

Pattern Recognition and Neural Networks

One of the early issues in AI research was the question of how human brains worked. Some people suggested that to make intelligent computers, the computers would have to work the same way as the human brain does. An important conclusion from this research is that humans are good at pattern recognition.

Humans use pattern recognition thousands of times a day. It enables people to recognize coworkers, to spot trends in data, to relate today's problems to last year's changes. Many problems in business could benefit from machines that can reliably recognize patterns. For example, what characteristics do "good" borrowers have in common? How will changes in the economy affect next year's sales? How are sales affected by management styles of the sales managers?

Pattern recognition is used by people to solve problems. It is one of the reasons teachers use cases to teach students to solve business problems. If you notice that a problem is similar to a case you have seen before, you can use your prior knowledge to solve the problem. Imagine how useful it would be if an expert system could recognize patterns automatically.

REALITY BYTES   The World Consists of More than Text

By now, everyone is used to looking for things using search engines. But search engines only index text, and the world contains way more interesting data. Computer systems today contain catalogs of objects for machine parts, buildings, and so on. Karthik Ramani, a professor at Purdue University, has developed a way to search those databases. The user simply draws an object, and the search system returns items that have a similar appearance. Caterpillar, like most companies, stores its designs in CAD systems. But the engine center alone has tens of thousands of different parts. Designers would have to manually search the database to find a part. Instead, many of them simply design a new part, adding to the mess. Boeing engineers invented a similar system to help improve the reuse of parts. A research group at Princeton has a 3-D model search engine you can test on the Web (shape.cs.princeton.edu/search.html).

Source: Adapted from "Researchers Develop 3-D Search Engine," *CNN Online,* April 16, 2004.

One current technique that is used to spot patterns is the use of neural networks. Initial study indicated that the brain is a collection of cells called *neurons* that have many connections to each other. Each of these cells is relatively simple, but there are approximately 100 million of them. In some respects, a neuron resembles a simple computer. It can be at rest (off), or it can fire a message (on). A neuron responds to other cells (input) to send messages to other neurons (output). A collection of these cells is called a **neural network.** Human neural cells are actually more complicated, but researchers have focused on this simplified form.

A common current example is a bank that uses a neural network to spot credit card fraud. In some cases, Mellon Bank's neural network identified fraudulent patterns even before the human investigators spotted them. It is faster and more accurate than an earlier expert system. The original expert system looked at a limited number of variables and indicated 1,000 suspects a day, which was far more than actually existed and too many for the investigators to keep up with. The new neural network system examines more variables, lists fewer false suspects, and adjusts its methods on its own.

A finance manager might use a form of pattern recognition to search for patterns in the financial markets to forecast future movements. Of course, with thousands of other people searching for patterns, the patterns would not last very long. Similarly, a banker might use pattern recognition to classify loan prospects.

Neural networks can be built with software. Also, computer chips are available today that function as neural networks. Neural networks can be measured in two ways by (1) the number of neurons and (2) the number of interconnections between the individual cells. It is fairly easy to increase the number of cells, but the number of possible interconnections increases very rapidly. For instance, if there are four cells, there are six possible connections. With 10 cells, there are 45 connections. With 1,000 cells, there are half a million connections. In general, if there are N cells, there are $N(N - 1)/2$ possible connections. For many purposes, not every connection is needed, but with millions of cells, a neural network would incorporate a large number of connections. Most existing networks use only a few thousand cells.

Figure 10.22 presents a version of how a neural network converts an array of input sensors into a hidden layer and then stores patterns on an output layer. One useful feature of the neural network approach is that it is fairly good at identifying patterns even if some of the inputs are missing.

What can neural networks do that cannot be done with traditional computers? The basic answer is "nothing." However, they provide a new way of thinking about problems. More important, with hardware specifically designed to process neural networks, some difficult problems can be solved faster than with traditional computers. The primary objective of neural networks is the ability to store and recognize patterns. A well-designed network is capable of identifying patterns (such as faces or sounds) even if some of the data is missing or altered. The army has designed a neural network system to process visual data that can drive a vehicle at speeds up to 55 miles per hour.

REALITY BYTES   Automated Customer Service

Everyone has dealt with automated customer service systems. In most cases, the systems are simplistic—offering a few options at the press of a phone button. Some are more sophisticated and can understand a limited number of spoken requests. Peter Plantec is attempting to change this world through the creation of virtual humans. In particular, he wants to give these online systems personalities to make them more interactive and more interesting. He has created software that he sells with his book that you can use to create your own virtual agents, although the technology has a long way to go and is ultimately limited to your programming ability.

In the short run, the goal is to provide customer service that is more knowledgeable and more available than a typical customer service rep. Since the systems would be rule-based, you could simply create new rules and the virtual reps would all follow the defined procedures. Working 24/7 with no paycheck, virtual humans could offer cost advantages in several situations. Of course, they would not be able to handle unexpected events, but even if they could handle the common inquiries, the cost savings could be worthwhile.

Source: Adapted from Michael Krey, "Is That Customer Service Rep Real or Virtual?" *Investor's Business Daily,* January 13, 2004; and Liz Stevens, "Build a Virtual Buddy," *The Star Telegram,* February 7, 2004.

FIGURE 10.22

Neural net for pattern matching: Input cells convert data to binary form. The required hidden layer recodes the inputs into a new internal representation. The connections represent outputs from the lower layers. When total input levels exceed some value, the receiving cell fires. Any cell can be connected to many other cells. Input weights are determined by training. The output cells are triggered when total input levels from the connections exceed some threshold. Note that a pattern can be recognized even if some input cells are wrong or not firing.

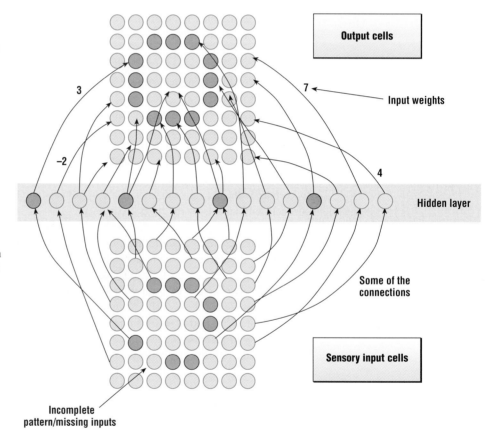

Another advantage that researchers hope to achieve with neural networks is the ability to simplify training of the computer. The discussion of expert systems noted that changes in the business often mean that knowledge engineers have to redesign the entire expert system. A neural network has a limited ability to "learn" by examining past data. Feeding it proper examples establishes the interconnection weights that enable the network to identify patterns. In theory, neural networks have the ability to learn on their own. In practice, the learning stage is the most difficult component of building a neural network. Most times the designer has to understand the problem and provide hints to the network, along with good sample data. In many ways, training a neural network uses basic properties of statistics related to data sampling and regression.

REALITY BYTES   Backseat Driver

In March 2004, the Department of Defense held its first robotic vehicle contest (The Grand Challenge)—offering a $1 million prize. The challenge: build a self-contained robotic vehicle that can drive itself on a course from Barstow, California, through the desert to near Las Vegas. Several teams vied for the prize. The favored was the Carnegie Mellon Red Team, led by William "Red" L. Whittaker, which spent about $3 million building an automated Hummer. The vehicles also had to navigate a simpler course before the race to prove their stability and control. To win the contest, a vehicle had to finish within a time limit—requiring approximately a 15 mph average speed. No one won the 189-mile contest. None of the vehicles finished. The Red Team Hummer went the farthest distance (7.4 miles, besting SciAu-

tonicsII at 6.7 miles). The Red Team Web site reports their result: "At mile 7.4, on switchbacks in a mountainous section, vehicle went off course, got caught on a berm and rubber on the front wheels caught fire, which was quickly extinguished. Vehicle was command-disabled." Despite the final results, the fact that vehicles were able to traverse several miles of treacherous desert roads is amazing. Another Grand Challenge is scheduled by DARPA for 2005. Of course, if you build a vehicle that can win the contest, you will be able to make substantially more than a million dollars.

Source: Adapted from John Markoff, "No Riders: Desert Crossing Is for the Robots Only," *The New York Times,* March 8, 2004; and redteamracing.org.

Machine Vision

Machine vision has many uses in manufacturing environments. Machines are used in optical character recognition, welding and assembly, and quality control. Mechanical sensors have several advantages over humans. They do not suffer from fatigue, they can examine a broader spectrum of light (including ultraviolet and infrared), and they can quickly focus at many different levels (including microscopic).

On the other hand, traditional computer systems are literal in their vision. It is hard for computers to compare objects of different sizes or to match mirror images. It is hard for machines to determine whether differences between objects are minor and should be ignored or if they are major distinguishing features.

Say you are shown a picture of your instructor, and someone adds or subtracts features to it, such as bigger eyebrows, longer hair, or glasses. In most cases, you would still recognize the face. Computers would have difficulty with that problem because they see pictures as a collection of dots (or lines). How does the computer know which changes are important and which are minor?

Machine vision systems are improving rapidly but still have a way to go to become commonplace. For example, companies are working on applications in facial recognition and facial expressions, body tracking (so you can use your hand as a computer pointer), visual tracking of handwriting for use in computer tablets, product inspections for defects, and shape identification.

Language Comprehension and Translation

Related to voice recognition is the issue of language comprehension, or the ability of the computer to actually understand what we are saying. Technically the two topics are separate, since it might be possible to have a machine understand what we type onto a keyboard. Language comprehension exists when the machine actually understands what we mean. One test of comprehension would be the ability of the computer to carry on a conversation. In fact, Alan Turing, a British pioneer in the computer field, suggested the Turing test for computer intelligence. In this test, a human judge communicates with a machine and another person in a separate room. If the judge cannot determine which user is the machine and which is a person, the machine should be considered to be intelligent. Some people have tested this concept (using specific topics). Other people have noted that perhaps you do not have to be intelligent to carry on a conversation.

Language comprehension would be useful because it would make it easier for humans to use computers. Instead of needing to learn a language such as SQL to access data, imagine being able to get answers to questions asked in English (or some other natural language). Of course, any natural language has its limitations. The greatest danger with

REALITY BYTES   But Can It Order Dinner?

The wars in Iraq and Afghanistan have raised several problems. Fighting small groups makes intelligence gathering and communication with citizens more critical. Yet few soldiers know Arabic, and there are not many translators available. To help, the army is turning to technology. Soldiers can carry a ruggedized handheld translator. A phrase spoken in English is translated, and the machine "speaks" the corresponding foreign-language phrase. The machine has a database of several thousand phrases geared to military requirements. Documents can be scanned and immediately translated. Soldiers can even take a photo of a street sign and have it translated. A more sophisticated device, although it is not portable, can translate a two-way real-time conversation. Of course, the technology is not as good as a human translator—but it is easier and cheaper to carry into the field. Most of the technology is not yet available publicly, but it represents a huge leap in capabilities over what was available a couple of years ago.

Source: Adapted from Patrick Chisholm, "Technology That Speaks in Tongues," *Military Information Technology,* March 15, 2004.

FIGURE 10.23

There are inherent problems with voice recognition. Punctuation and implicit meaning are two difficult areas. Even communication between people has frequent misinterpretations.

Language Comprehension Example

See what happens when you give a computer the first set of instructions, but it does not hear the commas correctly and thinks you said the second line:

1. Copy the red, file the blue, delete the yellow mark.

2. Copy the red file, the blue delete, the yellow mark.

Consider the following sentence, which can be interpreted by humans but would not make much sense to a computer that tries to interpret it literally.

I saw the Grand Canyon flying to New York.

---

language comprehension is that the machine will interpret your question incorrectly and give you the "right" answer to the "wrong" question. Figure 10.23 provides a simple illustration of the complexities of language comprehension. The first example involves the use of punctuation. A misinterpretation of the command can result in deleting the wrong file. Similarly, interpretation of a natural language involves understanding some basic concepts, such as the fact that the Grand Canyon cannot fly.

Ultimately, translating languages requires an understanding of the underlying meaning of a sentence and paragraph. Early translation systems can convert a word from one language into another. For example, check out babel.altavista.com, or any of the other online translators. Some high-end translation systems have been developed that do a better job by at least recognizing common phrases and idioms. Yet even these systems need to be supplemented by human translators.

Robotics and Motion

Modern manufacturing relies heavily on robots, and the capabilities of robots continually increase. Most existing robots are specialized machines that perform a limited number of tasks, such as welding or painting. In many firms, there is little need for a general-purpose robot that can "do everything." However, one area that remains troublesome is the ability of machines to move. Making a machine that can navigate through an unknown or crowded space is especially difficult. Some work is being done in this area. Liability is a major problem when robots attempt to move among people.

In 2000, Honda built a humanoid robot (Asimo) in Japan. The Asimo robot has two legs and arms. Its most impressive feature is the ability to walk like a human, including up and down stairs. It can also shake hands and hand objects to people. The multimillion-dollar project is the latest step of a 16-year evolution.

REALITY BYTES   A Robot Scientist

Biologists Ross King at the University of Wales and Stephen Oliver at the University of Manchester created a robot scientist. A combination of robotic hardware and sophisticated AI software, the system proved capable of formulating hypotheses, developing and running experiments, and arriving at conclusions. In the scientific process, it was able to achieve results equivalent to those achieved by humans.

The system is charged with trying to determine the role of different genes in baker's yeast. The special yeast has certain genes knocked out. The robot observes how the yeast grows or does not grow. It formulates hypotheses based on its database of biochemistry. It then plans an experiment to eliminate as many of the hypotheses as quickly as possible. The liquid-handling robot then sets up and conducts the experiment and monitors its results. In testing on a known problem, the system achieved the same result as a group of graduate students and staff workers. But as King and Oliver report, it "was both significantly cheaper and faster than just choosing random experiments or the cheapest experiments." The pair is testing additional experiments to see if the system can generate new knowledge.

James Collins, a biomechanical engineer at Boston University, notes that the system could provide several benefits by handling the tedious elements of scientific research. Even if the system is successful, Collins is not concerned about his job, because he notes that "there is still a significant role for imagination and creativity that is overlaid, coupled with the scientific knowledge in front of you for coming up with a non-obvious hypothesis."

Source: Adapted from John Roach, "'Robot Scientist' Said to Equal Humans at Some Tasks," *National Geographic News,* January 14, 2004.

In March 2004, DARPA held the first Grand Challenge contest for automated vehicles in the Mojave Desert. The challenge was to create an automated vehicle that could drive itself across 189 miles of desert hitting about 1,000 GPS waypoints in about 10 hours. The Carnegie Mellon $3 million Red Team vehicle (a modified Hummer) made it 7.4 miles, which is actually an amazing accomplishment. Congress has mandated that 30 percent of Army vehicles be automated by 2015, and DARPA is attempting to stimulate innovation with a $1 million prize.

As computer processors decline in size and price, it becomes easier to build intelligent mobile systems, making it possible to build robots and automated vehicles. Major automobile manufacturers are working on slightly less automated systems to provide assistance to drivers. For example, crash-warning sensors can automatically apply brakes for an inattentive driver. Slide-control systems to prevent spinouts on sharp turns have been installed in luxury vehicles for several years.

Machine Intelligence

What would it take to convince you that a machine is intelligent? The Turing test has been proposed as one method. Many other tests have been proposed in the past. At one time, people suggested that a machine that could win at chess would be intelligent. Today's chess-playing computers have beaten even the top human players. Another test proposed was the ability to solve mathematical problems, in particular, the ability to write mathematical proofs. An early AI program created in the 1950s could do that. Today, for a few hundred dollars, you can buy programs that manipulate mathematical symbols to solve equations.

Some people have suggested that intelligence involves creativity. Creativity is probably as hard to measure as intelligence. Even so, there are examples of computer creativity. A few years ago, a programmer developed a system that created music. The interesting feature of the program was that it allowed people to call on the phone and vote on the music. The computer used this feedback to change its next composition. Not only was the computer creative, but it was learning and adapting, albeit in a limited context.

Although there are limited business applications to much of this current research, there are two main reasons for staying abreast of the capabilities. First, anything that makes the computer easier to use will make it more useful, and these techniques continue to improve. Second, you need to understand the current limitations to avoid costly mistakes.

DSS, ES, and AI

What are the differences between DSS, ES, and AI systems? The differences among decision support systems, expert systems, and artificial intelligence can be confusing at first. Take a simple problem and see how a computer system based on each method might operate. A common financial problem is to determine how much money to lend to customers. Any firm that grants terms to customers—not just financial institutions—must make this decision. Figure 10.24 discusses the differences among a DSS, ES, and AI approach to the inventory problem.

In a relatively simple system, the computer would retrieve data about the customer and the prior loans to that customer. Historically, loan officers used basic data and personal factors to make the lending decision. In some instances, these rules of thumb led to problems—with bad decisions and sometimes discrimination. The DSS could also be used to monitor existing loans and payments. As part of a transaction-processing system, it can notify managers when customers continually make late payments and help identify problem loans.

To improve consistency and reduce the decision time, many firms have moved to expert systems to help evaluate loans. Statistical analysis of prior loans is used to establish a set of rules that are coded into the ES. In some cases, the ES can then be operated with push-button phones or over the Internet. In straightforward cases, the ES can make the final decision and approve the loan. In more difficult situations, the preliminary results and data can be forwarded to a human loan officer to factor in personal judgment and factors not considered by the ES.

Of course, the value of the ES depends heavily on the accuracy of the underlying rules (and the supplied data). These rules might change over time or as economic conditions change. A neural network can be used to examine the prior loans automatically to identify the factors that predict successful and unsuccessful loans. Once these factors are identified, they can be coded into the ES to automate the decision process. In this situation, the AI/neural network takes the place of (or supplements) the decisions of the human expert.

FIGURE 10.24

Comparison of techniques for a loan: A DSS can display background data for a loan officer and can also monitor customer payments. An ES could help managers decide if they should make the loan by evaluating more complex rules. An AI such as a neural network can analyze past loans and determine the rules that should be used to grant or deny future loans.

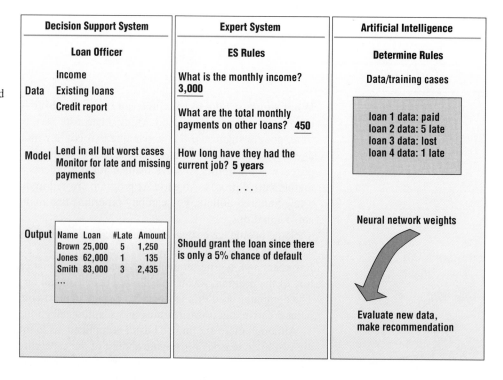

Technology Toolbox: Forecasting a Trend

Problem: You need a basic forecast of sales data.

Tools: Many statistical tools and packages exist to build models and estimate trends. The simplest technique is a linear regression. Excel has tools to calculate and display the results.

Open the Rolling Thunder database and create a query that computes the total sales by year and month. The Format function will convert the date into just the year and month: Format(OrderDate, "yyyy-mm"). Save this query within Access, and close the database. To import the data into Excel, open a new worksheet and choose the Data/Import/New Database Query option. This approach will build a dynamic link to the query.

Create a line chart of the data and add a trend line to the chart. Right-click the plotted line and select the option to add a trend line. You should stick with the linear trend, but you might want to test the other choices. You should also select the options to display the equation and the r-squared value on the chart.

To see the actual forecast values, select the entire column of data for SumOfSalePrice, but do not include the title row. Scroll down to the last row in the series and find the small square handle on the lower-right-side corner. Drag this handle to extend the series for six months. Add the appropriate months in the month column. Edit the chart and edit the series selections to include the new rows. Notice that the new points fall exactly on the trend line.

Excel includes more powerful statistical tools, including one that performs multiple regression when you want to examine the effect of

Sum of SalePr		1994	1995	1996	1997	1998	1999	2000	2001	2002	2003	2004	2005	2006	Grand Total
SaleState	ModelType														
AK		$24,715	$5,200	$5,190	$17,880	$13,320	$11,240	$6,530	$5,410	$10,300	$22,100	$13,920	$29,760	$19,780	$185,345
AL		$10,020	$28,430	$57,940	$63,430	$69,620	$98,370	$56,140	$56,820	$103,520	$119,070	$148,090	$128,980	$152,440	$1,092,870
AR		$18,760	$16,470	$24,640	$29,960	$33,470	$55,390	$34,760	$32,060	$52,590	$67,750	$97,110	$115,100	$98,400	$676,460
AZ		$48,455	$62,600	$93,960	$104,050	$128,790	$140,840	$37,090	$77,000	$144,090	$171,250	$256,970	$244,320	$251,510	$1,760,925
CA	Hybrid	$3,320	$29,150	$132,130		$28,720		$30,100	$27,220						$250,640
	Mountain	$4,055	$117,670	$312,750	$146,750	$262,280	$587,420	$305,390	$192,480	$286,160	$400,460	$152,290	$211,960	$212,600	$3,192,265
	Mountain full				$326,300	$561,040	$575,550	$320,570	$340,120	$430,990	$652,730	$659,508	$759,650	$719,940	$5,346,398
	Race	$8,620	$65,240	$255,110	$348,260	$128,880	$396,990	$151,510	$138,250	$289,630	$254,590	$437,070	$473,690	$456,110	$3,403,950
	Road	$19,040	$212,990	$72,020	$183,770	$300,950	$388,260	$119,370	$162,760	$302,760	$527,250	$529,340	$447,360	$476,450	$3,742,320
	Tour	$5,775	$153,620	$42,070		$36,980	$133,300			$47,450	$95,770	$52,210	$78,150	$95,500	$740,825
	Track		$32,200												$32,200
CA Total		$40,810	$610,870	$814,080	$1,005,080	$1,318,850	$2,081,520	$926,940	$860,830	$1,356,990	$1,930,800	$1,830,418	$1,970,810	$1,960,600	$16,708,598
CO		$33,682	$49,710	$53,220	$46,440	$62,750	$124,480	$54,280	$79,770	$83,600	$161,350	$254,520	$226,330	$240,170	$1,470,302
CT		$36,980	$46,830	$56,660	$95,610	$131,760	$177,840	$102,330	$93,830	$124,530	$221,950	$142,950	$161,620	$141,020	$1,533,910
DC					$16,090	$16,310	$36,290	$20,900	$5,180	$37,390	$31,470			$46,190	$292,915
DE					$8,280	$6,690	$7,260	$3,020	$7,470	$7,200	$17,550			$30,320	$168,370
FL					$273,150	$329,220	$462,580	$270,470	$279,740	$357,780	$603,300			$96,780	$5,064,050
GA		$49,287	$38,560	$53,770	$52,860	$88,070	$135,670	$70,790	$68,290	$111,800	$134,830	$87,760			$1,416,907
HI		$8,380	$9,740	$10,530	$36,040	$32,900	$73,130	$37,760	$12,900	$46,510	$42,250	$90,030			$526,880
IA		$22,272	$20,740	$43,970	$47,460	$58,220	$103,170	$30,210	$27,660	$93,060	$83,380	$106,690			$894,042
ID		$9,580	$10,940	$7,540	$22,390	$15,610	$26,660	$12,310	$26,060	$19,340	$23,420	$93,500			$311,210
IL		$27,605	$180,790	$214,820	$256,650	$357,010	$509,580	$247,340	$246,100	$336,960	$531,290	$141,680			$4,864,795
IN		$11,120	$54,840	$52,710	$106,330	$133,920	$242,020	$78,980	$72,370	$143,130	$203,150	$87,490			$1,872,830
KS		$44,658	$28,840	$34,670	$58,130	$41,310	$99,820	$36,110	$36,730	$80,240	$104,980	$66,390			$1,001,898
KY		$605,794	$31,760	$45,890	$121,950	$79,120	$114,170	$32,930	$62,640	$119,530	$97,850	$35,930			$1,663,764
LA		$25,385	$52,540	$41,960	$77,690	$78,790	$138,230	$54,460	$73,190	$85,350	$136,290	$91,760			$1,318,815
MA		$30,866	$71,680	$117,910	$181,590	$203,380	$322,920	$169,610	$142,070	$211,730	$430,880	$53,530			$2,896,806
MD		$41,234	$70,980	$75,790	$125,500	$115,830	$207,120	$135,820	$106,740	$175,530	$272,710	$36,890			$2,089,624
ME		$1,625	$14,890	$7,630	$18,830	$42,670	$37,910	$5,420	$14,840	$22,540	$26,830	$61,920			$362,715
MI		$82,707	$86,970	$118,480	$199,970	$240,500	$349,250	$98,500	$121,170	$295,660	$332,990	$69,550			$3,154,207
MN		$75,626	$61,750	$57,640	$76,740	$112,370	$142,080	$82,730	$96,900	$113,310	$143,620	$24,810			$1,697,956
MO		$72,765	$27,460	$80,080	$93,610	$115,880	$153,820	$66,390	$77,910	$129,200	$176,920	$77,910			$1,643,505
MS		$12,314	$23,620	$36,620	$28,310	$49,330	$93,890	$28,100	$30,600	$43,640	$92,820	$106,150	$99,940	$100,060	$745,394
MT		$39,935	$2,450	$14,040	$16,520	$9,640	$23,240	$2,420	$5,810	$5,190	$27,630	$58,550	$29,250	$38,420	$273,095

many variables. Although this dataset contains only one variable, you can still use it to test the tool. First, insert a new column that numbers the months as 1, 2, 3, and so on. You can use the Fill command, or just enter the first couple of rows and use the forecast trick to create the rest. Check the Tools/Add-Ins option to ensure the Analysis ToolPak is loaded. Then select Tools/Data Analysis and pick the Regression tool. As the Y range, select the sales column including the title row but excluding the six rows you forecast earlier. Select the month column as the X range. Be sure to check the Labels box, and then run the regression. This tool provides the standard regression coefficients, probabilities, and diagnostics.

Quick Quiz:

1. Why is a linear forecast usually safer than nonlinear?
2. Why do you need to create a new column with month numbers for regression instead of using the formatted year-month column?
3. What happens to the trend line r-squared value on the chart when you add the new forecast rows to the chart?

The Importance of Intelligent Systems in e-Business

How can more intelligent systems benefit e-business? Disintermediation is a primary aspect of e-business. Businesses can interact directly with customers, with less need for middle levels such as retail stores. However, these middle levels often existed because they provided more explanations and support to customers. If you remove that level, how are you going to deal with thousands or millions of customers? If you have to hire hundreds of workers to answer customer questions, you will lose most of the potential benefits of disintermediation. One of the solutions to this problem is to implement more intelligent systems that can provide automated support to customers.

In many ways, the Internet adds complexity to the daily lives of customers and managers. The Internet provides access to huge amounts of data—and it is growing constantly. The growth adds more data, but it also means that the availability and use of information is constantly changing.

Agents

A recent application of AI techniques has arisen in the context of the Internet. A key issue of the Internet is searching for data. Although the Internet dramatically improves communication, there are problems with maintaining the "interpretation" of the information from various systems. Originally, most data on the Web was stored as standard pages of text using HTML. Search engines would simply scan these pages and build searchable indexes.

Increasingly the Internet is being used to store and transmit objects composed of data, pictures, spreadsheets, sounds, and video. From a pure transmission standpoint, any object can be decomposed into raw data bits and sent between computers. Where we run into problems is searching for the objects. Consider a simple example where you want to find a new printer, so you search the Internet for prices. Today, many vendors store the product descriptions and prices in a database, and then build the HTML page on demand when you go to the site. Since the page is not static, the search engines do not index it.

One solution to this problem is to create software agents. **Agents** are object-oriented programs designed for networks that are written to perform specific tasks in response to user requests. The concept of object orientation is important because it means that agents know how to exchange object attributes, and they have the ability to activate object functions in other agents. The tasks could be simple, such as finding all files on a network that refer to a specific topic. One key feature of agents is that they are designed to communicate with each other. As long as your agent knows the abilities or functions of another agent, they can exchange messages and commands. General Magic is a pioneering company that created a standard programming language for agents. With this language, agents can transfer themselves and run on other computers. Agents also have a degree of "intelligence." They can be given relatively general commands, which the agents reinterpret and apply to each situation they encounter.

Consider an example illustrated by Figure 10.25. You have been working hard and decide to take a vacation. You want to go to a beach but do not have much money to spend. You are looking for a place where you can swim, scuba dive, and meet people at night. But you also want the place to have some secluded beaches where you can get away from the

FIGURE 10.25

Software agents: A personal software agent might be used to book a vacation. It would take your initial preferences and communicate with other agents to find sites that matched your preferences. It might also be able to negotiate prices with competing resorts.

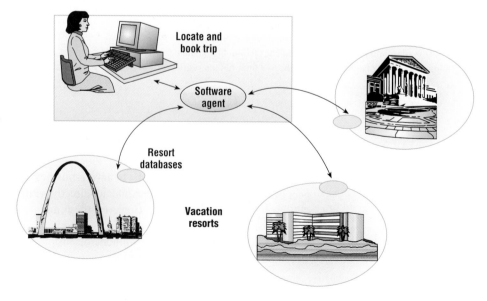

crowds and relax. You could call a travel agent and buy a package deal, but every agent you call just laughs and says that next time you should call three months ahead of time instead of only three days ahead. You suspect that a beach resort probably has last-minute cancellations and you could get in, but how do you find out? There are thousands of possibilities. If all of the resort computers had automatic reservation agents, the task would be fairly easy. You would start an agent on your computer and tell it the features you want. Your agent sends messages to all of the automated resort agents looking for open spots at places that matched your features. When your agent finds something close, it brings back details and pictures to display on your screen. When you decide on a resort, the agent automatically makes the reservations.

Notice three important features of software agents. First, the agents need to know how to communicate. It is not as simple as transmitting raw data. They must understand the data and respond to questions. Second, imagine the amount of network traffic involved. In the vacation search example, your agent might have to contact thousands of other computers. Now picture what happens when a thousand other people do the same thing! Third, all of the agents are independent. You, as well as other computer owners, are free to create or modify your own agent. As long as there are standard methods for agents to exchange attributes and activate functions, they can be modified and improved. For instance, you might program your agent to weight the vacation spots according to some system, or you might teach it to begin its search in specific locations.

Programmers have begun to incorporate expert system and other AI capabilities into these agents. By adding a set of rules, the agent becomes more than just a simple search mechanism. The more complex the rules, the more "intelligent" it becomes, which means you have to do less work. In fact, software agents have the potential to dramatically increase the research in AI. Currently, because of limited standards and the difficulty of creating them, there are few examples of useful agents. As increasing numbers of people use agents and begin demanding more intelligence, it will become profitable for researchers to work harder at building reliable, intelligent software.

Support and Problem-Solving Applications

Increasingly, your customers want personalized attention to help in both selecting products and solving problems. Yet it is expensive to provide individual personal support to every customer. Instead, firms are developing expert systems and other intelligent applications to help customers with a more personalized touch. For example, look at Amazon.com's recommendation system. It began with books but has been expanded to most of their products. As you purchase items at Amazon.com, the system gives you a list of similar products that you might be interested in. For instance, if you purchase several science fiction books, it will suggest new releases of similar books. The system can increase sales because it helps show customers items that they might not have found otherwise.

More complex products can benefit from more sophisticated expert systems that help analyze customer needs and help configure the correct components. For example, a computer vendor could build a system that asks questions to help identify the applications that a customer will run. It could then suggest specific enhancements such as adding RAM or a second disk drive to improve performance.

Similarly, many firms are building expert systems to help customers with problems. If a customer has a problem installing a new product, he or she can turn to the Web site. The system asks questions to identify the problem and then make suggestions. The advantage of the expert system is that it is available 24 hours a day, can solve most of the easy problems, and is less embarrassing to customers who might think their questions are too "silly" to ask a human troubleshooter.

Intelligent systems can also be useful for B2B and other forms of e-business. The systems might analyze past purchases and suggest new products, or automatically analyze sales patterns and help managers develop new products and close out unprofitable lines. They can be used to develop automated ordering systems that predict customer demands, schedule production, and generate automated sales orders and payments.

It can be difficult to develop these applications, but firms that build powerful systems will attract customers and increase the level of sales to each customer. Ultimately, these systems could be the primary reason people switch to buying items over the Internet.

Summary

Managers make many different decisions. Every business discipline builds models to help people analyze problems and make decisions. Without models and tools, people rarely make good decisions. Many tools have been created to help you analyze data and make decisions. In many cases, you will want to build a data warehouse to retrieve and organize the data. You can build a DSS, building a model in a spreadsheet or more advanced statistical analysis tool. A good DSS extracts the needed data from the database, evaluates the model, and displays the results in a form that helps managers visualize the problem and quickly choose a solution. The biggest difficulty with DSS tools is that you generally need to be trained to create the models and understand the results.

A Manager's View

It is hard to make good decisions. You need fast access to huge amounts of data, the ability to evaluate various models, and a way to visualize the problem and the solution. Various levels of tools are available to help. The tools provide different types of intelligence and support. As a manager, you need to understand the context of the problem and know which tools can be applied to solve a problem. You also need to be enough of an expert to recognize when a system provides useless or bad answers so that you can avoid disasters.

More sophisticated data mining tools can be employed to semiautomatically search for correlations and other relationships within the data. Common regression, clustering, and classification tools use statistical measures to identify the importance of various attributes and to build forecast equations. Market basket analysis identifies items that customers purchase together. The information provided by this analysis is a powerful tool for cross selling related products. Data mining tools are powerful techniques, but the results are not always useful, and you must carefully evaluate the implications of the results to ensure that they are realistic and repeatable.

Expert systems provide a different level of decision automation. They analyze data based on rules defined by an expert. They can handle complex and missing data. They are particularly useful at helping novices reach a better decision. They are excellent tools for specialized, narrowly defined problems. The biggest concern arises when someone tries to build an ES for a problem that is too large, too variable, or unstructured. The ES is not likely to work, and it will cost money and time to build. Worse, the proposed decisions might be nonsensical.

Scientists are continually working on ways to automate even more decisions. Neural networks are incredible tools for analyzing pattern data. They have been successfully applied to problems ranging from speech recognition to lending analysis. You can purchase software that will quickly build a neural network to analyze data. One drawback to neural networks is that the relationships tend to be highly nonlinear and difficult to interpret. So, you might reach an answer, but you might not be able to explain the relationships. Other tools that are increasingly useful in business applications are machine vision, robotics, and language comprehension.

Automated tools can help you provide better service to customers and suppliers, particularly when the intelligent systems can be reached online. If you can help a customer solve a problem 24 hours a day without having to pay hundreds of humans, you can gain happier customers with little additional cost. Several companies are working on building intelligent agents that will enable customers and vendors to interact automatically by following rules that you specify.

Key Words

agent, *380*	geographic information	online analytical processing
artificial intelligence	system (GIS), *362*	(OLAP), *356*
(AI), *350*	global positioning system	optimization, *354*
data marts, *356*	(GPS), *363*	parameters, *353*
data mining, *364*	knowledge base, *369*	prediction, *353*
data warehouse, *355*	knowledge engineer, *369*	rules, *369*
decision support system	market basket	simulation, *354*
(DSS), *358*	analysis, *365*	Turing test, *375*
decision tree, *369*	metadata, *356*	
expert system, *350*	models, *352*	
extraction, transformation,	natural language, *375*	
and loading (ETL), *355*	neural network, *373*	

Web Site References

Expert Systems and AI Tools

A.L.I.C.E. conversation	www.alicebot.org
CLIPS (started by NASA)	www.ghg.net/clips/CLIPS.html
ExSys (commercial)	www.exsys.com
International Neural Network Society	www.inns.org
Jess (Java)	Herzberg.ca.sandia.gov/jess/
Mathworks neural network toolbox	www.mathworks.com/products/neuralnet

Machine Vision

CalTech	www.vision.caltech.edu/html-files/research.html
Carnegie Red Team	www.redteamracing.org
Vision 1	www.vision1.com/indapps.shtml

Additional Readings

Barabba, Vincent, and Gerald Zaltman. *Hearing the Voice of the Market.* Cambridge, MA: Harvard Business Press, 1991. [Overcoming design biases at GM.]

Dangermond, Jack, and Adena Schutzberg. "Engineering, Geographic Information Systems, and Databases: A New Frontier." *Journal of Computing in Civil Engineering,* July 1998, pp. 121–122. [Uses of GIS.]

Franses, Philip Hans. *Time Series Models for Business and Economic Forecasting.* Port Chester, NY: Cambridge University Press, 1998. [An introduction to forecasting.]

Krill, Paul. "Analytics Redraw CRM Lines." *Computerworld,* December 3, 2001. [A summary of vendors developing products to analyze customer data.]

Neil, Stephanie. "Blue Cross Dissects Data to Improve Care." *PC Week,* February 8, 1999. [BCBS uses data warehouse and online application processing DSS to improve service.]

Wilkinson, Stephanie. "PC Apps Help to Take a Byte Out of Crime." *PC Week,* February 23, 1998. [GIS and imaging tools help police predict and solve crimes.]

Review Questions

1. Why is it so important to build models and analyze data using a scientific process?
2. What is the purpose of a data warehouse?
3. How is an OLAP cube browser better than using queries?
4. List the three major components of a DSS.
5. How can a GIS help managers make better decisions?
6. How can data mining help you make better decisions and what are some of the primary methods?
7. What is an expert system and what are the characteristics of the problems that it is designed to solve?
8. What types of problems are best suited for a neural network?

9. How can you use the advanced intelligence capabilities and research in business?

10. What are the differences between DSS, ES, and AI features?

11. Why are intelligent systems so important for e-business?

Exercises

1. Talk with managers or use research to identify three expert systems (that are not described in the textbook). What tools were used to build the expert system? What problem is it designed to solve?

2. A marketing manager has asked you to help design a DSS for the marketing department. Every month marketers need to evaluate the effectiveness of their advertising campaigns and decide how to allocate their budget for the next month. They advertise only in the local area and have four basic choices: radio, television, local newspapers, and direct mail. Each month, they conduct random phone interviews to find out who sees their advertisements. They can also purchase local scanner data to determine sales of related products. Each month, the media salespeople give them the Arbitron ratings that show the number of people (and demographics) who they believe saw each advertisement. They also receive a schedule of costs for the upcoming month. As a first step in creating the DSS, identify any relevant assumptions and input and output variables, along with any models that might be useful.

3. Interview an expert in some area and create an initial set of rules that you could use for an expert system. If you cannot find a cooperative expert, try researching one of the following topics in your library: fruit tree propagation and pruning (what trees are needed for cross-pollination, what varieties grow best in each region, what fertilizers are needed, when they should be pruned); requirements or qualifications for public assistance or some other governmental program (check government documents); legal requirements to determine whether a contract is in effect (check books on business law).

4. A government official recently noted that the government is having difficulty processing applications for assistance programs (welfare). Although most applications are legitimate, several facts they contain have to be checked. For instance, welfare workers have to check motor vehicle and real estate records to see whether the applicants own cars or property. The agency checks birth, death, and marriage records to verify the existence of dependents. They sometimes examine public health data and check criminal records. It takes time to check all of the records, plus the agency needs to keep track of the results of the searches. Furthermore, a few applicants have applied multiple times—sometimes in different localities. The office needs to randomly check some applications to search for fraud. Every week, summary reports have to be sent to the state offices. A key feature of these reports is that they are used to convince politicians to increase funding for certain programs. Describe how a DSS could help this agency. (*Hint:* Identify the decisions that need to be made.)

5. Obtain an expert system (e.g., Jess and CLIPS are free). Create a set of rules to evaluate a simple request for a car loan.

6. Identify a problem that would be well suited for a neural network. Explain how the system would be trained (e.g., what existing data can be used?). Explain why you think the problem needs a neural network and what benefits can be gained.

7. For the following problems identify those that would be best suited for an expert system, decision support system, or a more advanced AI system. Explain why.

a. Helping students create a degree program.

b. Determining how many cooks are needed each night at a large restaurant.

c. Identifying potential criminals at an airport.

d. Investing in the stock market.

e. Hiring an employee for a technical job.

f. Troubleshooting the cause of power problems on a ship.

g. Predicting the impact of government economic policies.

h. Evaluating crime trends within a city.

8. Who will pay for the creation of software agents? What about the use of the agents? Should (or could) users be charged every time their agent calls another one? What about network usage? What would happen if your agent used your telephone to connect to thousands of other agents?

9. Use a spreadsheet to create the example from the Human Resources Management example. Fill in the market adjustment column so that raises match the performance appraisals. Remember, total raises cannot exceed $10,000.

DeptStor.mdb

You are a midlevel manager for a small department store. You have collected a large amount of data on sales for 2004. Your transaction system kept track of every sale (order) by customer. Most customers paid by credit card or check, so you have complete customer data. Walk-in customers who paid cash are given a separate customer number, so you still have the sales data.

You are trying to determine staffing levels for each department. You know that the store becomes much busier during the end-of-the-year holiday season. For summer months, you have thought about combining staff from the departments. From conversations with experienced workers, you have determined that there is a maximum number of customers that can be handled by one person in a department. These numbers are expressed as monthly averages in the table.

You are thinking about combining workers from some of the departments to save on staffing—especially over the spring and summer months. However, working multiple departments makes the sales staff less efficient. There are two considerations in combining staff members. First, if any of the departments are reduced to a staff of zero, sales in that department will drop by 10 percent for that month. Second, total staffing should be kept at the level defined by the monthly averages. If average staffing (total across all departments) falls below the total suggested, then sales in all departments will fall by 2 percent for each tenth of a percentage point below the suggested average.

10. Using the database and a spreadsheet, determine how many workers we need in each department for each month. Present a plan for combining departments if it can save the company money. Assume that sales members cost an average of $1,000 a month. Two queries have already been created by the MIS department and are stored in the database: SalesbyMonth and SalesCountbyMonth. The first totals the dollar value; the second counts the number of transactions.

11. Write a report to upper management designating the appropriate sales staff levels for each department by month. Include data and graphs to support your position. (*Hint:* Use a spreadsheet that lets you enter various staffing levels in each department in each month, and then calculate any sales declines.)

Technology Toolbox

12. Create the pivot table report for Rolling Thunder Bicycles. Briefly summarize any patterns or problems you identify.

13. Using the Rolling Thunder Bicycles query, create a pivot chart and compare sales of the different models over time. Identify any patterns that you see.

14. Interview a manager (or research a case study), and identify a problem that could benefit from the use of a pivot table or cube browser. Be sure to identify the main data elements and the purpose of the system. Sketch the primary screen for the pivot table or pivot chart.

15. Compute the average number of days it takes to build a bicycle (ShipDate − OrderDate) for each month. Import the data into Excel and forecast the trend. First, forecast it based on all of the data. Second, forecast it for three time periods: (a) the early years, (b) the middle years, and (c) the most recent years. Look at the initial chart to estimate the breaks between these three sets, or just divide it into three equal-size groups if you do not see any good break points. Comment on any differences or problems.

16. Using federal data (start at www.fedstats.gov), compute a regression analysis of Rolling Thunder sales by state by year compared with at least population and income.

Teamwork

17. Have each person find and describe a problem that could benefit from a GIS. Make sure it needs a GIS, not just a mapping system. Combine the results and compare the types of problems to identify similarities.

18. Go to the Department of Transportation Web site (http://www.transtats.bts.gov/ DL_SelectFields.asp?Table_ID=247) and download airline data for a few different time periods. Include origin, destination, year, quarter, number of passengers, operating carrier group, and market fare. (*Warning:* The files are big.) Create a database table to hold the data. Build a pivot table to analyze the data. Have each person work with the cube to spot any patterns or trends. Report any interesting information you find.

19. Using Rolling Thunder Bicycles, have each person forecast the sales by one model type for six months. Combine the individual model results and compare this value to the forecast based only on total sales.

20. Select an economic data series (check www.fedstats.gov). Place members into one of three subgroups. Have each group forecast the series using a different methodology. Compare the results. If you have sufficient data, leave out the most recent data, and then forecast those values and compare the forecasts to the actual.

21. Define a problem that could benefit from an expert system. As a team, develop the basic rules that would be applied to the problem.

22. Have each person find a problem that could benefit from a neural network. Describe how the system would be trained. Combine the individual comments and identify any commonalities.

Rolling Thunder Database

23. Identify shipments where receipts do not match the original order. Provide a count and value (and percentages) by supplier/manufacturer.

24. Analyze sales and discounts by employee and by model type. Are some employees providing higher discounts than others? Are we discounting some models too much or not enough?

25. Identify an area in which an expert system could help. Be specific and explain the advantages of using an ES for that area. Where would you find an expert to assist with creating the knowledge domain?

26. Describe how new technologies might be used to improve decisions at the Rolling Thunder Bicycle company. What experimental and future technologies should we watch closely? If you could create an "intelligent" computer system for the company, what would it do and how would it be used to increase profits?

27. What pattern-matching types of decisions arise at Rolling Thunder that could benefit from the use of neural networks?

28. What aspects of customer service might be automated with expert systems? What are the potential advantages and disadvantages?

Cases: Financial Services Industry

The Industry

The financial industry is interesting. It is huge and everyone interacts with the trillions of dollars a day handled by the global financial system. It is also complex, with many different types of firms involved, and constantly creating new financial tools. At one point, the financial industry was driven by banks. Today, banks still play important roles, but where do people put their money? In the stock market or other investments. So brokerage firms have a strong role. How do consumers pay for things? With debit cards and credit cards. So the card-processing sector, led by Visa and MasterCard, plays a huge role in the industry. As the national laws have changed, mostly relaxed, over the past few years, the industry has become even more complex. Banks can once again sell stocks and investments, as well as insurance. And brokerage firms and insurance companies can perform banking functions.

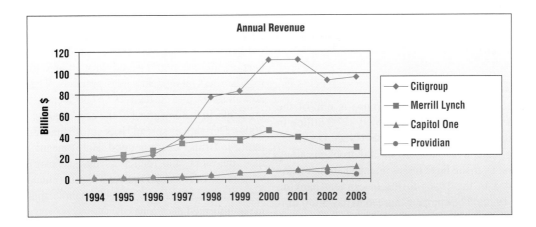

Making Money

How do brokerage firms make money? They used to make a profit on transaction commissions, as much as several percentage points per trade—amounting to hundreds or thousands of dollars every time a client bought or sold a stock. With the advent of online trading, pushing the discount brokerage firms, commissions fell to fixed rates of $10 to $20 per trade, a tiny fraction of what they were and under 10 cents a share. The big firms tried to convince customers that their higher fees were worthwhile because they also provided investment advice. But with tainted advice, and a huge amount of data available free to customers online, the full-price firms suffered.

How do banks make money? Banks make money in two ways: interest rate spreads and fees. Interest rate spreads are the difference between the rates the banks charge borrowers and the amount the bank has to pay to obtain the money. Banks select different lending markets (consumer versus business) and have diverse ways of obtaining funds (deposits or loans from other banks). Likewise, fees vary depending on the type of bank. Consumer-oriented banks receive fees from customers (such as checking account fees). Business or investment banks charge fees for more sophisticated services.

How do credit card companies make money? Here the answer is trickier, because there are several types of companies involved. The transaction-processing organizations (Visa and MasterCard) receive a fee for every transaction handled through the clearing system. However, banks ultimately issue the cards and are responsible for the money. A consumer bank issues a card to customers and is responsible for paying vendors for legitimate transactions. The consumer bank makes money on consumer fees (usually low today) and interest charges to customers on outstanding balances. It also uses the cards as a marketing tool to attract customers and encourage them to purchase other services. The merchant bank is responsible for ensuring that the merchant is legitimate. It makes money by taking a percentage cut of all the merchant's credit card (or debit card) sales.

Brokerage Firms

More than three-fourths of Americans' liquid assets ($12 trillion) are in stocks, bonds, and money market funds (Rev-

ell 2002). How safe are these assets? Do you trust your broker? Do you trust the advice from brokers? In April 2003, forced by a lawsuit led by New York attorney general Eliot Spitzer, 10 of the largest Wall Street investment banks paid $1.4 billion (Nocera 2004). The money was a settlement for providing misleading investment analysis. The brokerage firms usually wrote glowing reports of companies—urging people to buy stock in specific companies. Many of the reports were written because the firms were vying for investment banker contracts with the same companies. In exchange for glowing reports, the companies provided more business (and fees) to the brokerage firms. James Freeman, a former research director, notes that analysts "went from having investment banking deals pushed on them in the 1980s to becoming the greedy pigs at the center of it" (Nocera 2004).

Credit Cards

At one time, the credit card industry was neatly divided into three main segments: the upper end controlled by American Express, the middle tier targeted by Citicorp, and the subprime market pursued by Providian. As a fourth group, MBNA targeted a wide swath of customers with its affiliate cards. Most card companies gained market share by blindly sending 5 billion solicitations a year to U.S. consumers (Gross 2002). Capital One grew by using targeted marketing and thousands of marketing tests with different groups of potential customers. Nonetheless, with competition at a peak for high-end customers, profits were squeezed. Companies were increasingly tempted to go after the subprime market—where they could charge higher interest rates in exchange for greater risk. But as the economy turns down and interest rates increase, this strategy results in greater losses when customers do not pay their bills or even file for bankruptcy (Dugas 2003). Providian lost 90 percent of its stock market value from mid-2001 to mid-2002. Capital One also faced greater losses, but not as large as many other companies. The 2003 settlement with Visa and MasterCard will ultimately affect profits for the industry. Wal-Mart had sued the two credit card companies to break up their power to force merchants to accept higher costs for debit cards. The win by the merchants reduces the power of the card companies and banks and should ultimately reduce fees paid by merchants (www.cardweb.com).

Banks

Citibank (or the parent company Citigroup) is one of the largest banks in the world. In 2003, it earned $17.9 billion in profits, the most ever by a single bank ("Just Deserts?" 2004). Over the years, it has suffered several problems along with other banks, from the huge losses on international loans to South America in the 1980s to the investment banking scandals in the 1990s. The company agreed to pay $400 million as part of the $1.4 billion investment banking settlement in 2003, the largest payment by any of the companies involved. Also like other banks, the company grew through acquisitions of other banks (Primerica in 1988), insurance companies (Travelers in 1993), brokerage firms (Shearson and Salomon in 1998), and credit cards (Sears in 2004) (Rosenberg 2003). In fact, the last decade of banking in the United States can be best characterized by the mergers. A handful of banks control a huge number of deposits (Citibank, Bank of America, J.P. Morgan Chase, Wells Fargo, and Wachovia) along with a few large regional banks (Stone 2003). Ultimately, one limiting factor to mergers is that federal law currently prohibits a single U.S. bank from holding more than 10 percent of the consumer deposits. Banks have also been one of the big beneficiaries of the loose federal monetary policy of the early 2000s—making it easy to borrow money at almost no cost.

Decisions

All aspects of the financial industry heavily utilize information technology. All firms face difficult daily questions on how to balance risks and profits. Overall, banks have profited because they have become more adept at identifying potential bad loans and diversifying risk. The entire industry has become more interconnected through new financial devices to share risk and create new products. The use of credit-default swaps and derivatives has been credited with protecting banks in the downturn of the early 2000s ("Just Deserts?" 2004). Derivatives spread risks across the entire industry and multiple firms, which is good. But it means that all companies, investors, and regulators have to carefully monitor a wide range of financial indicators and evaluate large-scale effects. How can anyone possibly handle this much data to make informed decisions?

Additional Reading

Dugas, Christine. "Bankruptcy Filings Set Record in 2002." *USA Today,* February 14, 2003.

Gross, Daniel. "Capital One, What's in Your Wallet?" *Slate,* October 25, 2002.

"Just Deserts?" *The Economist,* April 15, 2004.

Nocera, Joseph. "Wall Street on the Run," *Fortune,* June 1, 2004.

Revell, Janice. "How Much Do Brokers Have to Hide?" *Fortune,* April 28, 2002.

Rosenberg, Yuval. "Sandy Hands Over the Keys to Citi." *Fortune,* July 16, 2003.

Stone, Amey. "Will Citi Upstage BofA's Big Deal?" *BusinessWeek,* October 29, 2003.

www.cardweb.com

Case: Citigroup

Charles Prince III, general counsel of Citigroup, explains the overall challenges facing management: "You've got five or six or seven businesses—credit cards to mortgages to personal loans to investment banking to commercial insurance. They relate in important ways, but they're different. And they're all over the place. No one has ever had a company as broad in geographic scope [101 countries], as broad in product set, and as deep in size" (Loomis 2001). Sandy Weill gained control of Citigroup (ticker: C), the parent company, in 2000 after a merger between his company (Travelers) and Citibank. In 2001, most of the top-level management was reorganized, but the structure is a little nontraditional. Robert Willumstad is head of consumer business. Michael Carpenter runs the corporate division including the Salomon Smith Barney brokerage and Citi's commercial bank. Thomas Jones runs the investment management and private bank. Bictor Menezes heads the emerging markets section. Charles Prince and Jay Fishman, technically co-chief operating officers, also report directly to Weill. Prince handles operations and administra-tion, Fishman risk and finance. Neither has any direct authority over the other business leaders. One of Fishman's jobs is to synthesize the overall risk picture of the business (into a 54-page monthly book), so that everyone can see the current issues and risks. The lines in many cases are somewhat blurry. Prince, for example, has a responsibility to promote cross selling of products. Because most of the company growth has come from acquisitions, few people down in the hierarchy know much about the other divisions and options. Chief financial officer Todd Thomson also has oversight of cross selling. Yet neither Prince nor Thomson has direct authority over the businesses that do the cross selling. Weill points out that "this company is too big to micromanage, but it's not so big that you can't know what's going on" (Loomis 2001). Overall, the combination of a huge bank and brokerage firm creates significant advantages over the competitors. When necessary, Citigroup can swing an investment underwriting deal by offering a Citibank loan—something that is much harder to do at brokerage firms like Merrill Lynch.

One controversial step Weill has taken is to minimize the use of the Internet. Instead of trying to run it separately, he moved the projects into the subdivision units and asked them to merge them into their own operations—while trying to reduce costs. Similarly, the Salomon Smith Barney retail brokerage is a full-service company and does not offer low-cost Internet trading. On the other hand, Deryck Maughan, CEO of E-Citi, worked hard to establish an electronic foreign-exchange market called Atriax in partnership with three other large banks. "We are saying that we would rather disintermediate ourselves in partnership with others and grab a large share of the new market than sit around in some pre-Information Age factory" (Loomis 2001). In October 2003, Weill remained chairman but made Prince CEO and Willumstad president (Stone 2003).

American financial institutions were hammered by the recession of the early 1990s; even Citibank came close to going under. Yet with the recession of the early 2000s, most banks, including Citigroup, increased profits. Average return on bank assets jumped from 8 percent in the 1990s to 16 percent in the 2000s. One reason is that the 2001 recession was not as deep, and banks are not as tied to corporations as before, supplying 40 percent of the funds today versus 50 percent a decade earlier. Banks also profited from the drop in interest rates engineered by the Fed. But banks are still the biggest source of funds for companies. The big change: a substantial improvement in risk management at American banks. Doug Woodham of Moody's observes that "there has been a step change in risk management" ("Just Deserts?" 2004). For example, mortgages have been turned into securities that are sold on a national market—spreading the risk away from the issuing bank. Credit-default derivatives have accomplished the same task for corporate loans, with the market reaching $350 billion in 2003.

The Hispanic population represents a growing market—particularly for Citibank with its international reach and reputation. In 2004, Citibank created a checkless checking account specifically for Hispanic customers. Many workers from South America come to the United States to make money, which they send back to their families. Yet many of them do not realize the importance of banks and ATMs in the U.S. economy. Most have difficulty opening checking accounts. The Citibank account relies on a debit card and Citibank's international collection of ATMs. Workers can deposit money in the account, and family members can withdraw it almost anywhere in the world through a local ATM (Wentz 2004).

Citibank is one of the largest issuers of credit cards in the United States. Yet that market is stagnant with intense competition and little opportunity for profit. Some firms have tried to expand profits by going after the subprime market, but Citigroup has resisted. Instead, it is aiming to expand its reach globally. Leveraging its experience in emerging markets, it began offering Visa cards to Chinese consumers in February 2004. The charges can be paid using either dollars or Chinese yuan. Charles Prince and other dignitaries opened the service with parades through the streets of Shanghai. In 2003, only 25 million of the 1.3 billion Chinese citizens held credit cards. Some experts expect the number to easily triple in 10 years. Although the untapped market seems to offer incredible benefits, the risks are enormous. There is only one credit bureau in the entire country, minimal market research, and high bank fraud. Similar expansions of credit in Hong Kong and Korea resulted in huge losses from personal bankruptcies. Citigroup is mitigating the risk by performing their own background checks, only issuing cards to clients older than 21, and requiring an annual income of at least $6,000 (restricting the market to only 10 percent of Shanghai's 16 million residents). Citibank has also devised a mathematical scoring system to assess each individual's credit risk. The McKinsey consulting firm notes that the current default rate in China is 1.5 percent compared with 5 percent in the United States. An interesting twist to the risk problem is that the customers tend to pay off their card in full each month, so the bank has to make its money on fees instead of interest charges (Baglole 2004).

Questions

1. How does Citigroup use models and information systems to make decisions in the credit card market?

2. How is the Chinese and Southeast Asian market for credit (especially in Korea) different from that in the United States?

3. How could Citigroup make better use of the Internet?

4. How can models, expert systems, and other information tools help Citigroup manage such a large organization?

Additional Reading

Baglole, Joel. "Citibank Takes Risk by Issuing Cards in China." *The Wall Street Journal,* March 10, 2004.

"Just Deserts?" *The Economist,* April 15, 2004.

Loomis, Carol J. "Sandy Weill's Monster." *Fortune,* April 1, 2001.

Stone, Amey. "Will Citi Upstage BofA's Big Deal?" *BusinessWeek,* October 29, 2003.

Wentz, Laurel. "Banks Tailor Efforts to Homesick Hispanics." *Advertising Age,* April 5, 2004.

Case: Capital One

As a newcomer to the credit card industry, Capital One (ticker: COF) needed an edge. The company created the edge by building the Information Based Strategy (IBS). The system is highly focused on testing and evaluating various options before offering them to the public. The three-step approach is to (1) create a new product and find a target population, (2) create a test by changing the variables and seeing how the group members react, and (3) use the test results to further divide the segment, and then test specific campaigns against those segments. By specifically targeting rates, fees, and options to each market, Capital One was able to obtain high response rates, reducing the costs of acquiring a customer. The company conducted 45,000 tests in 2000 alone (120 per day). The company extended the process to its Web site, tracking visitor activity, tailoring options to each specific customer, and using the background data to buy ads on other sites with the appropriate demographics. For example, if sports enthusiasts responded well to certain features, those features would be advertised on sporting sites. With this process, the company opened 2 million new accounts online (Cohen 2001).

The company uses the test results and marketing to tailor interest rates and fees to individual customers. In effect, it has created 100,000 different segments or product combinations. The process extends to the customer call center. Capital One uses Cisco Systems Global Service Logistics (GSL) system to route calls. The system retrieves information about the customer and routes the call to the most appropriate representative. For example, a customer who routinely pays off the monthly charges might be routed to a representative to sell a platinum card with a higher balance.

In a different twist, Capital One uses a similar process to hire and promote employees. It records specific data on every hire, including scores on a timed math test and a behavioral test. During promotions, the characteristics of successful employees are listed for each job. These characteristics, and the initial test scores, are used to refine the hiring process for each type of job. The process fits employees to jobs and reduces hiring costs (Cohen 2001).

For several years, Capital One had enviable growth rates with revenue growing from $95 million in 1995 to $4.97 billion in 2001, from 6 million customers to 33 million (Cohen 2001). Yet because of the extremely competitive nature of the industry, Capital One had to extend into the subprime market to capture more customers. With the economic downturn, the subprime market crashed in 2002. Capital One suffered along with the others in the industry. For the first time, managers also revealed how dependent Capital One was on the subprime market. In 2002, 40 percent of its cards were in the hands of subprime customers (Albergotti 2003), far above what most investors had believed. The market punished Capital One's stock. Yet, ultimately, Capital One's system worked. The company's risk management techniques gave it one of the lowest levels of bad loans—until 2003. The company wrote off bad debt, but earnings eventually rose and the company survived. The company has reduced its exposure in the subprime market. Federal oversight also forced companies to reevaluate the subprime market—regulators have been attempting to limit fees and penalty charges (Smith 2002). But the strategic shift leaves Capital One facing more competition in the higher quality markets. Its profit margins have shrunk accordingly—down to 16 percent in 2004, half their earlier levels (Byrnes 2004).

Searching for new markets, Capital One is widening its search into more traditional banking areas. Richard D. Fairbank, the CEO, knows that growth in the card market will be slow. "A lot of the different financial markets are evolving, but the most evolved is the credit card business. This is pretty close to the endgame. We've really got to work for a living these days in the credit card market." His new target: auto loans, installment loans, and even international loans. In particular, he wants to target small businesses. Capital One's lending to small businesses has grown from $400 million in 1999 to $3.3 billion in 2003. At the end of 2003, the company managed $46.3 billion in credit card loans, $8.5 billion in autos, $5.4 billion in installment loans, and $7.6 billion in international loans (Kuykendall 2004).

In the meantime, the company is cutting expenses, eliminating as many as 2,500 of its 9,000 positions in its Richmond, Virginia, headquarters. Fairbanks told employees he needed to cut expenses by 20 percent. "Our businesses need to improve their cost positions to compete in the future against leading players in the financial-services industry" (Hazard 2004). Capital One is also interested in using the Internet to reduce costs. Processing payments online instead of paper checks reduces costs by $1 a year per customer. Persuading customers to accept electronic statements instead of mail cuts costs an additional $5 per customer per year. Rick Long, director of U.S. card operations at Capital One, notes that "our ROI [return on investment] models are built on lowering costs" (Wade 2004). He was emphasizing that Capital One is primarily interested in using the Internet only where it is cost effective. The company is also concerned that customers have to be enticed to use the Internet instead of coerced. "If we drive them to the site, they may not stay" (Wade 2004). Most customers who are interested in using the Internet enroll within the first six months.

Questions

1. How does Capital One use decision support systems to reduce risk and increase sales?

2. With its advanced systems, how did Capital One lose so much money in 2003?

3. How can Capital One use technology to reduce its costs?

Additional Reading

Albergotti, Reed. "Fewer Credit-Card Solicitations Are in the Mail." *The Wall Street Journal,* November 5, 2003.

Byrnes, Nanette. "Coming of Age at Capital One." *BusinessWeek,* February 16, 2004.

Cohen, Jackie. "Growth Formula." *Computerworld,* July 2, 2001.

Hazard, Carol. "Capital One Shifts Focus; Firm to Cut Richmond, Va., Jobs to Reduce Costs." *Richmond Times,* April 29, 2004.

Kuykendall, Lavonne. "Amex, Capital One Talk about the Future." *The American Banker,* June 7, 2004.

Smith, Geoffrey. "The Bill Comes Due for Capital One." *BusinessWeek,* November 4, 2002.

Wade, Will. "Coming Full Circle on E-Strategies." *The American Banker,* June 15, 2004.

Case: Providian

The credit card industry has changed in the decades since the 1960s when Bank of America flooded households with millions of cards. Today, trillions of dollars of transactions are paid with credit cards, with 1.2 billion in use in the United States alone. The average cardholder has 2.7 bank cards, 3.8 retail cards, and 1.1 debit cards for a total of 7.6 cards per person. Despite the huge variety, the top 10 issuers handled about 78 percent of the total value at the end of 2002. About 24 percent of all consumer retail transactions are paid with credit and debit cards (www.cardweb.com).

A huge percentage of the U.S. population already holds several credit cards, and banks are constantly competing to give more cards to high-income customers. To most observers, the market appears to be saturated. Customers will switch banks if one offers a better rate or different benefits. Providian Financial (PVN), a San Francisco–based company, looked at this market and decided to find a new niche: the subprime market. According to cardweb, approximately 25 percent of the population has weak credit ratings. The objective was to find low-income people with poor or no credit, offer them a credit card, and then charge huge fees and high interest rates. Shailesh Mehta, who eventually became CEO, developed a complex mathematical model that allowed the company to identify the subprime customers who would be most likely to use the cards, but not default on the loans. One executive characterizes the process as "we found the best of the bad." Since other banks refused to serve this market segment, Providian had solid growth rates and, despite the 24 percent and higher interest rates, was able to claim that it was providing a useful service to the customers. Eventually, other banks (notably Capital One and Household International) jumped into the market. By 2000, 20 percent of the cardholders were classified as subprime (cardweb), and Providian was the fifth largest card issuer in the nation (Koudsi 2002). In 2000, the company was ordered to pay $300 million in restitution for misleading, unfair, and deceptive business practices. To keep growing, the company had to find a new market. It failed in an experiment to go after the platinum market. So, it went after increasingly risky customers. By 2001, when the economy faltered, the subprime market felt the impact first, and the company saw its default rates jump—to a huge 12.7 percent. Amid claims of misleading accounting, the stock price plummeted 90 percent. Cardweb notes that 1.3 million cardholders declared bankruptcy in 2001—which generally erases unsecured credit card debt. Other banks focusing on the subprime market faced similar problems. Bernhard Nann of Fair Isaac, which evaluates consumer creditworthiness, notes that "data used in traditional behavioral models is not quite as powerful as we would like. We'd like to go and expand the universe of data that can be looked at to produce better predictions. That's particularly important in the subprime area." In particular, the company wants to include utility and rent payments in its calculations (Punch 2003).

With the economy improving in 2003 and 2004, Providian was able to sell off some of its loans and write off the really bad ones. The company also refocused its efforts to go after the middle market, people with a FICO score between 600 and 720 (Albergotti 2003). Although weak, the company was able to report a profit in late 2003 ("UBS" 2003). By 2004, some experts saw an improvement in the credit card industry profits. Many homeowners had already refinanced their mortgages—and paid down credit card debt. But, that leaves them free to increase the borrowing—hence increasing profits (Stovall 2004).

Yet with increasing competition for the platinum and midmarket segments, banks continue to search for ways to make money on credit cards. With low balances and low interest rates, and few new customers, banks turned to fees. Income from late fees and penalties was predicted to reach $13 billion for 2004, with total fees likely to account for 39 percent of revenue (Simon 2004). Providian joined in the parade and increased its fees annually. However, the company also created a "Real Rewards" program, where cardholders accumulate points for cash rebates that can also be used to offset late fees.

In 2004, Providian settled the accounting and insider-trading lawsuits for $65 million (Kuykendall 2004).

Questions

1. Why is the subprime market so risky and how does Providian use information technology to minimize the risks?

2. How are the platinum and midmarket accounts different from the subprime market, and can Providian use the same models?

3. How can Providian use information technology to increase its revenue from fees?

Additional Reading

Albergotti, Reed. "Fewer Credit-Card Solicitations Are in the Mail." *The Wall Street Journal,* November 5, 2003. http://www.cardweb.com/cardlearn/stat.html.

Koudsi, Suzanne. "Sleazy Credit." *Fortune,* February 19, 2002.

Kuykendall, Lavonne. "Providian Says It Can Move On after Settling Class Action for $65M." *The American Banker,* June 9, 2004.

Punch, Linda. "Subprime Cards, Act II." *Credit Card Management,* November 2003.

Simon, Ruth. "Credit-Card Fees Are Rising Faster; As Economics of Industry Change, Issuers Seek to Boost Income from Penalties; $35 Late Charge." *The Wall Street Journal,* May 31, 2004.

Stovall, Sam. "A Rising Rating for Consumer Finance." *BusinessWeek,* February 24, 2004.

"UBS Financial Cuts Providian to 'Neutral'." *BusinessWeek,* October 30, 2003.

Case: Merrill Lynch

For decades, Merrill Lynch (ticker: MER) was the premier brokerage firm. It led the industry in sales and innovations. The firm helped create hundreds of modern companies with its access to capital and the ability to sell stocks. In the 1970s and 1980s, its innovations in money market funds rocked the financial world and resulted in substantial changes to the federal banking laws. It accomplished many of these innovations through technology—and the recognition that money is really data. It expanded its reach overseas, and became the largest retail brokerage and the largest underwriter of stocks and bonds in the world. Through the stock market bubble of the 1990s, Merrill prospered—at least in terms of market share. They helped finance several start-ups, and retail stock brokerage revenues grew by $3 billion from 1996 to 1998. But the growth carried equally huge costs: only $100 million of that money made it to the bottom line. By 1998, Merrill's profit margins were 10 percentage points lower than its competitors. At the same time, the growth of online account management and discount brokerage firms had chipped away at the retail end of Merrill's operations. By 2001, even the directors knew that Merrill was in trouble and might not survive. Being the largest was not very useful if the company was not making money (Rynecki 2004). In 2001, the board made the surprising move of appointing Stan O'Neal, the CFO, to become the new CEO of Merrill. Recognizing the importance of profits, and seeing limits on the ability to increase revenue, he began focusing on cutting costs. Ultimately, he eliminated 24,000 jobs, including 20 percent of investment banking and analyst positions. He closed 300 field offices and completely pulled out of Australia, Canada, New Zealand, and South Africa. He reduced the number of stocks traded directly by the firm by 75 percent. He replaced almost all of the management from the top down—largely replacing them with younger staffers looking to make their marks. He reportedly often states that "ruthless isn't always that bad" (Rynecki 2004). The result: in 2003, the firm earned a record $4 billion in profit, and pretax margins reached 28 percent—vastly exceeding the high-growth years of the 1990s.

Despite the profitability, the firm still has to worry about revenue. In 2004, with the slow economy and shaky financial markets, Merrill ranked last in sales growth among the Newsday Top 100—with a three-year sales decline of 14.8 percent (Murray 2004). Merrill Lynch is refocusing its retail brokerage operations—on wealthy customers. The company pays higher interest rates to customers with balances over $10 million (McGeehan 2004). Merrill also jumped into the credit card market in 2004. The company realized that customers withdrew $3 billion from their accounts in 2003 to pay off credit card debt. Co-branded with MBNA, the card is designed to provide one-stop shopping for its customers. Merrill is targeting its wealthier customers—in an effort to provide more services, but also to keep control over a larger percentage of their money. The company is offering a variety of awards to entice customers to use them for large transactions (Lieber 2004).

Despite the renewed emphasis on cost, Merrill still has to handle business, and that requires technology. In 2003, the company began the first steps of a $1 billion upgrade to their broker workstation systems. The new Client 360 system is designed to be a total wealth-management tool—largely focused on customer relationship management. It is designed to provide a complete view of customer data to the broker. John Killeen, the chief technology officer, notes that "the tool suite around wealth management is pretty well established across the industry, still what will make this unique is that we are facilitating the relationships for our financial advisers with their clients. . . . It's a single-screen representation of the most important and most prevalent questions that a client may ask a financial adviser when they have them on the phone. It will talk to balances; it will talk to progress towards plans, and any important notices that affect that client. And within one or two clicks, we can drill down to greater and greater detail. It represents a huge productivity gain for our financial advisers" (Pallay 2004). Most of the front-end system being developed is installed by Thomson Financial, which is overseeing the integration of work from 400 vendors. The back-end system remains Merrill's proprietary system, largely running on Microsoft software. The company built a framework that separates the back-end and middle tier systems from the front end. This approach enables the company to alter various components on either end without having to rebuild the entire system. Despite the complexity of the project, Killeen's focus has been on the end-use applications: "I think the lynchpin around the tools will be client data—who has the greater understanding of the total client relationship, what is important to the client at the different phases of their financial life cycle, and how do we put all of that together so that our advisers are best positioned to work with their client?"

Questions

1. How can Merrill Lynch survive as a full-service broker, particularly with the regulatory changes in investment research?

2. How can Merrill Lynch use information technology to attract and keep the high-end investors that it wants?

3. How can the company use technology to reduce its costs and improve its profit margins?

Additional Reading

Lieber, Ron. "A New Contender for Your Wallet; Merrill Jumps into Card War with No-Fee Rewards Offer, but Does It Beat Platinum?" *The Wall Street Journal*, April 20, 2004.

McGeehan, Patrick. "Schwab Tells Less-Affluent Customers They Have to Pay More Than Richer Clients to Make Trades." *The New York Times,* May 26, 2004.

Murray, Christian. "Top 100; After a Low, Merrill Looking Up." *Newsday,* June 14, 2004.

Pallay, Jessica. "An Interview with Merrill Lynch's John Killeen." *Wall Street & Technology,* May 2004.

Rynecki, David. "Putting the Muscle Back in the Bull." *Fortune,* April 5, 2004.

Summary Industry Questions

1. What information technologies have helped this industry?

2. Did the technologies provide a competitive advantage or were they quickly adopted by rivals?

3. Which technologies could this industry use that were developed in other sectors?

4. Is the level of competition increasing or decreasing in this industry? Is it dominated by a few firms, or are they fairly balanced?

5. What problems have been created from the use of information technology and how did the firms solve the problems?

CHAPTER ELEVEN

Strategic Analysis

Chapter Outline

Introduction
The Competitive Environment
External Agents
   Buyers
   Suppliers
   Rivals, New Entrants, and Substitutes
   Government Regulations
IS Techniques to Gain Competitive Advantage
   Barriers to Entry
   Distribution Channels
   Switching Costs
   Lower Production Costs
   Product Differentiation and New Products
   Quality Management
   The Value Chain
The Search for Innovation
   Research
   Engineering and Design
   Manufacturing
   Logistics and Supply
   Marketing
   Sales and Order Management
   Service
   Management
Costs and Dangers of Strategies
   High Capital Costs
   When the Competition Follows
   Changing Industry
   Sharing Data
   Government Intervention
The Role of Economics
Entrepreneurship
Idea
   Strategy
   Research
Plan
   Strategy, Competition, and Market Analysis
   Forecasts, Cash Flow, and Investment
   Budget
   Marketing
   Organization and Timetable

Implementation
   Ownership Structure
   Financing
   Accounting and Benchmarks
   Flexibility
Starting an e-Commerce Firm
Summary
Key Words
Web Site References
Additional Reading
Review Questions
Exercises
Cases: The Airline Industry

What You Will Learn in This Chapter

- How can you use information technology to improve your organization and make it better than your competitors?
- How competitive is your world?
- What are the main factors affecting a firm's competitive advantage? Where do you begin looking for an edge?
- How can you use IT to gain a competitive advantage? Where do you begin your search?
- How can IT support the operations of the firm to provide a competitive advantage?
- Why is it so difficult to convince management to make strategic changes? What are the risks of strategic decisions?
- Why did so many dot-com firms fail? Do their failures mean there is no viable Internet strategy?
- How do you start a business? How do you start an online business?
- How will your business be different from the existing firms?
- How do you turn an idea into money?
- Is it true that genius is 1 percent inspiration and 99 percent perspiration?
- What additional steps are required to start an EC firm?

How can you use information technology to make your company better than your rivals? Delta is one of the original airlines in the United States. Only a handful of the original remain, and most of them, including Delta, are flirting with bankruptcy. Many of the airline executives blame September 11, 2001, the SARS scare of 2002–2003, and the oil price increases of 2003–2004 for their problems. But if you look at revenue and profits over time, it is clear that the big airlines were getting their butts kicked long before these events. The discount airlines, led by Southwest and joined by JetBlue and AirTrans, have been profitable over the last few years—because they have found a way to attract customers and hold down costs.

Discounters and upstarts are not new to the airline industry. In a classic case, American Airlines was able to drive away People Express in the early 1980s with its Sabre reservation system. American pioneered yield management—charging everyone on the plane different prices—trying to get as much money from each person as possible, meaning that businesses paid through the nose while tourists who book in advance get cheap seats. The advantage generated from this system was refined with frequent flier miles and kept American, Delta, and the others on top for 15 years. But Southwest, with a radically different strategy, has slowly grown to challenge the entire industry. Is there another rabbit in the hat for the big, traditional airlines? Can Delta find a new way to use information technology to save the day?

Introduction

How can you use information technology to improve your organization and make it better than your competitors? Can technology make your company the best in the industry? These questions are still being debated, but it is clear that in some cases information technology has provided the ability for companies to dramatically change industries. Figure 11.1 shows that all of these changes came about because the technology enabled firms to alter the business practices. The reengineering provided by the technology creates the benefits. It is critical that you remember that technology by itself is not a magic wand. Now, for the important question: How can you use information technology to find new opportunities and gain a competitive advantage? Strategy is particularly important if you want to start a new business. Starting a business requires an idea, a plan, and implementation. Starting an e-business adds several steps, including developing software and selecting an ISP.

In some ways, information systems designed for competitive advantage are not much different from transaction-processing and decision support systems. In many cases, advantages over your rivals can result from changes in the basic transaction-processing systems and business methods. The real difference with strategy lies in its goal: to change the way the business operates and gain an advantage over the other firms in the industry.

Creating strategic systems requires that you understand the entire firm and its relationships with external agents in the environment, such as suppliers, consumers, workers, and rivals. Many systems have been devised to help you analyze and create corporate strategies. A common thread in gaining a competitive advantage is to improve the ties and communication with suppliers and consumers. Electronic communication can provide automatic data collection, minimize errors, and create faster responses.

Information systems can provide a competitive advantage through increasing the barriers to entry and controlling distribution channels. Services from information systems can be used to differentiate your product from the others in the market or even to create entirely

TRENDS

Ideas and concepts for managing businesses are constantly changing. Many current practices are often traced to Alfred Sloan, who drove the consolidation and expansion of General Motors from 1920 to 1956. Management techniques evolve over time and ideas come from many sources. Through the 1950s, many companies focused on making production more efficient. In the 1950s and 1960s, U.S. firms expanded into wider markets, both nationally and internationally. In the 1970s, managers were preoccupied with the economic changes brought on by oil price rises and consequent shocks of high inflation and high interest rates. The 1970s and 1980s also saw the emergence of increased international competition—for example, between 1960 and 1985, U.S. imports as a percentage of GDP increased from 5.6 percent to 11.5 percent.

Despite these general trends, most companies find it difficult to change. As a result, as the business environment changes, a company might lose its focus or new competitors may appear. Periodically, executives need to examine the overall position of the firm to see whether there might be a better strategy or a new way to gain an advantage over rival firms. Michael Porter, in his book *Competitive Strategy: Techniques for Analyzing Industries and Competitors*, took the lead in showing executives how to reexamine their business and search for competitive advantages.

Through the 1960s and 1970s, the use of MIS was largely governed by its capabilities and the immediate needs of the organizations. The most common MIS objective was to save money and time by automating transaction-processing tasks. The projects were evaluated on the basis of how much money they could save. Eventually, managers came to realize that computer systems have other advantages. A new technology might enable the firm to provide better service to customers. The company that is the first implementer of a technology might find it easier to attract customers, giving it a competitive advantage over the other firms. For example, the first banks that installed ATMs to provide 24-hour access gained an advantage over their competitors. Warren McFarlan was one of the first writers to analyze how information technology could be used to gain a competitive advantage.

FIGURE 11.1

Strategies: Managers are increasingly being asked to find ways to give their firm an advantage over the competition. Information systems can help identify areas that can provide a competitive edge. Information systems can also directly provide services and advantages that are not offered by your rivals.

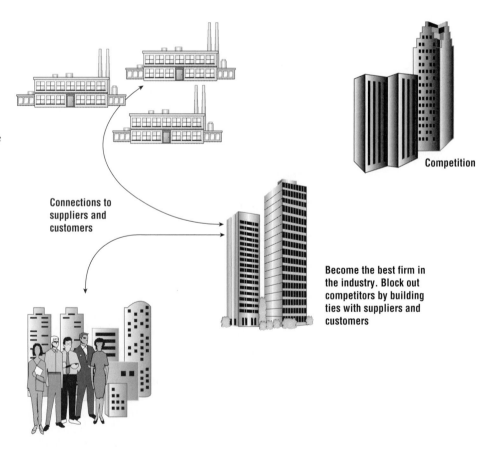

Connections to suppliers and customers

Competition

Become the best firm in the industry. Block out competitors by building ties with suppliers and customers

new products. Computer systems might give you an edge through low-cost production or improved quality management.

Designing strategic systems can be a dangerous task with many opportunities to fail. One complication is that development costs are high. Some strategic systems use new technology, which carries higher costs and a greater risk of incompatibilities and other prob-

REALITY BYTES | Business Trends

Business statistics indicate a clear trend toward the increased importance of service-oriented firms. Service firms are well suited to certain strategic uses of information systems. In particular, product differentiation, product quality, and new products are typically useful strategies. In many service industries, information is the primary product, so technology is especially valuable.

The financial industry provides several strategic examples, such as the Merrill Lynch *Cash Management Account,* ATMs, or new financial instruments created by brokers. Similarly, Federal Express uses tracking information to differentiate its service from its rivals' offerings. Likewise, the airlines used their reservation systems to give them a competitive advantage in transportation services.

lems. It is also important to remember that attempts to monopolize a market are illegal, and strategic systems can sometimes come close to breaking the antitrust laws.

The most difficult aspect of strategic systems is coming up with ideas that might give you an advantage. One way to get ideas is to see what firms in other industries have done. You never know when some of the techniques and tricks used by other companies might be useful to you.

The Competitive Environment

How competitive is your world? One of the important trends facing most businesses today is the increased level of competition. Improved telecommunications and faster delivery services mean that local firms face competition from regional, national, and international firms. Local firms have to compete against national mail-order companies, which offer wide selections, next-day delivery, and low prices. The Internet, home shopping channels, and toll-free phone numbers make it easier for consumers to compare prices, putting pressure on all firms.

Large national retailers and franchises put pressure on local stores. They also compete against themselves for market territories. Their size gives them leverage in dealing with manufacturers. By purchasing in large quantities, they can negotiate lower prices. Their high volume also makes it easier for them to buy from foreign producers.

Several international trends are creating increased competition. The international search for lower manufacturing costs puts pressure on firms to cut their costs. For instance, the Japanese have moved production to other Asian nations to build television sets. Decreasing trade barriers throughout the world also creates larger markets. As eastern European economies rebuild, as the European Union takes shape, and as Mexican incomes increase, consumers will be able to buy more products. Although the prospect of these increased sales is enticing to U.S. manufacturers, there are some complications. If a competitor becomes established first, it will be a stronger and tougher competitor in the United States. New firms will arise or expand in these international markets, giving them a stronger base to increase sales in the United States, providing for increased competition.

External Agents

What are the main factors affecting a firm's competitive advantage? Where do you begin looking for an edge? Competitive advantage can be gained by establishing or changing relationships between the firm and its **external agents.** External agents consist of suppliers, customers, rivals, potential new entrants, substitute products, and sometimes the government. Figure 11.2 portrays these relationships in Porter's **Five Forces model.** From a systems perspective, each of these entities is outside the control of the firm. Yet they strongly affect the company. Through improved ties to these agents, they become part of your system, which can be used to improve the competitive position of the firm.

FIGURE 11.2

Porter's Five Forces model: Strategies often involve external agents: customers, suppliers, competitors, the threat of new entrants, and substitute products.

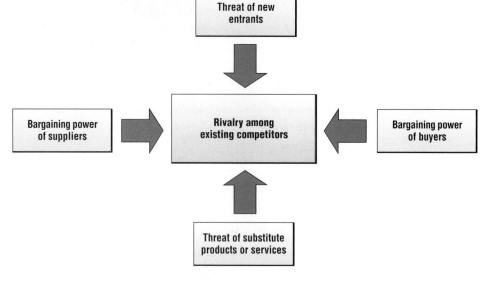

FIGURE 11.3

Production chain: Modern companies have ties to hundreds or thousands of entities. Sometimes a company will own several pieces of the production chain (vertical integration). Sometimes the company might expand horizontally by building related businesses. Each linkage requires communication and offers the possibility for strategic gain.

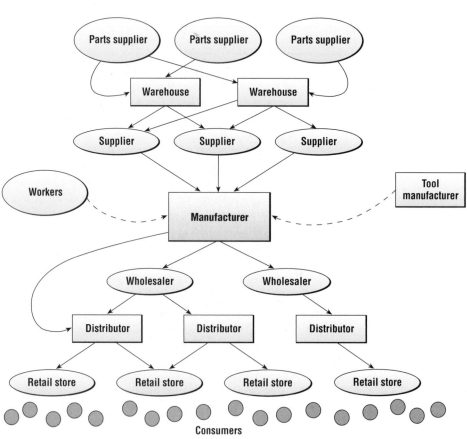

Buyers

Who are your customers? This famous question is used to highlight the issues in an industry. The answer might seem obvious, but many firms have layers of customers. To a retail outlet, customers are likely to be individual people. As shown in Figure 11.3, a large manufacturer may have several levels of customers, ranging from wholesale firms that buy in bulk, then sell to distributors, which deliver products to retailers, where the final customer purchases the product. Having more intermediate levels between the manufacturer and the customer can make it much harder to manage the firm. It also makes it more difficult to identify the needs of your customers—particularly when information from the various levels conflicts. For instance, an end consumer might want more features, while a retail store might want simpler products and fewer models to reduce stocking problems.

An important goal in any company is to satisfy the customers. If there are many layers of buyers between the company and the ultimate consumer, it can be difficult to determine what the customer wants. Similarly, the layers create delays that make it difficult for the retailer to order and obtain the products. For example, with older, slower manufacturing processes, merchants have to place most orders for the Christmas season around July—five or six months before the sales would occur. What happens if the economy changes or some event causes people to suddenly demand a different product? The retailer, manufacturer, and customers all suffer as a result of these long lead times.

A common strategic goal is to "get closer to the customers." Information systems can be used to strengthen the ties among the customers, manufacturers, and various intermediaries. For example, you could build electronic ordering systems, with terminals in the retail stores to capture current sales levels. The systems could also be used to send new product information to the customers, or collect feedback on various attributes, or provide immediate answers to questions from retailers and customers.

The issue of buyer's power is critical in Porter's model. For example, if you are a small company selling parts to General Motors, then you have little power in that relationship. So, you will need to look at the supplier side for strategic options.

Suppliers

Suppliers can provide individual parts, entire products, or even services (such as a bank that lends money). Three major issues involving suppliers are price, quality, and delivery schedules. Just as with customers, problems can arise when many layers of suppliers exist. For instance, increased layers can result in longer delays between ordering and delivery because the supplier has to contact its supplier, who contacts its supplier.

Quality management is also more difficult when there are several layers of suppliers. A fundamental element of **total quality management (TQM)** states that quality must be built into every process and item. Picture the problems that arise if quality is measured only in terms of the output at the manufacturer. When a defective product is found, there is no information about the cause. How can the problem be corrected? Managers need to know where each component came from and evaluate the quality as soon as possible. For instance, if there is a defective product, you could check each component to determine its original manufacturer. The manufacturer could be notified of problems, and you could search other items for similar defects. The manufacturer could use this data to identify problems with individual production lines.

Information systems can be used to build electronic ties to suppliers. Common uses of these systems include placing orders, tracking shipments, monitoring quality control, notifying partners of changes in plans, and making payments. Electronic links provide faster responses, better record keeping, and fewer errors. They also offer the potential strategic benefits described in the next section.

Rivals, New Entrants, and Substitutes

The goal of a strategic approach is to derive a competitive advantage over the **rivals,** or other firms in the industry. There could be many competitors or just a few larger rivals. The competition could take place in a small town, across a nation, or worldwide. One of the first steps in any strategic analysis is to identify the primary competitors and to assess their strengths and weaknesses. Is the industry rivalry intense with constant price movements and attempts to gain market share? Or do companies rarely adjust prices and are largely content to service existing customers?

One issue to remember about competition is that it never stops. Coming up with one strategic idea is not good enough. For example, American Airlines and United Airlines spent millions of dollars to build reservation systems as strategic systems. Today, all major airlines have access to these systems, and each airline must continually work to improve its

Problem: You need to identify locations and characteristics of your customers.

Tools: A geographic information system (GIS) helps you analyze and display relationships based on location. ESRI's ArcInfo and Microsoft's MapPoint are two leading products for displaying overlays of geographical information. ArcInfo is relatively expensive, but is widely used for large projects. MapPoint is not included with Office, but is affordable and demonstration copies are available. GIS software is designed to display basic maps, showing boundaries and major infrastructure items such as roads and rivers. You can choose the level of detail you want to see by zooming in or out. The critical feature of a GIS is the ability to display geo-coded data. Data is usually displayed using shading or differ-

ent circles or other icons. You can also overlay pie or bar charts in each location, but you need to keep the number of charts relatively low to remain readable.

Some common governmental data is available already encoded. For example, the census data is associated with various geographical levels including zip codes, counties, and states. Income is a common economic data item to display. The census data contains more obscure statistics, such as the percentage of adults who traveled on cruise ships in the last three years, and the percentage of households that spent more than $150 per week in a food store. The resulting map reveals clusters of customers. If these are your strategic target, then you should design advertising, distribution, and sales systems to these specific locations.

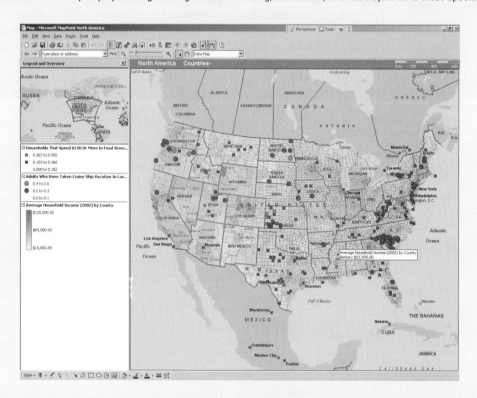

To further refine your strategies, you can add your own data, such as sales, factories, or competitor locations. Advanced systems also provide optimization routines that help select distribution routes.

One of the greatest strengths of a GIS is the ability to persuade others. Even if you already know the general relationships, a map is a powerful tool to convince executives. Instead of reading through pages of data, they can quickly see the spatial relationships on the map.

Quick Quiz:

1. How often does the U.S. Census Bureau update its data?

2. Why is location an important element in business decisions.

3. How many location-based pie charts do you think could be placed on a map?

system to provide new enticements to customers. Similarly, automobile companies designed computerized diagnostic systems to improve services offered by repair shops. Today, all of the manufacturers have essentially the same systems. In some cases, they might offer improvements over your ideas, which will put the originator at a disadvantage. However, the firm that first implements a new strategy can gain recognition and market share. It is important to remember that companies must continually improve and seek new opportunities.

A related issue is the concept of potential competitors or entrants in the business. In some cases, you might identify the major rivals, implement a strategy, and then immediately lose everything as new firms enter your business. Entrants might build their firms from scratch, such as the way Burger King built new stores in the same areas as McDonald's restaurants. Alternatively, other firms may increase the sales of products that are similar to your products. Substitute products are related economically by the degree to which consumers are willing to use one product instead of the other. A classic example comes from the late 1970s, when the U.S. economy faced high inflation rates and banks were subject to limits on the interest rates they could pay on deposits. Merrill Lynch, the stock brokerage firm, introduced a service enabling customers to store their money in a wide variety of financial instruments that paid significantly higher interest rates than checking accounts, and still write checks on the account. Many larger customers took their money away from banks and put it in these asset accounts. These new accounts were perceived as close substitutes for traditional bank services, and people transferred huge sums of money out of the banking system.

The key point is that you need to take a broad look at your firm and the industry. Know who your competitors are and how they operate. Are other products or services offered by other industries that might attract your customers? If you make a change in the way you do business, find out how it will affect your rivals. Determine how changes will alter the industry. Will they provide an opening for firms in other industries?

Government Regulations

In any economy, government intervention has a strong influence on the firm. There are myriad government agencies, regulations, taxes, and reports. The situation multiplies for multinational firms that are subject to the regulations of many nations. These agencies and regulations can have strong effects on the profitability of a firm. Generally, an individual firm has no control over government regulations, but sometimes suggestions can lead to modifications. For instance, it is now possible to submit some documents to government agencies in computer form. In fact, some reports (such as 10K or 10Q financial reports) are *required* to be filed electronically. Electronic forms can decrease your storage costs and make it easier to find documents that have been stored for long periods of time.

IS Techniques to Gain Competitive Advantage

How can you use IT to gain a competitive advantage? Where do you begin your search? These questions are difficult to answer. Keep in mind that your competitors are asking the same questions every day. Competitive advantage may be achieved with many techniques in business. Information technology is one area that may provide several opportunities. In general, MIS techniques may not be better than other methods. However, some firms have experienced considerable success from using these techniques, so they are well worth considering. Moreover, the rapid changes in technology often lead to competitive advantages if your firm is the first to find a creative use for the new technology. The other side of the coin is that untested new technologies may not work as planned. Hence, the pioneer is taking a risk: If the project fails, the development costs may put the firm at a competitive disadvantage.

The fundamental mechanisms for gaining competitive advantage are barriers to entry, switching costs, lower production costs, product differentiation, control over distribution channels, innovation, and quality control. These techniques are illustrated in Figure 11.4. The question we wish to examine is how information systems can take advantage of these techniques.

Barriers to Entry

A fundamental concept of economics is that in order to make extra profits, you need some mechanism to prevent other firms from entering the industry. Otherwise, as soon as your firm develops a strategy that pays higher returns, other firms will flock to the industry and drive the prices and profits down. Figure 11.5 summarizes the common **barriers to entry**.

REALITY BYTES   People Express Airlines (Classic Case)

In 1981, Donald Burr's People Express Airlines was the darling of the airline industry and American management. In four years the fledgling airline grew to a $2 billion company. People Express was cited in *In Search of Excellence* as an ideal American business because of its flat organizational structure and compensation plan that based reward on stock growth. All employees, whether "customer representatives" or pilots, were viewed as equally valuable to the company. Growth seemed to be unlimited and the airline could not process applications or reservations fast enough. Yet on January 18, 1985, People Express Airlines declared bankruptcy. Soon thereafter, the parts of the empire that Burr constructed were auctioned off and the routes redistributed.

The basic philosophy driving People Express was to make air travel available to everyone. At its peak, People's low fares brought thousands of students, the elderly, and the middle class through Newark, New Jersey. The waits were horrendous and the service was chaotic. Yet the $29 fare made the hassle worth it, particularly when the other airlines were charging five times as much. People's fairs allowed the carrier to book and fly full planes.

As long as the flights were full, the profits were easy to calculate: determine the price of the fuel and the equipment and employee cost per flight of the plane; determine a per flight fare that would provide a profit when the expenses were subtracted; and repeat this formula across the flight pattern. Keep the fares so low that the flight would always be booked. By developing the demand in this new market segment, Burr felt that he had found a formula for success that could not be broken.

This approach looked promising until American Airlines used its Sabre reservation system to implement "yield pricing." Through ad-

vance ticketing and other restrictions, American was able to discount seats that would otherwise have gone unsold because of People's low fares. The flying public now had a choice. They could continue to fly on People Express Airlines and deal with the chaos and the crowds, or they could make reservations and fly on American Airlines with comfort. Besides, they could fly directly and not go through Newark. The snack and soft drink were free. The remainder of the seats were sold at full price to business people who could not plan far enough ahead to make advance reservations.

People's vision was a good one. It centered on cost cutting and motivating the workforce. Certainly overexpansion and the lack of a marketing focus contributed to the failure of People Express. However, a third major factor was the failure to integrate technology into solving its business problems. Before its first plane left the ground, People Express decided not to duplicate American and United Airline's sophisticated reservation systems. Instead, the carrier opted for "a big, dumb computer" that stored passengers' names but could not do sophisticated pricing.

Another reason People Express shied away from technological development was that the airline lacked the internal expertise to build or even buy a reservation system. In 1983, the carrier contracted with NCR Corporation to build a system to handle yield management. After 18 months, the project failed. According to Burr, the failure was due to poor communication on both sides and a lack of management attention.

Source: Richard Pastore, "Coffee, Tea and a Sales Pitch," *Computerworld,* July 3, 1989, p. 1; Clinton Wilder, "Don't Blame the System," *Computerworld,* July 3, 1989, p. 42.

One way that information systems create barriers to entry is from their cost. Consider what happens when you create a new information system that provides additional services, like banks did with ATMs. Customers soon expect all firms to offer those services. If a new company wishes to enter the industry, it will have to spend additional money to buy the computers and create the systems to offer those services. The information system raises the cost of entering the industry. A classic example of this situation was the introduction of People Express Airlines in 1981. The CEO of People Express stated that he knew the airline needed a reservation system to compete effectively with other airlines, but after raising $100 million to start the airline, top management found it impossible to raise the additional $100 million needed to create the reservation system.

Computer systems might also be used to create more direct barriers to entry. For instance, as a manufacturer you could build a computer system that is tied to retail stores. The stores would use the system to place orders and to inquire about products, warranties, and delivery schedules. You might be able to forbid the stores from using the system to connect to any other manufacturers. If the stores gain advantages from the new system, they will end up placing more orders from you, and you will keep out potential competitors. However, you will have to be careful not to violate antitrust regulations.

Distribution Channels

Controlling **distribution channels** is a method of gaining competitive advantage that is similar to creating barriers to entry. The Japanese economy has long been a classic example of controlling distribution channels, although the role of information systems is mini-

FIGURE 11.4

Methods to gain competitive advantage: Examining the production chain highlights several useful techniques. Barriers to entry keep out potential competitors and substitutes. Ties to suppliers can cut costs, improve quality, and lock out competitors. Control over distribution provides stronger markets and keeps out competitors. Building ties to customers builds loyalty, improves products, and increases margins. Creating switching costs keeps customers loyal.

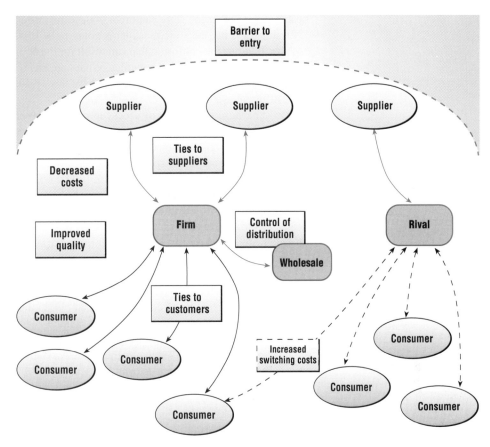

FIGURE 11.5

Several methods can build barriers to entry. Be careful. Many attempts to erect barriers are considered illegal under antitrust legislation.

Sources of Barriers to Entry
Economies of scale (size).
Economies of scope (breadth).
Product differentiation.
Capital requirements.
Cost disadvantages (independent of size).
Distribution channel access.
Government policy.

mal. In Japan, sales relationships are developed over long periods of time, and companies have many interrelationships and ties. In particular, distribution of products from manufacturers to retailers is controlled by a few large companies that are loosely organized into support groups (keiretsu). If you want to sell products in Japan, you must build a relationship with one of these companies. American executives have often complained about the problems they experience in dealing with these distributors, which creates a barrier to selling U.S. products in Japan. Although there is disagreement on the cause of the problems, the ability to control distribution channels can be an effective strategy for maintaining market share and deterring rivals. The distributors gain power through their close personal ties to the customers. For example, in Japan, most new automobiles are sold by salespeople who call on customers at their homes.

Information systems can be used to control distribution channels. As a manufacturer, you could build a computer link to the retail stores. In addition to providing faster ordering and more information, you encourage the store to order directly from your company and avoid competitors. For example, Levi Strauss, the jeans manufacturer, has installed such a system in some retail chains. Assume that you work for a competitor and you call on the retail store to convince the buyers to carry your products. Probably the first question you will be asked is whether the store can order your jeans through the Levi Strauss computer link. If the answer is no, the store manager is going to be less willing to buy your products.

Now, imagine the confusion that can result for the poor retail manager who wishes to sell similar products from three companies. What happens if each company has its own private computer link? Does the manager need to have three different computer terminals and learn three different systems?

Partly because of the loss of access to distribution channels and partly because of the confusion resulting from having multiple systems, attempts are being made to standardize some electronic relationships. An important component of electronic data interchange (EDI) is to define standards so that managers have to work with only one system and everyone has reasonable access to that system. If EDI does become standardized, there will be fewer opportunities to control distribution channels with information systems. However, businesses might still be able to gain a competitive edge by providing better, more sophisticated electronic services through the links. For example, expert systems might be used to provide faster responses to retailer and consumer questions.

One of the interesting aspects of the Internet is its ability to alter traditional distribution channels. In particular, the Internet could eventually become the major distribution system for digital data such as books, music, software, and videos. Some traditional organizations fear this change as a loss of control. For example, in the U.S. music industry, a handful of firms have controlled the production and distribution of most music. In 1998, the firms attempted to stop the expansion of digital music (e.g., MP3 format), but the courts did not support this interference. Consequently, it is now relatively easy for anyone to create music in a commercial format and distribute it cheaply over the Internet. The same industry-altering effects can occur within the book industry—if a standard digital reader ever becomes acceptable.

Switching Costs

An interesting strategic capability of information systems is their ability to create **switching costs** for your consumers. Consider the case of a brokerage firm that creates a system that enables you to manage your accounts with your personal computer. You buy and sell financial instruments and write checks against your account. The computer automatically tracks your portfolio, notifies you of major changes, and automatically sweeps uninvested cash into interest-bearing assets. At the end of the year, it prints a complete summary of your transactions for tax purposes.

Now, what happens if another broker offers you the same capabilities? Will you switch to a new firm? You might, but it depends on what other incentives the company offers. If everything else is the same, most people would be reluctant to change since they incur costs to switch. For example, you would have to learn how to use the new system. Besides, you would have to reenter your investment data and program new reports and graphs. If you are one of the first firms to create a new system, the deterrence of switching costs can be a powerful tool to maintain your market share. Figure 11.6 summarizes the tools to create competitive advantages as practiced by companies in the classic cases.

Lower Production Costs

In some cases, an effective strategy is to become the lowest-cost producer. If you can consistently sell your product for lower prices than your competitors do, you will have an important advantage. However, consumers need to believe that your products are as good as the competition's.

Computer systems have long been used to decrease costs. Transaction-processing and accounting systems decrease administrative costs. Robots and process-control systems can be used to control manufacturing costs. Inventory systems are used to track parts and reduce inventory ordering and holding costs. Marketing systems might be used to create better target marketing, with the advantages of improved response and lower marketing costs. Financial systems that control investments and cash flow also can result in decreased costs.

REALITY BYTES — Merrill Lynch Cash Management Account (Classic Case)

Until the 1970s, banks and other financial institutions were treated differently by the government than stock brokers such as Merrill Lynch. Financial institutions could not sell stocks, and there were limits on interest rates that could be paid to depositors. Brokerage companies focused on investments in stocks. In this environment, Merrill Lynch created its *Cash Management Account* (CMA). For a minimum sum of $25,000, investors could open a new account with Merrill Lynch. The account was similar to a bank account. The money could be placed in risk-free government bonds or it could be used to purchase stocks and bonds. The money could be obtained with minimal problems, including writing checks against the account. In short, the CMA became a bank account for medium and large investors. The primary advantage to the CMA over traditional bank accounts was that there were no government restrictions on the interest rates. As commercial interest rates rose in the late 1970s and early 1980s, huge sums of money left the banking industry and were deposited in the CMA.

Merrill Lynch used its information system to offer additional features, such as automatic transfers between accounts, overnight repurchases and sales of government bonds, and automatic investments and sales of stocks. All the investment options were controlled by individual investors. Banks could not offer these services because of governmental restrictions, and other brokerage firms did not have the information systems. This use of information technology gave an advantage to Merrill Lynch.

While Merrill Lynch was not known for other innovations, it is one of the largest financial institutions in the United States with a balance sheet comparable to Citicorp's. In 1995, the brokerage firm had 44,000 employees and operated in 31 countries. The 1994 profit amounted to 18.6 percent return on equity.

FIGURE 11.6

Classic cases: Several classic cases illustrate some important methods of acquiring a competitive advantage. Understanding these cases will help you identify potential strategies in other situations. They will also help you communicate with IS professionals.

Gaining a Competitive Advantage

Barriers to Entry
The additional costs of creating a sophisticated information system make it harder for firms to enter the industry. Classic case: People Express.

Distribution Channels
Control over distribution prevents others from entering the industry. Case: Napster.

Switching Costs
Consumers are reluctant to switch to a competitor if they have to learn a new system or transfer data. Classic Case: Baxter Healthcare.

Lower Production Costs
Using technology to become the least-cost producer gives an advantage over the competition. Classic case: Wal-Mart.

Product Differentiation
Technology can add new features to a product or create entirely new products that entice consumers. Classic cases: Federal Express and Merrill Lynch.

Quality Management
Monitoring production lines and analyzing data are important aspects of quality control. Improving quality leads to more repeat sales. Classic case: Digital Equipment Corp.

The Value Chain
Evaluating the entire production process identifies how value is added at each step. Combining steps or acquiring additional stages of the value chain can lead to greater profits. Case: Boeing Information Systems.

Product Differentiation and New Products

Another strategic use of information systems is the ability to create new or different products. If you can add features to your product so that consumers believe it is different from the competition, you will be able to make more money.

A classic case of using technology to create a new product is portrayed by Merrill Lynch.

A classic case of using information systems to modify a product for competitive advantage came from Federal Express—an overnight package delivery company. Federal Express was the first major delivery company to track individual packages. The service places bar codes on every package and scans them every time the package is moved. By storing this

REALITY BYTES   FedEx vs. UPS Part 1

UPS delivers 13.6 million packages a day. FedEx handles 6 million. In both cases, operating efficiently is a critical aspect of holding costs down and reducing delivery times. FedEx began by focusing on next-day deliveries and has gradually expanded through acquisitions into ground deliveries. UPS began with ground deliveries with an emphasis on reduced costs and has expanded into next-day deliveries. Both use technology, but in different ways. FedEx has been on the leading edge of network technologies, including wireless ties to the drivers. Both developed nationwide wireless connections to drivers in the 1980s, but now that wireless technology is commercially available, they are both switching to standards-based systems. For example, FedEx deployed wireless networking (801.11b) as soon as it was available in 1999. FedEx deploys technology as soon as it can show a return on investment. UPS takes a slower approach and cycles its technologies every five to seven years, phasing in the new technologies as they become more stable. Consequently, UPS did not begin installing wireless networks until 2004. FedEx is now looking for ways to make additional information available to drivers through wireless technology. For example, customers might ask questions about packaging rules or report procedures. Currently, drivers have to return to the truck and look up the details in a book. Both FedEx and UPS are working at embedding GPS units to reroute delivery trucks if a customer calls with a last-minute pickup request. Wireless technology is also heavily used in the distribution centers. Human sorters wear ring scanners that capture the bar code data and send it back to the central computer over wireless connections. UPS is switching to a newer Symbol Technologies where the ring scanner has a Bluetooth wireless connection to a transmitter on the sorter's waist—eliminating the cables that get caught as the person loads a box.

Source: Adapted from Galen Gruman, "UPS vs. FedEx: Head-to-Head on Wireless," *CIO*, June 1, 2004.

data in a central database, Federal Express employees can tell customers exactly where any package is located. Besides decreasing the number of lost packages, this system provides a new service for customers. Nervous customers can use the information to determine when a package will be delivered. The information system tracks the current location of each package. When the system was created it provided a unique service to customers. To consumers, Federal Express is offering not just package delivery but also information on the location of the package. This **product differentiation** will help attract customers and might allow the company to charge higher prices.

In some cases, information systems can be used to create entirely new products or services. For example, many banks offer "sweep accounts" to customers who place large sums of money in their bank accounts. There are variations, but the purpose of a sweep account is to automatically place money into higher-interest-bearing assets. For instance, you might need cash available during the day to cover any withdrawals. But if you do not make major withdrawals at night, the bank could lend your money to someone for overnight use. The bank needs a sophisticated information system to keep track of which customers are participating, monitor what limits they have imposed, and automatically transfer the money to the borrower's accounts. (As a side note, you might wonder who wants to borrow money for just one night. There are many possibilities, but two major players are governments and large banks. Some interesting international possibilities also arise by lending across time zones.) Customers receive more interest, borrowers have access to more funds, and banks make money on the transaction fees and interest differentials. These accounts can be provided only by investing in new information systems.

Quality Management

Firms can gain a competitive advantage by offering higher-quality products. Through the 1980s, surveys indicated that owners reported fewer problems with automobiles manufactured by Japanese firms compared with those produced by U.S. manufacturers. This difference in quality gave the Japanese firms a competitive advantage. Similarly, Motorola is one of the leading proponents of total quality management. The company is constantly encouraging its suppliers to work at improving quality through the entire manufacturing process.

Information systems have a role in improving quality management. For starters, they can be used to collect data about quality measures. If quality measures come directly from production machines, there can be an overwhelming amount of data. In other cases, quality measures might be collected electronically from your suppliers. Collecting data seems like an obvious idea, but the huge amount of data complicates the process. In many cases, manufacturers have trouble identifying the original source when a component fails. Often, just knowing which suppliers cause the most problems is a useful step in quality management. This data can also help the supplier. Failure data can be used by the supplier to pinpoint the source of problems. Since 1992, nations in the European Union (EU) have been requiring firms to improve quality by complying with the statements in the ISO 9000 (International Organization of Standards) directive. ISO 9000 requires companies to measure quality at all stages of production. Any firm that wishes to sell products or parts to firms in the EU must build an information system to monitor quality and provide information to customers.

No machine is perfect. There is always an element of error in the output. The difficult part is to determine which errors imply that the machine needs to be readjusted. Decision support systems can be used to improve quality. **Statistical quality control (SQC)** is an important tool. Several statistical calculations and graphs are used to determine whether fluctuations are purely random or represent major changes that need to be corrected.

Expert systems can also be employed to control errors and locate the source of the problems. Consider a production line that has 50 major machines. In addition, several hundred parts are purchased from external suppliers. The final product has thousands of parts and hundreds of assembly operations. Total quality management requires that quality be monitored at each step of the process. A typical problem facing a machine operator is that a machine might stray off the baseline and need to be corrected. The operator faces several questions, such as: Which adjustment should be made? Should we overcorrect to compensate for the prior errors? Was the problem caused by this machine, or did earlier operations contribute? If corrections are made now, how will they affect other machines down the line? An experienced operator might be able to answer some of these questions. On the other hand, an expert system might be helpful at solving the more complex problems. Digital used expert systems to improve quality and cut the cost of installing minicomputers. Digital's weak performance in the 1990s also illustrates the difficulty in maintaining a competitive advantage as the market changes.

The Value Chain

One method of searching for areas that might provide you with strategic benefits is to examine the entire **value chain** of the industry. As shown in Figure 11.7, the key feature of a value chain is to examine each step of production and determine how value is added at each step. If some steps show larger increases in value than others, they will be key points to target for strategic action. The second objective of value chain analysis is to encourage

FIGURE 11.7

Value chain: The value chain illustrates the essential operations in a business. Every firm has operations for purchasing, production, shipping, marketing, and customer service. These processes are supported by the organization of the firm, human resources management, technology development, and procurement services. Providing services desired by customers contributes to the profit margin of the firm.

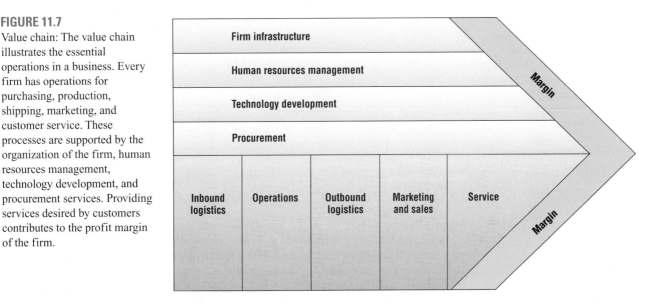

decision makers to examine the bigger picture in the industry. In many cases, a firm can benefit by expanding its operations beyond its traditional activities. For instance, an automobile manufacturer (Ford) might buy a car rental agency (Hertz). Now the manufacturer can control a large consumer of its products and control the sale of the used vehicles.

The Search for Innovation

How can IT support the operations of the firm to provide a competitive advantage? Industry and academic leaders are constantly searching for ways to improve organizations and gain a competitive advantage. Illustrated by Figure 11.8, one method to organize the search is to examine the primary processes of the firm: research, engineering and design, manufacturing, logistics and supply, marketing, sales and order management, service, and general management. Each of these processes has its own inputs, outputs, and objectives. Analyzing them in detail enables managers to spot problems and to search for innovative opportunities.

The following sections present general ideas for each of these processes that have generated interest and some success. Most of them use technology to improve the process or to help the processes work together better. Keep in mind that in any firm, there can be many ways of improving processes. Relying on information technology is not always the best answer.

Just coming up with a new corporate strategy is difficult, but it is not enough. As indicated by Figure 11.9, an effective strategic plan must also describe the changes in the process, identify the new data needs, and describe how the information system will be changed to support the new strategy. Figure 11.10 summarizes the capabilities of IT to support innovation.

Research

Research in firms varies enormously depending on the industry and the overall corporate strategy. At a minimum, most firms at least have a product development team that is constantly searching for new products or improvements in existing products. Some companies—such as 3M, DuPont, AT&T, and Intel—spend considerable sums of money on basic research to create entirely new products. To these firms, strategic advantage comes from being the leader in the industry with a constant cycle of new products.

IT support for research takes the form of computer analysis and modeling, statistical analysis of data, project management and budgeting, and workgroup technologies that make it easy for researchers to collaborate and share information with each other and with managers throughout the company.

FIGURE 11.8

Process innovation: Production consists of the processes of supply logistics, manufacturing, and sales management. These processes are directly supported by design, engineering, and marketing. Research and customer service support all of the processes; top management organizes and controls the firm. Technology can provide innovations in all of these processes.

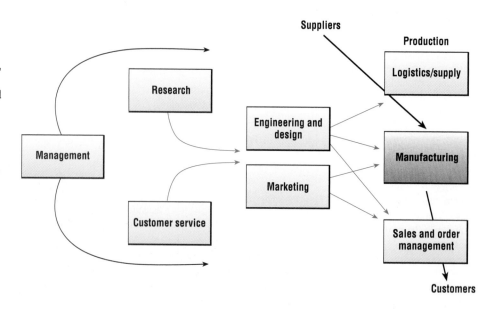

FIGURE 11.9

Developing strategies: Market measures and firm performance measures are used to highlight problems and opportunities. Corporate strategies are developed from process improvements and innovations. Potential strategies are evaluated and prioritized. Processes are reengineered and new systems are designed and implemented.

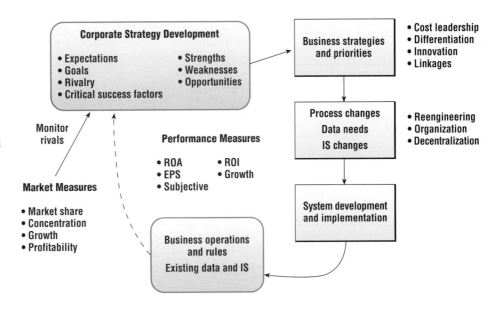

FIGURE 11.10

The search for innovation: Information technology provides many opportunities for improving the fundamental business processes. IT is used to improve communication, decrease costs, reduce design times, monitor customers and rivals, and improve customer service.

Area	Information Technology Support
Research	Analysis and modeling, project management, workgroup support, databases, decision support.
Engineering and design	CAD/CAM, testing, networks, workgroup support.
Manufacturing	Mass customization, links from customers and suppliers, robotics, quality monitoring, expert systems for maintenance, production databases, business integration tools.
Logistics and supply	Just-in-time linkages, forecasts, models, links for design, transaction processing.
Marketing	Frequent buyer databases, target market and media analysis, survey design and analysis, multimedia promotion design, links between customers and design teams.
Sales and orders	Portable computers for salesperson contact, expert systems for order customization and configuration, workgroup tools for customer support.
Service	Phone support systems, location monitoring and scheduling of service people, expert system diagnostics, databases.
Management	Enterprise information systems, links to service providers (accountants, consultants, etc.), e-mail, bulletin boards, decision support systems, personal productivity tools, workgroup support.

Engineering and Design

Engineering and design processes are responsible for converting theoretical research into new products. Engineers establish manufacturing procedures, design new equipment, and coordinate suppliers with production. In particular, the design process must optimize the production line to minimize costs and retain high quality.

Support for engineering and design takes the form of CAD/CAM systems that make it easy to create, modify, store, and share new designs. If these systems are coupled to integrated design databases, engineers can more easily reuse prior results. Tying into production databases enables the engineers to model and test various aspects of their designs. Engineers can also be supported with expert systems that help them analyze production aspects of their designs. As General Motors engineers design new cars, software helps them improve the layout to simplify production and to use existing components. Engineers are also being supported by workgroup technologies that make it easy to share designs and receive input from teams of workers throughout the company.

REALITY BYTES   Musical Balance of Power

The music and entertainment industry is somewhat unique. Consumers have faced the power of the record companies in the death of peer-to-peer file sharing (aka stealing music). But why do the record companies still exist? At one point, they exercised control over the old distribution channels. But today, anyone can create a decent song or collection of songs and have them professionally produced and distributed on the Internet. But how does anyone find those songs? Marketing, particularly through radio play, is a critical element. Changing FCC rules are resulting in a shift in power within the music industry. Clear Channel Communications, Inc., with 1,200 stations, is the largest holder of radio stations in America. And they are using that clout. In the industry, the radio stations have to pay the record companies (and artists) every time they play a song. But the radio stations get to choose which songs to play. In 2002, Clear Channel brought in 27 pop-radio programmers for meetings. A perfect opportunity for record companies to pitch new artists. Clear Channel allowed record companies in—but only if they sponsored lunch of cocktails to the tune of $40,000. Direct payola (payments to play specified songs) was banned after scandals in the 1950s and 1960s. But record companies still hire independent promoters who find legal ways to encourage stations to play their songs. Record labels say that they pay about $250,000 per song and sometimes as much as $1 million to get airplay. Some promoters, like Jeff McClusky & Associates in Chicago, have locked up exclusive access to programmers at some of the biggest stations. Another, Bill Scull of Tri-State Promotions in Cincinnati, notes that "because of the size of the radio groups, the power has shifted and record companies now feel like they're not getting full value."

Source: Adapted from Anna Wilde Mathews and Jennifer Ordonez, "Record Labels Say It Costs Too Much to Get Radio Play," *The Wall Street Journal*, June 10, 2002.

Manufacturing

There are four key features to production: costs, speed or timing, quality, and flexibility. Competing through lower costs and higher quality is a time-honored means of gaining a competitive advantage. It might not be sufficient today. Increasingly, firms are turning to **mass customization** in an attempt to gain market share. Twenty or thirty years ago, the large firms in an industry were content to build huge plants, gain economies of scale, and aim at the mass market. This approach tended to leave niches open for competing firms. The problem with this strategy is that it allows rival firms to gain a toehold, which they might use to build market share and eventually compete directly against your primary market. Today's firms are trying to shift production fast enough so that they can cover virtually all of the niche markets.

Mass customization requires an IT system that links the sales system directly to the production line and through to supply. It also involves heavy use of robotics that are configurable directly from one computer. Other uses of IT include expert systems for maintenance and diagnostics. Japanese firms have long been proponents of preventive maintenance. If you wait until a machine breaks, it is too late. Expert systems can be used to schedule routine maintenance and spot problems before they cause problems. IT systems are also heavily used to monitor quality and suggest improvements.

Logistics and Supply

The implementation of just-in-time (JIT) inventory systems is largely credited to Japanese manufacturers. Today they are used by manufacturers worldwide. Manufacturers attempt to cut costs by holding minimal inventories. Instead, inventories are maintained by the suppliers, who deliver the products to the assembly line just as they are needed. The system can work only if the suppliers and factories are linked electronically—often there is only a one- or two-hour delay between ordering and delivery.

Suppliers are often involved in the design phase. Their knowledge is useful in identifying supply availability, costs, and substitutability of components. Sometimes, it is difficult to locate suppliers for equipment. Computer networks such as IndustryNet help firms connect with potential suppliers and identify equipment, parts, and prices.

Marketing

A well-known application of IT to improve marketing is the use of frequent-buyer databases that identify major customers. More traditional point-of-sale transaction systems can be

REALITY BYTES   Disintermediation

The story of Dell Computer has been told so many times it has taken on mythical elements. Dell rose to the top of the industry by focusing on direct sales using the Internet and building each product to order, while taking advantage of supply chain efficiencies. But a big part of the story involves the elimination of the middleman and traditional retail channels. But it turns out that Dell is unique. Most manufacturers prefer to keep the existing distribution system. Retail stores add value—by purchasing in bulk and by dealing directly with the customer. Still, the Internet raises problems for these traditional manufacturers. Maytag, the appliance manufacturer in Newton, Iowa, gets 400,000 visitors a month to its Web site. Yet the company does not want to undercut sales at the 10,000 retail stores. Instead, the company found a way to sell products through the Web site but still involve the local store. Shoppers read the detailed literature and select their appliances. When they check out, based on their zip code, the site recommends the closest retailers and checks on price and availability. Shoppers then arrange delivery with the local store.

Source: Adapted from Michael Totty, "The Dell Myth," *The Wall Street Journal,* September 16, 2002.

leveraged by identifying preferences and rapidly spotting patterns or trends. At the tactical level, expert systems are used to help analyze data and perform statistical trend analysis. Geographic information systems are being used by leading firms to identify patterns and possibilities for new sales. Information systems can also be used to link firms more closely to external marketing firms for research data, communication, and development of promotional materials.

Multimedia tools are being used by leading firms to develop initial ideas for advertising and promotional campaigns. Companies such as General Motors are also using video tools and computer dissemination of video to link customers and marketing departments closer to the design team.

Sales and Order Management

Sales and order management are often handled simply as an operations or transaction-processing area. However, in the last 10 years, several firms have used technology to gain a competitive advantage by improving the way they handle sales and orders. Frito-Lay's use of handheld computers is a classic example. The systems enable managers to more closely track their own sales, sales of competitors, and other external factors, because salespeople can enter data immediately. For certain industries, the concept can be extended further to installing workstations at the customer sites that tap into your central databases. Federal Express and Baxter Healthcare both used this technology to gain a leadership position.

Leading firms are also using expert systems to assist customers in choosing the products and options that best match their needs. These systems assist order takers and improve sales by matching customer needs. Expert systems are similarly used to improve configuration and shipping.

Workgroup technologies, e-mail, and expert systems all combine to give more power to the frontline workers dealing directly with customers. Resolving problems and meeting customer needs faster improve customer satisfaction and cut costs.

Service

Service industries and service-based processes (like accounting, MIS, and law) have their own problems and opportunities. Technology is used to support services with on-site, portable computers. These systems enable workers to have complete access to information almost anywhere in the world. Leading companies are building specialized databases to support their service workers, such as the "answer line" databases that support General Electric and Whirlpool customer service representatives.

Systems are built that monitor locations of service personnel, enabling firms to identify the closest workers to problems and to fine-tune schedules throughout the day. Complex products are increasingly being sold with internal diagnostic systems that automatically notify service departments. Similarly, companies are cutting costs and reducing repair time by building expert systems to diagnose problems.

REALITY BYTES   FedEx vs. UPS Part 2

In 2001 UPS expanded its operations by acquiring Mail Boxes, Etc. This purchase gave UPS a presence in thousands of neighborhoods across the United States. In 2003, FedEx announced that it was acquiring Kinko's. The ultimate goal in both cases is tighter access to the small and medium business (SMB) sector. Since Kinko's also operates in 10 countries with 100 international locations, the purchase gives FedEx broader reach into international markets. Because FedEx had an ongoing relationship with Kinko's since 1988, operating full-service counters in 134 stores, the immediate effect on sales will likely be minor. Some analysts were concerned that the benefits would be too limited. Alan Graf Jr., chief financial officer at FedEx, responded that "I guarantee you we're going to get a high return on our investment here." FedEx officials added that the deal would increase delivery volumes as well as broaden the company's mix into photo-copying, computer rentals, and large-format printing for banners.

Source: Adapted from Betsy McKay and Rick Brooks, "FedEx Will Buy Kinko's for $2.4 Billion in Cash," *The Wall Street Journal*, December 30, 2003.

Management

One of the more dramatic IT support mechanisms for management is an executive information system. Giving top managers better access to data allows them to identify and correct problems faster. More sophisticated models can be built to examine alternatives—especially to analyze the potential reactions of rivals in a competitive situation.

Larger firms are building electronic links to their strategic partners, for instance, by providing electronic access to corporate data to accounting and legal firms. These links enable the external partners to keep a closer eye on the firm, speeding the identification of problems and assisting them in spotting broad patterns and opportunities.

Executives are also increasingly turning to electronic conferencing tools and workgroup software, even e-mail. Executives can cover more areas and deal with more people with these systems than they can by phone or through face-to-face contact. Some studies have shown that, in traditional conversations, managers spend as much as 50 percent of the time on personal chitchat. Electronic systems (although they might be less personal) tend to be more efficient. On the other hand, some companies have been restricting employee access to electronic networks (especially the Internet) because they waste too much time on personal communications.

Another approach taken by management is the move toward standardization: the effort to make all jobs similar, routine, and interchangeable. By reducing jobs to their most basic level, they become easier to control and easier to support or replace with information technology. Franchises make good use of this concept. At the same time, management jobs in some companies are being reformulated as teams of knowledge workers. In the past, managers worked on fixed tasks within the corporate hierarchy. Today, you are more likely to be hired for your specific skills and knowledge. As the needs of the company change, you will work with different teams at solving problems and creating new products and services. Personal computers and client-server technologies are often used to support these management teams. Instead of relying on one central computing facility, each team has its own set of resources, which are shared over networks throughout the company.

Costs and Dangers of Strategies

Why is it so difficult to convince management to make strategic changes? What are the risks of strategic decisions? Strategic uses of information systems can be seductive. There are many interesting cases in which companies have created innovative information systems. Inventing strategic alternatives requires a considerable amount of creativity. It is easy to get caught up in the excitement of designing new approaches and to forget about the risks. Evaluation of any project requires weighing the risks against the potential gains. Although it is often difficult to measure the potential gains and risks, it is important to consider all consequences. By their nature, strategic changes can alter the entire course of the

FIGURE 11.11

Implementing strategy can be difficult, costly, and time consuming. Firms generally choose one primary strategy and then build the resources and shape the organization to best support that strategy.

Strategy	Skills and Resources Required	Organizational Requirements	Risks
Differentiation	• Strong marketing. • Product engineering. • Basic research skills. • Distribution channel acceptance and cooperation.	• Internal coordination, R&D, production, and marketing. • Incentives for innovation. • Resources to attract creative and skilled labor.	• Competitors imitate. • Customers do not accept differences. • Cost is too high.
Cost leadership	• Continued capital investment. • Process engineering. • Continuous quality improvement. • Tight supervision of labor and costs. • Products designed for low-cost production. • Low-cost distribution.	• Tight cost control. • Frequent, detailed control reports. • Highly structured organization. • Incentives based on quantitative measures.	• Competitors imitate. • Technology changes. • Lose production or distribution advantage.
Customer–supplier links	• Influence with partners. • Communication channels. • Standards or agreements.	• Flexibility to respond to customers. • Service culture. • Ability to adapt to emergencies.	• Security threats. • Changing standards. • Competitors copy with more links.

firm. Figure 11.11 summarizes the skills, organizational effects, and risks involved with several strategies.

Robert Morison and Kirtland Mead ("A Hard Look at Strategic Systems" 1989) pointed out that it is easy to misinterpret the various classic cases regarding strategic use of technology. For example, in many cases, the true strategy does not lie in the computer system; instead, the gains came from changing the way the business operates. For instance, the gains experienced by American Hospital Supply (Baxter Healthcare) came about because they improved the way their customers (hospitals) handled supplies and inventory. The computer system facilitated this change but was not necessarily responsible for it. In other words, rather than search for a *killer* strategic computer system, it is wiser to identify ways to improve the overall business.

High Capital Costs

One of the important considerations in strategic analysis is the cost. Strategic changes often involve implementing new technology before any of your competitors. Yet new technology tends to carry high costs. Manufacturers of technology may not have reached economies of scale, and they might have monopoly power over prices through patent rights. Furthermore, the IS teams will have less experience with the technology, so it will take longer to implement and may result in missteps and require additional testing. For instance, Morison and Mead (1989) report that "it took six years and $350 million before American Airlines' Sabre travel agency reservation system started paying off." As Figure 11.12 implies, these costs might take away money from other projects.

It can be difficult to estimate the cost of major projects, especially when they involve new technologies. There are many examples of MIS projects going over budget and beyond

FIGURE 11.12

Dangers of strategy: When developing and choosing strategies, you must always remember that innovations can be risky and often carry high capital costs. Although it may be exciting to spend millions of dollars on technology, it can destroy the firm if you do not have enough resources to support research and operations.

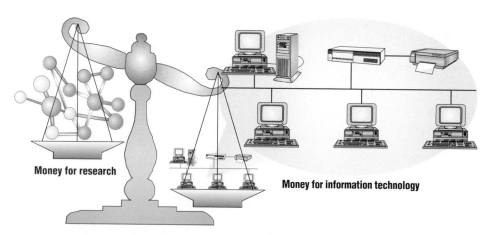

Money for research

Money for information technology

deadlines. Moreover, strategic projects often require major capital outlays up front, but increased revenues do not appear until much later.

A big question with new technology is trying to decide when it should be implemented. There is an inherent conflict. If you offer an innovative service from the technology before your competitors, you can gain a competitive advantage. However, if you wait, the costs will be lower. In making this decision, you will also have to guess what action your competitors will take.

When the Competition Follows

Another difficulty with strategic systems is that much of the advantage comes from creating a service that is not offered by your rivals. Once you introduce the service, your rivals will watch the customer response closely. If the customers begin to switch to your firm, your rivals will undoubtedly create a system to offer the same services. At that point, you lose most of the competitive advantage. Even worse, you might end up with an escalating "war" of technology. Although the competition is good for the customer, the increased expenditures can cause problems for the company if the ideas do not work as well as you expected.

The gains to technology occur from when you first implement the strategy to the point that your rivals follow. For example, almost all of the major overnight delivery services now provide the ability to track shipments. If the system is easy to create, you may not gain much. However, it is likely that customers who switched to your firm will stay, so you can gain a larger share of the market.

On the other hand, if your strategic ideas do not pay off, your rivals will gain, because you will likely lose most of the money invested in the project. Some firms use this tactic to great advantage. They allow smaller firms to take the risk and experiment with new technologies. If the project succeeds, the large firm steps in with more money and more clout and creates its own, improved version. About the only risk it takes is that the smaller firm might become successful enough to grab a serious share of the market.

Changing Industry

An intriguing problem that can arise is that even if your strategic project succeeds, the company might lose because your project has changed the industry. Consider an insurance company that sells software to companies to allow them to track insurance deductions and payments to workers. The insurance company decides that it can add a program to compute payroll, so the companies could drop their existing payroll software. These features appear to give the company an edge over its rivals in the insurance industry. The problem is that there are many more companies that create payroll software, and it is very simple for these companies to add insurance capabilities to their existing software. The actions of the insurance company encourage the payroll software firms to move into the insurance market. As illustrated in Figure 11.13, the insurance company suddenly has hundreds of new competitors and could lose customers.

FIGURE 11.13

Changing industry and government intervention: A complication with strategy is that it might alter the industry. A firm in Industry 1 might use IT to attract customers from a different industry. Because of this expansion, the firm gains new competitors (from Industry 2). While competition is often beneficial, you must thoroughly analyze the effect of the new competition before embarking on changing the industry. In a related manner, sometimes changes in government regulations alter relationships between industries, as in the telephone and cable TV markets.

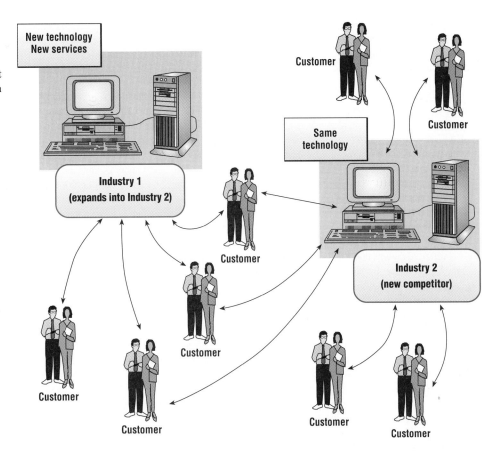

Sharing Data

One common technique in strategic systems is to share your data with customers and suppliers. Two questions arise from this situation. First, do you really want suppliers and customers to have access to the data? Second, can you control their access to protect other data? Security and control issues are examined in detail in Chapter 14. The main point to think about here is what might happen as your customers gain access to your data. Consider the situation of a supplier to General Motors. To save costs and improve communications, GM wants you to connect your computer to the GM factory computers. GM intends to use the links to place orders, monitor quality data, and track shipments. Are you willing to give GM access to your computer? Can you control the information that the large corporation is allowed to see? Maybe when checking on their orders, GM will also be able to determine how much you are producing for other companies. Or maybe GM will gain access to your supplier lists and raw material prices. Even if the GM managers are ethical and do not reveal this data to anyone else, you still might worry. What happens when you have to negotiate prices with GM the next time? If the corporation has access to your data, you might be concerned that it could influence the negotiations. Figure 11.14 illustrates the need for security systems that will enable you to control the access to your data.

Government Intervention

You have to be careful when considering strategic maneuvers. Many potential strategies violate **antitrust laws.** For example, many barriers to entry are illegal, as is price discrimination. In fact, attempts to monopolize a market are forbidden by the Sherman Antitrust Act. Price fixing and other forms of collusion are also outlawed. Information system agreements between competitors could be scrutinized by the Justice Department or the Federal Trade Commission.

If government agents choose strict interpretations of the laws, it could complicate many information system issues. For instance, firms might be discouraged from forming consortiums

REALITY BYTES   IT Kills AT&T Wireless

AT&T was one of the classic American brands. Even when the company was divided into multiple organizations to break up the telephone monopoly, a vestige of pride remained with the AT&T name. AT&T Wireless was a relatively new division—focused on selling nationwide cellular service. In 2003, the company began to fall apart. On November 24, 2003, federal regulations took effect—enabling cell phone customers to switch to a different company and keep the same phone number. AT&T was in the middle of converting to a new CRM system from Siebel. The conversion failed. AT&T was fined for not supporting the new law, and customers left the company in droves. In early 2004, Cingular agreed to purchase AT&T Wireless.

In 2001, AT&T was the leading cell phone provider with a 25 percent market share. By the end of 2003, the company was in third place with a 17 percent share. To help regain share, the company decided to install new CRM software. On average, customer service reps needed about 20 minutes to work through six screens, fetching data from 15 legacy systems, to set up one new customer. The goal was to switch to Siebel 7.5 and put all of the basic data on one screen that would then transfer the necessary data to the underlying systems. The process was difficult and required rewriting complex back-end point-to-point transfer code. Teams of 20 or more people were often created to handle connections for just one system. Communication among the teams was nonexistent. In April 2003, Mike Benson, a 15-year AT&T veteran and the CIO, retired. Christopher Corrado, head of security solutions for Wipro, an Indian

offshore outsourcing company, was named as the new CIO. Employees were concerned that the entire project would be outsourced. Corrado did not help things when at his first IT presentation he announced, "Come in every day and expect to be fired." The conversion was not going well, and they were facing the FCC-mandated November 24 deadline.

Two weeks before the deadline, there was some talk of rolling back to the Siebel 6 system, but no one had kept enough of the old system to be able to restore it. On Halloween, the project team tried to test the new system for the first time. A former employee notes that "it went down and stayed down. They could not get it working again." Rumors of layoffs and outsourcing were confirmed and IT morale plunged. On November 24, for several reasons, the number portability code did not mesh with the code from the other providers and it crashed the system. At one point 50,000 AT&T customers per week lost service. The company is estimated to have lost $100 million in sales. In January and February, the CIO assigned Indian outsource workers to follow around the AT&T workers. Essentially, the workers about to be fired were supposed to train their lower-cost replacements. On February 17, Cingular announced that it was purchasing AT&T Wireless for less than half the stock price value the company had in 2000.

Source: Adapted from Christopher Koch, "AT&T Wireless Self-Destructs," *CIO,* April 15, 2004.

FIGURE 11.14

Security complications: Improving communication and sharing data are common themes in using technology for competitive advantage. This need to share data with "outsiders" makes it more difficult to protect your internal data. Some data you will want to share; other data must be kept secret. Security systems can provide some protections, but the more outsiders who are involved, the more difficult it is to provide adequate security.

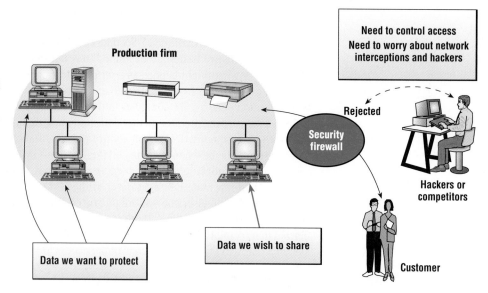

that define standards. Agreements to share disaster backup facilities might be outlawed. Computer links to customers might be seen as limiting competition. So far, the U.S. agencies have allowed all of these activities to proceed without interference. However, there is always the chance that other nations or different political administrations will view the issues differently.

In the 1980s, the government was relatively lenient about antitrust issues, including those regarding information systems. However, one interesting case arose with the airline reservation systems. For many years, American Airlines and United Airlines had the leading reservation systems. Other airlines could list flights on the systems, but they had to pay money for each ticket sold through the system. A conflict eventually arose because the airlines that created the system programmed it to list their flights first. Flights from other airlines were often listed on separate screens, so travel agents and customers were encouraged to choose flights from the airline that built the system. Although this mechanism did not directly violate antitrust laws, Congress decided to pass a new law, making the practice illegal. Lawmakers decided that as long as the other airlines had to pay for access to the system, everyone should have an equal chance at being listed first. The point is that even though the initial action was not illegal, Congress has the ability to pass new laws and remove the advantages, so you cannot assume that the benefits will last.

The Role of Economics

Why did so many dot-com firms fail? Do their failures mean there is no viable Internet strategy? The main lesson from the failures of the early dot-com firms in 2000 and 2001 is that no matter what anyone tries to tell you, to succeed in business, you must make a profit on operations. The second lesson is that it takes time to acquire loyal customers—longer if you want to change the world. Many of the early e-commerce managers felt that to become the dominant player, they had to be the first and biggest firm. So their primary strategy was to sell products below cost and spend huge amounts of money on national advertising. The advertising was successful at attracting investors, whose cash kept the firms alive for a year or so. But when the sales failed to generate profits, there was no way to keep the companies running.

The advertising strategy also created an interesting domino effect in the early industry. By pushing the importance of name recognition (and a good domain name), many of the early firms were able to survive by attracting advertising money from other firms. For example, Excite was a leading Web-portal firm. With its easy name and relatively popular search engine, many people used the site on a regular basis. Based on the number of people visiting the site (known as eyeballs), Excite was able to sell advertising space on its pages to other Web firms. Over 80 percent of Excite's revenue came from advertising. As the other firms in the industry fell apart, they stopped their advertising spending and Excite's revenue plummeted. Many other firms faced the same problem, and the chain reaction caused hundreds of firms to fail.

Despite the early setbacks, there is still uncertainty about what will become a successful Web strategy. Will consumers really buy enough products over the Internet to make e-commerce profitable? Should firms concentrate on publishing strategies—where they provide useful content for free or low cost, making profits by selling advertising space to other (preferably non-e-commerce) firms? Television stations and magazines survive under this model—is there room for Internet sites?

The strategic options in e-business are increasing as new tools are created, wireless capabilities improve, and people begin to adopt connectivity as a way of life. At this point, there is no single answer, which makes it even more important that you carefully define your goals, analyze the profits, evaluate your competition, and build a creative business plan.

Entrepreneurship

How do you start a business? How do you start an online business? Entrepreneurship is the act of building and running a business. The term is generally applied to new businesses, but it is becoming common for large businesses to encourage entrepreneurship within the main organization. For instance, a manager who comes up with an idea for a product might seek support to run a new project within the larger company.

Entrepreneurship is built on three broad fundamentals: (1) an idea, (2) a business plan, and (3) implementation. Risk is a fourth important element. You should not consider

REALITY BYTES   The New Economy?

In the late 1990s, particularly with the enormous growth and excitement generated by the Internet, many people were arguing that a new economy was being shaped. Some of their arguments were used to "explain" the sky-high prices being paid for Internet IPO stocks. Other people used the analysis to claim that business strategy needed to change. While there might have been some truth to the statements, it was dangerous to base your entire company on them—as some managers and entrepreneurs who followed the hype learned. The problem is that there are no easy answers to business success. The basic myths/statements were:

1. Grow or die.
2. You must be virtual.
3. Go global.
4. Capital is easy.
5. Everybody is an entrepreneur.
6. Technology makes life easier.
7. You must be on the Web in a big way.

The *Inc.* article presents many examples of managers who attempted to follow these ideas and encountered problems. For example, Jonathan Katz is CEO of Cinnabar, a $17 million company that creates scenery and special effects for movies, commercials, and theme parks. The company was enthusiastic about technology. Managers and employees quickly realized the value of cell phones and e-mail. Whenever a problem cropped up, employees used the electronic communication to contact clients and production studios to straighten it out. The problem is that at the start of 1997, Cinnabar's commercial and film business started to drop. After a great deal of thought, Katz realized that "my people had become complacent and too reliant on the conveniences of electronic communication like faxes, e-mail, and telephones. The real heart of our business, which came out of direct contact with our clients, was not happening." He told the employees to put away the cell phones and e-mail, and pay personal visits with directors, producers, and art directors. In the last quarter of 1998, Cinnabar's commercial business increased by 50 percent.

Source: Adapted from "Some of the Smartest CEOs Around Bought into the Myths of the New Economy," *Inc.,* February 1999.

becoming an entrepreneur unless you are willing to accept a high risk of loss—loss of time and loss of money. However, having a good idea, building a solid business plan, and managing the implementation carefully can reduce risk.

Flexibility is another important characteristic of successful entrepreneurs. The problem with having a new idea is that it is difficult to forecast exactly how it will be received by customers. Hence, many ideas and plans began in one direction, and only succeeded when the managers used the information to change directions and find a more profitable solution. Along the same lines, a thousand unforeseen obstacles can leap into the path of any good plan; flexibility and perseverance are important to circumventing these problems.

Idea

How will your business be different from the existing firms? Ideas are the foundation of entrepreneurship. There is little point in starting a business or project just to copy someone else. The idea could be a new product or service, or it could be a better method of production, or a better marketing or financial system.

Ideas are closely tied to strategy. As a start-up firm, yours will be small and must have a clear focus. Are you trying to be the least-cost producer to attract customers from older firms? Or are you planning to offer radically new products and services that provide greater benefits than the competition? A successful strategy will depend on a careful analysis of the industry and your role within it.

Strategy

The key as an entrepreneur is to examine the many aspects of strategy to find and clarify an idea. For entrepreneurs, three key strategic issues are (1) an understanding of where you will stand on the production chain, (2) identification of the competition and substitute products, and (3) barriers to entry.

As a new firm, yours will most likely be one of the smallest. Even if you start an entirely new concept or industry, you will be dealing with an entrenched base of suppliers and

Technology Toolbox: Creating a Business Plan

Problem: You want to start a business.

Tools: You can buy templates and software that will help you organize your ideas and generate business plans. You need a detailed plan that you can present to potential investors and bankers. However, the canned plans tend to be too generic. In most cases, you can use a spreadsheet or accounting software to design your own plan. The overall structure of the plan should follow a standard organization: Introduction (a summary of the company), Marketing (market analysis and pricing), Historic Analysis (sales and profits in the industry), Organization (structure of the firm and the management team), Financing (detailed budgets and cash needs), and Projections (estimates of sales, costs, and accounting statements).

Forecasting is often the most important but challenging aspect to creating a plan. You need to create a complete set of accounting statements (income statement, balance sheet, and cash flow) that reflect the anticipated position of the firm for the first few years. But how are you going to estimate all of the numbers required to generate these statements? The key lies in understanding that the numbers depend on the size of the company, which depends heavily on sales. Consider the Rolling Thunder Bicycles company. If it anticipates selling only 100 bicycles, you could run the company with a couple of employees. If sales grow to 2,000 bicycles, you will need more employees to build and sell the bicycles. Consequently, you will need bigger facilities and more managers. So, begin with a detailed forecast of the sales. In the case of RT, you would estimate sales of each type of bicycle and multiply by the average sale price to obtain an estimate of revenue. The sales number also tells you the materials and tools you need, which gives estimates of the major expenses. Now you can estimate the start-up costs to build or lease space and buy equipment. Combining these numbers with the sales revenue gives you assets and cash flow. Initially cash flow will probably be negative. This number tells you how much you have to finance. If you borrow money, your statements will have to incorporate the interest costs as well. When you build the spreadsheet, you should set up a page of constants (such as percentage increase in sales) and build the formulas to refer to these cells. Then you can see the effect of your assumptions on the financial picture by simply entering new values.

Building the accounting statements yourself (perhaps with the assistance of an accountant) forces you to identify the primary financial information items you will want to see. It also helps you see the financial relationships and internal structure that you will have to build.

Quick Quiz:

1. How can you forecast sales? What information would you want to collect?

2. How would the financial statements be different for an EC firm (for example, a Web site that sells photographs)?

3. What key element would you place in the marketing section for a service firm (e.g., dentist)?

Rolling Thunder Estimated Sales—Number of Bicycles

Year	Increase	Hybrid	Mountain	Race	Road	Tour	Track	Annual Total
1		250	250	350	200	350	50	1450
2	10%	275	275	385	220	385	55	1595
3	10%	302	302	423	242	423	60	1752
4	10%	332	332	465	266	465	66	1926
5	10%	365	365	511	292	511	72	2116

Average Sale Price of a Bicycle

$1,000	$1,500	$2,500	$2,000	$1,000	$2,000

Estimated Sales Value

Year	Hybrid	Mountain	Race	Road	Tour	Track	Annual Sales
1	$250,000	$375,000	$875,000	$400,000	$350,000	$100,000	$2,350,000
2	$275,000	$412,500	$962,500	$440,000	$385,000	$110,000	$2,585,000
3	$302,000	$453,000	$1,057,500	$484,000	$423,000	$120,000	$2,839,500
4	$332,000	$498,000	$1,162,500	$532,000	$465,000	$132,000	$3,121,500
5	$365,000	$547,500	$1,277,500	$584,000	$511,000	$144,000	$3,429,000

Income Statement—Projected	Year		
	1	2	3
Sales	$2,350,000	$2,585,000	$2,839,500
Material	822,500	904,750	993,825
Labor	550,000	550,000	550,000
Lease	60,000	60,000	60,000
Advertising/promotion	500,000	250,000	250,000
Tools depreciation	50,000	60,000	70,000
Cost of merchandise sold	1,932,500	1,764,750	1,853,825
Operating and administrative expenses	100,000	100,000	100,000
Operating profit	317,500	720,250	885,675
Other income (expense)			
Interest income	0	0	93
Interest expense	0	0	0
Shareholder related expense	(10,000)	(10,000)	(10,000)
Earnings before income taxes	307,500	710,250	875,768
Federal and state income taxes	(123,000)	(284,100)	(350,307)
Net earnings	$184,500	$426,150	$525,461

Balance Sheet—Projected at Year End	Year		
	1	2	3
Assets			
Current assets			
Cash	($193,550)	$3,095	$302,395
Receivables	235,000	258,500	283,950
Inventories	98,700	108,570	119,259
Prepaid expenses	1,000	1,000	1,000
Total current assets	141,150	371,165	706,604
Property, plant and equipment			
Land	0	0	0
Buildings	0	0	0
Fixtures and equipment	250,000	50,000	50,000
Subtotal	250,000	50,000	50,000
Less accumulated depreciation	50,000	110,000	180,000
Net property, plant and equipment	200,000	(60,000)	(130,000)
Total assets	$341,150	$311,165	$576,604
Liabilities and shareholders' equity			
Current liabilities			
Accounts payable	82,250	90,475	99,383
Accrued payroll and benefits	0	0	0
Income taxes payable	(123,000)	(284,100)	(350,307)
Other current liabilities	0	0	0
Total current liabilities	(40,750)	(193,625)	(250,925)
Other liabilities	0	0	0
Long term debt	0	0	0
Total liabilities	(40,750)	(193,625)	(250,925)
Shareholders' equity	0	0	0
Additional paid-in capital	0	0	0
Retained earnings	(193,550)	196,645	299,300
Total shareholders' equity	(193,550)	196,645	299,300
Total liabilities and shareholders' equity	($234,300)	$3,020	$48,375
Money to be raised (equity or debt)	$575,450	$308,145	$528,229

Cash Flow—Projected	Year		
	1	2	3
Net earnings	$184,500	$426,150	$525,461
Depreciation	50,000	$110,000	$180,000
Net (gain) loss on asset sales	0	0	0
Other	0	0	0
Subtotal from sales	50,000	$110,000	$180,000
(Increase) decrease in current assets:			
Receivables	$(235,000)	(23,500)	(25,450)
Inventories	98,700	9,870	10,689
Prepaid expenses	(1,000)	0	0
Subtotal from assets	(137,300)	(13,630)	(14,761)
Increase (decrease) in current liabilities			
Accounts payable	82,250	8,225	8,908
Other current liabilities	0	0	0
Accrued payroll	0	0	0
Income taxes payable	(123,000)	(284,100)	(350,307)
Total change in current liabilities	(40,750)	(275,875)	(341,400)
Total adjustments	(128,050)	(179,505)	(176,161)
Net cash provided by operations	56,450	246,645	349,300
Cash flows from Investing:			
Expended for property, plant, equipment	(250,000)	(50,000)	(50,000)
Proceeds from sale of assets	0	0	0
Net cash used in investing	(250,000)	(50,000)	(50,000)
Cash flows from financing:			
Proceeds (payments) from long-term debt	0	0	0
Stock or additional paid-in capital	0	0	0
Cash dividends	0	0	0
Net cash provided by financing	0	0	0
Net increase (decrease in cash)	(193,550)	196,645	299,300
Cash and cash equivalents:			
Beginning of year	$0	(193,550)	3,095
End of year	($193,550)	$3,095	$302,395

customers. As a newcomer, your business clout will be small, so you will not be able to count on discounts or goodwill from your suppliers.

Figure 11.3 showed the production chain. When you are looking for ideas, you should examine the production chain for various industries. Get information on the leading firms in each step of the chain. Determine the concentration ratios. Do four firms control 50 percent of the market at a given level, or are there many small firms with no dominant player? Look at the final price and profit of the product or service, and then trace backward and identify the various costs and profits at each level. Then combine your analyses. For example, if there is a reasonable profit at the consumer level, it might appear to be a good opportunity. But if only a few dominant firms supply the product, then these firms might be thinking about expanding into consumer sales—or they might make it difficult for you to create a new retail firm.

Even if you have an idea that creates an entirely new industry, your firm will face competition. You must carefully identify your closest competitors and also specify any potential substitute products. You can also use this analysis to generate new ideas. As a consumer, look at the products and services you buy and identify the main competitors and the potential substitutes. E-commerce specifically looks at the steps that consumers must go through to purchase an item. Can these steps be simplified? Can additional services or products be offered at the same time using information technology?

When searching for ideas, expand your focus to include different aspects of the problem. For instance, perhaps you can create an expert system to help customers select features of a product. You might think about creating a retail store or a Web site to sell that product. But perhaps a few large firms dominate the retail side, or it requires expensive advertising to enter the market. In this situation, as shown in Figure 11.15, it might be more profitable to build your system and sell or lease it to the existing retail firms. Or you could create a service Web site that other sites can connect to and pay a fee for each use of your system.

When evaluating ideas, you must always consider the issue of barriers to entry. If you do have a great idea, and your company makes a profit, how are you going to keep rivals from entering your industry and taking away your customers? If you create a new business process or new software, what will stop others from emulating your system? Figure 11.5 listed some of the typical areas firms consider to create barriers to entry. As a new, small firm, the economies of scale, capital requirements, and control over distribution are not likely to apply to you, except negatively. Also, remember that there is a fine line between creating barriers to entry and violating antitrust laws. So far, most IT barriers have been considered acceptable as long as you do not coerce people to use them.

In the United States it is still possible to obtain patents on business processes. These patents were popular in the early days of the dot-com expansion, but the patent office began to take a closer look and deny some obvious ideas. If you have a truly new process, you might be able to patent the concept—preventing anyone else from copying it for 20 years. Of course, a single patent can cost $10,000 to $30,000 or more to obtain.

FIGURE 11.15

Expand your focus: When searching for ideas, it might be better to partner with a large firm instead of competing head-on.

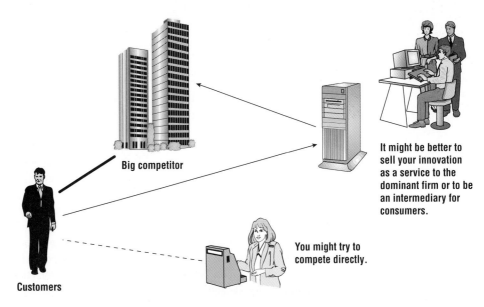

Big competitor

It might be better to sell your innovation as a service to the dominant firm or to be an intermediary for consumers.

You might try to compete directly.

Customers

FIGURE 11.16

Business research: You need to collect data on competitors, the size of the market and how it is growing, production costs, and the legal environment.

- **Competition**
  - **Number**
  - **Concentration ratios**
  - **Sales by firm**
  - **Technology plans**

- **Size of the market**
  - **Number of customers**
  - **Amount of revenue**
  - **Growth rate**
  - **Market comparison for substitute products**
  - **Consumer focus group interviews**

- **Production costs**
  - **Start-up/fixed costs**
  - **Operating costs**

- **Legal environment**

Research

Research is closely tied to idea generation. As you evaluate alternatives, you need to obtain current data on several items. Figure 11.16 summarizes some of the basic data that you will need.

Broad industry information can be obtained from various government Web sites or publications. More specific data can be obtained from the companies themselves, if they are publicly traded. Sales data and more detailed comments on rivals can often be purchased from marketing companies. A few companies monitor Web site traffic, so you can obtain basic online activity data for some of the larger firms. Customer focus interviews are important. At some point, you need real-world feedback on your ideas.

Production costs and other hints can be obtained from suppliers and salespeople. If you are serious about developing a presence in a particular area, scour the trade journals and find some of the leading suppliers. Call the regional sales representatives and they will provide detailed information on items that you will need. But be sure to compare prices from several firms.

Even for retail firms, several legal hurdles must be cleared. Some industries have more complications than others, so you need to carefully investigate all laws and rules that might apply to your business. Find out if there are restrictions on what you will be allowed to do. In terms of permits, identify the permits you need to obtain, exactly where to get them, how often they need to be renewed, the cost of the permits, and the time frames between application, inspection, and approval.

Plan

How do you turn an idea into money? Millions of people have ideas; only a few are able to create new businesses and turn them into money. Once you have identified a reasonable idea and done the basic research so that you understand the industry, you need to write a business plan. The purpose of the plan is to create a road map that will help you set up, manage, and evaluate your progress. It is also critical to obtaining external financing. In 2000, the heyday of Web start-ups, there were stories of entrepreneurs obtaining financing on the basis of a short PowerPoint slide show. Those days are gone. A detailed business plan will convince prospective investors that you are serious and that you know what you are doing. It will also help them evaluate the true potential of your ideas.

You can purchase software that will help you organize the business plan, but you must still collect the data and write the descriptive sections. You must also be careful when using some software templates. When potential investors see plans that are simple fill-in-the-blank templates with little additional content, they do not believe you spent much time on the plan.

FIGURE 11.17

Business plan: A business plan helps you organize your ideas, provides a road map and schedule, and provides financial targets to use as benchmarks as you move forward. It is also critical for obtaining investment funding.

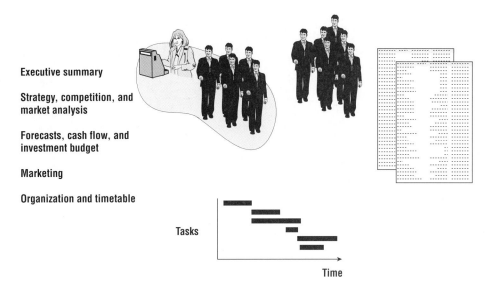

Executive summary

Strategy, competition, and market analysis

Forecasts, cash flow, and investment budget

Marketing

Organization and timetable

Tasks

Time

As shown in Figure 11.17, the goal of the plan is to precisely describe the business you wish to start (or expand), the market environment, and your strategy. You must include financial analyses using forecasted sales and costs. You should include a timetable that indicates how the company will need to grow. Based on these projections, you will be able to determine the amount of money you need to raise to run the company over the next three to five years. In terms of presentation, you must also include an executive summary that is a one-page review of the major points.

Strategy, Competition, and Market Analysis

The strategy section is based on your research of the market. It contains several subsections that describe exactly what products or services you will produce. It should identify the major competitors and estimate the size of the market and how it will change over time.

If you are creating or distributing products, you need to identify your suppliers, including backup suppliers if something happens to your primary source. For products, it is also critical that you describe your distribution network. Will you distribute through standard retail stores? Ship products by UPS? If there are multiple layers, it is particularly critical that you identify how you will track shipments and sales through the process.

Forecasts, Cash Flow, and Investment Budget

The financial section is a primary component of the business plan. For a start-up firm, it can also be one of the most difficult to create. This section includes estimates of sales and costs. You will have a separate section for start-up costs and ongoing costs—this section is relatively straightforward, but you have to contact several suppliers and contractors to get good estimates of the costs.

The more challenging aspect of the financial section is the need to forecast sales by month for at least three years, and annual sales for five years. Figure 11.18 shows that the sales forecast is the foundation for the other financial data. The level of sales directly determines the revenue, the marketing costs, and the cost of goods sold. Once you know the sales level, you can determine the scale of the infrastructure needed to support those sales, for instance, the size of the Web server and Internet connection speeds in an e-commerce world, or size of distribution facilities in a traditional retail environment. The size of the firm also determines the number of employees needed, which identifies the cost of salaries. Salaries can be a significant component of some firms. Note that for e-commerce firms, you might require a larger number of contract employees to develop software in the beginning. Once the system is operational, you may be able to run with a smaller core group of employees. These costs should be recorded in a separate start-up cost statement.

FIGURE 11.18

Estimating financial statements: The estimate of sales determines the size of the infrastructure and the marketing and purchasing costs. The number of employees needed can be determined from the size of the firm and provides the estimate for salaries. With these major points, the financial statements can be projected to identify the cash flow and the amount of investment money needed.

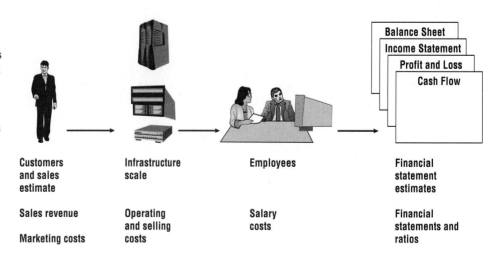

Customers
and sales
estimate

Infrastructure
scale

Employees

Financial
statement
estimates

Sales revenue

Marketing costs

Operating
and selling
costs

Salary
costs

Financial
statements and
ratios

FIGURE 11.19

Break-even analysis: If it is too hard to forecast sales, you can choose an infrastructure size and estimate fixed costs. Then estimate variable costs and revenue per unit sold. Compute total cost and total revenue for varying levels of sales. Look for the break-even point. That is the minimum level of sales you must be able to reach to be profitable.

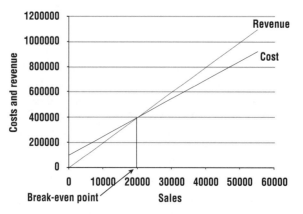

With sales, cost of goods sold, infrastructure costs (leases and so on), and salaries, you have estimated the primary costs and can create projected financial statements. You need to estimate a growth factor for each month or year. This growth factor is one of the most subjective elements in the projection. However, you should try to estimate growth rates of similar firms and keep your numbers in a reasonable range. Also, higher growth rates will mean that you need greater marketing expenses to obtain that increase in sales.

With the basic financial statements estimated, you can concentrate on cash flows. When will money arrive? Will there be delays in payments? Many of your costs occur up front or on a monthly basis, so calculate these and estimate the firm's cash position for each month. You will need a source of funds to cover times when the cash flow is negative. You should do the same for profit, so that you have an estimate of when the firm will become profitable.

Of course, you still face the problem of estimating the level of sales, which can be next to impossible for new products or services. If there is no way to generate a plausible sales forecast, it might be better to start with an estimate of the infrastructure size. From there it is generally easy to estimate the fixed costs. Now, examine various levels of sales to pick up revenue, cost of goods sold, and marketing costs. As shown in Figure 11.19, you can now compute total cost and revenue for varying levels of sales. The point where the two are equal (where the lines cross) is the break-even point. You must reach this level of sales before you can make a profit. Now, compare that sales number to similar firms. If the sales number is too high, it is unlikely that your venture will be profitable. Conversely, if it is substantially lower than for other firms, you are probably overestimating the price you can charge, or you are missing some costs. If the lines never cross—you have a major problem: the firm will never be profitable based on your estimates.

Marketing

As part of the business plan, you will have to create a marketing plan. The marketing plan will begin with the anticipated sales level. Then it will identify the target customers with as much demographic detail as you can obtain. Income level is critical. Regional location could be important for some businesses. It is also desirable to find out what magazines, newspapers, television shows, and radio programs the consumers prefer. If you are selling to other businesses, you should identify trade groups that are likely to represent the target businesses.

The marketing plan should contain an analysis of pricing. At a minimum, you should survey consumers, or create a focus group, and find out how much the potential customers are willing to pay for your product or service. You should also identify points for quantity discounts, particularly if you are selling to other businesses.

You then need to create an advertising plan. You need to find prices and viewer demographic data for newspapers, magazines, radio, television, and Web sites. You might also consider alternatives such as direct mail, billboards, and tie-ins with other products. For local promotions, you can contact advertising managers directly. For nationwide campaigns, you will want to hire an advertising design and placement firm. While it increases your costs, the experience and contacts of the firm will save you time and help focus your campaign.

You will also need to create a sales management plan, where you focus on the internal structure of the marketing department. How many salespeople will you need? How will they be paid and what additional incentives will you provide? How will you handle customer complaints? What tools will you use for customer relationship management? How will you identify and build cross sales of products?

Organization and Timetable

You need to specify the organizational structure and create a project timetable to provide a road map and benchmarks so that you can evaluate your progress. For the management, you need to identify who will fill each of the primary roles. If you are using the plan to raise money, you need to include a brief biography of each person. If there will be more than a handful of employees, you need to draw an organizational chart. You also need to indicate how the structure will change as the firm grows.

For complex start-ups, a project management timetable can be invaluable. The thousands of management tasks from government filings, construction, purchases, writing programs, hiring people, managing advertising, and dealing with suppliers can quickly bury you in details. You need a timetable to record when tasks should be started, and which tasks depend on others, and to track which tasks have not been completed. A project management package is a useful tool to handle all of these details. It can also track assignments by employees and has tools to help you identify bottlenecks and times when you might need to hire additional people.

The timetable should also be integrated with the financial forecasts so that as the company moves forward, you can evaluate your progress. If you do not reach a certain sales level at the forecasted time, you can adjust your future growth rates and recalculate the amount of investment money you will need in the future.

Implementation

Is it true that genius is 1 percent inspiration and 99 percent perspiration? Yes, most likely, Edison was correct. Ideas and planning are only the beginning of creating a business. The real work begins with implementation. The true job of an entrepreneur is to devise the rules and procedures that make a business successful. Once the plans are in place and you know how much it is going to cost to get started, you need to form the legal company and obtain financing. You probably need to hire an initial staff, and you need to create an accounting system to record all transactions and monitor your progress.

FIGURE 11.20
Primary forms to start a business: Companies are incorporated by the state, and states have different requirements and filing fees. Companies must also obtain an EIN from the IRS. The S corporation election is optional but popular with small businesses.

State forms
 Articles of Incorporation
 Corporate Bylaws
 Registered Agent (self)
 Business Registration Form
  State Employer Number
  Withholding ID
  Sales Tax ID
 Additional licenses
Federal forms
 SS-4 Application for Employer Identification Number (EIN)
 2553 Election by a Small Business Corporation

Starting a firm requires a considerable amount of paperwork. Some of the basic steps are shown in Figure 11.20. Some types of firms require dozens of licenses, and if you need to construct or remodel facilities, you will need additional permits. One of the first decisions you must make is to choose a state in which to incorporate. Each state has different rules, procedures, and fees. Delaware is a popular choice because of the way its laws are written. But small businesses may find it easier to file with the state in which they are located. Then the company can be its own registered agent and can avoid paying franchise fees to two states. Even if you incorporate in Delaware, you will still have to register in each state that you have a physical presence. A few companies specialize in helping you incorporate a new company for a fee. You answer a few basic questions, and the firm fills out boilerplate articles of incorporation and bylaws and files them with the state of your choice.

Ownership Structure

One of the more difficult decisions to make is the legal structure of the firm. Simple partnerships are relatively easy to create and to register with the state. However, partnerships generally cannot issue stock and it can be harder to protect the partners from lawsuits. Corporations stand as separate entities and can issue stock, but the accounting requirements are a little more time consuming, and you face a double-taxation issue. Any money the company makes is subject to corporate income taxes, and dividends that you pay to owners are subject to personal taxes. Most states enable you to create a **subchapter S corporation** or a **limited liability company (LLC)** to combine features of partnerships with those of corporations.

Most small business start-ups choose one of these two structures. With both forms, income and losses flow directly to the owner's income statements and are only taxed once. Both protect the owners from lawsuits, as long as you keep a solid line between company business and personal funds. The primary difference between them is that the LLC is not a corporation and cannot sell stock. The S corporation is also easier to convert into a standard (chapter C) corporation. States have different interpretations of the LLC, so your choice of structure depends on the state in which you incorporate.

Financing

Obtaining financing is related to the type of business structure and the size of your firm. The two choices are debt and equity (stock). However, as a start-up, you will find it difficult to find a bank willing to lend you money. Banks will lend money for relatively liquid assets, such as inventory. But they will generally not lend over 80 percent of the value. Most start-up businesses find investors and grant them partial ownership through shares of stock.

Debt

Firms can borrow money to finance certain things, but it is difficult to borrow money for a start-up. Banks know that many small businesses fail within the first year, so they prefer to lend to an established business. Some banks specialize in merchant loans to cover some of the costs of buying products that will be sold at retail. But even in these cases, the company will have to

FIGURE 11.21

Start-up financing: Venture capital firms and partners are given ownership positions and sometimes provide management control in exchange for development funding. If the firm is successful, it issues an initial public offering of stock, which funds additional operations and rewards the original investors.

Venture capital
Angel investor
Partners

Become owners with some control over management

Sucessful firm IPO:
Additional funds
Reward to original investors

Funding for development and operations

provide cash to cover some of the costs. Larger firms can sell bonds on the market for long-term debt, but it is unlikely that anyone would be willing to buy bonds from an unknown start-up company. Borrowing money also entails interest payments, so the cost can be relatively high.

Equity

Most entrepreneurs search for investors willing to provide start-up capital in exchange for partial ownership in the form of shares of stock. Figure 11.21 shows that **venture capital (VC)** firms exist specifically to provide funding to start-up firms. An entrepreneur generally presents the business plan to a VC firm, with a detailed budget and a request for the money to cover development and operating costs for the first year. VC firms evaluate hundreds or thousands of proposals in terms of the strength of the idea, the ability and track record of the management, and the potential profits. VC firms expect many of the small companies to fail, but to cover the losses by having a few firms with enormous returns.

Once the firm is established and potentially profitable, the managers take the firm public by issuing stock at an **initial public offering (IPO).** The public stock raises additional money and eventually gives the entrepreneur and the VC firm an opportunity to sell some of their shares for a personal gain.

In a hot market, start-up firms can often trade initial private shares of stock for many items they need. For example, many managers are willing to accept smaller salaries in exchange for stock options. **Stock options** are granted by the firm at a specific price. If the firm goes public and the stock price increases, the employee buys the stock from the company at the option (low) price and sells it for the higher public price. As an employee, keep in mind that this transaction is taxed as current income and can take one-third or more of the profit. But you need to offer stock options, because you need experienced employees willing to work for low pay in exchange for future rewards if the company succeeds.

Although equity has many advantages, remember that you give some control of the firm to the investors in exchange for their money. How much control depends on your negotiating skills, on the number of firms interested, and on the amount of money.

Accounting and Benchmarks

Careful accounting is an important requirement in a start-up firm. You need to be particularly careful at tracking expenses. A good accounting system is important, but you must also establish procedures and policies. In the hectic day-to-day world of starting a firm, there is little time to stop and analyze every transaction. You need procedures in place so that everything gets recorded as soon as possible. If several managers have purchasing authority, a Web-based accounting system might be helpful to ensure that all items are recorded immediately—wherever the managers are located.

Your accounting system needs to run comparisons to benchmarks that you established in the business plan. For example, if your cash flow is running below projected levels, you will need to cut expenses or find additional funding. You need to closely monitor these numbers so that you have more time to react and make corrections.

If your firm requires developing software, you need to track the development progress. Estimating design and programming time is notoriously difficult, but you should still track the progress because you will need to update your target completion dates. Project management software shows how each task depends on others, and it can identify bottlenecks and highlight which tasks need additional resources.

The entrepreneur also needs to provide feedback to investors. Beyond standard quarterly accounting reports, you will need to keep investors apprised of development progress, marketing campaigns, and sales data.

Flexibility

One theme repeatedly echoed by entrepreneurs is that you need to be flexible. Many times your initial idea just will not work. Perhaps consumers are not ready, or development costs are too high, or the competitors respond too quickly and take away the market. Whatever the cause, you need to constantly reevaluate the progress and be prepared to redirect your efforts to related areas.

For instance, in 1999, Nvest, a Boston investment firm, created a company around the URL mutualfunds.com. It began with a huge business plan to build the site as a portal for mutual fund companies, advisers, and investors. The ambitious plan was to make the site a central source for many aspects of mutual funds. By May 2000, the company realized that it would not be able to achieve all of its goals. The CFO went back to the investors to see if they could raise more money. But the plan was too aggressive (and the dot-com market was beginning to crash), so the firm filed for bankruptcy. However, several of the employees used the technology to get funding from a different set of investors to create a smaller site focused on providing online training for financial services professionals. Hundreds of similar stories exist. You must constantly reexamine your strategy, your performance, your rivals, and your customers—searching for an even better plan.

Starting an e-Commerce Firm

What additional steps are required to start an EC firm? An EC start-up faces the same paperwork, financing, and organizational issues as any other firm. However, it faces several additional hurdles. As shown in Figure 11.22, one of the biggest challenges is the innovation factor—few investors and managers have experience with EC firms. The problem is compounded since many EC firms are unique. It is even more complicated with the over 80 percent failure rate of the early EC firms in 2000–2001. All of these factors add to the risk and uncertainty. To attract funding and succeed, you will need a solid business plan that demonstrates traditional business emphasis on sales and profits.

Site development time and cost are important challenges. For simple retail sales, you can generally purchase software or lease a site that provides standard sales software. This approach is preferred for situations where you want to focus on marketing a new product, and the Web is simply the sales channel. You will still have to allocate time to customize the site and enter all of the product and pricing data; but the process is relatively organized and predictable. More complex EC service sites usually require custom software. And building custom software is still a time-consuming, somewhat unpredictable process. If you are not the lead programmer, you will have to find one willing to work with you, generally in exchange for money and stock.

You will also need to find a company to host your Web site. While there are many ISP hosting companies, you will have to talk to several to find one that can handle the complexity of your site and offer the bandwidth you need at reasonable rates. It can take several weeks to negotiate a contract, so you need to start early. On the other hand, if you need to

FIGURE 11.22

Additional e-commerce start-up tasks: An EC start-up requires several tasks on top of the traditional steps. Developing software is difficult, time-consuming, and unpredictable. Finding a Web hosting company can take several weeks. Processing credit cards is harder than it looks because many banks do not like dealing with small start-up firms.

- Additional risk and challenge of obtaining funding.
- Web site development.
    - Programming cost.
    - Time and management.
    - Purchase or lease merchant software if possible.
- Find a Web hosting ISP.
    - Site complexity.
    - Internet connectivity.
    - Costs.
- Host site yourself.
    - Time to get leased line.
    - Choose site location based on Internet access.
- Obtain digital security certificate (Verisign).
- Find bank that will provide merchant account services to accept credit card payments.
    - Setup fee.
    - Monthly fee.
    - Transaction fee.
- Find a credit card processing firm that works with your bank and your software.
    - Setup fee.
    - Monthly fee.
    - Transaction fee.

host the site at your own facilities, you have even more hurdles to clear to obtain the leased line you will need from the phone company. In fact, if at all possible, you should probably avoid choosing a site for your company until after you contact the phone company and several ISPs. Some cities have firms that offer high-speed Internet connections at relatively low cost—as long as your offices are within certain buildings (sitting on top of existing fiber-optic connections). If you do need to order a leased line, be prepared to wait six months or more for the installation.

To conduct business over the Internet, you will also have to obtain a digital security certificate. While this process is fairly easy, you need to budget for the annual cost and you might have to build your software to support the processing company's procedures. Likewise, you will have to contact a bank to establish a merchant account so that you can accept credit cards. Most banks price their services depending on the number and value of transactions you conduct monthly. They also tend to charge higher fees to start-up firms, because the start-up firms have no established credit rating. Note that to process transactions over the Internet, you will have to pay setup and monthly fees to the merchant bank and to the data processing company.

Summary

Information systems can provide benefits beyond traditional cost saving. Competitive advantages can be gained by creating barriers to entry and gaining control over distribution channels. Using information systems to build ties to suppliers and customers can provide lower costs and better quality products. Computer systems also provide incentives for customers to remain with your company if they incur costs of learning new systems and transferring data when switching to a competitor. Information systems can also be used to differentiate your products from the others in the marketplace. Similarly, innovative services offered with the help of technology can entice customers and expand your market.

You can search for competitive advantages by examining Porter's external forces of rivals, customers, suppliers, substitute products, and new entrants. You can also search for strategies in research, engineering, and design. In manufacturing, you can look for ways to decrease costs and improve logistics. In marketing, potential gains can be found in better understanding of customer wants, as well as sales and order management. Services can be

> ### A Manager's View
>
> With increased competition, every manager is being asked to identify ways to improve the company and find an advantage over the rivals. Gaining a competitive edge is not easy. Examining the entire value chain is a useful place to start. Information systems can provide data and evaluate models to help you identify strategic applications. Information systems can also provide direct advantages by creating a barrier to entry, gaining control over distribution, cutting costs, improving quality, and improving ties between suppliers and customers. Choosing an effective strategy is a critical task in e-business. Creating a plan and successfully implementing it are critical steps in strategy and entrepreneurship.

supported through better information flows and workgroup products. Management can be helped with better data and better decision tools.

Strategic systems face many risks. They tend to be expensive and difficult to create. Any gains created may disappear when competitors pick up the technology and imitate your offerings. In addition, making strategic changes to your firm might alter the industry, which might adversely affect your firm. And if these problems are not enough to discourage you, remember that attempts to monopolize a market are illegal, so you have to make sure that your plans do not violate governmental regulations.

Entrepreneurship requires a good idea and a detailed plan, followed by implementation. The plan should include financial details and budgets. You then have to raise the money needed to start the business and keep it operational until it generates sufficient revenue to be self-sustaining.

Key Words

antitrust laws, *415*	limited liability company (LLC), *426*	subchapter S corporation, *426*
barriers to entry, *401*	mass customization, *410*	switching costs *404*
distribution channels, *402*	product differentiation, *406*	total quality management (TQM), *399*
entrepreneurship, *417*	rivals, *399*	value chain, *407*
external agents, *397*	statistical quality control (SQC), *407*	venture capital (VC), *427*
Five Forces model, *397*	stock options, *427*	
initial public offering (IPO), *427*		

Web Site References

Management Consulting

Accenture	**www.accenture.com**
Bain & Company	**www.bain.com**
Boston Consulting Group	**www.bcg.com**
Booz Allen & Hamilton	**www.bah.com**
McKinsey & Company	**www.mckinsey.com**

Additional Readings

Applegate, Lynda M., and F. Warren McFarlan. *Creating Business Advantage in the Information Age.* New York: McGraw-Hill/Irwin, 2002. [Business strategy in information technology from a Harvard perspective.]

Melymuka, Kathleen. "State Street Bank's Change in Direction Required a New IT Approach." *Computerworld,* February 15, 1999. [Changing strategy with information technology.]

Morison, Robert E., and Kirtland C. Mead. "A Hard Look at Strategic Systems." *Indications,* January 1989. [Myths and issues in IT strategy.]

Porter, Michael E. *Competitive Advantage: Creating and Sustaining Superior Performance.* New York: Free Press, 1985. [Early discussion of strategy and competitive advantage.]

Porter, Michael E. "Strategy and the Internet." *Harvard Business Review,* March 2001, Vol. 79, Issue 3.

Strassmann, Paul A. *The Squandered Computer: Evaluating the Business Alignment of Information Technologies.* New Canaan, CT: Information Economics Press, 1997. [A detailed, but controversial, discussion of the value of information technology, with some excellent cases.]

Review Questions

1. Briefly describe four techniques that can be used to gain competitive advantage.
2. What are external agents?
3. What are the risks and costs of strategic implementations?
4. For a large manufacturing firm, who are the customers? How many different types of customers can there be?
5. Why are barriers to entry important to gain a competitive advantage?
6. How does control over distribution channels give a firm a competitive advantage?
7. How can information systems be used to gain control over distribution channels?
8. How might EDI limit firms from gaining control over the distribution channels?
9. What are switching costs, and how can they give a company a competitive advantage?
10. How can information systems be used to enhance product differentiation and create new products?
11. What role is played by information systems in improving quality management?
12. Within management, how can information technology provide a competitive advantage?
13. What are the major elements of an entrepreneurship plan?
14. How do the elements of strategic analysis relate to entrepreneurship?
15. What are the main choices for firm structure and financing?
16. What additional steps are needed to start an EC firm?

Exercises

1. Consider a small service firm such as a physician, dentist, accountant, or lawyer. Is it possible for such an office to use computers to gain a competitive advantage? To start, identify the customers, suppliers, and rivals. Do you think the "natural" switching costs are high or low; that is, how often do customers switch to competitors? Which of the major techniques do you think would be the most successful (barriers to entry, switching costs, quality control, lower prices, ties to customers or suppliers, etc.)?

2. How long can firms maintain an advantage using an information system? Research one of the classic cases and find out how long it took for the competitors to implement a similar information system (for example, Merrill Lynch and its Cash Management Account, American Airlines and the Sabre System, Levi-Strauss and its Levi-Link ordering system, or Federal Express and its tracking system). Find out when the system was implemented, identify the competitors, and find out when they implemented similar systems. Did the original company continue to update its strategy? Collect data on sales and profits for the firms to see whether there were major changes.

3. Pick an industry. Find two firms in the industry—one a technology leader, the other a follower. Get the financial information on those firms for the last five years. Find analyst summaries of their operations. Compare the two firms. Are there differences in finances, operating methods, or customers?

4. Find information on two e-commerce firms in the same industry: one failing and one still operating. What differences are there between the firms? What strategies did the firms follow?

5. Write a business plan for a new company. Choose an existing small company if you do not have ideas for a new firm.

6. Research the detailed steps needed to start a Chapter S corporation in your state. Obtain the necessary forms (most states have them on Web sites).

7. Choose an area of management, such as marketing, manufacturing, or logistics. Find an example of a firm that you believe is doing a good job applying IT in this area. Briefly explain how this usage could provide strategic benefits to the firm.

8. Choose one of the IS techniques to gain a competitive advantage. Identify a firm (not one of the examples in the text) that is using that method. Briefly describe the financial position of the firm and how it is using information systems.

Technology Toolbox

9. Using a GIS tool, compare the sales for Rolling Thunder Bicycles against population and income.

10. As a team assignment, interview as many students as possible to obtain their home zip codes (or try to obtain the data from your institutional research office). Store the data in a spreadsheet or DBMS by zip code. Use a GIS to display the data.

11. Create sample sales data by state. Use a GIS tool to compare the sales against population and income.

12. Select a small business that you might want to start. Choose the type of business structure and where it will be located. Explain your choices.

13. Choose a company that you would like to start, write the overall strategy section, and build the projected accounting statements for the first three years.

14. Assume that you have been hired by a physician who wants to start a Web site to help dieters. Create a business plan that focuses on the competition, marketing, and Web aspects of the business.

Teamwork

15. Each team member should read through at least two industry cases in the chapters of this book. Identify whether the firm is a leader or a follower in terms of strategy and technology. Compare each firm's financial data to that of the industry (for example, by sales and number of employees). Combine the individual analyses and summarize them. Identify any patterns you might see. For example, do the larger firms tend to be leaders or followers in technology?

16. Choose a firm that provides reasonable amounts of management information (such as a local firm or a well-documented public firm). Have each team member choose one area (research, engineering, marketing, and so on). Identify the strengths of the firm in the area. Create a short plan to improve the company's use of IT within that area. Make sure the usage fits with the overall strategy of the company.

17. Choose an industry. Assign each team member to investigate a level within the production chain. Each person should identify the tasks that occur at the specified level along with the major firms. Identify the rivalry and any dominant firms at each level. Identify the use of IT at each level and any ties across levels. Combine the results and briefly discuss where on the chain you would prefer to enter as a new firm.

18. Choose a firm that the team might want to start. Create a brief business plan for the company by assigning one section to each team member.

19. Choose an existing firm. Using Porter's model, identify how the company could use information technology to gain a competitive advantage.

Rolling Thunder Database

20. Identify the competition in the industry. Who are existing rivals? Who are potential rivals? Be sure to define the industry carefully. Consider using North American Industrial Classification System (NAICS) codes.

21. Perform a value chain analysis of the company. Could they improve profits by expanding vertically or horizontally? Are there additional products they should consider offering?

22. The management has the opportunity to purchase a chain of retail bicycle stores. Evaluate the strategic aspects of this proposed acquisition. What will be the effect on the information systems? Can the existing information system be used to improve the operations of the retail stores? What additions and improvements would be needed?

23. Is there any way to increase ties to the customers using technology to gain a competitive advantage?

24. Examine the value chain in the bicycle industry. How many levels are there and which levels are the most profitable?

25. Using the existing data, write a business plan to obtain venture capital to expand the operations of Rolling Thunder—focusing on the need to develop a marketing campaign and a Web-based ordering system.

26. Using the spreadsheet for the Rolling Thunder Bicycle start-up situation shown in the figures, choose a financing method and complete the projected accounting statements.

27. Assuming the salaries and capital costs are fixed to start Rolling Thunder Bicycles, and assuming the average price of a bicycle is $2,250, compute the break-even number of bicycles.

Cases: The Airline Industry

The Industry

To understand the state of the airline industry, you have to look at some of the history. The most important historical issue is that the airline industry was heavily regulated until 1978. Until then, the civil aeronautics board (CAB) controlled all of the business aspects of the airlines, including landing rights and fares. Several large airlines were established and grew during that time. In 1978, the CAB was disbanded and the airlines were free to select routes and set prices as they chose, without government oversight. However, the FAA still controls several safety issues, including work rules for flight crews, the number and spacing of flights into airports, and national flight lanes, as well as several other details.

So, what happened when flights were deregulated? This is a good time for you to start thinking like an airline executive. Were you making money? Did your passenger mix suddenly change? Are your revenue and costs any different initially? The simple answer is that initially very little changed. As an established company, with procedures and a system that works and makes money, you would not be inclined to change anything.

Deregulation and Competition

But all it took was a little time. A few airlines started offering new flights on high-demand routes. Then, Donald Burr founded People Express, the airline that scared every other business manager, starting in 1981. As a no-frills airline (they charged $3 to check luggage and sold snacks on the plane), the airline charged incredibly low prices to fly tourists. You no longer had to be in the upper class or funded by a business to fly. Based out of the unused international terminal in Newark, New Jersey, the company picked up nonunion crews, negotiated with the FAA to fly with only a pilot and copilot (no flight engineer), and charged fares of a paltry $59 to Chicago or $99 to London—a tiny fraction of the fares charged by the traditional airlines.

With their substantially higher cost structures, the mainstream airlines could not compete. So, why did People Express disappear and some of the other airlines survive? Part of the answer is mismanagement—People Express tried to grow too rapidly and did not have a solid management structure in place to handle the problems. But a big part of the answer is that American Airlines fought back with information technology. The company quickly realized that People Express appealed to tourists who were very price sensitive. Business people stayed away from the discounter and wanted the amenities and reliable service provided by the mainstream airlines. So, American Airlines turned to its reservation system (Sabre) and estimated the number of people on every flight who were business people. It then came up with the differential pricing system (yield management) that is still in use today. Business people, those who book a couple of days before the flight and do not want to stay Saturday night, get charged thousands of dollars. Tourists, who book early, are offered low fares that compete with the discounters. The basic premise is that the large airlines want to charge higher prices and fly business people, but there is no point in flying empty seats, so they discount the seats until they are all sold. Today, it is likely that almost every passenger on a flight has paid a different price (McCartney 2003).

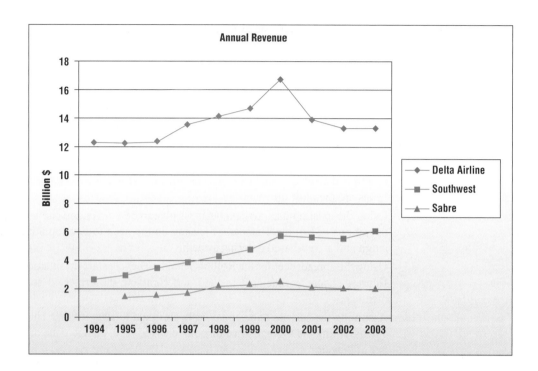

Growth of the Discounters

People Express did not have the information systems and could not compete. The big airlines had won—but only for a while. They did learn to adopt the hub-and-spoke system pioneered by People Express. Small feeder flights brought passengers to a few major airports, where passengers made connections to the next hub. The cost advantage of the hubs is that at the end of the day, all the planes and flight crews returned to a hub city. Consequently, maintenance facilities are centralized into a few key airports instead of scattered around the country. Plus, the key airports handle multiple flights each day, simplifying routing decisions.

But the story is not over. Southwest Airlines was also an upstart—beginning in Texas in 1971. By flying within the state, the airline was not subject to CAB regulations. Founded and largely run by Herbert D. Kelleher, the airline grew slowly to maintain control. Part of the simplicity lies in its fee structure—far simpler than the major airlines, Southwest prices flights so that they are profitable. By supporting several daily flights to each destination, with reasonable fares, Southwest promotes itself as the "company plane." By holding down costs (flight attendants often help clean the airplane, and the company flies only Boeing 737s to minimize maintenance costs), the company grew steadily. More important, Southwest Airlines has been profitable every single year for over 30 years—a statement that no other airline can match (www.southwest.com).

Recent Changes

To understand the current state of the airline industry, you also have to look at September 11, 2001. The event shocked the American people. The industry and government response provided almost as much of a shock to the industry. Suddenly, flying became considerably more complicated—passengers and airlines wrestled with long security lines and new rules. The U.S. government bailed out most of the airlines by providing billions of dollars in grants and loan guarantees.

Yet the major airlines were still saddled with strict working rules and high wages through negotiated contracts. In December 2002, United Airlines filed for reorganization under Chapter 11 of the bankruptcy code. In 2004, the company was still struggling to obtain financing to emerge from bankruptcy (www.pd-ual.com). Several other large airlines, including Delta, are running close to the margin and rumors continue to circulate about which airline might be next to go under. A large reason for filing for bankruptcy (or at least threatening to) appears to be a negotiation strategy aimed at reducing labor contract costs.

Several other airlines were created in the early 2000s to pick up passengers on highly traveled routes. JetBlue, founded in 2003, is one of the largest. JetBlue is based out of JFK airport in New York City and initially focused on East Coast destinations. It has expanded to cross-country flights and is slowly adding some Western cities to its routes. It has been successful (passengers like the DirectTV broadcasts available on the seat-back sets) and profitable (www.jetblue.com). AirTran, a successful start-up from 1998, has been hammering Delta's fares in the Atlanta airport—Delta's home base (www.airtran.com). While still only carrying a fraction of the passengers of the big airlines (maybe 10 percent), JetBlue and AirTran have been growing ("The New Normal" 2002). The secret to success, as explained by Joe Leonard, the CEO of AirTran, to a congressional committee "is not to be a low-fare airline, but to be a highly efficient airline, whether you are a big airline or small, and to adapt to the changing marketplace" (Leonard 2004).

The obvious question at this point is that since Southwest has been so successful with its strategy, why don't the airlines simply copy their formula? Yes, September 11 and the resulting gasoline price increases due to the war with Iraq have put added pressure on the airlines. But the big airlines were struggling even before these events. The answer is that it might not be possible for the big airlines to make the huge changes needed. Delta and United have started some experiments. Delta created a subsidiary called Song in 2003 designed to compete directly with the discounters—focusing on leisure travel between high-demand cities (www.flysong.com). United formed Ted (a part of United) in early 2004 for the same purpose (www.flyted.com). Although the fare rules for Song and Ted are usually simpler than for the parent company, the interesting part is that it is sometimes cheaper to fly the parent airline. In 2004, the CEO of Delta, Leo Mullins, resigned, and the interim CEO suspended any expansion of the Song airline.

Airline Costs

If airlines are going to cut costs, it helps to know where those costs are. The Air Transport Association (ATA) tracks these costs and releases summary data. The easiest way to understand the costs is to examine them as a percentage of the total. By far, labor costs are the largest share (38.4 percent). All other costs, mostly administrative overhead, are second (23.7 percent). Fuel costs vary over time, but most airlines use futures markets to hedge their costs (11.6 percent). The cost of the planes seems reasonable (10.2 percent), but you also have to add in the interest costs of the debt for the planes. Since interest rates were at historical lows, the cost was relatively small (3.0 percent). Maintenance material (2.5 percent) is usually steady, unless an airline is running a large percentage of older planes. Passenger food costs have been declining as airlines drop their food programs (2.3 percent). Airlines still pay some commissions to travel agents, but that number is dropping steadily (2.2 percent). Airlines have to pay landing fees to airports to use their gates (2.1 percent). Insurance costs (1.5 percent), communication (1.5 percent), and advertising (1.0 percent) are all relatively small components (McCartney 2002). These industry averages conceal the differences between the airlines. Through cheaper labor contracts, newer planes that need less maintenance and use less fuel, and a focus on costs, the discount airlines average a cost of 7.3 cents per mile, compared with 11.7 cents for traditional airlines (Rosato 2004).

The Possible Future

A large part of the differences with Song and Ted are the union contracts. The major airlines and the flight crews need to find some way to negotiate contracts that enable the carriers to compete with the discounters. The airlines also need to find a way to reduce costs and provide a service that people are willing to pay for. The good news for passengers is that airlines should be more willing to try innovations and search for ways to provide better service.

For business travelers, some new options are on the near horizon. Several companies are building small, "personal" jets that will cost less than $1 million. Some companies will purchase the jets for company use, but the annual upkeep and crew costs still make them expensive. On the other hand, they might enable a type of air taxi service to be created. Flying from small regional airports, the jets could offer quick service directly from one city to another, bypassing the big airline hubs and their driving, parking, and security hassles. This service will probably be too expensive for leisure travelers, but would appeal to a business person who is currently being charged $2,000 for a major airline flight. That would leave the big airlines running a type of low-cost mass-transit bus service (McCartney 2003).

Additional Reading

Leonard, Joe. "U.S. Government Subsidizes Inefficiency in Airline Industry." *Aviation Week & Space Technology,* June 21, 2004, Vol. 160(25), p. 86.

McCartney, Scott. "Which Costs Airlines More: Fuel, Labor or (Ugh) Meals?" *The Wall Street Journal,* November 6, 2002.

McCartney, Scott. "Airline Visionary Burr Sees Future in 'Personal' Travel." *The Wall Street Journal,* June 4, 2003.

"The 'New Normal': Big Carriers Lose Market Share to Upstarts." *The Wall Street Journal,* May 14, 2002.

Rosato, Donna. "The Plane Truth about Flying Cheap." *Money,* May 2004, Vol. 33(5), pp. 83–86.

www.airtran.com

www.flysong.com

www.flyted.com

www.jetblue.com

www.pd-ual.com

www.southwest.com

Case: Delta Air Lines

Delta (ticker: DAL) is one of the original airlines—tracing its history back to its first passenger flight in 1929. The company, headquartered in Atlanta, had revenues of $13 billion in 2003—a steady decline from 2000. With over 60,000 employees, the company flew about 100 million passengers in 2003. The company, and its code-share partners, fly to almost 500 cities in 86 nations (www.delta.com). Delta's books showed a net profit in 2000, but the company has been in the red since that time. Delta has reported a total loss of $3.7 billion in 2001, 2002, and 2003. For most quarters, the company is losing money even on operations (annual report). Fred Reid, president of Delta, knows the problems: "There's no question whatsoever in Delta's mind that we are in the midst of a profound, fundamental and truly irreversible series of changes in which the value proposition to the investors and the customers is changed unalterably. In this new world some airlines are winning and some airlines are losing, and I would say that Delta is still positioning for long-term success" (Bond March 2004).

Pilots and Costs

As of 2004, Delta's pilots are the highest paid in the industry. After acrimonious negotiations, then-CEO Leo Mullins granted the union huge pay raises. In 2004, Leo Mullins was removed as CEO. The airline is attempting to renegotiate all salaries. The company executives have discussed the possibility of filing bankruptcy to force the union to negotiate lower salaries (Bond May 2004). Many of Delta's older pilots are abandoning ship before it sinks. In mid-2004, 288 pilots applied for retirement—266 of them were for early retirement. An additional 300 had already applied for retirement in September 2003. Despite the retirements, Delta has plenty of pilots available: 8400 on active duty, plus 1,060 on furlough ("Delta Pilots" June 2004). Delta's total costs of flying domestically are 30 percent higher than Southwest's (McCartney October 2002).

Subsidiaries

To fight the discount airlines, Delta has established or purchased several subsidiary airlines. Delta Express and Skywest are two regional subsidiaries that operate out of Delta hubs. These airlines fly smaller planes or regional jets and deliver passengers to the hub, providing access to Delta in smaller cities. A key arrangement with the pilot's union allows the regional airline pilots to be paid less and fly under less limiting rules—as long as the planes carry a limited number of passengers.

In 2003, Delta launched service on Song. Although the goal was to keep fares relatively low, Song was competing more with JetBlue than with Southwest. In particular, the airline offers seat-back television for satellite programs, pay-per-view movies, and video games. However, the company had trouble getting the systems installed and had to begin operations without the technology for several months. Another drawback faced by Song was that they used the same Delta personnel, with the same contracts and lack of focus on cost cutting (Melymuka 2003). When Leo Mullins was replaced by Gerald Grinstein as CEO in 2004, Grinstein halted expansion of the Song division.

Information Technology

Information technology has an impressive role in the history of airlines. At the pure transaction level, IT is necessary to handle the millions of reservations a day. Running from huge databases, the large systems find flights, check seats, and bill customers when seats are reserved. When American Airlines used its system to create yield management and differentiate prices, it represented a milestone in the competitive use of technology. But today, the reservations systems have been moved out to subsidiaries and passengers can book online or through third-party reservation systems. Although the systems are still used by some of the major airlines to jockey prices, companies are increasingly looking at simpler fare structures. In 2004, Qantas, the Australian airline, decided it was pointless to run its own system. CIO Fiona Balfour said, "I don't think airlines get a competitive advantage from IT anymore. They get competitive advantage from how they use it. Running IT at a low unit cost becomes a competitive advantage" (Kontzer 2004). Nonetheless, Delta (and most of the other major airlines) continues to run its own systems. Delta's CIO, Curtis Robb, believes that outsourcing will not necessarily reduce costs or improve service. He observes that "we get payback on a yearly basis for in-house IT work and we get it at a fraction of the cost" (McDougall 2003).

Away from the reservation system, Delta is working harder to use the transaction to increase the operational efficiency. For example, the company runs the Delta Nervous System (DNS) that pushes data from the transaction system out to the desktop and even handheld computers. For example, as a plane arrives at an airport, the gate agent and luggage handler are notified electronically. A first step in creating the DNS was to set common definitions for data stored in over 70 different databases and place every item into one of 15 subject categories. This system forms the foundation of all the real-time applications. For example, the gate information display simply queries the DNS data layer for real-time information about the specific flight, formats it, and presents it to the customers. New applications can be built relatively quickly—programmers need only identify the data they require and can focus on the application and display. At Delta hubs, the DNS data is supplemented with data from the federal air traffic control (ATC) system. This data is examined for late flights and enables managers to spot problems and reschedule flights. DNS is a $1.8 billion project started in 1998 ("Technology Leadership" 2004).

The company also installed customer relationship management software for the call center. The CRM system enables clerks to see the entire picture of the customer who called (McDougall 2003). In the process, the company consolidated 30 customer databases into one, with three data warehouses to support analytical functions (Gareiss 2003). The newer jets offer additional ways to save money through integrating with information technology. The Boeing 777 collects information from various subsystems electronically. This telemetry is collected and transmitted to the maintenance engineers. If a problem arises, such as excessive vibration in an engine, managers can spot the problem and correct it before it causes additional problems. The company is also working to create electronic documents for all of the maintenance procedures. Electronic versions can be provided instantly to maintenance workers—saving search time (McDougall 2003b).

Like other airlines, Delta has installed kiosks to encourage departing passengers to record their own check-in, saving money by reducing the number of ticketing agents. Delta has also created a telephone system that customers can use to check in. More important, the IT system automatically monitors late flights and missed connections. If a passenger is not going to make a connection, the system automatically re-books the flight (Schwartz 2004).

Questions

1. Why do people fly on the discount airlines? What do they not like about the discounters? Can Delta combine these answers with IT to regain market share and profits?

2. How does Delta use technology to reduce costs? Is it enough to make a difference?

3. Can Delta use IT to become more like Southwest? Is that the best strategy?

Additional Reading

Bond, David. "Work in Progress." *Aviation Week & Space Technology,* March 1, 2004, Vol. 160(9), p. 45.

Bond, David. "Bankruptcy's Siren Song." *Aviation Week & Space Technology,* May 17, 2004, Vol. 160(20), p. 24.

Delta Annual Report 2003.

"Delta Pilots in New Retirement Application Spike." *Aviation Week & Space Technology,* June 14, 2004, Vol. 160(24), p. 17.

Gareiss, Robin. "Technology Takes to the Air." *Information Week,* April 21, 2003.

Kontzer, Tony. "Airline Taps IBM for Flexible Pricing Deal." *Information Week,* May 24, 2004.

McCartney, Scott. "Southwest Sets Standard on Costs for Airlines." *The Wall Street Journal,* October 9, 2002.

McDougall, Paul. "Tough Climb." *Information Week,* April 21, 2003.

McDougall, Paul. "Prevention: The Cure for High Maintenance Costs." *Information Week,* April 21, 2003b.

Melymuka, Kathleen. "Delta's Test Pilot: IT at Song, Delta's New Low-Cost Airline Unit." *Computerworld,* August 18, 2003.

Schwartz, Adele C. "On the Wings of IT." *Air Transport World,* March 2004, Vol. 41(3), pp. S7–9.

"Technology Leadership." *Air Transport World,* February 2004, Vol. 41(2), p. 32.

www.delta.com

Case: Southwest Airlines

One of Herb Kelleher's favorite stories is that back when they started flying to West Texas, the competitors tried to fight back by matching his fares. Herb's answer was to start offering a bottle of whiskey to every Southwest passenger. Within a few weeks, Southwest (ticker: LUV) became the largest liquor distributor in West Texas. Knowing the customers and not being afraid to take chances (or play jokes) became hallmarks at Southwest. At one point in 2002, domestic traffic at the nation's five largest airlines fell by 10 percent. At the same time, travel on the five biggest discount airlines increased by 11 percent. In 2002, the discounters accounted for 20 percent of U.S. passenger traffic (Trottman 2002). Within California, Southwest flew a whopping 63 percent of the passengers (Leonhardt and Maynard 2002). To traditional airline executives, the amazing aspect of this change is that even business people are flying on the discount airlines. Southwest pushed this concept hard for many years—emphasizing that a manager could get on the plane at the spur of the moment and fly to a business meeting at a reasonable fare. One executive, Brent Harris, managing director of Pacific Investment Management, notes that he now flies JetBlue for business instead of one of the big carriers for transcontinental flights. He observes that "while I could afford to pay more, there's a certain sense of satisfaction," in getting the discounts (Trottman 2002). Southwest began adding transcontinental flights (from Baltimore) in 2002 ("The 'New Normal'" 2002].

Southwest is an incredibly efficient airline, turning a plane around in as little as 20 minutes. Other airlines average 50 minutes. As a result, Southwest is able to fly its Boeing 737s an average of nine hours a day, compared with six hours for Delta and United (Trottman 2002). In general, the major airlines would have to cut 29 percent of their costs ($18.6 billion) to match the cost structure of Southwest (McCartney 2002). In 2002, Southwest had become the nation's sixth largest airline.

Not all is rosy in the Southwest family. In 2004, Herb Kelleher had to step in to negotiate a new contract with the flight attendant's union. Normally, negotiations are friendly at the employee-centered company, but these took two years to settle. In the end, the workers gained an average 31 percent raise spread over six years ("Business and Finance" 2004). In July, James F. Parker resigned as CEO.

Information Technology

Even in the early days, Southwest managed to avoid many of the hassles of reservation systems. For years, the company was able to list its flights for free on the industry reservation systems. It required travel agents to call the company to book the flight—the systems carried listings for free but charged when flights were booked. One estimate places the cost of booking through the Sabre system at $12 to $14 per transaction (Hoffman 2002). Today, Southwest has benefited considerably from the Internet. Customers can see all fares quickly and make their own reservations. Southwest gets over 40 percent of its bookings online, compared with United's 5 percent (Trottman 2002). The Internet also makes air fares more transparent. Even business people can quickly see the difference in the prices across airlines. Using the online tools, travelers can arrange flights to avoid the huge fares that airlines are trying to hoist onto business fliers. David Weiner, corporate travel manager for DaimlerChrysler, explains that although the company has preferred discounts with Northwest, most of his managers would rather fly Southwest. He claims that "with companies like Southwest, their fares are affordable as is. It's not like you would require any additional discounts" (Leonhardt and Maynard 2002).

Southwest also pioneered business reservations on its Web site (www.swabiz.com). In addition to letting managers and workers book flights, the system tracks companywide data for travel managers. Kaiser Permanente, a major health care organization, spends $6 million on Southwest travel. The business site enables Margy Skinner, the travel manager, to identify all tickets and use them to obtain quarterly bulk rebates (Kontzer 2004).

The Web site is so critical to Southwest that it rebuilt the system in 2002. The new UNIX-based system uses servers from Fujitsu in a cluster to ensure that the system keeps running and can scale up. Steve Taylor, director of interactive marketing, observes that "the bedrock of customer service in the online world is always being there. That's what we're aiming for with this clustering project" (Greenemeier 2002). The online marketing team consists of 70 employees, with 50 of them IT professionals and the rest marketing specialists.

Southwest does use information technology to help analyze its data. Since it does collect a large share of the transaction data directly, it has purchased business intelligence tools to help analyze it. In particular, the company is using Hyperion's Essbase OLAP application and budgeting software to make financial forecasts. Mike Van de Ven, vice president of financial planning and analysis at Southwest, notes that after the September 11 attacks, the company knew it faced huge uncertainty and needed help. He adds that "we were asked to give some sort of financial insight for a variety of decisions the company might make" (Songini 2002). Before installing the $1 million software, managers relied on writing custom database queries and evaluating the data in spreadsheets. Essbase provides immediate analysis and charts, cutting analysis time to as little as two minutes. Managers use the system to evaluate best and worst case scenarios to determine how to respond to problems. The software paid for itself within the first year by providing more accurate forecasts and saving time for managers.

Unlike the other big airlines, Southwest is growing—that means it needs to hire more workers. Growth is good for both the company and the employees, but how can Southwest deal with the 200,000 résumés a year that it receives? Southwest is turning to Deploy software to handle the major tasks of hiring. The software tracks everything from job requests by departments, to application progress, and candidate matching and ranking. The tool also integrates with the U.S. government system for verifying job candidate fingerprints and validating drug-test results (Hayes 2003).

Radio systems in airlines are ancient. Even if the planes and radios are new, they use technology developed in World War II. As one of the few airlines making money, Southwest is one of the first to install a new digital technology (VDLM2) to transmit data between its dispatchers and aircraft captains. Because the technology is restricted to a portion of the VHF bandwidth allocated to airlines, it provides a data rate of 31.5 K bits/second. But that rate is 15 times the rate of the company's old system. The system primarily handles short text messages—often instructions on the best route around weather problems. Ultimately, the system will be used to transmit high-resolution weather radar images to the cockpit. The company is also planning to collect telemetry information on the plane's performance and route it to maintenance personnel at the next airport if problems are detected (Brewin 2004).

Questions

1. How does Southwest use information technology to establish fares?
2. How has Southwest used the Internet to gain at least a short-term competitive advantage?
3. Can Southwest maintain its competitive strengths as it continues to grow? What risks will the company face?

Additional Reading

Brewin, Bob. "Data Takes Flight." *Computerworld,* June 21, 2004.

"Business and Finance." *The Wall Street Journal,* July 2, 2004.

Greenemeier, Larry. "IT Pros Plus Marketing Experts Equal Better Service." *Information Week,* March 18, 2002.

Hayes, Mary. "Southwest's People Plan." *Information Week,* September 8, 2003.

Hoffman, Thomas. "IT Investments Grounded at USAir, Other Carriers." *Computerworld,* August 19, 2002.

Kontzer, Tony. "Low-Cost Airlines Build Portals for Business." *Information Week,* April 5, 2004.

Leonhardt, David, and Micheline Maynard. "Troubled Airlines Face Reality: Those Cheap Fares Have a Price." *The New York Times,* August 18, 2002.

McCartney, Scott. "Southwest Sets Standard on Costs for Airlines." *The Wall Street Journal,* October 9, 2002.

"The 'New Normal': Big Carriers Lose Market Share to Upstarts." *The Wall Street Journal,* May 14, 2002.

Songini, Marc L. "Southwest Expands Business Tools' Role." *Computerworld,* July 12, 2002.

Trottman, Melanie, and Scott McCartney. "The Age of 'Wal-Mart' Airlines Crunches the Biggest Carriers." *The Wall Street Journal,* June 18, 2002.

Trottman, Melanie, and Scott McCartney. "Southwest's CEO Abruptly Quits a 'Draining Job.'" *The Wall Street Journal,* July 16, 2004.

Case: Sabre

Sabre (ticker: TSG) is the monster real-time reservation system originally created by American Airlines. The first system went live in 1960 and handled 84,000 telephone calls a day. In 1964, the system ran on its own private network—reducing American Airlines' staff by 30 percent in the first year. In 1976, the system was installed into travel agent offices—quickly reaching 130 locations. In 1985, preceding the Internet adoption by several years, easySabre gave dial-up access to users with personal computers. In 2000, the company was spun off as a separate entity, but tracking-stock data is available back to 1996. In 2004, the system handled $70 billion of travel products and connected 53,000 travel agents. It also forms the foundation of the Travelocity Web site (www.sabretravelnetwork.com).

Technology

For years, the Sabre system ran on large IBM computers. Much of it was jointly developed with IBM, since the demands and technologies needed continually pushed the available hardware and software. The system handles 15,000 transactions per second and tracks 79 million air fares. In 2001, the company announced it would migrate the massive system to a completely new architecture—based on a UNIX platform (Anthes May 2004), but the transfer would take several years.

Throughout its history, Sabre has been a leading-edge system, handling huge transaction volumes and providing detailed data for analysis. Almost all of the code has been custom written. In 2000, Sabre produced Release 8 of its Air-Flite Profit Manager. The modeling and forecasting package is used by airlines to estimate demand for seats on every flight. It is the core of the yield management system. Release 8 had about 500,000 lines of code. The problem is that it was four months late because final system testing turned up 300 bugs. The first customer found 26 more bugs in the first three days, and additional joint testing turned up another 200 defects. Sabre and its development team were embarrassed. However, the situation mirrored other development projects. The catch is that Sabre has 62 software products with 13 million lines of code. It cannot afford defect rates that high. For Release 10, shipped in December 2002, Sabre turned to extreme programming (XP). With XP, programmers work in pairs, but more important, they define testing procedures for each module before writing the code. The final version turned up only 100 defects after 16 months of use. At the same time, programmer productivity increased. The reduced defect rate also cut the number of support programmers needed (Anthes March 2004).

Competition

Despite the technological advances and prowess of Sabre, it faces competition. Its biggest competition is undoubtedly the Internet. Although the company runs Travelocity, one of the big Internet travel sites, the site is not profitable yet. Furthermore, when customers book flights through Travelocity, the airline or hotel pays a fee to Sabre. Consequently, airlines have been encouraging customers to book their flights directly at the airline Web sites—bypassing Sabre entirely. The Orbitz Web site was created by the five largest airlines specifically for that purpose. It searches the company's individual databases and routes the customer's choice directly to the airline's server.

In 2004, Alaska Airlines, tired of waiting for new services from Sabre, decided to create its own itinerary-planning and fare-searching system on a Linux-based system. Alaska simply purchased the system from Cambridge, Massachusetts, ITA software. Steve Javris, vice president of e-commerce at Alaska, noted that "we couldn't wait on Sabre. ITA's algorithms are widely regarded as the best in the industry" (Verton 2004). Alaska will continue to use Sabre to book reservations, but will use the new system for data analysis. The ITA system is primarily used as the back-end processor for Web sites—helping customers identify routes. Jeremy Wertheimer, ITA's founder and CEO, comments that "it processes and confirms availability for [trip] pricing in less than one-tenth of a second" (Verton 2004).

But Sabre is not standing still. The company is creating new tools to encourage airlines to continue using the system and new products that will help travel agents. In terms of helping the airlines, Sabre launched its interline e-ticketing (IET) hub in 2004. Since Sabre serves multiple airlines, it is in an ideal position to provide links between them. Previously, customers had trouble booking e-tickets for flights that involved multiple airlines. Each system was separate and the airlines had to reidentify the passenger at each step. With the interline system, the passenger data and validation are shared across airlines. Essentially, Sabre serves as an EDI consolidator and translates data from each system into a common format that is accessible to all systems. The system is based on Web services, making it easy to expand and change as airline systems change (Rosencrance 2004).

Sabre also introduced a new feature for travel agents in 2004. What happens if a customer wants an aisle seat, but the only seat available is a middle seat? A good travel agent would book the available seat to keep it, and then periodically check the flight to see if a more desirable seat opens up. But that requires considerable time and effort by the travel agent. Sabre's answer was to create an event model that will alert the travel agent when a seat opens up. Loren Brown, CIO of Carlson Wagonlit Travel, a company with 8,000 agents, notes that agencies would likely pay extra for that feature alone, stating "that would be a much more elegant solution than we have in place now" (Kontzer June 2004).

Sabre also faces competition from more traditional rivals: Amadeus Global Travel Distribution, Cendant's Galileo International, and Worldspan. All of these were originally developed by other airlines and spun off as well. All of them are facing similar problems and working to cut costs and offer new services. That is one of the main reasons driving the switch in servers. Sabre estimates that by running the open-source MySQL database on open-source Linux servers, the new system will cost 80 percent less to operate [Kontzer June 2004].

The Future

With so many competitive factors, it is difficult to guess who is going to win the battles for customer reservations. Sabre and its direct rivals have some amazing technology as well as the developers to build complex systems. One of the things that might be changing is that passengers will want to book package deals. But not quite like the old "here's a tour—take it or leave it." Instead, customers will want to go to a site and select their own custom bundle: pick low-cost air fares, choose hotels that offer the desired amenities at an acceptable price, then add in some adventure excursions. Yes, the big travel sites support these steps in a limited way now. However, they rarely allow anything more than limited customization. Ultimately, customers want a more intelligent system that can create desired bundles—at a discount. So, airlines, hotels, and other providers will need to cooperate. Then, the reservation sites will have to become sophisticated enough to balance the various choices and compute all of the package deals (Kontzer May 2004).

Questions

1. Who are Sabre's competitors?
2. What risks does the company face? Will travel agents continue to exist and will they use Sabre?
3. What factors are needed for an intelligent agent reservation system to be created? Who would create these elements?

Additional Reading

Anthes, Gary H. "Sabre Takes Extreme Measures." *Computerworld,* March 29, 2004.

Anthes, Gary. "Sidebar: Sabre Timeline." *Computerworld,* May 31, 2004.

Kontzer, Tony. "Travel Execs Get a Glimpse of Their Future." *Information Week,* May 7, 2004.

Kontzer, Tony. "Bound for Industry Upheaval—with a Layover in Dallas." *Information Week,* June 7, 2004.

Rosencrance, Linda. "Sabre Launches Interline E-Ticketing Hub." *Computerworld,* February 3, 2004.

Verton, Dan. "Alaska Airlines Switches to Linux-Based Fare Searching." *Computerworld,* February 2, 2004.

www.sabretravelnetwork.com

Summary Industry Questions

1. What information technologies have helped this industry?
2. Did the technologies provide a competitive advantage or were they quickly adopted by rivals?
3. Which technologies could this industry use that were developed in other sectors?
4. Is the level of competition increasing or decreasing in this industry? Is it dominated by a few firms, or are they fairly balanced?
5. What problems have been created from the use of information technology and how did the firms solve the problems?

PART FOUR

Organizing Businesses and Systems

12 SYSTEMS DEVELOPMENT

13 ORGANIZING MIS RESOURCES

14 INFORMATION MANAGEMENT AND SOCIETY

How do managers organize and control businesses and information systems?

How are information systems created? How do you organize the information system resources? How do information systems affect society?

Information technology provides new ways to organize businesses. In particular, the Internet makes it possible for firms of any size to conduct business around the world. But creating these new structures requires thought, effort, and time. Experience shows that it is easy to make mistakes and waste huge amounts of money. Organizing and planning are critical to avoiding these problems.

Because of their importance in a modern firm, information systems must be carefully planned, designed, and maintained. Business managers are increasingly involved in designing and organizing MIS resources. Managers need to understand the difficulties faced in systems development to understand the rules and processes. As technology changes, the organization of business operations and the MIS resources is changing. By identifying these changes, business managers can improve their operations and make better use of new information technologies.

Changes in technology and business cause fundamental changes in society. These changes affect everything from education to government to our daily lives as employees and citizens. Changing technology brings new responsibilities and problems. As managers and citizens we will face many new decisions. We must always remember our ethical responsibilities to other members of society.

CHAPTER TWELVE

Systems Development

Chapter Outline

Introduction
Building Information Systems
  Custom Programming
  Outsourcing and Contract Programmers
  Assemble Applications from Components
  Purchase an External Solution
Systems Development Life Cycle
  The Need for Control
  Introduction to SDLC
  Feasibility and Planning
  Systems Analysis
  Systems Design
  Systems Implementation
  Maintenance
  Evaluation
  Strengths and Weaknesses of SDLC
Alternatives to SDLC
  Prototyping
  Developing Systems Requires Teamwork: JAD and RAD
  Extreme Programming
  Open Source Development
  End-User Development
  Development Summary
Process Analysis
  Input, Process, Output
  Divide and Conquer
  Goals and Objectives
  Diagramming Systems
  Summary: How Do You Create a DFD?
Object-Oriented Design
  Properties and Functions
  Object Hierarchies
  Events
  Object-Oriented and Event-Driven Development
Distributed Services
Summary
Key Words
Web Site References

Additional Reading
Review Questions
Exercises
Cases: Government Agencies

What You Will Learn in This Chapter

- How do you create the software tools needed for your organization?
- What main options exist for building information systems?
- How do you control a major development project? Why is control so important?
- Is SDLC always the best approach? What other methodologies could be used?
- How do you analyze and annotate a process-based system?
- How is object-oriented design different from process design?
- Can software be located in different places?

Why is it so difficult to develop software? Developing software for complex systems is a difficult task. Even bringing in outside contractors has not solved all of the problems for the FAA. Cost overruns and missed schedules have happened so many times in FAA (and other government) projects that completing a project on time is the rare exception.

The FAA is charged with controlling civilian and military uses of U.S. airspace. The FAA is also responsible for modernizing the airways, installing radar, and training air traffic controllers. Probably their best-known function is control over commercial flights and routes to maintain safety and efficiency. With 50,000 flights a day among 300 major airports, the FAA has a huge task.

The FAA has a computer system to help it control the thousands of daily flights. However, the system was created in the early 1960s. It has been patched and upgraded, but most of the hardware and software are based on decades-old technology. On several occasions, the FAA attempted to upgrade the facilities, but complications have forced the agency back to the old technology.

The FAA systems are particularly difficult since they entail high-risk operations that have to be performed accurately. Also, the technology is relatively unique and development often requires state-of-the-art skills in areas that are rarely taught or researched in schools. Also, large-scale projects are always difficult to forecast, because any number of things can go wrong.

FIGURE 12.1

It is not easy to create information systems to support business needs (strategy, tactics, and operations). Three basic development techniques are systems development life cycle, prototyping, and end-user development. As a manager, you will participate in each of these methods. You will sometimes have to choose which method to use.

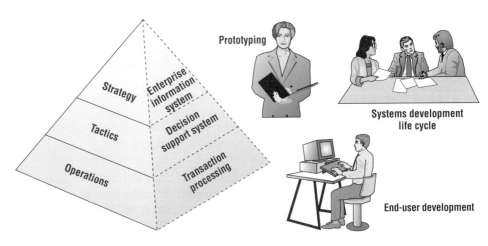

Introduction

How do you create the software tools needed for your organization? Can you simply buy them? Do the tools need to be customized? How is software developed? Why is the process so difficult? To answer these questions, you need to examine how software is developed. As a business manager, you will probably not become a developer. On the other hand, you will have to interact with developers to ensure that you get the systems you need. You need to be able to communicate with the developers, and you need to understand their constraints. Furthermore, as a manager, you need to understand the costs and management issues facing MIS departments. You might have to choose among development methodologies, so you need to know the options and their strengths and weaknesses.

Anyone developing computer applications faces a fundamental dilemma. Most problems are so large they have to be split into smaller pieces. The difficulty lies in combining the pieces back into a complete solution. Often each piece is assigned to a different team, and

TRENDS

Internally, computer processors have limited capabilities. The processor has a set of a few hundred internal instructions that it knows how to perform, such as moving a number to a new place in memory or adding two numbers together. Initially, all computer programs were written at this low level; but writing programs at this level is difficult and time consuming. Over time, two major innovations were created to reduce the difficulty of programming at these low levels: (1) higher-level languages were created that handle many details automatically for the programmer, and (2) common algorithms used by many applications were created and sold as operating systems. These advances enable programmers to focus on the applications instead of machine-specific details.

Despite many advances, writing programs is still complex and time consuming. Large-scale applications require the teamwork of millions of hours of programmer time and cost hundreds of millions of dollars to build and maintain. These high, fixed development costs underlie the growth of the commercial software industry. By making the software relatively generic and selling it to hundreds or thousands of firms, the development costs are spread over a wide group.

Increasingly, firms are moving away from custom-written software. They are purchasing packages and hiring outside programmers to develop many components. In these situations, design issues generally consist of choosing and customizing the software to meet the individual needs of the organization.

sometimes it takes months to complete each section. Without a solid plan and control, the entire system might collapse. Thousands of system development projects have failed or been canceled because of these complications.

Partly because of the problems that have been encountered in the past, and partly because of technological improvements, several techniques are available to develop computer systems. The most formal approach is known as the **systems development life cycle (SDLC)**. As indicated by the Reality Bytes boxes, large organizations that develop several systems use this method to coordinate the teams, evaluate progress, and ensure quality development. Most organizations have created their own versions of SDLC. Any major company that uses SDLC also has a manual that is several inches thick (or comparable online documentation) that lays out the rules that MIS designers have to follow. Although these details vary from firm to firm, all of the methods have a common foundation. The goal is to build a system by analyzing the business processes and breaking the problem into smaller, more manageable pieces.

Improvements in technology also improve the development process. The powerful features of commercial software make it easier to build new applications. Programmers and designers can work with larger, more powerful objects. For example, instead of programming each line in COBOL, a report can be created in a few minutes using a database management system or a spreadsheet. **Prototyping** is a design technique that takes advantage of these new tools. The main objective of prototyping is to create a working version of the system as quickly as possible, even if some components are not included in the early versions. The third method of creating systems, **end-user development**, relies on users to create their own systems. This method typically uses advanced software (such as spreadsheets and database management systems) and requires users who have some computer skills.

It is important to be careful when you implement any new system. Case studies show that major problems have arisen during implementation of systems. In fact, some organizations have experienced so many problems that they will deliberately stick with older, less useful systems just to avoid the problems that occur during implementation. Although changes can cause problems, there are ways to deal with them during implementation.

There have been some spectacular failures in the development of computer systems. Projects always seem to be over budget and late. Worse, systems are sometimes developed and never used because they did not solve the right problems or they are impossible to use. Several design methods have been created to help prevent these problems. All methods have advantages and drawbacks. As a result, they tend to be suitable for different types of problems.

REALITY BYTES   System Development Methodologies

Accenture is the largest worldwide consulting firm in management information systems. It conducts major installations using a proprietary methodology called Method/1. Method/1 uses four phases in the development process: plan, design, implement, and maintain.

McKinsey and Co., a strategic consulting firm, examines organizations with a copyrighted "Seven S" model. The Seven S's are structure, systems, style, staff, skills, strategy, and shared values.

Electronic Data Systems (EDS), started by Ross Perot, purchased by GM, and now independent, is the largest outsourcing company. It also develops systems using a traditional SDLC methodology. The detailed methodology has thousands of individual steps spelled out on separate pages that must be signed off at each step.

Rational Rose, a tool to support object-oriented development, was designed by the leading OO gurus. It is a graphical tool designed to show the object details and their relationships. It supports reverse engineering, by reading existing code and converting it into the corresponding diagrams. The Rose tool can also generate the final code from the diagrams.

Microsoft, as a commercial software vendor developing highly complex systems used by millions of people, has developed its own methodologies for quickly creating code. The company has been a proponent of Rapid Application Development to reduce the time it takes to complete large projects. The methodology is designed to segment the code so that hundreds of programmers can work on it simultaneously. The methodology also relies on creating code that can be modified later, for improvements and patches.

With *Open Source,* led by Richard Stallman and the GNU project, thousands of programmers around the globe are building complex projects in a loosely knit organization. Generally, one person is a project leader responsible for setting strategies and resolving disputes. All of the source code is publicly available to anyone (hence the name). Interested programmers suggest improvements and submit the modifications. Some complex systems have been built this way with minimal central control.

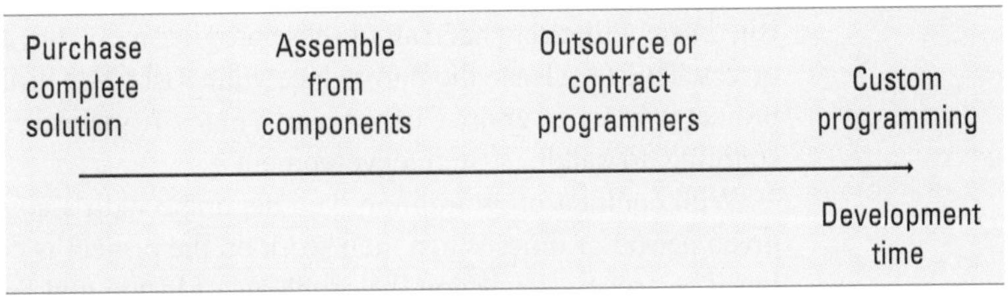

FIGURE 12.2
Development choices: Longer development time means more risk, possibly higher costs. But it also enables you to create a more customized solution.

Building Information Systems

What main options exist for building information systems? Several methods exist to build information systems, but all of them can be challenging. The key to understanding the different methods is to realize that ultimately developers have to write detailed program code. The primary difference in the methods lies in who writes the code. Figure 12.2 shows the four basic methods: (1) program the entire application from scratch, (2) pay an outside company to develop the application, (3) assemble an application by customizing various purchased components, or (4) purchase the entire application from another company. These methods apply to virtually any type of software development project, from small one-person applications to complex e-commerce solutions.

Custom Programming

Ultimately, all applications are created by teams of programmers writing detailed code. Writing your own custom program gives you complete control over the application. You can include any features, build in special routines unique to your company, and integrate the data with your existing systems. The problem with creating your own code is that programming is difficult, time consuming, hard to control, and expensive. Even when the application is completed, you will still need groups of programmers to fix problems, add new features, and develop future versions of the software. Modern development tools make it easier to write programs today, but every application still requires intense development efforts, and the tools never seem to provide all of the features you need.

REALITY BYTES — Rent a Programmer

Most cities have a location where day laborers (often Mexican immigrants) stand around and wait for contractors to drive up in their trucks and hire them. Now there is a Web site (www.2rentacoder.com) where you can hire a programmer for small projects. Coders register their skills and check the listings for potential jobs. Buyers describe the projects and suggest a maximum price. Developers can then bid on the projects they are interested in working on. Once an agreement is reached, the buyer pays the money into escrow. When the project is completed, the site takes 15 percent of the money and gives the rest to the programmer. Sounds like a perfect free market. Many programmers are based in countries where a $100 bid represents a substantial income. But glancing through the solicitations, many of the initial offers have unrealistically low prices. The site also contains requests for language translations and some hardware work.

Source: Adapted from Lee Gomes, "Hearing 'I Work Cheap' from across the Globe," *The Wall Street Journal,* June 3, 2002.

Quality and security are two critical issues with any type of development. If you build a custom application, you must leave sufficient time to build in quality tests and to correctly build security controls. Employees also have to be trained in these two areas, and you generally need specialized managers to oversee each of these two areas.

Outsourcing and Contract Programmers

One of the other problems with creating your own software is that you generally have to hire many programmers at some point in the development. But when the development is finished, you will rarely need all of these programmers. So, either you find new tasks for them or you have to release them to reduce your costs. But hiring and firing workers for a single project is frowned upon. Consequently, many firms use contract programmers, or even outsourcing, to handle system development.

With contract programming, you negotiate with a company to provide specialists for a given period of time. When their work on the project is complete, they move on to another job. The process saves you the problems of hiring and firing large numbers of employees. On the other hand, contractor salaries are usually higher than traditional employees. More important, several lawsuits have made it critical that you clarify the exact role of contractors—otherwise they can sue to be classified as regular employees to gain additional benefits such as stock options.

Outsourcing goes a step further than contract programming. When you outsource project development, you transfer most responsibility to the outside firm. Typically, you negotiate a development price, provide detailed specifications, and the outsourcer hires workers and develops the system. A huge variety of outsourcing arrangements are available, including situations where the outsourcers run your entire MIS department or just your servers or networks, or handle PC maintenance.

The primary advantage of outsourcing is that the external company takes responsibility for managing the process and producing the application. You still have the responsibility to clearly define exactly how the application should work, but the outsourcer bears more of the risk—particularly with fixed-fee contracts. The one thing you want to avoid with contractors and outsourcers is uncontrolled hourly fees.

Assemble Applications from Components

A good way to reduce development time and costs is to buy portions of the system from other companies. Even if you need a custom solution, you can purchase a variety of software components that handle many of the difficult tasks for you. Components are a powerful feature of modern operating systems. They are blocks of code that are integrated into custom applications. For instance, you could purchase a security control to handle encryption on a Web site. Whenever your application needs to encrypt or decrypt some data, it simply calls the component's methods. Similarly, if you need to process a credit card

Technology Toolbox: Analyzing Businesses

Problem: You are presented with a business problem to solve.
Tools: You need an analytical methodology to evaluate the problem, focus on the causes, and identify appropriate solutions. If the situation is based on business processes, you can use the data flow diagram techniques to show how the firm is organized and how data is supposed to move. Because it is a graphical approach, it is good for spotting the cause of problems and for communicating relationships to others. You can also adapt database and object-oriented tools to help you understand design details for data-intensive problems. Ultimately, every manager needs to develop a methodology for approaching business problems and cases. When you encounter a new situation, where do you start?

Foundation	Business Plan	Expectations
Solve the right problem.	Problem description	Measurable goals.
Choose the right tools.	State facts and problems.	Financial implications.
Divide the system.	Identify most important problems and causes.	Effect on human resources.
Make a decision.	Plan	Strategic effects.
Consider the consequences.	Describe the new system.	Critical success factors.
Detail the implementation.	Detail how to implement the plan.	Potential risks.
	Provide a contingency plan.	
	Advantages	
	Show how your plan will solve the problems.	
	List additional advantages and strategic effects.	

The most important first step is to solve the right problem. Most businesses encounter multiple problems. Often, you see only the symptoms, and you need to trace your way back to the cause. This work requires detective and diagnostic skills—which are usually acquired through experience with cases and real-world problems. Once you have identified the root problems, you have to choose the correct tools. There is an old saying: When all you have is a hammer, everything looks like a nail. Make sure you examine all of the available tools before pounding away.

You need to develop a structure for your business plan. A good starting point is the old debating approach: problem description, plan, and advantages. Use the problem description to identify the most important problems and the cause of the problems. This section must clearly communicate the need for a change. The plan itself must be detailed and as specific as possible. You should include implementation issues, costs, and alternatives or contingency plans. Be sure to include a section that explains how your plan is going to solve the problems you identified. You should also include additional advantages such as strategic implications.

Your analysis also needs to include a section on the expected outcomes. In particular, identify any measurable goals and financial implications. If the goal is to reduce costs or save time, try to quantify those numbers. Also consider the effects on human resources. Will the technology reduce the number of employees? Will you retrain employees, or need to hire more within the MIS department? What are the critical success factors for the firm and the project? How will the project affect those factors? Also, what are the potential risks of the project? Cost is obviously an issue, but could the project alienate employees or customers? Identifying these risks up front makes it easier to find ways to mitigate them later.

Quick Quiz:

1. Why is practice so important in learning to diagnose business problems? Where will you get this practice?

2. Where do you place the expectation elements in the business plan?

3. How is the problem description for a business case compared with an actual business problem?

application, you can install a component (or link to a Web service) that handles everything for you. Thousands of useful components are available for a few hundred dollars each or less. You simply install the component on your server and your programmers can begin using the functions within their code. This approach relies on the capabilities of **commercial off-the-shelf software (COTS).** As the number and quality of software packages have increased, it has become easier to build a system based on COTS.

Increasingly, tasks currently performed by components are being offered as services over the Internet. The same principles will apply, but the external company will maintain the application, install upgrades, and add new features. In addition, new services will become available. For example, services provide instant exchange rate conversions so that you can list prices in any currency. The conversion rates will always be current with no effort on your part.

Components have many substantial advantages and only minor drawbacks (primarily the price hassles with upgrades). They can significantly reduce development time and provide powerful features that are beyond the capabilities of many staff programmers. In fact, many outsource specialists develop their own collection of components to use in developing custom solutions. By integrating commonly used features, they can build new applications faster with fewer errors.

Purchase an External Solution

Taking the concept of components and outsourcing a step further, many commercial software companies sell prepackaged applications. Some are *turnkey* systems where you simply load your data, select a few preferences, and the system runs (much like buying an automobile, you turn the key and no assembly is needed). Other applications require detailed customization. The ERP packages (such as SAP) are classic examples. The system handles all of the basic operational data of the firm, including generation of financial reports. You purchase the software from the vendor and install it on top of a database management system. You still have to set up your accounts and some custom details for reports. The application can then be used by your company to track all financial and manufacturing data and produce standardized reports.

On the other hand, you can also customize most of the features. If you need unique manufacturing reports, you can write code to generate them. The degree of customization often depends on the attitude of management. The drawback to extensive customization is that it requires specially trained programmers and delays the entire project. Moreover, when the DBMS vendor or the ERP vendor upgrades the underlying software, you may have to rewrite all of your custom programs.

Prewritten packages can have high price tags (SAP costs can easily run into millions of dollars). But it could take millions of hours of programmer time to create a custom system with the same functionality.

In general, it is almost always preferable to buy solutions, but keep a close eye on prices. The commercial software essentially spreads the development costs across thousands of firms. Unless you have a truly unique application and are willing to pay a staff of top-notch programmers, it is better to share the development costs. And if you do have a radically different application, you should consider packaging it and selling it to other firms to reduce your costs.

Systems Development Life Cycle

The Need for Control

How do you control a major development project? Why is control so important? Runaway projects are a substantial problem in any development effort, but they are particularly important for new designs. Building a project from scratch (particularly an EC project) means it is hard to estimate the amount of time and effort needed to build the system. As projects become larger, they become more difficult to monitor and control. Several e-commerce firms failed because they were unable to produce a working system.

A factor in many runaway projects is the concept of scope creep or expanding features. Once development starts, users and programmers start thinking of new ideas that they would like to see in the project. So a simple, two-month project for one division suddenly expands into a two-year companywide project costing millions of dollars. A key role of any IT project manager is to politely avoid adding "features" that are not immediately necessary.

SDLC was designed to overcome the problems that arose with large projects that involve many users and require thousands of hours of development by multiple analysts and programmers. Difficulties with runaway projects are shown in Figure 12.3.

FIGURE 12.3

Runaway projects: Managers fear runaway projects, but they still occur. Some projects end up two to five times over budget and behind schedule. Some projects are canceled because they never meet their objectives. Some fail because of design problems and conflicts among users, management, and developers. An important step in managing projects is to identify when the project becomes a runaway project.

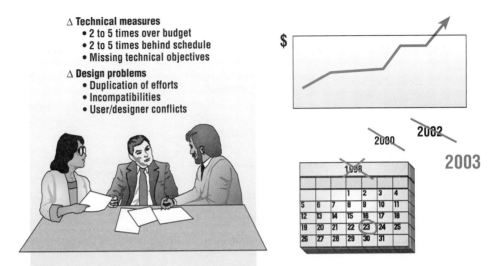

Before the use of the SDLC method, several related problems were common. It was hard to coordinate and control the various programmers and analysts, so efforts were duplicated. Individual programmers created portions of a system that would not work together. Users did not always have much input into the process. When they did have input, there were conflicts between users, and analysts did not know which approach to use. With long-term projects, programmers were promoted to other areas or left for different companies. New employees had to learn the system and determine what others had done before they could proceed. Similarly, new users would appear (through promotions and transfers), and existing users would change the specifications of the system. These problems often lead to runaway projects—projects that are significantly late and over budget. Even today, there are many instances of runaway projects.

These problems are related through the issue of control. It is impossible to prevent users from changing the specifications and to prevent employees from taking other jobs. Likewise, large projects involving many analysts and programmers will always have problems with coordination and compatibility. The goal of SDLC was to design a system that can handle all of these problems.

A key value in SDLC is project management. An important aspect of project management consists of identifying the dependencies among the various tasks. Project management tools exist to help evaluate these dependencies and show how the overall schedule is affected by delays in individual tasks.

Introduction to SDLC

An important feature of the SDLC approach is that it is a comprehensive method. Some organizations (such as EDS) that specialize in systems development have hundreds of pages in manuals to detail all the steps and rules for using SDLC. Fortunately, it is possible to understand SDLC by looking at a smaller number of steps. As illustrated in Figure 12.4, the SDLC approach encompasses five basic stages: (1) feasibility and planning, (2) systems analysis, (3) systems design, (4) implementation, and (5) maintenance and review.

Actually, just about any systems-development methodology uses these five steps. They differ largely in how much time is spent in each section, who does the work, and the degree of formality involved. The SDLC approach is by far the most formal method, so it offers a good starting point in describing the various methodologies.

Feasibility and Planning

The primary goal of systems analysis is to identify problems and determine how they can be solved with a computer system. In formal SDLC methodologies, the first step in systems analysis is a feasibility study. A feasibility study is a quick examination of the problems,

FIGURE 12.4

Systems development life cycle: Sometimes SDLC is known as the waterfall methodology because each step produces outputs that are used in the next step. The existing system is studied for problems and improvements. A new design is analyzed for feasibility. In-depth analysis generates the business requirements. Systems design turns them into a technical design that is implemented, creating a new system. This new system is analyzed and the process continues.

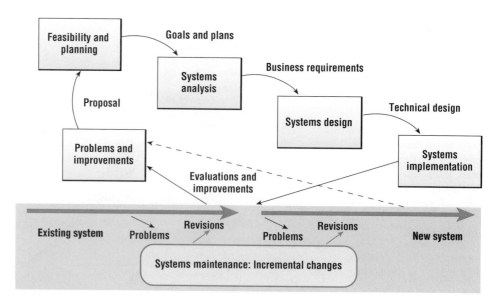

goals, and expected costs of the system. The objective is to determine whether the problem can reasonably be solved with a computer system. In some cases, maybe there is a better (or cheaper) alternative, or perhaps the problem is simply a short-term annoyance and will gradually disappear. In other cases, the problem may turn out to be more complex than was thought and to involve users across the company. Also, some problems may not be solvable with today's technology. It might be better to wait for improved technology or lower prices. In any case, you need to determine the scope of the project to gain a better idea of the costs, benefits, and objectives.

The feasibility study is typically written so that it can be easily understood by nonprogrammers. It is used to "sell" the project to upper management and as a starting point for the next step. Furthermore, it is used as a reference to keep the project on track and to evaluate the progress of the MIS team. Projects are typically evaluated in three areas of feasibility: economical, operational, and technical. Is the project cost effective or is there a cheaper solution? Will the proposed system improve the operations of the firm, or will complicating factors prevent it from achieving its goals? Does the technology exist, and does the firm have the staff to make the technology work?

When the proposal is determined to be feasible, the MIS team leaders are appointed, and a plan and schedule are created. The schedule contains a detailed listing of what parts of the project will be completed at each time. Of course, it is extremely difficult to estimate the true costs and completion dates. Nonetheless, the schedule is an important tool to evaluate the status of the project and the progress of the MIS teams. Figure 12.5 summarizes the role of planning and scheduling in providing control for projects.

Systems Analysis

Once a project has been shown to be feasible and is approved, work can begin on a full-fledged analysis. The first step is to determine how the existing system works and where the problems are located. The technique is to break the system into pieces. Smaller pieces are easier to understand and to explain to others. Also, each piece can be assigned to a different MIS team. As long as they work from the same initial description and follow all of the standards, the resulting pieces should fit back together. Of course, it still takes time and effort to integrate all of the pieces.

Diagrams are often created to illustrate the system. The diagrams are used to communicate among analysts and users, other analysts, and eventually the programmers. Data flow diagrams are a common method to display the relationships that were determined during systems analysis. The diagrams represent a way to divide the system into smaller pieces.

Graphics tools provide a useful way to communicate with the user and to document the user requirements. However, they do not speed up the development process. Producing,

REALITY BYTES   Converting 10 Million Lines of Assembler Code

Sabre, the original giant travel reservation system, has a problem: 10 million lines of code written in assembler language over the last 40 years. The mainframe system used flat files and 8,337 programs to handle searches by travel agents. But as agents and now customers on the Internet expanded use of the system, it cost too much to run on the big mainframe computers. The company does not get paid until people actually book a flight and was spending a huge amount of processing power just doing searches. The answer was to rewrite the programs as a distributed system using C++ and Java with modern object-oriented techniques and tools. The four-year project is projected to cost at least $100 million but will recover the money by running on horizontally scaled server farms that provide enormous computing power for substantially less money than the existing system.

But there are problems. The legacy (older) people who designed and built the original system do not know the new tools. And the new just-out-of-school programmers do not understand the business issues. Craig Murphy, the chief technology officer, notes: "The legacy guys tend to favor the subject-matter experts and don't trust the kids. That's a problem for me because the kids are always forcing me to go faster." The company is using Agile RUP, a version of IBM's Rational Unified Process software, to help design and test the new system. It is based on an iterative approach to development and frequent testing. Murphy observes that "it's based on the notion that no one knows what to do, so do something. Make some pudding and see what it tastes like. Less sugar, more chocolate, make another batch."

Source: Adapted from Gary H. Anthes, "Culture Clash between Veteran Programmers and Younger Coders," *Computerworld,* May 31, 2004.

FIGURE 12.5

Development controls: A complex system requires careful management. Without planning and control, any project will become a runaway. Control begins with a detailed plan and performance targets that enable managers to evaluate progress and identify problems. System control is provided by standardized practices and procedures to ensure that teams are producing compatible output. User input and control ensure that the final project will actually be useful?

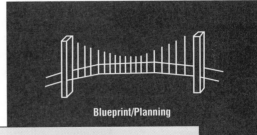

- **Detailed work plan**
- **Performance targets**
- **Practices and procedures**
- **User input and control**

Blueprint/Planning

changing, and storing documentation can be a significant problem. Yet these tools are necessary because they make it easier for the user to control the final result. One increasingly common solution is to keep all of the documentation on the computer. This method reduces the costs, makes it easier for everyone to share the documentation, and ensures that all users have up-to-date information for the system.

At the end of the analysis phase, the MIS team will have a complete description of the business requirements. The problems and needs are documented with text, data flow diagrams, and other figures depending on the methodology followed.

Systems Design

The third major step of the SDLC approach is to design the new system. During this step, the new system is typically designed on paper. The objective of systems design is to describe the new system as a collection of modules or subsystems. By subdividing the total project, each portion can be given to a single programmer to develop. As the pieces are completed, the overall design ensures that they will work together. Typically, the diagrams created during the analysis phase can be modified to indicate how the new system will work. The design will list all of the details, including data inputs, system outputs, processing

REALITY BYTES · Garbage In, Steel Out

A steel company in the 1980s decides to upgrade its manual quality control system. Line managers carry around production control cards that define the optimal control settings for each machine. The managers check off each setting and mark the machine as compliant with the settings. A programmer is charged with automating the cards so that the setting data is collected electronically. The project is moving along well, and the programmer reaches the final system-testing phase. In talking with the line managers, the programmer quickly learns that "the common reply throughout the plant was that they always mark the card as being in compliance, even though the settings identified on them were incorrect." Apparently, the "cor-

rect" settings were dictated by management. But the line managers knew that if those settings were used, the steel would never pass the final quality control evaluation. Since the line managers knew what the machine settings needed to be, they used those and simply marked the cards as being compliant—instead of challenging management. The new electronic system was implemented—and line managers used it the same way as the card-based system—marking everything as being in compliance. And management is happy (but no wiser).

Source: Adapted from "Shark Tank: Sure, It's Useless—but What a Success Rate!" *Computerworld,* November 18, 2003.

steps, database designs, manual procedures, and feedback and control mechanisms. Backup and recovery plans along with security controls will be spelled out to ensure that the database is protected.

In traditional SDLC methods, managers and users will be shown various components of the system as they are completed. The managers will have to *sign off* on these sections to indicate that they meet the user needs. This signature is designed to ensure that users provide input to the system. If there are many diverse users, there can be major disagreements about how the system should function. Sign-offs require users to negotiate and formally agree to the design. It is relatively easy to make design changes at this stage. If everyone attempts to make changes at later stages, the cost increases dramatically.

In terms of physical design, some of the hardware and software will be purchased. Programmers will write and test the program code. In most large projects, the actual coding takes only 15 to 30 percent of the total development time. Initial data will be collected or transferred from existing systems. Manuals and procedures will be written to instruct users and system operators on how to use the system.

Design tools can be used to create prototypes of major system elements. For example, a designer can quickly piece together displays that illustrate how each screen might look and how the user will see the system. These prototypes can be used to help users walk through aspects of the proposed system and make changes while it is easy and inexpensive. The walk-throughs also provide management with feedback regarding the time schedule and anticipated costs of the project, because they are often scheduled in the original feasibility study.

The output of the design stage consists of a complete technical specification of the new system. It includes as many details as possible, sometimes leading to thousands of pages (or computer files) of description.

One of the difficulties in the design stage is sometimes called *creeping elegance.* As the system is being built, analysts, programmers, and users all want to include additional features. Although many of the features are good ideas, the continual evolution of the system causes additional delays. It also complicates testing, because changes in one section can affect the rest of the system.

Systems Implementation

Systems implementation involves installation and changeover from the previous system to the new one, including training users and making adjustments to the system. Many nasty problems can arise at this stage. You have to be extremely careful in implementing new systems. First, users are probably nervous about the change already. If something goes wrong, they may never trust the new system. Second, if major errors occur, you could lose important business data.

A crucial stage in implementation is final testing. Testing and quality control must be performed at every stage of development, but a final systems test is needed before staff en-

REALITY BYTES — Even Experts Have Bad Days (Years)

The Navy was looking for a new network to connect 4,000 locations across the world to securely link 345,000 computers. The work included configuring and installing thousands of personal computers. EDS, a leading outsourcing firm, won the $8.8 billion contract in 2000. As of 2004, EDS had lost $1.6 billion in the process. Navy Secretary Gordon R. England notes that "this was a very difficult program, more complex than either of us thought. We've both had some problems with the program." The contract itself was unusual. EDS purchased the individual computers, configured them, and was paid by the Navy after they were installed. EDS soon learned that the Navy wanted 67,000 different software programs transferred to the machines—not the 5,000 originally estimated. Originally, EDS planned to tailor each machine to a single employee. Of course, that process took forever, so commanders quickly decided that employees within

a group could get a similar package of software. EDS initially fought the decision—arguing that the extra software increased the licensing costs. Other difficulties arose. Several service members ordered desktop computers and then changed their minds and asked for laptops. With no penalty for the change, and limited tracking, EDS personnel simply created two computers for one person. But since the original desktop was never "installed," EDS was not paid for the work. At one point, an EDS employee found 1,500 personal computers already assembled, sitting in a Navy warehouse in San Diego. Some had been there for months.

Source: Adapted from Gary McWilliams, "After Landing Huge Navy Pact, EDS Finds It's In over Its Head," *The Wall Street Journal*, April 6, 2004; and "Mired in Big Computer Job, Company Loses $1.6 Billion," *The Wall Street Journal*, April 6, 2004.

---

trust the company's data to the new system. Occasionally, small problems will be noted, but their resolution will be left for later. In any large system, errors and changes will occur. The key is to identify them and determine which ones must be fixed immediately. Smaller problems are often left to the software maintenance staff.

Change is an important part of MIS. Designing and implementing new systems often cause changes in the business operations. Yet many people do not like changes. Changes require learning new methods, forging new relationships with people and managers, or perhaps even loss of jobs. Changes exist on many levels: in society, in business, and in information systems. Changes can occur because of shifts in the environment, or they can be introduced by internal **change agents.** Left to themselves, most organizations will resist even small changes. Change agents are objects or people who cause or facilitate changes. Sometimes it might be a new employee who brings fresh ideas; other times changes can be mandated by top-level management. Sometimes an outside event such as arrival of a new competitor or a natural disaster forces an organization to change. Whatever the cause, people tend to resist change. However, if organizations do not change, they cannot survive. The goal is to implement systems in a manner that recognizes resistance to change but encourages people to accept the new system. Effective implementation involves finding ways to reduce this resistance. Sometimes, implementation involves the cooperation of outsiders such as suppliers.

Because implementation is so important, several techniques have been developed to help implement new systems. Direct cutover is an obvious technique, where the old system is simply dropped and the new one started. If at all possible, it is best to avoid this technique, because it is the most dangerous to data. If anything goes wrong with the new system, you run the risk of losing valuable information because the old system is not available. The various methods are displayed in Figure 12.6.

In many ways, the safest choice is to use parallel implementation. In this case, the new system is introduced alongside the old one. Both systems are operated at the same time until you determine that the new system is acceptable. The main drawback to this method is that it can be expensive because data has to be entered twice. In addition, if users are nervous about the new system, they might avoid the change and stick with the old method. In this case, the new system may never get a fair trial.

Several intermediate possibilities are called *phased implementation.* For example, if you design a system for a chain of retail stores, you could pilot-test the first implementation in one store. By working with one store at a time, there are likely to be fewer problems. But if problems do arise, you will have more staff members around to overcome the obstacles. When the system is working well in one store, you can move to the next location. Similarly,

FIGURE 12.6

Conversion options: When you implement a new system, there are several possible conversion methods. In most cases, direct cutover should be avoided because of the disruptions and potential for lost data. Parallel conversion entails running both systems simultaneously, which is safe but can become expensive and time consuming. With multiple stores or business units, pilot introductions of phased implementations are common. For pilot testing, designers can bring extra workers, managers, and systems designers to one location and work out the problems with the system. Once the system is running well, it can be implemented at other locations. With a phased implementation, a system can be introduced slowly throughout the company (e.g., by department). Projects can also be phased in by modules.

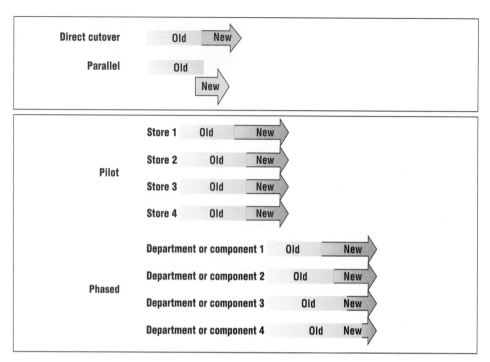

even if there is only one store, you might be able to split the implementation into sections based on the area of business. You might install a set of computer cash registers first. When they work correctly, you can connect them to a central computer and produce daily reports. Next, you can move on to annual summaries and payroll. Eventually the entire system will be installed.

Maintenance

Once the system is installed, the MIS job has just begun. Computer systems are constantly changing. Hardware upgrades occur continually, and commercial software tools may change every year. Users change jobs. Errors may exist in the system. The business changes, and management and users demand new information and expansions. All of these actions mean the system needs to be modified. The job of overseeing and making these modifications is called **software maintenance.**

The pressures for change are so great that in most organizations today as much as 80 percent of the MIS staff is devoted to modifying existing programs. These changes can be time consuming and difficult. Most major systems were created by teams of programmers and analysts over a long period. In order to make a change to a program, the programmer has to understand how the current program works. Because the program was written by many different people with varying styles, it can be hard to understand. Finally, when a programmer makes a minor change in one location, it can affect another area of the program, which can cause additional errors or necessitate more changes.

One difficulty with software maintenance is that every time part of an application is modified, there is a risk of adding defects (bugs). Also, over time the application becomes less structured and more complex, making it harder to understand. At some point, a company may decide to replace or improve the heavily modified system. Several techniques can be used to improve an existing system, ranging from rewriting individual sections to restructuring the entire application. The difference lies in scope—how much of the application needs to be modified. Older applications that were subject to modifications over several years tend to contain code that is no longer used, poorly documented changes, and inconsistent naming conventions. These applications are prime candidates for restructuring, during which the entire code is analyzed and reorganized to make it more efficient. More important, the code is organized, standardized, and documented to make it easier to make changes in the future.

FIGURE 12.7

Evaluation of completed projects: When projects are completed, the design team should evaluate the project and assess the development procedures. Cost and time estimates can be used to improve estimates for future projects. System performance issues can be addressed with future upgrades. It is important that the system achieve project goals and provide users with necessary tools and support.

Feasibility Comparison	
Cost & Budget	Compare actual costs to budget estimates.
Time Estimates	Was project completed on time?
Revenue Effects	Does system produce additional revenue?
Maintenance Costs	How much money and time are spent on changes?
Project Goals	Does system meet the initial goals of the project?
User Satisfaction	How do users (and management) evaluate the system?
System Performance	
System Reliability	Are the results accurate and on time?
System Availability	Is the system available on a continuous basis?
System Security	Does the system provide access only to authorized users?

Evaluation

An important phase in any project is evaluating the resulting system. As part of this evaluation, it is also important to assess the effectiveness of the particular development process. There are several questions to ask: Were the initial cost estimates accurate? Was the project completed on time? Did users have sufficient input? Are maintenance costs higher than expected? The assessment items are summarized in Figure 12.7.

Evaluation is a difficult issue. As a manager, how can you tell the difference between a good system and a poor one? In some way, the system should decrease costs, increase revenue, or provide a competitive advantage. Although these effects are important, they are often subtle and difficult to measure. The system should also be easy to use and flexible enough to adapt to changes in the business. If employees or customers continue to complain about a system, it should be reexamined.

A system also needs to be *reliable.* It should be available when needed and should produce accurate output. Error detection can be provided in the system to recognize and avoid common problems. Similarly, some systems can be built to tolerate errors, so that when errors arise, the system recognizes the problem and works around it. For example, some computers exist today that automatically switch to backup components when one section fails, thereby exhibiting **fault tolerance.**

An important concept for managers to remember when dealing with new systems is that the evaluation mechanism should be determined at the start of the project. Far too often, the question of evaluation is ignored until someone questions the value of the finished product. It is a good design practice to ask what would make this system a good system when it is finished, or how we can tell a good system from a bad one in this application. Even though these questions may be difficult to answer, they need to be asked. The answers, however incomplete, will provide valuable guidance during the design stage.

Recall that every system needs a goal, a way of measuring progress toward that goal, and a feedback mechanism. Traditionally, control of systems has been the task of the computer programming staff. Their primary goal was to create error-free code, and they used various testing techniques to find and correct errors in the code. Today, creating error-free code is not a sufficient goal.

We have all heard the phrase "The customer is always right." The meaning behind this phrase is that sometimes people have different opinions on whether a system is behaving correctly. When there is a conflict, the opinion that is most important is that of the customer. In the final analysis, customers are in control because they can always take their business elsewhere. With information systems, the users are the customers and the users should be the ones in control. Users determine whether a system is good. If the users are not convinced that the system performs useful tasks, it is not a good system.

Strengths and Weaknesses of SDLC

The primary purpose of the SDLC method of designing systems is to provide guidance and control over the development process. As summarized in Figure 12.8, there are strengths

FIGURE 12.8

Strengths and weaknesses of SDLC: The SDLC methodologies were created to control large, complex development projects. They work fairly well for those types of processes. They do not work as well for small projects that require rapid development or heavy user involvement with many changes.

Strengths	Weaknesses
Control.	Increased development time.
Monitor large projects.	Increased development costs.
Detailed steps.	Systems must be defined up front.
Evaluate costs and completion targets.	Rigidity.
Documentation.	Hard to estimate costs, project overruns.
Well-defined user input.	User input is sometimes limited.
Ease of maintenance.	
Development and design standards.	
Tolerates changes in MIS staffing.	

FIGURE 12.9

Capability maturity model: Based on standard management techniques. A development organization should strive to install processes, measure progress, and improve the development methodology.

1. **Initial.** Ad hoc development with undefined processes. Often driven by individual programmers.
2. **Managed.** Standard project management tools to track costs and schedules. Basic processes to ensure development is repeatable.
3. **Defined.** Management and development is defined and standardized. Processes are documented and followed.
4. **Quantitatively Managed.** Detailed measures are collected and evaluated.
5. **Optimizing.** Continuous improvement methods are applied to fine-tune and improve the development process.

and weaknesses to this methodology. SDLC management control is vital for large projects to ensure that the individual teams work together. There are also financial controls to keep track of the project expenses. The SDLC steps are often spelled out in great detail. The formality makes it easier to train employees and to evaluate the progress of the development. It also ensures that steps are not skipped, such as user approval, documentation, and testing. For large, complex projects, this degree of control is necessary to ensure the project can be completed. Another advantage of SDLC is that by adhering to standards while building the system, programmers will find the system easier to modify and maintain later. The internal consistency and documentation make it easier to modify. With 80 percent of MIS resources spent on maintenance, this advantage can be critical.

In some cases the formality of the SDLC approach causes problems. Most important, it increases the cost of development and lengthens the development time. Remember that often less than 25 percent of the time is spent on actually writing programs. A great deal of the rest of the time is spent filling out forms and drawing diagrams.

The formality of the SDLC method also causes problems with projects that are hard to define. SDLC works best if the entire system can be accurately specified in the beginning. That is, users and managers need to know *exactly* what the system should do long before the system is created. That is not a serious problem with transaction-processing systems. However, consider the development of a complex decision support system. Initially, the users may not know how the system can help. Only through working with the system on actual problems will they spot errors and identify enhancements.

Although some large projects could never have been completed without SDLC, its rigidity tends to make it difficult to develop many modern applications. Moreover, experience has shown that it has not really solved the problems of projects being over budget and late. As a result of this criticism, many people are searching for alternatives. One possibility is to keep the basic SDLC in place and use technology to make it more efficient. Other suggestions have been to replace the entire process with a more efficient development process, such as prototyping. Consider the assistance of technology first.

Several researchers at Carnegie Mellon University have created (and trademarked) the **capability maturity model integration (CMMI)** to help development organizations evaluate their abilities. Figure 12.9 shows the various levels of maturity. The goal is to improve the development process within an organization so that everyone follows a process that is measurable and sustainable. In standard management terms, quantifying the development process makes it possible to fine-tune and improve. Possibly the greatest strength of the CMMI approach is also one of its weaknesses. The overall approach is designed to support and encourage mediocrity in development. Programmers are considered interchangeable—an organization that succeeds by relying on "star" programmers is considered to be inferior. For some large organizations (particularly governments), this characterization makes sense—the system should function even with staff turnover. The weakness is that some software development requires creativity and flexibility to create new approaches.

Alternatives to SDLC

Is SDLC always the best approach? What other methodologies could be used? The two primary drawbacks to SDLC are that (1) it takes a considerable amount of time, and (2) all of the system details have to be specified up front. The project management and control features add paperwork and delays, making SDLC unsuitable for small projects. SDLC worked reasonably well for transaction-processing systems that were well defined and the design elements could be specified up front. It does not work well for decision support systems particularly when users do not really know exactly what they want the system to do.

Object-oriented programming (OOP) was developed in the computer science field to improve software programming. One of the main goals is to create relatively independent objects that can be reused for multiple applications. This concept was extended to components, where developers could create their own components or purchase them as needed from commercial vendors. Overall, the tools have been helpful for some projects, but the methodology does not really replace SDLC. Developers still need to design the system, and then reuse, buy, or build the components needed. In many cases, programmers tend to simply build new components—even if they duplicate existing objects.

Prototyping

Prototyping has been proposed as a method to use for systems that are not overly complex and do not involve too many users or analysts. Just as automobile engineers design prototypes before attempting to build the final car, MIS programmers can build early versions of systems. These systems are then continually modified until the user is satisfied.

The first step in designing a system via prototyping is to talk with the user. The analyst then uses a fourth-generation language and a DBMS to create approximately what the user wants. This first step generally requires only a couple of weeks. The business user then works with the prototype and suggests changes. The analyst makes the changes and this cycle repeats until the user is satisfied or decides that the system is not worth pursuing. The emphasis is on getting a working version of the system to the user as fast as possible, even if it does not have all the details. Figure 12.10 illustrates the cycle involved in prototyping.

The major advantage of prototyping is that users receive a working system much sooner than they would with the SDLC method. Furthermore, the users have more input so they are more likely to get what they wanted. Finally, remember that a large portion of MIS time is spent making changes. A system designed with the prototyping method is much easier to change because it was designed to be modified from the start.

Developing Systems Requires Teamwork: JAD and RAD

Designing and developing systems are much easier if the entire system can be built by one person. In fact, that is one of the strengths of recent tools—they enable a single person to build more complex systems. However, many information systems, especially those that affect the entire organization, require teams of IS workers. As soon as multiple designers, analysts, and programmers are involved, we encounter management and communication problems. MIS researchers have measured the effects of these problems. One study by DeMarco and Lister showed that on large projects, 70 percent of a developer's time is spent working with others. Jones noted that team activities accounted for 85 percent of the development costs. There seem to be substantial areas for improvement in systems development by focusing on teamwork.

FIGURE 12.10

Prototyping: Prototyping typically involves one user and one developer. The developer interviews the user and designs an initial system using a DBMS. The user works with the prototype and suggests changes. This process repeats until the user or developer is satisfied or gives up.

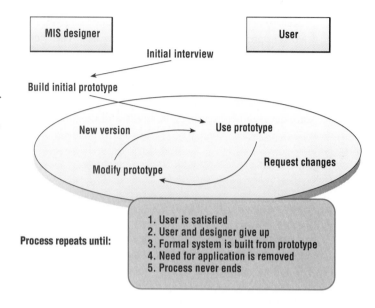

Process repeats until:
1. User is satisfied
2. User and designer give up
3. Formal system is built from prototype
4. Need for application is removed
5. Process never ends

FIGURE 12.11

Joint application design: Application design can be accelerated and simplified by putting key users and developers together for a few days. By focusing on the single project, everyone gets input and can reach a consensus in a shorter time.

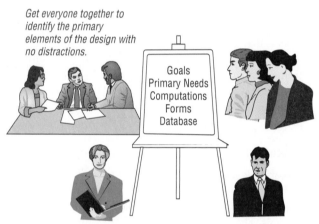

One of the most difficult steps in creating any new system is determining the user requirements. What does the system need to do and how will it work? This step is crucial. If the designers make a mistake here, the system will either be useless or need expensive modifications later. Prototyping and SDLC take different approaches to this problem. With SDLC, analysts talk with users and write reports that describe how the system will operate. Users examine the reports and make changes. This approach is time consuming and difficult for users because they only see paper notes of the proposed system. Prototyping overcomes some of the problems by letting users work with actual screens and reports. But use of prototyping is hard to expand beyond one or two users.

Some companies overcome the problems of SDLC by prototyping each input screen and report with one or two primary users. Once the main concepts have been designed, the analysts formalize the system and get approval from other users. The designs are then given to programmers to create with the traditional SDLC development methods.

Recall that an important reason for using SDLC is to obtain the views and agreement of many users. Using traditional interview methods and paper documentation, this process often takes several months. Each change has to be reexamined by other users, and disagreements have to be resolved.

A technique known as **joint application design (JAD)** was created to speed up the design stage. With JAD the main system is designed in an intense three- to five-day workshop. As shown in Figure 12.11, users, managers, and systems analysts participate in a series of intense meetings to design the inputs (data and screens) and outputs (reports) needed by the new system.

By putting all of the decision makers in one room at the same time, conflicts are identified and resolved faster. Users and managers gain a better understanding of the problems and limitations of technology. The resulting system has greater value for users and managers because it more closely matches their needs. There is less need for changes later, when they become more expensive, so the system is cheaper to create.

The biggest drawback to JAD is that it requires getting everyone together at the same time for an extended period of time. Even for moderately complex systems, the meetings can run eight hours a day for three to five days. Most managers (and users) find it difficult to be away from their jobs for that length of time. Higher-level managers are also needed at these meetings to ensure the system provides the appropriate reports and information. Finally, the meetings can succeed only if they are led by a trained facilitator. The facilitator keeps the discussions moving in the right direction, minimizes conflicts, and encourages everyone to participate. At the end of the sessions, the systems development team should have a complete description of the proposed system.

Rapid application development (RAD) applies the value of teamwork to the developers. By providing advanced development tools, prebuilt objects, and collaboration tools, some companies have found it is possible to reduce the overall development time. The key is to target steps that can overlap and be performed by multiple teams. By improving the collaboration tools, more steps can be compressed. Many e-commerce projects were developed with RAD techniques. Firms were concerned about being the first in the market and felt they needed to develop software rapidly. The goal of being first was later shown to be pointless, but the techniques of using small groups of programmers with advanced tools, collaboration, and intense programming sessions were relatively successful at quickly producing thousands of new applications.

Extreme Programming

In some ways, **extreme programming (XP)** is a new concept; in other ways it is an extension of the earlier work in prototyping and RAD. The main premise of XP is that SDLC and its variants are too large and cumbersome. While they might provide control, they end up adding complexity, taking more time, and slowing down top programmers. XP simplifies the development process by focusing on small releases (similar to prototyping) that provide value to the customer. Note, Microsoft's Windows XP name is not related to extreme programming.

One new aspect to XP is paired programming, where two programmers work together constantly. Generally, one is the lead programmer and the other is responsible for testing, but the jobs can overlap and be defined by the team. Making testing a key element of programming is an important part of XP. However, paired programming is seen by many as an inefficient use of resources. The second programmer is often a less experienced developer and can slow down an experienced developer. Besides, it can be more efficient to have one person test large sections of code at a time, instead of multiple people testing separate pieces.

One of the most challenging aspects to development is that there is a tremendous difference between individual programmers—in subject area knowledge, speed of programming, number of defects, and code maintainability. Some methodologies work well when an organization has top-notch developers, but fall apart in other companies. In choosing a methodology, managers must be aware of the capabilities of the individual programmers—and beware of turnover.

Open Source Development

Open source development is an interesting new method of developing complex software. With this approach, developers from virtually any company or location work on portions of the code. Usually, one person coordinates the efforts and identifies major changes and structure. The individual programmers write, debug, or test sections of code. If a programmer finds a better way to implement a function, the newer version is incorporated into the code. Hundreds or even thousands of programmers can contribute to the development of a project.

Technology Toolbox: Programming a New Function in Excel

Problem: You need to add a tricky function to a spreadsheet.

Tools: Microsoft Office contains a programming language that enables you to create your own tools and functions. To use this tool, you need to learn a little about programming. Many programming languages exist for different jobs, but they all have similar features. The common tasks you need are (1) define variables and perform calculations, (2) create functions and subroutines, (3) use conditional (if) statements to make choices, (4) write loops that perform the same steps many times, and (5) input and output data (to the spreadsheet in this case). You use these building blocks to build functions and applications.

Assume you need to evaluate the price of a financial option. An option is a contract that enables you to purchase (or sell) shares of stock in the future for a specified exercise price. The stock currently trades at some other price, so you are essentially gambling the price will increase or decrease. The Black-Scholes equation is often used to calculate a value for option prices (you will learn more about it in your finance course).

To begin, you need a place to write your new function. Open a new worksheet. Choose Tools/Macro/Record New Macro. Start recording, click a cell in the worksheet, and stop recording. Now choose Tools/Macro/Visual Basic Editor, and delete the Macro1 subroutine you created. Add the new BlackScholes function. A sample spreadsheet is on the Student CD if you do not want to type the formula.

```
Function BlackScholes (CallPut As String, StockPrice As Double, ExercisePrice As Double,_
    TimeLeft As Double, rate As Double, volatility As Double) As Double
    Dim d1 As Double, d2 As Double
    d1 = (Math.Log(StockPrice / ExercisePrice) + (rate + volatility ^ 2 / 2) * TimeLeft) /_
    (volatility * Math.Sqr(TimeLeft))
    d2 = d1 − volatility * Math.Sqr(TimeLeft)
    If (Left(CallPut, 1) = "c") Then
        BlackScholes = StockPrice * Application.WorksheetFunction.NormSDist(d1) _
        − ExercisePrice * Exp(−rate * TimeLeft) * Application.WorksheetFunction.NormSDist(d2)
    Else
        BlackScholes = ExercisePrice * Exp(−rate * TimeLeft) * _
        Application.WorksheetFunction.NormSDist(−d2) − StockPrice * _
        Application.WorksheetFunction.NormSDist(−d1)
    End If
End Function
```

Return to the spreadsheet and enter some sample data for stock price (60), exercise price (65), time left (0.25), rate (0.08), and volatility (0.3). To determine the value of a call option, enter the formula: = BlackSholes ("call", B2, B3, B4, B5, B6), where the cell values match the locations you put the sample data. The spreadsheet will call your new function and return the results.

stock price	60	call	2.133368
exercise price	65	put	5.846282
time left	0.25		
rate	0.08		
volatility	0.3		

Quick Quiz:

1. What does the statement If(Left(CallPut, 1)="c") do in the code?
2. What security setting do you need for this function to work?
3. How can a function directly alter several cells in a spreadsheet?

So far, this methodology has been used only to develop "free" software that is available for everyone's use. Many of the techniques were pioneered by Richard Stallman, who developed emacs, a programmer's text editor. He later founded the GNU project (www.gnu.org) that uses the same methods to create and distribute tools and systems software. Linus Torvalds uses a similar approach to create and distribute the Linux operating system.

Open source development is interesting in terms of both the sophisticated software that has been created and the development methodology. Using Internet communications,

REALITY BYTES Software Development

Ameritrade is one of the largest online discount brokerage firms and has purchased most of its rivals, including Datek. It is based in Omaha, Nebraska, and handles over 110,000 trades a day. For years, the company developed software following the traditional waterfall approach. Projects were managed in nine-month cycles, with new versions rolled out to customers each fall. When Asiff Hirji became CIO in April 2003, he changed the entire process, focusing on smaller

projects of 6 to 10 weeks. He notes that they were able to release an entirely new application (QuoteScope) in four months. He also observes that if a competitor launches a new service, "we're 12 weeks away from responding to it under a worst-case scenario."

Source: Adapted from Thomas Hoffman, "IT Execs Push New Governance Models to Speed Up Projects, Improve Visibility," *Computerworld,* February 20, 2004.

and only a small team to coordinate and review the work, thousands of individuals have been able to work together to create complex software that rivals commercial products costing millions of dollars to create. In theory, similar techniques could be used to improve development within business. On the other hand, the technique requires the cooperation of hundreds of developers, often some of the best programmers in the world. It might be possible to hire these programmers on a freelance basis. A few companies have proposed Web sites that would enable you to auction contracts for various portions of a programming job. But it is not entirely clear that this approach would be cheaper than just hiring the best programmers.

Another issue with open source development also affects your decision about whether to use open source products such as Linux. How is the software going to be maintained and updated? Creating the initial software is only the first step. Bugs have to be fixed and new features added on a regular basis. As long as there is a core group of people willing to continue working on the project, these issues can be handled. Or if you have a staff with the skills to modify the software, you can make any changes you want—because you have the source code. But what happens 20 years later? Or even in the short run, can open source projects devote the time and money to usability testing and radical improvements as hardware changes? A commercial company has a financial incentive and the cash flow to keep products moving forward. Open source development has only the personal motivations of the prime organizer and the world developer community. Sometimes these motivations are enough to ensure the longevity of a product; sometimes they are not.

End-User Development

The term *end user development* simply means that users do all of the development work themselves. In many ways, it resembles prototyping, except that users (instead of analysts from the MIS department) create and modify the prototypes. Clearly the main advantage is that users get what they want without waiting for an MIS team to finish its other work and without the difficulty of trying to describe the business problems to someone else.

Two basic reasons explain why end-user development is increasingly popular. First, most MIS organizations are facing a two- or three-year backlog of projects. This means that if you bring a new project to MIS, the designers will not even start on it for at least two years (unless you give up some other project). In fact, with the Year 2000 changes, many MIS departments simply gave up on other modifications. The second reason is that software tools are getting more powerful and easier to use at the same time. Today it is possible for users to create systems with a spreadsheet in a few hours that 10 years ago would have taken MIS programmers a month to build with third-generation languages. As tools become more powerful and more integrated, it becomes possible to create even more complex systems. Reread the discussion of software integration in Chapter 7 and picture the reports you can create using off-the-shelf software. Five years ago, most users would not dream of being able to create these reports. Today, with windowing software you can build systems that share data with many users across the corporate networks, simply by pointing to items with a mouse. The advantages of end-user development are similar to those in prototyping. In particular, users get what they want, and they get working systems sooner.

The potential problems of end-user development are not always easy to see. Most of them arise from the fact that users generally lack the training and experience of MIS analysts and programmers. For instance, systems produced by end users tend to be written for only one person to use. They are oriented to working on stand-alone personal computers. The systems are often customized to fit the needs of the original users. Moreover, most users do not write documentation, so others will have difficulty using the products. Because of lack of training, users rarely perform as much testing as they should. The systems lack security controls and are hard to modify. Think about the problems you encounter when you are given a spreadsheet that was created by the person who held the job before you.

Other problems stem from the bottom-up approach inherent in end-user development. People in different areas of the company will wind up working on the same problem, when it could have been solved once by MIS. Data tends to be scattered throughout the company, making it hard to share and wasting space. Not following standards generates incompatibilities among systems, making it difficult to combine systems created by different departments or even by people within the same department.

End users are limited by the capabilities of commercial software. The initial systems may work fine, but as the company grows and changes, the commercial software might be unable to support the necessary changes. As a result, some users have created systems that produce incorrect answers, take too long to run, or lose data.

The last, and possibly most important, complication is that end-user development takes time away from the user's job. Some users spend months creating and modifying systems that might have been created by MIS programmers in a fraction of the time. One of the reasons for creating an MIS department is to gain efficiency from using specialists. If users are spending too much time creating and revising their own applications, the company needs to consider hiring more MIS personnel.

Development Summary

As a manager, one of the more difficult IT decisions you make is the choice of development methodology. As a business manager in a large organization, you might not have a vote. But within a smaller company, you will certainly have to look at the alternatives to help identify the most efficient means of creating projects. Even within a larger company, you might be in a position to suggest alternatives when price tags or time frames get too high.

Figure 12.12 summarizes the characteristics of the primary development methodologies. The chart is basically organized on a scale of formality. Large, formal projects are built using SDLC to control the development and record progress. Small-scale reports and analy-

FIGURE 12.12

Comparison of methodologies: Each methodology has different strengths and weaknesses. You need to understand these differences so that you can choose the right tool for each project. Note that you can combine methodologies on large projects. For example, you could use prototyping to develop initial forms and reports that are incorporated into a larger SDLC project.

	SDLC	RAD	Open Source	Objects	JAD	Prototyping	End User
Control	Formal	MIS	Weak	Standards	Joint	User	User
Time frame	Long	Short	Medium	Any	Medium	Short	Short
Users	Many	Few	Few	Varies	Few	One or two	One
MIS staff	Many	Few	Hundreds	Split	Few	One or two	None
Transaction/DSS	Transaction	Both	Both	Both	DSS	DSS	DSS
Interface	Minimal	Minimal	Weak	Windows	Crucial	Crucial	Crucial
Documentation & training	Vital	Limited	Internal	In objects	Limited	Weak	None
Integrity & security	Vital	Vital	Unknown	In objects	Limited	Weak	Weak
Reusability	Limited	Some	Maybe	Vital	Limited	Weak	None

ses can be created with end-user development. Prototyping is similar to end-user development, but is a step toward more control and formality because it uses trained MIS developers who follow established procedures and internal standards.

Remember that the various methodologies can be combined. For example, a JAD session might be used to define the initial goals and attributes of a large project. The forms might be refined through prototyping. But the overall project could be controlled through an SDLC project management system. Remember that each technology has different costs. SDLC provides the most control, but adds overhead costs that you have to recognize. On the other hand, prototyping might appear to be inexpensive, but the costs could skyrocket if the project is never completed or requires huge amounts of developer and management time. One key issue in modern development is to identify these possible risks and threats up front. Then, each day, managers should evaluate the risks and see if the project has headed in the wrong direction. It might be impossible to prevent all risks, but at least if you are alert to the symptoms and recognize the problem earlier, you can correct it before the costs escalate and kill the project.

Process Analysis

How do you analyze and annotate a process-based system? If you are examining a transaction-processing system or dealing with a system that is largely noncomputerized, you should consider creating a process diagram. The purpose of a process diagram is to describe how the individual processes interact with each other. It concentrates on the business activities instead of the objects.

A data flow diagram is a process-oriented technique used for investigating information systems. The method can be used to look at the "big picture" and see how a system works in total. It also can be used to examine the details that occur within each process. Examining organizations at both levels provides a relatively complete picture of the problems and potential solutions. The use of systems analysis is illustrated by evaluating a small system for a zoo.

Input, Process, Output

One useful approach to systems is to look at them as a collection of processes or activities. The most important step in solving problems is to find the cause of the problems. Identifying the major processes in a system will help you understand how the system works. Examining input and output objects helps you spot problems and trace them back to their source. As illustrated in Figure 12.13, systems receive *input,* which is *processed* to produce *output.* The process could be mechanical, such as manufacturing using raw materials, workers, and power. Alternatively, it might be a process involving symbolic processing instead of physical activity. For example, accounting systems receive sales data and process it into cash-flow statements. In many cases, there are two types of input and output: physical and data. Physical flows are often accompanied by data. For instance, raw materials are shipped with an invoice that describes the products and the shipping information. Systems theory can be used to examine both types of flow. However, this is an MIS text, so most of the problems presented here deal with flows of data.

Systems are described by collections of these processes. Each system operates in an environment that is somewhat arbitrarily defined by the boundaries of the system. For most problems, anything directly controlled by the firm is considered part of the relevant system. Everything else exists in the environment outside of the firm. The environment typically

FIGURE 12.13

Each system can be decomposed into three major components: input, process, and output.

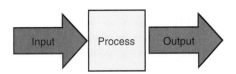

FIGURE 12.14

System boundary at the zoo: As we build systems, we must identify the components that make up the primary system. There will be many other entities that interact with the system. However, these entities are beyond our control, so they are outside of the system.

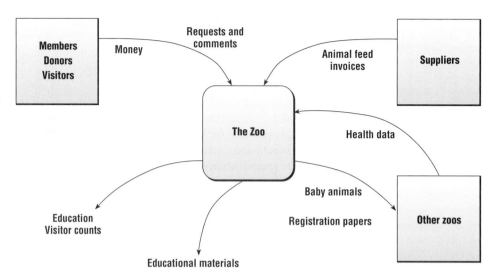

includes at least the physical space, laws, customs, industry, society, and country in which the firm operates. The firm can influence the physical environment, laws, and customs, but it does not have direct control over them.

Consider the example of a zoo: input and output are less concrete because a zoo primarily produces services instead of products. Figure 12.14 shows the basic inputs of food, money, and health data for potential new animals. Output objects include education, educational materials, and baby animals for other zoos. For most purposes, the system boundary is relatively clear. Visitors, suppliers, and other zoos are outside the direct control of the zoo, so they are in the environment. If the zoo was operated by a governmental agency, it would be harder to identify the boundary. Government systems tend to reach into many different areas, and it can be hard to identify their exact limits, especially since they can be extended or contracted by political decisions.

If a system is entirely self-contained and does not respond to changes in the environment, it is called a *closed system.* An *open system* learns by altering itself as the environment changes. Systems are almost never completely closed because closed systems cannot survive for long. However, some systems (or companies) are more responsive to changes in the environment than others.

Most large firms face a certain amount of inertia. It is easier for these firms to keep operating the way they always have than to continually introduce changes. But if a firm becomes too static, it can no longer respond to changes in the environment. Much like the U.S. railroad companies in the 1960s, closed firms will lose ground to firms that are more open and responsive to the environment. Remember that a key component of strategy is to search the environment for potential advantages.

Divide and Conquer

Most problems are too complex and too large to deal with all at once. Even if you could remember all the details, it would be hard to see how everything was supposed to fit together. A crucial step in analyzing a system is to carefully break it into smaller pieces or a collection of subsystems. Each subsystem is separate from the others, but they are connected and interdependent.

Figure 12.15 shows the five primary subsystems within the zoo. Of course, there could be many possible subsystems for the zoo. The actual division depends on how the organization operates. Each subsystem is defined by identifying the input and output flows. How do you know how to divide a system into smaller parts? Fortunately, most complex systems have already been subdivided into different departments and tasks. Many companies are organized by business functions: accounting, finance, human resources, marketing, MIS, and production. Others are split into divisions according to the type of product.

FIGURE 12.15

Primary subsystems of the zoo: The first step in analyzing a system is to identify the major subsystems. In most organizations, this step is relatively easy because the organization will consist of several departments or functions.

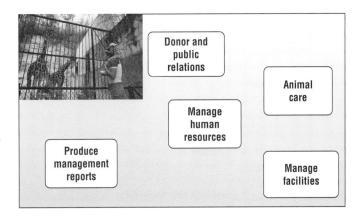

Once you have determined the major components of the system, each subsystem can be divided into even smaller pieces. An accounting department, for example, might be split into management reporting, tax management, quarterly reporting, and internal auditing groups. Each of these areas might be split into even more levels of detail. At each step, the subsystems are defined by what they do (process), what inputs are used, and what outputs are produced.

There are some drawbacks to the divide-and-conquer approach. It is crucial that you understand how the components work together. If a project is split into small parts and given to independent teams, the teams might lose sight of the overall goals. Important components might not be completed, or the individual pieces might not meet the overall objectives of the system.

Goals and Objectives

Subsystems have goals or purposes. A goal of a manufacturing firm might be to sell more products than any rival (increasing sales). Or it might be to make as much money as possible for its owners (increasing revenues). Another goal might be to find an entirely new area in which to sell products (new market segments). The owners of the system should define its goals. If the system does not have a goal, it has no purpose and there is no way to evaluate it. In fact, by definition, it would not be a system. When you observe a system, you will need to evaluate performance, which means you have to identify the goals.

Typical spreadsheets give us the ability to ask "what-if?" questions. For example, you might want to know what happens if you increase sales commissions by 10 percent. Goals help focus the answer by providing the ability to ask *Why?* and *So what?* The answer to the *What-if?* question involving commissions might be that revenue increases by 5 percent. But what does that result mean? If we also know that a goal of the company is to increase profits, we could look more carefully and find that increasing commissions by 10 percent leads to a 3 percent increase in profits. That result is important because it brings the system closer to one of its goals. Hence, it would make sense to increase the commissions.

It is clear that to solve business problems, you must first identify the organization's goals. The catch is that there are often conflicting ways to measure the goals. For instance, improved customer satisfaction or product quality might be useful goals. But how do we measure them? Managers who measure customer satisfaction by the number of complaints they receive will make different decisions than those who actively survey customers. In other words, the measurement of our performance with respect to the goals will depend on the data we collect.

Diagramming Systems

We often represent systems graphically to gain insights and spot problems. We also use diagrams to communicate. Communication is of critical importance in MIS and all areas of business. Users describe their problems to systems analysts, who design improvements and describe them to programmers. Ideas and comments can be misinterpreted at any step. We

FIGURE 12.16
Only four or five objects are used to create a data flow diagram. External entities are objects that are independent and outside the system. Processes are functions and actions applied to data. A data store or file is a place to hold data. Data flows are shown as solid lines with arrows to indicate the data movement. Control flows are marked with dashed lines.

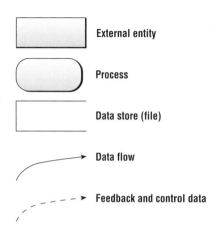

External entity

Process

Data store (file)

Data flow

Feedback and control data

can minimize problems by using a standard diagramming technique. The data flow diagram approach presented in this section is commonly used because it focuses on the logical components of the system and there are few rules to remember, so almost anyone can understand the diagrams.

Although you could invent your own diagramming technique, a method called a **data flow diagram (DFD)** has been developed to represent information systems. It is designed to show how a system is divided into smaller portions and to highlight the flow of data between those parts. Because there are only three graphical elements (five if you count the dashed control flows separately), it is an easy technique to learn. The DFD illustrates the systems topics in this chapter.

The basic elements of a DFD are external entities (objects), processes, data stores (files), and data flows that connect the other items. Each element is drawn differently, as shown in Figure 12.16. For example, data flows are shown as arrows. Feedback and control data are usually drawn as dashed lines to show that they have a special purpose.

Figure 12.17 presents the main level of subsystems for the zoo. Notice that it contains external entities, processes, and data flows. This level generally does not show data files or control flows. They can be incorporated in more detailed presentations.

External Entity

When you identify the boundary of a system, you will find some components in the environment that communicate with your system. They are called *external entities*. Although each situation is different, common examples include customers, suppliers, and management. External entities are objects, so they are labeled with nouns.

In the zoo example, the primary entities are management, certification agencies, other zoos, and members of the public (visitors, donors, and members). All relevant external entities need to be displayed on the first-level diagram.

Process

In a DFD, a process is an activity that involves data. Technically, DFDs are used to show systems that involve data, not products or other materials. However, in business today, virtually all physical processes have data-processing counterparts. When customers buy something, they get a receipt. In a manufacturing process, the amount of raw materials being put into a machine, measures of the volume of output, and quality control values are recorded. The DFD process is used to represent what happens to the data, not what occurs with the raw material.

Because processes represent actions, they are typically labeled with verbs, such as *sell products* or *create tax reports for management*. There are two important rules involving processes. First, a process cannot invent data. That means every process must have at least one flow of data entering it. Second, a process cannot be a black hole; every process must transfer data somewhere else. If you look at your DFD and find one of these two problems, it usually means that you missed a connection between the processes. On the other hand, processes that do not export data might be data stores or external entities.

FIGURE 12.17

The zoo: Level 0: The primary processes and data flows of the zoo.

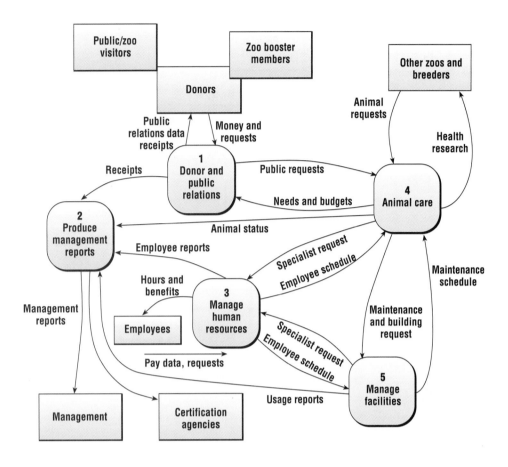

Data Store

A data store or file is simply a place to hold data for a length of time. It might be a filing cabinet, reference book, or computer file. In a computerized system, data is likely to be stored in a database management system (DBMS). Chapter 4 provides more detail on the capabilities and uses of a DBMS. For now, it is important to remember that data is a valuable resource to any company. In drawing a DFD, try to list exactly what needs to be stored, how long it should be held, and who should be able to read or change the data.

Data Flow

The data flows represent the inputs and outputs of each process or subsystem. The data flows are easy to draw. They are simply arrows that connect processes, entities, and data stores. Be sure to label every data flow. The diagram might seem obvious *now*; however, if someone else reads it or you put it away for several months, it can be hard to figure out what each flow represents.

Division of the System

A DFD provides an excellent way to represent a system divided into smaller components. First, each task is shown as a separate process. The data flows between the processes represent the inputs and outputs of each subsystem. Second, the DFD for a complex system would be too large to fit on one page. Hence, the DFD is displayed on different pages or levels. The top level, or *context diagram,* acts as a title page and displays the boundaries of the system and the external entities that interact with the system. The next level (*level zero*) shows the primary subsystems. Figure 12.17 is an example of a level zero diagram. Each of these processes is then exploded into another level that shows more detail. Figure 12.18 is the exploded detail for the first process (donor and public relations). These explosions can continue to any depth until you have displayed all the detailed operations needed to explain the system.

FIGURE 12.18

Each process can be expanded into more detail. This diagram shows the interactions with various members of the public. Note that data flows from the higher level must appear on this level.

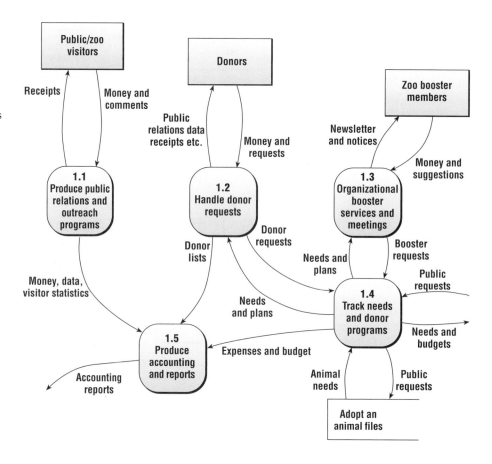

Data Dictionary

In any project, you need to remember additional pieces of information about each object. You might want to keep a sample report for a *management tax report* data flow, along with any deadlines that must be met. For data stores, you need to record information such as who controls it, who needs access to the data, how often it should be backed up, and what elements it contains.

A **data dictionary,** or repository, contains all of the information that explains the terms you used to describe your system. A good computer-aided software engineering (CASE) tool will maintain the dictionary automatically and help you enter longer descriptions for each item. Without these tools, you will have to keep a notebook that contains the full descriptions. For convenience, the entries should be sorted alphabetically. A word processor can be used to hold and print the dictionary. Figure 12.19 shows sample entries for the zoo system.

Summary: How Do You Create a DFD?

The first step in creating a DFD is to identify the environment and boundaries of the system by asking the following questions: What problems do you need to solve? What areas do you want to avoid? What are the goals? What are the main external entities? The second step consists of identifying the primary processes that define the system. Keep the list short (fewer than 10). Then answer these questions: What are the main activities in the system? What are the inputs and outputs of each process? How are these processes interconnected by the data flows? The third step is to look at each process in more detail and draw an expanded subsystem on a new page. What activities take place within a given process? What detail is needed in the reports and data inputs? The fourth step is to build the control flows. What processes are used to monitor progress toward the goals? What additional data is collected to monitor the environment and the system's performance?

FIGURE 12.19

A few sample entries from the zoo's data dictionary: A data dictionary records details on all of the organization's objects. It is typically organized by type of object. It is easiest to maintain if it is stored in a computer database.

Processes	Description . . .
Animal care	Feed, clean, and vet care
Donor and public relations	Handle public requests and provide educational information
Employee relations	Schedule employees, process benefits, handle government reports
Facility management	Handle maintenance, new construction, planning
Produce management reports	Collect data and produce summary reports for management
Entities	
Certification agencies	Government and private agencies that create rules and regulate zoos
Donors	People and companies who donate money to the zoo
Employees	Primary (paid) workers, full-time and part-time
Other zoos and breeders	Zoos we trade with and share data with
Public/zoo visitors	Daily visits, we rarely keep data on individuals
Zoo booster members	Members who donate money and time for minor benefits
Data	
Accounting reports	Standard (GAAS) accounting reports for management
Certification reports	Reports for certification agencies; produced annually
Facility reports	Summaries of work done and plans, mostly weekly
Needs and budgets	Budgets and special requests from animal care
Public requests	Suggestions and comments from the public

The key to analyzing systems is to start small. You can begin with one detailed subsystem and build your way up, or you can describe the general system processes and work down by adding increasing levels of detail.

Object-Oriented Design

How is object-oriented design different from process design? One way to begin your analysis of a business is to focus on the business objects: what they are and what they do. Objects could be anything from people to raw materials to data files or schedules. The key to **object-oriented design** is to focus on defining what an object is and what it can do. A *class* is a generic description of a set of objects. This distinction is not crucial in this book, but you might want to know there is a difference. For example, the Bicycle class describes any bicycle that could be built by the company. A specific bicycle (e.g., serial number 15) is an object.

Properties and Functions

Objects are defined by a set of properties (or attributes). The properties define the object. They also represent data that will be collected for each object. Consider the small example of a banking system. One primary object will be Accounts. A generic account object would have basic properties such as Account Number, Account Name, Client, Manager, Date Opened, Beginning Balance, Current Balance, and Interest Rate.

Each object also has functions, which describe actions that can be performed by the objects and define how to alter the object. In the bank example, there would be functions to Open Account, Close Account, Accept Deposits, Pay Withdrawals, and Pay Interest. Note that each type of account could have a different method for computing interest payments. One account might compound them daily, another weekly, and so on. With the object-oriented approach, the properties and functions are combined into the definition of the object. The goal is to describe a system so that if you change a function, you only have to change one object. All of the other objects and processes remain the same.

FIGURE 12.20

Objects: encapsulation, hierarchy, inheritance, polymorphism: Object-oriented design focuses on individual objects and the data within the organization. Processes are secondary and they are usually embedded in the object. By encapsulating these definitions, the objects can be used to develop related systems with less effort. It is also easier to modify a system by making small changes to an object's behavior.

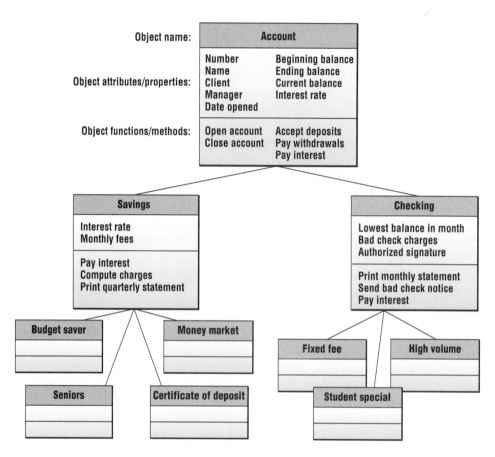

Object Hierarchies

Objects are related to each other. Typically there is a base class of objects, and other objects are *derived* from the base definitions by adding properties and altering functions. This process results in an **object hierarchy,** illustrated in Figure 12.20, that shows how the classes are derived from each other. The bank example has several types of accounts with each of these categories containing further subdivisions.

Figure 12.20 also shows detail in the classes by including some of the properties and member functions. The accounts have elements in common that are an **inheritance** from the base class (account), such as the balance attributes. Each level adds additional detail. Each account class also contains member functions to perform operations, such as paying interest. Because the interest computations can be different for each of the accounts, the method is stored with the original definition of each account.

Events

Another aspect of modeling objects is that they are often used in an **event-driven approach.** When some business event occurs, an object function is called or a property is modified. As a manager, you need to think about possible events and how they influence the objects you control. In the banking example, a customer's deposit triggers a credit to her account. This change might then force an update in a daily report object. This chain of events defines the business operations. As a manager, you are likely to be asked to identify the major objects and the events that affect your area of expertise in the company.

To see the usefulness of the object approach, consider what happens if the bank decides to collect additional data for the checking accounts. The only change needed is to add the new data items (and the associated functions) to the checking account class. All checking accounts will then inherit those properties and functions. None of the other operations are affected. Changes to the information system will only affect the specific accounts; the rest of the system will remain the same.

FIGURE 12.21
SDLC versus object oriented: Initial design of an object-oriented approach takes more effort than an SDLC approach. However, once the objects are properly defined, it is much easier to create and implement a new system.

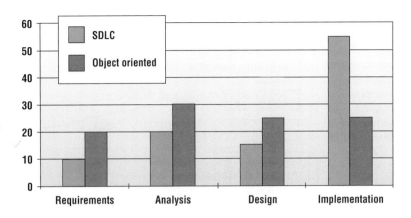

Object-Oriented and Event-Driven Development

The concept of object-oriented design has received considerable attention during the past few years. In some ways, the base design techniques are not much different from traditional SDLC techniques. In other ways, object orientation requires a completely new way of thinking about systems development. The ultimate goal of the object-oriented approach is to build a set of *reusable* objects and procedures. The idea is that eventually, it should be possible to create new systems or modify old ones simply by plugging in a new module or modifying an existing object.

One key difference between object orientation and other development methods is the way processes or functions are handled. With objects, all functions are embedded in the definition of the object—the object comes first. The object approach reverses the treatment of processes and data. With SDLC, illustrated by a data flow diagram, the emphasis is on processes, and data (attributes) is passed between processes.

One goal of an object-oriented approach is to create a set of information system building blocks. These objects and procedures could be purchased from commercial software companies (such as a spreadsheet from Microsoft or a database system from Oracle). MIS programmers or consultants can create additional objects tailored for your specific company or department. Once the basic blocks are in place, end users or MIS analysts can select the individual pieces to create a complete system. Hence, as Figure 12.21 indicates, less time is needed for implementation, as long as the analysis and design are performed carefully. On the other hand, the up-front costs of designing and building these objects can be quite high. Furthermore, the tools and techniques tend to require substantial retraining of the existing MIS staff. Both of these types of costs have caused some companies to avoid object-oriented methods.

Distributed Services

Can software be located in different places? A major question in decentralization is where the software needs to be located. Substantial benefits arise from centralizing data—providing access across an intranet or the Internet. But users need some type of distributed hardware to access the data. Does that mean all of the software has to be installed on each machine? Some new technologies are being developed that provide support for distributing software functions across the network. While basic tools such as a word processor are still needed on individual machines, the complex business and analytical tools can be installed on central servers.

One of the primary technologies is the **simple object access protocol (SOAP)**. It is a standard being pushed by several vendors to define how objects can be used across the Internet. It relies heavily on the **extensible markup language (XML)** to transfer data between diverse computers. As a general manager, you do not need to know the details of how these two technologies work, but you should remember their purpose. Ultimately, you will

FIGURE 12.22

Simple object application protocol: SOAP enables firms to offer application object services that other firms can use across the Internet. In this example, your application can call the bank's currency converter object to get the correct exchange rates.

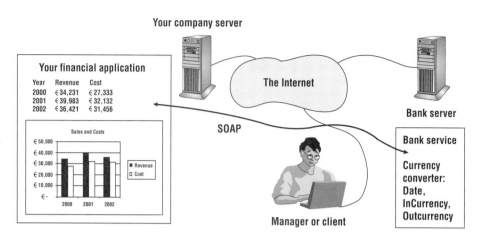

want to select applications that fully support these standards so that you can build and use systems that work transparently across the Internet.

The purpose of SOAP is to enable firms to build application services that can be used by other organizations across the Internet. For instance, as shown in Figure 12.22, a bank (e.g., www.oanda.com) might offer a currency conversion application. Your company's accounting application could call the bank's program whenever it needed to convert money to a different currency.

Applications that use the SOAP and XML protocols will be able to interact with other services across the Internet. However, a big question that remains to be resolved is how firms will price their services. Firms that create service objects will ultimately be able to bill clients a usage fee or a monthly charge with unlimited access. But a standardized billing mechanism has not been implemented yet.

Summary

Systems development can be a difficult task. Many projects have failed because they cost much more than anticipated or they did not produce useful systems. Large projects are especially difficult to control because there can be conflicting goals, it is hard to ensure that subsystems work together, business needs change during the development process, and there is turnover among the MIS employees. The systems development life cycle evolved as a means to deal with the complexity of large systems and provide the necessary controls to keep projects on track.

A Manager's View

As a manager in a large company, you will work closely with the MIS department to modify and build systems that support your operations. You need to be aware of the problems facing MIS staff to understand the reasons for their rules and methods. Managers are increasingly being asked to develop their own systems and to participate more heavily in the design of new reports and forms. The details of analysis, design, testing, and implementation will be useful regardless of the method used. As a manager, you also need to know the advantages and drawbacks of various development methods; you will often have to choose the method that is best suited to solving your problems.

Systems analysis techniques are used to break projects into manageable pieces. Various graphing tools, such as data flow diagrams, are used to display the relationships between the components. Systems design techniques use the results of the analysis to create the new system. The new system consists of interconnected modules. Each module has inputs, outputs, processing steps, database requirements, manual procedures, and controls. At various stages in the design process, managers and users are asked to sign off on the proposed system, indicating that they will accept it with no further changes.

In contrast to the rigid control embodied in the SDLC method, the prototyping approach is iterative and creates an early working model of the system. Users and managers can see the proposed input screens and reports and make changes to them. As the project develops, the prototype goes from a simple mockup to a working system. Prototyping is sometimes used in conjunction with SDLC during the design phase to lay out input screens and reports.

A third way to build systems is for end users to develop their own projects using fourth-generation tools such as database management systems, spreadsheets, and other commercial software. As the capabilities of commercial software tools increase, users can develop more complex systems. The backlog facing MIS also encourages users to develop their own systems. The potential dangers of user development—such as lack of testing, incompatibilities, and unnecessary duplication—can be controlled by having MIS teams available to assist end users.

All three methods of developing systems involve five basic steps: feasibility and planning, systems analysis, design, implementation, and maintenance. Prototyping and end-user development typically focus on the design stage. However, managers need to remember that implementation problems can arise with any new system. regardless of how it was created. Similarly, there will always be a need to maintain and modify existing applications. It is easy to forget these steps when users develop their own software.

Key Words

capability maturity model integration (CMMI), *456*	extreme programming (XP), *459*	open source development, *459*
change agent, *453*	fault tolerance, *455*	outsourcing, *446*
commercial off-the-shelf software (COTS), *447*	feasibility study, *449*	prototyping, *444*
data dictionary, *468*	inheritance, *470*	rapid application development (RAD), *459*
data flow diagram (DFD), *466*	joint application design (JAD), *458*	simple object access protocol (SOAP), *471*
end-user development, *444*	object hierarchy, *470*	software maintenance, *454*
event-driven approach, *470*	object-oriented design, *469*	systems analysis, *449*
extensible markup language (XML), *471*	object-oriented programming (OOP), *457*	systems development life cycle (SDLC), *444*

Web Site References

Computer Industry News

ACM Digital Library Portal	portal.acm.org/portal.cfm
CNet News	news.com.com
Computer Economics	www.computereconomics.com
Computerworld	www.computerworld.com
eWeek	www.eweek.com
Federal Computer Weekly	www.fcw.com
Gartner Group	www.gartner.com
IDG	www.idg.com
IEEE	www.ieee.org
Infoworld	www.infoworld.com
Internet.com	www.internet.com
PC World	www.pcworld.com
The Industry Standard	www.thestandard.com

Additional Readings

Brooks, Frederick P. *The Mythical Man-Month, Anniversary Edition.* Boston: Addison-Wesley, 1995. [Classic book on software development problems and why adding people to a project often slows it down.]

DeMarco, T., and T. Lister, *Peopleware.* New York: Dorset House, 1987. [Hints and problems developing useful systems.]

Jeffries, Ronald, Ann Anderson, and Chet Hendrickson. *Extreme Programming Installed.* Boston: Addison-Wesley, 2001. [A detailed explanation of how to use extreme programming. Also look at other books in the series for theory.]

Jones, T. C. *Programming Productivity.* New York: McGraw-Hill, 1986. [Evaluating and measuring productivity, costs, and teamwork.]

McConnell, Steve. *Rapid Development: Taming Wild Software Schedules.* Redmond: Microsoft Press, 1996.

Naumann, Justus, and Milton Jenkins. "Prototyping: The New Paradigm for Systems Development." *MIS Quarterly,* Spring 1982. [Description, uses, and advantages of prototyping.]

Paulk, Mark C., Bill Curtis, Mary Beth Chrissis, and Charles V. Weber. *Capability Maturity Model for Software.* Carnegie-Mellon University, Software Engineering Institute, 1993. http://www.sei.cmu.edu/pub/documents/93.reports/pdf/tr24.93.pdf. [Description of how to evaluate software development programs in terms of their capabilities on a relatively standardized maturity scale—essentially an evaluation of how well an organization follows the SDLC.]

Wallnau, Kurt, Scott Hissam, and Robert C. Seacord. *Building Systems from Commercial Components.* Boston: Addison-Wesley, 2002. [Description and cases of developing systems using commercial off-the-shelf software components, from the Carnegie-Mellon Software Engineering Institute.]

Review Questions

1. What fundamental methods are available to build information systems?
2. What is the primary purpose of the systems development life cycle methodology?
3. What are the main steps in the systems development life cycle methodology?
4. What drawbacks are created with the systems development life cycle methodology?
5. What alternative methods are being used to develop information systems?
6. What is the role of a data flow diagram in analyzing systems?
7. What are the main components of a data flow diagram?
8. What is the role of object-oriented design, particularly class diagrams, in analyzing systems?
9. How do data flow diagrams and object-oriented techniques differ in the way they divide systems?

Exercises

1. Interview a local manager to determine the requirements for a new system. Explain which method would be the best approach to develop the system. Estimate how long it would take to complete the project and how much it would cost. Advanced option: Illustrate the new system with a data flow or object-oriented diagram. More advanced: Create the system.

2. Using the example of the zoo, along with any other information you know about zoos, define an initial list of objects that would be used to create an information system.

3. A regional bank office generates loans for builders. The office has several bankers who form alliances with regional builders and negotiate loans and other services. The manager wants a system to track the leads, including the potential amount of the loan and the probability of the loan going through. Every month, the main office sends a spreadsheet file with current loan information. The manager and the main office want the regional bank officers to project the amount of money that will be loaned in the coming months. The manager wants a system to help collect and track this data. Identify the best development methodology. Assuming no one in the regional office has the skills to create the application, do some research to find at least two firms that could handle the job for a reasonable price.

4. You have been hired to create a new checkout system for a grocery chain. It wants to put scanners into the shopping carts and have shoppers scan their own products. The system will track the basic purchases by customer so that it can offer discounts and recommend related products based on current and past purchases. You need to find a way for people to pay for their purchases. You want to minimize theft, but one of the goals is to reduce costs by using fewer checkout clerks. Create an initial design for this system.

5. For each of the following information system projects, identify the method that would be the best approach for most companies.

a. A new system to track customer requests and comments for the marketing department at a large ski manufacturer.

b. A system to help managers evaluate regional sales data, from the existing sales system running on an Oracle database.

c. A system to track current location and maintenance status of thousands of baggage carts at an airport.

d. A Web site to sell "homemade" dog treats over the Internet for a small business.

e. A scientific system to help astronomers collect data from colleagues, track specific items (e.g., comets), and send announcements and questions over the Internet to a group of registered users.

f. A system to help a group of financial managers monitor client transactions and observe them for potentially illegal patterns such as insider trading.

g. A system running on one PC that connects to a truck scale and records incoming shipments of recyclable materials.

h. A system for a manager that pulls data on cell phone usage from all of her workers. It groups the calls and costs so that she can see if workers are making too many personal phone calls.

6. Assume that you are on a project to build a new Web site for a midsize company. The firm sells materials to home builders—usually contractors, but some individual sales as well. The company wants to take orders over the Web and enable customers to track the status of current orders. Contractors also want the ability to look at old orders when placing new ones. For example, if they build the same style of house twice, they will need approximately the same materials. The manufacturer is not completely certain on many of the details yet, and you will have to interview customers to get additional details and feedback. Set up a schedule for developing this system using the SDLC approach. Then, identify ways that RAD might be used to reduce the overall development time.

7. You work for a company that is increasingly asking employees to develop their own applications using Microsoft Office tools connected to the corporate database. This process has not been working very well, and employees are grumbling. But the company has decided it cannot afford to hire all of the MIS people that would be needed to develop all applications and reports within the MIS department. How can the company improve the process? What tools and capabilities should the company add?

Technology Toolbox

8. Write a short macro program in Excel that adds all of the numbers between the values in cell A1 and cell A2 and puts the result in cell A5. For example, if A1 = 1 and A2 = 5, then add 1 + 2 + 3 + 4 + 5 to get 15. *Hint:* You can read or write to a cell with the command Range("A1").

9. Write an Excel macro that looks at each item selected to see if any cells are blank. If any are blank, display a message notifying the user how many blank cells there are. (*Hint:* Use the IsEmpty function to test and the MsgBox command to display a message.)

10. Create a form in Microsoft Access (or Visual Studio). Place text boxes on the form for amount to borrow, interest rate, and number of months. Add a fourth text box to hold the resulting payment amount. Set the properties to format and name each of the

boxes. Add a button to calculate and display the payment amount based on the entered data. Use the Pmt function to do the calculation.

11. Assume that you need to analyze an IS problem at a business. Create an outline that you could use for a final report. You do not actually have to do the entire analysis at this point; just write the general outline that you would use.

12. Choose one of the cases in this book and identify the main problem and the cause of the problem. Why is it often difficult to identify the cause of business problems?

Teamwork

13. Interview computer users to determine how they feel about their current system. Do they like it? What are the major advantages and drawbacks? How long have they used it? When was it changed last? Are there changes users want to see? Are they willing to accept changes? How are relations with the MIS workers? Who initiates changes, users or MIS? If users proposed a new project, how long would it take for MIS to get to it (how long is the backlog)? Each team member should interview a different person (some users, some in MIS). Combine your results to get a picture of the entire company. Do users agree with each other? Does the MIS department agree with the users? Do they see the same problems? (*Hint:* If you do not have access to another company, you can always find computer users in the university.)

14. Choose one person in the team who has an interesting job. Create a data flow diagram for the job and organization. Be sure to label everything and provide a data dictionary.

15. Begin by having each person think about an application that would be useful for some task. Split into pairs with one person as the business manager and one as the systems analyst. The analyst has to interview the manager to identify the details and create an initial system design. Trade partners and repeat the process until everyone has had a chance to be a manager and an analyst. Combine the results and identify any difficulties you experienced and how you might avoid those problems in the future.

16. Choose a problem that needs a new application, or find an existing business application. For example, consider a bank, a retail store, or a small manufacturer. Split the team into two groups. One group diagrams the system with a process approach (DFD), the other with an object-oriented approach. Combine the two results and briefly discuss any differences or advantages.

17. Choose a problem that needs a new application, or find an existing business application. Have each team member choose an alternative development methodology (prototyping, JAD, RAD, XP, and so on) and describe how it might be used and the effect on the development process. Combine the results and recommend a methodology or combination of methodologies.

Rolling Thunder Database

18. Rolling Thunder Bicycles needs a new Web site to sell its custom bicycles. How should it be developed? What methodology could be used?

19. Using the help system and Web site description of Rolling Thunder, create a data flow diagram to show the main processes directly involved with the customers (taking orders, sending notices and bills, and receiving payments).

20. Rolling Thunder bicycles needs a new system to generate and track electronic orders (EDI) to its suppliers. What methodology should be used to develop the system?

21. Assume that the managers of Rolling Thunder bicycles have decided to purchase and implement an enterprise resource planning system. You have been selected to help determine which system the company should purchase. Outline the steps you will have to perform to select a vendor.

Cases: Government Agencies

Most U.S. citizens know the overall structure of the federal government: the president, Congress, and the Supreme Court. These groups are responsible for creating and interpreting the laws to govern the nation. What many people do not realize is that both the president and Congress are supported by a huge set of government agencies. These organizations form a bureaucracy that is ultimately responsible for carrying out the laws. Governmental agencies have several unique problems. The most important one is that funding is subject to changes in the political climate. With each election, an agency runs the risk of having to change direction, cancel projects, or provide support for new tasks.

On the other hand, from an economic perspective, most government agencies are not subject to economic pressures. Consequently, they have not been faced with the same incentives to economize and minimize costs that have faced businesses. Another critical feature of most government agencies is that they tend to serve large numbers of people, especially at the federal level. These large organizations collect huge amounts of data. Even today, much of this governmental information is stored on paper.

Most governmental agencies have dealt with the size issue by maintaining large staffs and combining decentralized management with centralized controls. Traditionally, government organizations have paid lower salaries than commercial businesses. Although the salaries are supplemented with benefits and job security, governmental agencies often face high turnover rates and changes in personnel. To compensate for these problems, the agencies rely heavily on procedures. These rules seek to predict and then direct what to do in circumstances that may arise. As new situations and decisions present themselves, new rules are created. Given these challenges, there is no surprise that most people perceive government agencies as large bureaucracies, filled with endless forms and strange rules.

There are many obvious uses for computers in government agencies. During a few minutes of observation, anyone can generate ideas that could improve agency performance, making life easier for the workers and citizens. However, the real challenges have always come in creating and implementing these ideas.

Although there are many success stories regarding computer implementation within government agencies, there are also some costly failures. The Federal Aviation Administration and the Internal Revenue Service cases present some of the difficulties that have arisen.

Be careful when you read these cases. Do not simply blame the problems on "typical government mismanagement." Many of these problems also exist within businesses. Always remember that the challenge is to search for and implement answers and methods that will overcome the obstacles and complications.

Size and Growth

The federal government employs 2 percent of the U.S. workforce. In 2003, it spent $757 billion. With the tax cut of the early 2000s, federal receipts declined in 2002 and 2003, while expenditures continued to increase about 6 percent a year. The federal debt rose to 2.7 percent of GDP in 2003. Part of the economic balance is due to the war in Iraq; part is due to the attempts to prevent a major recession.

Overall, the size of the federal government is shrinking. The number of elected officials remains constant but the rest of the federal government is downsizing. Federal government employment peaked in 1990 and since has fallen by over

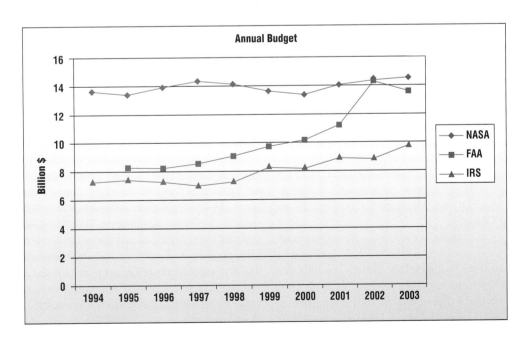

530,000 jobs from 1990 to 2002. On the other hand, several widely circulated reports from most federal agencies indicate that by 2008, over 50 percent of the federal workforce will be eligible for retirement. Not all of them will actually retire immediately, but over the course of a few years, a substantial percentage of the federal workforce will need to be replaced. A considerable amount of internal knowledge could potentially be lost in the process.

In comparison, for the United Kingdom in 2003, public spending amounted to 41.1 percent of its GDP. Deficits in European nations routinely run about 5 percent of GDP ("Has Tony" 2004). However, remember that the UK pays for health care. In the United States, if you include state and local government spending, total government spending was over $2 trillion in 2003 or 18.7 percent of GDP. If you include current health care spending, the total would be about 35 percent of U.S. GDP.

Information Technology

Like any business, government agencies increasingly rely on technology to improve productivity. Most agencies are under constant pressure to reduce costs—often to the point of having their funding cut. In large agencies, such as the IRS and the FAA, monster technology projects are funded separately. Consequently, the agencies have often been able to obtain funds specifically set aside to acquire or build new systems.

Most tasks performed by government agencies are unique. As a result, they require custom-developed software. Since the projects are huge and involve a large number of users, they are difficult to develop. Throw in a few bureaucratic turf battles, and it is amazing that anything gets done. Unfortunately, the result has been that many agencies are operating with technology that is 10, 20, or more years out of date. These archaic systems create their own ongoing problems. The government cannot just stop what it is doing, throw the old systems away, and build new ones. Instead, most of the government IT workers keep the old systems running. So, who is going to build the new systems? And how do you obtain the detailed knowledge from the users and workers of the old systems? Then, how do you transfer all of the data and keep both systems updated and running while testing the new system? However, we know that information technology constantly changes. Somehow, agencies have to balance the costs against the capabilities of the new systems.

Oversight

Congress is charged with appropriating all federal money and controlling spending. Yet members face an enormous bureaucracy, plus constant reelection worries to distract them. Consequently, the General Accounting Office (GAO) was created to help monitor the spending and procedures at the various agencies. As a nonpartisan office, the GAO is free to collect whatever data it wants from the agencies and yell at them as necessary. You can obtain GAO reports directly from www.gao.gov. The reports often contain detailed information on specific projects and audits. The agencies generally provide responses to GAO concerns within the report. These responses are always interesting because the agency director tiptoes a line. No one wants to accept all of the GAO criticisms (and look like there is no control), yet no one wants to totally disprove the GAO, because that would mean no more funding is needed.

Additional Reading

Bureau of Economic Analysis, www.fedstats.gov/key_stats/BEAkey.html.

"Has Tony Wasted Your Money?" *The Economist,* July 10, 2004, p. 12.

Statistical Abstract of the United States, www.census.gov/statab/www.

Case: Federal Aviation Administration (FAA)

The FAA is charged with overseeing all public (nonmilitary) flight operations in the United States related to safety and access to the air. They establish safety criteria, issue licenses for pilots, and create air worthiness certificates for planes. They also operate the air traffic control system throughout the United States. Funding for the agency is generated through user fees and taxes on aircraft fuel, tires, and airline tickets. The FAA is an executive agency that operates under the budgetary control of the president. Appropriations and organizational structure for the agency are approved by the Congress.

The increase in air traffic in the United States has made air traffic control a complex issue. In 1990, 466 million passengers a year were flying on U.S. airlines. In 2002, the airlines carried 714 million paying passengers. With more airlines and more daily flights, the air traffic control system is dealing with more difficult problems every year. The busiest airports (Atlanta tops the list) cause even more complications—trying to schedule hundreds of flights per hour.

Traffic control is organized into three levels: nationwide U.S. airspace, 20 regional air traffic centers, and individual airports. Air traffic control operators at each airport have immediate control over takeoffs and landings. Regional operators watch traffic within their defined airspace. They "hand off" planes as they fly across the country into the next airspace. Systemwide control is provided by the Central Flow facilities located in Washington, D.C. The Central Flow managers examine traffic across the entire United States and resolve conflicts and problems that arise among regions. The 40 traffic management specialists plan each day in advance, devising alternative routings for aircraft that may be needed because of problems arising from snowstorms, accidents, and closed runways.

Early Systems and Ongoing Problems

The early traffic control system was built with hardware and software from Sperry-Rand/Univac, a computer company that was purchased in the mid-1980s by Burroughs, and now named Unisys. The airport-based traffic control computers were based on 256K bytes of main memory and performed 500,000 instructions per second. The original systems were installed in the early 1960s. The 20 regional centers had their own computers—IBM 9020 machines that were custom made for the FAA in the 1960s.

Air traffic controllers have been reporting problems with existing systems for years:

- In 1992, West Coast air traffic was delayed for several hours. An IBM 3083 at the regional station crashed. In the process, it removed the identification labels from the radar screens of controllers from Oregon to Los Angeles. The controllers switched to an older backup system but had to increase plane separation from the typical 3 miles to up to 20 miles. Pilots and controllers used radio communication and manually filed flight plans to compensate for this loss. Ron Wilson, a spokesman for the San Francisco airport, noted that although there were frequent disruptions, "the FAA computer failures generally don't last long, just long enough to screw things up."

- In Oakland, California, the controller screens fail an average of three times a month. When this happens, the controllers have only a few seconds to memorize the position, speed, course, altitude, and destination of the 12 planes they are typically directing. Then their screens go blank for at least 10 seconds. Sometimes when the screens come back online, they are missing critical data.

- Joel Willemssen, assistant director of the U.S. GAO's Information Management and Technology Division, reported that 70 percent of the 63 largest airports in the United States have experienced problems with blank or flickering computer screens. John Mazor, a spokesman for the Airline Pilots Association, notes the problems cause "delays, diversions, and—in the worst possible cases—accidents. It's not as dangerous as you might think, but it's not something you want to have happen to you."

- The Los Angeles basin region consists of 21 airports handling 6.5 million flights a year. The GAO notes that the FAA computers in the region have repeatedly suffered from the loss of critical data and slow responses because of the overload.

Improvements

In 1981, the FAA was given approval to upgrade to a comprehensively new computer system. New airports, such as Dallas–Fort Worth, and the deregulation of the airline industry in 1978 led to huge increases in air traffic. The $12 billion plan called for replacement of 12 major systems over the course of 12 years. An additional 80 smaller projects were included in the plan.

By 1990, only 1 of the 12 systems had been replaced and the project was $15 billion over the original budget. The one project that was completed was known as Host, because it called for replacement of the mainframe computers at the 20 regional control centers. IBM installed its 3083 mainframes on schedule but was $16 million over budget. The 3083s were technologically obsolete at the time they were installed because the newer IBM 3090-class machines had already replaced them over a year before.

The FAA has been criticized for a lack of oversight and control in developing new systems. In 1980, the Senate Appropriations committee noted that "the FAA has no ongoing, well-defined, and systematic management approach to evaluating software and operational cost, capacity, and performance of the current system to meet projected short-range workloads." The General Accounting Office (GAO), the watchdog of Congress, echoed that sentiment several times later.

Advanced Automation System

One of the more visible components of the plan to refurbish the system is the Advanced Automation System (AAS). It was designed to provide updated tracking displays for the controllers. It was supposed to be completed by 1990, but at that time was delayed until 1993. The system was designed to use IBM RS-6000 computers to display flight information, schedules, and current location along with weather fronts. The color systems were to have higher resolution, be easier to read, and carry more information.

In 1994, an internal study of the AAS showed that the project was still two years behind schedule and probably would fall back another two years before completion. Up until that time, the project had cost $2.3 billion. It was estimated to eventually cost about $7 billion. David Hinson, FAA administrator, announced that he was replacing top managers on the project, dropping portions of uncompleted work, and demanding performance guarantees from the contractors. The Area Control Computer Complex was canceled at this time. It was designed to interconnect the host computers at the airport with those at the regional levels.

Global Positioning System (GPS)

GPS is a satellite-based navigation system that was developed by the Pentagon and previously available for use only in connection with military air travel. GPS allows pilots to navigate based on satellite signals instead of radar signals. It allows real-time flight planning for pilots. As more satellite technology becomes available, the integration of air traffic as well as weather information and other data communication will become a necessary technological step. Four-dimensional GPS readings—longitude, latitude, altitude, and time—enable an aircraft to come within a few feet of any given target. Encryption technology is currently in place to protect security in the transmission of the satellite messages.

In 2004, the FAA began testing GPS tracking for air traffic control in Alaska. Because of the vast rugged terrain, it would be impossible to put radar stations across Alaska. Moreover, the onboard GPS units can report position data every second, while radar hits a plane only once every six seconds. The ADS-B technology GPS systems connect through the Iridium satellite system (Jackson April 26, 2004).

Standard Terminal Automation Replacement System (STARS)

"STARS is the next big step in the FAA's comprehensive effort to upgrade air traffic control facilities across the nation. The new system will provide the platform for improvements to handle the ever-growing volume of air traffic safely and efficiently well into the 21st century," said FAA administrator David R. Hinson (Dorr 1996). STARS will standardize all air traffic control equipment at the 172 FAA facilities as well as the 199 Department of Defense facilities. STARS will supply new hardware and software to these facilities. The program will be a complete replacement for the aging systems currently in use.

The most important feature of the STARS system will be the ability to display transmissions. The Automated Radar Terminal System (ARTS) that is currently in place was developed in the 1970s and 1980s. The FAA believes that interim programs are limited in their ability to extend the ARTS life in the short term. It is generally accepted that this system does not have the capabilities to take air traffic into the next century. ARTS software contains various versions and languages that are very labor intensive as well as expensive to support.

The STARS program includes a commercial standard system that the FAA believes will be much cheaper and easier to maintain. A key feature is the ability to extend and advance the capacity of the system without reengineering the basic architecture. By building on commercially available hardware and software, the development time for the software will be reduced significantly. The resulting maintenance costs will also be lower than those associated with the current ARTS system.

By 2003, the STARS project was behind schedule by at least six years and millions of dollars. The system was supposed to be completed in 1998 for $12 million. But after more than six years of development the system was still not implemented (McCartney 2003). However, an initial version of the system was installed in Philadelphia in late 2002. The system gathers data from several radar systems on color displays. However, not everyone was happy with it. Controllers in El Paso noted that the system could not distinguish between planes sitting on the runway and trucks on a nearby highway ("New Air" November 17, 2002). In mid-2004, the FAA announced that it was ready to begin implementing the new system. The Phase I rollout would take place at airports with the oldest equipment and cost $1.4 billion. Nineteen of the fifty sites were online as of 2004. But the last of the 50 airports were not scheduled to receive the new equipment until the end of 2007. There was no budget or schedule for the remaining 100 plus airports. In 2004, the GAO and inspector general urged the FAA to gain control over costs. The project was already seven years behind schedule and estimated costs had risen to $1.9 billion (Mosquera April 26, 2004).

Wide Area Augmentation System (WAAS)

The Wide Area Augmentation System is used in conjunction with GPS. Using a network of 36 ground stations to "distill" satellite GPS signals, WAAS will allow commercial aircraft to pinpoint a location within seven meters. With the use of WAAS/GPS, the FAA hopes it can close many of its ground control centers and allow pilots to fly more direct routes. Consolidated, these tools are projected to lead to the concept of free flight.

The WAAS system fell even further behind than the STARS project. The satellite-based system was pushed back by five years and the estimated costs were tripled (McCartney 2003).

Free Flight

Free flight is a consolidated goal toward which the FAA is working. Free flight would enable pilots to control their own navigation procedures. The pilot would use the WAAS and GPS systems for navigational purposes and choose their own routes, speed, and altitude. Ground support will be held to a minimum and would be most important when flights are in congested airport areas, when airplanes approach restricted airspace, or when safety is at stake.

Two principles that drive the free flight plan are the protected and the alert airspace zones. The sizes of these zones are determined based on aircraft speed, performance characteristics, communications, navigation, and surveillance equipment. The protected zone is the zone closest to the aircraft. No aircraft should overlap the protected zone of another aircraft. The alert zone is one that extends far beyond an aircraft's protected zone. The distance between planes will be monitored closely. If a plane touches another plane's protected zone, the pilots and the air traffic controllers will determine the course corrections that are needed. Under the free flight system, interference will be minimized until the alert zones collide.

Of course, after September 11, the issue of free flight is probably obsolete. The FAA and security agencies are even more interested in controlling and restricting flights. Nonetheless, the FAA and the GAO continue to investigate free flight options. A main step in the process is the Traffic Management Advisor. This software helps controllers efficiently regulate the space between airplanes as they arrive at airports. Under Phase I of the free flight program, five software tools are being tested at various sites. Phase II represents the expansion of the systems—if they work. One system, the User Request Evaluation Tool (URET), was deployed late, so it will require additional testing. It is designed to identify conflicts and respond to pilot requests for route changes. Another tool, the Final Approach Spacing Tool (FAST), has been abandoned because of risks found in testing. It was designed to assign runways and schedule landings (Langlois October 2001).

Some researchers note that reducing flight times will not be sufficient to speed up the system. Delays are also created by slow operations at the terminals, including refueling, baggage handling, and unscheduled gate changes. These researchers suggest that significant changes are needed to improve communications among airport terminals. One possibility is wireless PDAs carried by all personnel and updated by the airlines.

The September 11 attacks caused the FAA to delay implementing some aspects of the free flight (CPDLC) deployment. A major reason for the delay was due to the costs that would be imposed on the airlines. The FAA was also not ready to implement the new technologies (Vasishtha 2002).

Technology Innovations

The FAA has suffered through several failed projects over the years, including the Advanced Automation System (AAS) that was designed in the mid-1990s and thrown away in favor of the STARS project. The FAA also designed and implemented new radio communication technology. The goal was to transfer data by text, to reduce the use of voice communications. The Aircraft Monitory System (ACMS) was designed to collect data on the plane and send it to controllers. The Aircraft Communication Addressing and Reporting System (ACARS) was introduced to cut down on the use of spoken radio messages to transmit information to the ground. It was thought that if the flight crew could save time by transmitting data to the ground rather than conveying it by voice to the air traffic controllers, they would be better able to concentrate on flying the plane. ACARS directly interfaces with ACMS and sends and receives messages directly to and from the pilot. The pilot punches the message, such as flight plans, in an alphanumeric keypad or touch screen. Both systems operate on the Aeronautical Radio system (ARINC) that runs on VHF radio waves and handles the data transmission between the plane and the ground controllers. The system is owned and operated by the major airlines. The main drawback to ARINC is that because of limited bandwidth, the system transmits data at 2.4 kbps. In 2004, some airlines (notably Southwest) began installing a newer data service called VHF Digital Link Mode 2 (VDLM2), which can transmit data at rates up to 31.5 kbps (Brewin 2004).

Network

In 1998, the FAA replaced its mainframe-based system for acquisition management with a distributed architecture. The old system ran on 1980s-era minicomputers at 12 centers nationwide and processed more than 200,000 purchases per year. It was not updated for more than three years and was not Year 2000 ready. Mounting problems in the old system led many FAA officials to revert to paper to track agency purchases.

The new system is called Acquire. It uses Oracle Corporation's Alert software and the Discoverer/2000 querying tool. The FAA must also use Oracle Federal Purchasing software to get Acquire to run on a network that links headquarters to regional offices and field centers.

The FAA also began preparing a communications system overhaul aimed at readying the agency's infrastructure to meet the needs of the 21st century. The FAA Integrated Communications Systems for the 21st century (FICS-21) program is projected to cost an estimated $2.75 billion.

FICS-21 will provide ground-to-ground transmission switching and network management control for voice, data, and video communications. The new initiative will replace at least 11 major programs, including FAA-owned and leased networks. FAA FICS-21 program manager Jeff Yarnell says it is a good time to rebuild the FAA's telecommunications infrastructure because many telecommunications contracts expired at the turn of the century.

In 2004, the FAA finally began rolling out its new communication backbone. The new FTI system was installed at 27 facilities. Steve Dash, FAA telecom manager, said that the system is replacing five disparate networks. He noted that "it's the first phase. The backbone will tie together the major operation facilities" (Jackson January 26, 2004). Ultimately, the system will be connected to the other 5,000 FAA facilities and save $700 million in telecommunication costs over 15 years. Installation of the system was contracted to Harris at an estimated total cost of $3.5 billion. As much as possible, the system will use off-the-shelf networking and telecommunication products.

The FAA also provides services to pilots (and the public) through its Web site. Pilots account for 30 percent of the site traffic. To provide faster service, the FAA installed an expert system from RightNow Technologies that examines questions posed by visitors. The software compares the question to answers that have been provided to other users. Matches that are close are immediately displayed to visitors. Other questions are forwarded to the appropriate FAA authorities. Greg Gianforte, CEO with RightNow, comments that "we use a series of both implicit and explicit learning capabilities, which include artificial intelligence and machine learning, to observe the historical usefulness of each knowledge item and provide greater visibility to knowledge." Typically, the system can automatically handle 90 percent of the inquiries (Chourey April 26, 2004).

In conjunction with NASA, the FAA is using a simulation system called FutureFlight to test changes to airport control systems. Researchers testing configurations of the LAX airport found that safety could be improved by moving a taxiway to one end of the airport. John Bluck, speaking for the Ames Research Center, notes that "the idea is to try it [changes] in a safe way that's as close to reality as we can make it. You don't have to try something new on a real airport, where you have thousands of flights coming and going" (Langlois October 2001).

The Future

The FAA has faced considerable criticism over the delays and cost overruns associated with replacing its primary systems. The agency makes heavy use of outside contractors, which is probably a necessity. However, the agency needs to write better contracts so that it can maintain control over costs and schedules.

The successful implementation of STARS is becoming critical. Like other federal agencies, by 2014, as many as half of the air traffic controllers can retire (about 7,000 people) (Chourey July 5, 2004). These workers require intensive training, and their salaries represent a significant expense. In 2002, more than 1,000 controllers earned over $150,000 (McCartney 2003). The FAA is going to need better automated systems that are easier and safer. With increased traffic demands, the FAA will have to find a way to improve productivity.

Questions

1. After 20 years, why is the FAA still having so many problems building new systems?

2. What tools or methodologies might be useful to help the FAA complete its remaining tasks?

3. How could you speed up the STARS implementation schedule?

4. Will outside contractors (Computer Science Corporation) help the projects? How can you monitor and control the work by the contractors?

Additional Reading

"Air Traffic Control—Good Progress on Interim Replacement for Outage-Plagued System, but Risks Can Be Further Reduced." *GAO Report,* October 17, 1996.

Brewin, Bob. "Data Takes Flight." *Computerworld,* June 21, 2004.

Chourey, Sarita. "Getting an Instant Response." *FCW,* April 26, 2004.

Chourey, Sarita. "Air Traffic Controllers Head to the Beach." *FCW,* July 5, 2004.

Dorr, Les. "FAA Selects Raytheon for Next-Generation Air Traffic Control System Upgrade." *FAA News,* September 16, 1996.

"FAA Radar Glitches Found." *Computerworld,* November 2, 1998, p. 12.

"FAA Ready for Free Flight." *Advanced Transportation Technology News,* April 1996.

"FAA's $500 Million Navigation Contract Takes Flight." *Federal Computer Week,* April 10, 1995.

Jackson, Joab. "FAA Considers Commercial Satellites for Traffic Control." *Government Computer News,* April 26, 2004.

Jackson, William. "FAA and GSA Renew Their Dogfight over Air Traffic Control Modernization." *Government Computer News,* September 18, 1995, p. 73.

Jackson, William. "FAA Clears Rollout of Net Backbone." *Government Computer News,* January 26, 2004.

Langlois, Greg. "Researchers: Don't Forget Airport Ops." *Federal Computer Week,* September 10, 2001.

Langlois, Greg. "Data Determining Free Flight Future." *Federal Computer Week,* October 2, 2001.

Langlois, Greg. "NASA: Simulation Proves Its Worth." *Federal Computer Week,* November 5, 2001.

Leopold, George. "Study: GPS Can Fly as Commercial Air Navigator." *Electronic Engineering Times,* February 8, 1999, p. 18.

McCartney, Scott. "Labor Costs, Mismanagement: Airlines Again? No, the FAA." *The Wall Street Journal,* February 19, 2003.

Mosquera, Mary. "FAA Slows Down Display System Deployment." *Government Computer News,* April 26, 2004.

"New Air Traffic Control System Tested." *CNN Online,* November 17, 2002.

Tiboni, Frank. "FAA Begins Upgrade Project on Its Controller-Pilot Comm System." *Government Computer News,* February 8, 1999, p. 8.

Vasishtha, Preeti. "FAA Defers CPDLC Deployment." *Government Computer News,* January 4, 2002.

Case: The Internal Revenue Service (IRS)

Counting both personal and business returns, the IRS processes more than 130 million personal tax returns and another 10 million business returns a year. Many of the returns are simple one-page forms; others run to thousands of pages of supporting documents. Overall, the service handles more than 1 billion information documents a year. The IRS processes more than $1 trillion in tax revenue a year. The IRS has 10 regional service centers that are responsible for processing and storing individual forms. In 1989, it cost the IRS $34 million just to store the paper documents.

Until 1990, all documents at the IRS were stored as paper records in a central warehouse. Documents were organized according to the year of filing. As a result, if a taxpayer had a problem or question that covered multiple years, the citizen had to schedule multiple meetings with IRS officials to correct problems for each of the years. In some cases, it could take weeks or months just to get the files. Occasionally, the IRS found it was faster to ask the taxpayer for a copy of the return. By the early 1990s, this problem was resolved by having each of the 10 service centers store digital images of the tax returns, making them available to agents on their terminals. While a step in the right direction, this approach did not give the IRS the flexibility it would receive from the ability to scan the returns directly into a computerized information system.

Automation sometimes causes problems in addition to solving them. Such was the case of Dickie Ann Conn. The

IRS determined that she owed $67,714 in back taxes. She was sent a bill for more than $1 billion in interest and penalties. After being challenged, the IRS admitted that there was an error in the interest computation.

A History of Automation Problems

The IRS seems like a logical candidate for improved automation. The benefits of faster processing, fewer mistakes, and easier access to data ought to save a considerable amount of money. The computer's ability to search the data, automatically match transactions, and analyze each return presents several additional opportunities that can either cut costs or raise additional revenue. Managers at the IRS are fully aware of the potential, and they have proposed several systems over the years. The problem has been in implementation of the plans and in getting Congress to financially support the changes.

In the late 1960s, the IRS knew it needed to redesign its basic systems. In response, it began to plan for a system to be installed in the 1970s. The IRS did not get the needed support in Congress because of fears that it would be too expensive and too invasive into individual security and taxpayer privacy. As a result of this lack of support, the IRS turned its attention toward keeping its existing computers running.

In 1982, the existing system was nearing capacity and the IRS established the Tax System Redesign program. It promised a complete redesign of the system. According to the GAO, changes in management resulted in the system never getting past the design stage. A new assistant commissioner in 1982 embarked on the design of a new system that promised to carry the IRS through the 1990s. Initial costs were estimated at $3 billion to $5 billion over the entire project. The primary objective was to replace the old central tape-based system with an online database. Eventually, optical technology would be used to scan the original documents and store the data in the database. A new communication system would carry the data to any agent's workstation. By 1989, initial planning had already cost the IRS more than $70 million, with no concrete proposal or results.

The main computer systems were replaced at the IRS service centers in 1985. The change in the systems was almost disastrous for the IRS. It delayed returns processing and led to delays in refunds that cost the IRS millions of dollars in interest payments. IRS employees worked overtime but still could not keep up. Rumors were flying that some employees were dumping returns to cut down their backlog. Because of the delays and backlogs, the IRS managed to audit only about half the usual number of returns on which it conducted audits.

In 1986, the IRS initiated a plan to provide 18,000 laptop computers to enable its field auditors to be more productive with its Automated Examination System (AES). Unfortunately, the service bought the Zenith laptops a full year before the software was ready. The system was written in Pascal and was delivered to agents in July 1986. It was designed to examine Form 1040 returns. The biggest drawback was that it used 18 different diskettes. This required agents to be constantly swapping disks. Based on the privatization directives from the Reagan administration, the system was subcontracted to outside developers. As IRS funding was cut, programmers with experience in Pascal were cut. This led the system to be rewritten in C.

A survey in 1988 revealed that 77 percent of the agents were dissatisfied with the software. Only 33 percent said that they used it. By 1989, the IRS revised the software and managed to reduce it to eight disks. By this time, the AES project was more than six years behind schedule and, according to the GAO, was $800 million over the original budget. The IRS originally anticipated that the AES would produce $16.2 billion in additional revenue over nine years by making agents more productive. The GAO disputed those numbers, noting that "the IRS has been unable to verify that the use of laptops has actually resulted in the examination of additional returns or increased tax revenues." In 1990, the White House cut the funding for the program from $110 million to $20 million.

In 1999, the IRS implemented a new network to connect computers throughout the organization. Twenty staffers were dedicated to the project and took four years to complete it. IBM's Tivoli software is a key tool to manage the 132,000 networked devices in 87 locations. The software enables network managers to continually monitor all aspects of the network. They can also push changes down to the desktop computers if problems arise or they need upgrades. Before the system was available, it took an IRS staff member 20 minutes to update each device. With Tivoli live in 2003, a single network administrator sent one update to 400 desktops in one minute. Jim Kennedy, program manager for enterprise systems management at the Austin, Texas, support center, estimates that the system has saved $2.6 million in the first quarter alone (Dubie 2003).

Technology Innovations

By 1989, the IRS knew that it desperately needed to redesign its entire system for collecting taxes and processing information. In hearings before Congress, Senator David Pryor (D-Ark.) noted that the 1960s-era IRS computers were headed for a "train wreck" in the mid-1990s. The GAO estimated the total project would cost between $3 billion and $4 billion. The projected date for implementation slipped from 1995 to 1998.

The overall design for the Tax System Modernization program (TSM) called for a centralized online database, smaller departmental systems containing local information, and linkage through a nationwide network. Tax return data would be entered through a combination of electronic filing and optical scanners.

By 1991, the estimated cost of the plan had expanded to $8 billion. Although the IRS projected that the system would cut $6 billion in costs, the plan was rapidly attacked by members of Congress. Three studies of the TSM plan by the GAO were released in early 1991:

- The GAO was concerned that optical technology was not sufficiently advanced to perform the tasks demanded by the IRS. The GAO urged greater emphasis on electronic filing.

- The GAO was concerned that management issues such as transition planning, progress measurement, and accountability were not sufficiently addressed by the plan.
- The GAO and Senator John Glenn (D-Ohio) voiced concerns about data security and integrity.

GAO official Howard Rhile noted, "This is a serious omission in view of the fact that the IRS intends to allow public access . . . to some of its systems and because concerns over the security of taxpayer information helped doom the first [IRS] modernization effort in the late 1970s."

Despite these misgivings, the IRS was committed to the TSM plan. Fred Goldberg, IRS commissioner, agreed with the GAO findings but observed that

> We have been running our business essentially the same way, using essentially the same computer and telecommunications systems design for 25 years. [Existing systems] will perform well and achieve incremental improvements for the next few years. . . . Our best judgment is that [OCR] technology will be there when we need it, by the end of the decade.

By 1992, the situation grew worse. Shirley Peterson, the new commissioner of Internal Revenue, stated at a congressional hearing that

> Our systems are so antiquated that we cannot adequately serve the public. The potential for breakdown during the filing season greatly exceeds acceptable business risk. . . . Some components of these computers are so old and brittle that they literally crumble when removed for maintenance.

In December 1991, the IRS awarded a 12-year, $300 million contract to TRW to help manage the process and provide planning and system integration services. The recommended system was ambitious. It called for 60 major projects, two dozen major purchases, 20 million lines of new software, and 308 people just to manage the purchasing process. Despite the best efforts of the administrators, elements of the IRS modernization plan were stalled because of purchasing difficulties. In July 1991, the IRS awarded a billion-dollar Treasury Multiuser Acquisition Contract (TMAC) to AT&T. The goal was to standardize purchasing for the IRS and the Treasury Department by routing all purchases through one vendor. The contract was challenged by other vendors and overturned. The contract was rebid and AT&T won the second time. IBM (one of the original protesters) again objected to the process, noting that the IBM bid of $708 million was less than the $1.4 billion bid by AT&T.

In 1993, the IRS acknowledged that the TSM Design Master Plan needed to be rewritten. In particular, it had to focus on business aspects instead of technology elements. To better coordinate technical planning with IRS needs, the agency established a research and development center funded by $78.5 million of federal money but run by the private sector. The center was responsible for providing technical assistance and strategic planning for the TSM. The IRS also established a high-level "architect office" to evaluate technologies and direct their proposed uses.

Throughout calendar year 1992, the IRS spent $800 million on TSM. In 1993, new IRS estimates indicated that TSM would cost $7.8 billion above the $15.5 billion needed to keep existing systems running. The new system was projected to generate $12.6 billion in total benefits by 2008 through reduced costs, increased collections, and interest savings. Moreover, the improved process was supposed to save taxpayers $5.4 billion and cut 1 billion hours from the collective time they needed to spend with the IRS.

In 1996, the IRS asked Congress for a $1.03 billion appropriation. This was a substantial increase over the $622 million it spent on automation in 1995. Hazel Edwards from the General Accounting Office noted, "After eight years and an investment of almost $2 billion, the IRS's progress toward its vision has been minimal."

IRS Commissioner Margaret Milner Richardson denied the GAO claims. She noted, "I think we have made significant progress, not minimal progress . . . but we do know we can and must do more" (Birnbaum, 1998).

The IRS situation represented a dilemma for Congress. The IRS claims that the only way to make a system that works is to spend more money. The GAO has set forth that it is impossible to complete the entire project envisioned by the IRS. The GAO believes the IRS should, instead, concentrate on smaller, more focused projects that can be completed in a one- to two-year timeframe.

In 2001, Congress passed tax-cut legislation to stimulate the economy and ordered the IRS to send "refund" checks to all taxpayers. It took several months to create and mail the tens of millions of checks, but most of them were correct. On the other hand, about 523,000 taxpayers received notices that they would be getting a check for the full refund amount, when they were actually eligible for only part of the refund. The mistake was attributed to a programmer error, and the final checks were correct; but some taxpayers were confused by the misleading letter.

Electronic Filing

The IRS introduced electronic filing in 1986, when 25,000 forms were filed electronically. By 1990, 4.2 million people filed for tax refunds electronically. In 1992, the number increased to 10 million filers. In 2003, 49 percent of the personal tax returns were filed electronically (www.irs.gov).

The primary target for electronic filing is the millions of individual taxpayers who are slated to receive refunds. To control the process and ensure that documents are properly filed, electronic filing is available only through authorized tax preparers. The IRS is deliberately avoiding providing access to individual taxpayers. As a result, taxpayers who use the system pay an additional charge to the preparer. However, the electronic filing system provides refunds within a few days.

Forms that have been electronically filed cost the IRS one-tenth the processing cost of paper forms. This approach also eliminates the cost of paper storage. The IRS notes that it is able to store 800,000 returns on one side of a 12-inch optical disk.

For taxpayers with easy returns, the IRS is simplifying the process even further. Short forms can now be filed over the telephone. In a 1992 pilot, 117,000 Ohio taxpayers filed for refunds using push-button phone calls. The system was expanded nationwide in 1994. The push-button system can be used only by taxpayers who are able to use the 1040EZ form. A replacement form (1040-TEL) must still be signed and filed with the IRS, along with the W-2 (withholding) statements.

In the 1998 IRS Restructuring and Reform Act, Congress required the IRS to encourage the use of electronic filing. The IRS has made it easier for people to file electronically—particularly for those who use computer software to compute their taxes. In 1998, about 20 percent of individuals filed electronically; in 2000 the number was 28 percent; in 2001 about 32 percent (45 million). The IRS goal is to increase this number to 80 percent by 2007 (Dorobek 2001). For the 2001 tax year (filing in early 2002), the IRS used the Digital Signature law to send PINs to several million taxpayers, enabling them to legally sign their tax forms electronically. However, the one important catch is that taxpayers who file electronically must pay an additional fee to do so. Hence, only those who receive refunds (about 70 percent of the filers) are interested in paying the fee, because it enables them to get their money faster. Most experts believe it is unlikely that the IRS will meet the congressional goal of 80 percent by 2007.

The Internet

In late 2001, the IRS announced plans to offer electronic payments by businesses over the Internet. A major portion of the money received by the IRS comes from withholdings collected by businesses. This money has to be forwarded to the IRS at regular intervals, so the IRS is trying to reduce handling costs by moving these transactions online. The Electronic Federal Tax Payment System (EFTPS) is a Web-based system that can also be used by small businesses and by taxpayers who make estimated quarterly payments. Using modern strong encryption technologies, the IRS is confident the system will be secure.

Relatively early in the dot-com and dot-gov restructuring, the IRS realized the importance of putting information on its Web site. In fact, a huge amount of information is available online. And that is a problem. In 2001, IRS executives were asked to search the site for common tax information. It generally took 20 or 30 clicks to find any piece of information. To improve its Web site, the IRS hired Gregory Carson, a designer from private industry who helped to launch the Priceline.com Web site.

The IRS also signed a contract with the consulting group Accenture to redesign the IRS Web sites. In 2001, the site received 80 million hits a day. Gregory Carson, director of electronic tax administration modernization at the IRS, notes that "the development of an intuitive, intentions-based design will make it considerably easier for taxpayers and tax preparers, who pull forms from the site, to obtain the information and documents they need to file tax returns" (Rosencrance August 2001). Accenture's goal is to make the site easier to use so that users can reach the desired information within three clicks. Furthermore, Accenture will be hosting the site on its servers.

In 2003, more people turned to the Internet to file their tax returns. Several companies provide online systems that automatically e-file the data with the IRS. A few offer free filing. In 2003, 3.4 million taxpayers used the Free File service. In total over 14 million people used their personal computers to e-file their taxes (Mosquera May 10, 2004).

Automated Under-Reporter (AUR)

The Automated Under-Reporter (AUR) is another component of the TSM plan. The AUR is a system designed to monitor returns and identify people who are most likely to underpay their taxes. The system was first installed in 1992 at the Ogden, Utah, regional center. The system pulls data from the service center's Unisys 1180 mainframe. The data is downloaded across a local area network to a Sequent Computer System S-81 minicomputer. From there the information is sent to one of 240 networked UNIX workstations on the employees' desks.

The system automatically matches distribution documents (such as 1099s and W-2s) with the filings of individual taxpayers. Mark Cox, assistant IRS commissioner for information systems development, noted that in trials with the AUR, "we've been able to cut down the rework of cases from 25 percent to less than 5 percent. We see this type of work enabling us to share in more of a connectivity mode" (Quindlen, 1991).

The system uses an Oracle database running SQL to match data from various sources. It also performs basic tax computation and helps agents send notices to taxpayers. Managers have noted that even though the new system has not improved the speed of the agents, it has cut down on the error rates. As agents become familiar with the system, productivity is expected to improve.

In 1991, the Ogden center processed 26 million tax returns and collected $100 billion in tax payments. It processed $9 billion in refunds. In 1992, it won the Presidential Award for Quality for improved tax processing by saving the government $11 million over five years.

The Currency and Banking Retrieval System

In 1988, Congress passed a new law in an attempt to cut down on crime (notably drug dealing) and to provide leads to people who significantly underreport their income. Every cash transaction over $10,000 is required by federal law to be reported to the IRS on a Form 8300. The IRS created the Currency and Banking Retrieval System to match these forms against the filer's tax return. The system automatically identifies people who had large cash purchases but claimed little income. Because of a programming error, the system missed forms covering $15 million in cash transactions between 1989 and 1990.

The problem stemmed from the fact that the IRS used the same code number on the 8300 forms that it used on other cash transaction forms. The IRS later assigned separate codes for each form. When programmers wrote the new matching programs, they did not realize there were two codes for each transaction. The system was corrected in 1991. By 1992 it was used to process more than 1 million queries a year.

Jennie Stathis of the GAO noted there were additional problems with Form 8300. In particular, the filings were incomplete or contained incorrect taxpayer identification numbers. The IRS is developing software to enable businesses to verify the taxpayer ID numbers automatically before the customer completes the purchase.

Document Processing System (DPS) and Service Center Recognition/Image Processing System (SCRIPS)

In 1994, the IRS awarded a $1.3 billion contract to the IBM Federal Systems division to design a document processing system. The goal was that by the late 1990s, the system would convert virtually every tax return to a digital format. A day after the contract was awarded, IBM sold the Federal Systems division to Loral Corporation for $1.52 billion.

The 15-year systems integration contract was to have the system running online in 1996. The plan called for scanning incoming tax forms. Special software digitally removed the form layout and instructions, leaving just the taxpayer data. OCR software was to then convert the characters (including handwritten numbers) into computer data.

The system was scheduled for initial installation at the Austin, Texas, regional center in August 1995. Plans called for installing it at Ogden, Utah; Cincinnati, Ohio; Memphis, Tennessee; and Kansas City, Missouri, by 1998. Despite the popularity of electronic filing, the IRS still sees a need for the OCR system. The IRS received 222 million filings in 2003. Of those, 53 million were electronic.

SCRIPS was the first scanning project. Presented at a cost of $17 million, it was approved to cost $88 million when it was awarded in 1993 to Grumman Corporation's Data Systems unit. SCRIPS was designed to capture data from four simple IRS forms that are single-sided. SCRIPS was supposed to be an interim solution that would support the IRS until the Document Processing System (DPS) could be fully deployed. However, delays pushed back the delivery of the SCRIPS project. By the time it was declared finished, the project cost $200 million (Birnbaum 1998).

DPS was the second scanning project. It has a projected cost of $1.3 billion. Interestingly, Grumman Data Systems was the loser in the contest for the DPS contract. The IRS noted that Grumman failed a key technical test. When completed, DPS was quite complicated to use. In this program, the IRS developed nine separate databases, most of which could not communicate with each other.

In 1996, Art Gross, a veteran of the New York State revenue department, became the new IRS chief information officer. He stated that the IRS's computers didn't "work in the real world" and that its employees lacked the "intellectual capital" to transform them. When he arrived in 1996, the IRS's Year 2000 conversion project had a budget of $20 million and a staff of three; by 1998, it had grown to a $900 million project with 600 workers, many of them consultants (Birnbaum 1998).

Gross tried to get control of the system. He ended the DPS or "Bubble Machine" project as being over budget and behind schedule. With help from TRW, he devised a new top-to-bottom computer architecture. The architecture was built around a centralized database to coordinate information at the IRS.

When Charles Rossotti arrived as the new commissioner, he proposed an even more ambitious plan. In addition to Year 2000 changes, computer updates from the 1997 tax law, and the overall modernization, Rossotti proposed to restructure the entire organization. This proved to be too much for Gross, who resigned.

In 1998, Congress passed the Government Paperwork Elimination Act, part of which forces the IRS to move to more electronic transactions. Since then, the IRS has created electronic versions of its forms that can be downloaded from its servers. In 2001, the IRS signed a contract with ScanSoft Inc. for OmniPage Pro 11 for use in its federal tax offices around the nation. The goal is to convert the masses of paper files into electronic documents. Instead of taxpayer files, the system is designed more to convert internal forms and documents so that all employees will have immediate access to up-to-date forms and policies on the IRS intranet.

Customer Relationship Management

In late 2001, the IRS began installing customer relationship management (CRM) software that it purchased from People-Soft. A key element of the kinder, gentler approach is the ability to track customer issues. CRM software can collect all of the customer interactions into one location—making it easier for multiple agents to see the entire history of a particular problem. The system will also enable the agency to create Web portals for professional tax preparers, IRS employees, and taxpayers. The portals will securely provide individual information to these groups over the Web. In addition to faster service, the IRS hopes to reduce the costs of its call centers by moving more access online.

Security Breaches

In 1983, Senator John Glenn (D-Ohio) released an IRS report indicating that 386 employees took advantage of "ineffective security controls" and looked through tax records of friends, neighbors, relatives, and celebrities at the Atlanta regional IRS office. Furthermore, five employees used the system to create fraudulent returns, triggering more than 200 false tax refunds. Additional investigations turned up more than 100 other IRS employees nationwide with unauthorized access to records. Glenn observed that the IRS investigation examined only one region and looked at only one of 56 methods that have been identified to compromise security. Glenn expressed the concern that "this is just the tip of a very large iceberg."

The IRS noted that the TSM program "greatly increases the risk of employee browsing, disclosure, and fraud," because of the online access to the centralized databases.

Margaret Richardson, commissioner of the Internal Revenue Service, noted that the system used by the perpetrators was 20 years old and was used by 56,000 employees. It met all federal security standards, including the use of passwords and limited access based on job descriptions. The IRS found the problems in Atlanta by examining records of database access from 1990 to 1993. Because the system generates 100 million transactions a month, the data is stored on magnetic tape, making it difficult to search.

In 1989, the IRS arrested Alan N. Scott, of West Roxbury, Massachusetts, for allegedly submitting 45 fraudulent returns via the new electronic filing system. The IRS claims Scott received more than $325,000 in refunds.

The IRS requires tax return preparers to fill out an application before it issues an access code. Scott apparently used a fake taxpayer ID number and lied on the application form to gain the access number. The IRS claims he then submitted false returns using bogus names and taxpayer ID numbers to get refund checks ranging from $3,000 to $23,000.

IRS officials noted that the electronic filings actually made it easier to identify the problem, because the computer could scan the data earlier than the data had been scanned if it had been submitted by hand. Once the situation was identified, the IRS was able to immediately lock out further transactions from Mr. Scott's access number.

Modern Disasters

In 1998, the message in congressional hearings was to "Do something. Anything." The hearings into IRS dealings with the public revealed several problems within the IRS. They emphasized the negative perceptions the public has toward this important agency. After listening to these criticisms, the IRS eventually agreed to change some of its policies to improve its treatment of citizens. The 1998 IRS Restructuring and Reform Act was aimed at changing IRS attitudes and providing citizens with more control in the tax-collection process. Charles Rossotti, the new IRS commissioner, described the process of upgrading the vacuum tube–era technology as being similar to "rebuilding Manhattan while we're still living in it." The $7 billion agency has attempted the same gargantuan task of modernizing its computers for 25 years and continues to fail. The total cost in the 1990s alone has been projected to be nearly $4 billion (Birnbaum 1998).

In 2002, the system included 80 mainframes, 1,335 minicomputers, and 130,000 desktop boxes that were largely unable to communicate with each other. Before his appointment as commissioner of the IRS in November 1997, Rossotti served as chairman of the computer consulting firm American Management Systems. In early 1998, Arthur Gross, the chief technology officer, who drafted the latest modernization blueprint, resigned in frustration. Shortly thereafter, Tony Musick, the chief financial officer, re-signed to become deputy CFO at the Commerce Department (Birnbaum 1998).

Unfortunately, the IRS has been even less successful at implementing new technologies. By 1998, nearly all of the earlier systems development efforts were canceled. In late 1998, the IRS signed a 15-year development contract with Computer Science Corporation (CSC) that was worth $5 billion. By contract, CSC is responsible for helping design new systems, indicating that the ultimate goal is still to be determined. Outside experts note that the contract does not necessarily solve all the IRS problems. The IRS must still deal with the contract management issues, which have proved difficult to the IRS in the past.

In 1999, the IRS launched yet another attempt to modernize its systems. The $8 billion Business Systems Modernization (Bizmo) program was supposed to replace the infrastructure and over 100 applications. A key element is to replace the Master File system—which is an ancient tape-based system that holds customer data that the IRS has been using for over 40 years. The system runs an archaic programming language with code written in 1962. The heart of the new system is the Customer Account Data Engine (CADE) designed to run on IBM's DB2 database system. As of 2004, the project is way over budget and years behind schedule. Even the system to process the simple 1040EZ form is three years late and $36.8 million over budget (Varon 2004).

The system design actually started out well. The IRS hired CSC as the prime contractor. But the IRS did not maintain control of the contract, and there are serious doubts that even CSC was capable of handling the complex project. Paul Cofoni, president of CSC's Federal Sector business, testified to the U.S. House Ways and Means Oversight Subcommittee that "I have never encountered a program of the size and complexity as the Business Systems Modernization program at the IRS" (Varon 2004). Several times, the IRS considered firing CSC, but kept deciding that it would not be cost effective. One of the problems is that the IRS is not providing sufficient oversight of CSC or the project. They originally planned a relatively hands-off approach to let the company use best practices in its development. The problem is that CSC needed the expertise of the IRS agents and IT workers. The other problem is that the IRS went through five CIOs in seven years. In the meantime, CSC has gone through four managers to lead the project.

The CADE system is an impressive piece of technology—if it ever works. Once the database is active, the IRS will use a customized version of the Sapiens eMerge rule-processing engine. Congressional tax laws are coded as business rules that the system applies to evaluate each tax return. The system includes an XML-based RulesScribe layer that handles changes and additions to the rules. The simplest 1040EZ tax form requires about 1,000 rules. Red Forman, associate IRS commissioner for business systems modernization, notes that "we are certain we will have tens of thousands of business rules once CADE rolls out, and that's just for individual filers" (Mosquera May 17, 2004).

In May 2003, Mark Everson was appointed IRS commissioner, and three weeks later, he appointed W. Todd Grams as the CIO. As of 2004, the project is nowhere near completion. The IRS and CSC have been repeatedly blasted by congressional reports. Relationships between CSC and the IRS are tense. CSC has been banned from participating in additional IRS projects (Perez 2004). On the other hand, in mid-2004, the FAA did hire CSC for up to $589 million to help build an enhanced Traffic Flow Management system (McDougall 2004).

The Future

In the meantime, the IRS still has to process taxes. So far, electronic filing is probably the only thing keeping the agency alive. Yet if anything goes wrong with the ancient Master File system, the IRS is dead in the water. The IRS, CSC, and IBM have no choice but to get CADE running correctly as soon as possible.

Talk to citizens about paying taxes and you get lots of interesting responses. Yet a critical feature of the system is that everyone has to believe that they are being treated fairly—meaning the same as everyone else. If people somehow perceived that millions of others are getting by without paying taxes, everyone will revolt. For years, since the 1980s, the IRS has relied on a relatively simple system to automatically scan returns and identify possible tax cheats. The problem is that the rules are based on data and an economy from 20 years ago. The system is no longer catching the real tax cheats. In 2002, the IRS began collecting new data and designing new rules to identify which returns should be scrutinized more carefully. With a 13 percent increase in tax returns and a 29 percent decline in the auditing staff since 1995, the IRS has to rely on automated systems to analyze the returns. Charles O. Rossotti, the IRS commissioner at the time, could not give details of the new rules but did note that "the fact is, people who make more than $100,000 pay more than 60 percent of the taxes, and we need to focus there" (Johnston 2002).

The electronic filing system is critical to improving productivity at the IRS. Without it, thousands of people have to enter data from the paper forms into the computer system. Yet the existing system has several problems. Notably, it often rejects 1040 forms because of errors. The errors are anticipated, because people often make simple mistakes while entering data into their systems. The problem is that the IRS system tends to reply with cryptic messages that users have trouble decoding. The IRS is aware of the problems, but cannot decide how to fix them. Terry Lutes, associate chief information officer for information technology services, notes that they cannot decide whether to fix the existing system or build a new one. He asks, "It's a question of how much money do you spend on a system that's going to be a throwaway?" But the drawback to a new system is that optimistically, it would not be in place until 2010 (Olsen 2004).

To top off all of the operational problems, the IRS is being criticized by the GAO because of problems with its internal accounting procedures. The GAO has been nagging the IRS about problems with their financial management system for a decade. Of 100 recommendations from the 2003 audit, the IRS has implemented only 24. The IRS is planning to address many of the other problems with another part of its modernization system, the Integrated Financial System (Mosquera April 30, 2004).

Questions

1. What problems have been experienced by the IRS in developing its information systems?

2. How are these problems related to the service's systems development methodologies?

3. How is the IRS going to get more people to file electronically? Is there an upper limit?

4. Are there any ways to speed up the development of systems for the IRS? What would be the costs and risks?

5. Are the IRS's problems the result of technology or management difficulties?

6. Why was the IRS unable to manage and control the CSC contract? What can the managers do differently to get the projects finished?

Additional Reading

"All 208 Million Tax Returns Get Electronic Scrutiny on Arrival." *Government Computer News,* March 6, 1995.

"Automation Failed to Meet Requirements." *Government Computer News,* July 17, 1995, p. 6.

Birnbaum, Jeffrey H. "Unbelievable! The Mess at the IRS Is Worse Than You Think." *Fortune,* April 13, 1998.

Dorobek, Christopher J. "IRS: E-File Goal Is a Stretch." *Federal Computer Week,* April 9, 2001.

Dubie, Denise. "IRS Touts Savings Project." *Network World,* April 15, 2003.

GAO. "Tax Systems Modernization—Management and Technical Weaknesses Must Be Corrected If Modernization Is to Succeed." GAO/AIMD-95-156, July 1995.

Hasson, Judi. "IRS Takes On Old-Style Paperwork." *Federal Computer Week,* December 10, 2001.

Johnston, David Cay. "Hunting Tax Cheats, I.R.S. Vows to Focus More Effort on the Rich." *The New York Times,* September 13, 2002.

Masud, Sam. "New Bells Are Ringing at IRS." *Government Computer News,* October 16, 1995, pp. 44–45.

Mayer, Merry. "Interim Systems Will Tide IRS Over as It Modernizes." *Government Computer News,* January 25, 1999, p. 21.

McDougall, Paul. "FAA Taps CSC to Ease Air Traffic Congestion." *Information Week,* July 2, 2004.

McNamee, Mike. "A Kinder Gentler IRS?" *BusinessWeek,* February 1, 1999, p. 128;

"Modernization," *Government Computer News,* January 25, 1999, p. 20.

Mosquera, Mary. "IRS Financial Management Weaknesses Linger." *Government Computer News,* April 30, 2004.

Mosquera, Mary. "E-Filers Just Shy of Half of All Tax Filers." *Government Computer News,* May 10, 2004.

Mosquera, Mary. "IRS Will Put Business Rules Engine to the Test." *Government Computer News,* May 17, 2004.

Olsen, Florence. "IRS Weighs E-Filing Upgrades." *FCW,* May 11, 2004.

Perez, Juan Carlos. "IRS Commissioner Bars CSC from Upcoming Projects." *Computerworld,* February 13, 2004.

Quindlen, Terrey Hatcher. "Recent IRS Award Puts TSM in Motion." *Government Computer News,* December 23, 1991, pp. 3–4.

Rosencrance, Linda. "IRS Sends Out 523,000 Incorrect Refund Check Notices." *Computerworld,* July 17, 2001.

Rosencrance, Linda. "Accenture to Redesign, Host IRS Website." *Computerworld,* August 13, 2001.

Rothfeder, Jeffrey. "Invasion of Privacy." *PC World,* November 1995, pp. 152–161.

Smith, James M. "IRS Spends $1b for Next Five Years of Systems Support." *Government Computer News,* July 17, 1995, p. 82.

Thibodeau, Patrick. "Private Sector to Tackle IRS Mess." *Computerworld,* January 4, 1999, p. 4.

Varon, Elana. "For the IRS There's No EZ Fix." *CIO,* April 1, 2004.

Weiss, Todd R. "Peoplesoft Sells CRM Software to a Friendlier IRS." *Computerworld,* August 23, 2001.

www.irs.gov

Case: National Aeronautics and Space Administration (NASA)

NASA has experienced some serious problems over the past decade. Some have been due to software development errors, such as the 1999 Mars Polar Lander that failed because a programmer made a calculation in miles instead of meters. Systems as complex as the ones that NASA builds are bound to have problems and most people are willing to tolerate the problems. But it turns out that rocket science must be easy compared to accounting. NASA has an ongoing problem with budgets and monitoring expenditures.

For years, NASA has routinely run over budget on projects. For years, the GAO has criticized NASA for poor accounting practices. One of the problems has been the decentralized nature of NASA—with offices scattered across the country and around the world. The financial system relied on 10 separate systems—some still written in decades-old COBOL. NASA knew it had to fix the financial reporting system, so it contracted with SAP to install their R/3 system to create a new Integrated Financial Management Program (IFMP). However, NASA has a target date of 2007 for completing the conversion, and even that number seems optimistic (GAO November 2003).

In 2004, the real nature of the mess was highly publicized by *CFO Magazine.* The article was largely driven by a disclaimed opinion by PriceWaterhouseCoopers (PwC), NASA's financial auditor. In that statement, PwC revealed that NASA's bookkeeping was so bad that they were unable to account for $565 billion in year-end adjustments. That is billions, not millions, of dollars. Patrick Ciganer, program executive officer for integrated financial management at NASA, explains that "we had people in each of the [10] NASA centers who knew they had to make the year-end adjustments. The problem was, they had never done them before. They had been trained, but in some cases, that was six or eight months before, and they did it wrong" (Frieswick May 2004). The data was so bad that PwC had no choice but

to discredit the data and note that it could not be fixed. PwC later declined to bid for the right to audit NASA in the following year.

In echoes reminiscent of Parmalat's financial scandal, PwC also discovered that NASA was $2 billion short in its cash account with the Treasury Department. NASA's books claimed $2 billion that did not exist. After seven months, NASA CFO Gwendolyn Brown was still unable to find the missing money. In testimony before the House Subcommittee on Government Efficiency and Financial Management, she denied that the loss was the result of "fraud, waste, or abuse," but she had no clue about where the money went. Subcommittee chair Rep. Todd Platts (R-Pa.) retorted, "If my checkbook is off by 10 cents, I'll stay up all night until I find that 10 cents. Your checkbook is off by $2 billion" (Frieswick July 2004). Brown noted that the agency was going back and reconciling balances from 2000 onward. But it is unlikely that they will find the $2 billion. PwC found several other problems involving hundreds of millions of dollars and failure by NASA to follow its own procedures and those required by the government rules.

Decentralization is a huge source of NASA's problems. Each of the 10 centers (including Kennedy and Marshall space centers and the Glenn research center) is run independently, with separate financial systems and personnel. When Brown arrived, she attempted to integrate the financial procedures, noting, "I've told them that from now on, the agency will set policy, process, and procedure, and you, the centers, will do implementation. If we're going to be accountable and credible, that's what we have to do here" (Frieswick May 2004). One of the goals of the SAP implementation is to embed all of the central rules and consolidate the data so that all of the centers have to follow the same procedures. In particular, each center will have to reconcile its spending to the Treasury balances every month.

NASA has been extremely optimistic about implementation of the new IFMP system, or deliberately misleading—it can be hard to tell the difference. The GAO commented that "when NASA announced, in June 2003, that [the core financial] module was fully operational at each of its 10 centers, about two-thirds of the financial events or transaction types needed to carry out day-to-day operations and produce external financial reports had not been implemented in the module" (GAO November 2003). Many of the features that NASA claimed to implement had never been tested. The GAO was also concerned about NASA's lack of oversight of its contractors and its equipment. As of 2003, NASA planned to continue using manual journal entries to handle all transactions with respect to its $37 billion in property (GAO November 2003). About $11 billion of that equipment is located at contractor facilities, and NASA has almost no documentation or reports on the property.

Along the same lines, NASA is unable to apply costs to specific projects. In particular, the agency is supposed to report all costs of the International Space Station (ISS). In their 2003 report, NASA did not even list the ISS—allegedly an "editorial oversight." The GAO report indicates that the NASA system is incapable of correctly assigning costs to projects.

NASA has made several attempts to improve its accounting. The GAO notes that "NASA has made two efforts in the recent past to improve its financial management processes and systems but both of these efforts were eventually abandoned after spending a total of 12 years and a reported $180 million" (GAO November 2003). NASA is already over budget and behind schedule with the new IFMP system. The ERP system was originally budgeted at $982.7 million and is already $121.8 million over budget (Dizard 2004).

Purchases

NASA purchases billions of dollars of supplies a year. Desktop computers and accessories are important items for most of the offices. In 1998, to simplify purchases, NASA signed a nine-year $1.3 billion deal with seven companies to provide server, desktop, communication equipment, and support services. The Outsourcing Desktop Initiative for NASA (ODIN) required the vendors to maintain inventory at each major site. The vendors created ODIN catalogs that listed all of the parts available. Some NASA sites required workers to order only from the catalogs; others allowed workers to find different deals. Normally, you would expect a centralized system to provide negotiated discounts and better prices. In this case, NASA agencies were able to save thousands of dollars by not using the catalogs. The Goddard Space Flight Center purchased 5,000 copies of antivirus software without using the catalogs and saved $200,000. In 2003, the agency decided to tell all divisions that they were not required to purchase from the catalogs (Cowley 2003).

The Future

In terms of operations and projects, NASA is moving forward with new design ideas. In particular, NASA is working with Carnegie Mellon University on a major software dependability project. The goal is to create software that can tolerate hardware faults and security problems. These more intelligent systems would help prevent problems like those that affected the Mars Polar Lander (Thibodeau 2003).

NASA is also investing in tools to improve collaboration among researchers. Communication and information sharing have presented operational problems in the past. If everyone has the same data, it is easier to spot problems, as well as conduct new research. For the Mars rover mission, the Jet Propulsion Lab (JPL) installed the DocuShare content-management system from Xerox. Thousands of experts around the world have access to over 100,000 files. The system can handle up to 50 simultaneous projects and has search systems to help researchers find the data they need (Chourey June 2004).

NASA is also installing a new high-speed network to support operations. The system from Force10 Networks will support 10 gbps, making it possible to transfer huge files quickly. The data is carried on optical fibers. The high capacity is needed to handle even the local satellite data. Every day, NASA's 14 satellites in earth orbit transmit three terabytes of data (Chourey April 2004).

On June 20, 2004, NASA, along with the rest of the world, saw a new piece of the future: SpaceShipOne, designed and built by Burt Rutan, carried a man into space and back (Weil 2004). Partly to prove a point, partly to win the $10 million Ansari X Prize in October, the ship did one thing extremely well. It pointed out that it is possible to reach space on a budget of a paltry $30 million. It is not likely that Rutan's company, Scaled Composites, is going to compete with NASA anytime soon. However, it does indicate that something must be seriously wrong at NASA—when a civilian company can get to space on a budget that would not even be a round-off value in the money that NASA mysteriously loses each year.

Questions

1. How can an organization lose $2 billion?
2. Were the auditor problems ($565 billion) due to technology, management, individuals, or some other reason?
3. Will the new ERP system be completed? If it is, will it solve NASA's problems, particularly in terms of centralization?
4. How is NASA going to solve its problems with the development of mission software? Why is this such a challenging problem?
5. How can Congress get NASA to provide accurate progress information, and how can Congress determine if it is being told the truth?

Additional Reading

Chourey, Sarita. "NASA to Move Data Faster with Bigger Pipes." *FCW,* April 12, 2004.

Chourey, Sarita. "NASA Uses Xerox for Sharing." *FCW,* June 23, 2004.

Cowley, Stacy. "NASA Wastes Money with Desktop Outsourcing Deal, Audit Finds." *Computerworld,* August 1, 2003.

Dizard III, Wilson P. "NASA's ERP Project Goes Awry, GAO Tells Panel." *Government Computer News,* May 24, 2004.

Frieswick, Kris. "NASA, We Have a Problem." *CFO,* May 1, 2004.

Frieswick, Kris. "Canary Chorus." *CFO,* July 1, 2004.

GAO. *Business Modernization: NASA's Integrated Financial Management Program Does Not Fully Address Agency's External Reporting Issues.* November 2003, GAO-04-151, http://www.gao.gov/new.items/d04151.pdf.

"NASA's Finances in Disarray; Auditor Quits." *Space Flight News,* May 16, 2004.

Thibodeau, Patrick. "NASA Reinvents Troubled IT with Help of Private Sector." *Computerworld,* February 10, 2003.

Weil, Elizabeth. "Rocketing into History." *Time,* June 23, 2004.

Summary Industry Questions

1. What information technologies have helped this industry?
2. Did the technologies provide a competitive advantage or were they quickly adopted by rivals?
3. Which technologies could this industry use that were developed in other sectors?
4. Is the level of competition increasing or decreasing in this industry? Is it dominated by a few firms, or are they fairly balanced?
5. What problems have been created from the use of information technology and how did the firms solve the problems?

CHAPTER THIRTEEN

Organizing MIS Resources

Chapter Outline

Introduction
Managing the Information Systems Function
MIS Roles
    Hardware Administration
    Software Support
    Network Support
    Software Development
    Support for End-User Development
    Corporate Computing Standards
    Data and Database Administration
    Security
    Advocacy Role
MIS Jobs
Outsourcing
MIS Organization: Centralization and Decentralization
    Hardware
    Software and Data
    Personnel
Recentralization with Intranets
    Networks
    Hardware
    Data
Conflict Management
Summary
Key Words
Web Site References
Additional Reading
Review Questions
Exercises
Cases: The Energy Industry

What You Will Learn in This Chapter

- What tasks are performed by the MIS department?
- Is the MIS department doing a good job? Should the company be spending more money on MIS? Is it getting a good value for its current spending? Are there other methods that would be more efficient or save money?
- What roles and tasks does the MIS department perform?
- What MIS jobs are available, and how much will it cost to hire IT employees?
- Do you really need to run all of the MIS operations yourself?
- Who should control IT resources?
- How can Internet technologies be used internally to centralize data but still support decentralized user access?
- Why is the MIS department involved in so many conflicts? How do you solve them?

How do you create and manage an information system when the organization has offices and people around the nation or around the world? ExxonMobil and several other companies faced this question with an additional twist. They had to combine systems from two huge companies when they merged. Mobil also had to extend its SpeedPass RFID payment technology to all of the new stations. That meant installing new networks and extending the information system. Ultimately, the answer by ExxonMobil was to combine the SAP systems used by both companies and run on a single, centralized system.

ChevronTexaco took a similar approach when those two companies merged. The new firm has relied on centralization to control technology and reduce costs.

Royal Dutch Petroleum (Shell) faces similar global issues. It has not been as effective at managing its information and financial systems. The company has experienced difficulties dealing with multiple contract employment agencies. The company's stock also took a beating when the company had to restate its accounts because it had misstated its oil reserves.

FIGURE 13.1

Organizing information system resources: Making effective use of information systems requires organizing the MIS resources: hardware, software, data, and personnel. A key decision involves positioning the resources in the organization, which revolves around decentralization versus centralization. The goal is to balance the need for central control with the value of decentralized decisions.

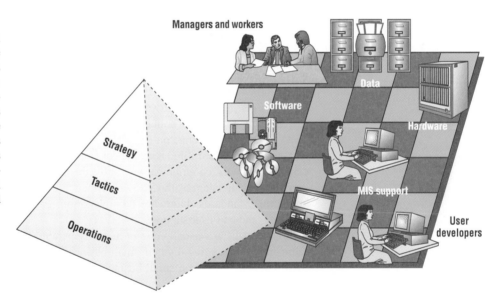

Introduction

What tasks are performed by the MIS department? What MIS jobs are available? What problems and issues will you have to handle as a manager? Why does the MIS department manager have so much power, compared with a typical business manager? As implied in Figure 13.1, the question of how MIS fits within an organization is difficult, and the answers have been changing along with the technologies. As a non-IS manager, you will encounter many issues and decisions that are affected by the MIS structure. You should learn to recognize common problems and possible solutions so that you can minimize the effect of some of these problems. When you are evaluating the CIO, MIS, and the overall structure, remember one rule: The job of MIS is to help the organization and the other managers.

The capabilities of application software are impressive. Because of these tools, business people using personal computers are solving problems in a few hours that never would have

TRENDS

In the early days, computers created few management issues. The large, expensive machines were placed in a central location and serviced by a centralized group of specialized employees. But as costs dropped over time, hardware spread throughout the organization. Soon, employees were collecting and creating data on hundreds or thousands of machines across the company. The local area networks of the late 1980s were installed in an effort to make it easier to share data and provide more centralized services. The initial spread of PCs and networks supported decentralization, where workers became responsible for handling their own data and computers.

Integrated packages (ERP), Web sites, and groupware tools make it easier to share data and support teamwork. These tools required corporatewide standards and began to encourage a recentralization of MIS resources. As companies periodically focus on cost control, the trade-offs between decentralization and centralization become a source of contention.

The increased attacks and renewed interest in security in the early 2000s generated additional interest in the management of information resources. Attempts to increase security led to even more demands for centralized control over resources. Centralized control and decentralized management are not necessarily good or bad. They both have strengths and weaknesses. The key is to find the appropriate balance for each organization. The challenge is that changes in technology and external events (such as security threats) sometimes cause organizations to leap to one solution without thinking about the consequences. Interesting arguments often follow.

been attempted five years ago. With these powerful tools available to the average business person, it is easy to wonder why a company needs an MIS department. That is a good question, and the answers keep changing through the years.

MIS departments provide many important services. For example, think about what happens when a new version of your word processor is released. Someone has to install the software, distribute the manuals, convert old document files to the new format, and show people how to use the new features. Now imagine the problems involved when there are 5,000 workers using this software.

According to statistics collected by *Computerworld,* large companies spend about 5 percent of their sales revenue on the MIS area. For a company with a billion dollars in sales, that amounts to $50 million a year spent on MIS. This money pays for personal computers, central computers, communications, software, and MIS personnel to manage it all. The primary tasks undertaken by the MIS department are software development, setting corporate computing standards, hardware administration, database administration, advocacy and planning, and end-user support.

Small businesses usually do not have a separate MIS department. That does not mean these duties are ignored. Even in small businesses, someone has to be responsible for these MIS functions. However, small businesses generally do not attempt to develop their own software. Even relying on commercial software requires that time be spent on determining data needs and evaluating software packages.

Probably the most important MIS decision facing business today is the issue of centralization. Because personal computers have a huge price/performance advantage over larger computers, there is a major incentive to decentralize the hardware. Yet there are some serious complications with complete decentralization. Several strategies for organizing information resources provide the advantages of both centralization and decentralization. The management goal is to find the combination that works best for each situation. Before examining the alternatives, you need to understand the basic MIS roles.

Managing the Information Systems Function

Is the MIS department doing a good job? Should the company be spending more money on MIS? Is it getting a good value for its current spending? Are there other methods that would be more efficient or save money?

Many times in your career you will find yourself heavily involved with members of the MIS department. In the case of a small business, you might be in charge of the one or two

REALITY BYTES   The Changing Role of MIS

The role of the MIS department has changed over time. In many respects, it is in the middle of a fundamental change. In the past, MIS departments focused on creating information systems and controlling data—particularly transaction data. Today, as explained by the Gartner Group (an IS consulting firm), the objectives of MIS are:

• Provide transparent access to corporate data.

• Optimize access to data stored on multiple platforms for many groups of users.

• Maximize the end-user's ability to be self-sufficient in meeting individual information needs.

These changes represent a shift in attitude. It moves toward the goal of increasing support for workers, not their replacement, so employees can do their jobs better on their own.

MIS personnel. At some time, you might be the company liaison to an outsourcing vendor, MIS contractor, or consultant. In all of these situations, you will be responsible for planning, monitoring, and evaluating the MIS organization.

As many companies have found, it is difficult to evaluate the MIS function. There are few objective measures. Changes in technology make the process more difficult. Innovations in hardware and software often make it easier to build and maintain information systems. However, there is a cost to buying new equipment. There is also a cost to continually retraining workers and modifying databases and reports. The goal of management is to find the appropriate balance between the need to update and the costs.

Management of information systems begins by understanding the roles of MIS. The MIS function is responsible for hardware and software acquisition and support. The MIS staff provide access to corporate data and build applications. They support end-user development with training and help desks. MIS workers set corporate data standards and maintain the integrity of the company databases. All of these functions have to be organized, performed, and evaluated on a regular basis.

The issue of new technology points out the importance of planning. The only way to control costs and evaluate MIS benefits is to establish a plan. Plans need to be detailed so that actual results can be compared to the plan. Yet plans need to be flexible enough to adapt to unexpected events and new technology. You also need to formulate contingency plans for events that might occur.

One key issue in managing information technology is organizing the MIS function so that it matches the structure of the firm. Centralization versus decentralization has been a key issue in the organization of MIS resources. Networks and powerful personal computers have led to more options supporting decentralization of information. The increased options are useful, but they create more issues that managers must examine. To understand the advantages and drawbacks of MIS options, we must first examine the roles of MIS.

Managing the MIS functions is a difficult job. Leaders must always remain focused on the primary goals. The primary job of the MIS department is to support and enhance the business. This mission is accomplished by enabling the sharing of data in a cost-effective manner but still providing adequate security controls to protect the information assets of the organization. An effective information system can create new methods of organizing and running the business. Of course, most of these goals are conflicting: security and sharing result in significant disagreements and trade-offs; holding down costs conflicts with just about everything.

MIS Roles

What roles and tasks does the MIS department perform? Good information systems do not simply materialize from thin air. Providing timely, accurate, and relevant information requires careful planning and support. Creating effective information involves maintaining

FIGURE 13.2

MIS roles: The MIS department is responsible for hardware administration, software development, and training and support. MIS staff establish corporate computing standards, provide access to corporate data, and support end-user development. The MIS department also plays an advocacy role, presenting the IT benefits and strategies to the executive office.

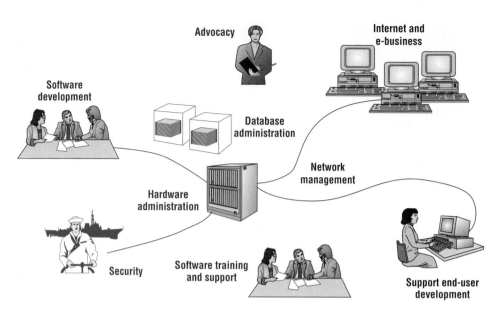

hardware, providing software training and support, supporting end-user development, defining and controlling access to databases, establishing corporate standards, and researching the competitive advantages of new technologies. The basic roles of MIS are outlined in Figure 13.2.

Hardware Administration

In some respects, hardware administration has become a little easier in the last few years. Computers are more reliable, more standardized, and cheaper. It used to be difficult to accommodate users who needed slightly different hardware. Many companies still prefer to standardize PC hardware to simplify purchasing and asset tracking. But with common three-year support contracts, standardized hardware, and low prices, it is less and less important to require that all employees have the exact same computer. Instead, most companies need to choose a time frame for updating their computers. For most purposes, three years has been shown to be a productive length of time to hold a PC. On the other hand, some companies require groups of employees to have exactly the same hardware. MIS can then make a standard copy of the configuration and software and reload this image if anything goes wrong with a user's computer.

Mobility has become an increasingly important issue for many business computer users. More managers are requesting the use of laptops instead of (or along with) desktops. Mobile systems like the PDAs and Internet-accessible cell phones change the picture even more. Fortunately, the cost of most of these devices has dropped as well. Consequently, purchasing is less of an issue. Instead, mobile systems present more problems in terms of security—beginning with loss of the equipment.

Purchase costs do not represent the entire cost of hardware. In the mid-1990s, a few companies began pushing a concept they called **total cost of ownership (TCO).** The basic issue is that someone has to configure the PC, install software, and troubleshoot problems. At the time, most of these tasks required an on-site MIS support person, which was expensive. Various attempts were made to estimate these additional support costs and derive the TCO. The slightly hidden objective was to show that centralized computers were not really more expensive than personal computers. While most of the numbers from this process were unreliable, the process did highlight the difficulties of maintaining personal computers. Consequently, several firms created tools to install software and troubleshoot PCs from a central location over the LAN.

The move toward Internet-based applications removes many of the issues of managing personal computer hardware. As long as the systems support the Internet standards, and as long as they can be purchased inexpensively, there is little need for detailed MIS oversight.

REALITY BYTES · Business Trends: Specialization

Just as in other areas of business, MIS jobs have become highly specialized. For instance, many advertisements for MIS jobs look like someone spilled a bowl of alphabet soup on the page. Companies often search for technical skills involving specific hardware and software.

Unfortunately, this approach to jobs causes problems for MIS personnel. In order to find other jobs or to advance in their current position, they have to acquire increasingly detailed knowledge of specific hardware and software packages. Yet with rapid changes in the industry, this knowledge can become obsolete in a year or two. These changes mean employees have to continually expand their knowledge and identify software and hardware approaches that are likely to succeed.

On the other hand, businesses need to keep their current applications running. With thousands of hours invested in current systems, companies cannot afford to discard their current practices and adopt every new hardware and software system that shows some promise.

On the other hand, the central servers that run the Web sites, databases, and applications become more important. MIS personnel need to monitor the performance of the servers, provide backup plans, maintain security, and plan for capacity increases.

Capacity planning is a major factor in MIS organizations. Building scalable systems is an important goal for most organizations. The objective is to purchase only the level of hardware that is needed. Then, as demand increases, add more servers or larger servers to handle the increased load. This process holds down central hardware costs, but it means that MIS has to carefully design the systems and carefully monitor the usage and predict future demands.

Software Support

Software generally requires more support than hardware does. MIS staff can help users decide which software to purchase and then install it. Users need to be trained to use various software features. Whenever workers change jobs or a company hires new workers, they need to be trained. Similarly, commercial software versions change almost every year, requiring more training for users. In addition, someone has to install the new copies on the machines, distribute manuals, and convert data files.

When users have difficulty getting the computer to do what they want, it saves time to have someone to call for help. Most commercial software companies provide telephone support for their products, although many of them charge extra for this support. In many cases, it is better for MIS to support users directly. Besides the possibility of lower costs, the MIS department has a better understanding of the business problems. Also, many users are now combining information from several packages. For example, you might put accounting data and a photograph into a word-processed document. If different companies created the three programs and you have trouble, which one of the three software companies do you call? Your own MIS department will have experience with all three packages and should be able to identify the cause of the problems.

Network Support

Both wired and wireless networks are critical to running a company. Managers rely on the networks being available 24 hours a day, 7 days a week. Fortunately, most modern network equipment is reliable and can run continuously for months. Moreover, network managers can build networks that can correct for failures and bottlenecks by routing traffic around a switch that has failed.

Network support becomes more complicated when managing Internet connections. Connecting to the Internet requires some specialized skills to configure the router. Once the connection is established, configuring the router for security becomes critical. Monitoring the connection and keeping up with current security advisories are even more challenging. Larger companies train specialized personnel to handle these tasks. Smaller companies often rely on consultants or contractors.

Wireless networks are relatively easy to install—several companies provide the hardware to install in your home. But they are much more difficult to configure if you are concerned about security. Several true stories exist of people sitting in parking lots or even passing commuter trains and establishing a wireless connection into a company's network. Network specialists are trained to configure networks to minimize these problems.

Software Development

Developing software and business applications is difficult. Projects can require teams of hundreds of developers. Even smaller projects and purchases of larger software applications require devoted attention to detail. Managing software development and purchases is a critical role in MIS. Beginning with project evaluation and feasibility studies, through project management and tracking progress, to evaluating the team efforts, someone has to be in charge of the details.

These tasks are some of the more traditional roles in MIS. They are also the most difficult. Unfortunately, most companies have poor track records in managing software projects. Many development projects fail, and even more are behind schedule and over budget. Consequently, many firms choose to buy software or use outside companies to help in development projects. Even in these cases, someone in MIS has to be responsible for evaluating choices and monitoring progress.

Support for End-User Development

Many application packages include programming capabilities. For example, a manager may create a spreadsheet to calculate sales commissions. Each week, new sales data is entered and the spreadsheet automatically produces summary reports. It would be better to have a clerk rather than a manager enter this new data. To make the clerk's job easier, the manager uses the macro capabilities in the spreadsheet to create a set of menus and help messages. Similarly, using a word processor's macro facilities, a legal department can create standard paragraphs for various contracts. With them, an assistant can type one word to display a prewritten warranty paragraph. In theory, even complex applications traditionally provided by the MIS department, such as accounting systems, could be programmed by end users with prepackaged software.

Several problems can arise from these end-user applications. Techniques that are acceptable for small projects may lead to errors and delays with large systems. Programming major applications requires obtaining information from users and managers. Applications designed for corporate use require extensive checking of data and security provisions to ensure accuracy. The software often needs to run on different operating systems and local networks.

The MIS department can provide assistance to minimize these problems. MIS personnel can assist end users in collecting ideas from other users. They can also help in testing the applications to verify the accuracy and make sure the software works with other applications. MIS can provide tools and help end users document their applications and move them to new operating systems or new hardware. Programmers can write special routines to overcome any limitations of commercial software that might arise. MIS staffs also maintain help desks or information centers to answer user questions and help users debug applications.

Corporate Computing Standards

Over time, MIS has learned that the firm gets into trouble if all of its people work independently. In the 1960s, applications such as payroll, accounting, and customer order processing were developed independently. During the 1970s, companies had to spend large amounts of money getting all of the pieces to work together. In the 1980s, personal computers arrived, and the problems got worse.

Reacting to the problems created by these incompatibilities, MIS professionals at different companies developed **standards.** If all vendors used standard formats for files, hardware connections, and commands, products from different vendors could be used together. Today, there are standards for everything: data, hardware, software, report layouts, and coffee pots.

REALITY BYTES   Clueless Management

In the 1990s, a new system administrator was hired by a company having problems with its systems. At least one major system would crash every week, wiping out minutes' or hours' worth of data. The senior manager gave the new administrator one command: "Do whatever it takes to make sure people can do their jobs and that systems do not go down anymore." Over several months, the new worker improved security, created automated backups, and improved system monitoring. He also added some modifications that would let processes roll over to another system if hardware failed. He documented all of the changes and reasons and explained the systems to other IT managers running crash-prone systems in other divisions. One day he gets called to a meeting with all of the senior IT staff members. The head of the IT department says, "All the de-partments are still having system problems, except for yours. In your area, the systems are always up, people are able to get on the systems anytime they need to, and the managers have no major complaints about the systems you're in charge of. It's like this little island that stands out." The system administrator is humble and explains he had help from many of the workers. He then offers to help the other administrators with their systems. Surprisingly, everyone is shocked. The head of IT breaks the silence, telling the administrator, "I'm afraid you don't understand. You can't run your systems this way. They're not configured to company standards. Put everything back the way it was."

Source: Adapted from Sharky (The Shark Tank), "An Island of Sanity in a Sea of Confusion," *Computerworld*, January 2, 2002.

It is unlikely that the computing world will ever see complete cooperation among vendors. Three factors prevent products from working together. First, standards are often ambiguous or incomplete. Human languages always have some ambiguity, and there is no way to determine whether the description actually covers every possible situation. A second problem is that standards incorporate what is known about a topic at the time the standard is developed. Computing technologies change rapidly. Often, vendors can produce better products by not following the standards. Then new standards have to be developed. A third problem occurs because vendors want to distinguish their products from the offerings of competitors. If there were standards that perfectly described a product, there would be only one way to compete: price. Many vendors find that it is more profitable to offer features beyond what is specified in the standards, enabling the developers to charge a higher price.

Even though it is not possible to create perfect industry standards, there are advantages to creating companywide standards. They enable firms to buy products at lower prices. Most large businesses have special purchase agreements with hardware and software vendors. Buying in bulk allows them to obtain better prices. Similarly, it is easier to fix hardware if all the machines are the same. Likewise, it is much more convenient to upgrade just one word processing package for 200 computers, instead of 20 different brands. Similarly, training is less expensive and time consuming if everyone uses the same software and hardware. Finally, standards make it easier for employees to share information across the company. The Internet and e-mail create additional demand for standards. To share a file on the Internet, you must store it in a standard format (e.g., HTML or PDF). People sometimes forget that a similar problem arises when attaching files to e-mail messages. Particularly when you send a file to someone in a different company, you need to remember that the recipient may not have the same version of software that you are using. If you attach a file in Word 2000 format, for example, the recipient needs to have Word 2000 to read it. Since some companies upgrade before others, it is generally safer to save attached files in either a standard format (HTML or RTF) or a previous version.

Some organizations forget that standards cannot be permanent. Hardware and software change almost continuously; new products arrive that are substantially better than existing standard items. Similarly, as the business changes, the standards often have to be revised. Also, there are exceptions to just about any policy. If one department cannot do its job with the standard equipment, MIS must make an exception and then figure out how to support this new equipment and software.

Data and Database Administration

Databases are crucial to the operation of any company. Keeping the databases up-to-date and accurate does not happen by chance. Larger organizations employ a **database administrator**

Problem: You need to track workers and schedules on a project.

Tools: Project management software such as Microsoft Project has becoming increasingly sophisticated. It is based on the fundamental concepts of project management—with an emphasis on Gantt charts. The strength of the computerized tools is that all of the information is stored in a database. The tools quickly provide you with different views of the data, including Gantt, network, and critical path charts. You can also see calendars and schedules by each worker.

The first step in any project is to identify the goal. Do you need to be finished by a specified date, or do you have a starting date and need to estimate the finish? The next step is the most important: break the project into multiple tasks. Tasks can be grouped and subdivided into even smaller activities for large projects. Each task should have a clear start-

ing and ending point. For each task, estimate the amount of time required to complete the task. Later, you can record when tasks begin and track their progress. Once the basic tasks have been defined, you need to specify the relationships: Which tasks cannot be started until a prior task has finished? For example, you cannot begin integration testing of software until after it has been written.

You can also assign resources to each task. Generally, you will assign people or outside contractors to particular segments. If technology or other hard resources are going to be a limiting factor, you should include them as well. Microsoft Project has a system to automatically "level" the project if resources are over allocated. For example, if you are scheduled to do three daylong tasks on one day, it will push the tasks forward to provide a better estimate of when the project will be completed.

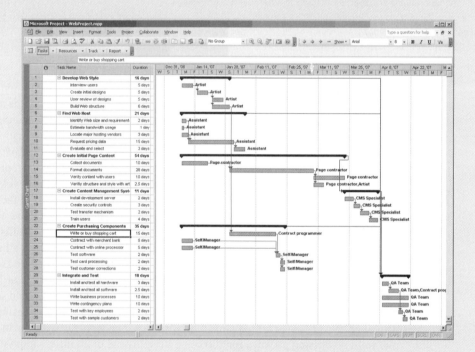

Most development projects involve multiple workers or contractors performing many tasks. Each task can be dependent on many other tasks. The Gantt chart highlights these dependencies. As the project progresses, you can add completion data to each task. If a task is delayed, the system will automatically push back the future tasks and show the new completion date.

Microsoft Project can also be integrated with a Web server, enabling each participant to check the progress and share calendars. The Web server acts as a groupware tool and can e-mail each person and record their comments.

Quick Quiz:

1. What advantages are provided by storing the project information in a DBMS?

2. Why is estimating development time one of the most difficult activities?

(DBA) to be responsible for maintaining the corporate databases, monitoring performance of the database management system, and solving day-to-day problems that arise with the databases.

Companies also need someone to coordinate the definition of the data. Large organizations might hire a separate **data administrator** (DA); smaller companies will pass this role to the DBA. The DA is responsible for defining the structure of the databases. The DA has to make certain the data is stored in a form that can be used by all the applications and users.

He or she is responsible for avoiding duplicate terms (e.g., customer instead of client). Furthermore, the DA provides for **data integrity,** which means that the data must contain as few errors as possible.

The DA is also required to maintain security controls on the database. The DA has to determine who has access to each part of the data and specify what changes users are allowed to make. Along the same lines, companies and employees are required by law to meet certain privacy requirements. For instance, banks are not allowed to release data about customers except in certain cases. European nations have much stricter privacy rules. If a firm operates a computer facility in many European countries, the company must carefully control access to all customer data. Some nations prohibit the transfer of customer data out of the country. The DA is responsible for understanding these laws and making sure the company complies with them.

Finally, because today's databases are so crucial to the company, the business needs a carefully defined disaster and recovery policy. Typically that means the databases have to be backed up every day. Sometimes, a company might keep continuous backup copies of critical data on separate disk drives at all times. MIS has to plan for things that might go wrong (fires, viruses, floods, hackers, etc.). If something does affect the data or the computer system, MIS is responsible for restoring operations. For instance, an alternate computing site might be needed while the original facilities are being repaired. All of this planning requires considerable time.

Security

Since most of today's business data is stored in computers, computer security has become a critical role for the MIS department. Often this role is shared with the accounting department to establish standards and procedures to ensure the integrity of financial data. Medium and large organizations have full-time computer security officers to set policies, establish controls, and monitor systems for attacks. Because of the constant evolution of new threats and the large number of systems and employees, the task can be immense. Attackers often search for one little hole in one system or one mistake by an employee. Security managers have to keep up with hundreds of different systems and applications to make sure that all of the holes are plugged.

Security administration also includes training users, testing system configurations, and monitoring networks for ongoing attacks. Establishing incident response plans and teams is also a major task. When things go wrong, you need a team and a plan to identify the problem, stop the attack, and restore business functions as quickly as possible. Along the way, you have to collect and maintain evidence that can be used in court cases, so that if you catch the attackers, you can file charges against them.

Advocacy Role

The MIS department is headed by a single manager, who often is called the chief information officer (CIO). The CIO position might be a vice president or one level below that. A major portion of this job involves searching for ways in which the information system can help the company. In particular, the CIO searches for and advocates strategic uses of MIS. The goal is to use the computer in some way that attracts customers to provide an advantage over the company's competitors.

The MIS goal is to help the organization and the other managers. But most business managers are not experts in technology. Whenever a new technology is introduced, someone has to be responsible for deciding whether it will be worth the expense to make a change. If there is no one in this **advocacy role** who evaluates the existing systems and compares them to new products, an organization is probably not often going to get new equipment. Even when many users are dissatisfied with an existing system, they will have a better chance of acquiring new technology if they can voice their complaints through one highly placed person. Along these lines, the CIO is responsible for long-run planning in terms of information technology.

FIGURE 13.3

IS salaries: As in any field, salaries depend on experience. However, in IS they also depend heavily on technical skills. Programmer/analysts with current skills and experience in new technologies find it easier to get jobs and obtain higher salaries. Note that there is a wide variety of jobs in IS, each requiring different types of skills.

IS Management	
CIO/VP IS/CTO	$154,000

Includes bonus

Systems Development	
Director	$127,000
Project manager	92,000
System analyst	68,000
Senior developer	76,800
Programmer/analyst	65,000
Junior programmer	45,000

Networks	
Manager	$67,000
Administrator	54,000
Network engineer	70,600
Junior analyst	34,000

Database	
Manager	$91,000
Architect	96,000
Analyst	67,900

Internet	
Director/strategy	$112,000
Manager	96,500
Application developer	56,000
EC specialist	70,100
EDI specialist	66,000

Security	
Chief security	$111,000
Manager	85,000
Specialist	75,000
IS audit manager	95,000
IS audit staff	53,000

User Support	
Manager	$88,300
Technical trainer	55,000
Help desk operator	45,800
PC technical support	43,000

Operations	
Director	$104,500
Manager	82,000
Systems administrator	61,000
Lead operator	40,500
Computer operator	35,000

MIS Jobs

What MIS jobs are available, and how much will it cost to hire IT employees? A wide variety of jobs are available in MIS. Some of the jobs require a technical education, such as that for programmers. Specialized positions are available in data communications and database management. On the other hand, **systems analysts** require an extensive knowledge of business problems and solutions. Some entry-level operator jobs require only minimal training. On the other end of the scale, analysts may eventually become team leaders or managers. The entire MIS function is coordinated by chief information officers.

As you might expect, salaries depend on experience, individual qualifications, industry, location, and current economic conditions. Six basic MIS job tracks are shown in Figure 13.3: systems development, networks, database, user support, operations, and other specialists. Systems development includes several levels of analysts and programmers. Network management involves installing network hardware and software, diagnosing problems, and designing new networks. Database management focuses on database design

FIGURE 13.4

Internationalization: In the past few years, U.S. and European firms have turned to using programmers in other nations. For example, U.S. programmers are paid about 20 times as much as Indian and Russian programmers. Both India and Russia have extensive educational programs and few jobs for local programmers.

Sources: www.statistics.gov.uk, www.payscale.com, www.cio.com/offshoremap. Differences can be affected by other factors, including benefits, cost of living, productivity, access to equipment, and transportation and communication costs.

Nation	Programmer/Analyst Salary
United States	61,500
Britain	59,600
Russia	11,000
Romania	6,500
China	9,000
India	6,100
India/Bangalore	10,000

Data in U.S. dollars.

FIGURE 13.5

MIS skills in demand: At any given time, some skills are in demand—reflecting demand for applications and a shortage of workers for new technologies. Other skills are also in demand, but workers with the listed skills generally received premium wages and bonuses.

Sources: Ware, "January 2004 IT Staffing Update," *CIO Magazine,* February 3, 2004; "In Demand: IT Starts Require Premium Pay," *Computerworld,* December 10, 2001; *Computerworld,* November 16, 1998; and Arnett and Litecky, *Journal of Systems Management,* February 1994.

Rank	2004	2001	1998	1994
1	Application development	ERP	ERP	Networking
2	Project management	Object engineering	Groupware	Database
3	Database management	Data warehouse and data visualization	Database	UNIX
4	Networking	Groupware	Networking	Visual Basic
5	Security	Wireless	COBOL	COBOL

and administration. End-user support consists of training users, answering questions, and installing software. Operations consists of day-to-day tasks such as loading paper, mounting tapes, and starting long computer tasks. Many of these tasks are being automated. Entry-level operator jobs do not require a college degree, but there is little room for advancement without a degree. Specialist positions exist in larger companies and generally evolve from new technologies. For example, Web masters who would create and manage Web sites were in high demand for two or three years; then as the Internet became more important to companies, all of the workers were trained in Web development, so there was less need for specialists.

Every year, *Computerworld* surveys workers in the industry and publishes average salaries. Job placement firms such as Robert Half also collect data on salaries. The *Wall Street Journal* and several other companies have Web sites that provide salary information for various jobs and locations. This data can be useful if you are searching for a job or thinking about a career in MIS. As a business manager, the numbers will give you an indication of the costs entailed in building and maintaining information systems. Basic averages are listed in Figure 13.3. As indicated by Figure 13.4, costs vary enormously by nation, which is leading some U.S. companies to use programmers from India and Russia.

One way to see the changes occurring in MIS is to look at the types of skills that businesses are looking for in MIS applicants. Figure 13.5 shows some of the top skills demanded in 1994, 1998, 2001, and 2004. Notice the demand for COBOL to fix date problems with old software. Then demand shifted to new technologies (ERP and groupware). In 2004, demand for applications development and management increased, along with a renewed interest in security.

Outsourcing

Do you really need to run all of the MIS operations yourself? In the past 20 years, many businesses have noted that it has become difficult to terminate or lay off employees. In MIS, it has also been expensive for firms to hire the best people. Consequently, many firms have chosen to outsource various aspects of their MIS functions. The basic premise is that specialized firms can offer more efficient service at better prices. For example, EDS runs huge data centers, and it is relatively easy to add more clients with only minor increases in costs. As a huge MIS organization, EDS also hires and trains thousands of workers. Outsourcing also is attractive to firms as a temporary measure. For example, firms might outsource their old accounting systems while designing and installing a new ERP system. The old system will continue to function and be ably supported by an expert company. The internal employees can focus on designing and installing the new system.

Outsourcing can take many forms. Firms might sell their entire computer center to an outsource specialist—and all of the data, software, and employees would move to the new company. Other firms might contract out other MIS functions such as network management, PC repair, training, security, or development. Some functions, particularly programming, can even be outsourced to companies based in other countries. India has several companies, led by Tata, that specialize in writing programs for American and European firms.

Two of the leading service providers are Electronic Data Systems (EDS) and Global Services, the IBM subsidiary. Some other leading outsourcing companies are listed in Figure 13.6.

FIGURE 13.6

Outsourcing revenue: In the latter half of the 1990s, outsourcing with the major providers accelerated as many companies chose to hire outside firms to run various MIS functions. For 2000 and beyond, much of the outsourcing is for ERP systems and Web housing. Data is taken from annual reports and company Web sites.

Company	1991	1995	1997	1999	2000	2003
IBM Global Services	0.4	17.7	24.6	35.0	37.0	42.6
EDS	1.2	12.4	15.2	18.7	19.2	21.6
Accenture	0.5	4.2	6.3	9.5	9.8	11.8
CSC	0.4	4.2	6.6	9.4	10.5	11.3
ADP	0.3	3.0	4.9	6.3	7.0	7.1
Affiliated Computer	0.16	0.4	1.2	2.0	2.1	3.8
Fiserv	0.23	0.7	1.0	1.4	1.7	2.7
Perot Systems	0.16	0.3	0.8	1.2	1.1	1.5
Total (billion dollars)	3.4	42.9	60.6	83.5	88.4	102.4

FIGURE 13.7

Outsourcing evaluation: Outsourcing entails many trade-offs. It means transferring control of a crucial resource to an outside company. If you are really interested in development of strategic applications and leading-edge applications, it is usually better to use an internal development team. If you are dealing with older technology used mostly for transaction processing, it can be cheaper to hire an outside firm to maintain your applications.

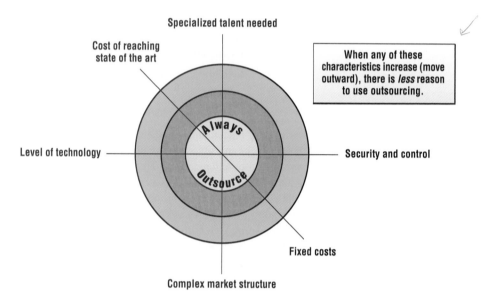

Note the huge growth in outsourcing in the 1990s. This trend was partly due to the desire to cut costs, the inability to hire IT workers, the increasing standardization of IT services, and the need to focus on core business management. In 1998, *Computerworld* reported that an average of 20 percent of IS budgets was spent on outsourcing. Generally, a company signs an agreement to use the services of the outsourcing firm for a fixed number of years. Depending on the agreement, the outsourcing firm can be responsible for anything from machine operation and maintenance, to development of new systems, to telecommunication services.

Outsourcing has primarily been used to decrease operating costs or to get the initial money from the sale of the machines. In particular, the company gains an infusion of cash through the sale of the machines. Some firms have stated that they chose outsourcing because it enabled them to focus on their core business and not worry about maintaining computers and designing systems. Today, outsourcing Web site hosting and development is relatively common. Few firms have the expertise to securely configure the networks and servers required for e-businesses; so they pay outside firms to handle the technical details.

Figure 13.7 illustrates conditions under which it is useful to consider outsourcing. As you move away from the center of the diagram, outsourcing becomes less useful. The most common uses of outsourcing are for straightforward applications of technology, including personal computer installation and servicing, legacy system maintenance, and network management.

On the other hand, situations that are unique or require advanced uses of information technology are best handled internally. For example, complex markets that benefit from strategic applications require the knowledge and experience of employees who work for the company. Likewise, situations that require tight security are easier to control if they remain in-house. Also avoid outsourcing when the outsourcing firm will have to pay the same costs

FIGURE 13.8

Outsourcing forces: Firms are being pushed to cut margins. Many are focusing on their core competencies, leaving little time for wrestling with technology. At the same time, as the large outsourcing firms gain customers, their efficiency improves and they can offer more services and more specialists at better rates.

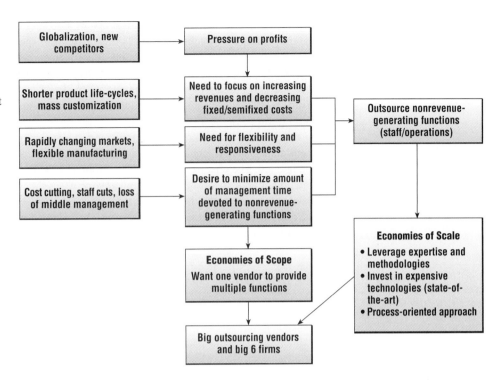

that you face—because they will charge for an additional profit margin, the final cost can be higher. Examples include applications with high fixed costs or those requiring high levels of expensive state-of-the-art equipment or specialized MIS talent.

Competitive pressures are also leading many managers to consider outsourcing their information systems. As technology continues to change, it becomes increasingly difficult for general business managers to keep up with the technology. Each change brings requests for new hardware and software, and the need to reevaluate the use of technology within the firm. Changing technology also requires continual retraining of the information systems staff. At the same time, middle-level management positions are being cut, and managers are asked to take on more tasks. Figure 13.8 shows why, in these circumstances, companies decide to transfer IS management to an expert through outsourcing.

There are drawbacks to outsourcing. First, there might be a slight increase in security risk because the MIS employees have weaker ties to the original company. On the other hand, outsourcing providers are likely to have stricter security provisions than an average firm does. A bigger question is the issue of who is responsible for identifying solutions and new uses of technology for the firm. If MIS workers are employed by an external firm, will it be their job to search for new applications? If not, who will?

In the past couple of years, some firms have begun to reconsider the costs of outsourcing. Although it results in a fixed charge for IS services, the hosting firm has little incentive to strive to reduce its prices. Moreover, it can be difficult to control the decisions of the outsourcing firm. Consequently, some firms have become more selective over which items are outsourced. As reported in *CIO Magazine,* a study by DiamondCluster in late 2002 revealed that 78 percent of IT executives had to terminate outsourcing contracts early.

Before you consider outsourcing, make sure you understand the answer to three critical questions: (1) How will you ensure adequate service? (2) How will you control costs? (3) Will it provide the flexibility you need if your strategies change? Most contracts establish base costs, but additional requests are charged at higher rates. The industry essentially created the concept of a **service level agreement (SLA).** An SLA is a defined performance measure that is specified in the contract. For example, a contract might specify that an outsource vendor must provide a new network port within 24 hours of the initial request. These agreements generally contain penalty clauses in the form of reduced payments. Some internal MIS organizations have mimicked the approach by writing SLAs for basic services.

The main benefit to an SLA is that it provides a defined measure of the organization's capabilities. The drawbacks are that (1) it is difficult to specify all of the detailed SLAs that you might need, and (2) contracts rarely encourage continuous process improvement.

Sometimes outsourcing contracts can backfire on the vendor. EDS won a contract with the U.S. Navy to supply computers and networks. According to *The Wall Street Journal* (April 6, 2004), EDS lost $1.6 billion on the contract and expected to lose about another half billion before it was completed.

Consultants and contract programmers are a simpler version of outsourcing. If you have a one-time task that requires workers you do not have on staff, you can simply hire them for the one job. The cost per hour might seem high, but you only pay for the specific job and you do not have to worry about firing anyone when the job is finished. One of the biggest issues with contractors is to ensure that your organization will be able to use and maintain the tools after the contractor leaves. You might need to arrange for access to the source code or for training sessions.

MIS Organization: Centralization and Decentralization

Who should control IT resources? Two broad trends are slowly creating significant changes in the way we perceive and organize information: (1) declining sizes and prices of technology, and (2) expanding access to the Internet—particularly wireless connections. Internet sites are slowly becoming repositories of information that is accessible any time from almost any location. External data on the economy, news, financial markets, consumers, competitors, and more is readily available on the Internet. Increasingly, you will have to pay for this data, but it is accessible. Advanced companies today are providing similar services in terms of internal organizational data. Data warehouses collect, clean, and present data to internal Web browsers. Ultimately, these databases will be integrated, so managers in a meeting can easily call up current sales data and combine it with economic forecasts on their handheld computers. The goal is to make integrated data available anywhere to authorized users. The question is, How should the MIS system be organized to provide these features?

When hardware was expensive, all data, software, and employees were centralized. As the use of midrange and personal computers expanded, hardware became decentralized and software and data began to follow it. For example, decision makers stored spreadsheets, analyses, and reports on their personal computers. But this decentralized data is more difficult to share, even with networks. At this stage the Internet technologies become important—the search engines and browsers were designed to make it easier to find and view data in many forms. Applying these technologies within the company (called an *intranet*) provides easier access to corporate data.

Almost none of the issues of centralization and decentralization are new—politicians, economists, and organizational theorists have debated them for hundreds of years. The basic argument for **centralization** revolves around the need to coordinate activities and efficiencies that can be gained from large-scale operations. Proponents of **decentralization** argue that moving control to smaller units produces a more flexible system that can respond faster to market changes, encourage individual differences, and innovate. Figure 13.9 summarizes the arguments for centralization and decentralization.

As with many arguments, there are different answers for different circumstances, and it is rare that the extreme choices are best. Wise managers will attempt to gain the advantages of both approaches. With information systems, four basic areas are subject to centralization or decentralization: hardware, software, data, and staffing. Determining the best way to organize information resources requires that managers understand the advantages and disadvantages for each of these areas.

Hardware

Today, hardware is relatively inexpensive. Even centralized servers have come down in cost, often using systems based on server farms consisting of hundreds or thousands of inexpensive computers.

FIGURE 13.9

Summary of benefits of centralization and decentralization: There are advantages to both centralization and decentralization of the MIS resources. The ultimate objective is to design an MIS organization to benefit from as many of the advantages as possible by combining both centralization and decentralization.

	Centralization	**Decentralization**
Hardware	Share data Control purchases Control usage Less duplication Efficient use of resources	Less chance of total breakdown Users gets personalized machines
Software	Compatibility Bulk buying discounts Easier training Ease of maintenance	Different user preferences Easier access Customization
Data	Easy backup Easier to share Less duplication Security control and monitoring	Only transmit data that needs to be shared Keeps user control and politics
Personnel	Similar worker backgrounds Easier training Straightforward career path Specialized staff Easier to see and control costs	Faster response to users More time with users Better understanding and communication Different career path

FIGURE 13.10

Complete centralization: For many years, computers were expensive and there were few communication networks. Consequently, hardware, data, software, and MIS personnel were centrally located. Data was sent to the computer for processing and printed reports were distributed throughout the company. Users only dealt indirectly with MIS.

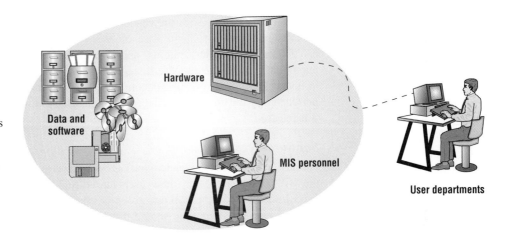

Similarly, on the user side, prices of personal computers have dropped substantially. Even portable devices are relatively inexpensive.

Centralization

The biggest advantage of centralized IS hardware is that it is easier to share hardware, software, and data with multiple users. Complete centralization is shown in Figure 13.10. Consider a simple example. If a company installs an expensive printer in one user's office, it will be difficult for other users to get access to the printer. On the other hand, with only one central computer, all of the hardware, software, and data will be located in one place. All users can be given equal access to these facilities. By keeping all hardware, software, and personnel in one location, it is easier to avoid duplication and keep costs down.

Along the same lines, centralized hardware also makes it easier to control user access to the information system. By storing all data on one machine, it is easy to monitor usage of the data. In a sense, all user access to data must first be approved by the MIS department. Any data alteration or transfer is much easier to control if it takes place on one machine.

Centralized purchasing can also be used to save money. It is easier to standardize equipment if it is all located in one place. It is generally possible to obtain discounts from vendors by buying larger quantities. Centralized purchases also make it easier to keep track of the amount of money spent on information technology. When user departments are responsible for all IT purchases, the lack of centralized control can lead to duplication of hardware.

Decentralization

Decentralization of hardware carries its own advantages. First, there is less chance of a total breakdown. If your computer breaks, everyone else can continue working. You might even be able to borrow someone else's machine.

With decentralization, users can obtain personalized equipment. Perhaps a financial analyst needs an extremely fast machine to process complex equations. Or maybe a marketing representative needs a portable computer to collect data from clients. An advertising specialist could use high-resolution graphics to help design promotions. In each case, the company saves money by buying each user exactly what he or she needs and not forcing everyone to use one standardized product.

Software and Data

Wherever there is hardware, it is also necessary to provide software. Nonetheless, it is possible to centralize some aspects of software, even though there are decentralized computers. The goal is to capture the advantages of both methods at the same time. Data files are similar to software files, but there are some additional features to consider when choosing where to store the data.

Software Centralization

If software applications are standardized and purchased centrally, it is possible to negotiate lower prices from software vendors. Besides, if everyone uses the same basic software, fewer compatibility problems arise and it is easy for users to exchange data with coworkers. Similarly, upgrades, training, and assistance are much simpler if there are a limited number of packages to support. Imagine the time and effort involved if the company needs to upgrade different spreadsheets on 5,000 separate machines. Some companies have reported that by the time they managed to upgrade the entire company, an even newer version was released.

Software Decentralization

Forcing users to choose identical packages can lead to major arguments between users and the MIS department. Many times users have different requirements or perhaps they simply have different preferences. If one group of users prefers the software that is different from the corporate standard, why should everyone in the company be forced to use the same tools? Cost becomes less of an issue as software prices drop. Support might be a problem, but major software packages today are similar. Data incompatibilities often can be resolved with conversion software.

To some extent, users should have the ability to customize their software to match their preferences. Today, most software packages enable users to choose colors, mouse or keyboard responsiveness, and locations to store personal files. If this software is moved to a centralized environment, you have to be careful to preserve this ability. One of the strengths of Windows XP is its ability to store individual user profiles on the server. Then from any machine, the desktop settings and preferences are retrieved from the server.

One complication with enabling users to choose different software is that it can be difficult to determine the configurations of each machine. If a user has a problem, the MIS support person needs to know what software is installed on the machine. When installing new hardware and software, the support team needs to know what software exists on each target machine. Managers also need to track software usage when they purchase upgrades and to verify compliance with software licenses. Several software tools exist to help the MIS department track software usage and report on the configuration of each computer. A small file is installed on each computer that reports on the software, hardware, and configuration of each machine.

Data Centralization

The most important feature of centralized data is the ability to share it with other users. Large central servers were designed from the ground up to share data. They were designed

REALITY BYTES
100 Days to the Flood

The FTC Do Not Call Registry is extraordinarily popular with citizens. The threat of $11,000 fines per call has reduced or eliminated those annoying dinnertime calls from telemarketers. Within 72 hours of its launch, more than 10 million phone numbers had been entered. By the end of the first week, there were 18 million. Today, more than half the adult population of America has signed onto the list with 58.8 million numbers. Developing the system to be foolproof and handle the huge load was a challenge. The system supports registration from the donotcall.gov Web site, from an automated phone system, and from operators. It also exchanges data with lists from 25 states. Moreover, the system accepts complaints from people who receive illegal calls, sorts them, and routes them to the appropriate state or federal prosecutor. It also has several subsystems to provide the data to more than 13,000 telemarketers to clean their lists. Telemarketers pay an annual fee to the U.S. Treasury to get the list. They can get the entire list, specific area codes, or mom-and-pop operations can log onto a Web site and test up to 10 numbers at a time.

This system has performed flawlessly. The main registration portion was built in less than 100 days. The project was headed by Stephen Warren, CIO of the FTC, and Lois Greisman, associate director of the Division of Planning and Information in the Bureau of Consumer Protection. Lacking the resources to complete the job on time, the team hired AT&T to handle the primary development, headed by Marjorie Windelberg. Marjorie estimates that she talked to or met more than 500 people during the project's implementation. An interesting twist to the project is that part of AT&T's payment was based on the number of people who successfully registered. To get the project done on time, rapid application development and extreme programming were used for many of the parts. Furthermore, the system was built as an N-tier application, where each subsystem is relatively independent and can be scaled up by adding more processors. Code can be rewritten and improved in a subsystem without affecting the other systems. Getting everyone involved in the design at the start was a key element to its success. Greisman notes that "for the first time, IT people sat down with policy and legal folks in the planning stage." Congress authorized about $18 million for the project, with about $3.5 million in payments to the contractor (AT&T) in 2003 and $2.5 million to cover FTC internal IT costs to upgrade the infrastructure.

Source: Adapted from Alice Dragoon, "How the FTC Rescued the Dinner Hour," *CIO*, June 1, 2004.

to solve the problems of allowing concurrent access and to protect the integrity of the data. Similarly, they have security facilities that enable owners of the data to specify which users can and cannot have access to the data. Centralized systems also monitor access and usage of the data to prevent problems.

Another important feature of centralized data is the ease of making backups. When all databases are stored on one machine, a single operator can be hired to maintain daily backups. If data files are lost, it is easy to restore them from the backups. With the data on one machine, it is easy to ensure that all files are regularly backed up. Contrast this situation with distributed personal computers, where users are generally responsible for making their own backup copies. How often do you personally make backups? Every night?

Data Decentralization

The strongest advantage to decentralizing data is that it gives ownership of the data to the group that creates and maintains it. Users also have complete control of the data and can prevent anyone else from even knowing that it exists. For data that does not need to be shared, this control presents no problems. However, scattered control of data can interfere with other users when many people need access to the data. An example of complete decentralization—including data, hardware, and personnel—is displayed in Figure 13.11.

Data replication is sometimes used to provide the advantages of decentralized data—and still provide companywide access. With replication, the database is copied to multiple servers throughout the company. Users work on their local copies, which provide fast access to the data. The changes are copied to the other servers at regular intervals, so everyone has access to the latest data. This technique is often used with groupware products to distribute spreadsheets and word-processed documents.

Personnel

When most users think about decentralization, they often forget about the information systems personnel. Traditionally, the MIS roles have been performed by centralized MIS staffs. However, the increased decentralization of hardware increases pressures to decentralize the personnel by having them report directly to user departments.

REALITY BYTES   Offshore IT Jobs

Bangalore, India, a city of 5.5 million people, is a hot spot for information technology. India's educational emphasis on mathematics and English, coupled with intense training of programmer specialists, and two decades of experience have created an opportunity for programmers. Companies in developed nations are looking for less expensive workers. Communication technology makes it possible for these workers to be located anywhere. By 2003, Coca-Cola was outsourcing 15 percent of its IT workforce and had a goal of hitting 70 percent. Some people are concerned about the trend—worried that American developers will lose jobs and be unable to compete with low-priced workers overseas. So far, the recession and downturn in corporate spending have cost considerably more jobs than offshoring. At the same time, with fewer students in U.S. computer science and MIS programs, the supply will ultimately decline. Companies might eventually have little choice but to hire programmers from other countries. Leading nations for programming include India, Israel, and Ireland. China, Russia, and Romania are also gaining ground, but English is a greater problem.

Source: Adapted from Scott Leith, "Jobs Take Trip Abroad," *The Atlanta Journal-Constitution,* April 5, 2003; and www.cio.com/offshoremap.

FIGURE 13.11

Complete decentralization: Each department maintains its own hardware, software, and data. Corporate standards and the network enable workers to utilize data across the company. MIS personnel are members of the user departments and support tasks within that department.

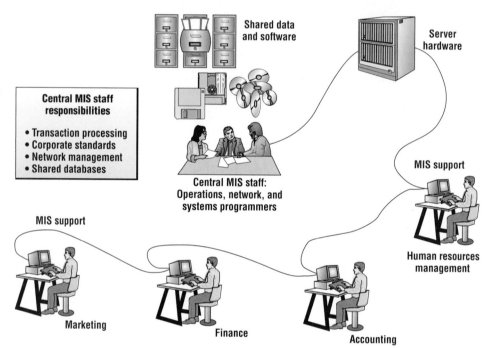

Centralization

Most of the advantages of a centralized MIS staff accrue to the MIS workers. For example, MIS workers often feel more comfortable with other MIS specialists. Centralization creates a group of homogeneous workers who share the same education and experiences. Moving MIS workers to user departments places them in a minority position.

One implication of this situation is seen by looking at the career path of an MIS worker. In a centralized environment, workers are typically hired as programmers. They eventually become systems analysts. Some move on to become team or project leaders, and a few can look forward to becoming managers of IS departments and perhaps a CIO someday. If programmers are moved to user departments (say, human resources), what career path do they have? Maybe they could become team leader or manager of the HRM department, but they would be competing with HRM specialists for those positions.

Centralization also makes it easier for the company to provide additional training to MIS staffers. Because hardware and software changes occur constantly, MIS employees need to continually learn new tools and techniques. If they are all located in a central facility, it is easy to set up training classes and informal meetings to discuss new technologies.

Problem: You get dozens or hundreds of messages a day.

Tools: Microsoft Outlook and other e-mail client packages have features to help you deal with the flood of e-mail. Even if you remove the junk e-mail, many business managers receive dozens of messages a day. Groupware tools and automated project management systems add to the list. Some are important; others are minor but still worth saving. But even if you save the messages, you need a way to organize and search them so that you can respond to the most important ones first and then search the others later.

The first step in organizing e-mail is to create additional folders. You can right-click the inbox folder and add new folders or a hierarchy of folders. The challenge is to create a list that makes it easy to find the messages you receive. You can manually move messages into the relevant folders. However, Outlook enables you to create powerful rules to automatically evaluate and handle your messages. It effectively allows you to build an expert system agent that deals with many of your messages automatically. The simplest type of rule is one that automatically moves messages from a specified sender into a designated folder. For example, messages from the CEO could be moved into a critical folder. As you receive new messages, you can deal with the most important folders first.

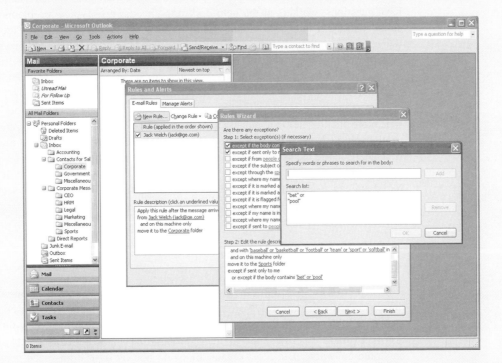

You can create sophisticated rules. The Tools/Rules and Alerts option has a wizard to help you, or you can create a rule from scratch. Rules have three basic components: (1) conditions that are evaluated for each message, (2) an action to take, and (3) exception conditions to exclude certain messages. You have a couple dozen types of conditions or exceptions, such as choosing people or matching words in the subject or body. You can select from a couple dozen actions, including moving the message to a folder, deleting it, forwarding it, or even running a custom script or opening an application on your desktop. This last option might be used to open a sales application and generate a new order when a specific message is received from a customer. Since you can control the order in which rules are applied to each message, you can create a decision tree of multiple rules.

Quick Quiz:

1. How is the e-mail system similar to an expert system? How is it different?

2. What is likely to be the most difficult part of creating a system for handling your messages?

Centralization also gives the firm the ability to hire MIS specialists. If there are 50 positions available, two or three can be set aside for workers specializing in areas such as database administration or local area networks. If all workers are distributed to user areas, the individual departments will be less willing to pay for specialists.

Finally, when the entire MIS staff is centralized, it is easier to see how much MIS is costing the firm. If the MIS functions are dispersed to user departments, they may be performed on a part-time basis by various employees. It is difficult to control the costs and evaluate alternatives when you do not know how much is being spent.

Decentralization

The primary advantage to decentralized MIS staffing is that the support is closer to the users. As a result, they receive faster responses to questions and problems. More important, as the MIS staffers spend more time with the users, they gain a better understanding of the problems facing the users' department. Communication improves and problems are easier to identify and correct. These are powerful advantages to the individual departments and have the potential to create much better development and use of information systems.

The Help Desk

One issue with decentralized MIS support is that it can be expensive to place MIS personnel in each department. Many companies compromise by creating a help desk that is staffed by MIS employees who specialize in helping business managers. When business managers have questions, workers at the help desk provide answers. Typical problems involve personal computers, networks, and access to corporate databases. One advantage for business managers is that they do not have to search for answers—they simply call one number. This system can also cut costs and ensure consistent support. The knowledge of the support workers is easily shared throughout the company. It is also easier to train and evaluate the workers.

To provide more decentralized support, some companies are using their networks to provide more detailed help to business departments. They set up a special program in the background on each personal computer. When someone calls for help, the microcomputer specialist can see the user's screen and take control of the user's machine. This method simplifies communication between the user and the specialist, making it easier to solve problems and make changes immediately. Of course, it also raises several security issues, because the help desk personnel could monitor any machine at any time.

Recentralization with Intranets

How can Internet technologies be used internally to centralize data but still support decentralized user access? No organization is completely centralized or completely decentralized. The true challenge is to create a system that matches the needs of the organization. Networks are a critical part of the solution. With reliable high-speed networks, data can be stored anywhere. But most organizations do not yet have high-speed networks everywhere. In particular, connections to offices in other cities or nations can be expensive and relatively slow. Consequently, bandwidth is a crucial factor in deciding centralization issues. Web-based intranets provide a solution to many of these problems.

Networks

Web technologies are particularly good at handling low-bandwidth connections to users. Web browsers are relatively efficient at displaying data. Many business pages contain only basic data and graphs, which can be easily and quickly sent to managers. Streaming media technologies can be used to send more complex data, such as speeches, to many users at the same time—even when the managers are connected through dial-up lines.

The capabilities of the Internet browser have led firms to consider a new approach to organizing the MIS resources. The **thin-client** approach, illustrated in Figure 13.12, uses a relatively simple computer to run a Web browser that is responsible for displaying data and getting input from the user. This approach recentralizes many of the MIS functions. All of the data and most of the applications reside on centralized servers. The use of Web standards simplifies many decisions. Users can choose almost any type of client hardware, including laptops, tablets, and PDAs. As long as the system runs a browser, it can access the corporate data. Of course, some client computers will have more capabilities than others.

The browser client is becoming a user interface device, with responsibility for displaying data and translating input to a standard form. This approach simplifies the development of applications and provides more flexibility to users and organizations. For example, some

FIGURE 13.12

Thin client: The thin client device is only responsible for displaying data and translating user input. The data and the application software reside on the central servers.

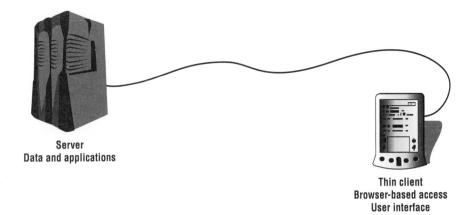

**Server
Data and applications**

**Thin client
Browser-based access
User interface**

FIGURE 13.13

Intranet networks: Server locations are connected by high-bandwidth networks to replicate data. Individual users obtain data using standard Internet connections.

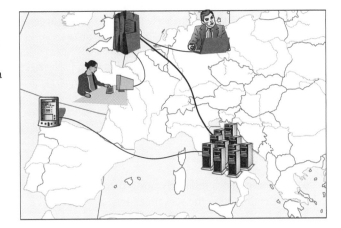

users or entire organizations might stick with standard desktops for years to save money. Others might move to wireless-based PDAs or Web-enabled cell phones that rely on voice input instead of keyboards. The key point is that the choice of the user device should no longer matter to the application developer. Regardless of the user device, the back-end data-bases are the same, the Web servers are the same, and the applications are the same. Note that currently, it does take a middle-ware component to strip down Web sites so that they are small enough for today's cell phones, but that limitation is likely to change in the near future. The simplicity of this approach is that it recentralizes the primary items that gain from centralization: the main business applications and the shared data. Users are free to use whatever devices they prefer and to load additional software on their computers. A key benefit of the thin-client approach is that the clients can be built from relatively simple hardware and software, reducing the cost and improving the reliability of the clients. With fewer problems, user support becomes easier and cheaper.

Keep in mind that some tasks can still be too hard to perform using pure Web-based solutions. For instance, standard personal productivity tools like word processors need to be running on the individual client computers. Several years ago, Corel built a suite of Internet-based personal productivity applications but stopped work on them because they ran too slowly. As technologies change, it might eventually be possible to run even these highly interactive applications over the Internet.

Similarly, large data transfers require high-speed connections. For example, bulk data transfers from one division to another will suffer if sent over dial-up lines. Since high-bandwidth Internet connections are expensive, companies will cluster their servers in a few key locations. As shown in Figure 13.13, these server locations will be connected with high-speed lines, and everyone else will use lower-priced basic services to connect over the Internet.

The network personnel still have to decide where to locate the servers and which data should be stored on each server. Many systems use data **replication,** where each server location holds the same data. Data changes are exchanged on a regular basis, often overnight,

REALITY BYTES   Offshore Development Challenges

ValiCert is a company that develops security software, mostly for banks, insurance companies, and the government. It is headquartered in Silicon Valley. In 2001, its sales slowed and it began laying off developers, instead, hiring $7,000-a-year replacements in India. Senior Vice President David Jevans says that the company had optimistic expectations, planning to "cut the budget by half here and hire twice as many people there." Using the time difference, developers could swap code overnight and "put more people on it and get it done sooner."

The result was far less valuable. The Indian engineers left out features that Americans considered intuitive and demanded detailed descriptions. U.S. programmers ended up spending months writing detailed instructions, delaying projects. Communication between the groups was limited. ValiCert contracted quality testing and some update functions to Infosys in India, but management remained in Silicon Valley. ValiCert frequently changed the tasks, and Infosys shuffled employees—making it difficult to create a single team. Within months, ValiCert formed its own Indian subsidiary with 60 employees and hired an engineer to manage the office in Banga-

lore. ValiCert was paying the Indian programmers about $10,000 a year. With benefits, operating expenses, and communication costs, it averaged to about $30,000 a year—substantially less than the $200,000 cost of Silicon Valley employees. Because of the communication issues, the Indian engineers grew frustrated. Suresh Marur, head of one programming team, worked on five projects in 2002. All of them were canceled or delayed. In 2002, a key project was returned to U.S. development. Yet because of the cost savings, ValiCert continued to refine the development process. In 2003, ValiCert merged with Tumbleweed, which also had offshore operations in Bulgaria.

Today, core development and architecture remain in California. Substantial development teams in Bulgaria and India do much of the development work, but management is coordinated across all three nations. Ultimately, Tumbleweed has survived, partly by reducing its engineering costs by 60 percent.

Source: Adapted from Scott Thurm, "Not Every Job Translates Overseas," *The Wall Street Journal*, March 3, 2004.

so each server has a relatively up-to-date copy of the data. The MIS department is responsible for maintaining the servers and the networks.

Hardware

Companies have several choices for the central server hardware. But the software environment is more important than the specific hardware. The servers need to run software that generates the Web data while interacting with the database management system. Several companies offer competing technologies for these services that run on diverse hardware platforms. The main issues are (1) cost, (2) scalability of the servers so that the system can be expanded without interfering with existing operations, and (3) reliability, maintainability, and backups to ensure the systems can remain operational at all times.

Data

Because of the challenges of running and securing servers, most companies lean toward centralizing the data. Certainly the basic financial data is consolidated in a data warehouse. This approach works well for managers retrieving data for analysis. The main problems arise in terms of creating or modifying the data. The workers who create and analyze the data to produce more useful information need more sophisticated tools. They also need greater access to the data, compared with users who simply view the data.

Giving users, even managers, the ability to create new data scares most MIS people. The security challenges are much greater when users need to add and change data. It is more difficult to control access and ensure that only authorized people can make the changes. Plus, if something goes wrong, the IS employee is the one who will be blamed. In the old days of simple transaction data, it was relatively straightforward to set up controls and procedures for the daily operations. And it was reasonably simple to keep transaction logs of all the changes so errors could be corrected. But in today's environment, teams of workers perform the analyses and information creation, so team members need access to work in progress. For instance, the financial budgeting team uses the marketing and production forecasts to generate estimates of future cash flows.

From the standpoint of data creation, the intranet approach requires two steps beyond traditional systems: (1) managers need tools that will create the final data and reports in a

REALITY BYTES   To Do It Right, Sometimes You Have to Do It Yourself

Since the late 1980s, outsourcing IT functions has been relatively popular—at least it receives a large amount of discussion. Companies hire external firms to run everything from PC maintenance, software development, servers, to even running all operations. A 2002 study by DiamondCluster International has found that 78 percent of executives who outsourced an IT function had to terminate the agreement early. The main reasons were poor service, a change in strategic direction, and costs. Professor Rudolf Hirschheim at the University of Houston notes that "many companies are finding that outsourcing simply doesn't provide the cost savings they had hoped for. Or they find themselves burdened by the contract, which doesn't allow them the flexibility they need."

Source: Adapted from "Bringing I.T. Back Home," *CIO Magazine,* March 1, 2003.

format suitable for the intranet browsers, and (2) managers need an easy method to securely transfer information to the intranet servers.

Better data creation tools have been created in the past few years, but in many cases they are still hard to use and can require specialized training. Likewise, several systems have been created to simplify transferring data to intranet servers. Some are relatively easy to use. As always, the challenge lies in providing security so that the transfer process is easy for authorized managers but impossible (or exceedingly difficult) for unauthorized users. Both of these conditions require that managers have more powerful tools and often higher-speed data connections. Managers will also need more support and technical assistance. Hence, portions of the MIS organization must be decentralized to handle these issues.

Conflict Management

Why is the MIS department involved in so many conflicts? How do you solve them? The answer to the first question should be relatively easy if you reread the sections on centralization and decentralization. Trying to resolve the issues is considerably more difficult because each organization is different. An answer that is often popular is to fire the CIO. But that rarely solves the underlying problems.

Centralization and decentralization are often causes of conflicts. Managers want the flexibility to respond to the changing environment. They often are willing to implement technology that helps them directly. But they rarely want to pay for the technology, and they generally dislike having to pay for infrastructure technology. The CIO and the MIS department provide and support IT, but they are usually squeezed by costs. Software and employee costs increase. Although hardware costs are declining, it simply means that organizations buy more hardware, and installing more hardware means more work. Leading edge MIS departments automate as many of the tasks as possible, from software installation to support to network monitoring. One way MIS departments try to reduce costs is to standardize as much of the technology as possible. The company purchases one machine and configures it the same for all users. Users are forbidden from customizing or adding any software or hardware. While this approach makes life easier for MIS, it does restrict the technology and applications available to the company. What is the goal of the company: To make life easier for MIS or to use technology to improve the business? At what cost? The issues are further complicated because no one really knows if the MIS department is efficient or wasting money. Hence, firms have an incentive to look at outsourcing—to provide a market price comparison.

The conflicts get even worse as MIS becomes more focused on security. Many restrictions have been imposed in the name of security. Yes, security is important, but remember that security requires a trade-off. For example, it is possible to "protect" a document so that it is 100 percent secure: all you have to do is completely destroy the document (and any copies). This action guarantees that no one can steal or read the document. But it also ensures that you cannot use the document. Be definition, security creates this trade-off, which pretty much guarantees there will be conflicts between the central security managers and the rest of the organization.

The answer to resolving these conflicts is to understand that they will arise and to build a mechanism to resolve the disputes. You could escalate all disputes to the level of the CIO or the board of directors, but that would waste an incredible amount of time. It is far better to establish a neutral committee to evaluate MIS progress and arbitrate conflicts. Just make sure the committee is chaired by a business leader and not an MIS manager.

Summary

Managing an MIS organization is difficult. Even as a business manager, working with MIS and choosing the proper role for technology can be challenging. Ideally, the goals of the MIS department should be aligned with the overall business goals. But with issues of centralization, cost control, and security staring you in the face, conflicts can easily arise. One of the more difficult problems facing MIS departments and company executives is the conflict between centralization and decentralization. These issues were involved in many decisions during the last 5 to 10 years, from politics to corporate organizations, to the way in which MIS fits into the organization. Although there is no single answer that applies to all situations, there has been a distinct trend during the last few years toward decentralization. In larger organizations, this propensity has been hampered by the highly centralized organizations and computer systems that have been in place for the last 30 years.

A Manager's View

It is difficult to manage and evaluate an MIS organization. With multiple roles and many different types of employees, IT departments can be expensive. You can try to use outsourcing and contractors to reduce costs. Ultimately, you have to decide on the strategic role of MIS. Is cost reduction your primary goal, or are you going to use technology to improve the business and gain a competitive advantage? Centralization and decentralization are key issues in managing information systems. Many conflicts arise when the IS departments are not aligned with the business practices. New Web-based technologies offer new methods of maintaining the cost advantages of centralization while still providing decentralized user access and control.

Decentralization of MIS can occur in any of four areas: hardware, software, data, and MIS personnel. Economics is driving the decentralization of hardware, because of tremendous price performance values in personal computers. The challenge is to accommodate this decentralization without losing the benefits of centralization. One option would be a completely decentralized information system, where each user and department is responsible for its own information. Today, the Internet standards provide new technologies to gain the benefits of both centralization and decentralization. Applications running on Web servers can retrieve centralized data to be displayed and modified using thin-client browsers. The goal is to gain the economies of scale and improved control and ease of sharing offered by centralized servers, yet provide users with the individual tools needed to perform their jobs. The simpler client hardware and software platforms offer the promise of less user support.

Managing servers and networks, as well as building applications, can be difficult tasks for many companies. It is hard to find and reward good IS workers, and continually solving technical problems takes time away from the daily business tasks. So, many organizations have chosen to outsource various IS functions—from development to maintenance to development and operation of the servers. Outsourcing provides a short-term increase in cash for the company, access to computer specialists, and the ability to concentrate on the company's primary business. However, firms requiring specialized talent, high security and control, high levels of recent technology, new state-of-the-art information technology, or complex market structures should avoid outsourcing and retain in-house management of the information function.

Key Words

advocacy role, *501*
centralization, *506*
data administrator, *500*
data integrity, *501*
database administrator, *499*

decentralization, *506*
outsourcing, *503*
replication, *513*
service level agreement (SLA), *505*

standards, *498*
systems analysts, *502*
thin client, *512*
total cost of ownership (TCO), *496*

Web Site References

Job Boards

Careerbuilder	**www.careerbuilder.com**
Computerworld	**www.computerworld.com/careertopics/careers**
Dice	**www.dice.com**
Information Week	**www.informationweek.com/career3**
Jobs.com	**www.jobs.com**
Kforce.com	**www.kforce.com**
Monster	**www.monster.com**
Riley Guide	**www.rileyguide.com**
Studentjobs.gov	**www.studentjobs.gov**
U.S. Government	**www.usajobs.opm.gov**
Wall Street Journal	**careers.wsj.com**

Additional Readings

Arnett, Kirk P., and C. R. Litecky. "Career Path Development for the Most Wanted Skills in the MIS Job Market." *Journal of Systems Management,* February 1994, pp. 6–10. [Job skills.]

Arnold, David, and Fred Niederman. "The Global IT Workforce." *Communications of the ACM,* July 2001, vol. 44, no. 7. [A special section on global issues in IT management.]

"Bringing I.T. Back Home." *CIO Magazine,* March 1, 2003. [Failure rate of 78 percent on outsourcing projects.]

Fryer, Bronwyn. "Difficult at Best." *Computerworld,* January 4, 1999, p. 38. [High demand for staff with ERP skills.]

"Managing Unruly Desktop Computers Costs Businesses Dearly." *The Wall Street Journal,* February 16, 1995, p. A1. [Maintenance costs of personal computers.]

McWilliams, Gary. "After Landing Huge Navy Pact, EDS Finds It's In over Its Head." *The Wall Street Journal,* April 6, 2004. [EDS loses $1.6 billion in trying to build a network for the Navy.]

York, Thomas. "Shift in IT Roles Ahead: Changes in Business and Technology Will Alter IT Careers." *Infoworld,* January 18, 1999, p. 75. [Predicting the future of IT jobs is hard, but useful.]

Review Questions

1. What are the basic roles of the MIS department?
2. What types of MIS jobs are available?
3. What are the potential advantages of outsourcing computer facilities? What are the drawbacks?
4. What are the advantages of centralizing computer hardware, software, and data? What are the advantages of decentralization?
5. How does the Internet/Web affect centralization and decentralization of information technology within a company?
6. Why do conflicts arise with MIS and how can you resolve them?

Exercises

1. Using salary surveys and local advertisements, find typical salaries for various MIS jobs in your area.

2. Make a list of symptoms you would expect to see in a company that has centralized databases and MIS personnel, but has just decentralized its departments and users have just bought hundreds of new personal computers in the last three years.

3. Make a list of symptoms you expect to see in a company that is "too decentralized." That is, company users are free to choose any hardware and software, and databases are maintained by each department. Data is shared through reports that are printed in each department and forwarded to other departments on paper. There is no central MIS staff and no CIO. Treat it as a company that started small using personal computers and grew but did not come up with a centralized information system approach.

4. Find at least two technologies that are being used to move data to centralized servers.

5. Find data on the number of computer science and MIS majors at your school for the past few years and identify any trends. How might these trends affect the job market?

6. Identify at least two tools that can be used to configure and manage personal computers from a central location.

7. Using the various salary surveys, compare salaries for small versus large businesses in your area. Briefly explain the differences. If possible, talk with employees at small and large businesses to see how the jobs might differ.

Technology Toolbox

8. Assuming that you work as a manager, create a set of mailbox folders to handle your expected mail. Create the rules that will move incoming mail to the appropriate folder.

9. Assuming that you are in charge of a sales division for a large company, create an e-mail rule to handle messages from customers. You have a couple of key clients that you have known for years, and they have a pattern of sending messages. For example, they send personal messages a few times a year, they send questions about price changes monthly, and once in a while they send complaints about late deliveries or quality concerns. Sometimes they send a new order directly to you, which you have to forward to the sales staff.

10. Create a project management analysis for starting a new company. Identify the major tasks and their dependencies. If possible, create the project in Microsoft Project (you can get a free demonstration copy). If it is not available, at least draw a Gantt chart by hand.

11. Create the Gantt chart for the development exercise using Microsoft Project. Assign resources at 100 percent as indicated and use resource leveling to determine the time it will take to complete the project.

Name	Duration	Depends on	Resources
1 Feasibility statement	5 days		
2 Get hardware list and costs	1 day		Analyst
3 Count forms and reports	1 day		Analyst
4 Estimate development time	1 day		Analyst
5 Get benefits from user	1 day		Analyst
6 Create statement	1 day	2, 3, 4, 5	Analyst
7 Management approval	1 day	1	
8 Analysis	17 days	7	
9 Interview users	7 days		Analyst
10 Evaluate competition	3 days		Analyst
11 Search for existing software	3 days		Analyst
12 Evaluate options	4 days	9, 10, 11	Analyst
13 Management approval	1 day	8	
14 Design	15 days	13	
15 Design and create database	2 days		Analyst
16 Build forms	8 days	15	Programmer

17 Create reports	4 days	15	Programmer
18 Design application	3 days		Programmer
19 User approval	1 day	14	
20 Management approval	1 day	19	
21 Implementation	10 days	20	
22 Purchase hardware	2 days		Analyst
23 Transfer data	3 days	22	Programmer
24 Integration test	4 days	23	Programmer
25 Train users	1 day		Trainer
26 Write procedures	1 day		Analyst
27 Transfer operations	1 day	24	Analyst, programmer
28 Review	1 day		Analyst, programmer

12. Using the data in the previous exercise, explore ways to complete the project earlier. Note that you can consider hiring more people, but there is a limit—adding more people to the project means you have to add more managers and increase some of the development times to compensate for the additional overhead.

Teamwork

13. Interview computer users and managers in a local firm (or your university) and determine the degree of decentralization in their information system organization. Talk to several users and see whether their perceptions agree. Are they receiving all of the advantages of centralization and decentralization? If not, how could the system be modified to gain these benefits without significantly increasing the drawbacks? Be sure to analyze hardware, software, data, and personnel.

14. Have each person select one country and find the average cost for programmers. Identify technology and telecommunication capabilities available. Identify social and cultural factors (such as education) that could affect programming abilities. Combine the data from each person and identify a nation in which you would want to establish an offshore outsourcing facility.

15. Assume that your organization wants to reduce costs of managing personal computers. Each person should identify one tool that can be used to improve centralized management control over the personal computers. Compare the costs and the potential benefits. Combine the recommendations for the products and select the most effective tools.

16. Have each person research one company and find examples of centralization versus decentralization conflicts or solutions. Combine the results and summarize them.

17. Assume that your team is managing a small company that needs a highly customized application to perform complex decision analysis. You have an initial guess that it will take a top-notch programmer at least six months to create the software. Assign team members to investigate the various methods of developing the software. Compare the costs and benefits and choose a method. Be sure to specify how the system will be maintained or modified later.

18. Write a plan for moving a midsize service company to an intranet and mobile-commerce-based information system, where as many applications as possible will run through browsers and data will be accessible from anywhere in the company. What technologies will you use? What functions will you centralize or decentralize? How will you provide adequate security?

Rolling Thunder Database

19. Describe the organization of the existing information system. What changes would enable the system to run better? If the company doubles in size in three years, what organizational changes do you recommend for the information system?

20. How should the company handle typical information system tasks such as backing up data, creating employee accounts, maintaining hardware, selecting new hardware and software, and so on?

21. Would you recommend a centralized or decentralized approach to information systems at the Rolling Thunder bicycle company? Who is currently in charge of the major components? What problems can we anticipate if we continue with the existing structure?

22. Assume users are complaining about lack of support from the MIS department. How can you improve MIS responsiveness? How can you do it without substantially raising costs?

Cases: The Energy Industry

The Industry

How do you control a huge organization geographically dispersed around the world? How do you choose and implement information technology to help workers perform tasks from simple communicating to advanced nonlinear analysis of seismic data? Then what happens when you merge two of these huge companies? Check the petroleum industry for different answers to these questions. The BP/Amoco, Exxon/Mobil, Chevron/Texaco, and Conoco/Phillips mergers of the late 1990s and early 2000s represented giant combinations. The mergers resulted in lower administrative costs. But they also made it more important to combine data and standardize processes across the new organizations.

The industry is also facing an eventual shortage of expertise, as the few industry experts retire. Many of the firms are turning to technology to leverage the knowledge of these workers. Communication technologies and high-resolution digital cameras make it possible for experts to diagnose problems remotely, reducing travel time. A few companies are experimenting with expert systems and knowledge management to store the accumulated knowledge of the experts.

Exploration

The energy sector contains a variety of companies and some interesting interrelationships and partnerships. The upstream process of oil exploration is notoriously variable. The exploration companies perform enormous data collection and analysis operations around the world. When oil prices are high, their services are in high demand. To spread the risk, most of the exploration companies are independent and provide services to all of the major petroleum companies. But that means rivals end up sharing data on some projects. Analytical tools that have been refined and improved over the years can provide a competitive advantage to a large company, so they are cautious about sharing techniques.

The exploration companies—such as Amerada Hess, Anadarko, and Schlumberger—work around the world. They invest billions of dollars in both mechanical and information technology. According to the Energy Department, the total cost of finding and producing a barrel of oil dropped from $15 in 1977 to $5 in 2001—primarily due to improved technology (Ricadela 2002). Randall Nottingham, an analyst at Strategy Analytics, says that the oil industry spends $9 billion a year on IT, not counting the oil field technology and robotics (Ricadela 2002).

The oil exploration side of the business generates petabyes of data. All major oil fields and potential fields around the globe have been examined with seismic sensors. Producing fields generate even more data collection. Amerada Hess has 100 terabytes of data in its Houston center alone. All of it is refined and analyzed through complex geological models. These models are proprietary to the various research firms. They require huge amounts of computational power. Mike Heagney, Sun's global energy manager, says that "oil companies are probably second to NASA in data volumes. The systems still aren't fast enough; they consume pretty much anything we put out" (Ricadela 2002).

To process that much data, Sun sells 106-unit server farms. IBM sells its monster symmetric processor systems as well as giant Linux cluster grids. John Sherman, executive vice president of marketing and systems for Landmark (a division of Halliburton), observes that "what we're trying to do in essence is look down in the earth. These [systems] are MRIs on supersteroids" (Weil 2002). Amerada Hess also runs a 200-node Dell cluster to run the huge analytical jobs. The PC-based systems cost about 10 percent of the price of the large IBM systems. A few companies perform the analysis as outsourcers—but the analytical tools are shared across the industry, reducing the competitive value.

Refineries

Refineries are some of the most complex chemical and mechanical systems in existence. Much of the systems are monitored and controlled through remote sensors coupled to computer systems. But the systems still need to be monitored by humans. It is critical to catch and repair a component before it fails. If something small fails, it can easily wipe out other components down the line.

Houston-based SAT corporation created a portable electronic system that managers can use to diagnose problems. Each component is given an RFID tag. Workers carry handheld computers that read the tag and provide device-specific data to check. For example, workers might be told to check the temperature, pressure, and vibration on a pump. The

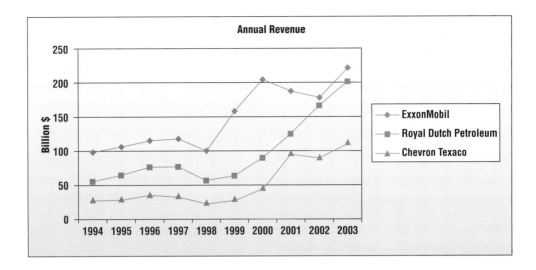

handheld expert system then provides instructions on what to do if problems exist. Bill Johnson, reliability manager at Lyondell-Citgo Refining LP, notes that "this thing will prompt some action. It allows us to identify problems earlier and do better troubleshooting when we identify those problems" (Thibodeau 2004). The data is eventually uploaded to the main computers to check for trends over time.

Because oil is so important to the current U.S. economy, the government and the firms are concerned about security from terrorists. Along with enhanced physical security measures, the companies are trying to create some type of network to help them share data and identify trends and threats. Protecting the IT infrastructure used to find and produce oil is also important. The main oil and gas companies have created the Energy Information Sharing and Analysis Center (ISAC). Users or outsiders can post warnings on the system. These warnings are analyzed and then threat notices are sent to the member companies.

The process is not that simple for the oil companies themselves. Mark Evans, CIO at Tesoro Petroleum Inc., notes that it is hard to retrieve information from the Supervisory Control and Data Acquisition (SCDA) systems that run the operations at most companies. "For a long time, we've been unable to share that information within our own company. That's really the first step" (Meehan 2002). Ultimately, the companies want to share security tips and best-practices information as well as notices of immediate threats.

Additional Reading

Meehan, Michael. "Energy Firms Move to Thwart Cyberattacks." *Computerworld,* February 25, 2002.

Ricadela, Aaron. "Pay Dirt." *Information Week,* March 18, 2002.

Thibodeau, Patrick. "SAT Corp.'s Handhelds Help Refineries Quickly Spot Problems." *Computerworld,* June 7, 2004.

Weil, Nancy. "IBM, Landmark Deal Takes Linux to Oil Industry." *Computerworld,* May 24, 2002.

Case: ExxonMobil

ExxonMobil (ticker: XOM) is the largest of the newly combined oil companies. With over $240 billion in revenue and 88,000 employees, it is the second largest company in the United States. The company is involved in all aspects of oil production and marketing, from exploration to refining, chemicals, and distribution and marketing. The company has several proprietary software tools to help find and analyze deposits, including its Stellar basin-modeling software (www.exxonmobil.com).

The oil glut of the late 1990s and early 2000s drove crude oil prices down to $10 a barrel, a number that quickly became nostalgic after the $40 and $50 a barrel prices in 2004 during the Iraq war. The unusual aspect to the price surge is that the oil companies have not dramatically expanded their exploration and production. In the past, companies would instantly respond to price signals, and the eventual increase in produc-

tion would lead to a drop in prices. In 2003, Exxon's spending on exploration and production rose by 15 percent, but was flat through 2004 (Warren 2004). One of the big questions is whether oil prices will remain high. The firms must forecast the price of oil for the near future.

Merger

Exxon's takeover of Mobil was a major milestone both for the industry and for the IT department. SAP was chosen as the main financial IT platform. Both companies had been running SAP software, but they were separate global systems and required changes so that the final system was using a single set of accounts and definitions. Plus, Mobil had only begun its conversion to SAP a few months before the takeover. Since the takeover occurred shortly before 2000, both IT departments were also busy working on Y2K updates (King 1998).

To promote competition, the FTC required the two firms to divest 2,431 gas stations in the United States. Mobil had more than 3,500 stations configured to use its Speedpass RFID system. Waving the key-ring device in front of the pump triggers the system to access the customer's credit record and authorize the charge via satellite. The newly joined IT system also had to install the system in the merged stores (Hamblen 1999).

In 2000, the company announced that it was implementing mySAP for all of its employees. mySAP is a Web-based platform that provides links into the company's main databases. A key goal was to integrate all of the data and provide a consistent interface. Suzanne McCarron, an ExxonMobil spokesperson, notes that "by consolidating and upgrading our systems, we will streamline our business processes, lower information system support costs and provide access to common consistent data—all of which will result in overall cost savings, rapid information technology project implementations and improved performance" (Songini 2000). The system provides access to supply chain management, plant maintenance, human resource, and accounting tools. It also contains industry-specific oil and gas applications. In particular, the specific functions include dispatch planning and optimization and inventory management. In terms of profits, the higher prices for exploration and production added to Exxon's profits. However, the increase in price at the pumps caused consumers to cut back on driving, reducing sales volume (Cummins and Warren 2004).

The oil business is closely tied to politics in many countries—which considerably increases the risks. In 2003, Exxon was in talks to invest in Russian oil fields through Russian oil baron Mikhail Khodorkovsky. Exxon would love to gain a foothold in the Russian oil production industry. Unfortunately for Exxon, Khodorkovsky was arrested and imprisoned before any deals could be reached. Russian president Putin charged Khodorkovsky with failing to pay taxes and had him arrested. Many observers believe Putin was more concerned about Khodorkovsky's political ambitions (White, Whalen, and Warren 2004).

Questions

1. What benefits did ExxonMobil gain by centralizing on SAP's ERP software?

2. How does ExxonMobil use technology to reduce costs?

3. What information technology problems can ExxonMobil expect if it tries to expand into Russia?

Additional Reading

Cummins, Chip, and Susan Warren. "High Prices Help Exxon Mobil, Shell." *The Wall Street Journal,* April 30, 2004.

Hamblen, Matt. "Merged Exxon Mobil Faces IT Issues." *Computerworld,* December 1, 1999.

King, Julia, and Kim S. Nash. "Exxon/Mobil Sets Up Mega SAP Project." *Computerworld,* December 7, 1998.

Songini, Marc L. "Exxon Mobil Adopts Mysap.Com As Its 'Primary Backbone,'" *Computerworld,* October 23, 2000.

Warren, Susan. "Oil Companies Curb Their Spending." *The Wall Street Journal,* June 1, 2004.

White, Gregory L., Jeanne Whalen, and Susan Warren. "A Global Journal Report; Tough Drill: For West's Oil Giants, Vast Fields in Russia Prove Hard to Tap." *The Wall Street Journal,* April 27, 2004.

www.exxonmobil.com

Case: Royal Dutch Petroleum (Shell)

Royal Dutch Petroleum (ticker: RD) is the main holding company for Shell Oil. It is headquartered in the Netherlands. Since the company did not participate as heavily in the late 20th century mergers, it has sales of about $120 billion and 71,000 employees. The company experienced a major public relations setback in 2004 when it was forced to restate its financial data for 2002 and 2003. The change was driven by an admission from Shell officials that they had overstated the company's oil and gas reserves by 22 percent. Four senior executives were fired as a result of the misstated information (Wang 2004). The company has fallen behind the other major producers in developing reserve fields. In 2004, Shell began pushing more money into exploration. Malcolm Brinded, head of exploration and production, said that he was going to focus on high-margin projects in the UK and the United States. The goal is to "re-establish the competitiveness of the portfolio" (Cummins and Warren 2004).

Shell spends a considerable amount of money on hiring temporary workers, as much as $100 million a year. Most of the departments used a homemade collection of paperwork to hire, track, and pay the workers. The company was working with 20 different organizations that supplied contract labor and needed to cut its costs. Shell reduced its outside service providers to four and then installed software from IQNavigator. The system automates most of the processes needed to hire, track, and pay the temporary workers. By consolidating the information, Shell can negotiate longer-term and volume discounts with the main suppliers. To cut costs even more, the outside suppliers are the ones who pay for the software, through a 5 to 8 percent assessment for each hire (Hoffman 2003).

Outsourcing and Standards

Since Shell is a smaller player in the market, it has found it necessary to partner with other companies to reduce costs and expand its capabilities. In particular, the company partnered with Chevron and Schlumberger Ltd. to define a vendor-neutral suite of applications for petroleum companies. Known as OpenSpirit, the technology should make it possible to integrate applications from multiple vendors into one framework (Ohlson 2000).

The OpenSpirit system is specifically designed to transform data from a variety of common sources, including seismic systems. It can scan databases, handle 2-D and 3-D projects, and maintain everything in a GIS database. The system supports multiple languages and platforms, including Java and C++ on Windows, Solaris (Sun), and Linux. It also contains connectors to ArcView (for GIS) and Excel (www.openspirit.com).

Shell has also turned to outside vendors to provide additional expertise in integrating data. In 2001, the company chose IBM to configure and set up three new data centers located in Houston, The Hague (headquarters), and Kuala Lumpur. Shell's general manager for IT projects, Alan Matula, said that "we were looking for a trusted technology partner to help us achieve aggressive TCO [total cost of ownership] targets in our MegaCentre project. [It is] one of the most important IT initiatives in Shell's history" (Vijayan 2001). Shell also worked with IBM to develop a high-performance Linux-based cluster to analyze seismic data. In 2004, Shell went even further and negotiated an agreement to outsource most IT functions to India-based Wipro and IBM. The company is trying to reduce its 9,000-employee IT workforce by 30 percent by 2006 in an effort to cut about $850 million a year (McDougall 2004).

Shell also realized that its communication network was "fragmented across business units," according to Rob van Zwieteren, the telecommunications manager. The goal is to save $50 million over three years by consolidating all communications into a single network infrastructure. The master contract is handled by Cable & Wireless (Cope 2001).

Knowledge Management

Solving problems in a huge company with experts scattered around the globe can be a challenge. Shell's Arjan van Unnik notes that "what we had was a community of expatriates who might link up when they encountered a problem. We had knowledge management, but not that much" (King 2001). To improve communication and sharing, Shell implemented a $1.5 million project using off-the-shelf collaboration software in 1999. The system evolved into 13 Web-based communities used by more than 10,000 employees. By sharing technical data and providing the opportunity for employees to ask questions, the system is estimated to have provided $200 million in benefits in less than two years (King 2001).

One challenge with KM projects is that the name has garnered a negative reputation. Several large projects were created that tried to capture wide levels of knowledge across an entire organization. Projects that large and broad tended to fail, giving KM a bad name. Yet the concept of KM is still important—particularly in a geographically diverse company, and in an industry facing retiring experts. Consequently, the KM label was discarded on the Shell project, and it was renamed "new ways of working." The group found that the system actually had to direct user discussions. It was not enough to just store and retrieve knowledge. People need more guidance. In particular, when the system splintered into more than 100 communities, the IT group had to redefine the groups and educate people to reduce the number of communities down to 12 (Kontzer 2003).

Questions

1. What problems has Royal Dutch experienced because of decentralization?
2. How is Royal Dutch using information technology to improve communications in its decentralized environment?
3. How is Royal Dutch's focus on reducing IT costs and centralizing services at three data centers going to solve its problems?

Additional Reading

Cope, James. "Shell to Set Up $250M Global Data Pipeline." *Computerworld,* October 15, 2001.

Cummins, Chip, and Susan Warren. "High Prices Help Exxon Mobil, Shell." *The Wall Street Journal,* April 30, 2004.

Hoffman, Thomas. "Contingent Workforce: Managing the Temporary Players." *Computerworld,* June 30, 2003.

King, Julia. "Shell Strikes Knowledge Gold." *Computerworld,* July 16, 2001.

Kontzer, Tony. "The Need to Know." *Information Week,* August 18, 2003.

McDougall, Paul. "Shell Objects to Reported $1B Outsourcing Price Tag." *Information Week,* May 5, 2004.

Ohlson, Kathleen. "Chevron, Shell and Schlumberger Team on Energy Software Venture." *Computerworld,* October 9, 2000.

Vijayan, Jaikumar. "Shell, IBM Agree to $100M E-Business Applications Deal." *Computerworld,* July 6, 2001.

Wang, Michael. "Shell Names Peter Voser as New Finance Chief." *The Wall Street Journal,* June 24, 2004.

www.openspirit.com

Case: Chevron Texaco

Chevron merged with Texaco at the end of 2001. The new firm (ticker: CVX) had sales of over $120 billion in 2003 with over 60,000 employees. It is headquartered in San Francisco. The merger created some issues with the ongoing Internet explo-

rations by both companies. But the dot-com crash at about the same time made those issues irrelevant (King 2000).

One of the more interesting aspects of the merger was the consolidation of their telecommunication networks. Because both companies had operations around the world, they had both contracted with AT&T to provide international telecommunication services. The merger provided the opportunity to consolidate the networks to reduce costs. In terms of financial systems, Chevron was using SAP software, while Texaco had an older custom system built over the years. Texaco replaced the system with SAP prior to the merger (Collett 1999).

Partly because of the merger, partly because of the expanded use of the Internet, from 1999 to 2001, Chevron's Internet demands increased by 200 percent a year for those three years. The company upgraded routers and servers to handle the new demands (Maselli 2001).

Managing desktops in a company scattered around the world is difficult. Dave Clementz, the CIO, standardized the company on a common network backbone. He also rolled out Windows XP early in 2002 to ensure that everyone had the same platform. For some cases, he installed thin-client terminals. The applications for the thin clients are stored on a central server, making it easier to update and troubleshoot the applications. The company is also planning to move to Web-based applications. Employees who need only simple tools, like e-mail, could run everything through a thin-client browser (Maselli 2001). IT directors at both companies were leaning to Web-based applications to provide more centralized management and reduced cost of applications.

In 2003, the combined ChevronTexaco signed an agreement to work with IBM and BearingPoint for supply chain management, procurement, and outsourcing. IBM was a lead contractor on merging the SAP systems of the two companies. IBM was also negotiating to provide outsource facilities and hosted services (McDougall 2003).

Big companies with multiple locations also generate issues with security. It is difficult enough to track IT assets. (Who is currently assigned to which computer?) It is also difficult to control user access to systems and applications. Chevron purchased eProvision Day One software from Business Layers to manage these processes. The system uses Lightweight Directory Access Protocol (LDAP) to track the user groups. It stores account data and access rights for voice mail, e-mail, and even cell phones. The system consolidates data from dozens of older databases used throughout the company—often including Excel spreadsheets. Centralizing the account data makes it easier to see and control user access rights. It also makes it easy to remove all permissions when an employee leaves the company (Verton 2001).

Questions

1. What benefits does ChevronTexaco gain with thin-client and Web-based applications?

2. Why is ChevronTexaco using LDAP to consolidate its user accounts instead of standardizing the underlying systems?

3. What did ChevronTexaco gain by consolidating its international telecommunication systems? Were there any other options?

Additional Reading

Collett, Stacy. "Chevron/Texaco Merger Could Recast AT&T Role." *Computerworld,* May 17, 1999.

King, Julia. "IT Implications Linger for Chevron/Texaco Merger." *Computerworld,* October 23, 2000.

Maselli, Jennifer. "Chevron Bolsters IT Infrastructure to Accommodate Growth." *Information Week,* September 17, 2001.

McDougall, Paul. "ChevronTexaco Prefers IBM for Services." *Information Week,* May 22, 2003.

Verton, Dan. "Chevron Adds Software to Control Network Access." *Computerworld,* July 27, 2001.

Case: Exploration

NuTec Energy Services is a specialty company that provides data and data visualization services for oil exploration. In particular, the Houston-based company takes raw seismic data and converts it into 3-D images. The company focuses on the Outer Continental Shelf (OCS) in the Gulf of Mexico. Customers purchase data by the OCS block, which is one square kilometer. The analyses use from 2 to 20 terabytes of data per project. Although profitable, the company was being squeezed between customers who wanted lower prices and increased computational and storage costs. NuTec solved its cost problems by moving to Linux-based servers and installing a dual-controller storage area network (SAN). The open-source system reduced costs by 84 percent. The challenge is that the servers have to deliver the massive data quickly to the 220 or more servers performing the computations. The system requires a high-speed network to move the data off the storage devices to the requesting computers. To solve the problem, NuTec installed two subsystems. One system serves the highly nonlinear analysis computers that perform intensive computations but pull data in bulk. Data for that system is stored on an EMC Clariion FC4700 linked to four servers running GFS. It feeds 130 Linux computational servers. The second analytical system performs a simpler calculation, but draws huge amounts of data quickly. Data for that time imaging system is stored on a MetaStor E4600 array from LSI, routed through McData 6140 SAN switches to 220 computational servers (Scheier 2004).

Anadarko Petroleum in Woodlands, Texas, faced similar problems with data storage. The company needed to consolidate the seismic 2-D and 3-D data used by its engineers, geologist, and geophysicists. The company installed network-attached storage (NAS) devices from Network Appliance. The new system uses EMC Symmetrix boxes to hold 110 terabytes of data. The conversion took 20 months. But CIO Morris Helbach notes that "an exploration and production company lives and dies by the way it acquires, manages and provides access to data" (Songini 2003).

British Petroleum (BP) faced a slightly different problem with similar data. The third-largest oil company has hundreds of leases in the Gulf of Mexico. But it does not have the staff to analyze all of the data. Steve Decatur, staff development deployment leader in the Houston office, observed that "it would take us four years with our current manpower to get all these properties analyzed" (Bryce 2001). The company found an innovative solution. It created a Web site and invited freelancers to analyze the data. Freelance analysts who develop suitable drilling plans get $50,000. If the wells produce oil, they receive a cash bonus. If BP does not drill, the analysts can take the plans to another company. The company initially provided data on five Gulf tracts. Based on the quality of responses, it eventually added 18 more to the site (Bryce 2001).

Questions

1. What are the benefits to outsourcing analysis of oil field data? What are the drawbacks?

2. What information technologies are important in the oil exploration industry?

Additional Reading

Bryce, Robert. "BP Drills Web." *eWeek,* July 9, 2001.

Scheier, Robert L. "Seismic Data Firm Boosts

Throughput, Cuts Costs with Super-Scalable SAN." *Computerworld,* January 6, 2004.

Songini, Marc L. "Profile: Joan Dunn." *Computerworld,* January 6, 2003.

Summary Industry Questions

1. What information technologies have helped this industry?

2. Did the technologies provide a competitive advantage or were they quickly adopted by rivals?

3. Which technologies could this industry use that were developed in other sectors?

4. Is the level of competition increasing or decreasing in this industry? Is it dominated by a few firms, or are they fairly balanced?

5. What problems have been created from the use of information technology and how did the firms solve the problems?

CHAPTER FOURTEEN

Information Management and Society

Chapter Outline

Introduction
Individuals
    Privacy
    Privacy Laws and Rules
    Anonymity
Jobs
    Loss of Jobs
    Physical Disabilities
    Telecommuting
Business: Vendors and Consumers
    Intellectual Property
    Balance of Power
Education and Training
Social Interactions
    Social Group Legitimacy
    Access to Technology
    e-Mail Freedom
    Liability and Control of Data
Government
    Government Representatives and Agencies
    Democracy and Participation
    Voting
    Information Warfare
    Rise of the World-State?
Crime
    Police Powers
    Freedom of Speech
Responsibility and Ethics
    Users
    Programmers and Developers
    Companies
    Governments
A Summary of Important Computer-Related Laws
    Property Rights
    Privacy
    Information Era Crimes

Summary
Key Words
Web Site References
Additional Reading
Review Questions
Exercises
Cases: Health Care

What You Will Learn in This Chapter

- How does your company affect the rest of the world? What influence does the outside world have on your company?

- How does information technology affect individuals? As a manager and a company, do you treat individuals the way you expect to be treated by other companies?

- How does technology affect jobs? If computers do more of the work, what jobs are left for people?

- How does technology change the relationship between businesses and consumers?

- Can information technology change education?

- How does technology affect different areas of society?

- Can information technology improve governments?

- Do criminals know how to use computers?

- How do your actions affect society? Is it possible to follow the laws and still be wrong?

- What major laws affect technology and the use of computers?

How do information systems affect society? From one perspective, health care organizations are simply another business. Yet because of their costs, importance to our daily lives, and widespread governmental involvement, health care has a special role in society. Not surprisingly, most physicians and other health care workers receive minimal training in information systems and are not comfortable with it. Consequently, information systems for medical care are being introduced slowly. On the other hand, information systems have the ability to reduce errors as well as costs. In particular, health care organizations like Sutter Health are working to implement electronic drug ordering and dispensing systems. Sutter is also working to implement paperless medical offices and already has 400 member physicians using a completely electronic system—including X-rays and prescriptions. The group is also working with telemedicine—particularly with intensive care units (ICUs) to reduce the costs of physicians and provide better care to remote locations. Of course, security and privacy issues become major areas of concern with medical information systems.

FIGURE 14.1

Information management and society: Every organization and individual exists in a social environment. Changes in the firm and changes in technology affect the environment. Changes in the environment can affect the firm. An understanding of these interactions will make you a better manager.

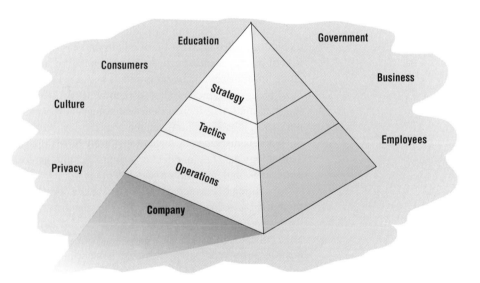

Introduction

How does your company affect the rest of the world? What influence does the outside world have on your company? Why should you care? Try an easier question: How much do your customers care about privacy? When you use information technology to help your company, it means you are collecting and analyzing data on customers and employees. As shown in Figure 14.1, your company lives within an environment. Companies influence the world through relationships with customers, employees, and other companies. In turn, your organization is affected by events in the world ranging from government laws to education and public opinion. When you make business decisions, you need to think about these interaction effects. Even if you cannot change the world yourself, you should be aware of the effects of your choices so that you are ready to deal with the consequences.

If nothing else, history has shown that technological change is inevitable. Competitive economics virtually guarantees that the search for new products, new manufacturing techniques, and other ways to gain competitive advantage will continue.

TRENDS

The industrial revolution in the late 18th century caused many changes to society. Before the revolution, workers were predominantly employed as craftsmen, farmers, or lesser-skilled laborers. Mechanization brought standardization and assembly lines, for which jobs were reduced to simple, repetitive tasks.

As transportation improved, people moved from farms to cities, and cities spread to suburbs. Communication systems improved and linked the populations back together. Better product distribution mechanisms changed the way products are sold. Companies (such as Sears, through its catalogs) began to distribute products nationally instead of relying on small local stores. National and international markets developed with every change in the communication and transportation systems.

These changes were so strong that philosophers and writers began to take note of how technological changes can affect society. From the bleak pictures painted by Dickens, Marx, and Orwell, to the fantastic voyages of Verne, Heinlein, and Asimov, we can read thousands of opinions and predictions about how technology might affect the political, economic, and social environments.

Changes in technology often affect society. Technology can change individuals, jobs, education, governments, and social interactions. As components of society, each group has rights and responsibilities to others, such as a right to privacy and obligations regarding ethics.

Technology effects on individuals can be beneficial or detrimental. Often a change in technology helps one set of individuals and harms another group. Typical problems include loss of privacy, depersonalization, and changing incentives or motivations. Advantages include lower prices and better products and service. The effect on jobs is hard to predict, but most observers conclude that workers will require more education and training. Most authorities think that increases in technology in the past generally led to an increase in the number of jobs. Now, however, many of the new jobs require higher levels of education, and the workers displaced by technology rarely have the qualifications needed for the new jobs. Technology also has an effect on crime. Technology creates new crimes, new ways to commit crimes, and new ways to catch criminals.

In addition to the increased demand, technology has provided new teaching methods. Although there is considerable debate over the costs and benefits of technology in education, there is usually a place for technology, even if only as a specialized technique. However, most educators remember the early claims of how television was going to revolutionize education. Fifty years later, television is beginning to play a role in education, but it is still hampered by the limited availability of two-way links.

Governments attempt to control these impacts of technology by creating laws, but laws often bring their own problems. Also, in times of rapid change, laws rarely keep up with the changes in technology. Governments are also directly affected by improved communication facilities. For example, technology makes it possible for governments to better understand the needs of the citizens and provide more avenues for communication.

Technology can alter any number of social interactions. Social groups can gain or lose power, and types or methods of criminals are altered. Furthermore, society can become dependent on technology, which is not necessarily bad, but it causes problems if the technology is removed or substantially altered.

Individuals

How does information technology affect individuals? As a manager and a company, do you treat individuals the way you expect to be treated by other companies? Information technology plays an important role in the lives of most individuals. Many jobs are directly involved in the collection, processing, and evaluation of data. Performance of many workers is continually monitored by computers. As consumers, virtually our entire lives are recorded and analyzed. Governments maintain massive files on all public aspects of our

FIGURE 14.2

Privacy: Businesses, employers, and governments all have reasons to collect data on individuals. The challenge lies in balancing these needs with the privacy of the individuals. Historically, there have been many instances of abuse and fraud when this balance is not achieved.

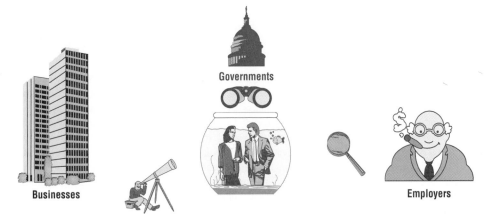

lives. **Privacy** is a delicate and controversial issue. Citizens must work together to live in a society, which requires giving up some elements of privacy. Businesses and governments often need to identify customers and employees to perform basic functions. Yet history reveals that individuals can be threatened or coerced if some people or organizations collect too much information.

Although data has been collected on citizens for many years, recent improvements in technology raise greater concerns about privacy. As computer capabilities increase, it becomes possible to collect, integrate, and analyze the huge volume of data. Using publicly available data, it is possible to collect an amazing amount of data on any person.

Privacy

As Figure 14.2 indicates, companies, governments, and employers collect data about many aspects of our lives. Most of the modern marketing efforts including data mining and building customer relationships require information about customers. Marketing and sales can be improved by maintaining databases of consumer information and tracking sales and preferences at the customer level. Combining government statistics and data from market research firms with geographical data can provide a precise picture of consumer demands. It also might represent an invasion of privacy for individuals. With databases available even to small companies, it is easy to acquire basic data on any individual. For instance, phone numbers and addresses are readily available online. Data collected by governmental agencies such as voter registration and property records can be purchased from several online sources. More comprehensive commercial databases are available from specialty marketing companies. Few laws exist that limit the use of personal data.

It is easy to obtain lists from universities, clubs and social organizations, magazine subscriptions, and mail-order firms. Statistical data can be purchased from the U.S. government. Although most U.S. agencies are forbidden to release specific individual observations until 50 years after the collection date, statistical averages can be highly accurate. By combining the statistical averages with your address, your actual income might be estimated to within a few thousand dollars.

Because most people prefer to maintain their privacy, companies have an ethical (and sometimes legal) obligation to respect their wishes. Individuals can always ask companies not to distribute personal data. Companies should give consumers the option of protecting personal data by building the option into their databases and informing consumers whenever companies collect data.

Consumer Privacy

As shown in Figure 14.3, a tremendous amount of data is collected on consumers. In the early years, consumer activists primarily worried about government data collection. Governments had more computers and the authority to force citizens to provide data. Today, businesses can easily collect, obtain, and integrate almost the same level of data available to government agencies. In fact, government agencies have begun using commercial

REALITY BYTES   Internationalization: Privacy

Different countries have different laws regarding protection of consumer data. In particular, some European nations have stricter controls than the United States. There has been some discussion among these nations (notably France) that firms should be forced to keep consumer data within the originating country; that way it is still subject to the local laws. If a U.S. firm transmits its local French database back to the United States, the data can no longer be controlled by French law. Although such restrictions would be difficult to enforce, companies have an ethical obligation to support the laws of the nation in which they operate.

The United Kingdom has a requirement that all databases involving personal data must be registered with the data protection agency.

The European Union in general has a restriction on trading data: personal data can only be transferred to another country if the nation supports "adequate" protection of personal data. According to *Network World,* the EU is considering a requirement that all businesses register databases containing personal data. Moreover, businesses would be required to obtain individuals' permission to collect or process the data. They would also have to notify the individual each time the data is reused or sold.

FIGURE 14.3

Privacy: Many businesses and government agencies collect data. With increasing computer capabilities, it is becoming possible to collect and correlate this data to track many aspects of individual lives.

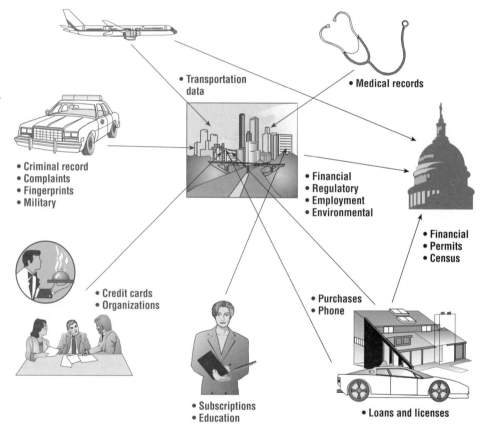

databases in some cases. Credit card and credit bureau data are the two most detailed sources of consumer data.

Consumers have little control over the collection of personal data. But it is interesting how cheaply people will give up their privacy. Grocery store loyalty cards collect a tremendous amount of personal purchase data. Customers routinely sign up for the cards in exchange for a tiny discount on prices. The purchase data is sold to marketing companies and manufacturers to track sales and the success of marketing campaigns.

A significant question remains as to whether consumers really care about their privacy. The loyalty card data and lack of concern over financial records indicate that many people do not care about privacy. Yet over 50 percent of U.S. households signed up for the national do-not-call list to stop telemarketing calls. Perhaps the conclusion is that customers do not mind having data collected, but they do not like being solicited directly.

FIGURE 14.4

Web cookies: Cookies are used to keep track of the user across page requests. Each time the user PC requests a page, it returns a small text file (cookie) containing an identification number.

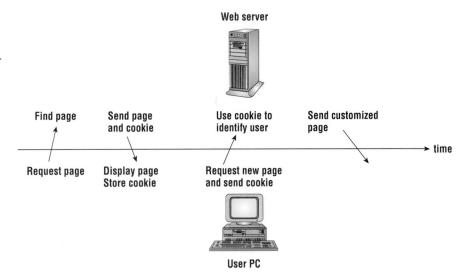

FIGURE 14.5

Misuse of Web cookies: Doubleclick.com as a third party places cookies onto visitor PCs. Every time the visitor sees an ad delivered by Doubleclick, Doubleclick records the user, the date/time, and the site visited. Doubleclick attempted to market this huge database.

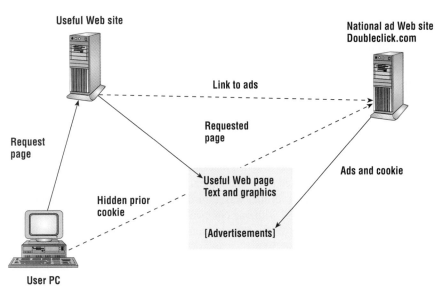

On the other hand, at times, consumers seem more concerned about online data collection. The technology for Web sites did not initially consider the demands of e-commerce. It was originally intended to simply display pages independently—every request for a page is independent of any other request. For e-commerce, the Web server needs to keep track of information about the person requesting a page. For instance, a shopping cart system needs to store items selected by the customer. Similarly, any site using security needs to track the user through a series of pages—otherwise it would force the user to log in for every new page. These problems were solved with the creation of "magic" **cookies.** A Web cookie is a small text file that the server asks the browser to store on the user's computer. As shown in Figure 14.4, whenever the browser requests another page from that server, it returns the cookie file containing an identification number. Hence, the server knows which user is returning. This use of cookies is common and relatively benign. Yes, the cookie could be used to track visitors, but presumably the visitor is purchasing items and already willingly provides more detailed information to complete the transaction.

Figure 14.5 shows a more troublesome use of cookies. In 2000, it was revealed that Doubleclick.com, the leading Web advertisement-placing firm, was using cookies as a third party to track page visits by millions of people. Leading Web sites register with Doubleclick to carry advertising. Companies wishing to advertise on the Web create the ad and pay Doubleclick to carry it on its servers. The original Web site includes a link to Doubleclick

REALITY BYTES — Would You Lie to a Computer?

Web sites are increasingly asking people to register to read the main content. Although the sites do not charge for the content, they do require you to enter your name and some personal information. Most use this demographic information to tailor advertising and help sell space to advertisers. But do you tell the truth? Darrell Kunken, vice president for marketing at the *Bakersfield Californian* newspaper, believes that 15 percent of his paper's registration data is false. Tim Ruder, vice president of marketing for the *Washington Post's* online division, believes that falsification is rare: "There are times when you look at the number of people in the 90210 zip code, and it's too high. But the numbers are so small in comparison to the aggregate that it's just noise in the equation." The *Augusta Chronicle* in Georgia found that only 208 of 80,600 registered users claimed to be from the 90210 zip code, made famous by the television series. Another 171 say they live in Schenectady, New York, with a 12345 zip code. *The New York Times* estimates that less than 1 percent of its data is false. Some sites, such as bugmenot.com, go further astray and enable users to share logins for various sites. Martin Nisenholtz, CEO of the digital unit at *The New York Times,* observes that "this is an attempt to defraud us of the thing we need to keep the site available for free."

Source: Adapted from Carl Bialik, "Web Users Thwart Sites' Efforts to Collect Personal Information," *The Wall Street Journal,* March 22, 2004.

software that delivers the ads and records page views so that the site owners can be paid the correct fee. However, Doubleclick also includes a cookie that is sent to the visiting PC with each ad placement. Anytime the user visits a site that deals with Doubleclick, the identifying cookie, date/time, and site visited are stored on Doubleclick's servers. Web users were understandably upset when Doubleclick attempted to market this data collection—particularly when the company wanted to tie the online identities to real-world names and addresses.

To prevent this loss of privacy, browsers enable you to turn off cookies—but then you will not be able to use many secure sites, such as those run by banks. With the XP release of Windows, Microsoft is offering another option: the ability to refuse third-party cookies, such as those placed by Doubleclick. The browser still exchanges the short-term cookies used to maintain identification across sessions, but it will not store or return cookies to any server that was a third party. This option is a useful compromise that allows customers to deal with one company and still maintain some control over privacy.

Wireless technologies offer even more methods for tracking people. Did you know that over 50 percent of emergency calls are made on cell phones? The federal e-911 law now requires cell phone operators to provide location data on cell phones. Manufacturers have begun embedding GPS locator chips within cell phones. Triangulation and signal strength are also used as backup methods. While this data is useful for emergencies, it could also be used for commercial purposes. One vendor was considering a locator system to notify you when a friend's cell phone is within a certain distance of yours. Imagine the commercial opportunities of broadcasting messages to consumer cell phones as they walk by your store. Now, ask yourself whether you want to be continually interrupted as you walk through the mall.

Employee Privacy

Computers have created other problems with respect to individual privacy. They are sometimes used to monitor employees. Computers can automatically track all of the work done by each person. Some employers post this data on public bulletin boards to encourage employees to work harder. Some software available for local area networks enables managers to see exactly what every employee is doing—without the employees knowing they are being watched. Some employers read their employees' electronic-mail messages. Currently, all of these activities are legal in the United States.

Many companies use electronic badges, which employees use to unlock doors. The systems are run by a centralized computer that can be programmed to allow access to specific people only during certain hours. These systems enable employers to track the daily movements of all employees—including the amount of time spent in the restroom.

Courts have repeatedly held that property owned by the employer is completely within its control. Hence, employers have the right to impose any controls or monitoring they wish; as long as they do not violate other laws, such as the discrimination laws.

REALITY BYTES   Car 54, Where Are You?

Sergeant John Kuczynski in Clinton Township, New Jersey, was hearing a lot of complaints that police officers were loafing on the job. As internal affairs officer, he installed a GPS tracking system in several patrol cars—without telling the police officers. He then tracked each car's movements with detailed maps on his laptop. He quickly caught five officers sitting at restaurants or hanging out in parking lots. The officer logs stated that they were patrolling streets or looking for speeders. Eventually, four of the officers pleaded guilty to filing false records. The fifth was caught napping and disputed the charges, but was convicted. Three of the officers are suing the town to get their jobs back.

In Massachusetts, snowplow operators were asked to carry GPS-enabled cell phones. Hundreds of them packed a legislative hearing in Boston, arguing that the satellite tracking might be used to cut their payments. The highway department compromised and will continue to use paper timesheets to record hours worked, but the drivers will carry the phones. C.J. Driscoll & Associates estimates that about 1 million fleet vehicles had GPS trackers installed in 2004.

Source: Adapted from Charles Forelle, "On the Road Again, but Now the Boss Is Sitting Beside You," *The Wall Street Journal,* May 14, 2004.

FIGURE 14.6

Government and privacy: Spying on "ordinary" people is not an issue. Spying on business and political leaders or journalists can cause problems. Collecting data on targeted individuals such as dissidents or minorities can stifle innovation.

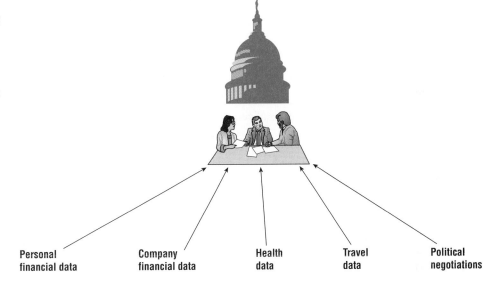

| Personal financial data | Company financial data | Health data | Travel data | Political negotiations |

It is easy to question why employers might feel the need to monitor their employees. At some point, you have to trust your employees to do their jobs. If an employee has so little work to do that he or she can "waste time using the Internet for personal use," the bigger problem is money the company is wasting on an unneeded employee. On the other hand, most major financial losses come from insiders such as employees and consultants. Furthermore, many companies have been burned by criminals when the companies were not careful enough in hiring and monitoring.

Government Privacy

Privacy from government agencies and their employees can be a touchy issue. As citizens, we agree to cooperate with government agencies to improve all of our lives. And to function properly, government agencies can require detailed personal data. For example, as shown in Figure 14.6, most governments collect health data, police records, driving records, international travel, and detailed financial data for taxes. Many people are also required to complete census surveys collecting detailed information about their lives. In the United States, much of this data is protected and can be shared or released only under specific conditions. But there have been several cases of government employees illegally browsing through records for their neighbors or even selling data. In 1991, 18 people were accused of selling Social Security information, including six government employees (*Government Computer News,* January 6, 1992, p. 58).

REALITY BYTES   You Expected Privacy in a Bar?

Most states have placed magnetic stripes on driver's licenses. The stripe contains basic data on the driver's birth date and address. Police can read the data into their portable scanners and have it instantly transmitted to a computer at headquarters. On the other hand, private businesses can also read the data on the licenses. The Rack, a bar in Boston favored by sports stars, gets 10,000 customers a week. To handle the influx, the doorman scans patrons' licenses, and the machine instantly indicates whether the person is old enough to enter the bar. Unknown to the customers, the box also collects the rest of the personal data on the card; sometimes even height, eye color, or social security number are retrieved and stored. Paul Barclay, the bar's owner, points out that he uses the data to determine information about his customers, identifying clientele by gender, age, and zip codes. He can track returning customers and even build mailing lists. Occasionally, police departments call bars to see if a suspect's name or SSN has shown up on their systems. Mr. Barclay also has a digital video camera at the door and can match faces to the data if he wants to. The system also enables him to reject certain people if they have caused problems in the past.

Kenny Vincent, who owns a bar in New Orleans that collects scanned data, observes that he can use the information for special promotions: "Let's say I'm doing an all-male-performer show. I could just mail to girls I want to target between 21 and 34. I have all that information. The whole reason to have a database is to advertise and market to your customers."

Source: Adapted from Jennifer Lee, "Finding Pay Dirt in Scannable Driver's Licenses," *The New York Times,* March 21, 2002.

In the United States, few laws or regulations control the use of data held by private organizations. However, several federal laws control the use of data collected by government agencies. For example, federal agencies are restricted from sharing databases except in specific situations. In most cases the FBI cannot access the IRS data without special permits. In terms of collection and use of data by private companies, there are few restrictions. Contrary to popular belief, there is no "right to privacy" specified in federal law. However, an element of privacy is contained in a few scattered federal laws and some state laws, and in some Supreme Court interpretations. For example, one federal law prohibits movie rental stores (and libraries) from disclosing lists of items rented by individuals.

As everyone was reminded on September 11, 2001, the flip side to privacy is the need for governments to identify and track individuals to prevent crimes and terrorism. As an open society, the United States has chosen to lean toward individual rights and privacy; but many people have suggested that more control and less privacy would make it easier to stop potential terrorists and criminals. Because of the capabilities of modern information systems and networks, it is now possible to build powerful systems that identify and track individuals within the nation and around the world. Some people have suggested that the United States should establish national identity cards, as used in many European nations. A single, unified database would make it easier to track individual actions.

People tend to be split on the issues of government privacy. Some hate the fact that they have to provide data. Others wonder what the problem is: if you tell your friends how much money you make, why not tell the government? In one sense, public information keeps everyone honest. And for many people, it probably does not matter if various government agencies collect personal data. No one really cares about the personal details of the housewife in Peoria. On the other hand, some people within governments have abused their positions in the past. Consider the tales of J. Edgar Hoover, longtime head of the FBI. He was obsessed with collecting data on people and built files on tens of thousands of people. Ostensibly he was attempting to remove "subversives" and was a leading cause of the McCarthy anticommunism hearings in the 1950s. He also collected thousands of secret files on politicians, journalists, and business leaders. He used these files to harass and blackmail leaders. Even if a modern-day data collector is not as blatant as Hoover, and even if modern politicians have fewer moral problems, there is still an important risk. What if a politician tries to spy on or interfere with political negotiations?

Protecting Your Privacy

Despite the shortage of laws, you can take several actions to protect your privacy and restrict access to personal data. First, it is your responsibility to direct employers and compa-

REALITY BYTES   Do National Databases Affect the Average Citizen?

On a June morning in 2004, Hope Clarke was dragged crying and in leg shackles from her cruise ship as it returned to Miami from Mexico. A wanted felon? A terrorist? No. She is a teacher's aide who had visited Yellowstone National Park the year before. While there, she was fined $50 for failing to put away her hot chocolate and marshmallows. Human food is considered a serious problem at Yellowstone because it attracts bears. Unfortunately, because Yellowstone is a national park, her citation was listed in a federal law enforcement database. Customs agents that meet all ships arriving from foreign ports ran a random check of the passenger list and Hope's name showed up with a note in the database that she had not paid the fine. After nine hours of detention and insisting that she paid the fine before she left the park, she appeared before U.S. Magistrate John O'Sullivan—who had a copy of the citation indicating that the fine had been paid. Zach Mann, a spokesman for U.S. Immigration and Customs Enforcement, said that "we were acting on what we believed was accurate information."

Source: Adapted from "Marshmallow Error Lands Woman in Shackles," *CNN Online*, June 18, 2004.

nies you deal with to not distribute your personal data. You can also ask them why they need personal data and whether it is optional or required. In particular, all federal agencies are required to explain why they need data from you and the purposes for which it will be used. You can also write to direct-marketing associations and file a request that your name not be included in general mailings or unsolicited phone calls. By using variations of your name or address, such as changing your middle initial, you can keep track of which organizations are selling personal data. In some cases, you can refuse to give out personal data (such as a Social Security or taxpayer identification number). If a private company insists, simply stop doing business with it. In a world where firms increasingly rely on a single number for identification, it is important that you protect that number.

With most government agencies and with banks, creditors, and credit-reporting agencies, you have the ability to check any data that refers to you. You have the right to disagree with any inaccurate data and request that it be changed. You can also file letters of explanation that are reported with the original data. In 1994, Congress updated the Fair Credit Reporting Act of 1970. The new version requires credit bureaus to verify disputed information within 30 days or delete it. Businesses that provide data to the credit agencies would also be required to investigate claims of incorrect information. The bill also limits who can have access to the data stored by the credit agencies and controls how it can be used in direct marketing campaigns. In 1994, according to the Associated Press, the bureaus processed 450 million files, selling 1.5 million records a day and handling almost 2 billion pieces of data every month.

Privacy Laws and Rules

The United States has few laws regarding privacy, although a few states do offer some stronger protections. On the federal level, the Bork Bill states that video rental stores and libraries cannot release their rental data. It was passed by Congress when some overzealous reporters obtained the video rental records of a judge nominee (Bork). The 1974 Family Educational Privacy Act prohibits schools from releasing grade data without permission from the student. The Privacy Act of 1994 placed some minimal limits on the sales of state and local driver's license data. The Privacy Act of 1974 limits what data can be collected and shared by federal agencies. However, various rules, interpretations, and practices have created enough loopholes to circumvent most of the original provisions.

In terms of financial data, various laws give consumers the ability to obtain their credit records (for a fee) and the right to dispute items in the report and have the dispute resolved within 30 days. In 2001, a federal rule took effect that was initiated by President Clinton to provide some control over the use of medical data. Health care providers are already complaining about the high cost of implementing the provisions, and it will take years to establish an accepted interpretation of exactly what is allowed and disallowed under the rules. Nominally, the rules state that transfer of data (particularly prescription drug data) requires permission from the patient.

REALITY BYTES   Opt Out Lists

Stop telemarketing phone calls:
www.donotcall.gov

Stop some junk mail:
Mail Preference Service
Direct Marketing Association
PO Box 643
Carmel, NY 10512

Stop credit agencies from selling your address to credit card companies:
Credit Bureau Screen Service
888-567-8688

In contrast to the United States, the European Union has solid consumer privacy laws. Most EU nations have adopted the European commission's 1995 Data Protection Directive. Since 1978, France has had its own strict Data Protection Act. The laws basically state that personal data can be collected only with the user's permission, the user must be clearly told how the data will be used, and the user has the right to see and to change any personal data. The laws have an additional important condition: personal consumer data cannot be moved to a nation with lesser privacy controls—notably the United States. The United States has negotiated a loose "safe harbor" provision, so that companies can bring European consumer data to the United States if the companies formally agree to abide by the EU directives and also agree not to resell the data. These provisions make it more expensive to collect data in Europe—sometimes beyond the price of small businesses. For example, in the United States, it is relatively easy to purchase e-mail lists of potential customers for a few hundred dollars. In Europe, these lists would generally be illegal to use, since the customer did not agree to the unsolicited use of his or her address.

Anonymity

Anonymity is the flip side of the privacy question. Until recently, it has been difficult or impossible to provide anonymous access to the Internet. Using advanced encryption, some firms now offer people the ability to use the Internet without revealing any data about themselves. For example, a proxy server can hide your IP address. Sites that you visit see only the address of the intermediate server. The server also intercepts all cookies and other files sent by some servers.

The ultimate question that you, as an important member of society, must answer is whether anonymity should be allowed, or how it should be controlled. Certainly it can be used to improve privacy. People who have a stronger belief in personal privacy will be willing to pay the fee—others will decide that privacy is not an issue. But what about drug dealers, terrorists, child pornographers, and other illegal activities that society wishes to stop? Or what about anonymous harassment? Someone could use the technology to harass and intimidate people on the Internet. Perhaps society should not allow anonymity? On the flip side, who makes that decision? If some nation chooses to ban dissenting viewpoints, or if a government whistleblower needs to protect a career, anonymous sites can be valuable tools to increase information and open discussions. Keep in mind that existing servers are anonymous only up to a point. With a court order, it is possible for existing anonymity servers to log and trace all current communications back to the real user.

Jobs

How does technology affect jobs? If computers do more of the work, what jobs are left for people? Technology can affect jobs in other ways as well. It opens up the world to people with physical disabilities. By removing location as an issue, networks make it possible

REALITY BYTES · Tell Me Where IT Hurts

Health care organizations have been slow to adopt digital information technology. Citing cost and privacy issues, everyone from hospitals to physicians have avoided electronic systems. Yet digital systems can offer tremendous improvements in health care and reductions in cost. In 2004, 60 percent of hospitals stated that they are either installing electronic medical record systems or planning to do so soon. Current systems are fragmented and contain large gaps in data. Many experts recommend that patients carry copies of all medical records—since that is the only way the data will be integrated in one location!

Standards are a major hurdle in establishing a medical record system. One group (Health Level 7) proposed a model in 2003, but it was rejected for being overly complex.

Even the moderately complex systems proposed will lack key data. For example, a medical record system might record that a physician prescribed a medication for a patient. But it will probably not indicate if the patient had the prescription filled, or if the drug had any beneficial effects. Throw in interoperability issues about trying to share data with different providers. Then note the new privacy provisions of the HIPAA rules, and it is clear that it will take years before much progress is made. President George Bush called for widespread adoption of electronic medical records in his 2004 State of the Union address. But the federal budget contains only $100 million for health care IT projects. The not-for-profit Health Technology Center suggests it will cost $5 billion over five years in state and federal money to create an integrated nationwide medical record system.

Source: Adapted from Laura Landro, "Three Imperatives for Digital Health Records," *The Wall Street Journal*, February 23, 2004.

FIGURE 14.7

Future jobs: Today there is no guarantee that your job will continue to exist. Demand for specialists changes constantly. Jobs that are well defined and require little innovation or thought can usually be performed easily by computers.

Source: U.S. Bureau of Labor Statistics.

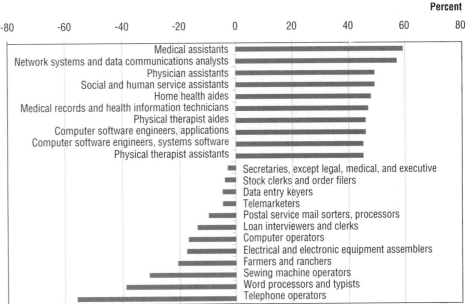

2002–20012 Job Gains and Losses

---

to work on jobs from almost anywhere in the world. You can telecommute or consult around the world without leaving your home.

Loss of Jobs

There is no question that technology causes some workers to lose their jobs. In the 19th century, Luddites reacted to textile automation by destroying machines. Information technology is no exception. Norbert Weiner, a computer pioneer in the 1940s, predicted a major depression would result from computers replacing workers. Despite these predictions, during the last 100 years technology has increased the number of jobs and raised the standard of living for most workers. Since the introduction of computers in the 1950s, the world's economies have grown and incomes have increased. However, individual workers can lose jobs in the short run. Even in the long run, lower-skilled workers experience greater difficulty in finding new jobs. Compare the automated shipyards of Singapore to those in the United States. In Singapore, one man using computer screens and a joystick moves hundreds of containerized cargoes without ever leaving his office. In the United States, each crane requires a crew of four workers, including one just to identify shipments and destinations that are handled by computer in Singapore. In Europe, the Dutch port in Rotterdam cut employment in half by installing robotic cranes and automated transfer vehicles.

The point is that some jobs will disappear, but others will take their place. In the shipyard example, more technical expertise will be needed to program and repair the equipment. Figure 14.7 shows the changes in jobs for the next few years that are anticipated by the Bureau of Labor Statistics. Some of the fastest growing jobs are in computer technology. But due to outsourcing and cost issues, the list is shorter now than it was a couple of years ago.

Most economic experts believe that technology increases the total number of jobs. New technology creates demand for people to design it, manufacturing firms to produce it, and people to maintain and repair it. Computer hardware also creates demand for software programmers. More important, technology can cause the economy to grow, creating more jobs in all sectors. By most indications, new jobs created by technology tend to be higher paying, physically safer, and less repetitive than those replaced by technology. Information technology can also reduce product prices, raising the standard of living by enabling people to buy more goods. On the other hand, technology typically causes some workers to lose their jobs. Unfortunately, many of these displaced workers cannot be retrained for the new jobs created by the technology. Similarly, the new jobs might pay less money, have lower status, or might have less desirable work environments.

Governments have created several programs to provide benefits of money, retraining, and relocation to workers who lose their jobs. As managers, we need to understand the effects on employees when we introduce new technology. Many corporations provide ongoing educational payments and training classes to help workers improve their skills. Others provide outplacement services to help unemployed workers in their job search.

As individuals, we need to remember that changing technology can eliminate virtually any job. One of the best plans is to continue your education and learn new skills. Remember that technology continually changes. Some of the skills you learn today will be obsolete in a couple of years. We must all continually learn new skills and adapt to changes. Applying these skills in your current job adds experience that will help you find a new job. It also benefits your current employer and might help you keep your job or stay with the company if new technology makes your current job obsolete.

The concept of continually acquiring new skills sounds straightforward. However, many times you will have to choose among multiple technologies. Guessing wrong can lead you to invest time and money in a technology or skill that fades away. As you become more involved with technology, you will increasingly find it necessary to "predict" the future. Identifying trends and deciphering fact from rumor are important skills to learn.

Physical Disabilities

Technology offers many possibilities to provide jobs for workers with physical disabilities. In fact, in 1992, the U.S. Congress passed the Americans with Disabilities Act, stating that companies are not allowed to discriminate against disabled employees. Common uses of technology include the use of scanners and speech synthesizers for visually impaired workers; voice input devices and graphics displays for workers who cannot use keyboards; and telecommuting for those who work from home. In 2001, the U.S. government began requiring that all software it purchases must be accessible to users with disabilities. Since the federal government employs hundreds of thousands of workers, this order should encourage all software providers to improve their software.

Most Windows-based software contains features to facilitate usage by people with various physical challenges. In some cases, additional accessibility tools can be downloaded or purchased to provide more features. Speech recognition packages are useful for many applications. Sometimes adaptive devices are needed to provide alternative ways to enter data and obtain the results.

Web sites still present accessibility problems, particularly for those with visual impairments. Many sites rely on color and graphics, which are difficult for the accessibility tools to interpret. These issues are being discussed by many vendors. Check Microsoft's accessibility site for more details.

Telecommuting

The fact that about 70 percent of U.S. jobs are service-based raises interesting possibilities for workers. Many services like accounting, legal advice, education, insurance, investments, data analysis, computer programming, and consulting are not tied to a physical location. As a service provider, you could be located anywhere and still perform your job—as long as you have the appropriate telecommunications system. As communication improves to include video links and faster document transfer, even more jobs can be performed from remote locations.

Some companies are experimenting with home-based workers, especially in cities such as Los Angeles and New York with long commute times. Some workers like the concept; others try it for a few months and return to a traditional workplace job. Several advantages and complications arise from the perspective of the worker, the firm, and society.

If a substantial number of workers choose to work from home, the firm gains two main advantages: (1) decreased costs through smaller offices, and (2) flexibility in hiring additional workers on a contract basis. Some people have predicted that companies might also gain from increased use of part-time workers, thus avoiding the cost of insurance and other benefits. The greatest complication to the firm is evaluating and managing employees. Without daily personal contact, including conversations, it is harder to spot problems and make informal suggestions as corrections.

To the worker, the most obvious benefit lies in reducing the time and expense of commuting to work. The biggest drawback lies in the loss of personal contact and daily ritual of a typical work schedule. Depending on your home environment, there can be substantially more interruptions and distractions at home. It is also more difficult to "get away" from your job. Working from home on a flexible schedule requires strong motivation and organization. Before you choose to work at home, talk to someone with experience.

A few firms have experimented with intermediate telecommuting options. As indicated in Figure 14.8, the firm leases smaller offices in city suburbs and workers operate from these satellite offices instead of one central location. The offices are linked by high-capacity telecommunication lines. Workers keep a traditional office environment but cut their commuting costs. Businesses maintain traditional management control but do not save as much money.

A few people have speculated about the effects on society if there is a large shift to telecommuting. At this point, there is not much evidence to support any of the hypotheses, but many of them focus on negative aspects. People could become isolated. Jobs could become highly competitive and short-term. Firms could list projects on the network and workers would compete for every job. Workers would essentially become independent contractors and bear the responsibilities and costs of insurance, retirement, and other benefits, with little or no job security. They would also have no loyalty to any particular firm. Firms could become loose coalitions of workers and teams that are constantly changing, with little control over future directions. It is hard to predict what will really happen, but by understanding the negative effects, they become easier to avoid.

Business: Vendors and Consumers

How does technology change the relationship between businesses and consumers? Business consists of transactions. Changes in the way transactions are handled can alter society. In particular, as digital content becomes more important, can the existing laws created decades ago still be applied? And if the laws are replaced, will they affect the balance of power in the relationship between vendors and consumers?

REALITY BYTES Telecommuting Benefits

Years ago, managers could constantly watch employees—simply by looking out over the rows of desks or wandering among the cubicles. Today, workers are scattered—visiting clients, working with salespeople, helping at factories or distribution centers, traveling, or even working from home. Managers need to learn how to support and guide this new type of worker. A study by Harris Interactive notes that about 25 percent of the U.S. workforce works from home at least some of the time. Another 25 percent is mobile or works at customer locations. In general telecommuting has been useful. A study by Work Design Collaborative shows that workers moving out of the main company become 15 percent more productive. The improvements come primarily from fewer distractions from colleagues—and unnecessary meetings.

For task-oriented jobs, software can monitor the working activities of the employees. For example, all 700 reservation agents for Jet Blue, the discount airline, work from home. The company monitors the amount of time required for each call, how long it takes before the employee handles the next call, and routinely plays tapes of the conversations to help employees become more efficient. Frankie Littleford, the vice president of reservations, notes that "we just want to make sure they're available and working when they're logged on. We're able to check from the second that they sign on to the second they sign off."

Other companies use more sophisticated tools to help traveling managers. Instead of spying on employees, they use tools to assist workers. In particular, collaborative tools help workers share their ideas and progress, and make it easy for managers to contribute and guide the work.

Source: Adapted from Riva Richmond, "It's 10 a.m. Do You Know Where Your Workers Are?" *The Wall Street Journal,* January 12, 2004.

FIGURE 14.8

Telecommuting: In the simplest form of telecommuting, individual workers connect to office computers from their homes. An intermediate method has been used to avoid the problems of distractions and the cost of creating a home office. Workers report to satellite centers in their suburban neighborhood. Workers retain a structured environment but reduce their travel time.

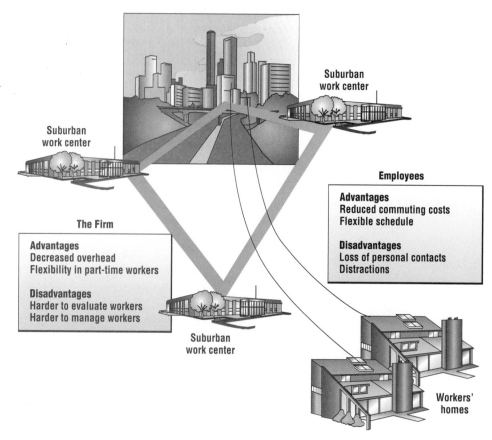

Suburban work center

Suburban work center

The Firm

Advantages
Decreased overhead
Flexibility in part-time workers

Disadvantages
Harder to evaluate workers
Harder to manage workers

Suburban work center

Employees

Advantages
Reduced commuting costs
Flexible schedule

Disadvantages
Loss of personal contacts
Distractions

Workers' homes

Intellectual Property

Intellectual property is the general term to describe ownership of ideas (patents) and creative expressions (copyrights). For many years, there was a solid distinction between the two: ideas involving physical items (such as machines) could be patented. A **patent** essen-

Problem: How do you deal with multiple languages and currencies?

Tools: Global business presents several challenges. Some, such as cultural issues, are too hard to handle with technology. Others, such as foreign exchange conversion and even some language translation, can be handled by automated systems. However, before you use these systems, you need to understand their features and limitations.

Items sold in one nation are usually priced in the national currency. Products in Europe might be priced in the national currency or in euros. Currencies exchanges are handled by banks or by specialty foreign exchange (FX) brokers. Due to international trade, large banks buy and sell currencies and record the going exchange rates. Currently, the United States uses a floating exchange rate, where the rate changes constantly in response to trade and interest rate differentials. Other nations, such as China or the member European Union countries, fix their exchange rates so that they change only when major economic conditions force a revaluation. Since the rates change, you need to convert currencies on a specific date. The other challenge with exchange rates is that the commonly cited rates are from large interbank transactions. Most people do not get to use those rates and have to pay additional fees to banks or brokers. For example, many credit card transactions use the interbank rates and then tack on 2 percent as a fee. Physically exchanging currencies at a border or airport kiosk will cost you even more in fees.

Oanda is probably the most powerful online FX converter (www.oanda.com/convert). It automatically converts between any two currencies (from 164) on a specified date, using interbank or typical credit card rates. You can use the system to convert prices on your Web site for customers in other countries.

Foreign Currency	1 U.S. Dollar Equals
Euro (EUR)	0.83724
Japanese yen (JPY)	106.650
British pound (GBP)	0.54975
Australian dollar (AUD)	1.32556
Mexican peso (MXN)	11.27800

Language translation is another challenge you need to solve to compete in world markets. Ultimately, you need to have Web sites (and product documentation) translated by human experts. However, if you happen to receive a note or see a Web site in a foreign language, or if you simply want to know the meaning of a few words, you can use the automated online translators. Several free translation systems are on the Web. The babel.altavista.com site is one that has been around for several years. Some experimental translation software is becoming good enough that it matches human translators. However, for now you are still better off hiring a person to translate Web sites and documents that will be read by customers. The online sites are useful for quick, approximate translations into your language. In most cases, you should be able to understand the gist of the document, even if it contains errors or poorly worded phrases. An interesting way to test the sites is to enter a phrase in your language (say, English); translate it to a second language (say, Spanish); and then ask the system to translate that phrase back (to English). See how far off it is from the original phrase.

To use this system, simply enter the text in English. Select the new language, then push the button to translate it. Then copy the text and translate it back to English.

Para utilizar este sistema, incorpore simplemente el texto. Seleccione la nueva lengua, después empuje el botón para traducirlo. Después copie el texto y tradúzcalo de nuevo a inglés.

In order to use this system, it incorporates the text simply. Select the new language, later pushes the button to translate it. Later it copies the text and tradúzcalo again to English.

Quick Quiz:

1. What cautionary messages do global Web sites use when converting currencies?

2. If you cannot afford a human translator, is it better to leave your Web site in English or to use a machine translation?

tially grants a monopoly to an inventor for a fixed period of time (originally 17 years in the United States but now 20 years). During that time, no other company can introduce a similar device—even if the second creator did not use any knowledge from the first inventor. A **copyright** is created for other creative works—traditionally writing and music. It protects the specific article from being copied and grants the owner the sole right to create derivative works (such as a sequel). But it does not prevent others from creating similar works. For example, one person could write a story about space explorers. Someone else could also write a story about space explorers, and it would not be an infringement on the first story. If the second story used the same characters and plot, it might be an infringement, but it might not, depending on the interpretation of the courts. In the mid-1990s, the U.S. patent office began granting patents for nonphysical items—specifically for business ideas. Patents were supposed to be granted only for nontrivial ideas, but for a while, the patent office got carried away and forgot that patents are only supposed to be granted for "nontrivial and nonobvious" inventions. For instance, it granted a business process patent to Amazon.com for one-click checkout of Web sales; so no other Web site was allowed to offer a checkout system with a single click without paying royalties to Amazon.

The goal of patents and copyrights is to encourage creativity by offering protected rewards to innovators. Remember from economics that without a barrier to entry, any firm

REALITY BYTES   Is Television Watching You?

Today, many people are aware of the privacy implications of credit data and even computer use. Few are knowledgeable about the new digital video recorders (DVRs), such as the TiVo service. Many people have fallen in love with the DVR technology that enables them to pause broadcasts and even replay various segments. The system digitizes the signal and stores it on a hard drive so that it can be replayed on demand. What many people do not realize is that TiVo and a few similar services provide viewer information back to a central system. Hence, TiVo was able to report that Janet Jackson's "wardrobe malfunction" in the 2004 Superbowl halftime was the most replayed event.

The TiVo system uses the feedback data to provide more information and options to customers. For example, it can suggest similar movies or automatically record shows that you might not have known about.

But there is nothing to stop the company from using the data for more sophisticated analysis. For example, researchers have been experimenting with statistically mining the viewer data along with Nielsen data to provide specific profiles of every viewer. For example, Dr. William Spangler notes that "we know, for instance, that people who tend to watch bass fishing shows weekly and golf and the sitcom *Friends* are men aged 45 to 50 with a certain income." The system could then deliver ads targeted specifically to each viewer.

Source: Adapted from Alison Bass, "Customer Care," *CIO,* January 12, 2004; and William E. Spangler, Mordechai Gal-Or, and Jerrold H. May, "Using Data Mining to Profile TV Viewers," *Communications of the ACM,* December 2003.

that makes a profit will attract competitors. Patents and copyrights are designed to be barriers to entry for a limited time. But the laws were written in decades when the goal was to protect companies from other companies. For instance, before computers, only a large company would be able to copy a book and reprint it. The laws made it clear that this action was illegal, and the injured party could easily find and sue the single violator for damages. Several exemptions to the copyright law were specifically created to support important noninfringing uses that are considered valuable to society. For example, educational institutions can make limited copies of items for discussion and research.

Digital content changes most of the underlying assumptions of the intellectual property discussion. First, it is easy for anyone to make perfect copies. Second, it is equally easy for everyone to distribute those copies—at virtually no cost. Instead of a large competitor, now the threat is millions of your own customers. Some of these issues are cultural and economic. For example, some industry-sponsored reports indicate that software piracy in Southeast Asia is huge: over 90 percent of software in use is copied. Nations such as Vietnam do not have the tradition of paying for creative works and do not have much money to pay for them.

The most famous case of these copyright issues involved the company called Napster. Napster was a pure Internet firm that ran a Web site to make it easy for consumers to find and share digital music files. In an attempt to stay within the copyright laws, Napster did not store any files and did not charge for its services. Instead, it was simply a giant directory. Individuals searching for specific songs went to the Napster site, found a fellow enthusiast with a desired file, and copied the file from the other's machine. Napster lost the ensuing lawsuit from the music industry. But the battle is far from over. Napster made it easy by providing a single target to sue. What if there is no central company directing the copying?

In response to these problems, the United States passed the Digital Millennium Copyright Act (DMCA). One of the most important changes in the act, and the most contested today, is a provision that makes it illegal to circumvent any copyright protection scheme. In existing cases, this provision has been interpreted to mean that any discussion of how to circumvent protection is illegal. The first case pursued under this provision relates to DVD movie disks and the DeCSS program. DVD files are encrypted so that they can be played only on specific machines with authorized software. The files are only weakly protected. Direct from the manufacturer, the files can be copied to other computers, but can only be viewed with the special software. Since that software did not originally exist for some computer systems (notably Linux), a few experts found a way to defeat the encryption. They posted this method (known as DeCSS) on the Internet. The movie studios promptly sued every Web site that carried the program for violating the DMCA. Many people are con-

FIGURE 14.9

Digital rights management: Authors create manuscripts that the publisher converts into an e-book format and transfers to a company running a digital asset server. The customer finds the book and purchases it at an e-commerce vendor. The vendor uses a typical bank system to collect the retail price and then sends the purchase information to the DAS. The DAS encrypts the book with the security specified by the publisher and transfers the book to the customer. The DAS keeps a percentage of the costs and settles the publisher account.

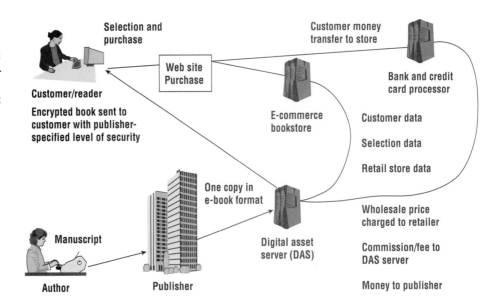

cerned that these actions violate the spirit of free speech and open discussion. Of course, whether or not the movie industry wins the case is almost irrelevant. One key factor of the Internet is that it is impossible to destroy knowledge once it has been created. Several Web sites in foreign nations that do not support the DMCA carry the information.

Digital books are soon going to face similar issues. Even printed books can be copied relatively easily today. However, it is hard to distribute them, so publishers have not been overly concerned. Digital books will exist online just as software and music files do today. To prevent mass copying, Microsoft and Adobe have created similar but incompatible systems utilizing **digital rights management (DRM).** Digital rights management systems provide copies over the Internet directly to the consumer and activate each copy for the specific machine. They also register the copy and the consumer with a central server. Ultimately, DRM could be used for any form of digital content. With DRM, the publisher can completely control the use and distribution of the copyrighted work, even to the point of specifying that the book cannot be loaned or even transferred to another person. These systems solve the problem from the perspective of the vendor—until someone breaks the protection system. Even though it would be illegal in the United States to break the system, many people will undoubtedly make the attempt. More important, will consumers accept the many restrictions and potential privacy invasion?

Figure 14.9 shows one of the DRM systems in use today. While Microsoft deliberately kept the traditional publisher, wholesaler, and retailer roles, it is possible for one firm to combine many of these steps. For example, a publisher could run the digital asset server (DAS) as well as the e-commerce store and maintain complete control over distribution.

The real issue that consumers and society must eventually face is the level of security applied to the digital content. Microsoft's method supports three levels: (1) sealed with a base encryption that prevents the contents from being modified, (2) inscribed with the purchaser's username, making it possible to track the source of any pirated copies, and (3) *owner exclusive* books that are encrypted so that they can be read only on machines activated by the specified owner. The book cannot be given to anyone else. Music publishers are evaluating even stronger security rules. For instance, it is possible to protect a song so that it can be played only one time—every time a customer wants to hear the song, he or she would have to pay an additional fee. Monthly subscription fees are a more common approach (e.g., www.pressplay.com). Customers pay a monthly fee that enables them to listen to a certain number of songs each month. If the customer drops the subscription service, he or she would no longer be able to play any of the downloaded material.

The flip side of copyrights is the argument that content should be free. But who would take the time to create useful content if it is free to everyone? Stephen King, the noted author, ran an experiment in the late 1990s. He wrote a novella and began writing a novel in installments. He distributed them through his Web site. He attracted hundreds of thousands of visitors and free downloads. He ultimately stopped the projects because of lack of revenue (it was more profitable for him to devote his time to paying projects).

Balance of Power

Some of the issues with intellectual property arise because of questions of balance of power between the creator, the publisher, the retailer, and the consumers. For instance, the Internet, with its digital content, provides the opportunity for authors and creators to circumvent the traditional publishers. Currently, authors receive only a small portion of the list price of an item. Retailers, distributors, and publishers take the majority of the money. In a world that requires distribution of physical items, these are the costs you must pay to reach consumers. In a digital world, anyone can sell products directly to consumers. Of course, it will be simpler and more cost-effective when consumers adopt a small-payments mechanism. The point is that the few large publishers in each industry have a strong interest in maintaining control over the distribution system, so most proposals have catered to these large firms. For example, the DRM systems keep the role of the retailers and the publishers, so the costs to consumers are likely to remain high.

The changing laws offer even more potential to change the balance of power between vendors and consumers. In particular, many larger software vendors have been pushing states to adopt the Uniform Computer Information Transactions Act (UCITA). The laws based on this system dramatically alter the balance of power between digital content vendors and customers. For instance, the laws make shrink-wrap licenses binding agreements—even though the customer cannot read them until after purchasing the product. It also makes it legal for the vendor to remotely disable any products if the vendor suspects the customer might be in violation of the "agreements." Traditional commercial law provides due process for handling disputes between vendors and customers. UCITA throws these processes away and gives substantial control to the vendor, including the ability to disclaim warranties. Many businesses and individuals are concerned about these provisions and are fighting the adoption of UCITA.

All of these issues are challenging with multiple perspectives. There is no question that society needs to protect and encourage innovation. There is no doubt that technology makes

FIGURE 14.10

Elasticity of demand: With zero marginal costs and a copyright "monopoly," firms can increase their revenue by reducing prices as long as the elasticity of demand is less than −1.

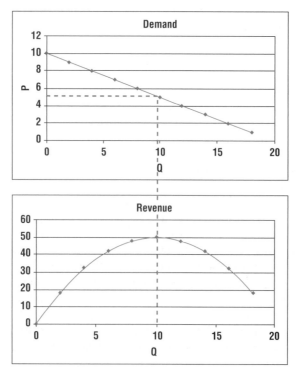

it easier for individuals to copy and distribute protected works. And it is economically infeasible for an innovator to sue millions of people over patent or copyright violations. The issues also revolve around important economic issues. Digital content essentially has zero cost to copy and distribute (but high fixed costs to create). Some people are willing to pay higher prices for the content than others are. So it is difficult to set prices on these products. Setting high prices restricts the product to an elite group of wealthy consumers and tempts people to break the law and copy the item. Setting low prices may not attract enough revenue to cover the development costs. As shown in Figure 14.10, the concept of elasticity of demand is a useful tool for identifying the best price point for digital products. Digital products have no marginal cost to produce or distribute, and generally have a "monopoly" granted by copyright laws. No one else can legally distribute the exact same product. Economics shows that this type of company makes the most money by reducing prices to the point where the elasticity of demand is equal to -1. In comparison to traditional paper-based books (or CD-based music) that do have marginal costs of production, the more traditional products will carry a higher price and lower sales. So eventually, digital products should cost less than their traditional counterparts. However, the analysis does not consider the issue of illegal copying, and it would ultimately require elimination of the middle distribution layers (retail outlets).

Education and Training

Can information technology change education? For hundreds of years, the principles and techniques of education have changed only slightly. As new technologies are introduced, people have often declared that the world of education would change markedly. Yet few technologies have had a lasting impact on education. Television is a classic example. Although movies and news reports are sometimes used for teaching purposes, the role of television in formal education is minimal. However, it is used for informal education and for training, especially with the availability of videotapes for teaching specific tasks.

One of the drawbacks to video education is the lack of interaction and feedback. Multimedia tools that combine video, sound, and computer interaction represent one attempt to surmount this limitation. However, three basic problems arise when applying technology to education. First, technology is often expensive, especially compared with traditional methods. Second, it is time consuming to create lessons that generally are difficult to change. Third, there is little conclusive evidence that the techniques are equal to or superior to existing techniques. Especially in light of the first two problems, it is difficult to test the new technologies. In many cases, by the time prices have fallen and lessons are created, an even newer technology emerges.

Despite these obstacles, technological innovations are often used for specialized teaching purposes. For instance, interactive and multimedia computer tools can be used to provide more in-depth study for advanced students or to handle repetitive drills for those students needing extra work. Increasingly available two-way video links are used to connect teachers and students in remote locations.

The main questions regarding technology in education are summarized in Figure 14.13. Note that nontraditional areas have been faster to adopt the technologies, for example, business training classes—partly to reduce the cost of hiring instructors and partly because the lessons are available to workers at any time and can be studied at whatever speed the student desires.

The Internet is increasingly being pushed as a means to expand the reach of higher education. Several universities are experimenting with offering individual courses over the Internet. The early examples often consisted of simple e-mail-based systems where students worked on their own and occasionally sent messages to the instructor. A few organizations, such as the University of the South, currently offer complete programs over the Internet. Eventually, these programs will evolve, particularly as Internet transmission speeds improve to offer more interactive communication.

The real key to online education is to use all of the power of the technology to develop entirely new applications. Communication is only one aspect of the Internet. Building more intelligence into the applications to create entirely new procedures will lead to more useful tools. Researchers have worked for years to develop computer-assisted instruction tools that will provide individualized attention to each student. While some individual products have been successful, these tools require considerable creativity and effort to create.

Social Interactions

How does technology affect different areas of society? As any good science fiction book illustrates, advances in technology can alter society in many different ways. Sometimes the responses are hard to predict, and they often occur gradually, so it can be difficult to spot patterns. At the moment, four patterns appear to be important: social group power, equal access to technology, e-mail freedom, and liability and control over data.

Social Group Legitimacy

One interesting feature of technology is that it has substantially lowered communication costs, including the costs of producing and distributing information to large public groups. For example, desktop publishing systems enable groups to create professional-quality documents at low cost. Furthermore, video production facilities are easily affordable by any group, and access to mass markets is provided free through *public-access channels* on cable television. Web sites can be created by anyone. These technologies enable small groups to reach a wider audience for minimal cost.

The only catch is that with growing professionalism of small-group productions, it becomes harder to distinguish fact from fiction, and it is harder for the public to tell the difference between mainstream, professional commentary and radical extremists. For example, do you believe stories that are printed in *The New York Times?* What about stories printed in supermarket tabloids that sport titles such as "Space Alien Eats Movie Star"? Now consider the Internet and run some searches on medical questions. You will find hundreds of Web sites and comments. Which ones do you believe? Web sites present the strongest challenge ever to trust and reliability issues. Literally anyone can create a site and say anything. Nonsensical comments will be found by the search engines and displayed along with accurate statements. Consider the examples in Figure 14.11 and see if you can determine which one to believe.

This issue has some interesting effects. For example, in several instances, disgruntled customers have created sites criticizing companies. If you search for a particular company, you are likely to encounter several of these sites. The Web makes it easy for people to criticize anyone—and the entire world can see the results. Of course, traditional defamation laws still apply, but in situations where there is an element of truth, companies will find it difficult to stop these activities.

The same issues can be applied to television broadcasts, except that for the moment, the high costs of broadcasts restrict this option to a few participants. With his "War of the Worlds" broadcast, Orson Welles shocked many listeners because they had come to accept radio broadcasts as fact. With existing technology, it is possible to create realistic-looking fictional broadcasts. It is not even necessary to resort to tricks such as hidden explosive charges. It is possible to create computer-generated images that exceed the quality of broadcast signals, so they appear to be realistic. Advertisers have made heavy use of these techniques. Every time you watch a commercial, you should remind yourself that a portion of what you are seeing is probably a computer-generated image. Now, imagine what would happen if an extremist organization used this same technology to create newscasts with altered pictures.

Access to Technology

Picture a world in which financial instruments are traded electronically, goods are purchased through computer-television systems, libraries are converted to electronic media,

FIGURE 14.11

A test of cynicism: Which Web site do you believe? Why? Would it help to know that the one on the left is from an independent chiropractor (ArthritisCure.com) and the one on the right from the BBC? With information technology, anyone can create a Web site. It can be difficult to determine the "truth." Of course, in many cases, truth may be only shades of gray, and there seldom are any "right" answers. All consumers must learn to challenge everything (even the report from the BBC).

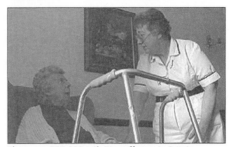

Sunday, 29 October, 2000, 17:34 GMT

Scientists closer to arthritis 'cure'

There are 750,000 arthritis sufferers in Britain

A new arthritis treatment developed by British scientists may lead to a cure for the crippling disease.

Initial trials of the drug treatment have exceeded all expectations with only two out of 20 patients showing no benefits.

A team from University College in London announced details of their treatment method at an international medical conference on Monday.

Astounding All-Natural Arthritis Breakthrough Gives Joint Pain Relief to Millions!!

Long Lasting Arthritis Relief...Naturally!

A local Doctor in Gaithersburg, Maryland has helped hundreds of his patients suffering with arthritis to drastically reduce (even eliminate in most cases!) their joint pain in 30 days or less! Here's his amazing secret weapon.. (Hint: It does not involve the use of arthritis medication!)

Dr. M. Kureshi, D.C.

- Clinical Director of Gaithersburg Pain Relief Center, P.A.
- Founder of Natural Medical Solutions, Inc.
- Has successfully helped thousands of Arthritis sufferers ease their pain naturally, without traditional arthritis medication.

FIGURE 14.12

International bandwidth: Access to the Internet requires more than computers; it requires high-speed communication lines between nations and continents. As noted by www.telegeography. com, most connections are between the United States and Europe.

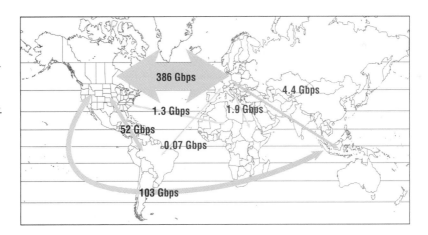

and businesses require suppliers to exchange data over computer links. Large portions of the United States and Europe are getting closer to this scenario every day. Now, what happens to the individuals in poorer nations who can barely afford to eat, much less invest in personal and national information systems? If the means of production are based on technology and certain groups do not have access, the gap between those who have access and those who do not (the **digital divide**) will widen. Although some groups will be content to live without technology, some will become upset at the imbalance.

Figure 14.12 shows that access to the Internet requires more than simple PCs and software. Individuals need access to telecommunication lines. More important, nations need high-bandwidth connections to other nations. The figure shows the currently installed bandwidth between major world regions. Note the major connections between the United States

FIGURE 14.13

Information technology in education: The technology has the potential to change education, particularly in terms of individualized attention, course management, and distance. But it is expensive and time consuming to provide the infrastructure and create new applications. Nontraditional areas such as continuing professional education (CPE), employer training, and the military have found several benefits in the technologies.

Can technology change education?
- Computer-assisted instruction to provide individual attention
- Course management
- Distance learning

Do people want more technology in education?
- Teachers
- Students
- Employers

Are the answers different for lifelong learning?
- Professionals
- Employers
- Military

and Europe, and the relatively small connections to Latin America and Africa. It takes time and money to install new fiber-optic connections across long distances. Telecommunication firms are reluctant to incur these high fixed costs until a region has enough paying customers to cover the costs with long-term usage.

Some companies have worked to give others access to technology. A few recycle older computers to libraries and citizen centers. On the international front, businesses can donate older personal computers to organizations for shipment to other countries. After three to five years, the technology is often out of date in the United States, but even old technology is better than nothing in some countries.

Wireless connections offer enormous potential to nations that cannot afford to install fiber-optic connections across their countryside. Wireless is particularly convenient and substantially cheaper to install in high-density areas.

e-Mail Freedom

Some organizations have observed an interesting feature when they first replaced paper mail with electronic-mail systems. The first people to use the technology are generally younger, more likely to take risks, and bolder than the typical employee. If the top management levels accept and respond to electronic messages, they are likely to get a different perspective on the organization, its problems, and potential solutions. E-mail systems provide a means for employees (and sometimes customers) at the lower levels to bypass the hierarchy of middle management. A few directed comments and words of encouragement can enhance this effect, which is useful if managers are searching for new approaches to solving problems.

Liability and Control of Data

Virtually all of our legal structures and interpretations were created before the advent of a computerized society. Although federal and state governments have passed a few laws specifically to address problems with computer interaction, most legal systems still rely on laws and definitions created for a paper-based world. Sometimes these concepts do not fit well in a computerized environment. For example, how would you classify the operator of a Web site? Is that person a publisher of information, like a newspaper? Or is the operator merely a vendor offering disk space to anonymous writers? In particular, are the owners of Web sites responsible for the content of messages posted on their systems? To date, the court systems have tended to make the decision based on whether the owners exercise "editorial control." In 1995, the New York supreme court ruled that Prodigy could be sued for libel. An anonymous writer posted a message that was highly critical of the financial status of a certain firm. The firm claimed that the comments were false and sued Prodigy for publishing false information. Since its inception, Prodigy maintained a policy of forbidding people to post "profane" messages. The Prodigy staff used software to scan messages. The court noted that these actions constituted editorial control, so Prodigy could be treated as any other publisher of information (like a newspaper). These concepts were later clarified into law. Now, Web sites that do not exercise control over the content are merely distribution channels (like booksellers) and cannot be held liable for the content. However, many Web hosting companies place restrictions on content (such as pornography) and will remove a site that is reported to violate its policies.

Government

Can information technology improve governments? Following the expansion of the Internet, the concept of e-government became popular. In some ways, government agencies are similar to businesses. Most federal and state agencies now provide data and communications via the Internet. Some are quite sophisticated.

Government Representatives and Agencies

Governments can be slow to adopt new technologies. Typically, government agencies have limited budgets, long procurement cycles, and requirements for special allocations to acquire new technology. They tend to have smaller IS staffs, who also receive less pay than their counterparts in private business. Moreover, government projects tend to be large and involve thousands of people, which makes them expensive, harder to create, and more difficult to implement.

In the United States, the federal government has begun to provide information and responses to questions via the Internet. It is even possible to send electronic mail to the president—although the mail is actually read and answered by assistants. Almost all federal data is available in computer form. Many agencies are positioning themselves as providers of economic data to facilitate business decisions. Fedstats (www/fedstats.gov) is one of the best starting points for finding data produced by federal agencies. Even municipal governments are beginning to post notices and data on the Internet. Most government agencies are still nervous about electronic commerce. One of the main problems they face is the inability to positively identify consumers over the Internet. Of course, government agencies operate on government time. Little has been done to reduce the time it takes to release government data. For example, data reports from the 2000 census are being released over a five-year time period. Data from many agencies is months or years out of date when it is released. Furthermore, many economic statistics are revised over time, so preliminary numbers you see one month may be replaced with different values several months later. Nonetheless, the government agencies are important sources for many types of data.

Politicians campaigning for office also use technology. For many years government officials have used databases to track letters and comments, solicit contributions, and tailor speeches to specific audiences. Politicians still rely on television to create images, but Web sites are commonly used to provide detailed position papers and background information that is too long to be covered in depth by traditional media.

Democracy and Participation

The U.S. Constitution and its amendments clearly recognize that democracy requires the participation of the citizens. And participation requires that citizens be informed—hence the importance of the press. Information is required to produce knowledge, which can lead to wisdom and better decisions. More important, it is not always clear exactly what information will be useful later. The Internet is a powerful source of information. Of course, distinguishing fact from fiction is critical. Yet today it is still possible for a nation to control the content available within its borders. China maintains its hold by owning and controlling all routers that connect to the Internet. Ultimately, it may become impossible for a nation to control all information. Between the massive data flows, encryption, automated document translation, and wireless capabilities, it will become increasingly difficult to control data.

Voting

With the fiasco of the 2000 U.S. election, people began to realize the deplorable status of existing voting systems. The level of mistakes due to machine, user, and counter error is

REALITY BYTES Controlling Access to the Internet

Although more than 1 billion people live in China, few have access to the Internet at their homes. Instead, Internet cafés became a popular method of getting information, sending e-mail, or playing games. The Chinese government controls the Internet through several mechanisms. For example, all routers connecting to the Internet are owned by the government. In March 2004, China closed 8,600 Internet cafés—most of them for illegally admitting juveniles. Xinhua, the official Chinese news agency, reported that "any such place allowing juveniles to enter or allowing unhealthy information to spread through the Internet will face rigid, severe penalty." Internet cafés are also banned within 200 meters of a school. The General Admin-

istration for Industry and Commerce argues that the cafés "have brought great harm to the mental health of teenagers and interfered with the school teaching, which has aroused strong reaction from the public." In one sad case in April 2004, two teenagers spent more than 48 hours playing an online video game in an Internet café in Chongqing. They were killed by a train when they fell asleep on a railroad track. Now, if the Chinese government could do something about the spam originating from Chinese servers, maybe the rest of the world would understand.

Source: Adapted from "China Shuts More Than 8,600 Internet Cafés," *eWeek*, May 6, 2004.

FIGURE 14.14

Electronic voting requirements: Electronic voting sounds convenient and easy to set up—until you look at the detailed requirements. Many avenues for fraud exist. Besides, complex systems are hard to create and susceptible to errors.

- Prevent fraud by voters (identify voters)
- Prevent fraud by counters
- Prevent fraud by application programmers
- Prevent fraud by operating system programmers
- Prevent attacks on servers
- Prevent attacks on clients
- Prevent loss of data
- Provide ability to recount ballots
- Ensure anonymity of votes
- Provide access to all voters
- Prevent denial of service attacks
- Prevent user interface errors
- Identify and let voters correct data entry errors
- Improve on existing 1 in 6,000 to 1 in 10,000 error rates

unacceptable in a modern society. Several people have mentioned the possibility of creating electronic voting systems to provide faster and more accurate tallies of votes. But many challenges exist as shown in Figure 14.14. Several experts have testified before Congress that they do not believe current technology is capable of surmounting all of the problems. But ultimately, the question comes down to whether a superior system can be developed, even though it may not be perfect, and whether it can prevent major problems. There is a long history of building and revising voting machines in an attempt to minimize fraud and abuse. But existing machines still miscount an average of one in 6,000 to 10,000 ballots. The other serious drawback to existing systems highlighted in the 2000 election was the usability issue, where thousands of ballots were disqualified and thousands more counted incorrectly because people did not understand them.

A few people have suggested that it would be nice to implement a voting system that works as easily as ATMs or even using their own PCs to connect over the Internet. But electronic voting has two main complications over traditional electronic commerce. First, it is critical to authenticate each voter. Current e-commerce handles this step with credit cards—which are not available to all voters and not secure enough to use as a public voting identifier. (What would stop a business from assuming your identity?) Second, the votes have to be auditable, but anonymous so that no votes can be traced back to an individual. This second condition is even trickier if you are concerned about vote selling. Ideally, voters should not be able to show their final vote to anyone else. If they can, it opens the possibility of buying votes. Currently, there is little incentive to buy votes because there is no way to prove how someone voted, so no way to enforce the agreement.

Voting from your home over the Internet might take years to develop, largely because of the challenge of protecting the client computers and denial of service attacks. Security ex-

REALITY BYTES   Unusual (At the Moment) Politics

Presidential election campaigns are a singular species. To a typical citizen, the process seems straightforward: you see a bunch of negative TV campaign ads, decide all politicians are the same, and skip the election. When only 50 percent of the population bothers to vote, much of the election hinges on which people actually show up at the voting booth. In the 2004 election campaign, both Republicans and Democrats are using information technology to target not just categories of voters but individual people. Combining commercial data, electoral data, and polling, political marketers are going door-to-door with handhelds loaded with data. They can contact people individually with a specific message tailored to each person. Once friendly voters have been identified and persuaded, the campaign workers take over. On election day, they can track who has voted and who has not (polling data is public, even though your actual vote is not). Workers can compare actual voters against the campaign list and contact no-shows to make sure they get to the voting booth on time. Will these techniques influence the outcome? Even the experts assume they can only affect a couple of percentage points. But, in a tight race, a few votes in key states could make the difference in the outcome.

Source: Adapted from John Heilemann, "Rewiring the War Room," *Business 2.0,* April 2004.

perts can protect the servers and data transmissions can be protected through encryption. But how can a government ensure the security of a PC in your house? Given the level of viruses, hoaxes, and false statements on Web sites, it would seem to be relatively easy to attack millions of home computers to control an election.

On the other hand, society has an additional critical objective in designing a new voting system: the need to make it easier for people to vote to increase participation rates. To combat this problem, several states have implemented paper-based ballots shipped to each person's home. Ultimately the point is that no system is perfect, so the question quickly becomes whether an electronic vote system is better than the existing methods, and whether it is possible to prevent significant fraud. In a test of electronic voting systems in the Georgia 2001 election, almost all said the system was easy to use and over 94 percent said the entire state should move to the electronic system.

Information Warfare

As firms and entire economies become more dependent on information systems, the underlying infrastructure becomes critical to the nation. Think about how the information society will work in 10 years or so. Communication will be based on Internet protocols. B2B e-commerce will take place over the Internet, with automated agents placing orders and handling most transactions. Private and government services will be provided through Web sites. Web services will be offered through interlinked sites.

Now, imagine what happens if some nation or group decides to attack this information system. Inexperienced people using software scripts found on various Internet sites have already attacked individual companies. These denial-of-service attacks can be mounted by anyone. If an experienced, dedicated group of experts attacked a nation, they could stop service to huge segments of the economy. This threat is one aspect of the Internet that scares many agencies.

The United States and other national defense departments have begun planning for **information warfare (IW)**—in terms of both potential defenses and attacks. The ultimate objective of information warfare is to control the information available to the other side so that you can encourage them to take certain actions. This definition includes the ability to intercept communications, as well as to provide new data that will be accepted as valid. IW goes way beyond hacking into a system or destroying enemy computers and networks. In many ways, IW has been a part of war and conquest for centuries. The increasing use of computers, both in the military and in economies, has made IW more important. IW has existed in many respects from the early centuries of warfare. Some aspects became prominent in World War II, such as code breaking, the Navajo code talkers, the use of the BBC to send coded signals, and misinformation. Misinformation and control of the press (domestic and worldwide) have become key aspects to IW, particularly given the worldwide reach of CNN.

REALITY BYTES   Digital Technology at War

The second U.S./Iraq war (2003) demonstrated the use of information technologies in battle. Sitting in their Humvees, U.S. soldiers had digital street maps, could download up-to-the-minute satellite images, and received instructions from their commanders. Soldiers can use touch screens to indicate the positions of enemies, and the data is instantly shared with the other troops. Meanwhile, the commanders at base could view real-time video images of battles and troop locations. Tracked by GPS locators and aerial drones, the dozens of components make up the Army Battle Command Systems.

The experimental system is credited with reducing incidents of "friendly fire" and providing faster responses to problems or changing conditions. For example, if a suspect is seen running to a new location, the information can be shared instantly with the attack troops. But it is not foolproof. Captain Nathan Saul notes, "They're waterproof and heat-resistant, but when you boil it down it's a computer. You're driving it in dust, sand, and rain, 130-degree heat. It's going to break down."

Source: Adapted from "Digital Warfare Adapted for Iraq," *The Globe and Mail,* January 2, 2004.

Some U.S. reports indicate that the Chinese military is attempting to develop viruses that can be inserted into foreign networks to disrupt the flow of data or provide false information. Information attacks can be targeted against military or civilian objectives. Military uses of information warfare are common today. One of the first steps the U.S. air force takes is to disable the enemy's air defense systems to gain control over the enemy airspace.

Civilian attacks are still new, but the potential is huge. The military goal would be to destroy the economic ability of a nation to build and deploy weapons, but an attack would also destroy the underlying infrastructure. The Internet was originally designed to survive military attacks through decentralization and the ability to route around broken links. However, as e-commerce has evolved, several vulnerabilities have been created that would enable governments or terrorists to disrupt major sections of the Internet by attacking some critical points.

In general, the same security controls that businesses use to protect systems on a daily basis are important to defend against international attacks. Ultimately, many aspects of the Internet infrastructure need to be improved to prevent attacks by terrorists, since the underlying components were not designed with security in mind. Several Internet committees are working on these new standards.

Rise of the World-State?

In ancient history (literally), communities of people formed into city-states to share common resources and provide a common defense. Because communication was limited and transportation costs were high, the city-states were largely self-sufficient. However, merchants traveled among cities to barter products that were only available in some locations. Over many years, transportation and communication costs declined, giving rise to nation-states. Through various battles and political arrangements, people accepted the role of the national governments, although some issues are still being fought.

For years, many writers have suggested that increasing international trade, declining transportation costs, and improving global communication will eventually lead to a world-state. National governments might still exist, but commerce would be more regional and global, and world laws would be more important than national policies. The rise of the European Union and other free trade areas (such as NAFTA) are sometimes seen as forerunners of this world.

International e-commerce provides some support for this hypothesis. In an environment where digital data and services can be transferred instantly around the world, it is easy to see the irrelevance of individual national laws. With encryption and a wireless (satellite) connection, how can a national government impose rules or taxes on the digital transfer? If a serious digital monetary system is developed and accepted, how will a nation impose its independent economic policies? Some of these issues are being addressed today by global political organizations. Nations are slowly learning to cooperate and create common procedures and laws.

REALITY BYTES   National Identity Cards in the UK

In 2004, David Blunkett, the home secretary of the UK, proposed a bill that would create a detailed national identity card program. Polls show that 75 to 85 percent of the people are in favor of the cards. However, only 10 percent are "very confident" that their data would be kept secure. Two-thirds believe that civil servants will share data with each other, and half suspect they will share it with outsiders. So, why would they want the cards? Basically, they want them to stop immigrants from using public services or taking jobs. Reducing fraud and fighting terrorism would also be nice benefits.

The proposed system would collect an ambitious amount of data. The central database would hold each person's name, date of birth, passport number, national insurance data, as well as current and former addresses. Ultimately, it would be linked to other government databases and hold biometric identifiers. Some question whether it is possible to create the advanced system. One of the challenges is to obtain clean, unduplicated data for everyone. Richard Barrington, head of government affairs at Sun Microsystems, observes that "if this [data cleaning] is not done in a disciplined way, the register will become like every other government database—that is, full of junk." The track record for ambitious tracking systems is not good. In 2001, the city of Southampton issued smart cards to every resident that were supposed to allow access to all basic services. Banks, transportation systems, and even the local councils did not cooperate very well. Today, the card is mostly used to check out library books.

Source: Adapted from "Identity Cards, Will They Work?" *The Economist,* May 1, 2004, pp. 57–58.

On the other hand, a world-state would be a massively complex system that would undoubtedly be politically unstable. There are still many regional tensions and periodic fights over physical resources. It would take many years of prosperity and economic growth before nations were willing to accept a truly global government. However, in the meantime, many issues will need to be negotiated in a global setting because they are beyond the control of any national government. Some international organizations facilitate these discussions, but most are somewhat cumbersome.

Crime

Do criminals know how to use computers? Crime has many aspects—both in the Internet/information world and in the "real" world. Security issues related to protecting information systems and Web sites are discussed in detail in Chapter 5. The issues in this chapter refer to questions of how governments can combat crime in society. Criminals today have access to the same technologies as everyone else. Drug dealers and weapons merchants use encrypted spreadsheets to track their sales. Terrorists use encrypted e-mail to transfer information. Con artists use the Internet to steal money from victims. Entirely new forms of harassment and stalking have been created with chat rooms, e-mail, cell phones, and other electronic communication systems. Most people want the government to protect them from these many forms of crime. The complication is that the electronic tools make it more difficult for police to work. So you as a citizen need to identify the trade-offs you are willing to accept.

Police Powers

For years, politicians have used the threat of crime to argue for granting increased powers to police agencies. Interception and decryption of communications (wiretapping) is a classic example. The United States passed the *Communications Assistance for Law Enforcement Act* in 1994. It has taken effect and requires that when requested by the government, any telecommunication company must route any communication that passes through its facilities to an off-site U.S. government facility. The FBI similarly created the Carnivore (DCS-10000) system to monitor and record all Internet communications of a targeted person. On a global scale, the National Security Agency (NSA), in cooperation with other national partners, routinely captures and monitors international communications. Under federal mandate, wireless providers are phasing in locator systems designed to route emergency crews to callers who use cell phones. Of course, these same locator systems could be used by police to monitor the locations of suspected criminals.

REALITY BYTES — Where Are You?

Cellular phone companies in the United States have invested millions of dollars upgrading their networks to be able to provide emergency location data. Since about 50 percent of emergency calls are made from cell phones, federal law requires companies to be able to provide location data to assist in emergencies. The phone companies would like to make a profit from this feature. One answer is to sell location data to customers—both cell phone users and businesses. For example, a restaurant might pay to be able to send a text message about specials to customers in the neighborhood. A business person might want to allow a customer to check on the location of a salesperson. A parent might want the ability to track the location of a child. Of course, privacy is an important consideration. You might be willing to let your spouse track your location, but not want to be bothered by constant advertisements from shops. Bell Labs has developed a rules-based system that will enable customers to specify how they want their location data released. One of the challenges is to store and process each person's preferences without bogging down the network. Bell Labs is negotiating with companies to make the technology available in 2005 or 2006.

Source: Adapted from Bruce Meyerson, "Bell Labs to Introduce New Location Engine for Cell Phones," *eWeek*, January 19, 2004.

Two questions must always be addressed with each new technology: (1) Is the technology effective or are there other ways to accomplish the same result? (2) How can society control the use of the technology and is it worth the loss of privacy? The technology press contains many stories of abuses of power and information—including those by IRS agents and state and local police agencies. The police can also tell stories of how the criminals use modern technology to thwart investigations, and how additional police powers can be used to reduce crime.

Freedom of Speech

As constitutional scholars have long known, freedom of speech is a difficult concept. In practice, many limits are placed on individual speech to protect society. The classic example: you are not allowed to yell "Fire!" in a crowded theater (when there is no fire) because the result is dangerous to many people. Similarly, there are restrictions on "speech" on the Internet. A big element is that you cannot defame or harass others. While this statement seems obvious, what happens when people sign up with an anonymity server? They could then use free e-mail services, chat rooms, and Web sites to attack other people or companies.

The flip side of this situation is the issue of how to control these problems. Should a police agency have the ability to routinely break the anonymity server to identify all people? But that raises the question of what constitutes defamation and harassment? It is legal for a person to report truthful information about a company or an individual, but sometimes marginal in whistleblower situations. But what if the person being criticized is a public official and uses the police power to retaliate and harass the original person? Of course that action would be illegal as well, but how do you prevent it?

The main thing to remember is that there are many sides to all of these discussions. Also remember that many people have strong personal preferences on each side, and debates are often filled with emotional and unsubstantiated claims. In the coming years, these topics will become increasingly important. It is critical that you form an educated opinion and make sure that your voice is heard.

Responsibility and Ethics

How do your actions affect society? Is it possible to follow the laws and still be wrong? In any society, but particularly in one with open information, ethics and morality are important. Laws do not always keep up with changes in society. Think about small towns a century ago. A few basic laws existed, but people generally behaved responsibly, in part because if you gained a negative reputation, people would not trade with you. In an Internet world where people can write almost anything about you for others to find, it is possible that your

REALITY BYTES | Software to Identify Plagiarism

Unscrupulous students have often turned to articles and the Internet when writing papers. Copying others' work without proper attribution is a serious violation of ethics. But many felt the probability of getting caught was low. In a survey of 30,000 undergraduates, 37 percent admitted to cut-and-paste plagiarism using the Internet. Unfortunately, a few people carried this technique into the business and professional world. Several newspaper publishers were embarrassed to find reporters who copied stories. In response, several companies now provide computer systems to compare documents and identify possible cases of plagiarism. Several universities have been using systems such as iParadigms, Glatt Plagiarism Services, MyDropBox, and CFL Software Development. These tools are also available for businesses. In 2004, the *Hartford Courant* concluded that Central Connecticut State University's president, Richard Judd, had stolen at least 11 percent of an op-ed piece from others. Other organizations have found additional uses. Police and military organizations are turning to the tools to check officers' applications for promotions.

Source: Adapted from "New Software Detects Plagiarized Passages," *CNN Online,* April 7, 2004.

reputation and honesty will become even more important. For example, eBay uses a ratings system to formalize these concepts. But even without worrying about your future prospects, you should strive to create an honest world.

Users

Computer users have certain responsibilities in terms of computer security and privacy. First, they have an obligation to obey the laws that pertain to computers. The U.S. government and some states, along with other nations, have laws against computer crimes. Most other traditional laws also apply to computer crimes. One law that has received much attention is the copyright law. European and U.S. copyright laws prohibit the copying of software except for necessary backup. It is the responsibility of users to keep up with the changes in the laws and to abide by them. In the last few years, software publishers have increased their efforts to stop illegal copying of software, called **software piracy.**

Although it might seem to be trivial, making illegal copies of software (or videotapes or other copyrighted works) can cause several problems. First, it takes money away from the legal owners of the software, which reduces their incentive to create new products. Second, you run the risk of hurting your employer. If employees illegally copy company-purchased software, the owners of the copyright can sue the employer. Third, copying software provides an illegal advantage over your competitors. A small design firm might decide to copy a $20,000 CAD design system instead of buying it. Consequently, honest firms are hurt because the original firm will be able to make lower bids on jobs because their costs are lower. Fourth, as an individual, you have a reputation to defend. If your friends, colleagues, or employers learn that you are willing to break the law by copying software, they can easily believe that you are willing to break other laws.

Users of computer systems also have an obligation as part of **computer ethics** to customers and clients. Most information in computer databases is confidential. It should not be revealed to anyone except authorized employees. Some nations have laws to protect this privacy. If you find a company violating these laws, it is your responsibility to question the practice.

Users have an obligation to use the information provided by computer applications appropriately. When a user sets up calculations in a spreadsheet, the user must realize that those calculations might be wrong. The calculations must be tested and the information produced should always be checked for reasonableness. You should not believe information solely because it comes from a computer. All data should be verified.

Programmers and Developers

Programmers would never get jobs if they could not be trusted. This trust is one of the most crucial requirements to being a programmer. As a programmer or developer, not only do you have to be honest, but you must also avoid any appearance of dishonesty. For example, practical jokes involving security violations can be dangerous to your career.

Programmers have more responsibilities than many other employees. Software is used in many critical areas. If a programmer attempts a job that is beyond his or her capabilities, crucial errors can be introduced. For example, consider what might happen if an underqualified person took a job programming medical life-support systems. If he or she made a mistake, a person might die. Although mistakes can be made by anyone, they are more likely to arise when a programmer attempts too difficult a job.

Along the same lines, programmers have an obligation to test everything they do. It also means that companies have the responsibility to provide adequate time for programmers to perform the tests. The important step is to identify components that are critical and to build in safeguards.

There have been enormous increases in the demand for software in the last decade. At the same time, new tools allow programmers to create much more complex applications. But our ability to create this new software has far outstripped our ability to ensure that it is error-free. Even commercial programs, such as word processors and spreadsheets, still have errors that can cause problems. In spite of the best efforts of conscientious, talented people, software used appropriately can produce erroneous information.

Liability for erroneous information produced by software has not been fully established yet. Laws and court decisions during the next few years should settle many aspects of who is responsible when software makes mistakes or fails. A related issue is the extent to which the user is responsible for correctly entering information needed by the program and for using the information produced by the program appropriately.

Companies

Every company has obligations to society, customers, employees, and business partners. In terms of society, a firm must obey all relevant laws. For customers, firms must ensure privacy of data. That means companies will collect only the data that they truly need. The data must be safeguarded so that only those who need it for their job have access. If customer information is sold or distributed for other purposes, customers should be notified. Consumers must be allowed to remove their names from any distribution lists.

For employees, a company must provide training and monitoring (compliance programs) to ensure they understand the laws and are following them. Firms must provide sufficient funds to allow the employees to meet their individual responsibilities. Companies must provide enough time and money to test software adequately. Firms have an obligation to allow their employees a certain amount of privacy. For instance, companies have no reason to routinely monitor and read employees' electronic mail messages.

Companies are required to abide by all partnership agreements. In terms of computers, they must safeguard all data acquired from partners. They must not use the data in a manner that would injure the firms involved.

Governments

Federal, state, and local governments have obligations to establish laws that provide a means for those unfairly injured to allow them to gain compensation from those who did the damage. Until the 1980s, relatively few laws at any level were specifically directed at computer usage. Instead, laws intended for other purposes were stretched to cover computer crimes. Frequently, citing mail fraud laws was the only recourse. Some criminals were not convicted because the crime was considered "victimless" by the jury, or the injured corporation declined to prosecute.

Starting in the mid-1980s, the federal government and nearly every state passed new laws concerning computer crime. In 1986, the Computer Fraud and Abuse Act and the Electronic Communications Privacy Act were enacted. The Computer Fraud and Abuse Act makes it a federal crime to alter, copy, view, or damage data stored in computers subject to federal law. The law provides fines of up to $100,000 and up to 20 years in prison. The Computer Abuse Amendments Act of 1994 expanded the original definitions to include transmission of harmful code such as viruses. It distinguishes between actions taken "with reckless disregard" for potential damages (misdemeanor) and intentionally harmful acts

REALITY BYTES   Would You Lie to Your Insurance Company?

Most people have heard of polygraphs ("lie detectors") that measure basic statistics such as heart rate and perspiration rate. They operate on the theory that people who lie undergo stress in the process. Most people know that polygraphs cannot be used against you in a criminal case in the United States—largely because of the unreliability. Several software companies offer software packages that claim to be relatively accurate at evaluating stress due to lies during a phone call. In 2004, several large UK insurance companies including Halifax General Insurance began testing the voice-risk analysis software, originally developed for Israeli security forces. When customers report losses, claims adjusters can monitor the system to see if they are making false claims or inflating the number of items lost. The claims adjuster uses the immediate responses to pinpoint possible issues and press the claimant for details. In a three-month trial, Halifax said the system resulted in 12 percent of the claims being withdrawn by the client, rejected by Halifax, or passed on for fraud investigation.

U.S. insurers are watching the technology closely. A study by consulting firm Accenture in 2003 revealed that up to 25 percent of policyholders believe it is acceptable to lie to insurance companies. Fraud is estimated to cost insurers $80 billion a year.

Although customers might be concerned about the invasion of privacy, the system can work to the benefit of honest policyholders. UK auto insurer Highway Insurance Holdings used the software for 18 months. With the 70 percent of the calls cleared by the system, claims were handled immediately, reducing settlement time from 14 to 10 days. The other 30 percent were passed to investigators for detailed follow-up. Of those, 60 percent were found to be fraudulent. One strength of the technology is that claimants are notified up front that they are being monitored—making it less likely for them to lie in the first place.

Source: Adapted from Charles Fleming, "Insurers Employ Voice-Analysis Software to Help Detect Fraud," *The Wall Street Journal*, May 17, 2004.

(felony). It also modified the language so that crimes causing damages of more than $1,000 or involving medical records are within federal jurisdiction. Furthermore, it placed controls on states in terms of selling driver's license records.

Most states have enacted similar laws for the few computers that might not be subject to federal law. European countries have been ahead of the United States in developing legislation to deal with computer crime.

Legislation, enforcement, and judicial interpretation have not kept up with changes in technology. A major question that is unresolved is the extent to which copyright law applies to the "look and feel" of software. For example, Lotus Corporation sued Borland because Borland's Quattro Pro spreadsheet used menu titles similar to those used by the Lotus 123 spreadsheet. Some people are calling for legislation making it illegal to *write* a computer virus program, although there is some question that such a law might be an unnecessary restriction on freedom of speech or freedom of the press. In fact, there is considerable discussion over whether electronic mail and Web site operators should be treated as members of the press and receive First Amendment protections.

In terms of enforcement, most federal, state, and local agencies have few, if any, officers devoted to solving computer crimes. In fact, many software piracy cases have been pursued by U.S. Secret Service agents. One complication is that most law enforcement agencies lack proper training in computer usage and investigation of computer crimes.

A Summary of Important Computer-Related Laws

What major laws affect technology and the use of computers? Laws form the foundation of society. They provide the structure that enables businesses to exist. As society changes, the laws must also be changed. Hence, as the use of computers grows, we can expect to see more laws governing their use. Existing laws will be extended and new ones created. To date, computer laws have been concerned with three primary areas: property rights, privacy, and crime. These areas overlap, and they cannot cover all possible issues. As information technology and robotics become entwined into all our activities, virtually any law can be applied or interpreted to the situation.

Laws continually change and new interpretations and applications regularly arise. You will generally need a lawyer to help you understand and apply the current laws. This short

REALITY BYTES   Governments Collect Huge Amounts of Data—And Resell It

Ambulance chasing has gone high-tech. Julie and Dennis Danielson's son suffers from a mental illness condition that requires medication. One night he did not come home, and they were concerned. He had been arrested on the mistaken belief that his erratic behavior at a casino was drug related. A couple of days later, Julie received at least a dozen letters—generated only hours after her son's arrest—from defense attorneys offering their services. The county sheriff routinely sends e-mail notices to lawyers. SpeedingTicket.net has turned the process into a business. The company pays states 10 to 30 cents for each courthouse record that it downloads—providing $1.7 million in revenue to the state of North Carolina. It then resells the data to attorneys for 50 cents to over a dollar. The company is expanding its operations into several other states. Company founder John White says that attorneys report that 10 percent of the people contacted end up calling—a solid advertising response rate. Defense attorney Charles Kish, whose southern California firm sent one of the letters to the Danielsons, sent 50,000 letters in 2003 and received 4,000 responses, generating 300 clients.

The Danielsons are concerned about the invasion of privacy, but even more upset that the sheriff's office notified attorneys but did not bother to call the parents—even though their son carried contact information. After several similar complaints, William Kenison, Riverside County's deputy counsel, asked the sheriff to stop e-mailing the daily arrest record to attorneys. He calls the lawyers "bottom feeders."

Although the automatic e-mails have stopped, other companies provide similar services. The data is available to the public. United Reporting Publishing Corp. stations employees at several California county courthouses. Dave Fisher, news director, states, "We send people to courthouses with laptops, digital scanners, even digital cameras. We have to convert it all, effectively digitize the information. If the person gets arrested before 11 (a.m.), we'll have it that day."

Source: Adapted from "Database Tech Helps Lawyers Scoop Up Clients," *CNN Online,* March 29, 2004.

---

appendix can provide you with only a limited background. You can find additional information in many places on the Web. This information will help you identify problems and generally enable you to obey the laws. However, a lawyer is still the best source of information—particularly if you anticipate problems or conflicts.

Property Rights

A property right gives you ownership and control over an object. While the term originated with physical property, the more important issues now involve intellectual property. If you write a book, a song, or a computer program, you should be able to receive money from sales of that item. Copyright, patent, trademark, and trade secret laws provide definitions of ownership and control transfer of these rights. They provide you with the opportunity to prevent others from using or stealing your work. Each of the four types of property-rights laws applies to different material.

Copyrights are used for books, songs, and computer software. The laws apply to the specific item, such as a book. You cannot copyright a general concept. For example, you can obtain a copyright for a specific word processing application. But other people are free to write similar applications, as long as they do not utilize your specific code or text. Copyrights generally last for 50 years after the death of the writer. In the case of a work produced by a group of workers in a company, the copyright lasts for 75 years after the publication of the work. After that time, the work falls into the public domain, where anyone can use or copy it with no restraints.

Patents were originally designed for mechanical devices, although today you can receive a patent for any device that is innovative and useful. For many years, computer software applications could not receive patents because "laws of nature" including mathematical algorithms were specifically excluded. In the last few years, the U.S. Patent Office has changed this interpretation and now grants patents for computer software. A U.S. patent right exists for 20 years from the date the application was filed. The strength of a patent is that it prevents other people from creating a similar product, even if they do not directly copy your work. Consequently, a patent is much more difficult to obtain than a copyright.

Trademarks are used to create a unique name. Once you find and trademark a name (or logo), no one else can use that name without your permission. It is relatively easy to obtain a trademark, except that you must find a name that no one else has already chosen.

Trade secret laws provide you with the ability to seek damages if someone steals your secret information. The catch is that you are responsible for protecting the information. The laws are generally used to enforce a nondisclosure agreement (NDA). If a company wants to work with another company or a consultant, it is a good idea to have the outsiders sign an NDA, in which they agree not to reveal any information you share. If you forget to have them sign an NDA and they release your "secret" information, you will have few options. It is your responsibility to protect the data.

These four basic protections have different purposes and different strengths and weaknesses. Copyrights and trademarks are relatively easy and inexpensive to obtain. You simply fill out a form, submit the material, and wait a few months for the agency to process the request. Actually, a copyright exists as soon as you create the material. You do not need to file the registration form. However, there are some legal and monetary advantages to registering the copyright. Patents require considerable documentation and a formal review to identify prior and related patents and to determine the legitimacy of the innovation. They usually require the help of a specialized law firm, take at least a year to obtain, and will probably cost about $10,000 in legal and processing fees. Trade secret protection requires no registration with the government, but requires you to create and enforce a security policy to ensure that your information is adequately protected.

In a digital age, copyright law is the most challenging to apply and to enforce. The first question is identifying ownership. Who owns a particular item? If you write a book on your own time with your own resources, then generally you own the rights. If you write a computer program for your employer as part of your job, the employer owns the copyright. Interestingly, if you are an outside contractor and create a program for a company, it is more likely that you own the copyright, unless you agree to transfer the rights.

There is an interesting exception to copyright law: mere collections of data cannot be copyrighted. Consider the example of *Feist Publications v. Rural Telephone Service* [499 U.S. 340 (1991)]. Feist wanted to publish a telephone directory, but Rural would not provide the data. So Feist copied much of the data from Rural's printed directory. The U.S. Supreme Court eventually ruled that Feist's action was not a copyright infringement because the directory contained only data, which is not sufficiently original to obtain a copyright. Now consider the case of *ProCD, Inc. v. Zeidenberg* [86 F3d 1447 (7th Cir. 1996)]. ProCD collects and publishes a CD-based list of phone numbers and addresses, which they generally obtain from printed phone directories. Zeidenberg purchased a copy of the CDs and transferred them to his Web site. He then charged people to access the site. ProCD sued for violating the copyright laws. Based on the Feist case, Zeidenberg was found innocent of copyright infringement. However, he was guilty of violating the shrink-wrap license agreement. Note that the data collection argument probably applies to most data collected by federal and state agencies.

Copyright protection gives you the ability to stop others from profiting from your work. There are a few minor exceptions—such as parody, excerpting short quotations, and educational "fair use," which allows educational institutions very limited provisions to make a limited number of copies for teaching purposes. A more interesting, unanticipated exception involves money. Consider the 1994 case of *U.S. v. LaMacchia,* who was a student running a bulletin board system on university computers. He routinely placed commercial software on the site and allowed people to download (steal) the software for their own use. The catch is that he did not charge access to the system and made no money from the process. Without this profit motive, the court ruled that LaMacchia could not be convicted on charges of criminal violation of the copyright laws. Of course, the commercial software vendors could sue him on civil grounds, but unless he was an unusually wealthy student, there would be little gain. On the other hand, the university could throw him out for violating university policy. Congress has proposed a law to modify the copyright provisions to cover this situation in the future.

Copying becomes a more serious problem every day. As more works are created and distributed in digital form, it becomes more difficult to protect them. Even though you might have a legal right to prevent copying, it becomes increasingly difficult to prevent the distribution of your work, particularly if individual ethics are weak. For example, say that you

Problem: How do you find public data and legal information?

Tools: The federal agencies and many of the state governments have established Web sites that provide a wealth of data and access to government officials. The first step in finding data is to realize that much of the actual data is not indexed by the public search engines, so you need to find a better starting point. The second step is to know that governments are organized into various departments and bureaus. Begin your search at a specific department. For example, www.census.gov is the main page for the federal Census Bureau. The Bureau of Labor Statistics (www.bls.gov), Bureau of Economic Analysis (www.bea.gov), and the IRS (www.irs.gov) are also common sites for business data. Of course, the EDGAR files by the Securities and Exchange Commission (www.sec.gov) are critical for business research. The Federal Trade Commission (www.ftc.gov) has imposed several rules that affect businesses—particularly online activities. The Patent and Trademark Office (www.uspto.gov) provides searches of patents and trademarks and helps you get started filing requests.

Useful Introductory Federal Web Sites

www.firstgov.gov	Official starting point for agencies
www.fedstats.gov	Best starting point for data searches
www.whitehouse.gov	The main White House/presidential site
www.whitehouse.gov/omb/egov	The e-government main site
thomas.loc.gov	Main legislative/congressional site
thomas.loc.gov/home/state.htm	Links to state home pages
www.loc.gov/law/guide/	Legal links for federal, state, and international
www.house.gov	House of Representatives home page
www.senate.gov	Senate home page
www.census.gov	Census Bureau home page

If you are interested in the use of information technology in government, you should periodically check two online specialty newspapers: *Government Computer News* (www.gcw.com) and *Federal Computer Week* (www.fcw.com). *Government Technology* (www.govtech.net) carries similar information on state and local governments.

In terms of pure legal resources, you can find full-text copies of legislation and proposed legislation on the government Web sites, particularly the Library of Congress (thomas.loc.gov). Several private sites offer detailed searches of laws and cases, but they usually charge for the service. Lexis and WestLaw are the largest providers. Many universities have subscriptions to these sites, so check with your library first. You can also try FindLaw (www.findlaw.com) and the Center for Regulatory Effectiveness (www.thecre.com), particularly the FedLaw site (www.thecre.com/fedlaw/default.htm). The Legal Information Institute at Cornell (www.law.cornell.edu) is also a good starting point for legal information and searches. Unfortunately, searching for laws and court cases is not as simple as Web searches. It takes practice and a little knowledge of how laws and cases are organized.

When searching for state government data, you can try starting at the state home page (see the Library of Congress list), or you can search for the specific state agency with a standard search engine. For example, most states have a Secretary of State office to handle business registrations. Unfortunately, there are almost 50 different names for the tax offices. Local governments are beginning to provide some data online, such as property tax records. You will have to search for them individually, or use a company such as KnowX (www.knowx.com) that collects and resells local and state data.

Quick Quiz:

1. Where can you find a list of government agencies and their online addresses?
2. Where can you find full-text copies of the U.S. Code? What is the U.S. Code?

write a story and sell it through your Web site. Once the first few people have read the story, they could copy it and e-mail it to their friends. What are you going to do? Arrest and sue your customers who first read the story? On the other hand, if a publisher took your story, printed it, and sold it, you clearly have the legal authority and monetary incentive to seek compensation. Consider a similar example. You build a Web site and create some interesting graphics and sound effects. Over time, other people routinely download your objects and use them on their own sites. Have they violated copyright laws? Can you stop them? Can you even find them? Would it be economically worthwhile to pursue them?

It is unlikely that individual motivations and ethics will improve. That is, despite the laws, many people will still copy anything they can (software, art, text, photos, video clips, and so on). Whatever technology might be applied, it is unlikely to be economically feasible to pursue them. Yet without incentive, why should you create and distribute new works? One possible outcome is that large, expensive content will disappear. Why should you write and distribute an entire book in one piece, when most people would steal it instead of paying $20 a copy? Instead, you could sell the book a section at a time, for a few cents per section. By releasing the sections over time, people would have to pay to receive the most recent (and organized) sections. Yes, some people might wait and have a friend pay for the section and e-mail it, but it is a question of economics. If the price is low enough, more people will opt to get the data earlier and directly from the source.

The federal white paper ("Intellectual Property and the National Information Infrastructure") contains an extended discussion of copyright issues and possible federal solutions. It is available online from the Information Infrastructure Task Force (IITF) bulletin board. You should also read Pamela Samuelson's criticism of the white paper proposal, which points out that the discussion strongly favors copyright holders as opposed to the public, particularly since the primary author (Bruce Lehman) was a lobbyist for the copyright industry.

Privacy

Privacy is an intriguing concept. Humans are a social group: we can accomplish far more by living in communities and sharing our talents. Yet individuals have a desire to keep some things private. More to the point, we have a desire to control what information we wish to share. For example, you might not want everyone to know exactly how old you are or how many times you were sick last year, but it is okay if your mother knows these things, and possibly essential that your doctor knows them.

Society has a vested interest in knowing some things about you and your life. For example, communities need to know how much you paid for your car and your house so they can fairly assess taxes. Society needs to track criminal behavior to help identify antisocial people who might harm us. Medical researchers need to track diseases to identify trends, causes, and potential solutions.

Businesses have an incentive to obtain considerable amounts of data on groups and individuals. And individuals have an incentive to provide some information to businesses. Whenever you make a purchase, you need information, and businesses are generally happy to provide you that information. The problem is how do you find the business or company that best matches your needs? Conversely, how can a company identify its potential customers? With no information, companies might resort to mass e-mail (spam) that clogs networks and irritates people who have no use for the services advertised.

The catch is that we do need to share information about ourselves, with government agencies, with researchers in various disciplines, and with businesses. Yet there is no reason that everyone in the world should be able to obtain every detail of our lives. The difficulty lies in determining where to draw this line. It is further complicated by the fact that every person (and social group) has different preferences.

First, it is important to realize that there is no constitutionally defined "right to privacy," especially with respect to data. A couple of Supreme Court rules have interpreted a right to privacy within the constitutional freedoms. A few laws have been enacted in the United States to provide minimal restrictions on the use and sharing of personal data. Figure 14.15 lists the most notable laws.

The Freedom of Information Act generally provides people with the ability to obtain information held by governmental agencies. There are limits for national security and on the release of data relating to individual personal data. For example, you cannot ask the IRS for personal information about your neighbor.

The most important feature of the Family Educational Rights and Privacy Act is that it limits the release of educational data. Institutions can release basic information such as the names of students (commonly sold to businesses), but they cannot release grades without the students' express written permission.

The primary purpose of the Electronic Communications Privacy Act was to extend traditional wiretap provisions to "electronic communication," which includes cellular phone and e-mail transmissions. Essentially, the law makes it illegal for individuals to intercept these conversations, and requires law enforcement agencies to obtain court permission to

FIGURE 14.15

Privacy laws: Only a few specialized laws exist to protect privacy in the United States. Some, like the Patriot Act, have actually removed earlier privacy protections.

- Freedom of Information Act
- Family Educational Rights and Privacy Act
- Fair Credit Reporting Act
- Privacy Act of 1974
- Privacy Protection Act of 1980
- Electronic Communications Privacy Act of 1986
- Video Privacy Act of 1988
- Driver's Privacy Protection Act of 1994
- Communications Assistance for Law Enforcement Act of 1994
- Health Insurance Portability and Accountability Act of 1996
- Children's Online Privacy Protection Act of 1998
- Graham-Leach-Bliley Act of 1999
- U.S. Patriot Act (antiterrorism) of 2001
- CAN-SPAM Act of 2003

intercept and record the conversations. On the other hand, it is specifically legal for an individual to record his or her transmissions (although a few states limit this right). Consequently, employers generally have the legal right (since they own the equipment) to monitor most communications by employees. Note that there may be some exceptions and an honest employer will always notify employees first.

The Fair Credit Reporting Act primarily gives consumers the right to inspect credit records—and it gives them the right to correct errors. The Driver's Privacy Act limits the use and release of state motor vehicle data. Its primary purpose was to prevent release of specific data to individual requesters. However, it has generous exceptions for insurance companies, research, and business use. The Video Privacy Act was created to limit the release of rental records from video stores and libraries.

The Privacy Protection Act of 1980 is primarily concerned with law enforcement investigations. It provides some definitions for when police searches are legitimate and when they are an invasion of privacy. The act predates the advances in information technology, so it is generally silent on the issue of privacy in terms of electronic data.

On the other hand, the Privacy Act of 1974 deals more directly with the collection and dissemination of information by the federal government. It specifically limits the collection of data by an agency to information that is relevant to its work. It provides citizens with the ability to examine and contest the data. The act initially limited agencies from sharing and matching data with other agencies, but most of these restraints have been removed by subsequent amendments. For example, the postal service is generally not permitted to disclose data on individual addresses. However, it does release data to a few large commercial service bureaus. Companies can submit address lists to these bureaus for correction of their mailing lists.

The Communications Assistance for Law Enforcement Act (CALEA) requires telecommunications firms to pay for wiretap facilities for police to listen to conversations. In 2004, the FTC began discussions to expand the coverage to nontraditional communication providers, such as ISPs.

The Health Insurance Portability and Accountability Act (HIPAA) is used to limit sharing of medical information. Many health care organizations now ask you to sign forms that give them the authorization to share the data. Since it is unlikely that consumers have the ability to refuse to sign or modify these preprinted agreements, the overall effectiveness is minimal.

The Children's Online Privacy Protection Act is much stronger, and if you run a Web site, you need to be aware of its provisions. As long as you make it clear that you are collecting data only from adults, the law does not apply. However, if you do collect data from children, you must be careful to minimize the personal data collected and generally have to obtain "verifiable parental consent."

The Graham-Leach-Bliley Act of 1999 primarily deregulated some financial services. In exchange, it imposed some trivial privacy clauses. In particular, it requires financial institutions to notify customers that they have the right to opt out of (1) selling their names to other companies and (2) marketing requests from the institution. Institutions reportedly spent hundreds of millions of dollars sending notices to customers, but many feel they deliberately made the process obscure and few consumers replied to the mass mailings. Consequently, businesses are basically free to continue using consumer data in any manner they want.

The U.S. Patriot Act was not directly concerned with privacy. However, it effectively repeals almost all governmental restraints. Someday it might result in some interesting lawsuits.

The CAN-SPAM Act is a halfhearted attempt to reduce the fraud involved with most unsolicited commercial e-mail (spam). Although it is a relatively weak law, you need to make sure that your messages conform to its provisions. For example, you need to include a physical address in each unsolicited message. The message must state that it is an advertisement. You cannot include false return addresses or message headers. And you must provide a working opt-out system. It also imposes limits on how you collect e-mail addresses. Individuals cannot sue violators, but ISPs do have the authority to sue for substantial sums of money. The most powerful aspect of the law is that it applies to the sender of the message and to the firm being advertised. To be safe, if you send unsolicited e-mail messages, be sure to send them yourself from a verified list. Do not purchase lists, and do not use third parties to send messages on your behalf.

The bottom line is that this piecemeal approach to privacy means that it is difficult for consumers to determine their rights and for businesses to identify their responsibilities. Consequently, except for the few specific limitations (e.g., credit and educational records), most businesses are free to collect and share information. On the other hand, you can improve relationships with customers by always asking them for permission to use and share personal data.

Information Era Crimes

As commerce moves to digital form, existing crime laws need to be extended and new ones need to be created. The biggest concerns are fraud, theft, and destruction of property. To understand the complications, consider what happens if someone steals your car. Why is that bad? Largely because you no longer have the use of the car. Now, what if someone steals your company's marketing plan? Why is that bad? You still have the use of the plan. Similarly, what if someone deleted your computerized customer database? Assuming that you are smart enough to keep a backup, what have you lost? The point of these questions is to show you that our traditional views on crime may not apply to crime related to information. Furthermore, computers create the prospect of new types of crime. For instance, what happens if someone writes a program that prevents you from obtaining access to your financial records? The alleged criminal did not steal or destroy anything, so what crime has been committed?

The Computer Fraud and Abuse Act of 1986 provides answers to many of the questions regarding crime in the digital realm. In particular, it outlaws (1) access to computers without authorization; (2) damage to computers, networks, data, and so on; (3) actions that lead to denial of service; and (4) interference with medical care. Interestingly, the act charged the U.S. Secret Service with enforcement.

Enforcement of the act has been challenging. It has been difficult to find qualified law enforcement personnel, including prosecutors. Besides, many businesses are reluctant to prosecute cases because they do not want competitors or shareholders to learn the details. On the other hand, sometimes companies and the Secret Service are too enthusiastic in their pursuit of alleged criminals. For example, one of the first cases supported by the Electronic Frontier Foundation (EFF) involved a bulletin board system (BBS) that supplied a document obtained from the telephone company that detailed information about the 911 system. The phone company complained that the document was stolen and that hackers might use it to break into its system. The Secret Service confiscated the BBS computer equipment and arrested the teenage owner. In court, with the help of the EFF, it was shown that the document could be purchased from the phone company for a few dollars.

If we examine crime historically, we see the same problems in preventing more traditional crime and enforcing the laws. In the United States, it was the introduction of the FBI and their professional investigative techniques that improved the detection and enforcement of various crimes. In the digital arena, until we gain more experience and improve training of police, attorneys, and judges, we will face the same problems of weak laws, difficulty in prosecution, and variable enforcement.

The Digital Millennium Copyright Act (DMCA) of 1998 changed some copyright provisions to synchronize the U.S. laws with the European laws. It also included a controversial provision that makes it a federal crime to create or to distribute devices that circumvent copy protection schemes. Part of its original purpose was to prevent people from advertising and selling black boxes to decode scrambled satellite TV signals. Many people believe that these provisions are too strict and that they infringe on the free speech rights in the Constitution. For instance, some researchers have been threatened with prosecution under the DMCA if they attempted to publish their work. The problem with copyright laws is that they can provide only limited legal protection. To enforce these laws, a copyright holder generally has to prosecute violators. But as the record industry was aware in the Napster case, it is virtually impossible to find everyone who copies a song—even more impossible to take them all to court. So, property owners are searching for ways to prevent casual theft. The problem is that in theory, it is impossible to completely prevent the copying of a digital work. So, portions of the DMCA are required to make it difficult for people to sell circumvention technology. By making it more difficult for people to copy a work, the laws essentially raise the cost of stealing. But there are fine lines between protecting copyright holders, protecting consumers' rights to use a work, and protecting everyone's right to study new ideas. It will take time and discussion to draw these lines.

Driven by the September 11 attack on the World Trade Center in New York, the U.S.A. Patriot Act (antiterrorism bill) of 2001 provides considerable new powers to federal, state, and local police agencies. Some of these provisions reduce privacy by making it easier for police agencies to monitor conversations, intercept e-mail and Internet messages, and detain people without cause. Law enforcement agencies are asking for even more flexibility to investigate people. These provisions do have some justifiable uses, and there are times when enforcement agencies have to jump through too many hoops to perform their jobs effectively. However, as J. Edgar Hoover proved, the challenge lies in preventing abuse of the laws, particularly preventing people from using them as political tools.

Summary

Technological change and increasingly aggressive use of information systems by businesses have several consequences. Technology affects individuals, their jobs, educational systems, governments, and society as a whole. Businesses have to be careful to protect the privacy of consumers and workers. Security provisions, disclosure policies, and audits are used to ensure that data is used only for authorized purposes. To ensure accuracy, it is crucial to allow customers (and workers) to examine relevant data and make changes.

A Manager's View

As a manager, you need to understand how businesses, technology, and society interact. Dealing with changes in privacy and security threats will become increasingly important to managing a company. Evaluating changes in society will also give you an advantage in the marketplace; it is important to know your customers. As a citizen, you need to be aware of the negative and positive effects of technology. In particular, changes in technology often lead to changes in political power and control. As a manager and a citizen, you are obligated to make ethical decisions and to understand the consequences of your actions.

Technology is generally believed to increase the total number of jobs available. However, the workers displaced by the introduction of technology are rarely qualified for the new jobs. Businesses and governments need to provide retraining and relocation to help those workers who lose their jobs. Sometimes technology allows physically disabled people to work in jobs they might not otherwise be able to perform.

Improved communication networks, huge databases, and multimedia tools provide possibilities for education and training in the public and business sectors. However, because of high development costs, technology tends to be used for specialized training.

Governments have long been involved in data collection, and technology enables them to work more efficiently. Of course, many political observers would argue that perhaps governments should not be *too* efficient. For example, it would be difficult for businesses to operate in an environment where the laws were changed every day. Technology also has the potential to improve communication between citizens and their representatives.

Technology and society produce other interactions. One feature is that lower prices, improved capabilities, and ease of use have made improved communication available to virtually any size group—providing a wider audience for small extremist groups. The new technologies also offer the ability to alter pictures, sound, and video, making it difficult to determine the difference between fact and fiction. Another important social issue is providing access to technology for everyone. It would be easy to create a world or nation consisting of *haves* and *have-nots* in terms of access to information. Those with information would be able to grow and earn more money, while those lacking the data continually lose ground.

Increasing dependence on technology brings with it new threats to the security of the firm. Managers need to recognize and evaluate these threats and understand some of the techniques used to minimize them. The most common threats come from inside the company, in terms of workers, consultants, and business partnerships. These threats are difficult to control, because firms have to trust these individuals to do their jobs. Training, oversight, audits, and separation of duties are common means to minimize threats. Depending on the communication systems used, there are threats from outsiders and viruses that can access computers with modems, over networks, or by intercepting communications. Dial-back modems, access controls, encryption, and antivirus software are common techniques to combat these threats.

Working in today's business environment means more than just doing your job. Each individual and firm has ethical obligations to consumers, workers, other companies, and society. In addition to obeying the laws, it is important for workers and companies to remember that the data in information systems refers to real people. The lives of people can be adversely affected by inaccurate data, poorly designed information systems, or abuse of the information.

Key Words

computer ethics, *555*	digital rights management (DRM), *543*	intellectual property, *540*
cookies, *531*		patent, *540*
copyright, *541*	information warfare (IW), *551*	privacy, *529*
digital divide, *547*		software piracy, *555*

Web Site References

Technology and Society

ACM/society	www.acm.org/usacm
Center for Democracy & Technology	www.cdt.org
Center for Information Technology and Society	www.cits.ucsb.edu
Center for the Study of Technology and Society	www.tecsoc.org
Computer Professionals for Social Responsibility	www.cpsr.org
Internet Society	www.isoc.org

MassMed	www.massmed.org
Privacy	
Electronic Frontier Foundation	www.eff.com
Electronic Privacy Information Center	www.epic.org
FTC advisory committee	www.ftc.gov/acoas
Kidz privacy	www.ftc.gov/bcp/conline/ edcams/kidzprivacy
Platform for privacy preferences	www.w3.org/P3P
Privacy, ACM	www.acm.org/usacm/privacy
Privacy International	www.privacyinternational.org
Privacy Rights	www.privacyrights.org

Additional Readings

Arkin, William, and Robert Windrem. "The U.S.-China Information War," *MSNBC,* December 11, 2001. http://www.msnbc.com/news/607031.asp. [Description of some aspects of the U.S. information warfare preparations.]

Government Computer News, January 6, 1992.

Grosso, Andrew. "The Individual in the New Age." *Communications of the ACM,* July 2001, Vol. 44(7), pp. 17–20. [A readable legal perspective on individual versus society.]

Jones, Douglas W. "Problems with Voting Systems and the Applicable Standards." May 22, 2001. http://www.house.gov/science/full/may22/jones.htm. [Issues on electronic voting systems.]

Machalaba, Daniel. "U.S. Ports Are Losing the Battle to Keep Up with Overseas Trade." *The Wall Street Journal,* July 9, 2001. [Effect of automation on jobs at the loading docks.]

Stoll, Clifford. *The Cuckoo's Egg: Tracking a Spy through a Maze of Computer Espionage.* New York: Doubleday, 1989. [Fascinating story of a spy searching U.S. networks.]

Review Questions

1. Do employees need to worry about the data collected by their employers?
2. If everyone is identified by some biometric measure, will that cause more dehumanization? Will it reduce individual privacy?
3. Do you think increasing use of computers causes a loss of jobs? What about in the past or in the future?
4. How are computers helping disabled people to perform jobs?
5. Do computers and digital content change the balance of power relationship between consumers and businesses? Should consumers have a right to make personal (backup) copies of digital works?
6. How does information technology add legitimacy to fringe groups?
7. Do you think state, local, and federal governments are making efficient use of computers? Will citizens ever be able to vote online?
8. In what ways have computers affected society and organizations? Will these patterns continue? Are there other important patterns that might arise?
9. Should governments be granted more powers to monitor and investigate people and transactions on the Internet?
10. What are the ethical responsibilities of users in terms of information systems?
11. Do we need additional privacy laws in the United States? What provisions would you add?
12. As a business manager running a Web-based company, which laws and rules do you need to pay careful attention to?

Exercises

1. Research the tools (hardware and software) available for a new employee of yours who is blind. List the sources, capabilities, and costs.
2. Should people be allowed to use the Internet anonymously? Should ISPs be required

to pay for hardware and software that can track individual usage in case of a lawsuit or criminal charge? Is it possible to prevent anonymous use of the Internet?

3. Do you think governmental agencies should share data about citizens? For example, should the FBI be able to access IRS records to locate suspected criminals? Should the FBI be allowed to access files from state and local governments? For instance, should all arrest records be automatically relayed to a central database? Should medical records be accessible to law enforcement agencies? Say that it is technically possible for the FBI to build a national database that contains DNA records for all citizens. If all medical records (from accidents, blood tests, and medical treatment) were computerized and automatically forwarded to the FBI, the agents could easily locate virtually any criminal.

4. Research the issues involved in electronic voting. What problems need to be overcome? What technologies could be useful? Does an electronic voting system have to be perfect, or simply better than the existing manual system?

5. Should vendors be allowed to charge different prices for online products, or should everyone pay the same price? Answer the question both from the perspective of the consumer and as a vendor or artist.

6. Should consumers be able to sue software companies for security failures or other problems with the software? What limits these lawsuits now?

7. What aspects of education would you prefer to have online or automated? What elements would you prefer to keep in person?

8. Should nations restrict the use of encryption technology? If that is not technologically possible, what other rules or actions can governments take to reduce problems due to encryption?

9. Find at least five news sites on the Web. Evaluate them in terms of (1) style/presentation, (2) accuracy, (3) believability, and (4) balanced news.

Technology Toolbox

10. Find at least two translation sites and test them with sample text. If you read the second language, comment on the results. Translate the text back to the original language and comment on the quality.

11. Find at least two foreign exchange sites and convert $100 (USD) into a different currency. Then convert that value into a third currency. Compare the results. How can they be different?

12. Assume that you have a Web site that needs to be written in at least one other foreign language. How much will it cost to have the pages translated? Can you use machine translation to reduce the costs?

13. Assume that you want to start a business in your state. Using the Internet, find the forms and cost to incorporate a new business. Choose a name and verify that the name is available. Find the IRS forms that you will need.

14. Find the text of the federal CAN-SPAM law and list the elements that must be included in an unsolicited commercial e-mail. What penalties can be applied if these items are missing? Research the current status of the national "do-not-spam" list.

Teamwork

15. Team project: Split into two groups. Individuals in each group will type a page of text into a word processor (pick any full page from the textbook). To start, everyone will work on the project independently, but there is a deadline of no more than two days. Second, team members will pair up and type the document a second time. This time, while one person types the document, the other one will time his or her performance and count mistakes at the end. The goal is to find the team member who is fastest and makes the fewest mistakes. The trick is that each person's work will be monitored at all times. Now, when all members of the team have completed their tasks, get the team back together and answer the following questions: Was there more pressure while you were being watched? Were you nervous? More attentive? Were you faster the second

time? Did you make more mistakes? Would you object to working under these conditions on a daily basis?

16. Assume that you are selling a new release for popular music. Create a silent auction and have everyone write down the price they are willing to pay for the music. Add up the numbers to get the total revenue you would obtain. Now, look up an average price for a similar item. Assume that each person who was willing to pay at least that amount would actually buy the item, and the others would not. Count the number of items sold and multiply by the fixed average price to get revenue. Compare the two values for total revenue.

17. Have each team member select a developing nation. Research the information technology available in that country. How do people get access to the Internet? What percentage of the people have used the Internet? Combine the results and create a list of options that might be used by other nations to improve Internet access.

18. Split the team into two groups to participate in a debate. The proposition is that programmers and developers should be licensed. One group should find evidence and arguments to support the proposition, the other to defeat it. If possible, conduct an actual debate. Otherwise, outline your arguments and compare them in writing.

19. Examine the arguments against electronic voting. Divide the arguments among the team members and have each person research existing technologies and proposals. Identify the methods used to avoid or minimize the stated problem. Combine the results and write a proposal defending the use of electronic voting.

 Rolling Thunder Database

20. What privacy problems might exist at Rolling Thunder? What rules or procedures should be enacted to avoid problems?

21. Your boss says that with the decline in sales, it would be wise to cut costs and suggests that you could buy only a single copy of some of the office software and install it on multiple machines. What do you do?

22. Find financial data for a publicly traded competitor to Rolling Thunder. Compare the basic financial ratios of the two companies.

23. The management at Rolling Thunder is thinking about trying to get a patent for an online process of configuring and ordering a custom bicycle. Search the patent records to see if anyone already has a similar patent, and estimate the probability of obtaining such a patent.

Cases: Health Care

The Industry

Health care makes up a substantial portion of expenditures in the United States. In 2004, health care expenditures were projected to be $1.8 trillion, a whopping 15.3 percent of gross domestic product. As the population ages, particularly the boomers, the U.S. government estimates that these values will rise to $3.4 trillion or 18.4 percent of GDP by 2013 (Brewin 2004). It is also a highly complex industry because the ultimate consumer, the patient, rarely bears the direct costs of the services. In 2000 (the most recent federal study), private medical insurance covered about 41 percent of total health care expenses, Medicare and Medicaid combined paid about 31 percent, and individuals paid 19 percent of the costs out of their own pockets (AHRQ 2003).

Federal Involvement in Care

Some people have heard about mistakes made in operating rooms—where the surgeon operated on the wrong knee or arm. Some patients have taken to writing on their limbs before surgery—just to make sure everyone knows which leg or arm to work on. Not as many people are aware of the problems that arise with drugs. Physicians sometimes prescribe the wrong drug. Nurses occasionally deliver the wrong drug or incorrect dose to a patient. The federal government has stepped in to reduce this problem. The Food and Drug Administration (FDA) in 2003 issued a ruling to take effect in 2004 for new drugs and 2006 for existing drugs. All individual doses of drugs will be required to have bar codes. Hospitals will then have to implement bedside

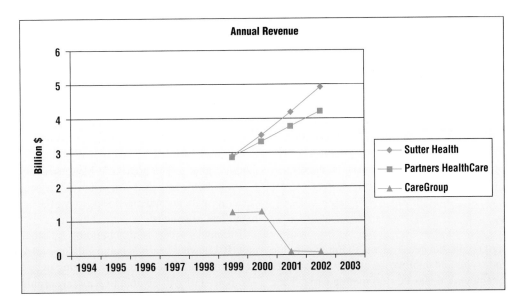

Annual Revenue

bar code readers that match patients and drugs before giving the drugs. Any errors will be flagged by the system. Hospitals are spending millions of dollars to add the new systems. In terms of those surgeries, new rulings require hospitals and physicians to adopt a marking system and mark every operating site on the body while the patient is conscious, to reduce mistakes. Apparently, they could not figure out a way to bar-code the body parts.

In 2004, President George Bush stated that he wanted the entire health care system to move to electronic records. Within 10 years, hospitals are supposed to have a system that allows electronic sharing of medical data (Brewin 2004). This push goes far beyond individual hospitals. It means that the entire health care and health informatics industry has to agree on standards and has to come up with a way to identify patients and transfer data securely.

The industry has been trying for several years to devise a health care information system that would work for the entire industry. Tommy Thompson, U.S. Secretary of Health and Human Services, had asked the industry to derive a blueprint for an electronic health-record system. In late 2003, the initial plan was rejected by the industry because it was overly complex. The original design was cumbersome, yet still did not address all of the potential issues. Part of the problem is that it tried to focus on a detailed level and include everything from medical records to billing to patient history. A bigger problem is that several proprietary systems already exist, and vendors are concerned that a government-designated system would be incompatible. At this point, there is not even a framework or structure for defining the overall approach (Landro, 2003).

Privacy

Privacy has become a more important issue. The Health Insurance Portability and Accountability Act of 1996 (HIPAA) has finally been given some teeth. Any organization that handles medical data has to comply with rules that prevent them from releasing medical data. The rules cover accidental releases, such as overheard conversations, and security breaches.

Actually, President Bush watered down the original medical privacy rules created by President Bill Clinton. The original rules required mandatory patient consent to disclose data, even for treatment and payment. The new rules simply require that patients be notified of the privacy policies ("Change" 2002). The main argument was that getting patient signatures might slow down the treatment process. Although privacy advocates were upset, the real-world effect was probably minimal. Most health care providers were simply requiring patients to sign a form that waives most privacy anyway.

The law has been useful at encouraging health care providers to tighten up the access to medical records. For example, hospitals cannot release or use patient data for charity solicitations. The billing system has to be separate from the medical system, so that a billing clerk could see that a patient was billed for a test but not see the test results (Tarkan 2003).

Additional Reading

AHRQ. *Statistical Brief #27: National Health Care Expenses in the U.S. Community Population, 2000.* Rockville, MD: Agency for Healthcare Research and Quality. http://www.meps.ahrq.gov/papers/st27/stat27.htm, November 2003.

Brewin, Bob. "Health Care IT Plans Get a Renewed Push." *Computerworld,* May 3, 2004.

"Change in the Air for Medical Privacy Rules." *CNN Online,* April 16, 2002.

Landro, Laura. "Plans for Health-Record System Need Work, Industry Players Say." *The Wall Street Journal,* September 15, 2003.

Tarkan, Laurie. "A Privacy Law's Unintended Results." *The New York Times,* June 3, 2003.

Case: Sutter Health

Sutter Health is one of the largest health care systems in northern California. In 2002, the not-for-profit organization had almost 40,000 employees and patient services revenues of almost $4 billion. Its 26-member hospitals with 5,773 beds recorded almost 240,000 discharges in 2002 and over 2.5 million outpatient visits (www.sutterhealth.com). Like any hospital group, Sutter works to improve the health of its community. And it struggles to balance costs, medical technologies, and information technology.

Quality Care

Sutter is working to build the new systems to implement the FDA drug bar code rules and improve the quality of drug prescriptions. It is deploying 6,000 PCs on mobile carts. They will be connected by Wi-Fi wireless networks because it would be too expensive to install wires in every hospital (Cuneo 2004). One advantage to the new system is that drug manufacturers will be required to put bar codes on individual doses. They have used them on bulk shipments in the past, but that still required hospitals to repackage and remark all of the drugs. John Hummel, CIO of Sutter Health, observed that those codes will save the company about $2 million a year (Brewin 2004).

Sutter recognized that a key part of the bar code point-of-care (BPOC) technology is that it had to be combined with a computerized physician order entry (CPOE) system. When the nurse scans patient and drug codes, the system has to verify the original drug order. That means the physicians need to enter the drug orders electronically. Sutter chose to implement a high-end BPOC system that also checks for patient allergies and asks nurses to double-check drugs if they have similar names or similar appearance to other drugs. Hummel involved nurses early in the selection process to ensure the system would be easy to use and that they would willingly adopt it. After implementation, nurses indicated a 42 percent improvement in satisfaction and a 64 percent improvement in perception of system efficiency (Johnson et al. 2004). Furthermore, the real-time dispensing data feeds directly into the charging system, so patient bills are more accurate.

One of the early challenges that Hummel faced was the need to integrate data from multiple medical systems. In 1999, he installed an interface engine from Century Analysis, now a division of Sybase. It serves as a hub and transfers data across systems. For example, the data from the Siemens Medical Health Services that handles picture archives can be transferred to or accessed from the Lawson ERP system. In 2003, he upgraded the engine to an eGate integration platform from SeeBeyond Technology Corporation. The new system utilizes XML to transfer data quickly between even more systems. His ultimate goal is to provide a single view of all patient data. The company is using Identity Hub software, an artificial-intelligence tool from Initiate Systems, that uses statistical techniques to match historical data. It is critical that physicians accurately identify patients to retrieve the proper records. Hummel observes that "if I go to the doctor, he needs to know the difference between John Hummel and John C. Hummel" (McGee September 2003).

As of 2004, more than 1,000 Sutter physicians store patient data electronically, and more than 400 of them have totally paperless offices. Even X-rays and prescriptions are stored digitally. The goal is to have data for all 4.5 million Sutter patients integrated in 2006. The system will make it easier for patients and physicians to use the health services—regardless of location.

Hummel's group is also building a virtual intensive care unit (ICU), where each hospital will have telecommunication links with real-time videoconferencing to an ICU physician. The ICU staff will be able to remotely monitor patients and collaborate with on-site staff. With the eICU system, one ICU physician and nurse monitor dozens of patients at hospitals that cannot afford full-time intensive care units. Keeping a physician online full-time provides additional supervision. Nurses do not have to worry about finding a doctor or surgeon for unnecessary cases. Dr. Daniel Ikeda, director of the system, notes that "when I'm in the eICU, I'm a lifeguard. I use the technology to look for troubling trends, before they become serious complications. A critically ill patient can turn sour in a matter of minutes" (McGee 2003).

Sutter Health is also rolling out Internet services to physicians and patients. By 2005, all Sutter physicians should have Web access, where they can download charts, check lab results, or order prescriptions. On the patient side, customers can use the Internet to communicate with doctors, view their records, order refills, or get additional instructions. The system is being used by 15,000 patients in Palo Alto (Cuneo 2004).

Sutter Health is using more sophisticated decision support and data analysis tools to help reduce errors and problems throughout the health care process. For example, a data warehouse tracks injuries that occur during childbirth, as well as the frequency of induced labor. The system is being used to reduce the instances of maternal tissue tears (McGee October 2003).

The California Pacific Medical Center in San Francisco is an affiliate of Sutter Health. The Center uses an automated Site of Care (SOC) system to enter data electronically at the bedside. The system saves time and money by reducing transcription costs. It also makes it easy to conduct studies and analyze the data. Reports can be generated quickly in response to physician queries. After a decade of use, the system contains substantial information and knowledge that can be used to improve patient care (Parker 2002).

Managing the Technology

John Hummel's IT department consists of almost 1,000 employees, with a budget of 3.9 percent of the hospital's net revenue, spending $105 million for operations (Cuneo November 2003). He still manages to send birthday and anniversary cards to each employee every year. But the department is busy, scheduling 750 large-scale projects for 2004 alone (Cuneo December 2003). The state of California essentially mandated the huge number of projects. In 1994, the state passed a law requiring all hospitals to be earthquake proof by 2008. Sutter Health has planned $5 billion in capital improvements. One of the big tasks for Hummel is building a new data center to consolidate all of the servers into one secure, safe location. By 2004, Sutter had completely replaced five hospitals and is planning to rebuild six more. Building the hospitals from scratch means that information systems can be built into them from the beginning (Brewin and Thibodeau 2004).

The hospital company operates in more than 100 communities and needs a network to connect all of the facilities. In 2003, the network team installed high-speed fiber-optic links to the new data center. The 50-micron multimode fiber cable can carry 10 gigabits per second. Chris Kennedy, network engineer for Sutter Health, notes that "we didn't want to impede our LAN system and therefore chose 10 Gbps multimode fiber. Most of our applications at the desk are pushing 100 Mbps though. With the new fiber backbone, we will be ready to easily push one gigabit from our desks without compromising our network." Category 6 cable was run to desktops in anticipation of the need to handle gigabit speeds (Oliver 2003).

Sutter Health is also spending money to improve privacy and protect data—partly driven by the HIPAA regulations. In addition to the common security and privacy controls, the IT department has a team of a half-dozen "white-hat hackers" to continually test the system to look for problems before real hackers can find them (McGee September 2003).

Costs

In 2002, Sutter Health raised its prices to Health Net insurance by 25 percent. After a public battle fought in newspaper ads, 20,000 Health Net members jumped to other insurers to avoid the battle. Ultimately, the two companies negotiated 15 percent annual increases.

In 2003, Sutter Health encountered a more serious public relations problem. Driven by ever-rising prices for health care, several large employers began examining prices at many of the large health care providers in California. Moreover, federal regulators have been examining overpricing claims against many hospitals. In 2003, the Service Employees International Union brought significant pricing data to the attention of several organizations, including Calpers, the large retirement investment agency. They found that five of the Sutter Health hospitals had inpatient charges that were up to 53 percent higher than the national average. Five of its hospitals were also being investigated by the federal Centers for Medicare and Medicaid Services for possible overbilling. In addition, nine of the Sutter Health hospitals had total profit margins exceeding 10 percent in 2001, compared to a state average of 3.5 percent on not-for-profit hospitals (Benko

2003). In early 2004, Calpers dropped 13 of the Sutter Health hospitals from its insurance coverage. It dropped 25 hospitals from other firms. A spokesman said, "We wanted to send a message to these providers that their costs are over the top." Calpers provides coverage for 1.2 million state employees, retirees, and their families (Wojcik 2004).

Questions

1. What obstacles will Sutter Health face to implement a completely digital health care information system by the end of 2006?

2. Why is Sutter using a data gateway to transfer information across machines instead of standardizing the underlying systems?

3. If Sutter is so advanced in its use of technology, why are its hospitals so expensive?

Additional Reading

Benko, Laura B. "Price Check." *Modern Healthcare,* April 21, 2003, Vol. 33 (16), pp. 6–8.

Brewin, Bob. "Sidebar: FDA Mandate Could Have $7B IT Price Tag." *Computerworld,* March 1, 2004.

Brewin, Bob, and Patrick Thibodeau. "Earthquake Law Pushes Hospitals to Spend Big on IT." *Computerworld,* February 16, 2004.

Cuneo, Eileen Colkin. "Uptick in Care." *Information Week,* November 3, 2003.

Cuneo, Eileen Colkin. "A Project for Every Problem." *Information Week,* December 22, 2003.

Cuneo, Eileen Colkin. "Mobile Care." *Information Week,* March 1, 2004.

Johnson, Van R., John Hummel, Terance Kinninger, and Russell F. Lewis. "Immediate Steps toward Patient Safety," *Healthcare Financial Management,* February 2004, Vol. 58(2).

McGee, Marianne Kolbasuk. "Mission Critical." *Information Week,* May 19, 2003.

McGee, Marianne Kolbasuk. "Health Care & Medical: Tech Innovation Keeps the Doctor In." *Information Week,* September 22, 2003.

McGee, Marianne Kolbasuk. "Putting a Clamp on Medical Mishaps." *Information Week,* October 13, 2003.

Oliver, Carol Everett. "A Cure for Bandwidth Bottlenecks." *Communications News,* September 2003, Vol. 40(9), p. 26.

Parker, Anne. "Tracking a Decade of CIS." *Health Management Technology,* April 2002, Vol. 23(4), pp. 28–30.

Weber, Joseph, and John Cady. "The New Power Play in Health Care." *BusinessWeek,* January 28, 2002.

Wojcik, Joanne. "Citing High Costs, Calpers Removes 38 Hospitals from Blue Shield Network." *Business Insurance,* May 24, 2004, Vol. 38(21), p. 4.

www.sutterhealth.com

Case: Beth Israel Deaconess Medical Center

Beth Israel Deaconess Medical Center (BIDMC) in Boston is a teaching affiliate of Harvard Medical School. It is a not-for-profit hospital that is part of the CareGroup Health System. The hospital has 534 beds and a Level 1 Trauma Center. It is a major biomedical research university (bidmc.harvard.edu). Like all hospitals, BIDMC has worked to install information technology to help patients, physicians, and nurses.

Information Technology

Emergency rooms in a major city are always hectic. The ER at BIDMC treats 60,000 patients a year (an average of 164 per day). Triage is the standard medical practice of identifying the most severe cases and treating those first (if the treatment can reasonably be expected to succeed). But with new patients arriving constantly, and nurses and physicians rotating among cases, it can be hard to keep track of the current situation. In the old days, hospitals used white boards to list major issues—but that sacrifices patient privacy and can lead to errors if the board is not updated or erased. At BIDMC, three doctors devised a new solution: an "electronic dashboard" that consists of a four-foot wireless plasma display. Patients are color-coded for severity (red for serious) and by gender (pink or blue). The entire ER was rebuilt with wireless technology in 2002. When a patient arrives, clerks enter registration data into a laptop, and the pertinent data is transferred to the plasma display identifying them by their initials. Unlike other hospitals, patients are immediately moved to beds. The wireless system enables clerks to come to the patients. Dr. John Halamka, CIO of CareGroup, notes that "if you think of a traditional emergency department, you walk in and immediately you're sitting at a triage desk. Maybe you're in pain, maybe you can't make it to the desk. Well, that's nuts. We put you in a bed, and then the registration people come to you and take your information" (Ewalt 2001).

Physicians treating patients enter orders and diagnoses into wireless laptops, with notations transferred to the display. When a procedure is completed, such as X-rays, the corresponding display element (XR) turns green. The physician's laptops also connect to the hospital's primary information system, so they can retrieve medical histories. In addition to improving care, the system has made the ER team more efficient. Nearby facilities averaged 450 hours in a six-month period where they had to turn patients away. BIDMC was overloaded only 40 hours in the same time period (MSNBC 2003).

The hospital has created wireless access in some other parts of the facility. In some wards, patients are even given laptops so that they can check their e-mail or surf the Web. Halamka observes that "unless I'm in critical condition, I need to access the outside world. People are there for a long time, so we give them PCs." To improve privacy and security, the hospital encrypts all wireless transmissions and requires that all wireless devices be registered before being granted access to the network (Ewalt 2001).

In terms of basic data and operations, BIDMC was an early adopter of computerized drug cabinets to monitor inventory levels throughout the hospital. The cabinets have a built-in PC board running a Sybase database and a flat panel display. Located throughout the hospital, they are tied to the central pharmacy to signal when an item needs to be refilled and to provide data for patient billing (Whiting 1999). With the new federal drug bar code regulations, the drug cabinet capabilities will probably not be needed.

Patient Care

As the U.S. population gets more comfortable with online interactions, it is only natural that patients want to be able to e-mail their physicians and obtain advice or renew prescriptions. Many physicians have resisted this technology. Some have claimed they are worried about privacy and liability issues. A few more cynical observers have noted that physicians do not usually get paid for these communications. Either way, few physicians embrace online interactions with patients. In 2004, Blue Cross Blue Shield of Massachusetts began a pilot study with several health care organizations, including 200 physicians at BIDMC. Blue Cross pays doctors $19 for each Web visit, and patients kick in a $5 co-payment. BIDMC anticipates participation by about 250 patients with perhaps two e-visits each for the first year. Contacts and billing are handled through a secure site by RelayHealth (McGee 2004).

Within the hospital, BIDMC is moving to electronic records. It is using a Web-based order-entry system for prescriptions, lab tests, and supplies. The system includes reminders for physicians and nurses and can electronically notify them when lab results come back. Massachusetts requires that all medical data be stored for 30 years, including images such as MRI, ultrasound, and X-ray scans. In addition to meeting state requirements, the system database can be used for data mining (McGee September 2003). Physicians can access stored images almost instantly through the network. Ronald Mitchell, CareGroup's director of radiation information systems, notes that "in the operating rooms, we're installing dual high-resolution flat-panel monitors so that surgeons can view the images prior to and during procedures" (McGee October 2003).

Network Disaster

One of the challenges to an electronic medical system is that it has to keep running—24 hours a day with no interruptions. In November 2002, the network at Beth Israel Deaconess crashed and had to be completely rebuilt in a matter of days. In the meantime, physicians and staff had to resort to paper records that had not been used for years. Dr. Halamka, the CIO, widely reported the problems he encountered, to show other hospitals how to improve their networks.

On Wednesday, November 13, 2002, Halamka noticed that the network was sluggish and taking too long to send and receive e-mail. He talked with the network team, and they had already noticed the problem. It appeared to be coming from a surge in one of the switches. They had experienced these spikes before, but happened to have a consultant on-site looking into the problem with that switch. To help identify the problem, network engineers began shutting down virtual LAN (VLAN) segments. That action was a mistake, because it forced the switches to recalculate the traffic distributions, and all data traffic ground to a halt while the switches continually reconfigured. They quickly turned everything back on, but the network was still sluggish. Around 9 p.m., the engineers spotted the problem: a loop in the spanning tree protocol. When data arrives at a switch, the switch computes the shortest path and directs the message to the destination. The problem was that the spanning tree could only look out to seven hops. Once data travels beyond seven jumps, it can lose its way and get redirected to the beginning—creating a loop. On Wednesday, a researcher had loaded several gigabytes of data into a file-sharing application, and it looped, clogging the network. The network team took standard steps to cut links and reduce the probability of loops and went home for the night.

The next morning, as usage ramped up, the network slowed to a crawl again. The team tried other options with no success. The network was beginning to cause problems for the physicians and patients. One physician was monitoring a critical patient and needed several lab reports to help spot the problem. But it was taking five hours to get lab reports completed. Fortunately, the patient survived. At 3:50 p.m., the hospital closed its emergency room for four hours.

At 4:00 p.m., Halamka called Cisco, their network provider. Cisco triggered its Customer Assurance Program (CAP) where the company commits every resource possible to solving the problem. A nearby team from Chelmsford moved in and set up a command center. Their first problem was that the network was so slow they could not get status information from the switches. They finally found some ancient 28.8Kbps modems to use to bypass the network and found the problem at 9 p.m. The image archive system was 10 hops away from the closest core network switch. Huge volumes of data were being abandoned because the spanning tree system could only go out to seven hops. The problem was that the network had been cobbled together since 1996 one piece at a time, using outdated switching technology. The team decided to upgrade the backbone to the image system with a Cisco 6509 router/switch. The router element provides more sophisticated communications by constantly evaluating bandwidth and rerouting traffic as needed.

Shortly after 9 p.m., Cisco loaded a 6509 onto a commercial flight from San Jose to Boston. Working through the night, the CAP team rebuilt the image network, a task that originally took six months.

The next morning, when the load increased again, the network still began to crash. By 10:00 a.m., Halamka decided to shut down the entire network and revert to paper. Most of the medical staff had already given up on the system anyway. Employees cranked up the copiers to generate blank forms. Some interns and physicians had never used paper prescription forms before and had to be trained. Runners were used to carry the paper and communicate orders.

By Saturday morning, the system was still down. The engineers decided the entire network was outdated. At 5 a.m., three additional Cisco engineers arrived from Raleigh. At 8 a.m., two more 6509 routers arrived by plane from Cisco. The team of 100 people spent the day building a new network. By Saturday night, the new core network was in place. But it took most of the night and Sunday to debug small glitches, such as a dead network card and out-of-date firmware. On Monday morning, the network was finally stable. At noon, Halamka declared the crisis over (Berinato 2003).

The main lesson from the disaster: networks have to be evaluated on a continual basis. You cannot just plug new items in and expect everything to work correctly. You need to have an overall architecture that supports the entire system. And you have to be willing to rebuild and replace core equipment as new technologies are introduced.

Questions

1. How does the emergency room system at BIDMC protect patient privacy?

2. Why have physicians been so slow to adopt online and e-mail communications from patients?

3. Why did the BIDMC network get so bad and fail? Why was it not fixed earlier?

Additional Reading

Berinato, Scott. "All Systems Down." *CIO,* February 25, 2003.

Ewalt, David M. "CareGroup's Wireless Hospital." *Information Week,* September 17, 2001.

McGee, Marianne Kolbasuk. "Health Care & Medical: Tech Innovation Keeps the Doctor In." *Information Week,* September 22, 2003.

McGee, Marianne Kolbasuk. "Putting a Clamp on Medical Mishaps." *Information Week,* October 13, 2003.

McGee, Marianne Kolbasuk. "E-Visits Begin to Pay Off for Physicians." *Information Week,* May 31, 2004.

MSNBC. "Next Frontiers: Using Technology to Get Ahead in Business." February 3, 2003.

Whiting, Rick, and Bruce Caldwell. "Data Capture Grows Wider." *Information Week,* June 14, 1999.

www.bidm.harvard.edu

Case: Partners HealthCare System

Partners HealthCare System, Inc., is an association of hospitals in the Boston area, including Brigham and Women's Hospital and Massachusetts General Hospital. The not-for-profit organization had revenues of $4.6 billion in 2003. Across the organization, the physicians and staff see 11,000 patients a day (annual report on the company Web site www.partners.org).

Telemedicine

With support from engineers at MIT, the hospitals in Partners were pioneers in the use of telemedicine. The system was created to expand the reach of the organization and provide quality care to patients in outlying areas. The system originally ran on ISDN phone lines with videoconferencing equipment. In 2000, the organization turned to an Internet-based system using Microsoft Windows 2000 Advanced Server. Dr. Joseph Kvedar, director of the Telemedicine Program, notes that "with the help of Windows 2000 Advanced Server, we will be able to extend the reach of our providers around the globe and to take the considerable body of knowledge within our organization and make it available virtually anytime, anywhere" (Microsoft 2000). The system is integrated into Microsoft's Internet Information Server (IIS) to exchange data and information as well as provide video streaming. The unit estimates that there are 20,000 potential users in one target group alone, and the system might eventually reach hundreds of thousands of users. Scalability and network load balancing were critical factors in upgrading the system. To access the system, users need only a Web browser and an Internet connection, as opposed to proprietary commercial lines that were needed with the old system (Microsoft 2000).

Telemedicine offers the possibility of providing detailed expert services to many new areas. However, some serious obstacles remain. Notably, insurance companies are reluctant to pay for the services. In part, they are concerned about fraud and billing abuse. Despite the obstacles, Kvedar says that Partners has seen e-visits increase by 25 percent a year McGee 2004). Some home-health nurses are turning to digital cameras and camera-equipped cell phones to treat basic skin problems. They take photos of skin wounds on diabetic patients and transfer them via the Internet to wound specialists. The specialists can examine the patterns using the digital history files. They can also check progress on many patients in one day. Partners is equipping up to 180 nurses with digital cameras or high-resolution cell phone cameras to provide care for 2,800 at-home patients (McGee 2004).

Knowledge Management

Medicine revolves around a tremendous amount of knowledge. Some of it is generated by research, some by best practices, some by experience. In the mid-1990s, medical researchers were concerned about the high error rates at Brigham and Women's and Massachusetts General hospitals. Sometimes simple things were causing huge problems—such as physicians not knowing a patient's allergies or forgetting that two drugs had bad interaction effects. So they built a knowledge management system to assist physicians prescribing drugs. Doctors enter orders into the computer and it examines patient data, test results, other drugs, and diagnostic information to evaluate the drug choice. It then makes recommendations. John Glaser, CIO at Partners, notes that serious medication errors have been reduced by 55 percent, and "about 400 times a day, a physician changes his mind on an order based on the computer" (Melymuka 2002). Although that is only 3 percent of the total drug orders, it can save lives. Because the system provides only concrete advice that is not debatable, physician acceptance has been fairly good—even though entering the data can add 30 minutes a day to their workload. One physician even thanked Glaser: "I just want to tell you our system has saved my ass a couple of times" (Melymuka 2002).

Unfortunately, Glaser notes that "only about 3 percent of hospitals have systems like this. That's because it's hard, but also because the ROI is fuzzy and messy" (Melymuka 2002). The low adoption rate is one of the reasons for the push by President Bush to force hospitals to move to electronic records and track drugs with bar codes. The Center for Information Technology Leadership backed by Partners notes that if the industry can standardize on electronic records, hospitals and insurers could save $86 billion a year (Brewin 2004).

Questions

1. Why did it require a federal law for hospitals to adopt bar code systems for drug prescriptions and delivery in hospitals?
2. What are the drawbacks to telemedicine?
3. What will it take for telemedicine to be used more often?

Additional Reading

Brewin, Bob. "Health Care IT Plans Get a Renewed Push." *Computerworld,* May 3, 2004.

McGee, Marianne Kolbasuk. "E-Health on the Horizon." *Information Week,* May 17, 2004.

Melymuka, Kathleen. "Knowledge Management Helps Cut Errors by Half." *Computerworld,* July 8, 2002.

Microsoft. "Partners HealthCare System, Inc." February 17, 2000.

www.partners.org

Summary Industry Questions

1. What information technologies have helped this industry?

2. Did the technologies provide a competitive advantage or were they quickly adopted by rivals?

3. Which technologies could this industry use that were developed in other sectors?

4. Is the level of competition increasing or decreasing in this industry? Is it dominated by a few firms, or are they fairly balanced?

5. What problems have been created from the use of information technology and how did the firms solve the problems?

10Base-T A system of connecting computers on a LAN using twisted-pair cable. The method relies on compression to increase raw transfer rates to 10 megabits per second.

A

access speed A measure of disk drive speed. Loosely, the time it takes a disk drive to move to a particular piece of data.

accounting journal Raw financial transaction data are collected by the accounting department and stored in a journal. Modern accounting requires the use of a double-entry system to ensure accurate data.

activity-based costing (ABC) ABC allocates costs by examining a detailed breakdown of the production activities. The cost of each process is computed for each different product. The detail provides a better picture of the production cost for each item.

advanced encryption standard (AES) A new U.S. standard for single-key encryption. Approved in 2001 by the government to replace DES and triple DES. With 128 bit keys, it is substantially more difficult to break; but still very fast to encrypt and decrypt.

advocacy role Someone in MIS, usually the chief information officer, who bears responsibility for exploring and presenting new applications and uses of MIS within the company.

agent An object-oriented program designed for networks that is written to perform specific tasks in response to user requests. Agents are designed to automatically communicate with other agents to search for data and make decisions.

American National Standards Institute (ANSI) An organization responsible for defining many standards, including several useful information technology standards.

American Standard Code for Information Interchange (ASCII) American standard code for information interchange. A common method of numbering characters so that they can be processed. For instance, the letter A is number 65. It is slowly being replaced by the ANSI character set table and the use of international code pages that can display foreign characters.

angel investor An individual who provides a limited amount of funding to start-up firms. Unlike a partner, the investor is rarely involved in management. The amount of funding is generally small—$25,000 to $100,000.

antitrust laws A variety of laws that make it illegal to use monopoly power. Some basic (economic) actions to achieve a competitive advantage are illegal. Strategic plans must be evaluated carefully to avoid violating these laws.

application service provider (ASP) A specialized Internet firm that provides an individual application to other businesses. For example, a reservation system can be run by an ASP to provide services to other companies.

artificial intelligence (AI) An attempt to build machines that can think like humans. Techniques evolved from this research help solve more complex problems. Useful techniques include expert systems, neural networks, massively parallel computers, and robotics.

assumptions Models are simplifications of real life, so they require assumptions about various events or conditions.

asynchronous transfer mode (ATM) A packet-based network system that uses high-speed transmission lines (150 megabits and over) and routers to maximize network efficiency and throughput.

attributes Descriptions of an object or entity. For example, a customer object would at least have attributes for name, phone number, and address.

auction In an e-commerce context, a Web-based system where individuals bid for items. Useful when you do not know the exact value of an item or have only a few items to sell. The auction site helps handle payments but charges a percentage fee.

audit trail The ability to trace any transaction back to its source. In accounting, transaction values are accumulated on the general ledger and used to create reports. An audit trail is a set of marks or records to point back to the original transaction.

authentication The ability to verify the source of a message. Dual-key systems are a useful technique. The sender uses a private key to encrypt the message. The recipient applies the sender's public key. If the decrypted message is readable, it had to have come from the alleged sender, because the keys always work in pairs.

B

backbone A high-speed communication line that links multiple subnetworks. It is usually a fiber-optic line.

backward chaining In an expert system, the user enters a "conclusion" and asks to see whether the rules support that conclusion.

barriers to entry Anything that makes it more difficult for new firms to enter an industry. Several possibilities would violate antitrust laws. An acceptable barrier is the increased use of information systems, which raises the cost of entering an industry because a rival would have to spend additional money on information technology.

Beginners All-purpose Symbolic Instruction Code (BASIC) An early computer programming language designed to be easy to program and to teach. Visual Basic is a current version for Windows programming.

benchmark A set of routines or actions used to evaluate computer performance. By performing the same basic tasks on several machines, you can compare their relative speeds. Benchmarks are especially useful when the machines use different processors and different input and output devices.

bill of materials Used in manufacturing, it is a list of components used to manufacture a finished product. In an ERP system, data from it is often used to trigger inventory deductions and to add the finished product to inventory.

bill presentation and payment Web-based software that automatically displays bills and invoices for customers. The payment side accepts various forms of payment including credit cards and electronic checks. Generally run as a Web service.

binary data A collection of ones and zeros called bits. Computer processors operate only on binary data. All data forms are first converted to binary.

biometrics A field of study that is trying to determine how to identify people based on biological characteristics. The most common devices are fingerprint and handprint readers.

bit The smallest unit of data in a computer. All data is converted to bits or binary data. Each bit can be in one of two states: on or off. Bits are generally aggregated into collections called a byte.

bitmap image A method of storing images. The picture is converted to individual dots that are stored as bits. Once a picture is stored in bitmap form, it is difficult to resize. However, bitmaps are good for displaying photographic images with subtle color shading.

blog Web log. Say it fast and you can hear the abbreviation. A special type of Web site with software that makes it easy for a user to enter comments. Typically used as a daily journal.

board of directors A group of people paid to oversee and evaluate the decisions of the company. Technically the CEO reports to the board of directors, but they are charged more with reviewing the CEO's decisions. Most boards have the authority to remove a CEO, but many board members are selected by the CEO.

Boolean search Searching for data by using the logic operators AND, OR, and NOT conditions in a WHERE statement; for example, find a list of customers where city = "Detroit" and age > 50 and do not own a car.

bottom-up development An approach to designing and building systems in which workers build system components to solve each problem as it arises. Eventually the pieces are combined to create an integrated system. The method relies on standards and controls to facilitate cooperation and integration. *See also* top-down development.

brainstorming A group technique in which each individual is asked to come up with possible suggestions to a problem. Any ideas are useful, regardless of how wild they are. Even fanciful ideas could stimulate someone else to improve it or to explore a related area.

broadcasts A technique of transmitting messages using radio, micro, or infrared waves. Broadcast messages are sent to all devices in a certain area. Others in the vicinity can also receive the messages.

browser A software tool that converts World Wide Web data into a graphical page with hypertext links. Using standard (HTML) commands, companies can offer data and additional links to users. Users simply click on individual words and pictures to retrieve additional data and move to other network sites.

brute force An attack on encrypted data that attempts to use every possible key. Can be stopped by using very long keys. For example, using a key or password of only three letters means there are only 26*26*26=17,576 possible values. Even a slow computer can test all combinations in a few seconds.

bulletin board system (BBS) Similar to a typical bulletin board, except that people access it from computers. The BBS enables users to store comments, pictures, and files for other people to retrieve. Bulletin boards are usually organized by topics and can be searched for specific phrases or comments. They are a useful way to disseminate information that is of interest to many different people.

bus Most computers have special slots called a bus to provide high-speed connections to other devices. Various manufacturers make boards that fit into these slots. The processor can exchange data with these other devices, but performance is sometimes constrained by the design of the bus.

bus network A network organizing scheme in which each computer is attached to a common transmission medium. Protocols are needed to determine when a machine can transmit and to recover from collisions.

business process management (BPM) *Also see* workflow software. The concept that business actions have to be performed in a specific sequence. Managing the process entails finding efficiencies through automating or reordering. For example, purchasing expensive items requires discussions and approvals by a variety of managers.

business to business (B2B) Business-to-business electronic commerce; sales by suppliers to other businesses over the Internet; often long-term relationships. *See* B2C and EDI.

business to consumer (B2C) Business-to-consumer electronic commerce; purchases by individual consumers similar to traditional mail-order systems, but conducted on secure Web sites over the Internet.

byte A collection of bits. Traditionally, 8 bits make up one byte. From binary arithmetic, an 8-bit byte can hold 2 to the 8th power, or 256, possible numbers. In many systems a byte is used to hold one character.

C

C A powerful programming language that is flexible and creates efficient code. A language commonly used to build complex applications and to create commercial software products.

C++ An object-oriented extension of the C programming language. It is commonly used to build commercial software. It produces efficient code and supports the development of reusable objects.

cable modem An Internet connection device that translates local area network protocols to run over a television cable line. It can provide transmission speeds around 1.5 Mbps. But the communication line is shared with other users.

cache A buffer between the processor and a slower device such as a printer, disk drive, or memory chips. The cache generally consists of high-speed memory. Data is transferred in bulk to the cache. It is then pulled out as it is needed, freeing up the processor to work on other jobs instead of waiting for the slower device to finish.

capability maturity model integration (CMMI) A system designed at the Carnegie Mellon Software Engineering Institute to help organizations improve their software development processes. A key element is to work toward a formal development model that is measurable and is continually upgraded. The CMMI system is an upgrade of the older CMM process.

Carrier-Sense, Multiple-Access/Collision Detection (CSMA/CD) A communications protocol that determines how computers will behave on a shared-medium network. Ethernet protocols rely on CSMA/CD. Other alternatives are Token Ring and packet switching.

case-based reasoning An expert system approach that records information in the form of situations and cases. Users search for cases similar to their current problem and adapt the original solution.

CD-ROM Compact disk-read only memory. Data is stored and retrieved with a laser. A special machine is required to create data on a CD-ROM. Used to hold data that does not change very often. Useful for multimedia applications because a disk can hold about 650 megabytes of data. The format used to store music CDs.

centralization A business scheme for performing most operations and making management decisions from one location in an organization. MIS organization can be examined in four areas: hardware, software, data, and personnel. *See also* decentralization.

certificate authority (CA) Dual-key encryption and authentication require that the public key be published and available to others. A certificate authority is an organization that validates the owner's identity, issues the keys, and runs the public directory. Almost anyone can run the software to be a CA, but others must trust that host.

change agents Objects or people who cause or facilitate changes. Sometimes the change agent might be a new employee who brings fresh ideas; other times change can be mandated by top-level management. Sometimes an outside event such as a competitor or a hurricane forces an organization to change.

change drivers Concepts or products that have altered the way businesses operate. Classic examples include bar code scanners in retail stores, handheld miniterminals or notebooks by delivery firms and salespeople, and reservation systems by travel and entertainment industries.

charge-back system A scheme for charging other internal departments for services. For example, some firms charge departments a fee based on how often they use the central computer. The goal was to ration a limited resource by avoiding free use.

chart of accounts A listing of all the accounts and subaccounts in the general ledger. It must be defined ahead of time for each business.

check in A step in version control systems. When a user is finished making changes to a file, the user checks in the file to the repository to make it fully available to other users. The user must first check out the file.

check out A step in version control systems. A user checks out a file or document to indicate that changes will be made. To prevent concurrency problems, the document is usually locked so that others cannot make changes at the same time. When finished, the user checks in the file.

chief executive officer (CEO) The head of a company. The person ultimately responsible for setting the direction and policies of the firm. Usually the CEO is also the chairperson of the board of directors.

chief information officer (CIO) The person who is in charge of the MIS organization within a firm, charged with overseeing operations, setting MIS priorities, and being a top-level advocate for MIS. Also develops and supports strategy for the firm.

circular reference In a spreadsheet, a set of cells that eventually refer to each other. In the simplest example, cell A1 would use values stored in cell A2, but cell A2 uses the value stored in A1. This technique is sometimes used to create an iterative solution to a model.

classes Base descriptions of objects. Technically, classes describe generic attributes and methods. Objects are a specific instance of a class.

click-through rate Used in Web advertising, the percentage of people viewing an online ad who actually click it to see the details on the advertised product or service. By 2000, the average click-through rates had declined to less than 1 percent. But it is not necessarily a good measure of advertising effectiveness.

client-server network A network configuration in which a few machines are used as file servers and the others (clients) are independent workstations. Shared data is first sent to a file server where it can be examined or transferred by another client.

client-server organization A method of organizing the MIS function so that some operations are centralized while others are decentralized. The client-server model separates all of the components into two categories: servers or clients. The functions associated with the server tend to be centralized, whereas the client components and tasks are dispersed among the users.

clip art Artwork created and sold to be used by nonartists. Hundreds of collections are available of people, places, buildings, and other objects. Clip art images are often used to create presentations and illustrate reports.

clipboard The method used to transfer data between software packages in windows-oriented operating environments. All objects that are cut or copied are placed onto the clipboard, ready to be pasted to another location or another package. Clipboard viewers exist to show the current contents of the clipboard. Some software systems allow a clipboard to hold several cuttings. Many automatically delete the older cuts—keeping only the most recent.

clipper chip An encryption method created by the U.S. top-secret National Security Agency (NSA). It uses a secret algorithm to encrypt and decrypt digital messages. It was particularly designed for digital voice communication. Its key feature is the use of two escrow keys assigned to each chip. If the police decide they want to listen to a conversation between two suspects, they can get a court order, collect the escrow keys, and instantly decrypt the call.

closed loop A system or piece of computer code in which every step in a control mechanism is contained inside the system and does not utilize external input. *See also* feedback.

closed system A system that is entirely self-contained and does not respond to changes in the environment. Most closed systems eventually fail due to entropy.

coaxial cable A cable used to transmit data. Cable television is a widespread application. The inner cable is surrounded by a plastic insulator, which is surrounded by a wire mesh conductor and an outer casing. The wire mesh insulates the internal signal wire from external interference.

cold site A facility that can be leased from a disaster backup specialist. A cold site contains power and telecommunication lines but no computer. In the event of a disaster, a company calls the computer vendor and begs for the first available machine to be sent to the cold site.

collision In networks, a collision arises when two computers attempt to broadcast messages at the same time. The network protocols need to identify the situation and determine which machine will go first.

column A vertical part of a table that holds data for one attribute of an entity in a database or spreadsheet. For example, a table to describe automobiles will have columns for make, model, and color.

command-line interface A method of controlling the computer by typing commands. The user must generally memorize specific commands. Older machines still use them because GUI systems require too much overhead. Some people prefer command lines, because it is faster to type one or two commands than to manipulate an image on the screen.

commerce server A software system that runs an e-commerce Web server. It handles the product catalog, searching, a shopping cart, and the payment mechanism. Several vendors sell versions to be run on your own server, or you can lease space on a hosting company.

commercial off-the-self software (COTS) Purchased software for building applications. Relatively popular because it is faster than building from scratch.

Common Business-Oriented Language (COBOL) An early programming language designed to handle typical transaction-processing tasks. Its death has been predicted for years, but it is hard to throw away billions of lines of code.

Common Object Request Broker Architecture (CORBA) A model largely developed in the UNIX community that will enable objects to communicate with each other across networks. In particular, it is designed to enable users to combine different data types from various software vendors into a single compound document. The data could reside on any server on the network.

competitive advantage Something that makes your company better or stronger than your rivals. Examples include lower costs, higher quality, strong ties to loyal customers, and control over distribution channels.

compound document A document that incorporates different types of data: text, graphics, sound, and video. The different objects might be transmitted across a network to be included in a final document.

computer-aided design (CAD) Programs that are used to create engineering drawings. CAD programs make it easy to modify drawings. They also make it easier to keep track of material specifications. They can perform spatial and engineering estimates on the designs, such as surface or volume calculations.

computer-aided software engineering (CASE) Computer programs that are designed to support the analysis and development of computer systems. They make it easier to create, store, and share diagrams and data definitions. Some versions even generate code. There are two categories of CASE tools: software development and maintenance of existing systems.

computer-integrated manufacturing (CIM) Using a computer to control most of the production equipment in a manufacturing environment. The computer can monitor the production statistics. It is also used to set individual machine controls.

computer ethics The concept that all of us have an obligation with respect to data. For example, managers have a responsibility to customers to protect personal data, to collect only data that is truly needed, and to give customers the ability to correct errors in personal data.

computer information system (CIS) *See* management information system (MIS).

composite key In relational databases, a key that consists of more than one column. The columns are combined to yield a unique primary key.

concurrency A situation that arises when applications attempt to modify the same piece of data at the same time. If two people are allowed to make changes to the same piece of data, the computer system must control the order in which it processes the two requests. Mixing the two tasks will result in the wrong data being stored in the computer.

context diagram The top level of a data flow diagram that acts as a title page and displays the boundaries of the system and displays the external entities that interact with the system.

continuous quality improvement The concept that any process can be improved by continually evaluating the system and making adjustments and refinements. The concept is also applied to service processes, but relies on a measurable performance objective.

converge The ability of an iterative model to stabilize on a fixed solution. The alternative is that values continually increase and never reach a solution.

cookies Small text files that a Web server sends to client computers. When the user returns to a site, the browser automatically returns the cookie file. Servers use them to keep track of transactions—so they know when the same user has returned. Marketers have used them to track individual users on the Web.

copyright A legal ownership right granted to the creators of intellectual property. All works are automatically copyrighted. Registering with the copyright office is not required but grants additional protection to the owner.

critical success factors A limited number of concrete goals that must be met for the organization to be successful. Identifying these key factors helps determine the strategic directions and highlights the areas that can benefit from improved information systems.

customer relationship management (CRM) A system for tracking and integrating all customer data. Salespeople, managers, and clerks all have access to the same data, so everyone has the same consolidated view of all customer interactions.

cut, copy, paste A common mechanism used to transfer and link data between different software packages. The data to be transferred is marked. When it is cut or copied, it is placed on the clipboard. Switching to the second package, the object is pasted into the appropriate location. Dynamic and static links are specified through options in the "paste special" menu. With the cut option, the original object is deleted. With copy, the original is unchanged.

D

data Consists of factual elements (or opinions or comments) that describe some object or event. Data can be thought of as raw numbers or text.

data administrator MIS manager who is charged with overseeing all of the data definitions and data standards for the company to ensure that applications can share data throughout the company.

data dictionary Contains all of the information to explain the terms used to define a system. Often includes report descriptions, business rules, and security considerations.

data encryption standard (DES) An older method of encrypting data that was commonly used by financial institutions. With current computer capabilities that can break a DES-encrypted message, DES is no longer considered a secure encryption system.

data flow diagram (DFD) A diagramming technique used to analyze and design systems. It shows how a system is divided into subsystems and highlights the flow of data between the processes and subsystems. It displays processes, external entities, files, data flows, and control flows.

data independence Separating programs from their data definition and storage. The main advantage is that it is possible to change the data without having to change the programs.

data integrity (1) A concept that implies data is as accurate as possible. It means the database contains few errors. (2) Keeping data accurate and correct as it is gathered and stored in the computer system.

data mart A small version of a data warehouse. A database designed to hold concise collections of data for retrieval and analysis by managers.

data mining An automated system that examines data for patterns and relationships. It is partly based on statistics, but also searches for more specific associations. The results are not always applicable to other situations.

data mirroring The ultimate backup technique where all data that is stored on one machine is automatically transferred and stored on a second computer. Useful to prevent loss of data and recover from disasters—particularly when the second computer is located many miles away.

data store A file or place where data is stored. In a realistic setting, a data store could be a computer file, a file cabinet, or even a reference book.

data types To humans, there are four basic types of data: text and numbers, images, sound, and video. Each data type must be converted to binary form for computer processing.

data warehouse A single consolidation point for enterprise data from diverse production systems. The data is typically stored in one large file server or a central computer. Because legacy systems are difficult to replace, some data is copied into a data warehouse, where it is available for management queries and analysis.

database A collection of related data that can be retrieved easily and processed by computers; a collection of data tables.

database administrator (DBA) (1) A person appointed to manage the databases for the firm. The DBA needs to know the technical details of the DBMS and the computer system. The DBA also needs to understand the business operations of the firm. (2) A management person in the MIS department charged with defining and maintaining the corporate databases. Maintaining data integrity is a key component of the job.

database management system (DBMS) Software that defines a database, stores the data, supports a query language, produces reports, and creates data-entry screens.

decentralization Moving the major operations and decisions out to lower levels within the firm. In MIS, decentralization has largely been led by the declining cost and improved capabilities of personal computers. *See also* centralization.

decision biases Without models and careful analysis, decisions made by people tend to be biased. There are several biases in each of the four systems categories: data acquisition, processing, output, and feedback.

decision process The steps required to make a decision. It includes problem identification, research, specification of choices, and the final selection. Midlevel managers are often involved in the initial stages and affect the outcome, even though they may not make the final decision.

decision support system (DSS) System to use data collected by transaction-processing systems to evaluate business models and assist managers in making tactical decisions. There are three major components: data collection, analysis of models, and presentation.

decision tree A graphical representation of logic rules. Each possible answer to a question or situation leads to a new branch of the tree.

default value A value that is automatically displayed by the computer. Users can often override the default by deleting the old value and entering a new one. The goal is to choose a value that will almost always be entered, so the user can skip that item.

dehumanization Some people feel that technology isolates people and decreases our contact with other members of society. Treating people as identification numbers and summary statistics can lead managers to forget the human consequences of their decisions.

denial of service (DoS) Preventing legitimate users access to systems and networks. A common Internet trick is to force thousands of zombie computers to flood a server with millions of meaningless messages—preventing anyone else from using the system.

descriptive model A model that is defined in words and perhaps pictures. Relationships between objects and variables tend to be subjective. Useful for an initial understanding of a system but difficult to evaluate by computer.

desktop publishing (DTP) The art of creating professional documents with personal computers and small laser printers. Beyond basic word processing, DTP software provides controls to standardize pages, improve the page layout, and establish styles.

detail section The section in a report that is repeated for every row in the associated tables. It is often used for itemized values, whereas group and page footers are used for subtotals.

diagnostic situations Spotting problems, searching for the cause, and implementing corrections. Examples include responding to exception reports to identify problems and potential solutions, and determining why the latest marketing approach did not perform as well as expected.

dial-back modem A special modem placed on a central computer. When a user attempts to log in, the dial-back modem breaks the connection and calls back a predefined phone number. Its use minimizes the threat of outsiders gaining access to the central computer.

digital cash An electronic version of money that is provided and verified by a trusted third party. It consists of an encrypted number for a specified value that can only be used one time. It provides for verifiable and anonymous purchases using networks.

digital certificate Part of an authentication mechanism used with dual-key encryption. Companies that host servers need to encrypt transactions over the Internet. They purchase a digital certificate from a certificate authority and install it on the Web server. The client browser recognizes the certificate key and encrypts the data.

digital dashboard A visual presentation of broad measures of current activity in an organization. The data is generally displayed as gauges, and the system must be customized for each organization. As part of an executive information system, managers can drill down to get more data.

digital divide The distance between those individuals or nations who have network capabilities and those who do not. Despite declining costs, many people and many nations cannot afford the hardware and software. If a large portion of the economy moves online, it could alienate those who cannot afford the network connection.

digital rights management (DRM) A combination of encryption and Internet validation for protecting vendor copyrights to prevent unauthorized copying of digital content (software, music, books, movies, and so on).

digital signature Any electronic signature technology that verifies the user. U.S. law now recognizes digital signatures as equivalent to handwritten ones. The most secure system is to obtain a digital certificate from a public company that verifies each person's identity. But the IRS accepts a simple PIN issued by the agency as a digital signature.

digital subscriber line (DSL) A special phone service connection available to customers within 3 miles of the phone company's switch. It provides about 1 Mbps transmission speed for Internet connections.

digital video/versatile disk (DVD) A digital format primarily used for storing video and movies. However, it can also hold audio and traditional computer data. One side of the disk can hold over 3 gigabytes of data.

disintermediation In an e-commerce context, using a Web-based system to skip over sections of the production chain, such as manufacturers selling directly to consumers. The approach can give the manufacturer a higher percentage of the sale price, but risks alienating retailers, resulting in lost sales.

distribution center A central point in a supply chain where incoming bulk goods are split and merged into multiple shipments to the final destination. For example, a truckload of bread would be unloaded and individual boxes placed on other trucks, along with other food items for distribution to a grocery store.

distribution channel The layers of distributors in between the manufacturer and the final customer. If a producer can gain control over this means of getting the product to the consumers, the producer can prevent new rivals from entering the industry. Improved communication systems offer the possibility of eroding control over some distribution channels.

diverge The property of an iterative model where successive computations keep leading to larger values (in magnitude). The model never reaches a stable solution. Generally due to insufficient or incorrect feedback mechanisms.

documentation Descriptions of a system, its components, the data, and records of changes made to the system.

domain name system (DNS) A set of computers on the Internet that converts mnemonic names into numeric Internet addresses. The names are easier for humans to remember, but the computers rely on the numeric addresses.

dot-com Abbreviation given to the many Internet firms formed in the late 1990s because their Internet names ended with the .com suffix. For a couple of years, having a dot-com name was prestigious and attracted funding. When hundreds of these firms failed in 2000 and 2001, they became known as dot-bombs.

download To transfer files from a remote computer to a local computer (usually a personal computer). *See also* upload.

drill down   To use an information system to get increasingly detailed data about a company. In an enterprise information system, the ability to look at overall company data, and then select breakdowns by regions, departments, or smaller levels.

dual-key encryption   A method of encrypting a message that requires two keys: one to encrypt and one to decrypt. One of the keys is a public key that is available to anyone. The other key is private and must never be revealed to other people. RSA is a popular dual-key encryption system. Dual-key systems can also be used to authenticate the users.

dynamic data exchange   An early method of linking data from multiple sources with the Windows operating system. The software packages literally send messages to other software packages, which enables them to combine and update data. *See also* dynamic integration as well as Object Linking and Embedding (OLE).

dynamic integration   A means of linking data from multiple documents. One compound document (or container) can hold data objects created by other software. As the original data is changed, it is automatically updated in the container document. *See also* static integration.

E

e-business   Electronic business. The process of conducting any type of business over the Internet. It includes all forms of e-commerce and m-commerce, as well as internal processes and Web services.

e-commerce   Electronic commerce. The process of selling items over the Internet. The most familiar form is business-to-consumer, but it includes business-to-business and auction sites like eBay.

e-mail   Electronic mail, or messages that are transmitted from one computer user to another. Networks transfer messages between the computers. Users can send or retrieve messages at any time. The computer holds the message until the recipient checks in.

EBCDIC: Extended Binary Coded Decimal Interchange Code A method of numbering characters so that they can be processed by machines. Used exclusively by large IBM and compatible computers. *See also* ASCII.

electronic data interchange (EDI)   Exchanging transaction data with entities outside the control of your firm. Private connections can be established directly between two firms. Public networks are also being formed where one provider collects data and routes it to the appropriate client.

encryption   A method of modifying the original information according to some code, so that it can be read only if the user knows the decryption key. It is used to safely transmit data between computers.

end-user development   Managers and workers are to develop their own small systems using database management systems, spreadsheets, and other high-level tools.

enterprise network   A network that connects multiple subnetworks across an entire firm. Often, the networks use different protocols and different computer types, which complicates transmitting messages.

enterprise resource planning (ERP)   An integrated computer system running on top of a DBMS. It is designed to collect and organize data from all operations in an organization. Existing systems are strong in accounting, purchasing, and HRM.

entrepreneurship   The act of creating and organizing a business. Generally, an entrepreneur takes the risks to create a new business in search of a profit.

ergonomics   The study of how machines can be made to fit humans better. One of the main conclusions of this research in the computer area is that individuals need to be able to adjust input (and output) devices to their own preferences.

escrow key   In an encryption system, it is a special key that can be used by government officials to decrypt a secret conversation. The Clipper chip uses escrow keys.

Ethernet   A network communications protocol that specifies how machines will exchange data. It uses a broadcast system in which one machine transmits its message on the communication medium. The other machines listen for messages directed to them.

ethics   The concept that various elements of society have obligations to the others. In IT, it focuses on the roles of users, developers, and vendors.

event-driven approach   A user-interface approach where the user controls the sequence or operations and the software responds to these events. Events can range from a simple key-press to a voice command. Modern, window-based software does not follow a sequential process. Instead, actions by users generate events. The programs respond to these events and alter data or offer additional choices. Typical events include mouse clicks pointing to items on the screen, keystrokes, changes to values, or transmissions from other systems.

exception report   Report that is triggered by some event to signify a condition that is unusual and needs to be handled immediately.

executive information system (EIS)   A type of decision support system that collects, analyzes, and presents data in a format that is easy to use by top executives. To achieve this objective, the EIS is based on a model of the entire company. In most cases the model is presented graphically and the executives retrieve information by pointing to objects on the screen.

exhaustive testing   Testing every possible combination of inputs to search for errors. Generally not a feasible option, so most computer systems will always contain errors.

expert system (ES)   System with the goal of helping a novice achieve the same results as an expert. They can handle ill-structured and missing data. Current expert systems can be applied only to narrowly defined problems. Diagnostic problems are common applications for expert systems.

expert system shell   A program that provides a way to collect data, enter rules, talk to users, present results, and evaluate the rules for an expert system.

export   An older method of exchanging data among various software packages. One package exports the data by storing it in a format that can be read by other software. Object Linking and Embedding is a more powerful way to exchange data.

extensible markup language (XML)   A tag-based notation system that is used to assign names and structure to data. It was mainly designed for transferring data among diverse systems.

external agents   Entities that are outside the direct control of your company. Typical external agents are customers, suppliers, rivals, and governments. Competitive advantages can be found by producing better-quality items or services at a lower cost than your rivals. Also, many firms have strengthened their positions by building closer ties with their suppliers and customers.

external entity   Objects outside the boundary of a system that communicate with the system. Common business examples include suppliers, customers, government agencies, and management.

extraction, transformation, and loading (ETL)   The process in data warehouses that involves taking data from existing systems, cleaning it up, and moving it into the data warehouse.

extranet   A network configured to give certain outsiders, usually customers and suppliers, limited access to data using Web-based systems.

extreme programming (XP)   A new version of development loosely based on prototyping. Pairs of developers rapidly build and simultaneously test applications. The goal is to build releases and then modify them to meet the changing needs of the users.

F

facsimile (fax)   A combination scanner, transmitter, and receiver that digitizes an image, compresses it, and transmits it over phone lines to another facsimile machine.

fault tolerance   The ability of a computer or a system to continue functioning properly even if some of the components fail. Fault-tolerant machines rely on duplication of subsystems with continuous monitoring and automatic maintenance calls.

feasibility study   A quick examination of the problems, goals, and expected costs of a proposed system. The objective is to determine whether the problem can reasonably be solved with a computer system.

feedback   Well-designed systems have controls that monitor how well they meet their goals. The information measuring the goals and providing control to the system is known as feedback.

fiber-optic cable   A thin glass or plastic cable that is internally reflective. It carries a light wave for extended distances and around corners.

file server   Computer on a network that is used to hold data and program files for users to share. To be effective, it should use a multitasking operating system.

file transfer protocol (FTP)   A standard method of transferring files on the Internet. If you control a computer, you can give other users access to specific files on your computer without having to provide an account and password for every possible user.

firewall   A small, fast network computer device that examines every packet entering a company. Rules or filters can be created that will reject certain packets that are known to be dangerous to the network.

Five Forces model Michael Porter's model used to search for competitive advantage. The Five Forces are rivals, customers, suppliers, potential competitors, and substitute products.

floating point operations per second (FLOPS) The number of mathematical calculations a processor can perform in one second. Typically measured in millions (mega-FLOPS) or billions (giga-FLOPS). Bigger numbers represent faster processors.

flow chart An old pictorial method for describing the logic of a computer program. It has largely been replaced by pseudocode.

font size An important characteristic of text is its size. Size of type is typically measured in points. For reference, a capital letter in a 72-point font will be approximately 1 inch high.

forward chaining In an expert system, the ES traces your rules from the data entry to a recommendation. Forward chaining is used to display questions, perform calculations, and apply rules.

frame A related set of information that humans group together. Sometimes groupings can be arbitrary. A concept used in discussing AI applications and human cognition.

frame relay A network communication system that uses variable-length packets. It is useful for high-speed, large bursts of data. It is being used for long-distance network communications.

franchise A means of organizing companies. Independent operators pay a franchise fee to use the company name. They receive training and benefit from the name and advertising of the parent company. They purchase supplies from the parent company and follow the franchise rules.

front-end processor A simple communications device for large central computers that accepted all of the terminal wires and then assigned each user to an open communications port on the computer. This device decreased the number of physical access ports required on the computer.

full duplex A method of transferring data, usually over phone lines, so that data is transmitted in both directions simultaneously. In terms of speaker phones, it means that people on both ends of a call can talk at the same time. With half duplex, the initial speaker blocks others from talking.

functions *See* methods.

fuzzy logic A way of presenting and analyzing logic problems that is designed to handle subjective descriptions (e.g., hot and cold).

G

general ledger A collection of accounts that break financial data into specific categories. Common categories include accounts receivable, accounts payable, inventory, and cash.

geographic information system (GIS) Designed to identify and display relationships among business data and locations. Used to display geographical relationships. Also used to plot delivery routes and create maps.

gigabyte Approximately 1 billion bytes of data. Technically, 1024 to the third power (or 2 to the thirtieth), which is 1,073,741,824. The next highest increment is the terabyte.

global positioning system (GPS) A system of 24 satellites created by the U.S. Department of Defense. The civilian receivers will identify a location to within about a few feet. Used for navigation, track vehicles, and plotting delivery routes.

graphical user interface (GUI) A system that is based on a graphics screen instead of simple text. Users perform tasks by clicking a mouse button on or manipulating objects on the screen. For example, copies are made by dragging an item from one location on the screen to another. Pronounced as "gooey."

grid computing A system that networks multiple computers so that they cooperatively process the designated tasks, effectively functioning as a single computer.

group breaks Reports are often broken into subsections so that data in each section is grouped together by some common feature. For example, a sales report might group items by department, with subtotals for each department.

group decision support system (GDSS) A type of groupware that is designed to facilitate meetings and help groups reach a decision. Each participant uses a networked computer to enter ideas and comments. Votes can be recorded and analyzed instantly. Comments and discussion are automatically saved for further study.

groupware Software designed to assist teams of workers. There are four basic types: communication, workflow, meeting, and scheduling. The most common is communication software that supports messages, bulletin boards, and data file transfers and sharing.

H

hacker Primarily used to indicate a person who devotes a great deal of time trying to break into computer systems.

hardware The physical equipment used in computing.

high-definition television (HDTV) Transmission of television signals in digital form. It provides clearer reception. It also supports encrypted transmissions so that broadcasters can control who receives the images. HDTV also supports compression, so that more data (better pictures or more channels) can be transmitted in the same frequency space.

hot links *See* dynamic integration.

hot site A facility that can be leased from a disaster backup specialist. A hot site contains all the power, telecommunication facilities, and computers necessary to run a company. In the event of a disaster, a company collects its backup data tapes, notifies workers, and moves operations to the hot site.

hub A network device used to connect several computers to a network. Commonly used in a twisted-pair LAN. A cable runs from each computer's NIC to the hub. The hub is often connected to a router.

hypertext markup language (HTML) The standard formatting system used to display pages on the Internet. Special tags (commands inside angle braces, e.g., <HTML>) provide formatting capabilities. Several software packages automatically store text in this format, so users do not have to memorize the tags.

I

icon A small picture on a computer screen that is used to represent some object or indicate a command. A classic example is the trash can used to delete files on the Apple Macintosh.

image A graphic representation that can be described by its resolution and the number of colors. They can be stored as bit-mapped or vector images.

import An older method of exchanging data among various software packages. Most software (e.g., a database management system) can export or store data in a text file format. Another software package (e.g., a spreadsheet) can import or retrieve this data. Object Linking and Embedding is a more powerful way to exchange data.

inference engine Within an expert system, the inference engine applies new observations to the knowledge base and analyzes the rules to reach a conclusion.

information Data that has been processed, organized, and integrated to provide insight. The distinction between data and information is that information carries meaning and is used to make decisions.

information center An MIS group responsible for supporting end users. It typically provides a help desk to answer questions, programmers who provide access to corporate databases, training classes, and network support people to install and maintain networks.

information rights management (IRM) A system to control exactly what each group can do with digital data, including documents, music, and video files. A good IRM system can prevent a document from being read by outsiders, even if the document is somehow shipped outside the company's computers.

information system A collection of hardware, software, data, and people designed to collect, process, and distribute data throughout an organization.

information technology (IT) The hardware and software used to create an information system. Sometimes used as an abbreviation for management information systems.

information threats There are two classes of threats to information: (1) physical, in the form of disasters; and (2) logical, which consists of unauthorized disclosure, unauthorized modification, and unauthorized withholding of data. The primary source of danger lies with insiders: employees, ex-employees, partners, or consultants.

information warfare (IW) The use of information in a conflict setting. It includes protecting your own information, providing misinformation to the enemy, and monitoring and disrupting the enemy's information.

inheritance Creation or derivation of objects from other object classes. Each derived class inherits the attributes and methods of the prior class. For example, a savings account object can be derived from an account object. The savings account object will automatically have the same attributes and methods. Attributes and methods specific to the savings account can be added.

initial public offering (IPO) The step when firms first sell stock to the public. A method of raising additional funds and a major step for most start-up firms.

input devices People do not deal very well with binary data, so all data forms must be converted into binary form for the computer. Input devices—for example, keyboards, microphones, and bar code readers—make the conversion.

input-process-output A shorthand description of a subsystem. Each subsystem receives inputs and performs some process. The output is passed to another subsystem.

instant messaging (IM) A two-way electronic communication in real time. Short comments that you type are immediately displayed on the recipient's screen. It generally requires that both parties run the same software.

integrated data The practice of combining data from different sources to make a decision. Data can come from different departments throughout the business, and it can come in many different forms. Networks, groupware, and products that support dynamic linking are all useful tools to integrate data to make better decisions.

Integrated Services Digital Network (ISDN) A set of services, and a transmission and control system, offered by telephone companies. It uses complete digital transmission of signals to improve transmission speed and quality.

intellectual property As defined by copyright laws, the concept that property such as music, books, software, and movies can be protected. The laws clearly define the owners of the property and specify that the owners can establish any type of copy protections they desire.

Internet A collection of computers loosely connected to exchange information worldwide. Owners of the computers make files and information available to other users. Common tools on the Internet include e-mail, FTP, Telnet, and the World Wide Web.

Internet Protocol version 6 (IPv6) A set of standards that define how raw data is transmitted on the Internet and how machines are addressed. Version 6 contains several improvements to the older version 4. For example, version 6 supports 128-bit addresses compared with 32 bits in version 4. It will take several years for people to move to version 6.

Internet service provider (ISP) A private company that provides connections to the Internet. Individuals pay a fee to the ISP. The ISP pays a fee to a higher-level provider (e.g., NSP) to pass all communications onto the Internet.

intranet A network within an organization that utilizes standard Internet protocols and services. Essentially, this includes Web sites that are accessible only for internal use.

intrusion detection system (IDS) A combination of hardware and software that monitors packets and operations on the network and computers. It watches for suspicious patterns that might indicate an attack.

iterative solution Building a model and evaluating it until the parameter values converge to a fixed solution. Sometimes an iterative model will diverge and never reach an acceptable solution. *See also* circular reference.

J

joint application design (JAD) A method to reduce design time by putting everyone in development sessions until the system is designed. Users, managers, and systems analysts participate in a series of intense meetings to design the inputs (data and screens) and outputs (reports) needed by the new system.

just-in-time (JIT) inventory A production system that relies on suppliers delivering components just as they are needed in production, instead of relying on inventory stocks. JIT requires close communication between manufacturers and suppliers.

K

Kerberos A security system created at MIT that enables systems to have a single sign-on. Users log into the Kerberos server and other systems can validate the user's identity from that server. Much simpler than requiring users to log in multiple times. Named after the hound that guards the gates of Hades (spelled Cerberus in Latin).

kilobyte Approximately one thousand bytes of data. Technically it is 2 to the tenth, or 1024.

knowledge A higher level of understanding, including rules, patterns, and decisions. Knowledge-based systems are built to automatically analyze data, identify patterns, and recommend decisions.

knowledge base Within an expert system, the knowledge base consists of basic data and a set of rules.

knowledge engineer A person who helps build an expert system by organizing the data, devising the rules, and entering the criteria into the expert system shell, trained to deal with experts to derive the rules needed to create an expert system. The engineer also converts the data and rules into the format needed by the expert system.

knowledge management (KM) A system that stores information in the context of a set of decisions. It contains cross-references and search methods to make it easy for workers to understand how and why decisions were made.

L

legacy system Information systems that were created over several years and are now crucial to operating the company. They probably use older technology, and the software is difficult to modify. However, replacing them is difficult and likely to interfere with day-to-day operations. Any changes or new systems must be able to work with the older components.

limited liability company (LLC) A legal variation of organizing a company. It protects the owners with the same separation of funds offered to corporations, but because it does not allow it to issue stock, the record keeping is somewhat easier.

local area network (LAN) A collection of personal computers within a small geographical area, connected by a network. All of the components are owned or controlled by one company.

M

magnetic hard drives Magnetic hard drives (or disk drives) consist of rigid platters that store data with magnetic particles. Data is accessed by spinning the platters and moving a drive head across the platters to access various tracks.

magnetic ink character recognition (MICR) A special typeface printed with ink containing magnetic ink. It can be read rapidly and reliably by computers. Banks are the primary users of MICR. Checks are imprinted with MICR routing numbers. MICR readers are more accurate than straight OCR because they pick up a stronger signal from magnetic particles in the ink.

mail filters Programs that automatically read e-mail and sort the messages according to whatever criteria the manager prefers. Junk mail can be discarded automatically.

management information system (MIS) An MIS consists of five related components: hardware, software, people, procedures, and databases. The goal of management information systems is to enable managers to make better decisions by providing quality information.

Manufacturing Resource Planning (MRP II) An integrated approach to manufacturing. Beginning with the desired production levels, we work backward to determine the processing time, materials, and labor needed at each step. These results generate schedules and inventory needs. Sometimes known as a demand-pull system.

market basket analysis A data mining technique pioneered to see if two items are commonly purchased at the same time. Can also be used to identify any pairs of items that are associated with each other.

mass customization The ability to modify the production line often enough to produce more variations of the main product. The goal is to cover virtually all of the niche markets.

materials requirements planning (MRP) An early production system, where at each stage of production, we evaluate the usage of materials to determine the optimal inventory levels.

mathematical model A model that is defined by mathematical equations. This format is easy to use for forecasts and for simulation analyses on the computer. Be careful not to confuse precision with accuracy. A model might forecast some value with great precision (e.g., 15.9371), but the accuracy could be quite less (e.g., actual values between 12 and 18).

media For transmissions, the means of connecting computers in a network. Common methods include twisted-pair and coaxial cable; fiber-optic lines; and radio, micro, and infrared waves.

megabyte Loosely, 1 million bytes of data. Technically, it is 1,048,576 bytes of data, which is 2 raised to the 20th power.

megaflops Millions of floating-point operations per second. A measure of the processor speed, it counts the number of common arithmetical operations that can be performed in one second.

megahertz One million cycles per second, a measure of the clock chip in a computer, which establishes how fast a processor can operate.

menu tree A graphical depiction of the menu choices available to users in a system.

metadata Describes the source data, and the transformation and integration steps, and defines the way the database or data warehouse is organized.

methods Descriptions of actions that an object can perform. For example, an employee object could be hired, promoted, or released. Each of these functions would necessitate changes in the employee attributes and in other objects. The methods carry out these changes.

microsecond One-millionth of a second. Few computer components are measured in microseconds, but some electrical devices and controllers operate in that range. One microsecond compared to one second is the same as comparing one second to 11.6 days.

million instructions per second (MIPS) A measure of computer processor speed. Higher numbers represent a faster processor. However, different brands of processors use different instruction sets, so numbers are not always comparable.

millisecond One-thousandth of a second. Disk drives and some other input and output devices perform operations measured in milliseconds. One millisecond compared to one second is the same as comparing 1 second to 16.7 minutes.

mirror drive A backup system where data is automatically written to a second disk drive. If the primary drive fails, operations can be switched instantaneously to the mirror drive.

model A simplified, abstract representation of some real-world system. Some models can be written as mathematical equations or graphs; others are subjective descriptions. Models help managers visualize physical objects and business processes. Information systems help you build models, evaluate them, and organize and display the output.

modem Modulator-demodulator. A device that converts computer signals into sounds that can be transmitted (and received) across phone lines.

morphing Digital conversion of one image into another. The term is an abbreviation of *metamorphosis*. True morphing is done with digital video sequences, where the computer modifies each frame until the image converts to a new form.

multimedia The combination of the four basic data types: text, sound, video, and images (animation). In its broadest definition, multimedia encompasses virtually any combination of data types. Today, it typically refers to the use of sound, text, and video clips in digitized form that are controlled by the computer user.

multitasking A feature of operating systems that enables you to run more than one task or application at the same time. Technically, they do not run at exactly the same time. The processor divides its time and works on several tasks at once.

Musical Instrument Data Interchange (MIDI) A collection of standards that define how musical instruments communicate with each other. Sounds are stored by musical notation and are re-created by synthesizers that play the notes.

N

nanosecond One-billionth of a second. Computer processors and memory chips operate at times measured in nanoseconds. One nanosecond compared to 1 second is the same as comparing 1 second to 31.7 years.

natural language A human language used for communication with other humans, as opposed to a computer programming language or some other artificial language created for limited communication.

network address translation (NAT) A network configuration where internal computers use nonroutable addresses (usually in the 10.0.0.0 range). When connecting to devices on the Internet, the boundary router temporarily assigns a real IP address and then directs the incoming messages to the original computer by changing the address within the packets.

network interface card (NIC) The communication card that plugs into a computer and attaches to the network communication medium. It translates computer commands into network messages and server commands.

network operating system (NOS) A special operating system installed on a file server, with portions loaded to the client machines. It enables the machines to communicate and share files.

network service provider (NSP) A high-level Internet service provider offering connections to ISPs. The NSP leases high-speed, high-capacity lines to handle the communication traffic from hundreds of ISPs.

neural network A collection of artificial neurons loosely designed to mimic the way the human brain operates. Especially useful for tasks that involve pattern recognition.

neuron The fundamental cell of human brains and nerves. Each of these cells is relatively simple, but there are approximately 100 million of them.

newsgroups A set of electronic bulletin boards available on the Internet. Postings are continuously circulated around the network as people add comments.

normalization A set of rules for creating tables in a relational database. The primary rules are that there can be no repeating elements and every nonkey column must depend on the whole key and nothing but the key. Roughly, it means that each table should refer to only one object or concept.

numbers One of the basic data types, similar to text on input and output. Attributes include precision and a scaling factor that defines the true size or dimension of the number.

O

object A software description of some entity. It consists of attributes that describe the object and functions (or methods) that describe the actions that can be taken by the object. Objects are generally related to other objects through an object hierarchy.

object hierarchy Objects are defined from other base objects. The new objects inherit the properties and functions of the prior objects.

Object Linking and Embedding (OLE) A standard created by Microsoft for its Windows operating system to create compound documents and dynamically link data objects from multiple software packages. You begin with a compound document or container that holds data from other software packages. These data objects can be edited directly (embedded). Most OLE software also supports dynamic linking.

object orientation An approach to systems and programming that classifies data as various objects. Objects have attributes or properties that can be set by the programmer or by users. Objects also have methods or functions that define the actions they can take. Objects can be defined from other objects, so most are derived from the four basic data types.

object-oriented DBMS A database system specifically created to hold custom objects. Generally supports developer-defined data types and hierarchical relationships.

object-oriented design The ultimate goal of the object-oriented approach is to build a set of reusable objects and procedures. The idea is that eventually, it should be possible to create new systems or modify old ones simply by plugging in a new module or modifying an existing object.

object-oriented programming (OOP) The process of writing software using sets of extensible objects. Programmers first create objects that encapsulate internal data structures with software methods. New objects can be created by inheriting properties and methods from more generic classes. A goal of OOP was to encourage reuse of objects to reduce the time it takes to create new applications.

one-to-many relationship Some object or task that can be repeated. For instance, a customer can place many orders. In database normalization, we search for one-to-many relationships and split them into two tables.

online analytical processing (OLAP) A computer system designed to help managers retrieve and analyze data. The systems are optimized to rapidly integrate and retrieve data. The storage system is generally incompatible with transaction processing, so it is stored in a data warehouse.

online transaction processing (OLTP) A computer system designed to handle daily transactions. It is optimized to record and protect multiple transactions. Because it is generally not compatible with managerial retrieval of data, data is extracted from these systems into a data warehouse.

open operating system An operating system that is supposed to be vendor neutral. It should run on hardware from several different vendors. When a buyer upgrades to a new machine, the operating system and software should function the same as before.

open system An open system learns by altering itself as the environment changes.

operating system A basic collection of software that handles jobs common to all users and programmers. It is responsible for connecting the hardware devices, such as terminals, disk drives, and printers. It also provides the environment for other software, as well as the user interface that affects how people use the machine.

operations level Day-to-day operations and decisions. In a manufacturing firm, machine settings, worker schedules, and maintenance requirements would represent management decisions at the operations level. Information systems are used at this level to collect data and perform well-defined computations.

optical character recognition (OCR) The ability to convert images of characters (bitmaps) into computer text that can be stored, searched, and edited. Software examines a picture and looks for text. The software checks each line, deciphers one character at a time, and stores the result as text.

optimization The use of models to search for the best solutions: minimizing costs, improving efficiency, or increasing profits.

output devices   Data stored in binary form on the computer must be converted to a format people understand. Output devices—for example, display screens, printers, and synthesizers—make the conversion.

outsourcing   The act of transferring ownership or management of MIS resources (hardware, software and personnel) to an outside MIS specialist.

P

packets   Network messages are split into packets for transmission. Each packet contains a destination and source address as well as a portion of the message.

packet switching network   A communications protocol in which each message is placed into smaller packets. These packets contain a destination and source address. The packets are switched (or routed) to the appropriate computer. With high-speed switches, this protocol offers speeds in excess of 150 megabits per second.

page footer   Data that are placed at the bottom of each page in a report. Common items include page totals and page numbers.

page header   Data that is placed at the top of every page in a report. Common items include the report title, date, and column labels.

parallel processing   Using several processors in the same computer. Each processor can be assigned different tasks, or jobs can be split into separate pieces and given to each processor. There are a few massively parallel machines that utilize several thousand processors.

parameter   Variables in a model that can be controlled or set by managers. They are used to examine different situations or to tailor the model to fit a specific problem.

patent   Legal protection for products (and sometimes business processes). It grants the owner sole right to sell or create modifications of the product for 20 years. No one can create the same product unless approved by the patent owner.

peer-to-peer communication   A method of sharing data and information directly with colleagues and peers, instead of transferring data through a shared central server.

peer-to-peer network   A network configuration in which each machine is considered to be an equal. Messages and data are shared directly between individual computers. Each machine continuously operates as both a client and a server.

personal digital assistant (PDA)   A small, portable handheld computer designed primarily to handle contacts, schedules, e-mail, and short notes. Some models have more advanced features to support documents, spreadsheets, photos, and music. A few have wireless connections; others have to be synchronized with desktops to transfer e-mail and update schedules.

photo-CD   A standardized system created by Kodak to convert photographs to digital (bitmap) form and store them on optical disks.

pivot table   A tool within Microsoft Excel used to extract and organize data. It enables users to examine aggregated data and quickly see the accompanying detail.

pixel   Picture element, or a single dot on an image or video screen.

point of sale (POS) system   A means of collecting data immediately when items are sold. Cash registers are actually data terminals that look up prices and instantly transmit sales data to a central computer.

polymorphism   In an object design, different objects can have methods that have the same name but operate slightly differently. For example, a checking account object and a savings account object could each have a method called pay interest. The checking account might pay interest monthly, whereas the savings account pays it quarterly.

portable document format (PDF)   A file format often used on the Internet. It can display documents with detailed precision, including special fonts and shading. Defined by Adobe, readers are freely available for many machines. Special software must be purchased to create the files.

precision (numeric)   In computers, numeric precision represents the number of digits stored to the right of the decimal point. So, 10.1234 is more precise than 10.12; however, it is not necessarily more accurate. The original value might not have been measured beyond two digits.

prediction   Model parameters can be estimated from prior data. Sample data is used to forecast future changes based on the model.

pretty good privacy (PGP)   A dual-key encryption system based on the Diffie-Hellman approach similar to RSA. Created by Philip Zimmermann and commonly used to encrypt e-mail. Free copies for noncommercial use are still available from MIT.

primary key   A column or set of columns that contains data to uniquely identify each row in a relational database table. For example, each customer must have a unique identifier, possibly a phone number or an internally generated customer number.

privacy   (1) The concept that people should be able to go about their lives without constant surveillance, that personal information about people should not be shared without their permission. (2) Collecting personal data only when you have a legitimate use for it, allowing customers to correct and remove personal data. Protecting confidential data so that it is not released to anyone. Giving customers the option so that you do not sell or lease their personal data.

private key   In a dual-key encryption system, the key that is protected by the owner and never revealed. It is generally a very large number.

problem boundary   The line that identifies the primary components of the system that are creating a specific problem. Subsystems inside the boundary can be modified to solve the problem or enhance the system. Subsystems outside the boundary cannot be altered at this time.

procedures   Instructions that help people use the systems. They include items such as user manuals, documentation, and procedures to ensure that backups are made regularly.

process   An activity that is part of a data flow diagram. Systems can be built to process goods or to process data. Most information system work focuses on processes that alter data.

process control   The use of computers to monitor and control the production machines and robots. Production lines generally use many different machines, each requiring several adjustments or settings. Computer control simplifies and speeds the setup.

process control system   A computerized system that monitors and controls a production line. Some systems are completely linked so that a central computer can set up machines on an entire assembly line.

process innovation   Evaluating the entire firm to improve individual processes, and to search for integrated solutions that will reduce costs, improve quality or boost sales to gain a competitive advantage. *See also* reengineering.

processor   The heart of a computer. It carries out the instructions of the operating system and the application programs.

product differentiation   The ability to make your products appear different from those of your rivals, thus attracting more customers. Information systems have been used to alter products and provide new services.

properties   *See* attributes.

protect document   A method of restricting changes to Microsoft Office files. A limited version of information rights management that will allow people to read a document but not make changes.

protocols   A set of definitions and standards that establish the communication links on a network. Networks are often classified by their choice of protocol. Common protocols include Ethernet, Token Ring, and TCP/IP.

prototyping   An iterative system design technique that takes advantage of high-level tools to rapidly create working systems. The main objective of prototyping is to create a working version of the system as quickly as possible, even if some components are not included in the early versions.

pseudocode   A loosely structured method to describe the logic of a program or outline a system. It uses basic programming techniques but ignores issues of syntax and relies on verbal descriptions.

public key   In a dual-key encryption system, the key that is given to the public. Each person wishing to use dual-key encryption must have a different public key. The key works only in tandem with the user's private key.

pure Internet plays   Dot-com firms that have no direct tie to traditional business. Firms that make all their revenue from Internet sales or other Internet firms. A popular concept in 1999, but most pure Internet firms failed in 2000 and 2001.

Q

query by example (QBE)   A visual method of examining data stored in a relational database. You ask questions and examine the data by pointing to tables on the screen and filling in templates.

query system   A method of retrieving data in a DBMS. It generally uses a formal process to pose the questions (1) what columns should be displayed? (2) what conditions are given? (3) what tables are involved? and (4) how are the tables connected? See query by example and SQL.

R

radio frequency identification (RFID)   Small, passive computer chips that are powered by radio waves. When triggered by a reader, the chip returns data stored in its memory by modulating the radio signals. Readable range is limited to a few feet or less. If price drops far enough, they might replace bar codes.

random access memory (RAM) High-speed memory chips that hold data for immediate processing. On most computers, data held in RAM is lost when the power is removed, so data must be moved to secondary storage.

rapid application development (RAD) The goal of building a system much faster than with traditional SDLC methods. Using powerful tools (database management system, high-level languages, graphical toolkits, and objects), highly trained programmers can build systems in a matter of weeks or months. Using workgroups, communication networks, and CASE tools, small teams can speed up the development and design steps.

Read Only Memory (ROM) A type of memory on which data can be stored only one time. It can be read as often as needed but cannot be changed. ROM keeps its data when power is removed, so it is used to hold certain core programs and system data that is rarely changed.

reduced instruction set computer (RISC) When designing a RISC processor, the manufacturer deliberately limits the number of circuits and instructions on the chip. The goal is to create a processor that performs a few simple tasks very fast. More complex problems are solved in software. Because RISC processors require fewer circuits, they are easier to produce.

redundant array of independent disks (RAID) A system consisting of several smaller drives instead of one large drive. Large files are split into pieces stored on several different physical drives. The data pieces can be duplicated and stored in more than one location for backup. RAID systems also provide faster access to the data, because each of the drives can be searching through their part of the file at the same time.

reengineering A complete reorganization of a company. Beginning from scratch, you identify goals along with the most efficient means of attaining those goals, and create new processes that change the company to meet the new goals. The term *reengineering* and its current usage were made popular in 1990 by management consultants James Champy and Michael Hammer.

relational database A database in which all data is stored in flat tables that meet the normalization rules. Tables are logically connected by matching columns of data. System data—such as access rights, descriptions, and data definitions—are also stored in tables.

repetitive stress injury (RSI) An injury that occurs from repeating a stressful action. For instance, several people have complained that constant typing damages their wrists. Ergonomic design, adjusting your work space, and taking breaks are common recommendations to avoid repetitive stress.

replication The intentional process of duplicating data in a database so that it can be transported and accessed in multiple locations. The DBMS has the ability to synchronize data changes between the master copy and any replicas.

report A printed summary or screen display that is produced on a regular basis by a database management system. The main sections of a report are report header, page header, group/break header, detail, group/break footer, page footer, and report footer.

request for proposal (RFP) A list of specifications and questions sent to vendors asking them to propose (sell) a product that might fill those needs.

resolution The number of dots or pixels displayed per inch of horizontal or vertical space. Input and output devices, as well as images and video, are measured by their resolution. Higher values of dots per inch yield more detailed images.

reverse engineering The process of taking older software and rewriting it to modernize it and make it easier to modify and enhance. Reverse engineering tools consist of software that reads the program code from the original software and converts it to a form that is easier to modify.

rivals Any group of firms that are competing for customers and sales. Similar to competitors, but "competition" carries an economic definition involving many firms. Even an industry with two firms can experience rivalry.

Rivest-Shamir-Adelman (RSA) Three mathematicians who developed and patented a dual-key encryption system. The term often refers to the encryption technique. It is based on the computational difficulty of factoring very large numbers into their prime components.

rocket scientists Mathematically trained financial analysts who build complex mathematical models of the stock market and help create and price new securities.

router A communication device that connects subnetworks together. Local messages remain within each subnetwork. Messages between subnetworks are sent to the proper location through the router.

row A horizontal element that contains all of the data to describe an entity or object in a relational database or spreadsheet.

rules A set of conditions that describe a problem or a potential response. Generally expressed as "If . . . Then" conditions. Used by expert systems to analyze new problems and suggest alternatives.

S

sampler An input device that reads electrical signals from a microphone and stores the sound as a collection of numbers. It measures the frequency and amplitude of the sound waves thousands of times per second.

scalability The ability to buy a faster computer as needed and transfer all software and data without modification. True scalability enables users to buy a smaller computer today and upgrade later without incurring huge conversion costs.

scrolling region On a data entry form, a subform or section that is designed to collect multiple rows of data. Much like a spreadsheet, the user can move back and forth to alter or examine prior entries.

secondary storage Data storage devices that hold data even if they lose power. Typically cheaper than RAM, but slower. Disk drives are common secondary storage devices.

secure sockets layer (SSL) A system that provides encryption for Internet transmissions. Commonly used to establish a secure connection between client browsers and e-commerce servers. It is established with dual-key encryption by installing a digital security certificate on the server.

serifs The small lines, curlicues, and ornamentation on many typefaces. They generally make it easier for people to read words and sentences on printed output. Sans serif typefaces have more white space between characters and are often used for signs and displays that must be read from a longer distance.

server farm A collection of dozens or hundreds of smaller servers. Software allocates tasks to whichever server is the least busy. This approach to scalability is fault-tolerant and easy to expand, but can be difficult to manage.

service level agreement (SLA) A formal written agreement between a user group and a service provider that specifies guaranteed levels of service and compensation for failure to meet those levels. SLAs are commonly used in outsourcing deals to ensure the contracted party is providing adequate levels of service, particularly with network providers.

SharePoint Microsoft's Web-based tool for teamwork. It supports file sharing, version control, discussion groups, and surveys.

sign-off In a systems development life-cycle approach, the approval that managers must give to forms, reports, and computations at various stages of the development. This approval is given when they sign the appropriate documents.

simple object access protocol (SOAP) A standard, easy-to-implement method of exchanging information and messages among different computers on the Internet. A protocol that works with XML to support Web-based services.

simulation Models are used to examine what might happen if we decide to make changes to the process, to see how the system will react to external events, or to examine relationships in more detail.

single sign-on A comprehensive security authentication system so that users can log in (sign on) one time. Once the user's identity has been established, all applications obtain the credentials from a central server to recognize the user and determine access rights.

social legitimacy At one time, mainstream organizations were identified by the quality of their presentation and their image. Large firms spend millions of dollars on graphic artists, professional designers, and professional printing. The decreasing cost of computers enables even small organizations to create an image that is hard to distinguish from large organizations.

software A collection of computer programs that are algorithms or logical statements that control the hardware.

software maintenance The act of fixing problems, altering reports, or extending an existing system to improve it. It refers to changes in the software, not to hardware tasks such as cleaning printers.

software piracy The act of copying software without paying the copyright owner. With few exceptions (e.g., backup), copying software is illegal. Companies and individuals who are caught have to pay thousands of dollars in penalties and risk going to jail. It is commonly accepted that piracy takes money away from the development of improved software.

software suites Collections of software packages that are designed to operate together. Theoretically, data from each package can be easily shared with data from the others. So word processors can incorporate graphics, and spreadsheets can retrieve data from the database management system. Suites are often sold at a substantial discount compared to buying each package separately.

sound One of the basic data types. There are two methods to describe sound: samples or MIDI. Digitized (sampled) sound is based on a specified sampling and playback rate, and fits into frequency and amplitude (volume) ranges.

spam Unsolicited commercial e-mail, or junk mail. Unwanted messages sent by commercial entities or hackers trying to steal your system or your money. It makes up over 50 percent of e-mail traffic. Most nations have made it illegal, but it is hard to stop. The name refers to a Hormel meat product, but its use is often attributed to a Monty Python sketch.

speech recognition The ability of a computer to capture spoken words, convert them into text, and then take some action based on the command.

SQL A structured query language supported by most major database management systems. The most common command is of the form: SELECT *column list* FROM *table list* JOIN *how tables are related* WHERE *condition* ORDER BY *columns.*

standard operating procedures A set of procedures that define how employees and managers should deal with certain situations.

standards An agreement that specifies certain technical definitions. Standards can be established by committees or evolve over time through market pressures. As technology changes, new standards are created.

static HTML Simple HTML pages that are changed only by humans, so they are rarely changed. Generally used only for the prepurchase information stage of e-commerce.

static integration A means of combining data from two documents. A copy of the original is placed into the new document. Because it is static, changes made to the original document are not automatically updated. *See also* dynamic integration.

statistical quality control (SQC) The statistical analysis of measurement data to improve quality. Several statistical calculations and graphs are used to determine whether fluctuations are purely random or represent major changes that need to be corrected.

stock options A right to purchase a specific stock at a given price. Often granted to workers and managers in start-up companies. If the company grows rapidly, its stock price should increase. The option owner can cash in the options and receive the difference between the current price and the option price.

storage area network (SAN) A method of storing computer data on devices attached to a high-speed local area network instead of placing them into each computer. Separating data from the computer and centralizing it makes it easier to upgrade, control, and provide backups.

strategic decisions Decisions that involve changing the overall structure of the firm. They are long-term decisions and are unstructured. They represent an attempt to gain a competitive advantage over your rivals. They are usually difficult and risky decisions. MIS support for strategic decisions typically consists of gathering, analyzing, and presenting data on rivals, customers, and suppliers.

structured decisions Decisions that can be defined by a set of rules or procedures. They can be highly detailed, but they are defined without resorting to vague definitions.

structured walkthrough A review process in which the objective is to reveal problems, inaccuracies, ambiguities, and omissions in the system's design before the program code is finalized. The users are presented with a prototype or mockup of the proposed system.

subchapter S corporation A legal variation of a corporation that can be chosen by the owners. The IRS and some states impose limits on the type of company that can elect this option. It avoids the problem of double taxation by passing income and losses directly to the owners' personal income tax statements.

supply chain management (SCM) Organizing the entire supply process including vendor selection, parts management, ordering, tracking, payment, and quality control.

switch A network device used to connect machines. Unlike a router, a switch creates a virtual circuit that is used by a single machine at a time.

switching costs The costs incurred in creating a similar information system when a customer switches to a rival firm. Information technology creates switching costs because customers would have to convert data, recreate reports, and retrain users.

synthesizer An electronic device to convert electrical signals into sound. One basic technique is FM synthesis, which generates and combines fixed waves to achieve the desired sound. A newer method combines short digitized samples of various instruments with waveforms to create more realistic sounds.

sysop System operator. Person in charge of an electronic bulletin board who organizes files and controls access and privileges.

system A collection of interrelated objects that work toward some goal.

systems analysis and design A refinement of the scientific method that is used to analyze and build information systems.

systems analyst A common job in MIS. The analyst is responsible for designing new systems. Analysts must understand the business application and be able to communicate with users. Analysts must also understand technical specifications and programming details.

systems development life cycle (SDLC) A formal method of designing and building information systems. There are five basic phases: (1) feasibility and planning, (2) systems analysis, (3) systems design, (4) implementation, and (5) maintenance and review.

T

T1, T3 An older communication link provided by phone companies. Used to carry digitized analog signals, it is being replaced with ISDN links. T1 refers to a group of 24 voice-grade lines and can carry 1.544 megabits per second (Mbps). A T2 trunk line is equivalent to 96 voice circuits providing 6.312 Mbps. T3 provides 44.736 Mbps, and T4 can carry 139,264 Mbps. Services can be leased at any of these levels, where greater bandwidth carries higher costs.

table A method of storing data in a relational database. Tables contain data for one entity or object. The columns represent attributes, and data for each item is stored in a single row. Each table must have a primary key.

tactical decisions Tactical decisions typically involve time frames of less than a year. They usually result in making relatively major changes to operations but staying within the existing structure of the organization. MIS support consists of databases, networks, integration, decision support systems, and expert systems.

Telnet A method supported on the Internet that enables users of one computer to log on to a different computer. Once logged on to the new system, the user is treated as any other user on the system.

terabyte Approximately 1 trillion bytes of data. Technically, it is 2 to the 40th power.

text The simplest of the four basic data types, it also includes numbers. In its most basic form, text is made up of individual characters, which are stored in the computer as numbers. More sophisticated text is described by its typeface, font size, color, and orientation (rotation).

thin client Simpler hardware than a full-blown personal computer, with minimal software. It is generally used to display applications running on the server and to accept input from the user.

Token Ring A communications protocol that describes when each machine can send messages. A machine can transmit only when it receives a special message called a token. When the message is finished or a time limit is reached, the token is passed to the next machine.

top-down development An approach to designing and building systems that begins with an analysis of the entire company and works down to increasing detail. A complete top-down approach is usually impossible because it takes too long to analyze everything. *See also* bottom-up development.

total cost of ownership (TCO) The cost of purchasing and running a client computer (personal computer). A highly subjective number, it typically includes the hardware cost, the software license fees, maintenance costs, and training costs.

total quality management (TQM) A management doctrine stating that quality must be built into every process and item. Every step and each person must be dedicated to producing quality products and services.

track changes A method in Microsoft Word that highlights the changes made by each person. The original author can then choose to accept or reject each change. A useful groupware tool when several people need to co-operate on writing a document.

transaction-processing system A system that records and collects data related to exchanges between two parties. This data forms the foundation for all other information system capabilities. MIS support typically consists of databases, communication networks, and security controls.

transborder data flow (TBDF) The transfer of data across national boundaries. Some countries place restrictions on the transfer of data, especially data that relates to citizens (and, of course, data related to "national security"). Some people have discussed taxing the flow of data.

triggered rule In an expert system, if a rule is used in an application, it is said to have been triggered or fired.

Trojan horse A special program that hides inside another program. Eventually, when the main program is run, the Trojan horse program might delete files, display a message, or copy data to an external computer.

true color Humans can distinguish about 16 million colors. Devices that can display that many colors are said to display true color. It requires the device to use 3 bytes (24 bits) for each pixel.

Turing test A test proposed by Alan Turing in which a machine would be judged "intelligent" if the software could use conversation to fool a human into thinking it was talking with a person instead of a machine.

twisted-pair cable Common dual-line wire. Often packaged as three or four pairs of wires. The cable can be run for only a limited distance, and the signal is subject to interference.

typeface A defined way to draw a set of text characters. Several thousand typefaces have been created to meet different artistic and communication needs. A common characterization is serif and sans serif typefaces.

U

Unicode An international standard that defines character sets for every modern (living) language and many extinct languages (e.g., Latin).

uninterruptible power supply (UPS) A large battery and special circuitry that provide a buffer between the computer and the power supply. It protects the computer from spikes and brownouts.

universal description, discovery, and integration (UDDI) A public Web-based directory system designed to enable computers to find and use Web services offered by other companies. For example, someday your computer could automatically find all companies that can use current exchange rates to convert prices.

UNIX A popular operating system created by Bell Labs. It is designed to operate the same on hardware from several different vendors. Unfortunately, there are several varieties of UNIX, and software that operates on one version often must be modified to function on other machines.

unstable model A model that cannot be solved for a single solution. The solution might continually diverge, or it could oscillate between several alternatives, generally due to insufficient or incorrect feedback mechanisms.

upload To transfer files from a local computer (usually a personal computer) to a distant computer. *See also* download.

Usenet *See* newsgroups.

user resistance People often resist change. Implementation of a new system highlights this resistance. Managers and developers must prepare for this resistance and encourage users to change. Education and training are common techniques.

V

value chain A description of the many steps involved in creating a product or service. Each step adds value to the product or service. Managers need to evaluate the chain to find opportunities to expand the firm and gain more sales and profits.

vector image A stored collection of mathematical equations, representing lines, circles, and points. These equations can be rescaled to fit any output device or to any desired size. Users deal with the base objects, not the mathematical definitions.

venture capital Money offered by specialized firms to start up companies. Banks rarely give money to start-ups, so venture capitalists finance risky ventures in the hope of high profits when the company goes public. Many strings can be attached to the money—including a loss of control.

version control Software that tracks changes made to other documents. Often used in software development to enable developers to go back to prior version. It is also available for common business documents and files. A limited version is embedded into Microsoft Word.

video One of the basic data types. Video combines the attributes of images and sound. An important attribute is the frames-per-second definition. U.S. standard video operates at 30 frames per second; movie films run at 24 frames per second. Digitizing video requires capturing and playing back the frames at the appropriate speed.

videoconference A meeting tool that transmits images and sound of at least one participant. Often, video cameras are available to everyone involved in the conference. High-end systems enable the participants to control the cameras.

view A stored query. If you have a complex query that you have to run every week, you (or a database specialist) could create the query and save it as a view with its own name. It is then treated much like a simple table.

virtual mall A collection of Web-based merchants who join together for marketing purposes. Generally they share a common Web host and the same commerce server software. By sharing costs, they can survive without a huge amount of sales.

virtual private network (VPN) Software installed on a company network and on each client that automatically encrypts all communications between the two; useful when workers travel or need to reach the company servers from home using the Internet.

virtual reality (VR) Virtual reality describes computer displays and techniques that are designed to provide a realistic image to user senses, including three-dimensional video, three-dimensional sound, and sensors that detect user movement that is translated to on-screen action.

virus A malicious program that hides inside another program. As the main program runs, the virus copies itself into other programs. At some point, the virus displays a message, shuts down the machine, or deletes all of the files.

Visual Basic A modern variation of the BASIC programming language created by Microsoft for application programming in Windows. A variation resides inside many of the Microsoft applications, enabling programmers to manipulate and exchange data among the database, spreadsheet, and word processor.

visual table of contents A graphical design method that shows how modules of a system are related. Versions of the technique are also used to display menu trees.

voice mail A messaging system similar to telephone answering machines but with additional features like message store and forward. You can use your computer to send messages to coworkers. There are tools that will read e-mail and fax messages over the phone, so managers can stay in touch while they are away from the computer.

voice over Internet protocol (VoIP) Connecting telephones to the network and using the Internet to transfer phone conversations—instead of traditional phone lines.

voice recognition The ability of a computer to capture spoken words and convert them into text.

W

Webmaster Specialized IS worker who is responsible for creating, maintaining, and revising a company's World Wide Web site. Webmasters use technical and artistic skills to create sites that attract browsers.

wide area network (WAN) A network that is spread across a larger geographic area. In most cases, parts of the network are outside the control of a single firm. Long-distance connections often use public carriers.

window A portion of the computer screen. You can move each window or change its size. Windows enable you to display and use several applications on the screen at one time.

wisdom A level above knowledge. Wisdom represents intelligence, or the ability to analyze, learn, adapt to changing conditions, and create knowledge.

workflow software A type of groupware that is designed to automate forms handling and the flow of data in a company. Forms and reports are automatically routed to a list of users on the network. When each person adds comments or makes changes, it is routed to the next process.

workstations Computers attached to a network, designed for individual use. Typically, personal computers.

World Wide Web (WWW) A first attempt to set up an international database of information. Web browsers display graphical pages of information, including pictures. Hypertext connections enable you to get related information by clicking highlighted words.

WYSIWYG What you see is what you get. With a true WYSIWYG system, documents will look exactly the same on the screen as they do when printed. In addition to format, it means that the printer must have the same typefaces as the video display. Color printers use a system to match the colors on the monitor.

Z

zShops Amazon.com offers small companies a relatively inexpensive e-commerce solution with little or no fixed costs. Useful for small firms, the system provides marketing, visibility, and a payment mechanism.

Organization Index

A. T. Kearney, 228
A&W, 33
AARP, 155
ABC, 13
ABC News, 275
Accenture, 149, 176, 445, 485, 504, 557
Adobe, 281, 543
ADP (Automated Data Processing), 249, 504
Advanced Micro Devices, 49
Advanced Research Projects Agency, 98
AeroComm, 33
Affiliated Computer, 504
Ahold's Stop & Shop division, 202
AHS (American Hospital Supply), 22–23, 75, 413
Air Transport Association (ATA), 435
Airborne, 338
Airtran, 434
AirTrans, 395
Alaska Airlines, 439
Albertson's, 8, 202, 203, 232–233, 280
Allegiance Corporation, 23
Allina Hospitals and Clinics, 21
Amadeus Global Travel Distribution, 439
Amazon.com, 57, 280, 284, 294–295, 302, 365, 381
Amerada Hess, 520
America Online (AOL), 13, 72, 99, 107
American Airlines, 117, 395, 402, 413, 416, 433
American Express, 123, 387
American Freightways, 340
American Hospital Supply (AHS), 22–23, 75, 413
American Management Systems, 487
American Stores, 232
Ameritrade, 461
Andarko Petroleum, 520, 524
Anderson Merchandisers, 229
Anheuser-Busch, 259
ANSI (American National Standards Institute), 95
AOL (America Online), 13, 72, 99, 107
Apple Computer, 56, 69, 70
Applebee's International, 28
Ariba, 160
Ark Digital Technologies, 195
Arkansas Aviation Sales, 340
Asia Vital Components (AVC), 50
ATA (Air Transport Association), 435
AT&T, 13, 56, 99, 341, 408, 416, 484, 509
AT&T Wireless, 416
AT&T WorldNet, 99
Atriax, 389
Augusta Chronicle, 532
Automated Data Processing (ADP), 249, 504

Baja Fresh Mexican Cuisine, 28
Bakersfield Californian, 532
Bandai Inc., 252
Bank of America, 63, 388, 391
Bank One, 215
Baxter Healthcare, 23, 24, 405, 411, 413
Bay Alarm Co., 311
Baylor Health Care System, 116
BearingPoint, 524
Bears, Chicago, 193
Bell Labs, 554
Benetton, 203
Berlitz, 230
Best Buy, 72, 344

Beth Israel Deaconess Medical Center (BIDMC), 572
Bigg's superstores, 202
BitPass, 204
Blue Cross Blue Shield of Massachusetts, 572
Boeing, 373
Boeing Information Systems, 405
Bonlat Financing Corp., 201
Borgata Hotel Casino and Spa, 128
Borland, 557
Boston Celtics, 194
Boston Market, 28, 29
BP (British Petroleum), 525
BP/Amoco, 520
Brigham and Women's Hospital, 574
Brightmail, 107, 110
Bristol-Myers Squibb, 159–160
Broadlane Inc., 21
Bureau of Customs and Border Protection, 143
Bureau of Economic Analysis, 560
Bureau of Labor Statistics, 6, 538, 560
Bureau of the Census, 362
Burger King, 27, 31, 401
Burroughs, 479

C. J. Driscoll & Associates, 533
CAB (Civil Aeronautics Board), 433
Cablevision, 99
Caliber System, 340
California Pacific Medical Center, 570
Callaway Golf, 294
Calpers, 571
Cap Gemini Ernst & Young, 341
Capable Toys factory, 252
Capital One, 387, 389–390, 391
Capital One Financial Corporation, 278
CAPTA, 267
Cardinal Health, 23, 75, 115
CareGroup Health System, 572
Caribbean Transportation Services, 340
Carlson Wagonlit Travel, 439
Carnegie Mellon University, 490
Carolina Panthers, 193
Carphone Warehouse Group, 354
Caterpillar, 373
CCH (Credit Clearing House), 368
CCITT. See ITU
CDISC (Clinical Data Interchange Standards Consortium), 161
Census Bureau (U.S.), 308, 560
Center for Information Technology Leadership, 574
Center for Regulatory Effectiveness, 560
Center for Science in the Public Interest, 30
Central Connecticut State University, 555
Century Analysis, 570
CERN, 103
Chase, 388
Chevron, 522–523
ChevronTexaco, 493, 520, 523–524
Chicago Bears, 193
Chipotle Mexican Grill, 28, 29
Cinergy Corp., 243
Cingular, 416
Cinnabar, 418
Cisco, 242, 573
Citibank, 388, 389
Citicorp, 215, 387
Citigroup, 158, 349, 388–389
Civil Aeronautics Board (CAB), 433
Claria Corp., 173
Clear Channel Communications, Inc., 410

Clear Channel Radio, 204
Clinical Data Interchange Standards Consortium, 161
CNN, 275, 551
Coca-Cola, 510
Coldwell Banker real estate company, 229
Comcast, 189
Commerce Department, 89
Compaq Computer, 17, 70, 277
CompTIA, 30
Computer Technology Industry Association. See CompTIA
Conoco/Phillips, 520
Covisint, 243, 251, 270
Credit Clearing House (CCH), 368
CSC (Computer Sciences Corporation), 231, 487, 488, 504
CSC Index, 17
CVS, 228
Cyrix/IBM, 49

Daewoo, 264, 267
DaimlerChrysler, 63, 264, 269–270, 322, 438
Darden Restaurants, 28
Dassault Systemes AG, 269, 270
Datek, 461
Dean Witter, 229
Defense Science Board, 82
Dell Computer, 17, 39, 68, 69, 70–72, 340, 411
Delta Air Lines, 395, 434, 435–437
Delta Express, 436
Denver Broncos, 193
Department of Defense, 82, 203, 362, 375, 377
Department of Health and Children (Ireland), 149
Department of Health and Human Services, 28
Department of Homeland Security, 176, 339
Deutsche Post, 338, 345
Deutsche Telekom, 35
DHL/Deutsche Post, 338, 339, 344–346
Diamondbacks, Phoenix, 195
DiamondCluster International, 515
Digital Equipment Corp., 405
Direct Satellite, 99
Disney, 13
dj Orthopedics, 246
Donato's Pizza, 29
DoubleClick, 289, 290, 291, 531–532
Dow Chemical, 243, 255
DuPont, 408
Dutch Ahold, 280

E. W. Scripps Co., 288
EarthLink, 99, 186, 310
EasyAsk, 230
EBay.com, 293
E-Citi, 389
EDS (Electronic Data Systems), 445, 453, 503, 504, 506
Edward Jones brokerage firm, 307
Electronic Frontier Foundation (EFF), 563
Elemica, Inc., 243
Eli Lilly and Company, 123, 157–158
Ellis & Everard, 118
EM, 231
eMachines, 39, 59, 69
Endeca, 230
Energy Department (U.S.), 520

England, Inc., 251
Escort Memory Systems, 267
Esker SA, 240
ESPN, 288
Evergreen International Airlines, 340
Excite, 417
Experian Marketing Services, 143
ExxonMobil, 493, 520, 521–522

FAA (Federal Aviation Administration), 443, 478–482
Fair Isaac, 391
Family Dollar, 217
FCC (Federal Communications Commission), 87, 89, 310
FDA (Food and Drug Administration), 156, 161, 568
Federal Computer Week, 560
Federal Trade Commission (FTC), 169, 509, 522, 560
FedEx Corp., 315, 338, 339, 340–342, 397, 405–406, 411, 412
Feist Publications, 559
Fiat, 264, 267
FindLaw, 560
First Data Corporation, 35, 228
First Genetic Trust, 159
Fiserv, 504
Flying Tigers network, 340
Food and Drug Administration (FDA), 156, 161, 568
Force10 networks, 490
Ford Motor Company, 235, 264, 265, 266–267, 279, 322
Fractal Edge, 354
France Telecom, 143
FreshDirect, 280
Frito-Lay, 411
FTC (Federal Trade Commission), 169, 509, 522, 560
Fujitsu, 59, 438
Fujitsu Siemens Computers, 69

Galileo International, 439
GAO (General Accounting Office), 478
Gartner Group, 213, 495
Gateway, 39, 59, 68–69, 70, 72
Genentech, 156
General Administration for Industry and Commerce (China), 550
General Electric, 411
General Magic, 380
Geological Survey (U.S.), 362
Gitano, 221
GlaxoSmithKline, 156, 158–159
Global Advisory Council on Healthy Lifestyles, 28
Global Services, 503
GM (General Motors), 169, 264, 265, 267–268, 279, 283, 322, 351–352, 396, 409
Google, 9, 230, 281
Government Computer News, 560
Government Technology, 560
Grant Thornton accounting firm, 201
Groxis, Inc., 9
Grumman Corporation, 486
GTE, 99

Halifax General Insurance, 557
Halliburton, 520
Harris Interactive, 540
Hartford Courant, 555
HCA Inc., 115

Health Net insurance, 571
Health Technology Center, 537
Hear Music, 36
Hewlett-Packard Co., 17, 39, 59, 69, 70
Highway Insurance Holdings, 557
Home Depot, 294
Honda, 264, 266–267, 376
Honeywell, 258
Hospital Logistics, Inc., 21
Household International, 391
Hyperion, 438

IAB (Interactive Advertising Bureau), 287
IBM, 56–57, 59, 69, 99, 116, 439, 486, 520, 523, 524
IBM Global Services, 504
ICANN (Internet Corporation for Assigned Names and Numbers), 97
ICC (Interstate Commerce Commission), 343
IETF (Internet Engineering Task Force), 97
Information Resources Inc., 259
Infosys, 514
Initiate Systems, 570
Intel, 49, 408
Interactive Advertising Bureau (IAB), 287
Internal Revenue Service (IRS), 309, 482–489, 554, 560
International Business Machines Corporation. See IBM
International Franchise Association, 13
International Telecommunications Union (ITU), 88, 95, 108
Internet Corporation for Assigned Names and Numbers (ICANN), 97
Internet Engineering Task Force (IETF), 97
Internet Storm Center, 189
Interstate Commerce Commission (ICC), 343
IQNavigator, 522
IRS (Internal Revenue Service), 309, 482–489, 554, 560
ISO, 95
Isuzu, 267
ITA software, 439
ITU (International Telecommunications Union), 88, 95, 108

J. P. Morgan, 240, 354, 388
Jack in the Box, 28
Jeff McClusky & Associates, 410
JetBlue, 395, 434, 436, 437, 540
Jewel-Osco grocery/drugstores, 232
Johnson & Johnson, 115
Johnson Controls, Inc., 269
Jupiter Media Metrix, 303

Kaiser Permanente, 438
Kendall Company, 115
KFC, 33, 34
Kimberly-Clark, 228
Kinko's, 217, 315, 341, 412
Kmart, 228
KnowX, 560
Kraft, Inc., 35
Kroger, 232

Labor Department (U.S.), 30
Laird Norton Financial Group, 232
Land Registry in the UK, 143
LandAmerica Financial Group, 104
Landmark, 520
Lands' End, 229–231, 279
La-Z-Boy, Inc., 251
LeapFrog Enterprises, Inc., 252
Legal Information Institute at Cornell, 560
Legato, 324
Levi Strauss, 403–404
LexiQuest, 160

Lexis, 560
Library of Congress, 560
Lilly. See Eli Lilly and Company
Liquid Audio, 229
Long John Silver's, 33
Loral Corporation, 486
Lotus Corporation, 557
Lyondell-Citgo Refining LP, 521

Magna Steyr, 269
MailBoxes Etc., 343, 412
Massachusetts General Hospital, 574
MasterCard, 278, 386, 387
MatrixOne, 269
Maytag, 411
MBNA, 387
McDonald's Corporation, 3, 12, 27–31
McDonnell Douglas, 260, 366
MCI, 13, 99
McKesson, 23, 115
McKesson Chemical, 118
McKinsey and Co., 389, 445
Mellon Bank, 373
Merchants Parcel Delivery. See UPS
Merrill Lynch, 18, 388, 392–393, 397, 401, 405
Meta Group, 243
Metreo Inc., 345
Metro Group, 205
Michelin, 231
Microsoft, 63–64, 73, 150, 176, 177, 281, 316, 324, 445, 543
Microsoft Network, 99
MIT, 157, 574
Mitsubishi Motors, 270, 281
Mobil, 493, 521, 522
Moody's, 389
Motion Picture Association of America, 63, 196, 283
Motorola, 49, 341, 406
Mrs. Fields Cookies, 11, 12
MyFamily.com, Inc., 275

Napster, 405, 542
NASA (National Aeronautics and Space Administration), 481, 489–491
National Bicycle Industrial Company (Japan), 241
National Football League, 165
National Hi-Tech Crime Unit (UK), 183
National Institute of Health, 159
National Restaurant Association, 30
National Science Foundation, 98
National Security Agency (NSA), 186, 553
Navy, 453, 506
NBA, 194–195
NCAA, 371
NCR Corporation, 31, 402
Neoforma, Inc., 246
Netegrity Inc., 116
netNumina, Inc., 161
Nets, New Jersey, 195
NetSuite, 169
Network Solutions, 286
Net-Zero, 310
New England Patriots, 193
New Jersey Nets, 195
New York city, 362
The New York Times, 288, 532
NHTCU. See National Hi-Tech Crime Unit (UK)
NSA (National Security Agency), 186, 553
NuGenesis Technologies Corporation, 160
NuTec Energy Services, 524
Nvest, 428

O&M. See Owens & Minor
Oanda, 541
Occupational Safety and Health Administration (OSHA), 249

OgilvyInteractive, 288
Omaha Steaks, 294
1edisource.com, 211
Online Publishers Association, 275
Opel, 267
Open Harbor, 339
Oracle, 239
Orlando Magic, 194–195
OSHA (Occupational Safety and Health Administration), 249
Owens & Minor, 23, 75, 115–116

Pacific Investment Management, 437
Pac-West Telecomm, Inc., 310
Panera Bread Company, 28
Panopticon Software AB, 354
Pantellos Group, 243
Panthers, 193
Parmalat, 201, 260
Partners HealthCare System, Inc., 574
Pasta Bravo, 34
Patent and Trademark Office, 560
Patent Office, 558
Patriots, New England, 193
Peapod, 278
Pentagon, 82
People Express Airlines, 395, 402, 405, 433, 434
PeopleSoft, 239, 486
Peppercoin, 204
PepsiCo, 34
Perot Systems, 116, 504
Petz Enterprises, 273, 308
Pew Internet, 327
Pfizer, 160–162
PGP, 171
Phoenix Diamondbacks, 195
Pizza Hut, 33, 34
Polycom, 320
Portland Trail Blazers, 194
Postini, Inc., 107
PRC, Inc., 249
Premier Health Partners, Inc., 246
Pret A Manger, 29
PricewaterhouseCoopers, 32, 489
Primerica, 388
Princeton, 373
ProCD, Inc., 559
Proctor & Gamble, 228
Prodigy, 548
Providian, 387, 391

Qantas, 436
Quintiles, Inc., 161
Quiznos Sub franchise, 13
Qwest, 99, 310

The Rack, 534
RealNetworks, 281
Redskins, Washington, 193
Regions Bank, 292
RelayHealth, 572
ReturnBuy, Inc., 294
Revenue Science, Inc., 288
RightNow Technologies, 481
Roadway Package System (RPS), 340
Robert Half, 503
Royal Dutch Petroleum (Shell), 493, 522–523
Royal Pakhoed, 118
Royal Van Ommeren, 118
Royal Vopak, 118
RPS (Roadway Package System), 340
RSA, 177
Rural Telephone Service, 559

Saab, 267
Safeguard Scientifics, 311
Safeway, 232, 280
Salesforce.com, 240
Salomon Brothers Capital Fund, 232
Salomon Smith Barney, 349, 389
SAP, 239, 489, 521

SAT corporation, 520
SBA (Small Business Administration), 273
Scaled Composites, 490
ScanSoft Inc., 486
Schlumberger Ltd., 520, 522–523
SCO, 63
SCP Private Equity Partners, 311
Sears, Roebuck and Co., 229–231, 274, 294, 388, 528
Season Ticket Solutions, 195
Seattle Coffee Company, 35
SEC (Securities and Exchange Commission), 560
Secret Service, 563
SeeBeyond Technology Corporation, 570
SenderBase, 189
Service Employees International Union, 571
7Safe Ltd., 183
Sharper Image, 294
Shearson and Salomon, 388
Shell Oil, 522. See also Royal Dutch Petroleum
Short's Travel Agency, 371
Siebel Systems, 240, 255, 416
Siemens, 59, 570
Sierra Beverage, 259
Skywest, 436
Small Business Administration (SBA), 273
Song airline, 435, 436
Southwest Airlines, 395, 434, 435, 436, 437–438, 481
SpeedingTicket.net, 558
Sperry-Rand/Univac, 479
Sprint, 99
Stanford Linear Accelerator Center (SLAC), 143
Starband, 99
Starbucks Corp., 31, 34
Strategy Analytics, 520
Subaru, 264
Sun Microsystems, 56, 73, 150, 520, 553
Sundance Institute, 36
Supervalu Inc., 202
Sutter Health, 527, 570–571
Suzuki, 264, 267
Sybase, 570

Taco Bell, 33, 34, 217
Tacoda Systems, Inc., 288
Target, 228
Tata, 503
TCI, 13
Ted airline, 435
Tesoro Petroleum Inc., 521
Texaco, 523
Thawte, 171
Thomson Financial, 392
3M, 408
Time/Warner, 13
Tivo, 365
TL Ventures, 311
T-Mobile USA Inc., 31, 35
Toshiba, 59
Toshiba Corporation, 69, 344
TowerGroup, 340
Toyota, 264, 266–267, 269
Toys "R" Us, 217
Trail Blazers, Portland, 194
Travelers, 349, 388
TriState Promotions, 410
TRW, 484
Tumbleweed, 514
Tyco International, 115

Unisys, 479
United Airlines, 416, 434, 435, 437
United Reporting Publishing Corp., 558
Univar, 118–120

UPS (United Parcel Service), 123, 338, 339, 340, 343–344, 406, 412
USPS (United States Postal Service), 338, 339
UUNet, 99

Valencia Group, 31
ValiCert, 514
ValueLink, 35
Van Waters & Rogers, 118–120
VantageMEd Corp., 17
Vauxhall, 267
Verifone, 33
Verisign, 171, 182, 286

Verizon, 106, 143
Vertex, Inc., 299
Viking Freight, 340
Visa International, 218, 278, 386, 387
Vivisimo, Inc., 9
Vopak, 118

W. W. Grainger, 116–118
Wachovia, 388
The Wall Street Journal, 288
Wal-Mart, 11, 199, 203, 217, 222, 226, 227–229, 232, 240–241, 275, 387, 405
The Washington Post, 302, 532

Washington Redskins, 193
Wayport Inc., 31
Webvan grocery delivery company, 8, 278, 280
Weight Watchers International Inc., 28
Wells Fargo Bank, 215, 388
Wendy's, 28, 31, 33
WestLaw, 560
Whirlpool, 411
William Blair Capital Partners, 311
Wipro, 416
Wired News, 63
Work Design Collaborative, 540
World Health Organization, 28

World Tariff, 340
World Trade Organization (WTO), 15
WorldCom, 13
Worldspan, 439

X.com corporation, 215
Xinhua, 550

Yaga, 204
Yahoo, 287, 300–301
Yan Can Chinese Restaurant, 28, 34
Yellow Transportation, 119
Yum! Brands Inc., 28, 33–34

Subject Index

Symbols and Numbers

% (percent sign), matching exactly one character, 130
* (asterisk)
  matching any characters, 130
  in SQL, 131
_ (underscore) as a SQL wildcard, 130
? (question mark) wildcard character, 130
3-D model search engine, 373
3G mobile phones, 88
4/3 aspect ratio, 45
10Base-T, 577
16/9 aspect ratio, 45
32-bit processors, 41
64-bit processors, 41

A

AAS (Advanced Automation System), 479, 481
ABC (activity-based coding), 577
Abell, Pete, 227
ACARS, 481
access
  controls, 150, 176–177
  to data on the Internet, 103–104
  speed, 577
  to technology, 546–548
Access software
  building forms in, 144
  QBE examples, 129–131
accessibility tools for software, 538–539
accounting
  audits, 260–261
  cycle, 246–247
  journal, 245, 577
  for a new business, 427–428
  statements, 420
  systems, 242, 244–247
accounting standards board (AICPA), 260
accounts
  categorizing data by, 245
  payable, 245
  receivable, 245
ACMS, 481
Acquire, 481
Active Directory (AD), 32, 116
activity-based coding (ABC), 577
acute mark, 60
Adams, S., 65
addresses on the Internet, 100–102
Adobe Acrobat, 322
Advanced Automation System (AAS), 479, 481
Advanced Encryption Standard (AES), 181, 577
"Advanced" searches on the Internet, 20
advertisers, Web advertising and, 288–289
advertising. See also Web advertising
  handling through an intermediary, 289, 290
  plan, 425
  revenue for e-commerce firms, 302–303
  traditional, 287
advocacy role, 501, 577
Aeronautical Radio system (ARINC), 481
AES (advanced encryption standard), 181, 577
agents, 380–381, 577
  external, 21–22, 397–401, 582
  features of, 381
  virtual, 374
Agile RUP, 451
Agnew, Marion, 120

AI (artificial intelligence), 350, 372, 378, 577
AICPA, 260
air traffic control, 436, 478–480
Aircraft Communication Addressing and Reporting System (ACARS), 481
Aircraft Monitory System (ACMS), 481
AirFlite Profit Manager, 439
airline industry cases, 433–440
airlines, shifting sales to the Internet, 276–277
AIX, 56
Albergotti, Reed, 390, 391
Albertson, Joe, 232
alert zone, 480
alerts, adding to shared items, 334, 335
Alexander, Max, 354
algorithms, common, 444
ALL keyword in SQL, 131
Amando-Blanco, Jose, 143
Amanovich, Andy, 176
Amazon MarketPlace, 294
American National Standards Institute (ANSI), 207, 208, 577
American standard code for information interchange (ASCII), 577
Americans with Disabilities Act, 538
amplitude, 45
analysts, 125
analytical methodology, 447
anchor tag, 96
AND conditions in QBE, 130
Anderson, Ann, 474
angel investor, 577
anonymity, 325, 536
Ansari X Prize, 490
ANSI X12, 207, 208
"answer line" databases, 411
Ante, Spencer E., 116
Anthes, Gary H., 223, 440, 451
Anthony, Robert, 18, 25
antitrust laws, 415–417, 577
antivirus software, 172
apnic.net (Asia), 101
Applegate, Lynda M., 430
applicability statement 2 (AS2) standard, 228
application generators, 146
application layer of TCP/IP, 97–98
application service providers (ASPs), 169, 296–297, 577
applications
  assembling from components, 446–448
  creating, 142–148
  improving existing, 454
  objects created by, 41
  prepackaged, 448
  programming capabilities in packages, 498
  software, 58–64
apprenticeship program for prospective project managers, 30
ArcInfo, 362, 400
area managers, 11
ARINC, 481
arin.net (America), 101
Arkin, William, 566
armed services, manual and electronic security role, 174
Army Battle Command Systems, 552
Arnett, Kirk P., 517
Arnold, David, 517
Arpanet, 98
art libraries, 60

artificial intelligence (AI), 350, 372, 378, 577
ARTS (Automated Radar Terminal System), 480
ASCII, 577
aspect ratios, 45
ASPs (application service providers), 169, 296–297, 577
Assheton, Alistair, 170
assumptions, 577
asterisk (*)
  matching any characters, 130
  in SQL, 131
asynchronous communication, 317
Atick, Joseph, 176
ATM (asynchronous transfer mode), 577
attacks on information systems, 551–552
attributes, 124, 577. See also properties
auction fraud, 169
auction sites, 114, 293, 295
auctions, 285, 577
audit trails, 179, 247, 577
auditing, 201
audits
  accounting, 260–261
  of data, 178
AUR (Automated Under-Reporter), 485
authentication, 181–182, 577
automated customer service systems, 374
Automated Examination System (AES), 483
automated inventory control systems, 246
Automated Radar Terminal System (ARTS), 480
automobile industry cases, 264–270
automobiles
  collaborating on, 322
  e-commerce and, 279–280
  production of, 267–268
AVG function in SQL, 131

B

B2B (business to business), 7, 275, 578
  auction sites, 251, 277
  auctions, 24, 285
  e-commerce and, 284–286
  Web sites, 114, 243
B2C (business-to-consumer), 7, 8, 274, 578
  e-commerce and, 278–284
  finding successful strategies for the Internet, 280–281
Babcock, Charles, 115
babel.altavista.com site, 541
Bacheldor, Beth, 116, 229, 233, 340, 342, 344
backbone, 91, 577
backup systems on networks, 81
backups, 55, 150, 174–175, 509
backward chaining, 577
"Bag a McMeal" nutrition tool, 30
Baglole, Joel, 389
balance of power, 544–545
balance sheets, 245
Balfour, Fiona, 436
Band, William, 36
Bandrowczak, Steve J., 345
bandwidth
  conserving, 104
  between major world regions, 547–548
  required to transmit realistic video data, 320
  scarcity of, 82
Bank, David, 173, 240
banking industry, 12

banks, making money, 387
bar chart, 61
bar code point-of-care (BPOC) technology, 570
bar code scanners, 201
bar codes
  for drug doses, 568–569, 570
  limitations of, 202
  versus RFID, 205
Barabba, Vincent, 352, 383
Barclay, Paul, 534
Baron, Talila, 195
barriers to entry, 401–402, 403, 405, 421, 541, 577
Barrington, Richard, 553
Bartels, Chuck, 229
bartleby.com, 6
baseball. See MLB
BASIC, 577
basketball, professional, 194
Bass, Alison, 542
Bass, Bill, 230
battle, information technologies in, 552
BBS (bulletin board system), 578
Becker, David, 309
Beckett, Paul, 278
Beckmann, Clems, 345
Beckwith, Harry, 29, 36
Beginners All-purpose Symbolic Instruction Code (BASIC), 577
Bell, Charles, 29
Bell, Wayne, 310
benchmark, 577
benefits, cafeteria-style, 249
Benko, Laura B., 571
Bennet, Michael, 193
Benson, Mike, 416
Bequai, August, 190
Berard, Jean-Michel, 240
Bergstein, Brian, 362
Berinato, Scott, 573
Berman, Dennis K., 87
BETWEEN statement in QBE, 130
Bialik, Carl, 288, 532
biases in decision making, 351–352
bill of materials, 220, 577
bill presentation and payment, 215, 577
Billpoint, 215, 293
binary data, 40, 577
biometrics, 176, 577
Birnbaum, Jeffrey H., 488
bitmap image, 44, 577
bits, 40, 577
Black-Scholes equation, 460
Bleakley, Fred, 223
blockbuster drugs, 157
blogs, 79–80, 289, 290, 319, 327, 577
Bluck, John, 481
Blum, Brady, 31
Blumenthal, Robin, 233
Blunkett, David, 553
board of directors, 577
Boehme, Alan, 345
Bond, David, 437
Booker, Ellis, 25
Boolean searches, 20, 577
Bork Bill, 535
Borkar, Shekhar, 50
Borzo, Jeanette, 304, 354
Boslet, Mark, 73
bottom-up development, 462, 577
boundaries of a system, 463, 464
Bounds, Gwendolyn, 308

BPM (business process management), 324–325, 578. *See also* workflow
brainstorming, 577
break-even analysis, 424
breaks in reports, 145
Brewin, Bob, 36, 73, 229, 342, 344, 438, 482, 569, 571, 574
Brinded, Malcolm, 522
BroadBand Access, 106
broadband connections, 91
broadcasts, 87, 577
brokerage firms, 387
Brolick, Emil, 34
Brooks, Frederick P., 473
Brooks, Rick, 412
Brown, Gwendolyn, 489
Brown, Laura, 118
Brown, Loren, 439
browsers, 57–58, 103, 512, 578
Brubaker, Bill, 157
brute force, 180, 578
Bryce, Robert, 525
Buczkowski, Tom, 270
BudNet, 259
bugmenot.com, 532
bugs
    adding, 454
    fixing, 461
built-to-order model, 70
Bulkeley, William M., 177
bulletin board system (BBS), 578
bullwhip effect, 226
Burr, Donald, 402, 433
Busch, August, III, 259
Bush, President George, 94, 537, 569
business(es)
    analyzing, 447
    combining data from operation, 237
    daily operation of, 7
    implementing new, 425–428
    integration in, 237–238
    needs, 443
    reengineering, 17
    responsibilities of, 556
    role of the Internet, 7–8
    selling to other, 114
    service-oriented, 16
    starting new, 307
    trends in, 10–16
    use of computers in, 4
business applications, creating, 142–148
business ideas, patents for, 541
business logistics industry.
    See package delivery industry
business operations. *See* operations
business partnerships as threats to information systems, 169
business plan, 422–425
    creating, 419–420
    for problem solving, 447
business process management. *See* BPM
business research. *See* research
Business Systems Modernization (Bizmo) program, 487
business to business. *See* B2B
business to consumer. *See* B2C
business transactions. *See* transactions
business travelers, options for, 435
Buss, Dale, 118
Butler, Betsy, 210
Buyer e-procurement software, 160
buyers, 253–254, 398–399
Buy-Me Button, 292
Byrne, David, 44
Byrnes, Nanette, 390
byte, 40, 578

C programming language, 578
C++ programming language, 451, 578

C2B, 275
C2C, 275, 276
c2it, 215
CA (certificate authority), 101, 182, 578
cable modems, 90–91, 578
cable television, 77
cache, 578
CAD (computer-aided design), 579
CAD/CAM systems, 409
CADE system, 487
Cady, John, 571
cafeteria-style benefits, 249
calculations
    application software for, 59–60
    in QBE and SQL, 131
calculators, 59
Caldwell, Bruce, 573
calendars
    application software for, 62–63
    on a network, 80
    in SharePoint, 329–330
Canada, purchasing drugs from, 156
CAN-SPAM law, 107, 563
Cantalupo, Jim, 29
capability maturity model integration (CMMI), 456–457, 578
capacity planning, 497
Carnivore (DCS-1000) system, 186, 553
Carpenter, Michael, 388
Carrier-Sense, Multiple-Access/Collision Detection (CSMA/CD), 92, 578
cars. *See* automobiles
Carson, Gregory, 485
Carter, Robert B., 341
CASE (computer-aided software engineering), 468, 579
case-based reasoning, 578
cases
    airline industry, 433–440
    automobile industry, 264–270
    computer industry, 68–73
    energy industry, 520–525
    entrepreneurship, 307–312
    fast-food industry, 27–36
    financial services industry, 386–393
    government agencies, 477–491
    health care industry, 568–575
    package delivery industry, 338–346
    pharmaceuticals industry, 155–162
    professional sports industry, 192–196
    retail sales industry, 225–233
    wholesale suppliers, 114–120
cash, 245
cash flow, 245, 424
Cash Management Account (CMA), 405
cash transactions, reporting to the IRS, 485
Cat 5 wiring, 86
catalog management system, 298
catalogs of objects, searching, 373
Catia software, 269
CD-ROM, 56, 117, 578
cell phone bill, small transactions on, 215
cell phones, 77
    middle-ware component for, 513
    providing location data, 532, 554
cellular frequencies, data transfers on, 105
central server
    hardware for intranets, 514
    running software on, 83
centralization, 578
    argument for, 506, 507
    as a cause of conflicts, 515
    of data, 508–509
    versus decentralization, 493, 494, 495
    of hardware, 507
    of MIS personnel, 510–511
    of purchasing, 507
    of software, 508

CEO (chief executive officer), 578
Cerf, Vincent, 44
certificate authority (CA), 101, 182, 578
Cesarano, Tony, 194
CFL Software Development system, 555
Chabrow, Eric, 340
Champy, James, 17, 589
Chan, Chi-wing, 110
change agents, 453, 578
change drivers, 578
change management strategy, 161
changes
    dealing with, 453
    tracking in Word documents, 322
character-based languages, 43
characters
    displaying, 43
    special, 60
charge-back system, 578
chart of accounts, 245, 578
charts, 60, 61. *See also* graphs
chat rooms, 79
check(s)
    electronic, 219
    validating and processing, 211
check number, item code numbers in, 216–217
checking in, 578
    documents, 333
    a file, 323
checking out, 578
    documents, 333
    a file, 323
checkout process in grocery stores, 202
chemical supply industry, 118
ChemPoint Web site, 119
chief executive officer (CEO), 578
chief information officer (CIO), 501, 578
Children's Online Privacy Protection Act, 562
Chinese government, control of Internet, 549, 550
Chisholm, Patrick, 376
Chourey, Sarita, 482, 491
Chrissis, Mary Beth, 474
CIA World Factbook, 6
Ciganer, Patrick, 489
CIM (computer-integrated manufacturing), 579
CIO (chief information officer), 501, 578
circular reference, 578
CIS (computer information system), 4, 579
Citrix terminal server system, 104
Citywide Geographic Information Systems Utility, 362
Civil Registration Modernization Program, 149
Clark, Don, 79
Clarke, Hope, 535
clash analysis, 269
classes, 578
clearinghouses for EDI transactions, 206
CLEC (competitive local exchange carrier), 310
Clementz, Dave, 524
click-through rate, 287, 302, 578
Client 360 system at Merrill Lynch, 392
client computers, 85
client-pull technology, Web pages as, 319
clients, 84
client-server network, 578
clinical trial registry, 156, 159
Clinton, President Bill, 535, 569
clip art, 60, 578
clipboard, 578
clipper chip, 579
Clips ES shell, 370
closed loop, 579
closed system, 464, 579

clothing, e-commerce prospects, 279
clustering as a data mining technique, 364–365
CMA (Cash Management Account), 405
CMMI (capability maturity model integration), 456–457, 578
CMYK standard, 62
CNET, search agent on, 283
cnet.com, 6
coaxial cable, 86, 579
COBOL programming language, 124, 579
Codd, E. F., 124
Cofoni, Paul, 487
Cohen, Jackie, 390
cold site, 167, 579
Colkin, Eileen, 118
collaboration, 316, 321–326
    in SharePoint, 331–333
    system, 119, 322
    tools, 7
collaborative planning, forecasting, and replenishment (CPFR) program, 227
collaborative software, 78
Collett, Stacy, 304, 524
Collins, James, 377
collisions, 92, 579
colors on display screens versus printers, 62
column chart, 61
columns, 123, 127, 579
combo box, 144
commerce server, 295, 296–297, 579
Commerce Server software, 282
commercial EDI providers and standards, 206–207
commercial e-mail, unsolicited, 106–107
commercial off-the-shelf software (COTS), 447, 579
commercial software versus open-source, 64
Common Business-Oriented Language (COBOL), 124, 579
Common Object Request Broker Architecture (CORBA), 579
communication
    costs lowered by technology, 546
    facilities for service industries, 15
    internal and external, 76
    methods, 316–321
    networks for, 78
    in SharePoint, 329–331
    standards for EDI, 206
    with team members, 316–321
Communications Assistance for Law Enforcement Act (CALEA), 553, 562
compact disk-read only memory. *See* CD-ROM
companies. *See* business(es)
companywide standards, 499
competition
    in discount retail, 228
    purely on price, 283–284
competitive advantage, 579
    gaining, 395, 396, 401–408
    searching for, 21–22
competitive environment, 397
competitive local exchange carrier (CLEC), 310
competitors, identifying, 399, 421
complete centralization, 507
complete decentralization, 510
compliance programs, 556
component devices of a computer, 48
components, assembling applications from, 446–448

composite key, 126, 579
compound document, 579
computations, 131–133
computer(s). *See also* personal
    computers
  in business, 4
  compared to humans, 372
  connected to a network, 84–85
  hardware components of, 47–56
  laws related to, 557–564
  programming, 41
  purchasing, 39–40, 47–48, 68
  resetting production lines, 204
  shelf life of, 39
Computer Abuse Amendments Act of
    1994, 556
computer crimes, 555, 556
computer ethics, 555, 579
computer forensics, 183
Computer Fraud and Abuse Act,
    556, 563
computer industry cases, 68–73
computer information system (CIS),
    4, 579
computer intelligence, Turing test
    for, 375
computer monitors versus television
    sets, 53
computer processors. *See* processors
computer security. *See* security
computer software. *See* software
computer-aided design. *See* CAD
computer-aided software engineering
    (CASE), 468, 579
computer-integrated manufacturing
    (CIM), 579
computerized physician order entry
    (CPOE) system, 570
computing standards, corporate,
    498–499
concentration ratios, 421
concurrency, 217–218, 579
conference telephone, 320
conferences, online, 320
conflict management, 515–516
Conn, Dickie Ann, 482
connections
  between cells in a neural network, 373
  electrical, 50–51
  to the Internet, 497
  for networks, 91–92
conservatism bias, 352
consultants, 168–169, 506
consumer electronics market, 69–70
consumer privacy, 529–532
consumer-oriented service sites, 283
contact points, sources of, 254–255
contacts in SharePoint, 329
content acceleration technologies,
    310
content management systems, 297–298
context diagram, 467, 579
contingency plans, 167
continuous backups, 55
continuous quality improvement, 220, 579
contract programmers, 446, 506
control flows, 466
converge, 579
conversion methods, 454
cookies, 531–532, 579
cooling computer components, 50
Cooney, Charles, 157
Cope, James, 523
Copeland, Lee, 152, 194
coporate computing standards, 498–499
copyright laws, 545, 555
copyrights, 540, 541–544, 558, 559, 579
CORBA (Common Object Request
    Broker Architecture), 579
corporate standards, reevaluating, 96
corporate strategies. *See* strategies
corporations, 307, 426
Corrado, Christopher, 416
correlation, 364

costs
  decreasing with computer
    systems, 404
  estimating in a business plan, 423
  of new technology, 413–414
  of switching, 404, 405
COTS (commercial off-the-shelf
    software), 447, 579
Cottrill, Ken, 120
COUNT function in SQL, 131
Covisint automotive auction system, 270
Cowley, Stacy, 491
Cox, Mark, 485
Craig, William, 196
creative destruction, 304
creativity, 377
Creativity Machine, 366
credit agencies, 535, 536
credit card companies
  fees on challenged transactions, 278
  making money, 387
  vendor risk assumed by, 210
credit cards
  drawbacks to, 214
  fees for, 219
  online transactions fraud, 213
  processing, 429
credit records, right to inspect, 562
CreditMap, 354
creeping elegance, 452
crimes
  computer, 555, 556
  information era, 563–564
  information technology and, 553–554
  technology-based, 183
Criteria row in Access, 130
critical success factors, 579
CRM (customer relationship
    management), 254–257, 579
  at AT&T, 416
  collecting necessary data, 256
  at Delta, 436
  at the IRS, 486
Cronin, Jeff, 30
CrossLink package, 308
cryptography, 179–180
CSMA/CD, 92, 577–578
cube browsers, 358
cubes, depicting data, 356–357
cultural issues for networks across
    international boundaries, 109–110
cultures, Lands' End versus Sears, 230
Cummings, Joanne, 194
Cummins, Chip, 522, 523
Cuneo, Eileen Colkin, 571
Cunningham, Joe, 204
Cuny, Tim, 120
Curley, Pat, 193
currencies
  converting in ERP systems, 242
  dealing with multiple, 541
  in spreadsheets, 60
Currency and Banking Retrieval
    System, 485
Curtis, Bill, 474
custom programming, 445–446
custom software, 59
Customer Account Data Engine
    (CADE), 487
Customer Assurance Program (CAP) at
    Cisco, 573
customer cards at Wendy's, 33
customer contact points, 254–255
customer definition, 29
Customer Fusion database at FedEx, 342
customer knowledge system (CKS) at
    Ford, 322
Customer Oriented Service and
    Management Operating System
    (COSMOS) at FedEx, 341
customer perspective on transactions, 210
customer relationship management.
    See CRM

customer service
  at Dell, 71
  providing better, 16
  providing direct, 256–257
  role of retailers, 225
customers
  establishing an interactive
    relationship with, 288
  identifying by location, 106
  layers of, 398–399
  locating with a GIS, 400
  opinion of, 455
customer-supplier links strategy, 413
cut, copy, paste, 579
Cyrnes, Brian, 35

DA (data administrator), 148,
    500–501, 579
DAI (Digital Access Index), 108
D'Ambrosio, Dan, 229
Dangermond, Jack, 383
Danielson, Dennis, 558
Danielson, Julie, 558
DAS (digital asset server), 543
Dash, Julekha, 342
Dash, Steve, 481
data, 4–5, 579
  availability bias, 352
  capturing, 200–209
  centralizing on intranet-accessible
    servers, 514–515
  collection for HRM systems,
    247–248
  compression, 47
  DBMS focus on, 127
  flows of, 463
  mirroring, 168, 580
  organizing, 5
  presentation bias, 352
  quality of transactions, 216–220
  replication, 509
  sharing in strategic systems, 415
  sharing on networks, 76–81
  summaries, 218–219
  templates in XML, 254
  transfers on cellular frequencies, 105
  transmission in e-commerce,
    183, 185
  types of, 40–47
  volume, 218
data administrator (DA), 148,
    500–501, 579
data backup. *See* backups
data dictionary, 127, 468, 469, 579
Data Encryption Standard (DES), 181,
    577, 579
data flow diagram approach, 466
data flow diagrams. *See* DFDs
data flows in a DFD, 466, 467
data independence, 127, 579
data input forms for applications,
    142–144
data integrity, 127–128, 216–217,
    501, 579
data management systems, 5
data marts, 356, 579
data mining, 364–365, 580
  at Anheuser-Busch, 259
  at Sears, 231
  systems, 350
Data Protection Act in France, 536
Data Protection Directive, 536
data store, 466, 467, 580
data types, 580
  characteristics of, 41
  in relational databases, 126
  storage space required for, 46–47
data warehouse, 128, 355–356, 580
  consolidating financial data in, 514
  at Lands' End, 230
  at Pfizer, 161
database administration, 148–150
database administrator. *See* DBA

database applications, 142–148. *See
    also* applications
  creating, 128
  at Dell, 71
database management approach,
    126–136
database management system. *See*
    DBMS
databases, 4, 580
  defining the structure of, 500
  designing, 137–142
  e-business and, 150–151
  massive size of corporate, 123
data-entry boxes in input forms, 142–143
data-interchange standard, 161
date formats, 143
dates
  international display of, 60
  storing, 126
David, Steve, 228
Davis, Nick, 35
DB2, 128
DBA (database administrator), 125,
    148, 150, 499–500, 580
DBMS (database management system),
    59, 123, 124, 580
DBMS input forms. *See* input
DC (distribution center), 221–222, 581
DCS-10000, 186, 553
debit cards, 210, 219
debt as financing, 426–427
Decatur, Steve, 525
decentralization, 580
  argument for, 506, 507
  of businesses, 13
  as a cause of conflicts, 515
  versus centralization, 493, 494, 495
  of data, 509, 510
  of hardware, 508
  of management, 10–11
  of MIS personnel, 512
  of software, 508
  as a source of NASA's
    problems, 489
decision(s)
  biases in making, 351–352
  keeping the knowledge gained
    from, 326
  levels of, 18
  making, 9
  making faster, 367–368
  making good, 350–355
  networks for, 77–78
  tactical, 349
decision biases, 580
decision process, 9, 580
decision support system. *See* DSS
decision tree, 370, 580
DeCSS program, 542
default values, 143, 580
defects. *See* bugs
dehumanization, 580
Delaney, Emma L., 159
Delaney, Kevin J., 240
delete permissions, 176, 177
Delivery Information Acquisition
    Device (DIAD) at UPS, 343
DELMIA, 270
Delta Nervous System (DNS), 436
demand, elasticity of, 544, 545
DeMarco, T., 473
demographic data, obtaining, 289
denial of service (DoS), 173, 580
  attacks, 166, 187–188, 551
dense-wave division multiplexing
    (DWDM), 87
department store, integrating data
    within, 237
Deploy software, 438
Derra, Skip, 162
Dervan, Vera, 149
DES (Data Encryption Standard), 181,
    577, 580

description biases, 352
descriptive model, 580
design
    object-oriented, 469–471
    process, 409
    tools, 452
Design View in Access, 144
desktop publishing (DTP), 580
detail section, 145, 580
developers, responsibilities of, 555–556
development, 498
    accounts at Dell, 71
    controls, 451
    encouraging mediocrity in, 457
    environments for Java and .NET, 300
    methodology, 462
    speed of, 128
    summary, 462–463
    techniques, 443
DeVincentis, John, 160
DFDs (data flow diagrams), 450,
    463, 579
    creating, 468–469
    elements of, 466–467
    methods, 466
    representing systems divided into
        smaller components, 467
diagnostic problems, 366–367
diagnostic situations, 20, 580
diagramming systems, 450, 465–468
dial-back modem, 580
diaries, creating on the Internet, 319
Dictation mode, 54
differentiation strategy, 413
Diffie, 181
Digital Access Index (DAI), 108
digital asset server (DAS), 543
digital books, 543
digital cash, 214–215, 580
digital certificates, 171, 182, 215, 580
digital content
    intellectual property and, 542
    level of security applied to, 543
digital dashboards, 256, 258–260,
    580. See also "electronic
    dashboard;" EIS
digital divide, 547, 580
digital information technology, health
    care organizations and, 537
digital map data, 362
Digital Millennium Copyright Act
    (DMCA), 283, 542–543, 564
digital music, 404
digital orders, 213
digital products
    in B2C e-commerce, 281–283
    international restrictions on, 300
digital rights management (DRM), 281,
    543, 580
digital security certificate, 101, 429
digital signatures, 182, 580
digital subscriber line (DSL), 90, 91, 580
digital video, 195
digital video/versatile disk. See DVD
Digitally Assisted Dispatch System
    (DADS), 341
digitized sound, 45–46
digitized video, 46
digitizer tablets, 52
Dillman, Linda, 227
direct cutover, 453, 454
Disabatino, Jennifer, 152, 223
disaster and recovery policy, 501
disasters as threats to information
    systems, 167–168
discussion group (listserv), 102–103
discussion sites, 79
discussion system in SharePoint, 329, 330
discussions, embedding, 332
disintermediation, 277, 379, 580
disk drives, 55, 585
distributed hardware and software, 244
distributed services, 285–286, 471–472

distribution center (DC), 221–222, 580
distribution channels, 402–404, 405, 580
distribution system, 411
distributors, electronically connecting
    to, 251
diverge, 580
divide-and-conquer approach, 464–465
Dizard, Wilson P., III, 491
DMCA (Digital Millennium Copyright
    Act), 283, 542–543, 564
DNS (Delta Nervous System), 436
DNS (domain name system),
    100–101, 580
Do Not Call Registry, 509
DoCoMo system, 110
document libraries, 331–332
document processing system, 486
documentation, 580
    for databases, 148–149
    storing, 451
documents
    checking in and out, 333
    controlling access to, 323–324
    embedding discussions within, 332
    hidden items in, 63
    revisions of, 323
    tracking changes in shared, 322
Dolby, Kent, 243
domain name system (DNS),
    100–101, 580
domain names, registration of, 100–101
Donde, Rajiv, 17
Dorobek, Christopher J., 488
Dorr, Les, 482
DoS (denial of service). See denial of
    service
dot-coms, 7, 8, 580
    advertising crash, 303
    failure of firms, 301–303
    failure of startups, 274
    failures, 417
dots per inch (dpi), 44
double-entry system for accounting,
    245, 247
download, 580
Dragoon, Alice, 509
Dreazen, Yochi J., 87
drill down, 258, 581
driver's licenses, magnetic stripes
    on, 534
Driver's Privacy Act, 562
DRM (digital rights management), 281,
    543, 580
drug cabinets, computerized, 572
drugs, prices of, 156
DSL (digital subscriber line), 90, 91,
    580
DSS (decision support system), 20,
    358–361, 581
    compared to ES and AI systems, 378
    tools, 356
DTP (desktop publishing), 580
dual-factor authentication, 193
dual-key encryption, 181, 581
Dubie, Denise, 488
Duetto, 35
Dugas, Christine, 388
Dunbar, Roy, 158
Dunst, Bob, 202, 233
DuPuy, Bub, 195
duties, separation of, 247
DVD (digital video disk or digital
    versatile disk), 56, 542, 580
dynamic data exchange, 581. See also
    Object Linking and Embedding
dynamic integration, 581. See also static
    integration
dynamic pricing, 284

e-911 law, 532
easySabre, 439
Eaton, Bob, 269
eBay, 275

EBCDIC, 581
e-business, 8, 273, 581
    computers in, 57–58
    databases and, 150–151
    intelligent systems in, 379–382
    strategic options in, 417
    at Univar, 119
Echelon, 186
e-commerce (EC), 7, 8, 76, 77,
    273–276, 581
    categories of, 275
    creating a Web site, 282, 291–298
    digital content over, 281
    international, 552
    production chain and, 276–286
    risk mitigation in, 212–213
    security challenges of, 166
    security issues, 183–189
    starting a firm, 428–429
    tracking information about the
        requestor, 531
economics, role in dot.com failures, 417
economies of scale, 250
EDGAR files, 560
EDI (electronic data interchange), 169,
    201, 205–209, 581
    creating transactions, 211
    data sharing and, 254
    defining standards, 404
    extending to the Internet, 284–285
    on the Internet, 208–209
    overall structure of messages, 207
    standards, 205, 207
    XML for, 209
Edifact standard, 207
"editorial control" on Web sites, 548
education
    continuing, 538
    effects of information technology on,
        545–546, 548
Edwards, Hazel, 484
e-government, navigating, 560
EIN, obtaining from the IRS, 426
EIS (executive information systems),
    256, 258–260, 412, 581
    advantages of, 260
    capabilities, 242
Eisenberg, Anne, 204
elasticity of demand, 544, 545
electric cables, 85–86
electromagnetic frequency spectrum, 88
electronic badges, 532
electronic business, 273
electronic calendars, 62–63
electronic checks, 219
electronic collaboration. See
    collaboration
Electronic Communications Privacy
    Act, 556, 561–562
electronic conferencing tools, 412
"electronic dashboard," 572. See also
    digital dashboards
electronic data interchange. See EDI
Electronic Federal Tax Payment System
    (EFTPS), 485
electronic forms, submitting to
    governments, 401
electronic links
    to strategic partners, 412
    to suppliers, 399
electronic mail. See e-mail
electronic payment mechanisms. See
    payment mechanisms
electronic records for health care
    systems, 537, 569
electronic refund originators
    (EROs), 308
electronic voting systems, 550
electronic workflow. See workflow
Elemica, 114, 119
emacs, 460
e-mail, 78, 317, 581
    attaching files to messages, 499

defining rules, 511
    drawbacks to, 78
    encrypting, 171, 185
    on the Internet, 102–103
    as least intrusive, 318–319
    messages as asynchronous, 78
    systems, 62
e-mail freedom, 548
emergency location data, 554
eMoneyMail, 215
employee privacy, 532–533
employees
    checking references and backgrounds,
        179, 180
    data transactions involving, 247–248
    monitoring, 532
    as threats to information systems,
        168–169
    training using expert systems, 368
employers, monitoring employees, 533
encapsulation, 470
encryption, 165, 179–182, 581
    controlled by governments, 213
    of e-mail, 171
    protecting credit card data, 212
    of wireless transmissions, 87
end user development, 444, 461–462,
    498, 581
energy industry cases, 520–525
Energy Information Sharing and
    Analysis Center (ISAC), 521
engineering and design processes, 409
England, Gordon R., 453
enterprise (or executive) information
    system capabilities. See EIS
enterprise networks, 92, 93–95, 581
enterprise resource planning. See ERP
enterprise systems, 235, 236, 237
entertainment industry, 410
entrants, 400–401
entrepreneurs, 307
entrepreneurship, 273, 307–312,
    417–418, 581
entry, barriers to, 401–402, 403, 405,
    421, 577
environment, responding to changes
    in, 464
eProvision Day One software, 524
equity as financing, 427
E-Rates program, 70
ergonomics, 52, 581
ERP (enterprise resource planning),
    239, 242, 581
    packages, 448
    software, 19, 240
ERP systems
    functions of, 239, 240
    installed at Grainger, 118
    selecting and evaluating, 241
    strengths of, 239
    summarizing data, 258–260
erroneous information from
    software, 556
error detection, 455
ES (expert system). See expert
    systems (ES)
escrow keys, 187, 581
Esposito, Victoria, 278
Essbase OLAP application, 438
Ethernet, 92, 581
ethics, 581
ETL (extraction, transformation, and
    loading), 355, 581
European Union
    consumer privacy laws, 536
    restrictions on trading personal
        data, 530
evaluation of completed projects, 455
Evans, Mark, 521
event calendar in SharePoint, 330
event-driven approach, 470, 581
events, 470
Everson, Mark, 488

evidence, collecting digital, 183
Evolution-Data Optimized (EV-DO), 106
Ewalt, David M., 158, 573
Excel
    creating a chart, 61
    pivot tables, 357
    programming a new function, 460
    statistical tools, 379
exception reports, 246, 581
exchange rates
    fixed, 541
    floating, 541
execute permissions, 176
executive information system. *See* EIS
executive-level decisions, 20–21
exhaustive testing, 581
expenses, tracking, 427
expert system shell, 370, 581
expert systems (ES), 5, 20, 350,
        365–368, 581
    agent in Outlook, 511
    building, 368–372
    compared to DSS and AI systems, 378
    controlling errors, 407
    creating, 370–371
    entering rules into the shell, 371
    at the FAA Web site, 481
    limitations of, 371
    management issues of, 372
    types of, 369
exploration for oil, 520, 524
explosions, DFD, 467–468
exports, 300, 581
ExSys, 367
Extended Binary Coded Decimal
        Interchange Code (EBCDIC), 581
extensible markup language. *See* XML
external agents, 21–22, 397–401, 581
external communications, 76
external entities, 466, 581
external software solutions, 448
extraction, transformation, and loading
        (ETL), 355, 581
extranets, 79, 581
extreme programming (XP), 439,
        459, 581
eyeballs, 302

FAA, 479, 481
Facelt, 176
face-to-face meetings, 320
facial-recognition software, 176
facilitator
    for a GDSS system, 325, 326
    required for JAD, 459
facsimile (fax), 581
fact, distinguishing from fiction, 546
failure data, 407
Fair Credit Reporting Act, 535, 562
"fair use," 559
Fairbank, Richard D., 390
Faltermayer, Charlotte, 190
Family Educational Privacy Act, 535
Family Educational Rights and Privacy
        Act, 561
fast-food industry, 27–36
fat content of McDonald's meals, 30–31
fault tolerance, 57, 455, 581
feasibility, areas of, 450
feasibility and planning stage of SDLC,
        449–450, 451
feasibility study, 449–450, 581
Fedele, Joe, 280
federal government
    involvement in health care, 568–569
    size and growth of, 477–478
Fedstats, 549
feedback, 581
    biases, 352
    system in Live Meeting, 321
fees for transactions, 210–211
Feig, Christy, 190
Feinbloom, William, 190

fiber networks, high-speed, 100
fiber optics, 86–87
fiber-optic cable, 581
FICS-21 program, 481
field, avoiding use as a term, 125
file server, 581
file transfer protocol (FTP), 102, 581
files, 467. *See also* data store
    attaching to e-mail messages, 499
    avoiding use as a term, 125
    checking in and out, 323
    transferring on the Internet, 102
Final Approach Spacing Tool
        (FAST), 480
final testing, 452–453
financial accounting in an ERP
        system, 242
financial audits, 260–261
financial data, collecting and storing, 245
financial records, accuracy of, 260
financial reports, responsibility for, 212
financial section of a business plan,
        423–424
financial services industry, 386–393
financial statements, estimating in a
        business plan, 424
financial transactions with external
        organizations, 246
financing a new business, 307–308,
        426–427
FindMRO division, 117
fingerprint readers, 176
Fireswick, Kris, 305
firewalls, 84, 187–188, 581
firms. *See* business(es)
first normal form, 139
first-level diagram, 466
Fisher, Dave, 558
Fishman, Jay, 388
Five Forces model, 22, 397, 398, 582
fixed costs, estimating, 424
fixed exchange rates, 541
fixed-fee contracts, 446
Fleming, Charles, 557
flexibility
    of entrepreneurs, 418, 428
    required by internationalization and
        decentralization, 16
Flexible Lineup Editor at UPS, 343
floating exchange rate, 541
FLOPS (floating point operations per
        second), 582
flow chart, 582
folders, creating for e-mail, 511
Foley, John, 342
Fonseca, Brian, 128
font size, 582
fonts, 43, 45
food
    distribution of, 278
    EC and, 278–279
football, professional, 193–194
Ford, Bill, 235, 266
forecasting
    in a business plan, 419
    process, 360
    trends, 379
foreign exchange (FX) brokers, 541
Forelle, Charles, 533
forensics, computer, 183
Form Wizard in Access, 144
formality of the SDLC approach, 456
Forman, Red, 487
format commands, 143
formatting data, 143
forms
    building in Access, 144
    required to start a business, 426
Forno, Richard, 190
fortune.com, 6
forward chaining, 582
Fowler, Geoffrey, 252
Fox, Pimm, 246

Fox, Prim, 152
frame relay, 582
frames, 371, 582
franchises, 582
    management by methodology, 11–12
    McDonald's, 30
Franses, Philip Hans, 383
fraud
    Internet-related, 169
    online, 278
Fraza, Victoria, 118
free flight, 480–481
Freedom of Information Act, 561
freedom of speech, 554
Freeman, James, 387
French, Barry, 71
frequency, 45, 87, 88
frequent-buyer databases, 410
Frieswick, Kris, 491
FROM clause in SQL, 131
front-end processor, 582
FrontPage, 102
Fryer, Bronwyn, 517
FTP (file transfer protocol), 102, 581
full duplex, 320, 582
Fuller, John, 120
function keys, predefining for
        databases, 148
functional areas, dividing businesses
        into, 353
functions. *See also* methods
    of an object, 41
    of objects, 469
    predefined for data types, 41
    SQL, 131
FutureFlight, 481
fuzzy logic, 583

Gallagher, Sean, 57
Gal-Or, Mordechai, 542
gambling on the Internet, 170, 213
GamePlus system, 193
Gantt charts, 500
Garbage In, Garbage Out (GIGO), 217
Gareiss, Robin, 437
Garfinkel, Simson, 105
Garnier, Jean-Pierre, 159
Garsten, Ed, 266
Gates, Bill, 316
Gator advertising system, 173
Gaynor, Scott, 195
GDP (gross domestic product), 359
GDSS (group decision support system),
        325–326, 582
Gene Anatomy Made Easy (Game)
        project, 158
General Agreement on Tariffs and
        Trade (GATT), 15
general ledger, 242, 245, 582
generally accepted accounting practices
        (GAAP), 260–261
geo-coded data, 400
geographic information system (GIS),
        361–364, 400, 582
geographical relationships, modeling, 361
George, Tischelle, 194
Gershon, Bernard, 275
Gianforte, Greg, 481
Gibson, Stan, 270
GIF
    files, 44
    format, 96
gigabyte, 582
giga-FLOPS, 582
Gilhooly, Kym, 345
GIS (geographic information system),
        361–364, 400, 582
Glaser, John, 574
Glatt Plagiarism Services, 555
Glenn, John, 484, 486
global bank, 349
global economy, 299–301
global environment, 541

Global Hawks, 82
global positioning system. *See* GPS
Global Service Logistics (GSL)
        system, 390
global shipping, 341
global standards, 97
global telecommunications, 107–110
Global Trade Manager system at
        FedEx, 341
GNU project, 64, 445, 460
goals, 465
Goff, Leslie, 195
Goldberg, Fred, 484
Golden, Charlie, 158
Gomes, Lee, 446
Google, 6
    search engine, 20
    search process on, 9
Gorry, G. A., 18, 25
Gory, Julie, 194
Gose, Joe, 233
Goss, Roger, 193
government(s)
    effects on the profitability of a
        firm, 401
    information technology and, 549–553
    intervention, 415–417
    perspectives on transactions, 212
    privacy and, 533–534
    responsibilities in terms of computer
        security and privacy, 556–557
government agencies, 477–491
Government Paperwork Elimination
        Act, 486
government statistics, 6
GPRS cellular wireless service, 341
GPS (global positioning system), 363,
        479–480, 582
    locator chips in cell phones, 532
    tracking system in patrol cars, 533
Graf, Alan, 342
Graf, Alan, Jr., 412
Graham-Leach-Bliley Act of 1999,
        562–563
grammar-checkers, 60
Grams, W. Todd, 488
Grand Challenge, 375, 377
graphical format, 44
graphical user interfaces (GUIs),
        129, 582
graphics
    application software for, 60–62
    devices, 44
    processor, 52
    tools, 450
graphs, 60. *See also* charts
Greenemeier, Larry, 158, 159, 438
Greenhouse, Steven, 217
Greenspan, Alan, 273
Greisman, Lois, 509
grid computing, 51, 82–83, 582
Griffin, Wally, 310
Grinstein, Gerald, 436
grocery stores, checkout process, 202
Grokker, 9
Gross, Art, 486
Gross, Arthur, 487
Gross, Daniel, 388
gross domestic product (GDP), 359
Grossman, David S., 268
Grosso, Andrew, 566
group breaks, 582
GROUP BY clause in SQL, 133
GROUP BY option in QBE, 132, 133
group decision support system (GDSS),
        325–326, 582
groupware, 80, 317, 582
    features of Office software, 316
    integrating tools with Office, 328
growth factor in a business plan, 424
Gruman, Galen, 406
GUI (graphical user interface), 129, 582
Gurden, Dereck, 259

Gusapari, John, 29
Guth, Robert A., 73
Guzman, David, 115, 116

hacker, 582
Halamka, John, 572, 573
Hall, Mark, 269
Hamblen, Matt, 522
Hammer, Michael, 17, 589
handhelds
    at FedEx, 341
    Frito-Lay use of, 411
handprint readers, 176
Hansen, Lloyd, 266
hard disk drives, 55, 583
hardware, 4, 40, 582
    administration, 496–497
    centralization versus decentralization,
        506–508
    components, 47–56
    distributed, 244
    sharing on networks, 81–83
    standardizing PC, 496
    trends in, 48
Harreld, Heather, 262
Harris, Brent, 437
Harriss, H., 190
Hasson, Judi, 488
Hauck, Walter, 161
Hausladen, Valerie, 71
HAVING label in SQL, 136
Hay, Jim, 344
Hayes, Mary, 438
Hazard, Carol, 390
HDTV (high-definition television), 45,
    109, 582
Heagney, Mike, 520
health, focus on, 28
health care
    industry, 568–575
    organizations, 537
    supply chain costs, 21
Health Insurance Portability and
    Accountability Act (HIPAA), 537,
    562, 569
"Healthy Lifestyle" program, 28
heat, generated in computers, 50
Heilemann, John, 551
Heim, Mike, 158
Helbach, Morris, 524
Hellman, 181
help desk, 512
Hendrickson, Chet, 474
Hessman, Tina, 366
Heun, Christopher T., 233
Hicks, Matt, 143
hidden items in Word documents, 63
hierarchical structure, 10
hierarchies, object, 470
Higday, Paul, 116
Higgins, Michelle, 202, 233
high-definition television (HDTV), 45,
    109, 582
high-frequency RFID chips, 202
high-speed connections
    for Internet 2, 104
    for large data transfers, 513
high-speed fiber networks, 100
high-speed laser printers, sharing, 81
Hillblom, Larry L., 339, 344
Hilson, Gary, 36
Hinson, David R., 479, 480
HIPAA, 537, 562, 569
Hiriji, Asif, 461
Hirschheim, Rudolf, 515
Hissam, Scott, 474
Ho, Arthur, 34
Ho, K. P., 112
Hoekstra, Arjan, 88
Hoffman, Thomas, 438, 461, 523
home buying, e-commerce and, 279
home-based workers, 539
Hoover, J. Edgar, 534, 564

horizontally integrated firms, 240–241
Host project, 479
hosting
    companies, 291
    software packages, 295–296
    Web sites, 428–429
hot links. See dynamic integration
hot site, 167, 582
hot-spot service, 35
Hovey, Hollister H., 159
Howard, Lisa, 30
HRM (human resource management)
    allocating raises, 360–361
    in an ERP system, 243
    transaction elements in, 247
    transaction processing and, 247–249
HTML (hypertext markup language),
    96, 291–293, 582
HTTP (hypertext transfer protocol), 97
hub-and-spoke system for airlines, 434
hubs, 91, 582
Hugos, Michael, 227
Hui, John, 72
Hulme, George V., 116
human biases, 351–352
human resource management. See HRM
humanoid robot (Asimo), 376
humans, compared to computers, 372
Hummel, John, 570, 571
hypertext markup language (HTML),
    96, 291–293, 582
hypertext transfer protocol (HTTP), 97

IBM Lotus Notes system at Daimler-
    Chrysler, 322
icons, 44, 582
iCraveTV Web site, 196
ICU (intensive care unit), virtual, 570
ideas, entrepreneurship and, 418,
    420–421
Identity Hub software, 570
identity management infrastructure, 32
Identity Minder from Netegrity
    Inc., 116
identity theft, 169
ideograms, 43
IDs
    assigning, 137
    generated by DRM systems, 281
IDS (intrusion detection system),
    189, 583
IEEE 1394 (firewire) standard, 51
Ikeda, Daniel, 570
illusory correlation bias, 352
IM (instant messaging), 79, 317, 583
images, 42, 582. See also pictures
    displaying in Web pages, 96
    storing, 44
importing, 582
imports, policies and taxes
    regarding, 300
impulse purchasing, 278
income statements, 245
inconsistency bias, 352
individuals, information technology
    affecting, 528–536
industrial revolution, 528
industry
    auction sites, 285
    changed by technology, 414, 415
    sources of information, 422
inference engine, 369, 582
information, 4, 5, 6, 582
Information Based Strategy (IBS) at
    Captial One, 389
information center, 582
information era crimes, 563–564
Information Infrastructure Task Force
    (IITF), 561
information resources, protecting,
    165–166
information rights management (IRM),
    323–324, 582

information systems, 5, 582
    effects on society, 527–528
    managing, 494–495
    options for building, 445–448
    organizing resources, 493
    role in improving quality
        management, 406–407
    supporting teams of workers,
        315–316
    threats to, 166–173
    using to control distribution channels,
        403–404
information technology. See IT
information threats, 582
information warfare (IW), 551–552, 582
infrared transmissions, 87–88
infrastructure, 182, 424
inheritance, 470, 582
initial public offering (IPO), 427, 582
ink jet printers, 54, 55
INNER JOIN clause in SQL, 133–134
innovation
    risks of, 414
    search for, 408–412
innovation factor, 428
Inouye, Wayne, 72
input, 463
    devices, 41, 48, 52–53, 583
    forms, 142–144
    for HRM systems, 247–248
    screens, 124, 148
input-process-output, 583
insiders, threats to information from, 167
instant gratification, 278
instant messaging (IM), 79, 317, 583
instant messenger service in
    SharePoint, 329
integrated data, 583
Integrated Financial Management
    Program (IFMP) at NASA, 489
Integrated Financial System at the
    IRS, 488
integrated reports, methods of
    creating, 238
Integrated Services Digital Network
    (ISDN), 583
integrated supply chain, 250
Integrated Supply division at
    Grainger, 117
integrated supply programs, 117
integrated system, benefits of, 235
integration
    in business, 237–238
    as a feature of ERP systems, 243–244
integrity. See data integrity
intellectual property, 540–545, 558, 583
    balance of power, 544–545
    rights, 281
intelligent mobile systems, 377
intelligent systems in e-business, 379–382
intensive care unit, virtual, 570
Interactive Advertising Board, 302
interactive Web sites, 300
interference, 86
interline e-ticketing (IET) hub, 439
internal communications in
    businesses, 76
internal documentation, 149
internal network technologies at
    Univar, 119
internal programming language of
    browsers, 57
internal systems at Grainger, 118
international environment, transactions
    in, 213–214
international market for the packaging
    industry, 339
international notations, 60
international trade
    importance of, 15
    on the Internet, 299–301
international transmission of data, 107
internationalization, 14, 15–16

Internet, 77, 98–107, 583
    access to data on, 103–104
    addresses on, 100–102, 105
    altering traditional distribution
        channels, 404
    anonymous access to, 536
    behavioral tracking and targeted
        data, 288
    complexity added by, 380
    connecting to, 98–100
    controlling access to, 550
    cost of connecting to, 89
    data transmission on, 183, 185
    EC features of, 280–281
    effect on the role of computers, 57
    electronic mail on, 102–103
    expanding access to, 506
    expanding the reach of higher
        education, 545
    finding information on, 6, 20
    fraud related to, 169
    gambling, 170, 213
    government information on, 549
    international trade on, 299–301
    interruptions and delays affecting
        EDI, 208–209
    IRS use of, 485
    languages on, 14
    managing connections to, 497
    marketing goods and services on,
        286–291
    moving business to, 273
    plagiarism using, 555
    protocols, 188
    role in business, 7–8
    solving business problems at
        McDonald's, 30–31
    as a source of information, 549
    speeds available, 89
    taxes on, 298–299
    transferring files on, 102
    tying to the real world, 101
    using for EDI, 208–209
Internet 2, 104–105
Internet cafes in China, 550
Internet Explorer, 103
Internet Information Server (IIS), 574
Internet layer of the TCP/IP reference
    model, 97
Internet Protocol (IP), 97
Internet Protocol version 6, 97, 100,
    105, 209, 583
Internet Relay Chart (IRC), 103
Internet search engines. See search
    engines
Internet service, launched by
    Gateway, 72
Internet Service Providers. See ISPs
interruptions, managing, 316, 317
interstate commerce, taxation of, 299
intranet sites, 79
intranets, 506, 512–515, 583
intrusion detection system (IDS),
    189, 583
inventory, 245, 246
    determining levels, 115
    DSS, ES, and AI approaches to, 378
inventory-management workbench, 230
IP (Internet Protocol), 97
IP addresses, hiding, 536
iParadigms software, 555
IPO (initial public offering), 427, 582
IPv6 (Internet Protocol version 6), 97,
    100, 105, 209, 583
IRC (Internet Relay Chart), 103
iris pattern recognition, 176
IRM (information rights management),
    323–324, 582
irrational firms, fear of, 284
irrelevant outcomes, learning
    from, 352
IRS Free Filing Program, 309
IRS Restructuring and Reform Act, 487

IS
  salaries, 502
  techniques, 401–408
IS NULL condition, 131
ISAC (Energy Information Sharing and
    Analysis Center), 521
ISDN (Integrated Services Digital
    Network), 583
ISO 9000 (International Organization of
    Standards) directive, 407
ISO 9001 quality standard, 327
ISPs (Internet service providers), 98,
    99, 583
  contracting to use Pac-West's
      network, 310
  identifying, 101
IT (information technology), 4, 582
  altering the organization of
      business, 10
  career tracks in, 30
  dramatically changing industries, 395
  effects on education, 545–546, 548
  effects on governments, 549–553
  effects on individuals, 528–536
  importance of, 5–7
  improving the fundamental business
      process, 409
  jobs offshore, 510
  staff at Sears, 231
  strategic uses of, 21
  uses in production management, 220
iterative solution, 583
ITU Web site, 108
IW (information warfare), 551–552, 583

J2EE, 150
Jackson, Janet, 542
Jackson, Joab, 482
Jackson, Peter, 320
Jackson, William, 482
JAD (joint application design),
    458–459, 462, 463, 583
Jaffe, Greg, 82
James, Geoffrey, 344
Jamison, Mark, 31
Java (J2EE), 300
Java object-oriented programming
    language, 73, 451
Javris, Steve, 439
Jeffries, Ronald, 474
Jenkins, Milton, 474
Jess ES shell, 370
Jevans, David, 514
Jezzard, Helen, 160
JIT inventory. See just-in-time
    inventory
JIT production, 221, 251
Joachim-Korber, Hans, 205
jobs, effects of technology on, 536–539
Johnson, Amy Helen, 229
Johnson, Bill, 521
Johnson, Dick, 267
Johnson, Ian, 201
Johnson, Van R., 571
Johnston, David Cay, 488
Johnston, Larry, 232
JOIN command in SQL, 131
joining multiple tables, 133–134
joint application design (JAD),
    458–459, 462, 463, 583
joint authorship on a network, 80
Jones, Douglas W., 566
Jones, Jeff, 231
Jones, T. C., 474
Jones, Thomas, 388
journal entries, 245
Joyce, Colum, 345
JPEG
  files, 44
  format, 96
Judd, Richard, 555
junk e-mail, 106, 107, 590
junk mail, stopping, 536

jurisdiction in international e-
    commerce, 214
just-in-time (JIT) inventory systems,
    410, 583
just-in-time approach, applied by Dell, 70
just-in-time inventory
  control, 246
  delivery service, 23
just-in-time production, 221, 251

Kahn, J. M., 112
Kahn, Robert E., 112
Kalb, Loretta, 17
kanban signals, 251
Kaplan, Robert S., 256
Katz, Jonathan, 418
Kaufman, Marc, 157
keiretsu (support group), 403
Kelkar, Bhooshan, 161
Kelleher, Herbert D., 434, 437
Kelleher, Kevin, 259
Kenison, William, 558
Kennedy, Chris, 571
Kennedy, Jim, 483
Kerberos
  security system, 583
  server, 175
keyboards, 52
Keyser, Richard L., 117
Khodorkovsky, Mikhail, 522
Kidd, Alan, 195
Killeen, John, 392
killer strategic computer system, 413
kilobyte, 583
King, Julia, 21, 162, 232, 522,
    523, 524
King, Ross, 377
King, Stephen, 543–544
Kinninger, Terance, 571
Kirby, Ned, 34
Kish, Charles, 558
Kline, Terry S., 268
KM (knowledge management),
    326–327, 583
  in SharePoint, 334–335
  at Shell, 523
knowledge, 5, 583
knowledge base, 316, 369
  at Grainger, 117
  modifying in an expert system, 371
Knowledge Centers at Dell, 71
knowledge engineer, 369, 583
knowledge management. See KM
knowledge-based systems, 5
Koch, Christopher, 416
Kolbasuk McGee, Marianne, 116, 574
Konicki, Steve, 118, 229, 232
Kontzer, Tony, 116, 195, 437, 438,
    440, 523
Koudsi, Suzanne, 391
Krazit, Tom, 59
Krey, Michael, 374
Krieger, Lisa M., 179
Krieser, John, 195
Krill, Paul, 262, 383
Krim, Jonathan, 107
Kuchinskas, Susan, 73
Kuczynski, John, 533
Kunken, Darrell, 532
Kurose, James F., 112
Kuykendall, Lavonne, 390, 391
Kvedar, Joseph, 574

labels in input forms, 142
Lacy, Alan, 231
Lacy, Ken, 343
Lail, Jarnail, 118
LaMacchia, 559
LAN cards, 84. See also network
    interface cards
Landro, Laura, 537, 569
Langlois, Greg, 482
language comprehension, 375–376

languages
  dealing with multiple, 541
  higher-level, 444
  on the Internet, 14
  translating, 376
LANs, 76, 583
  format and speed of, 89
  private wireless, 186
laptops, portability offered by, 58
laser printers, 54, 55, 81
Latour, Jose, 311–312
laws
  antitrust, 415–417, 577
  CAN-SPAM, 107, 563
  Communications Assistance for Law
      Enforcement Act (CALEA),
      553, 562
  computer-related, 557–564
  copyright, 545, 555
  e-911, 532
  privacy, 109, 110, 213, 535–536,
      561–563
  regarding protection of consumer
      data, 530
  trade secret, 559
layers of the TCP/IP reference model, 96
LCD tags at Albertsons, 233
LCD TV sales, 69
LDAP (Lightweight Directory Access
    Protocol), 524
Leavitt, Harold J., 25
Lee, Jennifer, 534
legacy costs in the automobile
    industry, 265
legacy systems, 161, 583
legal complications with international
    networks, 109
legal structure of a new business, 426
Lehman, Bruce, 561
Lehmann, Carl F., 243
Leith, Scott, 510
Leonard, Joe, 434–435
Leonhardt, David, 438
Leopold, George, 482
Leung, Shirley, 13
level zero diagram, 467
level-of-service quality, 104–105
levels of management, 18
Lewis, Russell F., 571
LexiQuest Guide, 160
liability
  control of data and, 548–549
  for erroneous information produced
      by software, 556
Liddle, Alan J., 36
Lieber, Ron, 371, 392
light as a transmission medium, 86
light pens, 52
Lightweight Directory Access Protocol
    (LDAP), 524
LIKE command in QBE, 130
limited liability company (LLC), 426, 583
line chart, 61
linear programming, 354
linear regression, 379
line-of-sight transmission, 87
Lingswiler, Michael, 31
links on a Web page, 96
Linux, 56, 64
  deciding to use, 461
  servers, 69
Lister, T., 473
lists, sharing, 329
listserv, 102–103
Litecky, C. R., 517
Little Touch LeapPads, 252
Littleford, Frankie, 540
Live Meeting, 119, 320–321
LLC (limited liability company),
    426, 583
local area networks. See LANs
location data, selling, 554
location role of retailers, 225

Lockyer, Bill, 63
logistics, 75, 242–243. See also SCM
  at Grainger, 117–118
  IT support mechanisms for, 409, 410
  by O&M, 115–116
  in the wholesale industry, 114–115
Lombardo, Carly, 309
Long, Rick, 390
"look and feel" of software, 557
Looksmart, 6
Loomis, Carol J., 389
Loshin, Pete, 223
lossy compression, 47
Lotus Notes, 317, 322
lower production costs, 405
lowest-cost producer, 404
loyalty card data, 530
Luddites, 537
Lutes, Terry S., 488
Luthans, Fred, 8, 25
Lynx, 159

Machalaba, Daniel, 566
machine intelligence, 377
machine vision, 375
Maddox, Kate, 118
magnetic hard drives. See hard disk
    drives
magnetic ink character recognition
    (MICR), 201, 583
magnetic stripes on driver's licenses, 534
magnetic tapes, 56
mail. See e-mail
mail filters, 62, 583
mail-order companies, 274, 279
maintenance, 410, 454, 586
maintenance, repair, and operations
    (MRO), 116
maintenance fees for ERP software, 240
Malone, Michael S., 242
malware, 173
management
  classifications of activities, 8–9
  decentralized form of, 10–11
  functional areas of, 19–20
  IT support mechanisms for, 412
  levels, 18–21
  by methodology, 11–12
  by rules and procedures, 16–17
  techniques, 396
  of temporary workers, 14
  traditional, 8–9
management information system.
    See MIS
managerial tasks, 8
managers, 125
  decision making by, 9
  duties of, 8–9
  jobs of, 6
  specialization of, 11
Mangalindan, Mylene, 270, 281
Mann, Zach, 535
manual and electronic security, 174
manual security precautions, 174
manufacturers, changing the ordering
    systems of, 275
manufacturing
  benefits from integrating data, 241
  collecting data from machines, 204
  IT support mechanisms for,
      409, 410
Manufacturing Resource Planning
    (MRP II), 583
many-to-many relationships, 126
Manzi, Jim, 280
MapInfo, 362
MapPoint, 400
Margolies, Ross, 232
market basket analysis, 365, 583
market research, 359
marketing
  data, 359
  forecasts, 359–360

IT support mechanisms for, 409, 410–411
phases of, 286–287
plan, 425
simple rules dominating, 278
MarketPlace system, 295
Markoff, John, 375
Martinez, Barbara, 157, 159
Marur, Suresh, 514
Maselli, Jennifer, 524
Mashburn, Sid, 231
masks for color printing, 62
mass customization, 205, 250, 251, 410, 583
mass production, 250, 266
massively parallel machines, 51
Master File system at the IRS, 487
Masud, Sam, 488
Matala, Alan, 523
materials requirements planning (MRP), 583
mathematical equations, representing a process, 353
mathematical models, 355, 583
Matthews, Anna Wilde, 410
Matthews, Robert Guy, 305
Maughan, Deryck, 389
MAX function in SQL, 131
maximizing inventory turnover, 226
May, Jerrold H., 542
May, Ned, 71
Mayer, Merry, 152, 488
Maynard, Micheline, 438
Mazor, John, 479
McAuliff, Robert, 195
McBrayer, Michael, 246
McCarron, Suzanne, 522
McCartney, Scott, 435, 437, 438, 482
McCausland, Richard, 309
McClenahan, Scott, 33
McCluskey, Jim, 342
McConnell, Steve, 474
McCullagh, Declan, 101
McDougall, Paul, 232, 437, 488, 523, 524
McFarlan, F. Warren, 396, 430
McGee, Marianne Kolbasuk, 571, 573
McGeehan, Patrick, 393
McGeever, Christine, 196
McGinty, Lee, 354
McKay, Betsy, 412
McMillan, Robert, 59
McMurchy, Lovina, 31
McNamee, Mike, 488
m-commerce, 106, 215, 283, 298
McWilliams, Gary, 453, 517
Mead, Kirtland, C., 413, 430
Meads, Mindy, 231
Mearian, Lucas, 232
mechanical sensors, 375
media, 583
medical data, use of, 535
medical record systems, 537, 569
medical supplies, 21, 22–24
Meehan, Michael, 229, 521
Meehana, Brian, 281
meetings
face-to-face, 320
online, 320
scheduling, 62
megabytes, 46, 123, 583
MegaCentre project, 523
megaflops, 583, 583
megahertz, 583
Mehta, Shailesh, 391
Melymuka, Kathleen, 430, 437, 574
memory chips, 49
memory stick, 55
Menezes, Bictor, 388
menu tree, 583
menus for business applications, 146–148
mergers, historical names of, 12–13

merit raises, determining, 360–361
Merrick, Amy, 232
messages on networks, 78–79
metadata, 356, 583
Method/1, 445
methodologies, 462
methods, 41, 583–584. See also functions
Meyerson, Bruce, 554
Miazga, Ron, 119
MICR (magnetic ink character recognition), 201, 583
micropayments, 204
microphone, 54
microsecond, 584
Microsoft Access. See Access software
Microsoft Excel. See Excel
Microsoft Exchange, 317
Microsoft Live Meeting. See Live Meeting
Microsoft .NET, 150, 300
Microsoft NetMeeting, 318
Microsoft Office. See Office
Microsoft Outlook. See Outlook
Microsoft Project, 500
Microsoft SharePoint. See SharePoint
Microsoft Windows. See Windows
Microsoft Word, 63, 322
microwave transmissions, 87–88
middle management
bypassing via e-mail, 548
over time, 238
middle-ware component for cell phones, 513
MIDI format, 46, 584
million instructions per second (MIPS), 584
milliseconds, 48, 584
MIN function in SQL, 131
Minges, Michael, 108
Minor, Bilmer, III, 115
Mintzberg, Henry, 8, 25
MIPS (million instructions per second), 584
mirror drive, 55, 584
mirrored sites, 174
MIS (management information system), 4, 583
jobs, 497, 502–503
roles of, 495
skills in demand, 503
MIS department
organization of, 506–512
roles of, 495–502
tasks performed by, 493–494
missing (null) data, 127
Mitchell, Ronald, 572
Mitchener, Brandon, 110
Mittra, Partha, 86
MLB (major league baseball), 195–196
mobile commerce, 105–106, 215, 283, 298
mobile devices, 85
mobile systems, 321, 377
mobility for business computer users, 496
models, 352–355, 584
building, 353
reasons for building, 353
modem, 584
Molecule Library, 158
money, making online, 275
monitoring access to data, 179
Moore's Law, 49
Morison, Robert E., 413, 430
morphing, 584
Morris, Gregory D. L., 120
Morse, Dan, 251
Morton, M. Scott, 18, 25
Mosquera, Mary, 482, 489
Moss Kanter, Rosabeth, 305
Mossberg, Walter S., 106
mouse, 52
movement of robots among people, 376

moving averages, 354
MP3, 46, 281
MRO (maintenance, repair, and operations), 116
MROverstocks at Grainger, 117
MRP (materials requirements planning), 583
MRP II, 583
Mullin, Bernie, 194
Mullins, Leo, 435, 436
multimedia, 584
multimedia messaging services (MMS), 88
multimedia tools, 545
multiple processors, 51–52
multiple regression, 364
multitable queries, 135, 136
multitasking, 217, 584
Murphy, Cheryl, 231
Murphy, Chris, 116, 158
Murphy, Craig, 451
Murray, Christian, 393
Murrell, Mack, 255
music industry, 404, 410
music publishers, 543
Musical Instrument Data Interchange (MIDI), 46, 584
Musick, Tony, 487
MyDropBox software, 555
mySAP, 522
mysimon.com, 6
myths/statements of the new economy, 418

name recognition, 287, 302
Nann, Bernhard, 391
nanoseconds, 48, 584
NAS (network-attached storage) devices, 524
NASDAQ market index, 301
Nash, Jim, 26
Nash, Kim S., 522
Nasser, Jacques, 235, 266
NAT (network address translation), 100, 105, 584
national identity cards, 534
National Information Technology Apprenticeship System, 30
natural language, 129, 375–376, 584
Naumann, Justus, 474
NDA (nondisclosure agreement), 559
negligence of employees, 169
Neil, Stephanie, 383
Nespoli, Harry, 362
.NET platform, 150, 300
NetMeeting, 318
Netscape, 103
network(s), 76. See also neural networks
across international boundaries, 107, 108–110
for communication, 78
communication across, 316
components of, 84–92
connecting, 92
connection devices for, 91
functions of, 76–84
intranets and, 512
peer-to-peer, 84
sharing hardware on, 81–83
sharing software on, 83
standards for, 95–98
structure of, 93–95
transmission media for, 85–91
voice and video communication on, 83–84
network address translation (NAT), 100, 105, 584
network cards, 84
network interface cards (NICs), 85, 584
network layer of the TCP/IP reference model, 97
network operating system (NOS), 584

network servers, sale of, 69
network service provider (NSP), 98, 99, 584
network support, 497–498
network technologies, FedEx on the leading edge of, 406
network-attached storage (NAS) devices, 524
networksolutions.com database, 101
neural networks, 350, 373, 378, 584
building with software, 373
learning, 374
spotting credit card fraud, 373
neurons, 373, 584
new economy, myths/statements of, 418
new services in B2C e-commerce, 283
news, selling, 275
newsgroups, 79, 102, 103, 584
next-day delivery, 339
Niccolai, James, 270
niche markets, 410
NICs. See network interface cards
Niederman, Fred, 517
Nirenberg, Walter, 204
Nisenholtz, Martin, 532
Nocera, Joseph, 388
nondisclosure agreement (NDA), 559
Nooyi, Indra, 34
Norihiko, Shirouzo, 266
normalization, 137, 584
North American Free Trade Area (NAFTA), 15
Norton, David P., 256
Norvig, Peter, 44
NOS (network operating system), 584
notations
international, 60
for tables, 138–139
Nottingham, Randall, 520
Novak, David, 34
NP-complete problem, 343
NSFnet, 98
NSP (network service provider), 98, 99, 584
N-tier application, 509
NULL value, 131
numbers, 42, 584
attributes of, 41
storage space required for, 46, 47
as written in European nations, 60
numeric data, storing, 126
numeric precision, 42
Nuss, Matthew, 31
nutrition databases, 30
nutrition information, Web-based, 30

Oakes, Chris, 191
obesity-related health problems, 28
object(s), 584
created by application packages, 41
derived from the base class, 470
searching for, 380
object hierarchy, 470, 584
Object Linking and Embedding (OLE), 584
object orientation, 41, 471, 584
objectives, 465
object-oriented DBMS, 124, 584
object-oriented design, 469–471, 584
object-oriented programming (OOP), 457, 584
object-oriented simulation, 355
Oblix NetPoint software, 32
OCR (optical character recognition), 52, 201, 584
O'Donnell, Anthony, 104
Office
groupware features, 316
groupware tools integrated with, 328
opening documents across Web connections, 321–322
voice input system built into, 54
offshore IT jobs, 510

off-site backups, 174
off-the-shelf software, 59
Ohlson, Kathleen, 523
oil exploration, 520, 524
OLAP (online analytical processing), 356–358, 584
OLE (Object Linking and Embedding), 584
Oliver, Carol Everett, 571
Oliver, Stephen, 377
Olsen, Florence, 489
OLTP (online transaction processing), 584
OmniPage Pro 11, 486
O'Neal, Stan, 392
one-to-many relationship, 584
connecting tables with, 133
identifying, 138
ongoing costs in a business plan, 423
online analytical processing (OLAP), 356–358, 584
online bookings at Southwest, 437
online conferences, 320
online fraud, 278
online meetings, 318, 320
online transaction processing (OLTP), 584
online translators, 541
online Web service system, 23–24
OnStar system, 283
OOP (object-oriented programming), 457, 584
open operating system, 584
open software, 63–64
Open Source, 445
open source
development, 459–461, 462
software, 57
open system, 464, 584
OpenSpirit, 523
operating systems, 41, 56–57, 217, 584
operations
combining data from, 237–238
level, 18–19, 584
opt out lists, 536
optical character recognition (OCR), 52, 201, 584
optical disks, 56
optimization, 353, 354, 584
opt-out links, 107
OR condition in QBE, 130
Oracle, 128
ERP license and fees, 240
Federal Purchasing software, 481
at FedEx, 342
Financials at Albertsons, 233
Oral-B CrossAction toothbrush, 366
Orbitz Web site, 439
ORDER BY clause in SQL, 131
order processing with static pages, 292
OrderZone at Grainger, 117
Ordonez, Jennifer, 410
organizational memory, 327
organizational structure, 10, 425
ornamental typefaces, 43
OS X operating system, 56
O'Sullivan, John, 535
Outlook
defining rules for, 511
setting digital signing and encryption, 171
output, 53–55, 463
biases, 352
component devices, 48
control over, 128–129
devices, 41, 585
for HRM systems, 248–249
types of, 53–55
outsiders as threats to information systems, 170
outsourcing, 503–506, 585
drawbacks to, 505

forces pushing, 505
IT functions, 515
programmers, 446
tradeoffs, 504
Web site hosting, 297
Outsourcing Desktop Initiative for NASA (ODIN), 490
Overby, Stephanie, 158, 162
owner exclusive books, 543
ownership
identifying, 559
of a new business, 426
Ozanian, Michael K., 193

package delivery industry, 338–346
package tracking, 339, 341
packet switching network, 587
Packeteer, 104
packets, 83, 97, 585
packet-switched networks, 83
page footers, 145, 585
page headers, 145, 585
paired programming, 459
Pallay, Jessica, 393
Pantone color standard, 62
paper, usage of, 60, 63
paperless office, 63
paperwork, required to start a business, 426
parallel implementation, 453, 454
parallel processing, 82, 585
parallel processors, 51–52
parameters, 353, 585
of a model, 353
parentheses, indicating repeating sections, 138–139
Parker, Anne, 571
Parker, James F., 437
partnerships, 307, 426
password generators, 175–176
passwords, 175
Pastore, Richard, 402
patents, 540–541, 558, 559, 585
on business processes, 421
for nonphysical items, 541
pattern matching, 374
pattern recognition, 372–373
Patti, Joe, 259
Paulk, Mark C., 474
Paxil, 159
payment card pilot test at Wendy's, 33
payment mechanisms
for digital products, 281
for transactions, 214–215
payment method, costs of, 219
payments for transactions, 219
payola, 410
PayPal, 215
payroll in an ERP system, 243
PC hardware, standardizing, 496
PCI bus, 51
PDA (personal digital assistant), 585
PDF (portable document format), 96, 585
peer-to-peer
communication, 585
networks, 84, 585
Peltz, James F., 233
pen-based computers, 53
PeopleSoft, 252, 253, 257
percent sign (%), matching exactly one character, 130
Pereira, Joseph, 252
Perez, Juan Carlos, 18, 489
performance evaluation, 361
peripheral devices, 48
PERL, 300
permissions, enforcing, 324
Perot, Ross, 445
personal communication service (PCS) bands, 87
Personal Computer Interconnect (PCI) bus, 51

personal computers (PCs), 59. See also computer(s)
personal data, collection of, 530, 533
personal digital assistant (PDA), 585
personal identification numbers (PINs), 175
personal software agent, 380–381
personnel, decentralizing MIS, 509–512
Petersen, Donald, 235
Peterson, Shirley, 484
Petz, Charles, 308
Petz, Leroy, Sr., 273, 308, 309
PGP (pretty good privacy), 181, 585
pharmaceuticals industry, 155–162
phased implementation, 453–454
Philpotts, John, 119
phishing, 186
phone. See conference telephone; telephone
phone numbers, internationalization of, 138
"phone" systems on the Internet, 102
photo-CD, 585
photocopiers, operating like laser printers, 55
PHP/PERL/PYTHON, 300
physical access to computers, 178–179
physical disabilities, workers with, 538–539
physical flows, 463
physical layer of TCP/IP, 96–97
picture elements, 44, 587
pictures, 44–45. See also images
attributes of, 41
storage space required for, 46, 47
pie chart, 61
pilot testing, 454
pilots, Delta's as the highest paid, 436
PINs (personal identification numbers), 175
piracy. See software piracy
Piszczalski, Martin, 266
pitch (frequency), 45
Pitsch, Peter K., 89
Pittman, R. J., 9
pivot table, 357, 358, 585
Pivot Table interface, 357
pixels, 44, 585
PKI (public key infrastructure), 181–182
plagiarism, 555
Plamondon, Scott, 73
plan. See business plan
planning in SDLC, 449–450, 451
Plantec, Peter, 374
Platts, Todd, 489
PLM (product life cycle management), 268
Plunkett Research, 266
PNG
files, 44
format, 96
point of sale. See POS
pointing devices, 52
points, 43
police powers, 553–554
political complications for networks across national boundaries, 109
polling tool in Live Meeting, 321
polygraphs, 557
polymorphism, 470, 585
Pooters, Drew, 217
pop-up form, 144
portability, 58, 87
portable data access, 274
portable document format (PDF), 96, 585
portable Internet connections, 298
Porter, Michael, 21, 22, 26, 396
Porter, Michael E., 431
ports, created by TCP, 97
POS (point of sale), 200, 585
advantages of, 203
capturing data at, 201–203
terminals at Burger King, 31–32

Post, Gerald, 152
postal telephone companies (PTTs), 108
Postelnicu, Andrei, 311
postpurchase phase of marketing, 286–287
potential competitors, 400–401
PowerPad, 341
PowerPoint, 44
Pratt, Mary K., 118
precision (numeric), 585
Predators, 82
prediction, 353, 354, 585
prepackaged applications, 448
prepurchase phase of marketing, 286–287
presentation, application software for, 60–62
Pretty Good Privacy (PGP), 181, 585
price competition
in e-commerce, 283–284
for PCs, 69
PriceLine, 275
pricing
analysis in a marketing plan, 425
at auction sites, 293
dynamic, 284
primary entities in a DFD, 466
primary key, 126, 137, 585
primary management level, 18
Prince, Charles, III, 388, 389
printers, 54
evaluating, 55
sharing on networks, 81–82
privacy, 529–535, 585
advertising and, 291
CRM systems and, 255
government and, 533
laws and rules, 535–536
laws relating to, 561–563
protecting, 534–535
regarding medical records, 569
versus security, 166, 189
Privacy Act of 1974, 535, 562
Privacy Act of 1994, 535
privacy laws in Europe, 109, 110, 213
Privacy Protection Act of 1980, 562
private key, 181, 585
problem boundary, 585
problems, diagnostic, 366–367
problem-solving applications, 381–382
procedures, 4, 585
process(es), 585
in a DFD, 466
documenting for services, 327
identifying in a system, 463
process analysis, 463–469
process control, 200, 203–205, 585
software, 19
system, 585
process design, 469
process diagram, 463
process innovation, 408, 585. See also reengineering
process reengineering, 327
processing biases, 352
processors, 48–52, 444, 585
building, 49
evolution of, 49, 50
multiple, 51–52
parallel, 51–52
speed of, 48
product differentiation, 405–406, 585
product life cycle management (PLM), 268
production
chain, 276–286, 398, 420–421
costs, 404
ERP and, 249
key features to, 409
line, 203–204
making more efficient, 249
management, 220–222, 266–267

productivity, 5–6
  improving, 6, 7
  measuring, 58–59
products
  creating new or different, 405–406
  descriptions and IDs of, 228
  success in B2C e-commerce,
    278–280
professional basketball, 194
professional football, 193–194
professional sports industry, 192–196
profit margins for e-commerce
    firms, 302
programmers, 125
  differences between individual, 459
  hiring for small projects, 446
  international salaries for, 502
  outsourcing, 446
  responsibilities in terms of computer
    security and privacy, 555–556
programming
  computers, 41
  custom, 445–446
  languages, 128
project management
  enhancing information technology, 30
  in SDLC, 449
  software, 425, 428, 500
  tools, 319
project timetable, 425
projects
  evaluation of completed, 455
  managing, 500
  runaway, 448–449
properties. See also attributes
  defining objects, 469
  of an object, 41
property rights, 558–561
proprietary EDI, 206
proprietorships, 307
protect document, 322, 585
protected zone, 480
protocols, 92, 585. See also Web
    protocols
prototyping, 444, 457, 458, 462, 585
Pryor, David, 483
pseudocode, 585
PTTs (postal telephone companies), 108
public carriers, links controlled by, 94
public key, 181, 585
public key infrastructure (PKI), 181–182
public-access channels on cable
    television, 546
Punch, Linda, 391
purchase order, 251–252, 324–325
purchase phase of marketing, 286–287
purchasing, 251–252, 507
pure Internet plays, 301, 585
"pure" managers, 5
push communication technologies,
    318–319
PYTHON, 300

QBE (query by example), 129, 585
  checking SQL statements in, 133
  computations in, 132
  example queries, 134–136
  joining multiple tables, 133
QSC formula, 29
quality control measures, 220
quality improvement, continuous,
    220, 579
quality management, 405, 406–407
quality of an information system, 5
quality of service (QOS), 79
quantum effects, 49
Quantum View Manage software at
    UPS, 344
quarterly reports, 246
queries
  creating output, 128
  examples of, 134–136
  multitable, 135

questions to create, 129
  single-table, 129–131
query by example. See QBE
query system, 124, 585
question mark (?) wildcard character, 130
quick casual restaurants, 28
Quindlen, Terrey Hatcher, 489
QuoteScope, 461

RAD (rapid application development),
    445, 459, 462, 586
radio frequency identification.
    See RFID
radio transmissions, 87–88
RAID, 55, 586
RAM (random access memory), 48,
    49–50, 55, 586
Ramani, Karthik, 373
Rand, Jonathan, 231
rapid application development (RAD),
    445, 459, 462, 586
raster format. See bitmap image
Rational Rose, 445
Rational Unified Process software, 451
Read Only Memory (ROM), 56, 586
read permissions, 176
real estate, e-commerce and, 279
real-time enterprise computing (RTEC)
    systems, 242
recentralization with intranets, 512–515
recommendation system at
    Amazon.com, 381
records
  avoiding use as a term, 125
  unauthorized access to IRS, 486
recovery, 150
recycling of computer equipment, 39
reduced instruction set computer
    (RISC), 586
redundant array of independent disks
    (RAID), 55, 586
reengineering, 16–18, 586
referential integrity, 142
refineries, 520–521
Regan, Keith, 305
registration
  of domain names, 100–101
  of Web sites on search engines, 287
regression, 353, 354
Regression tool in Excel, 379
regulation of the airline industry, 433
Reid, Fred, 436
relation, 124
relational DBMS, 123–124, 586
relational model, 124
reliability of a system, 455
Rendleman, John, 229
repeating sections
  of database forms, 137
  indicating, 138–139
  splitting out all, 139, 140
replication, 586
  of data on servers, 513–514
  of decentralized data, 509
Report Wizard, 147
report writers, 128, 145
reports, 586
  for business applications, 145–146
  in COBOL, 124
  creating database, 147
  in a DBMS, 124
  for human resources management
    systems, 248–249
  modifying without changing data, 127
  standards for, 149
request for proposal (RFP), 251, 586
research, 59, 408, 409, 422
reservation agents for JetBlue, 540
resistance to change, 453
resolution, 44, 45, 586
resources, assigning to tasks, 500
restaurant chains, 27

restaurants, quick-casual, 28
restrictions, entering in QBE, 130
retail distribution channel, 277
retail sales industry, 225–233
retail Web site template, 282
reusable objects and procedures, 471
Revell, Janice, 388
revenue
  management at Ford, 266
  from Web advertising, 288
reverse engineering, 586
Reviewing toolbar in Word, 322
revisions of documents, 323
Reynolds, L., 65
RFID (radio frequency identification),
    202–203, 585–586
  versus bar codes, 205
  chips, 199, 227
  at DHL, 345
  standard, 227
  tags at Ford, 267
RFP (request for proposal), 251, 586
Rhile, Howard, 484
Rhone, Steven, 232
Rhyne, Mary Anne, 159
Ricadela, Aaron, 521
Richardson, Margaret Milner,
    484, 487
Richardson, Marvin, 120
Richmond, Riva, 540
right to privacy, 534, 561
Rimnac, George, 117
ripe.net (Europe), 101
RISC (reduced instruction set
    computer), 586
risk factors for transactions, 209, 210
risk mitigation in e-commerce,
    212–213
rivals, 586
  analyzing, 399–400
  creating similar technical systems, 414
Rivest, Ron, 204
Rivest-Shamir-Adelman (RSA), 586
Roach, John, 377
Robb, Curtis, 436
Roberts, Paul, 189
robot scientist, 377
robotic vehicle contest, 375
robotics, motion and, 376–377
rocket scientists, 586
Rogers, Nat S., 118
ROM (Read Only Memory), 56, 586
Rosato, Donna, 435
Rosemier, R., 65
Rosenberg, Yuval, 388
Rosencrance, Linda, 120, 196, 229,
    232, 269, 322, 336, 342, 344,
    346, 440, 489
Ross, Keith W., 112
Rossotti, Charles, 486, 487, 488
Rothfeder, Jeffrey H., 489
Round function, 42
routers, 84, 91, 92, 586
routes, optimizing, 343
Rovell, Darren, 196
rows, 586
  dividing into groups, 132
  in a table, 123
Rozewell, Carol, 117
RSA, 581, 586
RSI (repetitive stress injury), 52, 586
RTEC systems, 242
Ruder, Tim, 532
rules, 586
  coded into an ES, 378
  defining for e-mail, 511
  devising for expert systems, 368
  organizing an expert system,
    369–370
  of thumb, 352, 378
runaway projects, 448–449
Rutan, Burt, 490
Rynecki, David, 393

S corporation election, 426
Sabre reservation system, 395, 402, 433,
    439–440, 451
salaries, IS, 502
sales
  estimating in a business plan, 423
  forecasting, 359, 360, 379, 424
  management plan, 425
  risk role of retailers, 225
  support mechanisms for, 409, 411
  taxes on the Internet, 298
Sample Identification Database, 158
sampler, 53, 586
Samuelson, Pamela, 561
SAN (storage area network), 58, 82,
    231, 524, 587
Sanchez, Rafael, 32
sans serif typefaces, 43
SAP software, 448
  access to Burger King's, 32–33
  installed at Grainger, 118
  at Lilly, 158
Sapsford, Jathon, 278
Sarbanes-Oxley Act, 212, 260
satellite centers for telecommuters, 540
satellites, microwave transmissions
    through, 108–109
Saul, Nathan, 552
scalability, 84, 586
  methods for providing, 84–85
  of Web servers, 58
scale effects bias, 352
Scaleable Processor Architecture
    (SPARC) microprocessors, 73
scanners, 52
scanning projects at the IRS, 486
scanningattack software, 170
scatter chart, 61
SCDA (Supervisory Control and Data
    Acquisition) systems, 521
scheduling, 319
  application software for, 62–63
  on a network, 80
  in SharePoint, 329–331
Scheier, Robert L., 229
Schiavone, Louise, 157
Schiesel, Seth, 103
Schlender, Brent, 336
Schmadel, Joseph C., Jr., 161
Schoenhals, Rick, 193
Schofman, David, 294
Schonfeld, Erick, 280
Schrage, Michael, 229
Schumpter, Joseph, 304
Schutzberg, Adena, 383
Schwartz, Adele C., 437
Scientific Data Management System
    (SDMS), 160
SCM (supply chain management), 205,
    249–254, 587
  obstacles to, 251
  at Wal-Mart, 227–228
scope creep, 448–449
Scott, Alan N., 487
Scott, Tony, 267
SCRIPS at the IRS, 486
script kiddies, 170, 187
script pages, 150–151
script typeface, 43
scrolling region, 143, 586
Scull, Bill, 410
SDLC (systems development life cycle),
    444, 448–457, 462, 587
  alternatives to, 457–463
  introduction to, 449
  versus object-oriented
    development, 471
  stages of, 449–455
  strengths and weaknesses of,
    455–457
  systems implementation in,
    452–454
Seacord, Robert C., 474

search engines, 20, 104
  choosing, 6
  at Lands' End, 230
  listing Web sites on, 287
search for extraterrestrial intelligence (SETI) project, 51
searches on the Internet, 20
Sears, Richard, 229
second normal form, 139–140, 141
secondary storage, 48, 55–56, 586
secure sockets layer (SSL), 185, 586
SecurID card, 177
security
  at Burger King, 32–33
  controls, 173–178, 501
  as a critical role of the MIS department, 501
  at O&M, 116
  permissions, 184
  versus privacy, 166, 189
  provided by non-computer-based tools, 178–179
  safeguards, 150
  systems, 415, 416
  trade-off required by, 515–516
Seideman, Tony, 120
SELECT command in SQL, 131
selection clauses, 132
self-service checkouts, 232–233
self-service portals in ERP systems, 256–257
Selig, Bud, 195
sellers, exchanging information with buyers, 253–254
separation of duties, 247
sequential storage, 56
serial ATA, 51
serif typefaces, 43
serifs, 43, 586
server farm method, 57
server farms, 58, 85, 451, 586
servers, 58, 84
  for intranets, 514
  on a network, 84–85
  sale of network, 69
  securing, 187
  theft of data from, 187
service(s)
  IT support mechanisms for, 409, 411
  many not tied to a physical location, 539
  sales taxes on, 299
service firms, 327
service industries, 15
service level agreement (SLA), 505, 586
service processes, 327, 329
service-oriented business, 16
service-oriented firms, 397
service-oriented Web sites, 283
"Seven S" model, 445
shared connections, 90–91
shared documents, tracking changes in, 322
shared folder, 184
shared-media networks, 92–93
SharePoint, 328–335, 586
  holding team documents, 321–322
  services, 102
SharePoint Portal, 328, 334–335
shelf life
  of computers, 39
  of PCs, 68
Sherman, Craig, 275
Sherman, John, 520
Sherman Antitrust Act, 415
Shill, Walt, 294
Shirouzo, Norihiko, 267
Shiver, Jube, Jr., 89
"shop with a friend" at Lands' End, 230
shopping cart system, 531
short message service (SMS) messages, 110

shrink-wrap licenses as binding agreements, 544
Siegel, Danny, 161
sign-offs, 452, 586
Silwa, Carol, 152, 205
Simonds, D., 65
Simons, George, 196
Simons, Mark, 344
Simons, Ruth, 391
simple object access protocol (SOAP), 286, 471–472, 586
simple static HTML, 291–293
simulation, 353, 354–355, 586
single sign-on, 177–178, 586
single-key encryption, 180–181
single-table queries, 129–131
single-unit sales, 293–295
Site of Care (SOC) system, 570
sites. See Web sites
Skillings, Jonathan, 73
skills, learning new, 538
Skinner, Margy, 438
SKU (stockkeeping unit), 227
SLA (service level agreement), 505, 586
Sleeman, P., 65
Sliwa, Carol, 229, 232, 346
Sloan, Alfred, 26, 265, 396
SMB (small and medium business) market, 241, 412
Smith, Craig, 115
Smith, Frederick W., 340, 342
Smith, Geoffrey, 390
Smith, Jack, 268
Smith, James M., 489
SOAP (simple object access protocol), 286, 471–472, 586
social engineering, 170
social interactions, 546–549
social legitimacy, 546, 586
social pressure bias, 352
society, effects of information systems on, 527–528
sofas, mass customization for, 251
software, 4, 40, 41, 586
  centralization, 508
  custom, 59
  decentralization, 508
  developing for complex systems, 443
  distributed, 244
  functions, 471
  "look and feel," 557
  making illegal copies, 555
  open, 63–64
  patents for, 558
  running on a central server, 83
  sharing on networks, 83
  suites, 587
software agents. See agents
software development. See development
software maintenance. See maintenance
software piracy, 542, 555, 586–587
software support. See support
software tools, 443
Solaris software, 56, 73
Songini, Marc L., 195, 262, 438, 522, 525
sound, 42, 45–46, 53, 587
  attributes of, 41
  components of, 45, 46
  sampling, 46
  storage space required for, 46, 47
sound waves, digitizing, 45–46
spam, 106, 107, 587
Spangler, William, 542
spanning tree protocol, 573
special characters, 60
specialization, applied to managers, 11, 12
Specialty Operations at Starbucks, 35
speech, freedom of, 554
speech recognition, 53, 202, 587
speeds of component devices, 48
speedy decisions, 367–368
Spitzer, Eliot, 159, 387
spoofed sites, 185

sports industry, 192–196
spread spectrum, 91
spreadsheets, 59–60, 124, 350
Springhill, Judy, 115
spy planes, unmanned, 82
spyware, 172, 173
SQC (statistical quality control), 407, 587
SQL query language, 129, 131, 587
  command words, 131
  computations in, 132–133
  example queries, 134–136
  functions, 131
  joining multiple tables, 133–134
SQL Server, 128
SSL (secure sockets layer), 185, 586
Stahl, Stephanie, 116, 229
Stallman, Richard, 64, 445, 460
standard operating procedures, 587
Standard Terminal Automation Replacement System (STARS), 480, 481
standardization, management move toward, 412
standardized reports, accounting system, 245
standards, 498–499, 587
  for authentication data, 177–178
  for biometric security devices, 176
  in a changing environment, 95–96
  companywide, 499
  for databases, 148–149
  for EDI, 205, 207
  global, 97
  for medical records systems, 537, 569
  for networks, 95–98
  organizations setting, 95
  for RFID, 227
  for Web advertising, 289
Starbucks Card program, 35
Starbucks Experience, 34
Stark, Jason, 87
STARS (Standard Terminal Automation Replacement System), 480, 481
start-up capital, 307
start-up cost statement in a business plan, 423
start-up costs, 423
start-up financing, 427
Stathis, Jennie, 486
static HTML, 291–293, 587
static integration, 587. See also dynamic integration
static memory chips, 55
statistical quality control (SQC), 407, 587
statistics capabilities of spreadsheets, 60
STDEV function in SQL, 131
Stedman, Craig, 118
Steermann, Hank, 231
steganography, 179
Steigers, Chad, 119
Stellar basin-modeling software, 521
Stepankowsky, Paula L., 233
Stewart, Martha, 160
stock options, 427, 587
stockkeeping unit (SKU), 227
Stoll, Clifford, 566
Stone, Amey, 388, 389
Stone, Martha L., 305
storage
  of exploration data, 524
  secondary, 55–56
storage area network (SAN), 58, 82, 231, 524, 587
storage devices, sharing, 82
storage space for data types, 46–47
stored-value card at Starbucks, 35
Stovall, Sam, 391
Strassmann, Paul A., 431
strategic decisions, 18, 20–21, 587
strategic systems
  creating, 395
  designing, 396–397

strategies
  costs and dangers of, 412–417
  developing, 409
  for an entrepreneur, 418, 420–421
  implementing, 413
  introduction to, 21–24
strategy section of a business plan, 423
Strattera, 157–158
streaming media technologies, 512
stress bias, 352
structured decisions, 19, 587
structured walkthrough, 587
Stuart, Anne, 312
style sheet, 96, 254
subchapter S corporation, 426, 587
subform, 143. See also scrolling region
subnet layer. See physical layer of TCP/IP
subprime market, 390, 391
subsystems, 464–465
success/failure attributions, 352
suffixes to Internet addresses, 100
Sullivan, Brian, 269
Sullivan, Laurie, 229, 342, 346
SUM function in SQL, 131
summaries of data, 218–219
summarizing ERP data, 258–260
Sumpter, John, 311
Sundance Film Festival, Starbucks and, 36
supercomputers, sharing access to, 81, 82
SuperTrackers, 341
Supervisory Control and Data Acquisition systems (SCDA), 521
suppliers, 399
  connecting to customers, 75
  electronically connecting to, 251
  layers of, 399
supplies
  delivered by Owens and Minor, 115
  logistics and, 410
supply chain management. See SCM
SupplyPower at GM, 322
support
  applications, 381–382
  calls rerouted by Dell to the U.S., 71–72
  software, 497
support groups (keiretsu), 403
SurfStats, 290
surveys in SharePoint, 330–331
SVG (scalable vector graphics) format, 44
Sviokla, John, 118
Swanson, Sandra, 232
sweep accounts, 406
Swisher, Kara, 305
switchboard.com, 6
switched networks, 90, 93
switches, 77, 84, 91–92, 587
switching costs, 22, 404, 405, 587
SXGA, resolution of, 45
Symbol Technologies, 406
synthesizer technology, 53
synthesizers, 45, 587
sysop, 587
System Idle Process, 49
systems, 587
  diagramming, 465–468
  improving existing, 454
  techniques for implementing, 453–454
systems analysis, 450–451, 587
systems analysts, 502, 587
systems design, 451–452, 587
systems development life cycle. See SDLC
Szygenda, Ralph, 264, 266, 268

T1, 587
T3, 587
tables, 123–124, 125, 587
  defining, 126

joining multiple, 133–134
notation for, 138–139
storing data in different, 125–126
tactical decisions, 18, 19–20, 349, 587
tapes, 56
targeted Internet ads, 288
Tarkan, Laurie, 569
tasks
in a project, 500
scheduling in SharePoint, 330
Taurel, Sidney, 158
Tax Return Logging System, 308
tax returns, electronic filing of, 484–485
Tax System Modernization program (TSM), 483–484
Tax System Redesign program, 483
TaxBrain Web site, 273, 308–309
taxes on the Internet, 298–299
TAXOL, 159–160
Taylor, Alex, III, 266, 267, 269, 270
Taylor, Sam, 230
Taylor, Steve, 438
TBDF (transborder data flow), 109, 588
TCO (total cost of ownership), 496, 587
TCP (transport control protocol), 97
TCP/IP reference model, 96–98
teaching methods, provided by technology, 528
team members, communicating with, 316–321
teams, 76, 315
teamwork, 6–7, 315
at DHL, 345
at FedEx, 342
fundamental concepts of, 316
on a network, 80
in the packaging industry, 340
required for developing system, 457–459
technical problems for networks across international boundaries, 108–109
technology
access to, 546–548
cost of new, 413–414
declining sizes and prices, 506
effects on individuals, 528
effects on jobs, 536–539
managing at Sutter Health, 570–571
trends in, 10–16
using to add value, 40
technology road mapping process at GM, 267–268
technology workers, future demand for, 17
telecommunication lines, access to, 547
telecommunications, global, 107–110
telecommunications industry
major collapse, 310
mergers in, 13
telecommuting, 539, 540
telemarketers, 509
telemarketing phone calls, stopping, 536
telematics, 265
telemedicine, 527, 574
telephone
cables, 86
calls, 83
conference, 320
system, 77
television sets versus computer monitors, 53
Telnet, 587
temporary workers, 12, 13–14, 522
Tennant, Don, 152
terabytes, 123, 587
Teresko, John, 269
testing
DBMS software changes, 150
final, 452–453
text, 42, 43, 587
attributes of, 41
converting to voice, 45
storage space required for, 46, 47

Thaler, Stephen, 366
Thibodeau, Patrick, 489, 491, 521, 571
thin-client, 587
approach, 512–513
at ChevronTexaco, 524
PDAs, 85
third normal form, 140–142
third-party cookies, 532
Thompson, Tommy, 569
Thomson, Todd, 388
Thurm, Scott, 514
Thurman, Mathias (pseudonym), 191
Tiboni, Frank, 153, 482
Tieman, Larry, 342
TIGER, 362
Tilton, Helga, 120
time as an aspect of information quality, 219–220
time bombs in software, 168
time shaving, 217
timetable in a business plan, 425
TiVo system, 542
Tivoli software, 483
T-Mobile HotSpot window signs, 35
Token Ring, 587
top-down development, 587
Torvalds, Linus, 56, 64, 460
total cost of ownership (TCO), 496, 587
Totty, Michael, 275, 411
touch screens, 52
toys, SCM for, 252
TQM (total quality management), 399, 407, 587
tracking, changes, 322, 587–588
trade secret laws, 559
trademarks, 558, 559
trade-off, required by security, 515–516
traditional advertising, 287
traffic, analyzing to Web sites, 289
Traffic Management Advisor software, 480
Trainer, Tom, 158
training, using expert systems, 368
transaction processing, 200
data capture, 200–209
as a major function of the accounting system, 245
systems, 19, 239, 588
transaction risks in e-commerce, 212–213
transactions, 200, 209
accuracy of, 260–261
collecting data about, 200
data quality of, 216–220
elements of, 209–213
encrypting, 185
fees for, 210–211
handling on Web sites, 295
increasing number of, 218
in an international environment, 213–214
paying for, 219
payment mechanisms for, 214–215
processing, 76–77, 199
recording in retail sales, 226
risk factors, 209, 210
verifying, 201
transborder data flow (TBDF), 109, 588
translation systems, 376, 541
translator, handheld, 376
transmission capacity, 88–90
transmission media for a network, 85–91
transport control protocol (TCP), 97
transport layer of TCP/IP, 97
transportation
costs for international orders, 300
e-commerce and, 279
transporters, connecting to, 251
trap doors, 168
Travelocity Web site, 439
trends
changing businesses, 11–16
forecasting, 379

triage, 572
triggered rule, 588
Trojan horses, 173, 588
Trombley, M., 223
Trombly, Maria, 153
Trotman, Alex, 235
Trottman, Melanie, 438
true color, 588
TSM Design Master Plan, 484
Tufte, Edward, 61
Tufts, Bob, 195
tuple, 124
Turing, Alan, 375, 588
Turing test, 375, 377, 588
turnkey systems, 448
twisted pair cable, 85–86, 588
twisted-pair wires, 86
typefaces, 43, 588

UCCnet registry, 228
UCITA (Uniform Computer Information Transactions Act), 544
UDDI (universal description, discovery, and integration), 286, 588
UDP (user datagram protocol), 97
Ulfelder, Steve, 243, 340, 342
ultra-high frequency RFID chips, 202
ultra-wideband (UWB), 51, 79
underscore (_) as a SQL wildcard, 130
UNEs (unbundled network elements), 311
Unger, Susan, 270
Unicode, 43, 588
Uniform Code Council (UCC), 228
Uniform Computer Information Transactions Act (UCITA), 544
uninterruptible power supply, 175, 588
United Kingdom
databases involving personal data, 530
public spending compared to U.S., 478
universal description, discovery, and integration (UDDI), 286, 588
UNIX, 56, 69, 588
unstable model, 588
UPCs (universal product codes), 201
upload, 588
UPS (uninterruptible power supply), 175, 588
UPS Exchange Collect, 344
U.S. Patriot Act, 563, 564
U.S. Visitor and Immigrant Status Indicator Technology (US-VISIT), 176
USB, 51
authentication key, 193
drives, 55
use taxes, 299
Usenet. See newsgroups
user datagram protocol (UDP), 97
user interface device, 512
User Request Evaluation Tool (URET), 480
users
as customers, 455
determining requirements, 458
identifying, 175–176
resistance, 588
responsibilities of, 555
USVisaNews.com, 312
UXGA, resolution of, 45

V Tax, 308
Valdes-Perez, Raul, 9
value chain, 405, 407–408, 588
VAN (value added network), 211
Van Armun, Patricia, 120
Van de Ven, Mike, 438
van Unnik, Arjan, 523
Van Waters, George, 118
van Zwieteren, Rob, 523
VAR function in SQL, 131
Varon, Elana, 489
Vasishtha, Preeti, 482

VC (venture capital) firms, 427
VDLM2 digital technology at Southwest, 438
vector images, 44, 588
vector tracing software, 52
vendor perspective on transactions, 209–210
venture capital, 588
venture capital (VC) firms, 427
version control, 323, 588
maintaining for Web sites, 298
in SharePoint, 333, 334
vertical integration, 398
vertically integrated firms, 240
Verton, Dan, 336, 440, 524
VGA, resolution of, 45
VHF Digital Link Mode 2 (VDLM2), 481
video, 42, 46, 588
attributes of, 41
bandwidth needed for, 79
capture, 53
communication on networks, 83–84
conference systems, 320
education, 545
output, 53
standards, 109
storage space required for, 46, 47
Video Privacy Act, 562
videoconference, 588
views, 136, 588
Vijayan, Jaikumar, 116, 194, 229, 523
Vincent, Kenny, 534
virtual 3-D model on the Lands' End Web site, 230
virtual agents, 374
virtual mall, 588
virtual private network. See VPN
virtual reality (VR), 588
viruses, 588
for information attacks, 552
as threats to information systems, 170, 172–173
Visual Basic, 170, 588
Visual Source Safe, 333
visual table of contents, 588
visualization software, 354
Vivisimo, 6
voice, converting to text, 45
Voice Command mode, 54
voice communication on networks, 83–84
voice mail, 62, 78, 318, 588
voice recognition, 54, 375, 376, 588
voice-risk analysis software, 557
VoIP (voice over Internet protocol), 83–84, 588
volume (amplitude), 45
voters, targeting individual, 551
voting systems, 549–551
VPN (virtual private network), 95, 102, 185, 588
VR (virtual reality), 588

WAAS (Wide Area Augmentation System), 480
Wade, Will, 390
Wagoner, Rick, 268
Waitt, Ted, 72
The Wall Street Journal, 281
Wallace, Bob, 194
Wallnau, Kurt, 474
Waltner, C., 112
Walton, Sam, 227
WAN (wide area network), 94–95, 588
Wang, Michael, 523
Want, Roy, 224
"War of the Worlds" broadcast, 546
Waraniak, John, 269
Wardani, Ladd, 79
warehouse-management system at O&M, 116
Warner, Fara, 266
Warren, Stephen, 509

Warren, Susan, 522, 523
waterfall methodology, 450
Web advertising, 287–289. *See also* advertising
  handling, 289
  return of, 281
  revenue, 288
Web broadcasts of baseball games, 195
Web browsers. *See* browsers
Web commerce servers. *See* commerce server
Web cookies. *See* cookies
Web hosting
  company, 295–296
  options, 297
Web logs. *See* blogs
Web mall, 296
Web of Trust, 171
Web pages, 89, 96, 319
Web protocols, 329. *See also* protocols
Web publishers, perspectives on Web advertising, 289
Web servers, 58
  code engines for, 300
  detailed logs maintained by, 289
Web sites, 79
  building interactive, 300
  connecting to databases, 150
  creating e-commerce, 282, 291–298
  creating entire, 96
  critical to Southwest, 438
  development time and cost, 428
  establishing, 100
  hosting, 428–429
  information on the IRS, 485
  maintaining a database of products for sale, 298
  ordering directly from, 201
  performance of, 297
  profitable for products, 280–281
  provided by federal and state governments, 560
  providing specific services, 285
  registering with search engines, 287
  service-oriented, 283
  spoofing, 185
  traffic analysis, 289–290

Web transactions. *See* transactions
Web-based intranets, 512–514
WebDAV service, 102
Weber, Charles V., 474
Weber, Jeffrey, 170
Weber, Joseph, 571
Web-hosting methods, 291
Webmaster, 588
Weed, Brian, 158
Weil, Elizabeth, 491
Weil, Nancy, 521
Weill, Sandy, 388, 389
Weiner, David, 438
Weiner, Norbert, 537
Weiss, Todd R., 162, 232, 302, 336, 489
Welles, Orson, 546
Wells, Melanie, 36
Wentz, Laurel, 389
Wertheimer, Jeremy, 439
Wessel, Jay, 194
Weston, Randy, 262
Whalen, Jeanne, 522
"what-if?" questions, 465
Wheeler, Eric, 288
WHERE clause in SQL, 131
WHERE criteria in QBE, 136
Whisler, Thomas L., 25
White, Gregory L., 522
White, John, 558
White, Joseph B., 266, 267
whiteboard in NetMeeting, 318
Whiteside, Thomas, 191
Whiting, Rick, 118, 162, 232, 340, 573
Whitman, Meg, 294
Whittaker, William L., 375
Whois facilities, 101
wholesale suppliers, 114–120
Wide Area Augmentation System (WAAS), 480
wide area network (WAN), 94–95, 588
Wi-Fi, 106
  "hot spot" technology, 31
  public-access, 344
  at Starbucks, 35–36
  wireless, 79
Wiggins, R., 112

wikipedia.org, 6
Wilder, Clinton, 196
Wildstrom, Stephen H., 63
Wiles, Russ, 309
Wilkinson, Stephanie, 383
Willemssen, Joel, 479
Williams, Sam, 176
Willumstad, Robert, 388, 389
Wilson, Ron, 479
Windelberg, Marjorie, 509
window, 588
Windows, 56
  accessibility tools, 538–539
  server market, 69
Windows XP Professional, setting security permissions, 184
Windrem, Robert, 566
Wingfield, Nick, 294
Winslow, Ron, 224
wireless access, 77
wireless connections, 298, 548
wireless networks, 105–106, 186, 498
wireless radio connections, 91
wireless technologies
  at McDonald's, 31
  tracking people, 532
wisdom, 5, 588
wishful thinking bias, 352
Witt, Douglas, 342
Wojcik, Joanne, 571
Woodham, Doug, 389
Word, 63, 322
word processing, 60
workers
  home-based, 539
  scheduling, 62
  temporary, 12, 13–14
workflow, 324
  in SharePoint, 333–334
  software, 588
workgroup software, 412
workstations, 73, 588
World Wide Web (WWW), 103, 588
world-state, rise of, 552–553
WorldWide Clearance System (WCS) at DHL, 345

worm, 172
Wright, Brian, 193
Wright, Maury, 36
write permissions, 176
writing, application software for, 60
WWW (World Wide Web), 103, 588
Wyden, Ron, 173
WYSIWYG, 588

X12 standard, 207, 208
XGA, resolution of, 45
XML (extensible markup language), 209, 471–472, 581
  for EDI, 209
  integration across systems, 253–254
  sharing data in B2B e-commerce, 284
  supporting distributed services, 286
XP (extreme programming), 439, 459, 581
XP Professional, setting security permissions, 184

Yahoo, 6
Yan, Martin, 34
Yandow, Laura, 269
Yarnell, Jeff, 481
Yasin, Rutrell, 160
yield management, 395, 433, 439
yield pricing, 402
York, Thomas, 517
Youndt, David, 21
Young, Ian, 120
Young, Matthew, 267

Zaltman, Gerald, 352, 383
Zarley, Craig, 269
Zarrella, Ron, 268
Zeidenberg, 559
Zimmerman, Michael R., 73
zip codes
  in database tables, 141–142
  internationalization of, 138
zombie computers, 187, 188, 189
zooming, 62
zShops, 294, 588